PSYCHOLOGY

FIFTH EDITION

PSYCHOLOGY

FIFTH EDITION

HENRY GLEITMAN
ALAN J. FRIDLUND
DANIEL REISBERG

W·W·NORTON & COMPANY·NEW YORK·LONDON

Copyright © 1999, 1995, 1991, 1986, 1981 by W. W. Norton & Company, Inc.

Editor: Cathy Wick
Developmental Editor: Jane Carter
Project Editor: Margaret Farley
Production Manager: Roy Tedoff
Photograph Editor: Ruth Mandell
Editorial Assistants: Elana Passman, Claire Acher
Book and Cover Designer: Antonina Krass
Layout Artist: Roberta Flechner
Compositor: TSI Graphics
Manufacturer: Quebecor, Kingsport

The text of this book is composed in Bembo with the display set in Machine.
Cover illustrations: (*Left*) Michelangelo Buonarroti, *David,* detail of head in profile. Accademia, Florence, Italy. Photograph courtesy Scala/Art Resource, NY. (*Right*) Michelangelo Buonarroti, *Studies for the Libyan Sibyl* (copy). Uffizi Gallery, Florence.
Frontispiece: Tommaso de 'Cavalieri, *Bust of a Youth in Fantastic Dress.* Ashmolean Museum, Oxford.

Further acknowledgments and credits appear on pp. C85–C90, which constitute a continuation of the copyright page.

Library of Congress Cataloging-in-Publication Data
Gleitman, Henry.
    Psychology/Henry Gleitman, Alan J. Fridlund, Daniel Reisberg.—5th ed.
        p.   cm.
    Includes bibliographical references and index.
    ISBN 0-393-97364-6
        1. Psychology.   I. Fridlund, Alan J.   II. Reisberg, Daniel.   III. Title.
BF121.G58   1998
150—dc21   98-29515

W. W. Norton & Company, Inc., 500 Fifth Avenue, New York, N.Y. 10110
                    http://www.wwnorton.com
W. W. Norton & Company Ltd., 10 Coptic Street, London WC1A 1PU
1 2 3 4 5 6 7 8 9 0

THE CONTENTS IN BRIEF

CONTENTS

CHAPTER **3** | MOTIVATION 71

CHAPTER **8** | THOUGHT AND
KNOWLEDGE 301

CHAPTER **9** | LANGUAGE 345

PART FOUR | DEVELOPMENT 531

CHAPTER 13 | PHYSICAL AND COGNI-
TIVE DEVELOPMENT 533

CHAPTER **18** | PSYCHOPATHOLOGY 757

PREFACE

This is the fifth edition of *Psychology.* One reason for this revision is the obvious fact that, like any other discipline, psychology advances and develops. Fifty years ago, psychologists tended to be rather defensive about the status of the field and were perhaps a bit too loud in proclaiming that "Psychology is a science!" But by now there is no need for such defensive proclamations, for that assertion has become a simple statement of fact. In the last half a century, psychology has assuredly become a real and vigorously progressive science.

As a field advances, so must all attempts to describe it. These advances, together with the suggestions by the many students and colleagues who have used this text, prompted a number of changes that we describe below.

In addition, this volume is now coauthored for the first time. Alan Fridlund and Daniel Reisberg played an important role as advisors on the previous editions, but up until now, this book has in important ways been Henry Gleitman's alone. This change in authorship has been driven by the increasing breadth and sophistication of our field, which make it difficult for any one individual to know the full span of psychology and to write about this material with the precision of an expert. The added perspective of the two new authors adds a depth and richness that our field now demands.

This edition has been a full collaboration, with all three of us deeply involved in every chapter. Each of us has brought our own background and experience to the project, but we have tried our very best to weave these strands together to ensure a unified and cohesive treatment. That unity is enhanced by our shared allegiance to the broad aims that have characterized this book from its very first edition.

THE OVERALL AIM: COHESION IN A DIVERSE FIELD

In writing *Psychology,* Gleitman sought to present the field in all its diversity while conveying the sense in which it is a coherent intellectual enterprise. In pursuit of this goal, he did the following:

1. To present the different subareas of psychology, the book was organized around five main questions: How do humans (and where relevant, nonhuman animals) act, how do they know, how do they interact, how do they develop, and how do they differ from each other?

2. To provide intellectual cohesion, each topic was considered against the backdrop of one or two major ideas that could serve as an organizing and unifying framework. Thus the chapter on the biological bases of behavior showcases Descartes' conception of the organism as a machine, and the next chapter treats various aspects of motivated behavior as manifestations of negative feedback. To relate the material across chapters, several overarching themes are carried over from chapter to chapter. For example, the various chapters that deal with cognition ("Sensory Processes," "Perception," "Memory," "Thought and Knowledge," and "Language") all consider variations on the two controversies of nature versus nurture and psychological atomism versus organization.

3. In many cases, integration requires taking a step backward to look at psychology's intellectual history, for a number of the field's endeavors are hard to explain unless one points out the paths that led up to them. Why did Thorndike study cats in puzzle boxes? Why did his conclusions have such an important effect on American psychology? Why were they challenged by Köhler and Tolman? It still pays to take a serious look at the work of such pioneers before turning to the present. Much as a river's water is clearer when it is taken from its source, so issues that have become more and more complex as detail has been piled upon detail become plainer and more evident when traced back to their origin.

GENERAL ORGANIZATION

These essential themes are preserved from earlier editions. At the same time, though, much is new. In the last two decades, psychology has developed a rich partnership with the neurosciences, and much of this new and exciting material is now included. Likewise, our field has benefited in recent years from an increased understanding of non-Western cultures and how the feelings, thoughts, and behavior of people in these cultures differ from those of people in the West. Our discussion of many topics in this edition now reflects the power of these cross-cultural comparisons. Similarly, evolutionary considerations, often fueled by comparisons across species, have provided new insights into many psychological questions, and this is also emphasized in this new edition.

All three of these topics—coverage of neuroscience, cross-cultural comparisons, and evolutionary insights—have been included in previous editions of *Psychology,* but our treatment of them in the Fifth Edition is much expanded. This might have entailed a celebration of these new domains by setting them off in their own chapters, distinct from the discussion contained elsewhere in the text. We have chosen not to do this, however, because we believe that students are not well served by placing these topics in a sort of intellectual quarantine, separate from the issues and arguments that constitute the rest of psychology. Instead, we have woven these new materials into the overall narrative of the book, where they can illuminate, and be illuminated by, long-standing psychological claims and evidence.

For this reason, the structure of the book remains largely as it was in earlier editions—despite the introduction of a very large quantity of new material. After an introductory chapter, the book is still divided into five parts that reflect the perspectives from which most psychological phenomena can be regarded: "Action," "Cognition," "Social Behavior," "Development," and "Individual Differences." In brief outline, they cover the following topics:

PART I: ACTION

This part focuses on overt behavior and its physiological basis. It begins by considering the biological underpinnings of human and animal action, leading to a discussion of the nervous system and its operation (Chapter 2) and some basic phenomena of motivation (Chapter 3). It then asks how organisms can modify their behavior to adapt to new circumstances, a topic that leads to a discussion of classical and instrumental conditioning, modern learning theory, and more recent approaches that take a cognitive slant (Chapter 4).

Chapter 2 ("Biological Bases of Behavior") has been extensively revised for this edition. The chapter now begins by explaining the methods by which the nervous system is investigated, then turns to the evolution and development of the nervous system. The section on the physiology of neurotransmission has been updated and clarified, and a new section covers the recovery of function following brain damage. Chapter 3 ("Motivation") uses the concept of potentiation as an overall organizational principle; this chapter has been extensively updated, particularly in light of new findings about the mechanisms of hunger and their implications for obesity and eating disorders. Chapter 4 ("Learning") stresses modern approaches to animal learning, including work on contingency and cognitive approaches to classical and instrumental conditioning. The discussion of reinforcers has been expanded to include work on intrinsic motivation; a new section on the neural basis for learning has also been added.

PART II: COGNITION

This part deals with knowledge and how it is gained and used. It begins by asking how the senses provide us with information about the world outside (Chapter 5) and how this information is organized and interpreted to lead to the perception of objects and events (Chapter 6). Further questions concern the way this knowledge is stored in memory and retrieved when needed (Chapter 7), the way it is organized through thinking (Chapter 8), and the way it is communicated to others through the medium of language (Chapter 9).

Chapter 5 ("Sensory Processes") contains a discussion of evolution and sensory equipment, as well as an expanded section on signal detection theory emphasizing the application of this theory to other problems and other domains. Chapter 6 ("Perception") contains a new section on the neural bases of form perception, as well as a new discussion of the evolutionary significance of redundant mechanisms in perception. Also new in this edition is an expanded discussion of the perception of motion. Chapter 7 ("Memory") focuses primarily on episodic memory, including the modern emphasis on encoding and retrieval, the role of schemas in memory, the issue of repressed memories, and the difference between explicit and implicit memory. A new section explores what we can learn from the neuropsychology of memory, and, with that, the various forms of amnesia. Chapter 8 ("Thought and Knowledge") begins with the database on which thinking rests, including analogical representations (imagery and spatial thinking) and symbolic or digital representations. A new section concludes the chapter with discussion of some of the neural mechanisms that underlie thinking and with a discussion of the relation between cognition and consciousness. Also new to this chapter is a discussion of how education can improve critical thinking. Chapter 9 ("Language") explores what it means to know a language and also how a language is learned. New sections examine the relation between language and thought, and place language in a social context by examining the role of context and conversation in guiding understanding.

PART III: SOCIAL BEHAVIOR

This part concerns our interactions with others. It begins with a discussion of built-in social tendencies in humans and animals, a topic to which ethology and evolutionary theory have made major contributions (Chapter 10). It then turns to modern social psychology, considering how people try to understand the social situation in which they find themselves, how they interpret their own internal states and emotions, and how they interact with others (Chapters 11 and 12).

There have been several changes in this section. In Chapter 10 ("The Biological Bases of Social Behavior") we have expanded and updated our consideration of natural selection, the evolution of behavior, and "fitness." New sections cover alternative mating systems and strategies, and current thinking about why so many organisms rely on sexual reproduction. Chapter 11 ("Social Cognition and Emotion") continues to focus on the way individuals interpret social events, including discussions of attitudes and attitude change, attribution, impressions of others, and the interpretation of one's own internal states, but it now also has an expanded discussion of emotions and facial expression, as well as a new section detailing how cultural comparisons produce dramatic insights into key phenomena in attribution, person perception, and compliance. Also included is a section on the neural basis of emotion, emphasizing the role of the amygdala in emotional appraisal. Chapter 12 ("Social Interaction") continues to treat the way individuals deal with others. In addition to discussions of social exchange, attraction and love, conformity, obedience, and crowd behavior, it has a new discussion of communal and exchange relationships.

PART IV: DEVELOPMENT

This section contains two chapters on development. Chapter 13 ("Physical and Cognitive Development") continues to focus on recent, post-Piagetian approaches to mental growth and includes material on counting and numerical skills in infants and preschoolers, and work on social cognition in infants and preschoolers, including studies of false beliefs and their bearing on the child's development of a "theory of mind." Chapter 14 ("Social Development") discusses such topics as moral development, empathy, sex, and gender. Among new developments treated in this chapter are an updated discussion of the effects of institutional day care, a new treatment of the psychological consequences of divorce, and a consideration of the physical aggression observed in boys versus the relational aggression observed in girls. New data are also presented that bear on intersexuality, nature versus nurture in gender identity, and the outcomes and ethics of sex reassignment surgeries.

PART V: INDIVIDUAL DIFFERENCES

This part begins with a chapter on mental testing in general and intelligence testing in particular (Chapter 15) and then continues with two chapters on personality assessment and theory (Chapters 16 and 17). It continues by looking at several varieties of psychopathology and asking how they arise (Chapter 18), and concludes by examining various methods of treatment and therapy (Chapter 19).

Chapter 15 ("Intelligence") is updated in various ways, including a section on recent attempts to understand intelligence in information-processing terms, including the role of working memory and attention. *The Bell Curve* also receives increased coverage, as does the impact of social environment on intelligence and the need to understand intelligence within an appropriate cultural context. Chapter 16 ("Personality I") considers methods of personality assessment and discusses trait theory and behavioral-cognitive theory as two of five theoretical approaches to personality, with particular attention to the trait-situation controversy and to recent attempts to look for biological and genetic bases of personality differences. Chapter 17 ("Personality II") takes up three other theoretical approaches to personality—the psychodynamic, humanistic, and sociocultural. It includes a full treatment of psychoanalytic formulations, beginning with Freud's original theories, continuing with more recent psychodynamic approaches, and concluding with a discussion of technical and sociopolitical critiques of psychoanalysis.

Both Chapter 18 ("Psychopathology") and Chapter 19 ("Treatment of Psychopathology") have been updated to include modern developments, such as new psychobiological theories, new pharmacological approaches to treatment, and new approaches to the evaluation of treatment outcome. A new section in Chapter 18 also discusses the prevalence of subsyndromal disorders and the dangers of "cosmetic" psychopharmacology. Chapter 19 also includes updated discussions of how the criteria for what makes a treatment "effective" have changed with the new emphasis on therapy accountability, and managed care and cost-containment measures.

APPENDICES

An entirely new appendix ("Methods of Scientific Research") has been added to this edition. This appendix covers experimental, correlational, and observational designs, and concludes with a discussion of research ethics. Many commonsense examples are employed throughout the appendix to convey the important message that the methods of scientific research can also be used to improve critical thinking in everyday life. Extensive cross-referencing to the rest of the volume makes it possible to use the appendix piece by piece over the course of the term or to present the appendix as a stand-alone unit either early or late in the semester.

A second appendix discusses the statistical methods used by psychologists to summarize and analyze their data. This appendix has been revised to maximize its clarity and accessibility, and also to ensure that it works well with the newly added appendix on research methods.

THE READER AND THE BOOK

It is sometimes said that students in the introductory course want to learn about things that are relevant to their own lives, and, in truth, this seems an entirely sensible view. Psychology deals with the nature of human experience and behavior, the hows and whys of what we do, think, and feel. How could an exploration of these topics *not* be relevant to someone's life? Everyone has perceived, learned, remembered, and forgotten, has been angry and afraid and in love, has given in to group pressure and stood up to it. In short, everyone has experienced most of the phenomena that psychology tries to explain. This being so, psychology cannot fail to be relevant.

But we can easily lose sight of this relevance amid the torrent of facts, theories, and methodological lessons that constitute our field. To keep the relevance in view, therefore, we rely on a liberal use of everyday examples and a frequent resort to metaphors of one kind or another, providing a succession of bridges between the psychological phenomena we discuss and the reader's own life.

In this effort, and, indeed, throughout the book, our most important guide has been our own experience as teachers (with a combined total of over eighty years in the classroom). This experience leaves us with no doubt that one of the best ways of learning something is to teach it, for in trying to explain something to others, you first have to clarify it for yourself. This holds for the subject matter of every course we have ever taught, but most especially for the introductory course. Students in an advanced course will come at you with tough and searching questions; they want to know about the evidence that bears on a theory of, say, color vision, language acquisition, or the placebo effect, and about how that evidence was obtained. But students in an introductory course ask the toughest questions of all. They ask why anyone would ever want to know about color vision (or language acquisition or the placebo effect) in the first place. And they also ask what any one topic has to do with any other. They ask such questions because they—unlike advanced students—have not as yet accepted the premises of the field. They wonder whether the emperor is really wearing any clothes. As a result, they make us ask ourselves again and again what the field of psychology is all about—what the emperor's clothes are really like when you look at them closely.

This edition, as well as its predecessors, reflects our attempts to answer such questions and to answer them not only to satisfy the students but also to satisfy ourselves.

SUPPLEMENTARY MATERIALS

To help serve the needs of students, instructors, and teaching assistants, several supplementary materials are available with this text.

1. For the student:

There is a complete study guide for students, prepared by John Jonides of the University of Michigan and Paul Rozin of the University of Pennsylvania. This study guide, a revised version of the guide the same authors wrote for previous editions of *Psychology,* should prove very useful to students who want some help and guidance in mastering the material in the text. Moreover, for every chapter, it provides experiments and observational studies that students can carry out on their own to get some first-hand experience with psychology's subject matter.

In addition, for this edition we introduce the *Psychology* WebBook—an on-line study guide designed to reinforce key ideas presented within each chapter of the fifth edition. This guide provides chapter summaries, an interactive tutorial for each chapter, animated diagrams, on-line quizzes, Web exploration activities, and a glossary. (Passwords to this Web site can be packaged at a considerable discount with new copies of the text; they can also be ordered separately from W. W. Norton & Company.)

2. For the instructor:

The instructor's manual, prepared by Ed Kako of the University of Pennsylvania, Kimberly Cassidy of Bryn Mawr College, Christine Massey of Swarthmore College, Hilary Schmidt of New Jersey Medical School, and Henry Gleitman, offers specific suggestions for every textbook chapter, including discussion topics, a bibliography, an annotated film and media guide, and classroom demonstrations. Included in the demonstrations are materials for some thirty in-class experiments covering a range of topics that include the speed of the nervous impulse, perceptual demonstrations, the Stroop effect, reasoning problems, the perception of personality, and gender stereotypes. Transparencies, student worksheets, data summaries, and detailed instructions for the teacher are included. These demonstrations are adapted from those that we and our collaborators, Paul Rozin and Lila Gleitman (both of the University of Pennsylvania), have used in our own teaching.

A test-item file of approximately 3,000 questions has been prepared for the fifth edition by Su Boatright-Horowitz of the University of Rhode Island, Kingston, and Susan Rakowitz of Fairfield University. Paul Cornwell, late of Pennsylvania State University, Richard Day of McMaster University, and John Jonides of the University of Michigan have also contributed to this test bank. These questions span all nineteen chapters and the two appendices. Of course, this test-item file is also available on diskette in Windows and Macintosh formats and is free to all qualified adopters.

In addition, instructors will receive Norton Presentation Maker, a practical, easy-to-use CD-ROM that allows instructors to create dynamic multimedia presentations quickly and easily, drawing on all the line art in the text, selected photos, brief excerpts from Norton's *Introduction to Psychology* video (described below), and some of the interactive tutorials from the student Web site. Norton Presentation Maker is available to adopters on request.

We also continue to publish a set of over one hundred transparencies, many in color, and these are free to qualified adopters as well.

New for this edition is the Norton *Introduction to Psychology* video, a fifty-minute videocassette produced in cooperation with a team of six Norton authors: the three authors of this book as well as David Funder, Lyle E. Bourne, Jr., and Nancy Felipe Russo. These thirteen original short sequences can be integrated easily into lectures to introduce a topic, illustrate difficult or counterintuitive material, or emphasize a particularly important point. The contents of the video correspond roughly to the contents of *Psychology,* Fifth Edition, and include "Classical Research: Bandura's Bobo Doll Study," "The Brain and Behavior," "Sleep and Sleep Disorders," "Sensing and Perceiving Our World," Limitations of Classical Learning Theory," "Methods and Mistakes in Memory," "Building Complex Cognitive Processes," "Detecting Lies Nonverbally," "Culture and Social Behavior," "Dimensions of Development," "Exploring Personality," "Stress and Health," "Psychopathology: Dissociative Identity Disorder."

Finally, as a new resource for this edition, instructors will be able to use the data obtained from student participation in many of the interactive tutorials available in the *Psychology* WebBook described earlier. Each tutorial ends with a request for students to send their responses to the instructor or teaching assistant; in several cases, these responses are actually data derived from standard psychological procedures that we have reproduced in the tutorials (generally in shortened versions). Instructors can discuss these data with the class, putting the class's own results side by side with the published data discussed in the text.

ACKNOWLEDGMENTS

There remains the pleasant task of thanking the many friends and colleagues who helped so greatly in the various phases of writing this book and its predecessors. Some read parts of the manuscript and gave valuable advice and criticism. Others talked to us at length about various issues in the field. We are very grateful to them all. The many helpers on earlier editions, and the main areas in which they advised us, are listed first. The names of those who guided us in the production of the present edition follow.

BIOLOGICAL FOUNDATIONS

Elizabeth Adkins-Regan, Cornell University; Norman T. Adler, Yeshiva University; Robert C. Bolles, University of Washington; Brooks Carder; Dorothy Cheney, University of Pennsylvania; John D. Corbit, Brown University; Alan N. Epstein, late of the University of Pennsylvania; Steven Fluharty, University of Pennsylvania; Charles R. Gallistel, University of California, Los Angeles; Harvey J. Grill, University of Pennsylvania; Jerre Levy, University of Chicago; Martha McClintock, University of Chicago; Peter M. Milner, McGill University; Douglas G. Mook, University of Virginia; Allen Parducci, University of California, Los Angeles; Judith Rodin, University of Pennsylvania; Paul Rozin, University of Pennsylvania; Jonathan I. Schull, University of Rochester and Swarthmore College; Robert Seyfarth, University of Pennsylvania; Paul G. Shinkman, University of North Carolina; Peter Shizgall, Concordia University; W. John Smith, University of Pennsylvania; Edward M. Stricker, University of Pittsburgh.

LEARNING

Ruth Colwill, Brown University; Frank Costin, University of Illinois; Richard B. Day, McMaster University; Paula Durlach, McMaster University; Richard C. Gonzales, Bryn Mawr College; Robert Henderson, University of Illinois; Werner Honig, Dalhousie University; Francis W. Irwin, late of the University of Pennsylvania; Nicholas Mackintosh, Cambridge University; Robert Rescorla, University of Pennsylvania; Paul Rozin, University of Pennsylvania; Jonathan I. Schull, University of Rochester and Swarthmore College; Barry Schwartz, Swarthmore College; Richard L. Solomon, late of the University of Pennsylvania; John Staddon, Duke University.

SENSATION AND PERCEPTION

Linda Bartoshuk, Yale University; Michael Gamble, Malaspina College; Julian E. Hochberg, Columbia University; Leo M. Hurvich, University of Pennsylvania; Dorothea Jameson, late of the University of Pennsylvania; R. Duncan Luce, University of California, Irvine; Neil A. MacMillan, Brooklyn College; James L. McClelland, Carnegie-Mellon; Jacob Nachmias, University of

Pennsylvania; Edward Pugh, University of Pennsylvania; Irwin Rock, late of the University of California, Berkeley; Burton S. Rosner, Oxford University; Robert Steinman, University of Maryland; Denise Varner, University of Washington; Brian Wandell, Stanford University; Jeremy M. Wolfe, Massachussetts Institute of Technology; James L. Zacks, Michigan State University.

COGNITION

Lynn A. Cooper, Columbia University; Robert G. Crowder, Yale University; Lila R. Gleitman, University of Pennsylvania; Douglas Hintzman, University of Oregon; Francis C. Keil, Cornell University; Deborah Kemler, Swarthmore College; Stephen M. Kosslyn, Harvard University; John Jonides, University of Michigan; Michael McCloskey, Johns Hopkins University; Douglas Medin, University of Illinois; Morris Moscovitch, University of Toronto; Ulric Neisser, Cornell University; Daniel N. Osherson, Massachusetts Institute of Technology; David Premack, Emeritus, University of Pennsylvania; Miriam W. Schustack, University of California, San Diego; Myrna Schwartz, Moss Rehabilitation Hospital; Michael Turvey, University of Connecticut; Rose T. Zacks, Michigan State University.

LANGUAGE

Sharon L. Armstrong, Drake University; Anne Fowler, Bryn Mawr College; John Gilbert, University of British Columbia; Roberta Golinkoff, University of Delaware; Barbara Landau, University of Delaware; Elissa Newport, University of Rochester; Ruth Ostrin, Medical Research Council, Cambridge, England; Ted Suppala, University of Rochester; Kenneth Wexler, Massachusetts Institute of Technology.

SOCIAL PSYCHOLOGY

Solomon E. Asch, late of the University of Pennsylvania; Joel Cooper, Princeton University; Phoebe C. Ellsworth, University of Michigan; Frederick J. Evans, Carrier Foundation, Bellemead, N.J.; Larry Gross, University of Pennsylvania; Michael Lessac; Clark R. McCauley, Jr., Bryn Mawr College; Stanley Milgram, late of City College of New York; Martin T. Orne, University of Pennsylvania; Albert Pepitone, University of Pennsylvania; Dennis Regan, Cornell University; Lee Ross, Stanford University; John Sabini, University of Pennsylvania; Philip R. Shaver, University of California, Davis; R. Lance Shotland, Pennsylvania State University.

DEVELOPMENT

Justin Aronfreed, University of Pennsylvania; Thomas Ayres, Clarkson College of Technology; Renée Baillargeon, University of Illinois; Edwin Boswell, Ardmore, Pennsylvania; Anne L. Brown, University of Illinois; Adele Diamond, Eunice Kennedy Shriver Center; Carol S. Dweck, Columbia University; Margery B. Franklin, Sarah Lawrence College; Rochel Gelman,

University of California, Los Angeles; Frederick Gibbons, Iowa State University; Ellen Gleitman, Devon, Pennsylvania; Susan Scanlon Jones, Indiana University; Ed Kako, University of Pennsylvania; Philip J. Kellman, University of California, Los Angeles; Ellen Markman, Stanford University; Elizabeth Spelke, Massachusetts Institute of Technology; Douglas Wallen, Mankato State University; Sheldon White, Harvard University.

INTELLIGENCE

Jonathan Baron, University of Pennsylvania; James F. Crow, University of Wisconsin; Daniel B. Keating, University of Minnesota; Robert Sternberg, Yale University.

PERSONALITY

Hal Bertilson, Saint Joseph's University; Jack Block, Massachusetts Institute of Technology; Nathan Brody, Wesleyan University; Peter Gay, Yale University; Lewis R. Goldberg, University of Oregon, Eugene; Ruben Gur, University of Pennsylvania; Judith Harackiewicz, Columbia University; John Kihlstrom, University of California, Berkeley; Lester B. Luborsky, University of Pennsylvania; Carl Malmquist, University of Minnesota; Jerry S. Wiggins, University of British Columbia.

PSYCHOPATHOLOGY

Lyn Y. Abramson, University of Wisconsin; Lauren Alloy, Temple University; Kayla F. Bernheim, Livingston County Counseling Services; John B. Brady, University of Pennsylvania; Gerald C. Davison, University of Southern California; Leonard M. Horowitz, Stanford University; Steven Mathysse, McLean Hospital; Sue Mineka, Northwestern University; Ann James Premack, Somis, California; Rena Repetti, University of California, Los Angeles; Martin E. P. Seligman, University of Pennsylvania; Larry Stein, University of California, Irvine; Hans H. Strupp, Vanderbilt University; Paul L. Wachtel, College of the City University of New York; Ingrid I. Waldron, University of Pennsylvania; Richard Warner, University of Southern California; David R. Williams, University of Pennsylvania; Julius Wishner, late of the University of Pennsylvania; Lisa Zorilla, University of Pennsylvania.

INTELLECTUAL HISTORY

Mark B. Adams, University of Pennsylvania; David DeVries, New York University; Claire E. Gleitman, Ithaca College; Alan C. Kors, University of Pennsylvania; Elisabeth Rozin, Upper Darby, Pennsylvania; John Sabini, University of Pennsylvania; Harris B. Savin, Philadelphia, Pennsylvania.

Several colleagues reviewed the fourth edition carefully to give us guidance on the fifth. These include Emir Andrews, Memorial University; Gregory Ball, Johns Hopkins University; Mary Crawford, West Chester University; and Kathie Galotti, Carleton College.

Other colleagues read and commented on draft chapters for the current edition, and we're grateful for their input: Su Boatright-Horowitz, University of Rhode Island; Bruce Goldstein, University of Pittsburgh; Mark Hauser, Harvard University; John Henderson, Michigan State University; and James Russell, University of British Columbia.

Finally, a small number of friends and colleagues deserve special thanks for their roles in many contexts, including—but not limited to—this edition. First, our thanks to Wendy and Art Kohn and everyone else at Kwamba Studios, for their fine work on the new Web site and video.

Thanks also to Neil Macmillan, who wrote "Statistics: The Collection, Organization, and Interpretation of Data," an appendix for *Psychology,* with a fine sense of balance between the twin demands of the subject matter and expositional clarity.

Lila R. Gleitman not only wrote Chapter 9, "Language," she also has read virtually every chapter in every edition of this text and in all cases has done what she always does with the things we think and write about: She makes them better.

Paul Rozin has likewise read every chapter of the book, and his insightful and wide-ranging comments testify to his extraordinary breadth of knowledge and depth of thought. He has helped us see many facets of the field in a new way, especially those that involve issues of evolutionary and cultural development.

Friderike Heuer and Amy Jaffey have also served as advisors, consultants, and critics, helping us to find ways to think about difficult issues and ways to write about them. Their intellectual and personal support have been immeasurably valuable; the book is far better for their input.

Further thanks go to many people at W. W. Norton & Company: To Roy Tedoff, who managed the production of the book with his usual aplomb; to Antonina Krass, whose brilliance as a book designer always astounds us; to John McAusland and Frank Forney, who executed some fine new drawings and illustrations; to Ruth Mandel, who provided her sharp artistic eye in the supervision of the photo and art research and gave so generously of her time in so many useful and pleasant discussions; to Roberta Flechner, for her remarkable efforts in arranging the layouts; and to Claire Acher and Elena Passman, who helped in many phases of the editorial and graphic aspects of the book.

We are especially indebted to three highly competent and indefatigable Norton editors. One is Cathy Wick, who provided invaluable advice and continual encouragement, and whose personal contact with many psychology instructors throughout the country was of enormous benefit. The second is Margaret Farley, whose care and skill are everywhere evident and whose patience was unflagging no matter how we taxed her. The third is Jane Carter, a person of superb literary taste and judgment, who combines the skills of a first-rate organizer with those of a fine critic. We hope they all know how deeply we appreciate them.

Our final thanks go to Norton's chairman of the board, Donald Lamm. Neither Fridlund nor Reisberg has had the pleasure of working closely with Lamm, but the loss plainly is theirs, and even by proxy, they are aware of and immensely grateful for his talents and his enormous and continuing contribution to this book. As Gleitman put it in the previous edition, "Age has not withered nor custom staled his infinite variety. His ideas are as brilliant and outrageous as ever; his puns are as bad as ever. And my esteem and affection for him are as great as ever."

Merion, Pennsylvania
Santa Barbara, California
Portland, Oregon

October, 1998

P S Y C H O L O G Y

FIFTH EDITION

CHAPTER **1**

INTRODUCTION

THE SCOPE OF PSYCHOLOGY 1

ELECTRICALLY TRIGGERED IMAGES ■ AMBIGUOUS SIGHTS AND SOUNDS ■ THE PERCEPTUAL WORLD OF INFANTS ■ DISPLAYS AND THE EVOLUTION OF COMMUNICATION ■ COMPLEX SOCIAL BEHAVIOR IN HUMANS

A SCIENCE OF MANY FACES 5

DREAMS AS MENTAL EXPERIENCES ■ DREAMS AS BEHAVIOR ■ DREAMS AS COGNITION ■ DREAMS AND NATURAL SELECTION ■ DREAMS AND SOCIAL BEHAVIOR ■ DREAMS AND CULTURE ■ DREAMS AND INTERNAL CONFLICT ■ DREAMS AND HUMAN DEVELOPMENT ■ DREAMS AND INDIVIDUAL DIFFERENCES ■ PERSPECTIVES ON PSYCHOLOGY

THE TASK OF PSYCHOLOGY 11

hat is psychology? It is a field of inquiry that is sometimes defined as the science of the mind, sometimes as the science of behavior. It concerns itself with how and why organisms do what they do; why wolves howl at the moon and children rebel against their parents; why birds sing and moths fly into the flame; why we remember how to ride a bicycle twenty years after the last attempt; why humans speak and gesture and make love and war. All of these are kinds of behavior, and psychology is the science in which all of these are studied.

THE SCOPE OF PSYCHOLOGY

The phenomena that psychology takes as its province cover an enormous range. Some border on biology; others touch on social sciences such as anthropology and sociology. Some concern behavior in animals; many others pertain to behavior in humans. Some are about conscious experience; others focus on what people do regardless of what they think or feel. Some involve humans or animals in isolation; others concern what they do when they are in groups. A few examples will offer a glimpse of psychology's scope.

ELECTRICALLY TRIGGERED IMAGES

Consider the relation between biological mechanisms and psychological phenomena. Some investigators have developed a technique of electrically stimulating the brains of human patients who are about to undergo brain surgery. Such operations are generally conducted under local rather than general anesthesia. As a result, the patients are conscious, and their reports are often used to guide the neurosurgeon during the operation.

These and other procedures have shown that different parts of the brain have different psychological functions. For example, when stimulated in certain portions of the brain, patients have visual experiences—they see streaks of color or flickering lights. When stimulated in other regions, they hear clicks or buzzes. Stimulation in still other areas produces involuntary movement of parts of the body (Penfield and Roberts, 1959; Penfield, 1975).

Related findings come from studies that look at the rate at which blood flows through different parts of the brain. When any part of the body is especially active, more blood flows to it—to deliver oxygen and nutrients and to carry away waste products—and the brain is no exception. Thus when the patient reads silently, certain regions of the brain receive more blood (and are thus more active) than others. A different blood-flow pattern is found when the person reads aloud, yet another when he watches a moving light, and so on (Lassen, Ingvar, and Skinhoj, 1978).

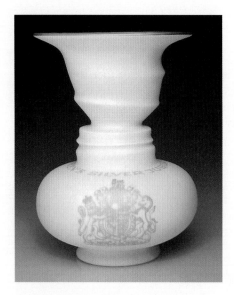

1.1 Reversible figure *Photograph of a vase celebrating the twenty-fifth year of the reign of Queen Elizabeth in 1977. Depending on how the picture is perceptually organized, we see either the vase or the profile of Queen Elizabeth and Prince Philip. (Courtesy of Kaiser Porcelain Ltd.)*

1.2 Perceptual bias *(A) An ambiguous form that can be seen either as (B) a rat or (C) a man with glasses. (After Bugelski and Alampay, 1961)*

AMBIGUOUS SIGHTS AND SOUNDS

Many psychological phenomena are best studied not biologically but at the psychological level. An example is the perception of ambiguous visual patterns. Consider Figure 1.1, which is a photograph of a vase created for Queen Elizabeth on the occasion of her Silver Jubilee. It is usually seen as a vase, but it can also be seen as the profiles of the queen and her consort, Prince Philip.

The way ambiguous figures are perceived often depends on what we have seen just before. Take Figure 1.2, which can be seen as either a rat or an amiable gentleman with glasses. If we are first shown an unambiguous figure of a rat, the ambiguous picture will be seen as a rat. If we are first exposed to an unambiguous face, the ambiguous figure will be perceived as a face.

What holds for visual patterns also holds for language. Many utterances are ambiguous. If presented out of context, they can be understood in several different ways. Take the following sentence, for example:

> The mayor ordered the police to stop drinking.

This sentence may refer to a command to enforce sobriety among the population at large. It may also be a call to end drunkenness among members of the police force. Just how it is understood depends on the context. A prior discussion of panhandlers and skid row probably would lead to the first interpretation; a comment about alcoholism among city employees would likely lead to the second.

THE PERCEPTUAL WORLD OF INFANTS

Phenomena of the sort we've just discussed document the enormous effect of prior experience on what we see and do. But this does not mean that all psychological accomplishments result from past experience. Some seem to be part of the equipment that all of us bring into the world when we are born. Take the infant's reaction to heights, for example.

Crawling infants seem to be remarkably successful in noticing the precipices of everyday life. A demonstration is provided by the visual cliff. This consists of a large glass table, which is divided in half by a wooden center board. On one side of the board, a checkerboard pattern is attached directly to the underside of the glass; on the other side, the same pattern is placed on the floor three feet below. To adults, this arrangement looks like a sudden drop-off in the center of the table. Six-month-old infants seem to see it in much the same way. When the infant is placed on the center board and called by his mother, his response

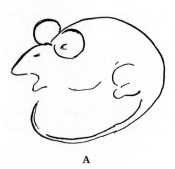

A

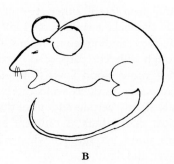

B

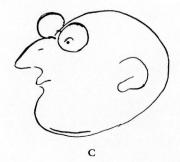

C

A

B

1.3 The visual cliff *(A) An infant is placed on the center board that is laid over a heavy sheet of glass, and his mother calls to him. If he is on the "shallow" side, he will not crawl across the apparent cliff. (Courtesy of Richard D. Walk) (B) A similar reaction in a kitten. (Courtesy of William Vandivert)*

depends on where she is when she beckons. When she is on the shallow side, he quickly crawls to her. But when she calls from the apparent precipice, discretion wins out over valor and the infant stays where he is (see Figure 1.3).

This result suggests that, to some extent at least, the perception of depth is not learned through experience but is built into our system from the very start.

DISPLAYS AND THE EVOLUTION OF COMMUNICATION

Thus far, all our examples have dealt with the behavior of individuals. But much of the subject matter of psychology is inherently social. This holds for animals no less than humans. For virtually all animals interact with others of their species, whether as mates, parents, offspring, or competitors.

In animals, many social interactions depend on largely innate forms of communication. An example is courtship in birds. Many species of birds have evolved elaborate bodily structures or rituals by which one sex—usually the male—woos the other. Just what this wooing consists of depends on the species. Some males court by making themselves conspicuous. The peacock spreads his magnificent tail feathers, the blue bird of paradise displays his plumage while hanging upside down from a branch, and the red frigate bird inflates his red throat pouch. Other males take a more romantic approach: The bower bird builds a special cabin that he decorates with colored fruit and flowers. The males of other species offer gifts. In all cases, the fundamental message is the same: "I am a male, healthy, and willing peacock (or bird of paradise, or frigate bird, or whatever), and hope that you will choose me as your mate" (see Figure 1.4).

Such social communications are based on displays that are specific to a particular species and that have arisen as a consequence of natural selection. They are ways by which individuals inform one another of their status and current intentions. Some are mating displays, as in the case of courtship rituals. Others are

1.4 Courting birds *Birds have evolved many diverse patterns of courtship behavior that are essentially built-in and characteristic of a particular species. (A) The peacock displays his tail feathers. (Photograph by Robert Estall/Corbis) (B) The blue bird of paradise shows off his plumage while hanging upside down from a branch. (Photograph by David Gillison/Peter Arnold, Inc.) (C) The frigate bird puffs up his red throat pouch. (Photograph by Wolfgang Kaehler/Corbis)*

A

B

C

threats ("Back off or else!"; see Figure 1.5A). Still others are attempts at appeasement ("Don't hurt me. I mean no harm!"). Some built-in displays form the foundation of expressions in humans. An example is the smile, a response found in all babies, even those born blind who couldn't have learned it by imitation. It is often considered a signal by which humans tell each other: "Be good to me. I wish you well" (see Figure 1.5B).

COMPLEX SOCIAL BEHAVIOR IN HUMANS

Human social interactions are generally much more subtle and flexible than those of other animals. Peacocks have just one way of courting: They spread their tail feathers and hope for the best. Human males and females are more complex, in courtship and many other social interactions. For much of human social life is based on one person's rational appraisal of how another person will respond to her actions: "If I do this . . . he will think this . . . then I will have to do this . . . ," and so on. Such subtleties are beyond the peacock. If his usual courtship ritual fails, he has no alternate strategy. He won't try to build bowers or offer flowers; all he can do is to display his tail feathers again and again.

While human social behavior has a strong element of rationality, there are some cases in which we seem to act with little thought or reason. This is especially likely when we are in large groups. An example is panic (see Figure 1.6). When someone shouts "Fire" in a crowded auditorium, the resulting stampede may claim many more victims than the fire itself would have. At the turn of the century, a Chicago theater fire claimed over six hundred victims, many of whom were smothered or trampled to death by the frantic mass behind them. In the words of a survivor, "The heel prints on the dead faces mutely testified to the cruel fact that human animals stricken by terror are as mad and ruthless as stampeding cattle" (Brown, 1965). The task for psychology is to try to understand why the crowd acted differently from the way each of its members would have acted alone.

A

B

1.5 Displays (A) Threat display of the male mandrill, a large West African baboon. (Photograph by George H. Harrison/Grant Heilman) (B) The human smile. (Photograph by Peter Hendrie/The Image Bank)

1.6 Panic Richard Bosman, 1982. (Collection of Robert H. Helmick; courtesy Brooke Alexander, New York)

A SCIENCE OF MANY FACES

These illustrations document the enormous range of psychology, whose territory borders on the biological sciences at one end and on the social sciences at the other. This broad range makes psychology a field of multiple perspectives, a science of many faces.

To make this point concrete, we will focus on one psychological phenomenon and show how it can be approached from several different directions. This phenomenon is dreaming. Dreaming is an interesting topic in its own right, but it is also an especially good illustration of how psychology approaches any single phenomenon, not just from one point of view but from several.

Let us start out by describing dreaming as we all experience it. A dream is a kind of nocturnal drama to which the only price of admission is falling asleep. It is usually a series of scenes—sometimes fairly commonplace, sometimes bizarre and disjointed—in which the dreamer often figures as a participant. While the dream unfolds, it is generally experienced as real. It sometimes seems so real in fact, that on waking one may wonder whether the dream events might have happened after all. As a Chinese sage wrote over two thousand years ago, "Once upon a time, I, Chuang-tzu, dreamed I was a butterfly, fluttering hither and thither. . . . Suddenly I was awakened. . . . Now I do not know whether I was a man dreaming I was a butterfly, or whether I am a butterfly now dreaming I am a man" (MacKenzie, 1965).

How can such intangible, fleeting events ever be a suitable topic for scientific inquiry?

DREAMS AS MENTAL EXPERIENCES

One way of looking at dreams is as conscious, mental experiences. According to an account that goes back to the Greek philosopher Aristotle, the dream happenings are mental evocations of sights and sounds that occurred during the dreamer's waking life. Aristotle believed that the succession of these dream images from the past is experienced as real while it occurs because there is no competition from the clamor of waking reality and because the intellect is "dulled" during sleep (Aristotle, ca. 330 B.C.).

Later investigators tried to relate what people dream about to what happens to them both before and during sleep. One question concerns the effect of recent waking experiences. Aristotle was apparently correct in his belief that they often reemerge in dreams, especially if they were highly emotional. For example, people who have just gone through an earthquake may relive their experience in nightmares (Wood et al., 1992).

Some writers have suggested that the dream images from the past are supplemented by external events that impinge upon the sleeper in the present. A widely cited example is the alarm clock, which is often said to turn into a peal of church bells or a fire engine in the dream. To test this hypothesis, several investigators have studied the effects of applying various forms of external stimulation during sleep. Numerous sleepers have been shaken, tickled, splashed with water, and shouted at, all to discover whether they would later report a dream that referred to these experiences. Sometimes they did, as in the dream reported on awakening after an experimenter shouted "Help" into the sleeper's ears: "I was driving along the highway at home. Heard yelling and we stopped. A car was turned sideways in the road. I went down and saw the car was turned over on the side of the road. . . . There was a woman badly cut. We took her to the hospital" (Hall, 1966, p. 6). It is hard to resist the conclusion that the dreamer heard and somehow understood the shout "Help" even while asleep and then incorporated it into his dream narrative.

DREAMS AS BEHAVIOR

Dreams as conscious, mental experiences are essentially private; they go on inside the individual. As such, dreams can be regarded as a form of behavior that is looked at from within, as if the actor were observing his own actions. Yet psychologists study most aspects of behavior from outside, for much of what we do is directly apparent and can therefore easily be seen by others. Humans and animals act. They run and fly and scurry about; they eat and fight and mate; they often perform new acts to attain their ends.

OVERT BEHAVIOR

Can we study dreaming from the outside by taking this action-oriented view? On the face of it, the prospects don't seem too bright, for during sleep the body is by and large immobile. Even so, there is a way. For there is one thing the sleeper does while dreaming that can be observed from the outside: She moves her eyes.

This fact emerged after it became clear that there are two kinds of sleep: slow-wave and REM (rapid eye movement) sleep. During slow-wave sleep, both breathing and heart rate are slow and regular, and the eyes roll slowly back and forth. But during REM sleep the pattern is different. Breathing and heart rate accelerate, and—most characteristic of all—the eyes dart back and forth irregularly behind closed eyelids. Periods of slow-wave and REM sleep alternate throughout the night, with periods of REM sleep ensuing about every ninety minutes (see Figure 1.7).

During REM sleep we experience vivid visual dreams. When participants—the persons whose behavior is being studied—are aroused during REM sleep, about 80 percent of the awakenings lead to reports of a vivid dream (Dement, 1974), although why the eyes move in REM sleep remains a mystery.

NEUROLOGICAL UNDERPINNINGS OF BEHAVIOR

Another clue to the nature of dreaming concerns its neurological basis. Most psychologists take it for granted that whatever we do or think has some physical basis in the activity of our brains. But how should we study the sleeping brain? One important tool is the electroencephalograph, or EEG, which measures the brain's overall electrical activity. The EEG's graphic record depicts the patterns often called brain waves (see Figure 1.8).

EEG patterns of sleeping and waking differ markedly. As an individual falls into deeper and deeper stages of sleep, the brain waves become slow, large, and rather regular, indicating a lower level of brain activity. But this holds only for periods of slow-wave sleep. When this is interrupted by REM sleep, the EEG becomes quite similar to that found when the person is awake. This makes good sense, for it suggests that during REM sleep the brain is reasonably aroused and active—as well it should be, since we are busily engaged in vivid dreaming.

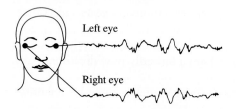

1.7 Eye movements and REM sleep
Record of eye movements picked up by electrodes at the side of each eye. The record shows the eye-movement pattern during REM sleep, a period when sleepers have vivid pictorial dreams. (After Dement, 1974)

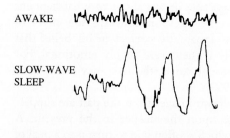

1.8 Sleep and the EEG *The figure shows EEG records during waking, slow-wave sleep, and REM sleep. (Courtesy of William C. Dement)*

DREAMS AS COGNITION

Like many other psychological phenomena, dreams reflect what we know and what we have experienced, remembered, or thought about—activities that psychologists call *cognition*. To be sure, the dream happenings didn't really take place. We didn't really fly through the air or have tea with Queen Elizabeth. But the components of the dream were surely drawn from the dreamer's own knowledge, which contains information about flying and the queen of England. How was this knowledge retrieved and woven into the dream story? How was the dream recalled on later awakening? And why is it that most of us remember so few of our dreams?

Some psychologists have tried to answer these and related questions by asking about the factors that promote better dream recall. They have collected some evidence that people who remember more of their dreams are more likely to have better and sharper visual mental images in their waking life; perhaps their dreams are more memorable because they are experienced in a more vivid pictorial form (Cory et al., 1975). Another factor is the extent to which the dream experience is interfered with by what happens immediately after the sleeper awakes. In one study, subjects were asked to call the weather bureau immediately after waking up; after this, they had to write down a detailed description of any dreams they had that night. The results showed that the weather reports interfered with the dream recall. The participants who made the call generally remembered having a dream, but most of them could not remember what they had dreamed about (Cohen and Wolfe, 1973).

DREAMS AND NATURAL SELECTION

Humans may not be the only dreamers. Many dog owners have watched their pets twitch, whimper, and bark while sleeping. Are their dogs dreaming? Do other animals dream, too? And if dreaming is widespread among non-human animals, then does it provide some evolutionary advantage?

We cannot ask other animals whether they dream, but we *can* find out whether they have REM sleep. Studies on this subject use the comparative approach in which many species are surveyed for insights about a behavior's possible functions and evolutionary history. Such studies show that amphibians and fishes do not show REM sleep, that reptiles may, and that birds and mammals do (with only two exceptions so far—the spiny anteater and the dolphin). But whether the REM sleepers of the animal kingdom actually have dream lives is entirely a matter of conjecture.

DREAMS AND SOCIAL BEHAVIOR

Human life is rarely solitary but is spent, instead, among a world of others—strangers and friends, partners and rivals, potential and actual mates. What holds for waking existence, holds for dreams as well. Some dreams feature themes of aggression, such as competition, attack, and submission. Others concern friendship and sometimes sex. But whatever the plot, the cast usually includes other people. More than 95 percent of our dreams are peopled with others, and most revolve around our relations with them (Hall and Van de Castle, 1966).

1.9 Iroquois cornhusk mask for dream ceremony *The Iroquois Indians regarded dreams as an important means for revealing hidden desires and held formal dream-remembering ceremonies during which special masks were worn. (Courtesy of Staatlicher, Museum für Völkerkunde, Munich)*

DREAMS AND CULTURE

Dreams concern major themes in the person's own life, but they take place within a larger framework, the dreamer's own culture. In our society, a common dream is of appearing naked among strangers and being embarrassed. But in a culture where it is normal to wear no clothes, such a dream would be unlikely. Nor are many urban Americans likely to have nightmares in which they are chased by cows, which happens to be a common dream in western Ghana (Barnouw, 1963).

Culture affects not only what the dream is about but also how the dreamer thinks about it when she recalls it. In some societies, including our own, dreams are generally dismissed as nonsensical fantasies, irrelevant to real life. Many pre-literate cultures have a different view (see Figure 1.9). Some regard dreams as supernatural visions and behave accordingly. Others take dreams very seriously even though they think of them as naturally occurring events. The Senoi, a tribe in Malaya, act as if they had all taken several courses in psychoanalysis. They believe that dreams indicate something about their inner lives and can provide clues for heading off problems before they become serious. Every morning Senoi children tell their fathers what they dreamed about the night before. The fathers then help the children interpret their dreams. These may reveal some incipient conflict with others, as in a dream of being attacked by a friend. If so, the father may advise the child on how to correct matters, for example, by giving the friend a present (Stewart, 1951).

DREAMS AND INTERNAL CONFLICT

The social aspect of dreaming lies at the heart of a famous (and controversial) theory of dreams proposed by Sigmund Freud. According to Freud, dreams are the product of a clash between two contending forces—the unconscious primitive urges of our biological heritage and the civilizing constraints imposed by society. In dreams we sometimes see one, sometimes the other side of the battle. Various forbidden impulses—mostly sexual and aggressive—emerge, but they are soon opposed by the thou-shalt-nots of our early upbringing. The result is a compromise. The forbidden material breaks through but only in a censored form (see Figure 1.10). This disguise explains why dreams are so often odd and senseless. Their senselessness is only on the surface, a cunning mask that lets us indulge in the unacceptable wish without realizing that it is unacceptable (Freud, 1900).

DREAMS AND HUMAN DEVELOPMENT

Thus far, we have discussed dreams as they are experienced by adults. But of course dreams occur in childhood as well. Psychologists who are concerned with the course of human mental development have considered the different ways in which children and adults think about their dreams.

Developmental psychologists want to know how children acquire the basic intellectual operations that are part of adult human thought—how they learn to count, to understand that events have causes, and so on. For example, they ask how children learn that there is a difference between two realms of phenomena, those that we call *subjective* (thoughts, beliefs, and, of course, dreams) and those

1.10 Symbolism in dreams *A film about Freud's early career includes a dream sequence in which he enters a deep tunnel that eventually leads him to a cavern where his mother sits, smiling, on a Cleopatra-like throne. The dream is a compact symbolic expression of how Freud saw himself: an explorer of subterranean unconscious motives who uncovered the hidden childhood lusts of all men and women. (From John Huston's 1963 film,* Freud, *with Montgomery Clift. Courtesy The Museum of Modern Art/Film Stills Archive)*

That very night in Max's room a forest grew

and grew—

The distinction between dreams and waking reality is not always clear in childhood
(From Sendak, 1963)

that we call *objective* (the world of tangible things "out there"). To ask how this distinction is made is another way of asking how we attain our adult notion of objective reality, how we come to know that the tree in the garden—unlike a dream—will still be there after we blink our eyes.

This distinction is by no means clear in early childhood. Thus, young children initially have great trouble in distinguishing dreams from waking life. A three-year-old awakes and tells her parents how much she loved the elephants at the circus yesterday. The parents correct her; she was not at the circus yesterday. But the child defiantly sticks to her story and appeals to her brother for corroboration, for "he was there, too." When her brother shakes his head in denial, she begins to cry, angrily insisting that she told the truth. Eventually, she learns that there is a whole group of experiences that older people call "just dreams," no matter how real they seem to her (Levy, 1979).

The fact that the child finally recognizes the circus elephants—and the nightmare monsters and witches—as dreams does not mean that she has acquired an adult conception of what dreams are. Young children tend to think of them as physical objects. When asked whether dreams can be tall, a four-year-old replied, "Yeah. How tall? Big, big, big, (spread arms). Where are dreams? In your bedroom. In the daytime? No they're outside. . . . What are they like? They're made of rock. Could they be heavy? Yeah; and they can't break either" (Keil, 1979, pp. 109–10).

It's quite a while before children think of dreams the way adults do. By six or seven, they believe that dreams are sent through the air, perhaps by the wind or by pigeons. Eventually they recognize that, as one eleven-year-old put it, "You dream with the head and the dream is in the head" (Piaget, 1972).

9

This realization that dreams are subjective events is no small achievement. As we will see later, the recognition that some experiences are subjective, inner happenings is not limited to dreams but extends to many other conceptual attainments about the basic nature of the physical and psychological universe.

DREAMS AND INDIVIDUAL DIFFERENCES

There is a further aspect of dreams: They reflect the fact that people are different. People vary in what they characteristically do and think and feel. And some of these differences are reflected in their dreams. Some simply pertain to the differing circumstances in the dreamers' lives. This point was made some two thousand years ago by the Roman poet Lucretius, who noted that at night lawyers plead their cases, generals fight their battles, and sailors wage their war with the winds (Woods, 1947).

More interesting are differences that reveal something about the personalities of the dreamers. An example is a comparison of the dreams of normal people and of patients with schizophrenia, a serious mental disorder. The difference between the two groups was enormous. The schizophrenics reported dreams that were bizarre and often morbid: The dreamer is eaten alive by an alligator; there are nuclear wars and world cataclysms. Themes of bodily mutilation were fairly common, as in a dream in which a woman killed her husband and then stuffed parts of his body into a camel's head. In contrast, the normals' dreams were comparatively mild and ordinary. This result fits what we know about many cases of schizophrenia. Schizophrenics often jump from one idea to the other without maintaining a coherent line of thought. As a result, their behavior often appears bizarre. And they often report great personal turmoil and distress. It seems that their extremely bizarre and morbid dreams are simply an exaggeration of a condition already present in their waking lives (Carrington, 1972).

PERSPECTIVES ON PSYCHOLOGY

We have seen that dreams can be looked at as conscious, mental experiences, as overt behaviors, as aspects of cognition, as a consequence of natural selection, as indications of social patterns, as reflections of human development, and as expressions of the dreamer's individuality. What holds for dreams holds for most other psychological phenomena: They can all be viewed from several perspectives. Each perspective is valid, but none is complete without the others, for psychology is a field of many facets, and to see it fully, we must look at them all.

Given the multifaceted character of psychology, it is not surprising that those who have contributed to it came from many quarters. Some had the proper title of *psychologist* with appropriate university appointments in that discipline, including two of its founding fathers, Wilhelm Wundt of Germany and William James of the United States. But psychology was not built by psychologists alone—far from it. Among its architects are philosophers, beginning with Plato and Aristotle and continuing to our own time. Physicists and physiologists played important roles and still do. Physicians contributed greatly, as did specialists in many other disciplines, including anthropology and, more recently, linguistics and computer science. Psychology, the field of many faces, is by its very nature a field of many origins.

The Dream *by Pablo Picasso, 1932 (Courtesy of the Ganz Collection/Scala/Art Resources)*

In presenting the subject matter of psychology as it is today, we must try to do justice to this many-sidedness. In an attempt to achieve that, this book has been organized around five topics that emphasize somewhat different perspectives on the field as a whole and that mirror the different ways in which we have just looked at dreams: action, cognition, social behavior, development, and individual differences.

THE TASK OF PSYCHOLOGY

Psychology is sometimes popularly regarded as a field that concentrates on the secret inner lives of individual persons—why Mary hates her mother and why George is so shy around women. But questions of this sort are really not psychology's main concern. The primary questions psychology asks are of a more general sort. Its purpose is not to describe the distinctive characteristics of a particular individual. Its main goal is to get at what is true for all of humankind.

The reason is simple. Like all other sciences, psychology looks for general principles—underlying uniformities among different events. A single event as such means little; what counts is what any one event—or object or person—shares with others. Ultimately of course, psychology—again, like all other sciences—hopes to find a route back to understanding the individual event. It tries to discover, say, some general principles of adolescent conflict or parent-child relations to explain why George is so shy and why Mary is so bitter about her mother. Once such explanations are found, they may lead to practical applications: to help counsel and guide, and perhaps to effect desirable changes. But, at least initially, the science's main concern is with the discovery of the general principles.

Is there any field of endeavor whose primary interest is in individual persons, with the unique George and Mary who are like no other persons who ever lived or ever will live? One such field is literature. The great novelists and playwrights have given us portraits of living, breathing individuals who exist in a particular time and place. There is nothing abstract and general about the agonies of a Hamlet or the murderous ambition of a Macbeth. These are concrete, particular individuals, with special loves and fears that are peculiarly theirs. But from these particulars, Shakespeare gives us a glimpse of what is common to all humanity, what Hamlet and Macbeth share with all of us. Both science and art have something to say about human nature, but they come to it from different directions. Science tries to discover general principles and then to apply them to the individual case. Art focuses on the particular instance and then uses this to illuminate what is universal in us all.

Science and art are complementary. To gain insight into our own nature we need both. Consider Hamlet's description:

> What a piece of work is a man, how noble in reason, how infinite in faculties; in form and moving how express and admirable, in action like an angel, in apprehension like a god: the beauty of the world, the paragon of animals! (*Hamlet,* Act II, scene ii).

To understand and appreciate this "piece of work" is a task too huge for any one field of human endeavor, whether art, philosophy, or science. What we will try to do here is to sketch psychology's own attempts toward this end, to show what we have come to know and how we have come to know it—and perhaps even more important, how much remains to be learned.

Wilhelm Wundt (1832–1920) *(Courtesy of Archives of the History of American Psychology)*

William James (1842–1910) *(Courtesy of The Warder Collection)*

PART ONE

ACTION

CHAPTER **2**

BIOLOGICAL BASES OF BEHAVIOR

Why should psychologists study the brain and nervous system? Why not leave such bodily details to the biologists and just study the mind? There are several reasons. First, it is a simple historical fact that much in psychology has been learned from the study of how our brains and bodies work. Second, it is important that we aren't just minds; we are minds embodied. Our knowledge about the world enters through our sensory apparatus, we act in the world using our neuromuscular equipment, and we think and reason about the world using the circuitry of our nervous system. This means that psychology cannot be disentangled from biology, and the fullest picture of our behavior requires an understanding of the hardware that enacts it. To be sure, psychologists don't study this hardware as an end in itself but as a way to learn more about the fundamental questions of psychology: What do we humans know? How do we come to know it? What do we want? Why do we act in the ways we do? In this section we present a biological perspective that emphasizes the ways in which the study of our brains, nervous systems, and hormones can help us understand these broad psychological questions.

hat are the biological foundations of mental life? The first steps toward an answer came from the study of human and animal action. The ancients, no less than we, wondered why humans and other animals behave as they do. What is it that impels the crab to crawl or the tiger to spring? Prescientific peoples could only answer animistically: There is some inner spirit in the creature that impels it to move, each creature in its own fashion. Today, we know that any question about bodily movement must inevitably call for some reference to the nervous system, for to us it is quite clear that the nervous system is the apparatus that most directly determines an organism's reactions to the world in which it lives.

THE ORGANISM AS A MACHINE

The idea that the brain is really some kind of complicated machinery to be analyzed like any other—by taking it apart, by seeing how the parts connect, and by testing what each of the parts does—was first raised seriously by the French philosopher René Descartes (1596–1650). His answer provides the broad outline for our thoughts about such matters even now.

Descartes lived in a period that saw the beginning of the science of mechanics. Kepler and Galileo were beginning to develop ideas about the movements of the heavenly bodies that some thirty years later led to Newton's *Principia*. Radically new views of the universe were being put forth. Laws were discovered that could explain natural phenomena ranging from the drop of a stone to the

1 5

motions of planets. These same laws could be seen operating—rigidly, precisely, immutably—in the workings of ingenious mechanical contrivances that were all the rage in the wealthy homes of Europe: cuckoo clocks that sounded on the hour, water-driven gargoyles with nodding heads, statues in the king's garden that bowed to visitors who stepped on hidden springs. The turning of a gear, the release of a spring—these simple mechanisms could cause all kinds of clever effects. With all these intellectual and technical developments in place, and with so many complex phenomena explicable in such simple terms, it was only a matter of time before someone asked the crucial question: Could human thoughts and actions be explained just as mechanically?

DESCARTES AND THE REFLEX CONCEPT

To Descartes all action, whether human or animal, was essentially a response to some event in the outside world. Something from the outside excites one of the senses. This, in turn, excites a nerve that transmits the excitation upward to the brain, which then relays the excitation downward to a muscle. The excitation from the senses thus eventually leads to a contraction of a muscle and thereby to a reaction to the external event that started the whole sequence. In effect, the energy from the outside is *reflected back* by the nervous system to the animal's muscles. The term **reflex** finds its origin in this conception (Figure 2.1).

Seen in this light, human and animal doings could be regarded as the doings of a machine. But there was a problem. The same external event produces one reaction today and another tomorrow. The sight of food might lead to reaching movements on one occasion (if we are hungry) but to some entirely different response in some other circumstance. It seems, therefore, that excitation from the senses can stimulate a nerve leading to one muscle on one occasion but an entirely different nerve, and a completely different set of muscles, on some other occasion. This suggests that Descartes' mechanism must have a central switching system, supervised by some operator who sits in the middle to decide which incoming pipe to connect with which outgoing one.

How did Descartes explain this switching system? A strictly mechanical explanation would be both difficult and dangerous. For one thing, Descartes was deeply concerned over the theological implications of this argument. If all human action was to be explained mechanically, then what role was left for the soul? For another, he was prudent—he knew that Galileo had had difficulties with the Inquisition because his scientific beliefs threatened the doctrines of the Church. So he shrank from taking the last step in his own argument. Instead, he proposed that human mental processes were only semimechanical. Many processes within the brain did function in a mechanical way, but what distinguished us from other animals, what made reason and choice possible, was the soul—operating through a particular structure in the brain and choosing among the nervous pathways that would determine our actions.

But as theology's grip on science loosened, later thinkers went further. They believed that the laws of the physical universe could ultimately explain all action, whether human or animal, so that a scientific account required no further "ghost in the machine"—that is, no reference to the soul. They ruthlessly extended Descartes' logic to human beings, arguing that humans differ from other animals only in being more finely constructed mechanisms.

It should be emphasized that Descartes' thinking was guided both by theology and by his perception of a key analogy—the analogy between human action and the workings of a machine. This is a common pattern in science, with inves-

René Descartes *(Courtesy National Library of Medicine)*

2.1 Reflex action as envisaged by Descartes *In this sketch by Descartes, the heat from the fire, A, starts a chain of processes that begins at the affected spot of the skin, B, and continues up the nerve tube until a pore of a cavity, F, is opened. Descartes believed that this opening allowed the animal spirits in the cavity to enter the nerve tube and eventually travel to the muscles that pull the foot from the fire. While the figure shows that Descartes anticipated the basic idea of reflex action, it also indicates that he did not realize the anatomical distinction between sensory and motor nerves. (From Descartes, 1662)*

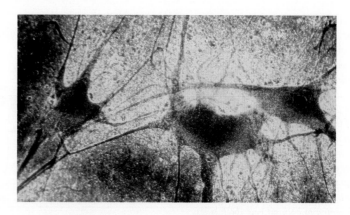

2.2 Observing the nervous system through a microscope *Nerve cells in the spinal cord. (Photograph by Cabisco/Visuals Unlimited)*

tigators often gaining enormous insights from one analogy or another. Of course, Descartes' analogy drew on the technology of his day, and so he envisioned the human "machine" as one in which fluid pressures and levers and gears led eventually to the actions we see. Later theorists improved upon this idea, although they, too, drew on the technology that surrounded them. Thus, in the 1950s, many scholars likened the brain to a giant telephone switchboard; in more recent years, many have suggested that the brain is like a complex computer. In all these cases, though, Descartes' key insight remains: that we can explain mental processes in terms of machinery in which some kind of energy (say, electrical or chemical) is transformed, first, into some other form and then eventually into bodily movement. The details of the proposed machine have changed drastically over the years, but the basic idea remains.★

HOW THE NERVOUS SYSTEM IS STUDIED

The total number of neurons in the human brain has been estimated to be as high as a thousand billion, with each neuron connecting to as many as ten thousand others (Nauta and Feirtag, 1986). Considering that all these interconnections occur in an organ that weighs only three to four pounds, it is no wonder that the human brain is sometimes said to be the most complex object in the universe.

How can such a complex object be studied? Neuroscientists have developed many ways to approach the basic questions of how the brain works and which parts of the brain affect (and are affected by) which aspects of behavior. These investigative techniques have told us much about our brains and our behavior. Some of the new techniques allow us to observe the operations of the **neurons,** the individual nerve cells that act as the information processors of the nervous system (see Figure 2.2). Others permit us to eavesdrop on the workings of living

★ In the final analysis, though, believing that humans are just machines—of whatever kind—will always be an act of faith (as is believing that we aren't just machines), because no one knows how to test for the existence of an immaterial (and hence unmeasurable) soul. What is undeniable, however, is that the strategy of acting *as though* humans are machines has led to dramatic breakthroughs in understanding ourselves and our fellow animals.

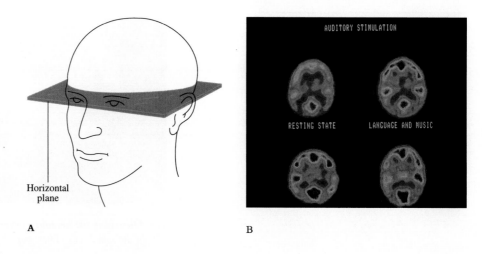

2.3   Observing the living brain with PET scans   *(A) Horizontal plane of brain used in taking the PET (positron emission tomography) scan. (B) Four PET scans taken while the participant rests, listens to someone talk, listens to music, or both. These scans indicate the degree of metabolic activity in different parts of the brain, viewed in horizontal cross section as shown in the diagram with the front of the head on top. Red indicates the most intense activity and blue the least. Listening to speech activates the left side of the brain, listening to music activates the right side, and listening to both activates both sides. (PET scans taken by Dr. John Mazziotta, UCLA School of Medicine, et al./Science Photo Library/Photo Researchers)*

human brains without seriously disturbing their owners (see Figure 2.3A and B). These techniques are often used in combination to give the fullest picture of brain function. We discuss them next.

CLINICAL OBSERVATION

Probably the first technique to be used for studying the brain was the direct **clinical observation** of patients with brain damage or disease. The object is to try to link physical brain abnormality with observable changes in behavior. Sometimes the brain abnormality is self-evident, and the effects on behavior must be evaluated. Such was the celebrated (and grisly) case of Phineas Gage, who in 1848 was working as a construction foreman. While preparing a site for demolition, some blasting powder misfired and launched a three-foot iron tamping rod into his cheek, through the front part of his brain, and out the top of his head (Figure 2.4). Gage lived, though not well. As we will see below, he suffered intellectual and emotional impairments that gave valuable clues about the roles of the brain's frontal lobes (Valenstein, 1986).

In other clinical cases, the behavioral effects are known but the brain damage can't be assessed until after death. The search for the brain regions responsible for speech is one example. They were first isolated during autopsy by examining the brains of adults who had suffered traumatic losses of speech years before (see pp. 35–37 below).

Clinical observation is not without its problems, however, and the major one concerns how generalizable it is. For example, would Phineas Gage's case tell us how *everyone* with frontal lobe damage behaves? Unfortunately, the answer is no. No two people ever suffer exactly the same brain damage, show exactly the same changes in behavior following the damage, or have exactly the same pattern of abilities before the damage. Thus, more definite statements about brain-behavior relationships often require more precise investigative techniques.

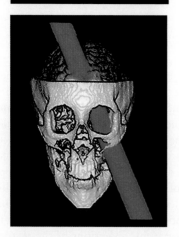

2.4   Phineas Gage's skull   *(A) A photograph showing the damage to Phineas Gage's skull. (Courtesy of the Warren Anatomical Museum, Harvard Medical School) (B) A computer reconstruction showing the path of the rod. (From Damasio et al., 1994; © 1994 by American Association for the Advancement of Science; courtesy of Hanna Damasio)*

INVASIVE TECHNIQUES

Since about 1850, experimenters have gone beyond clinical observation and begun to deal with the brain directly, by opening the skull and "invading" the brain matter (hence, the term *invasive*) while the subject is alive. Once inside, the investigator can activate a given region of the brain—or inactivate it —and watch for any changes in behavior. Tissue can be stimulated with weak applications of electricity, chemicals, heat, or cold, or it can be *lesioned* (destroyed in place) using more potent forms of each. Brain tissue can also be *ablated* (removed) with a vacuum or scalpel, and if the connecting pathways to that tissue are known, then the tissue can be isolated by cutting—technically, *transecting*—the relevant pathways.

Although such procedures are most frequently employed on laboratory animals, they have also been used in some special circumstances on humans. For example, patients who suffer epileptic seizures but are unresponsive to medication can sometimes be helped if the particular brain cells prone to seizure are destroyed, but it is crucial that this surgery not destroy the healthy surrounding cells. In this case, the neurosurgeon is aided by a little-known fact about the brain, namely, that its own tissue is largely insensitive to pain. This allows neurosurgery to be conducted under local anesthesia, with the patient conscious throughout. It also lets the surgeon determine the precise boundaries of various brain regions by electrically stimulating the tissue and observing the effects. For example, the patient's "speech areas" can be precisely located by observing whether stimulation of the tissue causes the patient to halt and stutter while trying to talk. This tissue can then be spared when the diseased cells are finally destroyed.

Still other techniques provide clues to brain function by *intracranial recording* of brain activity during some behavior. In some cases, both the monitoring and stimulation are electrical; in others, the stimulation is chemical. For example, neuroscientists have implanted tiny tubes called *cannulas* that permit the injection or withdrawal of small quantities of brain chemicals that may be involved in the behavior.

Obviously, these invasive techniques engender a host of ethical quandaries— especially when the humans involved cannot give full consent or when disabling and possibly painful procedures are conducted with animals. Some ethical lapses deserve, and have resulted in, professional censure or criminal prosecution. Nevertheless, when used advisedly, invasive techniques have their place and are invaluable not only in producing basic knowledge, but also in treating a variety of both human and animal disorders.

NEUROIMAGING TECHNIQUES

In the last few decades, our understanding of the linkage between brain and behavior has been revolutionized by a number of *neuroimaging instruments.* These provide us with remarkable views of the brain's anatomy (structure) or its physiology (function), with absolutely no invasion of brain tissue and with the brain's owner awake and fully conscious.

One technique for imaging brain anatomy is the *CT (computerized tomography) scan* (or *CAT scan,* an abbreviation for *computerized axial tomography*). It employs a narrow beam (an "axis") of X rays that is aimed through the patient's head and hits a detector on the opposite side. This beam moves in a slow circular arc, and the detector moves along with it. Since different brain tissues vary in density, they block the X rays to different degrees. A computer eventually constructs a composite picture based on the X-ray views from all the different angles (see Figure 2.5).

The most widely used neuroimaging technique currently is *magnetic resonance imaging (MRI).* MRI scans are safer because they use no X rays, relying instead upon a physical principle called *nuclear magnetic resonance.* This refers to the fact

2.5 CT scan The CT scan shows a subarachnoid hemorrhage (the arachnoid is one of the meninges, membranes that envelop the brain), resulting from a ruptured blood vessel. The hemorrhage is the light area over the right side of the brain (left on image). It looks white because there was considerable bleeding; blood absorbs more radiation than ordinary brain tissue. (Courtesy Radiography Dept., Royal Victoria Infirmary, Newcastle-upon-Tyne. Photo by Simon Fraser, Science Photo Library/Photo Researchers, Inc.)

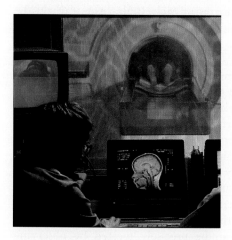

2.6 Magnetic resonance imaging (MRI)
A patient goes through the MRI procedure, while a medical specialist watches the image on a screen. (Photograph © Paul Shambroom)

that the nuclei at the center of atoms have their own resonant frequencies: If you perturb them, they sing like tuning forks as they bounce back to normal. Because the different structures of the brain have different chemical compositions, the nuclei of their atoms sing differently. An MRI scan disturbs these atoms by passing a very high frequency alternating magnetic field through the brain by means of electromagnets surrounding the patient's head. As the magnetic field fluctuates, the chorus of atomic voices is detected by magnetic sensors within the scanner. A computer then assembles the data to form a magnificently detailed picture of the brain that can show tumors, sites of tissue degeneration, and the blood clots and leaks that may signal strokes (see Figure 2.6).

CT and MRI scans typically allow only anatomical depictions: They can reveal brain structures but not whether those structures are active or are participating in a given behavior. To reveal function, experimenters use several techniques that measure brain physiology. The earliest developed was *electroencephalography.* The electroencephalograph (or *EEG*) detects tiny electrical currents generated by neurons on the surface of the brain and only requires taping tiny metal electrodes to the top and sides of the head. The EEG's reaction to a repeated stimulus can also be averaged by a computer, yielding *event-related potentials* (sometimes called *evoked potentials*). EEGs find their greatest use today in diagnosing epilepsy and sleep disorders; event-related potentials are valuable in verifying the intactness of our sensory and neuromuscular pathways.

For a time, it seemed that investigators could view anatomy in depth (with the CT and MRI scans) but could observe physiology only from the brain surface (using EEG's or event-related potentials). The breakthrough that allowed in-depth, three-dimensional localization of brain function was the *positron emission tomography* (or *PET*) *scan.* In PET scans, the participant is injected with a safe dose of radioactive sugar that resembles glucose (the only metabolic fuel the brain can use) but which emits subatomic particles called *positrons.* Brain cells that are particularly active at any moment will take up more of this substance and thus give off more positrons, which are then detected and from which an image is assembled in much the same way as CT and MRI scans. The resulting PET scan can thus tell the physician that a certain region within the brain is abnormally active or inactive, and this may suggest a tumor, a lesion, or a psychological disorder (see Figures 2.7 and 2.8).

2.7 PET scans and mental disorders
The scans show the difference in metabolic levels in normal, schizophrenic, and depressed individuals. Red indicates highest metabolic activity, with yellow next, followed by green, and then blue. During depression, for example, brain activity is considerably reduced, especially in the frontal areas. (NIH/SPL/Photo Researchers)

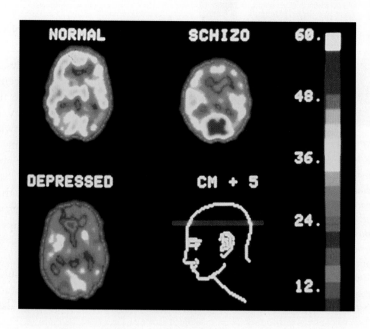

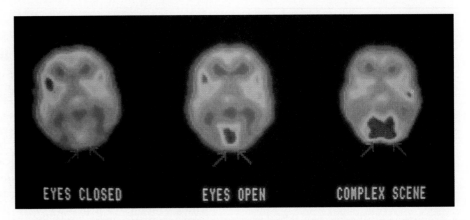

2.8 PET scan and visual stimulation *PET scans also show the difference in metabolic brain activity in healthy subjects. This scan shows metabolic activity when the patient's eyes were closed or when she was viewing a simple or complex scene. (Photograph by Dr. John Mazziotta et al./Photo Researchers)*

As powerful as this technique is, the PET scan has some liabilities. Since radioactive material must be injected, a given PET scan session cannot last too long lest the patient receive too much radiation. Moreover, the radioactive material takes time to be absorbed by active brain cells and to wash out later. This means that PET scan images change too slowly to capture fast-changing brain events. Both of these problems are avoided, however, by a still newer technique called ***functional MRI (fMRI) scanning*** (Figure 2.9). This technique adapts standard MRI procedures to provide exquisite depictions of anatomy. It can also be used to measure fast-changing physiology (mostly blood flow and oxygen use in the brain). Already, neuroscientists have connected fMRIs to three-dimensional virtual reality displays to give an in-depth view of a brain at work on a cognitive task or of a damaged brain that may require neurosurgical correction.

2.9 fMRI *This fMRI scan shows activation in the visual cortex after visual stimulation. The colored activation map is superimposed on a high-resolution anatomical scan, which is rendered in 3-D. (Image generated by Dr. Krish Singh)*

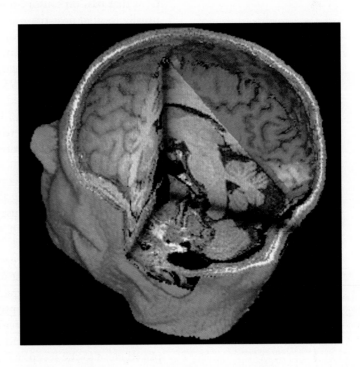

THE ARCHITECTURE OF THE NERVOUS SYSTEM

Our studies of the nervous system, whether based on clinical observation or invasive or neuroimaging techniques, have taught us much. In the following we will discuss some of what we have learned, starting with what we now know about the evolution and development of the nervous system, next discussing how the nervous system communicates with the rest of the body, and finally turning to the gross structures of the nervous system.

Of course, describing *the* nervous system is impossible, because there is no generic nervous system. The nervous system of a roundworm or a cockroach differs greatly from that of a dog or a human. Nonetheless, the architectural principles of all nervous systems—the genes that dictate their designs, the cells and chemicals that make up their circuitry—are quite similar. All nervous systems, from the cockroach's to the human's, appear, in fact, to be offshoots of one basic design. The divergences from this design, however, are what make the dog uniquely dogish and ourselves uniquely human.

THE EVOLUTION OF NERVOUS SYSTEMS

One important way in which nervous systems differ from one another is in their degree of regional versus central control. Generally, more complex animals show more central control, whereas in simpler animals, like many invertebrates, regional rule predominates. For example, sea anemones (flowery-looking animals that latch onto the ocean bottom and strain seawater for food) have networks of nerves with no obvious focus of connection. Slightly more complex invertebrates like mollusks (for example, snails, oysters, clams, and octopuses) have neurons that control individual movements, with these neurons clumping together to form **ganglia** (singular, *ganglion*). These ganglia serve primarily as relay stations that pass on sensory messages from the sense organs to the muscles and are usually located near the muscles they control. One mollusk, the sea snail *Aplysia,* has five ganglia that control the animal's entire repertoire of behaviors: sucking food in and out of its siphon, moving its eyes and tentacles, working its sticky foot to enable motion, and managing circulation, gill-breathing, and reproduction (Krasne and Glanzman, 1995; Rosenzweig et al., 1996; see Chapter 4).

As evolution continued, the initial loose federation of ganglia became increasingly centralized, and some ganglia gradually began to control others. The dominant ganglia were those located in the head, and it's not hard to see why: Most organisms, starting with the evolutionarily ancient flatworms, have a body plan organized front to back. Forward movement proceeds head first, making it sensible that receptors for light or chemicals be situated in the animal's head. Even the lowly flatworm already knows something about what's at its rear, for it was there just a moment ago. What lies ahead, however, is still unknown and often worth scrutiny. In addition, the worm's head contains its mouth; the terminus of the digestive tube is at the animal's other end. This also makes it useful for the receptors to be located in the head: Taste receptors near the beginning of the digestive tube can be used to signal edibility, thus allowing an animal to determine whether food should be accepted or rejected before it's eaten. All in all, then, receptors at the head are obviously of enormous utility.

To integrate the messages from the various receptors in the head, organisms needed to evolve more and more neural machinery. This machinery was best placed close to the receptors, so it too needed to be in the head. These ganglionic centers became increasingly complex as organisms evolved and eventually started to coordinate the activity of ganglia elsewhere in the body. Over millions of years of evolution, these centers emerged as the "head" ganglia in status as well as in location. In short, they became the brain.

This tendency toward increasing centralization continued within the brain itself. The brain's various structures tend to function hierarchically; as we will see, there are higher centers that command lower centers that in turn command still lower centers and so on.

But centralization is not the whole story, for there are also some important advantages to regional rule. Brains are heavy and require a great deal of energy to build and maintain. And much can get done quickly and economically by avoiding a distant, bureaucratic chain of command. For example, although cockroaches have a small brain (with the biggest chunk of their brain dedicated to their compound eyes), they also have a chain of large ganglia spanning nearly the length of their body. One of these ganglia connects to nerve endings in the tail and can trigger quick escape when the tail is stimulated by even the faintest air movement. This decentralized reflex is one reason cockroaches are some of Earth's longest survivors, defeating even large-brained mammals who can wield both rolled-up newspapers and cans of pesticide.

THE DEVELOPING NERVOUS SYSTEM

In many modern organisms, and certainly across all the vertebrates, centralized rule is the norm, and the vast majority of the body's neural cells are located in the processing center we call the brain. This pattern emerges very early in the development of each individual (see Figure 2.10). The nervous system first begins to appear at about the third week of embryonic life. It starts as a small thickening atop the embryo that runs from the head to (nearly) the tail. Within a few days, the left and right edges of this *neural plate* zip together and

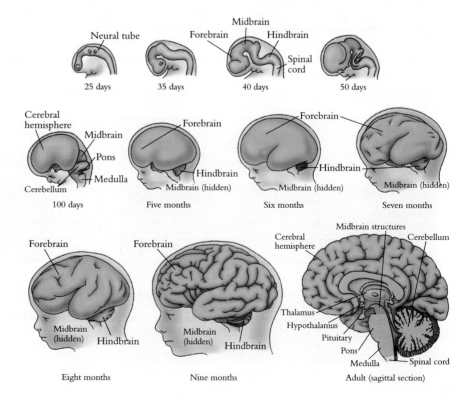

2.10 Embryonic-fetal development of the human brain

fuse lengthwise to form the **neural tube.** By one month of embryonic life, the head end of the neural tube develops three thickenings. These three thickenings—which will develop into the **hindbrain** (the thickening nearest the tail), the **forebrain** (that nearest the head), and the **midbrain** (the thickening between the two)—become enclosed by the cranial bones and form the **brain.** The lower end of the hindbrain marks the beginning of the spinal cord, which is discussed further below. But while we separate them in our discussion, the brain and the spinal cord function as one integrated unit, and the two together make up the **central nervous system (CNS).**

THE MAJOR STRUCTURES OF THE CENTRAL NERVOUS SYSTEM

During the first few months of prenatal development, the brains of all vertebrate species look remarkably alike, but they soon diverge in how the different portions develop. For example, birds begin to develop large midbrains, whereas primates develop large forebrains. Despite these species-specific differences, one can still make generalizations about the involvement of each portion in behavior. Here, we focus on the major structures of the human brain (Figure 2.11). The hindbrain is a good place to start.

THE HINDBRAIN: MEDULLA, PONS, AND CEREBELLUM

At the bottom of the hindbrain is the **medulla,** which lies directly above the spinal cord. The medulla is crucial in controlling many basic biological functions. First, it regulates the cardiovascular and respiratory systems, determining each second how rapidly and heavily we should breathe, how quickly our hearts should beat, and how much blood we should pump. Second, it integrates a number of important reflexes such as swallowing, coughing, and sneezing. Third, it helps in maintaining balance by controlling head orientation and limb positions with respect to gravity.

Just above the medulla the hindbrain thickens, and this thickened area is known as the **pons.** The pons contains special regions that integrate movements

2.11 The human brain *(A) A photograph of the brain cut lengthwise. (Photograph by Biophoto Associates, Photo Researchers) (B) A diagram of the brain, cut lengthwise. The hindbrain is shown in dark blue, the midbrain in aqua, and the forebrain in light green. (After Keeton, 1980)*

A

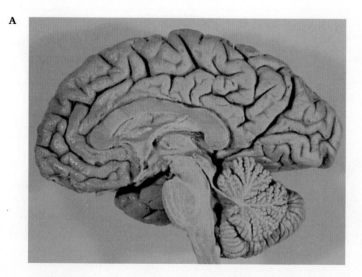

B

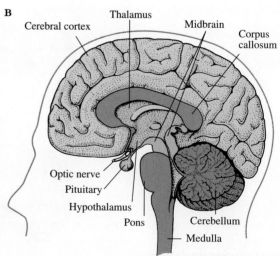

of, and sensations from, the facial muscles, tongue, eye, and ear. Other regions in the pons are important in regulating the brain's level of attentiveness and in initiating sleep and dreaming.

The most visually striking portion of the hindbrain is the *cerebellum,* a massive cauliflowerlike structure that hangs directly behind the pons and overlaps the medulla. This structure seems to act as a specialized computer whose thirty billion or more neurons integrate information from our gravity-sensing (balance) mechanisms, as well as data from the muscles, joints, and tendons of the body. This deeply convoluted structure has several separate regions. One portion controls overall bodily balance. Damage to this part—whether caused by injury, disease, or the temporary toxin alcohol—results in a wide stance and staggering gait. (This is why traffic officers ask suspected drunk drivers to walk a straight line.) Another portion manages the performance and timing of precise skilled movements, whether the execution of a well-practiced tennis swing or an arpeggio on the piano. Damage here can cause tremors during movement and an inability to perform rapidly alternating movements (for example, tapping alternate fingers).

One way of determining just what functions are served by the hindbrain is to disconnect it surgically from the higher portions of the brain. It turns out that a cat whose brain has been transected at a point just above the hindbrain (thus leaving only the hindbrain and spinal cord in primary control) can still make the various limb and trunk movements that are required for standing, crouching, or walking. Nonetheless, this *low-decerebrate animal* can't put the movements together and will collapse without physical supports. Reduced to a hindbrain, the animal "can move, but it cannot act" (Gallistel, 1980).

THE MIDBRAIN

The midbrain is crucial for targeting auditory (sound) and visual stimuli. Portions of the midbrain appear to control the eye movements and—in floppy-eared animals—to prick up the ears when encountering novel or important events. Birds have proportionately large midbrains—it appears to take lots of fast midbrain machinery to target prey from high above and to swoop down for the catch. Mammals have small midbrains, having shifted much of the control of vision and hearing to their forebrains. Other areas within the midbrain help regulate body temperature and pain perception, and they cooperate with the pons in controlling the sleeping-waking cycle.

The midbrain also coordinates the simple movements organized by the hindbrain to form larger wholes. When a transection is made just above the midbrain (creating a *high-decerebrate animal*), the animal can now stand without support, and it can walk, shiver, chew, and swallow. But while these acts are certainly broader and more organized than the discrete movements observed in the low-decerebrate animal, they are much less so than those seen in an intact animal. For the high-decerebrate animal's acts don't cohere into a broader behavioral scheme. If starved, it won't look for food; if attacked, it won't flee. It acts, but it acts without point or purpose. Such observations suggest that the midbrain contains circuitry that coordinates lower level building blocks such as reflexes, forming them into the organism's most basic acts. But the orchestration of these basic acts into patterns of purposeful action is conducted at a higher level still.

Occasionally, and tragically, human infants are born with brains missing most of the forebrain and can be roughly considered high-decerebrate humans. Most such infants look normal except for a flattened head, and they can suck, yawn, cry, and track visual stimuli. However, they seem not to learn and appear drowsy unless actively stimulated. Perhaps fortunately, most of these children die of natural causes within weeks or months (Kolb and Whishaw, 1996).

THE FOREBRAIN

The forebrain comprises everything above the midbrain. In reptiles, amphibians, and most fish, the forebrain is about the size of the midbrain or hindbrain. Mammals—particularly the primates—have the largest forebrains. Indeed, in humans the forebrain is so large that it surrounds and hides from view all of our midbrain and half of our hindbrain (Figure 2.12). In mammals, the most obvious portion of the forebrain is that part on the surface, which is wrinkled like a prune. This is the mammalian *cortex,* and it is so important that it (and the reason for the wrinkles) will be discussed separately below.

Like the rest of the brain, the forebrain is bilaterally symmetrical. This symmetry is especially obvious on the surface of the cortex, which shows a deep front-to-back cleavage called the *longitudinal fissure.* On either side of this fissure, and underneath the cortex, lies the rest of the forebrain, including a number of *subcortical structures.* Of these, four are specifically worth mention. First, buried deep within the forebrain and shaped like a fist atop the midbrain, lies the *thalamus.* The thalamus incorporates a large number of centers that appear to act as relay stations for nearly all the sensory information going to the cortex. A second major structure in this region, lying directly underneath the thalamus, is the *hypothalamus,* which is intimately involved in the control of motivated behavior such as feeding, drinking, maintaining an appropriate body temperature, and engaging in sexual activity (see Chapter 3).

Directly astride the thalamus in each hemisphere lie the *basal ganglia.* They are crucial in regulating muscular contractions during movement (especially smooth movements) and keep our movements from being jerky. Just how crucial they are is obvious when observing individuals with basal ganglia disorders. One such disorder is *Parkinson's disease,* which involves the degeneration of certain cells in the basal ganglia. Sufferers from Parkinson's disease often show a loss of muscle tone, an immobile masklike face, slow movements, and tremors when the limbs are at rest. Parts of the basal ganglia also degenerate in *Huntington's disease,* a progressive, hereditary disorder that can cause jerky limb movements, facial twitches, and uncontrolled writhing of the body.

A fourth set of interconnected structures surrounds the thalamus and basal

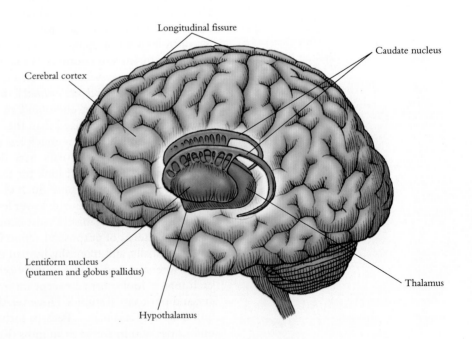

2.12 **Important structures of the forebrain** *Three of these subcortical structures are the basal ganglia, which is comprised of the caudate and lentiform nuclei; the hypothalamus; and the thalamus.*

Longitudinal fissure

Caudate nucleus

Cerebral cortex

Lentiform nucleus
(putamen and globus pallidus)

Hypothalamus

Thalamus

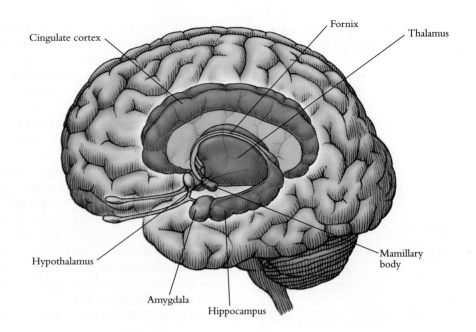

Cingulate cortex · Fornix · Thalamus · Hypothalamus · Amygdala · Hippocampus · Mamillary body

2.13 The limbic system *This system is made up of a number of subcortical structures, including the limbic lobe (consisting of the fornix, the hippocampus, the cingulate cortex, and the mammilary bodies); the thalamus; the hypothalamus; the basal ganglia; and the amygdala.*

Motor control of reptiles *The motor control system provided by the midbrain and basal ganglia are normally quite sufficient for the limb movements of alligators. Only those alligators that come out of Walt Disney Studios have motor control precise enough to allow dancing. (From* Fantasia, *1940; courtesy of Photofest)*

ganglia and lies directly beneath the cortex. These are often grouped together under the term **limbic system** (from the French *limbique,* "bordering"). The limbic system, which includes structures such as the *amygdala* and the *hippocampus,* has close anatomical ties with numerous other parts of the brain, especially the hypothalamus, cortex, and regions controlling the sense of smell (Figure 2.13). It is involved in emotional and motivational activities, and some aspects of learning and memory (see the discussions of the amygdala in Chapter 11 and of the hippocampus in Chapter 7).

Some experimenters have wondered just what changes would occur if a mammal were deprived of its cortex, leaving only its basal ganglia, limbic system, and other subcortical structures in command. A cat whose cortex is surgically disconnected in this way can still direct its actions toward simple goals. Thus, it can forage when it is hungry, look for a warmer place when it's cold, try to escape when it's threatened, and so on. In these circumstances, the cat seems normal. But increase the challenge, and the cat begins to appear inept. For example, when trying to fend off another cat, it tries to retaliate, but its blows are poorly directed and easily avoided. This is typical: although the cat can coordinate its acts into a coherent sequence, it cannot apply those sequences tactically. The animal can act without a cortex, and its acts have some purpose. But lacking a cortex, it acts stupidly (Bard and Rioch, 1937; Wetzel and Stuart, 1976; Gallistel, 1980). Such experiments, though unpalatable, give us a glimpse of the functions served by both the cortex and the structures below it.

THE CENTRAL NERVOUS SYSTEM'S CONNECTIONS WITH THE BODY

The CNS connects with the rest of the body through nerve fibers that conduct excitation either toward the brain and spinal cord or away from them. Nerve fibers that transmit information from the sense organs to the brain and spinal cord are called **afferent nerves.** Nerve fibers that transmit their

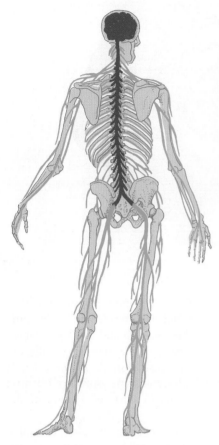

2.14 Central and peripheral nervous systems *The central nervous system (in dark red) and the peripheral nervous system (in orange). (After Bloom, Lazerson, and Hofstadter, 1988)*

messages from the CNS to the **effectors,** the muscles and glands that are the organs of action, are called **efferent nerves.**

The spinal cord itself is a major trunk line of nerve fibers: some afferent, some efferent, with still others just making local internal connections within the spinal cord. These local connections can initiate or regulate movements on their own and can modulate sensory information as it proceeds to the brain.

But not all nerves between brain and body run through the spinal cord. Separate nerves, twelve pairs in all, enter and exit directly from the hindbrain (from the pons and medulla, specifically—see below) and poke through holes in the skull. These **cranial nerves** have both afferent and efferent functions. They control the movements of the head and neck, carry sensations from them—including vision, olfaction (smell), and audition (hearing)—regulate the various glandular secretions in the head (e.g., tears, saliva, and mucus), and control life-sustaining visceral functions, such as digestion and excretion.

Together, the cranial nerves and the nerves that connect to the spinal cord—in other words, all the nerve fibers, ganglia, and so forth that lie outside the central nervous system—are called the **peripheral nervous system** (Figure 2.14). Anatomists distinguish between two divisions of the peripheral nervous system based upon their function. The **somatic division** is the set of nerves that control the skeletal musculature and the transmission of information from the sense organs; the **autonomic division** (typically called the **autonomic nervous system,** or **ANS**) is the set of spinal and cranial nerves that regulate and inform the brain about the viscera (including the heart and lungs, the blood vessels, the digestive systems, the sexual organs, and so on).

A final line of communication between brain and body is indirect, occurring via hormonal secretions. For example, the **pituitary gland,** commonly known as the "master" gland because of its supervisory role among the glands of the body, is an extension of the hypothalamus, receiving not only nerve fibers but also neurochemical channels from it. The brain also has sensors responsive to chemicals circulating in the bloodstream, and these chemical receptors are important in regulating states like hunger and thirst. These hormonal connections receive more discussion later (pp. 62–63) and in Chapter 3 as well.

THE CORTEX

We now turn to the outermost layer of the cerebral hemispheres, the mammalian **cortex.** (The term *cortex* comes from the Latin for "bark"; see Figure 2.15.) For primates and other complex mammals, the cortex is the most massive single portion of the brain, accounting for more than half the brain's volume (in humans, 80 percent).

What about the animals that rank in complexity just below the mammals, the birds and the reptiles? By and large, these animals have little in the way of a cortex (birds have more than reptiles, but much less than mammals). Moreover, the cortex that they do possess is comparable, both anatomically and functionally, to regions that in the mammalian brain are *sub*cortical. For this reason, in mammalian brains these subcortical forebrain structures—including the hippocampus and the basal ganglia—are sometimes called the "old cortex," because they are the outermost layer—that is, the cortex—in the animals that predated mammals. Similarly, the new, expanded cortical tissue seen in mammals is often called the "new cortex," or *neocortex,* reflecting the fact that, in evolutionary terms, this bit of the brain is relatively new. For the sake of simplicity, though, we will use the term *cortex* to mean the new, mammalian cortex.

Traditionally, the cortex has enjoyed a reputation as the part of the brain that makes us intelligent, but that's only part of the story. As we mentioned, many functions performed in nonmammals by subcortical regions, like parts of the limbic system and the midbrain, are in mammals predominantly cortical. These include complex sensory perception and coordinated muscular action. Indeed, this is a clear trend in mammalian brain evolution: As the cortex enlarges and becomes more of a supervisor, the subcortical structures and the midbrain begin to act more as relay stations or middle managers.

What do the mammals gain from their massive cortex, especially when its functions can be performed by other structures? The answer is flexibility in behavior. The frog that has a fly-sized object waved in front of it will try to swallow it. But we humans are different. If someone waves a chocolate truffle in front of *us,* there's no guarantee that we'll gobble it immediately. We might decide otherwise, because we're on a diet or want to save our appetite for dinner. Likewise, a chimpanzee might encounter a fresh banana but hide it until all the other chimps who might grab it have left. This flexibility underlies the cleverness that typifies many mammals, most primates, and now and then, us humans.

Remarkably, although the cortex has an enormous volume (as we said, it makes up 80 percent of the human brain), it is only 2–3 mm thick. This is made possible by the cortex's most striking anatomic feature—its many wrinkles (technically, its **convolutions**). If someone could iron the wrinkles out of a human cortex, it would occupy an area of 2,500 cm^2 (about two square feet). Housing this structure in uncompressed form would take an odd-sized head indeed (and, just as important, would require much longer nerves to connect all its regions). But all crumpled up, this large surface can be jammed into the limited volume of a human skull.

Some of the convolutions in the cortex are actually very deep grooves or *fissures* (see Figure 2.15). The deepest fissure was already mentioned—the longitudinal fissure, which runs from front to back and separates the left and right cerebral hemispheres. Other fissures mark off several large sections of each hemisphere, called *lobes.* There are four such lobes, each named for the cranial bone nearest to it. Within each hemisphere, the *frontal* and *parietal* lobes form the front and topmost parts of the brain, respectively, and the groove separating them is the *central fissure.* The earflap-like *temporal lobes* press against the frontal lobes, forming a groove between them called the *lateral fissure.* The *occipital lobe* is the rear-most lobe; it is smoothly adjoined to the temporal and parietal lobes.

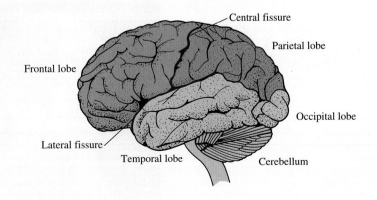

2.15 The cortex of the cerebral hemispheres Side view, showing its convolutions, fissures, and lobes.

LOCALIZATION OF FUNCTION IN THE CORTEX

We have now identified a number of different brain regions. But how does each region contribute to thinking and behavior? This question is known as the problem of *localization of function,* and the predominance of the cortex in the human brain made it the first candidate for localization efforts.

Early investigators approached this problem in a fashion that had more in common with palm reading than neuroscience. Their method was to feel the bumps on a participant's head and make pronouncements, based on the size of these bumps, about that person's personality and intellectual capacities. The assumption here was that the size of any cortical area would be reflected by bumps or indentations on the surface of the skull, thus indicating whether the participant had a surfeit of or deficit in the associated mental function. This practice, known as *phrenology,* became popular in the early 1800s. It took on many of the trappings of science, with a jargon of its own and elaborate charts that depicted small regions with the ostensible mental functions controlled by each. For example, love of one's children (*philoprogenitiveness,* according to one chart) was located at the back of the head, self-esteem near the top, sense of history at the front, and destructiveness just above the ear (Figure 2.16).

The founder of phrenology, Franz Joseph Gall, was a respected Viennese doctor and anatomist, but his followers were rather reckless, promulgating phrenology as the scientific way to know oneself and finding more and more ways to apply it. In the United States, phrenology became a craze. Phrenology parlors were opened in several cities, and "having one's head examined" (a phrase still

2.16   Cerebral localization then and now *(A) According to phrenology, a nineteenth-century theory that is now totally discredited, the degree to which people possessed such characteristics as foresight, courage, and the desire to have children could be assessed by looking at the shape of their skulls. The figure shows a model of a human head, indicating the supposed functions of the brain regions below. (Courtesy of The Science Museum/Science & Society Picture Library) (B) Modern neuropsychologists try to determine brain function by correlating activity with psychological processes. The figure shows data from a high-precision, 124-electrode electroencephalogram (EEG) superimposed upon a 3-D computer model of the participant's head obtained using magnetic resonance imaging (MRI). Here the participant is shown a letter on a computer screen and must compare its location on the screen to three previous letters. One half-second later, the white patch appears over the prefrontal area, indicating heightened activity that is associated with working memory (see Chapter 7). (Photograph courtesy Alan Gevins, EEG Systems Laboratory)*

A

B

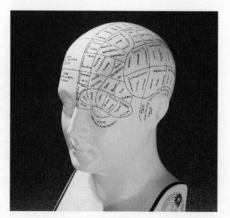
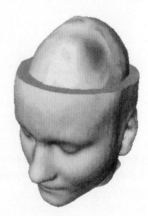

used today) was recommended both as a condition of employment and as an aid in choosing marriage partners (Hothersall, 1990).

It is now known that Gall's theory far outstripped his evidence and that the relationship of bumps on the head to convolutions on the cortex is nil. Nonetheless, neuroscience owes phrenology a great debt. Phrenology acquainted the mid-nineteenth-century public with the somewhat radical idea that our mental functioning might be understood by directly studying our brains. Phrenology's most important contribution was in inspiring carefully conducted experiments that clarified aspects of brain function, some of which we discuss next.

PROJECTION AREAS

Among the first discoveries in the study of cortical function was the existence of sensory and motor *primary projection areas.* The *primary sensory projection areas* serve as the receiving stations for information arriving from the eyes, ears, and other sense organs. The *primary motor projection area* is the departure point for nerve cells that enter lower parts of the brain and spinal cord and carry directives that ultimately result in muscle movement. The term *projection* is borrowed from cartography, because the sensory and motor primary projection areas seem to form maps in which particular regions of the cortex correspond roughly to the parts of the body they represent or influence.

PRIMARY MOTOR AREA

The discovery of the primary motor projection area dates back to the 1860s, when investigators began to apply mild electric currents to various portions of the cortex of anesthetized animals. The effects were often quite specific. Within the frontal lobe, stimulating one point led to a movement of the forelimb, while stimulating another made the ears prick up, and so forth. These early studies also pointed to what neuroscientists call *contralateral control:* Stimulating the left hemisphere led to movements on the right side of the body; stimulating the right hemisphere caused movements on the left. Contralateral control appears to operate in nearly all nervous systems. It is also evident anatomically, because most of the major efferent pathways from the brain cross over to the opposite side within the hindbrain.

Perhaps the best studies of stimulation-elicited movements were obtained in the 1880s by the British researcher David Ferrier who succeeded in producing the first detailed localization "maps" for motor function in the cortex. His mapping of the monkey's motor functions was precise enough to encourage him to extrapolate it to humans, and it led to a medical breakthrough: the first localization of a brain tumor prior to neurosurgical removal (Hothersall, 1990).

Some fifty years later, Canadian neurosurgeon Wilder Penfield began similar mapping studies using humans who were suffering from severe epilepsy and needed neurosurgery to remove the diseased cells. For these surgeries, Penfield capitalized on a fact about the brain that was mentioned earlier: its near total insensitivity to pain. (This is attributable to the fact that while the brain—obviously—has an enormous number of nerve cells, it contains very few sensory receptors.) This allowed Penfield to operate on patients under local anesthesia, leaving them fully awake throughout the experience. From surgeries on over four hundred patients, Penfield confirmed that the cortical motor area in humans lies within the frontal lobe. Stimulation there led to movement of specific parts of the body, much to the surprise of patients who had no sense of willing the action or of performing it themselves. Systematic exploration

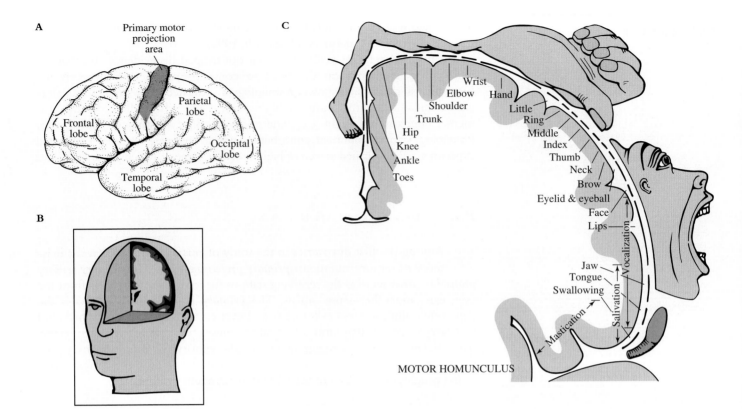

A

Primary motor projection area

Frontal lobe

Parietal lobe

Occipital lobe

Temporal lobe

B

C

Wrist
Elbow
Shoulder
Hand
Trunk
Little
Hip
Ring
Knee
Middle
Ankle
Index
Toes
Thumb
Neck
Brow
Eyelid & eyeball
Face
Lips
Vocalization

Jaw
Tongue
Swallowing
Salivation

Mastication

MOTOR HOMUNCULUS

2.17 **The primary motor projection area of the human cortex** *(A) The location of the motor projection area in a side view of the brain. (B) The head shows the plane of the cross section of the figure. (C) The primary motor projection area of one hemisphere shown in a cross section of the brain. The location and relative amount of cortical space allotted to each body region is graphically expressed as a motor homunculus. (After Penfield and Rasmussen, 1950)*

showed that for each portion of the motor cortex, there was a corresponding part of the body that moved when its cortical counterpart was stimulated, with each hemisphere exhibiting contralateral control. The map generated from such surgery is sometimes depicted graphically by drawing a "motor homunculus," a schematic picture of the body with each part depicted on the motor projection area that controls its movement (see Figure 2.17).

The human motor homunculus shows that equal areas of the body do not receive equal cortical space. Instead, parts that we are able to move with the greatest precision (for instance, the fingers, the tongue) receive more cortical space than those over which we have less control (for instance, the shoulder, the abdomen). Evidently, what matters is function, the extent and complexity of use (Penfield and Rasmussen, 1950). This generalization seems to apply across species. Unlike the dog, the raccoon is a manual creature that explores the world with its forepaws; neatly enough, the forepaw cortical area in raccoons dwarfs its counterpart in dogs (Welker, Johnson, and Pubols, 1964).

PRIMARY SENSORY AREAS

Methods similar to Penfield's revealed the existence of sensory projection areas. Adjacent to and directly behind the primary motor projection area is its sensory counterpart, the primary ***somatosensory*** area. This area, located in the parietal lobe in each hemisphere (see Figure 2.18) is the receiving area for sensory information from the skin senses. Patients stimulated at a particular point of this area usually report tingling somewhere on the opposite side of their bodies. (Less frequently, they report experiences of cold, warmth, or movement.) The somatosensory projection area resembles its motor counterpart in several ways. First, it shows a neat topographic projection, with each part of the body's surface sending its sensory information to a particular part of the cortical somatosensory area. Second, the assignment of cortical space is disproportionate, with the parts of the body that are most sensitive to touch, such as the index finger and the

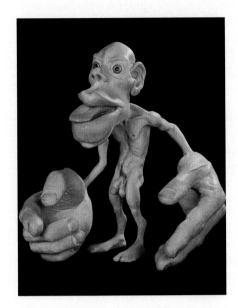

The sensory homunculus *An artist's rendition of what a man would look like if his appearance were proportional to the area allotted by the somatosensory cortex to his various body parts. (Courtesy of The Natural History Museum, London)*

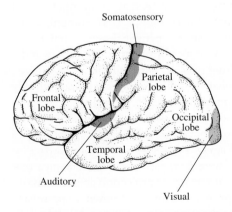

2.18 Primary sensory projection areas of the human cortex *The location of the primary somatosensory, auditory, and visual projection areas in the human brain. (After Cobb, 1941)*

tongue, receiving more cortical space. Finally, sensation—like motor control—is contralateral, with sensory information from each extremity of the body proceeding to the hemisphere on the side opposite to it: the right thumb onto the left hemisphere, the left shoulder onto the right hemisphere, and so on (information from the trunk of the body close to the body's midline is represented in both hemispheres).

Similar primary projection areas exist for vision and for hearing and are located in the occipital and temporal lobes, respectively (see Figure 2.18). Here, too, the representation is topographical: In the occipital lobe (especially the area known as the "visual cortex"), adjacent brain areas represent adjacent locations in visual space. In the temporal lobes, adjacent areas represent similar ranges of pitch. These projection areas are contralateral as well. For vision, objects seen on the left are processed by the right visual area, while those seen on the right are processed by the left visual area. Similarly, sounds entering the left ear are represented mostly in the right auditory projection area and vice versa. Patients who are stimulated in the visual projection area report optical experiences, vivid enough, but with little form or meaning—flickering lights, streaks of color. Stimulated in the auditory area, patients hear things, but again the sensation is rather meaningless and chaotic—clicks, buzzes, booms, and hums.

NONPRIMARY (ASSOCIATION) AREAS

The primary projection areas constitute less than one-quarter of the human cortex. What about the rest? These areas were originally referred to as "association areas" because they did not seem to show any kind of fixed sensory mapping and were implicated in such higher mental functions as planning, perceiving, remembering, thinking, and speaking. While there is good reason to believe that these regions are indeed crucial for these higher mental functions, some of them are now known to function as still further projection areas, over and above the primary ones we have just described.

Thus, just ahead of the primary motor projection area are large nonprimary motor regions that appear critical to initiating and coordinating complex skilled movements. On the sensory side, it appears that each sensory modality may have dozens of secondary projection areas located in the temporal and parietal lobes, with each showing topographical and contralateral representation and each involved in processing different aspects of sensation. For example, the monkey cortex has at least twenty-five nonprimary projection areas for vision, with each area specialized for different visual qualities, such as form, color, or movement (Kolb and Whishaw, 1996). In addition, there are also areas that integrate multiple sensory modalities, such as touch and vision, so that we can, for example, recognize by sight an object that we have previously only touched.

Collectively, these nonprimary areas serve to organize and relate the various messages that come from the primary sensory projection areas or that go to the primary motor projection areas. To that extent, they do indeed provide the integration and organization that is crucial for the so-called higher mental functions. But despite their involvement in these "higher" functions, we cannot point to any particular brain location and assert that it is *the* organizing center for, say, planning, or visual memory, or thinking. For these higher tasks seem to depend on many different cortical locations, and so the control of each task is said to be distributed across these various locations.

Most of our knowledge about these functions has come from the study of individuals who suffer from malfunctioning caused by cortical lesions. By studying the disorders caused by such lesions, neuropsychologists have been able to make inferences about the functions of the cortical areas that have been damaged.

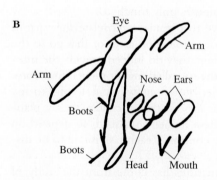

2.19 Drawings by a patient with visual agnosia *(A) Trying to copy an elephant. (B) Production when asked to draw a man. (From Luria, 1966)*

DISORDERS OF ACTION

Some lesions in the frontal lobe of the cortex produce *apraxias,* which are serious disturbances in the initiation or organization of voluntary action. In some apraxias, the patient is unable to perform well-known actions, such as saluting or waving good-bye, when asked to do so. In other cases, actions that normal persons regard as quite simple become fragmented and disorganized. When asked to light a cigarette, the patient may strike a match against a matchbox and then strike it again and again after it is already burning; or he may light the match and then put it into his mouth. These deficits are in no sense the result of simple paralysis, because the patient can readily perform each part of the action in isolation. His problem is in initiating the sequence or in selecting the right components and fitting them together (Luria, 1966; Kolb and Whishaw, 1996).

Some of the apraxias may represent a disconnection between the primary and nonprimary motor areas. The primary motor area is responsible for producing the movements of individual muscles, but the nonprimary motor areas must first organize and initiate the sequence. Evidence consistent with this idea comes from an experiment in which EEG monitoring electrodes were placed on the scalps of participants who were then asked to press a button in response to various stimuli. The EEG data showed that the neurons in the nonprimary areas fired almost a second before participants actually moved their fingers, suggesting that these areas play a role in preparing that action (Deecke, Scheid, and Kornhuber, 1968). In short, the nonprimary areas seem to be responsible for "Get ready!" and "Get set!" while at "Go!" the primary motor area takes over (Roland et al., 1980; Bear, Connors, and Paradiso, 1996).

DISORDERS OF PERCEPTION AND ATTENTION

In several other disorders the patient suffers a disruption in the way she perceives the world or attends to it.

Agnosias   One such group of disorders is the *agnosias* in which the sufferer cannot identify familiar objects using the affected sensory modality. Patients with visual agnosia, for example, can recognize a car key by grasping it but not by looking at it. Some of these patients can identify each separate detail of a picture, but they are unable to identify the picture as a whole. When shown a drawing of a telephone, one patient painstakingly identified several parts but when asked to tell what the object was, could only venture a guess: "A dial . . . numbers . . . of course, it's a watch or some sort of machine!" (Luria, 1966, p. 139). Sometimes the guess leads to a correct inference, as in the case of a patient shown a drawing of two giraffes: "The way this comes down, this could be an animal, four legs and a tail . . . a long neck comes up, an awfully long neck . . . here's a head because here's an eye . . . not a mouse God knows . . . what would have such an extraordinarily long neck? . . . a giraffe" (Wapner, Judd, and Gardner, 1978, p. 347).

Agnosic patients have similar difficulties when asked to copy drawings. The individual parts are rendered reasonably well, but they cannot be integrated into a coherent whole (see Figure 2.19). Visual agnosia tends to result from damage to the occiptal area of the cortex and to the rearmost part of the parietal area that borders the occipital area, the primary and nonprimary projection areas for vision.

One striking and complex kind of agnosia, technically known as *prosopagnosia,* seems to involve areas of both the temporal and parietal lobes. In prosopagnosia, the main difficulty is in recognizing faces. Some of these patients are unable to distinguish familiar faces; others cannot even recognize a face as a face. When walking down the street, one such patient would pat the tops of fire hydrants, which he thought were the heads of little children. On one occasion he

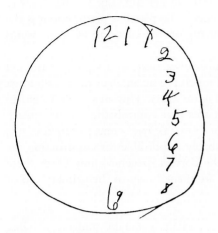

2.20 Neglect syndrome *A patient with damage to the right parietal cortex was asked to draw a typical clock face. In his drawing, the left side was ignored, and all the hours were squeezed into the right. (From Rosenzweig and Leiman, 1989)*

mistook his wife's head for a hat (Sacks, 1985; for further discussion, see Chapter 6). But the problems suffered by individuals with prosopagnosia are typically not confined just to faces. They may not be able to identify their own car, or particular types of clothing or food. A dairy farmer who could formerly recognize every cow in his herd lost the ability to tell them apart.

Neglect syndrome In agnosia, the patient can see (or feel or hear), but he is unable to make sense of what his senses tell him. In some other disorders, the patient's problem is one of attention, and he systematically ignores certain aspects of the world.

A striking example is the **neglect syndrome,** which typically results from damage to certain areas on the right side of the parietal lobe. Its main characteristic is the patient's systematic neglect of the left side: He acts as if it does not exist. When asked to read compound words such as *toothpick* or *baseball,* such a patient will read "pick" and "ball," ignoring the left half of each word; when asked to draw the face of a clock, he will squeeze all of the numbers onto the clock's right side (see Figure 2.20). When eating, he will select and eat food only from the right side of his plate. A similar neglect applies to the left side of the patient's own body. When dressing, he will ignore the left shirt sleeve and pants leg; when shaving, he will leave the left side of his face unshaven (Heilman and Watson, 1977; Kolb and Whishaw, 1996).

What accounts for the neglect syndrome? According to some theorists, the reason is essentially a failure of attention, caused by the disruption of a cortical arousal system that orients us to what is new (Heilman and Watson, 1977). Others believe that the person with the neglect syndrome loses the ability to integrate the spatial properties of stimuli or hold the properties in memory (Rafal, 1994).

Gerstmann syndrome One of the mysteries of the neglect syndrome is that, almost universally, the left side is what gets neglected, as a consequence of damage to the right parietal lobe. But what does damage to the left parietal lobe cause? Rather than neglect, the most common consequence of damage to the left parietal lobe is the **Gerstmann syndrome,** a cluster of difficulties that includes the inability to perform mathematical calculations, the loss of handwriting, confusion about which direction is left and which is right, and "finger agnosia"—the inability to recognize the fingers on either hand (Kolb and Whishaw, 1996).

DISORDERS OF LANGUAGE

Certain lesions in the cortical nonprimary areas lead to disruptions of the most distinctively human of all human activities—the production and comprehension of speech. Disorders of this kind are called *aphasias.* In right-handers, they are almost always produced by lesions (strokes, typically) in the left hemisphere.

Nonfluent aphasias Disorders of speech take different forms. Which particular form they take depends heavily on the particular sites of brain damage. In the so-called **nonfluent aphasias,**★ the patient's primary difficulty is with the production of speech. In extreme cases, a patient with this disorder becomes virtually unable to utter or to write a word. In less severe cases, only a part of the normal vocabulary is lost, but the patient's speech becomes labored and fragmented, as finding and articulating each word requires special effort. The result is a

---

★ An older set of terms contrasted "expressive" with "receptive" aphasias, but this dichotomy was unsatisfactory because many individuals with damage to Broca's area (who were formerly labeled "expressive" aphasics) also show comprehension difficulties (Goodglass, 1973; Cummings, 1985).

staccato, spoken telegram: "Here . . . head . . . operation . . . here . . . speech . . . none . . . talking . . . what . . . illness" (Luria, 1966, p. 406).

The similarity to the apraxias we have discussed before is striking. There is no paralysis of speech muscles, because the patient can move her lips and tongue quite well. What is impaired is her ability to organize and plan these movements into a unified sequence, her ability to coordinate her individual movements to form a word or to create a coherent sentence. The patient's predicament is the enormously frustrating and often demoralizing one of knowing what she wants to say but being unable to say it.

Nonfluent aphasias are generally produced by lesions in a region of the left frontal lobe called **Broca's area** (after the French physician, Paul Broca, who first noted its relation to speech in 1861; see Figure 2.21). This area lies adjacent to the part of the primary motor projection area that controls the various speech muscles (jaw, tongue, lips, larynx, and so on). Broca's area seems to function like other nonprimary motor areas, and is probably responsible for constructing the patterns of movements that will lead to the correct speech sounds. Once these **speech plans** are formulated, though, they are turned over to the primary motor area, which then executes them.

Fluent aphasias   In the nonfluent aphasias, patients generally understand what they hear but cannot answer. In the fluent aphasias, the patients suffer from what is in some ways the reverse problem—they don't understand what is said to them, though they usually answer anyway. The fluent aphasias are essentially language agnosias, in which the ability to recognize speech sounds is impaired. Unlike patients with nonfluent aphasias, those with fluent aphasias talk freely and rapidly, but while they utter many words, they say very little. The sentences they produce are reasonably grammatical, but they are "word salad," largely composed of the little filler words that provide scant information. A typical example is, "I was over the other one, and then after they had been in the department, I was in this one" (Geschwind, 1970, p. 904). The poor recognition of speech sounds extends to the written symbols of those sounds, and so the writing of fluent aphasics is usually impaired as well. The psychological impact of all this is enormous. The afflicted person is traumatically cut off from language: She hears gibberish everywhere and can only produce gibberish when she tries to speak.

Fluent aphasias are usually associated with left-hemisphere lesions in various nonprimary auditory areas of the left temporal and parietal lobes. Many authorities believe that the crucial locus is **Wernicke's area,** a region that borders on the auditory primary projection area, named after the nineteenth-century neurologist Carl Wernicke (see Figure 2.21). And what of the right auditory projection areas? People with damage to these areas have problems with musical pitch perception, and it has been suggested that a right-side counterpart to Wernicke's area may be responsible for sensitivity to tone of voice. Whether there is a right-side counterpart to Broca's area responsible for singing and making speech inflections is more speculative (Ross, 1981; Zatorre and Halpern, 1993; Kolb and Whisaw, 1996).

Aphasia and sign language   In all cases of aphasia we've discussed thus far, there is a disruption of a spoken language, such as English, or Hindi, or Swahili. If the sufferer is multilingual, then all the languages suffer. But what happens to congenitally deaf people who suffer a stroke in the left hemisphere? Many of these persons communicate through sign languages, which are as complex and sophisticated as any of their vocal counterparts (see Chapter 9; Klima and Bellugi, 1979). How is a sign language affected by left-hemisphere brain damage?

The general finding is that, in these cases, the deaf individuals show sign-language deficits that correspond closely to the spoken-language deficits observed in hearing persons. If there is damage to Broca's area, they exhibit the

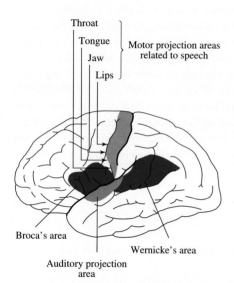

2.21 Broca's and Wernicke's areas   *The diagram shows the two association areas most relevant to language. Destruction of Broca's area generally leads to nonfluent aphasia; destruction of Wernicke's area leads to fluent aphasia. Note the proximity to the relevant projection areas: Broca's area is closest to the regions that control the speech muscles, while Wernicke's area borders on the auditory primary projection area.*

signing equivalent of nonfluent aphasia. They can move their hands and fingers but have serious difficulties in using them effectively to produce signs. Some lesions seem to impair the ability to produce particular signed words. Others impair the ability to put these signs together to form grammatical signed sentences. With lesions involving Wernicke's area, the deaf suffer the signing equivalent of fluent aphasias: They sign smoothly but with many errors, and they are deficient in their comprehension of others' signing. Thus, it appears that the left-hemisphere lesions that produce the aphasias of spoken language affect some mental function that is not specific to the ear-mouth channel. Instead, these lesions seem to disrupt human language itself, no matter what its form. Apparently, then, language depends on some cerebral machinery that is pretty much the same whether the language is produced by tongue and mouth or by hands and fingers (Bellugi, Poizner, and Klima, 1983; Mayeux and Kandel, 1991; Bear, Connors, and Paradiso, 1996).

Dyslexias **Dyslexia** refers to any reading difficulty not associated with obvious problems like bad eyesight. Dyslexias occur more often in boys and among left-handed individuals. Common dyslexias include the inability to name letters, to read words or sentences, or to recognize words directly even though they can be sounded out. Each kind may reflect different deficits, such as in speech-sound processing or memory for word meanings. Likewise, the different dyslexias are probably associated with different brain regions, and most theories focus on nonprimary areas in the frontal and temporal lobes (Galaburda, 1994; Rosenzweig et al., 1996; see also Shaywitz et al., 1995).

Neuroimaging and aphasia As we noted earlier, trying to infer the functions of different parts of the brain from the deficits that result from damage to those areas is always an uncertain business. Fortunately, though, this uncertainty can be reduced by combining the data from studies of patients suffering certain lesions with other sorts of evidence. For example, PET scans show that Broca's area is indeed more active (that is, PET scans show more blood flow in that area) when individuals generate words than when they merely listen to them. Wernicke's area shows the opposite pattern.

But the PET scans also suggest that the way we process language is quite complex. It matters whether the sounds we hear are meaningful words, whether we have rehearsed our words in advance or are choosing them on the spot, and whether we speak spontaneously or are merely reading from a script provided for us. With each of these changes, the pattern of brain activation (as revealed by PET scans) is altered. Thus, there is not a single pattern of brain activation broadly associated with language use. Instead, the pattern observed depends on exactly how language is being used on that occasion. Moreover, each of the patterns involves many different brain sites. Similar complexities are found in the study of lesions; the resulting aphasias are rarely found to be pure textbook types (Peterson et al., 1988; Kimura and Watson, 1989; Demonet, Wise, and Frackowiak, 1993).

DISORDERS OF PLANNING AND SOCIAL COGNITION

Earlier we referred to the famous case of Phineas Gage. After his head was shot through by the tamping iron, Phineas could still speak and move fairly normally. But something subtler had changed. As the original medical report on Gage stated:

> He is fitful, irreverent, indulging at times in the grossest profanity (which was not previously his custom), manifesting but little deference for his fellows, impatient of

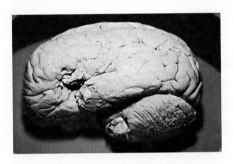

Tan's brain *The embalmed brain of a famous aphasic patient of Broca's called "Tan" because this was the only syllable he was able to utter. Note the area of damage on the lower side of the left frontal lobe, now known as Broca's area. (Photograph by M. Sakka, courtesy Musée de l'Homme et Musée Dupuytren, Paris)*

restraint or advice when it conflicts with his desires, at times pertinaciously obsti-nate, yet capricious and vacillating, devising many plans of future operation, which are no sooner arranged than they are abandoned in turn for others appearing more feasible. Previous to his injury . . . he possessed a well-balanced mind . . . was ener-getic and persistent in executing all his plans of operation. In this regard his mind was radically changed, so decidedly that his friends and acquaintances said he was "no longer Gage." (Valenstein, 1986, p. 90)

Just what was different about Gage? It is now known that his problems were typical of what can occur with damage to the front-most part of the frontal lobe, the *prefrontal area.* The prefrontal area is disproportionately large in primates, especially in humans. The effects of prefrontal damage vary, but a number of the same effects are found in many patients (Milner and Petrides, 1984).

One common consequence is a lack of spontaneity. The patients have few facial expressions and gestures, speak rather little, and what they do say is not flu-ent. If asked, for example, to write a list of five-letter words that begin with "s," they will write very few and neglect the five-letter rule—even though they can state that they are breaking that rule as they write. Another common problem suffered with prefrontal damage is in strategy formation. Asked to run a simple series of errands (say, "first, put the pencil on the table, then close and lock the door, and finally, bring me the newspaper"), they will skip some tasks, linger over others, and make mistakes while discharging even the simplest—again, even though they can recall what they are supposed to do.

Still another problem concerns a deficiency in response inhibition. The patients often break rules because they seem unable to use the rules to control their behavior. This obviously causes many problems for them, including prob-lems in the social realm.

Depending upon the exact site of brain damage, these individuals may appear uninvolved, depressed, and apathetic. Alternatively, they may seem like psy-chopaths, acting flagrantly and crudely, being sexually promiscuous, and perhaps engaging in criminal conduct. In fact, one hypothesis about actual criminal psy-chopaths suggests that these individuals may suffer from subtle prefrontal dam-age (see Chapter 18).

ONE BRAIN OR TWO?

At first glance, the brain's left and right hemispheres look quite similar to each other, but as differences resulting from damage to the two hemispheres suggest, their functions are often rather different. This asymmetry of function is called *lateralization,* and its manifestations influence such diverse phenomena as lan-guage, spatial organization, and handedness—the superior dexterity of one hand over the other (Springer and Deutsch, 1998).

Despite their superficial similarity, both autopsies and neuroimaging studies show that the two cerebral hemispheres are different in both structure and func-tion. The convolutions have different patterns, and they develop differently as well, appearing much earlier in infancy on the left than the right. In addition, the portion of the temporal lobe that includes Wernicke's area is larger on the left side in most people. The left and right hemispheres differ in many other ways as well, such as in blood volume, occipital lobe size, concentrations of vari-ous hormones and other neurochemicals, and in the microscopic wiring of their nerve cells (Geschwind and Levitsky, 1968; Geschwind and Galaburda, 1985; Steinmetz et al., 1991; Kolb and Whishaw, 1996).

Functionally, the overriding difference between the hemispheres involves language. It has already been noted that in right-handers, aphasia is usually associated with lesions in the left hemisphere. Until fairly recently, neuroscientists interpreted this fact to mean that one hemisphere is dominant over the other. As a result, they called the (right-hander's) right hemisphere the "minor hemisphere," for they believed that it was essentially a lesser version of the left hemisphere, a hemisphere that lacks language functions, has less capacity for fine motor control, and so forth.

The right hemisphere has now been relieved of this poor-relation status, because it appears to have its own specializations. Right-handers with lesions in the right hemisphere often suffer from difficulties in the comprehension of various aspects of space and form; in many tasks, they concentrate on details but cannot grasp the overall pattern. And as we've seen, damage to the left temporal lobe can result in a fluent aphasia, whereas damage to the right temporal lobe results in deficits in music perception.

The results are more ambiguous for the 12 percent or so of the population that is left-handed (and also generally left-footed and, to a lesser extent, left-eyed and left-eared as well; Porac and Coren, 1981). About 70 percent of left-handers have speech predominantly lateralized in the left hemisphere; the other 30 percent divide equally between those whose language is represented in both hemispheres and those for whom language seems to be represented just in the right (Rasmussen and Milner, 1977). More generally, there seems to be less lateralization in left-handers than in most right-handers. In line with this view, aphasia in left-handers is sometimes produced by lesions to *either* hemisphere. But by the same token, left-handed aphasics have a greater chance for recovery, apparently because the intact hemisphere is better able to assume the responsibilities that formerly belonged to the damaged one (Brain, 1965; Springer and Deutsch, 1998).

Does gender matter? Some investigators have reported that males are more lateralized than females—that is, that there is more of a left-right difference in the male brain than there is in the female brain. However, some other studies have contradicted these claims, and the jury is still out on whether these gender differences truly exist (Kolb and Whishaw, 1996).

EVIDENCE FROM SPLIT BRAINS

In the normal, intact brain, the two hemispheres communicate via a massive bundle of nerve fibers called the *corpus callosum.* This structure allows the two halves of the brain to communicate so that they can pool their information and function collaboratively. In some cases of severe epilepsy, however, this neurological bridge (and some other subsidiary ones) is cut so that seizures will not spread from one hemisphere to the other (Bogen, Fisher, and Vogel, 1965; Wilson et al., 1977). The surgery clearly relieves suffering, but it has a side effect—the two hemispheres of the brain are now functionally isolated from each other and in some ways act as two separate brains (see Figure 2.22; Gazzaniga, 1967; Sperry, 1974, 1982).

The effect of the split-brain operation is well demonstrated by tasks that pose a question to one hemisphere and require an answer from the other (see Figure

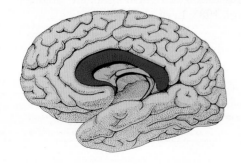

2.22 The split brain *To control otherwise intractable epilepsy, neurosurgeons sometimes sever the two hemispheres. This is accomplished by cutting the corpus callosum (in blue) and a few other connective tracts. The corpus callosum is shown here in a lateral cross section.*

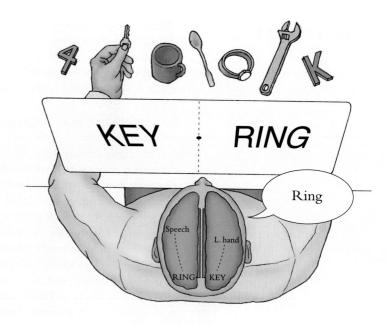

2.23 A setup sometimes used in split-brain studies *The participant fixates a center dot and then sees a picture or a word on the right or left side of the dot. He may be asked to respond verbally, by reading the word or naming the picture. He may also be asked to respond without words, for example, by picking out a named object from among a group spread out on a table and hidden from view, so that it can only be identified by touch. (This figure illustrates both types of response. Ordinarily, only one type at a time is required.) (After Gazzaniga, 1967)*

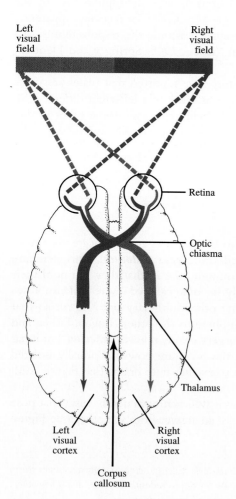

2.23). One method is to show a picture so that the message only reaches one hemisphere. This is done by flashing the picture for a fraction of a second to either the right or the left side of the patient's field of vision. The anatomical pathways of the visual system are such that if the picture is flashed to the right, it is processed by the left hemisphere; if presented to the left, it is processed by the right hemisphere (see Figure 2.24). When the picture is on the right, the patient is easily able to identify what he sees, because the information is transmitted to the left hemisphere, which readily formulates a spoken response. The situation is different when the picture is flashed on the left. Now the image is sent to the right hemisphere, but this hemisphere can neither provide a spoken reply nor relay the information to the left hemisphere (which has the language capacity), because the bridge between the two has been cut (Gazzaniga, 1967). In fact, in this circumstance, the patient may announce that he saw *nothing*—a response coming from the (more verbal) left hemisphere and correctly reporting what that hemisphere saw (or, in this case, didn't see).

These studies indicate that language is largely the province of the left hemisphere. But this doesn't mean that language is completely absent in the right hemisphere. A ready example is provided by a split-brain patient who was asked to name a picture (say, of a planter) flashed to the left side (that is, to the right hemisphere). He sometimes ventured a haphazard guess ("coffee cup?") and then frowned or shook his head immediately afterward. The left hemisphere generated the guess, but the right hemisphere—which saw the object—had evidently understood the question well enough to know that the guess was mistaken (Gazzaniga, 1967; for further discussion of right-hemisphere language abilities, see Zaidel, 1976, 1983; Gazzaniga, 1983; Levy, 1983).

2.24 The contralateral connections in the visual pathways *The visual pathway is so arranged that all points in the right visual field send their information to the left hemisphere; all those in the left field send theirs to the right hemisphere. Information from one hemisphere is transmitted to the other by way of the corpus callosum.*

HEMISPHERIC LATERALIZATION IN NORMAL PARTICIPANTS

Most of the evidence for hemispheric lateralization we've discussed thus far has come from patients with neurological deficits: some with lesions in one or another hemisphere, others with a severed corpus callosum. Can lateralization be demonstrated in normal populations? A considerable amount of research shows that it can.

One approach uses the same experimental procedure that was so successfully employed with the split-brain patients. Various stimuli are briefly presented to either the right or the left visual field of normal participants. Some stimuli are items that are presumably better dealt with by the left hemisphere: words or letters. Others are items that call on the special capacities of the right hemisphere: faces or other complex forms. The participant's task is to recognize the items and indicate his response as quickly and as accurately as he can. In studies of this sort, the experimenters' primary interest is in the participant's *response time,* that is, how long it takes him to respond. The logic of the experiment is simple. Suppose the stimulus is presented to the hemisphere that is most appropriate to it: words to the left, faces to the right. If so, this hemisphere can get to work immediately, decipher the stimulus, and come up with an answer. But suppose the stimulus is sent to the wrong cerebral address: words to the right and faces to the left. This calls for an extra step, because the visual message must be forwarded to the other hemisphere by way of the corpus callosum. This additional transmission step takes a certain amount of time—not very much time, to be sure, but enough to be clearly measurable. As a result, we would expect participants to be slightly faster in recognizing words presented to the left hemisphere than to the right hemisphere. By the same token, we would expect them to respond more quickly to faces shown to the right hemisphere than to the left. By and large, this is just what happens (Geffen, Bradshaw, and Wallace, 1971; Moscovitch, 1972, 1979).

More direct evidence of hemispheric lateralization has also been provided by neuroimaging techniques, such as PET scans. Such studies generally show that speech tasks produce predominantly left-hemisphere activity, whereas right-hemisphere predominance occurs on musical and spatial tasks (Kolb and Whishaw, 1996).

TWO MODES OF MENTAL FUNCTIONING

The preceding discussion indicates that language and spatial organization are usually handled in two different areas of the brain. Some psychologists believe that this difference in hemispheric localization coincides with a distinction between two fundamentally different modes of thought: one involving words, the other spatial processes. This distinction certainly accords with everyday observation. We often express our thoughts in words—about our work, about politics, about who likes whom; the list is endless. But we also mentally manipulate the world with little benefit from language—as when we visualize a room with rearranged furniture or when we do a jigsaw puzzle. Many problems can be solved by either mode. We may find our way to a friend's home by referring to a mental map or by memorizing a verbal sequence, such as "first right turn after the third traffic light." But the two modes are not always interchangeable. How a corkscrew works is hard to describe in words; the pros and cons of a

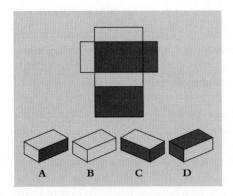

2.25 An item from a test of spatial relations *The participant has to decide which of the figures, A, B, C, or D, can be made by folding the pattern above. (The correct answer is D. After Cronbach, 1970a)*

political two-party system are impossible to convey without them. (For more on the distinction between words and images, see Chapter 8.)

The difference between verbal and spatial modes of thought is explicitly recognized in many tests of intelligence. Different test items are provided to assess each mode separately. Verbal aptitude is often gauged by vocabulary questions ("What does *formulate* mean?") or abstraction tasks ("In what ways are dinosaurs and horse-drawn carriages alike?"). Testing spatial ability may require the subject to construct a design by arranging a set of colored blocks or to visualize how a two-dimensional shape will appear when folded into a box (see Figure 2.25).

For some theorists, the verbal-spatial distinction defines the difference in the functioning of the two cerebral hemispheres, with the left hemisphere the "linguist," and the right hemisphere the "map maker." This model neatly fits the fact that performance on the various verbal tests is more impaired by lesions to the left hemisphere, while performance on spatial tests is more impaired by lesions to the right hemisphere (Levy, 1974). But other theorists suggest that the distinction between the hemispheres must be conceived differently. In their view, the right hemisphere is specialized for the organization of space, whereas the left hemisphere's specialty is organization in time. Thus, if language functions are found more in the left hemisphere, it is not because of a specialization for language per se. Rather, it is because language, like many other functions, depends crucially on precisely timed sequences of elements. The person who is insensitive to what comes first and what comes second cannot possibly speak or understand the speech of others. *Tap* is not the same word as *pat,* and the sentence "The dog bit the man" is crucially different from "The man bit the dog." To summarize this view, the right hemisphere is more concerned with what goes where, the left more with what comes when (Bogen, 1969; Tzeng and Wang, 1984).

Although the space versus time hypothesis is rather speculative, it fits in well enough with the facts we have described in this chapter. The same is not true of the many accounts written for the general public. Some authors go so far as to equate left-hemispheric function with western science and right-hemispheric function with eastern culture and mysticism. In the same vein, others have argued that western societies overly encourage left-brained functions at the expense of right-brained functions and that we need special efforts to train the neglected right hemisphere (e.g., Ornstein, 1977). One author recommends "Ten Ways to Develop Your Right Brain," one of which involves drowning out the presentation of information with music (Prince, 1978, cited in Springer and Deutsch, 1998). There is, however, no persuasive evidence for any of these popular claims. In many cases, the distinctions being proposed—between the rational and the intuitive, the analytic and the artistic, or between western and eastern philosophies of life—are not so clear cut. In other cases, the distinctions fit badly with, or go wildly beyond, the available evidence. And even if these distinctions are sometimes useful, there is little reason to believe that each mode corresponds to the functioning of one of the brain hemispheres. After all, despite the mythic appeal of two modes of thinking, there may turn out to be five, or ten, or a hundred modes of thought, and this obviously would not map neatly onto the two hemispheres (Levy, 1985; Efron, 1990).

The popular misconceptions are particularly misleading when they imply that the two cerebral hemispheres, each with its own talents and strategies, endlessly vie for control of our mental life. Instead, each of us has a single brain. Each part of the brain (and not just the cerebral hemispheres) is quite differentiated and so contributes its own specialized abilities to the activity of the whole. But in the end, the marvelously complex, extraordinarily sophisticated skills that we each display depend on the whole brain and on the coordinated actions of all these components. Our hemispheres are not cerebral competitors. Instead, they pool their specialized capacities to produce a seamlessly integrated single mental self.

BRAIN FUNCTIONS AND NEURAL HIERARCHIES

Most nervous systems combine the advantages of central control—flexibility and complexity of behavior—with the speed and economy of regional rule. To combine these levels, nervous systems are invariably organized in a hierarchical fashion, with higher centers coordinating lower centers, which themselves coordinate yet lower ones.

HIERARCHIES IN SMALL NEURAL CIRCUITS

Hierarchies of nerve cells operate in even the simplest of nervous systems. In some instances, just one cell acts as the controller within the hierarchy, coordinating the activity of several others. This is the case with the sea snail *Aplysia,* whose blood circulation is governed by a total of seven neurons, with one supervisory cell coordinating the activities of the other six (Kandel, 1979).

In *Aplysia,* the lower level of the hierarchy involves single cells. More typically, the lower levels of the hierarchy consist of groups of cells that form small circuits called **central pattern generators** (or **CPGs**). These instigate rhythmic actions such as chewing, swallowing, breathing, and locomotion. For example, consider how a dog or cat walks: The four legs have to act in concert; when two of the legs are lifted off the ground, the other two have to exert special force to hold the body up. This intricate rhythmic interplay of individual limb movements is orchestrated by CPGs, many of them in the hindbrain. These CPGs initiate and orchestrate lower-level reflexes (and other neural activities) into organized rhythmic acts (Gallistel, 1980; Grillner and Wallén, 1985).

DISINHIBITION

CPGs provide one example of hierarchical control in the nervous system; another example comes from cases in which one part of the nervous system holds another in check. This process is most visible when this inhibition is interrupted—a phenomenon known as **disinhibition.** A classic example involves the spinal reflexes in frogs, which are more vigorous when all brain structures have been removed. This reflects the fact that these brain structures normally inhibit these reflexes; with the inhibition removed, the reflexes are correspondingly strengthened.

Another instance of disinhibition is seen in the mating behavior of the praying mantis (see Figure 2.26). The female mantis is a rapacious killer. She seizes and devours any small creature unfortunate enough to move across her field of vision. Since the male mantis is considerably smaller than the female, he too may qualify as food.★ This cannibalism is quite puzzling. How can the mantis survive as a species given a behavioral tendency that counteracts successful fertilization?

★ One study suggests that this cannibalistic pattern may only occur under artificial conditions of captivity and when the female is virtually starved. Under more natural circumstances, males seem to manage to mate quite successfully without losing their heads in the process. But even if induced artificially, the phenomenon is an interesting if macabre illustration of the effect of disinhibition (Liske and Davis, 1984).

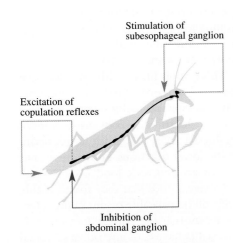

Stimulation of
subesophageal ganglion

Excitation of
copulation reflexes

Inhibition of
abdominal ganglion

2.26   The disinhibitory mechanism in the praying mantis Excitation of the abdominal ganglion leads to copulatory movements in the male. But the sight of the moving female stimulates the subesophageal ganglion in the male's head, which inhibits the abdominal ganglion so that copulation stops. Decapitation severs the subesophageal ganglion. The result is disinhibition and copulation resumes. Here, dark green indicates excitation and dark red inhibition. (Roeder, 1967)

According to one hypothesis, the female's predatory pattern is triggered almost exclusively by moving visual stimuli, and the male's mating behavior is delicately attuned to this fact. As soon as he sees her, he becomes absolutely immobile. Whenever she looks away for a moment he moves toward her ever so slowly, but freezes immediately when her eyes wheel back toward him—an inhibitory effect upon overall reflex activity. When close enough to her, he suddenly leaps upon her back and begins to copulate. Once squarely upon the female's back he is reasonably safe (her predatory reflexes are elicited only by moving visual stimuli, and he is mostly out of sight). But the dangers he must surmount to reach this place of safety are enormous. He must not miss her when he jumps; he must not slip while upon her. Should he fall, he will surely be grasped and eaten. Fairly often he does lose his balance, but even then his generative efforts will not have been in vain—for his genes, if not for him. The female will eat her fallen mate from the head down. In almost all instances, the abdomen of the male continues its copulatory movements despite the loss of the head. Why?

It appears that the intact male's copulatory reflexes are ordinarily held in check by a ganglion located in his head. When this nerve cluster is experimentally removed, the animal will engage in endless copulatory movements even when no female is present. The same thing happens if the female chances to seize her mate. She first chews off his head and with it the ganglion that inhibits his copulatory movements, thus disinhibiting the male's copulatory pattern, which now resumes in full force, thus demonstrating the benefits of hierarchical organization (Roeder, 1935).

WHO IS IN CHARGE?

We have noted that the nervous system is organized along the lines of a hierarchy, with higher centers controlling lower centers, which control yet lower ones. But, ultimately, who is in charge? Some nineteenth-century neurologists supposed that some regions of the cortex are at the very top of the hierarchy and hand down orders to all the rest. This notion fits in with our view that those functions that are most severely disturbed by cortical lesions—language, thinking, memory, and perception—are the "higher" mental processes and that these "higher" processes presumably govern the "lower" ones. But many modern neuroscientists believe that this conclusion doesn't really follow, for in important ways, the cortex does not control many of the lower functions. For example, rats —and for that matter, humans—continue to eat and seek food even though they may have suffered extensive cortical damage. Foods that they found highly palatable or distasteful before the lesion will still be palatable or distasteful afterward (Grill and Berridge, 1985). This not to say that the cortex does not play any role in food seeking (or drinking, or sexual behavior, or any other so-called lower functions). But there is no evidence that it governs them.

The best guess is that the nervous system is not organized according to a single hierarchy. Rather than having an absolute monarch, a cortical queen who governs all else below (e.g., Arbib, 1972), it is composed of a number of hierarchies whose controls and functions overlap, with some in the cortex and some in subcortical structures. These hierarchies interact continuously, with one in charge on one occasion but not on another. So it probably makes no sense to say that any one of them is the ruler. The operation of the nervous system may well be analogous to that of a complex twentieth-century society such as ours. The United States, for example, is not governed by one hierarchy, but by a number of interlocking ones. There are the three branches of the federal government, as well as the armed forces. The bureaucracies of the government agencies, the hierarchies of the large corporations, the labor unions, the media, and so on each have a large measure of control over their own domains, but they are all shaped and influenced by each of the others. Thus, the country as a whole is governed by a complex interaction of all these institutions, each with its own control mechanisms. For any individual decision, who will decide depends on many factors, including what is to be decided.

So who's in charge of the nervous system? As yet, we know too little to be sure of any answer. But the best guess is: It depends.

BUILDING BLOCKS OF THE NERVOUS SYSTEM: NEURONS AND NERVE IMPULSES

We now have some understanding of the general structures of the nervous system and how they function. But how do these structures accomplish their tasks? To answer this question we must first look at the building blocks of which the system is composed—the individual nerve cells called **neurons** and the **nerve impulses** by which they communicate. We will now drop down to this cellular level, discussing the kinds of circuitry that can result from interactions among different nerve cells and the neurochemistry that makes such interactions possible. Along the way, we will show how the analysis of this circuitry has begun to help us understand some aspects of mental illness, the effects of drugs, and the effects of and recovery from brain damage.

THE NEURON

The neuron is a single cell with three subdivisions: the **dendrites,** the **cell body** (or **soma**), and the **axon** (see Figure 2.27). The dendrites are usually branched, sometimes so much that they resemble a thick Medusa-like bush. The axon, which extends like a wispy thread, may fork out into several **axonal branches** at its end. The dendrites receive nerve impulses from other neurons; the axon transmits that impulse.

A

Nucleus

Dendrites

Cell body

Nodes
of
Ranvier

Axon

Myelin sheath

Terminal
endings

2.27 The neuron   (A) A schematic diagram of the main parts of a motoneuron. Part of the cell is myelinated; that is, its axon is covered with sets of segmented, insulating sheaths formed by encircling glial cells. (After Katz, 1952) (B) Highly magnified nerve cell in the human brain showing cell body and several dendrites. The long vertical bands are branches from other nerve cells. (Photograph by Manfred Kage/Peter Arnold, Inc.)

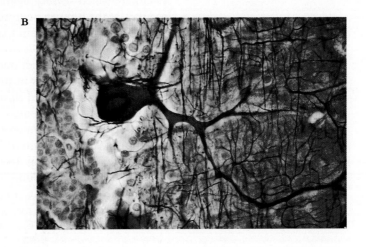

B

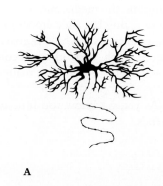

A

B

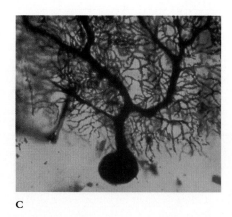

C

2.28 *Different kinds of neurons* *(A) A motoneuron of the human spinal cord. (B) A neuron in the human cerebral cortex, the part of the brain concerned with such mental functions as perception and planning. (After Kolb and Whishaw, 1996) (C) A specialized neuron in the cerebellum, a part of the brain that controls motor coordination. This kind of cell has been said to gather impulses from as many as 80,000 other neurons. The photomicrograph is from the cerebellum of a twelve-month-old infant. It has been stained by a special chemical that shows the extent of the branching of the cell's dendrites. (© Guigoz/ Dr. A. Privat/Petit Format/Science Source/ Photo Researchers)*

A few details about neurons will give a feeling for their size and number. The diameter of an individual neuron is very small; cell bodies vary from 5 to about 100 microns in diameter (1 micron = 1/1,000 millimeter). The average hair on your head, in contrast, has a diameter of about 100 microns. Dendrites are typically short, say a few hundred microns. But axons can be much longer.

The easiest neuron to describe is the motor neuron, or **motoneuron** (Figure 2.28). It provides an efferent pathway that begins within the CNS, exits through the spinal cord or a cranial nerve, winds up on a muscle fiber, and makes that muscle fiber contract. The axon of the motoneuron transmits the nerve impulse initiated at its dendrites to the muscle fiber and at this neuromuscular juncture produces a chemical that triggers the fiber's contraction. Some motoneuron axons are quite long, extending from the head to the base of the spinal cord, others from the spinal cord to the limbs. Our longest axons run from our spinal cords to our legs; these are about a meter long. To get a sense of the cell body relative to the axon in such a motoneuron, imagine a basketball attached to a garden hose that stretches the whole fourteen-mile length of Manhattan.

The muscle contractions initiated by motoneurons are but one kind of efferent control. Other efferent neurons control the endocrine and digestive glands or the smooth muscle fibers that surround the digestive tract and blood vessels.

Still other neurons convey information inward, keeping the nervous system informed about the external world and the body's internal environment. Some of these are afferent neurons attached to specialized receptor cells that respond to various external energies, such as pressure, chemical changes, light, and so on. These receptor cells translate (more technically, **transduce**) these physical stimuli into electrical changes, which then trigger a nervous impulse in other neurons.

Neurons that convey impulses from receptors toward the rest of the nervous system are called **sensory neurons.** Sometimes the receptor is actually a specialized part of the sensory neuron, as in the neurons that are responsible for sensing pressure on the skin. But in many cases, transduction and transmission are separate functions that are entrusted to different cells. In vision and hearing, for example, receptor cells transduce optical stimulation and air pressure, respectively, into electrical changes in the cell, which in turn trigger impulses in sensory neurons that then proceed through the nervous system.

Thus far we have discussed two kinds of neurons: those that trigger some action (such as the motoneurons) and those that receive information (the sensory neurons). This is consistent with Descartes' simple stimulus-response conception of reflex action (see p. 16–17), which works well enough for simple actions like knee jerks and eye blinks.

But more complex behavior needs more complex neural circuitry, and indeed the pathways that carry our sensations and produce our actions are typically quite indirect. In fact, in complex organisms the vast majority of nerve cells are neither sensory neurons nor motoneurons. Rather, they are *interneurons,* neurons that are *inter*posed between two or more other neurons. Interneurons vary widely in both form and function. They often show considerable branching, which produces an enormous number of contacts between different neurons.

In the vast majority of cases, these interneurons transmit their message to yet other interneurons, and these send theirs to still other interneurons. Typically, many thousands of such interneurons must interact before the command is finally issued and sent down the path of the efferent nerve fibers. These interneuronal connections form the *microcircuitry* of the central nervous system. The microcircuitry is where the brain conducts most of its information processing, and the bulk of the brain structures we have reviewed consist of just such microcircuitry.

GLIAL CELLS: UNSUNG HEROES OF THE NERVOUS SYSTEM

Besides neurons, nervous systems are also full of *glial cells* (from the Greek word for "glue"), and in some areas of the brain, glial cells outnumber neurons by ten to one (Shepherd, 1994). Their functions are crucial to neuronal communication. To begin with, they act as guidewires for growing neurons, much like beanpoles that guide bean shoots in the garden. Later in development, they provide a supportive scaffolding for mature neurons and assist in the repair process when brain tissue is damaged.

Yet another function of glial cells is to increase the speed at which neurons can communicate. The specialized glial cells that accomplish this are mostly made of the fatty substance known as *myelin.* Beginning shortly after birth, they spiral and wrap their fatty tentacles around neurons that have long axons, such as those that proceed from distant sensory organs or travel to distant muscles. Each spiral creates a myelin "wrapper" around a portion of the axon, and soon the entire length of the axon is covered by a succession of these wrappers. As we will see, the uncoated gaps between the wrappers, called the *nodes of Ranvier,* are crucial in speeding up the nerve impulses traveling along these myelinated axons (see Figure 2.27).

The fact that myelin is white explains why brains are made up of both *white* and *gray matter.* What anatomists call the white matter is the myelinated axons traversing long distances either within the brain or to and from the body (hence the need for speed). Conversely, the gray matter consists of cell bodies, dendrites, and unmyelinated axons and the interneurons that comprise the nervous system's microcircuitry.

HOW THE NERVOUS SYSTEM MAKES ITS OWN CIRCUITRY

Within the huge complexity of the brain, it is crucial that each neuron send its neuronal messages to the right targets, so that, at the coarsest level, information intended to move the leg doesn't halt digestion instead. The primary projection areas on the surface of the cortex, by themselves, suggest an exquisite mapping of pathways between the brain and the body, and connections within the brain require even more precise navigation. But how does each developing neuron come to know its eventual target? How do the microcircuits that do the brain's information processing organize themselves?

As yet, we have only the beginning of an answer to these questions, drawing what little we know from observations of animals with much simpler nervous systems than ours. First, nerve cells begin to reproduce early in the embryo's life, migrate to key areas in the brain-to-be, and begin to differentiate into different kinds of neurons by sprouting axons and dendrites. Some of the budding axons attach themselves to glial-cell guidewires and follow them to the far reaches of the brain where they attach themselves to distant neurons. Interneurons proliferate and interconnect. This budding and connecting of neurons occurs in spurts as the embryo develops, with wave after wave of axon proliferation interspersed with periods of microcircuitry construction.

All these developmental processes are under genetic control and are automatic, although they can be distorted by influences like drugs, genetic defects, or poor nutrition. The possibility of wiring errors is minimized through competition among neurons. Many more neurons are created than are needed, and each neuron tries to form many more connections than are required. But if a neuron's connections prove either wrong or redundant, that neuron must either withdraw its connections and find suitable targets or wind up dying.

It is entirely normal for between 20 and 80 percent of neurons to die as the brain develops, depending upon which region of the brain is under discussion. (In humans, this decimation occurs at between 4 and 6 months after conception.) By birth, most creatures are left with just about all the neurons they will ever have (Rosenzweig et al., 1996). Overall, it seems that the nervous system's circuitry organizes and corrects itself as it grows.

THE ELECTRICAL ACTIVITY OF THE NEURON

Neurons communicate by receiving and transmitting nerve impulses. But just how do they do this? How do they transmit signals, influence each other, and cause us to sense, to think, to act? We now know that they do so electrically and chemically. But the unraveling of this mystery was hard won. It required advances both in our knowledge of the anatomy of neurons and in the measurement of tiny quantities of electrical current—the movements of charged particles. One crucial advance was in the production of ever finer microelectrodes, some of which have tips so small (less than 1 micron in diameter) that they can puncture a neuron without squashing it and detect weak electrical currents without disrupting them. A related advance was the invention of a device that could display tiny currents that the microelectrodes could now detect. This device was the *oscilloscope,* which could amplify weak electrical fluctuations and depict them as wavy lines on a fluorescent screen. Every bit as important a contribution was made by natural selection. It gave us the squid, an animal endowed with several giant axons up to 1 millimeter in diameter, which—compared to the smaller neurons found in most other species—could be poked, prodded, and measured much more easily.

NEURONAL POTENTIALS: THE RESTING AND ACTION POTENTIALS

The neuron is, in most respects, just a cell. It has a nucleus on the inside and a cell membrane that defines its outside. In the middle is a biochemical stew of ions, amino acids, proteins, DNA and RNA, and so forth, and a collection of

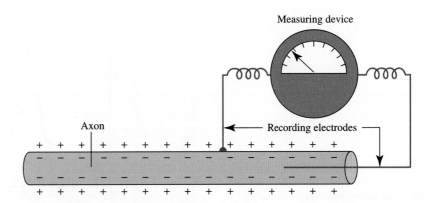

2.29 Recording the voltage within a neuron *A schematic drawing of how the impulse is recorded. One electrode is inserted into the axon; the other records from the axon's outside. (After Carlson, 1986)*

smaller structures like mitochondria. What makes the neuron a neuron, though, is the peculiarity of its cell membrane. It is irritable. Poke it, shake it, stimulate it electrically or chemically, and the neuronal membrane may destabilize, producing a cascade of changes that form the nerve impulse—that is, make the cell fire. Some neurons even fire on their own, at regular intervals, and seem to act as pacemakers for behavior such as wing-flapping, breathing, and sleeping-waking. Whether elicited or self-induced, it is this irritability that makes neurons the fast communicators of the nervous system. Figure 2.29 shows how the neuron's irritability (and its effects) are studied. Two microelectrodes are used: one is inserted into a nerve axon while the other contacts its outer surface. In this manner, any electrical activity near the cell membrane can be detected. As it turns out, there is activity even when the cell is not firing, as shown by a voltage difference between the inside and the outside of the fiber. Like a miniature battery with a positive and a negative connection, the inside of the axon is electrically negative with respect to the outside, with the difference measuring about −70 or so millivolts (a standard AA battery, at 1.5 volts, has over twenty times this voltage). Because this small negative voltage occurs when the neuron is stable, it has traditionally been called the neuron's ***resting potential,*** although, as we shall see, maintaining this voltage takes work, and in its stable state the neuron is anything but at rest.

What happens when the neuron is irritated and is made to fire? To find out, neuroscientists stimulate the surface of the fiber by means of a third microelectrode, which applies a brief electrical pulse. This pulse reduces the voltage difference across the membrane. If the pulse is weak, nothing further will happen, and the membrane will work to restore itself to its usual −70 millivolt charge. But if the pulse is strong enough to push the voltage difference past a critical ***excitation threshold*** (about −55 millivolts in mammals), something dramatic happens. The voltage difference between the inside and outside of the cell abruptly collapses to zero, and, in fact, begins to reverse itself. Now, instead of the inside of the membrane showing a negative voltage compared to the outside, suddenly it swings positive, up to +40 millivolts. This marks the neuron's destabilization, a cataclysm that completely disrupts the cell's membrane. Fortunately, the chaos is short-lived; the membrane restabilizes itself within about 1 millisecond and returns to its −70 millivolt state.

This entire destabilization-restabilization sequence is called the ***action potential*** (Figure 2.30), and its influence can spread far beyond the point of irritation.

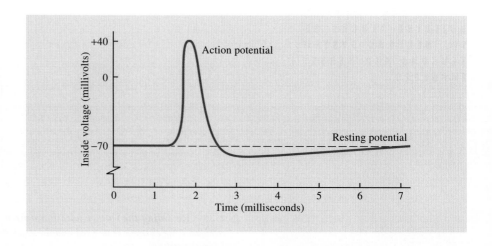

2.30 The action potential *Action potential recorded from the squid's giant axon. (After Hodgkin and Huxley, 1939)*

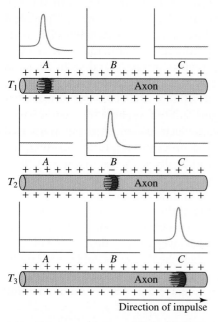

2.31 The action potential as it travels along the axon *The axon is shown at three different moments—T₁, T₂, and T₃—after the application of a stimulus. The voltage inside the membrane is shown at three different points along the axon—A, B, and C. (After Carlson, 1986)*

Figure 2.31 shows a longer segment of an axon, with microelectrodes inserted at several points. An *adequate stimulus*—that is, one that pushes the voltage difference past the excitation threshold—is applied to point *A,* and the voltage difference is measured at point *A,* as well as at points *B* and *C.* At first, an action potential is observed at *A,* while *B* and *C* are still stable and retaining their normal negative voltage. A moment later, *A* returns to normal, while *B* has destabilized and shows an action potential. A moment after this, *B* returns to normal but an action potential is found at *C.* (Of course, the time intervals between each period of destabilization are exceedingly brief.) The action potential is evidently contagious, with each region quickly destabilizing its neighbor.

Explaining neuronal potentials The resting and action potentials are the key to explaining nearly all neuronal communication. What creates them? Neurobiologists have concluded that they derive from chemical processes at the neuron's membrane, as well as from the structure of the membrane itself. It turns out that there are electrically charged particles (ions) dissolved in the fluid both inside and outside the neuronal membrane. In general, ions are defined as molecules (or single atoms) that have lost or gained electrons and have thus acquired a positive or negative charge. The membrane controls which ions are allowed to remain inside the neuron and which ones are shoved outside. It does this using biochemical portholes, known as *ion channels,* that let certain ions pass through, as well as *ion pumps* that suck them in or push them out. This is the key to understanding the neural impulse, because the relative concentrations of ions inside and outside the cell are what determine the voltages and voltage changes associated with the resting and action potentials.

When the membrane is stable, positively charged sodium ions are forcibly pumped from the inside of the membrane to the outside, while channels that might otherwise let sodium ions back in are shut. This excess of positively charged sodium ions on the outside of the cell—as well as imbalances of other ions, especially potassium—creates the voltage difference known as the resting potential—negative on the inside and positive on the outside (see Figure 2.32). Maintaining this stable state takes constant work, because the membrane is leaky and the pumps are imperfect. Indeed, probably most of the metabolic energy used by the brain is expended on maintaining these so-called resting potentials (Rosenzweig et al., 1996). When the membrane is sufficiently irritated (such as by reducing the voltage difference to the threshold), the sodium channels spring open temporarily, and sodium ions rush in. This creates a temporary excess of positively charged particles on the inside of the membrane, which produces the positive swing of the action potential. But immediately afterward, the membrane restores itself to stability, closing its ionic channels and pumping out the excess sodium ions.

Propagation of the action potential   These electrochemical events explain what happens at a single region of the membrane, but why does this excitation spread to neighboring regions? The reason is that the temporarily positive voltage inside the axon induces the opening of ion channels at adjacent regions, which first changes the voltages at these regions and then induces more distant channels to open, and so on. The upshot is that the impulse—the cascade of events that creates the action potential—moves down the entire length of the axon and throughout the rest of the neuron as well. This is known as the **propagation** of the action potential. The whole thing is like a spark traveling along a fuse, except that while the fuse is consumed by the spark, the ion channels rapidly reclose and the membrane restores itself within milliseconds. As a consequence, the neuron is soon ready to fire again, and if a superthreshold stimulus is still present, then fire it will.

At the microscopic level, the chain reaction that produces the propagation of the action potential seems fairly fast, but it actually travels at a rate of only about 1 meter per second—about average walking speed. If this was the fastest that action potentials could propagate, then all our actions would slow to a crawl, and faster-paced acts like speaking and jumping would simply be impossible. Enter the nodes of Ranvier, which, as we mentioned, are the spaces between the glial cell tentacles that wrap axons with myelin. On these myelinated axons, only the nodes must be destabilized, and thus the changes that produce the action potential can skip from node to node. Myelinated axons can propagate their action potentials at speeds up to 120 meters per second (about 260 miles per hour). Myelination, found only in vertebrates, allows us to move much faster than, say, a jellyfish or a snail.

The importance of intact myelin is underscored by the deficits suffered when myelination breaks down in the brain. This happens in **multiple sclerosis** (**MS**), a disease in which the body's immune system mistakenly regards the brain's

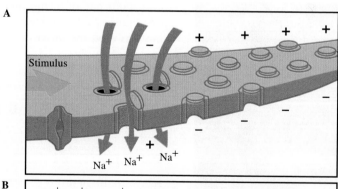

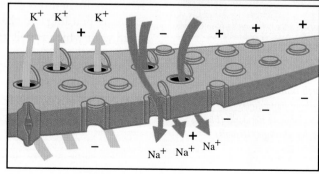

2.32   Ion channels and the action potential   *(A) When a stimulus is above threshold, special ion channels of the membrane open, and positively charged sodium ions (Na^+) surge inside. (B) Immediately thereafter, the gates that admitted Na^+ close, and the electrical balance is restored, because some other positively charged ions—specifically potassium ions (K^+)—are now forced out. The whole process is repeated at an adjacent point in the axon. (After Starr and Taggart, 1989)*

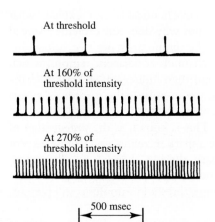

At threshold

At 160% of
threshold intensity

At 270% of
threshold intensity

500 msec

2.33 Stimulus intensity and firing frequency *Responses of a crab axon to a continuous electric current at three levels of current intensity. The time scale is relatively slow. As a result, the action potentials show up as single vertical lines or "spikes." Note that while increasing the current intensity has no effect on the height of the spikes (the all-or-none law) it leads to a marked increase in the frequency of spikes per second. (After Eccles, 1973)*

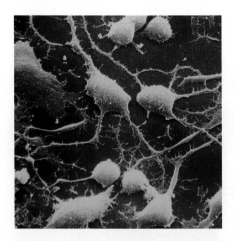

Interaction among nerve cells *An isolated nerve cell. The cell body is in contact with other cells through numerous extensions. The figure illustrates how nerve fibers cross each other to form an elaborate network. (Photograph by David M. Phillips / Visuals Unlimited)*

myelin as an intruder and attacks it. The manifestations of MS are highly variable, but can include blindness, numbness, and paralysis.

All-or-none law Once a stimulus is strong enough to destabilize the neuronal membrane sufficiently, an action potential will propagate. The action potential will be the same size, and will be propagated just as rapidly, whether the stimulus just meets threshold or exceeds it by two, three, or twenty times. This phenomenon is sometimes referred to as the ***all-or-none law***—either there is an action potential or there isn't. There's no compromise possible, and no variations allowed in the size or speed of the action potential. Thus, just as pounding on a car horn doesn't make it any louder, a stronger stimulus doesn't produce a stronger action potential. A neuron either fires or does not fire. It knows no in-between.★

Stimulus intensity Neurons obey the all-or-none law, and stimulus intensity has no effect once the threshold is exceeded. But how can we reconcile this fact with our everyday experience? The world isn't all black or all white, and sounds aren't simply on or off. We can obviously see shades of gray (not to mention colors) and tell the difference between the buzz of a mosquito and the roar of a jet plane. How can this be? There are two answers.

First, more intense stimuli can simply excite greater numbers of neurons. This is because different neurons vary enormously in their thresholds. As a result, a strong stimulus will stimulate more neurons than a weak stimulus: The weak stimulus will stimulate all neurons whose thresholds are below a given level, while the strong stimulus will stimulate all of those plus others whose threshold is higher.

The second mechanism applies to individual neurons. While remaining strictly obedient to the all-or-none law, they are nevertheless affected by stimulus intensity. This becomes apparent when we apply a continuous stimulus for a longer interval. When bombarded with such a sustained stimulus, most neurons don't just fire once and retire. Instead, they generate a whole stream or "volley" of action potentials, by repeated cycles of destabilization and restabilization. In accordance with the all-or-none principle, the size of each of the action potentials remains the same; what changes is the impulse frequency—the stronger the stimulus, the more often the axon will fire. This effect holds until we reach a maximum rate of firing, after which further increases in intensity have no effect (see Figure 2.33). Different neurons have different maximum rates; the highest in humans is on the order of 1,000 impulses per second.

INTERACTION AMONG NERVE CELLS

In a way, the neurons of our nervous system are like a thousand billion speakers, endlessly prattling and chattering to one another. But each of them has only one word with which to tell its story. It can choose only whether to speak or remain silent, to speak often or almost never. Looked at in isolation, the individual speakers seem like imbeciles with a one-word vocabulary, babbling and being babbled at. But when taken as a whole, this gibbering becomes somehow harmonious. The trick seems to be in the integration of the individual messages and the ways that the single syllables become an ensemble. The really interesting

★ The all-or-none law holds for the action potential—that is, for conduction along the axon. As we will see shortly, however, the situation is different at the dendrites and cell body, where potentials are graded, being built up or lowered in a continuous rather than an all-or-none fashion.

question for psychology, then, is not how a neuron manages to produce its word, but rather how it connects to others and participates in the neuronal conversation.

INFERRING THE SYNAPSE

Neurons can interact in many ways. We begin with the simplest illustration of such interactions—the reflex. From Descartes on, it was widely believed that reflexes were formed from a long and essentially continuous strand of nervous tissue—in essence, along one neuron. According to this view, the incoming sensory information triggers a response at one end of this neuron, and then the response is initiated at the other end of the same neuron. By the end of the nineteenth century, however, most observers were convinced that the pathway between stimulus and response wasn't direct and that the neurons must therefore be communicating across some kind of gap. This gap, together with the membranes of the neurons that form it, is called the *synapse.*

The critical studies establishing the role of the synapse and its place in nerve interaction were performed at the turn of the century by the English physiologist Sir Charles Sherrington (1857–1952). Amazingly, Sherrington's work was conducted at the level of behavior rather than that of electrophysiology. What he observed directly was reflex action in dogs, cats, and monkeys. How the synapse worked, he inferred. In this sense Sherrington acted more like a psychologist than a physiologist: He focused on behavior in order to gain insight into its underlying mechanisms.

Sherrington set out to study the *simple reflex,* isolated from the influence of other neurons. To achieve this, he used *spinal animals,* usually dogs, whose spinal cords had been severed in the neck region. This cut all connections between the body (from the neck down) and the brain, leaving the spinal reflexes free of higher influences.

EXCITATION

Sherrington's method was simple. He applied mild electric shocks to some point on the animal's skin and observed whether this stimulus evoked a particular reflex response (Figure 2.34). In one series of experiments, Sherrington showed that although one stimulus below threshold might not elicit the reflex, two or more stimuli (all of them subthreshold) might do so if presented successively. Such *temporal summation* could occur even when the individual stimuli were separated by as much as half a second (see Figure 2.35). How could this be?

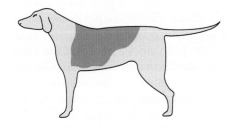

2.34 Saddle-shaped area of spinal dog *When a stimulus whose strength is above threshold is applied at any point in the "saddle," the animal will perform a scratching movement. (After Sherrington, 1906)*

2.35 Arguments for synaptic transmission *(A) Temporal summation. A subthreshold stimulus will not elicit the reflex, but two or more stimuli will if presented successively at intervals of up to half a second. This indicates that the effects of the first stimulus were somehow stored and added to the effects of the second. (B) Spatial summation. Subthreshold stimuli applied to different points in the saddle area will not evoke a reflex if presented separately, but they will if presented simultaneously. This indicates that the excitatory effects from different regions are all funneled into the same common path.*

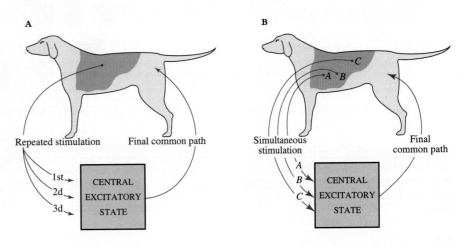

Sir Charles Sherrington *(Courtesy National Library of Medicine)*

Sherrington supposed that there is some kind of excitation created at the end of the axon. This excitation would accumulate at some junction between neurons (at the synapse), gradually building up until it reached a level high enough (the threshold level) to trigger the next neuron into action. Thus, every time cell *A* fires, a tiny quantity of this excitation is liberated into the gap at the synapse of cell *A* and cell *B*. This quantity might not be enough by itself to trigger a response from *B,* but with enough repetitions of the stimulus, the accumulated total amount of excitation would exceed the threshold of cell *B,* which would then fire (Figure 2.35A).

Sherrington discovered another phenomenon, namely ***spatial summation,*** using the same approach. He first stimulated two nearby points on a dog's flank, *A* and *B,* either of which would elicit a particular reflex if the stimulus was intense enough. Sherrington showed that if the stimuli at points *A* and *B* are weakened, then neither one might elicit the reflex by itself, but the simultaneous combination could. Sherrington reasoned that the nerve fibers from *A* must be converging with those from *B,* so that they could jointly contribute their excitation to the nerve fibers that trigger the response. Once again, the hypothetical excitation released by the converging neurons was piling up, and so its effects were summating (Figure 2.35B).

INHIBITION

So far it would appear that neurons either vote "yea," thus adding to the excitation at the synapse, or else abstain altogether. However, some neurons may signal "nay" and set up an inhibitory effect, actively opposing and preventing excitation. One of the clearest demonstrations of such an effect is the phenomenon of ***reciprocal inhibition.*** Skeletal muscles typically come in flexor and extensor pairs (Figure 2.36). In most cases, one member of the pair causes a joint (say, the knee or the elbow) to bend; the other causes the same joint to straighten. Clearly, these muscles must not both contract at the same time, lest they act like two wrestlers pitted against each other. In fact, for maximum efficiency, the excited muscle should encounter little or no opposition. A mechanism that, upon the contraction of a flexor, would automatically relax the extensor would promote this efficiency.

Using a spinal animal, Sherrington provided an experimental demonstration of this effect. He stimulated a sensory site that caused the flexor to contract, but

2.36 An example of muscle antagonists
The figure shows how the members of a flexor-extensor pair (biceps and triceps) oppose each other in flexing and extending the forearm.

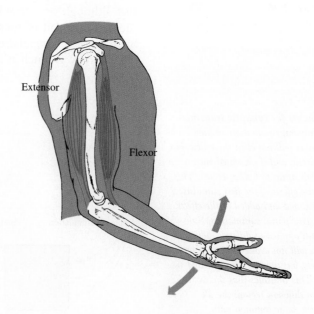

that single stimulus also caused the extensor to relax and actually go limp—limper than in its normal resting state. Sherrington concluded that another process was countermanding the messages to the muscle fibers that maintained normal muscle tone—inhibition.

Apparently, a neuron can receive both excitatory and inhibitory messages. The two processes appear to summate algebraically, such that the effect of a positive (excitatory) influence can be weakened, neutralized, or even reversed by a negative (inhibitory) one. In Sherrington's study of flexor and extensor pairs, a single sensory input caused excitation in one motoneuron and inhibition at another. Such interplays of excitatory and inhibitory influences occur throughout the nervous system. In the motor systems, they promote the mechanical efficiency of flexor-extensor pairs. In our sensory systems, they may enable us to pay attention to one stimulus and ignore another. And in our microcircuitry, they allow us to use complex stimulus patterns to construct complex behavior patterns.

THE SYNAPTIC MECHANISM

Sherrington could only guess at the specific physical mechanism that governs transmission at the synapse, but he did sketch some guidelines. There had to be excitatory and inhibitory processes, accumulating over time, pooling effects from various neural inputs, and adding algebraically. But what was their nature?

Sherrington and some of his contemporaries guessed that the excitation by which neurons communicated with their neighbors is actually a chemical substance released when the impulse reaches the end of the axon. The first direct evidence came in 1920 when Otto Loewi performed a crucial experiment. He dissected two frogs, removed their hearts, and placed each of the two hearts in separate, fluid-filled jars. Both hearts continued to beat, but one of the hearts still had part of the vagus nerve attached to it. One of the functions served by the vagus nerve is to slow the heartbeat. Loewi electrically stimulated the vagus nerve for half an hour or so. All this time the other heart stayed in its own jar, and beat at its own, quicker pace. After a while, Loewi performed the crucial step. He took some fluid from the jar that held the first heart (whose beat had been slowed down by the vagus nerve) and poured it into the jar in which the second heart was kept. Almost immediately, that second heart slowed down as well. The implication was clear. The stimulation of the vagus nerve had apparently released some substance that could inhibit the heart muscle (see Figure 2.37); that substance had mixed in with the fluid in the jar, and when the fluid

2.37 Schematic illustration of Loewi's discovery of the action of neurotransmitters The hearts in two jars, I and II, are beating. (A) The vagus nerve that is still attached to the heart in jar I is stimulated, thus inhibiting the muscle and slowing down the heartbeat. (B) After an interval, the fluid in jar II is replaced by the fluid from jar I. The heart in jar II will now slow down almost immediately. (After Groves and Rebec, 1988)

A

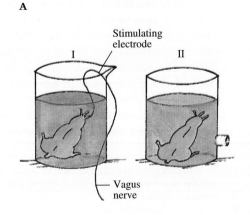

B

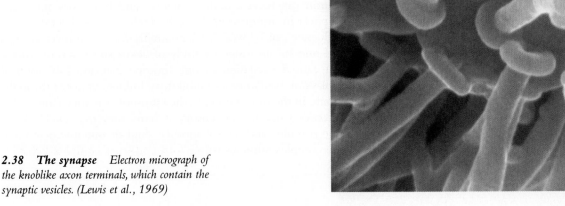

2.38 The synapse *Electron micrograph of the knoblike axon terminals, which contain the synaptic vesicles. (Lewis et al., 1969)*

was poured into the other jar, so was this controlling substance. Lowei called that substance "vagus stuff." We now call it *acetylcholine* (usually abbreviated ACh), the first of a hundred or more chemical substances now identified as *neurotransmitters* (Loewi, 1960; Eccles, 1982).

Loewi's experiment showed only that the transmission of the neural message involves a chemical substance. We now know quite a bit more about the way in which this transmission occurs. Let's begin by distinguishing between the *presynaptic* neuron—the cell that sends the message—and the *postsynaptic* neuron —the one that receives it. The actual transmission process begins in the tiny knoblike *axon terminals* of the presynaptic neuron (see Figure 2.38). Within these swellings are numerous tiny sacs, or *synaptic vesicles* ("little vessels"), which are like water balloons filled with neurotransmitters. When the presynaptic neuron fires, some of the vesicles literally burst and eject their contents through the terminal's membrane into the *synaptic gap* that separates the two cells. The transmitter molecules then diffuse across this gap and impinge upon the *postsynaptic membrane* (see Figure 2.39A and B). Usually the postsynaptic membrane is part of a dendrite, but it can also be a cell body or even another axon.

Once across the synaptic gap, the transmitters activate specialized molecular receptors in the postsynaptic membrane.★ When one of these receptors is activated, it opens or closes certain ion channels in the membrane. For example, some neurotransmitters open the channels to sodium ions. As these ions enter the postsynaptic cell, the voltage difference maintained across the membrane is decreased (that is, shifts in the direction of zero volts), rendering that part of the membrane less stable (see Figure 2.39C and D). As more and more transmitter molecules cross at the synapse, they activate more and more receptors, opening more and more channels, which further reduces the voltage difference. These effects accumulate and spread along the membrane of the postsynaptic neuron. When the voltage difference is reduced enough, the excitation threshold is reached, the action potential is triggered, and the impulse speeds down the postsynaptic cell's axon.

A similar mechanism accounts for inhibition. At some synapses, the presynaptic cell liberates transmitter substances that produce an *increased* voltage differ-

---

★ In contemporary neuroscience, the term *receptor* is used both at the cellular level (referring to neurons that transduce a physical stimulus), and at the molecular level (referring to the synaptic receptors described here).

ence across the membrane of the postsynaptic neuron. The heightened voltage difference acts to fortify the membrane against other, destabilizing influences. Since most neurons have synaptic connections with neurons that excite them as well as with others that inhibit them, the response of a given postsynaptic cell depends on a final tally of the excitatory and inhibitory "yeas" and "nays" that act upon it. If the net value is excitatory, and if this value exceeds the threshold, the cell will fire.

These synaptic mechanisms readily account for Sherrington's discovery that conduction within neurons is governed by different principles than conduction between neurons. Within neurons, conduction occurs via action potentials, which are all-or-none. Between neurons, conduction depends upon levels of neurotransmitters that can accumulate gradually with repeated stimulation. Most neurons also receive inputs from a great many presynaptic cells—in the brain, often from a thousand or more. Thus, the synapse serves as the common final path for all these presynaptic signals, a gathering point at which these various inputs can accumulate. This provides a ready account of spatial summation.

What happens to the transmitter molecules after they have affected the postsynaptic neuron? It wouldn't do just to leave them where they are, because they might continue to exert their effects long after the presynaptic neuron had stopped firing, thus making any input permanent. There are two mechanisms that prevent such mishaps. First, some transmitters are inactivated shortly after they've been discharged by special "cleanup" enzymes that break them up into their chemical components. More commonly, though, neurotransmitters are not destroyed but reused. In this process, called *synaptic reuptake,* used neurotransmitter molecules are ejected from the receptors, vacuumed by molecular pumps back into the axon terminals, and repackaged into new synaptic vesicles.

In some cases, the postsynaptic neuron can be bombarded so rapidly with bursts of neurotransmitter that the mechanisms of enzymatic cleanup and reuptake are momentarily overwhelmed. Such rapid-fire stimulation results in an accumulation of neurotransmitter that can fire the postsynaptic neuron; this explains the process of temporal summation.

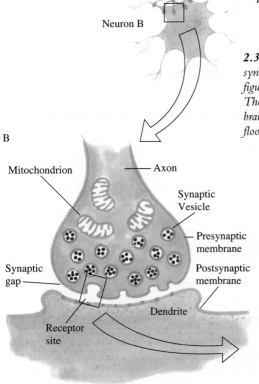

A

Neuron A

Impulse

Neuron B

B

Mitochondrion — Axon

Synaptic Vesicle

— Presynaptic membrane

Synaptic gap

Postsynaptic membrane

Receptor site

Dendrite

2.39 Schematic view of synaptic transmission (A) Neuron A transmits a message through synaptic contact with neuron B. (B) The events in the axon knob (the mitochondria shown in the figure are structures that help to produce the energy the neuron requires for its functioning). (C) The vesicle is released, and neurotransmitter molecules are ejected toward the postsynaptic membrane. (D) Neurotransmitter molecules settle on the receptor site, an ion channel opens, and Na^+ floods in. (After Bloom, Lazerson, and Hofstadter, 1988)

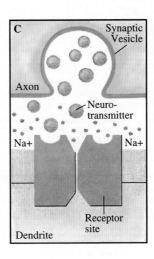

C

Synaptic Vesicle

Axon

Neuro-transmitter

$Na+$ $Na+$

Dendrite

Receptor site

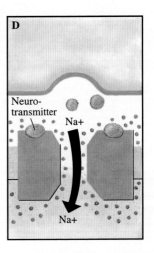

D

Neuro-transmitter

$Na+$

$Na+$

NEUROTRANSMITTERS

One the face of it, one might think that the nervous system only needs two transmitters: one excitatory and the other inhibitory. But nature, as so often, turns out to be exceedingly generous, for in actual fact there are a great number of different transmitter substances. About a hundred or so have been isolated thus far, and many more are sure to be discovered.

We will mention just a few of these neurotransmitters here. *Acetylcholine (ACh)* is released at many synapses and at the neuromuscular junction (itself a kind of synapse); the release of ACh makes muscle fibers contract. *Serotonin (5HT)* is a transmitter that is involved in many of the mechanisms of sleep, mood, and arousal. *Glutamate* is a critical neurotransmitter in the retina of the eye and appears to be important for long-term memory as well as for the perception of pain. *GABA* (or to give its full name, gamma-amino butyric acid) is the most widely distributed inhibitory transmitter of the CNS. Still others are *norepinephrine (NE)* and *dopamine (DA),* to which we will refer in later discussions of drug effects and certain mental disorders (see Chapters 3, 18, and 19).

NEUROTRANSMISSION: THE LOCK-AND-KEY MODEL

Individual neurons are quite selective in what neurotransmitters they will respond to. One attempt to understand some differences in chemical responsiveness is the *lock-and-key model* of transmitter action. This theory proposes that transmitter molecules will only affect the postsynaptic membrane if the molecule's shape fits into certain synaptic receptor molecules much as a key must fit into a lock (see Figure 2.40). But the mere fact that a given molecule fits into the receptor is not enough to qualify it as a transmitter. The key must not just fit into the lock; it must also turn it. In the language of neurophysiology, the transmitter molecule must produce the changes in membrane potential that correspond to excitatory and inhibitory processes.

NEUROTRANSMISSION: BEYOND LOCK-AND-KEY

Not surprisingly, recent findings suggest that neurotransmission is more complicated than the simple lock-and-key model would suggest. Neuroscientists now regard the various transmitters released by the presynaptic neuron as the brain's *primary messengers,* responsible for neuron-to-neuron communication. But increasingly, investigators are focusing on various chemical processes that occur *within* the postsynaptic neuron after it has been stimulated by a primary messenger and that can render the neuron more or less responsive thereafter. These chemical processes regulate such mechanisms as the creation of receptor sites for

2.40 Lock-and-key model of synaptic transmission Transmitter molecules will only affect the postsynaptic membrane if their shape fits the shape of certain receptor molecules in that membrane, much as a key has to fit into a lock. The diagram shows two kinds of transmitters and their appropriate receptors. (From Rosenzweig and Leiman, 1982)

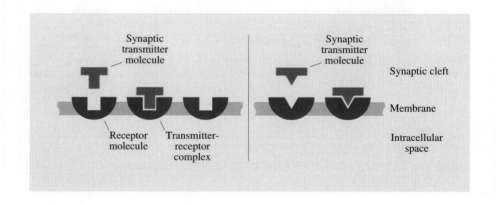

INTERACTION AMONG NERVE CELLS

A   **B**

Curare, the black widow's venom, and paralysis (A) This Cofan man from Colombia is using a curare-tipped dart to hunt. The curare acts as an acetylcholine antagonist: It inhibits this neurotransmitter's action, which leads to paralysis and death. (Photograph by B. Malkin/Anthro-Photo File) (B) The venom of the black widow spider also affects its victim's acetylcholine level, but instead of inhibiting acetylcholine action, it acts as an acetylcholine agonist, quickly exhausting the victim's supply of this neurotransmitter. For small prey at least, the end is the same: paralysis and death—for humans, a painful but usually nonlethal illness. (Buddy Mays/Corbis)

specific neurotransmitters and the synthesis of the neuron's own neurotransmitter, and they are set in motion by a set of substances known as the neuron's *second messengers* (Shepherd, 1994).

Finally, neurons involved in the control of very high speed acts (such as eye movements) may circumvent chemical neurotransmission altogether. They may communicate via narrow electrical synapses, with the action potential of one neuron directly inducing an action potential in the next (Shepherd, 1994).

All of these added complexities reflect relatively recent discoveries, and it is likely that other additions to the simple lock-and-key model of chemical neurotransmission will be found. Clearly, the brain may have many other tricks up its metaphorical sleeve.

POISONS, MEDICATIONS, AND NEUROTRANSMITTERS

The fact that communication between neurons depends on different neurotransmitter substances (and possibly different processes) has wide implications for both psychology and pharmacology. Drugs that enhance a transmitter's activity are technically called *agonists,* a term borrowed from Greek drama in which the agonist is the name for the hero. Drugs that impede such action are *antagonists,* a term that refers to whoever opposes the hero (so to speak, the villain).

Some agonists enhance a transmitter's effect by blocking its synaptic reuptake, thus leaving more transmitter within the synapse. Others act by counteracting the cleanup enzyme or by increasing the availability of some *precursor* (a substance required for the transmitter's chemical manufacture). Conversely, some antagonists operate by speeding up reuptake, others by augmenting cleanup enzymes, and still others by decreasing available precursors.

Other drugs affect the synaptic receptors. Some are agonists that activate the receptors by mimicking the transmitter's action. Antagonists of this type prevent the transmitter effect by binding themselves to the synaptic receptor and blocking off the transmitter, thus serving as a kind of putty in the synaptic lock.

Acetylcholine, curare, and the black widow's venom An example of an antagonist that works by blocking receptors is *curare,* a substance discovered by certain South American Indians who dipped their arrows in a plant extract that contained it, with deadly effect on animal prey. Curare blocks the action of acetylcholine at the synaptic junctions between motor neurons and muscle fibers. The result is total paralysis and eventual death by suffocation, since the victim is unable to breathe.

The venom of the black widow spider, while actually an agonist, achieves a similar result. This substance initially enhances the production of acetylcholine at the neuromuscular junction, but does it so rapidly that the neuron's supply of the transmitter is quickly exhausted. The ultimate result is the same muscular paralysis produced by a direct antagonist such as curare.

Norepinephrine and amphetamine   Amphetamines act as agonists that enhance the release of norepinephrine from the presynaptic neurons and also inhibit its reuptake. Norepinephrine turns out to be an important transmitter for neurons that regulate general bodily and psychological arousal. The greater the activity of such neurons, the more active and excited the individual is likely to be. It is therefore understandable that amphetamine ("speed") acts as a powerful stimulant. In moderate doses, it leads to restlessness, insomnia, and loss of appetite; larger doses and continued use may lead to paranoia. Certain other stimulants, cocaine in particular, have similar effects.

Serotonin and the SSRIs   A class of agonist medications called **selective serotonin reuptake inhibitors (SSRIs)** act specifically, as the name suggests, to block the reuptake of serotonin and thereby increase its availability within the synapse. These medications, which include Prozac and Zoloft, have demonstrated effectiveness in treating numerous disorders, including depression, obsessive-compulsive disorder, other anxiety disorders, and bulimia nervosa. We discuss the SSRIs more fully in Chapter 19.

Dopamine, schizophrenia, and Parkinson's disease   Some transmitter antagonists, like curare, lead to catastrophic results. But other such antagonists may be beneficial. An example is the effect of various antipsychotic medications, such as Thorazine or Haldol, on the symptoms of schizophrenia, a group of serious mental disorders that afflicts about 1 percent of the population. In its more extreme forms, schizophrenia may be characterized by delusions (believing what isn't so, such as conspiracies and persecution), hallucinations (perceiving what isn't there, such as hearing voices), or bizarre mannerisms and unusual postures that may be maintained for many hours. According to one hypothesis, many cases of schizophrenia are produced by an oversensitivity to the transmitter dopamine. Support for this theory comes from the fact that the effectiveness of medications for these cases depends upon the degree to which they block dopamine (again, see Chapter 19).

If the dopamine theory of schizophrenia is correct, then schizophrenia is caused, at least in part, by an excess of (or an oversensitivity to) dopamine. In other disorders, the problem is the very opposite. An important example is Parkinson's disease, which we mentioned earlier in the discussion of the basal ganglia. Here, too, the cause is related to dopamine, but now as a case of too little rather than of too much, for in Parkinson's disease there is a gradual degeneration of dopamine-releasing neurons in a part of the brain crucial for movement. Some of the symptoms of Parkinson's disease are counteracted by the administration of L-dopa, a dopamine precursor that increases the supply of dopamine in the brain and allows the patient's surviving dopamine-releasing neurons to function more effectively. Other patients derive benefits from electrical stimulation of the brain using surgically implanted electrodes. While these therapies can alleviate many patients' symptoms, they do not constitute cures, for the progressive destruction of the dopamine-releasing neurons continues (Marsden, 1985). Brain tissue transplants do offer some hope of reversing the process of cell destruction, however (see p. 65).

Identifying new neurotransmitters   As we have seen, some of the drugs that have substantial effects on the nervous system turn out to work either by mimicking or by blocking the actions of neurotransmitters. This fact has led some scientists to wonder just how many new neurotransmitters might be discovered using existing drugs to probe the brain. This strategy has been successful in several cases. A celebrated example is the discovery of endorphins, which are important in how we perceive and cope with pain (see Chapter 3).

Similar logic led to the discovery of a brain receptor for THC (tetrahydrocannibinol), the active ingredient in marijuana. A team of researchers injected a THC-like chemical into the brains of rats and found that it latched onto receptors located especially in the midbrain and in limbic structures, such as the amygdala and the hippocampus (Devane et al., 1988). Four years later the same team reported isolating a compound produced by the brain itself with many of THC's properties (Devane et al., 1992). They named this neurotransmitter *anandamide* (from the Sanskrit word *ananda,* for "bliss") because of the giddy euphoria many marijuana users experience. Will anandamide turn out to be the brain's own marijuana, responsible for our natural euphoric moments? Research is ongoing in an attempt to answer this question. If it is, then anandamide may offer a new tool for understanding the effects of marijuana. Already, some investigators suspect that anandamide may help explain our reactions to a substance that is not usually considered a drug—chocolate. Chocolate contains both anandamide and some closely related compounds, and it may produce a mood elevating effect by activating anandamide neurons (Tomaso, Beltramo, and Piomelli, 1996).

INTERACTIONS THROUGH THE BLOODSTREAM

Although our discussion of the nervous system has emphasized the neurons and nerve pathways that compose it, two other aspects of the nervous system deserve special mention: blood circulation and the channels of chemical communication within the body.

BLOOD CIRCULATION

The cells that make up the central nervous system require considerable energy to function and are thus nutrient gluttons. In fact, the brain, which amounts to only about 2 percent of our body weight, consumes about 15 percent of our metabolic energy (Rosenzweig et al., 1996). This fact makes the circulation of blood—which supplies the brain its diet of oxygen and glucose—particularly crucial. Several arteries enter the brain separately and join up once inside the brain, probably to provide redundancy in the event that any one artery should malfunction.

THE BLOOD-BRAIN BARRIER

The cerebral blood vessels not only assure that the blood supply to the brain is constant; they also make sure that it is pure. The cells making up the nervous system are quite sensitive to toxins, so the cerebral vasculature filters these out to protect the brain from harmful chemicals. To accomplish this, the blood vessels within the brain develop specialized membranes which form the **blood-brain barrier.** This barrier is remarkably effective. Indeed, it sometimes seems *too* effective to investigators trying to design medicines to help people with brain disorders. For them the task is twofold—to design an effective medicine *and* to design one that can outwit the barrier and reach the brain cells.

THE ENDOCRINE SYSTEM

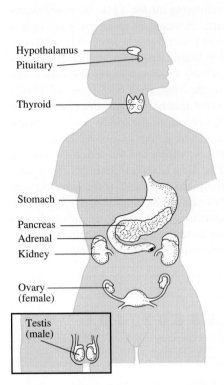

Hypothalamus
Pituitary

Thyroid

Stomach

Pancreas
Adrenal
Kidney

Ovary
(female)

Testis
(male)

2.41   Location of major endocrine glands and hypothalamus

An enormous volume of information flows to and from the brain via the nervous system. But the body also has another avenue of internal communication: *the endocrine system* (see Figure 2.41 and Table 2.1). Various *endocrine glands* (such as the *pancreas, adrenal glands,* and the *pituitary*) release certain chemical secretions, *hormones,* directly into the bloodstream and thus exert effects upon structures often far removed from their biochemical birthplace. As an example, take the pituitary gland. One of its components secretes a hormone that tells the kidney to decrease the amount of water excreted in the urine, a useful mechanism when the body is short of water (see Chapter 3). Another part of the pituitary gland controls the thymus gland in the chest, which in turn produces the T-lymphocyte cells so important in fighting widespread systemic infections (including those from the human immunodeficiency virus, or HIV).

On the face of it, the communication and control provided by these endocrine glands seems very different from that provided by the nervous system. In the nervous system, neurotransmitters are sent to particular addresses through highly specific channels. In contrast, the chemical messengers employed by the endocrine system travel indiscriminately throughout the bloodstream, reaching virtually all parts of the body. There is also an enormous difference in the distance these messengers have to travel. While neurotransmitters must only cross the synaptic gap, which is less than 1/10,000 mm wide, the endocrine messengers may have to traverse half the length of the body. But despite these differences, the two communication systems have a good deal in common, because both systems deliver their messages by the release of chemical substances. In the

TABLE 2.1 THE MAIN ENDOCRINE GLANDS AND SOME OF THEIR FUNCTIONS	
Gland	*Functions of the released hormones*
Anterior pituitary	Often called the body's master gland because it triggers hormone secretion in many of the other endocrine glands.
Posterior pituitary	Prevents loss of water through kidney.
Thyroid	Affects metabolic rate.
Islet cells in pancreas	Affects utilization of glucose.
Adrenal cortex	Various effects on metabolism, immunity, and response to stress; some effects on sexual behavior.
Adrenal medulla	Increases sugar output of liver; stimulates various internal organs in the same direction as the sympathetic branch of the ANS (e.g., accelerates heart rate).
Ovaries	One set of hormones (estrogen) produces female sex characteristics and is relevant to sexual behavior. Another hormone (progesterone) prepares uterus for implantation of embryo.
Testes	Produces male sex characteristics; relevant to sexual arousal.

nervous system, neurotransmitters excite or inhibit the postsynaptic cell; in the endocrine system, hormones affect specially sensitive cells in the target organ.

The relationship between neural and endocrine communication is further underlined by the fact that a number of substances serve both as hormones and as neurotransmitters. For example, norepinephrine is the transmitter released by certain neurons that make blood vessels constrict; it is also one of the hormones secreted by the adrenal gland and has similar results. The adrenal gland's release of norepinephrine, and its close relative epinephrine (known commonly as adrenaline), is controlled by pituitary hormones.

Considering these many relationships, it is understandable that a number of investigators argue that neurons and the cells of the endocrine glands evolved from a common chemical messenger system (LeRoith, Shiloach, and Roth, 1982).

RECOVERY FROM BRAIN INJURY

We have said a great deal in this chapter about the effects of various brain lesions. The people suffering from such lesions have been an important source of our current knowledge about brain function. But this knowledge has been derived from cases that are often tragic, from individuals who have been massively disabled by brain damage. Can these people recover? Clearly, this topic is of vital medical and general importance. But the facts about recovery also have considerable scientific importance, because they throw further light on how the human brain works.

REPAIR FROM WITHIN

In some cases, there is considerable spontaneous recovery from brain damage; a stroke patient with aphasia may regain normal fluency and comprehension after a couple of months, though a certain difficulty in finding words (sometimes called *anomia*) usually remains. When shown a picture of a key, the patient may be unable to think of its name and say, "I know what it does . . . you use it to open a door" (Kolb and Whishaw, 1996). In other cases, though, the recovery is considerably less, and the prospects for improvements are not bright; if the victim of brain damage has not recovered by a year or so after the brain injury, the hopes for further gains are relatively small.

RECOVERY OF INJURED NEURONS

How can we explain these great variations in the degree to which patients recover from brain damage? A critical factor is whether the neurons in the affected area were damaged rather than destroyed outright. If there is damage but little or no destruction, many of the symptoms may be reversible. For example, if the pressure brought on by swelling following a head injury, an infection, or a tumor is reduced by, say, draining some cerebral fluid, the damaged neurons may recover and the patient's symptoms become less severe or even disappear (Moscovitch and Rozin, 1989).

SPROUTING OF COLLATERALS

The outlook is much less favorable when neurons have been destroyed. There is no replacement warranty for dead neurons—neurons lost are typically lost

6 3

forever with little chance of regeneration.★ Even so, improvements can still occur. One reason is that the remaining neurons can form new connections: The axons of healthy neurons adjacent to the damaged cells can grow new branches, called **collateral sprouts,** that may eventually attach themselves to the synapses left vacant by the cells lost through injury (Veraa and Grafstein, 1981). Consider the effects of a certain lesion in the hypothalamus of a rat. In the first few days after the lesion, the animal just lies on its belly, unable to stand, let alone walk around, but after a few weeks there is recovery (Golani, Wolgin, and Teitelbaum, 1979). Some authors believe that some of the axons cut by this lesion gradually sprout new collateral branches that fill in for cells that were permanently destroyed. As a result, a smaller number of neurons can now do the work formerly done by many (Stricker and Zigmond, 1976).

Whether such sproutings will always be beneficial is by no means clear. Recovery will occur only if the newly grown branches attach themselves to the appropriate terminals. If the connections are made willy-nilly, the animal may end up worse off than it was before. This is analogous to what happens if a cable of telephone wires is cut. The trick is to reconnect the wires appropriately, otherwise there will be telephonic chaos. As yet, we don't know exactly when sprouting will be helpful and when it won't, though there is evidence that both kinds of results can occur (Scheff and Cotman, 1977; Wall, 1980).

SUBSTITUTION OF FUNCTION

Another factor that can produce recovery is substitution of function. This occurs when undamaged portions of the brain take over the functions previously controlled by parts that have been damaged. For example, we have discussed the fact that many language functions are normally supported by the left hemisphere and that damage to this hemisphere often results in aphasia. In some cases, though, aphasic patients recover because their right hemisphere comes to perform some of the tasks originally handled by the left. Evidence comes from patients who show nearly complete recovery of language function subsequent to left-hemisphere lesions; in most of these cases, there is an increase in the blood flow to the *right* hemisphere, reflecting its increased role (Knopman et al., 1984, cited in Rosenzweig and Leiman, 1989).

The most dramatic cases of substitution of function occur when an entire cerebral hemisphere is removed. Such hemispherectomies are sometimes performed in cases of childhood epilepsy that are so severe that neither medications nor more precise neurosurgery are effective. When the left hemisphere is removed early enough, the right hemisphere will assume a good many of the responsibilities of its missing counterpart—even speech (Kolb and Whishaw, 1996). Remarkably, these children live—quite literally—with half a brain but can function at an almost normal level.

It appears, then, that the brain has a certain flexibility (technically, **plasticity**) of function: Jobs performed by one region can be taken on by other parts when injury requires it. This plasticity is generally greater in the young. At least up to age eight, children who become aphasic regain speech function, even if their impairment immediately after the brain injury was quite severe (Woods and Teuber, 1978). For anyone becoming aphasic at a later age, however, chances of recovery are correspondingly reduced.

★ But some findings sound a more optimistic note, at least for male songbirds. Their brains shrink in the winter (when they don't sing) and expand in the spring (when they do). This annual increase in brain size is partially caused by the formation of new neurons during the spring to replace old neurons that die off in the fall (Nottebohn, 1987).

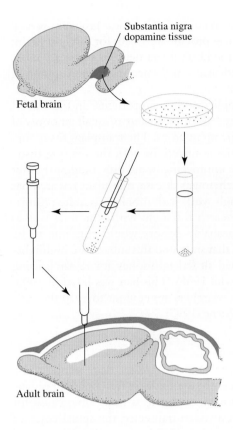

Substantia nigra dopamine tissue

Fetal brain

Adult brain

2.42 Steps in the grafting procedure *Fetal brain tissue is dissected from a fetal brain, transferred to a dish with a saline solution, and then treated to separate the fetal brain cells from connective tissue, blood vessels, and other tissue. It is then transferred to a syringe and injected into the appropriate region of an adult brain. (After Björklund et al., 1983)*

REPAIR FROM WITHOUT

Thus far, we've talked about cases in which the nervous system manages to repair itself, at least to some extent. Is there a way to help that repair along?

Although we've seen that the brain cannot ordinarily replace dead neurons, certain chemicals, known as *nerve growth factors,* do seem to spur neurons to form new connections (Bothwell, 1995). Work is underway to determine whether these growth factors can aid in recovery of function. Other studies suggest that someday neurologists may be able to transplant neural tissue. Thus far, this work is still largely experimental, but initial results give grounds for hope for several conditions, such as Parkinson's disease and Alzheimer's disease (Fine, 1986; Young, 1996).

PARKINSON'S DISEASE

In one group of studies, investigators partially destroyed a pathway of dopamine-releasing fibers in the midbrain of rats. This pathway projects upward to a region at the base of the cerebral hemispheres that is intimately involved in the control of voluntary movement, the same pathway whose gradual degeneration produces Parkinson's disease in humans. The effect of the lesion on rats is similar to that found in humans: a serious drop in the level of dopamine concurrent with massive motor disturbances (see p. 60). The investigators then grafted tissues from the brains of rat fetuses into the affected areas (see Figure 2.42); the donors were fetuses rather than adults because fetal tissue is still relatively unformed and plastic. This implantation led to an increase in the host brains' level of dopamine and considerable improvement in motor performance.

ALZHEIMER'S DISEASE

Another group of studies is of potential relevance to Alzheimer's disease, which afflicts 5 to 10 percent of all people over age sixty-five (Kolb and Whishaw, 1996). This devastating disease is characterized by a progressive decline in intellectual functioning that begins with serious memory problems, continues with increasing disorientation, and culminates in total physical and mental helplessness. Alzheimer's disease leads to degenerative changes throughout the brain. In most cases, the destruction is worst along a pathway of acetylcholine-releasing neurons that originates at the base of the forebrain and extends to the hippocampus (a structure that is important for memory) and many cortical areas as well. When enough of these cells are dead or dying, the cortical and hippocampal regions to which they project are no longer activated. As a result, there is loss of memory and cognitive functioning (see Figure 2.43; Coyle, Price, and DeLong, 1983).

Can degenerative changes of this sort be reversed by brain transplants? They can in rats, at least to some extent. Some investigators worked on rats that had been subjected to lesions in acetylcholine-releasing pathways analogous to those destroyed in Alzheimer patients. Others used animals of a fairly advanced age (in rats, this is about two years of age). Both the lesioned and the aged rats showed substantial impairments on various tests of memory and spatial learning. Initially, they couldn't learn certain simple mazes or retain what they had learned from one occasion to the next. But after appropriate brain transplants, there was significant improvement (Björklund and Stenevi, 1984; Gage and Björklund, 1986).

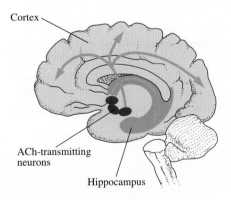

Cortex

ACh-transmitting neurons

Hippocampus

2.43 Acetylcholine pathways apparently involved in Alzheimer's disease *Acetylcholine-transmitting neurons located in regions at the base of the forebrain activate many regions of the cortex as well as the hippocampus. The degeneration of these neurons may be a major cause of Alzheimer's disease. (After Coyle, Price, and Delong, 1983)*

Just how do these brain grafts lead to recovery? There are probably several answers. In part, the transplanted tissue may provide new cells for the host brain; in part, the graft may stimulate some of the host's intact neurons to release more transmitter substances; finally, the grafted tissue may encourage axon sprouting (Freed, de Medicacelli, and Wyatt, 1985).

Can these or similar techniques be applied to human patients? In the case of Parkinson's disease, a few patients have received transplants of small amounts of fetal brain tissue rich in dopamine-producing neurons. The transplant tissue survives in the patients' brains and establishes connections with the existing tissue (Kordower et al., 1995). But, thus far, the improvements are only modest (Hoffer and van Horne, 1995). In the case of Alzheimer's disease, transplant research has yet to achieve clinical application, although work with monkeys is quite promising (Kordower et al., 1994). But such research is fraught with ethical (as well as political) problems, because the most probable donors would continue to be aborted human fetuses. The many issues that surround this subject are highlighted by a 1988 federal decision that denied all federal money for research using fetal tissue obtained from abortions (Lewin, 1988). This ban was lifted in 1993, but the controversy remains, and many researchers are content to keep the procedures experimental (Hoffer and van Horne, 1995).

SPINAL CORD INJURY

Perhaps nowhere is interest in recovery of function greater than among those paralyzed by spinal cord injury. Until recently, the outlook for obtaining regeneration of function in such cases was dismal, but there is now some cause for hope. In a dramatic study, researchers in Sweden transected the spinal cords of rats, leaving their hind limbs completely paralyzed. The researchers then spliced the gaps they had created using axons taken from the rats' own peripheral nerves and applied a glue containing a nerve-growth factor. Over the year following the surgery, the rats regained the ability to stand on their hind legs. In contrast, a separate group of rats that were transected but did not receive the nerve splices showed no recovery of hind limb function. When the researchers inspected the spinal cords of the repaired animals, they found clear evidence that the splices worked: They had become functional bridges between the disconnected portions of the spinal cord (Cheng, Cao, and Olson, 1996). The import of this study is considerable, and follow-up research is expected to determine the procedures optimal for recovery (Wise, 1996).

To sum up, scientists investigating the recovery of brain and spinal cord function now believe they are on the verge of discovering how to reconnect neuronal pathways lost to injury or disease, using neuron transplants and growth-promoting chemicals. For the first time, there is hope for those who were thought to be hopelessly disabled. The same applies to degenerative brain disorders such as Alzheimer's disease. Considering the ever-growing proportion of senior citizens in the population, help can come none too soon.

REHABILITATION

Recovery through processes of self-repair can only go so far, especially in adults. What factors enhance recovery? Brain-damaged rats show greater recovery if they are exposed to other rats and to highly stimulating environments, and rehabilitation programs now stress mental stimulation as well as physical therapy (Rosenzweig et al., 1996). Patients can sometimes be taught—very slowly and very patiently—to regain functions that were impaired or to learn skills that compensate for what is lost or damaged. For example, a stroke patient may place her good arm in a restraint to force herself to use her semiparalyzed

2.44 Rehabilitation *Sometimes sheer persistence (and no doubt some good fortune in the site and extent of the lesion) leads to remarkable results. An example is the case of Patricia Neal, an Academy Award–winning actor who had a stroke at the age of thirty-nine. The stroke paralyzed one leg and left her unable to speak, read, or write. But an intensive rehabilitation program enabled her to recover sufficiently so that four years later she could star in other films. (Neal, 1974; courtesy of Rex USA)*

one. Days and weeks of practice will bring slow gains, but these gains can accumulate to help the patient become more self-sufficient. How much this rehabilitation can accomplish depends on the injury and on the patient's motivation to continue the training (see Figure 2.44).

SOME FINAL COMMENTS

We have obviously come a long, long way since Descartes. Today we know a great deal about the biological foundation on which all human striving rests: the thousand billion or so neurons whose collective firings make up our human mind. Without these aggregates of neurons, there would be no *Hamlet,* no Great Wall of China, no Ninth Symphony, no atomic physics, no space travel, no hi-tech medicine. Nor would there be—to mention our darker side—any genocide or nuclear warfare.

The nervous system and its operation clearly underlie whatever we do and think and feel. But does this mean that all psychological questions are at bottom neurological ones? Does it mean that the answers to all of our questions will ultimately be phrased in terms of action potentials and neurotransmitters?

The answer is no. As this chapter has tried to make clear, many psychological questions do lend themselves to physiological answers, but many others do not. Suppose, for example, that a journalist or historian or legal scholar asks why a criminal jury acquitted O. J. Simpson of murder. To answer with a paragraph—or a book—about the jurors' neurons and synaptic connections would be absurd. Better answers might be found in the jury's interpretation of the evidence, their personal attitudes toward the defendant, the racial climate of the times, and so on. Any of these answers might prove inadequate or incomplete, but at least they are aimed at the right level of explanation. In contrast, a statement about neuronal firings in the frontal cortex of each juror seems off the mark. This is not because we simply don't know enough yet about the nervous system. Even if we could analyze all the neuronal firings in all the jurors throughout the trial, this analysis would not provide adequate answers for the journalist, the historian, or the legal scholar—let alone the ordinary man and woman on the street.

What holds for historians asking questions about a particular event holds for psychologists asking about the mind. When they ask about how humans and animals act, perceive, think, remember, and feel, they often want answers at a different level from that offered by a neurophysiologist. Of course, they're aware that all our actions take place within a framework set by our nervous systems. But even so, they believe that many psychological explanations are more appropriately offered in other terms. Just how such psychological explanations are formulated will be the topic of many subsequent chapters.

One of the oldest of old and tired riddles is "Why did the chicken cross the road?" The answer—"to get to the other side"—is exceedingly silly, but it is surely much less silly than the answer "Because its neurons fired that way."

SUMMARY

1. Since Descartes, many scientists have tried to explain human and animal movement within the framework of the *reflex* concept: A stimulus excites a sense organ, which transmits excitation upward to the spinal cord or brain, which in turn relays the excitation downward to a muscle or gland, and thus produces action.

2.   Neuroscientists have developed numerous ways to investigate the links between brain and behavior. The traditional techniques included human *clinical observation* and *invasive techniques,* usually performed on animals. Modern *neuroimaging* techniques such as the *CT scan,* the *PET scan, MRI,* and *functional MRI* make it possible to diagnose and study *lesions* in the brains of living patients, as well as to study the brain activities of normal participants.

3.   Across species, brains vary in their degree of central versus regional control, with more complex animals showing more centralized control. Decentralized nervous systems act inflexibly but quickly, and many animals thrive with them. More complex brains are costly to build and maintain, and their centralized control means that they act more slowly, but they permit very flexible behavior patterns. All vertebrates have brains that begin to develop early in embryonic life as a simple tube that develops three thickenings, which mature to form the *hindbrain* (including the *pons, medulla,* and *cerebellum*), the *midbrain,* and the *forebrain.* The forebrain is well-developed in primates, especially humans, and includes the *thalamus, hypothalamus,* and structures such as the *cerebral hemispheres,* the *basal ganglia,* and the *limbic system.*

4.   The role played by each of the three major subdivisions of the brain is shown by studies of animals with transections at various points. An animal whose brain is cut so that only the hindbrain remains can still move but can't integrate its movements. An animal that has a hindbrain and midbrain but that lacks a forebrain shows integrated movements but without any goal. An animal that only lacks the cortex integrates its movements and goals but pursues those goals ineptly.

5.   The *brain* and *spinal cord* together form the *central nervous system (CNS).* The CNS connects with the body in two main ways: through the *afferent* and *efferent nerves* of the *peripheral nervous system* (both the *somatic* and *autonomic divisions*) and (indirectly) through the bloodstream, by virtue of the brain's control of hormonal secretions and internal receptors that monitor hormone levels in the blood.

6.   The *cerebral cortex* is generally believed to underlie the most complex aspects of behavior. The *primary projection areas* of the cortex act as receiving stations for sensory information or as dispatching centers for motor commands. Early studies of the *primary motor projection area* indicated that the brain exhibits *contralateral control* (that the right side of the body is primarily controlled by the left side of the brain and vice versa).

7.   The *primary sensory projection areas* for vision, hearing, and the bodily senses are respectively located in the *occipital, temporal,* and *parietal lobes; nonprimary sensory projection areas* adjoin each primary area and perform more complex analysis and identification of stimuli. The primary motor projection area is in the *frontal lobe.* It controls single muscle actions, while the adjoining *nonprimary motor projection areas* coordinate complex acts involving multiple muscles. The remaining regions of the cortex seem to link multiple kinds of sensations (for example, sights with sounds).

8.   Certain lesions of the frontal lobe lead to *apraxias,* serious disturbances in the organization of voluntary action. Other lesions produce *agnosias,* the disorganization of perception and recognition. Still others cause *aphasias,* profound disruptions of language, which may involve speech production, speech comprehension, or both. A lesion in *Broca's area* leads to *nonfluent aphasia;* one in *Wernicke's area* leads to *fluent aphasia. Prefrontal lesions* can produce deficits in planning and problem solving that have consequences for social behavior.

9.   The two hemispheres of the human brain look superficially similar but are somewhat different in both structure and function. In most right-handers, the left hemisphere handles the bulk of the language functions, while the right hemisphere is more relevant to spatial comprehension. One source of evidence for this difference in hemispheric function, or lateralization, comes from the study of *split-brain patients* in which the main connection between the two hemispheres, the *corpus callosum,* has been surgically cut. Further evidence is provided by the response times of normal subjects when stimuli calling on verbal or spatial abilities are presented to one hemisphere or the other.

10.   The hierarchical organization of the nervous system is seen at all levels, from *central pattern generators* (or *CPGs*) in the brainstem and spinal cord up through the projection areas of the cortex. Destruction of higher centers can produce the *disinhibition of*

reflexive behavior. But hierarchies in the brain do not have the neatness of a corporate organizational chart. Instead, the brain is an assemblage of structures that probably do not show clear division of labor. Understanding the brain's *microcircuitry* may hold the key to how the brain processes information.

11. The basic unit of communication in the nervous system is the *neuron*, whose primary components are the *dendrites, cell body,* and *axon. Glial cells* are crucial for enabling neurons to find the right connections and to communicate at high speeds.

12. The main function of a neuron is to produce a *nerve impulse,* an electrochemical disturbance that is propagated along the membrane of the axon when the cell's normal *resting potential* is disrupted by a stimulus whose intensity exceeds the *excitation threshold.* This stimulus produces a brief destabilization and restabilization of the cell membrane, which constitutes the *action potential.* The action potential obeys the *all-or-none law:* Once threshold is reached, further increases of stimulus intensity have no effect on its magnitude. But the nervous system can nevertheless distinguish between different intensities of stimuli all of which are above threshold. One means for doing this is *frequency:* The more intense the stimulus, the more often the neuron fires.

13. To understand how neurons communicate, investigators have studied *reflex action,* which is necessarily based on the activity of several neurons. Results of studies with *spinal animals* led Sherrington to infer the processes that underlie conduction at the *synapse,* the junction of neuronal membranes at which communication occurs. Conduction within neurons was shown to obey different laws than conduction between neurons (that is, at their synapses). Evidence included the phenomena of *spatial* and *temporal summation.* Sherrington concluded that the excitation from several neurons funnels into a common reservoir to produce a *central excitatory state.*

14. Further studies argued for a process of inhibition. Evidence came from *reciprocal inhibition* found in flexor-extensor muscle pairs. Further work showed that a reflex can be activated either by increasing excitation or by decreasing inhibition.

15. Sherrington's inferences of synaptic functions have been confirmed by modern electrical and chemical studies. Today we know that transmission at most synapses is accomplished by *neurotransmitters,* chemical substances that are liberated at the axon terminals of one neuron and exert excitatory or inhibitory effects on the dendrites and cell body of another. These transmitters cross the *synaptic gap* and affect *receptor molecules* located on the *postsynaptic membrane.* This creates *graded potentials* that summate and spread. When they reach threshold, they produce an action potential in the axon of the second neuron.

16. Important examples of neurotransmitters include *acetylcholine, serotonin, glutamate, GABA, norepinephrine,* and *dopamine.* The effect of transmitters is enhanced by *agonists* and reduced or blocked by *antagonists.* Understanding the role of neurotransmitters has increased our knowledge of mental disorders and how to use medications to treat them. Recent studies suggest that neurons communicate not only through chemical neurotransmitters, but also through *electrical synapses,* with the action potential of one neuron inducing an action potential in the next directly, without a chemical go-between.

17. Blood circulation also plays a vital role in the functioning of the brain and as an instrument of communication. Not only does the blood bring energy to the nutrient-hungry brain, it also carries the hormones secreted by the endocrine glands to the various target organs throughout the body.

18. Recovery from cerebral lesions varies considerably from one patient to another, depending in part on whether the affected neurons were destroyed or only injured. Damaged neurons can recover and symptoms can be alleviated through the reduction of pressure on the brain. Destroyed neurons cannot be replaced, but some recovery can be produced by *collateral sprouting,* whereby healthy neurons adjacent to the region of injury grow new branches. In addition, some functions of the damaged regions may be taken over by other, undamaged parts of the brain. Recent work on the transplanting of neural tissue and on spinal cord repair offers some hope that neurobiologists may ultimately be able to replace damaged tissue and restore function.

CHAPTER

MOTIVATION

I In this chapter, we will examine some of the motives that characterize human behavior. Our focus here will be on relatively simple motives, such as hunger and thirst—motives that, it turns out, we share with most other animals. (We will turn to other, more complex motives, such as the need for friendship and love, in later chapters.) Some of these simpler motives can be understood as attempts at self-regulation, reflecting the organism's tendency to maintain a temperature that stays within certain limits, a water supply sufficient for circulation and digestion, and nutrient levels adequate for providing energy. Other motives are attempts at self-preservation, such as the body's response to pain or its preparation to respond to a threat. Yet another motive is the need for sleep, which is sometimes thought to reflect the need for self-restoration.

These motives are obviously different from one another, but they nevertheless share the property of making some acts more probable than others. For example, when we are hungry, we are more likely to eat than to wash our hair or read a book. When we are thirsty, we are more likely to drink than not. Likewise, these motives tune our perceptions: When we are hungry, we become more alert to food-related stimuli like the smell of popcorn or the sight of a package of cookies. And when we finally do eat, our hunger makes us more likely to savor the taste. That some behaviors and perceptions become more probable than others is sometimes called **potentiation** (an increase in the potential for an action). This chapter is an attempt to show how modern psychologists try to account for all these phenomena.

MOTIVATION AS DIRECTED ACTION

Most human and animal actions are directed. We don't simply walk, reach, shrink, or flee; we walk or reach toward some objects and shrink or flee from others. Sometimes what the organism approaches or avoids is physically present, as when a dog fetches a ball or runs from a honking car. At other times, though, the motivating object is not yet present but exists only in the organism's expectations—as, for example, when a hawk circles in search of prey or a lizard changes color to camouflage itself in case a predator ventures by.

Such directed actions seem difficult to reconcile with Descartes' notion that the actions of humans and animals are just simple sensory-motor reflexes. This problem is most pronounced for actions that are directed toward some future goal, but the same point applies even when the action is directed toward an immediately present object. Consider the dog fetching the ball. Dogs don't fetch robotically, moving the same muscles each time. Rather, their movements depend on the ball—where it is in relation to them, whether it is in motion and, if so, where it is likely to land, whether they need to scoop the ball off the ground or grab it in the air.

Motivation as directed action This painting was commissioned by a man dramatically
rescued from a shark attack in Havana harbor.
As here depicted, every member of the small
boat's crew directs his efforts toward the
swimmer's rescue. (Watson and the Shark
by John Singleton Copley, 1778; gift of
Mrs. George von Lengerke Meyer; courtesy of
the Museum of Fine Arts, Boston)

In an important sense, then, the dog's behavior seems to be directed by the
goal. If the goal (the ball) moves, the dog's behavior changes appropriately. If the
path toward the goal is blocked, the dog seeks an alternative path. This seems a
far cry from the water-driven statues that inspired Descartes. These always
moved in exactly the same way and never altered their actions to match the circumstances. In Descartes' time, this was the best that machines could do. But can
machines be modified to overcome this deficiency? The answer is yes.

CONTROL SYSTEMS

Unlike the machines of Descartes' time, those of today can monitor and
control their own activities and are in that sense directed. Many of the
methods that make this possible rely upon the notion of *feedback.*

As a machine operates, it changes its environment, whether that change is
mechanical, electrical, thermal, or whatever. If these changes can in turn influence the further operation of the machine—if they "feed back" upon it—we
have a **control system** based on feedback. In **positive feedback systems,** the feedback amplifies the response that produced it. The result is that a small effort can
exert a great change. Take, for example, what happens when a microphone is
held too close to its amplifier. The microphone picks up whatever noise is generated by the amplifier. It then feeds this static back to the amplifier, which
makes the noise yet louder (that is, amplifies it). This louder noise is picked up
by the microphone, is again fed back to the amplifier, which makes it even louder, and so on, until it produces an unbearably loud wail that is the bane of poorly designed public address systems.

The opposite case is **negative feedback,** in which the feedback slows, stops, or
even reverses, the response of the machine that produced the original change
(Figure 3.1). A simple example is the system that controls most home heating
systems. A thermostat turns on the heater when the house's temperature falls
below a given setting (its **setpoint**). The heater then causes the temperature to

rise, and this provides the negative feedback signal to the thermostat: With the house no longer cold, the thermostat turns the heater off.

In a sense, one could say that the thermostatically controlled heater has a goal: It wants to maintain a particular temperature, so to speak. Similar negative feedback systems exist at all levels of most nervous systems and are responsible for much of the directedness we observe in living organisms. Many examples of this pattern involve the organism's regulation of its own internal environment.

HOMEOSTASIS

Descartes' account of behavior focused on the external environment—the stimuli that impinge on our senses and the reactions that are triggered in our muscles. Some two hundred years after Descartes, another Frenchman, the physiologist Claude Bernard (1813–1878), emphasized that the organism has not only an external environment but an internal one as well—the organism's own bodily fluids. As Bernard noted, even with great fluctuations in the outside environment, these fluids remain strikingly constant—in the concentrations of various salts, the level of dissolved oxygen, the quantities of nutrients like glucose, and their pH (that is, their acidity). In addition, many creatures (including all birds and mammals) maintain a relatively constant body temperature as well.

In healthy organisms, all of these conditions fluctuate within very narrow limits. And indeed they must stay within these limits, because otherwise the organism is at severe risk. In healthy humans, for example, the acceptable concentration for glucose in the blood is about 75 to 140 milligrams per 100 cubic centimeters. A drop below this range means fatigue, coma, and eventual death; a prolonged elevation above it can produce eye and kidney disease, heart attacks, and strokes. These examples of internal equilibrium reflect a process that achieves **homeostasis** (literally, *equal state*), a process so awe inspiring in both its complexity and effectiveness that it is sometimes said to reflect a "wisdom of the body" (Cannon, 1932).

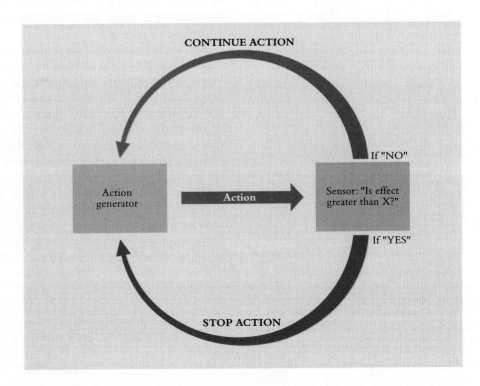

3.1 Negative feedback In negative feedback systems, the feedback slows, stops, or reverses the action that produces it. A sensing device indicates the level of a certain stimulus. If that level exceeds a certain setpoint, the action stops. The effect is self-regulation.

TEMPERATURE REGULATION

A clear example of homeostasis is provided by temperature regulation (or, more technically, **thermoregulation**), and natural selection has provided us with two methods for it. Birds and mammals are **endotherms,** animals that employ adjustments that are mostly internal or physiological to maintain stable body temperatures. Some of these adjustments involve large-scale bodily changes, such as gaining weight and growing an insulating coat of fur in preparation for the cold months, and losing both over the warm months. Other changes involve more directly reflexive actions, which we will describe in a moment.

The second kind of thermoregulation is found in **ectotherms** such as reptiles, which lack these internal mechanisms and must maintain their body temperatures with externally directed behavior (usually, choosing sunny or shady environments). Endothermic animals used to be called "warm-blooded," in contrast to ectotherms, which were said to be "cold-blooded." But these terms are misleading, because the internal temperatures of endotherms and ectotherms are about the same. What distinguishes the two is their capacity for internal thermoregulation (Rosenzweig et al., 1996).

TEMPERATURE CONTROL BY INTERNAL ADJUSTMENT

Endothermic animals generally have metabolisms that generate considerable heat within their bodies. If too much of this heat accumulates, sending their internal temperature too high, then various reflexive reactions come into play to get rid of the excess heat. One such reaction is peripheral **vasodilatation,** a widening of the skin's capillaries. This sends warm blood to the body's surface and results in heat loss by radiation. Other reactions that lead to cooling are sweating (in humans) and panting (in dogs), both of which produce heat loss by evaporation.

The opposite pattern comes into play when the animal's internal temperature dips too low. Sweating and panting stop, and there is **vasoconstriction,** a contraction of the capillaries that squeezes blood away from the cold periphery and keeps it, instead, in the body's warmer core. Other reflexive reactions include a ruffling of the fur to create a thick envelope of protective air, known technically as **piloerection.** We humans possess this reflex, too, but in our relatively hairless state we see only a remnant of it, in the reaction called "goosebumps."

Like all homeostatic adjustments, these reflex reactions are directed at maintaining physiological constancy. Heat is exhausted when the core body temperature is too high and conserved when it begins to drop too low. In this regard, these adjustments are completely analogous to the thermostatically controlled heater; both act to maintain some optimal temperature, or **setpoint** (see Figure 3.2).

Although we have presented the internal body temperature as relatively fixed, in a few animals it can change markedly. For example, some ground squirrels

Vasodilatation
Sweating
Panting, etc.

Parasympathetic

Upper set-point

Lower set-point

Sympathetic

Vasoconstriction
Shivering
Fur-ruffling, etc.

3.2 Reflexive temperature regulation in mammals *When the temperature deviates from an internal setpoint, various reflexive reactions occur to restore the temperature.*

External temperature control and mother love in rats After rat pups are born, they huddle under the mother's belly for warmth. Why does the mother allow this? It's not just maternal affection. The hormones circulating through the mother after she gives birth overheat her, so she is quite content to have the cool bodies of her offspring against her own. She also leaves her offspring for brief periods when the group snuggling itself begins to overheat her. (Photograph by Jane Burton; © 1987, Bruce Coleman, Inc.)

spend the winter in hibernation. When the outside temperature falls, their internal setpoint drops, and they find secluded burrows and settle into a winter torpor—a useful mechanism in times when food is very scarce. But while this new setpoint is low, they can still function. When the weather gets cold enough, they wake up to keep from freezing to death (Heller, Cranshaw, and Hammel, 1978).

Nonhibernating animals like humans show more stable temperature setpoints; ours averages about 98.6 degrees Fahrenheit (37 degrees Celsius). But these setpoints show predictable variations. For example, our body temperatures peak in the late afternoon and reliably drop a degree or two when we fall asleep. Similarly, strenuous exercise can temporarily raise our body temperatures a degree or two. These variations still leave us with relatively stable temperatures, but even these limits can be exceeded in emergencies, as in fever, when our body temperatures can rise for short periods to well above 100 degrees Fahrenheit (38 degrees Celsius) (Sewitch, 1987; Rosenzweig et al., 1996).

TEMPERATURE CONTROL BY EXTERNALLY DIRECTED BEHAVIOR

The homeostatic mechanisms we have just described are essentially involuntary. But endotherms also supplement these adjustments with voluntary action. This is especially true in very young animals, who have immature thermoregulatory systems and so typically huddle together or stay next to their mothers to keep warm. But at least in rats, mothers limit the duration of this contact with their young lest their own body temperatures rise too high (Leon et al., 1990). Other kinds of thermoregulatory behavior are also available. In many circumstances, endothermic animals rely on the strategies regularly used by ectotherms—lounging in the sun to keep warm or lurking in the shade to stay cool. Another strategy is nest building, which, among its other advantages, provides an insulating layer around the inhabitants. And humans, of course, have their own variations on these techniques: we wear coats, wrap ourselves in blankets, and snuggle up with partners during the winter, and we wear light (or very little) clothing and shower more or swim during the summer. All of these actions serve the same goal—preserving the internal environment whose constancy is so crucial to our survival.

THE AUTONOMIC NERVOUS SYSTEM AND TEMPERATURE CONTROL

What controls the various mechanisms that regulate our internal temperature? The most direct control is exerted by the ***autonomic nervous system (ANS).*** In general, this is the part of the peripheral nervous system that sends commands to the ***glands*** and the ***smooth muscles*** ★ of the viscera (internal organs) and blood vessels. The ANS has two divisions, the ***sympathetic*** and the ***parasympathetic,*** and these divisions often act reciprocally. The excitation of the sympathetic division leads to an acceleration of heart rate and inhibition of peristalsis (rhythmic contractions) of the intestines, while parasympathetic activation has the opposite effects: slowing of the heart rate and stimulation of peristalsis. The same relationship is seen in temperature regulation. The sympathetic division acts to conserve internal heat; it triggers vasoconstriction and fur-ruffling. In contrast, the parasympathetic division helps to exhaust heat; it stimulates panting, sweating, and vasodilatation (see Figure 3.13, p. 93).

SENSING THE INTERNAL ENVIRONMENT: THE HYPOTHALAMUS

What governs the ANS itself? A crucial center is the hypothalamus, which is located at the base of the forebrain (see Figure 3.3). This brain structure is a triumph of anatomical miniaturization; it contains over twenty clusters of neurons that regulate many of the biological motives, yet it is only about the size of a pea.

Among its many functions, the hypothalamus appears to contain a control mechanism, akin to a thermostat, that detects when the body is too cold or too hot. This was shown in cats who had wires implanted in their anterior hypothalamus. When the wire was heated gently, the cats panted and vasodilated as though they were too hot and needed to cool themselves, even though their body temperature was well below normal (Magoun et al., 1938). As we now know, the warm wire stimulated specialized neurons called ***thermoreceptors,*** which normally respond to the temperature of the bodily fluids that circulate throughout the brain. The warm wire mimicked warm bodily fluids and tricked the thermoreceptors into triggering behavior designed to cool the animal and restore a normal body temperature. The effect is analogous to what would happen if a blow dryer were directed at a home thermostat. The heater would be shut off even if the house were actually freezing.

Does the hypothalamus also control externally directed behavior, such as moving into the sun, huddling, nesting, or even putting on a jacket? In many cases, it appears so. One experiment showed this by using the fact that rats in a cold chamber can learn to press a bar for a brief burst of heat (Weiss and Laties, 1961; see Figure 3.4). The question was whether rats with this skill would press the bar if their brains were cooled rather than their bodies. To find out, an investigator ran cold liquid through a tiny tube implanted near the anterior hypothalamus (Satinoff, 1964). The answer was clear: Even when the outside temperature was comfortable, the rats turned on the heat lamp when their brains were cooled.

It seems that the hypothalamus (and certain regions adjacent to it) plays a crucial role in instigating both reflexive behavior, such as vasodilatation, and voluntary behavior, such as seeking warmth. We hasten to add, however, that different

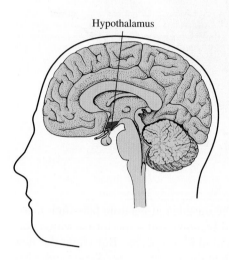

3.3 The hypothalamus *Cross-section of the human brain with the hypothalamus indicated in blue. (After Keeton, 1980)*

3.4 Performing a learned response to keep warm *A rat kept in a cold environment will learn to press a lever that turns on a heat lamp for a few seconds after each lever press. (Weiss and Laties, 1961)*

★ The individual fibers of these muscles look smooth when observed under a microscope, in contrast to the fibers of the skeletal muscles, which look striped.

brain areas seem to control which of the two kinds of responses are triggered by the thermoregulatory commands of the hypothalamus. When rats trained to lever-press for heat had one area destroyed just in front of the hypothalamus, the animals stopped pressing levers to turn heat lamps on or off, but still showed involuntary reactions such as shivering and vasoconstriction. The result was reversed when another region was destroyed, this time an area at the side of the hypothalamus; now the autonomic reactions were abolished but the voluntary behaviors remained (Satinoff and Rutstein, 1970; Satinoff and Shan, 1971; Van Zoeren and Stricker, 1977). The implication is that there must be separate circuits to handle the two different ways of solving the problem of thermoregulation. Here, as in many other areas, natural selection has provided multiple safeguards to protect the organism's vital functions (Satinoff, 1978).

Interestingly, the hypothalamus also turns out to be the main instigator of fever. Fever appears to be triggered by chemicals called **pyrogens,** which are released into the bloodstream at sites of bacterial or viral invasion. These chemicals then stimulate special receptors in the anterior part of the hypothalamus, leading to a temporary change in the body's temperature setpoint. What function does this serve? It probably represents the body's effort to kill off invading pathogens by temporarily overheating (Rosenzweig et al., 1996).

THIRST

What holds for temperature holds for most other homeostatic regulations as well. Consider the body's water supply, which is crucial to every aspect of normal functioning. We continually lose water—primarily through urination, but also through respiration, sweating, defecation, and, occasionally, through vomiting or bleeding. So our bodies must monitor this water loss carefully and take steps, when needed, to replace what is lost and to conserve when supplies are low.

How does the body know when it needs water? The commonsense answer is, of course, that our mouths get dry. But it turns out that a dry mouth is only part of thirst. This was discovered from studies in which rats were implanted with tubes that drained water out of their stomachs as fast as they could drink it. The rats still drank despite the fact that their mouths were thoroughly moistened (Blass and Hall, 1976).

The evidence indicates that our bodies independently monitor two separate aspects of our internal water balance. One is the water volume that exists inside our cells. The other is the volume of the fluids that circulate outside our cells, in

"This looks like a good spot." (Drawing by Chas. Addams; © 1987, The New Yorker Magazine, Inc.)

bodily fluids like saliva, blood, lymph, cerebrospinal fluid, and so forth. Each of these aspects of our water balance—extracellular and intracellular—is controlled by its own set of receptors and makes its own set of internal homeostatic adjustments.

EXTRACELLULAR WATER VOLUME

Cells that sense the volumes of extracellular fluids are located throughout the body. Some of the most important receptors, though, are in the heart and surrounding blood vessels. These detect the drops in blood pressure that occur whenever there is a drop in the total amount of bodily fluid. These pressure receptors send messages, via their axons, directly to the brain, which then orchestrates various attempts to restore normal blood pressure. One major route for this restoration is through a hormone called **vasopressin** (or sometimes *antidiuretic hormone*), which is manufactured by the hypothalamus and secreted by the pituitary gland into the bloodstream. Vasopressin causes the blood vessels to constrict and thus drives up blood pressure; it also instructs the kidneys to retain water instead of excreting it.

The pressure receptors also have behavioral effects, as shown by studies on dogs in which a small balloon was inserted into the large vein that leads to the heart. When this balloon was inflated, the dogs drank copiously. The balloon impeded the blood flow into the heart and caused a decrease in fluid pressure, so the pressure receptors signaled the brain to initiate drinking (Fitzsimons and Moore-Gillow, 1980; Rolls and Rolls, 1982).

Other receptors located in the kidneys also detect the volume of extracellular fluids. They deliver their messages indirectly to the brain by modulating the amount of a hormone called **angiotensin II** circulating in the bloodstream. Once in the brain, this hormone seems to act on receptors located just in front of the hypothalamus and in various regions bordering the fluid-filled ventricles of the brain (Epstein, Fitzsimons, and Rolls, 1970; Epstein, 1982; Rosenzweig et al., 1996). Whether injected into the bloodstream or directly into the brain, angiotensin II is an extremely powerful and immediate motivator of drinking.

Osmotic dehydration *Although surrounded by water, sailors in a lifeboat are nevertheless dying of thirst, for drinking the seawater would only lead to further dehydration. (Scene from* Mutiny on the Bounty, *1935; courtesy Photofest)*

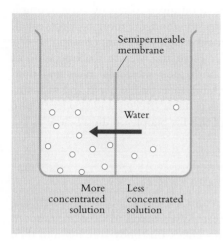

3.5 Dehydration by osmosis *If two so-lutions are separated by a membrane that al-lows the free flow of water but impedes the flow of substances that are dissolved in the water, water flows from the less concentrated region into the more concentrated one.*

INTRACELLULAR WATER VOLUME

Still another group of receptors keeps track of the water *within* the body's cells. These receptors depend upon the chemical process of osmosis and are thus called **osmoreceptors.** The role of these osmoreceptors is shown by a number of studies in which tiny drops of salt water were injected into regions in or around the hypothalamus of a rat. The injections immediately led to drink-ing: They increased the concentration of sodium ions in the fluid surrounding the receptor cell, which induced water to leak out of these cells by osmosis (to equalize ion concentrations in the two areas); this in turn caused the cell to deflate somewhat, which caused the receptor to fire (Figure 3.5; Blass and Epstein, 1971; Rolls and Rolls, 1982).

Why are there so many different receptor systems, all monitoring the levels of bodily fluids? Here, as in the case of temperature regulation, we find that natural selection has provided us with multiple defenses, so that if one system fails, another can take its place. And again as with temperature regulation, internal compensatory readjustments can only restore the bodily balance up to a point. Eventually, the cor-rective measures must involve some behavior by which the organism reaches out to the external world. In the case of thirst, this behavior is obviously drinking—in humans, an average of two to three quarts of water per day.

We will find even greater redundancy when we turn to another complex sys-tem of self-regulation: maintaining the body's nutrient levels by feeding.

HUNGER

All animals have to eat, and much of their lives revolve around food—searching for it, hunting it, ingesting it, and doing their best not to be food for others. All of these acts are, of course, related crucially to homeostasis, because each serves the broader purpose of maintaining appropriate nutrient supplies in the animal's internal environment. But what are the mechanisms that determine when humans and animals eat or stop eating?

BODY WEIGHT, NUTRITION, AND ENERGY

Through the process of digestion, nutrients are extracted from food and then converted when needed into energy that supplies body heat, enables the muscles to contract, and, in general, supports all life functions (Rosenzweig et al., 1996). Animals with big brains also devote considerable energy—up to 20 percent—to the maintenance of resting potentials in the neurons.

Animals vary greatly in how fast they need to "burn" food—that is, in their **basal metabolic rate**—to gain the energy and raw materials they need. With their faster metabolisms, endotherms, who eat almost constantly, need much more food than ectoderms, who sometimes go for weeks or months between meals. In addition, smaller animals generally have faster metabolisms than larger ones, which means that they have to eat proportionately more food to maintain their normal body weights.

When food is readily available, adult animals usually eat just about the right amount both to satisfy their immediate nutritional needs and to keep their weight roughly constant. Interestingly, the "right amount" here refers not to the volume of food, but to the number of calories—and hence, the potential metabolic energy—contained in it. This was demonstrated in a study in which the experimenter varied the caloric level of the food given to rats by adulterating it with nonnutritive cellulose. The more diluted the food, the more of it was eaten, in a quantity that kept the total caloric content roughly constant (Adolph, 1947).

But what happens if food is unavailable? Here, too, we see the operation of homeostasis: Animals immediately lower both their metabolic rates and their activity levels so that they can continue to fulfill their bodily needs and to maintain their normal body weights for as long as possible (Keesey and Powley, 1986). (We will discuss the obvious implications of this for people on diets below.)

THE SIGNALS FOR FEEDING

What makes us hungry and want to eat? What makes us sated and want to stop? Most of us don't step on a scale, check our body weights, and then adjust our food intake accordingly. (Certainly, nonhuman animals don't.) Instead, we maintain our body weight by our response to numerous internal signals of our nutritional state. Some signals indicate the state of our short-term energy reserves, used in emergencies or other bursts of activity; others indicate the state of our long-term reserves, needed for sustained exertion.

SIGNALS FROM THE LIVER

A major source of information on our nutritional needs is the liver, which has the crucial job of monitoring and controlling the major nutrient used for short-term energy: the blood sugar known as *glucose.*

Immediately after a meal, glucose is plentiful. While some is used right away, much is converted into *glycogen* (often called animal starch) and various fatty acids, which are stored for later use. Later on, when this stored energy is needed, this process will be reversed, and the glycogen and fatty acids will be turned back into usable glucose.

The liver manages this reversible conversion process and informs other organs in which direction the metabolic transaction is going, from glucose cash to glycogen deposits or vice versa. If the balance tips toward storage (supply currently exceeds demand, so that the excess can be converted into glycogen), the liver sends a satiety signal and the animal stops eating. If the balance tips toward glucose production (demand exceeds supply, so that reserves are being used), the livers sends a hunger signal and the animal eats (Figure 3.6). The evidence for the liver's role comes from hungry dogs that were injected with glucose. When the glucose was injected into the vein that goes directly to the liver, the dogs stopped eating. When the glucose was injected anywhere else, there was no comparable effect (Russek, 1971; Friedman and Stricker, 1976).

Notice, though, that this regulatory system must deal with a considerable time lag. Imagine that the liver waited until glucose supplies were low and only then gave the signal that initiated eating. Since food metabolism is a slow process, many minutes would then elapse between the time the "Need glucose!!" signal was given and the time that the needed supplies finally arrived. This situation could be quite dangerous for the animal and so must be avoided. The liver must anticipate the body's future needs, so that eating is initiated well in advance. That way, the nutrients will arrive in a timely fashion.

How does the liver manage to do this? It does so by responding to a charac-

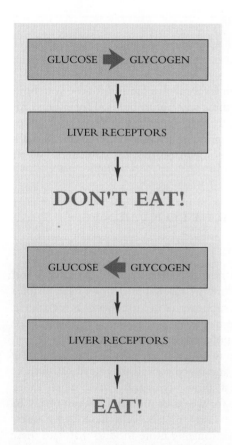

3.6 The relation between the glucose-glycogen balance in the liver and eating

teristic drop and rise in the glucose level: When an organism hasn't eaten for a while, the level of glucose in the blood begins to drop. Before these levels drop too far, the liver takes action, drawing some glycogen out of storage and converting it to glucose. As a result, blood glucose levels bounce back to normal. This sequence of events produces an easily identifiable pattern—a gradual drop in blood glucose levels, usually lasting many minutes, followed by a quick rise, resulting from the liver's compensatory action.

This slow drop–quick rise pattern does not indicate that the energy account is empty; instead, it indicates that the organism is drawing on its reserves, making it a good time to make a deposit. When this pattern of blood glucose levels occurs in rats, the animals start to eat (Campfield and Smith, 1990a, b). When it occurs in humans, they say they're hungry and want something to eat (Campfield and Rosenbaum, 1992).

RECEPTORS IN THE BRAIN

The liver is only one component in regulating food intake. Many researchers believe that the brain itself contains cells sensitive to glucose levels in the blood, with these cells concentrated, once again, in the brain structure responsible for so much of homeostasis: the hypothalamus. Evidence for such glucose receptors comes from studies in which the hypothalamus was injected with a chemical that made its cells unable to respond to glucose. The result was ravenous eating. This treatment presumably silenced the glucoreceptors; their silence was then interpreted by other brain mechanisms as indicating a fuel deficiency, which led to feeding (Miselis and Epstein, 1970).

SIGNALS FROM THE STOMACH AND INTESTINES

We have now discussed why an animal *starts* eating, but what causes it to stop? The receptors in the brain can't be the reason, because they respond to a fuel deficiency in the bloodstream that isn't corrected until after the meal has been at least partially digested. Yet humans and animals stop eating much before that. Why?

The common belief that we eat until we're full turns out to be only partly true. An animal will stop eating when its stomach is only partially full, if it has ingested something nutritious; if its stomach is filled with an equal volume of nonnutritive bulk, it will continue to eat. This suggests that the stomach walls contain receptors that are sensitive to the nutrients dissolved in the digestive juices. These receptors signal the brain that nutrient supplies are on their way, and the result is satiety (Deutsch, Puerto, and Wang, 1978).

SIGNALS FROM THE SMALL INTESTINE

Further satiety signals come from the duodenum, the first part of the small intestine. When food passes out of the stomach into the intestines, the duodenum begins to release a hormone from its mucous lining. There is good evidence that this hormone—***cholecystokinin,*** or ***CCK***—sends "stop eating" messages to the brain (Gibbs and Smith, 1984). When CCK is injected into the abdominal cavity of hungry rats and dogs, they stop feeding (Stacher, Bauer, and Steinringer, 1979). If an animal eats a food that contains CCK, the animal swiftly learns to avoid that food (Chen, 1993). Rats will also stop eating if they smell the kind of food they were given when they were injected with CCK (Weller et al., 1995). Unfortunately, dieters won't like taking CCK; humans given this hormone experience abdominal cramping, nausea, and sometimes vomiting (Miaskiewicz, Stricker, and Verbalis, 1989).

Peasant Wedding Feast *(Peter Brueghel the Elder, 1568; courtesy the Kunsthistorisches Museum)*

SIGNALS FROM FATTY TISSUE

Because they cannot be sure that food will be available the next time they need energy, animals don't just eat for the moment. Instead, they eat enough to satisfy both their current needs and to create a store of potential nutrients for later on. Part of this store is for the short-term future, so food is converted to glycogen, which can quickly be converted to glucose when needed. Another part of this store is for the long haul. Animals use the fatty or *adipose cells* of their bodies for long-term storage. These cells absorb the fatty acids created by the liver and swell in the process. When the animal's glycogen supplies are exhausted, it turns to these longer-term reserves. Fatty acids are drained from the adipose cells into the bloodstream and then converted into glucose.

Although adipose tissue used to be regarded as a kind of inert storage, it now appears that adipose cells play a role in governing hunger. Fat cells generate a chemical called **leptin,** which they secrete into the bloodstream, where it is sensed by receptors in the hypothalamus and areas near the brain's ventricles (Maffei, 1995; McGregor, 1996). Some speculate that leptin may provide a signal indicating that there is plenty of fat in storage and no need to add more and that this may diminish eating. The fact that certain strains of genetically obese mice lose marked amounts of weight when given leptin injections supports this conjecture (Pelleymounter et al., 1995). Research is underway to determine how leptin works in the hypothalamus and whether leptin or related compounds can be beneficial in treating some kinds of human obesity.

SIGNALS FROM THE OUTSIDE

Humans and animals eat to maintain homeostasis; in other words, they eat because their bodies need food. But they also eat for other reasons. For example, external stimuli—say, the smell of pizza—can be a powerful inducement to start eating. The time of day is also important: Organisms are more likely to eat at their habitual mealtime. Yet another influence is the company of fellow eaters. A hen who has had her fill of grain will eagerly resume her meal if joined by other hens who are still hungry (Bayer, 1929).

But the effectiveness of these external cues depends on the internal state of the organism. If we have just eaten an enormous meal, or if we are enduring the stomach flu, even the tastiest dessert will no longer be tempting. These commonsense claims can be confirmed in the laboratory: In one group of studies, investigators implanted microelectrodes in the hypothalamus of waking monkeys and found neurons that fired when the animal was shown a peanut or a banana. But these cells only fired when the monkey was hungry. When the animal was first fed to satiety and then shown the same foods, the hypothalamic neurons did not respond. It would seem that at least in the hypothalamus, the eye is not bigger than the stomach (Mora, Rolls, and Burton, 1976; Rolls, 1978).

The fact that the attractiveness of food depends on the degree of hunger calls our attention once again to the manner in which all of the motives work—by potentiating certain responses. After all, animals have no way of knowing exactly what their bodies need at any particular moment; neither they nor most of us have ever read a text on digestive physiology. But, helpfully, nature has built that information into their (and our) nervous systems so that specific needs guide perception, making food particularly attractive to the hungry. That the most enjoyable dessert becomes cloying after two or three portions is yet another demonstration of the potentiating role of motives that determine what we experience no less than what we do.

HYPOTHALAMIC CONTROL CENTERS

We have now seen that there are many different signals for food intake, with some arising in the liver, others in the intestine and fatty tissue, and still others hinging on nutrient levels in the bloodstream. It seems natural to suppose that these various messages are all integrated at some point in the nervous system, where a final decision is made to eat or not to eat. For many years, the natural candidate for such a feeding center was considered to be the hypothalamus, which was already known to contain controls for temperature regulation and water balance. Physiological psychologists devised a *dual-center theory* of hypothalamic control of feeding that was analogous to the temperature system. It postulated two antagonistic centers, one corresponding to hunger, the other to satiety.

DUAL CENTERS FOR FEEDING

According to dual-center theory, the hypothalamus contains an "on" and an "off" command post for eating. The "on" center was hypothesized to be in the lateral region of the hypothalamus; it was said to function as a hunger center whose activation led to eating. The "off" center was hypothesized to be in the ventromedial region and was thought to constitute the mechanism whose stimulation stopped eating.

The evidence for these claims came from the effects of various brain lesions. Rats whose lateral hypothalamus has been destroyed suffer from *aphagia* (from the Greek for "no eating"). They refuse to eat and drink and will starve to death unless forcibly tube-fed for weeks (Teitelbaum and Stellar, 1954). Interestingly enough, eventually there is some recovery of function. After a few weeks the animals begin to eat again, especially if tempted first by such delectables as eggnog (Teitelbaum and Epstein, 1962).

Lesions to the ventromedial region produce effects that are in many ways the very opposite. Animals with such lesions suffer from *hyperphagia* (from the Greek for "excess eating"). They eat voraciously and keep on eating. If the lesion is large enough, they may become veritable mountains of rat obesity, finally reaching weights that are some three times as great as their preoperative levels. Tumors in this hypothalamic region, although very rare, have the same effect on humans (Miller, Bailey, and Stevenson, 1950; Teitelbaum, 1955, 1961).

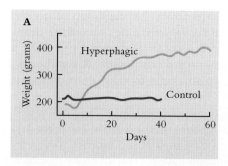

A

B

3.7 Hyperphagia *(A) Curve showing the weight gain of hyperphagic rats after an operation creating a hypothalamic lesion. The weight eventually stabilizes at a new level. (After Teitelbaum, 1955) (B) Photograph of a rat several months after the operation. This rat weighed over 1,000 grams. (Courtesy Neal E. Miller, Rockefeller University)*

While ventromedial lesions lead to rapid weight gain, this weight increase levels off in a month or two. From that point forward, the animal's weight remains stable at a new (and of course much greater) level. The animal eats enough to maintain this weight, but no more (Figure 3.7; Hoebel and Teitelbaum, 1976). This suggests that the lesion produces an upward shift in a setpoint for weight regulation—a point that defines a kind of target value that determines food intake. As we shall see, this interpretation may apply to certain aspects of human obesity (Nisbett, 1972).

DUAL CENTERS RECONSIDERED

The dual-center theory of feeding has held center stage for several decades. But recent years have seen it fall out of favor, partly because research on the neurochemicals involved in feeding has shown it to be far too simple. For example, consider the role of the lateral hypothalamus in feeding. True, certain neurochemicals called *orexins* initiate eating when injected into the brain, and they are secreted in the lateral hypothalamus (Sakuriam et al., 1998). But another neurochemical, called *neuropeptide Y (NPY),* turns out to be the most potent appetite stimulant yet discovered (Gibbs, 1996), so potent that, when it is injected into the brain, it can make even fully sated rats resume eating (Stanley, Magdalin, and Leibowitz, 1989). But NPY exerts its strongest effects outside the lateral hypothalamus, which suggests that this region cannot be the main "feeding" center (Leibowitz, 1991).

Another problem concerns the effects of ventromedial lesions. According to the original dual-center view, rats with such lesions overeat because of damage to some off switch for feeding. But there may be a better way to think about this overeating. One effect of ventromedial lesions is that they produce an overreaction of certain branches of the parasympathetic system. This triggers an oversecretion of the hormone insulin, which in turn increases the proportion of usable nutrients, especially glucose, that are turned into fat and cached away as adipose tissue. The trouble is that so much is stored that not enough is left over to serve as metabolic fuel. As a result, the animal stays hungry; it has to eat more to get the fuel it needs. But since most of what it eats is turned into fat and stored away, the process continues and the animal has to keep eating. The animal is in the position of a rich miser who has buried all his possessions and so has no money to live on. Evidence comes from studies showing that animals with ventromedial lesions get fatter than normals, even when both groups are fed the identical amount (Stricker and Zigmond, 1976). So the ventromedial hypothalamus may not be the satiety center at all. Lesions here may cause overeating, not because they have destroyed the "stop eating" center, but rather because they have severely disrupted how the body uses (or saves) the nutrients it has ingested.

These findings and others have gradually undermined the idea of two hypothalamic centers controlling feeding. These brain sites are certainly relevant to food intake but probably do not control feeding in any simple or direct sense. There are probably multiple hunger and satiety systems, some specialized for short-term energy needs, others for long-term storage. All of this provides another example of the elegance and sophistication of homeostasis, with a rich and sometimes redundant set of mechanisms precisely and powerfully controlling the organism's internal state.

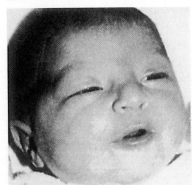

A

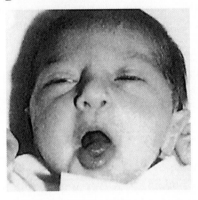

B

3.8 The response of newborn human babies to different tastes *Drops of different solutions were placed in the infants' mouths to record their reaction to (A) a sweet taste (sugar solution) and (B) a bitter taste (quinine solution). (From Steiner, 1977; photographs courtesy of Jacob Steiner)*

FOOD SELECTION

The mechanisms that determine feeding are at least partially under the control of homeostasis, and, in this regard, they resemble those that govern drinking and temperature regulation. But in many ways the mechanisms controlling hunger are considerably more complex. One reason is that the control of food intake depends on two decisions. The animal must not only decide whether to eat, but also what to eat. How do humans and nonhuman animals make this selection?

Part of the answer is built into the nervous system. For example, there appears to be a set of hardwired taste preferences in human infants, among them ones that lead the infants to prefer sweet tastes over bitter or salty ones. This particular preference appears quite early: the rate at which newborns suck at a nipple depends on the degree of sweetness or saltiness of the solution in the bottle (Lipsett and Behl, 1990). The preference is also seen in newborns' facial reactions. When a human newborn's mouth is moistened with a sweet solution (say, sugar water), the infant's face appears receptive; when the solution is bitter (say, quinine water), the newborn contorts his face and turns away (Steiner, 1974; see Figures 3.8A and B). This selectional bias makes good biological sense, since in the natural environment, sweet substances generally have more nutritional value than others. In contrast, bitter tastes are found in many poisonous plants. With artificial sweeteners, though, the nutritional bet is lost: Saccharin is sweet and is generally preferred to less sweet substances, but it contains no calories.

Can built-in preferences of this sort account for all of an animal's food choices? They might, if the animal lives on one (or only a very few) food items, such as the koala, whose diet consists almost entirely of eucalyptus leaves. But the majority of animals are less specialized than the koala; their diet is made up of all sorts of foods (Figure 3.9). How do these animals know which substances provide calories and which do not? Furthermore, how do they identify food that will supply the specific nutrients they require: various vitamins, minerals, amino acids, and so on? And in humans, there is yet another layer of complexity—taste preferences: Why do some humans prefer spaghetti over sushi? Why do some prefer spicy foods and some bland? All of these are issues of food selection.

For most carnivores, the food selection problem is relatively easy. In general, carnivores feed on animals that have nutritional needs like theirs, and this assures

3.9 Food selection *(A) Some animals such as zebras eat only plants. (Photograph by Laura Riley/Bruce Coleman) (B) Others such as lions eat only other animals. (Photograph by Stan Osolinski/Oxford Scientific Films) (C) A few others subsist on a diet of just one food substance. In the case of the koala of Australia, this consists of eucalyptus leaves, which provide the animal with water as well as nutrients. (Photograph by Helen Williams/Photo Researchers)*

A

B

C

them a balanced diet. Lions run no risk of vitamin deficiency unless they insist on eating vitamin-deficient zebras (Rozin, 1976c, 1982).

But how do herbivores (plant eaters) like the zebra or omnivores (everything eaters) like us manage their own nutritional needs? One difficulty lies in the fact that many plants lack nutrients that animals need for survival. Worse, some plants contain poisons, an adaptation that they use to protect themselves from plant eaters. To get the necessary nutrients, therefore, herbivores and omnivores must avoid the toxic plants while ingesting a large range of edible plants that, taken together, will satisfy their dietary needs. How can this be done? Part of the answer lies in a simple solution adopted by many species. When it comes to food, they are **neophobic**—that is, afraid of anything new. When rats (who, like humans, are omnivores) are confronted with some substance they've never tasted before, they will initially shy away from it altogether. But eventually, they'll taste-test just a very small amount. If it is poisonous, they will get sick. But since they only ate a little, they will most probably recover. They will later associate the taste of that food with their sickness and will avoid this taste from now on.★ On the other hand, if the food turns out to be safe, the animals will return in a day or two, take larger bites, and add this particular taste to their repertoire of acceptable food flavors (Rozin, 1976c).

Many children exhibit a similar neophobia about foods once they are about two years old. From then on, they tend to be culinary conservatives who stick to foods they know and make sour faces if confronted with something new. But in humans this neophobia is less pronounced than it is in rats and is not very hard to override. One contributing factor is the built-in taste preferences we've already mentioned. Three-year-olds may dislike new foods, but they are certainly willing to make an exception for chocolate pudding. But even more important is the fact that people live in a culture that allows them to benefit from the pooled experience of previous generations. Most animals have to learn anew whether a given food is safe, but a child can rely on her parents.† She may fuss and fume about the spinach and cauliflower on her plate, but at least she doesn't have to worry that they might be poisonous. After a while, she will learn to eat the foods her culture prefers (Mom's apple pie) and to avoid those to which her culture has aversions or taboos (pork to Muslims and Jews).

Food choices also serve other functions as well. For some of us, they can be a source of aesthetic satisfaction. The choices are sometimes used to make various symbolic statements, may underline social distinctions, and can help to cement social and family groups. After all, is there any American who believes that there are special metabolic needs that arise in late November requiring the specific nutrients a turkey provides? In these ways, also, food selection is heavily influenced by our cultural and social context.

Inborn aversions? (This FAR SIDE cartoon by Gary Larson is reprinted by permission of Chronicle Features, San Francisco, California, all rights reserved)

OBESITY

All of these determinants of food intake are relevant to a problem partially created by the affluence of modern industrialized society—obesity. Obesity is sometimes defined as a body weight that exceeds the average for a given height by 20 percent. Judged by this criterion, about 35 percent of American women

---

★ Such acquired taste aversions have some important implications for our understanding of learning, which will be discussed in the next chapter.

† To some extent this is true even of rats. Young rats rely on the smell of their mothers' breath to decide whether to eat a novel food. When a new food item is encountered, rat pups will only eat it if they can smell it when sniffing at their mothers' mouth (Galef, 1988).

over the age of twenty are obese, as are 31 percent of men over age twenty. By this same criterion, about 25 percent of American children and adolescents are also obese (Stern et al., 1995). Even if we adopt a less-inclusive criterion, the fact remains that a huge number of individuals desperately want to be slimmer than they are, and their desperation offers a ready market for a vast number of diet foods and fads. In part, the reason is health (at least it is sometimes said to be). But more important are social standards of physical attractiveness. There are no corpulent teen heartthrobs, no fat sex goddesses (Stunkard, 1975).

There are many reasons why people become obese. In some cases, the cause is a bodily condition, sometimes related to genetic factors. In others, it is simply a matter of how much they eat.

BODILY FACTORS IN OBESITY

Most of us take it for granted that body weight is a simple function of caloric intake and energy expenditure. This is undoubtedly true, but it is not the whole story. Constitutional factors may predispose one person to get fat, even if he eats no more (and exercises no less) than his slender next-door neighbor. What are these factors? One may be a more proficient digestive apparatus, since the person who manages to digest a larger proportion of the food he ingests will necessarily put on more weight than his digestively less efficient fellows. Another may be a lower metabolic level; the less nutrient fuel that is burned up, the more that is left for fatty storage. In still other individuals, too much of the nutrient intake may be converted into fat, leaving too little to burn as metabolic fuel. These and other constitutional differences may help to explain why some people gain weight much more readily than others (Sims, 1986; Friedman, 1990a, b).

GENETIC FACTORS IN OBESITY

But where do these constitutional factors come from? Part of the answer is genetics, and one's genetic makeup does have a great influence on the predisposition to obesity. Evidence comes from studies of identical twins reared apart, whose weights are as much alike as when they are reared together (Price and Gottesman, 1991). In addition, one specific kind of severe human obesity seems due to a defect in a gene that regulates the manufacture of leptin in both mice and men (Reed et al., 1996).

One's genetic makeup cannot cause obesity directly, since anyone on a near-starvation diet will lose weight. But our genetics can predispose us to obesity, most likely by producing the constitutional differences in metabolic efficiency we just discussed. This possibility appears to fit the results of a study of twelve pairs of male identical twins. Each of these men was fed about 1,000 calories per day above the amount required to maintain his initial weight. The activities of each participant were kept as constant as possible, and there was very little exercise. This regimen continued for a period of one hundred days. Needless to say, all twenty-four men gained weight, but the amount they gained varied substantially, from about ten to thirty pounds. A further difference concerned the parts of the body where the newly gained weight was deposited. For some participants, it was the abdomen; for others, it was the thighs and buttocks. The important finding was that the amount each person gained was very similar to the weight gain of his twin (see Figure 3.10). Similarly for the location on the body where the weight was deposited. If one gained in the abdomen, so did his twin; if another deposited the fat in his thighs and buttocks, his twin did too. These findings are a strong indication that people differ in how their bodily machinery handles excess calories and that this metabolic pattern is inherited (Bouchard et al., 1990).

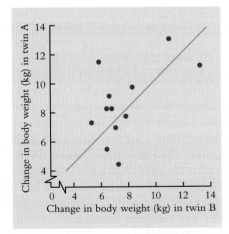

3.10 Similarity of weight gains in identical twins *Weight gains for twelve pairs of identical twins after 100 days of the same degree of overfeeding. Each point represents one twin pair, with the weight gain of twin A plotted on the vertical axis and the weight gain of twin B plotted on the horizontal axis. Weight gains are plotted in kilograms (1 kg = 2.2 lbs). The closer the points are to the diagonal line, the more similar the weight gains of the twins are to each other. (After Bouchard et al., 1990)*

Does such metabolic efficiency indicate a genetic defect? Not for proponents of the "thrifty gene" hypothesis, who argue that our ancestors may have benefited from efficient metabolisms in times when feasts were occasional and famines frequent (Fujimoto et al., 1995; Groop and Tuomi, 1997; Ravussin, 1994, 1997). In such circumstances, a tendency toward storing as much fat as possible may well have promoted survival, much as a bear is well served by storing excess fat in preparation for its winter-long fast. But the same tendency does not serve us well now, especially those of us in affluent cultures where obtaining food—high-fat food, at that—means just a trip to the supermarket.

BEHAVIORAL FACTORS

In some people, obesity is evidently a constitutional condition. But for many others, the cause lies in behavior: They simply eat too much. Why is this? It is virtually certain that there is no one answer, for chronic overeating has not one cause but many.

The externality hypothesis Some years ago, a number of investigators subscribed to the **externality hypothesis,** which held that obese people are comparatively unresponsive to their own internal hunger state. Instead, the hypothesis claimed, they are much more influenced by food-related signals from outside (Schachter and Rodin, 1974). And, of course, we are all regularly deluged with the sights or smells of food, or food-associated cues (Schachter, 1971). If someone were particularly sensitive to these external cues, and correspondingly insensitive to the fact that, at that moment, his body needed no calories, he might well overeat and eventually grow obese.

Indeed, several studies seem to show that obese participants are quite sensitive to these external signals and, in particular, quite sensitive to the sensory properties of food. If offered a premium grade of vanilla ice cream, they eat more than normal participants. But if offered vanilla ice cream that has been adulterated with bitter-tasting quinine, they actually eat less than do normals (Nisbett, 1968; see Figure 3.11). In line with the externality hypothesis, then, it appears that the obese participants, while obviously eating far more than their comrades, were nonetheless fussier about what they ate.

But more recent studies have cast some doubt on the externality hypothesis. To begin with, the evidence for the greater sensitivity of obese people to external cues turns out to be rather inconsistent. And to the extent that this oversensitivity does exist, its explanation may be different from what was originally supposed; it may be an effect of the obesity rather than its cause (Nisbett, 1972; Rodin, 1980, 1981). In our society people who are overweight generally try to restrain their eating. Since obesity is a social liability, they go on diets, buy low-calorie foods, and do what they can to clamp a lid on their intense desire to eat. But keeping the lid on is difficult, because any external stimulus for eating threatens the dieter's resolve (Herman and Polivy, 1980).

These suggestions offer a different perspective on the "fussiness" often observed in obese eaters. Their resolve *not* to eat is easy to maintain when the food is not at all tempting. But when exposed to delectable foods, they fall prey to strong temptation—perhaps the same strong temptation that led them to become obese in the first place. So what looks like fussiness may actually reflect how the participants handle temptation and not some excess sensitivity to external cues.

The setpoint hypothesis What makes some people obese while others stay thin, regardless of what they eat? One possibility is that people differ in their weight setpoints. These may reflect differences in constitution, which may in part be genetically determined (also see Foch and McClearn, 1980).

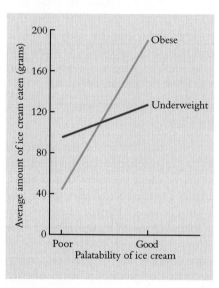

3.11 Eating, palatability, and obesity
In the experiment, obese and underweight participants were given the opportunity to eat ice cream. If the ice cream tasted good, the obese participants ate more than the underweight ones. The reverse was true if the ice cream did not taste good. (After Nisbett, 1968)

That we may be predisposed toward a certain weight is suggested by the fact that obese people who go on crash diets return rapidly to their starting weights as soon as they break their diets. Moreover, such dieters don't lose nearly as much weight as would be expected based on their reduced caloric intake. The reason for this lies in something we have already discussed: the body compensates for the caloric loss by reducing its basal metabolic rate. The situation is worse with "yo-yo" dieting, in which people repeatedly go on diets, break them, regain their starting weights, and then start dieting again (Carlson, 1991). Although the evidence is contradictory on this, for these dieters there may be further metabolic reduction with each successive diet, such that it takes longer to achieve the desired weight each time (Brownell et al., 1986).

THE TREATMENT OF OBESITY

What can be done to help people who are overweight? Attempts to treat obesity have taken many forms, including psychoanalysis, various forms of behavior therapy (techniques for modifying the individual's behavior by the systematic use of certain principles of learning; see Chapters 4 and 19), and self-help groups (such as Weight Watchers International). There is considerable dispute over the extent to which any of these methods leads to long-term change, although there is some suggestion that the self-help groups do a fairly good job, especially for those who are only mildly overweight (Booth, 1980; Stuart and Mitchell, 1980; Stunkard, 1980; Wilson, 1980).

Surveys suggest that "going on a diet" is the most popular method of weight control. In the United States, dieting is nearly the norm, since at any one time up to 40 percent of women and 25 percent of men report that they are trying to lose weight (National Institutes of Health, 1995). Others increase their average amount of exercise, a better option all around, since it accomplishes more fat reduction, reproportions body weight, and has positive effects on health and life expectancy (Blair, 1993).

In extreme cases, physicians resort to more drastic measures, arguing that being overweight is a health hazard that must be treated medically if psychotherapy or behavioral interventions do not work. Certainly, gross obesity usually leads to early death, and for the worst cases physicians resort to surgical procedures such as stapling the stomach (to limit its capacity) or cutting out some of the small intestine (to reduce caloric absorption from food). Much more commonly, physicians prescribe various appetite-suppressing medications. These can produce dramatic weight loss, but they all have side effects, which in rare circumstances can be lethal. Moreover, these medications clearly illustrate the degree to which our bodies defend a weight setpoint, because the medications are effective only as long as they are taken; when they are stopped, gluttonous hunger ensues and the lost weight rapidly returns.

But apart from cases of gross obesity, the relation between overweight and life expectancy is actually a matter of debate (Fitzgerald, 1981; see Figure 3.12). One complication in interpreting the evidence is that obesity is associated with inactivity, which itself is a health risk. Indeed, one study tracked over 25,000 men and 7,000 women for eight years and found that obese men who were physically fit had lower mortality rates than normal weight men who were sedentary. A similar (although smaller) result was found for women (Kampert et al., 1996).

Some authors argue, therefore, that obesity is more a social and aesthetic problem than a problem of physical health. This is especially so for women, who are much more likely to regard themselves as overweight than are men (Gray, 1977; Fallon and Rozin, 1985). Seen in this light, being slender is merely a social ideal, and one held by only some societies. Other cultures set quite different standards. The women painted by Rubens, Matisse, and Renoir were considered

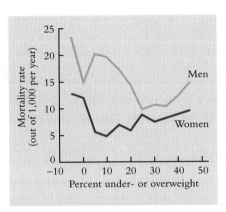

3.12 Relation of obesity to mortality
The figure presents the mortality rate in a sample of 5,209 people in Massachusetts for men and women from 45 to 74 years old between 1948 and 1964. The percent overweight is calculated by reference to mean weights for a given height. The figure shows that overweight does not increase overall mortality risk, at least not for overweight percentages that are less than 50. (From Andres, 1980)

beautiful by their contemporaries, who would judge today's supermodels to be undernourished and unappealing. Conversely, a modern woman who fit Rubens's ideal would simply be considered obese.

Of course, the forces sustaining a society's ideal body weight—including an incessant barrage of media images reinforcing the idea that the ideal body is a thin body—are forces of enormous power. This makes it immensely difficult for overweight individuals simply to accept their bodies as they are. They might fully understand that there is nothing sacred about a society's ideal body weight and that there is no law (or any medical reason) requiring each individual to match this ideal. But this knowledge is a flimsy shield against a world filled with social pressures, Hollywood images, and fashion advertisements, all celebrating a level of thinness that is, for many of us, unnatural and probably unhealthy (for further discussion, see Smith, 1996).

ANOREXIA NERVOSA

In some cases, the desire to be thin may be so extreme that it leads to eating disorders whose health hazards are serious indeed. One such condition is *anorexia nervosa,* which afflicts up to 1 percent of young people in industrialized societies. Its defining feature is "the relentless pursuit of thinness through self-starvation, even unto death" (Bruch, 1973, p. 4). Over 90 percent of anorexics are females. The disorder typically begins in midadolescence and is most common in societies in which food is plentiful but thinness is the ideal of attractiveness (American Psychiatric Association, 1994).

Anorexics are intensely and continually preoccupied by the fear of becoming fat. They eat only low-calorie food, if they eat at all. In addition, they may induce vomiting to purge whatever they do eat, and they may use laxatives to speed weight loss. Moreover, they often engage in strenuous exercise, sometimes for many hours each day. Of course, this regimen leads to extreme weight loss, sometimes reaching levels that are less than 50 percent of the statistical ideal. Further symptoms include the cessation of menstruation, hyperactivity, sleep disorders, and avoidance of sex.

For up to 40 percent of those with anorexia nervosa, treatment—which can range from outpatient care all the way to forced hospitalization and intravenous feeding—is successful. Less happily, the largest percentage of patients suffer chronically. Most tragically, in about 10 percent of the cases, the end result of this self-starvation is death (Andreasen and Black, 1996).

What leads to anorexia nervosa? Some authorities believe that the primary causes are psychological and center on not eating simply because of our modern obsession with slimness (Logue, 1986). In some patients, the main cause may be a fear of sexuality. In others, the primary focus involves a rebellion against the parents and a fierce desire to exercise some degree of autonomy and control. As one patient put it: "When you are so unhappy and you don't know how to accomplish anything, then to have control over your body becomes a supreme accomplishment. You make out of your body your very own kingdom where you are the tyrant, the absolute dictator" (Bruch, 1978, p. 61).

Other authors believe that the problem is primarily organic, involving some of the regulatory pathways in the hypothalamus. The fact that anorexics tend to have unusually low levels of reproductive and growth hormones, as well as abnormal levels of certain neurotransmitters, supports this view. As yet, we don't know whether these imbalances are the effect or the cause of the psychological problems (Garfinkel and Garner, 1982). But one clue that the hormonal problems may be primary is provided by the fact that about one-fifth of anorexic females cease menstruation before they lose any weight (Andreasen and Black, 1996).

Thin is beautiful—or is it? *The Boston organization Boycott Anorexic Marketing is a group of women who believe that the glamorization of ultrathin models in advertising tends to encourage the development of eating disorders in young women. To call attention to this relationship, such groups sometimes annotate the ads of those they see as culprits. (Kate Moss in an advertisement for Calvin Klein; photograph courtesy of Jane Carter, 1994)*

A

B

C

Changing conceptions of the relation between body weight and attractiveness *An underlying cause of many eating disorders in Western women is their belief that being slender is beautiful. But is it? It depends. (A) The Venus of Willendorf, a prehistoric statuette unearthed near Willendorf, Austria, that was sculpted some 30,000 years ago. Some archeologists believe that it depicts a fertility goddess; others, that it represents the female erotic ideal of the Ice Age. (Courtesy Naturhistorisches Museum, Wien) (B) The Three Graces, painted by the Flemish master Peter Paul Rubens in 1639. (Courtesy Museo del Prado) (C) Naomi Campbell, a 1990s "supermodel." (AP Photo/Laurent Rebours)*

Whether anorexia nervosa proves to be primarily organic or psychological, a genetic predisposition to it appears likely. Between 6 and 10 percent of female relatives of anorexics also have anorexia nervosa. The same rates apply to the siblings of anorexic individuals. For identical twins, if one twin has anorexia nervosa, the other has more than a 50 percent chance of being anorexic herself (Andreasen and Black, 1996).

BULIMIA NERVOSA

Another eating disorder is **bulimia nervosa,** characterized by repeated eating binges followed by attempts to purge the calories just consumed by self-induced vomiting or by taking laxatives. Unlike those with anorexia nervosa, individuals with bulimia are of roughly normal weight. Still, they suffer both physically and emotionally from the repeated binging and purging. The repeated binges may produce disruptions of electrolyte balance that can ultimately result in cardiac and kidney disease, as well as urinary infections. And their self-induced vomiting often causes erosion of their fingernails and tooth enamel. Most bulimic individuals also suffer from serious depression, and antidepressant medications such as Prozac are typically successful not only in relieving the depression but in halting most of the binge-and-purge behavior (Fluoxetine Bulimia Nervosa Collaborative Study Group, 1992).

Bulimia nervosa is fairly common among college students; in one survey, it was found in 19 percent of the women and 5 percent of the men. The binge-and-purge cycle is a perfect expression of our contradictory attitudes toward food and eating. On the one hand, print ads and television commercials urge us constantly to buy high-calorie foods that are easily available and chemically formulated for palatability; on the other hand, we are constantly reminded that to be sexually attractive we must be thin (Logue, 1986).

9 1

Together, the eating disorders show us that, despite tight homeostatic adjustments that regulate food intake, our species is quite susceptible to social and psychological factors that can in some cases cause these mechanisms to fail, resulting in grave bodily harm and even death.

THREAT

Thus far, our emphasis has been on motives that are largely based on internal, homeostatic controls. A disruption of the internal environment impels the organism to perform some action that ultimately restores its internal balance. As we have seen, though, these so-called internally regulated motives are not entirely internally regulated. Delectable food can cause us to eat even when we're not hungry; the anticipation of cold can trigger nest building even though the organism is not yet cold.

Other motives take this one step further, since their primary triggers are largely external (although, as we will see, internal factors matter as well). One such motive concerns our reaction to intense threat. In this case, the instigation is usually external—the threatening event or object—but the adjustment is largely internal, as the body prepares to escape, retaliate, or negotiate.

THREAT AND THE AUTONOMIC NERVOUS SYSTEM

What are the biological mechanisms that underlie our reactions to threat? We have already discussed the fact that the autonomic nervous system is divided into two branches: sympathetic and parasympathetic (p. 76). According to the American physiologist Walter B. Cannon (1871–1945), these branches serve two broad and rather different functions. The parasympathetic system handles the *vegetative* functions of ordinary life: the conservation of bodily resources, reproduction, and the disposal of wastes. In effect, these reflect an organism's operations during times of peace—a low, steady heart rate, peristaltic movements of stomach and intestines, secretions by digestive glands, and the like. In contrast, the sympathetic system has an activating function. It summons the body's resources in times of crisis and gets the organism ready for vigorous action (Cannon, 1929).

This opposition of the two autonomic divisions is seen in many bodily activities. For example, parasympathetic excitation slows down the heart rate and reduces blood pressure. Sympathetic excitation, as we have mentioned, has the opposite effect and also inhibits digestion and sexual activity. In addition, it stimulates the inner core of the adrenal gland, the ***adrenal medulla,*** to pour epinephrine (adrenaline) and norepinephrine into the bloodstream. These have essentially the same effects as sympathetic stimulation—they accelerate the heart rate, speed up metabolism, and so on. As a result, the sympathetic effects are amplified yet further (see Figure 3.13).

THE EMERGENCY REACTION

Cannon argued that intense sympathetic arousal serves as an emergency reaction that mobilizes the organism for a crisis—for "flight or fight," as he described it.

Walter B. Cannon *(Courtesy National Library of Medicine)*

3.13   The sympathetic and parasympathetic branches of the autonomic nervous system   *The parasympathetic system (shown in red) facilitates the vegetative functions of the organism: It slows the heart and lungs, stimulates digestive functions, permits sexual activity, and so on. In contrast, the sympathetic system (shown in blue) helps ready the organism for emergency: It accelerates the heart and lung, liberates nutrient fuels for muscular effort, and inhibits digestive and sexual functions.*

Note that the fibers of the sympathetic system are interconnected through a chain of ganglionic fibers outside of the spinal cord. As a result, sympathetic activation has a somewhat diffuse character; any sympathetic excitation tends to affect all of the viscera rather than just some. This is in contrast to the parasympathetic system, whose action is more specific and which operates through the vagus nerve, a cranial nerve that emerges from the skull and permeates the chest and abdomen. (After Cannon, 1929)

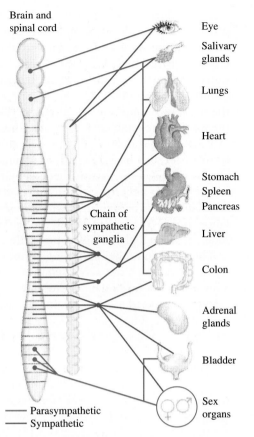

Brain and spinal cord

Eye
Salivary glands
Lungs
Heart
Stomach
Spleen
Pancreas
Liver
Colon
Adrenal glands
Bladder
Sex organs

Chain of sympathetic ganglia

—— Parasympathetic
—— Sympathetic

PARASYMPATHETIC SYSTEM

Constriction of pupil

Secretion of tear glands

Salivation

Inhibition of heart action

Constriction of respiratory passages

Stomach contraction: secretion of digestive fluids

Intestinal peristalsis

Contraction of bladder

Erection

SYMPATHETIC SYSTEM

Dilation of pupil

Inhibition of tear glands

Inhibition of salivation

Acceleration of heart action

Opens respiratory passages

Inhibits stomach contractions and digestive secretion

Inhibits intestinal peristalsis

Relaxes bladder

Inhibits erection

3.14   Sympathetic emergency reaction
A cat's response to a threatening encounter. (Photograph by Walter Chandoha)

Consider a grazing zebra, placidly maintaining homeostasis by nibbling at the grass and vasodilatating in the hot African sun. Suddenly it sees a lion closing in for the kill. The vegetative functions must now take second place, for if the zebra doesn't escape, it will have no internal environment left to regulate. Escape will require pronounced muscular exertion, with the support of the entire bodily machinery, and this is exactly what intense sympathetic activation provides. Because of this activation, more nutrient fuel is available to the muscles and can be delivered rapidly through wide-open blood vessels. At the same time, waste products are jettisoned and all less-essential organic activities are brought to a halt. If the zebra does not escape, it is not because its sympathetic nervous system did not try.

Cannon produced considerable evidence suggesting that a similar autonomic reaction occurs when the pattern is one of attack rather than of flight. A cat about to tangle with a dog shows accelerated heartbeat, piloerection (its hair standing on end, normally a heat-conserving device), and pupillary dilation—all signs of sympathetic arousal, signs that the body is girding itself for violent muscular effort (Figure 3.14).

But Cannon's fight-or-flight formulation is too simple to account for the full pattern of evidence, since organisms respond to threat in many different ways. For example, rats try to escape when threatened but fight when finally cornered. Some animals stand perfectly immobile, so that predators are less likely to notice them. Other animals have more exotic means of self-protection: Some species of fish pale when threatened, which makes them harder to spot against the sandy ocean bottom. This effect is produced by the direct action of adrenal epinephrine on various pigments in the animal's skin (Odiorne, 1957).

In fact, it's relatively rare that animal encounters result immediately in fight *or* flight, for either participant. Instead, there is usually a period of heightened vigilance during which each animal senses the behavioral signals given by the other. These signals—whether paling, piloerection, or paralysis, vocalizations or facial expressions—serve as cues to the signaler's status and intentions (see Chapter 10). This allows for a kind of negotiation in which the ultimate outcome might be fight or flight, but might just as well be mating or playing (Smith, 1977; Hinde, 1985). In all these cases, though, the pattern of reaction in the nervous system remains the same: The outcome may differ, but in all cases the readiness for immediate response must be in place.

What about humans? When we are threatened, we also respond autonomically: We pant, our hearts pound, our palms sweat, and we sometimes get goosebumps or shiver—all sympathetic activities. In fact, such autonomic responses can be used as indicators of emotional status. The *galvanic skin response (GSR),* for example, is a particularly favored measure. A brief drop in the electrical resistance of the skin, caused largely by activity of the sweat glands, it is a sensitive index of general physiological preparation.

The GSR and other indices of autonomic activity are often used as part of the set of measures of the *polygraph,* a machine commonly called a "lie detector." This name is a misnomer, because no machine can detect lies. What the polygraph does instead is detect autonomic arousal when examinees are asked certain key questions. The responses to these critical items (e.g., "Did you stab anyone with a knife on . . . ?") are then compared with the responses to control items—questions that are likely to produce an emotional reaction but are irrelevant to the issue at hand (e.g., "Before age nineteen did you ever lie to anyone?").

The fundamental assumption on which the lie-detection enterprise rests is that innocent people will feel more upset about the control items than the critical questions and will therefore show more intense autonomic arousal to the former than to the latter (Figure 3.15). But this assumption is in serious dispute (Lykken, 1979, 1981). By and large, while polygraph operators do rather well in identifying guilty individuals, certain people—especially those called *antisocial personalities,* or *psychopaths*—seem to have a special knack for beating polygraph tests (Waid and Orne, 1982; see Chapter 18). In addition, the polygraph does rather poorly in clearing the innocent. If, for example, an innocent person is particularly anxious about the key questions, or particularly troubled by the events being probed, this will show up as arousal in the polygraph test, and this pattern may be indistinguishable from the reaction of an individual who is truly guilty of the offense in question (Saxe, Dougherty, and Cross, 1985). Concerns of this kind, as well as ethical considerations, led the U.S. Congress to pass legislation in 1988 that severely restricted the use of lie-detector tests in the courts, in government, and in industry.

3.15   Lie detection by use of autonomic measures   *(A) Various devices measure autonomic arousal—a tube around the chest measures respiration rate, electrodes attached to the hand measure GSR, and an arm band measures blood pressure and pulse. (Photograph by Mary Shuford) (B) A recording of respiration, GSR, and a measure of blood pressure and pulse. The record was obtained from a store employee caught stealing merchandise. At issue was the amount of the theft. To determine this, all parties agreed to be guided by the results of a lie detector test. The employee was asked questions about the amount, such as "Did you steal more than $1,000?" and "Did you steal more than $2,000?" The record shows a high peak just after $3,000 and before $5,000. Later the employee confessed that the actual amount was $4,000. (After Inbau and Reid, 1953)*

A

B

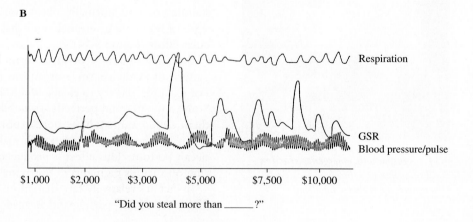

Respiration

GSR
Blood pressure/pulse

$1,000 $2,000 $3,000 $5,000 $7,500 $10,000

"Did you steal more than _____?"

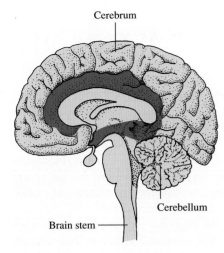

Cerebrum

Cerebellum

Brain stem

CENTRAL CONTROLS

Thus far, we have focused on the autonomic nervous system, in both its sympathetic and parasympathetic branches. But various areas of the brain are also crucial to an organism's response to threat. These areas are concentrated in the so-called old cortex of the brain, the portions underneath the neocortex that are sometimes collectively called the **limbic system** (Figures 3.16 and 3.17). Electrical stimulation within the limbic system can transform a purring cat into a spitting, hissing Halloween figure. Stimulation of the same region in humans often produces feelings of great anxiety or of rage, as in a patient who said that she suddenly wanted to tear things to pieces and to slap the experimenter's face (Magnus and Lammers, 1956; King, 1961; Flynn et al., 1970).

Different brain areas also seem to initiate different kinds of attack. In cats, the stimulation of one hypothalamic region produces predatory attack: quiet stalking followed by a quick, deadly pounce. The stimulation of another region leads to the Halloween pattern: a counterattack in self-defense (probably related to what in humans is called rage). When this rage pattern is triggered, the cat ignores a nearby mouse and will spring viciously at the experimenter, by whom it presumably feels threatened (Egger and Flynn, 1963; Clemente and Chase, 1973). Predatory attack is another matter entirely: the lion who pounces on and then disembowels a zebra is probably not at all enraged but is merely engaged in the everyday business of food gathering. (Whether the zebra is comforted by the fact that the lion is not angry at it is another question.)

3.17   The limbic system and some related structures   *The brain is pictured here as if the hemispheres were essentially transparent. One of the structures particularly relevant to emotional reactions is the amygdala, a walnut-sized structure that has been implicated in the production of aggressive behavior and threat reactions, and in the perception of certain situations as emotional. (After Bloom, Lazerson, and Hofstadter, 1988)*

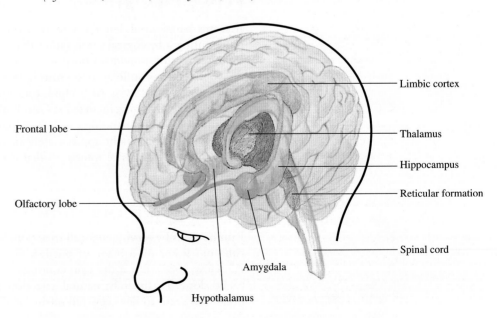

Frontal lobe

Olfactory lobe

Hypothalamus

Amygdala

Limbic cortex

Thalamus

Hippocampus

Reticular formation

Spinal cord

DISRUPTIVE EFFECTS OF AUTONOMIC AROUSAL

Our preceding discussion emphasized the biological value of the emergency system. But strong arousal of the sympathetic branch of the ANS can also be disruptive and even harmful to the organism. This negative side of the matter is especially clear in humans. In our day-to-day lives we rarely encounter emergencies that call for violent physical effort. But our biological nature has not changed just because our modern world contains no saber-toothed tigers. We still have the same emergency system that served our primitive ancestors, and its bodily consequences can take a serious toll.

The disruptive effects of threat upon our digestion or sexual responses are common knowledge. During periods of acute anxiety, diarrhea or constipation are widespread, and it is difficult to achieve or maintain sexual arousal. This is hardly surprising, since our digestive functions and many aspects of our sexuality (for example, erections in males and vaginal lubrication in females) are largely controlled by the parasympathetic system and are thus inhibited by intense sympathetic arousal. Moreover, the aftereffects of threat can sometimes be disabling, causing disorders such as stomachaches and headaches. In more extreme cases, the psychophysiological effects are severe and chronic, as in cases of hypertension and coronary disease, which can lead to strokes, heart attacks, and death (see Chapter 18).

PAIN AND THE ENDORPHIN SYSTEM

We've now said a great deal about how an organism responds to threats of various sorts, but what about the stimuli that set off this response in the first place? Some of these stimuli have surely acquired their significance through learning (to which we will turn in the next chapter). But some of them seem to produce the emergency reaction we have described without any prior experience. An important example of such a built-in trigger is *pain*.

PAIN AS AN AID TO SURVIVAL

It seems paradoxical, but the sensation of pain has considerable survival value, representing a biological boon rather than a burden. This fact is highlighted by the rare cases of individuals born with a virtual insensitivity to pain. They often die young, having suffered numerous injuries and showing considerable scarring (Manfredi et al., 1981). As a child, one such individual bit off the tip of her tongue while chewing, incurred serious burns when kneeling on a hot radiator, and suffered severe pathological dislocations in her hips and spine because she failed to shift her weight appropriately or turn over in her sleep. Such traumas eventually led to massive infections that caused her death at the age of twenty-nine (Melzack, 1973).

PAIN RELIEF THROUGH ENDORPHINS

Pain helps us by serving as a call to action, leading us to withdraw from a flame, run cold water on a burn, or put less weight on a sprained ankle (Bolles and Fanselow, 1982). But if the pain continues, it may interfere with whatever needs to be done. Fortunately, natural selection has confronted this problem, since organisms seem to have evolved means of alleviating much of their own pain.

A

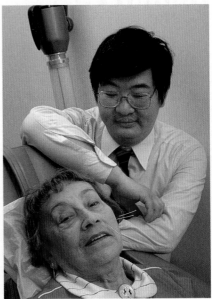

B

3.18 Acupuncture *Acupuncture is a complex system of treatment that grew up in ancient China and was based on the idea that disease is a disturbance of vital energies that circulate in particular channels. Their balance was to be restored by manipulating metal needles at special points along these channels. (A) From a seventeenth-century Chinese treatise illustrating the liver tract with twenty-eight special points. (From Blakemore, 1977) (B) A contemporary dental patient receiving treatment in place of novocaine. (Copyright © Dan McCoy, 1994/Rainbow)*

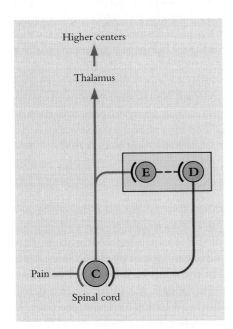

3.19 Pain and pain relief *Highly schematic diagram of a proposed neural circuit to explain certain pain relief phenomena, with dark green indicating excitation and dark red indicating inhibition. Pain stimuli excite neurons in the spinal cord (C) that carry pain information upward to the thalamus. But they also excite endorphin-releasing neurons (E) in the midbrain, which, through several intermediate steps, excite descending neurons (D) that inhibit the pain pathway in the spinal cord. This pain-relief system can also be activated by the administration of morphine or by the electrical stimulation of the region of the midbrain that contains the endorphin-releasing neurons. (After Groves and Rebec, 1988)*

There are many stories of athletes who suffer injuries but don't feel the pain until the game is over; similar accounts are told of soldiers in battle or parents rescuing their children from accidents. These stories seem to suggest that internal mechanisms are available that can produce **analgesia,** or pain relief. Various laboratory experiments support this conclusion. Rats subjected to various forms of stress, such as being forced to swim in cold water, actually become less sensitive to pain (Bodnar et al., 1980). Similar results have been shown in humans: Paradoxically enough, mild electric shock to the back or limbs can serve as an analgesic. So can acupuncture, an ancient Chinese treatment in which needles are inserted in various parts of the body (see Figure 3.18; Mann et al., 1973); this procedure seems to suppress pain in animals as well as humans (Nathan, 1978).

What mechanisms underlie these effects? The answer seems to lie in brain chemistry. It has long been known that the experience of pain can be dulled or entirely eliminated by drugs, such as morphine and other opiates. These drugs are typically applied from the outside. But on occasion, the brain is its own pharmacist. When assailed by various kinds of stress (including pain), the brain produces its own brand of opiates, which it then administers to itself. These are the **endorphins** (a contraction of the word *endogenous*—that is, internally produced—and the word *morphine*), a group of neurotransmitters that are chemically very similar to opiates like morphine and that modulate pain messages going to the brain through nerve tracts in the spinal cord (see Figure 3.19). It appears, then, that the opiate compounds dispensed by physicians work by mimicking the body's own analgesics, though, in fact, some of the brain's endorphins are considerably more powerful than the artificially produced drugs (Snyder and Childers, 1979; Bloom, 1983; Olson, Olson, and Kastin, 1995).

Placebos Many investigators believe that the endorphins play a role in the pain reduction produced by **placebos,** chemically inert substances that nonetheless actually diminish pain and promote healing (see Chapter 19 for a discussion of placebos in the context of psychotherapy). The power of placebos is readily demonstrated. In one experiment (Evans, 1974) some patients were given a sugar pill described as aspirin; others were given a sugar pill described as morphine. In both cases, the pills produced substantial relief—about 50 percent of the relief produced by the actual drugs.

Do endorphins play a role in these placebo effects? To find out, investigators turned to opiate-blocking drugs such as naloxone or naltrexone. These drugs are generally given to addicts who have overdosed on heroin; they have also become powerful investigative tools. A number of studies have shown that naloxone blocks the pain alleviation produced by acupuncture (Mayer et al., 1976) and also blocks the effects of placebos. In one such study, patients were given a placebo after having a wisdom tooth extracted. This helped some of the patients, but had no effect when the patients were given naloxone in addition to the placebo (Levine, Gordon, and Fields, 1979). The implication, of course, is that placebos work by triggering endorphin production; the effect of the naloxone is then to block the effects of the endorphins.

Some later studies have shown, however, that although naloxone can lessen such placebo effects, it does not abolish them. This indicates that there are some avenues to pain relief that do not involve the endorphin system (Watkins and Mayer, 1982; Grevert and Goldstein, 1985). In humans, a clear example of pain relief provided by nonendorphin systems is hypnosis. Hypnotic pain relief is sufficiently powerful to be used sometimes in surgery, but its analgesic effect is not abolished by naloxone (De Beneedittis et al., 1989; Moret et al., 1991).

Why does the body have multiple pain-relief systems? The answer seems to depend, at least in part, on the duration of the pain: Short-term pain seems to be alleviated by endorphins, but if the pain continues, then nonendorphin systems take over. And if stressors are especially prolonged, then the endorphin system appears to reemerge to help control the pain (Terman et al., 1984; Olson et al., 1995).

ENDORPHINS AND EXERCISE

Some researchers believe that the exhilarating effect of repeated stressful exercise, such as jogging and marathon running, is also related to the endorphins. The runner continues to exert herself until she is exhausted and in pain. This builds up endorphins, which counteract the pain produced by the exercise itself and simultaneously produce a mood swing in the opposite direction. Eventually there may be something like an addiction—the jogger has to have her jogging fix to enjoy the endorphin-produced euphoria. Whether this interpretation is correct is still unknown, though there is evidence that stressful exercise does increase the secretion of endorphins (Carr et al., 1981; Thoren et al., 1990; Hawkes, 1992).

Observing sleep *All-night EEG recordings of patients in sleep labs have revealed the several stages of sleep. (Photograph by Grant Leduc/Monkmeyer)*

SLEEP AND WAKING

We turn next to a rather different sort of motivation: the need for sleep. Sleep is actually just one phase of what researchers called the **sleep-wake cycle,** a daily rhythm that reflects a continuum of both brain and bodily arousal that ranges from alert hypervigilance to the near-total deactivation of deep sleep.

WAKING

The sympathetic branch of the autonomic nervous system serves as an arousal system for many processes in the body. Another set of arousal systems operates to alert the brain, waking the animal if it is asleep or bringing an already-awake animal to full alertness. These arousal systems involve structures in the mid- and hindbrain, and pathways that ascend to the rest of the brain (Aston-Jones, 1985).

Apart from these subcortical structures, the brain's state of arousal is also regulated by the cortex itself. The role of the cortex in rousing itself is shown by the fact that some complex stimuli whose recognition requires cortical involvement—a baby's cry, the smell of burning wood, the sound of our own name—are more likely to wake us than others, regardless of their intensity. Furthermore, signals from the cortex can excite subcortical structures, which then reciprocate and activate the cortex further. This arc—cortex to lower systems to cortex—plays an important role in many phenomena of sleep and waking. We sometimes have trouble in falling asleep because we can't "shut off" our thoughts. Here, cortical activity triggers the subcortical arousal system, which activates the cortex, which again excites the lower level subcortical system, and so on.

SLEEP AND PHYSIOLOGICAL ACTIVITY

The same circuits that enhance arousal can also lower it, as when we listen to the drone of a monotonous lecturer or fixate on the median line of the highway during long hours of late-night driving. Such low levels of stimulation can cause our arousal levels to drop so low that we are tempted to nod off into a state that seems the very opposite of high arousal—sleep. What can we say about this state in which we spend about one-third of our lives?

Eavesdropping on the brain of waking or sleeping participants is possible because, as we saw in Chapter 2, the language of the nervous system is partly electrical. When electrodes are placed at various points on the scalp, they pick up electrical fluctuations that result from the activity of the millions of neurons in the cortex just underneath. In absolute terms these changes are very small, so they are fed through highly sensitive amplifiers before being graphed on a scrolling paper chart or displayed directly on a computer screen (Figure 3.20). The resulting record is an *electroencephalogram,* or *EEG,* a picture of voltage changes over time occurring at the surface of the brain.

Figure 3.21 shows an EEG record that begins with the participant in a relaxed state, with eyes closed and "not thinking about anything in particular." The record shows alpha waves, a regular waxing and waning of electrical potential, at some 8 to 12 cycles per second. This *alpha rhythm* is very characteristic of this state (awake but resting) and is found in most mammals. When the participant attends to some stimulus with open eyes or when he is involved in active

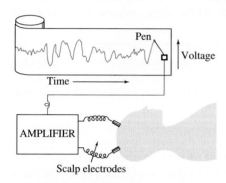

3.20 Schematic diagram of an EEG recording *A number of scalp electrodes are placed on a research participant's head. At any one time, there are small differences in the electrical potential (that is, the voltage) between any two of these electrodes. These differences are magnified by an amplifier and are then used to activate a recording pen. The greater the voltage difference, the larger the pen's movement. Since the voltage fluctuates, the pen goes up and down, thus tracing a brain wave on the moving paper. The number of such waves per second is the EEG frequency.*

3.21 Alpha waves and alpha blocking *(After Guyton, 1981)*

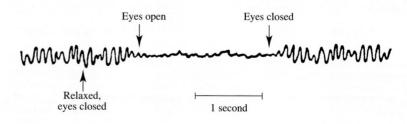

thought (for instance, mental arithmetic) with his eyes closed, the picture changes. Now the alpha rhythm is blocked, and the participant mainly shows a **beta rhythm:** the voltage is lower, the frequency is much higher (12 to 14 cycles per second), and the pattern of ups and downs is nearly random.

Sleep researchers most often obtain continuous, all-night recordings not only of brain waves, but also of other kinds of physiological activity that have proven quite informative about both sleep and wakefulness. These usually include respiration rate, heart rate, muscle tension, and eye movements.

THE STAGES OF SLEEP

Such physiological recordings demonstrate that there are two quite distinct kinds of sleep. The first kind, called **slow-wave sleep,** ensues as we first fall asleep; the second kind, called **REM sleep,** occurs intermittently throughout the night.

Let's begin with slow-wave sleep, which shows various stages based on the sleeper's EEG patterns. At bedtime, as a participant begins to relax in bed and becomes drowsy, his EEG pattern tends to slow from its jittery waking frequency and develops an accentuated alpha rhythm. He is now in a light, dozing sleep from which he is easily awakened and in which he experiences fleeting daydream-like imagery; this is the lightest stage, or Stage 1, of slow-wave sleep (Figure 3.22). After a few minutes in Stage 1, the participant passes a "point of no return" in which he feels himself drop off to sleep (perhaps with a few muscle twitches). This signals the start of Stage 2 of slow-wave sleep. Over the next hour, as his sleep deepens, he passes from Stage 2 to Stages 3 and 4 of slow-wave sleep. His heart rate and respiration slow, and his eyes drift slowly and no longer move in tandem. His EEG shows fluctuations of increasingly higher voltage and lower frequency (Stages 2 through 4 in Figure 3.22). At this point he is virtually immobile, curled up in semifetal position, and hard to wake up. Indeed, trying to wake up a person from slow-wave sleep takes sustained effort; the person will protest, appearing disoriented, mumbling incoherently or thrashing around, even if shaken or shouted at. Some people enter such a confused half-sleep, half-awake state spontaneously, and this accounts for slow-wave sleep disturbances such as sleepwalking and childhood night terrors (Hauri, 1977).

The sleeper will typically spend about 90–100 minutes in uninterrupted slow-wave sleep, shifting up and down among Stages 2, 3, and 4. After that, her quality of sleep changes dramatically. Her heart rate and respiration rate quicken, almost as if she were awake and exercising. Her EEG returns to the high-frequency activity associated with wakefulness (Jouvet, 1967). Her eyes stop rolling lazily and begin jittering back and forth under her closed eyelids. According to all these physiological signs, she should be awake and alert. But she doesn't wake up, and her skeletal muscles show sudden flaccidity—her jaw goes slack and she moves from a semifetal position to a sprawl, with arms and legs draped haphazardly. And despite the active EEG, in this sleep stage she is least

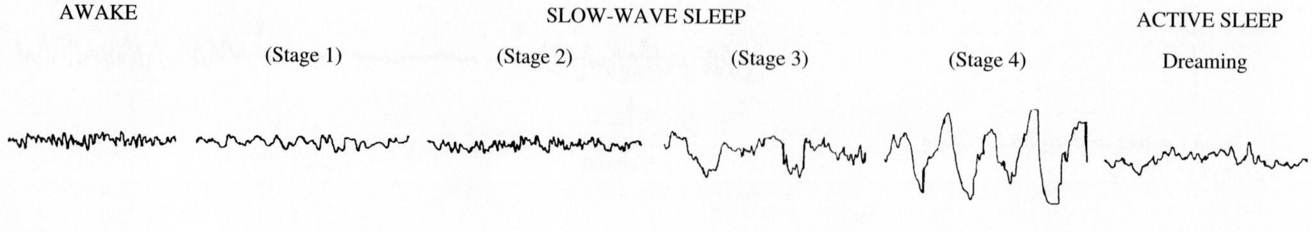

3.22 The stages of sleep *The figure shows EEG records taken from the frontal lobe of the brain during waking, slow-wave sleep, and REM sleep. (Courtesy of William C. Dement)*

AWAKE	SLOW-WAVE SLEEP			ACTIVE SLEEP
(Stage 1)	(Stage 2)	(Stage 3)	(Stage 4)	Dreaming

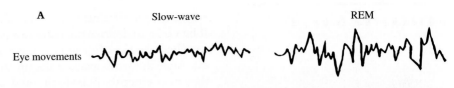

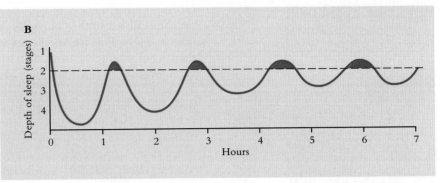

3.23 REM and slow-wave sleep *(A) Eye movements during slow-wave and REM sleep. (B) The alternation of slow-wave and REM sleep periods throughout the night (REM periods are in color). Rapid eye movements begin as the person repeatedly emerges from deeper sleep to the level of Stage 2. More vivid and visual dreams are recalled after awakening from REM sleep. (After Kleitman, 1960)*

sensitive to external stimulation (Williams, Tepas, and Morlock, 1962). But if awakened, she leaps to attention instantly. This odd state is REM sleep, named for the participant's rapid eye movements (Figure 3.23). Participants in this state are both physiologically activated and muscularly inactivated, and because of this contrast, REM sleep is often called *paradoxical sleep.*

This first REM period of a night's sleep usually lasts only about 5 minutes, after which people switch back to slow-wave sleep. After another 90–100 minutes, a second REM period ensues. This pattern continues, with alternating slow-wave and REM sleep periods. The average night's sleep includes 4 to 5 REM periods with the REM periods lasting longer each time, and the final REM period of the night as long as 45 minutes. Because REM sleep is so physiologically active, these latter REM periods can be strenuous, explaining why people who decide to "sleep in" and ignore the alarm clock often wake up extra tired: They have exhausted themselves REMing. They may also be more susceptible to the frightening but harmless state known as **sleep paralysis** (Hauri, 1977), in which the muscular paralysis of REM sleep persists for a few moments past awakening, leaving the person conscious but temporarily unable to move.

THE FUNCTIONS OF SLEEP

Why does sleep show such a complex architecture? What functions are served by slow-wave and REM sleep? Surprisingly enough, the answers are still unknown. But attempts to find the answers are ongoing.

SLEEP DEPRIVATION

One way to assess the benefits of sleep is to observe what ills befall us without it. This is the logic of sleep-deprivation experiments in which humans and animals are kept awake for days on end. The results confirm that the need for sleep is powerful indeed. If deprived of sleep, we seek it just as we crave food when we are famished. When sleep is finally allowed, we typically collapse wherever we can and try to regain the sleep we have lost.

Sleep-deprived people don't just need sleep; they need adequate amounts of both slow-wave and REM sleep. This is shown by studies in which the

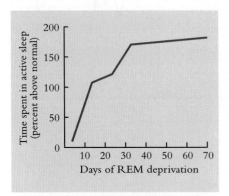

3.24 **The effect of lost REM sleep** *The figure shows an increase in the time cats spend in REM sleep after various periods of REM-sleep deprivation. The animals were deprived of REM sleep (but not non-REM sleep) for from 5 to 72 days by being awakened as soon as their EEG indicated the beginning of a REM period. On the day when the animals were finally allowed to sleep undisturbed, there was an increase in the proportion of time spent in REM sleep rather than non-REM sleep. (Data from Cohen, 1972)*

experimenter prevents one kind of sleep (for example, REM) but not the other. If he wants to deprive the participants of REM sleep only, he simply wakes them up whenever the EEG and eye movements signal the beginning of a REM period. After the participants wake up, they go back to sleep, are reawakened when they next enter the REM state, and so on through the night. After a few nights of this, the participants are allowed to sleep freely. They will now spend more time in REM than they normally do, apparently making up for their deprivation (Figure 3.24). This **REM rebound** is commonly seen after taking, and then withdrawing from, medications that selectively suppress REM sleep—a group that includes some of the commonly prescribed sleeping medications.

The same compensation holds for selective deprivation of Stages 3 and 4 of slow-wave sleep. If lost one night, they are made up on another (Webb, 1972).

Clearly, sleep deprivation is a serious problem, which makes it all the more unfortunate that only 5 percent of people with chronic insomnia seek professional help—despite the fact that the disorder is quite treatable (Dement and Mitner, 1993; National Commission on Sleep Disorders, 1993; Kupfer and Reynolds, 1997). Many cases of insomnia respond readily to simple sleep regimens: making the bedroom quiet and dark; keeping bedtimes and waking times constant; refraining from vigorous exercise, stressful thinking, or stimulants like caffeine or nicotine after the evening meal. Even alcohol, which makes most of us sleepy, actually produces troubled, fragmented sleep and results in less total sleep time (Hauri and Linde, 1991).

How much sleep do we truly need? The answer varies from person to person, and certainly varies with age. Infants take brief naps throughout the day, with 50 percent of their sleep devoted to REM periods (they average sixteen hours of sleep a day, eight of those REM sleep). It is not until four to six months of age that infants begin to consolidate their sleep into one nighttime period. As children age, they need less sleep, and less of that sleep is spent in REM periods. Adolescents average eight hours per night, two of which are REM sleep; senior citizens, on the other hand, average six hours per night, of which only one hour is spent in REM (Rosenzweig et al., 1996). These numbers, however, are just averages; some people need more and some much less. One researcher found a seventy-year-old nurse who reported, accurately, that she slept only about one hour per night; she was nonetheless attentive and cheery, and apparently suffered no ill effects from what would, for most people, constitute acute sleep deprivation (Meddis, 1977).

SLEEP AS A RESTORATIVE PROCESS

Sleep-deprivation experiments demonstrate the need for sleep, but they do not tell us *why* we must sleep. One possibility is that sleep is restorative, a period during which some vital substance is replenished in the nervous system. In one form or another, this view was held at least as early as the Renaissance. Shakespeare regarded sleep as "a balm of hurt minds" that "knits up the ravel'd sleave of care."

But if sleep is restorative, then what is being restored? Some researchers focus on slow-wave sleep (especially Stages 3 and 4), since much evidence suggests that slow-wave sleep is enhanced under conditions such as physical fatigue, where there is a greater need for bodily recuperation. For example, marathon runners sleep longer during the two nights after the race largely because they spend more time in slow-wave sleep (Shapiro et al., 1981). What function does this serve? Some clues come from the fact that a growth-promoting hormone that boosts protein synthesis (and thus helps to repair body tissue) is secreted primarily during slow-wave sleep (Takahashi, 1979). But whether this hormone (or some other form of bodily repair) is the key to sleep's function is a matter of

WHAT DIFFERENT MOTIVES HAVE IN COMMON

In this chapter, we have dealt with a number of motives that impel us to action—hunger, thirst, threats, and so on. Some of these motives, such as hunger, serve to maintain the internal environment. Others, such as threats, are triggered by factors in the external environment and serve the goal of self-preservation. For a few others—the main example is sleep—the functions are still unknown. These various motives are clearly very different, as are the goals toward which they steer the organism—food, water, coping with predators or enemies, a good night's sleep. But we might also ask: What do all these motives have in common? To be sure, they all potentiate behavior, organizing what we do, what we see, and what we feel. But do these motives share any more specific features?

THE PSYCHOLOGY OF REWARD AND THE AROUSAL LEVEL

A number of theorists have suggested that all—or at least most—motives can be described as a search for some optimum level of arousal or of general stimulation. One of the early controversies in this area was over the question of what the optimum level is.

DRIVE-REDUCTION THEORY

According to the **drive-reduction theory** proposed some fifty years ago by Clark L. Hull (1884–1952), the optimum level of arousal that organisms seek is essentially zero. Hull and his students were impressed by the fact that many motives seem directed at the reduction of some internal state of bodily tension, which he called a *drive*. Hunger drives an animal to behave in such a way that would diminish its hunger (eating); likewise, pain drives an animal to find some way to alleviate the pain (for example, leaving the briar patch). For Hull, each of these acts was rewarding precisely because it reduced the drive that instigated it. By extension, he inferred that what organisms strive for is the reduction of all drives —an absolute minimum of arousal and stimulation, a biopsychological version of the eastern search for Nirvana (Hull, 1943).

AN OPTIMUM AROUSAL ABOVE ZERO

Hull's drive-reduction theory suggests that, in general, organisms seek minimum levels of stimulation, preferring peace and quiet to states of tension and arousal. But, in fact, this doesn't seem to be true, for there is little doubt that some experiences are actively sought after, like the taste of sweets, sexual foreplay, athletic workouts, and roller-coaster rides. These activities make little sense if the organism is truly seeking to reduce its arousal level and to avoid stimulation.

This pattern of stimulation-seeking can be seen even in the rat, who prefers drinking artificially sweetened water to plain water, even though the sweetener has no caloric value and does not quell hunger (Sheffield and Roby, 1950). A similar conclusion emerges from work on curiosity and manipulation. Monkeys

3.26 Curiosity and manipulation
Young rhesus monkeys trying to open a latch. The monkeys received no special reward for their labors but learned to open the devices "just for the fun of it." (After Harlow, 1950; photograph courtesy of University of Wisconsin Primate Laboratory)

will go to considerable lengths to figure out how to open latches that are attached to a wooden board (see Figure 3.26), even if opening the latch gets the animal absolutely nothing. The act of solving the puzzle seems to be its own reward. In this regard, monkeys act much like human beings, who buy jigsaw puzzles, solve crossword puzzles and anagrams in the newspaper, and in countless other ways seeks out stimulation rather than trying to reduce it (see Chapter 4).

These observations suggest that the optimum level of arousal may in fact be above zero. If we find ourselves above this optimum, we act as Hull suggested and attempt to reduce stimulation. But if we are below the optimum level, we disobey Hull and instead seek stimulation to regain our optimum level.

What is this optimum level? It undoubtedly varies from time to time and from motive to motive. The optimum level for hunger is presumably rather low, such that we tolerate very little hunger before being driven to eat. That for sex is likely to be higher, since most animals are choosy about their mating partners even when in states of sexual readiness and arousal (see Chapter 10). There may also be variation from one individual to the next: According to some authors, some people are sensation seekers who generally look for stimulation, while others prefer a quieter existence (Zuckerman, 1979; see Chapter 16).

DRUGS AND ADDICTION

Ordinarily, people seek to optimize their arousal levels through the expected routes—eating when hungry, sleeping when tired, looking for interesting people or exciting situations when bored. In some cases, though, our desire for stimulation can lead us to seek drastic changes of arousal through the use—and abuse—of drugs.

Drugs that change arousal level   Two major classes of drugs are used precisely to change arousal level: ***depressants,*** which reduce arousal, and ***stimulants,*** which heighten it.

The depressants include various sedatives (for example, barbiturates), alcohol, and the opiates (opium, heroin, and morphine).★ Their general effect is to

★ Strictly speaking, the opiates belong to a separate class. For unlike alcohol and other sedatives, they serve as narcotics (that is, pain relievers) and act on separate opiate receptors. In addition, one of their number—heroin—seems to be able to produce an unusually intense euphoric "rush," sometimes likened to intense sexual excitement, when taken intravenously.

depress the activity of all the neurons in the central nervous system. This may seem surprising, since all of us have seen loud and aggressive drunks; they hardly seem lethargic or depressed. But this paradox is resolved if we recognize that the drunken person's hyperexcitability is a case of disinhibition. After just a drink or two, the inhibitory synapses in the brain seem to be depressed, but at these (relatively) low doses, the excitatory ones aren't yet affected. As a consequence, the usual constraints on behavior are relaxed, and the individual may act completely out of character, feeling euphoric and loosening his sexual or aggressive inhibitions. But if he keeps drinking, the depressive effects will spread to all his cerebral centers. Now the disinhibitory excitement will give way to a general slowdown of activity. His attention and memory will blur, his movements will become clumsy and his speech inarticulate, until finally he falls down and loses consciousness.

The effects of the behavioral stimulants, such as amphetamine and cocaine, are of course rather different. These drugs produce effects like rapid heart rate and high blood pressure, insomnia, lowered appetite, and—perhaps as a result of internal stimulation—behavioral quieting. This last finding has led to the widespread use of low doses of amphetamine-like stimulants such as Dexedrine, Cylert, and Ritalin to treat individuals suffering from hyperactivity or attention deficit disorders (Andreasen and Black, 1996).

Stimulants also heighten mood. With cocaine in particular, the mood elevation can be intense—a euphoric "rush" or "high" accompanied by feelings of enormous energy and increased self-esteem, a fact that led some turn-of-the-century physicians (including Sigmund Freud) to tout cocaine as a miracle drug that produced boundless energy, exhilaration, and euphoria with no untoward side effects. This is unfortunately far from true, for the initial euphoria is bought at a considerable cost. Contrary to early claims, amphetamines and cocaine often produce addictions that can become the user's primary focus in life. In addition, chronic use of these drugs can lead to irrational states that resemble certain kinds of schizophrenia, in which there are delusions of persecution, irrational fears, and hallucinations (Siegel, 1984). Some of the chemical cousins of these drugs have other toxic effects; methamphetamine, for example, is a powerful **neurotoxin** that can obliterate neurons.

Seeking stimulation   People have invented many activities to experience the paradoxical joy of fear and danger. (A) Some of these activities induce excitement but are known to be safe in reality, such as riding on roller coasters. (AP Photo/HO) (B) Others are more dangerous but provide greater thrills, such as skydiving. (Photograph by Guy Sauvage, Agence Vandystadt/Photo Researchers) (C) In yet other activities the fear and danger are experienced vicariously, as in watching horror movies. A scene from 1996's Scream, *with Drew Barrymore. (Photo courtesy of Photofest, copyright © Dimension Films)*

A

B

C

Tolerance and withdrawal Many drugs, not just amphetamines and cocaine, can produce addiction. In general, the pattern of addiction is characterized by two important features. First, the addict acquires an increased ***tolerance*** for the drug, so that she requires ever-larger doses to obtain the same effect. Second, when the drug is withheld, she suffers from ***withdrawal.*** In general, withdrawal symptoms are the opposite of the effects produced by the drug itself. Thus, heroin produces relief from pain. Heroin addicts deprived of their drug, in contrast, are extremely irritable, are restless and anxious, and suffer insomnia. The stimulants are similar: Cocaine and amphetamines produce elation and energy; withdrawal from these substances gives rise to catastrophic depression coupled with profound fatigue. The same holds for many of the physical symptoms produced by these drugs: One characteristic of the opiates is that they lead to marked constipation. (They've been used for centuries to relieve diarrhea and dysentery.) But when the drug is withdrawn, the addict suffers acute diarrhea and related gastrointestinal symptoms (Julien, 1985; Volpicelli, 1989).

THE OPPONENT-PROCESS THEORY OF MOTIVATION

What accounts for the phenomena of drug use and drug addiction? Some suggestions come from the ***opponent-process theory,*** which offers a broad outline of how many motives are acquired.★ The basic premise of this theory is a homeostatic one, that the nervous system has a general tendency to counteract any deviation from normal. Thus, an organism that is too cold seeks means of gaining warmth; an organism that is too warm seeks means of cooling off. The same is true, this proposal claims, for the dimensions of arousal and of pleasure versus pain. If there is too much of a swing toward joy and ecstasy, an opponent process is called into play that seeks to restore mood neutrality. Conversely, if the initial swing is toward terror or revulsion, there will be an opponent process toward the positive side, in order to return the individual to a more balanced state.

A further assumption of this theory is that, in each of these cases, the opponent process grows more effective with practice. So the first time one is frightened, it may take some time before balance is restored. But as the frightening experience is repeated, balance will be restored more and more quickly (Solomon and Corbit, 1974; Solomon, 1980).

This "practice effect" may explain the development of tolerance and withdrawal, as well as the resulting cycle of addiction. According to the theory, the reaction produced by a drug triggers a process that pulls in the opposite direction, restoring the body's initial state. The more often the drug is taken, the stronger this opponent process becomes. The result is increased tolerance, thanks to the fact that the opponent process has now become quite effective and so is able to counter the drug's effects quickly and fully. As a consequence, ever larger doses of the drug are required to overcome the opponent process and thus to produce the desired "high."

What happens when the drug is withheld? Now there is obviously no drug effect, but there is still the opponent process, whose strength has increased with every dose. The opponent process pulls the addict in the direction opposite to the withheld drug's, and this is what creates the anguish of withdrawal—with a set of traits, as we have seen, the opposite of those associated with the drug (Solomon, 1980; see Chapter 4).

★ The term *opponent process* was originally used in the field of color vision where it designates neural processes that act in opposite directions (see Chapter 5).

THE BIOLOGY OF REWARD

Our discussion of optimum arousal levels and of opponent-process theory has drawn attention to what the various motives might have in common *psychologically.* All involve some optimal level of arousal (even if that optimum varies from motive to motive); all may involve an opponent process, serving to maintain the body's steady state. But are there also some *physiological* commonalities underlying the various motives? Might there be some single region of the brain whose activation gives rise to what we humans call "pleasure," whether that pleasure is from having sex, listening to great music, or eating a hot fudge sundae? Investigators have tried to answer this question by studying the rewarding effects of electrically stimulating various regions in the brain.

This general area of study had its beginnings in 1954 when James Olds and Peter Milner discovered that rats would learn to press a lever if rewarded with only a brief burst of electrical stimulation in certain regions of the hypothalamus and limbic system (Olds and Milner, 1954; see Figure 3.27). Similar rewarding effects of self-stimulation have been demonstrated in a wide variety of other animals, including cats, dolphins, monkeys, and human beings. To obtain such stimulation, rats will press a lever at rates up to 7,000 presses per hour for hours on end. When forced to choose between food and self-stimulation, hungry rats will often opt for self-stimulation, even though it literally brings starvation (Spies, 1965).

SPECIFIC AND GENERAL PLEASURE CENTERS

What explains the rewarding effect of self-stimulation? One possibility is that brain stimulation mimics specific natural rewards. Thus, stimulating one region might fool the brain into assuming there had been eating, stimulating another that there had been copulation, and so on. A different account is that self-stimulation provides a more general, nonspecific kind of pleasure, something that all rewards share. Drinking, eating, and copulating are obviously different, but perhaps the different messages they send to the brain ("have just drunk, eaten, copulated") ultimately feed into a common neurological system that responds to all of them in much the same way ("that sure felt good").

In general, the evidence seems to favor the first of these possibilities—namely, that stimulation of these brain areas provides rather specific rewards. For example, animals will work to obtain electrical stimulation of the lateral zone of the hypothalamus (which often stimulates hunger), but how much they will work to get this reward depends on their hunger level. If they haven't eaten for a while, they will work much harder than they would otherwise. This suggests that the brain regards stimulation in this region as equivalent to food. Analogous effects are found in regions that are concerned with drinking or sexual behavior (Olds and Fobes, 1981).

THE DOPAMINE HYPOTHESIS OF REWARD AND DRUG EFFECTS

What is the physiological basis for the self-stimulation effect? A number of investigators believe that the key lies in some dopamine-releasing pathways in the brain. It is known that self-stimulation is most effective when applied to a bundle of nerve fibers called the ***medial forebrain bundle (MFB).*** These fibers course from the midbrain to the hypothalamus and, according to some theorists, trigger activity of other cells that extend from one part of the midbrain

3.27 Self-stimulation in rats *The rat feels the stimulation of a pulse lasting less than a second. (Courtesy of Dr. M. E. Olds)*

111

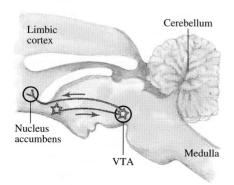

3.28 Pathways implicated in the rewarding effect of brain stimulation *The figure is a schematic cross section of the lower part of a rat's brain, showing a descending pathway that stimulates dopamine-releasing neurons in the ventral tegmental area (VTA) that ascend to the nucleus accumbens. (After Rosenzweig, Leiman, and Breedlove, 1996)*

(the *ventral tegmental area,* or *VTA*) to an area in the forebrain known as the *nucleus accumbens* (see Figure 3.28). These pathways rely on dopamine as a neurotransmitter. This is shown by the fact that when drugs that serve as dopamine antagonists are injected into the relevant brain regions, brain stimulation is much less effective. Conversely, if drugs that serve as dopamine agonists are injected into that same area, the opposite effect occurs: Brain stimulation is much more effective (Gallistel, Shizgal, and Yeomans, 1981; Stellar and Stellar, 1985; Wise and Rompre, 1989).

To explain these findings, some authors assume that the activation of fibers originating in the nucleus accumbens is interpreted by the brain as the neurological equivalent of "Good—let's have it again." This may actually help to explain some of the phenomena of drug addiction. Both cocaine and amphetamine enhance the levels of dopamine at the synapse. Cocaine does so by blocking dopamine reuptake (so that the transmitter stays around longer); amphetamine does the same and also enhances the release of dopamine at the axon terminal. Once in the bloodstream, both drugs will eventually enter the nucleus accumbens and trigger the "Good—let's have it again" fibers.

There is much in this domain that we still do not understand. It is clear that dopamine plays a crucial role in the physiology of reward, and we have identified some of the brain structures crucial for reward. But we still don't know how to put all the various findings on brain stimulation together to create a coherent picture of the biological basis for reward or, more ambitiously, the biological basis for pleasure. When we do, we may understand much more than why rats (and dogs and dolphins) press levers that give certain portions of their brains small jolts of electric current. We may understand the neurological basis of natural rewards and motives, what it is in the brain that makes humans and animals record certain events as events they want to reexperience (such as eating when hungry, copulating when sexually aroused, and so on). And we may also understand something about the underlying biology of certain "unnatural" rewards, like drugs, to which some individuals become addicted.

THE NATURE OF MOTIVES

During the past fifty years, there has been enormous progress in our understanding of the psychology and physiology of the biological motives. These motives are enormously diverse. Some, including temperature regulation, thirst, and hunger, involve negative feedback mechanisms; others, such as sleep or sex, do not. For some motives, such as threats, the optimum arousal level is high; for others, such as sleep, it is low. We have identified some features—both psychological and physiological—that may unite the motives, but in the end, the diversity of motives remains. Perhaps our quest for simplicity and commonality is misguided. Like all scientists, psychologists are much happier with neat explanations. But Mother Nature did not design organisms to make psychologists happy; she designed organisms to do what they need to do to survive and to propagate their genes.

A final point: This chapter has been concerned with motives that arise from largely innate mechanisms. These are, after all, motives concerned with the biological goals we must attain in order to survive. But whenever we look at a motive in detail (as in the case of human food selection), we find that our motivated behavior depends not only on our biology, but also on what we have learned about the environment in which we behave. Thus, what we drink is not only a matter of our water balance, it is also a matter of acquired preference and, in some cases, culturally encouraged aversions. For example, most members of western culture would be averse to drinking a cup of their own saliva, even though it came directly out of their own mouths. By the same token, while we have to maintain certain nutrient levels, most of us would not be satisfied with a diet of grasshoppers. Likewise for other motives, such as what catches our curiosity, threatens us, or arouses us sexually. In all these cases, our experience builds on our biology like a weaver who takes our genetic yarn and weaves the ultimate fabric that is *us*.

In the next chapter we will begin our discussion of just how the warp and woof of this weave is formed. This is the intricate process by which we gain information about our environment and how to navigate it called *learning*.

SUMMARY

1. Most human and animal actions are motivated. *Motives* are two-fold: First, they ready the organism to engage in a particular behavior. Second, they *potentiate* certain perceptions, behaviors, and feelings rather than others, impelling the organism toward or away from some goal.

2. One biological basis of directed action is *negative feedback,* in which the system "feeds back" upon itself to stop its own action. Built-in negative feedback is responsible for many reactions that maintain the stability of the organism's internal environment, or *homeostasis.* Special cells in the hypothalamus sense various aspects of the body's internal state, such as temperature. If this is above or below certain *setpoints,* a number of self-regulatory reflexes controlled by the *sympathetic* and *parasympathetic* divisions of the *autonomic nervous system* are triggered (for example, shivering). In addition, externally directed actions (such as moving into or out of the sun) are also brought into play.

3. Similar homeostatic mechanisms underlie a number of other biological motives, such as *thirst.* The organism is informed about its water balance by *volume receptors* that monitor the total volume of its bodily fluids and by *osmoreceptors* that monitor water levels within the cells. Water losses are partially offset by reflex mechanisms, including the secretion of *vasopressin,* the antidiuretic hormone, which instructs the kidneys to reabsorb more of the water that passes through them. In addition, the organism readjusts its own internal environment by directed action—drinking.

4. The biological motive that has been studied most extensively is hunger. Many of the signals for feeding and satiety come from the internal environment. Feeding signals include nutrient levels in the bloodstream (which probably affect *glucoreceptors* in the brain) and metabolic processes in the liver (especially the *glucose-glycogen balance*). Satiety signals include messages from receptors in the stomach, the small intestine (particularly a satiety hormone called *cholecystokinin,* or *CCK*), and the adipose tissue, which secretes *leptin.* Other feeding and satiety signals are external, including the palatability of the food.

5. Researchers once believed that the control of feeding was lodged in antagonistic hunger and satiety centers in the hypothalamus. As evidence, they pointed to the effects of lesions that produced *aphagia,* a complete refusal to eat, or *hyperphagia,* a vast increase in food intake. This original *dual-center theory* has been supplanted by findings suggesting a greater role for the digestive organs and adipose tissue in hunger, as well as multiple hunger and satiety pathways in the brain.

6. Homeostatic factors determine whether and when an animal eats but not what it eats. Food selection is determined by a variety of factors, including built-in preferences and learning. Many animals are *neophobic*—afraid of anything new. They will only sample new foods in small amounts, developing a *learned taste aversion* if those foods turn out to be poisonous and adding them to their diet if they prove to be safe.

7.   One feeding-related disorder is *obesity*. Some cases are produced by various constitutional factors, including metabolic efficiency. The obesity seen in some people may represent the operation of "thrifty genes" that code for slower metabolisms, which are optimal for sparse diets but deleterious for modern abundance. Other cases of obesity result from various behavioral factors. According to the *externality hypothesis,* overweight people are comparatively insensitive to internal hunger signals and oversensitive to external ones such as palatability. A more compelling alternative is the *setpoint hypothesis,* which asserts that overweight people have a higher internal setpoint for weight.

8.   Other eating disorders are *anorexia nervosa,* in which there is a pattern of relentless and sometimes lethal self-starvation, and *bulimia nervosa,* which is characterized by normal weight despite repeated binge-and-purge bouts.

9.   In contrast to thirst and hunger, which are largely based on homeostatic factors from within, a number of motives are instigated externally. An example is the preparatory reaction to threat. Its biological mechanisms include the operations of the *autonomic nervous system (ANS).* The ANS consists of two antagonistic branches. One is the *parasympathetic nervous system,* which serves the vegetative functions of everyday life, such as digestion and reproduction. It slows the heart rate and reduces blood pressure. The other is the *sympathetic nervous system,* which activates the body and mobilizes its resources in response to threat. It increases the available metabolic fuels and accelerates their utilization by increasing the heart rate and respiration. Intense sympathetic activity is an *emergency reaction* that makes us vigilant and able to deal with the momentary contingencies imposed by threatening situations.

10.   The sympathetic emergency reaction is not always adaptive. It can produce temporary disruptions of digestive and sexual functions, and can also lead to more permanent psychophysiological disorders.

11.   Among the stimuli that set off the sympathetic emergency reaction is pain, which though unpleasant, is a signal to react to danger. But since continued pain may interfere with appropriate action, counteracting processes intervene to alleviate it. One pain mechanism involves the *endorphins,* a group of neurotransmitters secreted within the brain that act to block the transmission of pain messages. The endorphins may explain the pain-relieving effect of *placebos,* chemically inert substances that induce well-being and healing because the patient believes in their effectiveness.

12.   While the sympathetic nervous system arouses many processes in the body, several cortical and subcortical structures activate the brain. These waking systems are opposed by antagonistic processes that lead to sleep. During sleep, brain activity changes as shown by the *electroencephalogram,* or *EEG.* Each night, we oscillate between *slow-wave sleep,* during which the cortex is less active and bodily functions are relatively quiescent, and *REM sleep,* characterized by considerable cortical and bodily activity, rapid eye movements (or REMs), and a near-complete flaccidity of the trunk and limb muscles. Dreaming occurs in both slow-wave and REM sleep. Highly visual dreams are more associated with REM sleep, but this may be because participants awaken more quickly from REM sleep and thus are able to report more detailed dreams.

13.   Sleep-deprivation studies show that when one or the other kind of sleep is prevented, it tends to be recovered on successive nights. This suggests that there is a need for each of the two sleep states, but the biological functions served by either are as yet unknown. One hypothesis is that one or both forms of sleep serve a restorative function, but this can't be the only reason, since sleep is a *clock-driven process* that partially depends on the time of day, regardless of the individual's state of exhaustion.

14.   According to *drive-reduction theory,* all built-in motives act to reduce stimulation and arousal. Today, most authors believe instead that organisms strive for an *optimum level of arousal.* If below this optimum, they try to increase arousal by various means.

15.   One way of coping with an arousal level that is too high or too low is by the use and abuse of drugs. Some drugs act as *depressants,* including alcohol and the opiates. Others, such as the amphetamines and cocaine, act as *stimulants.* In many individuals, repeated drug use leads to *addiction,* accompanied by increased *tolerance* and *withdrawal* if the drug is withheld.

SUMMARY

16. The *opponent-process theory of motivation* tries to explain drug tolerance, withdrawal, and many other phenomena by arguing that all shifts of arousal level produce a counteracting process that acts to moderate the ups and downs. When the original instigator of the shift is removed, the opponent process is revealed more clearly, as in withdrawal.

17. Work on the rewarding effects of certain regions of the brain has led to speculations about possible *pleasure centers* in the brain. There is evidence that stimulation of certain areas leads to specific reward effects. According to the *dopamine hypothesis of reward,* the neural underpinnings of such reward effects lie in the activation of fibers that originate in a brain structure called the *nucleus accumbens* and are triggered by dopamine. According to the hypothesis, their activation is the neurological equivalent of "Good—let's have it again!"

CHAPTER

LEARNING

uch of our discussion so far has centered on the neural equipment provided for us by our biological inheritance. But much of what we do goes beyond these built-in mechanisms and depends instead on experience acquired during our lifetime. In other words, organisms *learn*. A human being learns to grasp a baby bottle, to read and write, to love or hate his neighbors, and, eventually, to face death. In other animals, the role of learning may be less dramatic, but it is enormously important for them, too.

In the preceding chapters, we discussed Descartes' conception of the organism as a reflex machine. In this view, behavior depends on built-in links between one set of neural messages, triggered by stimuli outside the organism, and another set, sending commands to the muscles or glands. Can we preserve this simple architecture and still accommodate the organism's potential for learning? A number of investigators, often called ***learning theorists,*** believe that we can: The organism is born, they argue, with a limited repertoire of hard-wired reflexes, but this set can be supplemented through learning. In some cases, the learning creates new connections between stimuli, so that, for example, the sight of the mother's face may come to signify the taste of milk. In other cases, the learning involves new connections between acts and their consequences, as when a toddler learns that touching a hot radiator is followed by a painful burn. In all cases, though, the basic arrangement of things stays the same, with identifiable stimuli eliciting identifiable responses. The intellectual challenge for this view lies in discovering how exactly these bits of "rewiring" come about.

The learning theorist's perspective continues to contribute to our understanding of learning, but the greatest blossoming of this perspective occurred during the first part of the twentieth century, especially in the United States. This was, in part, a reflection of the intellectual and political climate of the times: These were years in which society was deeply committed to the belief that each individual could improve herself by means of greater effort and by acquiring new skills. There was an enormous faith that humans were extraordinarily malleable and perhaps infinitely perfectible if only the proper changes could be made in the environment and in education. Under the circumstances, it was hardly surprising that learning became one of the great concerns of American psychology.

How should the learning process be studied? At least initially, most learning theorists believed that there were some basic laws that come into play, regardless of what is learned or who does the learning—whether it is a dog learning to sit on command or a college student learning calculus. To be sure, some examples of learning seem quite complicated, but these, it was argued, are actually made up of simpler bits of learning, much as complex chemical compounds are made up of basic elements. Given this belief, it was only natural that the early investigators concentrated their efforts on trying to understand learning in simple situations and in relatively simple creatures such as dogs, rats, and pigeons. In this way, the investigators hoped to strip the learning process down to its essentials, so that its basic laws might be revealed. With this done, these "learning elements" could then be reassembled as needed to account for the more complex cases.

As we will see, the early learning theorists never succeeded in finding one set of laws that covered all cases of learning in all organisms. But even so, their search for these laws led to a series of important discoveries, discoveries that form the basis of much of what we know about learning today.

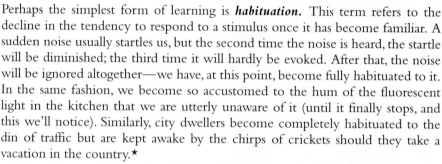

HABITUATION

Habituation in Siamese fighting fish
Male Siamese fighting fish (Betta splendens) adopt a fighting posture when they see another male, but after a while they habituate to his presence. (Photograph by Oxford Scientific Films)

Perhaps the simplest form of learning is **habituation.** This term refers to the decline in the tendency to respond to a stimulus once it has become familiar. A sudden noise usually startles us, but the second time the noise is heard, the startle will be diminished; the third time it will hardly be evoked. After that, the noise will be ignored altogether—we have, at this point, become fully habituated to it. In the same fashion, we become so accustomed to the hum of the fluorescent light in the kitchen that we are utterly unaware of it (until it finally stops, and this we'll notice). Similarly, city dwellers become completely habituated to the din of traffic but are kept awake by the chirps of crickets should they take a vacation in the country.★

One of the major benefits of habituation is that it narrows the range of stimuli that elicit alarm. A sudden and unfamiliar stimulus may well indicate danger, and so it makes sense to attend fully to such an input. But there's usually no point in scrutinizing something familiar, especially since this would probably distract the animal away from more vital activities. Habituation solves this problem by allowing organisms to ignore the familiar, which in turn allows them to focus instead on more important, and informative, events (Wyers, Peeke, and Herz, 1973; Shalter, 1984).

Habituation plainly relies on memory. The animal must somehow compare what it now hears and sees with what it has previously heard and seen. To the extent that the current stimulus matches what is in memory, it is judged to be familiar and thus not startling (Wagner, 1979; Whitlow and Wagner, 1984). Of course, we still need to ask what the nature of this memory is, an issue to which we will turn in Chapter 7. For now, we simply note that habituation, as simple as it seems, surely does count as an example of learning and clearly relies on what the organism remembers about its previous experiences.

CLASSICAL CONDITIONING

In habituation, an organism learns to recognize an event as familiar, but it doesn't learn anything new about that event. Much of our learning, however, does involve new information, and often this information is concerned with the *relationship* among events or between an event and a particular behavior. Learning theorists (and many other investigators) talk about these relationships in terms of

★ There is some debate about whether habituation is really a different kind of learning from certain others we'll describe later, such as classical and instrumental conditioning. According to some authors, it only refers to a certain experimental procedure used to establish the effect (Rescorla and Holland, 1982).

associations, with the proposal that much learning can be understood as the formation (or strengthening) of associations, or the weakening of already existing associations. Thus, we learn, for example, to associate thunder with lightning, a smile with friendly behavior, and tigers with zoos.

The importance of associations in learning and thinking has been emphasized since the days of the Greek philosophers, but the experimental study of associations did not begin until the end of the nineteenth century. A major contribution was the work on conditioning performed by the great Russian physiologist, Ivan Petrovich Pavlov (1849–1936).

PAVLOV AND THE CONDITIONED REFLEX

Ivan Petrovich Pavlov had already earned a Nobel prize for his research on digestion before he even began to study conditioning. In that earlier work, Pavlov was exploring the neural control of various digestive reflexes, and his laboratory studies focused on the secretion of saliva in dogs.

Pavlov knew from the start that this salivation is typically triggered by food (especially dry food) placed in the mouth. In the course of his research, however, a new fact emerged: The salivary reflex could be set off by a range of other stimuli as well, including stimuli that were at first totally neutral. Dogs that had been in the laboratory for a while would salivate, not only to the taste and touch of meat in the mouth, but in response to the mere sight of meat, or the sight of the dish in which the meat was ordinarily placed, or the sight of the person who usually brought the meat, or even to the sound of that person's footsteps. Pavlov decided to study these effects in their own right, for he recognized that they provided a means of extending the reflex concept, so that it could embrace learned as well as innate reactions.

Pavlov's initial observations were serendipitous—a particular pattern of footsteps, for example, just happened to have been associated with food. To study this learning, however, Pavlov didn't rely on accidents. Instead, he created patterns for

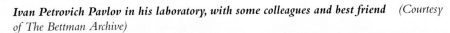

Ivan Petrovich Pavlov in his laboratory, with some colleagues and best friend   *(Courtesy of The Bettman Archive)*

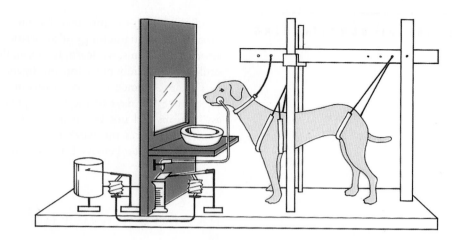

4.1 Apparatus for salivary conditioning
The figure shows an early version of Pavlov's apparatus for classical conditioning of the salivary response. The dog was held in a harness; sounds or lights functioned as conditioned stimuli (CS), while meat powder in a dish served as the unconditioned stimulus (US). The conditioned response (CR) was assessed with the aid of a tube connected to an opening in one of the animal's salivary glands. (After Yerkes and Margulis, 1909)

the animal to detect and learn about. Thus, he would repeatedly sound a bell and always follow it with food. Later, he observed what happened when the bell was sounded alone, without any food being given (Pavlov, 1927; Figure 4.1).

The result was straightforward: Repeated pairings of bell with food led to salivation when the bell was presented by itself (that is, unaccompanied by food). To explain this finding, Pavlov proposed a distinction between **unconditioned** and **conditioned reflexes.** Unconditioned reflexes, he argued, were essentially inborn—a product of the organism's biology and largely independent of any learning. An example is food in the mouth, which unconditionally elicits salivation. In contrast, conditioned reflexes were acquired through learning; they were conditional upon the animal's experience.

Pavlov proposed that every unconditioned reflex is based upon a hardwired connection between an **unconditioned stimulus (US)** and **unconditioned response (UR).** Likewise, a conditioned reflex involves a connection between a **conditioned stimulus (CS)** and a **conditioned response (CR).** The connection between CS and CR, however, is learned, not innate. Thus the CS (in our example so far, the bell) is initially a neutral stimulus—it does not elicit the CR. The CS comes to elicit the CR (in this case, salivation) only after some presentations of the CS (again, the bell) followed by the US (in this case, food in the mouth). These various relationships are summarized in Figure 4.2 and constitute the basis of what is now known as **classical conditioning.★**

Early research on classical conditioning focused on dogs salivating to bells, lights, and metronomes. However, conditioning would be of little interest if it applied only to these cases. As it turns out, though, the scope of conditioning is much wider than this and encompasses a vast range of cases—both inside and outside the laboratory.

To begin with, classical conditioning has been found in a large variety of animal species, including ants and anteaters, cats and cockroaches, pigeons and people (to name just a few). Crabs have been conditioned to twitch their tail spines, fish to thrash about, and octopuses to change color, using the appropriate US in each case. Responses conditioned in studies with human research participants include the galvanic skin response (where the US is typically a loud noise or electric shock) and reflexive eye blink (with the US consisting of a puff of air on the open eye; Kimble, 1961).

Outside of the laboratory, classical conditioning touches many aspects of our everyday lives. Many of our feelings and urges, for example, are probably the

---

★ The adjective *classical* is used, in part, as dutiful tribute to Pavlov's eminence and historical priority and, in part, as a way of distinguishing this form of conditioning from *instrumental conditioning,* to which we will turn later.

result of classical conditioning: We tend to feel hungry at mealtimes and less in between; this is so even if we have fasted for a whole day. This probably reflects a conditioning process in which the CS is a particular time of day and the US is the presentation of food (which normally is paired with that time of day). Another example is sexual arousal, which can often be produced by a special word or gesture whose erotic meaning is very private and is surely learned.

We will say more about these cases, and the great breadth of classical conditioning's effects, in later sections. For now, however, we simply note that this is a phenomenon with wide application and correspondingly great importance.

THE MAJOR PHENOMENA OF CLASSICAL CONDITIONING

Pavlov was able to document, fully and accurately, many of the central phenomena of classical conditioning, and his findings laid the foundation for subsequent theories in this domain. We begin, therefore, by describing some of Pavlov's empirical findings.

ACQUISITION OF CONDITIONED RESPONSES

Initially, the conditioned stimulus (CS) does not elicit the conditioned response (CR). But after several pairings with the unconditioned stimulus (US), the CS (say, the bell) is able to elicit the CR (salivation). Clearly then, presenting the US (food) together with (or more typically, just after) the CS is a critical operation in classical conditioning. These pairings are said to *reinforce* the connection; trials in which the CS and US are both presented are therefore called **reinforced trials;** trials in which the CS is presented without the US are called **unreinforced trials.**

Measuring the strength of the CR There are a number of ways in which the strength of a CR can be measured. One is **response amplitude:** In Pavlov's experiments, this was the amount of saliva secreted when the CS was presented without the US. Another measure is **probability of response:** the proportion of trials on which the CR is made when the CS is presented alone. Yet another measure is **response latency:** the time from the presentation of the CS to the eliciting of the CR. In contrast to amplitude and probability of response, which increase as CR strength increases, response latency decreases as the CR grows in strength. Thus, after many pairings of bell and meat powder, a dog, upon hearing the bell alone, is quite likely to salivate

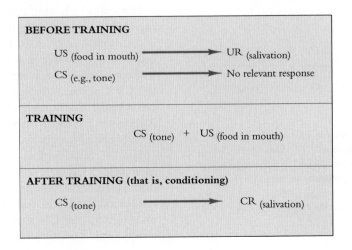

4.2 *Relationships between CS, US, CR, and UR in classical conditioning*

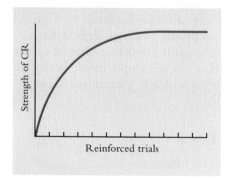

4.3 An idealized learning curve
Strength of the CR is plotted against the number of reinforced trials. The curve presents the results of many such studies, which by and large show that the strength of the CR rises with increasing number of trials, but each trial adds less strength than the trial just before it.

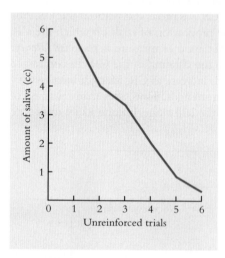

4.4 Extinction of a classically conditioned response *The figure shows the decrease in the amount of saliva secreted (the CR) with increasing number of extinction trials—that is, trials on which the CS is presented without the US. (After Pavlov, 1928)*

(high probability), will produce a lot of saliva (strong response), and will probably start salivating soon after hearing the bell (short latency).

Figure 4.3 shows an idealized **learning curve** in which the strength of the CR (y–axis) is plotted against successive reinforced trials (x–axis). The pattern of these data is very clear: The strength of the CR is initially zero, grows rapidly, and then levels off at some nonzero level. This pattern can easily be demonstrated with dogs salivating in response to bells but also with other organisms, other CSs, and other CRs. This is, in short, a highly typical pattern for virtually all instances of classical conditioning.

Second-order conditioning   Once the CS–US relation is solidly established, the CS can serve to condition yet further stimuli. To give one example, Pavlov first conditioned a dog to salivate to the beat of a metronome, using meat powder as the US. Once this was done, he presented the animal with a black square followed by the metronome beat, but without ever introducing the food. This pairing of black square and metronome was repeated several times, and soon the sight of the black square alone was enough to produce salivation. This phenomenon is called **second-order conditioning.** In effect, the black square had become a signal for the metronome, which in turn signaled the appearance of food.

EXTINCTION

The adaptive value of conditioning is self-evident. Imagine a wolf that has often found many mice to eat at a particular site. It would serve the wolf well to learn about this conjunction of mice and location; that way, it would know where it's likely to find a good meal the next time it's hungry. But it would be unfortunate if this connection, once established, could never be undone. The mice might leave the area, or might all be eaten up, so that the wolf would now waste time and energy revisiting this barren spot.

These considerations fit well, however, with what we know about classical conditioning. Pavlov was able to show that a conditioned response can be undone via a process not so different from the one in which the reaction was established in the first place. To be precise, he demonstrated that the CR will gradually disappear if the CS is repeatedly presented by itself—that is, without the US. In Pavlov's terms, the CS–US link undergoes **extinction.** Figure 4.4 presents an extinction curve from a salivary extinction experiment. As in Figure 4.3, response strength is measured along the y-axis, while the x-axis indicates the number of trials (in this case, extinction trials—trials without reinforcement). As extinction trials proceed, the salivary flow dries up. In effect, the dog has learned that the CS is no longer a signal for food.

But extinction itself can also be undone. One means is through **reconditioning,** that is, by presenting further reinforced trials. Reconditioning typically proceeds more quickly than the initial acquisition did: The speed of *relearning,* in other words, is faster than the original speed of *learning.* This remains true even if the extinction trials were continued until the animal stopped responding to the CS altogether. Apparently, extinction does not work by "erasing" the original learning; after extinction, the animal does not return to its original "naive" state. Instead, it retains some memory of the learning, and this memory provides it with a head start in the reconditioning trials.

Similar conclusions about extinction can be drawn from the phenomenon of **spontaneous recovery.** This phenomenon is observed in animals who have been through an extinction procedure and then left alone for a rest interval. After this rest period, the CS is again presented, and now the CS will often elicit the CR—even though the CR was fully extinguished earlier. The interpretation of this effect is still a matter of debate, but many accounts focus on what it is that the animal is learning during the extinction trials. According to one view, the extinction trials lead the animal to recognize that a once-informative stimulus is no longer informative. The bell used to signal that food would be coming soon, but now the bell signals nothing. As a consequence, the animal ceases to pay any attention to the bell. However, the animal remembers that the bell was *once* informative, and so when a new experimental session begins, the animal checks to see whether the bell will again be informative in this new setting. Thus, the animal resumes responding to the bell, producing the result we call spontaneous recovery (Robbins, 1990).

GENERALIZATION

So far our discussion has been confined to situations in which the animal is trained with a particular CS—a bell, or a metronome, or whatever—and then later tested with that exact same stimulus. In the real world, however, things are more complicated than this. The master's voice may always signal food, but his exact intonation will surely vary from one occasion to another. The sight of an apple tree may well signal the availability of fruit, but apple trees vary in size and shape. These facts demand that animals be able to respond to stimuli that are not identical to the original CS; otherwise, they will obtain no benefit from their earlier learning.

It is not surprising, therefore, that animals show a pattern called ***stimulus generalization***—that is, they respond to a range of stimuli, provided that these stimuli are sufficiently similar to the original CS. For example, a dog might be conditioned to respond to a yellow light. When tested later on, that dog will respond most strongly if the test light is still yellow. However, the dog will also respond (although a bit less strongly) to an orange light. The dog will probably also respond to a red light, but the response will be weaker still. In general, the greater the difference between the new stimulus and the original CS, the weaker the CR. Figure 4.5 illustrates this pattern, called a ***generalization gradient***. The peak of the gradient (the strongest response) is typically found when the test stimulus is identical to the stimulus used in training; the response gets weaker and weaker (and so the curve gets lower and lower), as the stimuli became more dissimilar.

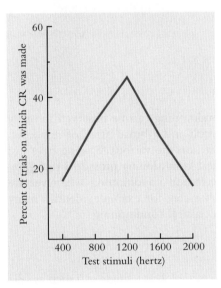

4.5   Generalization gradient of a classically conditioned response   *The figure shows the generalization of a conditioned blinking response in rabbits. The CS was a tone of 1,200 hertz, and the US was electric shock. After the conditioned response to the original CS was well established, generalization was measured by presenting various test stimuli, ranging from 400 hertz to 2,000 hertz and noting the percent of the trials on which the animals gave the CR. The figure shows the results, averaged over several testing sessions. (After Moore, 1972)*

DISCRIMINATION

Stimulus generalization is obviously beneficial but can be carried too far. A tiger may be similar to a kitten, but someone who generalizes from one to the other is likely to regret it. What he must do instead is discriminate—and not try to pet the tiger.

The phenomenon of ***discrimination*** is readily demonstrated in the laboratory. A dog is first conditioned to salivate to a CS—for example, a black square. After the CR is well established, reinforced trials with the black square are randomly interspersed with nonreinforced trials with another stimulus, say, a gray square. This continues until the animal discriminates perfectly, always salivating to the reinforced stimulus (referred to, generally, as the CS⁺) and never to the nonreinforced stimulus (referred to as the CS⁻). Of course, the dog does not reach this point immediately. During the early trials it will be confused, or more precisely, it will generalize rather than discriminate and salivate equally to both the CS⁺ and the CS⁻. However, these errors gradually become fewer and fewer until perfect discrimination is finally achieved.

Not surprisingly, the discrimination will be more difficult if the CS⁺ and the CS⁻ are quite similar to each other. With similar stimuli, the tendency to respond to the CS⁺ is quite likely to generalize to the CS⁻, while the tendency *not* to respond to the CS⁻ will probably generalize to the CS⁺. As a result, the dog will require many trials before it learns to respond without error.

Whether with similar stimuli or easily distinguishable ones, it is important that the animal learns the significance of *both* the CS⁺ and the CS⁻. It learns, of course, that the CS⁺ signals the approach of the US. What about the CS⁻? One might think that the animal learns that this stimulus conveys no information—after all, this stimulus is not followed by the US. But there *is* information here: The CS⁻ signals a period in which the US is likely *not* to arrive. If the US is a loud noise, then the CS⁻ signals the start of a period of time that will be noise free. If the US is food, then the CS⁻ indicates that food is not coming soon.

In essence, then, the CS⁻ takes on a significance opposite to that of the CS⁺. It means "no noise," or "no food," or, in general, "no US." Correspondingly, the animal's response to the CS⁻ tends to be the opposite of its response to the CS⁺. If the US is a noise blast, then the CS⁺ elicits fear, and the CS⁻ seems to inhibit fear. If the US is food, then the CS⁺ elicits salivation, and the CS⁻ causes the animal to salivate somewhat less than it ordinarily would. Thus, the CS⁻ takes on the role of ***inhibitor***—it inhibits the response elicited by the CS⁺ in that procedure.

EXTENSIONS OF CLASSICAL CONDITIONING

We have mentioned that classical conditioning can be observed in many organisms, with a wide range of stimuli and a broad array of responses. The evidence for this depends, in large part, on the various facts we have just reviewed. The major phenomena of classical conditioning provide a recognizable profile that we can use to identify classical conditioning whenever we encounter it. By recognizing this profile, we can, for example, identify many emotional reactions that are attributable to classical conditioning.

CONDITIONED FEAR

In many procedures, the conditioned response involves a single act, such as salivating or blinking. Sometimes, though, the CR is more complex than this. For example, we have mentioned procedures in which the US is some aversive stimulus, such as a very loud noise. In these procedures, the CS will come to elicit a multifaceted response, including changes in the animal's behavior and also in its bodily state (heart rate, hormone secretions, and so on). In short, the animal will become fearful and will do all the things that animals do when they are afraid.

Many studies have examined these conditioned emotions, especially fear. Often, these studies employ the ***conditioned emotional response (CER)*** procedure. In this procedure, a rat, say, is first taught to press a lever for a food reward. After a few training sessions, it learns to press at a steady rate, and now fear conditioning can start. While the animal is pressing, a CS is presented—perhaps a light or a tone that will stay on for, say, three minutes. At the end of that period, the CS stops and the rat receives a brief electric shock (the US). This causes the rat to pause in its lever pressing, but soon it restarts, and the CS–US sequence is repeated. Then, after another period of lever pressing, the CS–US pairing is again repeated, and so on (Estes and Skinner, 1941; Kamin, 1965).

In this procedure, the fear response is superimposed on an ongoing activity—namely, the pressing of the lever. This is crucial, because it allows us to measure the fear. Early in training, the animal essentially ignores the CS, so when the CS is presented, lever pressing goes on uninterrupted. Later on, the animal learns that the CS signals the approach of the US (shock). At this stage, the CS (and the

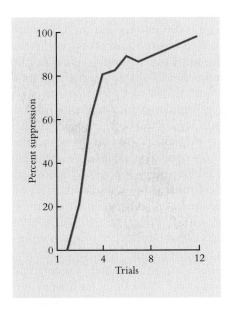

4.6 Response suppression *A rat is trained to press a lever at a steady rate to gain food. The figure plots the extent to which this response is suppressed after successive presentations of a three-minute light (CS) that is immediately followed by electric shock (US). After twelve such trials, suppression is at 100 percent, and the animal doesn't respond at all during the three minutes when the CS is presented. (Data from Kamin, 1969)*

anticipation of the shock) seems to distract the animal from its chore of lever pressing, so it presses less often during the CS (while afraid) than otherwise. By measuring this *response suppression,* we can measure the strength of the conditioning (see Figure 4.6).

This technique can be used for many purposes, including the study of inhibitory learning. In one experiment, a tone (the CS$^+$) was associated with shock, and a light (the CS$^-$) was associated with *absence* of shock and thus signaled a period of relative safety. After some learning, the CS$^+$ elicited fear from the animal, but the CS$^-$ (the "safety signal") inhibited fear. All of this was evident in the animal's lever pressing: Response rates went down during the CS$^+$ (this is the standard pattern of response suppression) but *up* during the CS$^-$. Clearly, then, the CS$^-$ had taken on a meaning opposite to that of the CS$^+$ and had an opposite effect on the animal's lever pressing (Reberg and Black, 1969).

Are human emotions shaped in the same manner? In many cases, they probably are. A frightful experience in a particular room can lead to fear of that room; falling off a bicycle can lead to fear of bike riding. These cases are easily understood in terms of classical conditioning. A number of psychologists have also proposed that the extreme fears we call *phobias* can be understood in the same terms, although other researchers are skeptical of this suggestion (Schwartz and Robbins, 1995). No matter how this debate is resolved, however, most researchers agree that classical conditioning can usefully be employed in the treatment of phobias, a point to which we will return in Chapter 19.

THE RELATION BETWEEN CR AND UR

The phenomenon of fear conditioning brings us to an important question that we have neglected up to now: What is the relation between CR and UR? In salivary conditioning, the CR and UR seem rather similar: Pavlov's dogs salivated both when they heard the CS and when they experienced the US. But even if similar, the CR and UR are rarely identical. When meat is placed in the mouth (the US), the dog's salivation is more copious and much richer in digestive enzymes, in comparison to salivation in response to a tone or bell (CS).

The difference between CR and UR is even more pronounced in the case of fear conditioning. When exposed to electric shock, the animal makes little jumps and its heart beats faster; this is the UR. When the same animal hears or sees a CS that signals the shock, its response (the CR) is quite different: The animal stops moving, tenses itself, and its heart beats more slowly. This is not an escape-from-shock reaction; it is, instead, a manifestation of fearful anticipation.

All of this makes good biological sense. An animal can't eat a tone that has been paired with food, and no tissue damage is produced by a light that has been paired with shock. Therefore, it would make no sense for the animal to treat the CS and US in exactly the same fashion. Instead, the animal seems to treat the CS as a "Get ready!" signal, an indication that the US is about to arrive. On this view, the CR is nothing more than the animal's *preparation* for the US. If a bell has been reliably followed by food, then the bell now signals that the animal should moisten its mouth, so that it will be ready to eat when the food does arrive. If a light has been followed by a shock, then it's a signal that the animal should tense its muscles, so that it's ready to jump when the shock begins (see Zener, 1937; Holland, 1984; Hollis, 1984).

CONDITIONING AND DRUG EFFECTS

Preparation for a US can take many forms. Consider, for example, a person who has received many doses of insulin, a drug that depletes blood sugar. After a number of these injections, the individual begins to respond to the various stimuli that accompany the drug, such as the mere sight of the needle. The reaction to these stimuli, though, is the exact opposite of the response to the drug itself: When these stimuli are presented (with no insulin injection), the blood-sugar level goes *up.*

In conditioning terms, the US in this case is the insulin, and the UR is the unlearned, biologically determined, decrease in blood sugar, produced by the insulin. The CS is the sight of the needle (or some other stimulus that generally accompanies the injection). And apparently, the CR is an *increase* in blood sugar level.

This CR actually makes perfect sense if we think of it as preparation for the upcoming US. In general, various mechanisms within the body try to maintain a stable, unchanging, internal environment. (In Chapter 3, we discussed these as ways of maintaining *homeostasis.*) Insulin disrupts this stability, by dropping blood-sugar levels. How, therefore, might stability be preserved? By increasing blood-sugar levels, through some other mechanism, just as the insulin arrives. This *increase* will offset the insulin-produced *decrease,* leading to no change overall and, thus, stability.

The body's preparation for insulin, therefore, can be thought of as a **compensatory reaction,** compensating for the drug effects to come. As a rough analogy, this is similar to a bear's stuffing itself just before it begins its winter hibernation: The animal is taking in a calorie overload so that it will be all set for the upcoming calorie shortfall. Of course, in the bear's case, this compensatory response is deliberate and relies on external food sources. In the case of the insulin reaction, the response is automatic and entirely dependent on internal mechanisms.

Classical conditioning plays a crucial role in creating and sustaining these compensatory mechanisms. For insulin and many other drugs, these mechanisms come into being because of repeated pairings between some CS (for example, the sight of the needle) and the US (the drug). These mechanisms can be eliminated by a conventional extinction procedure. We can also observe a generalization gradient, if we vary the CS. In short, these effects show the full profile of classical conditioning, strongly suggesting that conditioning is in fact the mechanism behind them (Siegel, 1977, 1983, 1989; but also see Baker and Tiffany, 1985; Poulos and Cappell, 1991).

CONDITIONING AND DRUG ADDICTION

There is obviously a parallel between these compensatory mechanisms and the opponent-process mechanisms described in Chapter 3. Opponent processes, in general, compensate for bodily changes and thus promote homeostasis. The point being added here concerns the *mechanism* through which opponent processes are created and maintained. The mechanism is classical conditioning.

We can see the full importance of this by returning to an example we introduced in Chapter 3, namely drug addiction and, in particular, addiction to drugs such as morphine or heroin. These drugs have many effects, such as relief from pain, euphoria, and relaxation. But after repeated exposures to these drugs, all of these effects weaken. In other words, the drug user develops a *tolerance*—a diminished response to the drug—and with that, a need for a greater and greater dose to achieve the drug's full effects. In Chapter 3, we suggested that this tolerance is the consequence of an opponent-process reaction, but we can now recast this idea more precisely in terms of classical conditioning: The sight of a hypodermic needle (for example) serves as a CS, signaling that heroin is about to arrive. This triggers the compensatory CR through which the body counteracts the drugs effects. The CR (the compensatory response) and UR (the drug effect) then cancel each other out, yielding no effect overall.

This same account can be used to explain the craving that is central to an

The compensatory-reaction hypothesis and drug use *Addicts often inject their drug in a particular setting. Many features of this setting therefore become associated with the drug and can function as conditioned stimuli, signaling the drug's arrival and triggering the compensatory reaction. If the same dose is taken in an unfamiliar setting, the compensatory reaction may not set in, and the addict may overdose. (Courtesy of the Museum of the City of New York)*

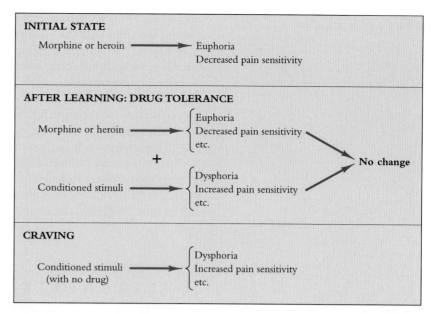

4.7 A classical-conditioning view of addiction *Morphine and heroin are unconditioned stimuli, producing a complex UR that includes (among other features) euphoria and decreased pain sensitivity. After learning, stimuli associated with the drug administration (such as the sight of the needle) trigger a compensatory CR, opposite in its qualities to the drug effects, and therefore canceling out these effects. This cancellation produces the pattern known as drug tolerance. If no drug is available, sight of the needle nonetheless triggers the CR, and so the addict experiences a pattern of changes opposite to the drug's effects.*

addiction. Imagine that the addict sees the hypodermic needle or approaches the site where the drug is usually injected but, for one reason or another, can't get the drug. In this case, the CS is present, triggering the CR, but the US is not, and thus there is no UR. The addict's body will therefore be preparing for a drug that does not arrive and so will experience the compensatory reaction with nothing to balance it (see Figure 4.7). And the compensatory reaction, we have hypothesized, is the very opposite of the drug reaction. This, then, is the source of the drug craving.

Consistent with these hypotheses, addicts generally report that their craving is greatest when they perceive stimuli that signal the injection of the drug but don't, in fact, get the drug—a situation with a CS but no US (Siegel, 1979). And the feelings and symptoms associated with drug craving are indeed the opposite of those associated with the drug itself. Thus, heroin or morphine produce euphoria, calmness, and diminished sensitivity to pain, while the craving involves depression, restlessness, and an increased sensitivity to pain.

This account in terms of classical conditioning explains many aspects of drug addiction, tolerance, and craving (Figure 4.7). Further—and rather strikingly—support for this account comes when we consider the most dangerous aspect of drug abuse: the potential for a lethal drug overdose. Suppose a drug addict has a long history of injecting heroin in her own apartment. She has gradually developed a tolerance to the drug, thanks to the compensatory reaction triggered by various cues in the apartment. But now suppose that on one occasion she injects heroin in some new environment—perhaps at a friend's house. This is, in effect, a change in the CS, since many of the cues normally associated with the injection are now absent. In keeping with what we know about generalization gradients, this will lead to a diminished CR—that is, a weaker compensatory response—and the consequences of this may be deadly: With a diminished ability to compensate for the drug's effects, the addict may, in the new environment, be unable to tolerate the amount of the drug normally injected.

Support for this account comes from interviews with addicts who have survived heroin overdoses. These addicts often report that their near-fatal overdose occurred on an occasion in which they had injected themselves with a dose no greater than their usual. What was different about these occasions was the setting in which they had taken the drug—the place, the company, and so on. Parallel results come from laboratory studies with rats: The rats are better able to tolerate a high dose of heroin if they receive it in an environment in which they have already experienced heroin. If they receive it in a novel setting, the rats cannot tolerate the same high dose (Siegel et al., 1982; Siegel, 1983).

It appears, therefore, that classical conditioning offers us some new and rather surprising insights into drug addiction. We should note, though, that the idea of compensatory reactions is itself a subject of continuing research and debate. Why is it that some CRs resemble the corresponding UR, while others are the very opposite? By the same token, why is it that we develop a tolerance to some drugs but not to others? These questions remain unanswered. But whatever the ultimate explanation, it is clear that classical conditioning is much more than a laboratory curiosity limited to dogs, metronomes, and saliva. It is a phenomenon of enormous scope, a basic form of learning that pervades much of our everyday life, and is clearly shared by flatworms and people alike (Eikelboom and Stewart, 1982; Hollis, 1982; Rescorla and Holland, 1982).

INSTRUMENTAL CONDITIONING

Habituation and classical conditioning are two of the forms of simple learning. Another is *instrumental conditioning* (also called *operant conditioning*). An example of instrumental conditioning comes from the zoo. When a seal learns to turn a somersault in order to get a fish from the zoo attendant, it has learned an instrumental response. The response is instrumental in that it leads to a sought-after effect—in this case, the fish.

Instrumental conditioning is different from classical conditioning in several ways. The most important is the fact that, in instrumental learning, reinforcement (that is, reward) depends upon the proper response. For the trained seal, no somersault means no fish. This is not true for classical conditioning. There the US is presented regardless of what the animal does—the meat powder, for example, arrives whether the animal salivates to the metronome or not. Another difference concerns the selection of the response. In instrumental learning, the response must be selected from a (sometimes large) set of alternatives. The seal's job is to select the somersault from among the numerous other things a seal could possibly do. Not so in classical conditioning. There the response is forced, for the US unconditionally evokes it: In response to meat, the animal salivates; this is not a matter of choice.

THORNDIKE AND THE LAW OF EFFECT

The experimental study of instrumental learning began a century ago, as a consequence of the debate over Darwin's theory of evolution by natural selection (see Chapter 10). Supporters of Darwin's theory emphasized the continuity among species, both living and extinct: Despite their apparent differences, a bird's wing, a whale's fin, and a human arm, for example, all have the same basic bone structure. This continuity buttressed the argument that these diverse organisms all descended from common ancestors. But opponents of Darwin's theory pointed to something they perceived as the crucial *discontinuity* among species: the human ability to think and reason, an ability that animals did not share.

In response, Darwin and his colleagues argued that there *was* continuity of mental prowess across the animal kingdom. Yes, humans are smarter than other species, but the differences might be smaller than we sometimes think. In sup-

Edward L. Thorndike (*Courtesy of The Granger Collection*)

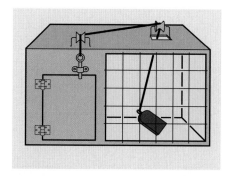

4.8 Puzzle box   *This box is much like those used by Thorndike. The animal steps on a treadle attached to a rope, thereby releasing the latch that locks the door. (After Thorndike, 1911)*

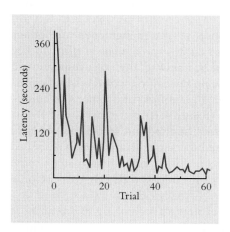

4.9 Learning curve of one of Thorndike's cats   *To get out of the box, the cat had to move a wooden handle from a vertical to a horizontal position. The figure shows the gradual decline in the animal's response latency (the time it takes to get out of the box). Note that the learning curve is by no means smooth but has rather marked fluctuations. This is a common feature of the learning curves of individual subjects. Smooth learning curves are generally produced by averaging the results of many individual subjects. (After Thorndike, 1898)*

port of this idea, Darwinian naturalists collected stories about the intellectual achievements of various animals. These painted a flattering picture, as in the reports of cunning cats who scattered bread crumbs on the lawn in order to lure birds into their reach (Romanes, 1882).

In many cases, however, it was unclear whether these reports were genuine or just bits of folklore. If genuine, it was unclear whether the reports had been elaborated or polished by the loving touch of a proud pet owner. What was plainly needed, therefore, was more systematic, more objective, and better-documented research. That research was made possible by a method described in 1898 by Edward L. Thorndike (1874–1949) in a doctoral dissertation that was to become one of the classic documents of American psychology (Thorndike, 1898).

CATS IN A PUZZLE BOX

Thorndike's method was to set up a problem for an animal—in his experiments, usually a hungry cat. The cat was placed inside a **puzzle box,** an enclosure from which it could escape only by performing some simple action that would unlock the door, such as pulling a loop of wire or pressing a lever (Figure 4.8). Once outside, the cat would be rewarded with a small portion of food. Then it was placed back into the box for another trial, so that the procedure could be repeated, over and over, until the task was mastered.

On the first trial, the typical cat struggled valiantly, meowing, clawing, and biting at the bars. This continued for several minutes until, finally, by pure accident, the animal hit upon the correct response. Subsequent trials brought gradual improvement. The moments of struggle grew shorter, and the animal took less and less time to produce the response that unlocked the door. By the time the training sessions were completed, the cat's behavior was almost unrecognizable from what it had been at the start. Placed in the box, it immediately approached the wire loop, yanked it with businesslike dispatch, and hurried through the open door to enjoy its well-deserved reward.

If one merely observed the cat's sophisticated final performance, one might well credit the animal with reason or understanding. But Thorndike argued that the problem was solved in a very different way. For proof he examined the learning curves. He plotted how much time the cat required on each trial to escape from the puzzle box—that is, the animal's response latency—and charted how these latencies changed over the course of learning. Thorndike found that the resulting curves declined quite gradually as the learning proceeded (Figure 4.9). This is not the pattern one would expect if the cats had achieved some understanding of the problem's solution. If they had, their curves would show a sudden drop at some point in the training, when the cat finally got the point. ("Aha!" muttered the insightful cat, "It's the lever that lets me out" and henceforth howled and bit no more.) Instead, these learning curves suggest that the cats achieved the correct response pattern in small increments, with no evidence at all of understanding and certainly no evidence of any sudden insight into the problem's solution.

THE LAW OF EFFECT

In Thorndike's view, the cats' initial responses to this situation were likely to be a result of prior learning or perhaps a result of some built-in predisposition. As it happened, however, virtually all of these initial responses led to failure. Therefore, as the trials proceeded, the tendency to produce these responses gradually weakened. In contrast, the animal's tendency to produce the correct response was initially weak but, over the trials, gradually grew in strength. In Thorndike's

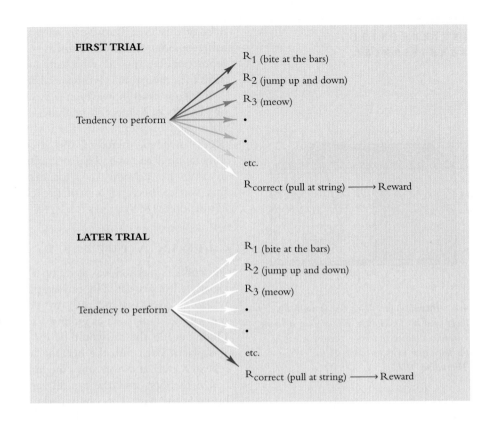

4.10 The law of effect *The figure is a schematic presentation of Thorndike's theory of instrumental learning. On the first trial, the tendency to perform various incorrect responses (biting the bars, jumping up and down) is very strong, while the tendency to perform the correct response (pulling the string) is weak or nonexistent. As trials proceed, the strength of these responses changes. The incorrect responses become weaker and weaker, for none of these responses is immediately followed by reward. In contrast, there is a progressive strengthening of the correct response because this is followed more or less immediately by reward.*

terms, the correct response was gradually "stamped in," while futile ones were correspondingly "stamped out."

But what is it that causes some responses to get strengthened and others weakened as learning proceeds? Thorndike's answer was the **law of effect.** Its key proposition is that, if a response is followed by a reward, then that response will be strengthened. If a response is followed by no reward (or, worse yet, by punishment), it will be weakened. In general, then, the strength of a response is adjusted according to that response's *consequences* (Figure 4.10).

Thus, we don't need to postulate any sophisticated intellectual processes to explain the cat's performance. We don't need to assume that the animal noticed a connection between act and consequence, or that it was trying to attain some goal. If the animal made a response and reward followed shortly, that response was more likely to be performed later.

Thorndike's proposal fit neatly into the evolutionary thinking so dominant at that time. First, the law of effect emphasized the adaptive nature of an animal's activity, which is gradually shaped to serve the creature's biological ends. Second, and more importantly, Thorndike pointed out that the law of effect is a close analogue of the Darwinian principle of natural selection. In the life of the species, individuals with successful adaptations will live long enough to transmit these adaptations to the next generation; creatures without these adaptations are likely to die off, leaving few offspring. In the life of the individual, the law of effect provides a virtually identical selection process for behaviors: The successful responses are preserved; the unsuccessful ones "die off." As Thorndike put it, "It is a process of selection among reactions . . . by eliminating the unsuitable reaction directly by discomfort, and also by positively selecting the suitable one by pleasure. . . . It is of tremendous usefulness. . . . He who learns and runs away, *will live to learn another day . . . "* (Thorndike, 1899, p. 91).

B. F. Skinner *(Photograph by Nina Leen, Life Magazine, © Time Warner, Inc.)*

SKINNER AND OPERANT BEHAVIOR

Thorndike initiated the experimental study of instrumental behavior, but the psychologist who shaped the way in which most modern learning theorists think about the subject is B. F. Skinner (1904–1990). Skinner was one of the first theorists to insist on a sharp distinction between classical and instrumental conditioning. In classical conditioning, the animal's behavior is *elicited* by the CS; salivation, for example, is set off by an event outside of the organism. But in instrumental conditioning, Skinner argued, the organism is much less at the mercy of the external situation. Its reactions are *emitted* from within, as if they were what we ordinarily call *voluntary*. Skinner called these instrumental responses **operants:** They operate on the environment to bring about some change that leads to reward. This reward was crucial for Skinner just as it was for Thorndike, and Skinner endorsed Thorndike's proposal of the law of effect, insisting that the tendency to emit an operant is strengthened or weakened by the behavior's consequences (Skinner, 1938).

Skinner believed, however, that Thorndike's procedure for studying learning was inefficient. Rather than placing animals in a puzzle box, Skinner sought a procedure in which the instrumental response could be performed repeatedly and rapidly. Many of his studies, therefore, employed an experimental chamber (popularly called the "Skinner box") in which a rat presses a lever or a pigeon pecks at a lighted key (Figure 4.11). In these situations, the animal remains in the presence of the lever or key for, say, an hour at a time, pressing or pecking at whatever rate it chooses. All of the animal's responses are automatically recorded, and stimuli and reinforcements are typically controlled by a computer. The usual measure of response strength is the **response rate,** that is, the number of responses per unit of time.

THE MAJOR PHENOMENA OF INSTRUMENTAL CONDITIONING

Many of the central phenomena of instrumental learning parallel those of classical conditioning. Consider reinforcement. In classical conditioning, the term refers to an operation (establishing a CS–US contingency) that strengthens

4.11 Animals in operant chambers
(A) A rat trained to press a lever for water reinforcement. (Photograph by Mike Salisbury) (B) A pigeon pecking at a lighted key for food reinforcement. Reinforcement consists of a few seconds' access to a grain feeder that is located just below the key. (Photographs by Susan M. Hogue)

A

B

the CR. In instrumental learning, reinforcement refers to an analogous operation: strengthening a response by following it with some attractive stimulus or situation. This often involves the presentation of something good, such as grain to a hungry pigeon. Alternatively, reinforcement may involve the termination or prevention of something bad, such as the cessation of an electric shock.

In other words, reinforcement can involve either the presentation of an **appetitive stimulus** (a stimulus for which the animal has an appetite), or the termination of an **aversive stimulus** (a stimulus that the animal will typically seek to avoid). From the animal's point of view, both of these are improvements over the status quo, and both will reinforce the previously occurring behavior.

Just as in classical conditioning, the probability of an instrumental response increases with an increasing number of reinforcements. And again as in classical conditioning, the response suffers extinction when reinforcement is withdrawn.

GENERALIZATION AND DISCRIMINATION

The instrumental response is not *elicited* by external stimuli but is, in Skinner's terms, *emitted from within*. But this doesn't mean that external stimuli have no role. They do exert considerable control over behavior, for they serve as **discriminative stimuli.** Suppose a pigeon is trained to hop on a treadle to get some grain. When a green light is on, hopping on the treadle will pay off. But when a red light is on, treadle hopping will gain no reward. Under these circumstances, the green light becomes a positive discriminative stimulus and the red light a negative one (usually labeled S^+ and S^- respectively). The pigeon will swiftly learn this pattern, and so will hop in the presence of the first and not in the presence of the second.

Let us be clear, though, about the relationship among these stimuli. A CS^+ tells the animal about events in the world: "No matter what you do, the US is coming." The S^+, on the other hand, tells the animal about the impact of its own behavior: "If you respond now, you'll get rewarded." The CS^- indicates that no US is coming, again independent of what the animal does. The S^-, in contrast, tells the animal something about its behavior—namely, that there's no point in responding right now.

Despite these differences, generalization and discrimination function quite similarly in classical and in instrumental conditioning. For example, consider the generalization gradient. We saw earlier that, if trained with one CS (perhaps, a high tone) but then tested with a different one (a low tone), the CR will be diminished. The greater the change in the CS, the greater the drop in the CR's strength. The same pattern can be observed in instrumental conditioning: In one experiment, pigeons were trained to peck at a key illuminated with yellow light. Later, they were tested with lights of varying wavelengths, and the results show an orderly generalization gradient (Figure 4.12). As the test light became less similar to the original S^+, the pigeons were less inclined to peck at it (Guttmann and Kalish, 1956).

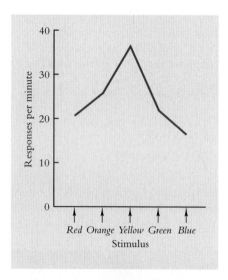

4.12 Stimulus generalization of an instrumental response *Pigeons were originally reinforced to peck at a yellow light. When later tested with lights of various colors, they showed a standard generalization gradient, pecking more vigorously at colors more similar to yellow (such as green and orange) than at colors farther removed (such as red and blue). Prior to being reinforced on the yellow key, their tendency to peck was minimal and roughly equal for all colors. (After Reynolds, 1968)*

SHAPING

The law of effect tells us that once a response has been made, then reinforcement will act to strengthen it. But what causes the animal to perform the desired response in the first place? Some responses are no problem: Pecking is the sort of thing pigeons do all the time, providing frequent opportunities for the animal trainer to reinforce (and thus encourage) this response; likewise for rats pressing and manipulating easily reachable objects in their environment.

But what about more complex responses? For example, we could set a lever so high on the wall that the rat must stretch up on its hind legs to reach it. Now

Shaping *The routines of circus animals are generally established through the method of successive approximations. (Photograph © Hank Morgan)*

the rat might never make the lever-pressing response on its own. Nonetheless, it can learn this response if its behavior is suitably *shaped.* This is accomplished by the method of *successive approximations.*

How would we train a rat to press the elevated lever? First, we must teach the animal to collect its food rewards. At random intervals, a click sounds, and a food pellet drops into a little cup. Initially, the rat might be afraid of this sound, but habituation quickly quells this fear, so that, before long, the rat approaches the food tray and collects the pellet as soon as it hears the click. Shaping can now begin. At first, we reinforce the animal merely for walking into the general area where the lever is located. As soon as the rat is there, we deliver food: The rat hears the click and devours the pellet. Very soon, the rat will have learned to remain in this neighborhood virtually all the time, allowing us to increase our demand: From this point forward, the rat is reinforced only if it is in the area *and* facing the lever. This response also is soon mastered, and so again we increase our demand: Now the rat is reinforced only if it is facing the lever *and* stretching its body a little bit upward. We continue in this fashion, reinforcing the rat only when it stretches all the way up to the lever, then when it actually touches the lever, and so on. Step by step, we move the rat toward the desired response. Throughout, the guiding principle is immediacy of reinforcement. If we want to reinforce the rat for standing up on its hind legs, we must do it the instant after the response; even a one-second wait may be too long, for by then the rat may have fallen back on all fours, and if we reinforce it then, we will reinforce the wrong response.

By means of this technique, animals have been trained to perform exceedingly complex behaviors (see Figure 4.13). Pigeons have been trained to play Ping-Pong and dogs to plunk out four-note tunes on a toy piano. In fact, this technique has allowed some enterprising psychologists to develop live advertising exhibits, featuring such stars as Priscilla the Fastidious Pig, who promoted the sale of certain farm feeds (Breland and Breland, 1951). Priscilla turned on the radio, ate breakfast at a kitchen table, picked up dirty clothes and dropped them in a hamper, vacuumed the floor, and finally selected the sponsor's feed in preference to Brand X—a sequence of behaviors that stands as a convincing tribute to both the sponsor and the power of reinforcement.

A

B

4.13 Animals in show business (A) A pig trained by means of operant techniques to push a market cart. The animal was first reinforced for putting its front feet up on the handle, until it could raise up on the handle and push the cart while walking on its hind feet. (Photograph courtesy of Animal Behavior Enterprises) (B) Squirrels trained to stand on their hind legs and hold onto the bar and, hence, to water ski for a fixed interval so as to get reinforced. (Photograph by Gerald Davis / Contact Press Images)

CONDITIONED REINFORCEMENT

So far, our examples of reinforcement have included food, water, and termination of electric shocks. But instrumental learning is not always reinforced by events of such immediate biological consequence. For example, piano teachers rarely reinforce their students with food or by turning off a shock; a nod or the comment "good" is all that is usually required. How does the Thorndikian approach explain why the word *good* is reinforcing?

Thorndike or Skinner would answer that a stimulus acquires reinforcing properties if it is repeatedly paired with another reinforcer. In this way, a stimulus can become a **conditioned reinforcer** and will then function just as any other reinforcer would.

Numerous experiments demonstrate that neutral stimuli can acquire reinforcing properties in this way. For example, chimpanzees in one study were first trained to insert poker chips into a vending machine to acquire grapes. Having learned this, they then learned to operate another device that delivered poker chips (Cowles, 1937; see Figure 4.14). Examples of this kind indicate that the critical factor in establishing a stimulus as a conditioned reinforcer is its association with a primary reinforcer. It is not surprising, then, that this effect increases the more frequently the two are paired. As we might also expect, a conditioned reinforcer will gradually lose its power if it is repeatedly presented alone, unaccompanied by some primary reinforcement.

All of this argues that conditioned reinforcement is established by a process that is akin to, if not identical with, classical conditioning. In short, conditioned reinforcers (tokens, smiles, nods) are similar to CSs. In both cases, these initially neutral stimuli become associated with a biologically important event, and once this is accomplished, the CS or the conditioned reinforcer takes on motivational significance.

4.14 Conditioned reinforcement in chimpanzees *Chimpanzee using a token to obtain food after working to obtain tokens. (Courtesy Yerkes Regional Primate Research Center of Emory University)*

WHAT IS A REINFORCER?

If all reinforcers were stimuli that met basic biological needs, such as food, water, or warmth, or stimuli that have been associated with these biologically important stimuli, then reinforcement might be explained in terms of the homeostatic mechanisms described in Chapter 3: Reinforcers, in essence, would always be stimuli that help an organism satisfy its biological needs.

However, much evidence indicates that this suggestion is too simple by far. Pigeons, for example, will peck in order to gain *information* about the availability of food (e.g., Bower, McLean, and Meachem, 1966; Hendry, 1969). Monkeys will work merely to open a small door through which they can see a moving toy train (Butler, 1954). And, in general, animals will respond simply to gain the opportunity to engage in some other, more preferred, activity—e.g., press a lever in order to run inside an exercise wheel (Premack, 1965).

These (and many other) examples make *reinforcement* difficult to define. Some reinforcers meet biological needs, but many do not. As a consequence, this term is generally defined only after the fact. Is a glimpse of a toy train reinforcing? We can find out only by asking whether an animal will work to obtain this glimpse. Remarkably, no other more informative definition of a reinforcement is currently available.

Behavioral contrast The issues are just as complicated when we consider the *magnitude* of a reinforcer. It is no surprise that an animal will respond a little bit for a small reward, but will respond more (more quickly, more strongly, more often) for a large reward. But what counts as small or large depends on the context: If a rat is used to getting sixty-four food pellets for a response, then sixteen pellets will seem measly, and the animal will respond only weakly for this puny reward. But if a rat is used to getting only four pellets, then sixteen pellets will seem like a feast, and its response will be fast and strong (e.g., Crespi, 1942). Thus, how effective a reinforcer will be depends to a large extent on what other rewards are available and also on what other rewards have been *recently* available. This pattern is often referred to as ***behavioral contrast.***

Intrinsic motivation   Behavioral contrast may provide a partial explanation for another phenomenon called ***intrinsic motivation.*** In an early study of this phenomenon, nursery-school children were given an opportunity to draw pictures. The children seemed to enjoy this activity, and they produced drawings at a steady pace even though no reinforcers for this activity were in view. Apparently, they were drawing because the activity was *fun,* or, put differently, because drawing was its own reward. The reward was intrinsic to the activity, not separate from it.

In this study, though, the experimenters added an extrinsic reward: The children were now rewarded with an attractive "Good Player" certificate for producing their pictures. Then, sometime later, the children were again given the opportunity to draw pictures, but this time with no provision for "Good Player" rewards. Remarkably, these children now showed considerably less interest in drawing than they had at the start, choosing to spend their time on other activities instead (e.g., Lepper, Greene, and Nisbett, 1973; see Kohn, 1993, for a review of subsequent related studies).

At one level, these data illustrate the power of behavioral contrasts. At the start of the study, the intrinsic reward involved in drawing was by itself sufficient to motivate the children. Later on, though, this same reward seemed puny when compared to the (greater) prize that consisted of the intrinsic reward plus the "Good Player" certificate. As a consequence, the smaller seeming reward was now insufficient to motivate continued drawing.

More fundamentally, though, these results imply that there may be two different types of reward. One type is merely tacked on to a behavior and is under the control of the experimenter. The other is intrinsic to the behavior and is independent of the experimenter's (or anyone else's) intentions. Moreover, some authors have suggested that intrinsically motivated behaviors—behaviors that we do for their own sake—may have a special status. Think about an artist who continues in her creative endeavors, even though her art wins her no tangible rewards. Think about a scientist who perseveres in testing an unpopular hypothesis, despite the criticism of skeptical colleagues; or an individual who insists on taking a firm moral stance, despite the financial incentives tempting him toward a morally dubious alternative. In all of these cases, important human activities seem to be sustained only by intrinsic motivation, with no accompanying extrinsic reinforcement. Indeed, the scientist and the moralist stay the course despite extrinsic rewards favoring an alternative course of action. Cases such as these lead one to wonder: How many activities are intrinsically motivated? Do intrinsically motivated acts have a special status, as these examples suggest? These are crucial questions to pursue if we are to understand the nature of reinforcement and reward, and, indeed, the nature of human motivation (for discussion, see Cameron and Pierce, 1996; Eisenberger and Cameron, 1996; Lepper et al., 1996).

SCHEDULES OF REINFORCEMENT

Let us return, though, to the issue of how extrinsic reinforcements work, since, on anyone's account, extrinsic reinforcement plays a huge role in governing human (and other species') behavior. We do, after all, work for money, buy lottery tickets in hopes of winning, and act in a fashion that we believe will bring us praise. How do these extrinsic rewards govern our behavior?

Note that, in these examples, reinforcement comes only occasionally: We aren't paid after every task we perform at work; we rarely (if ever) win the lottery; we do not always get the praise we seek. In fact, this is the usual pattern outside the laboratory. The fisherman does not hook a fish with every cast, and even a star tennis player occasionally loses a match. All of these are cases of ***partial reinforcement*** in which a response is reinforced only some of the time.

In the laboratory, partial reinforcement can be arranged in different ways. Reinforcement might be delivered after a certain number of responses are made or after some interval has passed. These different patterns can each be described in terms of a ***schedule of reinforcement.*** In essense, the schedule defines the rules that determine when, and under what conditions, a response will be reinforced.

Ratio schedules   One example of such a rule is the ***fixed-ratio schedule*** (or ***FR***) in which the research participant must produce a specified number of responses in order to receive each reward. The number of responses required determines the number following "FR": If two responses are required for each reinforcement, the schedule is FR 2. If three or four responses are required, then it's FR 3 or FR 4 (and so on). Such schedules can generate very high rates of responding, especially if the ratio is high, but to reach these high rates, the ratio must increase gradually, beginning with FR 1 (each response is rewarded) and then slowly increasing the requirement.

When the fixed ratio gets high enough, a specific pattern of responding emerges: Following each reinforcement, the animal will pause for a while; the higher the ratio, the longer the pause (see Figure 4.15). In a way, the laboratory pigeon pecking a key resembles a student who has just finished one term paper and has to write another. It is very hard to start again, but once the first page is written, the next ones come more readily.

The pause following each reinforcement can be eliminated by changing the schedule to a ***variable ratio (VR).*** In VR schedules, reinforcement still comes after a certain number of responses, but the number of responses needed varies from one reinforcement to the next. VR schedules are typically described in terms of the average number of responses required, so that a VR 10 (for example) is a schedule in which, on average, the animal receives a reward for every ten responses. However, within this schedule, it might turn out that the first five responses were enough to earn one reward, but fifteen more were needed to earn the next.

In a VR schedule, there is no way for the animal to know which of its responses will bring the next reward. Perhaps one more response will do the trick, or perhaps it will take a hundred more. This uncertainty helps explain why VR schedules produce such high levels of responding, in humans and in other creatures. This is easily demonstrated in the laboratory, but more persuasive evidence comes from any gambling casino. There the slot machines pay off on a VR schedule, with the "reinforcement schedule" adjusted so that "responses" occur at a very high rate, ensuring that the casino will be lucrative for its owners and not for its patrons.

4.15 *Performance on two fixed-ratio schedules* *The figure records the pigeon's cumulative responses—how many key pecks it made after five minutes in the operant chamber, after ten minutes, and so on. The steeper the record, the faster the response rate. The left-hand panel shows performance on FR 65, the right on FR 185. The small diagonal slashes indicate times when the animal received reinforcement. Note the characteristic pause after the fixed ratio has been run off and that the duration of this pause increases with increasing ratios. (Adapted from Ferster and Skinner, 1957)*

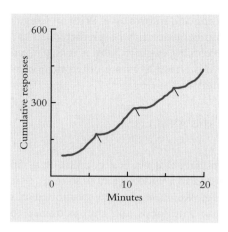

4.16 *Performance on a fixed-interval schedule* *The cumulative record of a pigeon's performance on a fixed-interval schedule, FI 5. The small diagonal slashes indicate reinforcements. Note the scalloped shape that is characteristic of performance on an FI schedule after the animal has been on that schedule for a few sessions. (After Ferster and Skinner, 1957)*

Interval schedules Ratio schedules are based on numbers of responses. Interval schedules are based on time. In a **fixed-interval schedule (FI),** reinforcement becomes available only after a certain interval has passed since the last reinforcement. Responses during that interval are not rewarded. Once the interval is completed, the very next response earns a reward. An example of an FI schedule is looking in the mailbox. No matter how many times you check the box, your effort will go unrewarded if you look *before* the mail has been delivered. But once the mail has been delivered, your very next response is certain to be reinforced. Since most mail delivery occurs daily, this would be a schedule of FI 24 hours.

After an animal has been on an FI schedule for a while, it shows a characteristic response pattern. Immediately after reinforcement, its response rate is very low. The rate then gradually picks up, getting faster and faster as the end of the interval approaches (see Figure 4.16).

The response pattern will be different, though, if the animal is put on a **variable-interval schedule (VI)** (see Figure 4.17). A VI schedule differs from an FI schedule in essentially the same way that a VR schedule differs from an FR. For a VI schedule, reinforcement occurs *on average* only after some specified interval. However, the actual interval varies unpredictably from trial to trial. An example from everyday life would be an employer who requires periodic drug tests of her employees. These might be administered, on average, every month, but to preserve the element of surprise, the timing of each drug test is unpredictable.

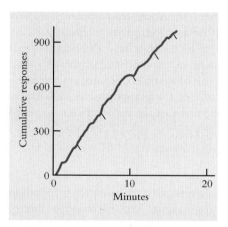

4.17 *Performance on a variable-interval schedule* *The cumulative record of an animal's performance on a variable interval schedule. Again, the small slashes indicate reinforcements. As the record shows, response rates are very high, and there are no pauses after reinforcement.*

Partial reinforcement and extinction The various schedules of reinforcement, as we have now seen, have different influences on behavior. But one of the most important effects of partial reinforcement is seen only during extinction. The basic fact can be stated simply: Partial reinforcement leads to slower extinction. This phenomenon is often called the **partial-reinforcement effect** (Figure 4.18; Humphreys, 1939).

On the face of it, the partial-reinforcement effect is paradoxical. If each reinforcement increases the strength of the instrumental response, then a greater number of reinforcements should lead to a more strongly established behavior. We should expect, therefore, that a group reinforced 100 percent of the time would continue to respond for longer than one reinforced only one-third of the time. But the very opposite is true. Why? Speaking informally, we might say that the partially reinforced animal has learned that not every effort leads to success; it has learned that "if at first you don't succeed, try, try again." This animal might not even notice initially that extinction trials have begun, since it has responded without reinforcement many times before.

Consistent with this idea, studies show that it is more difficult to extinguish a response that was established with an *irregular* sequence of reinforcements. With a regular sequence, the animal knows when reinforcement will be delivered, so

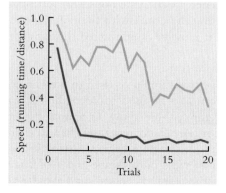

4.18 *The partial-reinforcement effect* *The figure shows runway speeds during extinction trials on two groups of rats. One group had previously been reinforced on every trial; the other had only been reinforced on 30 percent of the trials. The figure shows that the group trained under full reinforcement (in dark red) stops running considerably before the group that was trained under partial reinforcement (in blue). (After Weinstock, 1954)*

the absence of reinforcement can be surprising and informative. With an irregular sequence, though, the delivery of reinforcement can't be predicted, so the absence of reinforcement is less informative. This explains why it is that fixed schedules (fixed ratio or fixed interval) are more readily extinguished than variable schedules (variable ratio or variable interval).

THE BREADTH OF INSTRUMENTAL CONDITIONING

In our earlier discussion, we emphasized the fact that classical conditioning can be observed in a wide variety of organisms and in a wide variety of settings. The same is true for instrumental conditioning. We have already mentioned rats trained to press levers, cats trained to pull on wire loops, and chimps trained to operate vending machines. Other examples are easy to enumerate, and instrumental conditioning has been observed in species as simple as honeybees and as sophisticated as humans.

The breadth of instrumental conditioning is also visible in the many applications of these techniques in nonlaboratory settings. A number of prisons use instrumental conditioning to shape prisoners' behavior; many parents employ similar techniques to teach their children. (Children's etiquette is almost certainly acquired in this fashion.) And instrumental techniques have also been applied in many clinical settings, including treatment in psychotherapy (the so-called behavior modification techniques) and the use of token economies among institutionalized patients. We will return to some of these applications in Chapter 19, when we discuss the methods used to treat people with various forms of mental disorder.

AVERSIVE CONDITIONING

Our discussion so far has centered on cases of reward, cases in which responding brings something good. But what about punishment? This is the other side of the coin, in which a response is followed by some aversive stimulus, be it a startling noise for laboratory rats or a stern "No!" for a naughty child. There is little doubt that organisms learn whatever they must to minimize such unpleasantness, a form of learning called ***aversive conditioning.***

Punishment   Aversive stimuli can play a number of different roles in instrumental learning, but the most obvious is ***punishment.*** Here, a response is followed by an aversive stimulus, and this will make that response less likely to occur on subsequent occasions. As with rewards, though, the timing of the punishment is crucial: Consider a cat that has developed the unfortunate habit of using a large indoor planter instead of its litter box. The irate pet owner discovers the misdeed an hour or so later and yells at the cat when he sees it in the kitchen. It's hardly surprising that this punishment will not produce the hoped for learning, because the animal has no way of connecting the crime with the punishment. For punishment to have its desired effect, it must be administered shortly after the unwanted response is performed.

Escape and avoidance   In punishment, an aversive stimulus is used to weaken an unwanted behavior. But aversive stimuli can also be used to strengthen a response. Consider ***escape responses,*** for example; these allow an animal to get away from, or terminate, an aversive situation. ***Avoidance responses*** have an even better outcome: They prevent the aversive stimulus from ever occurring in the first place. Clearly, from the animal's point of view, both escape and avoidance bring about a good result; it is no surprise, therefore, that escape and avoidance responses are swiftly learned. As an example of escape, a rat can easily be trained

Avoidance learning   *No doubt the infant will learn to avoid the flame. (Photograph by Erika Stone)*

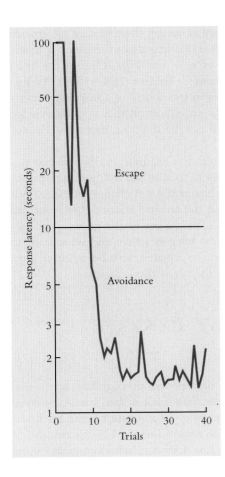

4.19 The course of avoidance learning in a dog *The figure shows response latencies of one animal in a shuttle box (where latency is the time from the onset of CS to the animal's response). A warning stimulus indicated that shock would begin 10 seconds after the onset of the signal. For the first nine trials the dog escaped. It jumped over the hurdle after the shock began. From the tenth trial on, the dog avoided: It jumped before its 10 seconds of grace were up. The jumping speed increased until the animal jumped with an average latency of about 1.5 seconds. (Latency is plotted on a logarithmic scale. This compresses the time scale so as to put greater emphasis on differences between the shorter response latencies.) (After Solomon and Wynne, 1953)*

to press a lever in order to turn off an electric shock. As an example of avoidance, a dog can readily learn to jump from one chamber to another, whenever it hears a tone that signals impending shock. If it jumps within some grace period, it will manage to avoid the shock entirely (see Figure 4.19).

Aversive conditioning and the law of effect The effects of punishment are easily accommodated by the law of effect. As we have already noted, good consequences strengthen the tendency to produce a behavior, and bad consequences weaken it. Likewise, the interpretation of escape learning is also straightforward: The escape response is followed by the termination of something bad, and this serves as a reward, making that same response more likely in the future.

But the interpretation of avoidance learning is more difficult. Consider a dog who jumps back and forth in order to avoid an electric shock. In the early stages of learning, the dog didn't jump until after the shock had begun, and so each jump was rewarded by the termination of shock. Later on, however, the dog has learned to jump early enough so that it avoids the shock altogether. On the face of things, this means that the reinforcement for jumping (the termination of the shock) is no longer being delivered, and this should lead to extinction of the response. Yet the animal continues to jump. Why is this?

Of course, each of the dog's jumps is followed by *absence of shock,* and this is probably what reinforces the jumping response. But let's be clear about what this involves: The dog must know that there's a real threat of shock in this situation; otherwise, absence of shock wouldn't be rewarding. To see this, consider the fact that each of the dog's jumps is also followed by the absence of earthquakes, just as it is followed by the absence of shock. But there is surely no reason to believe that earthquake avoidance is why the animal continues to jump. That's because there was never any reason to fear (or even to think about) earthquakes in this situation, and so the absence of earthquakes provides no relief, no release from fear, and hence no reward.

Hence, it is not absence of shock by itself that is the reward. This absence is rewarding only when shock is realistically threatened. Only in that context is the absence of shock a relief and a reward. To explain avoidance learning, therefore, we need somehow to acknowledge that the animal knows what threats are present in a situation and knows what will happen if it doesn't respond. It is these complexities that demand an account fuller than that provided simply by the law of effect. This account is readily developed within a more cognitive approach to learning.

COGNITIVE LEARNING

To the early theorists, the essential thing about classical and instrumental conditioning was that both procedures modify behavior. In classical conditioning, a new response (the CR) is created. In instrumental conditioning, responses are strengthened or weakened by the mechanical effects of reinforcement and punishment.

Edward C. Tolman *(Courtesy Psychology Department, University of California, Berkeley)*

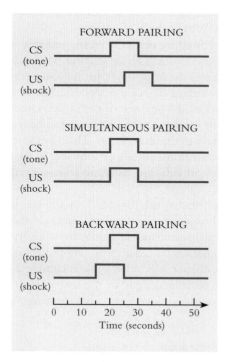

4.20 *Some temporal relationships in classical conditioning*

From the earliest days of learning theory, however, there was an alternative view of conditioning, one which asserted that learning is not the *change in behavior* as such but is instead the acquisition of new *knowledge.* One of the most prominent exponents of this view was Edward C. Tolman (1886–1959). As Tolman saw it, the response an animal acquires in the course of a learning experiment is crucial, because it provides us with an indication that new knowledge has been gained. But it is the **cognition,** and not the response, that is the essence of what is learned (Dickinson, 1987).

Tolman's view is supported by many results. For example, in one experiment, rats were ferried from one end of a large room to another, riding in transparent trolley cars. During these rides, the rats' behavior did not change, but there was learning nonetheless: Later tests showed that the rats had learned the layout and the general features of the room (Gleitman, 1963). They had acquired what Tolman called a "cognitive map" that represents what is where and what leads to what (Tolman, 1948). Thus learning cannot be equated with behavior change, because here the passenger rats showed the former without the latter.

A COGNITIVE VIEW OF CLASSICAL CONDITIONING

Classical conditioning can also be understood in cognitive terms—in terms of what the animal *knows* rather than what it *does.* Pavlov believed that the conditioned stimulus gradually becomes a substitute for the unconditioned stimulus, so that the animal comes to respond to the CS just as it did to the US. But as we have seen, this is not the case. Even in Pavlov's original experiment, the UR and CR were not identical, and in other experiments (such as those involving opiate drugs), the CR and UR appear to be exact opposites. It seems, therefore, that the CS does not become a substitute for the US but, instead, becomes a sign that the US will soon follow, leading the animal to make appropriate preparations for the US. In other words, what the animal acquires in classical conditioning is an understanding of the relation between two stimulus events (Tolman, 1932; Rescorla, 1988).

TEMPORAL RELATIONS BETWEEN THE CS AND THE US

The cognitive approach to learning is also pertinent to another crucial issue: What is it that produces classical conditioning? What causes the CS to become associated, in an animal's mind, with the US? Pavlov believed that the key was **temporal contiguity,** that is, togetherness in time. The CS and US occur together, and that is why they become associated. But as we shall see, the answer is more complicated than this.

A number of studies have examined the role of contiguity by varying the interval between the CS and the US, as well as the order in which they are presented. In some studies, the CS precedes the US **(forward pairing),** in others it follows the US **(backward pairing),** and in yet others the two stimuli are presented at the same time **(simultaneous pairing).** (See Figure 4.20.)

These procedures generally show that conditioning is best when the CS *precedes* the US by some optimum interval (see Figure 4.21).★ If the interval

★ The precise value of the optimum interval depends on the particulars of the situation; it usually varies from about half a second to about ten seconds. In one form of classical conditioning, learned taste aversion, the CS-US is very long and may be of the order of an hour or more. This phenomenon poses obvious difficulties for a contiguity theory of conditioning—and much else besides—and will be discussed in a later section (see pp. 149–50).

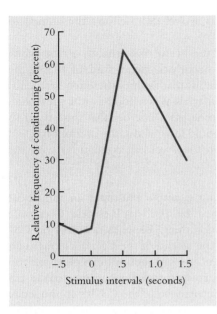

4.21 The CS-US interval in classical conditioning *The figure shows the results of a study of the effectiveness of various CS-US intervals in humans. The CR was a finger withdrawal response, the CS a tone, and the US an electric shock. The time between CS and US is plotted on the horizontal axis. Negative intervals mean that the US was presented before the CS (backward pairing), a zero interval means that the two stimuli were presented simultaneously, and a positive interval means that the CS began before the US (forward pairing). The vertical axis indicates the degree of conditioning. (After Spooner and Kellogg, 1947)*

between the CS and US is increased beyond this optimum, the effectiveness of the pairing declines sharply. In addition, presenting the CS and US simultaneously is much less effective in establishing an association, and the backward procedure is even worse (Rescorla, 1988).

These facts make perfect sense if we understand the CS as a signal, allowing the organism to prepare for the US. To see how this works, imagine a driver setting out on an unfamiliar road, en route from Denver to Salt Lake City. Let's say that there is a dangerous hairpin turn about 150 miles out of Denver. How should the driver be warned of the impending curve? Ideally, the highway department would place a "hairpin turn" sign just a bit before the turn (analogous to forward pairing with a short CS-US interval). This would be informative and would give the driver time to prepare for the relevant maneuver. It's important that the sign not appear too much before the turn, because then the driver would not connect it with what it signifies. Surely she would lose faith in the highway department if it set up the sign just outside the Denver city limits, while the turn itself is three hours away (forward pairing with a long CS-US interval). Things would be worse still, though, if the sign were prominently displayed right in the middle of the hairpin turn, because now the sign's warning comes too late to be of any use (simultaneous pairing). Worst of all, the driver would suspect a degree of malevolence if she discovered the sign innocently placed on the road a hundred feet *beyond* the turn (backward pairing), though she would probably be grateful that she did not find it at the bottom of the ravine.

CONTINGENCY

According to the cognitive learning approach, in classical conditioning an organism learns that one stimulus signals another. But what does this signaling involve? Consider a dog in a conditioning experiment. Several times, it has heard a metronome and, a moment later, received some food powder. But of course many other stimuli were also present. Simultaneous with the metronome, the dog heard some doors slamming and some voices in the background. It saw the laboratory walls and the light fixtures hanging from the ceiling. At that moment, it could also smell a dozen different scents, and could feel a similar number of bodily sensations.

What, therefore, should the dog learn? If it relies on mere contiguity, then it will learn to associate the food powder with all these stimuli—metronomes, light fixtures, and everything else that's on the scene. After all, these were all together in time with the US.

We have already suggested, though, that the conditioned response is an act of *preparation* for the upcoming US. It would seem, then, that what the animal needs is the ability to *predict* the US, so that it knows when to launch this preparation and when not to bother. For this purpose, an association between the US and, say, the light fixtures would be of no value: The fixtures were on the scene just before the food powder arrived, but they were also on the scene during the many minutes in which no food was on its way. Likewise for the smells and most of the sounds in the laboratory: These were all associated with food but also associated with the absence of food. Therefore, none of these provides any information about when food is about to arrive; none allows the animal to predict the food's approach.

What the animal needs, obviously, is some event that reliably occurs when food is about to appear, and which *doesn't* occur otherwise. And, of course, the metronome beat in our example is the stimulus that satisfies these requirements, for it never beats in the intervals between trials when food is not presented. Therefore, if the animal hears the metronome, it's a safe bet that food is on its way. If the animal cares about *signaling,* it should learn about the metronome, and not about these other stimuli, even though they were all contiguous with the target event.

Contingency versus contiguity   The preceding example illustrates an influential analysis of classical conditioning developed by Robert Rescorla (Rescorla, 1967). According to Rescorla, classical conditioning depends not only on CS-US pairings, but also on pairings in which the *absence* of the CS goes along with the *absence* of the US. These two experiences—say, metronome/meat and no metronome/no meat—allow the dog to discover that the occurrence of the US is *contingent* (that is, dependent) upon the occurrence of the CS. It's contingency that allows the animal to forecast what is going to happen next, and according to Rescorla, it's contingency that's crucial for conditioning, and not contiguity.

Contingency need not be perfect, and in nature it rarely is. A dark cloud generally precedes a storm, but it doesn't always. As a result, while weather predictions are never perfect, they are nevertheless usually informative, because it's far more likely to rain when the sky is dark than when the sun is shining.

The same imperfect contingency holds in the conditioning laboratory. Here, for example, we can arrange things so that a tone (the CS) is followed by food on 80 percent of the trials, but on the remaining 20 percent the tone is followed by nothing. In addition, we can occasionally arrange that food arrives with no warning. We have now created an imperfect contingency: The probability of receiving food after a tone is less than 100 percent; the probability of receiving food in the absence of a tone is greater than zero. But there is a contingency here even so, for food is more likely after the CS than otherwise. Therefore, there is information to be gained by attending to the CS and by increasing one's preparations for food when the CS occurs.

In short, a contingency depends on a comparison between two probabilities: (1) the probability of a US, given the fact that the CS has occurred, and (2) the probability of a US, given the fact that *no* CS has occurred. If these two probabilities are equal, then there's no point in paying attention to the CS. If the first of these is greater than the second, then the CS does provide information that the US is likely to be on its way.

Can animals make such comparisons? Apparently, they can. To demonstrate this, Rescorla exposed rats to various combinations of a tone (CS) and a shock (US). For one group of rats, the presentation of a tone signaled a 40 percent chance that a shock was about to arrive, but shocks also arrived 40 percent of the time without any warning. For this group, there was no conditioning. This is a case in which the two probabilities are equal. For another group of rats the number of signaled shocks remained at 40 percent but the number of unsignaled shocks was reduced, so that the likelihood of a shock was smaller (below 40 percent) when the tone was off than when it was on. For this second group, conditioning did take place. And the greater the difference in these probabilities, the stronger the level of conditioning the animal achieved (see Figure 4.22).

Notice that for both groups, the number of CS-US pairings was the same. Likewise, the degree of contiguity between CS and US was the same for all groups. But neither of these was the critical factor for conditioning. What mattered, instead, was whether the tone was informative, whether the shock was

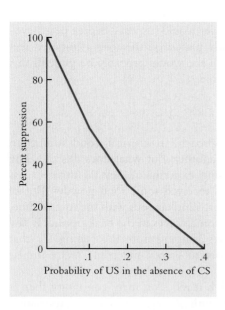

4.22   Contingency in classical conditioning   *The figure shows the results of fear conditioning as a function of contingency. The probability of the US in the presence of the CS was always .40, but the probability of the US in the absence of the CS varied from 0 to .40. Conditioning was measured by the degree of response suppression. (After Rescorla, 1966)*

more likely following the tone than at other times (Rescorla, 1967, 1988; but see also Papini and Bitterman, 1990).

The absence of contingency   What happens when there is no contingency whatsoever? This is the case in which *probability of shock, given the tone* is equal to *probability of shock, without the tone.* On the face of it, there is nothing to learn here, since the tone provides no information. But the animal does learn something in this situation: It learns that there is danger in this setting, and, crucially, it learns that it can never feel safe.

To see how this works, consider two contrasting situations. In the first, the CS signals that shock is likely to follow. When the CS appears, the animal will become fearful. But when there is no CS, the animal can relax, for now shock is less likely. The absence of the CS has become a safety signal, an inhibitor of fear (see pp. 124–25).

In the second situation, the arrangement is different. This time, no stimulus predicts when shock will occur. Now, there is no CS to elicit fear, but from the animal's point of view, this makes things worse, not better. Without the CS, there is no safety signal, and as a result, the animal must be afraid all the time.

The difference between signaled and unsignaled shock may also be related to a distinction frequently made between *fear* and *anxiety.* Fear is elicited by a specific situation or object, whereas anxiety is chronic, objectless, and occurs in many situations. A number of authors suggest that such unfocused anxiety is in part produced by unpredictability—in essence, by an absence of safety signals (Seligman, 1975; Schwartz and Robbins, 1995).

THE ROLE OF SURPRISE

How do animals manage to learn about contingencies? A pigeon is obviously not standing by with a calculator, tallying trials on which the CS was followed by a US and dividing this by the number of trials on which the US occurred alone. How, therefore, does it learn?

Researchers have proposed a number of mechanisms through which an organism might learn about contingencies. These mechanisms involve simple trial-by-trial adjustments in the strength of association between CS and US; there's no need for the animal to compute any sort of overall tally, comparing probabilities in one situation to probabilities in another. While there is some disagreement over the details, most researchers agree that a critical ingredient driving this process forward is the extent to which the US is surprising (that is, unexpected). If the US is unsurprising, then the animal's expectations were in line with reality, and so there is no point in adjusting those expectations. But when surprises occur, it's time to adjust: If a CS has been paired with a US in the past, but now appears alone, this will be something of a surprise, and will lead to a weakening of the CS–US connection; conversely, if the animal hasn't associated a CS with a US and now the two are paired, this will also be a surprise and so will lead to a strengthening of the association (Kamin, 1968; Rescorla and Wagner, 1972; but see also Miller, Barnet, and Grahame, 1995).

Blocking   Evidence for the role of surprise comes from a series of studies performed by Leon Kamin, who discovered a phenomenon called the **blocking effect.** Kamin's basic experiment was run in three stages. In Stage 1, the rats heard a hissing noise that was followed by a shock. As one might expect, this noise became a CS for conditioned fear. In Stage 2, the shock was preceded by two stimuli presented simultaneously: One was the same hissing noise used in Stage 1; the other was a light. In Stage 3, the light was presented alone to see whether it would also produce a conditioned fear reaction. The results show

TABLE 4.1 BLOCKING				
Group	Stage 1	Stage 2	Test	Result
I	Noise → shock	(Noise + Light) → shock	Light alone	No conditioned fear
II	—	(Noise + Light) → shock	Light alone	Conditioned fear

that it did not. Even though the light had been paired many times with the shock, no learning took place. Why? Because the light provided only redundant information: The animal already knew that a shock was coming; the hissing noise told it so. No new information was associated with the light, and no surprise was evoked by the light. Therefore, there was no learning.

In support of this interpretation, Kamin's study also included an important control group. These rats never went through Stage 1, beginning, instead, at Stage 2 (that is, light plus noise followed by shock). When these animals were later tested with the light alone, they exhibited a substantial conditioned fear response (Kamin, 1969; see Table 4.1 and Figure 4.23).

Humans are similarly alert to redundancy. Consider the practice among many U.S. radio stations of announcing the day's temperature in both Fahrenheit and Celsius. Initially, many educators hoped that this would teach listeners to use the Celsius scale—they would learn that an announcement of 1° (Celsius) is predictive of a cold day; an announcement of 25° is predictive of warmth. But this learning never happened: Listeners got all the information they needed from the familiar Fahrenheit number, and so they ignored, and learned nothing about, the Celsius numbers.

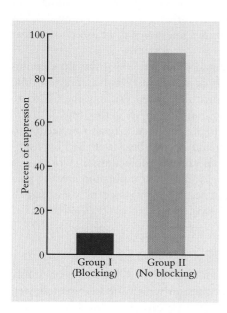

4.23 The effect of blocking *Results for the test phase of Kamin's blocking experiment in which the animals were presented with the light alone. Group I (in dark red) showed virtually no response suppression (and hence no fear conditioning), indicating that the initial pairing of noise and shock in Stage 1 had blocked the recognition of the light-shock contingency during Stage 2. Group II (in blue) had no such prior pairings and showed no blocking effect. (After Kamin, 1969)*

A COGNITIVE VIEW OF INSTRUMENTAL CONDITIONING

The cognitive perspective provides many insights into classical conditioning, helping us to understand both what is learned and what produces the learning. A similar cognitive account applies to instrumental conditioning. Here, too, learning involves more than the mere strengthening or weakening of a particular response. Instead, what the animal acquires is an internal representation of the relationship between the response and the reinforcer that follows it. It doesn't just learn to press a bar; it learns that the bar press leads to a food pellet. In effect, the animal learns to associate an act with its outcome, an association referred to as an ***act-outcome representation*** (Tolman, 1932).

EVIDENCE FOR ACT-OUTCOME ASSOCIATIONS

Many studies demonstrate that new knowledge can be acquired without a corresponding change in behavior. The organism will demonstrate its new knowledge only when that knowledge acquires significance for the organism. Psychologists use the term ***latent learning*** to describe this pattern—learning that is not yet evident in the animal's behavior.

Latent learning can be demonstrated in many contexts. A classic example is an experiment in which rats were allowed to explore a maze without any reward for ten days. There was no detectable change in their behavior during these days, but latent learning was nonetheless taking place: The rats were learning how to navigate the maze's corridors. This became obvious on the eleventh day, when food was placed in the maze's goal box for the first time. The rats learned to run to this goal box, virtually without error, almost immediately. The knowledge they had acquired earlier now took on motivational significance, and so the animals swiftly displayed what they already knew (Tolman and Honzik, 1930).

Act-outcome associations can also be displayed directly. In an elegant study, rats were trained to make two different responses, each of which produced a different reward. On some days, their experimental chamber contained a standard Skinner-box lever that projected from one wall. If the animals pressed this lever, they were rewarded with a food pellet. On other days, instead of the lever a chain dangled from the ceiling. If the rats pulled this chain, they were rewarded with a few drops of sugar water.

After a few days of training, the rats were busily lever pressing and chain pulling, indicating that instrumental learning had been effective. But exactly what was it that had been learned? One possibility is that the rats had simply acquired a tendency to perform these two responses. Another is that they acquired some knowledge—that bar pressing leads to food pellets and chain pulling leads to sugar water.

To decide between these alternatives, the experimenters changed the attractiveness of one of the rewards. They allowed the rats to drink some of the sugar water, but then gave them injections of a mild toxin. This created a taste aversion for the sugar (but not for the pellets), so that the rats no longer found the sugar water desirable. (For more on taste aversions, see pp. 149–51.) What effects would this have when the animals were next given the chance to press a lever or pull a chain? The results showed that the rats continued to press the lever to obtain food, but they no longer pulled the chain. Clearly, the animals had learned which response led to which reward (Colwill and Rescorla, 1985; Rescorla, 1991, 1993a, b; see Figure 4.24).★

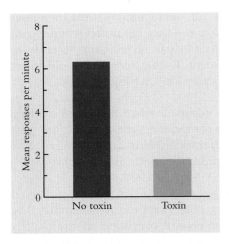

4.24 Act-outcome cognitions *The figure shows the results on the final test of an experiment in which two different responses were reinforced by two different food rewards. Subsequently, one of the two rewards was paired with a toxin. There was a marked decline in the response leading to the reward that was devalued by the toxin (in blue) as compared with the response leading to the reward that was not devalued (dark red). (After Colwill and Rescorla, 1985)*

CONTINGENCY IN INSTRUMENTAL CONDITIONING

We have seen that classical conditioning depends on the contingency between the CS and the US, and not their mere contiguity. A similar relation holds for instrumental conditioning. Here, the relevant contingency is between an act and its outcome. If the act is lever pressing and the outcome is a food pellet, then the contingency depends on the probability of getting a pellet when the lever has been pressed, compared to the probability of getting one when the lever has not been pressed. If the first probability is greater than the second, getting food is contingent upon lever pressing. If the two probabilities are equal, there is no contingency—lever pressing and getting pellets are independent.†

Response control in infants One line of evidence for the importance of contingency in instrumental conditioning comes from studies of human infants. In one study, the infants were placed in cribs above which a colorful mobile was suspended. Whenever the infants moved their heads, they closed a switch in their pillows, and this activated the overhead mobile, which spun merrily for a second or so. The infants soon learned to shake their heads about, making their mobiles

---

★ For half the rats, a taste aversion was established for the pellets rather than the sugar water. When subsequently tested, these rats pulled the chain (which led to the sugar water) and did not press the lever (which led to the pellets).

† If the second probability is greater than the first, then getting the pellet is contingent upon *not* pressing the lever. This kind of contingency is common whenever one wants the learner to refrain from doing something, for example: "I'll give you a cookie if you stop whining."

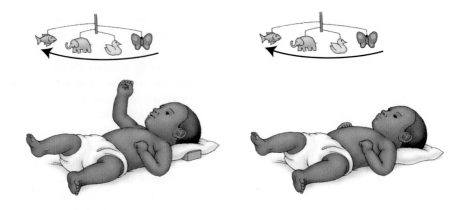

4.25 Response control *Infants who can make a mobile move smile and coo at it, while those who have no control over its motion stop smiling.*

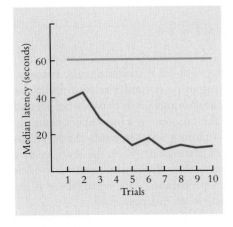

4.26 Learned helplessness *The figure shows the shuttle-box performance of two groups of dogs. On each trial, the animal could escape or avoid a shock. If it jumped within ten seconds after the CS, it avoided the shock altogether; if it did not jump within sixty seconds, the trial was terminated. The figure shows how quickly the animals jumped. The animals in Group A (dark red) had previously received electric shocks that they could escape by performing an instrumental response. The animals in Group B (blue) received the same shocks, but were unable to do anything about them. (After Maier, Seligman, and Solomon, 1969)*

turn. They evidently enjoyed this, smiling and cooing at their mobiles, clearly delighted to see them move.

A second group of infants was exposed to a similar situation, but with one important difference: Their mobile turned just as often as the mobile for the first group, but it was moved for them, not by them. And this turned out to be crucial: After a few days, these infants no longer smiled and cooed at the mobile, nor did they seem particularly interested when it turned. This suggests that what the first group of infants liked about the mobile was not that it moved but that they made it move. Clearly, then, infants can distinguish between response-controlled and response-independent outcomes—they can detect when a contingency is present and when it is absent. And infants, no less than we, prefer to exercise some control over their environment. Even a two-month-old infant wants to be the master of her own fate (Watson, 1967; see Figure 4.25).

Helplessness in dogs The mobile-turning infants illustrate the joy of mastery. Another highly influential series of studies demonstrates the despair of no mastery at all. The focus of these studies is on ***learned helplessness,*** an acquired sense that one can no longer control one's environment, with the sad consequence that one gives up trying (Seligman, 1975).

The classic experiment on learned helplessness used two groups of dogs, *A* and *B,* who received strong electric shocks while strapped in a hammock. The dogs in group *A* were able to exert some control over their situation. They could turn the shock off whenever it began simply by pushing a panel that was placed close to their noses. The dogs in group *B* had no such power. For them, the shocks were inescapable. But the number and duration of these shocks were exactly the same as for the first group. This was guaranteed by the fact that, for each dog in group *A,* there was a corresponding animal in group *B* whose fate was yoked to that of the first dog. Whenever the group *A* dog was shocked, so was the group *B* dog. Whenever the group *A* dog turned off the shock, the shock was turned off for the group *B* dog. This ensures that the physical suffering meted out to both groups was precisely the same. What was different was what they could do about it. Group *A* was able to exercise some control; group *B* could only endure.

What do the group *B* dogs learn in this situation? To find out, both groups of dogs were next presented with a standard avoidance learning task in which they had to jump from one compartment to another to avoid a shock (Figure 4.26). The dogs in group *A* learned this task easily. During the first few trials, these dogs ran about frantically when the shock began but eventually scrambled over the hurdle into the other compartment. Better still, they soon learned to jump before their grace period was up, thus avoiding shock entirely. Things were different, though, for the dogs in group *B,* the dogs who had previously experienced the inescapable shock. Initially, these dogs behaved much like any others, running about, barking, and so on. But they soon became much more passive. They lay down, whined quietly, and simply took whatever shocks were delivered. They neither avoided nor escaped; they just gave up trying. In the first phase of this experiment, they really had been objectively helpless; there truly was nothing they could do. But in the shuttle box, their helplessness was only subjective, for there was now a way in which they could make their lot bearable. But they never discovered it. They had learned to be helpless (Seligman and Maier, 1967).

Helplessness and depression   Martin Seligman, one of the discoverers of the learned helplessness effect, asserts that a similar mechanism underlies the development of certain kinds of depression in humans. (For further discussion of depression, see Chapter 18.) Just like animals who have been rendered helpless, these patients show no initiative, and "just sit there." Both are slow to learn that something they did was successful; both lose weight and have little interest in others. To Seligman and his associates these parallels suggest that the underlying cause is the same in both cases. Like the helpless dog, the depressed patient has come to believe that his acts are of no avail. And Seligman argues that, like the dog, the depressed patient was brought to this morbid state by an initial exposure to a situation in which he really was helpless. While the dog received inescapable shocks in its hammock, the patient found himself powerless in the face of bereavement, some career failure, or serious illness (Seligman, Klein, and Miller, 1976). In both cases, the outcome is the same—a belief that there is no contingency between acts and outcomes and so no point in trying. (For more on this theory of depression, and for some discussion of the theory's limitations, see Chapter 18.)

VARIETIES OF LEARNING

Until fairly recently, investigators were primarily interested in discovering general laws of learning—laws that would apply to all organisms, all behaviors, and all situations. We know, of course, that humans and other primates are capable of behaviors and cognitions more complex than those produced by other animals, but it's still plausible that these behaviors are learned and maintained by the same broad rules, rules that emphasize (for example) the role of contingency, the importance of discrimination, and so on.

As we have seen, this perspective has much to recommend it. Some principles of learning do seem remarkably general, and we have commented in this chapter on the many parallels between human and nonhuman behavior. Recognition of this generality has allowed us to gain insights into human depression by studying helplessness in dogs; it has increased our understanding of human drug addiction, thanks to research on classical conditioning in rats. Different species share many biological traits and, it seems, many psychological traits as well.

During the last few decades, though, researchers have begun to place more and more emphasis on the differences, from one species to the next, in how learning proceeds. This emphasis is urged, in particular, by investigators who have adopted an *evolutionary perspective* on learning (e.g., Roper, 1983; Bolles and Beecher, 1988; Rozin and Schull, 1988).

BIOLOGICAL CONSTRAINTS ON ASSOCIATIVE LEARNING: BELONGINGNESS

In the early days of learning theory, there was a widespread belief that animals are capable of connecting any CS to any US (in classical conditioning) and of associating virtually any response with any reinforcer (in instrumental conditioning). A dog could be taught that a tone signaled the approach of food or that a flashing light or a particular smell did. Likewise, a rat could be trained to press a lever to get food, water, or access to a sexually receptive mate.

This broad claim is sometimes called the **equipotentiality principle**—the idea that there is an "equal potential" for producing any association we might choose. But much evidence speaks against this idea. Instead, each species seems to have certain predispositions toward forming some associations and not others. These put **biological constraints** on that species' learning, governing what it can learn easily and what it cannot learn at all. These constraints are probably hardwired and help each species adjust readily to the requirements of the environment in which it evolved (Rozin and Kalat, 1971, 1972; Seligman and Hager, 1972).

CS-US RELATIONS IN CLASSICAL CONDITIONING

An important constraint on learning comes from the fact that, from an animal's point of view, some stimuli belong together and some do not—a pattern clearly contrary to the equipotentiality principle. Much of the evidence for this phenomenon of **belongingness** comes from an effect we have already touched on: **learned taste aversion** (Garcia and Koelling, 1966; Domjan, 1983).

Belongingness and learned taste aversions   As we described in Chapter 3, rats are remarkably adept at learning to avoid foods that, in the past, have made them sick. This is the reason why it is so difficult to exterminate wild rats with poison: The rat takes a small bite of the poisoned food, becomes ill, generally recovers, and thereafter avoids that particular flavor: The animal has become bait shy. Similar effects are easily observed in the laboratory. The subjects (usually rats) are presented with a given flavor, such as water containing the artificial sweetener saccharin. After drinking some of this sweetened water, they are exposed to X-ray radiation—not enough to injure them but enough to make them ill. After they recover, if they are given a choice between, say, plain water and the saccharine solution, they will refuse to drink the sweetened water even though they much preferred this sweet-tasting drink prior to their illness.

This sort of learned taste aversion seems to be based on classical conditioning. The CS is a certain flavor (here, sweetness) and the US is the sensation of being sick. In this case, though, the classical conditioning is quite rapid, and one pairing of CS and US is enough to establish the connection between them. Researchers call this **one-trial learning.**

In addition to their rapidity, learned taste aversions are also remarkable for their specificity. In one early study, thirsty rats were allowed to drink sweetened water through a drinking tube. Whenever the rats licked the nozzle of this tube, a bright light flashed and a clicking noise sounded. Thus the sensations of sweetness, bright light, and loud noise were always grouped together; if one was presented, all were presented. Some time later, one group of these rats received an electric shock to the feet. A second group was exposed to a dose of X rays strong enough to produce illness.

Arbitrary learning by operant techniques
Animals can be trained to perform all manner of arbitrary responses by operant techniques, as in the case of this cat that plays the piano. But there are important biological constraints that make some responses more difficult to learn than others. The cat has trouble learning to press the piano keys for food because its natural tendency is to importune people (or as a kitten, its mother) to feed it. (Photograph courtesy of Animal Behavior Enterprises)

TABLE 4.2 BELONGINGNESS IN CLASSICAL CONDITIONING

Training	In all groups: CS = saccharine taste + light + sound			
US:	Shock		X-ray illness	
Test: water with	Saccharine taste	Light + sound	Saccharine taste	Light + sound
Results	No effect	Aversion	Aversion	No effect

Notice, then, that we have two different US's—illness for one group, and foot-shock for the other. In addition, both groups have received a three-part CS: sweet + bright + noisy. The question is: How will the animals put these pieces together? What will get associated with what?

To find out, the experimenters tested the rats in a new situation. They gave some of the rats water that was saccharin-flavored but was unacccompanied by either light or noise. Rats who had received foot-shock showed no inclination to avoid this water; apparently, they did not associate foot-shock with the sweet flavor. However, rats who had been made ill with X rays refused to drink the sweet water, even though the light and noise were absent. They associated their illness with the taste (Table 4.2).

Other rats were tested with plain, unflavored water accompanied by the light and sound cues that were present during training. Now the pattern was reversed: Rats who had become ill showed no objection to this water; they did not associate illness with sights and sounds. Rats who had been shocked refused it. In their minds, pain was associated with bright lights and loud clicks (Garcia and Koelling, 1966).

These results clearly undermine the equipotentiality principle. For the rat, taste goes with illness, sights and sounds with externally induced pain. And for this species, this pattern makes good biological sense. Illness, for many creatures, is likely to have been caused by some novel or perhaps tainted food. And in the wild, the rat selects its food largely on the basis of flavor. With this setup, it's sensible for rats to avoid tastes they associate with illness; this will ensure that they do not resample the harmful berries or tainted meat. There is survival value in the rat's tendency to ask itself, whenever it has a stomachache, "What did I eat?"

By this logic, one might expect a different pattern with a species that chooses its foods based on another sense. For example, many birds make their food choices largely on the basis of vision; how will this affect the data? In one study, quail were given blue, sour water to drink and were then poisoned. Some of the birds were later tested with blue, unflavored water; others were tested with water that was sour but colorless. The results showed that the quail had developed a drastic aversion to blue water, but they drank just about as much sour water as they had before being poisoned. Here, the learned aversion was evidently based on color rather than taste (Wilcoxin, Dragoin, and Kral, 1971).

Clearly, what belongs with what depends on the species being studied. Birds are generally disposed to associate illness with visual cues. Rats (and many other mammals) associate illness with taste. In each case, this bias makes the animal more prepared to form certain associations and far less prepared to form others (Seligman, 1970).

Learned taste aversions and the CS-US interval   Taste-aversion learning is remarkable in yet one more way. In most examples of classical conditioning, the interval between CS and US must be relatively short; if more than a few seconds separate these two events, learning proceeds much more slowly. But for taste aversions, the

Learned food aversions in birds *In contrast to rats and humans, whose learned food aversions are usually based on taste and odor, most birds rely on visual cues. The figure shows the reaction of a bird who has just eaten a monarch butterfly, which contains distasteful and poisonous substances. The distinctive wing pattern of this butterfly provides the cue for an immediately acquired food aversion, for after one such mistake the bird will never again seize another monarch. (Courtesy of Lincoln P. Brower, University of Florida)*

optimum CS-US interval seems to be about an hour; if the interval between CS and US is much shorter than this, learning will actually be retarded. Similarly, taste-aversion learning will still occur if the interval is as long as twenty-four hours (Garcia, Ervin, and Koelling, 1966; Rozin and Kalat, 1971; Logue, 1979).

There is still debate over how an animal manages to associate events so distant in time from each other (see Revusky, 1971, 1977, 1985; Rozin and Kalat, 1971; Domjan, 1980). But whatever the mechanism, the biological utility of this phenomenon is clear enough: Food ingested now won't affect an animal for many minutes (or hours), thanks to the fairly slow processes of digestion and absorption. Under the circumstances, a mechanism that allows an animal to connect its internal malaise with tastes experienced some time before makes excellent adaptive sense.

Taste aversion in humans Imagine a person who enjoys a delicious bowl of strawberry ice cream. Unfortunately, this person also has the flu, and so later that night, he becomes acutely nauseated. He knows he has the flu (there are, after all, many other symptoms). And he knows that the ice cream itself was innocent (after all, the rest of his family ate the same dessert, without ill effects). But despite these beliefs, this individual is likely to develop a taste aversion, just as a rat would. The mere thought of strawberry ice cream is now utterly revolting, a reaction that may last for years (Logue, 1986).

Human taste aversions provide important information about learning, but they also have important practical implications. Cancer patients undergoing chemotherapy often experience intense nausea, a side effect of the therapeutic drugs. This nausea may lead to a taste aversion for foods eaten prior to the treatment, which in some cases can lead to a total refusal to eat. This pattern was demonstrated in a study in which cancer patients were given a novel tasting ice cream before a chemotherapy session. Many of these patients developed a strong aversion to that particular flavor, even though they knew that their nausea was caused by the chemotherapy and not the ice cream. This study suggests that cancer patients' reluctance to eat might be minimized by their avoiding meals—especially meals including novel foods—shortly before treatment (Bernstein, 1978).

ACT-OUTCOME RELATIONS IN INSTRUMENTAL CONDITIONING

Clearly, then, the CS-US relation in classical conditioning is far from arbitrary. A CS belongs with certain USs and not with others. Similarly for instrumental learning: From an animal's point of view, certain responses belong with some rewards and not others (Shettleworth, 1972).

Consider a pigeon pecking away in a Skinner box. Pigeons can easily be taught to peck a lit key in order to obtain food or water. But it is exceedingly difficult to train a pigeon to peck in order to escape or avoid electric shock (Hineline and Rachlin, 1969). In contrast, pigeons can easily be taught to hop or flap their wings in order to get away from shock, but it is difficult to train the pigeon to produce these same responses in order to gain food or water.

According to Robert Bolles, these results reflect the fact that most animals have built-in reactions to danger. For the pigeon, the ***species-specific defense reaction*** is speedy locomotion, preferably by flying away. There's no need therefore to *teach* a pigeon to fly away whenever danger comes; this is the bird's natural reaction. Likewise, birds easily learn to hop or flap their wings in the face of danger, because these responses are close cousins to the innate defense pattern. The pecking response, however, is quite distant from this innate defense pattern, making it difficult for the pigeon to learn pecking as an escape response (Bolles, 1970).

Similar logic explains why it's easy to teach pigeons to peck a key to gain food. Pecking is what pigeons do naturally when they consume food, so the pigeon's response to a lit key in the animal chamber merely reflects its normal behavior. In essence, the pigeon is reacting to the key in the same way that it reacts to the reward. And, in fact, their key-pecks in this situation actually resemble the key-pecks observed with eating. The key-pecks are different if thirsty pigeons are trained to peck at a key to obtain water; those pecks resemble the beak movements pigeons make while drinking (Figure 4.27). The pattern of key-pecking is still different if the pigeon's pecks are rewarded with access to a sexually receptive mate. Now the pigeons coo as they press the key. It seems, then, that the pigeon "eats" the key when working for food, "drinks" it when working for water, and "courts" it when working for sex. Clearly, the relation between the response and its reinforcer is intimate and nonarbitrary (Schwartz and Robbins, 1995).

A number of psychologists have argued that these findings indicate a role for classical conditioning within instrumental conditioning. The pigeon's peck may be a CR, rather than an instrumental response; the food (or water or access to the mate) may be a US, rather than a reward for a response. Given this view, it's entirely sensible that different rewards (USs) yield different responses (CRs).

Support for this suggestion comes from a study in which naive pigeons were placed in a box with a response key that lit up periodically. The key stayed lit for six seconds, and if the pigeon didn't peck the key during this interval, food was

A

B

4.27 Key pecking for food and water (A) The pictures show a pigeon's beak movements as it pecks a key to obtain water. The movements resemble those the bird makes when it drinks. (B) These pictures show quite different beak movements made when the bird pecks a key for food. Now the movements resemble those the animal makes when it eats. (Photographs by Bruce Moore, from Jenkins and Moore, 1973)

delivered. But if it did peck the key, the light went out and no food was presented. Here, food reward was contingent upon *not* pecking. But the pigeons pecked anyway (Williams and Williams, 1969). The CS-US contingency (here, lit key and food) evidently outweighed the response-outcome contingency (here, not pecking and food). This may be another way of saying that the response was in large part a classically conditioned CR, elicited by the CS, rather than an operant under the animal's control (Schwartz and Gamzu, 1977; Burnes and Malone, 1992).

THE "MISBEHAVIOR" OF ORGANISMS

Still further evidence against the equipotentiality principle comes from observations by psychologists who train animals to perform as live advertising exhibits. We mentioned these cases earlier, in our discussion of shaping (see pp. 132–33), and, by and large, this training can accomplish a great deal. In some cases, however, the trained animals "misbehave" in an interesting fashion. An example is a raccoon that was supposed to pick up several coins and then deposit them into a small piggy bank. To create this response, the animal was first rewarded merely for picking up a coin; the reward was a bit of food. Once this was established, the raccoon was reinforced only if it picked up the coin and dropped it into a container. This was more difficult, for the raccoon refused to let the coin go. It would rub the coin against the container, pull it back out, clutch it for a while, and release it only after considerable hesitation.

The next step was even worse. Now the animal was required to pick up two coins and deposit them both. The raccoon refused. Instead of acting like a model savings-bank customer, it rubbed the two coins together, dipped them into the container, pulled them out again, rubbed them together, and so on. It appeared that the raccoon had reverted to a species-specific behavior pattern: Raccoons in the wild tend to rub food objects together and dunk or "wash" them. This same behavior emerged in the training, despite reinforcement contingencies to the contrary. Here, as in our previous examples, the relation between the instrumental response and its reinforcer is not arbitrary. The trainers wanted the animal to learn a novel response (deposit two coins). But the animal's behavior drifted instead toward the response it was biologically predisposed to perform under these conditions (Breland and Breland, 1961).

ADAPTIVE SPECIALIZATIONS OF LEARNING

As we have now seen, animals come biologically prepared to make certain associations and not others. Clearly, the laws of learning must somehow be modified to encompass the relationship between a particular CS and a particular US or between a particular reinforcer and a particular response. But some theorists go further than this. They contend that it's not enough merely to modify the laws of learning; we may also need some new laws. That's because, according to their view, some forms of learning are not general at all, but instead are specific to the species that does the learning and to what it is that gets learned.

DIFFERENCES IN WHAT DIFFERENT SPECIES LEARN

Different animals have vastly different anatomies and also different behaviors: lions stalk, antelopes run, and hyenas wait around to scavenge for leftovers. A similar diversity may arise when we consider the processes of learning. Propo-

A

B

Biological constraints on learning *(A) The chicken pulls the loop on the jukebox to start the music, then "dances" on the platform by scratching the floor. The scratching is not reinforced but is a built-in tendency of the chicken when it seeks food. (B) The "gold-mining pig" tends to toss the nuggets around and root them even though this delays its reinforcement. Rooting is a natural tendency of the pig in food-seeking situations; in this case, it leads to "misbehavior," since it interferes with the desired operant response. (Photographs courtesy of Animal Behavior Enterprises)*

Adaptive specialization of learning A black-capped chickadee hiding a seed in one of many holes in a specially constructed laboratory tree. This bird has been shown to have a remarkable spatial memory: It hides over a hundred seeds per day, each in a different location, and remembers where these seeds were deposited for up to fourteen days. (From Dr. David Sherry; photograph courtesy of Susan Bradnam)

nents of the evolutionary perspective argue that some animals learn in ways that others cannot (Roper, 1983; Gallistel, 1990).

An often cited example is the Clark's nutcracker, a bird that makes its home in the American Southwest and is a distant cousin of jays and crows. In the summer this bird buries thousands of pine nuts in various hiding places over an area of several square miles. Then, throughout the winter and early spring, the nutcracker flies back again and again to dig up its thousands of caches. The bird does not mark the burial sites in any special way. Instead, it relies on memory—a prodigious feat that few of us could duplicate.

We know that the Clark's nutcracker has a number of anatomical features, not shared by other birds, that support its food-hoarding activities. For example, this bird has a special pouch under its tongue that it fills with pine nuts when flying to find a hiding place. The bird's remarkable spatial memory, and its extraordinary ability to learn a huge number of geographical locations, is probably a similar evolutionary adaptation, with obvious survival benefits. And like the tongue-pouch, this learning ability is a specialty of this species: Related birds, such as jays and pigeons, don't store food in this way, and when tested, they have a correspondingly poorer spatial memory (Shettleworth, 1983, 1984, 1990; Olson, 1991).

The nutcracker's memory specialization is also visible in another way. There is reason to believe that the hippocampus is the part of the bird's brain essential for this learning. When lesioned in the hippocampus, food-storing birds can't locate their caches. And in line with the evolutionary perspective, it turns out that food-storing species possess a hippocampus that's twice the size of those found in species that don't store food.

Many phenomena of animal learning—in birds, fish, and mammals—reveal similar specializations. In each case, the organism has some extraordinary ability not shared even by closely related species. In each case, the ability has obvious survival value. And in each case, the ability seems interestingly narrow: The nutcracker has no special skill in remembering pictures or shapes; instead, its remarkable memory comes into play only in the appropriate context—hiding, and then relocating, buried pine nuts. Similarly, many birds show remarkable talent in learning the particular songs used by their species, but this skill can be used for no other purpose: A zebra finch easily masters the notes of the zebra-finch song but is utterly inept at learning any other (nonmusical) sequence of similar length and complexity.

Truly, then, these are specialized learning abilities—possessed just by a single species and applicable just to a particular task crucial for its members' survival (Marler, 1970; Gallistel, 1990; we will have much more to say about specialized learning abilities in humans in Chapters 9 and 13).

SIMILARITIES IN WHAT DIFFERENT SPECIES LEARN

The evolutionary perspective raises an interesting question for us: Different species live in different environments with different survival needs. They need different skills and may need to learn in different ways. But if this is the case, why are there so many similarities in learning from one species to the next? To put this in more concrete terms, rats and pigeons don't gather food the way a honey bee does; they don't communicate with their fellows the way the bee does; they also have nervous systems that are vastly different from the bee's and have an entirely different evolutionary history. So it would not be surprising to discover that they learn in different ways as well. And yet, as we have repeatedly noted, the major phenomena of conditioning are found in honey bees just as they are in rats and pigeons (Couvillon and Bitterman, 1980).

We can understand the *specialized* forms of learning with reference to a species' ecological niche and its evolutionary history. But how should we think about the equally important fact that there are also *general* forms of learning, shared from one species to the next?

The answer to this question lies in the fact that various creatures, while living in very different environments, all live in the same physical world. Thus, all are subject to the laws of gravity. All require energy in order to survive. And all need to learn certain things: In our shared world, it pays to be prepared for upcoming events, and that preparation is made possible by the fact that some events are predictable from (contingent upon) other events. Similarly, in the world we all share, important outcomes are often influenced in a systematic way by one's behavior. As a result, it will be useful for all creatures to learn about the consequences of their actions and to adjust their future acts accordingly.

All creatures share certain ways of learning, therefore, because the environment poses analogous challenges for them all. A porpoise, a porcupine, and a person all increase their chances of survival if they can learn to anticipate, and prepare for, upcoming events. No wonder then that each is capable of classical conditioning. The specific brain processes supporting this learning might differ from species to species, but the characteristics of the learning are the same, a natural consequence of the relationships among events in the world. As one example, consider the superiority of forward to backward conditioning—a natural consequence of the fact that, in our world, time only flows in one direction, with the cause always preceding the effect.

Likewise for instrumental conditioning: For all species, it pays to repeat actions that have worked well in the past and to abandon actions that have not been successful. Hence, we might expect natural selection to favor mechanisms that allow creatures to detect the relationships between their own actions and the consequences of those actions. It is these mechanisms that allow instrumental conditioning.

Thus, there are pragmatic reasons why principles of learning are (and perhaps must be) shared from ones species to the next. So while our account of learning must include some important species-specific differences in how learning proceeds, it must also include some general principles, such as those governing classical and instrumental conditioning. Organisms do differ in their learning capacities, but we can also find important principles—often rather specific principles—that describe learning in an extraordinary range of species and settings.

THE NEURAL BASIS FOR LEARNING

In the previous section, we asked *why* so many creatures show the capacities we call classical and instrumental conditioning. A related question is *how* they achieve these forms of learning. What mechanisms make this learning possible?

It is almost certain that learning involves changes in how neurons function, both internally and in their communication with each other. In some cases, learning may involve the growth of new synapses or the inactivation of existing ones. In other cases, neurons may change in their sensitivity to stimulation, or they may change the amount of neurotransmitter they secrete when they are stimulated. In all cases, though, learning depends on **neural plasticity**—a capacity for neurons to change the way they function as a consequence of experience. But how do these changes in function come about?

To study the neural bases of learning, scientists have employed a common investigative strategy: exploring first the functioning of a relatively simple system and then building on what they've learned to understand more complex cases. Thus, much of what we know about neural plasticity has come from the study of the marine mollusk *Aplysia*.

Aplysia has an extremely simple nervous system, with a mere twenty thousand neurons or so (compared to the one-thousand billion or so in the human brain), and therefore has been a good candidate for detailed scrutiny and analysis. *Aplysia*'s behavior is also rather simple. Mostly, these animals just crawl and eat seaweed. If threatened, though, by a touch or a poke, *Aplysia* retracts both its gill, which is usually spread across its back, and its tubular siphon, which sucks in water and circulates it over the gill.

PRESYNAPTIC FACILITATION

What makes *Aplysia* especially valuable to investigators, however, is the fact that this animal is capable of a simple form of classical conditioning: In each learning trial, the animal is first touched lightly on its siphon (CS) and then, a moment later, shocked on its tail (US). Initially, the light touch is not enough to trigger a response but the tail shock is. But after a number of these CS-US pairings, the animal will respond to the CS alone. It has developed a new response—in effect, a CR.

What neural mechanisms make this possible? The tail shock activates a number of sensory neurons, which in turn activate the motoneurons that cause *Aplysia*'s gill to contract. These same motoneurons also receive activation from the sensory neurons triggered by the light touch (see Figure 4.28), but prior to learning, this is not enough to produce a response. Therefore, at the outset, the light touch (CS) does not trigger gill contraction.

Sensory neurons in *Aplysia* also stimulate *other* sensory neurons. Thus, to continue our example, the sensory neurons carrying the tail-shock message also end up stimulating the sensory neurons carrying the light-touch message. This stimulation

4.28 A mechanism for neural plasticity
Initially, the sensory signal resulting from tail shock is sufficient to cause gill contraction, but the signal resulting from a light touch on the siphon is not. However, the sensory neuron carrying the tail-shock message (via the modulatory neuron) also stimulates the other sensory neurons, including the one carrying the light-touch message. As a result, the light-touch neurons are eventually able to release enough neurotransmitter to activate the motoneurons on their own.

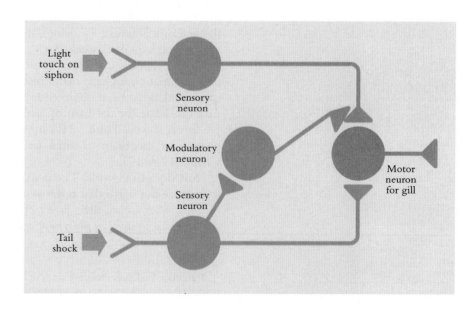

causes the light-touch neurons to increase the amount of neurotransmitter they release each time they fire, and impressively, investigators have been able to chart—molecule by molecule—the mechanisms through which this change takes place. As a result of this change, the light-touch neurons eventually release enough transmitter to activate the motoneurons on their own—and so the CS (light touch) eventually comes to produce a CR (gill contraction).

To be sure, what *Aplysia* learns is extremely simple. And there is reason to believe that some aspects of *Aplysia*'s neural functioning may be specific to *Aplysia*; other organisms may use somewhat different mechanisms. But even so, there is no question that our understanding of neural plasticity in *Aplysia*—in this case, an increase in neurotransmitter release as a result of experience—represents a tremendous step forward. It was one of the very first cases in which investigators could describe in detail how experience causes neurons to change their functioning, and the lessons learned from *Aplysia* have provided an enormously important stepping stone, as we seek to understand plasticity in more complex systems.

As we have discussed, both classical and instrumental conditioning involve learning about contingencies between events. In classical conditioning, the organism learns that the occurrence of one event (the CS) is correlated with the occurrence of another event (the US). In instrumental conditioning, the organism learns that the occurrence of a response (the operant) is correlated with the occurrence of an external event (the reinforcer). In both cases, the essence is the same: The organism learns about patterns of correlation—when event 1 happens, event 2 is more likely; in the *absence* of event 1, event 2 is *less* likely.

Thanks to the mechanism described above, even lowly *Aplysia* can learn about correlated events, and this is why these mechanisms are so important. In our example, *Aplysia* learned that a light siphon touch is correlated with tail shock: When the first occurs, the second is likely to follow. Thus the simple neural circuit shown in Figure 4.28 serves as a correlation detector, a crucial building block for more complex forms of learning.

LONG-TERM POTENTIATION

Other neural mechanisms may also serve as correlation detectors. One particularly important mechanism is **long-term potentiation (LTP)** (Bliss and Lømo, 1973; Martinez and Derrick, 1996)—"potentiation" because the mechanism involves an increase in the responsiveness of a neuron (an increase in the neuron's potential for firing), and "long term" because this potentiation lasts for days, perhaps even weeks.★

LTP is of special interest to investigators for two reasons. First, the longevity of this potentiation suggests that it may actually serve as the neural basis for memory. Second, it has been observed in a wide range of organisms, making it a plausible candidate for the basis of learning in all vertebrates, and perhaps in other life forms as well. Third, LTP can be easily demonstrated in the hippocampus, a portion of the brain essential for the creation of long-term memories (see Chapters 2 and 7).

How does LTP work? The neural mechanisms we described in *Aplysia* serve to increase the signal that is released from a sensory neuron. These mechanisms, in other words, have their direct effect on the sending side of the synapse, and are thus said to involve **presynaptic facilitation.** LTP, in contrast, is a **postsynaptic**

★ Another important building block of learning is *long-term depression (LTD)* through which the postsynaptic neuron becomes less sensitive as a function of experience.

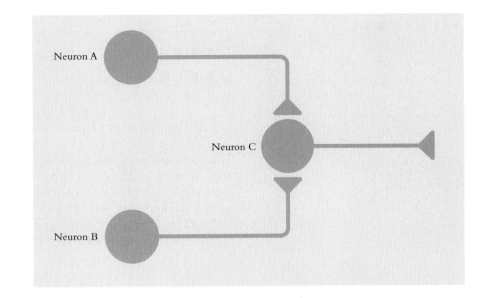

4.29 Long-term potentiation If neuron A fires over and over, neuron C will become more responsive to A than it was initially. This is the potentiation effect. If neuron B tends to fire at the same time as neuron A, then it too will benefit from this potentiation. In this way, the spread of potentiation is activity dependent—spreading only to neurons that were active at the same time as the neuron that caused the potentiation in the first place.

mechanism, influencing the receiving side of the synapse. Its main effect is to increase the receiving neuron's sensitivity, as a consequence of repeated stimulation. Thus, if neuron *A* (in Figure 4.29) fires rapidly, over and over, within a brief period of time, neuron *C* will become more responsive to *A* than it was initially. Moreover, and crucially, this potentiation can spread to other neurons with synapses on neuron *C,* such as neuron *B* in the figure.

To see how this happens, let us say that neuron *A* fires repeatedly within a short period of time. As a result, the receptors on neuron *C* that receive the neurotransmitter from neuron *A* will become more sensitive. This is the **potentiation effect.** But *C* also has other receptors, receiving input from other neurons. These receptors, too, will become more sensitive provided that these other neurons fire at the same time as neuron *A.* In other words, the spread of potentiation is **activity dependent** and will spread to neuron *B* only if *B* was active at the same time as the neuron that caused the potentiation in the first place, in this case, neuron *A* (McNaughton et al., 1978; Levy and Steward, 1979).

In this fashion, a single synapse can detect the fact that the activity of neurons *A* and *B* are correlated—they tend to fire together. As a consequence, the postsynaptic neuron (*C* in our example) now reacts more vigorously to both of them: If potentiation is produced for one, then it is produced for both.

It appears, therefore, that LTP provides a cellular mechanism through which associations can be detected and recorded in the brain. And remarkably, neurobiologists can provide a reasonably complete account of how this takes place. As with the presynaptic mechanism that underlies *Aplysia*'s plasticity, we now know, molecule by molecule, chemical reaction by chemical reaction, how LTP occurs (Kandel and Hawkins, 1992; Martinez and Derrick, 1996).

However, we need to voice the same caution here that we did in our discussion of *Aplysia:* There is, without question, a substantial gap between this very simple step of detecting an association and, say, the achievement of learning an act-outcome relationship. Nonetheless, many investigators have argued that LTP is indeed the basic building block of which more complex forms of learning are constructed. In fact, one article declared that LTP is likely to be "the primary cellular process of synaptic change that underlies learning and memory in the vertebrate brain" (Martinez and Derrick, 1996; for a more skeptical view, see Gallistel, 1995).

COMPLEX COGNITION IN ANIMALS

Let us pull away, though, from these microscopic events and return to a larger issue that we met earlier: As we have discussed, animals often know something without manifesting this knowledge in their actions. But what is the nature of this knowledge? How is it maintained and used? These will become crucial questions in Chapters 7 and 8, when we turn more fully to the topics of memory and thinking. But we can also examine the intellectual capacities relevant to the tasks we have already considered in this chapter. (For further discussion of the role of memory in the tasks we've been discussing, see Tarpy, 1997.)

COGNITIVE MAPS

In our earlier discussion of latent learning, we mentioned Tolman's claim that an animal can create a cognitive map, a mental representation of spatial layout, indicating what is where and what leads to what. It turns out that this spatial knowledge can be quite complex. Some of the evidence comes from studies of rats in radial-arm mazes, mazes with a central platform from which a number of pathways extend outward, like spokes in a wheel (Figure 4.30). In one experiment, each arm of the maze contained a food pellet. A hungry rat was placed on the center platform and allowed to move about freely. It generally explored a bit, then chose one of the arms, ran to its end, found the food pellet, and ate it. After a while, the rat returned to the maze's center.

What would it do next? The rat's optimal strategy is not to revisit the arm in which it had just eaten, for this arm is now empty. Instead, the rat should visit each arm just once, thus getting the most food for the least effort. To accomplish this, though, the rat must learn the maze's layout, and it must remember where it has been and where it hasn't. This is no problem for the rat, and performance in this task is nearly perfect: Given a radial maze of 8 arms, on average rats choose 7.9 different arms in 8 choices (Olton and Samuelson, 1976; Olton, 1978, 1979).

What rats can do, chimpanzees can do even better. Proof comes from a chimpanzee version of an Easter-egg hunt. The experimenter carried one animal at a time along an irregular route across a large open area. The experimenter's assistant accompanied them on this tour, and as they moved along, the assistant hid pieces of fruit at various locations. The chimpanzee was not allowed to do anything during this tour but merely watched as the bits of food were hidden. Nonetheless, the moment it was set down and allowed to move on its own, it dashed from one hiding place to the next, locating and eating the fruit. It had obviously learned, and remembered, the eighteen locations after just one trial of passive watching (Menzel, 1973, 1978; for evidence of cognitive maps in other creatures, including invertebrates, see Gallistel, 1994; Gould, 1990).

INSIGHTFUL BEHAVIOR

It seems, then, that the notion of a cognitive map is more than a figure of speech: There really is some representation of spatial layout in the animal's mind. Once again, therefore, our account of learning cannot rely only on descriptions of behavior and behavior change. Instead, we must make reference

4.30 A radial-arm maze *One pellet is placed at the end of each arm, so the rat earns the greatest reward for the least effort by choosing each arm once. (From Olton and Samuelson, 1976)*

COMPLEX COGNITION IN ANIMALS

Wolfgang Köhler *(Courtesy The Warder Collection)*

4.31 Tool using in chimpanzees *(A) Using a stick as a pole to climb up to a banana. (B) Using a stick as a club to beat down a banana. (C and D) Erecting three- and four-story structures to reach a banana. (From Köhler, 1925)*

to cognition—and perhaps complex cognition—occurring within the animal. The role of cognition is equally clear in another domain: the study of insightful learning.

Recall that Thorndike had argued that nonhuman animals solve problems through a process guided only by trial and error: The law of effect strengthens behaviors produced on the successful trials and weakens behaviors on the failed trials. But this claim was soon challenged by the German psychologist Wolfgang Köhler (1887–1968).

Köhler contended that some animals, at least, can behave intelligently. To be sure, Thorndike's cats had shown little sign of understanding the puzzle box, but perhaps cats are not the best subjects for determining the upper reaches of animal intellect. Animals more closely related to human beings, such as chimpanzees, might prove a better choice. Even more important, Köhler believed that Thorndike had loaded the dice in favor of blind trial and error by giving his cats problems that were impossible to solve in any other way. Thus, even an intellectual supercat could hit on the idea of yanking the wire that pulled the door latch only by chance; there was no other way to solve this problem, for all the strings and pulleys were hidden from the animal's view. To Köhler the real question was whether animals would behave intelligently when the conditions were optimal, when all of the ingredients of the solution were visibly present.

Köhler's procedure was simple. A chimpanzee was placed in an enclosed play area. Somewhere out of its reach was a desirable lure (usually a piece of fruit, such as a banana); to obtain this lure, the ape had to employ some nearby object as a tool. The animals had no problem with this task. They learned to use sticks as rakes to haul in bananas placed on the ground just outside the cage but beyond the reach of their arms. They also learned to use these sticks as clubs, to knock down fruit hung too high overhead. Some chimpanzees used the sticks as a pole as well. They stood it upright under the banana, frantically climbed up its fifteen-foot length, and grasped their reward just as the stick toppled over (a considerable intellectual as well as gymnastic feat, demonstrating the virtues of a healthy mind in a healthy body). The chimpanzees also learned to use boxes as "climb-upon-ables," dragging them under the banana and then stepping atop them to claim their prizes. Eventually they even became builders, piling boxes on top of boxes and finally erecting structures that went up to four (rather shaky) stories, as Köhler spurred them on to ever-greater architectural accomplishments by progressively raising the height of the lure (Figure 4.31).

A

B

C

D

4.32 Tool making in chimpanzees
Sultan making a double stick. (From Köhler, 1925)

Occasionally the apes became tool-makers as well as tool-users. For example, when in need of a stick, they might break a branch off a nearby tree. Even more impressive was one feat by a particularly gifted chimpanzee named Sultan, who was faced with a banana far out of his reach. There were two bamboo sticks in his cage, but neither of them was long enough to rake in the lure. After many attempts to reach the banana with one stick or another, Sultan finally hit upon the solution. He pushed the thinner of the two sticks into the hollow inside of the thicker one and then drew the banana toward himself, his reach now extended by the length of two sticks (Figure 4.32).

Köhler argued that these achievements were not the result of trial and error, nor the product of some mechanical strengthening of response tendencies. On the contrary, the animals behaved as if they had attained **insight** into the problem and into the relationship crucial for solving the problem. In support of this conclusion, Köhler offered several observations. To begin with, the insightful solution often came quite suddenly, sometimes after a pause during which the chimpanzee only moved its head and eyes, as if studying the situation. In addition, once each problem had been solved, the animals could smoothly and easily solve it again and again, as if they knew what they were doing. This stands in marked contrast to Thorndike's cats who went on fumbling for many trials, even after their first success.

But the most convincing evidence for Köhler's claims came from tests in which the situation was changed somewhat, in order to determine what skills the animals would transfer from the original task to the new setting. Such **transfer of training tests** are, in general, a useful means of finding out what has been learned in a situation. Teachers use just this approach to find out what their students have understood. Consider a young child who quickly answers "7" when confronted by the symbols "3 + 4 = ?" Has he really grasped the notion of addition? A simple test might be to present him with another problem, "4 + 3 = ?" If he is now bewildered, he presumably has learned merely to give a specific answer to a specific question. But is his reply again is "7," he may be on the way to genuine arithmetic insight.

Köhler used similar tests on his chimpanzees. For example, he took animals who had previously learned to use a box as a platform and presented them with yet another high lure, but now with all the boxes removed from the scene. The animals were untroubled by this. They were quick to find other objects, such as a table or a small ladder, which they promptly dragged to the proper place, allowing them to climb up and grab the fruit. On one occasion, Sultan did something even more impressive: He came over to Köhler, pulled him by the arm until he was under the banana, and then showed that in a pinch even the director of the Prussian anthropoid station would do as a climb-upon-able.

In one way, this pattern of transfer might seem to be just another example of stimulus generalization. We know that a dog who has been conditioned, say, to salivate to a tone of 1,000 hertz will also salivate when presented with a tone of 1,500 hertz. Köhler argued, though, that the transfer displayed by his chimpanzees was quite different from this. Stimulus generalization ordinarily depends on perceptual similarity. An animal will generalize its prior learning to a novel stimulus if that stimulus looks or sounds or feels like the stimulus used in the earlier training. But things are different with the chimpanzees. When Sultan figured out that he could reach the high banana by climbing on Köhler, this was not because Köhler looked like the climbed-upon box used during training. Instead, the key relationship was conceptual: Sultan saw that, despite their perceptual differences, boxes and human experimenters were alike in just the crucial way: Each was capable of supporting Sultan's weight, allowing him to climb up. This attention to conceptual elements, and the ability to focus on just the attributes that matter, ignoring the perceptual differences, was for Köhler the mark of genuine understanding.

COMPLEX PERCEPTUAL CONCEPTS IN ANIMALS

Köhler was duly impressed by his apes' attention to conceptual categories—for example, the category of climb-upon-ables. But perceptually based categories can also grow quite complex. For example, pigeons in one study were trained to peck a key whenever a picture of water was in view, but not to peck otherwise. Some of the water pictures showed flowing water; some showed still water. Some showed large bodies of water photographed from far away; some showed small puddles photographed close-up. Despite this diversity, pigeons rapidly mastered this discrimination task and so seemed to have grasped the category *water* (Herrnstein, Loveland, and Cable, 1976). Similar procedures have shown that pigeons can discriminate between pictures of trees and pictures not showing trees, with (as before) considerable diversity in the tree pictures actually shown. Thus, pigeons can learn to peck in response to a picture of a leaf-covered tree or a tree bare of leaves, but they won't peck in response to a picture of a telephone pole or a picture of a celery stalk. Likewise, pigeons can learn to peck whenever they are shown a picture of a particular human, whether photographed from one angle, close-up, from a very different angle, wearing different clothes, or from far away (e.g., Herrnstein, 1979; Lea and Ryan, 1983).

Some investigators conclude from these studies that pigeons have the concept *water,* or *tree,* and so on. If they do, it is surely a concept very different from the concept humans hold. Humans recognize pictures of water, but they also understand a great deal about water and about the relationship between water and many other concepts. What the pigeons have learned to do is complex to be sure, but it is a far cry from the sort of concepts we hold. (For further discussion of concepts, see Reisberg, 1997.)

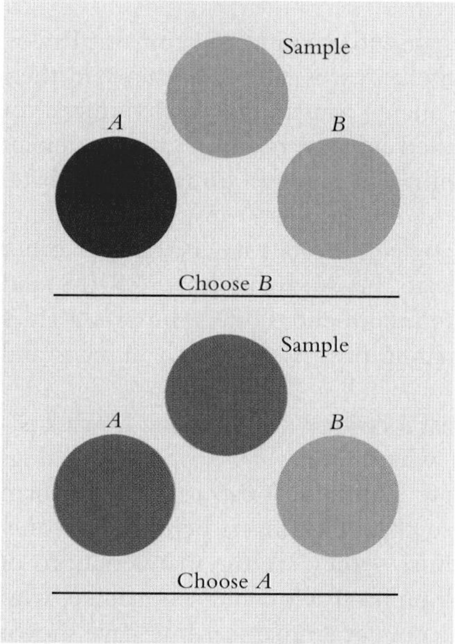

ABSTRACT CONCEPTS IN ANIMALS

What about more abstract concepts and more abstract relationships? Much research has scrutinized this point, focusing on the relationships of *same* and *different*.

Some of the evidence comes from studies by Ann and David Premack, who have tried to map the cognitive capacities of several chimpanzees, including their prize pupil, Sarah (Premack, 1976; Premack and Premack, 1983). In one procedure, the chimpanzee is shown three items. One of these serves as the sample, the other two as alternatives. The animal's task is to choose the alternative that matches the sample. Suppose the alternatives are a triangle and a square. If the sample is also a triangle, then for this pair triangle is the correct choice. If the sample is a square, then with the same alternatives square is correct. This procedure is called **matching to sample** (see Figure 4.33). Chimpanzees easily master this task. After just a few trials, Sarah (and a few of her comrades) plainly got the point and understood that this was a task involving the relationship *same.* This was evident in the fact that they readily handled a variety of new problems, performing perfectly on the very first trial.

What about pigeons? Can they also master this task? The answer is yes, with enough training. Thus, pigeons can be taught to peck at a green rather than a yellow key if the sample is green and to peck at the yellow key if the sample is yellow. But what exactly has the pigeon learned here? Has it learned the specific rules: "When you see yellow, peck yellow; when you see red, peck red?" Or has it learned something broader: "Peck the key that's the same as the sample."

To find out, we might employ a transfer of training test. Take the pigeon that has learned to match green with green and yellow with yellow. The evidence indicates that this pigeon might choose correctly if now asked to match red with red. But the bird is likely to fail if now asked to match triangle with triangle. It appears, then, that the bird has not grasped the broader concept of *same,* but has

4.33 Matching to sample *The figure shows the procedure of a typical matching-to-sample experiment. The top circle in each panel represents the sample. The animal's task is to choose the one circle from the two at the bottom that matches the sample's color. In the top panel of the figure, the correct choice is B; in the bottom panel, it is A.*

Means *same*

Means *different*

4.34   The same–different problem
(*After Premack and Premack, 1972*)

instead grasped only the narrower idea of *same color* (Premack, 1978; but see also Zentall and Hogan, 1974; Cook, Cavoto, and Cavoto, 1994; Wasserman, Hugart, and Kirkpatrick-Steger, 1995).

How do chimps perform in such transfer of training tests? Some, at least, do quite well. Sarah, for example, learned to use two special plastic tokens to indicate *same* and *different*. She was first shown two identical objects, such as two cups, and was then given a token whose intended meaning was *same*. Her task was to place this token between the two cups. She was then presented with two different objects, such as a cup and a spoon, and was given yet another token intended to mean *different*. In this setup, she was required to place this token for *different* between the cup and the spoon. After several such trials, she was tested with several pairs of items, some identical and some different, and had to place the correct token between them. It was as if the experimenter was asking, "same or different?" and Sarah was answering by providing the correct plastic "word." Sarah was able to master this task perfectly (see Figure 4.34).

It is no surprise that the conceptual attainments of the pigeon are limited in comparison to those of the chimpanzee, just as the achievements of the chimpanzee are limited in comparison to our own achievements. More importantly, though, these experimental procedures allow us to explore the differences among species, providing a firm base of evidence from which we can explore the diversity of animal cognition and how the complexities of both animal and human cognition evolved.

TAKING STOCK

The scientific study of animal learning began with the investigations of Pavlov and Thorndike some one hundred years ago, and it is clear that they and their intellectual descendants have discovered many fundamental phenomena of learning. But were these investigators justified in their faith that the principles they uncovered underlie all forms of learning? This is still a matter of debate. Some intellectual achievements in animals and in humans—insightful learning, abstract concepts, and especially human language—seem to cry out for other explanations. But there is no question that the study of how CS–US and response-reinforcer relations are acquired and represented offers important clues about the fundamental nature of basic learning processes in both humans and nonhuman animals.

When we began our discussion, our initial focus was on *action*, on how classical and instrumental conditioning change what animals *do*: how Pavlov's dogs came to salivate to ticking metronomes; how Thorndike's cats came to perform all sorts of novel tricks. But as we saw, these changes of overt behavior are only one aspect of what happened to these animals—they are the manifestations of having learned rather than its essence. For unlike Pavlov and Thorndike, who focused on overt behavior, modern investigators of animal learning have shown that, at bottom, classical and instrumental conditioning (and many other forms of learning, too) depend on cognition. Rats, fish, pigeons, even mollusks all learn which events predict which other events and which actions produce which outcomes. These and other phenomena demonstrate that psychological functions involve not just what animals *do*, but also what they *know*.

Psychology must necessarily deal with both action and knowledge. In our discussion of animal learning we have straddled both, for the field represents a kind of bridge between these two major concerns. We will now cross the bridge completely and move on to the study of cognition as a topic in its own right.

SUMMARY

1. The simplest of all forms of learning is *habituation,* a decline in the response to stimuli that have become familiar through repeated exposure. In habituation the organism learns that it has encountered the stimulus before.

2. In *classical conditioning,* first studied systematically by Ivan Pavlov, animals learn about the association between one stimulus and another. Prior to conditioning, an *unconditioned stimulus* or *US* (such as food) elicits an *unconditioned response* or *UR* (such as salivation). After repeated occasions in which the US follows a *conditioned stimulus* or *CS* (such as a buzzer), this CS alone will begin to evoke the *conditioned response* or *CR* (here again, salivation) that is often similar to the UR.

3. The strength of conditioning is assessed by the readiness with which the CS elicits the CR. This strength increases with the number of *reinforced trials,* that is, with occasions on which the CS is followed by the US. When a CS-US relation is well established, the CS can be preceded by a second, neutral stimulus to produce *second-order conditioning.*

4. Nonreinforced trials (when the CS is presented without the US) lead to *extinction,* a decreased tendency of the CS to evoke the CR. Some contend that *spontaneous recovery* shows that the CR is masked, not abolished, by extinction.

5. The CR can be elicited not only by the CS but also by stimuli that are similar to it. This effect, *stimulus generalization,* increases the more the CS resembles the new stimulus. To train the animal to respond to the CS but not to other stimuli, one stimulus (CS^+) is presented with the US, while another (CS^-) is presented without the US. The more similar the CS^+ is to the CS^-, the more difficult this *discrimination* will be.

6. Classical conditioning can involve many responses other than salivation, including fear, as assessed by the *conditioned emotional response (CER)* procedure. The CR is never identical, and sometimes not even similar to the UR, which suggests that the CS serves as a signal and not a substitute for the US. In some cases, the CR is not just different from the UR but is its very opposite. One example is found in the development of drug tolerance. According to some authors, this is partially caused by a *compensatory reaction* conditioned to stimuli that habitually accompany drug administration.

7. When training an animal using classical conditioning, the US occurs regardless of whether the animal performs the CR. When training an animal using *instrumental* (or *operant*) *conditioning,* a reward or reinforcement is only delivered upon performance of the appropriate instrumental response.

8. An early study of instrumental conditioning was conducted by E. L. Thorndike using cats that learned to perform an arbitrary response to escape from a *puzzle box.* Thorndike believed that their learning reflected no understanding but was based instead on a gradual strengthening of the correct response and a weakening of the incorrect one. To account for this, he proposed his *law of effect,* which states that the tendency to perform a response is strengthened if it is followed by a reward (reinforcement) and weakened if it is not.

9. During the past seventy years or so, the major figure in the study of instrumental conditioning was B. F. Skinner, one of the first theorists to distinguish sharply between classical conditioning, in which the CR is elicited by the CS, and instrumental (or operant) conditioning, in which the instrumental response, or operant, is emitted from within. *Operants* are strengthened by reinforcement, but their acquisition may require some initial *shaping* by the method of *successive approximations.*

10. While some reinforcers are stimuli whose reinforcing power is unlearned, other *conditioned reinforcers* acquire their power from prior presentations with stimuli that already have that capacity. One of the factors that determines the strength of instrumental conditioning is the delay of reinforcement: The more quickly the response is followed by the reinforcer, the stronger the response.

11.   During *partial reinforcement,* the response is reinforced only some of the time. Responses that were originally learned under partial reinforcement are harder to extinguish than those learned when the response was always reinforced. The rule that determines when a reinforcer is given is called a *schedule of reinforcement.* In *ratio schedules,* reinforcers are delivered after a number of responses that may be *fixed* or *variable.* In *interval schedules,* reinforcers are delivered for the first response made after a given interval since the last reinforcement, which again can be fixed or variable.

12.   Reinforcers can include the presentation of *appetitive stimuli* or the termination or prevention of *aversive stimuli.* Aversive stimuli can weaken or strengthen instrumental responding, depending on the relation between the aversive stimulus and the response. In *punishment training,* the response is followed by an aversive stimulus; as a result, responding decreases or is extinguished. In *escape learning,* the response stops an aversive stimulus that has already begun; in *avoidance training,* the response averts the aversive stimulus altogether. In both cases, the animal will learn to make the desired response.

13.   Pavlov, Thorndike, and Skinner believed that the essence of both classical and instrumental conditioning was that they modified action. Cognitive theorists such as Köhler and Tolman believed that when humans and animals learned, they acquired new bits of knowledge, or *cognitions.* According to many theorists, what is learned in classical conditioning is an association between two events, the CS and the US, such that the CS serves as a signal for the US. One line of evidence comes from studies of the effect of the CS-US interval. The general finding is that conditioning is more effective when the CS precedes the US by some optimal, usually short, interval.

14.   A number of investigators have asked how the animal learns that the CS is a signal for the US. The evidence shows that CS-US pairings alone will not suffice; there must also be trials on which the absence of the CS predicts the absence of the US. This allows the animal to discover that the US is contingent (depends) on the CS. The discovery of this *contingency* seems to depend on the extent to which the US is unexpected or surprising, as shown by the phenomenon of *blocking.*

15.   Unlike Thorndike and Skinner, who argued that instrumental learning involves the strengthening of an instrumental response, cognitive theorists believe that it is based on an association between an act and its outcome. Evidence for this view comes from studies in which animals are trained to perform two responses that lead to two different outcomes, after which one of the outcomes is made less desirable. Subsequent tests indicate that the animals learned which response led to which result.

16.   Contingency is as crucial to instrumental conditioning as it is to classical conditioning. In instrumental conditioning, the relevant contingency is between a response and an outcome. When there is no such contingency, the organism learns that it has no response control. Threatening conditions in which there is no response control may engender *learned helplessness,* which often generalizes to other situations.

17.   According to Pavlov, Skinner, and other early learning theorists, the connections established by classical and instrumental conditioning are essentially arbitrary: Just about any CS can become associated with any US, and just about any response can be strengthened by any reinforcer. This *equipotentiality principle* is challenged by the fact that certain CSs are more readily associated with some USs than with others, as shown by studies of *learned taste aversions.* These studies suggest that animals are biologically prepared to learn certain relations more readily than others. Similar effects occur in instrumental conditioning, with some responses more readily strengthened by some reinforcers than by others.

18.   According to some investigators, certain forms of learning are *species-specific;* they cite evidence that some animals can readily learn what others cannot. Various birds, for example, have specialized adaptations that include remarkable memory for hoarded food, song learning, and navigational abilities, whereas other, closely related birds lack these abilities.

19.   In recent years, investigators have made enormous progress in understanding the neural bases for learning. One neural mechanism involves a change in how much neurotransmitter a neuron releases. This mechanism serves as a primitive correlation detector

SUMMARY

and may be a crucial building block for more complex learning. A different mechanism—*long-term potentiation*—involves changes in a neuron's sensitivity to stimulation. Because this potentiation is *activity dependent,* it is also sensitive to patterns of correlations among events.

20.   Cognitive theorists point out that animals are capable of rather complex cognitions. Evidence comes from work on spatial memory in rats and chimpanzees which shows that these animals can form elaborate *cognitive maps.* Further work concerns the ability to abstract conceptual relationships. Early evidence came from Köhler's studies of insightful learning in chimpanzees, who showed remarkable *transfer* to novel situations. Later work showed that some chimpanzees can acquire certain higher-order concepts such as *same-different.*

PART TWO

COGNITION

CHAPTER

5

SENSORY PROCESSES

The approach to mental life we have considered so far emphasizes action; our focus has been on what organisms do and how they do it. We now turn to another approach to mental functioning, one that asks what organisms know, how they come to know it, and how, finally, they use what they know—to direct their own actions or to guide the actions of others.

Many kinds of animals are capable of knowledge, but in our species, knowing (or cognition) is immensely complex. We know about the world directly around us, perceiving objects and events that are in our here and now, like the rose that we can see and smell. We also know about events in our past. The rose may fade, but we can recall what it looked like when it was still in bloom. Our knowledge can be transformed and manipulated by thinking, as we somehow sift and analyze our experiences to emerge with new and often abstract notions. We can, for example, think of the faded rose petals as but one stage in a reproductive cycle, which in turn reflects the procession of the seasons. We can also communicate our knowledge to others by the use of language, a uniquely human capability that allows us to transmit vast quantities of knowledge, with each of us building upon the discoveries of the preceding generations. In this chapter and the next four, we will examine all of these forms, and uses, of knowing.

T o survive, we must know the world around us, for most objects in the world are charged with meaning: Some are food; others are mates; still others are mortal enemies. The ability to distinguish among these—say, between a log and a crocodile—is literally a matter of life and death. To make these distinctions, we have to use our senses. We must do our best to see and hear the crocodile so that we can recognize it for what it is before it sees, hears, smells, and (especially) tastes us.

THE ORIGINS OF KNOWLEDGE

The study of sensory experience grows out of an ancient question: Where does human knowledge come from? One suggestion is straightforward: Our senses receive and record information, much as a camera receives light or a microphone receives sound. On this view, our eyes and ears are sensitive to the relevant information, just as film (for example) is sensitive to light. According to this approach, the collection of information is a relatively passive affair. The camera, after all, does not choose which light beams to receive, nor does it do much

169

interpretation of the light it detects. Instead, it simply records the light available to it. Likewise, a tape recorder does not interpret the speech or appreciate the music; again, in a passive fashion, it simply records. Could this be the way vision and hearing work?

THE EMPIRICIST VIEW

Many philosophers have argued that our senses are passive in this way, and this position is associated with the philosophical view known as *empiricism,* according to which all knowledge is acquired through experience. A major proponent of this position was the English philosopher John Locke (1632–1704). Locke argued that there are no innate ideas: At birth, the human mind is simply a blank tablet, a *tabula rasa,* upon which experience leaves its mark.

> Let us suppose the mind to be, as we say, a white paper void of all characters, without any ideas:—How comes it to be furnished? Whence comes it by that vast store which the busy and boundless fancy of man has painted on it with an almost endless variety? Whence has it all the materials of reason and knowledge? To this I answer, in one word, from experience. In that all our knowledge is founded; and from that it ultimately derives itself. (Locke, 1690)

Locke's position was based on philosophical arguments, but it also fit well with political views that were emerging during the eighteenth century. The merchants and manufacturers of western Europe had little use for the hereditary privileges of a landed aristocracy or for the divine right of kings to govern (and worse, to tax) as they chose. Under the circumstances, the middle class readily seized upon a doctrine that proclaimed the essential equality of all people. If all people enter life with a tabula rasa, then the aristocracy had no intrinsic advantages, and each person could (in principle) prove as worthy as any other, given suitable opportunities and education.

DISTAL AND PROXIMAL STIMULI

The notion that knowledge comes from experience implies that all of what we know derives from what we have seen, heard, and felt during our lifetimes. This leads us to ask: What kinds of knowledge come through the senses? What exactly is the information the senses receive? Consider vision. We look at a tree some distance away. Light reflected by the tree's outer surface enters through the pupil of the eye, is gathered by the lens, and is cast as an image upon the *retina,* the photosensitive region at the rear of the eye. The stimuli that are involved in this visual sequence can be described in either of two ways. We can talk about the tree itself—that is, the object or event in the world outside of us. This is the *distal stimulus.* (The distal stimulus is typically at some distance from the perceiver, hence the term *distal.*) Or we can talk about the pattern of stimulus energies that actually reaches the eye—in our example, the optical image cast onto the retina by the light reflected by the tree. This is the *proximal* (or "nearby") *stimulus.*

As perceivers, our interest obviously centers upon the distal stimulus, the real object in the world outside. We want to know about the tree, not its retinal image. Our interest is in the tree's real size, its distance from us, the kind of leaves it has, and so on. But we have no direct access to the distal stimulus. Instead, our only information about the distal stimulus lies in the energies that actually reach us—namely, the proximal stimulus. If the tree cast no retinal image, it would be invisible to us. The same holds for the other senses. We can only smell a rotten

John Locke *(Courtesy of the National Portrait Gallery, London)*

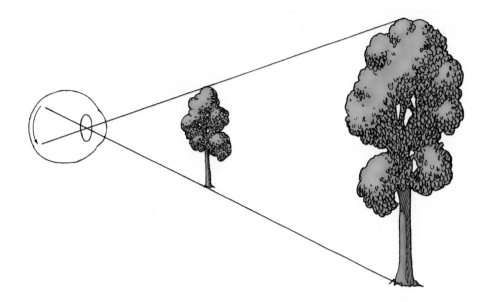

5.1 Distal and proximal stimuli *The two trees are distal stimuli, real objects in the world outside. One is small and close to the viewer; one is larger and more distant. But the proximal stimuli they give rise to—the images they cast on the retina—are identical. This highlights the potential ambiguity of the proximal stimulus.*

Bishop George Berkeley *(Detail from* The Bermuda Group *by John Smibert; courtesy of Yale University Art Gallery, gift of Isaac Lothrop of Plymouth, Mass.)*

egg (the distal stimulus) because of hydrogen sulfide molecules suspended in the air that flows over the sensory cells in our nasal cavities (the proximal stimulus).

Notice, though, that this distinction between distal and proximal stimuli raises questions for the empiricist. The senses are the only portals we have to the world outside, and the proximal stimuli are the only messengers allowed to pass through these gates. How, therefore, can we know the true qualities of the distal stimulus? Consider, for example, points raised by another empiricist philosopher, Bishop George Berkeley (1685–1753). Berkeley pointed out that we cannot tell the size of the physical object from the size of its retinal image. Our tree might be a miniature plant nearby or a giant one in the distance (see Figure 5.1). By the same token, we cannot tell, merely by inspecting the retinal image, whether an object is in motion or at rest, for motion of the image may be caused either by motion of the external object or by movements of our eyes. Likewise, since the retina is a two-dimensional (flat) surface, Berkeley argued that our vision cannot directly inform us about the three-dimensional world. How, then, does perception of depth proceed? In actual life, we seem to have little difficulty in telling how far away an object is from us, and we can generally perceive the size of an object with some accuracy. After all, even Berkeley would have to admit that we have little trouble in distinguishing between a tiger in the distance and a kitten close by. How can these observations be reconciled with the empiricist view?

SENSATIONS

The empiricists claimed that knowledge comes from the senses, but these give us access to the proximal stimulus, not the distal. How, therefore, do we know the distal world? In addition, the empiricist view invites another concern: The empiricists assumed that all knowledge is constructed out of simple sensory experiences, or **sensations.** These are the building blocks out of which all complex experiences and all complex ideas are constructed. Green and brown are examples of visual sensations. An example of an auditory sensation would be a loud A-flat. An example of a gustatory (that is, taste) sensation would be bitterness. According to the empiricists, all our perceptual experience is ultimately composed of such sensations—a mosaic of colored patches, tones of different pitch and loudness, sweets and sours, and so on.

5.2   *The use of linear perspective in Renaissance art* The School of Athens *by Raphael, 1509–1511. (Stanze della Segnatura, Vatican; courtesy Scala/Art Resource)*

Can this description possibly do justice to the richness of our perceptual world? For the fact is that we see trees and coffee cups (and innumerable other objects) and not mere patches of green and brown. What glues the pieces of the mosaic together?

THE ROLE OF ASSOCIATION

We have raised several questions about the empiricist view, but to all of these questions, the empiricists offered a single answer: learning. They argued that prior experience plays a crucial role in creating the meaningfulness and organized character of our perceptual world. The key mechanism of this learning was held to be ***association,*** the process whereby one sensation is linked to another. The basic idea was very simple: If two sensations occur together often enough, eventually one of them will evoke the idea of the other. According to the empiricists, this associative linkage is the cement that binds the separate components of the perceptual world together.★

An example is provided by the various ***distance cues.*** Some of these had been noted by the painters of the Renaissance who discovered several techniques for rendering a three-dimensional world on a two-dimensional canvas. One of these techniques was linear perspective—objects appear to be farther away as they decrease in size (Figure 5.2). But how does perspective convey depth? To an empiricist, the explanation is a matter of prior association. We see the visual cues of perspective (see Chapter 6), and a moment later we reach for or walk toward the object we are viewing. This experience creates an association in the mind between the visual cue and the appropriate movement, so that, eventually, the visual cue alone will produce the memory of the movement and thus the experience of depth.

★ It is obvious that the notion of association was at the root of many of the theories of learning we discussed in the last chapter. For example, Pavlov's conceptions of classical conditioning are in many ways derived from the views of the early associationists.

THE NATIVIST REJOINDER

The empiricists acknowledged that the perceiver must supplement her sensory inputs with associations. Other scholars, however, have suggested that the perceiver plays a role far more active than this.

The major alternative to the empiricist position is **nativism,** which asserts that many aspects of perceptual experience depend on our ability to categorize and interpret the incoming sensory information. This ability to understand the sensory input, the nativists claimed, is what makes perception possible. As a consequence, this ability must be in place *before* any perceptual experience can occur, and so it cannot possibly be derived *from* perceptual experience. Instead, this ability must be part of our natural (innate) endowment.

This general position has a long ancestry, with roots that go back as far as Plato. In more recent times, this position was advocated by the German philosopher Immanuel Kant (1724–1804). Kant argued that knowledge cannot come from sensory input alone; there must also be certain preexisting categories according to which this sensory material is ordered and organized. In particular, Kant claimed that the categories of space, time, and causality are built into the very structure of the mind, and these categories order all of experience, so that there is no way in which we can see the world except in terms of these categories. It is as if we looked at the world through colored lenses that we could never take off; if they were red, then redness would necessarily be part of everything we see. It is these categories, according to Kant, that make the sensory input interpretable. The categories themselves and the way in which they order the sensory information are part of our biological heritage.

PSYCHOPHYSICS

The dispute between the empiricists and the nativists—in the broadest of terms, a dispute over the nature, origins, and trustworthiness of our knowledge—focused attention on the role of the senses and prodded investigators to discover just how the senses function. The investigators' goal can be stated very simply: They wanted to uncover the chain of events that begins with a stimulus and leads to reports such as a "bitter taste," a "dull pressure," or a "brightish green." The details of this sequence are obviously very different for the different senses. Vision differs from hearing, and both differ from taste—in the stimuli that normally excite them, in their receptors, in the qualities of their sensations. But even so, we can analyze the path from stimulus to sensory experience in quite similar ways, whatever the particular sense may be.

In all cases, there seem to be three basic steps. First, there is the proximal stimulus. Second, there is the chain of events in the nervous system that is triggered by the stimulus. These events begin when the stimulus is converted (technically, **transduced**) into a nerve impulse.★ Once converted in this manner, the message is transmitted further (and often modified) by other parts of the nervous system. Third, there is some sort of psychological response to the message, often in the form of a conscious sensory experience (or sensation).

The sequence can be looked at from several perspectives. For now, we will focus on the psychophysical perspective. **Psychophysics** is the study of the relation between the properties of the (physical) stimulus and the (psychological) sensory experience the stimulus ultimately gives rise to. Its object is to uncover, for example, what physical attribute of a sound makes us hear the sound as loud or soft, what dimensions of a light make that light appear red rather than green.

Immanuel Kant *(Courtesy of Culver Pictures, Inc., New York)*

★ This is typically a two-stage affair. The transduction process produces a graded potential in specialized receptor cells, which in turn triggers a nerve impulse in other neurons.

Gustav Theodor Fechner   (Courtesy
National Library of Medicine)

E. H. Weber   (Courtesy National Library
of Medicine)

Broadly put, research in psychophysics seeks to address four questions. First, there is the question of **detection:** What stimuli is an organism able to detect? Second, there is the question of **discrimination:** Which stimuli can an organism tell apart, and which stimuli are indistinguishable? From the organism's point of view, this is a question of "Is this one different from that one?" Third is the question of **scaling:** How loud is this sound? How bright is this light? How strong is this smell? Finally, there is the question of **recognition:** Is this a cat or a dog? a tree or a sculpture?

MEASURING SENSORY INTENSITY

How should we tackle these questions? To relate qualities of the stimulus to qualities of perception, we need first to measure the physical stimulus. This is easy enough; we can readily find out how many pounds this bowling ball weighs or how hot this water is in degrees centigrade. But how can we make the corresponding *psychological* measurements needed to assess the sensory experience of the subject? How can we quantify how something tastes, or sounds, or smells?

Gustav Theodor Fechner (1801–1887), the founder of psychophysics, argued that sensations and the stimuli that produce them belong to two totally different realms—the first belong to the mental world, the second to the physical world. Therefore, they cannot be directly compared to each other. But it is possible, Fechner noted, to make comparisons *within* each of these realms. Even if sensations can't be compared to physical stimuli, they can at least be compared to each other, and this can provide a basis for measuring them.

Consider the sensation of visual brightness produced by a patch of light projected onto the eye. We can ask, what is the minimal amount by which the intensity of this light must be increased so that the subject experiences a sensation of brightness just greater than the one he had before? This minimal change in the stimulus defines an observer's **difference threshold**—the smallest stimulus change that the observer can reliably detect—and if the stimulus is changed by this amount, it creates what psychophysicists call a **just noticeable difference,** or **jnd.** The jnd is a psychological entity, because it describes a subject's ability to discriminate. But it is expressed in the units of the physical stimulus that produced it. It would seem, therefore, that Fechner had found an indirect means to relate sensory magnitude to the physical intensity of the stimulus.

THE WEBER FRACTION

To Fechner, measuring jnds was only the means to a larger goal; his ultimate aim was to formulate a general law relating physical stimulus intensity to psychological sensory magnitude. He believed that such a law could be built upon a proposal made in 1834 by the German physiologist E. H. Weber (1795–1878). Weber had proposed that the size of the difference threshold is a constant fraction of the standard stimulus. Suppose that we can just tell the difference between 100 and 102 candles burning in an otherwise dark room. This does not indicate, Weber argued, that we are in general sensitive to differences of just 2 candles. What matters instead, he suggested, is the proportional difference—in this case, a difference of 2 percent. On this logic, we would not be able to distinguish 200 candles from 202 (a 2 candle difference but only a 1 percent change) or even 203. But we should be able to distinguish 200 candles from 204, or 300 from 306—in each case a 2 percent difference.

Fechner referred to this relationship as **Weber's law,** a label by which we still know it. Put algebraically, this law is usually written as

$$\frac{\Delta I}{I} = c.$$

TABLE 5.1 REPRESENTATIVE (MIDDLE-RANGE) VALUES FOR THE WEBER FRACTION FOR THE DIFFERENT SENSES

Sensory modality	Weber fraction $(\Delta I/I)$
Vision (brightness, white light)	1/60
Kinesthesis (lifted weights)	1/50
Pain (thermally aroused on skin)	1/30
Audition (tone of middle pitch and moderate loudness)	1/10
Pressure (cutaneous pressure "spot")	1/7
Smell (odor of India rubber)	1/4
Taste (table salt)	1/3

SOURCE: Geldard, 1962.

I is the intensity of the standard stimulus, the one to which comparisons are being made; ΔI is the amount that must be added to this intensity in order to produce a just noticeable increase; c is a constant (in our example, it was .02, or 2 percent). The fraction $\Delta I/I$ is referred to as the **Weber fraction.**

Fechner and his successors performed numerous studies to determine whether Weber's law holds—that is, whether the sensory apparatus is sensitive to percentage changes rather than absolute changes. The evidence suggests that this claim is correct for all of the sensory modalities, across most of the range of intensities to which a subject is sensitive.★ It seems that the nervous system is geared to notice relative differences rather than absolute ones.

Weber's law provides us with several advantages. Among them, it allows us to compare the sensitivities of different sensory modalities. Suppose we want to know whether the eye is more sensitive than the ear. We cannot compare jnds for brightness and loudness directly; the first is measured in millilamberts, the second in decibels, and there is no way to translate the one into the other. But we can compare the Weber fractions for the two modalities. If the fraction is small, then we know that the sense modality is able to make fine discriminations; put differently, relatively little must be added to the standard for a difference to be detected. And the smaller the Weber fraction, the more sensitive the sense modality. Using these comparisons, we can show that we are much keener at discriminating brightness (1/60) than loudness (1/10); the Weber fractions needed for this comparison, and fractions for other sense modalities, are presented in Table 5.1.

FECHNER'S LAW

By making a number of further assumptions, Fechner generalized Weber's finding to express a broad relationship between the sensory experience and the physical intensity of a stimulus. The result was **Fechner's law,** which states that the strength of a sensation grows as the logarithm of stimulus intensity:

$$S = k \log I.$$

S stands for psychological (that is, subjective) magnitude, I for the physical intensity of the stimulus, and k for a constant whose value depends on the value of the Weber fraction.

★ Weber's law tends to break down at the two extremes of the intensity range, especially at the lower end (for example, for visual stimuli only slightly above absolute threshold). At these intensities, the Weber fraction is larger than it is in the middle range.

This law has been challenged on several grounds, which are beyond the scope of this book. For our purposes, though, it is sufficient to note that this law does provide a reasonable approximation of the relationship between stimulus intensity and subjective impression. Moreover, a logarithmic law such as Fechner's makes good biological sense. The range of stimulus intensities to which we are sensitive is enormous. We can hear sounds as weak as the ticking of a watch twenty feet away and as loud as a pneumatic drill operating right next to us. Our nervous system has to have a mechanism to compress this huge range into some manageable scope, and this is precisely what a logarithmic transformation does.*

DETECTION AND DECISION

The goal of psychophysics is to chart the relationship between an individual's perceptions and various characteristics of the physical stimulus. But are these physical characteristics the only factors that determine what the research participant does or says in a psychophysical experiment? What if she is employing some clever strategy (consciously or nonconsciously) to figure out when the experimenter is changing the stimulus and when not? What if she is particularly eager to show off what a sensitive perceiver she is? The early psychophysicists believed that such factors could largely be disregarded. But a more recent approach to psychophysical measurement insists that they cannot. This is *signal-detection theory,* an approach that provides an influential and broadly useful way of thinking about how people make decisions, both in the psychophysics laboratory and in a wide range of other contexts. Indeed, this approach, developed to study elementary sensations, has been applied to cases as diverse as jury decision making and the memory effects of hypnosis. (We will consider some of these broader applications after first discussing the logic of signal detection.)

SIGNAL DETECTION

Psychophysical experiments actually involve a considerable element of judgment on the part of the research participant. This arises from the fact that the object of psychophysics is to explore the limits of our sensory apparatus: What is the dimmest light we can perceive? What is the smallest difference in pitch we can discern? As a consequence, psychophysical experiments routinely focus on very weak signals, be they dim lights, faint odors, or tiny increments in saltiness. Some of these signals are so weak, in fact, that they are barely greater than the background noise that comes from within the participant's own body. Take an experiment in hearing. Here the background noise might come from slight air currents wafting inside the participant's ears each time he moves his head, or from the sounds of his own pulse. These sounds are slight, of course, but they loom large when placed alongside the soft tones or the subtle distinctions he is trying to hear in a psychophysics experiment.

Because of these background noises, the research participant's task is not merely one of distinguishing tone from silence. Instead, the participant must hear the difference between the tone plus the background noise and the background noise alone. Put differently, there is really no such thing as a *zero stimulus.* Instead, all psychophysical judgments are superimposed on the background noise that is there with or without an incoming signal.

---

* Some of the challenges to Fechner's law have led researchers to believe that a power function provides a more accurate description of the psychophysical data than a logarithmic function does (Stevens, 1955). But this leaves unchanged the main conceptual point of Fechner's law: Both mathematical functions serve to compress a huge range of values into a more manageable form, and this is exactly what our sensory apparatus needs.

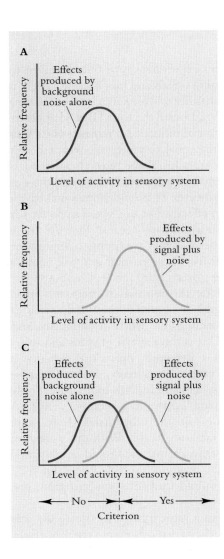

A

Effects produced by background noise alone

Relative frequency

Level of activity in sensory system

B

Effects produced by signal plus noise

Relative frequency

Level of activity in sensory system

C

Effects produced by background noise alone

Effects produced by signal plus noise

Relative frequency

Level of activity in sensory system

←——— No ——→|←—— Yes ———→
Criterion

5.3 *The decision process according to signal-detection theory* (A) A frequency distribution of the activation level in the sensory system when there is only background noise. The activation level is plotted on the horizontal axis and the frequency with which that intensity occurs on the vertical. (B) A frequency distribution of the activation level in the sensory system when the stimulus is presented; again, intensity fluctuates but the average intensity is greater than that produced by the background noise alone. (C) The two frequency distributions overlap: On some trials the intensity of the background noise alone exceeds that of the stimulus plus background noise.

The research participant's task, therefore, is to judge whether the level of activity in the sensory system comes from the stimulus plus noise or from the background noise alone—whether she hears a faint tone from outside along with her heartbeat or whether she hears only her heartbeat (or some other background noise). According to signal-detection theory, she will base this judgment on some criterion. If the level of activity is above this criterion, she will attribute the activity to an incoming signal; if the activity is below this criterion, she will attribute it to the background noise alone. It is as if she asked herself: "A strong level of activation? There must have been a signal. A weak level of activation? Probably background noise alone."

Of course, this criterion-based decision rests on the assumption that, in general, the stronger the activation, the more likely it is that the activation results from an incoming signal. This seems perfectly sensible, since the activation resulting from the stimulus plus the noise is usually stronger than that produced by the background noise alone. But not always: In any sensory modality, the intensity of the background noise varies. An individual's pulse waxes and wanes rhythmically; his head is sometimes moving, sometimes still. If the signal happens to arrive at a moment when the background noise is low, the resulting sum of noise plus signal may be relatively low. In fact, this sum may actually be lower than the level reached occasionally by the background noise alone: The activation resulting from (a low level of) noise plus the signal may be weaker than that resulting from (a high level of) noise without any signal.

There is some overlap, therefore, between the range of intensities caused by background noise alone and that caused by the signal plus the noise (see Figure 5.3). Because of this overlap, the research participant cannot avoid error completely. If her criterion is high, she will only respond when the activation level is strong. In this case, she is unlikely to indicate that she heard a tone when in fact there was none. That is, she will rarely produce a *false alarm*. But she is also likely to produce some *misses:* She will not indicate some tones that were actually presented because any criterion high enough to exclude all the noise-alone trials will also exclude some of the signal-plus-noise trials (see Figure 5.4). If, on the other hand, her criterion is low, there will be few misses—trials *with* signal are quite likely to exceed a low criterion. But a low criterion will also be exceeded in some trials with noise alone, ensuring a number of false alarms.

5.4 *The effects of changing the criterion* Whatever activation level the listener chooses as her criterion, some of her judgments will be in error. In (A), the participant has set her criterion level so high that it is never exceeded by the noise alone. However, many trials with a signal fall below the criterion. Therefore, this participant will never produce a false alarm but will often miss the signal. In (B), she has set her criterion so low that virtually all of the trials with a signal will exceed this criterion. But now many trials with noise alone also exceed the criterion. This participant will produce few misses, but many false alarms.

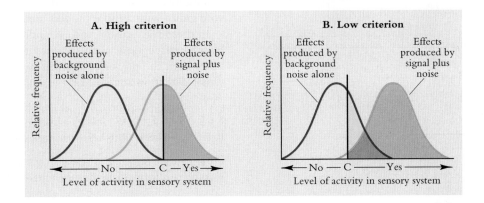

A. High criterion

Effects produced by background noise alone

Effects produced by signal plus noise

Relative frequency

←— No ——— C — Yes —→
Level of activity in sensory system

B. Low criterion

Effects produced by background noise alone

Effects produced by signal plus noise

Relative frequency

←— No — C ——— Yes —→
Level of activity in sensory system

RESPONSE BIAS

An individual's responses in a psychophysics experiment turn out, therefore, to depend both on his sensitivity to the incoming signals and his criterion. There is no way to respond without any criterion: He must choose some level of the sensory process at which he is willing to say, "Yes, I heard the tone." But what determines the placement of this criterion? A crucial influence is *response bias.* This refers to his inclination, all other things being equal, to prefer one response over another, quite apart from the nature of the stimulus. Some research participants will approach the task with great caution and will respond, "Yes, I heard the signal," only if they are quite certain they did hear it. These individuals will have a response bias toward the "no" response—in effect, a bias of "when in doubt, say no." Others will have a more casual attitude, perhaps because they are more inclined to trust their intuition or perhaps because they are trying to impress the experimenter with their perceptual sensitivity. These participants will adopt a rule of "when in doubt, say yes," producing a bias toward the "yes" response.

Response bias can also be influenced by the research participant's broad expectations about the experiment: Are signals presented in most of the trials? If so, then it seems appropriate to adopt the strategy of "when in doubt, say yes." Another influence is the *payoff matrix.* This is the pattern of gains and losses associated with the various responses in a detection procedure. Imagine a prospector digging for gold. Is that sparkle in the dirt perhaps a fleck of the precious metal? A false-alarm response (that is, deciding to look more closely, only to discover that the sparkle is just a bit of sand) costs only a moment's effort. A miss—not bothering to inspect the sparkle—on the other hand, seems more costly: The prospector might miss out on fabulous wealth. With this pattern of payoffs (high cost for a miss, low cost for a false alarm), one should sensibly tend toward a positive response—when in doubt, check the sparkle (see Table 5.2). This pattern of payoffs, in other words, should lead to a low criterion, one exceeded by even a weak signal.

As a related case, consider the situation of a juror trying to evaluate the evidence in a criminal trial. The juror might believe that prisons are cruel, horrible, and inhumane places, with little chance of reforming prisoners. From this perspective, a false alarm (voting guilty when the defendant is actually innocent) would have terrible consequences, and so the juror would be determined to avoid this error. As a result, he will set his criterion high, voting guilty only if the quantity of evidence is considerable.

Another juror might see things differently. She might be deeply concerned about cases in which the justice system has set guilty people free, allowing them to break the law again. For this juror, a miss (voting "not guilty" when the defendant is actually guilty) would be an unacceptable prospect; this would lead to a low criterion, with the juror voting to acquit the defendant only if she were absolutely certain of the defendant's innocence. As a result, the juror is willing to vote guilty with a more modest quantity of evidence.

In these ways, jurors, too, are influenced by a payoff matrix and, in particular, by their perceptions of the cost associated with a miss or a false alarm. This illustrates both the power of a payoff matrix and also the breadth of cases to which signal-detection analysis can be applied.

SEPARATING SENSITIVITY FROM RESPONSE BIAS

How can we separate a research participant's actual sensitivity to a signal—how well he can hear or see the stimulus—from his criterion or response bias? This is

TABLE 5.2 PAYOFF MATRIX THAT WILL PRODUCE A "YES" BIAS		
	Stimulus present	*Stimulus absent*
Responds yes	Find fabulous wealth	Waste a moment's effort
Responds no	Miss out on fabulous wealth	No change

the role of the **detection experiment,** in which experimenters present a stimulus on some trials but no stimulus on other trials. The trials without a stimulus, called "catch trials" (Green and Swets, 1966), allow the experimenter to ask how often the participant gives the four possible types of response. We have already encountered the two different kinds of errors: One is a miss, not reporting a stimulus when one is present; the other is a false alarm, reporting a stimulus when in fact there is none. There are also two kinds of correct responses: a **hit,** reporting a stimulus when it is actually there, and a **correct negative,** not reporting one when none is present (see Table 5.3).

To see how this information can be used, consider two research participants: Lynn is cautious in her responding but has exquisitely sensitive hearing. As a result, her hit rate (saying yes when the stimulus is present) is high. Charles, in contrast, is almost deaf but quite casual in his responding, and so he tends to say yes whenever he is in doubt. His hit rate is also high: He reliably says yes when the stimulus is present (because, in fact, he says yes most of the time). If we look only at hit rates, there is no way to distinguish the sensitive Lynn from the deaf Charles.

However, we have more information than just the hit rates. Charles, always inclined to say yes, also produces many false alarms (saying yes when the stimulus is absent). His responses, in other words, tend to be in the top two cells of Table 5.3. Lynn, in contrast, will produce few false alarms. With her acute hearing, she will probably realize when the stimulus is truly absent and will produce many correct negatives. Lynn's responses, in other words, will accumulate in the top-left and bottom-right cells of Table 5.3.

This sets the pattern for a signal-detection analysis. In general, if individuals differ in their sensitivity, then they will differ in their proportions of correct and incorrect responses—their total number of hits and correct negatives relative to their total number of misses and false alarms. If they differ in their criterion, then they will differ in their proportions of yes and no responses. As a result of all this, we can assess a research participant's sensitivity and criterion by looking at all four types of response, and calculating the relative numbers of each.

EXTENSIONS TO OTHER FIELDS

Signal-detection theory has applications to many areas outside of psychophysics. It is relevant whenever a person must decide between two alternatives but can't be sure of the outcome. We have already mentioned the example of a juror's decision making, in which a false alarm sends an innocent person to jail, a miss sets a guilty one free. Yet another example is medical testing: A false alarm on an HIV test will bring horrible anxiety to someone who is in fact healthy, but a miss might lead someone to neglect life-prolonging medical treatment and to infect others.

Signal-detection theory has been applied to these cases as a way of understanding and improving these (and many other) instances of decision making. These applications rest on the fact that in virtually all decisions some errors are inevitable. These errors can be either misses or false alarms, and there is always a trade-off between the two. In order to minimize the number of misses (for example, people with HIV whose tests yield a false negative), one has to shift the response bias toward yes, which inevitably increases the number of false alarms (people without HIV whose tests yield a false positive). Conversely, in order to minimize the number of false alarms, one necessarily must increase the number of misses. Just which trade-off is chosen depends on the particulars of the case, and the costs and benefits associated with the different errors and correct responses.

TABLE 5.3 THE FOUR POSSIBLE OUTCOMES OF THE DETECTION EXPERIMENT

	Stimulus present	Stimulus absent
Responds yes	Hit	False alarm
Responds no	Miss	Correct negative

SENSORY CODING

Thus far, our focus has been on the relationship between the physical properties of the stimulus and the sensory experience it gives rise to. But sensory psychologists are not content with this alone. They also want to learn something about the intervening neural steps. In particular, researchers strive to understand the nature of the **sensory code** through which the nervous system represents various sensory experiences. A code is a set of rules whereby information is transformed from one set of symbols to another. An example is the Morse code used by telegraphers, in which letters are transformed into patterns of dots, dashes, and spaces, so that *dot-dash* stands for *A*, *dash-dot-dot-dot* for *B*, and so on. What Samuel Morse did for telegraphy, the nervous system does for all the senses. Instead of dots and dashes, the nervous system encodes (that is, *translates*) the various properties of the stimulus into various characteristics of the nervous impulse. Many of the efforts of sensory psychophysiologists are directed at cracking these codes.

Some general issues apply to all the codes used within the different senses. One concerns the code for **psychological intensity,** such as changes in loudness and brightness. In general, the code for intensity used by the nervous system is firing frequency: the more intense the stimulus, the greater the rate of neural firing (and the more intense the subjective experience; Borg et al., 1967). Another signal for sensory intensity is the sheer number of neurons that are triggered by the stimulus: The more intense the stimulus, the more neurons it activates, and the greater the psychological magnitude.

Another question concerns the code for **sensory quality**—the attribute that distinguishes the sensation of pressure from the sensation of red or the sensation of sour. These sensations are obviously produced by very different stimuli, but this is not how the nervous system makes these distinctions. To be sure, visual sensations are usually produced by light waves, but occasionally other stimuli will serve as well. Strong pressure on the eyeballs leads us to see rings or stars (to the chagrin of boxers and the delight of cartoonists). Similarly, we can produce visual sensations by electric stimulation of various parts of the nervous system. In 1826, these facts led the German physiologist Johannes Müller (1801–1858) to formulate his famous **doctrine of specific nerve energies.** According to this law, the differences in sensory quality are not caused by differences in the stimuli themselves but by the different nervous structures that these stimuli excite. Thus, any event that stimulates the optic nerve—light waves or pressure or a chemical stimulus—will lead to the sensation of vision; any event that stimulates the auditory nerve will lead to a perceived sound.

Some of Müller's successors extended this doctrine to cover qualitative differences within a given sense modality. For example, blue, green, and red are qualitatively different even though all three are colors. To the heirs of Müller, such a qualitative difference could only mean one thing: There had to be some decisive difference in the neural processes that underlie these different sensations, perhaps at the level of the receptors, perhaps higher up.

Note, though, what is left unsaid by Müller's doctrine. Differences in sensory quality may well reflect a difference in some underlying neural process, but this leaves room for debate about what the particular process is. As one broad suggestion, **specificity theory** asserts that different sensory qualities are signaled by different neurons. These quality-specific neurons are somehow "labeled" with their quality, so that whenever they fire, the nervous system interprets their activation as "red" or "sour" or whatever their particular sensory quality might happen to be. The alternative position is **pattern theory.** This asserts that the code for quality comes from a pattern of activation across a whole set of neurons. In taste, for example, the same sensory neurons seem to be involved whether one is tasting "sweet" or "sour," and so it cannot be the identity of the individual neurons that distinguishes these two sensations. What differs between "sweet" and "sour" is the *pattern* of activation—which neurons are firing more and which less at any given moment—across a set of sensory neurons. The significance of a particular neuron's activity, therefore, can only be understood in relation to the broader pattern, and it is this pattern that gives rise to the sensory qualities. As we will see, the nervous system uses both specificity and pattern codes in different sensory systems (Goldstein, 1996; Rosenzweig, Leiman, and Breedlove, 1996).

A SURVEY OF THE SENSES

The development of psychological methods, coupled with various physiological techniques, has given psychology a powerful set of tools with which to study the senses. Our primary focus will be on vision, because, as we will see, there is reason to believe this is the dominant sense modality in human perception. But we will first look briefly at some of the other sensory systems that provide us with information about our world and our own position in it.

KINESTHESIS AND THE VESTIBULAR SENSES

One group of senses informs the organism about its own movements and its orientation in space. Skeletal movement (i.e., movement of the arms, legs, neck, and so on) is sensed through **kinesthesis,** a collective term for information that comes from receptors in the muscles, tendons, and joints. Another group of receptors signals all movements of the head, whether produced by deliberate motion or by a force from the outside. These are the receptors in the **semicircular canals,** which are located within the **vestibules** of the inner ear (Figure 5.5). The three canals contain a viscous liquid that moves when the head moves. This motion bends hair cells located at one end of each canal. When bent, these hair cells give rise to nervous impulses. The sum total of the impulses from each of the canals provides information about the nature and extent of the head's movements.

One vital function of the semicircular canal system is to provide a firm base for vision. As we walk through the world, our heads move continually. To compensate for this endless rocking, our eyes have to move accordingly. This adjustment is accomplished by a reflex system, closely coupled with the cerebellum in the hindbrain, which cancels each rotation of the head by an equal and opposite motion of the eyes. These eye movements are initiated by messages from the three semicircular canals, which are then relayed to the appropriate muscles of each eye. Thus, the visual system is effectively stable, operating as if it rested on a solid tripod.

THE SKIN SENSES

Stimulation of the skin informs the organism of what is directly adjacent to its own body. Not surprisingly, skin sensitivity is especially acute in those parts of the body that are most relevant to exploring the world that

A

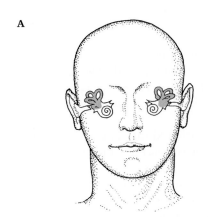

B

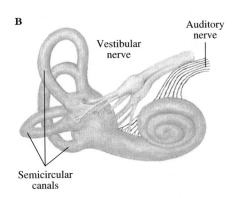

Vestibular nerve

Auditory nerve

Semicircular canals

5.5 The vestibular sense *(A) The location of the inner ears, which are embedded in bone on both sides of the skull. The vestibules are indicated in orange. The rest of the inner ear is devoted to the sense of hearing. (After Krech and Crutchfield, 1958) (B) Close-up of the vestibular apparatus. (After Kalat, 1984)*

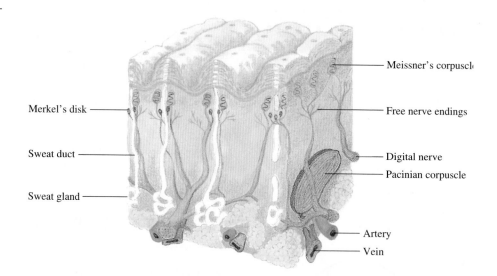

Merkel's disk
Sweat duct
Sweat gland

Meissner's corpuscle
Free nerve endings
Digital nerve
Pacinian corpuscle
Artery
Vein

5.6   A cross section through the skin
The figure shows a number of structures that serve as receptors in hairless skin; for example, on the fingertips and palms. (After Carlson, 1986)

surrounds us directly: in humans, the hands and fingers, the lips and tongue. These sensitivities are reflected in the organization of the cortical projection area for bodily sensations. As we have seen, the allocation of cortical space is quite unequal, with a heavy emphasis on such sensitive regions as face, mouth, and fingers (see Chapter 2).

How many skin senses are there? Aristotle believed that all of the sensations from the skin could be subsumed under just one rubric, that of touch. But today investigators believe that there are at least four different skin sensations: *pressure, warmth, cold,* and *pain.* Some would lengthen the list to include other sensations, among them *vibration, tickle,* and *itch.* How are these different sensory experiences coded by the nervous system? Here, as in the study of many other senses, the first line of inquiry was suggested by Müller's doctrine of specific nerve energies: If the sensory qualities are different, see whether there are different receptors that underlie them.

Are there different receptors that correspond to these different sensations? The answer is a qualified yes. There is reason to believe that various sensations of pressure, for example, are produced by specialized receptors in the skin (see Figure 5.6). Some of these receptors are wrapped around hair follicles in the skin and sense movements of the hair. Others are capsules that are easily bent by slight deformations of the skin. Some of these capsules respond to continued vibration, others to sudden movement across the skin, still others to steady indentation. It's clear that there is not one touch receptor but several.

Less is known about the receptor systems for warmth, cold, and pain. Some of these sensations are probably signaled by free nerve endings in the skin that have no specialized end organs. These free nerve endings have been thought to provide information about warmth, cold, and pain, but some of them may actually be additional pressure receptors (Sherrick and Cholewiak, 1986).

THE SENSE OF TASTE

The sense of taste acts as the gatekeeper for an organism's digestive system by providing information about the substances that should or should not be ingested. Its task is to keep poisons out and usher foods in. In most land-dwelling mammals, this function is performed by specialized receptor organs contained within the *taste buds,* which are sensitive to chemicals dissolved in water. The average person possesses about ten thousand such taste buds, located

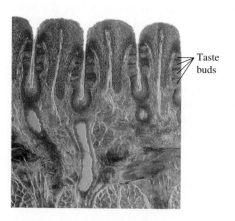

Taste buds

Section of a mammalian tongue   *The taste buds, which look like small hairy balls, are embedded in the walls of deep narrow pits in the tongue. (Courtesy of Ed Reschke)*

mostly on the tongue but also in other regions of the mouth. Fibers from these receptors convey the message to the brain—first to the medulla and then further up to the thalamus and the cortex.

TASTE SENSATIONS

Many investigators believe that there are four basic taste qualities: *sour, sweet, salty,* and *bitter.* In their view, all other taste sensations are produced by a mixture of these primary qualities. Thus, grapefruit tastes sour and bitter, while lemonade tastes sweet and sour.

Each of these basic tastes may have its own special biological role. Most organisms are attracted by sweet tastes, presumably because so many nutritive substances contain some form of sugar. And because so many toxic substances are bitter, we develop protective reflexes against ingesting them early in development, reflexes that include retching and vomiting, both coordinated by neural circuits in the hindbrain (Shepherd, 1994).

What are the stimuli that produce these four basic taste qualities? As yet, we don't have a full answer. We do know that the sour taste is produced by receptors sensitive to acidity, and that salty tastes emanate from sodium-sensitive receptors. The story is more complicated for sweet and bitter sensations. Both are generally produced by complex organic molecules, but as yet there are no clear-cut rules that summarize the relation between a molecule's structure and the resulting taste. Sweet tastes are, of course, produced by various sugars but also by the artificial sweetener saccharin, a chemical that is structurally very different from sugar. Bitter tastes are produced by a wide variety of chemicals, suggesting that there may be several different sensory receptors for bitterness.

CODING FOR TASTE QUALITY

What neural processes underlie the different taste qualities? According to specificity theory, these qualities are signaled by different neurons that carry the messages from the taste receptors to the brain. Electrical recording studies using rats and hamsters have shown that some of these neurons respond best when stimulated by sugar, others when stimulated by salt, still others by (very diluted) hydrochloric acid, and yet others by quinine, corresponding to the four primary taste sensations. According to specificity theorists, the neuron that responds best to sugar (the "sugar-best neuron") signals sweet, the "quinine-best neuron" signals bitter, and so on. To the extent that any substance stimulates several taste neurons (and most substances do), the result will be a taste mixture. Evidence for this view comes from a comparison of two sugars: sucrose and fructose. Both rats and humans prefer sucrose to fructose, even though both sugars stimulate the sugar-best neurons (the ones that presumably signal "sweet"). The preference probably comes about because fructose also stimulates the salt-best neuron. As a result, its taste is a mixture of sweet and salty, which is less preferred. Whether these results are best explained by the specificity theory or by some version of the pattern theory is still a matter of debate (Bartoshuk, 1988; see Figure 5.7, adapted from Nowlis and Frank, 1981).

TASTE AND SENSORY INTERACTION

The sense of taste provides an illustration of a principle that holds for most (perhaps all) of the other senses, a principle that we will here call *sensory interaction.* It describes the fact that a sensory system's response to any given stimulus generally does not depend just on that stimulus alone. The response is also affected by other stimuli that impinge, or have recently impinged, upon that system.

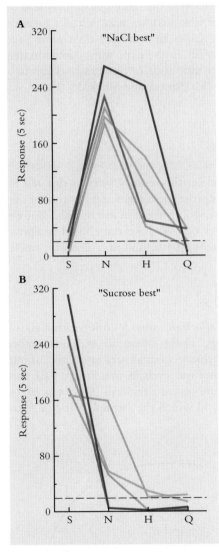

5.7 Response profiles of two kinds of taste neurons in the hamster The figures show the responses from two kinds of neurons when stimulated by sucrose (S), sodium chloride (N), hydrochloric acid (H), and quinine (Q). In humans these substances give rise to the sensations of sweet, salty, sour, and bitter respectively. (A) Five neurons that respond best to sodium chloride. (B) Five neurons that respond best to sucrose. (From Nowlis and Frank, 1981)

One kind of sensory interaction occurs over time. Suppose a taste stimulus is presented continuously for fifteen seconds or more. The result will be *adaptation,* a phenomenon that is found in virtually all sensory systems. For example, if the tongue is continually stimulated with a salty taste, sensitivity to saltiness will decline. Likewise, after continuous exposure to a quinine solution, the quinine will taste less and less bitter and may finally appear to be completely tasteless. This adaptation process is reversible, however. If the mouth is rinsed out and left unstimulated for, say, a minute, the original taste sensitivity will be restored in full.

In another form of interaction, the adaptation to one taste quality may lead to the enhancement of another, an effect that is sometimes regarded as a form of contrast. For example, adaptation to sugar makes an acid taste even more sour than before (Kuznicki and McCutcheon, 1979). In the same way, adaptation to a salty solution will make ordinary tap water taste sour or bitter; adaptation to a sweet solution will make water taste bitter (McBurney and Shick, 1971).

THE SENSE OF SMELL

Thus far, our discussion has centered on the sensory systems that tell us about objects and events close to home: the movement and position of our own bodies, what we feel with our skin, and what we put in our mouths. But we also receive information from much farther off. We have three main receptive systems that enlarge our world by responding to stimuli at a distance: smell, hearing, and vision.

THE OLFACTORY STIMULUS

Smell, or to use the more technical term, **olfaction,** provides information about chemicals suspended in the air around us. These chemicals excite receptors located in an area called the **olfactory epithelium**—a small area at the top of our sinus cavities, deep within our heads, behind our eyeballs (see Figure 5.8). But there is considerable debate about the nature of the chemicals that act as effective olfactory stimuli (*odorants*) and the way in which they stimulate the olfactory receptors.

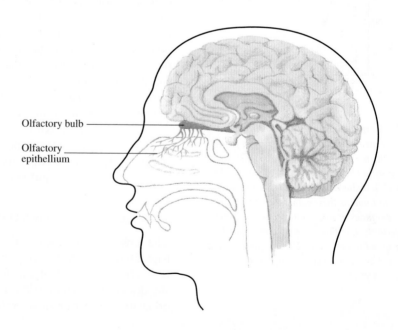

Olfactory bulb

Olfactory epithellium

5.8 The olfactory apparatus Chemicals suspended in the air that flows through the nasal passages stimulate receptors in the olfactory epithelium that relay their information to a structure in the forebrain, the olfactory bulb. (After Amoore, Johnson, and Rubin, 1964; Carlson, 1986)

Some researchers have suggested that there are a small number of primary smell sensations—for example, fragrant (rose), spicy (cinnamon), and putrid (rotten eggs). Other, more complex, smells would then be regarded as mixtures of these primary elements. Presumably, each one of these primary smells would correspond to a particular kind of receptor. More recent evidence speaks against this idea. There seems to be a very large number of different odor receptors—about a thousand—each of which responds to a specific set of odor molecules. Could it be that we have one receptor type for each odor we can detect? Clearly not, because humans can recognize approximately ten thousand different scents. It appears, therefore, that the sensory code for odor quality must be a pattern of excitation across the different receptor groups (Axel, 1995).

SMELL AS AN INTERNAL SENSE

Olfaction is an important distance sense, but smell is also a sense that can refer to things much closer by—in fact, to objects inside our own mouths (Rozin, 1982). We can smell the spaghetti on our plate, but we can also sense its flavor when we take a forkful in our mouths. That flavor—as indeed all flavors—depends largely on our sense of smell. For what we commonly call the "taste" of food is rarely the sensation of taste alone; it is almost always a combination of taste, texture, temperature, and—most important of all—smell. When our nose is completely stuffed up, food appears to be without any flavor. While we can still experience the basic taste sensations, the aroma is lost and so the food seems tasteless. If smell is gone, we can no longer distinguish between vinegar and a fine red wine or between an apple and an onion. For a gourmet (or a chef or a wine taster), a sensitive nose is even more essential than a sensitive tongue.

SMELL AS A DISTANCE SENSE

As a distance sense, smell is of vital importance for many species, serving as the primary means for locating food, predators, and mates. Smell plays a much smaller role for humans, our primate cousins, and birds. These are all creatures whose ancestors left the odor-impregnated ground to move up into trees, and in this arboreal environment, other senses, especially vision, become more critical. We can examine this contrast among species using psychophysical methods. It turns out, for example, that a dog's sensitivity to smells is about a thousand times greater than our own (Marshall and Moulton, 1981; Cain, 1988).

Compared to most other land-dwelling animals humans are olfactory incompetents. But that doesn't mean that smell is of no relevance to human life. It does warn us of impending danger (as when we sniff escaping gas), it greatly adds to our enjoyment of food, and it provides the basis of the perfume and deodorant industries. According to some reports, it even helps to sell luggage and used cars: Plastic briefcases saturated with artificial leather scents and second-hand cars permeated with a "new car" odor are said to have greater market value (Winter, 1976). In addition, smell evidently plays a role in identifying other people. In one study, a psychologist asked men and women to wear T-shirts for twenty-four hours without taking a shower or using perfumes or deodorants. After the twenty-four hours were up, each (unwashed) T-shirt was sealed in a separate bag. Every research participant was then asked to sniff the contents of three of these bags without looking inside. One contained his or her own T-shirt, a second the T-shirt worn by another man, a third the T-shirt worn by another woman. About three-quarters of the participants were able to identify their own T-shirt based only on its odor and could also correctly identify whether the other T-shirts had been worn by a man or a woman (Russell, 1976; McBurney, Levine, and Cavanaugh, 1977). This sensitivity to human odors starts in the nursery. Babies apparently respond to the odor of their own mother's breast and underarm in preference to the odors of a strange mother (Russell, 1976; Cernoch and Porter, 1985). Generally speaking, females perform better than males on these and other olfactory-related tasks (a difference that seems to be present from earliest infancy), and younger people do better than older ones (Balogh and Porter, 1986; Cain, 1988).

PHEROMONES

In many species, olfaction also has another important function. It represents a primitive form of communication. Certain animals secrete chemical substances called **pheromones** that trigger particular reactions in other members of their kind. In many mammal species, for example, the female secretes a chemical (often in the urine) that signals that she is sexually receptive. In some species, the male sends chemical return messages to the female. Boars, for example, apparently secrete a pheromone that renders the sow immobile so that she stands rigid during mating (Michael and Keverne, 1968).

Other pheromones signal alarm, so that, in effect, some animals can smell danger. To be more exact, they can smell a substance secreted by members of their own species that have been frightened. Thus, rats who suffer an electric shock seem to exude a chemical that induces fear in other rats when they smell it (Valenta and Rigby, 1968).

Communication via pheromones serves an important social and biological function in many species, and organisms capable of this communication would have an obvious evolutionary advantage. So it is unsurprising that most mammals possess a separate organ within the nose, physically distinct from the main olfactory epithelium, specialized for the detection of pheromones that govern reproductive and social behaviors. This organ is called the **vomeronasal organ,** but it is sometimes informally referred to as the "sexual nose" (Axel, 1995).

Is there a pheromone system in humans? We may indeed have the vestiges of one. One line of evidence concerns the development of **menstrual synchrony.** Women who live together—for example, in college dormitories—tend to develop menstrual cycles that roughly coincide with each other, even though their periods were very different at the start of the school year (McClintock, 1971). Some studies suggest that this synchrony is primed by olfactory cues. Female participants exposed to the body odor of a "donor" woman gradually shifted their menstrual cycles toward that of the donor, even though the participants and the donors never saw each other (Russell, Switz, and Thompson, 1980; McClintock and Stern, 1998).

Of potentially greater interest is the possibility of discovering an olfactory sex attractant that operates like a kind of pheromone. Thus far, there has been little to whet the financial appetites of perfume manufacturers or the erotic hopes of Lonely Hearts. At best, there may be some faint remnants. One line of evidence comes from olfactory thresholds to certain musklike substances similar to that secreted by boars. Sexually mature women are vastly more sensitive to the smell of these compounds than are men or sexually immature girls. This sensitivity fluctuates with the woman's menstrual cycle and seems to reach a peak during ovulation. An intriguing speculation is that the receptive female's greater sensitivity to this odor points to the existence of a human male pheromone in our evolutionary past. Perhaps it is still present in a greatly attenuated form, but if so, its effects are almost certainly too weak to be of any practical significance. Drenching himself in boar's musk and wearing Brad Pitt's or Will Smith's unwashed T-shirt will not transform the universally rejected male suitor into an idol pursued by all woman (even those—or especially those—near enough to smell him).

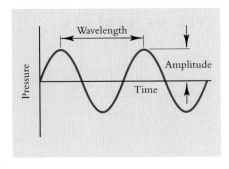

5.9 The stimulus for hearing *A vibrating object creates a series of pressure pulses in the molecules surrounding it; these pulses then spread outward like ripples in a pond into which a stone has been thrown. To describe this pattern, it is useful to measure the air pressure at a single point in space. The pressure of a sound wave waxes and wanes, as shown here. The extent of the pressure determines the height of the wave; the timing between points of maximum pressure determines the wavelength.*

HEARING

The sense of hearing, or **audition,** is a response to pressure, and in this way it is a close relative of the skin senses. However, unlike the skin senses, hearing informs us of pressure changes arising from events in the world many meters away from us.

SOUND

What is the stimulus for hearing? Outside in the world there is some physical movement—perhaps an animal scurrying through the underbrush or a set of vibrating vocal cords. This movement agitates the air particles that surround the moving object, causing these particles to jostle other particles, which in turn jostle still other particles. The actual movement of these particles is slight (about one-billionth of a centimeter) and short-lived (the particles return to their original position in a few thousandths of a second), but this motion is enough to create a momentary pressure moving outward from the moving object, similar to the ripples set in motion by a stone thrown into a pond.

If the movement continues for even a short time, it will create a series of pressure variations in the air, and when these **sound waves** hit our ears, they initiate a set of further changes that ultimately trigger the auditory receptors. The receptors then trigger various neural responses, which eventually reach the brain and lead to the experience of hearing.

Sound waves can vary in both **amplitude** and **frequency.** Amplitude refers to the amount of pressure exerted by each air particle on the next. This pressure waxes and wanes as the sound wave moves along. The amplitude we seek to measure is typically the maximum pressure achieved, at the crest of the sound wave. Frequency refers to the timing of the crests. How much time elapses between one point of maximum pressure and the next? This interval is called the sound wave's **wavelength.** More generally, though, sound waves are described by their frequency, which is the number of crests per second. Since the speed of sound is constant within any given medium, frequency is inversely proportional to wavelength (Figure 5.9).

Both amplitude and frequency are physical dimensions of the sound wave itself, but they correspond reasonably well to the psychological dimensions of **loudness** and **pitch.** Roughly speaking, a sound will be heard as louder as its amplitude increases and more high pitched as its frequency goes up.

Amplitude and loudness The range of amplitudes to which humans can respond is enormous, so investigators find it useful to measure these intensities with a logarithmic scale, which compresses this huge range into a more convenient form. Thus, sound intensities are measured in **decibels** (Table 5.4). Twenty decibels represents a tenfold increase in the physical stimulus intensity (that is, the amplitude). Psychologically, perceived loudness doubles each time the intensity of a sound increases by 10 decibels (Stevens, 1955).

Rock and roll and hearing loss *As rock guitarist Pete Townshend learned too late, prolonged exposure to loud noise, like that produced by his band, The Who, can cause serious hearing loss, as well as tinnitus, or ringing, in the ears. Many rock musicians, as well as fans, now wear ear plugs to prevent damage. (Photograph © RDR productions, 1981; Rex USA)*

TABLE 5.4 INTENSITY LEVELS OF VARIOUS COMMON SOUNDS

Sound	Intensity level (decibels)
Manned spacecraft launching (from 150 feet)	180
Loudest rock band on record	160
Pain threshold (approximate)	140
Loud thunder; average rock band	120
Shouting	100
Noisy automobile	80
Normal conversation	60
Quiet office	40
Whisper	20
Rustling of leaves	10
Threshold of hearing	0

Frequency and pitch   The frequency of a sound wave is generally measured in cycles per second, or **hertz** (named after the nineteenth-century German physicist Heinrich Hertz). The frequencies associated with various musical tones are shown in Table 5.5. Young adults can hear tones as low as 20 hertz and as high as 20,000 hertz, with maximal sensitivity to a middle region in between. As people get older, their sensitivity to sound declines, especially at the higher frequencies.

Simple and complex waves   Thus far we have only dealt with simple wave forms; when these waves are expressed graphically, with pressure change plotted against time, they yield curves that correspond to the plot of the trigonometric sine function. Accordingly, such curves are called **sine waves** (Figure 5.10).

   Sine waves can be produced by tuning forks or by special electronic devices. In normal life, however, the sounds encountered are rarely as simple as this.

TABLE 5.5 SOUND FREQUENCIES OF SOME MUSICAL TONES

Sound	Frequency (hertz)
Top note of grand piano	4214
Top note of piccolo	3951
Top range of soprano voice	1152
Top range of alto voice	640
Middle C	256
Bottom range of baritone voice	96
Bottom range of bass voice	80
Bottom note of contra bassoon	29
Bottom note of grand piano	27
Bottom note of organ★	16

★Can be felt but not heard
SOURCE: After Geldard, 1972.

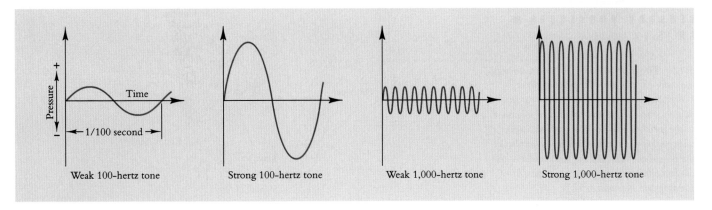

5.10 Simple wave forms vary in frequency and amplitude *These curves show the sine waves for a weak and a strong 100-hertz tone (relatively low in pitch) and a strong and a weak 1,000-hertz tone (comparatively high in pitch). (After Thompson, 1973)*

Below is an example of the kind of wave we might actually encounter:

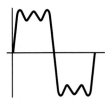

It can be mathematically demonstrated, however, that these complex waves can always be analyzed into simpler components, so that we can think of sine waves as the ingredients from which more complicated sounds are produced. The complex wave just shown can be produced by the acoustic mixture of these three simple sine waves:

Physicists studying sound often find it convenient to analyze a complex wave in terms of its sine-wave constituents. In hearing, the auditory system performs a similar sort of analysis, detecting the simpler components within the complex. However, this ability has its limits. If the sound is made up of a great number of unrelated waves, it is perceived as noise, which we can no longer analyze (Figure 5.11).

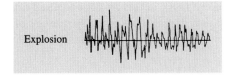

5.11 An irregular sound wave—an explosion *As in the previous figures, pressure change is plotted against time; but now there is no more regularity, so the wave form cannot readily be analyzed into its simpler components. (From Boring, Langfeld, and Weld, 1939)*

GATHERING THE PROXIMAL STIMULUS

Mammals have their receptors for hearing deep within the ear, in a snail-shaped structure called the **cochlea.** To reach the cochlea, sounds must travel a complicated path. The **outer ear** itself collects the sound waves from the air and directs them toward the **eardrum,** a taut membrane at the end of the **auditory canal.** The sound waves cause the eardrum to vibrate, and these vibrations are then transmitted to the **oval window,** the membrane that separates the **middle ear** from the **inner ear.** This transmission is accomplished by a trio of tiny bones known collectively as the **auditory ossicles.** The vibrations of the eardrum move the first ossicle, which then moves the second, which in turn moves the third, which completes the chain by imparting the vibratory pattern to the oval window to which it is attached. The movements of the oval window then give rise to waves

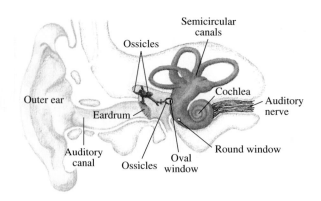

5.12 The human ear *Air enters through the outer ear and stimulates the eardrum, which sets the ossicles in the middle ear in motion. These in turn transmit their vibration to the membrane of the oval window, which causes movement of the fluid in the cochlea of the inner ear. Note that the semicircular canals are anatomically part of the inner ear. (After Lindsay and Norman, 1977)*

in the fluid that fills the cochlea, causing (at last) a response by the receptors (Figure 5.12).

Why this roundabout method of sound transmission? Sound waves reach us through the air, and the proximal stimulus for hearing is made up of minute changes in the air pressure. But the inner ear (like most body parts) is filled with fluid—cochlear fluid to be exact. Therefore, in order to hear, the changes in air pressure must cause changes in fluid pressure. This is a problem, because fluid is harder to set in motion than air is. To solve this problem, the pressure waves must be amplified on their way toward the receptors, and this is accomplished by various features of the ear's organization. For example, the ossicles work as levers, using leverage to increase the sound pressure. Similarly, the eardrum is about twenty times larger than that portion of the oval window moved by the ossicles. As a result, the fairly weak force provided by sound waves acting on the entire eardrum is transformed into a much stronger pressure concentrated upon the (smaller) oval window.

TRANSDUCTION IN THE COCHLEA

Throughout most of its length the cochlea is divided into an upper and lower section by several structures, including the **basilar membrane.** The actual auditory receptors are called **hair cells.** These cells—some fifteen thousand of them in each ear—are lodged between the basilar membrane and other membranes above it (Figure 5.13).

Motion of the oval window produces pressure changes in the cochlear fluid that in turn lead to vibrations of the basilar membrane. As the basilar membrane vibrates, its deformations bend the hair cells and provide the immediate stimulus for their activity. How do the movements of the hair cells lead to the sensory properties of auditory experience? Much of the work in this area has focused on the perception of pitch, the sensory quality that depends upon the frequency of the stimulating sound wave.

5.13 Detailed structure of the middle ear and the cochlea *(A) Movement of the fluid within the cochlea deforms the basilar membrane and stimulates the hair cells that serve as the auditory receptors. (After Lindsay and Norman, 1977) (B) Cross section of the cochlea showing the basilar membrane and the hair cell receptors. (After Coren and Ward, 1989)*

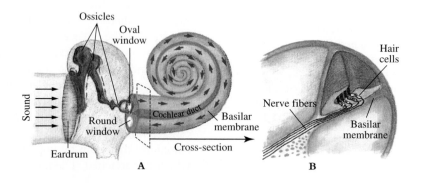

Hermann von Helmholtz *(1821–1894)*
(Courtesy National Library of Medicine)

Basilar place and pitch According to the **place theory** of pitch, first proposed by Hermann von Helmholtz (1821–1894), different parts of the basilar membrane respond to different sound frequencies. The nervous system is then able to identify a sound's pitch by detecting where the movement was strongest along the length of the basilar membrane. The stimulation of hair cells at one end of the membrane leads to the experience of a high tone, while the stimulation of hair cells at the other end leads to the sensation of a low tone.

Helmholtz's claim was explored in a series of classic studies by Georg von Békésy (1899–1972), whose work on auditory function won him the Nobel prize in 1961. Working with preserved specimens of both human and animal cochleas, Békésy was able to remove part of the cochlear wall so that he could observe the basilar membrane through a microscope while the oval window was being vibrated by an electrically powered piston. He found that such stimulation led a wavelike motion of the basilar membrane (Figure 5.14). When he varied the frequency of the vibrating stimulus, the peak of the deformation occurred in different regions of the membrane, as Helmholtz had proposed. For high frequencies, the peak was closer to the oval window; as the frequency dropped, the peak moved closer and closer to the cochlear tip (Békésy, 1957). As a result, high and low frequencies cause different hair cells to fire, and this stimulates different auditory nerve fibers, which in turn go to different places in the brain.

Sound frequency and frequency of neural firing The place theory of pitch faces a major difficulty. As the frequency of the stimulus gets lower and lower, the deformation pattern it produces on the basilar membrane gets broader and broader. At frequencies below 50 hertz, the wave set up by the stimulus deforms the entire membrane just about equally (although see Khanna and Leonard, 1982; Hudspeth, 1989). We can, however, discriminate frequencies as low as 20 hertz, so the nervous system must have some means for sensing pitch in addition to basilar location.

This second means for sensing pitch is likely to be tied to the firing frequency of the auditory nerve, a hypothesis referred to as **frequency theory.** For lower frequencies, the frequency of a stimulus tone may be directly translated into the appropriate number of neural impulses per second. This information would

5.14 *The deformation of the basilar membrane by sound* *(A) In this diagram, the membrane is schematically presented as a simple, rectangular sheet. In actuality, of course, it is much thinner and coiled in a spiral shape. (B) The relation between sound frequency and the location of the peak of the basilar membrane's deformation. The peak of the deformation is located at varying distances from the stapes (the third ossicle, which sets the membrane in motion by pushing at the oval window). As the figure shows, the higher the frequency of the sound, the closer to the stapes this peak will be. (After Lindsay and Norman, 1977; Coren and Ward, 1989)*

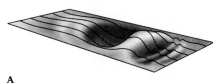

A

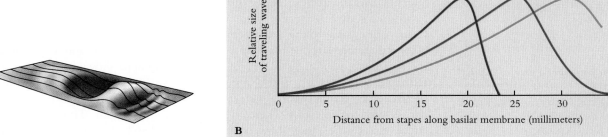

B

then be relayed to higher neural centers that would somehow interpret this information as pitch.

Current evidence indicates that both of these mechanisms contribute to pitch perception. It appears that higher frequencies are coded by the place of excitation on the basilar membrane and lower frequencies by the frequency of the neural impulses. Place of excitation plays little role in the perception of frequencies below 500 to 1,000 hertz, while impulse frequency has little effect for tones above 5,000 hertz. In the middle range, between 1,000 and 5,000 hertz, both mechanisms are operative, and in this range the discrimination of pitches is highly accurate (Green, 1976; Goldstein, 1989).

EVOLUTION AND SENSORY EQUIPMENT

Organisms differ in the stimuli to which they are sensitive, for the sensory equipment of any species is an adaptation to the environment in which it lives. Thus, it's hardly surprising that vision is exquisitely acute in eagles, who hunt from high in the air, but only rudimentary in moles, who live in lightless burrows. Many animals have senses that we lack altogether. Sharks are sensitive to electric currents leaking through the skin of fish hiding within crevices, and carrier pigeons use the earth's magnetic field to find their way home on cloudy nights when they can't navigate by the stars (Wiltschko, Nohr, and Wiltschko, 1981; Dyer and Gould, 1983; Gould and Gould, 1988).

Another example of natural selection fashioning a species' sensory system comes from studies of insect behavior. Researchers long believed that the praying mantis is deaf, for it doesn't seem to possess any ears. But electrophysiological evidence showed that some of the insect's nerve tracts fire in response to sounds in the ultrasonic region, between 25,000 and 50,000 hertz, which humans of course can't hear. So the mantis is evidently not deaf after all. But where are its ears? To find out, the investigators coated the entire animal with a layer of Vaseline, after which the nerve no longer responded to sound. They next scraped the Vaseline off different portions of the mantis until they finally found a critical groove in the animal's thorax. When the Vaseline was removed from this area, the nerve resumed its response to auditory stimulation.

An ear had been found, but this only deepened the puzzle. For there was only one ear, located in the animal's midline. In the animal kingdom, ears almost invariably come in pairs—a crucial prerequisite for sound localization. If the sound comes from the right, the right ear will be stimulated earlier and more intensely than the left; conversely, if the sound comes from the left. Information of this sort allows the possessor of two ears to determine where a given sound is coming from. Given its one-eared status, the mantis can't do that. What then is its one ear good for?

The answer is bats. Bats emit high-frequency sounds that operate like radar. These sounds echo back off the bodies of flying insects, enabling bats to locate their prey. The mantis's ear evidently serves as a bat detector. The single ear can't tell the mantis where the bat is coming from, but this turns out not to be a problem, since for the mantis, sensing the likely direction of attack doesn't really matter. In one study, investigators climbed onto a ladder holding a mantis and then (gently) threw it into the air. When the mantis was aloft and flying, the investigators triggered a device that emits brief pulses of ultrasonic sound, much like the screams of a hunting bat. High-speed photographs showed that whenever the device fired, the mantis adopted an evasive flight pattern reminiscent of those used by fighter pilots—a steep, spiraling power dive likely to get it out of harm's way regardless of where the bat was coming from. This technique is effective: A further study showed that, when attacked by real bats, all insects that went into the spiral escaped unharmed; those that did not were generally captured (Yager and Hoy, 1986; Yager and May, 1990).

Evasive flight pattern of a praying mantis
When a bat noise is produced (indicated by the arrow), the mantis takes evasive action, plummeting to the ground, away from what in nature would be a hungry bat. (From Yager and May, 1990)

THE SENSES IN OVERVIEW

We've presented a brief sketch of all the senses except for vision, which we will take up in detail below. But before moving on, we should say a few words about the senses in general.

In our discussion of the various senses, we have come across many ways in which they differ—from each other and, to some extent, among species. But we have also encountered a number of important general patterns.

First, in most sense modalities (and among many animals) the processing of external stimulus energies begins with various *accessory structures* that gather these physical energies and fashion a "better" proximal stimulus for the receptors to work on. A clear example is provided by the gathering and amplification of sound achieved by the mammalian ear.

Second, in all sense modalities, the next step involves the receptors that *transduce* the physical energy of the stimulus into a neural signal. In some sensory systems, particularly hearing and vision, the nature of this transduction process is reasonably well understood. In other systems, such as smell, there is still much to learn.

Third, the processing of the stimulus input continues in further neural centers, where the stimulus information is *coded* (so to speak, *translated*) into the various dimensions of sensation that are actually experienced. Some of these dimensions involve intensity. In taste, we experience more or less bitter; in hearing, more or less loud. Other dimensions involve differences in quality. In taste, we can tell the difference between bitter, sweet, sour, and salty; in hearing, we can discriminate differences in pitch.

Fourth, any part of a sensory system is in continual interaction with the rest of that system. We considered some examples of sensory interaction in the taste system, including the phenomena of adaptation (with continued exposure, quinine tastes less bitter) and taste contrast (adaptation to sugar makes acids taste even more sour).

VISION

We turn now to vision, which for humans is the distance sense par excellence. In describing vision we will focus on the same issues that have been our concern in describing the other senses. Specifically, we will describe the eye as a structure for gathering the visual stimulus, examine the transduction of light energies by the visual receptors, discuss some processes of interaction found in vision, and consider the coding processes that are involved in experiencing a particular sensory quality—in the case of vision, color.

THE STIMULUS: LIGHT

Many objects in our environment are sources of light; examples include the sun, a candle, or even a glow worm. These are objects that **emit** light in their own right. But most objects are sources of light only if some external light source illuminates them. They will then **reflect** some portion of the light cast upon them while absorbing the rest.

The stimulus energy that we call *light* travels in a wave form that is analogous to the pressure waves that are the stimulus for hearing. Like all waves, light can vary in its **intensity** and in its **wavelength.** The intensity—the amount of radiant energy per unit of time—is the major determinant of perceived brightness. Wavelength, the distance between the crests of two successive waves, is the major determinant of perceived color. As it turns out, the wavelengths we call *light* are just those wavelengths to which our visual system is sensitive and are only a tiny part of the broader electromagnetic spectrum. The **visible spectrum** extends from roughly 360 (violet) to about 750 (red) nanometers (1 nanometer = 1 millionth of a millimeter) between successive crests. Shorter wavelengths (like those of **ultraviolet light**) are invisible to us, as are longer wavelengths (although we feel these longer **infrared** waves as heat). Light consisting of just a single wavelength, however, is rare; the light we ordinarily encounter is made up of a mixture of different wavelengths.

GATHERING THE STIMULUS: THE EYE

Eyes come in many forms. Indeed, visual organs seem to have developed independently in many kinds of creatures. Some invertebrates have simple eyespots sensitive merely to light or dark, while others have complex multicellular organs with pinhole apertures or crystalline lenses. In vertebrates, the actual detection of light is done by cells called **photoreceptors,** located on the **retina,** a layer of tissue lining the back of the eyeball. Before the light reaches the retina, however, several mechanisms are needed to control the amount of light reaching the photoreceptors and, above all, to ensure a clear and sharply focused **retinal image.**

The human eye is sometimes compared to a camera, and in its essentials this analogy holds up well enough (Figure 5.15). Both eye and camera have a **lens,** which suitably bends (or *refracts*) light rays passing through it, thus projecting an image onto a light-sensitive surface behind—the film in the camera, the retina in the eye. (In the eye, refraction is accomplished by both the lens and the **cornea,** the eye's transparent outer coating.) In the camera, the image is focused by changing the position of the lens; in the eye, this is accomplished by a set of muscles that change the shape of the lens, contracting to curve the lens further when focusing on an object close by and relaxing to flatten out the lens when focusing on an object at a distance. Technically, this process is called **accommodation.** Finally, both camera and eye are able to govern the amount of entering light. In the camera, this function is performed by the lens aperture; in the eye it is

5.15 Eye and camera *The eye has a number of similarities to a camera. Both have a lens for bending light rays to project an inverted image upon a light-sensitive surface at the back. In the eye a transparent outer layer, the cornea, participates in this light-bending. The light-sensitive surface in the eye is the retina, whose most sensitive region is the fovea. Both eye and camera have a focusing device; in the eye, the lens can be thickened or flattened. Both have an adjustable iris diaphragm. And both finally are encased in black to minimize the effects of stray light; in the eye this is done by a layer of darkly pigmented tissue, the choroid coat. (Wald, 1950)*

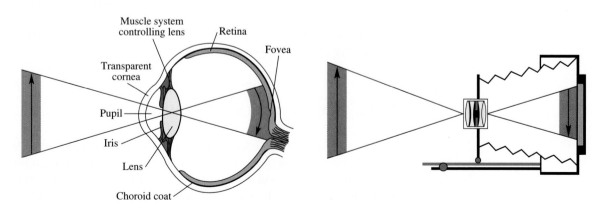

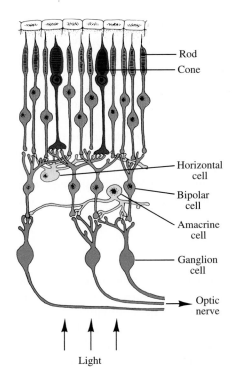

Rod
Cone

Horizontal cell
Bipolar cell
Amacrine cell
Ganglion cell
Optic nerve

Light

5.16 **The retina** *There are three main retinal layers: the rods and cones, which are the photoreceptors; the bipolar cells; and the ganglion cells, whose axons make up the optic nerve. There are also two other kinds of cells, horizontal cells and amacrine cells, that allow for lateral (sideways) interaction. As shown in the diagram, the retina contains an anatomical oddity. As it is constructed, the photoreceptors are at the very back, the bipolar cells are in between, and the ganglion cells are at the top. As a result, light has to pass through the other layers (they are not opaque so this is possible) to reach the rods and cones, whose stimulation starts the visual process. (After Coren and Ward, 1989)*

performed by the **iris,** a smooth, circular muscle that surrounds the pupillary opening and that contracts or dilates under reflex control as the amount of illumination changes.

THE VISUAL RECEPTORS

Once light reaches the retina, we leave the domain of optics and enter the domain of neurophysiology, for it is at the retina that the physical stimulus energy is transformed into a neural impulse. The retina contains two kinds of receptor cells, the **rods** and the **cones;** the names of these cells reflect their different shapes. The cones are plentiful in the **fovea,** a small roughly circular region at the center of the retina, but then become less and less prevalent as one moves away from the fovea, into the retina's periphery. The opposite is true of the rods; they are completely absent from the fovea but frequent in the periphery. In all, there are some 120 million rods and about 6 million cones in the normal human eye.

The rods and cones do not report to the brain directly. Instead, their message is relayed by several other layers of cells within the retina (Figure 5.16). The receptors stimulate the **bipolar cells,** and these in turn excite the **ganglion cells.** The ganglion cells collect information from all over the retina, and the axons of these cells converge to form a bundle of fibers that we call the **optic nerve.** The optic nerve leaves the eyeball carrying information, first, to an important way station in the thalamus, called the **lateral geniculate nucleus,** and then to the cortex. Where the optic nerve leaves the eyeball there is no place for photoreceptors, and so this region of the eyeball cannot give rise to visual sensations; appropriately enough, it is called the **blind spot** (Figure 5.17).

THE DUPLEX THEORY OF VISION

The fact that rods and cones differ in structure, number, and placement on the retina suggests that they also differ in function. Almost a hundred years ago, this notion led to the development of the **duplex theory of vision,** a theory that by now has the status of established fact. The idea is that rods and cones handle different aspects of the visual task. The rods are the receptors for night vision; they operate at low light intensities and lead to **achromatic** (colorless) sensations. The cones serve day vision; they respond at much higher levels of illumination and are responsible for sensations of color. The utility of this duplex arrangement becomes clear when we consider the enormous range of light intensities encountered by organisms like ourselves who transact their business during both day and night. In humans, the ratio between the stimulus energy at absolute threshold and that transmitted by a momentary glance at the sun is 1 to 100,000,000,000. Natural selection has allowed for this incredible range by a biological division of labor, with two separate receptor systems responsible for dim-light and bright-light vision.

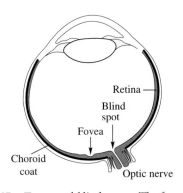

Retina
Blind spot
Fovea
Choroid coat
Optic nerve

5.17 **Fovea and blind spot** *The fovea is the region on the retina in which the receptors are most densely packed. The blind spot is a region where there are no receptors at all, this being the point where the optic nerve leaves the eyeball. (After Cornsweet, 1970)*

The enormous sensitivity of the rods, however, comes at a price. The rods are much worse than the cones at discriminating fine detail; *acuity,* the ability to perceive detail, is much greater in the cones. This is a major reason why we move our eyes whenever we wish to inspect an object. To "look at" a stimulus means to move the eyes so that the target's image falls on the foveas of both eyes. It is at the fovea that the cones are most closely bunched, so acuity is greatest when a stimulus is in foveal view.

Consider the fact that sailors, wishing to perceive a faint star in the night sky, know that they should not look directly toward the star but instead should look slightly to the left or right of the star's position. This ensures that the star's image will fall in the periphery, where the rods are most prevalent. This strategy sacrifices the ability to discern detail but, by relying on the more sensitive rods, maximizes sensitivity to dim light.

SPECTRAL SENSITIVITY

Further evidence for the duplex theory comes from the study of *spectral sensitivity.* The human eye is insensitive to light waves shorter than (about) 360 nanometers or longer than 700 nanometers. What is the sensitivity to the wavelengths in between? To answer this question, we can ask subjects to detect a faint test light of a specific intensity and wavelength. Then we can do the same with another test light at a slightly different wavelength, and then with another test light at still a new wavelength. If we continue in this fashion, we can determine in a systematic way how the eye's sensitivity varies as a function of wavelength. If we project these lights onto the rod-free fovea, this procedure will allow us to determine the sensitivity of the cones to each individual wavelength. If we project the lights onto the retina's periphery, we can do the same for the rods.

The results of this sort of experiment are usually summarized in terms of a *spectral sensitivity curve* in which sensitivity is plotted against wavelength. As the curve in Figure 5.18 shows, maximal sensitivity for the rods is toward the short-wave region, with a peak at about 510 nanometers. (This wavelength, if presented to the cones, appears green; it of course appears gray if presented to the color-blind rods.) The curve for the cones is lower overall, reflecting the cones' lesser sensitivity to light. In addition, the cones' region of maximal sensitivity is toward the longer wavelengths, with a peak at about 560 nanometers (seen as yellowish green). For rods, the blues are easier to detect than the yellows and reds (although, again, all appear gray to the rods); for cones, the opposite is the case.

VISUAL PIGMENTS

The rods and cones can be distinguished functionally (by what they do) and anatomically (by their shapes). They can also be distinguished chemically. Inside each photoreceptor is a *visual pigment,* a chemical that is sensitive to light, and it is the pigment that allows the transduction of light energy into a neural signal. When light enters the receptor, the light energy changes the chemical form of the visual pigment, setting off a chain of events that leads, ultimately, to an elec-

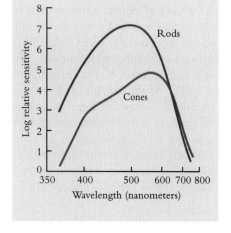

5.18 Sensitivity of rods and cones to light of different wavelengths Sensitivity was measured by determining the threshold for different frequencies of light projected on retinal areas rich in rods or cones. Sensitivity was then computed by dividing 1 by the threshold (the lower the threshold, the greater the sensitivity). Since sensitivity varied over an enormous range, the range was compressed by using logarithmic units. Note first that the cones, overall, are less sensitive than the rods. Note also that the point of maximal sensitivity is different for the two receptor systems. The cone maximum (560 nanometers) is closer to yellow, the rod maximum (510 nanometers) closer to green. (After Cornsweet, 1970)

trical signal. In this fashion, the light energy is translated into the language of the nervous system. The pigment itself is then reconstituted by other mechanisms, so that it will be ready to react when the next opportunity arises.

The visual pigment inside the rods is **rhodopsin.** The cones contain three different pigments, but their exact chemical composition remains uncertain. Still, the fact that they have three pigments rather than one is crucial to the cones' ability to discriminate colors, a topic to which we will turn shortly.

INTERACTION IN TIME: ADAPTATION

One might think of the rods and cones as mere detectors of light, passively receiving and recording the stimulus in just the fashion Locke proposed. Many observations, however, show that the visual system, even at this early stage, is not at all passive. The visual system actively shapes and transforms the stimulus input (as, indeed, do all sensory systems). This activity begins at the receptor level and continues at all subsequent levels, thanks to the fact that the components of the visual system interact constantly and never function in isolation from each other.

One kind of interaction concerns the relation between what happens now and what happened just before. The general finding is simple: There will be a gradual decline in the reaction to any stimulus if that stimulus persists unchanged. For example, after continued inspection of a green patch, its greenness will eventually fade away. Similar **adaptation phenomena** are found in most other sensory systems. Thus, the cold ocean water feels warmer after we have been in it for a while.

What does the organism gain by sensory adaptation? Stimuli that have been around for a while have already been inspected; if they posed a danger, this would have been detected already. Since these stimuli are of lesser relevance to the organism's survival, it pays to give them less sensory weight. What is important is change, especially sudden change, for this may well signify food to a predator and death to its potential prey. Adaptation is the sensory system's way of pushing old news off the neurophysiological front page.

An interesting adaptation effect in vision is provided by the **stabilized image.** In normal vision, the eyes move constantly. In consequence, no retinal region ever suffers prolonged exposure to the same stimulus; one moment it will be stimulated by a dark object, the next moment by a lighter one. Even if one tries to hold one's eyes steady to fixate a stationary picture, adaptation effects will be rather minor because we cannot truly hold our eyes motionless. Small tremors in the eye muscles lead to involuntary eye movements, and these necessarily alter the stimulus input for any given retinal region.

Several investigators, however, have developed a technique that achieves a truly stationary retinal image. The basic idea is as clever as it is simple. Since you can't stop the eye from moving, you move the stimulus along with the eye. One way to accomplish this is by means of a contact lens to which a tiny projector is attached. The projector casts a stimulus pattern onto the retina. The contact lens moves with every motion of the eyeball, and the projector moves with it, so the retinal position of the projected image does not change. Thus, no matter what eye movements are made, the retinal surface is continually exposed to the identical stimulus pattern (Figure 5.19).

At first, the image thus produced is seen very sharply, but after some seconds it fades away completely, usually piece by piece. This offers a dramatic demonstration of the system's adaptation to unchanging stimulation. We can conclude that, in humans, continual involuntary eye movements serve the crucial purpose of keeping the visual world intact. It is these eye movements that (ordinarily)

5.19 Stabilized-image device *The participant wears a contact lens on which a tiny projector is mounted. At the rear of the projector is the stimulus target, which is projected onto the retina. This target will remain fixed at one point of the retina, for as the eyeball moves, so does the contact lens and its attached projector. As a result, the image on the retina remains stabilized. (After Pritchard, 1961)*

Labels in figure: Eyeball, Contact lens, Microlens, Microlamp, Target, Ball-and-socket joint, 0 5 10 millimeters

5.20 Brightness contrast *Four (objectively) identical gray squares on different backgrounds. The lighter the background, the darker the gray squares appear.*

ensure that the retinal image is not stabilized in its position, guaranteeing that there is always change in the retinal image (Riggs et al., 1953).

INTERACTION IN SPACE: CONTRAST

Adaptation phenomena show that sensory systems do not really respond to stimulation; instead, they respond to *changes* in stimulation. If no change occurs, the sensory response diminishes. What holds for time holds for space as well. For here, too, the key word is change. In vision (as in some other senses), the response to a stimulus applied to any one region partially depends on how the neighboring regions are stimulated. The greater the difference in stimulation, the greater the sensory effect.

BRIGHTNESS CONTRAST

It has long been known that the appearance of a gray patch depends on its background. The identical gray will look much brighter on a black background than it will on a white background. This is **brightness contrast,** an effect that increases as the intensity difference increases between two contrasting regions (Figure 5.20).

Contrast is also a function of the distance between the two contrasting regions—the smaller that distance, the greater the contrast (Figure 5.21). This

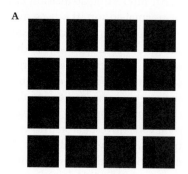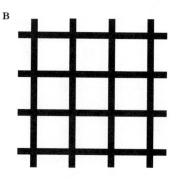

5.21   The effect of distance between contrasting regions   *(A) The white lines in the grid are physically homogeneous, but they don't appear to be—each of the "intersections" seems to contain a gray spot. The uneven appearance of the white strips is caused by contrast. Each strip is surrounded by a black square, which contrasts with it and makes it look brighter. But this is not the case at the intersections, which only touch upon the black squares at their corners. As a result, there is little contrast in the middle of the intersections. This accounts for the gray spots seen there.*
(B) The same point is made by the second grid. Here there seem to be whitish spots at the intersections. The explanation is the same: The black lines are bounded by white and thus look darker by contrast. There is less contrast operating on the regions in the middle of the intersections. As a result, they don't appear as dark as the streets, but rather like whitish spots. (After Hering, 1920)

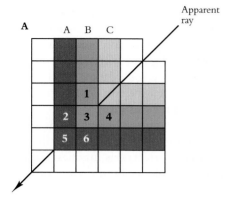

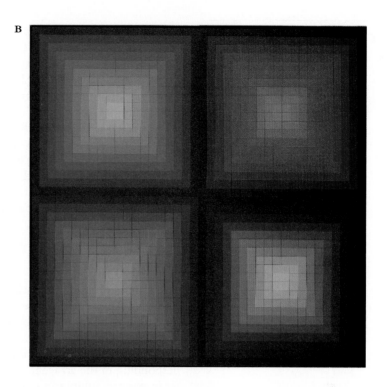

5.22 Contrast *(A) The figure focuses on three of the frames of the painting in (B) to show how the luminous rays are created. Consider squares 1, 3, and 4. Squares 1 and 4 each have an entire side next to the brighter frame C above them. As a result of brightness contrast, they look darker than square 3, which suffers little contrast, for it touches on the brighter frame only at its corner. For the same reason, squares 2 and 6 seem darker than square 5. Since this happens for all the squares at the corners, the observer sees four radiating luminous diagonals. (Jameson, 1975) (B) Arcturus (1966) by Victor Vasarely. (Courtesy of the Hirshhorn Museum and Sculpture Garden, Smithsonian Institution; gift of Joseph H. Hirshhorn, 1972. Photograph by Marianne Gurley)*

5.23 Mach bands *(A) The series of gray strips is arranged in ascending brightness, from left to right. Physically, each strip is of uniform light intensity, as shown graphically in (B), which plots position against physical light intensity. But the strips do not appear to be uniform. For each strip, contrast makes the left edge (adjacent to its darker neighbor) look brighter than the rest, while the right edge (adjacent to its lighter neighbor) looks darker. The result is an accentuation of the contours that separate one strip from the next. The resulting appearance—the way the figure is perceived—is described graphically in (C). (After Cornsweet, 1970; Coren, Porac, and Ward, 1978)*

phenomenon gives rise to a number of visual illusions and has been used by some contemporary artists to create striking effects (see Figure 5.22).

ACCENTUATING EDGES

Contrast effects have another consequence: They serve to accentuate the edges between different objects in our visual world, allowing us to see these edges more clearly. Consider Figure 5.23A, which contains strips of grays that range from very dark to very light. Within each strip, the physical light intensities are equal. That is, the figure shows a uniform dark gray strip, then a uniform slightly lighter strip, then another uniform slightly lighter strip, and so on. This pattern is summarized by Figure 5.23B, in which the actual light intensities for each strip have been plotted against stimulus position.

But the appearance of Figure 5.23A is different from what one might expect based on the pattern shown in Figure 5.23B. At the border between each strip and the neighboring one, there seems to be a band. On the dark side of each juncture, an even darker band is seen; on the bright side of the juncture, a brighter band is visible. This pattern is summarized in Figure 5.23C, which shows *perceived* brightnesses (as opposed to the physical brightnesses, shown in Figure 5.23B).

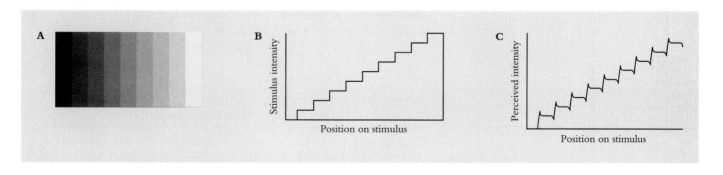

These illusory bands are usually called **Mach bands,** after the nineteenth-century physicist Ernst Mach who discovered them. They are produced by the same contrast effects we discussed before. When a light region borders a darker region, contrast makes the light region look even lighter; when a dark region borders a light region, contrast makes the dark region look darker still. In both directions, contrast accentuates the difference between the two adjacent regions and in this way highlights the edge where the two regions meet.

This sort of process helps vision overcome certain optical imperfections in the eye. Because of these imperfections, the retinal image is often fuzzy, even though the external stimulus is outlined sharply. Contrast corrects this fuzziness, for the visual system recreates, and even exaggerates, boundaries by the same mechanisms that generate Mach bands.

LATERAL INHIBITION AND BRIGHTNESS CONTRAST

Brightness contrast and Mach bands provide some initial basis for the perception of shape: They enhance the differences between adjacent regions and thus help to produce contours. But what is the physiological mechanism that creates them?

At many levels in the visual system, activity in one region tends to inhibit responding in the adjacent regions. This tendency is called *lateral inhibition*—it is, in essence, inhibition exerted sideways. This effect, anticipated by scholars a hundred years ago, has now been confirmed by recordings from single cells in the visual system. These recordings clearly document the fact that neighboring regions in the retina tend to inhibit each other. Similar effects can also be observed at higher levels in the visual system.

Thus, when any visual receptor is stimulated, it transmits its excitation to other cells that eventually relay it to the brain. But the receptor's excitation also has a further effect. It stimulates neurons that extend sideways along the retina. These lateral cells make contact with neighboring cells and inhibit the activation of these neighbors.

To see how this works, consider Figure 5.24. Receptor cell *A* is positioned so that it receives light reflected from a dark gray patch. This incoming light causes the cell to respond, and this response is then transmitted upward to the brain. Receptor cell *B* also receives light from a dark gray patch and so, initially, is stimulated in just the way cell *A* is. But the excitation from cell *B* will not be passed upward to the brain unimpeded. Cell *B* is next to cell *C*, which receives its light from a brightly illuminated patch and so is intensely excited. *C*'s excitation stimulates yet another cell, *D*, whose effect is inhibitory, blocking the excitation that *B* sends upward. Cell *D*, in other words, carries the lateral inhibition.

In short, receptors *A* and *B* are exposed to the same stimulus but do not send the same signal to the brain. Cell *B* is hushed by its excited neighbor and, as a result, sends a weaker signal to the brain than does cell *A*. This is the basis for brightness contrast, and it has the effect of sending the brain a visual message that is, in a sense, an exaggeration. Whenever a dark region is next to a lighter one, the dark one seems darker, and the light one seems lighter.

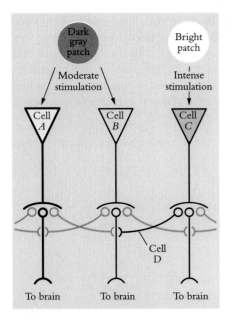

5.24 Lateral inhibition and contrast   *Two receptor cells,* A *and* B, *are stimulated by the same dark gray patch.* A's *excitation is transmitted to the brain unimpeded. But* B *is adjacent to cell* C, *which is intensely stimulated by a bright patch.* C's *excitation is transmitted to the brain, but* C *also excites a lateral cell,* D, *which exerts an inhibitory effect on the message being sent by* B. *As a result,* A *and* B, *receiving the same inputs, send different messages to the brain.*

5.25 **The visible spectrum and the four unique hues** *The visible spectrum consists of light waves from about 360 to 700. White light contains all of these wavelengths. They are bent to different degrees when passed through a prism, yielding the spectrum with the hues shown in the figure. Three of the four unique hues correspond to parts of the spectrum: unique blue at about 465 nm, unique green at about 500 nm, and unique yellow at about 570 nm. These values vary slightly from person to person. The fourth, unique red—that is, a red that has no apparent tinge of either yellow or blue—is called extraspectral because it is not represented by a single wavelength on the spectrum. It can only be produced by a mixture of wavelengths. (From Ohanian, 1993)*

COLOR

The foregoing discussion makes it clear that interaction among sensory elements can shape the sensory input and can, in fact, serve to highlight elements, such as boundaries and moments of change, that are of particular interest to the organism. This pattern of interaction is also evident when we consider a different aspect of vision, namely, the perception of color.

CLASSIFYING THE COLOR SENSATIONS

A person with normal color vision can distinguish over seven million different color shades. These many colors can be classified by reference to a few simple dimensions. The classification scheme concentrates on what we see and experience, on psychology rather than physics, and so it allows us to classify the color sensations rather than the physical stimuli that produce them. As a result, the classification scheme can provide some important insights into the nature of color vision, since the order we find in the classification of our sensations is at least partially imposed by the way in which our nervous systems organize the physical stimuli that impinge upon them.

The dimensions of color All of the colors we can discriminate can be classified according to three perceptual dimensions: hue, brightness, and saturation.

Hue is the attribute that distinguishes blue from green from red, and it is the attribute that is shared by, say, a bright orange, a middle orange, and a darker orange. This term corresponds closely to the way we use the word *color* in everyday life. Hue varies with wavelength (Figure 5.25) so that a wavelength of 465 nanometers is perceived as **unique blue,** a blue that is judged to have no trace of red or green in it; a wavelength of about 500 nanometers is perceived as **unique green** (green with no blue or yellow); a wavelength of 570 nanometers is perceived as **unique yellow** (yellow with no green or red).

Brightness is the dimension that differentiates black (low brightness) from white (high brightness), with various shades of gray in between. Black, white, and all of the grays are the **achromatic** colors; these have no hue. But brightness is also a property of the **chromatic** colors (purple, red, yellow, and so forth). Thus, ultramarine is darker (has a lower brightness) than sky blue, just as charcoal gray is darker than pearl gray (Figure 5.26).

Saturation is the "purity" of a color, the extent to which it is chromatic rather than achromatic. The more gray (or black or white) that is mixed with a color,

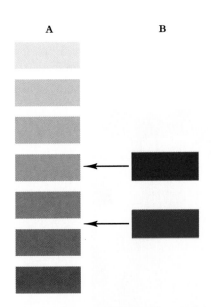

A   B

5.26 **Brightness** *Colors can be arranged according to their brightness. (A) This dimension is most readily recognized when we look at a series of grays, which are totally hueless and vary in brightness only. (B) But chromatic colors can also be classified according to their brightness. The arrows indicate the brightness of the blue and dark green shown here in relation to the series of grays.*

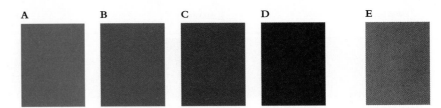

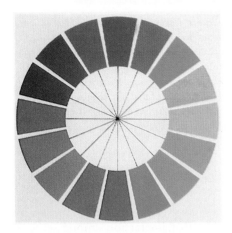

5.27 Saturation *The four patches A–D are identical in both hue and brightness. They only differ in saturation, which is greatest for A and decreases from A to D. The gray patch, E, on the far right matches all the other patches in brightness; it was mixed with the blue patch, A, in varying proportions to produce patches B, C, and D.*

the less saturation it has. Consider the various blue patches in Figure 5.27. All have the same hue (blue), and all have the same brightness. The patches differ only in one respect: the proportion of blue as opposed to that of gray. The more gray there is, the less saturated the color. When the color is entirely gray, saturation is zero. Red and pink differ largely in saturation, so that pink looks like a washed out red.

The color circle, color disk, and color solid   Consider the colors that look most chromatic—that is, colors whose saturation is maximal. If we arrange these on the basis of perceptual similarity, the result is the so-called **color circle,** in which red is followed by orange, orange by yellow, yellow-green, green, blue-green, blue, and violet, until the circle finally returns to red (Figure 5.28).

The color circle embodies the perceptual similarities among the different hues. For each of these hues, a range of saturations is possible, and these can all be depicted as a **color disk,** shown in Figure 5.29.

For each of these combinations of hue and saturation, a range of different brightnesses is also possible, requiring another dimension in our representation. The resulting three-dimensional form summarizing these perceptual attributes is called the **color solid** (Figure 5.30). By specifying a position within this solid, we can identify each of the seven million colors that humans can discriminate.

5.28 The color circle *The relationship between maximally saturated hues can be expressed by arranging them in a circle according to their perceptual similarity. Note that in this version of the color circle, the spacing of the hues depends upon their perceptual properties rather than the wavelengths that give rise to them. In particular, the four unique hues are equally spaced, each 90 degrees from the next. (Hurvich, 1981)*

5.29 The color disk *The two dimensions of a disk allow the representation of hue and saturation. The hues are positioned at the disk's perimeter. Fully saturated colors are shown at the edge of the disk, completely unsaturated (achromatic) colors at the center. (Courtesy Douglas Downing)*

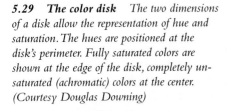

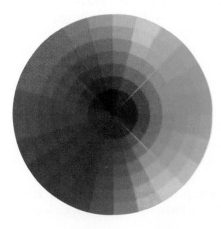

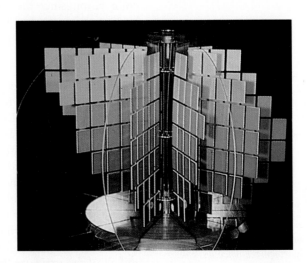

5.30 The color solid *To represent all colors, one needs three dimensions. Brightness is represented by the central axis, going from darkest (black) to brightest (white). Hue is represented by angular position relative to the color circle. Saturation is the distance from the central vertical axis: The maximal saturation that is possible varies from hue to hue; hence, the different extensions from the central axis. The inside of the solid is shown here by taking individual slices, each of which illustrates, for a single hue, the variations in brightness and saturation (Munsell Color, courtesy of Macbeth, a division of Kollmorgen Corporation)*

A

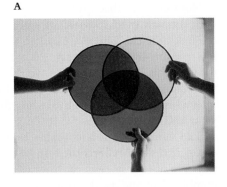

B

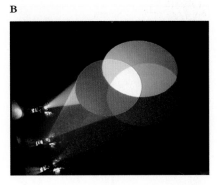

Color mixture *The effect of (A) passing light through several filters (subtractive mixture) and (B) throwing different filtered lights upon the same spot (additive mixture). (Photographs by Fritz Goro/Life Magazine, © Time Warner, Inc.)*

COLOR MIXTURE

With rare exceptions, the objects in the world around us do not reflect a single wavelength; rather, they reflect several different wavelengths, all of which strike the retina simultaneously. Let us consider the results of some of these mixtures.

Subtractive mixture   Before proceeding, we must recognize that the kind of color mixture sensory psychologists are interested in is different from the sort artists employ when they stir pigments together on a palette. Mixing pigments on a palette (or smearing crayons together on a piece of paper) is ***subtractive mixture.*** In subtractive mixture, one set of wavelengths is subtracted from another set.

This sort of mixing can be illustrated with colored filters, such as those used in stage lighting. Each filter allows some wavelengths to pass through, while absorbing others. For example, one such filter, blue in appearance, would absorb all light waves with frequencies below 420 nanometers and also all with frequencies above 520 nanometers. Only frequencies between 420 and 520 are allowed to pass. (A glance back at Figure 5.25 will show why this filter appears blue.)

Another filter, yellow in appearance, absorbs all light waves with frequencies below 480 nanometers or above 660 nanometers. Only the middle range, between 480 and 660, is allowed to pass (Figure 5.31).

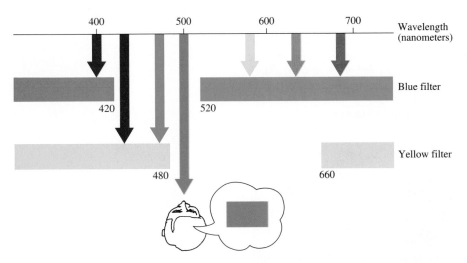

5.31 Subtractive mixture *In subtractive mixture, the light passed by two filters (or reflected by two mixed pigments) is the band of wavelengths passed by the first minus that region subtracted by the second. In the present example, the first filter passes light between 420 and 520 nanometers (a broad-band blue filter), while the second passes light between 480 and 660 nanometers (a broad-band yellow filter). The only light that can pass through both is in the region between 480 and 520 nanometers, which appears green.*

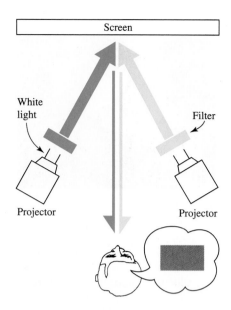

Now imagine that we put these two filters on top of each other and shine a light through them. Wavelengths between 420 and 520 nanometers would pass the first obstacle. The second filter, though, absorbs any light with a wavelength lower than 480 nanometers. As a result, the only light waves that can pass through this double barricade would be those between 480 and 520 nanometers, the only interval left unblocked by both filters. As it happens, light in this interval is seen as green. Thus, when the mixture is subtractive, mixing blue and yellow will yield green.

The same account also applies to artists' pigments. A pigment absorbs some wavelengths and reflects the rest. When two pigments are combined, each continues to absorb its own set of wavelengths. Therefore, if a light shines onto the combined pigments, the only light reflected will consist of those wavelengths not absorbed by *either* pigment. This creates a situation just like the one shown in Figure 5.31. If we mix a blue pigment and a yellow pigment, the blue will absorb all wavelengths above 520 nanometers; the yellow will absorb all below 480. The only wavelengths reflected will be those between 480 and 520, which are seen as green.

5.32 Additive mixture *In additive mixture, the light passed by two filters (or reflected by two pigments) impinges upon the same region of the retina at the same time. The figure shows two projectors throwing blue and yellow filtered light upon the same portion of the screen from which it is reflected onto the same region of the retina. In contrast to what happens in subtractive mixture, the result of adding these two colors is gray.*

Additive mixture In subtractive mixture, one set of wavelengths is removed from another set. This occurs before the light ever hits the eye. In **additive mixture,** the procedure is the very opposite. Additive mixture occurs when different bands of wavelengths stimulate the same retinal region simultaneously. Such additive mixtures can be produced in the laboratory by using light from two different projectors focused on the same spot. If the lights are blue and yellow, then the light reaching the eye will consist of wavelengths between 420 and 520 nanometers (i.e., those produced by the blue light) plus wavelengths between 480 and 660 nanometers. Think of this as the sum "blue plus yellow," in contrast to the subtractive mixture, "neither absorbed by blue nor absorbed by yellow" (Figure 5.32).

Additive mixture has many uses. One is color television, in which a wide range of colors is produced by adding together the emissions of just three phosphers in varying proportions. Another example is provided by the Pointillist painter Georges Seurat. His works are composed of dots of different colors too close together to be seen separately, especially when the picture is viewed from a distance (Figure 5.33). The result is that, while the colors remain separate on the canvas, they blend together in the viewer's eye.

5.33 Additive mixture in Pointillist art The Channel of Gravelines *(1890) by Georges Seurat. A detail of the painting (on the left) shows the separate color daubs which, when viewed from a distance, mix additively. The Pointillists employed this technique instead of mixing pigments to capture the bright appearance of colors outdoors. Pigment mixture is subtractive and darkens the resulting colors. (Courtesy Indianapolis Museum of Art, gift of Mrs. James W. Fesler in memory of Daniel W. and Elizabeth C. Marmon)*

B

A

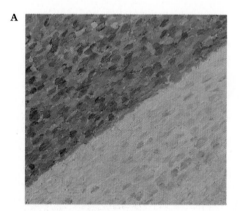

THE PHYSIOLOGICAL BASIS OF COLOR VISION

What is the physiological basis of color vision? We will consider this issue by subdividing it into two questions: How are wavelengths transduced into receptor activity? And how is the receptor output coded so that it yields the psychological attributes of color, such as the experience of blue or yellow?

COLOR RECEPTORS

Normal human color vision depends on three different kinds of cones; this is why our color vision is called *trichromatic*. Each of the three cone types responds to a very broad range of wavelengths in the visible spectrum, but their sensitivity curves differ in that one cone type is most sensitive to wavelengths in the short-wave region of the spectrum, the second to wavelengths in the middle range, and the third to wavelengths in the long range (Bowmaker and Dartnall, 1980; MacNichol, 1986; see Figure 5.34).

As we have already noted, all three cone types respond to some extent to a wide range of wavelengths. Therefore, we cannot discriminate among wavelengths simply by noting which cones are responding—generally all are. What is crucial is the relative *rates* of response by the three cone types. For an input of 480 nanometers, for example, the "short-preferring" and "middle-preferring" cones will respond equally, and their response will be approximately double the response of the "long-preferring" cones. It is this pattern of response that specifies the wavelength; other patterns indicate other wavelengths.

THE YOUNG-HELMHOLTZ THEORY

These observations are broadly consistent with a view proposed in the late nineteenth century by Thomas Young and Hermann von Helmholtz. According to the *Young-Helmholtz theory,* stimulation by red light strongly activates the long-preferring receptors and only weakly activates the other two receptors; it is this combination that gives rise to the experience of red. Similarly, stimulation by blue light strongly activates the short-preferring receptors and only weakly activates the other two; this is what gives rise to the perception of blue. And, finally, stimulation by green light strongly excites the medium-preferring receptors and only weakly activates the other receptors; this gives rise to the perception of green. All other colors are then derived from mixtures of these three primary experiences.

Young first proposed this view in 1802; Helmholtz's refinements of the theory arrived in 1866. Today, these claims fit reasonably well with what we know about receptor function and the spectral sensitivities of the three cone types. The claims also accord well with the fact that, in additive color mixture, we can recreate any hue by a suitable mixture of the three primary colors. (A color television, you will recall, uses just these three to create all of the hues you see on the screen.)

COMPLEMENTARY HUES

This trichromatic analysis of color vision allows us to explain how we discriminate between lights of different wavelengths. For each wavelength, there is an identifiable pattern in the relative firing rates of the three cone types. Strong firing only from the short-preferring cones? The wavelength is likely to be around 430 nanometers. Equal firing from the short-preferring and medium-preferring

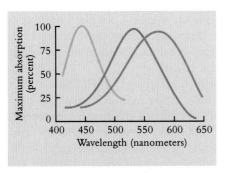

5.34 Sensitivity curves of three different cones in the primate retina   *The retinas of humans and monkeys contain three different kinds of cones, each with its own photopigment that differs in its sensitivity to different regions of the spectrum. One absorbs more of the shorter wavelengths (and is thus more sensitive to light in this spectral region), a second more of the middle wavelengths, a third more of the longer ones. The resulting sensitivity curves are shown here. (After MacNichol, 1964)*

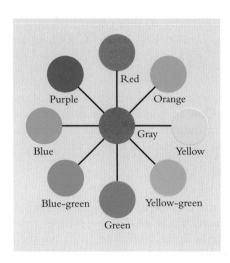

5.35 Complementary hues *Any hue will yield gray if additively mixed (in the correct proportion) with a hue on the opposite side of the color circle. Such hue pairs are complementaries. Some complementary hues are shown here linked by a line across the circle's center. Of particular importance are the two complementary pairs that contain the four unique hues: red-green and blue-yellow.*

cones, with only modest firing from the long-preferring cones? The wavelength is 480 nanometers.

But can these patterns tell us why the colors *look* the way they do? The Young-Helmholtz theory asserts that three colors—red, green, and blue—have special status, since these are the colors that maximally stimulate the three receptors. This fits with the fact that these colors do look relatively pure to most observers, in contrast to a color such as purple, say, which looks like a mixture of primary colors (in this case, red and blue). But what about yellow, which looks like a primary (does not look like a mixture) yet does not have primary status according to trichromatic theory (Bornstein, 1973)?

Trichromatic theory also does not explain the fact that, in important ways, colors come in pairs. For example, in additive color mixture every hue has a **complementary color**—another hue that, if mixed with the first in appropriate proportions, produces gray. (Things work differently in subtractive color mixing.) An easy way to find complementaries is by reference to the color circle. Any hue on the circumference will yield gray if mixed (additively) with the hue on the opposite side of the color circle (see Figure 5.35). Hues that are not complementary produce mixtures that preserve the hue of their components. Thus, the mixture of red and yellow leads to orange (which still looks like a yellowish red), while that of blue and red yields a violet (which looks like a reddish blue).

COLOR ANTAGONISTS

Complementary colors, such as blue and yellow, or red and green, seem to function as mutually opposed "antagonists," each able to cancel the other's hue. Some further phenomena lead to a similar conclusion. For example, consider the phenomenon known as **simultaneous color contrast,** the chromatic counterpart of brightness contrast. *Color contrast* refers to the fact that any chromatic region in the visual field tends to induce its complementary color in adjoining areas. For example, a gray patch will tend to look bluish if surrounded by yellow, yellowish if surrounded by blue, and so on (Figure 5.36).

In simultaneous contrast, the complementary relation involves two adjoining regions in space. A similar phenomenon occurs if two regions are appropriately related in time, rather than in space. Suppose we stare at a green patch for a

5.36 Color contrast *The gray patches on the blue and yellow backgrounds are physically identical. But they don't look that way. To begin with, there is a difference in perceived brightness: The patch on the blue looks brighter than the one on the yellow, a result of brightness contrast. There is also a difference in perceived hue, for the patch on the blue looks somewhat yellowish, while that on the yellow looks bluish. This is color contrast, a demonstration that hues tend to induce their antagonists in neighboring areas.*

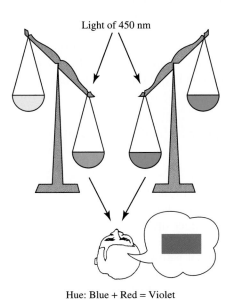

Light of 450 nm

Hue: Blue + Red = Violet

5.38 The opponent-process hue systems
The diagram shows how opponent-process theory interprets our response to light of a particular wavelength. In the example, the light is in the short-wave region of the visible spectrum, specifically, 450 nanometers. This will affect both the blue-yellow and red-green systems. It will tip the blue-yellow balance toward blue, and the red-green balance toward red. The resulting hue will be a mixture of red and blue (that is, violet).

Leo Hurvich and Dorothea Jameson
(Courtesy of Department of Psychology, University of Pennsylvania)

5.37 Negative afterimage   *Stare at the center of the figure for a minute or two, and then look at a white piece of paper. Blink once or twice; the negative afterimage will appear within a few seconds, showing the rose in its correct colors.*

while and then look at a white wall. We will see a **negative afterimage** of the patch, in this case, a reddish spot (Figure 5.37). In general, negative afterimages have the complementary hue of the original stimulus (which is why they are called *negative*). Thus, fixation on a brightly lit red bulb will make us see a dark greenish shape when we subsequently look at a white screen.

THE OPPONENT-PROCESS THEORY

What produces this pairing of hues? And why is it that yellow looks relatively pure to the human eye and not at all like a mixture? These observations can be accounted for by the **opponent-process theory,** first suggested by Ewald Hering but then developed in crucial ways by Leo Hurvich and Dorothea Jameson. According to this theory, the output from the three cone types is recoded by another layer of neural mechanisms into six psychologically primary color qualities—red, green, blue, yellow, black, and white. These six processes are themselves organized into three opponent-process pairs: red-green, blue-yellow, and black-white. The two members of each pair are antagonists. Excitation of one member automatically inhibits the other (Hurvich and Jameson, 1957).

The two hue pairs   According to the opponent-process theory, the experience of hue depends on two of the opponent-process pairs—red-green and blue-yellow. Each of these opponent-process pairs can be likened to a balance. If one arm (say, the blue process) goes down, the other arm (its opponent, yellow) necessarily goes up. The hue we actually see depends upon the position of the two balances (Figure 5.38). If the red-green balance is tipped toward red and the blue-yellow balance toward blue (excitation of red and blue with concomitant inhibition of green and yellow), the perceived hue will be violet. If the red-green system is in balance, and the blue-yellow system tips toward blue, unique blue is perceived (that is, blue with no trace of red or green). The three other unique hues are coded in a similar fashion. (For example, unique red is perceived when the blue-yellow system is in balance, and the red-green system tips toward red.) If both hue systems are in balance, there will be no hue at all, and the resulting color will be seen as achromatic (that is, without hue).

The relation between color receptors and opponent processes   There is no question that there are three types of cones, as predicted by trichromatic theory. How can we

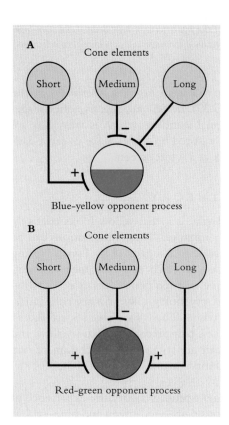

A

Cone elements

Short   Medium   Long

Blue-yellow opponent process

B

Cone elements

Short   Medium   Long

Red-green opponent process

5.39 *From receptors to opponent-process pairs* A simplified presentation of a neural system in which all three receptor elements feed into two color opponent-process pairs. One pole of each opponent process is activated by excitation, while its opposite pole is activated by inhibition. (A) The blue-yellow system. This is excited by the short-wave receptors and inhibited by the medium- and the long-wave receptors. If excitation outweighs inhibition, the opponent-process signals blue; if inhibition outweighs excitation, it signals yellow; if excitation and inhibition are equal, there is no signal at all and we see gray. (B) The red-green system. This is excited by both the short-wave and the long-wave receptor elements, and is inhibited by the medium-wave elements. If excitation outweighs inhibition, the system signals red; if inhibition outweighs excitation, it signals green; if excitation and inhibition are equal, there is no signal and we see gray. The assumption that this system is excited by both short- and long-wave receptors is made because the experience "red" occurs at the two extremes of the spectrum: Short wavelengths produce the hues of violet or purple, which are perceived as having some red in them, while long wavelengths produce various oranges, which of course are also seen as having red in them. (For discussion, see Hurvich and Jameson, 1957)

reconcile this fact with the suggestion that there are *four* chromatic color opponents? Hurvich and Jameson have suggested that the three receptor types provide the input to opponent-process neurons higher up in the visual system. The receptors have both excitatory and inhibitory connections with the opponent-process neurons, such that one pole of each opponent process will be activated by a receptor signal while its opposite pole will be inhibited by the same signal (see Figure 5.39).

THE PHYSIOLOGICAL BASIS OF OPPONENT PROCESSES

When first proposed, the opponent-process mechanism was only an inference, based on the perceptual phenomena of color vision. This inference was subsequently confirmed, however, by single-cell recordings (see Chapter 2), which show that some neurons, in the retina and higher up, behave very much as the opponent-process theory would lead one to expect.

As an example, consider studies of the visual pathway of the rhesus monkey, whose color vision seems to be very similar to ours. Some of the cells in this pathway behave as though they were part of a blue-yellow system. If the retina is stimulated by blue light, these cells fire more rapidly. If the same area is exposed to yellow light, the firing rate is inhibited (Figure 5.40). Other cells show a

5.40 *Opponent-process cells in the visual system of a monkey* The figure shows the average firing rate of blue-yellow cells to light of different wavelengths. These cells are excited by shorter wavelengths and inhibited by longer wavelengths, analogous to the cells in the human system that signal the sensation "blue." As the figure shows, shorter wavelengths lead to firing rates that are above the spontaneous rates obtained when there is no stimulus at all. Longer wavelengths have the opposite effect, depressing the cell's activity below the spontaneous firing rate. (Data from De Valois and De Valois, 1975)

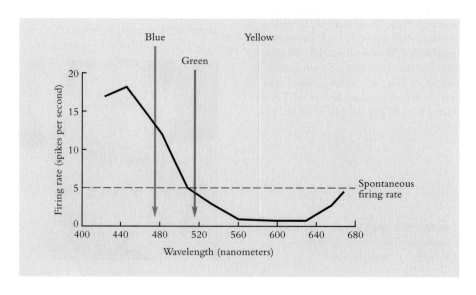

similar antagonistic pattern when stimulated by red light or green (De Valois, 1965). All of this is exactly what one might expect if these cells embody the mechanisms proposed by the opponent-process theory.

COLOR BLINDNESS

Most mammals have some degree of color vision (Jacobs, 1993), as do most humans. A small proportion of the population, however, does not respond to color as the rest of us do. Of these the vast majority are men, since many such conditions are inherited and sex linked. Some form of color-vision defect is found in 8 percent of all males as compared to only .03 percent of females.

Deficiencies in color vision come in various forms: Some involve a missing visual pigment, others a defective opponent process, and many involve malfunction at both levels (Hurvich, 1981). Most common is a confusion of reds with greens; least common is total color blindness in which no hues can be distinguished at all. Color defects are rarely noticed in everyday life, for color-blind people ordinarily use color names quite appropriately. They call blood *red* and dollar bills *green*, presumably on the basis of other cues such as form and brightness. To determine whether a person has a color defect, he or she must be tested under special conditions in which such extraneous cues are eliminated (Figure 5.41).

How do people with color defects see colors? This question long seemed unanswerable: The color-blind individual cannot know what sensory quality is lacking from his visual experience and thus has no way to compare his experience to that of an individual with normal color vision. However, one unusual person (one of the rare women with a color-vision defect) was red-green color blind in one eye but had normal color vision in the other. She was able to describe what she saw with the defective eye by using the color language of the normal one. With the color-blind eye she saw only grays, blues, and yellows. Red and green hues were altogether absent, as if one of the opponent-process pairs were missing (Graham and Hsia, 1954).

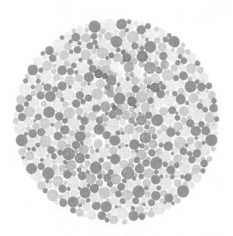

5.41   Testing for color blindness   *A plate used to test for color blindness. To pick out the number in the plate, an observer has to be able to discriminate certain hues. Persons with normal color vision can do it and will see the number 3. Persons with red-green color blindness cannot do it.*

PERCEIVING SHAPES

The perception of color and brightness is important to us—whether in enhancing our appreciation of art, or, more practically, in allowing us to distinguish a ripe fruit from one that's green. But other aspects of perception are at least as important. After all, a color-blind individual can live a perfectly normal life. But not so an individual who is unable to discriminate among shapes or forms, or an individual unable to recognize a square or a circle. These individuals (known as *visual agnosics*) are dramatically impaired in their functioning. We need to ask, therefore, how the visual system achieves the perception of shape. This achievement turns out to be quite complex; so while we begin addressing it in this chapter, the issues discussed here will carry over into Chapter 6.

FEATURE DETECTORS

How do we perceive the contours that outline and define the shape of any particular form? We do so through specialized detector cells that respond to certain characteristics of the stimulus and to no others—so some respond to curves, others to straight edges, some to contours angled upward, others to contours angled downward, and so forth. The discovery of these cells has been one of the most exciting achievements of visual physiology during the past five decades.

Electrophysiologists often record from single nerve cells (see Chapter 2) and,

5.42 Recording from the visual system of a cat *The experimental setup for recording neural responses from the visual system of a cat. An anesthetized cat has one eye propped open so that visual stimulation can be directed to particular regions of the retina. A microelectrode picks up neural impulses from a single cell in the optic system, amplifies them, and displays them on an oscilloscope. (After Schiffman, 1976)*

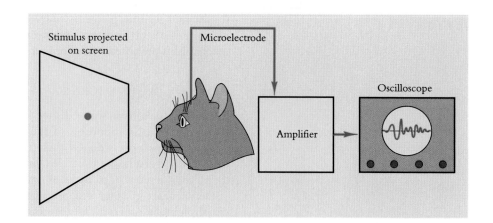

by such techniques, have discovered how particular cells in a sensory system respond to simple stimuli such as light of a given wavelength. More recently, they have applied the same approach to the perception of contours. In these studies, a microelectrode is placed into the optic nerve or, in some studies, the brain of an anesthetized animal. (Special care is taken to protect the well-being of the animal, both for ethical reasons and also to allow the investigators to assess how neurons function in an intact, healthy organism.) The eye of the animal is then stimulated by visual inputs of varying brightness and different shapes, at different locations (Figure 5.42). In this fashion, the investigator can learn which stimuli evoke a response (either an increase or a decrease in firing rate) from that cell.

Typically, results show that a cell responds maximally to an input of a certain shape and size at a certain position. This defines the **receptive field** for that cell—the region of a particular shape, size, and location within the visual field to which that cell responds (see Figure 5.43).

For example, certain ganglion cells in a frog's optic nerve respond intensely to a small, dark object that is moved into a particular retinal region and then moved around within that region. Stimuli that lack any of these features have little or no effect. Why should the frog possess such fussy cells? Ordinarily, the stimulus that excites these cells is a flying insect—a stimulus of some importance to the frog. It is no wonder, then, that natural selection has provided the frog with this prewired sensory mechanism—often called a "bug detector"—which responds specifically to buglike objects that move in a buglike manner, with a concomitant disregard for all other stimuli (Lettvin et al., 1959).

In the frog and in many other animals, this sort of visual analysis is carried out largely by specialized cells in the retina. In higher animals, such as cats and monkeys (and undoubtedly humans as well), the retinal detectors are relatively simple and not as specialized. In these creatures, most of the specialized visual analysis takes place at higher levels, primarily in the visual cortex.

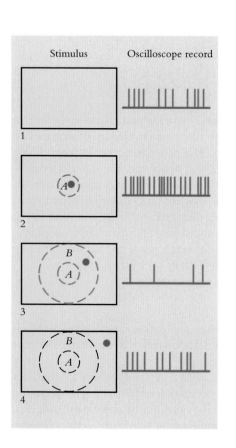

5.43 Receptive fields on the cat's visual system *Using the setup shown in Figure 5.42, stimuli are presented to various regions of the retina. The panels show the firing frequency of a particular ganglion cell. Panel 1 shows the baseline firing rate when no stimulus is presented anywhere. Panel 2 shows the effect when a stimulus is presented anywhere within an inner, central region, A, on the retina. When stimulated in A, the cell's firing rate goes up. Panel 3 shows what happens in response to a stimulus presented anywhere within the ring-shaped region, B, surrounding region A. Stimulation in B causes the cell's firing rate to go down. Panel 4, finally, shows what happens when a stimulus is presented outside of either A or B, the regions that together comprise the cell's receptive field. Now there is no significant change from the cell's normal baseline. (From Kuffler, 1953)*

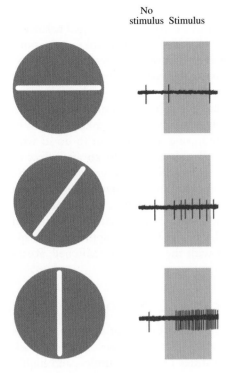

No stimulus Stimulus

5.44 Feature detectors in the visual system of the cat *The response of a single cortical cell when stimulated by a slit of light in three different orientations. This cell, a simple unit, was evidently responsive to the vertical. A horizontal slit led to no response, a tilted slit led to a slight response, while a vertical slit led to a marked increase in firing. (After Hubel, 1963)*

Much of what we know in this domain derives from the work of two physiologists, David Hubel and Torsten Wiesel, who won the Nobel prize for their work. They studied the activity of single cortical cells of cats in response to various visual stimuli and found that some cells react to lines or edges of a particular orientation. Such cells would be excited by a thin sliver of light slanted at, say, 45 degrees, regardless of the line's specific location (Figure 5.44). This sort of cell is called a ***feature detector;*** it analyzes the visual stimulus to detect a certain feature such as orientation; the cell selectively responds to this feature and not to other aspects of the stimulus pattern such as brightness (Hubel and Wiesel, 1959, 1968).

There are actually several different kinds of detectors. The so-called **simple cells** fire maximally when the input is a line or an edge of a specific orientation at a specific retinal position. One simple cell might respond to a vertical line at one position in the visual field, whereas another simple cell might respond to a line tilted to 45 degrees at the same position; still another cell might respond to a vertical line at some other position. In this fashion, the visual field is blanketed by receptive fields, so that lines of any orientation at any position will be detected by the appropriately tuned cell.

Other cells in the visual cortex have been dubbed **complex cells.** Like simple cells, these are also sensitive to the input's orientation, and so fire at their maximal rate only if the input is tilted appropriately. However, these cells are more sensitive to the direction of movement of the target.

Still other cells respond to yet more complex features, including corners and angles. In this way, information arriving from the retina passes from one processing layer to the next. Each layer adds to the sophistication of our perception of the stimulus until a complete coding of the input's contours, shapes, and motions is obtained.

ADAPTATION OF FEATURE DETECTORS

Recording from single cells provides us with exquisitely precise information about how such cells respond to the incoming stimulus information. But how do the cells work together? How do they pool their various bits of information to produce a perception of the whole? This is an issue to which we will return in Chapter 6, but an important source of information comes from the study of adaptation effects.

We have previously encountered the phenomenon of adaptation in the case of relatively simple sensory qualities such as hue. After prolonged fixation on a green patch, its apparent greenness will fade. If a neutral gray is now projected upon the same retinal region, it will look reddish. Effects of this sort laid the foundations for a theory of the opponent processes that underlie color vision. The same logic motivates the study of adaptation effects in more complex perceptual attributes (Anstis, 1975).

An example is the ***aftereffect of visual movement.*** If one looks at a waterfall for a while and then turns away to look at the riverbank, the bank and the trees upon it will seem to float upward, a dramatic effect that is readily reproduced in the perceptual laboratory (Figure 5.45). We can easily explain this result if we assume that the direction of perceived movement is signaled by the activity of two movement detectors that operate as an opponent-process pair. If these two detectors interact like the members of the color opponent-process pairs, then the stimulation of either one will automatically lead to the inhibition of the other.

Consider, therefore, what will happen if one member of this motion-detector pair has been stimulated for a long time (say, by exposure to a downward moving pattern). It will gradually adapt and will therefore fire less. As a result, the

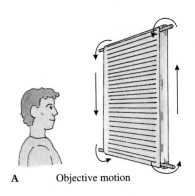

A Objective motion

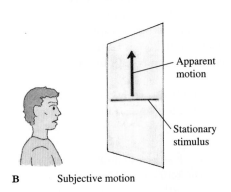

Apparent motion

Stationary stimulus

B Subjective motion

5.45 Aftereffect of movement *(A) The research participant first looks at a band of downward moving lines for a minute or two. (B) He then looks at a stationary horizontal line. This line will now appear to be moving upward. This effect is probably produced by the adaptation of a movement detector that signals downward motion.*

balance will swing toward the other member of the pair. This changed balance is revealed when the moving target is withdrawn and the subject looks at a stationary pattern. This objectively stationary pattern will now be perceived as moving upward. The effect is obviously analogous to the red afterimage that follows prolonged fixation on a green patch.

Evidence suggests that these motion-detector pairs are located in the brain and not in the retina. In a number of experiments, investigators asked subjects to look at a stimulus that moved continuously in one direction but to do so with one eye only; the other eye was covered. Would this lead to an aftereffect of movement when the subjects were then tested with the other eye? If so, the motion detectors that were adapted by the moving stimulus *must* be located at a point beyond the retina, in some region in the brain where the information from both eyes is somehow combined. The results showed that this was indeed the case. Looking at a moving stimulus with one eye led to an appropriate adaptation effect when the test was conducted with the other eye (Mitchell, Reardon, and Muir, 1975).

FEATURE DETECTORS OF COMPLEX FORMS?

The notion of opponent pairs provides some indication about how the nervous system begins to integrate the various features it detects. But we still need to ask how the visual system organizes all these features into the countless and highly complex objects that we can recognize. For some complex shapes, particularly those that have special significance for a species, there are prewired detectors of suitable design and sophistication. Something of this sort is clearly true for many lower animals, whose visual analyzers are tuned to detect those few objects that matter for the species; the frog's bug detector is a case in point.

But it is inconceivable that such built-in mechanisms could account for all the forms higher animals—and especially humans—perceive and recognize. For unlike frogs, humans must discriminate among a multitude of patterns, and it is hardly possible that we carry specialized detectors for all of them—triangles, squares, apples, apple pies, champagne bottles, cabbages, kings—the list is endless. Nevertheless, it may well be that even the primates—and indeed, we ourselves—possess some special cells geared to detect stimulus relationships appreciably more complex than color, edges, and direction of movement. In fact, certain cells in a monkey's cortex have been shown to respond to pictures of a monkey's face but not at all to nonface stimuli. Some other cells responded to pictures of a monkey's hand (Desimone et al., 1984). While there is no evidence that humans have analogous face or hand detectors, there is good reason to believe that the cortical systems that are responsible for recognizing faces are not the same as those that handle the perception of other visual forms. For as we saw in Chapter 2, certain cortical lesions may lead to a visual agnosia for faces (that is, to prosopagnosia) without affecting the perception of most other nonfacelike objects (Farah, 1990).

Perhaps, then, we do possess some cells that do for us what the bug detector does for the frog. But there is little doubt that the vast majority of the forms we recognize are assemblies of lower-level features glued together by experience. As we'll see in the next chapter, these lower-level feature detectors are the raw material out of which we construct the infinity of shapes we can perceive and recognize. But the way we glue the output of these detectors together is surprisingly complex and will be one of our main concerns in Chapter 6.

TAKING STOCK

We have looked at the way in which the different sensory systems respond to external stimuli, how they transduce the proximal stimulus and convert it into a neural impulse, how they code the incoming message into the various dimensions of our sensory experience, and how activity in any part of a sensory system interacts with the activity of other parts. All of this has led us to some understanding of how we come to see bright yellow-greens and hear high-pitched sounds. But it has not yet addressed the question with which we started. How do we come to know about the objects and events outside—not just bright yellow-greens but grassy meadows, not just high-pitched sounds but singing birds? That the sensory systems contribute the raw materials for such knowledge is clear enough. But how do we get from the sensory raw materials to a knowledge of the world outside? This question is traditionally dealt with under the heading of perception, the topic to which we turn next.

SUMMARY

1. The study of sensory processes grew out of questions about the origin of human knowledge. John Locke and other adherents of *empiricism* argued that all knowledge comes through stimuli that excite the senses. We can distinguish two kinds of stimuli. One is the *distal stimulus*, an object or event in the world outside. The other is the *proximal stimulus*, the pattern of physical stimulus energies that impinges on a given sensory surface. The only way to get information about distal stimuli outside is through the proximal stimuli these give rise to. This leads to theoretical problems, for we perceive many qualities—depth, constant size, and shape—that are not given in the proximal stimulus. Empiricists try to overcome such difficulties by asserting that much of perception is built up through learning by *association*. This view has been challenged by *nativism*, a view espoused by Immanuel Kant and others who believe that the sensory input is organized according to a number of built-in categories.

2. The path to sensory experience or sensation begins with a proximal stimulus. This is *transduced* into a nervous impulse by specialized receptors, is usually further modified by other parts of the nervous system, and finally leads to a sensation. *Psychophysics*, a branch of sensory psychology, tries to relate the characteristics of the physical stimulus to both the quality and intensity of the sensory experience.

3. The founder of psychophysics, Gustav Fechner, studied sensory intensity by determining the ability of subjects to discriminate between stimulus intensities. The *difference threshold* is the change in the intensity of a given stimulus that is just large enough to be detected, producing a *just noticeable difference,* or *jnd*. According to *Weber's law,* the jnd is a constant fraction of the intensity of the standard stimulus. Fechner generalized Weber's law to express a wider relationship between sensory intensity and physical intensity. This is *Fechner's law,* which states that the strength of a sensation grows as the logarithm of stimulus intensity.

4. A way of disentangling sensory sensitivity and response bias is provided by *signal-detection theory*. In a typical detection experiment, the stimulus is presented on some trials and absent on others. In this procedure, there can be two kinds of errors: *misses* (saying a stimulus is absent when it is present) and *false alarms* (saying it is present when it is absent). Their relative proportion is partially determined by a *payoff matrix*. According to signal-detection theory, distinguishing between the presence of a stimulus and its absence depends on a process in which the subject has to decide whether activation in a sensory

system is produced by the signal plus background noise or by the background noise alone.

5.   Investigations of the neural underpinning of sensation involve attempts to understand the *sensory codes* by which the nervous system represents sensory experiences. Of particular interest are qualitative differences that occur both between sensory modalities (e.g., A-flat versus red) and within them (e.g., red versus green). According to the *doctrine of specific nerve energies,* such qualitative differences are ultimately caused by differences in the nervous structures excited by the stimuli rather than by differences between the stimuli as such.

6.   Underlying neural processes are described by two alternative views: *specificity theory,* which holds that the different sensory qualities are signaled by different neurons, and *pattern theory,* which asserts that these differences are coded by the overall pattern of activation across a whole set of sensory fibers. The evidence indicates that the nervous system uses both specificity and pattern codes in different sensory systems.

7.   Different sense modalities have different functions and mechanisms. One group of senses provides information about the body's own movements and location. Skeletal motion is sensed through *kinesthesis,* bodily orientation by the vestibular organs located in the inner ears.

8.   The various skin senses inform the organism of what is directly adjacent to its own body. There are at least four different skin sensations: *pressure, warmth, cold,* and *pain.*

9.   The sense of taste acts as a gatekeeper to the digestive system. Its receptors are *taste buds,* whose stimulation generates the four basic taste qualities of *sour, sweet, salty,* and *bitter.*

10.   Smell, or *olfaction,* is both an internal sense that provides information about substances in the mouth and (with the sense of taste) gives rise to the experience of flavor, and a distance sense that gives information about objects outside of the body. In humans, olfaction is a relatively minor distance sense, but in many other animals it is a vital guide to food, mates, and danger. In many species, it permits a primitive form of communication based on *pheromones.*

11.   The sense of hearing, or *audition,* informs us of pressure changes that occur at a distance. Its stimulus is a disturbance of the air that is propagated in the form of *sound waves.* These can vary in *amplitude* and *frequency,* and may be simple or complex.

12.   A number of accessory structures help to conduct and amplify sound waves so that they can affect the auditory receptors. Sound waves set up vibrations in the *eardrum* that are then transmitted by the *ossicles* to the *oval window,* whose movements create waves in the *cochlea* of the *inner ear.* Within the cochlea is the *basilar membrane,* which contains the auditory receptors that are stimulated by the membrane's deformation. According to the *place theory,* the sensory experience of pitch is based on the place of the membrane that is stimulated, each place being responsive to a particular wave frequency and generating a particular pitch sensation. But since very low frequency waves deform the whole membrane just about equally, modern theorists believe that both the place of deformation and firing frequency of the auditory nerve are important. The perception of higher frequencies depends on the place stimulated on the basilar membrane, while perception of lower frequencies depends on neural firing frequency.

13.   Vision is our primary distance sense. Its stimulus is light, which can vary in *intensity* and *wavelength.* Many of the structures of the eye, such as the *lens* and the *iris,* serve to control the amount of light entering the eye and to fashion a proper proximal stimulus, the *retinal image.* Once on the *retina,* the light stimulus is transduced into a neural impulse by the visual receptors, the *rods* and *cones.* Acuity is greatest in the *fovea,* where the density of the receptors (here, cones) is greatest.

14.   According to the *duplex theory of vision,* rods and cones differ in function. The rods operate at low light intensities and lead to colorless sensations. The cones function at much higher illumination levels and are responsible for sensations of color. Further evidence for the duplex theory comes from differences in their *spectral sensitivity.*

SUMMARY

15.   The first stage in the transformation of light into a neural impulse is a photo-chemical process that involves the breakdown of various *visual pigments* that are later resynthesized. The pigment in the rods is *rhodopsin*. The cones contain three different pigments but the chemical composition of these pigments is still unknown.

16.   The various components of the visual system do not operate in isolation but interact constantly. One form of interaction occurs over time, as in various forms of *adaptation*. Visual adaptation is usually counteracted by eye movements, but their effects can be nullified by the *stabilized image* procedure.

17.   Interaction also occurs in space between neighboring regions on the retina. An example is *brightness contrast*. This tends to accentuate edges, as in the case of *Mach bands*. The physiological mechanism that underlies these effects is *lateral inhibition*.

18.   Visual sensations have a qualitative character—they vary in color. Color sensations can be ordered by reference to three dimensions: *hue, brightness,* and *saturation*. Colors can be mixed *subtractively* (as in mixing pigments) or additively (as in simultaneously stimulating the same region of the retina with two or more stimuli). The results of *additive-mixture* studies show that every hue has a *complementary* that, when mixed with the first, yields gray. Two important examples are red-green, and blue-yellow. These two color pairs are color *antagonists,* a fact shown by the phenomena of the *negative afterimage* and *simultaneous color contrast*.

19.   The fact that any color can be matched by mixing together three other colors fits well with the *Young-Helmholtz theory* of color vision. According to this theory, the qualities of color are specified by the relative firing rates of the three types of cones, each of which has its own somewhat different sensitivity curve.

20.   The output of the three cone types is recoded by subsequent neural systems; this recoding is described by the *opponent-process theory* of Hurvich and Jameson. This assumes that there are three neural systems, each of which corresponds to a pair of antagonistic sensory experiences: red-green, blue-yellow, and black-white. The first two determine perceived hue; the third determines perceived brightness. Further evidence for the opponent-process view comes from single-cell recordings of rhesus monkeys and some phenomena of *color blindness*.

21.   Attributes of visual contour are vital to the recognition of form. Many of these attributes are sensed by *feature detectors,* both in the retina and in the brain. These are cells that respond to certain relational aspects of the stimulus, such as edges and corners, as shown by single-cell recordings. The adaptation of such feature detectors may explain certain changes of perceptual experience after prolonged exposure to a certain kind of stimulus, as in the *aftereffect of visual movement*.

CHAPTER  **6**

PERCEPTION

I n the previous chapter, we discussed some of the simpler attributes of sensory experience, such as red, A-flat, and cold. The empiricist philosophers Locke and Berkeley thought that these experiences were passively registered by the senses, and then glued together, by means of associations, to form more complex perceptions. As they saw it, the creation of these associations was also a passive affair: Two ideas were associated in the mind, they argued, merely because these ideas had been experienced together in the past. Associations, like the sensations themselves, are imposed on us from the outside.

But the eye is much more than a camera, the ear more than a microphone. From the very start, both sensory systems actively transform their stimulus inputs, emphasizing areas of difference or contrast within the input and minimizing areas of uniformity. This active organization of the stimulus input is impressive enough when we consider the experience of simple sensory attributes. It becomes even more dramatic when we turn to the broader question of how we apprehend objects and events in the world around us—how we see, not just something bright, or something red, but a bright red apple.

THE PROBLEM OF PERCEPTION

What is actually involved in our seeing an apple? At first, we might think that the only problem is grasping the meaning of the visual input: Having perceived the apple, how do we manage to interpret it as an edible fruit—one that grows on trees, keeps the doctor away, caused the expulsion from Eden, and so on? But these are not the only questions, or even the most basic ones, for the student of perception. The fundamental issue is not why we see a particular kind of object, but rather why we see any object at all. Suppose we show the apple to someone who has never seen this type of fruit before. He will not know what it is or what it is for, but he will certainly see it as some round, red thing of whose tangible existence he has no doubt—in short, he will perceive it as an object.

How do we accomplish this feat? After all, the apple is known to us (at least visually) only through the proximal stimulus it projects upon our retina, and this proximal stimulus is two dimensional and constantly changing. It gets smaller or larger depending on our distance from the apple; it stimulates different regions of the retina each time we move our head or eyes. How do we see past these continual variations in the proximal stimulus to perceive the constant properties of the external object? For that matter, how does he manage to identify the apple's boundaries, treating all of the apple's parts as one unit, separate from those of the banana right beside it? How do we compensate for the fact that part of the apple's form is hidden from view by the edge of the fruit bowl? These achievements, simple as they seem, turn out to be impressively complicated, and they are achievements without which perception cannot proceed.

In short, before we can decide whether the object we are looking at is an apple (or a baseball or a human head or whatever), we must organize the sensory

2 1 7

The problem of perception *How do we come to perceive the world as it is—to see the flags as smaller than the boat, to see the wall extending continuously behind the people that block some portion of it from view, and so on? (Claude Monet,* Terrace at Sainte-Adresse, *1867; courtesy The Metropolitan Museum of Art, purchased with special contributions and purchase funds given or bequeathed by friends of the Museum, 1967)*

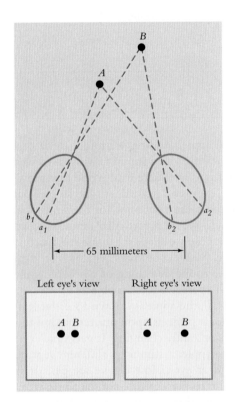

6.1 Retinal disparity *Two points, A and B, at different distances from the observer, present somewhat different retinal images. In the left-eye's view, the image cast by A and that cast by B are close together; in the right-eye's view, the images are further apart. This disparity between the views serves as a powerful cue for depth. (After Hochberg, 1978a)*

world into a coherent scene in which there are real objects (such as apples) and real events. Likewise, before we can take a walk down a hallway, we need to perceive the layout of the hallway—which obstacles are nearby and which far off, whether the people we see are standing still or moving across our path. To accomplish all of this, we have to answer three important questions about whatever it is we see (or hear or feel) in the world outside: Where is it? Where is it going? And, most important: What is it? Each of these questions is crucial, since our very existence (as well as our evolutionary success) demands that we act differently toward a potential mate than toward a lamppost, toward a tiger far away than one nearby, and toward a car streaking toward us than one zooming away.

Our discussion will begin with the question of where the object is and in particular how we determine whether it is nearby or far away.

THE PERCEPTION OF DEPTH: WHERE IS IT?

The perception of depth has intrigued scholars for over three hundred years. Their question has been simple: Since the image that falls upon the retina has only two dimensions, how is it that our perceptual world contains three? This question has led to a search for **depth cues,** features of the stimulus situation that indicate how far an object is from the observer or from other objects in the world.

BINOCULAR CUES

One important cue for depth comes from the fact that we are binocular creatures—that is, we have two eyes. Our eyes look out onto the world from slightly different positions; as a result, each eye has a slightly different view of the world, and this difference provides important information about depth relationships in the world (Figure 6.1). The difference between the two eyes' views is called **binocular disparity.**

6.2   Interposition   When one figure interrupts the boundary of another figure, it provides a monocular cue for depth. This is interposition. Because of interposition, the red rectangle in the figure appears to be in front of the blue one.

Binocular disparity can induce the perception of depth, even if no other distance cues are present. For example, the bottom panels of Figure 6.1 show the views that would be received by each eye while looking at a pair of nearby objects. If we separately present each of these views to the appropriate eye (for example, by drawing the views on two cards and placing one card in front of each eye), we can obtain a striking impression of depth. (The popular child's toy, the Viewmaster, works in the same way, presenting two slightly different pictures to the two eyes; many years ago, the stereopticon viewer used the same principle.)

MONOCULAR CUES

Binocular disparity is a powerful (and probably innate) determinant of perceived depth. Yet we can perceive depth even with one eye closed. Similarly, people who have been blind in one eye from birth are able to perceive the world accurately in three dimensions. Clearly, then, there are cues for depth perception that come from the image obtained with one eye alone. These are the **monocular depth cues.**

Some of the monocular depth cues have been exploited for centuries by artists in order to create an impression of depth on a flat surface. Such cues are therefore called **pictorial cues.** In each case, these cues exploit simple principles of physics. For example, objects that are farther away will inevitably be blocked from view by any other opaque object that obstructs their optical path to the eye. So we are able to use this pattern of blocking as a cue to which objects are more distant from us—a depth cue known as **interposition** (Figure 6.2). Similarly, distant objects necessarily produce a smaller retinal image than nearby objects of the same size; this provides the basis for the cues of **linear perspective** and **relative size** (Figures 6.3 and 6.4).

A different sort of pictorial cue is provided by **texture gradients.** Consider what meets the eye when we look at cobblestones on a road or clumps of grass in a meadow. The retinal projection of such objects shows a pattern of continuous

*6.3   Linear perspective as a cue for depth
(Photograph by Wolfgang Kaehler/Corbis)*

6.4   Relative size   (A) All other things being equal, the larger of two otherwise identical figures will seem to be closer than the smaller one. This is a consequence of the simple geometry of vision illustrated in (B). Objects a and b are equal in size, but because they are at different distances from the observer, they will project retinal images of different sizes.

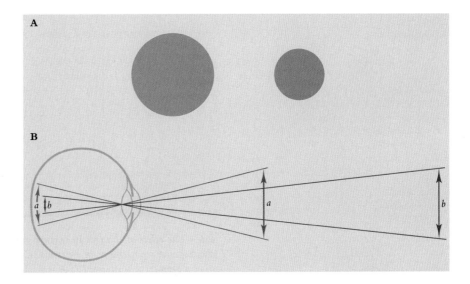

6.5 Texture gradients as cues for depth
Uniformly textured surfaces produce texture
gradients that provide information about
depth: As the surface recedes, the size of the
texture elements decreases, and the density of
these elements increases. Such gradients may
be produced by sand ripples (A), or stones in a
courtyard (B). (A: © Stephen J. Krasemann/
Allstock; B: Lee Snider/Corbis)

change, and this pattern can reveal the spatial layout of the relevant surfaces
(Figure 6.5). Thus, the discontinuity in the gradients in Figure 6.6A produces
the impression of a receding plane and then an upward tilt, whereas that in Figure 6.6B yields perception of a sharp drop, a visual cliff (Gibson, 1950, 1966).

THE PERCEPTION OF DEPTH THROUGH MOTION

Thus far we have considered situations in which both the observer and the
scene remain stationary. But in real life we are constantly moving through
the world, and this motion provides a vital source of visual information about
the spatial arrangement of the objects around us.

Whenever we move our heads, the images projected by the objects in our
world necessarily move across the retina. For reasons of geometry, the projected
images of nearby objects move more than those of more distant ones. The direc-

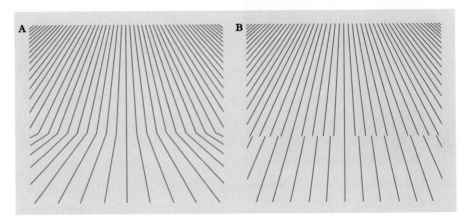

6.6 The effect of changes in texture gradients Such changes provide important information
about spatial arrangements in the world. Examples are (A) an upward tilt at a corner; and (B) a
sudden drop. (After Gibson, 1950)

Position 2 ◄———— Viewer ————— Position 1

6.7 Motion parallax *As the bicyclist moves forward, her position changes relative to stationary objects in her environment. As a result, these objects are displaced (and therefore seem to move) relative to her and each other. The rate of displacement is indicated by the dark red arrows: The thicker these arrows, the more quickly the objects seem to move. The direction of the observer's movement is indicated by the blue arrow. (For simplicity's sake, we assume that, as the bicyclist moves forward, she keeps her eyes fixed on the horizon.)*

tion of motion across the retina depends on where we are pointing our eyes. Points closer to us than the target of our gaze appear to be moving in a direction opposite to our own, while points farther away appear to be moving in the same direction we are. This entire pattern of motion in the retinal images provides a highly informative and enormously effective depth cue, called **motion parallax** (Helmholtz, 1909; see Figure 6.7).

A different motion cue is produced when we move toward or away from objects. As we approach an object, its image gets larger and larger; as we move away, it gets smaller. In addition, as we move toward an object, the pattern of stimulation across the entire visual field changes, resulting in a pattern of **optic flow,** which provides crucial information about depth and plays a large role in the coordination of our movements and our maintenance of balance (Gibson, 1950, 1979; Figure 6.8).

A   B

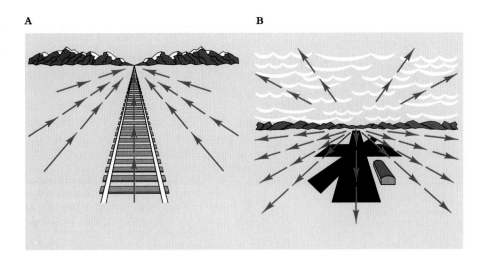

6.8 Optic flow *(A) The optic flow field as it appears to a person looking out of the rear window of a railroad car. (From Bruce and Green, 1985) (B) The optic flow field as it appears to a pilot landing an airplane. (From Gibson, 1950)*

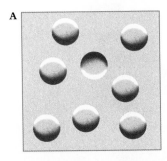

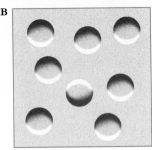

More monocular cues to depth: Light and shadow *Observers are sensitive to many different depth cues, including depth from shading. (A) shows eight circular objects. To most viewers the one in the middle looks concave, indented, whereas the other seven look as if they are bulging out. (B) shows the same figure rotated 180 degrees. Now the middle object looks convex, while the other seven seem concave. The reason is the location of the shadows. When the shadow is at the bottom, the object looks convex; when at the top, the object looks concave. This makes good biological sense, since light almost always comes from above. (Adapted from Beck, 1982)*

THE ROLE OF REDUNDANCY

We noted that the pictorial cues for depth reflect simple facts of geometry and optics. The same is true for the other depth cues. The information we call binocular disparity, for example, derives in a straightforward fashion from the position of the two eyes and the fact that light travels in a straight path. It is just a fact of our world, therefore, that these cues are available to us as potential sources of information about distance and depth.

What is perhaps surprising, however, is that we make use of *all* these cues (as well as some others we have not described). Why did natural selection favor a system influenced by so many cues, especially since the information provided by these cues is often redundant? After all, what we can learn from linear perspective is often the same as what we can learn from motion parallax. Why then should we be sensitive to both?

The most likely answer is that different distance cues become important in different circumstances. For example, binocular disparity is a powerful cue, but it is informative only for objects relatively close by. (For targets farther than thirty feet away, the two eyes receive virtually the same image.) Likewise, motion parallax tells us a great deal about the spatial layout of our world, but only if objects are moving. Texture gradients are informative only if there is a suitably uniform texture in view. So while these various cues are often redundant, each can provide information in circumstances in which the others cannot. By being sensitive to all, we are able to judge depth in nearly any situation we encounter.

THE PERCEPTION OF MOVEMENT: WHAT IS IT DOING?

To see a large, unfriendly Doberman in front of you is one thing; to see him bare his teeth and rush directly at you is quite another. We want to know what an object is and where it is located, but we also want to know what it is doing. Put another way, we want to perceive events as well as objects. And to do this, we must be able to perceive movement.

RETINAL MOTION

One might think that we see things move because they produce an image that moves across the retina. In fact, some cells in the visual cortex do seem responsive to such movements on the retina. These cells are ***direction specific,*** firing if a stimulus moves across their receptive field from, say, left to right but not if the stimulus moves from right to left. (Other cells, of course, show the reverse pattern.) These cells are therefore well-suited to act as ***motion detectors*** (e.g., Vaultin and Berkeley, 1977).★

★ Direction-specific cells play an important role in a phenomenon we considered in Chapter 5, namely, the aftereffect of visual movement. As we saw, prolonged inspection of a continuous motion leads to a motion aftereffect in which stationary objects appear to be moving in a direction opposite to the one just observed. This effect is readily explained in terms of adaptation of the relevant detectors and also carries the suggestion that these detectors are organized into opponent-process pairs (see pp. 211–12).

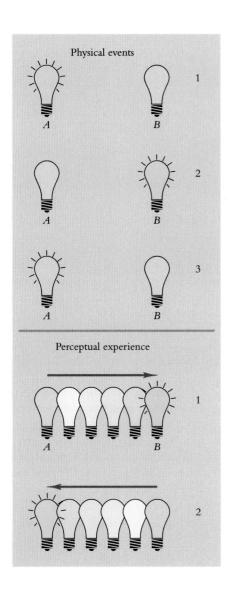

Physical events

A *B* 1

A *B* 2

A *B* 3

Perceptual experience

A *B* 1

2

Apparent movement created by a series of stills. *(© Globus Studios/The Stock Market)*

6.9 ***Apparent movement*** *The sequence of optical events that produces apparent movement. Light A flashes at time 1, followed by light B at time 2, then back to light A at time 3. If the time intervals are appropriately chosen, the perceptual experience will be of a light moving from left to right and back.*

APPARENT MOVEMENT

Further evidence makes it clear, however, that retinal motion is only part of the story. Suppose we turn on a light in one location in the visual field, then quickly turn it off, and after an appropriate interval (somewhere between 30 and 200 milliseconds) turn on a second light in a different location. The result is **apparent movement.** The light appears to travel from one point to another, even though there was no stimulation—let alone movement—in the intervening region (Figure 6.9). This phenomenon is perceptually overwhelming; given the right intervals, it is indistinguishable from real movement (Wertheimer, 1912). It is an effect that has numerous technological applications and is why, for example, people and objects seen in movies seem to move. (Movies, of course, actually consist of a sequence of appropriately timed still pictures.)

This phenomenon underscores the fact that motion can be perceived even when there is no motion of an image across the retina. Instead, all we need is an appropriately timed change in position: Something is here at one moment and there at the next. If the timing is right, the nervous system interprets this as evidence that this something has moved.

EYE MOVEMENTS

A further complication arises from the fact that our eyes are constantly moving, and this creates a continuous series of changes in the retinal image, even when we are inspecting a static scene. Given this fact, why do we perceive the world as stationary? One hypothesis is that the perception of motion depends on the *relative* positions of the objects in our view. If we move our eyes as we look at a chair, the retinal image of the chair is displaced, but so is the image of the lamp alongside the chair, the image of the floor beneath both chair and lamp, and so on. As a result, there is no relative displacement, and perhaps this is what signals the world's stability.

But this cannot be the entire story. As Hermann von Helmholtz showed a century ago, movement will be seen if the eyes are moved by muscles other than their own. Close one eye and jiggle the outside corner of the other eye (gently!) with a finger. Now the entire world will seem to move around, even

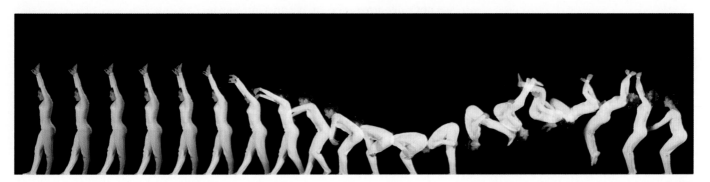

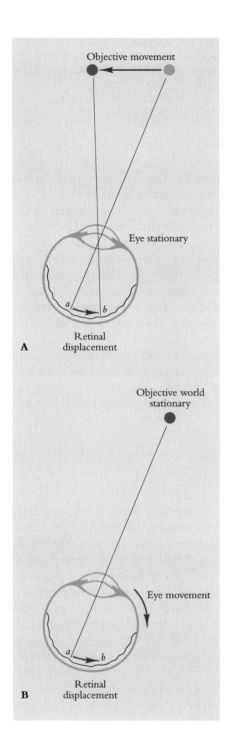

A

Objective movement

Eye stationary

Retinal
displacement

B

Objective world
stationary

Eye movement

Retinal
displacement

6.10 Compensation for eye movements In (A) an object has moved from right to left; as a result, its retinal image has shifted from location a to location b. In (B) there is no motion in the world; instead, the eye has moved from left to right. But here, too, the object's retinal image shifts from location a to location b. Based only on the retinal information, the displacements in (A) and (B) seem identical. But our brains allow for the displacements caused by changes in eye position. So in (B) the brain would decide that there had been no movement because the motion of the eye was precisely equal (and opposite) to the displacement on the retina.

though all relationships within the image remain intact. This shows that the perceptual system does respond to absolute displacement, not just relative displacement. So we must look elsewhere to explain the fact that we perceive a stable visual world.

A different hypothesis is that the nervous system actually compensates for the retinal displacements that are produced by voluntary eye movements. When the brain signals the eye muscles to move, it computes the retinal displacement that such a movement would produce and then cancels out this amount of movement in interpreting the visual input it receives (Figure 6.10). As a result, we perceive a stationary point as stationary, even though our eyes are moving (Bridgeman and Stark, 1991).

Proof for this claim comes from studies in which a number of heroic experimenters had themselves injected with drugs that cause temporary paralysis of the eye muscles. They report that, under these circumstances, the world did indeed appear to jump around whenever they tried to move their eyes, just as the canceling-out theory would predict. The brain ordered the eyes to move, say, 10 degrees to the right, and therefore anticipated that the retinal image would shift 10 degrees left. But the eyes were unable to comply with the command, and so no retinal shift took place. In this setting, the normal cancellation process failed, and as a result, the world was seen to jump with each eye movement—an unsettling but persuasive confirmation of the canceling-out theory (see Matin et al., 1982).

ILLUSIONS OF MOTION

As the preceding discussion showed, the perception of motion depends on several factors. As we've discussed, movement of an image across the retina stimulates movement detectors in the medial temporal cortex (Newsome et al., 1995). We've also discussed our sensitivity to changes in position; when the timing is right, these also cause the perception of movement without any motion on the retina. Finally, we saw that we compensate for changes in eye or head position, so that we can determine whether motion across the retina is produced by an object's movement in the environment or merely by a change in our viewing position. But even with all of this said, a further step is required. For we not only *detect* motion, we also *interpret* it.

The barber-pole illusion Think about an ordinary barber pole. The pole actually rotates from left to right, but we perceive the stripes on the pole as moving upward. Similarly, a spinning spiral shape drawn on a flat surface appears to be moving toward us (or away from us, depending on the direction of spin). These illusions derive from the way the perceptual system interprets the relationship between the view in front of our eyes right now and the view we had just a moment ago. Specifically, the perceptual system must solve the **correspondence problem**—the problem of determining which elements of our current view cor-

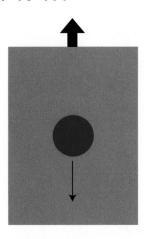

6.11 Induced movement *Research participants in an otherwise dark room see a luminous dot surrounded by a luminous frame. When the frame is moved upward, participants perceive the dot moving downward, even though it is objectively stationary. (Duncker, 1929)*

respond with which elements in our view a moment before (Wallach, Weisz, and Adams, 1956; Wallach, 1976).

Induced motion   A different sort of perceptual interpretation is illustrated by the phenomenon of **induced motion.** Consider a ball rolling on a billiard table. We see the ball as moving and the table at rest. But why not the other way around? To be sure, the ball is being displaced relative to the table edge, but so is the table edge displaced relative to the ball. One might guess that the reason we see this one way rather than the other is learning. Perhaps experience has taught us that balls generally move around while tables stay put. But the evidence indicates that what matters is a more general perceptual relationship between the two stimuli. The object that encloses the other tends to act as a frame, which is seen as stationary. Thus, the table serves as a frame against which the ball is seen to move.

In the billiard table example, perception and physical reality coincide, for the frame provided by the table is truly stationary. What happens when the objective situation is reversed? In one study research participants were shown a luminous rectangular frame in an otherwise dark room. Inside the frame was a luminous dot. In actual fact, the rectangle moved to the right while the dot stayed in place. But the subjects saw something else. They perceived the dot as moving to the left, in the direction opposite to the frame's motion. Participants had correctly perceived that the dot was moving closer and closer to the rectangle's left edge and further from its right edge. But they misperceived the source of this change. The physical movement of the frame had *induced* the perceived movement of the enclosed shape (Figure 6.11).

The induced motion effect is familiar from everyday life as well. The moon seems to sail through the clouds; the base of a bridge seems to float upstream, against the flow of the river's current. A related (and sometimes unsettling) phenomenon is **induced motion of the self.** If the participant stands on the bridge that he perceives as moving, he perceives himself moving along with it. The same effect occurs when sitting in a train that's standing in a station. If a train on the adjacent track pulls out, we tend to feel ourselves moving though in fact we (and the train we're in) are stationary.

FORM PERCEPTION: WHAT IS IT?

So far, we have considered how we know where an object is and where it is going. But we have not yet considered what is probably the most important question of all: How do we perceive and recognize what an object is? In vision, our primary means for recognizing an object is through the perception of its form. To be sure, we sometimes rely on color (a violet) and occasionally on size (a toy model of an automobile), but in the vast majority of cases, form is our major avenue for identifying what we see. The question is how? How do we recognize the myriad forms and patterns that are present in the world around us—triangles and ellipses, skyscrapers and automobiles, elephants and giraffes?

One simple hypothesis (ultimately derived from the work of the early empiricists) is that we have some sort of checklist in memory for each of the objects we are able to recognize. Does the object have four legs and a very long neck? Is it yellow and brown? If so, it is likely to be a giraffe. Does the object have four straight sides of equal length? If so, then it's a square.

6.12 **The variability of stimuli we recognize** *We recognize giraffes from the side or from the front, whether we see them close-up or from far away. This makes it unlikely that we have a checklist or template for recognizing giraffes; we would need a different template for each of the possible views.*

But a bit of reflection shows that things can't be quite so simple. One problem is the variability of most stimuli: We recognize giraffes from the side or from the front, whether we see them close-up or from far away, whether they are lying down or standing up (Figure 6.12). Do we have a different checklist for each of these views? Similarly, we often have only partial views of the objects around us, yet we recognize them nonetheless. We see television newscasters as intact human beings, even though we never see their legs; we identify the form in Figure 6.13 as a square, even though one corner is hidden.

A related point is that we can recognize a form even if its component parts are altered. The shapes in Figure 6.14 are all triangles. They differ in size, in color, in whether they are made up of solid or dotted lines. But this seems not to matter for our perception of the overall shape. The same phenomenon can be observed with sounds: A melody remains the same even when all of its notes are changed by *transposition* to another key, and the same rhythm will be heard whether played on a kettledrum or a glockenspiel.

Observations such as these were crucial for **Gestalt psychology,** a school of psychology whose adherents believed that *organization* is an essential feature of all mental activity. They insisted that a form is not perceived by somehow summing up all its individual components. Instead, they argued that a form is perceptually experienced as a coherent, intact *Gestalt,* a whole that is different from the sum of its parts. (The word *Gestalt* is derived from a German word that means "form" or "entire figure.") Thus the triangularity of the shapes in Figure 6.14 is not a property of any of the shape's elements. Rather, it is a property of the whole form, taken as a coherent unit.

The Gestalt psychologists clearly had an important point. There is little doubt that a form is not just the sum of its parts: Three angles alone do not make a triangle, no more than a mouth, a nose, and two eyes suffice to make a face. These

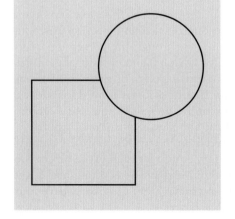

6.13 **Recognizing partially occluded figures** *We have no trouble recognizing the square, even though one of its corners is hidden. This further supports the argument that we do not have a checklist or template for every object we recognize.*

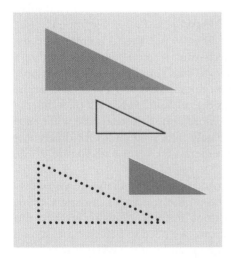

6.14 Form equivalence *The perceived forms remain the same regardless of the parts of which they are composed.*

forms are instead defined by the *relationships* among their elements, and so, to specify the nature of these forms, we need to specify how exactly the parts are bound together. This is a problem to which we will return later in the chapter. First, though, we need to consider what else is known about the broader issue of form perception.

THE INFORMATION-PROCESSING APPROACH

Many psychologists believe that perception involves a complex series of **information processing** steps. These steps begin with a visual input that is gradually transformed into the cognitive end product: our perception of objects in the world. This involves a series of successive stages in which the output of each stage is further transformed in the next.

In part, this information-processing approach grew out of an analogy between the operations of the mind and the workings of a computer. After all, computers do have some of the capabilities of human minds: They can acquire information, store it in memory, retrieve it, classify it, and manipulate it. In fact, the mind-as-computer has by now become a dominant scientific metaphor, replacing the metaphors of previous generations. These earlier metaphors—Descartes' water-powered statues as models of animal action or more recent analogies between the nervous system and a telephone switchboard—emphasized transformations of energy (hydraulic, chemical, or electrical) into bodily movements. In contrast, the mind-as-computer metaphor tries to explain the transformation of symbols into other symbols.

In the last two or three decades, the language of computers has become a regular element of psychological theorizing, and terms like *input, memory store,* and *coding* have become part of the psychologist's everyday vocabulary. Attempts to understand such mental operations as recognizing a shape, recalling a name, or trying to solve a puzzle are often cast in the form of a flowchart. In the world of computers, such flowcharts show the step-by-step operation of a computer program. Applied to the study of human cognitive processes, similar diagrams are meant to chart the flow of information as it is processed by the human mind. Much of our subsequent discussion of perception will be organized along the lines of this information-processing approach.

THE ELEMENTS OF FORM

Most investigators believe that the recognition of a form begins with the detection of **primitive features,** the building blocks of visual perception. This claim is based in part on the physiological findings we discussed in the previous chapter (see pp. 209–10). Various cells in the brain do seem to act as feature detectors, responding selectively to certain elements of visual form. In addition, a number of findings indicate that these simple features do have special priority in our perception of form.

FREE-FLOATING PRIMITIVES

In an influential series of studies, Anne Treisman argues that primitive visual features can be perceived in an immediate, effortless fashion. One doesn't have to

6.15   Pop-out in visual search   *An O embedded in an array of Vs pops out immediately. Here, the visual system does not have to inspect each figure in turn to determine whether it is the target. Instead, it conducts a parallel search, inspecting all of the items simultaneously.*

Anne Treisman   *(Photograph by Paul Haller)*

search the display or analyze its pattern to locate and identify these features. Instead, the features just "pop out" (Treisman, 1986a, b, 1988).

One way of demonstrating this is by means of a ***visual search task*** in which subjects have to indicate whether a certain target is or is not present in a display. When the target is an *O* amidst a field of *V*s, subjects find it very quickly (see Figure 6.15). What's more, the number of *V*s in which the *O* is embedded has very little effect on the search time: Subjects can locate an *O* hidden within a dozen *V*s almost as quickly as they can locate an *O* sandwiched between only two *V*s. This indicates that the visual system doesn't have to inspect each of the figures in turn to determine whether it has the relevant properties. (If it did, the larger number of figures would require more time.) Instead, the difference between the *O*s and *V*s jumps out immediately. The same holds for differences in color, orientation, or direction of movement (Treisman and Gelade, 1980; Treisman and Souther, 1985).

Of course, the objects we perceive are made up of more than one visual feature. A leaf on a tree has a certain shape and position, as well as a certain color. But it's not enough merely to detect all these features individually; they also need to be assembled into the correct packages. We need to perceive that it's the round apple that is red, and the leaf that is green, and not the other way around.

But unlike the identification of single features, perceiving a combination of features is not immediate or automatic. Treisman and her collaborators showed their subjects displays that contained items such as a red *F* and a green *X* for about 200 milliseconds, and then asked the subjects to report what they saw. On a fair proportion of the trials, the subjects reported ***illusory conjunctions***, such as having seen a green *F* or a red *X*. It seems that subjects were able to perceive the features of this display, but not able to figure out how these features were related to each other. Apparently, then, the coordination of features requires a separate step that occurs after the features are identified.

Treisman argues that the various primitive features are initially detected and identified in terms of their location within the visual image. However, each feature system (color, shape, and so on) seems to mark these locations on its own map, with the different maps separate and distinct from each other, so that the perceiver doesn't know immediately that this color goes with that contour, and so on (Treisman and Schmidt, 1982). Only later are the separate systems integrated and the various maps coordinated and superimposed. This later stage requires some time to work (although, in truth, it's just a matter of milliseconds—not enough for the perceiver herself to notice but certainly enough to have an effect in the relevant experiments). This later stage also seems to require the perceiver's attention—a point to which we will return later in the chapter. Crucially, though, this later step allows the perceiver to determine what goes with what—that the *F* is red and the *X* is green (rather than the reverse), that the same leaf is at once green, curved with jagged edges, and fluttering in the breeze.

PERCEPTUAL SEGREGATION

So far we have considered only the initial steps of form perception: deciding which features are present and how these features go together. The next step is to organize the overall scene, a process known as ***visual segregation***.

Suppose the observer looks at the still life in Figure 6.16. To make sense of the picture, the perceptual system must somehow group the elements of the scene appropriately. For one thing, it has to determine what is focal (in this case, the fruit and the bowl) and what can be ignored (at least for now) as background. And since some pieces of fruit will be blocking others, the perceiver

6.16   Perceptual segregation   (A) A still life. (Photograph by Jeffrey Grosscup) (B) An overlay designating five different segments of the scene shown in (A). To determine what an object is, the perceptual system must first decide what goes with what: Does portion B go with A, with C, D, or E? Or with none of them?

A

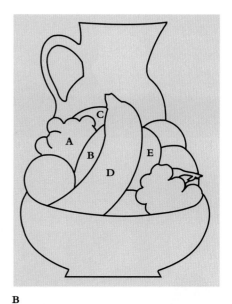

B

must also figure out what goes with what. Portion *B* (one half of the apple) must be united with portion *E* (the other half of the apple), even though they are separated by portion *D* (a banana). Portion *B* should not be united with portion *A* (a bunch of grapes), even though they are adjacent and approximately the same color. The bit of the apple hidden from view, or *occluded,* by the banana must somehow be filled in, so that we perceive an intact apple rather than two apple slices.

This process of visual segregation is sometimes called ***perceptual parsing***, because it performs the same function for vision that parsing performs for speech. When someone talks to us, our eardrums are exposed to a sound stream that is essentially unbroken. What hits the ears is a sequence of sounds such as:

Thestudentsaidtheteacherisafool

The listener parses the sound pattern by grouping some sounds together with others, forming units called words:

The student said the teacher is a fool.

He may then parse further by grouping the words into larger units called phrases, as in:

The student, said the teacher, is a fool.

In some cases, he may even discover that there are alternate ways of parsing, as in:

The student said, the teacher is a fool.

The important point is that the parsing is not primarily in the stimulus. It is contributed by the listener, for the sound stream itself has no pauses between words and contains no commas. (When we don't understand a language, we don't "hear" the pauses, which is why foreigners speaking in their own language often sound as if they speak much faster than we do.) Until at least some basic parsing has been performed, the listener has no hope of comprehending what

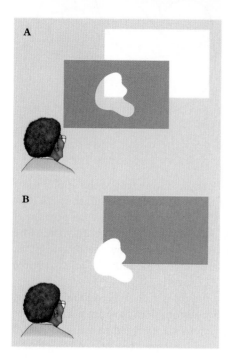

6.18   Edges belong to the figure   *If we perceive Figure 6.18 as a blue rectangle with a hole in it (A), the edge marks the contour of the hole. The situation is reversed in (B). Now the edge demarcates the white blob, not a break in the blue background. In this sense, the edge belongs to the figure, not the ground.*

6.17   Figure and ground   *The first step in seeing a form is to segregate it from its background. The part seen as figure appears to be more cohesive and sharply delineated. The part seen as ground seems more formless and to extend behind the figure.*

she has heard. To understand the meaning of the word *student*, she must first have segregated it from the surrounding sounds and heard it as a separate word.

What holds for words in speech, also holds for objects in the visual world. Visual segregation (or perceptual parsing) is the first step in organizing the world we see.

FIGURE AND GROUND

A crucial step in visual segregation is the separation of the object from its setting, so that the object is seen as a coherent whole, separate from its background. This separation of *figure* and *ground* allows us to recognize (as focal) the familiar shapes of an apple or banana, but the same process also occurs with figures that have no particular meaning. Thus in Figure 6.17, the white splotch appears as the figure and is typically perceived as in the foreground relative to the blue region (which is seen as the ground). The edge between the blue and white regions is perceived as part of the figure, defining its shape. The same edge does not mark a contour for the blue region, but merely marks the point at which this region drops from view (Figure 6.18).

Let us emphasize that this differentiation of figure and ground, like all aspects of parsing, is contributed by the perceiver and is not a property of the stimulus itself. This is most evident when the perceiver discovers that there is more than one way to parse a given stimulus, as with Figure 6.19, which can be seen either as a white vase or as two blue faces in profile. These *reversible figures* make it clear that the stimulus itself is neutral with regard to parsing. What is figure and what ground is in the eye of the beholder.

After we parse the input into figure and ground, different kinds of processing are applied to these two regions. We are sensitive to fine detail within the figure, but our perceptual analysis of the ground seems to employ a cruder analysis, appropriate to the perception of larger areas (Julesz, 1978). This was evident in one experiment in which subjects were briefly shown vertical or tilted lines, flashed in various positions on the vase-profiles figure (see Figure 6.20). Subjects were much more accurate in judging the orientation of the lines when they were projected onto an area the subjects happened to see as the figure; they were less accurate when the line was projected onto an area they perceived as the ground (Weisstein and Wong, 1986).

PERCEPTUAL GROUPING

If we happen to see a cat walking behind a picket fence, the stimulus that strikes our eye is not the image of an intact cat. Instead, at any moment, we might see a bit of the cat's head here, a bit of its body there, and a bit of its tail for good measure. Somehow, though, we fuse these bits together and perceive the animal as a whole. Likewise, we perceive the left half and right half of the apple as parts of the same whole, and the top half of a blouse as united with the bottom, even if it

6.19   Reversible figure-ground pattern   *The classic example of a reversible figure-ground pattern. It can be seen as either a pair of silhouetted faces or a white vase.*

Figure–ground reversal in the visual arts *The Trojan War as depicted by Salvador Dali. The scene of wild carnage conceals the image of the Trojan Horse, whose outline follows the gateway to the city. (Courtesy Esquire)*

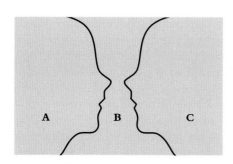

6.20 Fine detail is more readily seen in the figure than the ground *Research participants looked at the vase-profiles figure and had to determine whether lines that were briefly flashed at points A, B, or C were tilted or vertical. If the vase was seen as the figure, they did much better when the stimuli were presented at B than at A or C. If the profiles were seen as the figure, they did much better when the lines were presented in A or C rather than in B. (After Weisstein and Wong, 1986)*

is sundered by a striped pattern in the fabric. This **grouping** of a figure's parts seems a trivial achievement, but grouping, like the assignment of figure-ground, is often ambiguous. The resolution of this ambiguity once again signals that grouping is an achievement of the perceiver and not a property of the stimulus.

Several of the factors that guide visual grouping were first described by Max Wertheimer, the founder of Gestalt psychology. Wertheimer regarded these grouping factors as the laws of **perceptual organization** (Wertheimer, 1923). One factor he identified is **proximity:** the closer two figures are to each other, the more they tend to be grouped together perceptually (see Figure 6.21A). Another factor is **similarity:** Other things being equal, we group together figures that resemble each other. So in Figure 6.21B, we group blue dots with blue dots, red with red. Similarly, we are likely to group verticals with verticals and diagonals with diagonals. However, more complex properties, such as shape, are less effective guides to grouping, presumably because shape depends on more complex relations among the stimuli (Beck, 1982; see Figure 6.22). Not surprisingly, the stimulus attributes that support grouping tend to be the same features that pop out from a complex display. This is just what we would expect if parsing is an

6.21 Grouping by proximity and similarity *We perceive the six lines in (A) as three pairs, grouping the lines by proximity. We perceive the dots in (B) as organized into rows on the left and columns on the right, grouping by similarity.*

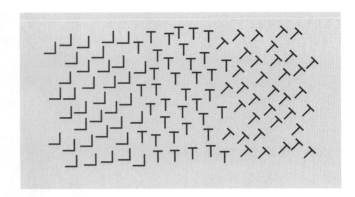

6.22 *The effect of orientation and shape on perceptual grouping* *The demarcation between the upright Ts and the tilted Ts is more easily seen than that between the upright Ts and the upright Ls. (From Beck, 1966)*

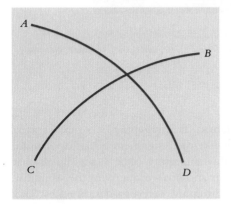

6.23 *Good continuation* *The line segments in the figure will generally be grouped so that the contours continue smoothly. As a result, segment A will be grouped with D and segment C with B, rather than A with B and C with D.*

early step in visual organization and thus dependent on the feature information available at that early stage.

Our visual system also seems to organize patterns in a fashion that suggests a preference for contours that continue smoothly along their original course (Figure 6.23). This principle of **good continuation** prevails even when pitted against prior experience (Figure 6.24), and is why camouflage can be an effective means of hiding a creature from view (Figure 6.25).

A dramatic extension of this principle is visible in **subjective contours**—contours that are perceived even though they don't physically exist (Figure 6.26). Some theorists interpret subjective contours as a special case of good continuation. In their view, the contour is seen to continue along its original path, even, if necessary, jumping a gap or two to achieve this continuation (Kellman and Shipley, 1991).

THE MAXIMUM-LIKELIHOOD PRINCIPLE

Can these grouping factors be united under some single general rule? One proposal to do so is referred to as the **principle of maximum likelihood** (Helmholtz, 1910; Gregory, 1974; Hochberg, 1981; Rock, 1983). The idea is that we know which configurations are likely and which not, and this knowledge guides us whenever we seek to determine what it is that gave rise to a particular proximal stimulus.

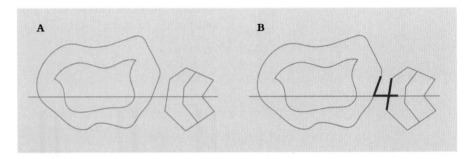

6.24 *Good continuation pitted against prior experience* *In (A), virtually all viewers see two complex patterns intersected by a horizontal line. Hardly anyone sees the hidden 4 contained in that figure—and shown in (B)—despite the fact that we have encountered 4s much more often than the two complex patterns, which are probably completely new. (After Köhler, 1947)*

6.25   Good continuation as the basis of camouflage   In (A) camouflage is achieved by providing artificial contours that break up the outlines of the soldier's face and body. (AP Photo/
Ricardo Choy Kifox) Good continuation helps to conceal the frog in (B) from predators who tend
to see it as continuous with its background. (Photograph © Michael Fogden, Oxford Scientific
Films)

For example, regions close together in the world have, in our experience,
often turned out to be parts of the same object. Our interpretation of the proximal stimulus is influenced by this knowledge, leading to the principle of proximity. The same holds for similarity. By and large, regions that are similar in
color and texture also belong to the same object. There may be some exceptions, such as a clown's costume or a patchwork quilt, but even with these
exceptions, it is generally a good bet to interpret the proximal stimulus pattern
as though it were produced by the distal stimulus that has most often produced it
in the past (Pomerantz and Kubovy, 1981; Hochberg, 1988).

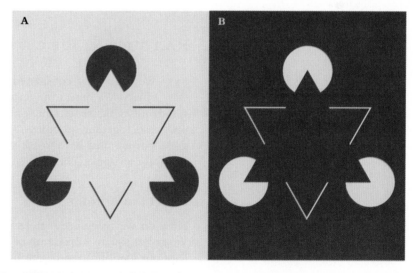

6.26   Subjective contours   Subjective contours are a special completion phenomenon in which
contours are seen even where none exist. In (A) we see a tan triangle whose vertices lie on top of
the three dark green circles. The three sides of this tan triangle (which looks brighter than the tan
background) are clearly visible, even though they don't exist physically. In (B) we see the same
effect with dark green and tan reversed. Here, there is a dark green triangle (which looks darker
than the dark green background) with subjective green contours (Kanizsa, 1976)

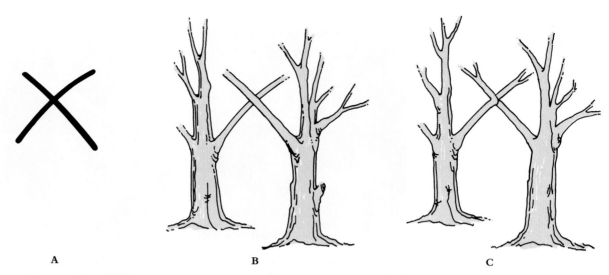

A   B   C

6.27 Good continuation and the maxi-mum-likelihood principle *(A) A figure that could be seen in two ways. (B) A likely alternative. (C) An unlikely alternative.*

Similar considerations apply to the principle of good continuation. Consider Figure 6.27A. Most observers perceive this as two smooth intersecting lines rather than as two triangular forms meeting at an angle (say, two fish kissing). To see why this should be so, let's ask what Figure 6.27A might correspond to in the external world. It could easily be an image cast by two elongated objects, such as the (more or less straight) branches of two trees (see Figure 6.27B). Alternatively, the figure might correspond to two angular objects, such as two elbow-shaped branches of trees that just happen to be viewed from an orientation that makes it look like they are touching (Figure 6.27C). Note, though, that in this latter case any slight change of vantage point would shift the angles and break the pattern. That makes this configuration exceedingly unlikely. Under the circumstances, the perceptual system draws the interpretation that is, in truth, most likely to correspond to external reality: It groups by good continuation.

PATTERN RECOGNITION

We have now considered several of the steps involved in perceiving an object: We detect the features of a scene and then parse the scene so that we identify a figure standing out against its background. We also bundle the figure's parts together, grouping them into a single object. But we are still far from done. For we next have to ask *what* the object is, whether it is the letter *A*, or a giraffe, or an apple. This next step is called ***pattern recognition***.

FEATURE NETS

How do we recognize patterns? To take an easy case, how do we recognize a square? A square is made up of four straight lines and four right angles, so perhaps our identification begins by checking for the presence of these elements. If they are on the scene, then the stimulus before us is probably a square.

But how do we recognize the elements themselves? How do we recognize, say, a right angle? We identified the square by looking for its constituent parts; why not do the same for the angle? So we might look for one vertical line and one horizontal line, in the correct positions relative to each other. If we find them, we know that a right angle is in view.

This simple proposal is at the heart of many theories of pattern recognition. The fundamental idea is that we are equipped with a series of detectors, each responsible for detecting a particular target. Low-level detectors respond to the simplest features; so, for example, there might be one detector for vertical lines and another for horizontals. Mid-level detectors, in turn, respond whenever the right combination of low-level detectors is firing. So our right-angle detector would not have to survey the visual world directly. Instead, it would fire only when triggered by both the vertical and horizontal line detectors (Figure 6.28). The response of the right-angle detector, in its turn, would then be one of the triggers for detectors in the next layer, that would perhaps include a square detector.

This sort of model is referred to as a ***feature net***, because it involves a *network* of detectors, with feature detectors at the bottom level. In the earliest feature nets proposed, activation flowed in a single direction—from feature detectors to more complex detectors, through a gradual series of larger and larger units (e.g., Selfridge, 1959). These models were therefore called ***bottom up*** or ***data driven***, to emphasize the fact that the pattern of response is determined almost entirely by the incoming stimulus information.

TOP-DOWN PROCESSING

Data-driven models can accomplish a great deal, but there are reasons to believe that pattern recognition also involves processes that are top down, or ***knowledge driven,*** in which the chain of events is influenced by one's beliefs and expectations, as well as by the incoming data.

For example, telling a research participant that the next word she will see is the name of something edible will usually speed up recognition of words such as *apple, steak,* and *carrot.* This benefit, called a ***priming effect***, requires a significant

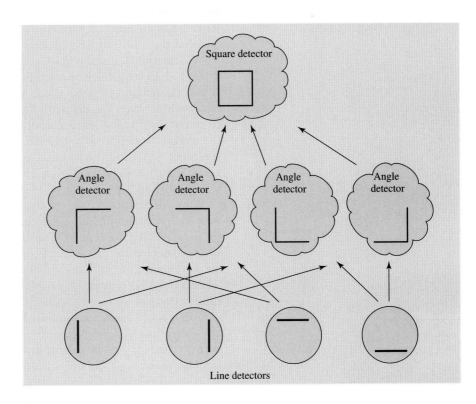

6.28 A feature net *We recognize a* square *by first identifying its components: four* right angles. *We recognize the right angles by first identifying* their *components: the line segments that make them up. Detectors for the simpler elements trigger detectors for the more complex elements, which, in turn, trigger detectors for the square.*

THE CAT

6.29 *The effect of context on letter recognition* (After Selfridge, 1955)

contribution from the participant: She must recognize all of the words in the priming sentence and put these together to derive the meaning of this sentence. Then, obviously, she must contribute some background knowledge about what sorts of things are edible and what things are not.

Other priming effects are simpler and can probably be accommodated by appropriate elaborations of the feature net. However, these effects still make it clear that pattern recognition is more than a simple pick-up of the available information. In Figure 6.29, for example, the second and fifth characters are physically identical. But, influenced by the context, subjects perceive the character as an *H* in *THE* and an *A* in *CAT*.

Similar **context effects** can make us hear speech sounds where in fact there are none. In one demonstration of this, subjects listened to tape-recorded sentences such as

The governor signed the bill passed by the legislature.

However, the experimenter carefully replaced the middle *s* in *legislature* with a coughlike noise. Almost none of the subjects noticed this alteration. When explicitly told that an alteration had been made and asked to identify it, most subjects could not. They had somehow restored the deleted sound and heard an *s* that was implied by the context (Warren, 1970).

BIDIRECTIONAL ACTIVATION

Top-down processing guides our perception in many ways. But top-down processing cannot work on its own: It is bottom-up processing that keeps us in touch with the stimulus input, ensuring that our perceptions stay faithful to the world around us.

It would appear, therefore, that perceptual processing must occur in both directions at once, guided both by the stimulus input and by our understanding and expectations. As an illustration of how this works, let's take a problem in word recognition (see Figure 6.30). Suppose a perceiver is shown a three-letter word in dim light. In this setting, the visual system might register the fact that the word's last two letters are *AT*, but, at least initially, the system has no information about the first letter. How, then, would it choose among *MAT*, *CAT*, and *RAT*? Let's suppose that the perceiver has just been shown a series of words, including several names of animals (*dog, mouse, canary*). This experience will activate the detectors for these words, and this activation is likely to spread out to the memory neighbors of these detectors, including (probably) the detectors for *CAT* and *RAT*. (See Chapter 8 for further discussion of spreading activation.) Activation of the *CAT* or *RAT* detector, in turn, will cause a top-down activation of the detectors for the letters in these words, including *C* and *R*.

While all of this is going on, the bottom-up analysis is continuing, so that by now the system might have registered the fact that the left edge of the target letter is curved (Figure 6.30B). This bottom-up effect will cause partial activation of the detector for the letter *C*; this will join up with the activation *C* has already received from *CAT*, so that the *C* detector becomes fully activated. Then, once *C* is activated, this will feed back to the *CAT* detector, activating it still further.

Many recent feature-net proposals incorporate inhibitory mechanisms, as well as mechanisms that produce activation. In these models, activation of the *CAT* detector would, in turn, inhibit the detectors for competing words—for example, the detectors for *RAT* or *MAT* (McClelland, Rumelhart, and Hinton,

6.30 Bidirectional activation (A) Top-down processing. Activation of the concept Animal activates the words CAT and RAT (among others), which then activate their constituent letters, including the first-position letters C and R. It also inhibits incompatible words such as MAT (again, among others). Activation is indicated in dark green; inhibition in dark red. (B) Bottom-up processing. Some milliseconds later, further perceptual analysis of the first letter of the stimulus word has activated the feature curved-to-the-left, which partially activates the letter C. This adds to the activation of the word CAT and inhibits the letter R and the word RAT. The result is that the word CAT is more intensely activated than all other words and will reach recognition threshold. Activation is again in dark green and inhibition in dark red. To keep things simple, many mutually inhibitory effects (e.g., between the words CAT and RAT) are not shown in the figure.

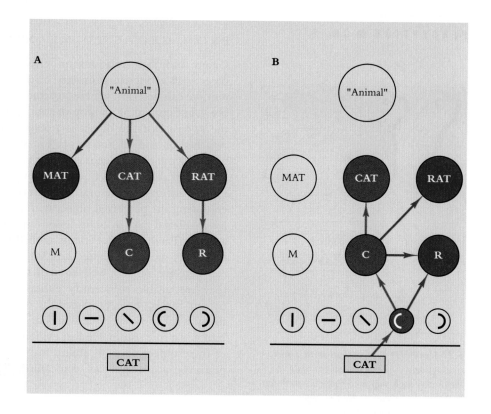

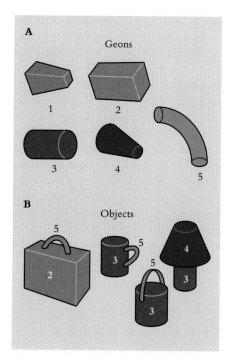

6.31 Some proposed geometric primitives (A) Some geons. (B) Some objects that can be created from these geons. (After Biederman, 1987)

1986). This makes it all the more likely that the *CAT* detector's response will be stronger than the response from any other detector, leading, finally, to a (correct) detection of the word.

In effect, then, the initial activation of *CAT* serves as a knowledge-driven hypothesis, making the visual system more receptive to the relevant data from the feature detectors. The arriving data would confirm the hypothesis, leading to the suppression of alternative hypotheses. Overall, we are left with a version of the feature net in which detectors at every level of the hierarchy—from above, below, and both sides—influence each other until a single detector finally wins out.

AN INTERMEDIATE STEP: PERCEPTUAL COMPONENTS

It is easy to construct a feature net for the recognition of simple targets, such as letters or numerals. But what about the vast variety of three-dimensional objects that surround us? For these, theorists believe that the recognition process must be more complex. In particular, object recognition may involve some intermediate levels of analysis, levels concerned with object parts broader than the features we have discussed so far.

A model proposed by Irving Biederman relies on some thirty geometric components that he calls **geons** (short for "geometric ions"). These are three-dimensional figures such as cubes, cylinders, pyramids, and the like. Just about all objects can be analyzed perceptually into some number of such geons. To recognize an object, therefore, we must first identify its features and then use these to identify the component geons and their relationships. We then consult our visual memory to see whether there's an object that matches up with what we've detected (Biederman, 1987; see Figure 6.31).

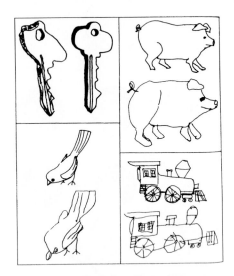

6.32 Drawings by a patient with associative agnosia *While the patient could see the models well enough to reproduce them fairly accurately, he was unable to recognize these objects. (From Farah, 1991)*

FROM GEONS TO MEANING

Geons and their relationships give us a complete *structural description* of an object—its complete geometry in three dimensions. Thus, in Biederman's system, we can describe, say, the structure of a lamp in terms of a certain geon (number 4, in Figure 6.31) on top of another (number 3). But that's not enough to tell the system that the object is a *lamp*, that it's an object that casts light, can be switched on and off, and so on. The structural description does a fine job of representing the object's geometry, but it says nothing about the object's meaning.

Remarkably, we can find cases in which the visual system succeeds in achieving an accurate structural description but fails altogether in this last step—endowing the perceived object with meaning. These cases involve patients who have suffered certain brain lesions, specifically cortical lesions leading to visual agnosia (Farah, 1990). Patients with this disorder can see but cannot recognize what they see (see Chapter 2, p. 34). In some cases of visual agnosia, the patients can perceive objects well enough to draw recognizable pictures of them, but they are unable to identify either the objects or their own drawings. One patient, for example, produced the drawings shown in Figure 6.32. When asked to say what these were drawings of, he couldn't name the key and said that the bird was a tree stump. He had evidently formed adequate structural descriptions of these objects, but his ability to process what he saw stopped there; what he perceived was stripped of its meaning (Farah, 1991).

THE PROCESSING SEQUENCE IN FORM PERCEPTION

At first it might have seemed that there is nothing simpler than seeing an apple and recognizing it for what it is. But, clearly, this is an achievement involving a number of steps. The first step is visual segregation: seeing the apple as a figure against the ground of whatever else is in the visual field and seeing it as a unified whole, even if it is partially obscured by other objects in the field. After this come several steps in pattern recognition: Lower-level features stimulate detectors that come together to stimulate higher-level detectors, which in turn are built up into geons that are then assembled to form a structural description of the object. The final step is the perception of the actual object.

These processing steps are described here as if they always occur one after another and in this precise bottom-up order. In actuality, these steps often occur simultaneously rather than in sequence. To use the technical terms, the processing may be *parallel*, rather than *serial*. If the steps do occur serially (that is, in sequence), their order may well be the reverse from the one we described, for as we've seen there is top-down as well as bottom-up processing. Nonetheless, our account provides a useful overview of the processing steps.

By George, you're right! I thought there was something familiar about it. (© The New Yorker Collection 1957, 1985 Chas. Addams from Cartoonbank.com. All rights reserved.)

PERCEPTUAL PROBLEM SOLVING

We noted earlier that models of pattern recognition describe the perceiver as if he is engaged in a peculiar form of problem solving, considering "What is this object now before me?" Expectations, prior knowledge, and early analyses of the stimulus together lead to a hypothesis about the object's identity. This hypothe-

6.33 Perceptual problem solving *This is a picture of something. What? (Photograph by Ronald James)*

sis is then checked against the evidence. That is, his perceptual system analyzes the stimulus further, searching for information that might confirm or disconfirm the hypothesis. If the stimulus information does not fit the hypothesis, a new hypothesis must be generated, and it too must be tested by searching the stimulus for yet other features.

Generally, this process goes smoothly forward outside of our awareness; we are conscious only of the finished product—our confident realization that the object is a tomato, or a taxi, or whatever. Occasionally, though, we are aware of the process of problem solving. Consider Figure 6.33. At first glance most observers don't know what to make of it. But as they continue to look at the figure, they develop hypotheses about what it might be (e.g., maybe this part is the leg of some animal; maybe the animal has a spotted hide). If they persist, they eventually hit on the correct hypothesis (a dalmatian, sniffing the ground). When they finally see the dalmatian, the top-down and bottom-up processes meet, and there is a perceptual insight, a visual "Aha!" (For other examples, see Figure 6.34.)

6.34 Perceptual puzzles *What are the objects shown here? These examples illustrate the role of problem solving in perception. (From Mooney, n.d.)*

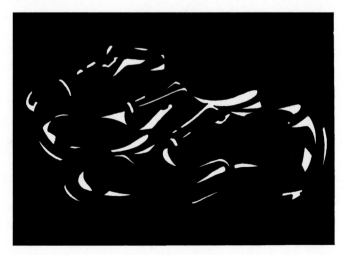

This sort of problem solving might seem quite different from the easy and swift processing needed for ordinary perception. According to some theorists, however, the same sort of steps are required whenever we identify an object. We may be unaware of our efforts as we solve the everyday perceptual puzzle, and the process proceeds at great speed. Nonetheless, they argue, there are striking parallels between commonplace perception and overt problem solving (Helmholtz, 1910; Rock, 1983).

THE LOGIC OF PERCEPTION

Irvin Rock argued that both everyday perception and overt perceptual problem solving seem to be governed by a series of logical principles. First, our solution of the perceptual puzzle must provide a coherent explanation for all the information contained within the stimulus. Second, it must try to avoid contradictions, such as perceiving a surface to be both opaque and transparent. Third, it must try to avoid interpretations of the world that depend on accident or coincidence.

An illustration of these principles comes from the study of stroboscopic (or apparent) movement. We have already described (p. 223) the standard demonstration of this form of movement: Viewers are first shown a light at one position; a moment later that light disappears and a second light appears at a nearby position (see Figure 6.9). If the timing is right, viewers do not perceive these as two stationary lights, coming one after the other. Instead, they perceive a single light, moving from the first position to the second.

To the perceiver, this interpretation of the display is quite reasonable: Why does the disappearance of the first light coincide with the second light's appearance? If there are two lights, then this is an odd coincidence that needs to be explained. But if there is just a single light moving between two points, then there is no coincidence, and the pattern of stimulation makes perfect sense.

But now let's add a complication. What if an obstacle is placed between the lights, apparently blocking the path between position 1 and position 2 (Figure 6.35); does this interfere with the perception of movement? It does not. Instead, viewers are likely to perceive motion in three dimensions: The light seems to hop in front of the obstacle, as it zooms from its starting point toward its goal. And again this is reasonable: It explains why one light disappears at just the moment that another appears, while avoiding the contradiction of a light passing through a solid obstacle.

Is the perceptual apparatus literally proceeding through these logical steps, weighing each consideration in turn? Surely not. Still, we can generally predict accurately how a display will be perceived by considering how this process of logical consideration might unfold. This implies that the perceptual processes somehow respect these principles, giving perception its logical character.

WHEN LOGIC FAILS: IMPOSSIBLE FIGURES

Our perceptual system is clever—able to interpret complex patterns, to reconstruct imperfect speech, and to discover hidden dalmatians. But even the cleverest system fails when it confronts a problem beyond its reach. By examining these failures, we can often learn a great deal about how the system operates.

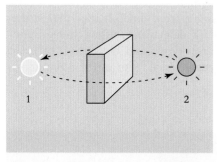

6.35 The logic of apparent movement
Adding an obstacle to block the path between the two lights in an apparent-movement display leads perceivers to "see" the light as zipping smoothly around the obstacle from position 1 to position 2.

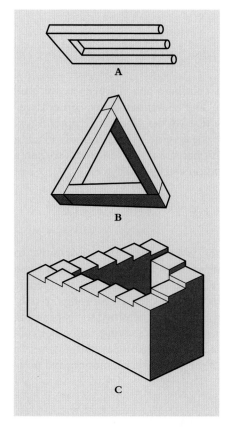

6.36 Impossible figures *(A) U-shape or three-pronged fork. (B) Impossible triangle. (C) Perpetual staircase. (Penrose and Penrose, 1958)*

Figure 6.36A shows one of the so-called *impossible figures*. The figure is drawn so that it appears three dimensional, but this form could not possibly exist in three dimensions (Penrose and Penrose, 1958). At the left end, it has two arms, at the right, three. Likewise, Figure 6.36B looks at first glance like a triangular, three dimensional object. The trouble is that the perspective is drawn differently at each corner. If we trace a path from one corner of the object to the next, then to a third, and finally try to return to the first, we find that the corners don't mate properly. Likewise for Fig 6.36C.

We could, of course, perceive these figures for what they are—two-dimensional drawings. But we tend not to. Instead, we see them as solid, three-dimensional shapes despite their impossibility. Apparently, there are limits to the logic of perception. In this case, the strong influence of the pictorial depth cues leads us to a perception that is most *illogical*.

FORM PERCEPTION AND THE NERVOUS SYSTEM

Our discussion of perception so far has revealed impressive complexity. How is all this complexity managed by the nervous system? And how does the nervous system manage to go through all the steps we've described swiftly, so that we perceive the approaching bus quickly enough to jump out of its path or the slice of apple pie soon enough to grab it before our younger brother or sister does? To answer questions like these, experimental psychologists have worked closely with neuroscientists in analyzing the anatomical and functional components of the visual system. By now we can trace many of the neurological steps that begin when individual photons of light excite retinal receptors and continue, neuron by neuron, tissue layer by tissue layer, ever upward into the brain.

EARLY STAGES OF VISUAL PROCESSING

As we saw in the previous chapter, the rods and cones pass their signals to the bipolar cells, which relay them to the ganglion cells. The axons of the ganglion cells form the optic nerve, which leaves the eyeball and begins the journey toward the brain. But even at this early stage, the neurons are specialized in important ways, with different cells responsible for detecting different aspects of the visual world.

The ganglion cells can be broadly classified into two categories: The smaller ones are called *parvo cells* and the larger are called *magno cells*. (The terminology derives from the Latin words for "small" and "large.") Parvo cells, far outnumbering the magno cells, blanket the entire retina. Magno cells, in contrast, are found largely in the retina's periphery. Parvo cells appear to be sensitive to color differences (to be more precise, to differences in hue), while magno cells, which are color-blind, respond to changes in brightness. (For more on the difference between hue and brightness, see Chapter 5.)

There is good reason to believe that magno and parvo cells play rather different roles within the sequence of visual processing. Parvo cells seem crucial for the perception of pattern and form, in part because their small receptive fields allow them to distinguish fine differences in position. In contrast, magno cells probably play a central role in the detection of motion and the perception of depth. Unlike their parvo counterparts, the magno cells do not continue to fire if the light stimulus remains unchanged. Instead, they fire when the stimulus appears and then again when it disappears. As a result, they are particularly sensitive to motion-produced changes in the visual scene.

VISUAL PROCESSING IN THE BRAIN

This pattern of neural specialization continues and sharpens as we look more deeply into the nervous system. The relevant evidence comes largely from the single-cell recording technique that we described in Chapter 5 (pp. 208–9). This technique lets investigators determine which stimuli elicit a response from a cell and which do not. This has allowed investigators to gain a rich understanding of the neural basis for vision cell by cell by cell.

SIMPLE AND COMPLEX CELLS IN THE VISUAL CORTEX

In the last chapter, we described cells in the visual cortex that are sensitive to simple characteristics such as the tilt of a line or its position. As we've seen, these so-called *simple cells* fire most strongly in response to a line or edge of a specific orientation and position. Other cells in the visual cortex, called *complex cells,* are also sensitive to the input's orientation but are less sensitive to its position. Complex cells are also sensitive to whether the target is moving. Still other cells respond to yet more complex features, including corners, angles, and notches. In this way, layer by layer, a complete coding of the input's shape, motion, and position is built up.

THE "WHAT" AND "WHERE" SYSTEMS

The cerebral processing of visual information begins in the occipital cortex; it is here that we find the simple and complex cells just described. But this information is then transmitted to two other brain areas, the temporal cortex and the parietal cortex (Figure 6.37). The pathway that carries information to the temporal cortex is often called the *"what" system* and plays a major role in the identification of visual objects, telling us whether the object is a cat, an apple, or whatever. The second pathway, which carries information to the parietal cortex, is often called the *"where" system*; it tells us where an object is located—above

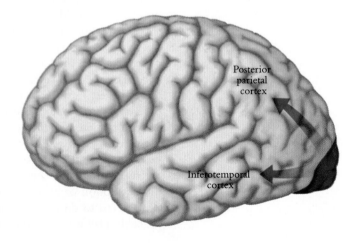

6.37 The "what" and "where" pathways Information from the primary visual cortex (located at the back of the head) is transmitted both to the inferotemporal cortex (the so-called "what" system) and to the posterior parietal cortex (the "where" system).

Posterior parietal cortex

Inferotemporal cortex

or below, to our right or left (Ungerleider and Mishkin, 1982; Ungerleider and Haxby, 1994; for a somewhat different conception of the "where" system, see Milner and Goodale, 1995).

Evidence for the contrasting roles of these two systems comes from studies of brain-damaged monkeys. The brain-damaged animals are given two tasks. One is a visual identification task, in which the monkey must learn to reach for one shape rather than another, for a cube, say, rather than a pyramid. The other task involves visual location, so that, for example, the monkey must learn to reach for a cube when it appears on the animal's left but not when it appears on the animal's right.

Monkeys who have suffered damage to the occipital-temporal pathway (that is, to the "what" system) show serious impairment on the identification task but do perfectly well on the location task. The reverse is true for monkeys with damage to the occipital-parietal pathway (the "where" system); they are impaired on the location task but behave normally on the identification task (Mishkin, Ungerleider, and Macko, 1983).

Similar observations have been made on humans. Patients with lesions in the occipital-temporal pathway show visual agnosia (see Chapter 2). They may be unable to recognize common objects, such as a cup or a pencil, and are often unable to recognize the faces of relatives and friends (although if the relatives speak, they can be recognized by their voices). On the other hand, these patients show little disorder in visual orientation and reaching. The reverse pattern is observed with patients who have suffered lesions in the occipital-parietal pathway—difficulty in reaching but no problem in object identification (Newcombe, Ratcliffe, and Damasio, 1987; Damasio, Tranel, and Damasio, 1989; Farah, 1990; Goodale, 1995).

THE HUMPTY-DUMPTY PROBLEM

It appears, then, that the visual system consists of an intricate network of subsystems, each specialized for a particular task. It seems clear that natural selection has favored a division-of-labor strategy for vision, with individualized processes responsible for each aspect of the whole.

This division into specialized subsystems allows us to perceive an extraordinary range of stimuli at different levels of illumination, in different colors and positions, in countless different shapes. It also helps to explain the sheer speed of visual perception, for example, our ability to recognize virtually any scene in a mere tenth of a second (Biederman, Mezzanotte, and Rabinowitz, 1982). The speed is made possible by the fact that different aspects of the scene are analyzed in parallel via different neural pathways, allowing processing to proceed simultaneously on several different fronts.

But this structure of the visual system raises a problem. How do we integrate these disparate pieces of information into one whole? (This is, of course, essentially the problem highlighted by the Gestalt psychologists.) When we see a ballet dancer in a graceful leap, the leap itself is registered by the magno cells, while the recognition of the ballet dancer depends on parvo cells. How are these pieces put back together? Likewise, when we reach for a coffee cup, but stop midway because we see that the cup is empty, the reach itself is guided by the occipital-parietal system (the "where" system); the fact that the cup is empty is perceived by the occipital-temporal system (the "what" system). How are these two streams of processing coordinated?

If we begin with a visual system that analyzes the scene into its constituents, how do we reunite the constituents to allow the perception of intact objects? To quote the nursery rhyme, "All the king's horses and all the king's men couldn't put Humpty-Dumpty together again." How does the nervous system solve its own version of the Humpty-Dumpty problem?

Neuroscientists call this the **binding problem**: how the nervous system manages to bind together elements that were initially detected by separate systems. We are only beginning to understand how the nervous system solves this problem, and it is a matter of intense interest to contemporary researchers.

PERCEPTUAL SELECTION: ATTENTION

While the binding problem remains unsolved, we do know one factor that helps enormously in gluing together the elements of our perceptual experience—namely, attention. Attention actually plays several roles in perception. One role is preparation: We are better able to perceive when we are paying attention. Attention also allows us to select some aspects of a scene for consideration, while ignoring others. We focus on the figure, not the ground, and if several figures are present, we choose the one to which we'll attend. And as we will see, attention also helps us knit together the sensations we receive to create a unified and coherent perceptual experience.

SELECTION THROUGH ORIENTATION

We are rarely the passive recipients of sensory information. We turn our head and eyes to look toward an interesting stimulus; we actively explore the world with our hands; we position our ears for better hearing. Other animals do the same, exploring the world with paws or lips or whiskers or even a prehensile tail. These various forms of *orienting* all serve to adjust the sensory machinery and to provide one of the most direct means of selecting input—a means through which we focus on the stimuli we care about, while disregarding those we do not.

In humans, movements of the eyes provide the major means of orienting. Peripheral vision informs us that something is going on, say, in the upper-left section of our field of vision. But our peripheral acuity is not good enough to tell us what it is precisely. To find out, we move our eyes so that the region in which the activity is taking place falls into the fovea. In fact, motion in the visual periphery tends to trigger a reflex eye movement, making it difficult *not* to look toward a moving object.

Other factors also influence our eye movements. One of them is interest. Figure 6.38 provides a record of subjects' eye movements when looking at a picture. In general, subjects directed their eyes toward regions that were visually informative, although the gaze pattern is different for different observers. This should not be surprising, since what interests one person may not interest another. Even for a single individual, interests change from occasion to occasion, so a picture will be scanned quite differently if the observer is asked to estimate the ages of the people in it than if she's asked to estimate their economic status (see Figure 6.39A, B, and C).

These results show that the act of looking is purposeful. People don't scan the world in the wistful hope that their foveas will hit on some interesting bit of visual news. They pick up some information from what they've vaguely seen in

A

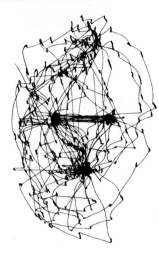

B

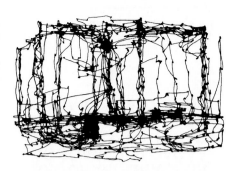

6.38 Eye-movement records when looking at pictures *Both (A) and (B) are pictures that were looked at for three and ten minutes respectively. With each picture is the record of the eye movements during this period. As the records show, most of the eye movements are directed toward the most visually informative regions. As a result, the eye-movement record is a crude mirror of the main contours of the picture. (From Yarbus, 1967)*

the periphery and also from their general notions of what the scene is all about. They then move their eyes to check up on what they've seen and to refine their visual knowledge further (Yarbus, 1967; Rayner, 1978; Stark and Ellis, 1981).

CENTRAL SELECTION

The selective control of perception also draws on central processes, which determine what inputs we will consider and what we will do with those inputs.

SELECTIVE LOOKING

A widely used method for studying visual attention is the visual search procedure, discussed earlier in this chapter. In this task, a subject is briefly shown an array of letters, digits, or other visual forms and asked to indicate as quickly as he can whether a particular target is present.

Searching for feature combinations As we noted earlier (p. 228), visual search seems almost effortless if the target can be distinguished from the field on the basis of just one feature—for example, searching for a vertical among a field of horizontals or for a green target amidst a group of red distractors. In such cases, the target pops out from the distractor elements, and search time is virtually independent of the number of items in the display.

6.39 Eye movements as a function of what the observer is looking for *(A) A picture shown to research participants. Three-minute eye-movement records when the viewers were asked to estimate the wealth of the family (B) and when they were asked to estimate the ages of the people in the picture (C). (From Yarbus, 1967)*

A

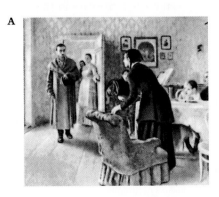

B

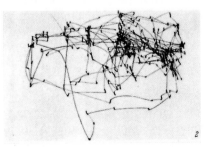

C

```
VOVOVOVVOVVVOVO
VOVOVVOOVVVOOVV
OVOVOVOVOOVVVOV
VVOVOVOVOVVOOOV
VOVOVVOOVVVOOVV
OVVOOVOVVOVVVOVV
OVOVOVOVOOVVVOV
VVOVOVOVVOVVOOOV
OVVOOVOVVOVVVOVV
OOVOVOVOVOOVVVO
VOVVOOVOVOVVOVVOV
OVVOOVOVVOVVVOVV
OVOVOVOVOOVVVOV
VVOVOVOVVOVVOOOV
OVVOOVOVVOVVVOVV
```

6.40 Serial processing in visual search
When the task is to find a target that is defined by a conjunction of features (here a red O), the search is conducted serially. Each item is inspected in turn, and the search time increases as the number of false alternatives (red or green V s, green O s) increases.

The situation is different, though, when the target is defined by a combination of features, for example, if one is searching for a red *O* among distractors that include green *O*s and red *V*s. Now it is not enough to search for redness or for the *O*'s roundness; instead, the subject must search for a target with both of these features. Under these conditions, the search process is serial rather than parallel. Search times are longer and increase with the number of items in the display.

Searching for a combination of features obviously requires more than searching for a single feature; it requires information about how the features are packaged together. In order to get that information, the perceiver must focus on one item at a time to figure out which features are present for just that item. By focusing a mental spotlight on just a single item, the perceiver can avoid any confusion about which features belong with which stimulus (Treisman, 1988; see Figure 6.40).

Priming What does it mean to say that we focus a mental spotlight? How is this selection achieved? Part of the answer lies in something we have already discussed: priming and top-down processing. If the circumstances lead the perceiver to expect, say, the word *CAT*, then the appropriate detectors will be partially activated. As a result, when the expected input actually arrives, it will be processed more efficiently: Since the detectors are primed, they need only slight additional activation to trigger a response. Notice, though, that the priming is selective: A subject who expects to see the word *CAT* will be unprepared for anything else. So if the stimulus turns out to be the word *BOG*, for example, it will be processed less efficiently. If the unexpected stimulus is weak (perhaps flashed briefly or only on a dimly lit screen), then it may not trigger a response at all. It's in this fashion that priming helps us to pay attention—selectively facilitating the perception of expected stimuli but simultaneously hindering the perception of anything else.

Priming can not only enhance the recognition of a particular stimulus; it can also prepare the perceiver for a broad class of stimuli—for example, any stimulus that appears in a particular location. In some experiments, subjects are asked to fix their eyes on a dot on a computer screen. Shortly thereafter, an arrow appears for an instant in that region and points either left or right. A moment later, the stimulus is presented. If it is presented in the location toward which the arrow pointed, the subjects respond more quickly than they do without the prime. If the stimulus appears in a different location (so that the prime was actually misleading), subjects respond more slowly than they do with no prime at all. Clearly, the prime influences how subjects allocate their processing resources.

This spatial priming is not simply a matter of cuing eye movements. In most studies, the interval between the appearance of the prime and the arrival of the target is too short to permit a voluntary eye movement.★ But even so (when it's not misleading) the arrow makes the task easier. Evidently, priming affects an internal selection process, as if the mind's eye moves even though the eyes in the head are stationary (Egeth, Jonides, and Wall, 1972; Eriksen and Hoffman, 1972; Gleitman and Jonides, 1976; Jonides, 1980, 1983; Posner, Snyder, and Davidson, 1980).

SELECTIVE LISTENING

Selective attention is also crucial for the other sensory modalities, including hearing. You may be at a noisy party, but you still manage to focus on just the voice of your conversational partner. Many other voices are audible, but these are some-

---

★ That interval is usually about 100 ms, while an eye movement takes about 150 to 200 ms to execute.

Attentional selection *(© Jeff Zamba/All-stock/PNI)*

how consigned to a background babble. This pattern, referred to as the ***cocktail party effect,*** is easily studied in the laboratory by asking research participants to attend to one of two simultaneously presented verbal messages. The usual procedure is ***dichotic presentation,*** in which the participant wears stereo headphones and receives different messages in each ear. To guarantee selective attention, the individual is asked to ***shadow*** the to-be-attended message. This means that she has to repeat it aloud, word for word, as it comes over the appropriate earphone. Under these conditions, the irrelevant message tends to be shut out almost entirely. She can hear speechlike sounds but notices little else. She is generally unable to recall the message that came by way of the unattended ear. In one classic study, research participants didn't even notice whether the speaker on the unattended ear shifted into a foreign language or read a passage backwards (Cherry, 1953).

However, participants are not totally deaf to the unattended message. If the voice reading the message changes from a male's to a female's, or if it changes pitch, this is noticed immediately. Occasional words from this message are also perceived. For example, research participants seem generally oblivious to the content of the unattended message but may register their own name if it is mentioned. Even with this salient stimulus, however, the effects of attention are visible: Only one-third of individuals notice their name, pronounced clearly in the unattended message; the majority do not (Moray, 1959).

These and similar results suggest that while attention may act as a kind of filter, this filter is not all-or-none, for it does not block irrelevant messages completely. It only attenuates them, as if a volume control is turned down but not off. If the item is important enough (or perhaps familiar enough), then it may pass through the attentional filter and be analyzed (Treisman, 1964).

PERCEIVING CONSTANCY

We have now considered a rich set of perceptual mechanisms, mechanisms that, in their normal operation, provide us with accurate information about the world around us. To be sure, the perceptual system occasionally leads us astray, as in illusions of distance or form or movement. But these are relatively rare occasions. By and large, the processes of perception serve us well as messengers about the real world outside.

To see the real world is to see the properties of distal objects: their color, form, size, and location; their movement through space; their permanence or transience. But as we have noted before, organisms cannot gain experience about the distal stimulus directly; instead, all information about the external world comes to us only from the proximal stimulus patterns that distal objects project upon the senses. And this creates a problem, because the same distal object can produce many different proximal stimuli. Its retinal image will get larger or smaller, depending upon its distance from us. Its retinal shape will change, depending upon its slant relative to our viewing perspective. The amount of light it projects onto our retinas will increase or decrease depending on the illumination that falls upon it.

Under the circumstances, it may seem surprising that we ever manage to see the real properties of objects at all. But see them we do. We are somehow able to distinguish changes in the proximal stimulus brought about by shifts in our viewing circumstances from changes created by an actual alteration in the world. We manage, in other words, to achieve ***perceptual constancy***. Thus, an elephant looks large even at a distance, a postcard looks rectangular even though its retinal image is a rectangle only when it is viewed directly head on, and a crow looks black even in sunlight. In all of these cases, we manage to transcend the vagaries of the proximal stimulus so that we can react to the world as it truly is. How do we accomplish this feat?

SIZE AND SHAPE CONSTANCY

Size constancy describes the fact that the perceived size of an object is the same whether it is nearby or far away. A house at the end of the street looks larger than a mailbox close by, even though the former produces a much smaller retinal image than the latter. An analogous phenomenon is *shape constancy*, which refers to the fact that we perceive the shape of an object more or less independently of the angle from which we view it. A rectangular door frame will look rectangular even though most of the angles from which we regard it will produce a trapezoidal retinal image (see Figure 6.41).

DIRECT PERCEPTION

How do we achieve these constancies? One explanatory approach is offered by James J. Gibson (1950, 1966, 1979). He believed that the vital characteristics of an object, such as its size, shape, and distance from the observer, are directly signaled by the visual stimulus. However, the relevant information is not the size or shape of the retinal image as such; instead, it is contained in *higher-order patterns*, patterns that usually depend on the *relationship* between the size (or shape) of the retinal image and various other attributes of the stimulus.

The size of the retinal image, for example, necessarily varies as the distal object changes its distance from the observer. But this does not mean that there is no size information in the stimulus that hits the eye. One reason is that objects are usually seen against a background that provides a basis for comparison with the target object. Often this comparison involves elements of the texture on which the target object sits: the pebbles or the clumps of grass that uniformly cover the surface on which the target is located. Size constancy, therefore, can be achieved by considering the number of these *texture elements* hidden from view by the target object or by considering the ratio between the size of the retinal image cast by the target and the size of the retinal image cast by its adjacent textural elements. The dog, sitting nearby on the kitchen floor, is half as tall as the chair and hides eight of the kitchen's floor tiles from view. If we take several steps back from the dog, none of these relationships changes, even though the size of

James J. Gibson *(Courtesy of E. J. Gibson)*

6.41 ***Shape constancy*** *When we see a door frame at various slants from us, it appears rectangular despite the fact that its retinal image is often a trapezoid. (After Gibson, 1950)*

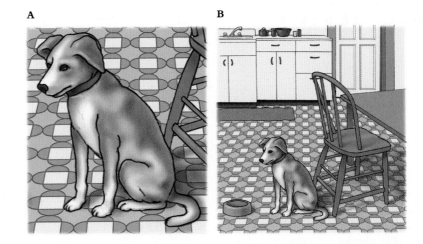

A   **B**

6.42 An invariant relationship that provides information about size (A) and (B) show a dog at different distances from the observer. The retinal size of the dog varies with distance, but the ratio between the retinal size of the dog and the retinal size of the textural elements (e.g., the floor tiles) is constant.

all the retinal images are reduced (Figure 6.42). In short, the retinal images change, but the higher-order information remains ***invariant***.

The evidence suggests that these relationships do contribute to size and shape constancy, but they are probably not the whole story. Size constancy is found even when the visual scene provides no basis for comparison, provided that other cues (such as binocular disparity or motion parallax) signal the distance of the target object. And these cues are not in the scene itself but, rather, are brought to the scene by the viewer, by the placement of his eyes or the point toward which his eyes are directed. Moreover, as the number of these distance cues diminishes, size constancy declines (Holway and Boring, 1947; Harvey and Leibowitz, 1967; Chevrier and Delorme, 1983). Likewise, if one of these cues is altered, indicating that the target object has moved further away, the perception of size changes, even though the relationship between the target and the background remains constant. These results are hard to reconcile with the view that our perception of a constant world depends entirely on higher-order relationships within the stimulus input.

UNCONSCIOUS INFERENCE

Invariant size relationships are apparently unable to explain all cases of size constancy. But what can? An influential hypothesis was formulated by Hermann von Helmholtz. Helmholtz started with the fact that there is a simple inverse relationship between distance and retinal image size. Thus, if an object doubles its distance from the viewer, the size of its image is reduced by half. If an object triples its distance, the size of its image is reduced to a third of its initial size (Figure 6.43).

This relationship makes it possible for perceivers to achieve constancy by means of a simple calculation. First, the perceiver needs to know the size of the image on the retina. Second, the perceiver needs to know how far away the object is (and, presumably, this information is provided by the distance cues we have already discussed). These two bits of information can then be combined via a process that somehow multiplies the size of the retinal image by the distance of the object from the viewer, and it is this calculation that leads to size constancy. Imagine an object that, at a distance of 10 feet, casts an image 4 millimeters across. The same object, at a distance of 20 feet, casts an image of 2 millimeters. In both cases, the product—10 × 4 or 20 × 2—is the same. Of course, Helmholtz knew that we don't go through any conscious calculation of this sort. But he believed that some such process—or something that produces the same result—was going on outside of our awareness, and so he called it ***unconscious inference*** (Helmholtz, 1909).

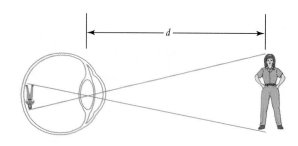

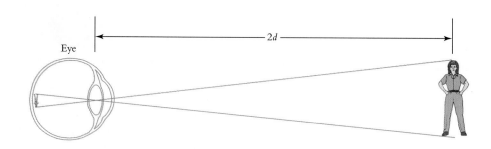

6.43 The relationship between image size and distance *If an object moves to a new distance, the size of the retinal image cast by that object changes. A doubling of the distance causes the retinal image size to be reduced by half. If the distance is tripled, the retinal image size is cut to one-third of its initial size.*

The heart of Helmholtz's view is that we somehow take distance into account in judging size. Likewise, for shape constancy, we somehow take the slant of the surface into account and make appropriate adjustments in our interpretation of the retinal image's shape. Much evidence indicates that this sort of adjustment is, in fact, an important element of our perception. For example, we have mentioned that size constancy is most accurate when there is a rich set of distance cues available. As the quality of distance information declines, so does constancy (Figure 6.44). As a result, many contemporary theorists agree that a taking-into-account process must be involved in size constancy and that some sort of unconscious inference must be drawn by our perceptual system (see for example Rock, 1977, 1983, 1986; Hochberg, 1981, 1988).

A

B

6.44 Perceived size and distance
(A) The actual image of the two men in the picture—which corresponds to the size of their retinal image—is in the ratio of 3 to 1. But this is not the way they are perceived. They look roughly equal in size, but at different distances, with one three times farther off than the other. In (B) there are no cues that indicate that one man is farther away than the other— on the contrary, the picture indicates that they are equally distant from the viewer. With this misinformation about distance, the men now look very different in size. The figure was constructed by cutting the more distant man out of the picture and pasting him next to the other man, with the apparent distance from the viewer equal for the two. (After Boring, 1964; Photograph by Jeffrey Grosscup)

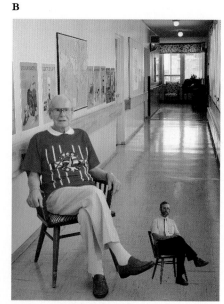

6.45 Lightness constancy and brightness contrast In (A) the illumination on both crow and wall is moderate; in (B) it is much greater. The fact that illumination goes up increases the amount of light reflected by the crow, but it also increases the amount of light reflected by the wall that serves as its background. The ratio between the light reflected from the crow and the light reflected from the wall remains constant. This leads to lightness constancy: The crow continues to look black even in brilliant sunshine.

A   B

LIGHTNESS CONSTANCY

Helmholtz in the nineteenth century, and Gibson in the twentieth, each hoped for a uniform account of perceptual constancies, a theory that would apply to size and shape constancy as well as lightness constancy. There is reason to believe, though, that the perceptual system may achieve different forms of constancy in somewhat different ways. Helmholtz's unconscious-inference theory seems to capture size and shape constancy, but Gibson's hypothesis, emphasizing the role of higher-order invariants, seems more plausible in the case of *lightness constancy*.

Lightness constancy refers to the fact that we are able to perceive an object's lightness, whether the object is white or gray or black, regardless of the illumination that falls upon it. On the face of it, this presents a problem. Virtually all objects reflect a certain proportion of the light that falls upon them. The exact proportion depends upon a physical property of the object itself, its *reflectance*. Some objects have a high reflectance (snow), others a low reflectance (coal). To say that an object is perceived as light or dark is really to say that we can tell something about its reflectance. Yet we cannot see the reflectance directly; all we get from the object is the amount of light it actually reflects on any given occasion. And this depends on both the object's reflectance and also the illumination that falls upon it. A white shirt in shadow may well reflect less light than does a gray shirt in brilliant sunlight. Nonetheless, we can tell that the first is lighter than the second. Similarly, a white shirt will not suddenly seem to turn gray when a cloud hides the sun; it appears just as white but in shadow.

How does this constancy come about? The answer was provided most persuasively by the work of Hans Wallach. As Wallach demonstrated, the perception of lightness seems to depend largely on the *ratio* between the amount of light reflected by the object and that reflected by the object's background. To see how this works, consider a black crow that stands in front of a gray garden wall (Figure 6.45). If the sun suddenly emerges from behind a cloud, the illumination on the crow will go up and so will the amount of light reflecting from the crow and reaching our eyes. But the same holds for the wall; it will also be more brightly illuminated and will also reflect more light. If the illumination of one is doubled, so is the illumination of the other; the relationship between them remains unchanged. Our visual system evidently responds to this relationship and thus accomplishes lightness constancy. This effect is probably produced by the same processes (presumably based on lateral inhibition) that are responsible

Hans Wallach (1904–1998)

for brightness contrast and related phenomena (Wallach, 1948; Richards, 1977; see Chapter 5).

EMPIRICISM AND NATIVISM REVISITED

Against this backdrop, let us return to the issues posed at the very beginning of the last chapter. What has happened to the debate between the empiricist heirs of Locke, on the one hand, and the nativist descendants of Kant on the other?

The empiricists, recall, argued that our perception is built up from a mosaic of elementary sensations—patches of color, brief tones, and the like. As we have seen, this is only partly correct, because it underestimates the richness of information actually contained in the visual input. The perceptual system is sensitive, for example, to many higher-order relationships; these play a role in constancy and also in the recognition of some forms, such as faces (e.g., Farah, 1995). The perceptual system is also influenced by patterns of organization within the stimulus; as we have seen, this plays a pivotal role in visual parsing. Finally, these patterns of organization can actually influence how we perceive the form's primitive elements, presumably via top-down processing (see Figure 6.46).

The empiricists also argued that the perceiver supplements her sensory explorations by means of associations. This is certainly true, but again, it understates the perceiver's activity. Our discussion of parsing, for example, emphasized the perceiver's role, guided both by past experience and also by more general principles, in dissecting a scene into its parts. Likewise, the perceiver's attention plays a pivotal role in assembling the sensations into wholes. Other examples of perceptual activity are easy to find.

The nativists, therefore, may have offered a more realistic conception of the importance of the perceiver's role in organizing and interpreting the perceptual input. But the nativists drew from this a strong claim about the *innateness* of the relevant mechanisms. Recall Kant's argument that, since perception can't occur without mechanisms of interpretation, these mechanisms must be in place prior to the perceptual experience and so must be innate.

This claim is certainly too strong. To be sure, we are born with an impressively sophisticated perceptual system. The basic architecture of the visual cortex, for example, is already evident in the newborn; similarly, size constancy can be documented in infants as young as six months old and, according to some authors, as young as one day old! (Slater, Mattock, and Brown, 1990; also see Bower, 1966; McKenzie, Tootell, and Day, 1980; Day and McKenzie, 1981; for more on perception in infancy, see Chapter 13). But it is also true that the perceptual system is massively influenced by learning. The visual cortex may be impressively mature even at birth; nonetheless, the receptive fields of the cortical neurons are tuned and sharpened during the early months of life. Other mechanisms must be continually refreshed and recalibrated. For example, the interpretation of binocular disparity must be shifted as the head grows (and the eyes grow farther apart). Other depth cues seem to provide the benchmark against which this recalibration is accomplished.

In fact, these last points highlight the difficulty of labeling any mechanism as learned or innate. Many of the mechanisms of perception do derive from structures and pathways present at birth. These shape the organism's experience and thus what it learns. What the organism learns, in turn, modifies, tunes, and calibrates the mechanisms already in place. It seems, therefore, that innate mechanisms shape learning, and learning shapes innate mechanisms. The achievements of perception, therefore, are, in their mature form, neither purely learned nor purely innate. Rather, they emerge from a complex and ongoing interaction between factors that are biologically given and those that are experience driven.

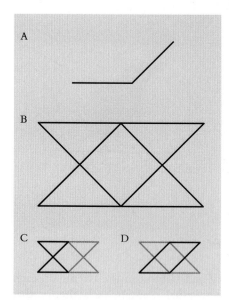

6.46 The status of sensations *The empiricists argued that our perceptions are built up from elementary sensations. Often, however, the reverse seems to be the case: The pattern of our elementary sensations depends on how we perceive an entire pattern. Is the corner shown in (A) present in the more complex pattern shown in (B)? If you perceive (B) as the Roman numeral twenty—as in (C)—you are unlikely to detect this corner. If you perceive (B) as two overlapping parallelograms—as in (D)—then you easily recognize the corner.*

THE REPRESENTATION OF REALITY IN ART

Throughout this chapter, we have emphasized the essential function of perception: It provides us with accurate and up-to-date information about the world around us. We obviously need this information to navigate through situations that are objectively dangerous (such as driving in heavy traffic), but the need is just as great in the ordinary circumstances that fill our day-to-day lives: We cannot walk across a room unless we know what objects surround us, where those objects are positioned relative to us, and whether they are moving or stationary.

The mechanisms of perception evolved to serve this essential function, and so it is crucial that these mechanisms allow us to see the world as it actually is. But it is part of our humanity that we have managed to turn these perceptual mechanisms to a use that goes beyond the necessities of survival: the representation of reality in art.

SEEING AND KNOWING

Consider Figure 6.47, a wall painting from Egypt some three thousand years ago. Why did the artist depict the figures as he did, with eyes and shoulders in front view and the rest of the body in profile? His fellow Egyptians were surely built as we are. But if so, why didn't he draw them "correctly"?

6.47 Horemhab offering wine to Annubis, ca. 1339–1304 B.C.E. The conventions of Egyptian art required the main parts of the human body to be represented in their most characteristic view. Thus, heads are shown in profile, arms and legs from the side, but eyes are depicted in full-face view, as are shoulders and chest. (Courtesy of the Metropolitan Museum of Art, New York, Rogers Fund, 1923)

The answer seems to be that Egyptian artists drew, not what they could see at any one moment or from any one position, but rather what they believed was the most enduring and characteristic attribute of their model. They portrayed the various parts of the human body from the vantage point that shows each in its most characteristic manner: the front view for the eyes and shoulders, the profile for the nose and feet. The fact that these orientations are incompatible was evidently of no concern; what mattered was that all of the components were represented as the artist knew them to be (Gombrich, 1961).

THE RENAISSANCE: SCENES THROUGH A WINDOW FRAME

The illustrations of Egyptian art show the enormous role of the known in the visual representation of the seen. This may simply reflect the fact that these artists never set themselves the task of mirroring nature as it appears to the eye. Does the artist copy more precisely if one of his main purposes is to do just that?

The most striking examples come from the Renaissance masters who conceived the notion that a picture should look just like a real scene viewed through a window from one particular orientation (see Figure 6.48). The painting's

6.48   Perspective in Renaissance art
The Annunciation *by Crivelli (ca. 1430–1495). Note the loving attention to perspective detail, such as roofs and arches extending far back. (Courtesy the National Gallery, London)*

6.49 The Cathedral of Rouen by Claude Monet, 1893 *Monet, one of the leaders of the Impressionist movement, was engaged in a life-long attempt to catch fleeting sensations of light. If this painting of the cathedral at Rouen is viewed from a distance or out of foveal vision, the form becomes clearer and less impressionistic. What is lost is the brilliant shimmer of light and color. The oscillation between these two modes of appearance contributes to the total esthetic effect. (Courtesy of Musée d'Orsay)*

frame is then the frame of this window into the artist's world. One major step toward achieving this end was the discovery of the geometrical laws of perspective, laws that were carefully codified by the Renaissance artists (Kubovy, 1986).

THE IMPRESSIONISTS: HOW A SCENE IS PERCEIVED

The Renaissance painters tried to represent a scene as it is projected on the eye. Other schools of painting set themselves a different task. Consider the French Impressionists of the late nineteenth century. They tried to recreate certain perceptual experiences that the scene evokes in the observer, the impression it makes rather than the scene itself. One of their concerns was to render color as we see it in broad daylight. Their method was to create a seeming patchwork of different daubs of bright colors (see Figure 6.49). These are clearly separate when looked at directly. But when viewed from the proper distance, they change appearance, especially in the periphery where acuity is weak. The individual patches now blur together and their colors mix. But when the eyes move again and bring that area of the picture back into the fovea, the mixtures come apart and the individual patches reappear. Some authors believe that this continual alternation between mixed colors and separate dots gives these paintings their special vitality (Jameson and Hurvich, 1975).

This patchwork technique has a further effect. It enlists the beholder as an active participant in the artistic enterprise. Her active involvement starts as soon as she tries to see the picture as a whole rather than as a meaningless jumble of colored patches. This happens when the separate patches blur; when they are

255

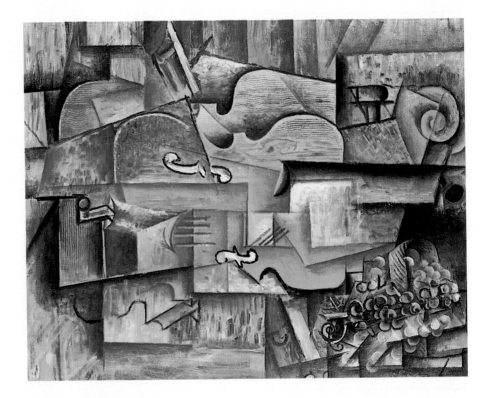

6.50 Violin and Grapes by Pablo Picasso, 1912 *(Courtesy Museum of Modern Art, New York, Mrs. David M. Levy bequest)*

viewed from the periphery or from a few steps back. Now the picture suddenly snaps into focus and a whole emerges. This is both similar to and different from what happens in ordinary life. There we move our eyes to bring some part of the world to a region of greater acuity, the fovea. In the museum, we sometimes move our eyes (or our entire body) to bring a picture to a region of lesser acuity, away from the fovea. In either case, active movement leads to the perception of a figural whole (Hochberg, 1978*b*, 1980).

THE MODERNS: HOW A SCENE IS CONCEIVED

The impressionists tried to engender some of the perceptual experiences a scene evokes in the observer. Later generations went further and tried to capture not just how the scene is perceived but how it is conceived, how it is known as well as seen. Modern art provides many examples, as in Pablo Picasso's still life showing superimposed fragments of a violin (Figure 6.50). Here perception and knowledge are cunningly merged in a sophisticated return to some of the ways of Egyptian artists (Gombrich, 1961).

Some Modern artists are not content just to add conceptual elements to their visual representations. They want to create ambiguity by setting up visual puzzles that can't be solved. One way is to pit knowledge against visual perception, as in Picasso's faces that are seen in profile and front-face at the same time. Another is to build contradictions into the perceptual scene itself. An example is a painting by the turn-of-the-century Italian Giorgio de Chirico (Figure 6.51). One reason for the disturbing quality of his work is the fact that de Chirico often used incompatible perspectives. In his *The Enigma of a Day*, the structure on the left converges to one horizon, the structure on the right to a different horizon, while the crate in the middle does not converge at all. The result is an insoluble visual problem, an eerie world that cannot be put in order.

De Chirico's streets do not look like real streets, and Picasso's violins are a far cry from those one sees in a concert hall. In this regard, these Modern painters appear quite different from many of their predecessors whose representations were closer to the world as it appears to the perceiver. But we have to realize that with few exceptions, no artists, whether Renaissance masters, Impressionists, or Moderns, ever try to fool the observer into thinking that he is looking at a real scene. They neither can nor want to hide the fact that their painting is a painting. It may spring to life for a moment and look like a real person or a real sunset, or it may briefly conjure up a vivid memory of what a face or a violin looks like when viewed from several angles. But whether it emphasizes the seen or the known, it is also recognized as a flat piece of canvas daubed with paint.

According to some authors, this perceptual duality is an important part of the beholder's esthetic experience as she looks at a work of representational art. In a well-known poem by Robert Browning, a duke points to his

> last duchess painted on the wall,
> Looking as if she were alive.

The key words are *as if.* One reason why visual art leads to an esthetic experience may be because it provides us with a halfway mark between seen reality and painted appearance, because it presents a visual *as if* (Hochberg, 1980).

In our discussion of visual art we have taken yet another step across the wide, shadowy region where perception and conception, seeing and knowing merge. In the next chapter we will cross the boundary altogether. There we will consider how we remember objects and events that no longer stimulate our senses.

6.51 **The Enigma of a Day** *by Giorgio de Chirico, 1914* (*Oil on canvas, 6′ 1 ¼″ × 55″, The Museum of Modern Art, New York, James Thrall Soby Bequest.*)

SUMMARY

1.   The fundamental problem of perception is how we come to apprehend the objects and events in the world around us. In the field of visual perception, the major issues concern the way in which we see *depth, movement,* and *form.*

2.   The visual world is seen in three dimensions even though only two of these are given in the image that falls upon the eye. This fact has led to an interest in *depth cues.* Among these are *binocular disparity* and *monocular cues,* such as *interposition* and *linear perspective, relative size,* and *texture gradients.* All of these cues are powerful determinants of perceived depth. More important still is the motion of our heads and bodies. This leads to *motion parallax* and various patterns in the *optic flow,* all of which provide vital information about how far objects are from each other and how far they are from ourselves.

3.   Some *direction-specific cells* do respond to movement of an image on the retina, but this alone cannot explain the perception of movement, as shown by the phenomenon of *apparent movement* and by the fact that the nervous system compensates for displacements produced by movements of the eye.

4.   Not only do we detect motion, we also interpret it. This is evident in the phenomenon of *induced motion,* in which we assume that smaller, enclosed objects are moving, whereas larger, enclosing frames are assumed to be stationary.

5.   In vision, our primary means for recognizing an object is through its form. An important phenomenon in the psychology of form perception is *transposition of form:* A perceived form may remain the same even if all of its constituent parts are altered. This phenomenon is the keystone of *Gestalt psychology,* a theory that emphasizes the importance of wholes created by the relationship among their parts.

6.   Many modern investigators believe that form perception is based on several steps of *information processing* that transform the initial visual input into its cognitive end product, the perception of objects in the world. This process begins with the detection of *primitive features,* which can be identified by the fact that they "pop out" in a *visual search task.* In the early stages of processing, these features are detected but not related to each other, as shown by *illusory conjunctions.*

7.   Before the perceiver can recognize a form, he must first engage in a process of *visual segregation* and *parse* the visual scene. This involves the segregation of *figure* and *ground,* which are not inherent in the proximal stimulus but are imposed by the perceptual system, as shown by *reversible figures.* Further segregation produces perceptual *grouping,* which depends upon factors such as *proximity, similarity,* and *good continuation.* Some authors believe that all of these parsing phenomena are manifestations of a *maximum-likelihood principle*—the tendency to interpret a proximal stimulus pattern as that external stimulus object that most probably produced it.

8.   *Pattern recognition* involves two kinds of processes. One is *bottom-up* (or data-driven) processing, which starts with the stimulus and subjects it to an analysis that begins with lower-level units (such as slanted lines) that then activate higher-level units (such as geometrical figures). The other is *top-down* (or knowledge-driven) processing, which is based on expectations and hypotheses, as shown by perceptual *context effects.* These top-down processes are able to prime lower-level detectors, so that they will respond even to weak inputs. Bottom-up and top-down processes work together, resulting in a process that allows lower-level units to activate higher-level units and also higher-level units to activate lower-level ones.

9.   To account for the recognition of ordinary, three-dimensional objects, theorists have proposed that pattern recognition also involves an intermediate level of analysis, in which features are assembled into object parts. One proposal is that these parts are *geons,* which are then assembled to form a structural description of the object.

10. Top-down processes provide perceptual hypotheses that are then tested by bottom-up processes. The result is sometimes described as *perceptual problem solving,* with the observer's perceptions apparently guided by a number of logical principles, including a principle that all the information within the stimulus must be explained, and an avoidance of interpretations that depend on accident or coincidence. This kind of *perceptual logic* sometimes fails, as in the case of *impossible figures.*

11. The neural processes that make perception possible involve a number of specialized subsystems. On the retina, two types of ganglion cells are sensitive to different aspects of the visual input: *Parvo cells* are sensitive to color differences and seem crucial for the perception of pattern and form; *magno cells* are color blind and play an essential role in the detection of motion and the perception of depth. In the visual cortex, different types of cells each respond to specific aspects of the stimulus. *Simple cells* fire most strongly in response to a line or edge of a specific orientation; *complex cells* are also sensitive to the orientation of the stimulus but, unlike simple cells, are less sensitive to its position. Still other cells respond to corners and angles.

12. The *"what" system* carries information to the temporal cortex and is crucial for the identification of visual objects. The *"where" system* carries information to the parietal cortex and conveys information about where a stimulus is located.

13. The fact that vision depends on multiple specialized subsystems raises a question: How are the separate pieces of information integrated to form a coherent perceptual whole? This question, called the *binding problem,* continues to be a subject of intense research.

14. Perception is selective. This selection is partially achieved by orienting, as in the case of eye movements. It is also achieved by a central process, *selective attention.* Methods for studying attention include *selective looking,* as demonstrated in *visual search procedures,* and *selective listening,* as shown by *dichotic presentation* in which the subject shadows one message while ignoring another.

15. The ultimate function of perception is to help the organism apprehend the outside world as it really is. This is illustrated by the *perceptual constancies* in which the perceiver responds to certain permanent characteristics of the distal object despite various contextual factors—including illumination, distance, and orientation—that lead to enormous variations in the proximal stimulus. In *size* and *shape constancy,* the perceiver responds to the actual size and shape of the object more or less regardless of its distance and orientation, apparently drawing unconscious inferences about size and shape based on *distance away* and angle of regard. In *lightness constancy,* however, the perceiver relies on higher-order information, responding to the object's reflectance and ignoring the level of illumination that falls upon it.

16. The current understanding of visual perception indicates that the *empiricists* understated the active role of the perceiver in organizing and interpreting the visual input. The *nativists' view* of this activity was more accurate, but they overstated the role of innate mechanisms. The visual system is impressively sophisticated at birth, but experience plays a crucial role in shaping the visual system's functioning. Overall, it appears that innate mechanisms shape learning, and learning shapes innate mechanisms.

17. The psychology of visual art is a further illustration of the overlap between perception and thinking. The artist represents both what she sees and what she knows. *Renaissance* painters represented scenes seen through a window frame; the *Impressionists* tried to recreate certain perceptual experiences the scene evokes in the beholder; while many *Modern* artists tried to represent the scene as they conceived and thought about it.

CHAPTER 7

M E M O R Y

O ur discussion of perception emphasized the way we organize the incoming sensory information in order to discern and accurately perceive objects in the world outside. Locke and Berkeley to the contrary, our perceptual world is not a jumbled mosaic of isolated fragments, glued together only by associations. Instead, it is an organized, coherent whole in which every piece relates to every other. We now turn to the subject of memory, in which organization plays an equally prominent part. Whereas perception concerns the organization of current stimuli, memory—at least, many aspects of memory—concerns the organization of past ideas and events.

Memory is the way we record the events of our lives and also the information and skills we glean from these events. It is hard to imagine humans (or any other animal) without this capacity. Without memory, there would be no *then* but only *now,* no ability to build or hone skills, no recall of names or recognition of faces, no reference to past days or hours or even seconds. We would be condemned to live in a narrowly circumscribed present, but this present would not even seem to be our own, for there can be no sense of self without memory for the events that shaped our lives. Each individual wakes up every morning and never doubts that he is he or she is she. This feeling of personal identity is necessarily based upon a continuity of memories that links our yesterdays to our todays.

STUDYING MEMORY

How do psychologists study memory? The first step is to realize that memory is not a single entity and that there is no single set of memory processes. Instead, the term *memory* is a blanket label for a large number of processes that work together to create a bridge between our past and our present.

SOME PRELIMINARY DISTINCTIONS

We rely on our memories to span a wide range of time intervals. In some cases, we need to remember something we learned just moments ago; on other occasions, we draw on knowledge gained days, months, or even years earlier. In some cases, we are asked to recall material that has never been out of our thoughts: You hear a bit of news, continue to think about it for a while, and then, without interruption, are asked to report what you had heard. Other cases are quite different: You learn something, then focus your attention on other matters for a time, and then, finally, dredge up what you learned earlier.

These different ***retention intervals*** are bridged by different memory systems. Information learned long ago is likely to be stored in ***long-term memory.*** This memory system allows materials to lie dormant for long periods of time. Other

Card games and memory *Many card games make considerable demands on memory. Pictured here are children hard at work "playing" the game of Memory. (Photograph by Kathy Hirsh-Pasek)*

information is stored in ***working memory.*** This is the memory system that stores information we are working on right now. For example, as you read this sentence, you must remember the sentence's beginning as you read through to its end; then you can combine the ideas you gained early in the sentence with those you gained later. In this situation, your memory of the sentence's start would be held in working memory.

Another distinction concerns the type of information we are remembering. Suppose someone asks us what we had for dinner last night. When we search our memories for that particular fact, we are drawing on ***episodic memory***—a memory for a specific event. But to have that conversation at all, we must also call on our memories in a different way: We must remember what the individual words in the conversation mean, and we must remember how to combine these words to form sentences. This requires information in our ***generic memory.*** Generic memory is our mental "reference library"—it holds our mental dictionary and is also the storehouse for all our commonsense knowledge. What color is the sky? How many months are in a year? Who is your favorite actress? In what room in a house would we find the oven? These facts, and millions more, are stored in generic memory.

A final distinction concerns our conscious awareness of remembering. When searching for the answer to "What did you have for dinner last night?" we are perfectly aware that we are trying to remember. (Whether we succeed or not is another question.) In such cases, we are dealing with ***explicit memory.*** Sometimes, though, we are influenced by the past without our realizing it at all. We solve puzzles more quickly the second time we encounter them, even when we have no recollection of ever having seen those puzzles before. We regard sentences we have heard before as being more credible, even if we don't recall having heard those sentences before. This sort of "memory without awareness" is called ***implicit memory.***

ENCODING, STORAGE, RETRIEVAL

Let us start by examining what the various types of memory all have in common. Any act of remembering implies success at three aspects of the memory process. First, in order to remember, one must have learned. This seems an obvious point, but it deserves emphasis because many failures of memory are, in fact, failures in this initial stage of ***acquisition.*** For example, imagine meeting someone at a party, being told his name, and moments later realizing that you no longer know it! This embarrassing experience is probably not the result of ultra-rapid forgetting. Instead, it is likely to stem from a failure in acquisition: You were exposed to the name but barely paid attention to it and, as a result, never learned it in the first place.

To understand acquisition, we must ask how the information was ***encoded*** into memory. The term *encoding* refers to the form (that is, the code) in which an item of information is to be placed in memory. Thus, a physician learning about a new medication might focus on its uses, without giving much thought to its side effects. Or she might focus on the biochemical mechanisms through which the drug works, without thinking about how a patient's life might be improved by it. Such differences in emphasis during encoding can have a profound effect on how (or whether) this information will be remembered later.

The next aspect of remembering is ***storage:*** To be remembered, the encoded experience must leave some record in the nervous system (the ***memory trace***); it must be squirreled away and held in some more or less enduring form for later use.

The final phase is *retrieval,* the point at which we "try to remember," try to dredge up a particular memory trace from among all the others we have stored. One way to retrieve material is through *recall.* This refers to our efforts to supply information from memory in response to a specific cue or question. Trying to answer questions like "What was the name of that medicine you learned about last year?" or "Can you remember where you read about that new medicine?" or "Do you know anything about drugs that help alleviate depression?" all require recall.

A different way to retrieve information is through *recognition.* In this kind of retrieval, we are presented with a name, fact, or situation and asked if we've encountered it before. "Was the medicine perhaps called 'Paxil'?" would be a question requiring recognition. When recognition is tested in the laboratory, subjects are usually asked to pick out the previously encountered item from a group of options ("Which of these is the name of a medicine you saw earlier?"). This obviously resembles a multiple-choice test, and in fact, multiple-choice testing in the classroom puts a premium on the ability to recognize previously learned material. In contrast, essay or short-answer examinations emphasize recall.

A failure to remember can result from mishaps during any of the three phases of the memory process. A doctor who thought only of a drug's peculiar name when first encountering it would have no memory trace of its other attributes, and so this other information would be unavailable later. Even if the other information had been encoded, it might have been "misfiled" in memory—stored, say, with information about chemically similar drugs rather than with information about treating depression. This would make it difficult to retrieve the information when it was needed subsequently. As we will see, many cases of memory failure can be understood in these terms—as failures of retrieval and not failures of storage. This becomes clear whenever we are unable to come up with the correct answer but then do recall it later on: "Of course, Paxil!"

In this chapter, we will focus on encoding and retrieval, because these can be studied more or less directly. But we will also touch on storage, looking at the brain mechanisms that make storage possible.

ENCODING

In our discussion of how memories are encoded, we'll start by considering an important theory of memory, which we will here call the *stage theory.* This theory has provided a foundation for current approaches, but as we will see, it also needs to be supplemented in several ways.

THE STAGE THEORY OF MEMORY

Memory has often been compared to a storehouse. This conception goes back to the ancient Greek philosophers and also to St. Augustine, who described the "roomy chambers of memory, where are the treasures of countless images. . . ." This metaphor likens memories to objects that are put into storage compartments, held for a while, and then searched for at a later time (Roediger, 1980; Crowder, 1985a).

The stage theory of memory, developed some forty years ago, represents a modern variation on this spatial metaphor. Unlike Augustine, who believed that there is one memory warehouse, this theory asserts that there are several storage systems, each with different properties (Broadbent, 1958; Waugh and Norman, 1965; Atkinson and Shiffrin, 1968).

Why might we need several kinds of memory? Think about the relationship between your desktop and your bookshelves. Your shelves hold many books and thus a great deal of information. But this information is not at your fingertips, so if you need some tidbit from the shelves, you may have to spend some time searching for it. Your desktop, on the other hand, offers limited space, so only a few books and a few papers can be on the desk at any one time. But what is on the desk is immediately available, with no time lost in searching for the information.

Obviously, each of these modes of storage has its advantages: Your bookshelves let you store a wealth of knowledge, including, of course, a great deal of information that you're not using right now. But your desktop gives you instant access to the small store of information pertinent to today's project.

This distinction, between desktop and bookshelves, parallels a distinction that is central to the stage theory of memory, a distinction between working memory (called ***short-term memory*** in the original theory) and long-term memory. Working memory holds information for short intervals—that is, while we are working with it. Long-term memory, in contrast, stores materials for much longer, sometimes for as long as a lifetime.★

THE STORAGE CAPACITY OF WORKING AND LONG-TERM MEMORY

Working memory and long-term memory differ in many important ways. One difference is in the ***storage capacity*** of each. The capacity of long-term memory is enormous: The average college student remembers the meanings of 80,000 words, thousands of autobiographical episodes, millions of facts, hundreds of skills, the taste of vanilla and the smell of lemon. All of this and much more are stored in long-term memory.

In contrast, the capacity of working memory is exceedingly limited. Traditionally, this capacity has been measured by a ***memory span task*** in which the individual hears a series of items and must repeat them, in order, after just one presentation. If the items are randomly chosen letters or digits, adults can repeat seven items or so without error. With longer series, errors are likely. This has led to the assertion that working memory's capacity is seven items, give or take one or two. In fact, many tasks, not just memory span, show this limit of seven plus-or-minus two items, leading psychologists to refer to this as the ***magic number*** (after Miller, 1956). Given the assumption that a wide range of tasks must rely on working memory, it is perhaps unsurprising that this limit—presumably, a reflection of the small size of this memory—sets a boundary on performance in a variety of settings.

WORKING MEMORY AS A LOADING PLATFORM

What is the relation between working memory and long-term memory? The stage theory asserts that the road to long-term memory necessarily passes through working memory. Seen in this light, working memory can be regarded as a loading platform, sitting at the entrance to the huge long-term warehouse.

Overloading capacity *The limited capacity of working memory has its physical analogue in the demands made upon us by modern society as caricatured in this scene from Charlie Chaplin's 1936 film,* Modern Times. *(Courtesy the Kobal Collection)*

★ The original theory asserted that an additional stage—a sensory register in which sensory material is held for a second or two—precedes the others (Sperling, 1960; Atkinson and Shiffrin, 1968).

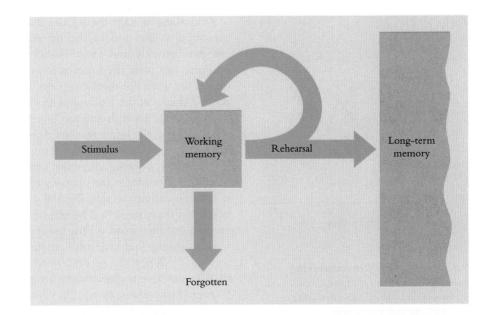

7.1   The relation between working memory and long-term memory as envisaged by stage theory   *The figure is a schematic representation of the relation between the two memory systems as stage theorists conceive of them. Information is encoded and enters working memory. To enter the long-term store, it must remain in working memory for a while. The means for maintaining it there is rehearsal. (Adapted from Waugh and Norman, 1965)*

A parcel that stays on the platform long enough may be picked up and placed in the warehouse, but the vast majority of parcels never make it.

Forgetting recent memories   Material in working memory is very short-lived. While reading the morning newspaper, we briefly note all kinds of extraneous matters: The coffee tastes bitter, a child is crying next door, there is a typo on the front page. But by and large these momentary experiences are instantly forgotten. One reason may be **decay:** The memory trace becomes eroded over time, so its details become gradually less distinct (see p. 280). Another possibility is **displacement:** Items are somehow pushed out of memory by other items that enter later. The best evidence to date suggests that both factors play a role, that some packages on the platform erode (decay), while others are shoved off by other packages (displacement). In either case, it is clear that they are generally not allowed to remain on the platform for long.

This rapid forgetting from working memory may be a blessing in disguise. Without it, our memory systems would soon become clogged with useless information. Given its limited capacity, the loading platform has to be cleared of the old packages quickly to make room for the new arrivals (Bjork, 1970).

Transfer into long-term memory   As we've just seen, most packages disappear from the platform before transfer to long-term storage. But a few remain on the platform for a while and thus become candidates for memorial permanence. One reason for this is memory **rehearsal:** When an item is repeated over and over again, it can be held in working memory, and this increases the probability that the item will be transferred to long-term storage (see Figure 7.1).

These suggestions fit rather well with some facts obtained by the method of **free recall.** In this procedure, research participants hear a list of unrelated items, such as common English words, presented one at a time. At the end of the list, the participants are asked to recall the items in any order they choose (hence the term *free*). If the items are presented only once, and if their number exceeds the participants' memory span, then they will not all be remembered. There is, however, a clear pattern for which words will be remembered and which not: Words that are presented at the beginning of the list are quite likely to be recalled; this is called the **primacy effect.** Likewise, the last few words on the list are also likely to be recalled; this is the **recency effect.** Likelihood of recall is appreciably poorer for words in the middle of the list (see Figure 7.2).

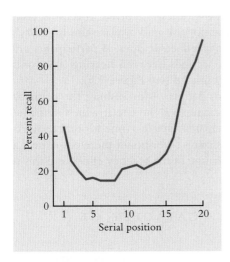

7.2   Primacy and recency effects in free recall   *Research participants heard a list of twenty common words presented at a rate of one word per second. Immediately after hearing the list, participants were asked to write down as many of the words on the list as they could recall. The results show that position in the series strongly affected recall: The words at the beginning (primacy effect) and at the end (recency effect) were recalled more frequently than those in the middle. (After Murdock, 1962)*

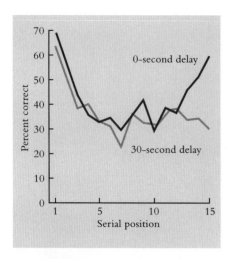

7.3 The recency effect and working memory *Research participants heard several fifteen-word lists. In one condition (dark red), free recall was tested immediately after they heard the list. In the other condition (blue), the recall test was given after a thirty-second delay during which rehearsal was prevented. The long delay left the primacy effect unaffected but abolished the recency effect, indicating that this effect is based on retrieval from working memory. (After Glanzer and Cunitz, 1966)*

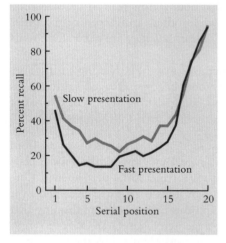

7.4 The primacy effect and long-term storage *The figure compares free-recall performance when item presentation is relatively slow (two seconds per item) and fast (one second per item). Slow presentation enhances the primacy effect but leaves the recency effect unaltered. The additional second per item presumably allows more time for rehearsal, which leads to long-term storage. (After Murdock, 1962)*

According to stage theory, the recency effect derives from the fact that items presented at the end of the list are still in working memory and so can be retrieved quickly and easily. Earlier words on the list passed through working memory but were then displaced by later arrivals. However, the last few words on the list were not displaced—no memory items arrived after these, so nothing pushed them off the loading platform. They are still available in working memory when the list ends and can be readily recalled.

In contrast, the items recalled from the beginning of the list must be retrieved from long-term memory. (This must be the case, since these words were displaced from working memory and so cannot be retrieved from that store.) What, then, produces the primacy effect? One hypothesis is that individuals have more opportunity to rehearse the earliest items in the list, increasing the likelihood that these items will be transferred into long-term storage. To see why, let's say that the first word on the list is *camera*. When research participants hear this word, they can focus their full attention on it, silently rehearsing "*camera, camera, camera. . .*" When the second word arrives, they will rehearse that one too, but they'll now have to divide their attention between the first word and the second ("*camera, boat, camera, boat, . . .*"). Attention will be divided still further after hearing the third word ("*camera, boat, zebra, camera, boat, zebra. . .*"), and so through the list. Notice, then, that earlier words get more attention than later ones. Put differently, as research participants hear more and more of the list, they must divide their attention more and more thinly. This provides our account of the primacy effect: Earlier words receive more attention and so are more likely to make it into the long-term warehouse. As a consequence, they are more likely to be recalled later.

Supporting evidence for these interpretations comes from various manipulations that affect the primacy and recency effects. For example, what happens if we require research participants to do some other task immediately after hearing the words but before recalling them? If our hypothesis is correct, this other task, which itself requires the use of working memory, should displace this memory's current contents and so disrupt the recency effect. It does: If participants are required to count backward for just thirty seconds between hearing the words and recalling them, the recency effect is eliminated (see Figure 7.3).

Other manipulations produce a different pattern—diminishing the primacy effect but having no effect on recency. An example is the rate at which items are presented. If this rate is relatively fast, participants have less time for rehearsal. As a result, there is less transfer to long-term storage. We should therefore expect a reduced primacy effect but no particular change in the recency effect, and this is what happens (see Figure 7.4).

RECODING TO EXPAND THE CAPACITY OF WORKING MEMORY

As we have seen, working memory has a limited capacity: It can handle only a small number of packages at any one time. However, what these packages contain is, to a large extent, up to us. If we can pack the input more efficiently, we can squeeze more information into the same number of memory units.

Recoding into larger chunks As an example, consider an individual who tries to recall a series of digits that he heard only once:

149162536496481

If he treats this as a series of fifteen unrelated digits, he will almost surely fail. But if he recognizes that the digits form a pattern, specifically

1   4   9   16   25   36   49   64   81

his task becomes much easier. He only has to remember the underlying relationship, "the squares of the digits from 1 to 9," and the fifteen components of the series are easily recreated.

A similar example is the letter series

CIAFBIIBMTWA

This will again be difficult to remember if interpreted as a series of twelve unrelated letters. But if it is reorganized by three-letter groupings,

CIA   FBI   IBM   TWA

the recall task is greatly simplified.

In both of these examples, the person repackages the material to be remembered, **recoding** the input into larger units that are often called **chunks.** This is crucial because working memory's capacity appears to be measured in chunks, rather than in bits of information. In general, working memory seems able to hold seven plus-or-minus two chunks. If each chunk contains only a single letter, then working memory can hold roughly seven letters. If each contains a trio of letters (*CIA, FBI,* and so on), then working memory can hold twenty-one letters (three letters per chunk) or seven chunks. The more information we jam into each chunk, the more information can be stored.

Much of the recoding of memory items, or chunking, happens quite automatically. To an adult, a word is already a coherent whole, not merely a sequence of sounds. Still higher units of memorial organization are involved in the memory of sentences. The memory span for random sequences of words is about six or seven items, but we can often recall a fairly long sentence after only a single exposure. This fact holds even for sentences that make little sense, such as *The*

The role of chunking in remembering a visual display   *Could you possibly remember all the figures in this bewildering array? You might, if you knew Netherlandish proverbs of the sixteenth century, for that is what the painting depicts. To mention only some, there is (going from left to right): a man who "butts his head against the wall," another who is "armed to the teeth" and "ties a bell to the cat," and two women of whom "one spins while the other winds" (malicious gossips). Going further left, we see a woman who "puts a blue cloak over her husband" (deceives him), a man who "fills the hole after his calf was drowned," and another who "throws roses [we say pearls] before swine." Recognizing these scenes as illustrations of familiar proverbs will organize the visual array and thus help you to remember its many parts. (Detail of Netherlandish Proverbs by Pieter Brueghel, 1559; courtesy Gemäldegalerie, Staatliche Museen Preussischer Kulturbesitz, Berlin)*

enemy submarine dove into the coffee pot, took fright, and silently flew away. This dubious bit of naval intelligence consists of fourteen words, but it clearly contains fewer than fourteen memorial packages: *The enemy submarine* is essentially one unit, *took fright* is another, and so on.

A CHANGED EMPHASIS: ACTIVE MEMORY AND ORGANIZATION

The stage theory dominated memory research for several decades. But as time went on, there was a reevaluation. The evidence indicated that stage theory had described the "architecture" of memory in roughly the right way. But what stage theory failed to encompass was the enormously important role of the learner—her strategies and goals, and, above all, the previous knowledge that she brings to the learning situation.

WORKING MEMORY AS AN ACTIVE PROCESS

One shortcoming of stage theory lies in how it explained the transfer of information from the short-term loading platform into the long-term warehouse. According to the theory, this transfer depends to a large extent on how long the information sits on the platform. The longer it sits there, the greater the probability of its being transferred. This implies that rehearsal promotes memory for a simple reason: It keeps information in working memory longer, increasing the likelihood of transfer into more permanent storage.

It turns out, however, that entering long-term memory is not this automatic and depends on more than the mere passage of time. Evidence comes from studies of **maintenance rehearsal,** a strategy that keeps information in working memory but with little long-term effect. As an everyday example, consider what happens when you look up a telephone number. You need to retain the number long enough to complete your call, but you have no need to memorize the number for later use. In this circumstance, you are likely to employ maintenance

Active memory at work *Cardplayers have to call on active memory to decide which cards were played most recently and which should be played next. (*The Cardplayers, *by Paul Cezanne; courtesy The Metropolitan Museum of Art, Bequest of Stephen C. Clark, 1960)*

rehearsal: You repeat the number to yourself while you dial. But what happens if the line is busy? A moment later, you try to dial the number again, but realize you've already forgotten it. Maintenance rehearsal kept the number in working memory long enough for you to dial it the first time but failed to establish it in long-term memory. As a result, the number is forgotten after just a few seconds.

Experimental evidence for this effect comes from an ingenious study. Research participants were asked to listen to a series of words and monitor it for words beginning with a certain letter. At the end of the series, they were to report the most recent word on the list that began with the designated letter. Suppose the letter was *G* and the list was:

daughter, oil, garden, grain, table, football, anchor, giraffe, pillow, thunder.

Subjects would initially try to remember the word *garden,* on the chance that no other *G*-words would follow. The moment they heard *grain,* though, they would stop thinking about *garden* and remember *grain* instead. *Grain* would later be replaced by *giraffe* and so on until the end of the list was reached, at which time they had to report the last *G*-word they heard—in this example, *giraffe.*

This arrangement guarantees that some of the *G*-words would be held only briefly in working memory, while others would reside in this memory system for a longer period. For example, *grain* was in working memory for a few seconds (until *giraffe* arrived); *garden,* in contrast, merely passed through working memory, abandoned the moment *grain* arrived. The interesting question, then, is whether this longer stay in working memory increased the chance that *grain* would be transferred to the long-term store. To find out, the experimenters gave an unexpected test at the end of the session, asking participants to report as many of the *G*-words as they could. The results showed strikingly poor memory overall and also showed that the time an item had been in working memory had no effect—*garden* was recalled just as often as *grain* (Craik and Watkins, 1973). It appears, therefore, that maintenance rehearsal confers little benefit in aiding recall. *Grain* received more of this rehearsal than *garden* did, but this had no impact on participants' performance: There's no advantage gained by doing more of an activity that, for this task, is basically without value.

This same pattern can also be observed outside of the laboratory. How often has the typical American seen a penny? Fifteen thousand times (roughly twice a day for twenty years)? In each of these encounters, though, there was no reason to scrutinize the penny, no reason to think about the penny's appearance. On the logic we have just developed, people's memory for the penny should be quite poor. And it is: In one study, subjects were asked whether Lincoln's profile, shown on the heads side of the penny, faced to the right or to the left. Only half of the subjects got this question right, exactly what one would expect if subjects were merely guessing. (Subjects would have done just as well if they had flipped a coin to choose their response, rather than trying to remember what the coin looked like.) This provides striking confirmation of the fact that memory requires mental engagement with a target and not mere exposure (Nickerson and Adams, 1979).

THE WORK IN WORKING MEMORY

The fact that maintenance rehearsal does not promote long-term retention tells us that the transfer to long-term memory cannot be automatic. We can't predict what a person will remember simply by asking how long the target information remained in working memory; we need, instead, to consider how that time was spent. Similarly, we should avoid thinking of working memory as some sort of passive receptacle in which materials rest on their way to long-term storage. Instead, we should conceive of working memory in more active terms, terms that reflect the work that is being done there.

In fact, this emphasis highlights the contrast between the stage theory and most contemporary views of memory. Current theorists emphasize the fact that long-term memories are formed by an active process in which the individual's own way of encoding and organizing the material plays a major role. As a result, they regard working memory not so much as a temporary storage platform but rather as a mental workbench on which various items of experience are sorted, manipulated, and organized. According to this view, how well information will be retained in memory does not depend on a simple transfer from one storage container to another. Instead, it depends on how this material is processed (that is, encoded and recoded). The more elaborate the processing, the greater the likelihood of recall and recognition.

Considerations of this sort provide one of the reasons why working memory is now named as it is, in place of the older term *short-term memory* (e.g., Crowder, 1982). The newer term appropriately draws our attention to the activity and processing made possible by working memory, rather than treating this memory merely as a box in which information is passively held.

Perhaps, therefore, the appropriate metaphor for working memory is not really a loading platform that can hold only so many parcels. It is, rather, an overworked operative at the memory workbench, an operative who can pack only so many parcels—can do only so much chunking and organizing—at any one time. It's as if he (or she or it) has only so many mental hands (Baddeley, 1976, 1986).

PROCESSING AND ORGANIZING: THE ROYAL ROAD INTO MEMORY

Our discussion invites an obvious question: If memories are formed by an active process, then what is that process? If some forms of encoding or rehearsal are more helpful than others, what identifies the more effective strategies?

Depth of processing   One influential position hypothesizes that success in remembering depends on the depth at which the incoming information is processed (Craik and Lockhart, 1972). For verbal materials, **shallow processing** refers to encoding that emphasizes the superficial characteristics of a stimulus, such as the typeface in which a word is printed. In contrast, **deep processing** refers to encoding that emphasizes the meaning of the material.

Many experiments suggest that deep processing leads to much better recall. In one study, research participants were told that the researchers were studying perception and speed of reaction and then were shown forty-eight words. As each word was presented, the participants were asked a question about it. For some words, they were asked about the word's physical appearance ("Is it printed in capital letters?"); this should produce shallow encoding. For others, they were asked about the word's sound ("Does it rhyme with *train*?"); this should engender an intermediate level of encoding. For the remainder, they were asked about the word's meaning ("Would it fit into the sentence: The girl placed the _____ on the table?"); this presumably would lead to deep encoding. After the participants had gone through the entire list of words, they were given an unexpected task: They were asked to write down as many of the words as they could remember. The results were in line with the **depth-of-processing hypothesis.** Words that called for the shallowest processing (typeface) were recalled worst of all; words that required an intermediary level (sound) were recalled a bit better; and words that demanded the deepest level (meaning) were recalled best of all (Craik and Tulving, 1975).

This example applies the depth-of-processing hypothesis to memory for words, with clear success in accounting for the data pattern. Other experiments have applied this approach to nonverbal stimuli, such as faces. Here, too, instructions for deep processing seem to promote memory (Shapiro and Penrod, 1986; Bloom and Mudd, 1991; Sporer, 1991; Reinitz, Morrissey, and Demb, 1994). However, we should note that it is sometimes difficult to apply this hypothesis to other, more complex cases, largely because the central term, *depth,* is not well defined (e.g., Baddeley, 1978). Even so, this approach does provide a useful rule of thumb: The more attention we pay to the meaning of what we hear and see and read, the better we will remember it.

Organization   The depth-of-processing hypothesis emphasizes the importance of meaning. A related view stresses *organization.* We encountered the importance of organization early on, when we considered chunking. Further evidence comes from a number of findings that elaborate on the nature of chunking and the organizational process.

Chunks—like the first nine squares, well-known acronyms such as *FBI,* and common English words—are taken from an individual's prior experience; all he has to do is to recognize them. But in many cases, the would-be memorizer will not be lucky enough to have all the material neatly prechunked; he has to perform some of the chunking himself if he wants to remember successfully.

Dramatic proof of the power of recoding came from a study in which a heroic research participant devoted more than 200 hours to the task of becoming a virtuoso at recalling strings of digits. In each session he heard random digits presented at a rate of one per second and then tried to recall the sequence. If his recall was correct, the sequence was increased by one digit; if it was incorrect, it was decreased by one digit. After more than twenty months of this, the digit span had risen enormously, from an initial starting point of seven to a final level of almost eighty (Figure 7.5). But this is not because his working memory somehow became larger. Instead, he had learned to recode the digit sequences into meaningful subparts, thus creating larger chunks. As it turns out, he was a long-distance runner who competed in major athletic events. This led him to express three- and four-digit groups as running times for various races (e.g., 3492 became "3 minutes 49 point 2 seconds, near world-record time"); other numbers were chunked as ages (893 became "89 point 3, very old man") or dates (1944 was "near end of World War II"). These recoded strings of digits became chunked groups in memory. This was neatly shown by the participant's pauses as he produced the digits in recall—virtually all of his pauses fell between the groups rather than within them (Ericsson, Chase, and Faloon, 1980).

Notice, then, that chunking often requires us to relate the materials we are learning to other things that we already know. This interweaving of new information with old certainly helps us to understand the things we see or hear, and it also has a powerful effect on memory. A further illustration of this comes from an experiment in which the following tape-recorded passage was presented:

> The procedure is actually quite simple. First you arrange things into different groups depending on their makeup. Of course, one pile may be sufficient depending on how much there is to do. If you have to go somewhere else due to lack of facilities that is the next step; otherwise you are pretty well set. It is important not to overdo any particular endeavor. That is, it is better to do too few things at once than too many. In the short run this may not seem important, but complications from doing too many can easily arise. A mistake can be expensive as well. The manipulation of the appropriate mechanisms should be self-explanatory, and we need not dwell on it here. At first, the whole procedure will seem complicated. Soon, however, it will become just another facet of life. It is difficult to foresee any end to the necessity for this task in the immediate future, but then one never can tell. (From Bransford and Johnson, 1972, p. 722)

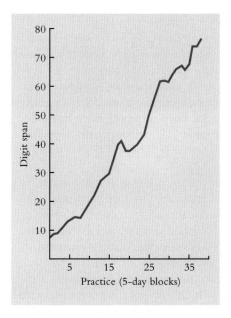

7.5   Chunking makes perfect   *The figure shows an enormous increase in memory span after twenty months of practice during which the research participant learned to code digit sequences into meaningful subparts. (After Ericsson, Chase, and Faloon, 1980)*

Half of the people heard this passage without any further information as to what it was about. The others were told: "The paragraph you will hear will be about washing clothes." Not surprisingly, the two groups performed very differently on tests of comprehension and tests of general recall (total number of ideas in the paragraph). Once they knew the sentences were about doing the laundry, the sentences in the paragraph could be related to what they already knew. This meaningful encoding dramatically improved later recall (Bransford and Johnson, 1972). A picture we met in the previous chapter (Figure 6.33) can be used to make a similar point with a nonverbal stimulus. This picture is immensely difficult to remember *unless* one detects the pattern. But if the pattern is detected, the picture becomes meaningful, and then it is effortlessly remembered (Wiseman and Neisser, 1974).

MNEMONICS

Memorial organization also underlies a practical endeavor whose roots go back to ancient times—the development of techniques for improving memory. These techniques are called **mnemonics** (or *mnemonic devices*). As it turns out, virtually all mnemonics build on the same base: We remember well what we have organized well.

Mnemonics through verbal organization The ancients were well aware that it is easier to remember verbal material if it is organized. Verse, with word sequences that maintain a fixed rhythm or rhyme, provides one way to achieve this organization, and this fact has been exploited by many cultures at many times. Without the use of verse, preliterate societies might never have transmitted their oral traditions intact from one generation to the next. Homeric bards could recite the entire *Iliad,* but could they have done so had it been in prose? Even in modern times, verse is still used as an effective mnemonic ("Thirty days hath September, April, June, and November").

Mnemonics based on visual imagery Some of the most effective mnemonics ever devised involve the deliberate use of mental imagery. One such technique is the **method of loci,** which requires the learner to visualize each of the items she wants to remember in a different spatial location (locus). In recall, each location is mentally inspected and the item that was placed there in imagination is retrieved.

The effectiveness of this method is easy to demonstrate. In one study, college students had to learn lists of forty unrelated concrete nouns. Each list was presented once for about ten minutes, during which the subjects tried to visualize each of the forty objects in one of forty different locations around their college campus. Tested immediately, they recalled an average of thirty-eight of the forty items; tested one day later, they still managed to recall thirty-four (Ross and Lawrence, 1968; Bower, 1970, 1972; Higbee, 1977; Roediger, 1980). In other studies, participants using the method of loci have been able to retain seven times more than their counterparts who learned in a rote manner.

Why does imagery help? Why are images such a powerful aid to remembering? One reason may be that images are yet another way of forming chunks in memory. By creating a mental image, two unrelated items are joined so that they form a new whole. When part of the chunk (the imagined locus) is presented, the entire chunk is retrieved, yielding the part required for recall.

Evidence for this view comes from studies that show that mental images facilitate recall only when they unify the items to be remembered into a coherent whole. Consider a person who has to learn a list of word pairs and is instructed to use imagery as an aid to memory. He might construct mental pictures that bring the items into some kind of unitary relationship. For example, to remember the pair *eagle-train,* he might imagine an eagle winging to its nest with a locomotive in its beak. But, alternatively, he might only imagine the eagle and the locomotive side by side, not interacting. Evidence indicates that images of the first (interacting) sort produce much better recall than nonunifying images (Wollen, Weber, and Lowry, 1972). A similar effect is found when the test items are pictures, rather than words: Pictures with interacting parts are remembered much more effectively than are pictures with their constituents merely side by side and not interacting (Figure 7.6).

The usefulness of mnemonics in everyday life Mnemonic systems provide an effective means for imposing an organization on otherwise disparate materials. These systems are therefore quite useful in memorizing a list of foreign vocabulary words or the unfamiliar materials sometimes encountered in the psychology laboratory. But what about memorizing more meaningful materials? A student reading a history text, for example, does not have to impose an arbitrary "external" organization on the to-be-remembered information. Instead, her job is to discover the organization already inherent in the text. When she does so, the various events and figures all fall into an appropriate mental scheme, linked not only to each other but also to other historical matters that she learned before. These links then provide a rich network of connections that will help the student remember the material.

In contrast, mnemonics lead the memorizer to focus on a much narrower set of memory links, and as a consequence, they often do *not* lead to the sort of remembering students want. For example, a visual image linking General Custer and Chief Sitting Bull will be helpful if the question: "With whom did General Custer do battle at Little Big Horn?" were to appear on a test. However, this image will not help a student answer most other questions about these two figures. ("Did Custer battle Sitting Bull before or after the American Civil War? Did these two negotiate in any way before the battle?") And the image will certainly do nothing to enhance the student's understanding of the conflict between the native Americans and the encroaching settlers.

In short, mnemonics are a useful tool in memorizing material devoid of internal organization. If the material to be learned is meaningful or already organized, however, the best approach is to seek an understanding of the material when it is being learned. This will lead to the best memory as well as to flexibility in how the target information can be retrieved.

7.6 Interactive and noninteractive depictions *Research participants shown related elements, such as a doll sitting on a chair and waving a flag (A), are more likely to associate the words* doll, flag, *and* chair *than participants who are shown the three objects next to each other but not interacting (B). (After Bower, 1970a)*

RETRIEVAL

When we learn, we transfer new information from working memory into our long-term store of knowledge. But successful encoding is not enough. We must also be able to retrieve the information when we need it; otherwise, what we've learned will be useless to us. The importance (and potential difficulty) of retrieval is obvious to anyone who has ever "blocked" on a familiar name. We may know the name (have encoded and stored it) but be unable to retrieve it when trying to introduce an old friend to a new one. In such cases, the memory trace is said to be *inaccessible*. Access to the trace can be restored, however, by an appropriate ***retrieval cue,*** a stimulus that opens the path to the memory.

Often retrieval seems effortless: You are asked your middle name and instantly respond. Sometimes, though, retrieval is more difficult, requiring effort and a deliberate search for retrieval cues: You walk out of the shopping mall and can't remember where you parked your car. But then you recollect that your first stop was at the drugstore, and this seems to trigger the memory of squeezing the car into a narrow space in the lot near the store.

In still other cases, retrieval initially seems impossible, as though the target information was truly lost. But then some cue is presented and suddenly the memory returns. A return to your home town, for example, after a long absence, may unleash a flood of recollection, as the sights and sounds of the place effectively trigger the relevant memories. A word, a smell, a visit from a school friend not seen for years—any of these may summon memories we thought were utterly lost.

THE RELATION BETWEEN ORIGINAL ENCODING AND RETRIEVAL

What makes a retrieval cue effective? Why do some reminders succeed, while others have no effect? One important determinant is whether the cue re-creates the context in which the original learning occurred. For example, if a subject focused on the sounds of words while learning them, then he will be well served by reminders that focus on sound ("Was there a word on the list that rhymes with *log*?"); if he focused on meaning while learning, then the best reminder would be one that again draws his attention toward meaning ("Was one of the words a type of fruit?"; Fisher and Craik, 1977).

To put this more broadly, retrieval is most likely to succeed when the cues and context during retrieval match those in place during the initial encoding. This principle is often referred to as ***encoding specificity,*** marking the fact that ideas and events are encoded from a particular perspective and within a particular context (Tulving and Osler, 1968; Tulving and Thomson, 1973; Hintzman, 1990). The optimal retrieval cue, therefore, is one that re-creates that perspective and that context.

A shift in mental context can thus impede retrieval: Someone who focused on meaning when learning a new word would not find a rhyme cue very helpful when trying to remember that word later on. The same is true for a shift in physical context. A dramatic illustration of this point is provided by a study of scuba divers who had to learn a list of unrelated words either on a boat or underwater. The divers were later tested for recall in either the same or the alternate environment in which they had learned. The results showed a clear-cut context effect:

Retrieval cues in the movies *A scene from Charlie Chaplin's 1931 film,* City Lights, *which shows the little tramp with a millionaire, played by Harry Myers, who befriends him one night while drunk, doesn't recognize him the next morning when he is sober, but greets him as an old friend when he gets drunk again the following night. While nowhere as extreme as this, such state-dependent memory effects have been observed in the laboratory. (Eich, 1980; courtesy Photofest)*

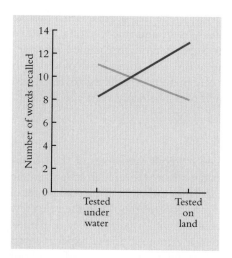

7.7 The effect of changing the retrieval situation *Scuba divers learned a list of thirty-six unrelated words above water (dark red) or twenty feet underwater (blue) and were then tested above or underwater. The figure shows that retention was better when the retrieval situation was the same as that in which encoding took place. (Godden and Baddeley, 1975)*

What was learned in the water was best recalled in the water, likewise for what was learned on deck (Godden and Baddeley, 1975; see Figure 7.7).

Similar effects can be obtained without going underwater. One experimenter presented subjects with a long list of words. A day later he brought them back for an unexpected recall test that took place in either the same room or a different one, one that varied in size, furnishings, and so on. Recall was considerably better for subjects who were tested in the same physical environment. But the investigator found a simple way of overcoming this context effect. A different group of subjects was brought to the new room, but just prior to the recall test they were asked to think about the room in which they had learned the lists— what it looked like, what it made them feel like. By doing so, they mentally re-created the old environment for themselves. On the subsequent recall test, these subjects performed no worse than those for whom there was no change of rooms. It appears, therefore, that a change in physical context influences memory because this change usually brings with it a corresponding change in mental perspective. If one changes physical context *without* changing one's mental perspective, the physical relocation has little or no effect (Smith, 1979).

ELABORATIVE REHEARSAL

The role of retrieval cues actually helps explain why some means of encoding are so much more effective than others. For example, we've seen that organization helps encoding, and so does attention to the meaning of the to-be-remembered materials. But why is this? One might think that these forms of encoding allow us to plant the memories more firmly or more fully. Evidence suggests, however, that these superior forms of learning actually help us in a different fashion: Rather than promoting encoding, they promote retrieval by making the material easier to find when we later need it. The key to good encoding, it seems, is to provide an effective means for retrieval later.

In the ancient world, all roads led to Rome, and so the traveler had no difficulty in finding the empire's capital; any path would lead to this target. A similar idea applies to memory: If many paths lead to the sought-after information, this will make the information easy to find from a variety of different starting points.

Support for this claim comes from studies of *elaborative rehearsal,* an activity in which the learner looks for connections within the to-be-remembered material or connections between this material and other things she already knows. (This is in contrast to maintenance rehearsal, in which, as we've discussed, material is simply held in a more-or-less passive fashion in working memory.) Elaborative rehearsal enhances learning because each step of elaboration builds another path by which the material can be accessed. The more such paths that are created, the easier retrieval will be.

The benefits of elaborative rehearsal are demonstrated by a study in which the degree of elaboration was varied. Research participants read sentences in which one word was missing. Some of these were rather simple, such as: "He cooked the _____." Others were more complex, such as: "The great bird swooped down and carried off the struggling _____." The task was to decide whether a given target word (such as *chicken*) could appropriately fit into the sentence frame. After sixty such trials, the participants were unexpectedly asked to recall as many of the target words as they could. In line with the elaborative rehearsal hypothesis, the more complex sentence frames led to better recall. The richer encoding contexts presumably built more and better retrieval paths (Craik and Tulving, 1975).

MEMORY SEARCH

Investigators believe that memory retrieval generally begins with a process of **memory search.** This search is usually swift and unconscious, as when we answer: "Which president of the United States had the first name *Abraham*?" But there are times when we do become aware that some kind of search is underway, as we consciously sift through our memories, seeking to recall just who it was that did what to whom on which occasion many years ago.

SEARCH STRATEGIES

In one study, research participants were asked to recall the names of their high-school classmates. Some of the participants had graduated from high school a mere four years earlier; others had graduated two decades earlier. In all cases, their recall accuracy was checked by consulting their high-school yearbooks. In their first few minutes of trying, participants generally came up with a fair number of names. After this, they said they couldn't remember any more. But the experimenters asked them to keep trying anyway. And so they did, for ten sessions of one hour each. As they continued their efforts, they surprised themselves by dredging up more and more names, until they finally recalled about a third of the names from a graduating class of three hundred (Williams and Hollan, 1982).

While going about this task, the research participants were asked to think aloud, and their comments suggest that they were hunting for names just as one might search for a tangible object, inspecting one likely memory location after another. Their efforts were rarely haphazard but, instead, often seemed based on well-formulated search strategies. For example, they mentally looked through their various classes, clubs, and teams, or scanned internal pictures to locate yet another person whom they would then try to name:

> . . . It's like I want to think of, sort of prototypical situations and then sort of examine the people that were involved in those. And things like P.E. class, where there was . . . Ah . . . Gary Booth. Umm, and Karl Brist . . . Umm . . . I can think of things like dances. I guess then I usually think of . . . of girls . . . Like Cindy Shup, Judy Foss, and Sharon Ellis . . . I mean it's sort of like I have a picture of the high school dance. . . . (Williams and Hollan, 1982, p. 90)

THE TIP-OF-THE-TONGUE PHENOMENON

Needless to say, memory search isn't always successful. Some forgotten names are never retrieved, no matter how hard we try. But occasionally, we experience a kind of halfway point, when we seem about to recall something but don't quite. When this occurs, we feel as if the searched-for memory is on the tip of the tongue, tantalizingly close, but inaccessible nonetheless. There is no better description of this phenomenon than that by William James:

> Suppose we try to recall a forgotten name. The state of our consciousness is peculiar. There is a gap therein; but no mere gap. It is a gap that is intensely active. A sort of wraith of the name is in it, beckoning us in a given direction, making us at moments tingle with the sense of our closeness, and then letting us sink back without the longed-for term. If wrong names are proposed to us, this singularly definite gap acts immediately so as to negate them. They do not fit into its mold. And the gap of one word does not feel like the gap of another, all empty of content as both might seem necessarily to be when described as gaps. (James, 1890, vol. 1, p. 251)

In one study of this phenomenon, college students were given the dictionary definitions of uncommon English words such as *apse, sampan,* and *cloaca.* The

External aids to memory *People often rely on external memory aids. Some remind us of events in our past, such as family albums and high-school yearbooks. Others remind us of plans for future actions, such as calendars, memo pads, and shopping lists. (Brockton High-School yearbook, class of 1975, p. 108)*

7.8 The tip-of-the-tongue phenomenon
This figure may provide an opportunity to demonstrate how something can be close to being retrieved from memory but not quite. (Adapted from Foard, 1975)

students were asked to supply the words that fit these definitions. In some cases, they simply did not know the words, and these trials were of no interest to the researchers. The experimenters were concerned instead with those occasions on which participants could not recall the target word but felt certain that they were on the verge of finding it (see Figure 7.8). Whenever this happened, participants were asked to venture some guesses about what the target word sounded like. These guesses turned out to be closely related to the target: Participants guessed the target's initial letter over 50 percent of the time and were generally able to guess the number of syllables. When asked to supply some other words that they thought sounded like the target, they were usually in the correct phonological neighborhood. Presented with the definition "a small Chinese boat," participants in the tip-of-the-tongue state offered these sound-alikes: *saipan, Siam, Cheyenne,* and *sarong*—all obviously similar to the actual word, *sampan* (Brown and McNeill, 1966; Koriat and Lieblich, 1974).

IMPLICIT MEMORY

Up to now, we've only considered methods of retrieval in which the research participant is asked questions that refer to her prior experience. She may be tested for recall: "Tell me the name of one of your former high-school teachers." Or she may be asked for recognition: "Was Mr. Halberdam one of your former high-school teachers?" These tests are said to rely on *explicit memory.* But we are also influenced by *implicit memory:* This term refers to cases in which we are affected by some past experience without realizing that we are in fact remembering. Implicit memory is also referred to as "memory without awareness" and has been a subject of intense research scrutiny (see Schacter, 1987, 1992; Roediger, 1990).

IMPLICIT MEMORY EFFECTS

Participants in one study were first shown a number of words. Later, they were given two tests of memory. The first was a test of explicit memory, employing a

*Answers for
tip-of-the-tongue
demonstration*

1. Vendetta
2. Amulet
3. Doubloon
4. Obsidian
5. Ambergris
6. Mosque
7. Scarab
8. Caduceus
9. Scimitar
10. Troika
11. Sextant
12. Isthmus

standard recognition procedure. The second was a test of implicit memory in which their task was simply to identify words that were flashed very briefly on a computer screen. Participants had no idea that many of the words in this identification task were taken from the list of words they had seen during the procedure's initial step.

The data from the word-identification task showed a pattern referred to as **repetition priming:** Words that had been on the original list were identified more readily than words that had not. Impressively, this priming effect was observed even for words that the participants failed to recognize as familiar in the recognition task. In other words, there was no relationship between the results of the explicit memory test (standard recognition) and the results of the implicit memory test (word identification). Thus, research participants showed evidence of implicit memory for items that they did not consciously—that is, explicitly—remember (Jacoby and Witherspoon, 1982).

Many other procedures also show this pattern of memory without awareness. In fragment-completion tasks, for example, participants are shown partial words (such as C__O__O__I__E) and asked to complete them to form actual words (CROCODILE). Success in this task is much more likely if the target word has been encountered recently; this advantage is observed even without conscious recollection of this encounter (Jacoby and Dallas, 1981; Tulving, Schacter, and Stark, 1982; Graf and Mandler, 1984).

A different example was produced in a study on "How to Become Famous Overnight." The research participants first performed in what they thought was a pronunciation test, reading aloud a long list of unfamiliar names. A day later, they were presented with a second list of names and were asked to assess how famous each of the people on the list was. As it turns out, half of the names on the list were of moderately famous people (Roger Bannister, Minnie Pearl, Christopher Wren). The other half were the names of people who were not famous at all but instead were picked randomly from a telephone directory (Sebastian Weisdorf, Valerie Marsh). Crucially, though, some of these nonfamous names had appeared on the original pronunciation list. How would this affect participants' judgments?

The participants in this study seemed to register that many of the test names were familiar, but they were unable to recall *why* they were familiar—they couldn't recall where or when they had encountered the names before. In other words, they had an implicit memory for their earlier reading of, say, Sebastian Weisdorf's name but no explicit memory for it. Under these circumstances, participants made a reasonable inference: I probably read his name in a newspaper, or heard it on TV, so he must be famous! Thus, familiarity in this case led to an erroneous judgment of fame.

We should mention an important control procedure needed in this experiment: In this condition, the second list (and the judgment of fame) was presented immediately after the original pronunciation list. Now there was little confusion. To be sure, Sebastian Weisdorf's name triggered a sense of familiarity, but since the pronunciation list had been read just minutes before, the participants knew exactly why his name was familiar and so decided that Sebastian was not famous after all (Jacoby et al., 1989).

Other studies show further ways in which implicit memory can affect our judgment. In one such study, researchers showed participants a series of sentences (e.g., "House mice can run an average of four miles per hour," or "Crocodiles sleep with their eyes open") and asked them to rate how interesting each sentence seemed. Some time later, they were shown a new series of sentences and had to judge the credibility of each, using a scale that ranged from "certainly true" to "certainly false." The evidence showed that this task, too, is influenced by implicit memory: Research participants were more likely to accept a sentence as true if they had encountered that sentence recently; this pattern was observed even if they had no conscious memory of this encounter (Begg, Armour, and Kerr, 1985; Brown and Halliday, 1990). Merely making a sentence familiar, it seems, can increase its plausibility. The relevance of this effect for propaganda and political innuendo should be quite clear.

DISTINGUISHING IMPLICIT FROM EXPLICIT MEMORY

Implicit memories are distinct from explicit memories in several ways. As we have seen, people can be implicitly influenced by events they cannot recall. In addition, some forms of brain damage impair explicit memory but spare implicit memory, whereas other forms of brain damage have the opposite effect. (See the discussion of amnesia later in the chapter.)

Implicit and explicit memories also seem to function differently. For example, we've seen that performance on a recall test (a test of explicit memory) is improved if participants pay attention to the meaning of the to-be-remembered material during encoding. Tests of implicit memory generally do not show this pattern; similar implicit-memory effects can be observed after shallow encoding or deep (Jacoby and Dallas, 1981; Graf, Mandler, and Haden, 1982).

Another difference concerns the effect of rather peripheral aspects of the stimulus. These aspects have little impact on explicit memory. Suppose, for example, a research participant is shown a series of words, and asked which of these were in a set he was shown earlier. If one of the original words was GIRAFFE, it won't matter if the test word looks the same (GIRAFFE) or different (*giraffe*). His response will be the same in either case.

Things are different, though, in many tests of implicit memory. If a participant initially sees GIRAFFE, then she'll show a priming effect if asked to complete the fragment: G_R_F_E. But she'll show little (or no) priming effect if tested with *g_r_f_e*. Apparently, implicit memory effects are often **stimulus specific,** and thus, once again, distinguishable from explicit memory effects.

All of these considerations combine to suggest that explicit and implicit memory tasks tap different kinds of memory. But how exactly we should distinguish the two is a matter of debate. Some authors suggest that the crucial distinction is one of consciousness, with implicit memories unconscious and explicit memories conscious. Others suggest that the crucial distinction lies in the fact that implicit memories are automatic—they influence our judgment whether we want them to or not. Explicit memories, in contrast, are controllable—we can choose whether or not we'll use information contained in the memory. Still other authors argue that the key lies in the type of content preserved by each memory, with implicit memory providing a repository for skills and procedures, whereas explicit memory stores so-called declarative knowledge (knowledge we can talk about, or *declare*). Currently, it is unclear which of these conceptualizations is correct. But it is fully clear that implicit memories can be distinguished from explicit memories and that they influence us in a surprisingly wide range of circumstances.

Very Bad Memory

(Cartoon by Abner Dean)

WHEN MEMORY FAILS

In popular usage, the word *forgetting* is employed whenever memory fails. But as we've seen, memory failures have many causes. Some arise from faulty encoding; others arise at the moment of recall. In this section, we will discuss three aspects of memory failure. One concerns the passage of time: Why is it easier to remember the recent past than it is to remember events from long ago? A second concerns memory error—cases in which events are *mis*remembered, so that the past as recalled differs from the past as it actually unfolded. The third topic concerns memory failure of a more extreme sort, as we consider what happens to memory in certain kinds of brain damage.

FORGETTING

Common sense tells us that yesterday's lesson is better remembered than last week's, and last week's better than last year's. In general, the longer the time between learning and retrieval—that is, the longer the ***retention interval***—the greater the chance of forgetting. An early demonstration of this fact was offered by Hermann Ebbinghaus (1850–1909). Ebbinghaus systematically studied his own memory in a series of careful experiments, examining his ability to retain lists of nonsense syllables, such as *zup* and *rif*.★ Ebbinghaus was the first to plot a ***forgetting curve*** by testing himself at various intervals after learning (using different lists for each interval). As expected, he found that memory did decline with the passage of time. However, the decline was uneven, sharpest soon after the learning and then more gradual (Ebbinghaus, 1885; see Figure 7.9).

DECAY

What accounts for the pattern observed by Ebbinghaus (and many other students of forgetting)? The most venerable theory holds that memory traces simply *decay* as time passes, like mountains that are eroded by wind and water. The erosion of memories is presumably caused by normal metabolic processes that wear down memory traces until they fade and finally disintegrate.

One line of support for this theory exploits that fact that, like most chemical reactions, many metabolic processes increase their rates with increasing temperature. If these metabolic reactions are responsible for memorial decay, then forgetting should increase if body temperature is elevated during the retention interval. This prediction is difficult to test with humans (or any other mammal), because internal mechanisms keep the temperature of our bodies relatively constant (see Chapter 3). However, this prediction has been tested with animals such as goldfish whose bodies tend to take on the temperature of their surroundings. By and large, the results are in line with the hypothesis: The higher the temperature of the tank in which the fish were kept during the retention interval, the more forgetting took place (Gleitman and Rozin, as reported in Gleitman, 1971).

Other findings, however, make it clear that decay cannot provide our entire explanation of forgetting. For example, several experiments have compared recall after an interval spent awake with recall after an equal interval spent sleeping. If the passage of time were all that mattered for forgetting, then performance would be the same in these two cases. But it is not: The group that slept during the retention interval remembered more than the group that stayed awake (e.g., Jenkins and Dallenbach, 1924). Presumably, the group that stayed awake experienced ***interference***—new ideas and events somehow interfered with their recall. This interference hypothesis is supported by the fact that less forget-

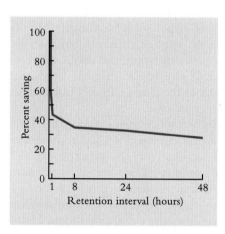

7.9 Forgetting curve *The figure shows retention after various intervals since learning. Retention is here measured in percent saving, that is, the percentage decrease in the number of trials required to relearn the list after an interval of no practice. If the saving is 100 percent, retention is perfect—no trials to relearn are necessary. If the saving is 0 percent, there is no retention at all, for it takes just as many trials to relearn the list as it took to learn it initially. (After Ebbinghaus, 1885)*

★ Ebbinghaus used nonsense syllables in order to study learning that was uncontaminated by prior associations. Modern psychologists, however, are skeptical about this approach. First, Ebbinghaus's nonsense syllables may not have been so meaningless after all. While *zup* is not an English word, it surely resembles several (e.g., *soup*). Second, the influence of prior associations is not a nuisance to be removed from studies of memory; instead, this influence is an important part of learning and remembering.

TABLE 7.1 RETROACTIVE INTERFERENCE EXPERIMENT

	Initial Period	Retention interval	Test period
Control Group	Learns list *A*	——————	Recalls list *A*
Experimental Group	Learns list *A*	Learns list *B*	Recalls list *A*

ting occurs after a period of slow-wave sleep than after more "active" forms, such as REM sleep (Ekstrand, 1972; Ekstrand et al., 1977). This again suggests that it is events and activities, and not the mere passage of time, that are crucial for forgetting. (For other evidence comparing the effects of time to the effects of interference, see Reisberg, 1997.)

INTERFERENCE

Memory is apparently vulnerable to some sort of interference, with the newly arriving information somehow interfering with the previously learned material. But what produces this interference? One hypothesis is that the forgotten material is neither damaged nor erased; it is simply misplaced. By analogy, consider someone who buys a newspaper each day and then stores them in a large pile in the basement. Each newspaper is easy to find when it is still sitting on the breakfast table; it can still be located without difficulty when it is on top of the basement stack. After some days, though, finding the newspaper becomes difficult. It is somewhere in the pile, but may not come into view without a great deal of searching. And, of course, the pile grows higher and higher every day; hence, interference will increase as the retention interval grows longer.

Memory interference is easily demonstrated in the laboratory. In a typical study, a control group learns the items on a list (*A*), and then is tested after a specified interval. The experimental group learns the same list (*A*) and is tested after the same retention interval. In addition, though, they must also learn the items on a second list (*B*) during the retention interval (Table 7.1). The result is a marked inferiority in the performance of the experimental group. List *B* seems to interfere with the recall of list *A* (McGeoch and Irion, 1952; Crowder, 1976).

The procedure just described demonstrates **retroactive interference** (sometimes called *retroactive inhibition*), in which new learning interferes with previous learning. A similar effect is **proactive interference,** in which old learning interferes with current learning. This can be demonstrated by having an experimental group learn list *A* followed by list *B,* and then testing for recall of list *B* after a suitable retention interval. The critical comparison is with a control group that learns only list *B* (Table 7.2). Here, too, the experimental group does worse on the recall test (e.g., Underwood, 1957).

TABLE 7.2 PROACTIVE INTERFERENCE EXPERIMENT

	Initial Period		Retention interval	Test period
Control Group	——————	Learns *B*	——————	Recalls list *B*
Experimental Group	Learns *A*	Learns *B*	——————	Recalls list *B*

The child's world is in many ways different from the adult's *According to some authors, childhood amnesia is partially produced by the enormous change in the retrieval cues available to the adult. (Photo courtesy of Suzanne Szasz)*

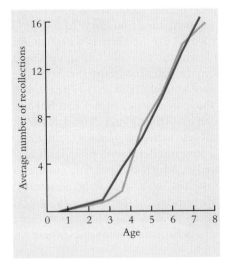

7.10 Number of childhood memories *College students were asked to recall childhood experiences. The figure plots the average number of events recalled as a function of the age at which they occurred for men (blue) and for women (dark red). Women recall a bit more at the earliest ages, which may reflect the fact that the maturation of girls is generally ahead of that of boys. (Data from Waldfogel, 1948)*

We should note that these interference effects (whether proactive or retroactive) depend on a number of other conditions. One such factor is similarity. If the material is dissimilar, there will be little interference—learning to skate does not interfere with one's memory for irregular French verbs. In addition, interference occurs only if the things to be remembered are essentially incompatible. The newly learned material will not interfere if it is consistent with earlier-learned material. In fact, just the opposite occurs: the subsequent learning helps memory, rather than hindering it.

RETRIEVAL FAILURE

We have suggested that interference does not "erase" memories; it simply renders them difficult to locate. With a suitable cue or prompt, these memories might be recovered. Could this be true of all forgetting? Or is some forgetting truly a matter of erasure (and thus permanent loss)? This is currently a matter of some controversy. It is clear, however, that much forgetting does involve **retrieval failure**: the memories are misplaced, but not erased.

This idea certainly fits several of our earlier claims. As we have discussed, elaborative rehearsal seems to promote recall by establishing multiple memory links, with each link providing access to the target memory. Maintenance rehearsal, on the other hand, establishes few links and therefore makes finding the target memory difficult. In other words, poor encoding makes retrieval failure more likely. We have also noted that memories can often be triggered by returning to the context (mental or physical) in which learning took place. Prior to that return, the target information might not be recalled—an apparent case of forgetting. The fact that this is retrieval failure and not a genuine memory loss is made clear once the right retrieval cues are available and the memory resurfaces.

Other phenomena can also be explained in these terms. Consider the fact that adults are usually unable to recall events before their third or fourth birthday, a phenomenon known as **childhood amnesia** (Waldfogel, 1948; Sheingold and Tenney, 1982; see Figure 7.10). This amnesia may derive from the fact that the world of the young child is different in many important ways from the world he will occupy some ten or fifteen years later. It is a world in which tables are hopelessly out of reach, chairs can be climbed upon only with great effort, and adults are giants in size and gods in ability. The child's memories, therefore, are formed and encoded within this context, and it is a context massively different from the circumstances of an adult. This virtually guarantees that the adult's perspective during retrieval, and the set of available retrieval cues, will be different from the perspective and cues in place during encoding, and it is this shift in context that leads to the observed amnesia (Schachtel, 1947; Neisser, 1967).

Other factors also contribute to childhood amnesia. For example, the hippocampus, a structure crucial for establishing coherent autobiographical memories, is not fully mature until the child is three or four years old (Nadel and Zola-Morgan, 1984). Thus, the very young child lacks the neural equipment needed to record memories in a full and orderly fashion. In addition, very young children have not yet developed the necessary schemas within which experiences can be organized, encoded, and rehearsed (White and Pillemer, 1979). Thus, while cue-change may account for some aspects of childhood amnesia, it almost surely does not account for all (see also Howe and Courage, 1993).

WHEN FORGETTING SEEMS NOT TO OCCUR

This emphasis on retrieval failure, rather than erasure, implies that memories may last for a long, long time. In fact, a number of studies have documented cases of remarkably little forgetting, even after very long intervals.

Childhood memories *While little is remembered from the first two or three years of life, some early memories do remain, often in a jumbled and kaleidoscopic fashion. Thus the paintings of the Russian émigré artist Marc Chagall (1887–1985) show composite images of his early life in a Russian village, including a cow being milked, his mother, a child's naive picture of a Russian village, and so on. (*I and the Village, *1911, oil on canvas, 6′3⅝″ × 59⅝″. Collection, The Museum of Modern Art, New York, Mrs. Simon Guggenheim Fund)*

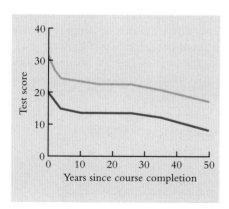

7.11 Forgetting a foreign language
The figure shows performance on a Spanish reading-comprehension test administered from zero to fifty years after taking Spanish in high school or college. The results from persons who had earned an A in the course are shown in blue; the results from persons who'd earned a C are shown in dark red. (After Bahrick, 1984)

Long-lasting memories If a student studied Spanish in high school, will she remember it five or ten or even fifteen years later? In one study, nearly 800 participants were given a Spanish reading-comprehension test; all of the participants had studied Spanish either in high school or in college. Not surprisingly, participants who had finished their Spanish classes just one week earlier did quite well on the test. Performance grew worse for those who had not studied Spanish for the past year, or for the past two or three years (Figure 7.11). Remarkably, though, performance then leveled off, and students who had taken their Spanish classes thirty years before remembered almost as much as students whose classes were just three years back. In essence, if the memories were established well enough to last three years, then they seemed to be virtually lifelong. (Performance levels did drop at retention intervals of forty and fifty years, but this may reflect the generalized effects of aging, rather than forgetting per se.)

It should also be noted that the degree of forgetting varied somewhat from one participant to the next, but in a predictable way: Students who had received A's in their Spanish classes forgot less than students who had received B's and C's (Bahrick, 1984). This pattern was observed even though the students had earned these grades a half-century earlier! Similar findings come from a more recent study on the retention of knowledge acquired in an advanced psychology course. Here, too, the basic concepts were retained for at least twelve years (Conway, Cohen, and Stanhope, 1991).

These results seem to conflict with Ebbinghaus's forgetting curve, described earlier in the chapter. In Ebbinghaus's case, forgetting grew worse and worse as time passed. In contrast, Bahrick's and others' data show some initial forgetting, but then the memories endure without change for many years. This invites a question about why some materials achieve this relatively permanent storage—why, in Bahrick's terms, some memories move into **permastore**—whereas other materials do not. Several factors contribute. We have already mentioned the importance of the initial learning: Material learned extremely well in the first place is much more likely to reach permastore. In addition, recall that Ebbinghaus's

Events that have produced flashbulb memories *(A) After the Kennedy assassination (Courtesy of the Bettmann Archive); (B) Princess Diana's funeral. (AP Photo/John Gaps III)*

forgetting curve was derived from studies using nonsense syllables, whereas the studies discussed here involve meaningful, structured information. This, too, matters for permastore, with inherently structured materials more likely to achieve this permanence than are, say, items on a shopping list (Neisser, 1989).

Flashbulb memories   Most examples of permastore involve generic knowledge, not memories tied to a specific episode or event. But can episodic memories be similarly immune to forgetting? Much of the evidence relevant to this question derives from studies of so-called *flashbulb memories,* extremely vivid and long-lasting memories that typically concern events that were highly distinctive, unexpected, and strongly emotional (Brown and Kulik, 1977). Sometimes flashbulb memories concern personal events, such as an early morning telephone call that tells of a parent's death. Others may involve news of national importance; many people have flashbulb memories of the *Challenger* space-shuttle disaster, the fall of the Berlin Wall, the reading of the O. J. Simpson verdict, or the news of Princess Diana's death.

One striking feature of flashbulb memories is their focus on immediate and personal circumstances. For example, many people remember exactly where they were when they first heard about the *Challenger* explosion, what they were doing at the time, who was with them, what words were spoken, and so on. This personalized focus, together with the level of detail and longevity of these memories, has led several authors to argue that there must be some special "flashbulb mechanism," distinct from the mechanisms that lead to the creation of other, more mundane memories (Brown and Kulik, 1977; but see also Winograd and Neisser, 1993).

The full pattern of evidence, however, suggests that such a special mechanism does not exist. For one thing, as vivid as they are, flashbulb memories are sometimes *incorrect,* straying from the actual facts in crucial ways (e.g., Neisser, 1982a, 1986; Thompson and Cowan, 1986; McCloskey, Wible, and Cohen, 1988). In addition, much of what is remembered may have been rehearsed in subsequent conversations with others, and it is this rehearsal, rather than some special encoding mechanism, that produces the memories' longevity. It should be said, though, that some episodic memories do seem extraordinarily accurate and virtually permanent; this is most likely for events that were deemed highly consequential for the rememberer at the time the event occurred (e.g., Conway et al., 1994). Thus, even for episodic memories, some sort of (relatively) permanent storage does seem possible—at least for this special set of episodes.

CONCEPTUAL FRAMEWORKS AND REMEMBERING

Thus far, our discussion of memory failures has focused on errors of *omission* in which we are simply unable to recall a name or recognize a face. We draw a blank and come up with nothing. We now turn to a different kind of failure in which the memory error is one of *commission*. These are errors in which we give a sincere but false account of the past, generally because we have unwittingly reconstructed an event based on what we think and know, rather than on what we really remember.

All remembering takes place against a backdrop of prior knowledge that necessarily colors whatever enters memory. Without prior knowledge, we could not understand the words we hear, their connections with each other, or their relations to events in the world. Without prior knowledge, we could not organize the material we encounter, because this organization is almost always based on connections between what we hear and see and what we already know. Thus, as we have seen, it's easier to recall the sequence 149162536496481 after discovering that it is actually the squares of the first nine digits; however, this discovery plainly depends on our knowing something about numbers and squares. Likewise, it's easier to recall some vague sentences when they're preceded by the title "Doing the Laundry" because we know about laundry routines and can use this knowledge to guide both our encoding and our retrieval. To give another example, consider a study in which subjects listened to a taped description of a fictional baseball game. Some of the subjects were very knowledgeable about the game; others were not (though they had a rough idea of the rules of the game). When later asked to write down as much of the taped account as they could, the more expert subjects did far better than the subjects whose knowledge of the game was slight (Spilich et al., 1979).

Using prior knowledge in memory is analogous to top-down processing in perception (see Chapter 6). As in perception, these top-down influences can be enormously helpful—increasing the efficiency of our processing and allowing us to compensate for incompleteness and ambiguity in the information we receive. But, as in perception, our knowledge and expectations can also lead us astray. For just as we can misperceive, so we can—and often do—misremember.

MEMORY DISTORTIONS

Classic experiments on memory distortions were performed by the British psychologist Frederic Bartlett sixty years ago. Bartlett's subjects were presented with folktales from other cultures; thus, the content of these tales often seemed rather strange. In subjects' recollection of these stories, though, the tales became less strange: Parts of the tale that had made no sense to the subjects (such as the supernatural elements) were either left out of the subjects' recall or were reinterpreted along more familiar lines. Similarly, subjects often added elements so that plot events that had initially seemed inexplicable now made sense (Bartlett, 1932).

The effect of schemas and scripts   Many studies have replicated and extended Bartlett's findings, showing in context after context that memory is strongly affected by the subject's conceptual framework: Elements that fit neatly within that framework are easily remembered; elements that are somewhat at odds with the framework are distorted in memory or omitted; and elements that are *absent* but typically present in events of that type may be added to the event in memory. For example, participants in one study were told about a person's visit to the dentist and then later asked to recall what they had been told. Many subjects falsely remembered hearing about the patient checking in with the receptionist and looking at a magazine in the waiting room, even though these details were not mentioned in the original account (Bower, Black, and Turner, 1979). In a different experiment, participants waited briefly in a professor's office and, seconds later, were asked to recall the contents of the office. One-third of the individuals "remembered" seeing books in the office, even though none were present (Brewer and Treyens, 1981). In this case, the error is a substantial one (bookshelves are large; the participants were actually in the office; the recollection took place just moments after leaving the office) but, again, is entirely in line with subjects' expectations of what "should" be in a professor's office.

We should mention that truly surprising elements are likely to be well remembered. If a waiter in a restaurant is wearing a bow-tie, this unexpected but hardly-shocking fact will soon be forgotten. But if a pig races through the restaurant in the middle of your dinner, this is certain to receive special attention and to be well remembered as a result. Once again, the relationship between an event and one's prior knowledge is crucial, but the relationship, it seems, is a complex one. (See Reisberg, 1997, for discussion.)

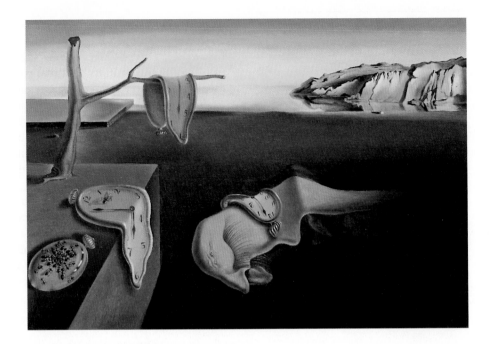

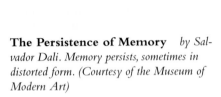

The Persistence of Memory *by Salvador Dali. Memory persists, sometimes in distorted form. (Courtesy of the Museum of Modern Art)*

In all these cases, then, memory is plainly and strongly affected by the research participants' broad knowledge of the world and by the conceptual framework they brought to the situation. Following Bartlett, many psychologists describe these frameworks as **schemas.** This term refers to a general cognitive structure into which data or events can be entered, typically with more attention to broad brush strokes than to specific details. Since many aspects of our experience are redundant—professors' offices do tend to contain many books, patients visiting the dentist do generally check in with a receptionist, and so on—a schema can provide a convenient summary of this redundancy and can therefore help us in interpreting and supplementing the details of our remembered experience. A special subcase of a schema is a **script,** which describes a characteristic sequence of events in a particular setting. The eating-at-a-restaurant script, for example, includes being seated, looking at the menu, ordering the meal, eating the food, paying the bill, and leaving; the visit-to-the-dentist script includes checking in with the receptionist and reading a magazine, among other things (Schank and Abelson, 1977).

Eyewitness testimony　Schematized remembering is in many ways beneficial: Its efficiency lets us package, store, and retrieve more material than we could ever manage otherwise. But this enhanced efficiency has a downside, for sometimes memory errors have serious consequences. Police investigators, judges, and juries all rely on the accuracy of eyewitness testimony, but witnesses (like anyone else relying on memory) do make errors. The details of an accident that occurred months ago have dimmed over time. As the witness tries to retrieve this past event, he may fill in the gaps by an inference of which he is quite unaware.

These schema-based inferences are entirely unconscious, so if the witness strays from the truth, he's not lying; he's simply mistaken. More, the witness may be entirely confident that his recollection is accurate, and this confidence may persuade a jury to take the testimony quite seriously. This is a troubling fact, since many studies have shown that the witness's confidence in the truthfulness of his testimony is nearly worthless as an indicator of accurate memory. Mistaken witnesses can be just as confident, and can offer testimony that is just as detailed and emotional, as accurate witnesses (Reisberg, 1997).

Elizabeth Loftus

In interpreting eyewitness testimony, it is crucial to consider how the witness has been questioned, both in court and in interviews prior to the courtroom appearance. This issue has been examined in a series of studies by Elizabeth Loftus and her associates. In one experiment, research participants watched a film of a car accident. Immediately afterward they were asked a number of questions. Some were asked, "Did you see the broken headlight?" Others were asked, "Did you see a broken headlight?" This small difference in wording had a large impact, and participants questioned about "*the* headlight" were much more likely to report having seen one than subjects asked about "*a* headlight," whether the film actually showed a broken headlight or not (Loftus and Zanni, 1975).

Another study showed that leading questions asked during one interrogation can change how an event is reported in subsequent interviews. Again, participants were shown film segments of a car accident. Shortly afterward some of them were asked leading questions, such as "Did you see the children getting on the school bus?" A week later, all participants were asked a direct (and unbiased) question, "Did you see a school bus in the film?" In actual fact, there was no school bus. But when compared to controls, those who were originally asked the leading question were three to four times more likely to say that they had seen one (Loftus, 1975; for similar data with children, see Ceci and Bruck, 1995).

The memory errors observed in these experiments are not small: We have mentioned "memories" for buses that weren't there and headlights that weren't broken. In other studies, researchers have planted memories for buildings that don't exist, and, indeed, memories for entire events that never occurred. While it is worth emphasizing that, in general, our memories are quite accurate—especially if appropriate, nonleading cues are provided—errors plainly do occur; they can be substantial in magnitude and, in some contexts, they can be frequent. The implications of this for the courts, or for any process that depends on memory-based testimony, are clear and deeply troubling.

What produces memory errors?   We have mentioned two broad types of memory errors. In one case, knowledge of a general sort intrudes into one's recollection of a specific event—for example, one's knowledge of the dentist's office script

shapes what one remembers about a particular visit to the dentist. In a second case, knowledge acquired on one occasion becomes mixed up with recollection of some other occasion, so that the bus mentioned by an interviewer gets added to one's recollection of the earlier film. Both of these cases are examples of *source confusion.* In both, relevant information is being drawn from memory and applied to a specific episode. But in both, the reporter is confused about the *source* of his knowledge, (falsely) believing that information acquired in one context had instead been encountered in some other context.

Source confusion can occur during initial encoding or during retrieval. If, during encoding, one's attention is focused on a few aspects of a scene, while other aspects are neglected, the neglected aspects can be filled in by relying on other knowledge. (This obviously resembles the perceptual inferences we described in Chapter 6.) If, during retrieval, one cannot remember all aspects of an event, gaps will be left in the memory records, and these can be filled in via a process of *memory reconstruction,* much as an archaeologist reconstructs an ancient city, based on a column here and a shard of pottery there. The archaeologist draws on knowledge she has about other cities of that time period; in the same fashion, memory reconstruction draws on outside knowledge to construct a persuasive memory edifice.

Can memories be altered after the event? Source confusion can influence both encoding and retrieval, but can it also influence memory storage? Put differently, knowledge can fill gaps in what we perceive or retrieve, but can it change what's already been recorded in our memories? This is a matter of some controversy. Some authors argue that newly arriving information can literally cause "destructive updating" of a memory. The old memory isn't just altered, it's *replaced* by a new memory entry. Other authors disagree, claiming instead that new information simply renders the old memory difficult to retrieve (Belli, 1989; Belli et al., 1992; Loftus, 1992, 1993; Zaragoza and Lane, 1994; Weingardt, Loftus, and Lindsay, 1995).

It is too soon to know how this debate will end, but for many purposes this may not matter. All sides agree that new information can dramatically change how participants report on earlier events, regularly incorporating suggestions and misinformation supplied after the target event occurred. More, all sides agree that these false reports are delivered in detail and with conviction. For many purposes, including those of the courtroom, this is damage enough. For these purposes, it may not matter whether or not an original, uncompromised memory still lies undetected, hidden somewhere in storage.

THE LIMITS OF MEMORY

Clearly, memory is fallible. Can this fallibility be overcome? Moreover, if a great deal of forgetting involves retrieval failure, can retrieval be improved?

Memory, hypnosis, and the courtroom A number of investigators have proposed using *hypnosis* as a technique for improving memory. The idea is that someone—for example, an eyewitness to a crime—can be hypnotized, given the suggestion that he is back at a certain time and place, and asked to tell what he sees. On the surface, the results of this procedure—in a police station or in laboratory studies—are quite impressive. A hypnotized witness mentally returns to the scene of the crime and is able to recall exactly what was said by the various participants; a hypnotized college student mentally returns to childhood and relives her sixth birthday party with childlike glee.

These hypnotized people are usually convinced that they are actually reexperiencing these events, and so they have full confidence in the accuracy of their recall. But upon investigation, these hypnotically evoked memories often turn

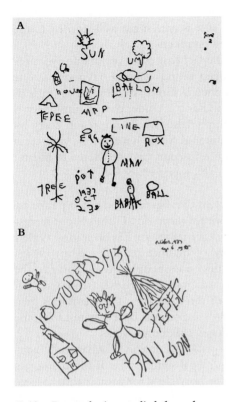

7.12 Remembering studied through drawings done while under hypnosis
(A) Drawings done at age six. (B) Drawings done while the participant was hypnotized and told that he was six years old. Note some interesting differences between the pictures, for example, the tepee, which is much more detailed in (B), the spelling of balloon, and a sense of overall design present in (B) but altogether lacking in (A). (From Orne, 1951)

out to be false. In one courtroom case, a witness recalled seeing the suspect during an assault, but investigation confirmed that he was out of the country at the time (Orne, 1979). Similar points apply to the description of childhood events elicited under hypnosis: Convincing details contained within these reports often turn out to be false when later checked against available records.

Moreover, the mental return to childhood itself turns out to be mere pretense. In one study, participants were asked to draw a picture while mentally "regressed" to the age of six. At first glance, their drawings looked remarkably childlike. But when compared to the participants' own childhood drawings made at that very age, it is clear that they are much more sophisticated. They represent an adult's conception of what a childish drawing is, rather than being the real thing (Figure 7.12; Orne, 1951). Similarly, these hypnotized adults answer questions and perceive the world, not as children would, but as they *believe* children would. When their (adult) beliefs about children are incorrect, then their simulation is correspondingly off the mark.

How can we explain these results? First of all, it is clear that hypnosis does not have the near-magical memory-enhancing powers sometimes attributed to it (Barber, 1969; Orne and Hammer, 1974; Hilgard, 1977). It does not enable us to relive our past any more than we can while awake (nor, for that matter, does it permit feats of agility or strength of which we are otherwise incapable). What hypnosis does do is make people unusually ready to believe in another person, the hypnotist, and to do what he asks of them—within the bounds of certain mutually understood limitations. If he asks them to remember, they will do their very best to oblige. They will doggedly stick to the task and rummage through their minds to find any possible retrieval cue. And so would we all, whether hypnotized or not, if we really wanted to remember badly enough. But what if we don't succeed? If we are not hypnotized, we will eventually concede failure. But hypnotized people will not. The hypnotist has told them to recall and has assured them that they can recall. And so, to please the hypnotist, they produce "memories"—by creatively adding and reconstructing on the basis of what they already know. As we have seen, such reconstructions are a common feature in much so-called remembering. The difference is that under hypnosis subjects become unusually confident that their memories are real.

Evidence for this interpretation comes from a study of the susceptibility of those under hypnosis to leading questions. The experimenter employed the familiar technique of showing participants videotapes of an accident and later asking them to recall certain details, in some cases while hypnotized and in others while not. Some of the probes were leading questions, while others were more objective in phrasing. As we have seen, such leading questions lead to errors even without hypnosis. But they lead to even more errors in hypnotized subjects than in controls. When asked whether they had seen "the license plate . . ." (which in fact was not visible), some of the hypnotized subjects not only said yes but actually volunteered partial descriptions of the license plate number. Findings of this sort cast serious doubts on the use of hypnosis in real-life judicial settings (Putnam, 1979; Smith, 1983), and, indeed, courts in America almost invariably reject testimony that has been "facilitated" by hypnosis.

The tape-recorder theory of memory In addition to what these findings tell us about hypnosis, they also have implications for what is sometimes called the **tape-recorder** (or, to update it, the *videotape-recorder*) **theory of memory.** According to this view, the brain contains a virtually indelible record of all we have ever heard or seen or felt. The only trick is to find a way to turn the recorder back to some desired portion of the tape. The evidence indicates, however, that this suggestion is exceedingly implausible. To be sure, there is much in memory that, under ordinary circumstances, we cannot retrieve. Nonetheless, all the evidence indicates that information will be recorded in memory only if we paid some attention, only if we engaged that information somehow, during our initial encounter with it. Without this engagement or attention, there is no memory record to be recovered. Likewise, we have seen that some information reaches the status of permastore and so can be remembered years and years after learning it. But information reaches this state only if it is extremely well learned in the first place; most information is not that well entrenched.

These observations are consistent with the fact that every technique ever proposed for "playing back" memories has been found wanting. Hypnosis is one example of these techniques, but the evidence is similar in other cases (including, for example, drugs alleged to improve memory). Under the circumstances, it appears that the tape-recorder theory is simply false. We do not retain every bit of sensory information we have ever encountered. Some never enters long-term storage, some enters but then is lost, and some, it seems, may be altered to fit later incoming material (Loftus and Loftus, 1980; Neisser, 1982b).

Are there repressed memories?   A special problem that has received much public attention concerns what have been called **repressed memories.** Claims about repression appear in many contexts, but in recent years, repression has been most widely discussed in connection with the recovery of traumatic childhood memories, often memories involving sexual abuse. In these cases, people often report that the traumatic memories were pushed out of consciousness—that is, repressed—for many years, sometimes for as long as two or three decades. The memories then surface much later, often while the person is being treated by a therapist for some problem not obviously connected to the alleged childhood events.

Are these memories accurate—that is, a true description of what really happened? This question has serious social and legal significance: If the memories are accurate, then they provide evidence for horrible wrongdoing and, indeed, for criminal prosecution. If, however, the memories are factually incorrect, then we must worry about the terrible consequences of these false accusations; we also need to worry about how these large-scale and painful false memories could ever come to be.

It is certainly clear that incest and childhood sexual abuse are far more prevalent than previously supposed. We also know that events—particularly emotionally significant events—are stored in memory for a very long time, perhaps permanently. Thus many memories of childhood abuse are likely to be entirely accurate. Still, we must be extremely careful in interpreting these memories of abuse, particularly those that were "repressed" for many years and then "recovered." As one broad concern, many investigators are skeptical about whether the phenomenon of repression exists at all (e.g., Holmes, 1990; Loftus, 1993, 1997). Highly emotional events, they argue, tend to be *better* remembered, in comparison to more mundane occurrences—exactly the opposite of the (alleged) repression pattern. Thus, rape victims are often haunted for years by the memory of their hideous experience; survivors of the Holocaust find it difficult to avoid thinking about the horrors they endured. (We return to these long-lasting memories in Chapter 18, when we discuss post-traumatic stress disorder.)

In addition, it is sadly plausible that memories "recovered" after a period of amnesia are, in many cases, false, fabricated through mechanisms we have already discussed. Thus, for example, we know that the possibility for error is greater in remembering the distant past than it is in remembering recent events. Likewise, we know that close questioning of a witness can create "memories" for entire events that never occurred, particularly if the questions are asked over and over (e.g., Ofshe, 1992; Ceci, Huffman, and Smith, 1994; Hyman, Husband, and Billings, 1995; Loftus, 1996; Zaragoza and Mitchell, 1996). We also know that false memories, when they occur, can be recalled just as fully, just as confidently, and, indeed, with just as much distress as memories for actual events.

It is also worth noting that many of these recovered memories emerge only with the assistance of a therapist who is genuinely convinced that the client's psychological problems stem from childhood abuse. Often, the therapist believes that these problems can be dealt with only if the client faces them squarely and uncovers the buried memories of that abuse (e.g., Bass and Davis, 1988). To help this process along, the therapist may rely on a variety of techniques aimed at improving memory, including hypnosis, drugs alleged to promote recollection, and guided imagination. In these cases, the therapist's intentions are good, but the techniques used magnify the risk of memory error. As we have noted, hypnosis and "memory-promoting" drugs (such as sodium amytal) do little to promote accurate recall, but they clearly do increase the risk of false memories. And while guided imagery is an effective way to increase recall, it is also a powerful source of false memories.

A therapist who is convinced that abuse took place may also ask suggestive questions that further increase the chances of memory fabrication. Even if the therapist scrupulously avoids leading questions, she can shape the client's memory in other ways—by giving signs of interest or concern if the client hits on the "right" line of exploration, by spending more time on topics related to the alleged memories than on other issues, and so forth. In these ways, the climate within the therapeutic session can subtly guide the client toward finding exactly the "memories" the therapist expects to find.

None of this is said to minimize the social and moral problems produced by childhood sexual abuse and incest. These offenses do occur and can have severe life-long consequences for the victim.★ But here, as in all cases, the veracity of our recollection cannot be taken for granted. We must always be careful in interpreting what seems like a memory of a long-past event, and that caution must be increased if the memory emerged through someone's (e.g., a therapist's) suggestions and hypnosis. (For further discussion of this difficult issue, see Holmes, 1990; Kihlstrom, 1993; Loftus, 1993; Pendergast, 1995; Schacter, 1996. For a sharply divergent position, see Bass and Davis, 1988; Freyd, 1996.)

THE LIMITS OF DISTORTION

Memory, it seems, is not a passive repository for our experience, recording the days of our lives and then permitting playback of these records later on. Instead, memory depends on a highly active set of processes, starting with the interpretation inherent in the initial encoding and continuing through the processes of reconstruction and interpretation used unwittingly to fill gaps in what we recall. There are numerous ways in which a memory can be distorted, but such distortions don't always occur—far from it. After all, we do remember many details of our experiences, and we can retain these details for a very long time. Even when errors do occur, some forms of testing, and some retrieval hints, seem capable of enabling recovery of the original record (Alba and Hasher, 1983).

In short, our memory is neither wholly distorted nor wholly accurate. The tape-recorder theory of memory is false, but so is the suggestion that everything we remember is changed and distorted. In these regards, memory is much like perception. Both are affected by processes that work from the top down as well

---

★ Some writers contend that people who were abused as children can develop a variety of symptoms, including eating disorders, inabilities to form close relationships, a variety of anxieties, and so on (e.g., Bass and Davis, 1988). But each of these symptoms can readily arise from other sources—that is, with no history of abuse. Therefore, we cannot interpret any symptom, or any pattern of symptoms, as evidence that abuse must have occurred at some prior point in an individual's life. In addition, it is important to note that we are a resilient species, and some children who have been abused emerge without subsequent symptoms (Kendall-Tackett, Williams, and Finkelhor, 1993; Kihlstrom, 1996). Let us be clear, though, that this takes nothing away from the ugliness of this offense: Abusing a child, sexually or otherwise, is a horrible deed, and a criminal offense, whether the child develops subsequent symptoms or not.

as by those that start from the bottom up. Perception without any bottom-up processing (that is, without any reference to stimuli) would amount to continual hallucination. Memory without bottom-up processing (that is, without any reference to memory traces) would amount to perpetual delusion, with the remembered past continually being constructed and reconstructed to fit the schemas of the moment. Thus, in both of these domains, bottom-up processes must play a crucial role.

The use of schemas—that is, top-down processing—clearly has a cost, for it can lead to distortions of memory. But it also confers great benefits. Our cognitive machinery is limited, and there's only so much that we can encode, store, and retrieve. Thus, we are forced to schematize, bringing order to the world we perceive and think about. Our mental shortcuts therefore serve us well, helping us to understand and remember, and this should be kept in mind when we realize that these same shortcuts occasionally backfire, leading to illusions and error.

DISORDERED MEMORIES

Thus far, our discussion has largely centered on people with normal memories. But over the last century, some intriguing questions about memory have been raised by studies of people with drastic defects in memory caused by various kinds of damage to the brain (Squire, 1987; Mayes, 1988; Squire and Shimamura, 1996).

ANTEROGRADE AMNESIA

Certain lesions in the temporal cortex (specifically, in the hippocampus and nearby subcortical regions) produce a memory disorder called **anterograde amnesia** (*anterograde* means "in a forward direction"). Patients with this disorder often have little trouble remembering events prior to the injury; their difficulty, instead, is in learning anything new. This kind of amnesia can occur as a result of various brain lesions. For example, it occurs in certain chronic alcoholics who suffer from **Korsakoff's syndrome** (named after the Russian physician who first described it). Anterograde amnesia is also one of the symptoms of Alzheimer's disease. And, in the famous case of a patient known as H.M., amnesia was a tragic side effect of neurosurgery undertaken to treat severe epilepsy (see Figure 7.13).

H.M.'s surgery occurred when he was twenty-nine. Following the surgery he had a normal memory span and thus, apparently, a normal working memory. But he seems incapable of adding any new information to his long-term storage. He

7.13 Regions of the brain where damage can cause memory loss *A cutaway section of the human brain showing regions of the hippocampus and associated structures whose destruction caused H.M.'s massive memory deficits. Patients with Korsakoff's syndrome tend to have lesions in regions that lie higher up, including the thalamus, while patients with Alzheimer's disease show damage in the base of the forebrain. (Adapted from Mishkin and Appenzeller, 1987)*

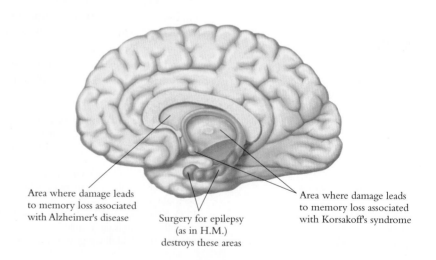

Area where damage leads to memory loss associated with Alzheimer's disease

Surgery for epilepsy (as in H.M.) destroys these areas

Area where damage leads to memory loss associated with Korsakoff's syndrome

A

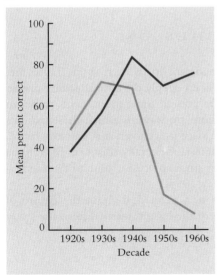

1960s   1970s   1980s   1990s

Remote and recent memory in amnesiacs
(A) Sample items adapted from the "famous
faces" test in which patients are asked to iden-
tify faces of individuals who reached fame in a
particular decade (Albert, Butters, and Levin,
1979; Butters and Albert, 1982). The names
of those pictured are listed on page 296.
(B) Results on the famous faces test for H.M.
(blue) and normal controls (dark red) for the
years from 1920 to 1960. Note that, as one
would expect, the performance of H.M. was
essentially equivalent to that of normal partici-
pants in identifying people who reached
prominence between 1920 and 1930. Like
normal participants, he did poorly for faces that
predate 1930 when he was still a preschool
child. But he performed much worse than the
two controls on faces from the period after his
operation (which was performed during the
early 1950s). (Adapted from Marslen-Wilson
and Teuber, 1975)

B

is unable to recognize individuals he first met after the surgery occurred, even if he saw them just a half-hour ago. His family moved to a new house after his operation, and he has been consistently unable to learn his new address or his new route home. When first told that his uncle had died he was deeply moved but then forgot all about it. Some time later, he asked again when his uncle would come to visit and was told again of his uncle's death. His grief was as intense as before. Each time he hears this sad news, it is as if he is hearing it for the first time—with all the shock and all the pain (Milner, 1966; Milner, Corkin, and Teuber, 1968; Marslen-Wilson and Teuber, 1975; Corkin, 1984).

H.M.'s long-term storage system seems almost completely closed to new memories, but his recollection of events prior to the operation remains largely intact, especially for events that happened more than a year or so before the surgery. His broad intellectual functioning also seems largely unimpaired, and he can, for example, still read, write, and engage in a conversation.

H.M.'s case is unique, but patients who have suffered damage to the hippocampus and related systems experience similar memory deficits. Korsakoff's original patient could play a competent game of chess but could not remember how the position now before him on the chess board had come to be.

This sort of memory loss is profoundly unsettling. Consider some of H.M.'s comments about his state:

> Right now, I'm wondering, Have I done or said anything amiss? You see, at this moment everything looks clear to me, but what happened just before? That's what worries me. It's like waking from a dream; I just don't remember. (Milner, 1966)

And on another occasion:

> . . . Every day is alone in itself, whatever enjoyment I've had, and whatever sorrow I've had. (Milner, Corkin, and Teuber, 1968; for more on H.M.'s case, see Hilts, 1995)

293

RETROGRADE AMNESIA

An opposite set of deficits occurs in **retrograde amnesia** (*retrograde* means "in a backward direction"), in which the patient suffers a loss of memory for some period prior to the brain injury. A brief period of retrograde amnesia always follows electroconvulsive therapy, a treatment for severe depression or mania that involves brief electric shocks applied to the head (Andreason and Black, 1996; also see Chapter 19). Patients receiving this therapy have no memories of their treatments or the events directly preceding.

Longer periods of retrograde amnesia, lasting weeks or even years, can result from brain tumors, diseases, or strokes. And in many cases, retrograde effects accompany anterograde amnesia. Thus H.M. has difficulty remembering events that happened one to three years before his operation, but his memory was perfectly normal for those that occurred before then (Mayes, 1988).

What accounts for retrograde amnesia? According to some authors, one cause is a problem with **trace consolidation,** a hypothetical process by which newly acquired memory traces gradually become firmly established. This might explain why this amnesia primarily affects memories that were formed shortly before the injury. These memories would not have had time to consolidate and would thus be more liable to destruction (Weingartner and Parker, 1984).

Whether retrograde amnesia can be explained in this manner, however, is still undecided. One trouble is that retrograde amnesia often extends back for several years prior to the injury. If so, consolidation could not explain the deficit unless one assumes—as a few authors do—that consolidation is an exceedingly drawn-out process, occurring over very long time periods (Squire and Cohen, 1979, 1982; Squire, 1987).

WHAT AMNESIA TEACHES US

The study of amnesic patients is important in its own right. These are, after all, individuals whose lives have been deeply disrupted, leading one to ask: What can we do to help them? At the present time, there seems to be no way to reverse anterograde amnesia, but there are ways in which these patients can be helped to lead productive lives (e.g., Glisky, Schacter, and Tulving, 1986). The prognosis is different for retrograde amnesia: Generally, this form of amnesia dissipates with the passage of time, although, in many cases, some of the memory loss is permanent (Campbell and Conway, 1995).

In addition, amnesic patients can teach us a great deal about the nature of memory. In this section, we consider some of the lessons learned from the study of amnesia.

WHAT TYPE OF MEMORY IS SPARED IN AMNESIA?

Many investigators have argued that patients with anterograde amnesia cannot acquire any long-term memories at all. But further study demonstrates that this isn't true. These patients can, for example, learn to trace the correct path through a maze and get faster each time they redo the same maze. They can also acquire skills such as learning to read print that has been mirror-reversed (Figure 7.14). In these and many other cases, the patients benefit from practice, and so they must have retained something from their previous experience. Nonetheless, each time

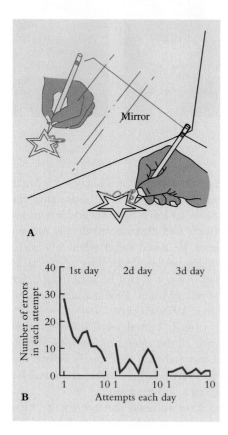

7.14   An example of what amnesiacs can learn   *(A) In mirror drawing, the research participant has to trace a line between two outlines of a figure while looking at her hand in a mirror (Kolb and Whishaw, 1996). Initially, this is very difficult, but after some practice the individual gets very proficient at it. The same is true for amnesics. The graphs in (B) show H.M.'s improvement on this task over a period of three days. (Milner, Corkin, and Teuber, 1968)*

they are brought back into the testing situation, they insist that they have never seen the apparatus or the test materials before, consistent with their diagnosis of profound amnesia (Corkin, 1965; Weiskrantz and Warrington, 1979; Cohen and Squire, 1980).

What can we make of these findings? Apparently, some sorts of memory are spared in anterograde amnesia: Skills, it seems, can be acquired in a perfectly normal way, while other sorts of memory are massively disrupted. What is the essential difference between these two kinds of memories? Some authors believe that the crucial distinction is between *procedural* and *declarative knowledge.* Procedural knowledge is knowing *how:* how to ride a bicycle or how to read mirror writing. Declarative knowledge, in contrast, is knowing *that:* that there are three outs in an inning, that automobiles run on gasoline, that March has thirty-one days. Declarative knowledge also includes episodic memory—the knowledge that you had chicken for dinner yesterday or that you woke up late this morning.

Procedural and declarative knowledge are surely different from each other, and one can have procedural knowledge in a domain without any corresponding declarative knowledge. Professional baseball players know how to swing a bat, but few can explain just what it is that they know. Conversely, most physicists probably know (and can describe) the underlying mechanics of a baseball swing, but few will be able to perform competently when given a bat and asked to hit a ball (especially one thrown at 90 miles per hour). The physicists, it seems, have declarative knowledge without the corresponding procedural knowledge.

Many neuroscientists argue that procedural and declarative memories depend on different neural systems and that only one of these systems is disrupted in amnesiac patients. As a result, the amnesiacs perform normally on most tasks of skill-learning, at the same time that they fail miserably on any task requiring the acquisition of declarative knowledge (Cohen and Squire, 1980; Squire, 1986).

A somewhat different description of amnesia centers on the distinction between explicit and implicit memory (see p. 277). Anterograde amnesiacs generally show their disruption on any task requiring explicit recollection of the past, and so they cannot answer questions like "Do you remember?" or "Do you recognize?" (at least not if the questions pertain to events that occurred after the cerebral damage). The patients perform normally, however, on tests of implicit memory. To put this in concrete terms, the patients will fail completely if they are shown a number of words and later asked to recall or recognize them. The results are quite different, though, if the patients are shown a list of words and later tested *implicitly*—say, with a word-fragment completion task. For example, the patients might be shown _ L _ P _ A _ T or B _ O _ C _ S _ and asked to complete these fragments to form English words. This task is quite difficult if the patient has not been primed in any way. But if the patient was previously shown a list containing the words ELEPHANT and BOOKCASE, he is likely to complete the fragments properly. Apparently, the patient does have some memory of seeing these words, and that memory facilitates performance with the word-fragment task (Warrington and Weiskrantz, 1978; Diamond and Rozin, 1984; Graf, Mandler, and Squire, 1984; Schacter, 1996).

Which, then, is the better account? Does anterograde amnesia disrupt declarative knowledge, while sparing procedural? Or does it disrupt explicit memory while sparing implicit? The evidence at this point is equivocal. As one complication, these distinctions overlap: Procedural knowledge is often implicit; declarative knowledge is generally explicit. In addition, it may turn out that different cases of amnesia require different explanations. Anterograde amnesia is probably not a single disorder, so which conception provides the better account may vary from patient to patient (Squire and Cohen, 1984). In either case, though, these cases of brain damage provide powerful reasons for distinguishing at least two types of memory, and continued research on amnesia is certain to sharpen our understanding of this distinction.

OTHER TYPES OF MEMORY

We have been focusing on a distinction that hinges on how a memory is revealed—implicitly or explicitly; in what the subject does (procedural knowledge) or what he says (declarative knowledge). But memories can also be distinguished according to the type of information contained within the memory, and here, too, the distinction can be illuminated by the study of amnesia.

For example, a patient known as Gene sustained a serious head injury in a motorcycle accident, damaging large areas of his frontal and temporal lobes, including his left hippocampus. As a result, he can recall no events at all from any time in his life. "Even when detailed descriptions of dramatic events in his life are given to him—such as the derailment, near his house, of a train carrying lethal chemicals that required 240,000 people to evacuate their homes for a week," Gene remembers nothing (Schacter, 1996, p. 150; Tulving et al. 1988). But he does remember some things: He remembers that he owned two motorcycles and a car; he remembers that his family has a summer cottage where he has spent many weekends; he remembers the names of classmates in a school photograph (Schacter, 1996). In short, Gene's *episodic* memory is massively disrupted, but his memory for *generic* information, including information about repeated events in his life, is intact.

Other patients show the reverse pattern: One such patient had suffered damage to the front portion of her temporal lobes as a result of encephalitis. As a consequence, she has lost her memory of many common words, important historical events, famous people, and even the fundamental traits of animate and inanimate objects. "However, when asked about her wedding and honeymoon, her father's illness and death, or other specific past episodes, she readily produced detailed and accurate recollections" (Schacter, 1996, p. 152).

Cases like these make it clear that episodic memory is truly different from generic memory, and the two are supported, it seems, by distinct brain systems. As a result, damage in some brain sites disrupts episodic memory, leaving generic memory untouched; damage in other sites has the opposite effect. But we should not think of these brain sites as the seat of memory, or, worse, as the "memory centers." This is because remembering involves many steps and many processes, starting with the moment of encoding and ending with the recollection of the target information some time later. These various steps each involve different regions of the brain, so that, in the end, many different brain sites play a role in remembering.

As an illustration of this multipart organization, consider the nature of memory retrieval. Some aspects of retrieval are swift and effortless, and the sought-after information simply "pops" into mind. This form of remembering is called **associative retrieval** and applies both to generic memory ("Who was the first president of the United States?") and to episodic memory—as, for example, when a song or a smell calls a particular event to mind. Other aspects of retrieval, however, require some effort. This **strategic retrieval** is needed whenever we must actively search for a memory ("How did you spend your summer vacation in 1996?") or whenever we must sort through various memories to locate the correct one ("Let's see . . . was that the summer I went hiking or the summer I worked at the bookstore?").

These two aspects of retrieval draw on different brain areas. Some of the evidence for this claim comes from brain-imaging studies (such as PET scans), which show much greater activation in the prefrontal cortex (especially in the right hemisphere) during strategic retrieval and greater activation in the hippocampus (and nearby temporal lobe structures) during automatic retrieval (Moscovitch, 1994; Schacter, 1996). This pattern is then confirmed by studies of patients with different types of amnesia: Damage to the right prefrontal cortex, for example, is associated not just with memory *loss,* but also with a peculiar pattern of memory *error.* The errors, referred to as **confabulations,** are sincerely offered, but utterly false, recollections. One patient recalled confidently that he and his wife had been married for only four months, when in fact they had been married for over thirty years. Remarkably, this same patient correctly remembered that he and his wife had four children, the youngest of whom was twenty-two (Moscovitch, 1995).

Why does prefrontal damage lead to confabulation? One proposal is that this kind of brain damage disrupts strategic retrieval. This leaves the patient unable to distinguish which thoughts are fantasies and which genuine memories, which remembered elements derived from this episode and which from that one. As a result, the patient's thoughts are "filled with all kinds of mnemonic flotsam and jetsam—fragments of experience that are not anchored to a proper time and place, and thus enter into peculiar alliances and marriages with one another" (Schacter, 1996, p. 121).

Other brain areas also play a crucial role in memory. We have just mentioned the role of the prefrontal cortex in memory retrieval; this same brain site is also essential for the operation of working memory. Damage to this area, therefore, impairs all of the tasks we earlier described as relying on working memory (also see Chapter 8). Likewise, a brain structure called the **amygdala** plays an important part in memory for emotional events. Damage to this structure has many effects; among them, the affected individual seems incapable of fear conditioning (Bechara et al., 1995; for more on fear conditioning, see Chapter 4; for more on the amygdala's role, see Chapter 11). And other forms of remembering seem to rely on still other brain areas. Damage to the occipital and temporal lobes can disrupt an individual's ability to retrieve specifically visual memories, such as the remembered face of a friend or the appearance of a previously visited landscape; damage elsewhere can disrupt the ability to remember words of certain types; and so on (e.g., Schacter, 1996). It is thus perfectly clear that no one brain area "handles" the job of remembering. Instead, remembering (like most cognitive operations) requires the close collaboration of many brain sites, each performing its own specific function.

TAKING STOCK

In looking back over this chapter, we are again struck by the intimate pattern of relationships among perception, memory, and thinking. It is often unclear where one ends and another begins. To give just one example, consider memory search. As we saw, trying to recall the names of one's high-school classmates apparently involves many of the same thought processes that are called upon when we try to figure out how to solve a geometry problem or look for our missing keys. To the extent that this is so, it is clear that much of memory involves thinking. And as we saw previously, the same is also true of perception. For there, too, the perceiver becomes a thinker as she tries to solve perceptual problems and make sense out of ambiguous or impossible figures. In the next chapter, we will turn to the topic of thinking in its own right.

SUMMARY

1.   Any act of remembering implies success in each of three phases: *encoding, storage,* and *retrieval.*

2.   According to the *stage theory of memory,* there are several memory systems. Of these, the most important are *working memory* (originally, short-term memory), in which information is held while one is actively working on it, and *long-term memory,* in which information is stored for much longer periods. According to stage theory, access to the long-term memory system requires that material first pass through working memory.

3.   The storage capacity of long-term memory is enormous; however, a search is sometimes required to locate information in this store. The capacity of working memory is quite limited—approximately seven items—but each of these items is immediately and easily available.

4.   When research participants are asked to recall lists of unrelated items, they are most likely to recall the first few items they heard and also the last few. The advantage for the first items is called the *primacy effect* and is associated with retrieval from long-term storage. The advantage for the last few items is called the *recency effect* and reflects retrieval from working memory.

5.   While the capacity of working memory is limited, research participants have considerable flexibility in how materials are packed into this memory. By recoding material into large memory *chunks,* a great deal of information can be held in working memory.

6.   In *maintenance rehearsal,* material is held passively in working memory. This form of rehearsal provides little benefit for subsequent recall, indicating that the transfer of information from working memory to long-term memory is not automatic. Instead, some mental activity is required to establish information in long-term storage, and this is one of the reasons why working memory is now conceived of as a mental workbench where items are sorted, manipulated and organized.

7.   Many studies demonstrate that memory is better after *deep processing* than after *shallow processing,* that it is helped by chunking and other organizational devices, and that it is further aided by relating the material to be remembered with what is already known. These general principles of memorial organization underlie *mnemonics,* techniques for helping memory, which include various forms of verbal organization and the use of *visual imagery.*

8.   Remembering depends in part upon the presence of appropriate *retrieval cues.* In general, retrieval cues will be most effective if they recreate the mental perspective that the individual held during the original encoding. As a result, remembering is most likely if the physical, mental, and emotional context at the time of retrieval matches the context at the time of learning, a principle often referred to as *encoding specificity.*

9.   One reason why certain forms of encoding (for example, organization and understanding) are so effective is that they help pave the way for later retrieval by establishing many retrieval paths leading to the target material. This same idea explains the effect of *elaborative rehearsal,* which, unlike maintenance rehearsal, helps in remembering because it provides appropriate retrieval paths.

10.   Retrieval from long-term memory is often preceded by a process of *memory search.* In some cases, the search reaches a point in which we are certain we know the target information and can recall some features of that information, but we cannot recall the target information itself. This pattern is called the *tip-of-the-tongue phenomenon.*

11.   When we seek to recall or recognize some material, we are drawing on *explicit memory.* In contrast, *implicit memory* includes cases in which we are affected by some past experience without realizing that we are in fact remembering. Laboratory methods to test for implicit memory include *repetition priming* and *fragment completion.* Explicit and

SUMMARY

implicit memory can be distinguished in several ways: Explicit memory (but not implicit) benefits from deep processing; implicit memory (but not explicit) is influenced by peripheral aspects of the stimulus, such as the typeface of a word.

12.   Other things being equal, forgetting increases the longer the *retention interval.* This point was first demonstrated by Ebbinghaus, who plotted the forgetting curve of associations between nonsense syllables. The causes of forgetting are still a matter of debate. One theory holds that traces gradually *decay* over time. Another view argues that the fundamental cause of forgetting is *interference* produced by other memories. Yet another theory asserts that forgetting is caused primarily by changes in *retrieval cues* at the time of recall. This position is sometimes used to explain the phenomenon of *childhood amnesia.*

13.   Under some circumstances, forgetting doesn't seem to occur, as in the case of a second language well-learned in school. Such material seems to reach a status called *permastore,* in which it is retained for many decades. Memories for events can also reach permastore. However, some of these so-called *flashbulb memories* turn out to be inaccurate, raising questions about the nature and reliability of flashbulb recollection.

14.   Remembering generally depends on prior knowledge, which affects both encoding and later retrieval. The prior knowledge often involves a general understanding about how events unfold or what a situation is likely to contain. The use of these general frameworks promotes accurate memory in many circumstances, but can also lead to memory distortions.

15.   Memory errors can also arise when an element experienced in one context is misremembered as having occurred in a different context. This point has been elaborated by studies of eyewitness testimony, which show that what is remembered can be extensively shaped by the questions posed to an eyewitness. The resulting errors are examples of *source confusion,* in which a witness is mistaken about the source of a particular remembered element.

16.   Hypnosis is sometimes offered as a means of improving memory accuracy. However, evidence indicates that hypnosis does nothing to improve memory and can actually increase the risk of memory error.

17.   There has been considerable controversy over the status of *repressed memories.* Evidence suggests that enormous caution is required in assessing these memories, especially if the memories emerged with the help of close questioning, hypnosis, or drugs alleged to promote recall.

18.   Certain injuries to the brain, particularly to the hippocampus and surrounding regions, can produce disorders of memory. In *anterograde amnesia,* the patient's ability to fix material in long-term memory is reduced. In *retrograde amnesia,* the loss is for memories prior to the injury and is sometimes attributed to a disruption of trace consolidation. An important current issue is why patients with severe anterograde amnesia can acquire certain long-term memories (learning a maze, benefiting from repetition priming) but not others (remembering that they have seen the maze or heard the word before). According to one hypothesis, the crucial distinction is between *procedural* and *declarative knowledge;* according to another, it is that between *implicit* and *explicit retrieval.*

19.   Amnesic patients can also be distinguished according to the type of information they are unable to remember. Some patients seem unable to recall generic facts (meanings of words, important historical events); others seem unable to recall specific episodes. This suggests that *generic* and *episodic memory* depend on different brain systems. But these brain systems are themselves complex, with many different brain areas contributing to any act of remembering. For example, retrieval from memory is sometimes automatic (*associative retrieval*) and sometimes effortful (*strategic retrieval*); these types of retrieval also seem to rely on different brain regions.

CHAPTER **8**

THOUGHT AND KNOWLEDGE

I n ordinary language, the word *think* has a wide range of meanings. It may be a synonym for *remember* (as in "I can't think of her name") or for *pay attention* (as in the exhortation "Think about it!"), or for *believe* (as in "I think sea serpents exist"). It may also refer to a state of vague and undirected reverie, as in "I'm thinking of nothing in particular." These many uses suggest that the word has become a blanket term to cover many different psychological processes.

But *think* also has a narrower meaning, which is wonderfully rendered in Rodin's famous statue *The Thinker.* Here, the meaning of *think* is best conveyed by such words as *reason* or *reflect.* Psychologists who study thinking are mainly interested in this sense of the term, which they call **directed thinking**—the mental activities we use whenever we try to solve a problem, judge the truth of an assertion, or weigh the costs and benefits in an important decision.

In each of these activities, we draw constantly on the foundation of what we already know. If the situation is one we have encountered before, then we can take into account how we reasoned or decided the last time we were in this setting. If the situation is unfamiliar, but resembles others we have encountered, then we can draw on more general knowledge: To make a pie, we call on our broad knowledge of cooking; to manage a difficult social situation, we rely on what we know about diplomacy and politeness.

Even in entirely novel situations, knowledge is still necessary in order to give meaning to our thoughts. Without a knowledge base, we could not think about dogs, say, because we would not know what dogs are, and likewise for any other thought, no matter how profound or how trivial, how complex or how simple. Hence, our knowledge provides the material we are able to think *about,* and so we begin our discussion of thinking with a consideration of the nature of knowledge.

ANALOGICAL REPRESENTATIONS

Many (perhaps all) of the components of our knowledge can be regarded as **mental representations** of the world and of our experiences in it. These representations are the main elements of thought. They are like the many external representations we encounter in ordinary life, those signs or symbols that stand for something else, such as maps, blueprints, menus, price lists, stories—the list is very large. In all these cases, the representation is not the same as what it stands for; instead, it signifies the real thing. We don't literally drive on the map, nor do we eat the menu.

Psychologists, philosophers, and computer scientists have found it convenient to distinguish between two broad classes of representations, the **analogical** and the **symbolic.**★ Analogical representations capture some of the actual characteristics

★Many psychologists and computer scientists use the term *digital* for what we here call *symbolic.* This is because computers usually encode such symbolic, nonpictorial representations in a discrete, all-or-none fashion by various combinations of the digits 0 and 1.

Thinking (Aristotle Contemplating the Bust of Homer, *1653, by Rembrandt; courtesy The Metropolitan Museum of Art, purchased with special funds and gifts of friends of the Museum, 1961)*

of (and are thus analogous to) what they represent. In contrast, symbolic representations bear no such relationship to the item they stand for. As we will see, human thought uses both kinds of representations.

Consider a picture of a mouse. The picture is in some ways quite different from the real animal; the real picture consists of marks on paper, whereas the actual mouse is flesh and blood. In this sense, the picture *represents* a mouse rather than actually being one. Even so, the picture has many similarities to the creature it represents, so that, in general, the picture *looks like* a mouse: The mouse's eyes are side by side in reality, and they're also side by side in the picture; the mouse's ears and tail are at opposite ends of the creature, and they're at opposite ends of the picture. It is properties like these that make the picture an analogical representation.

In contrast, take the word *mouse*. Unlike a picture, the word in no way resembles the mouse. It is an abstract representation, and the relation between the five letters *m-o-u-s-e* and the little animal that they represent is entirely arbitrary.

The same distinction holds for mental representations. Some of our mental representations are images that reflect more or less directly many of the attributes of the objects or events they represent. Other mental representations are more abstract, much as words in a language. We will begin our discussion by considering analogical representations: mental images and the related topic of spatial thinking.

MENTAL IMAGES

Imagine someone standing with her arms hanging loosely at her sides. Will her hands be higher than her hips or lower? Most people faced with this question will retrieve the relevant information from a mental image, easily

Some representations are pictorial, others—abstract (A) A photograph of Ambroise Vollard, a French art dealer at the turn of the century. (B) A cubist portrait of Monsieur Vollard by Pablo Picasso. Note that while Picasso's rendering is by no means literal, there is enough of a pictorial similarity to the model that the portrait is still recognizable. While this painting is a pictorial representation, the model's name—Ambroise Vollard—is not. It stands for him, but it is not like him, for both names and words are abstract representations rather than pictorial ones. (Picasso's Portrait of Ambroise Vollard, *1909. Pushkin Museum, Moscow; courtesy of Scala/Art Resource)*

discerning in the image that her hands will fall below her hips (but above her knees). Observations like these suggest that some of our knowledge is based on analogical representations called *mental images.* We seem to inspect these images with "our mind's eye," and read information from these images much as we would read information off of a picture. Similar claims have been made for other senses—including hearing with the "mind's ear," or feeling with the "mind's fingers." But far more is known about *visual imagery* than about imagery in these other modalities, and so our focus will be on visual images.

STUDYING ONE'S OWN IMAGES

The first attempt to study visual imagery goes back a hundred years to Sir Francis Galton (1822–1911). Galton asked people to describe their own images and to judge their vividness (Galton, 1883). Different people responded to this question in very different ways. Some said they could call up scenes at will and see them with the utmost clarity. Others (including some well-known painters) denied ever having images at all.

One might expect that these differences would correspond to differences in performance when using visual imagery: One might predict, for example, that people who claim to have vivid imagery have better memories for visual appearances or that they are better able to use their imagery in solving problems. But, surprisingly, the results on this issue are ambiguous. Some studies do find the expected relationship, others find a reverse effect, while still others find no relationship at all (Di Vesta, Ingersoll, and Sunshine, 1971; Baddeley, 1976; Marks, 1983; Reisberg and Leak, 1987).

How can this be? Why don't we observe a consistent performance advantage in imagery tasks for those people with particularly clear and vivid mental imagery? How is it possible for people who deny having imagery to perform an imagery task at all? Part of the answer to these questions lies in the inherent ambiguity of these *self-reported data.* For one thing, research participants often lack the vocabulary to describe the details or quality of the imaged form, and this obviously diminishes the precision of their imagery self-reports. In addition, the words that they use in describing their images are often of uncertain meaning: What does a participant's claims of having very vivid imagery mean? Perhaps his imagery is actually cloudy but he regards it as vivid because he has never experienced anything more. Another participant, also claiming to have vivid imagery, might actually be able to call up much more detailed images. These ambiguities make self-reports difficult to interpret. Perhaps it is no surprise, then, that imagery self-reports have at best an uncertain relationship to more objective measures of performance.

EIDETIC IMAGERY

8.1 Test picture for study of eidetic imagery This picture from Alice in Wonderland *was shown for half a minute to elementary schoolchildren, a few of whom seemed to have an eidetic image of it. (Illustration by Marjorie Torrey)*

However, one aspect of the self-report data is worth highlighting. As we have mentioned, Galton found that individuals vary widely in their imagery experience. Few individuals, however, reach the extreme clarity and detail of *eidetic imagery.* This is imagery characterized both by its extraordinary vividness and by the truly photographic quality of the image. Eidetic imagery is quite rare, and we know relatively little about it. But this extremely clear imagery does exist. In one study, a ten-year-old child with eidetic imagery was shown a picture from *Alice in Wonderland* (Figure 8.1) for thirty seconds. After it was taken away, the child was asked whether he could still see anything and, if so, to describe what he saw (Leask, Haber, and Haber, 1969). The boy's extraordinarily detailed imagery is evident in the following exchange, which took place while the child was looking at a blank easel.

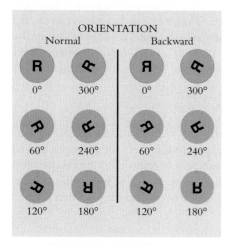

ORIENTATION

Normal   Backward

R	ᴚ	ᴙ	ᴚ
0°	300°	0°	300°

| 60° | 240° | 60° | 240° |

| 120° | 180° | 120° | 180° |

8.2   Mental rotation   *Normal and backward versions of one of the characters used in the mental rotation study, showing the orientations in which it appeared as a test stimulus. (Adapted from Cooper and Shepard, 1973)*

Experimenter:	Do you see something there?
Subject:	I see the tree, gray tree with three limbs. I see the cat with stripes around its tail.
Experimenter:	Can you count those stripes?
Subject:	Yes (pause). There's about 16.
Experimenter:	You're counting what? Black, white or both?
Subject:	Both.
Experimenter:	Tell me what else you see.
Subject:	And I can see the flowers on the bottom. There's about three stems but you can see two pairs of flowers. One on the right has green leaves, red flower on bottom with yellow on top. And I can see the girl with a green dress. She's got blonde hair and a red hair band. There are some leaves in the upper left-hand corner where the tree is (Haber, 1969, p. 38).

Researchers estimate that only 5 percent of all children are capable of eidetic imagery; the proportion is probably even smaller in adults. According to one author, this difference between children and adults may indicate that children rely more on imagery in their thinking, perhaps because their verbal and conceptual memory systems are not yet fully developed (Kosslyn, 1980, 1984). In any case, there is no reason to believe that this type of imagery is especially useful. Contrary to popular belief, memory experts generally don't have eidetic imagery (or "photographic memory" as it is sometimes called); their skill lies instead in their ability to organize material in memory, rather than in storing it in pictorial form.

PICTURELIKE ASPECTS OF VISUAL IMAGERY

We have described several of the hazards associated with the interpretation of self-report data, and these concerns have led researchers to seek more objective means of studying mental imagery. Their experiments typically ask research participants to *do* something with the image—to manipulate it in some fashion or to "read off" certain information from the image. These procedures indicate that, to a remarkable extent, visual images do function just like mental pictures.

In **mental rotation** experiments, for example, participants are shown a letter or a number, either in its normal version or mirror-reversed (that is *R* or *ᴚ*). In addition, the figures are tilted so that participants might encounter an *R* rotated by, say, 180 degrees or an *ᴚ* rotated by, say, 60 degrees (see Figure 8.2). Their task is to press one button if the stimulus is normal, another if it is mirror-reversed.

As the orientation of the letters changes from upright (that is, 0 degree rotation) through 60 degrees to 180 degrees, participants' response times for making this decision steadily increase (Figure 8.3). Apparently, they perform this task by imagining the test stimulus rotating into an upright position; only then can they judge it as normal or mirror-reversed. And it seems that mental rotation, just like actual movement, takes time: The more the character has to be rotated, the longer it takes (Cooper and Shepard, 1973; Shepard and Cooper, 1982).

Another line of evidence comes from studies on **image scanning.** In a classic study, research participants were first shown the map of a fictitious island containing various objects: a hut, a well, a tree, a meadow, and so on (see Figure 8.4). After memorizing this map, the participants were asked to form a mental image of the entire island. The experimenter then named two objects on the map (say, the hut and the meadow), and the participants had to imagine a black speck zipping from the first location to the second. The results showed that the time

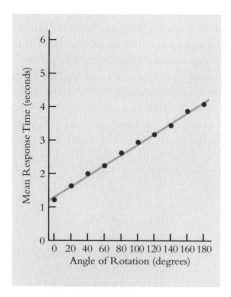

8.3   Data from a mental rotation experiment   *Research participants need to imagine a form rotating into an upright position in order to make a judgment about that form. The greater the degree of rotation required, the longer the response time. (After Shepard and Metzler, 1971)*

8.4 Image scanning *Research participants were asked to form a mental image of a map of an island and then to imagine a speck zipping from one location to another. (After Kosslyn, Ball, and Reiser, 1978)*

needed for this speck to "travel" from location to location was directly proportional to the distance between the two points. Of course, this is just what one would expect if participants were scanning a physical map with their eyes. That the same holds true when they scan a mental image with the mind's eye highlights the remarkable parallels between mental images and visual stimuli, between imaging and perceiving (Kosslyn, Ball, and Reisser, 1978).

IMAGES AND PICTURES

Clearly, then, visual images do share many properties with pictures. In particular, it seems that the spatial characteristics of the depicted scene are directly represented in the image, so that the image truly *depicts* the scene just as a picture does, rather than describing it in some symbolic fashion. Thus, if two points are close together in the to-be-represented scene, they will be functionally close together in the image; if they are far apart, they will be functionally far apart in the image. What holds for distance also holds for such spatial relations as *between*. If point *B* in the scene is between points *A* and *C,* this relation will be preserved in the image, and so one cannot mentally scan from point *A* to point *C* without passing through point *B*.

It is perhaps unsurprising, therefore, that images function just like pictures in many settings. For example, we discussed the role of mnemonic imagery in Chapter 7: Apparently, we can "discover" elements in a mental image and thus be reminded of them, just as we can with a picture. Similarly, mental images can help people solve problems, including problems that require creative solutions (Finke et al., 1992; Finke, 1993).

In addition, much evidence indicates that the process of *visualization* draws on many of the same brain areas as the processes needed for actual *vision*. Some of the evidence for this claim comes from neuroimaging techniques, using the procedures described in Chapter 2. These studies make it clear that many of the same brain regions (primarily in the occipital lobe) are active during both visual perception and visual imagery. Evidence also comes from studies of individuals with brain damage: Lesions that disrupt vision also seem to disrupt visual imagery and vice versa. Often these disruptions are quite specific. For example, patients who, because of a stroke, lose the ability to perceive color often seem to lose the ability to imagine scenes in color; patients who lose the ability to

305

8.5 **_Images are not pictures_** _The rabbit-duck figure, first used in 1900 by Joseph Jastrow._

perceive fine detail seem also to lose the ability to visualize fine detail (Foch, 1988; Isha and Sagi, 1995; Miyashita, 1995).

All of these findings point to considerable overlap between visualizing and perceiving, likewise between mental pictures and actual pictures. But alongside this overlap, there are also important contrasts here, for while images are picture*like,* they are *not* pictures. Some evidence for this view comes from a study in which research participants were shown a figure that they had never seen before. This figure is normally reversible: If it is seen as oriented toward the left, it looks like the head of a duck; if oriented toward the right, it looks like the head of a rabbit (Figure 8.5). The picture was then removed, and the participants were asked to form a mental image of this figure. They were then asked to inspect this image and describe what it looked like. All "saw" either a duck or a rabbit with their mind's eye, and some said they saw it very vividly. They were then asked whether their image might look like something else. Not one of the participants came up with a reversal, even after hints and considerable coaxing. The results were very different when they subsequently drew the figure and looked at their own drawing. Now everyone came up with the perceptual alternative. These results seem to indicate that a visual image is not a picture. It is based on a picture but is already encoded to some extent—perhaps as a duck, perhaps as a rabbit. To the extent that it is so encoded, it has lost its pictorial innocence. It is no longer ambiguous because it has already been interpreted (Chambers and Reisberg, 1985; for further discussion, see Finke, Pinker, and Farah, 1989; Reisberg, 1996).

SPATIAL THINKING

Closely related to mental imagery is **spatial thinking,** the kind that we use when we want to determine a shortcut between two locations or when we mentally try to rearrange the furniture in the living room. How are such tasks accomplished? One means is by way of mental images. By imagining the route, the traveler can find shortcuts just as she might from an actual map, and the decorator can save wear and tear on his back muscles by imagining the rearrangement before doing it.

MENTAL MAPS THAT ARE PICTURELIKE

Most people have a general conception of the layout of their environment. According to some investigators, part of this knowledge is based on mental maps that have pictorial qualities. In one study, students were asked to estimate the distances between various locations on their university campus—for example, between their dormitory and the gymnasium or between the student union and the library. The students were quite accurate in their estimates, but more important was the time it took to provide these estimates. The longer the distance, the longer the estimation time. It was as if the students measured distances with a mental ruler on a mental map, much as one might measure the length of a wall with a small ruler. The longer the wall, the more often the ruler would have to be moved from point to point, and the longer the process would take (Jonides and Baum, 1978).

MENTAL MAPS THAT ARE BOTH SYMBOLIC AND CONCEPTUAL

Other kinds of spatial thinking, however, involve processes that are symbolic, not analogical. In one study, research participants were asked to indicate the relative

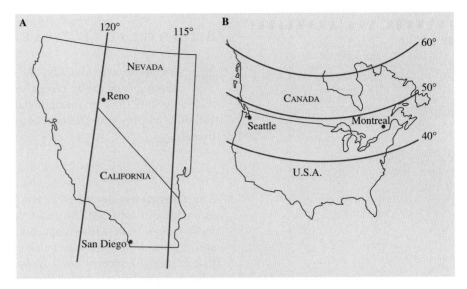

8.6 *Conceptual mental maps* *Participants tend to judge San Diego to be west of Reno and Montreal to be north of Seattle. But these judgments are in error. (A) A map of California and Nevada with colored lines of longitude (angular distance from an arbitrary reference point in Greenwich, England), which shows that, in fact, San Diego is east of Reno. (B) A map of the United States and southern Canada with colored lines of latitude (angular distance from the equator), which shows that Seattle is slightly north of Montreal. (Stevens and Coupe, 1978)*

locations of San Diego, California, and Reno, Nevada (Figure 8.6). The participants judged San Diego to be west of Reno, although it is actually farther east. Similarly, they judged Montreal, Canada, to be farther north than Seattle, Washington, although the reverse is true. These results suggest that they weren't basing their answers on mental maps at all. Instead, they seemed to be reasoning in this fashion:

> California is west of Nevada.
> San Diego is in California.
> Reno is in Nevada.
> Therefore, San Diego is west of Reno.

The knowledge being used here ("San Diego is in California") is clearly symbolic, not pictorial. Moreover, these symbolic formulations can (and in this case do) lead to error. Even so, most of us often store spatial information in such a rough-and-ready conceptual way. To the extent that we do store some geographical information under category rubrics, our spatial knowledge cannot be exclusively—or even largely—picturelike (Stevens and Coupe, 1978).

SYMBOLIC REPRESENTATIONS

Imagery is not the only kind of thinking, nor is it the most important kind. Around the turn of the century, several psychologists asked research participants to describe everything that went through their minds as they tried to solve various intellectual problems. The solution frequently came without a trace of imagery (and frequently also without words). Participants reported that they simply had a wordless, imageless sense of certain relationships, such as the experience of "this doesn't go with that" or a feeling of *if* or *but* (Humphrey, 1951).

Symbolic Elements

The attempt to describe the components of this more abstract type of thinking is relatively recent, at least in psychology. But other disciplines—including logic and linguistics—have wrestled with this issue for many years, and their progress provides crucial groundwork for psychological research in this domain.

CONCEPTS

The term *concept* describes a class or category that includes some number of individuals or subtypes. An example is *dog,* which includes *poodle, beagle, dachshund,* and *Alsatian.* Other concepts designate qualities or dimensions. Examples are *length* and *age.* Still other concepts are relational, such as *taller than.* Notice that relational concepts don't apply to any one item in isolation. One can't be *taller than* except in relation to something else to which one's height is being compared. We will have much more to say about concepts—what they are and how they are represented in the mind—in Chapter 9.

PROPOSITIONS

Concepts are what we generally think *about.* But in thinking, we combine concepts in various and sometimes complex ways. One means of combination, emphasized by the British empiricists, is *association*—a sense of "this goes with that." Often, though, our thoughts specify more precise relationships among concepts, and for this purpose, associative links may be inadquate. Many philosophers have argued, therefore, that our thoughts take the form of **propositions.** These are statements that relate a **subject** (the item about which the statement is being made) and a **predicate** (what is being asserted about the subject). Propositions can be true or false. For example, "Jacob loves to play the tin whistle," "Jennifer plays soccer," and "Squirrels eat burritos" are all propositions. But just the words "Susan," or "is squeamish" are *not* propositions—the first is a subject without a predicate; the second is a predicate without a subject.

KNOWLEDGE AND MEMORY

When we think, we often form new concepts and formulate new propositions. But many concepts and propositions are already stored in memory, where they constitute our accumulated knowledge, the "database" that sustains and informs our thoughts. How is this knowledge organized in memory, and how is it retrieved?

GENERIC MEMORY

In the previous chapter, we said a great deal about how information is stored in, and then retrieved from, memory. Many of the examples we considered in the earlier chapter were concerned with *episodic memory.* This term refers to the stored records of particular events (episodes) in one's own life, memory for what happened when and where. This contrasts with *generic memory,* which is memory for items of knowledge independent of the particular occasion on which one acquired that knowledge. For example, we remember that Paris is the capital of France, that three is the square root of nine, and that sugar is an ingredient of most cookies. Rarely, though, do we remember how or when we acquired these bits of knowledge; if we did, our recollection of these occasions would be episodic, not generic.

For each person, generic memory contains an extraordinary wealth of knowledge, including the meanings of words and symbols, countless facts about the world, what objects look like, and various general principles, schemas, and scripts. Within this huge archive, one of the important components is **semantic memory,** which concerns the meanings of words and concepts. As some authors conceive it, our entire vocabulary is in this store: every word, together with its pronunciation, all of its meanings, its relations to objects in the real world, and the way it is put together with other words to make phrases and sentences. How do we ever find information in this bulky mental dictionary? Clearly, there must be some sort of organizational system; otherwise, the hunt for an entry might last for days. But what is that system?

A HIERARCHICAL NETWORK

Several investigators have proposed **network models** of generic memory. In these models, words and concepts are linked through a complex system of relationships, so that it is possible to trace a path through these relationships from one concept to other related concepts. Within these networks, words or concepts are represented by **nodes,** while the associations between the concepts are indicated by **associative links** or **associative connections** (see Figure 8.7).

One hypothesis, proposed early on, was that the network has a hierarchical structure. Thus, words naming relatively specific concepts (say, *canary*) would be stored under the relevant higher-order category (in this case, *bird*), which in turn would be stored under a yet higher category (*animal*). Within this system, properties would be stored under the higher-order category, rather than the lower. Thus, "has wings" and "has feathers" would be associated with *bird*, and not with *canary, robin,* and each of the other kinds of birds. The feature "is yellow," however, would be associated with *canary,* since this is an attribute of canaries, but not of birds in general (see Figure 8.8; Collins and Quillian, 1969).

This hierarchical model is very neat, but as so often happens, nature is not as neat as theorists might wish. To mention only one problem, membership in many semantic categories does not seem to be an all-or-none affair. For example, Americans rate robins as highly typical birds, chickens as less typical, and penguins as less typical still (Rosch, 1973a, b). These differences in typicality are not a matter of whimsy; instead, typicality has a robust effect on the way semantic memories are accessed. For example, research participants are faster in agreeing that "*X* is a bird," if *X* is a typical bird, like a canary, rather than a marginal case, like a penguin or an ostrich (Rips, Shoben, and Smith, 1973; Rips, Smith, and Shoben, 1978). Such effects suggest that the relation between items of information in semantic memory is more complex than the hierarchical model indicates (e.g., Conrad, 1972; for further discussion, see Chapter 9).

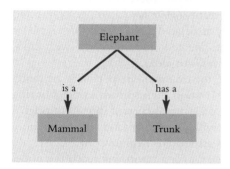

8.7 Network structure in semantic memory models *The figure shows a small section of a semantic memory model, with nodes (elephant, mammal, trunk) connected through associative links. Some networks employ labeled associations that indicate the particular relations between the nodes (such as, is a, has, and so on).*

8.8 A hierarchical theory of semantic memory *To decide whether the sentence "Ravens have feathers" is true, given the organization of the entries depicted here, one has to "look up" the information at the second level, under* bird.

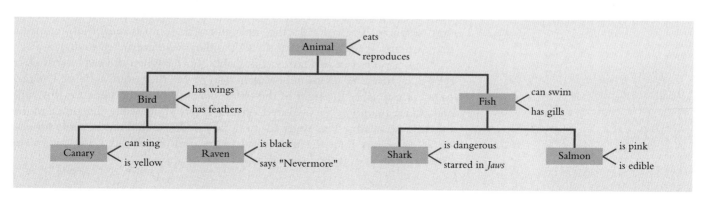

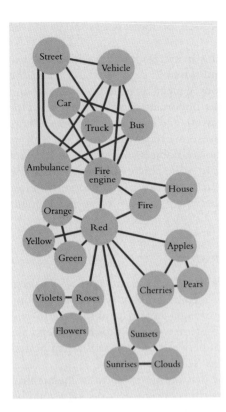

8.9   The spreading activation model
The figure shows a very small portion of the semantic network postulated by the spreading activation model. The shorter the path, the stronger the semantic relation. (After Collins and Loftus, 1975)

A NETWORK MODEL BASED ON SEMANTIC DISTANCE

Difficulties with the hierarchical model led to the formulation of several alternatives, one of which is the **spreading activation model.** In this model, concepts are still represented by nodes, with associative links connecting one node to the next. However, this model allows these links to represent many different kinds of relationships, including relationships based on hierarchical position (as in *canary-bird*) or based on similarity of meaning (*apple-orange*) or on well-learned associations (*peanut butter-jelly*). In addition, the links among these concepts can vary in strength, so that two frequently associated terms (*white-house*) will be connected via a strong linkage, whereas less frequently associated terms (*father-niece*) will be connected via a weak linkage or perhaps connected only indirectly (with links, perhaps, from *father* to *uncle* and then from *uncle* to *niece*).

In this model, nodes can be activated if, for example, the person is currently thinking about the node's content. This activation then spreads to neighboring nodes, through the associative links, much as electrical current spreads through a network of wires. The spread of activation will be stronger (and will occur more quickly) between nodes that are strongly associated. Moreover, the activation will dissipate as it spreads outward, so little or no activation will reach the nodes more distant from the activation's source (Collins and Loftus, 1975; see Figure 8.9; these ideas are also closely related to the notion of a feature net, which we discussed in Chapter 6).

How can these claims be tested? One line of evidence came from a study in which broad semantic categories were activated. Research participants were asked to think of a word that begins with a certain letter and that also belongs to a particular category, such as *G-fruit* (sensible answers would be *grape* or *grape-fruit*). Shortly thereafter, participants were tested again, and on some trials, the same category was requested, but with a different initial letter (perhaps *S-fruit*). The data showed that the time needed to retrieve a suitable word (*strawberry*) was shorter if the category was repeated in this way. Apparently, the first trial had activated words associated with the term *fruit,* and so the nodes for these words were already "warmed up" at the start of the second trial. This made it easier to activate these nodes when they were needed for the second trial, with a corresponding savings in response time (Loftus, 1973).

Further evidence comes from experiments on **semantic priming.** In the classic study in this area, participants were presented with two strings of letters, one printed above the other (Meyer and Schvaneveldt, 1971). Three examples are:

nurse   nurse   narde
butter   doctor   doctor

The participants' job was to press a "yes" button if both sequences were real words (for example, *nurse-butter* or *nurse-doctor*) and a "no" button if either was not a word (e.g., *narde-doctor*). Our interest is in the two pairs that required a "yes" response. (In these tasks, the "no" items serve only as **catch trials,** ensuring that participants really are doing the task as they were instructed to do.)

Response times in this task were reliably shorter when the two words were related in meaning (as in *nurse-doctor*) than when they were unrelated (*nurse-butter*). Presumably, the sight of the word *nurse* activated the node for this concept. Once the node was activated, activation spread out from this source to the other nodes nearby. This warmed-up nearby nodes, including the node for *doctor.* If *doctor* was then the next word to be dealt with, this warm-up led to easier activation of its node and thus to a faster response.

PARALLEL DISTRIBUTED PROCESSING

The network models we've discussed so far employ a system of *local representations.* This means that each concept—say, the concept *fire engine*—is represented by a particular node or set of nodes. When these nodes are activated, one is thinking about fire engines, and when one is thinking about fire engines, these nodes are activated.

The past two decades, however, have seen the development of a new type of network model, employing ***distributed representations.*** In these models, each concept is represented, not by a single node, but by a pattern of activation across the entire network. To take a highly simplified case, the concept *fire engine* might be represented by a pattern in which nodes *A, D, H,* and *Q* are firing, whereas the concept *ambulance* might be represented by a pattern in which nodes *D, F, L,* and *T* are firing. In this case, node *D* is part of the pattern that represents *fire engine* but also part of the pattern that represents *ambulance* and many other concepts as well. Thus, the *D* node, by itself, does not represent anything; the significance of this node is only interpretable in the broader context of other nodes' activities.

This representational format has important consequences for our understanding of how the network functions. Imagine being asked, "What equipment would you find in an ambulance?" To answer, the concept *ambulance* must trigger a number of other concepts (*stretcher, oxygen tank,* and so on). With distributed representations, this triggering must involve a process in which all of the nodes representing *ambulance* somehow manage collectively to activate the broad pattern of nodes representing (say) *oxygen tank.* In the (simplified) terms we used a moment ago, node *D* might trigger node *H* at the same time that node *F* triggers node *Q,* and so on, leading ultimately to the activation of the *H-Q-S-Y* combination that, let's say, represents *oxygen tank.* In short, then, a network using distributed representations must employ processes that are similarly distributed, so that one widespread activation pattern (e.g., that for *ambulance*) can have broad enough effects to evoke a different (but equally widespread) pattern. Moreover, the steps bringing this about must all occur simultaneously—in parallel—with each other, so that one entire representation can smoothly trigger the next entire representation. That is why this sort of model is said to involve ***parallel distributed processing,*** or ***PDP*** for short. Models of this type are also described as ***connectionist,*** highlighting the fact that the functioning of these models depends on having just the right connections at just the right strengths.

How do these distributed processes work? Consider an espionage story in which a master spy works out an ingenious plot to overthrow the government. The plot involves one hundred different operatives, but to ensure secrecy, the master spy has made certain that none of the operatives knows anything about the overall plan. Each knows only her own little part—just that small bit that she's been instructed to do. And now chance enters: Immediately after instructing the last operative, the master spy dies of a heart attack. This won't, however, terminate the scheme. All of the operatives have their orders and need no further supervision; the plot will presumably run by itself, even after the master spy's death.

Notice the peculiar status of the master spy's plan in this situation. As long as the master spy was alive, the overall plot was represented in her thoughts—there was, therefore, a local representation of the entire scheme. After the master's death, there is no local representation of the plan. There's surely none in the minds of the individual operatives, since each knows only a tiny part of the whole. Still, in a way, the overall plan continues to exist, and it would be seen if only we could view all the operatives simultaneously and understand how the actions of each fit into the whole. The plan is thus represented in a distributed fashion, manifest in the collective and simultaneous activity of all the operatives. And whether we perceive it or not, the plan will go forward, because of the distributed pattern of the operatives' actions (Reisberg, 1997). This fanciful arrangement is exactly the sort needed for a PDP model.

Working models of this type have been devised for many cognitive operations, including pattern recognition, memory processes, and aspects of thinking and language (McClelland and Rumelhart, 1986; Churchland and Sejnowski, 1992; Rumelhart, 1997). Indeed, proponents of this approach believe that eventually all cognitive operations will be described in these terms. They argue that, in general, the complex phenomena of mental functioning are best understood as the result of many much smaller events, much as an avalanche is produced by the movement of many small stones and rocks. These smaller events are each computationally simple, but that's okay, since each is responsible only for a fraction of the overall achievement, much as the operatives in the spy story were each responsible only for a bit of the overall scheme.

Proponents of this approach also argue that claims about distributed processing fit well with what we know about the cerebral machinery that underlies cognition. More specifically, they assert that the brain's functioning is more similar to that of PDP networks than it is to networks modeled along traditional lines (e.g., with local rather than distributed representations). For this reason, PDP models are sometimes referred to with the ambitious label of **neural networks.** Let us be careful, though, in understanding this label: These are not networks made up of neurons but, instead, networks hypothesized to function as we believe assemblies of neurons do.

These proposals have led to considerable debate, with some researchers strongly advocating neural net or connectionist models and other researchers claiming that these models are sharply limited in what they can accomplish (e.g., Pinker and Prince, 1988; Hetherington and Seidenberg, 1989; McCloskey and Cohen, 1989; Ramsey, Stich, and Rumelhart, 1991). How this debate will turn out remains to be seen. This is an exciting area of research, and new advances are coming at a rapid rate.

THE PROCESS OF THINKING: SOLVING PROBLEMS

Thus far, we have been describing what we mean by *thinking* and offering various models for how thinking works. We turn next to the question of how thought proceeds in a particular area: problem solving.

ORGANIZATION IN PROBLEM SOLVING

How do we proceed when we are trying to repair a broken bicycle, or for that matter, a damaged friendship? In some cases, the solution to quandaries like these is suggested by immediately available cues (you can see that the bike's chain has fallen off the gears) or perhaps a specific memory (you recall that the friend likes receiving flowers). In other cases, though, we must search for a solution, because the problem is one we have never solved before.

This search is far from random; it proceeds with constant reference to two anchors: the current situation, on the one hand, and the goal, on the other. Consider a taxi driver who is trying to choose the best route to the airport. His

NAGMARA

BOLMPER

SLEVO

STIGNIH

TOLUSONI

*8.10 **Anagrams*** *Rearrange the letters on each line to form a word. (For the solution, see p. 316.)*

*8.11 **Nine-dot problem*** *Nine dots are arranged in a square. Connect them by drawing four continuous straight lines without lifting your pencil from the paper. (For the solution, see p. 320.)*

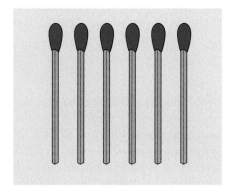

thoughts are guided both by his current location and by thoughts about his destination. Perhaps the taxi is close to the freeway, but this isn't enough to direct the driver toward the highway's on-ramp. Instead, he is likely to ask: "Will this path bring me where I want to go?" If the highway heads in the wrong direction, or if the driver remembers some road construction along that route, he's likely to seek an alternative path. This process of checking current options against one's goal is a central part of problem solving. In fact, some researchers argue that a crucial strategy for problem solving is a ***means-end analysis*** in which one asks, over and over as the problem solving proceeds, "How can I use the means now available to me to get closer to my goal?" (Newell and Simon, 1972).

In laboratory studies of problem solving, research participants have been asked to solve a variety of problems—deciphering anagrams (Figure 8.10), finding the solution to geometrical problems (8.11), or manipulating objects to produce a desired result (Figure 8.12). It is hardly surprising that people differ in how they attack and solve these diverse problems: A person who tries to join nine dots with one line will surely call upon a different set of skills than one who has to rearrange letters to form an English word. But in all cases, the problem solver's efforts are directed toward a goal.

HIERARCHICAL ORGANIZATION

Problem solving is not merely goal directed, it is also *hierarchical:* The effort to solve one problem often creates ***subproblems,*** so that one needs to reach certain ***subgoals*** on the way toward achieving the main goal. And here, too, means-end analysis is helpful: "I want to get to the store. What's the difference between my current state and my goal? One of distance. What changes distance? My automobile. My automobile won't work. What is needed to make it work? A new battery...." In this case, the initial problem (getting to the store) is replaced by a series of subproblems (e.g., getting the car to work). By solving these, one at a time, the larger problem gets dealt with (Newell and Simon, 1972).

Often, the subproblems one encounters are relatively straightforward. For example, the taxi driver might realize that his best path to the airport is indeed the freeway, and so the larger problem ("get to the airport") can be replaced with a simpler and more familiar ***routine*** ("take the freeway"). This routine is in turn composed of still simpler ***subroutines,*** such as "go to the on-ramp at Front Street," "accelerate when the light turns green," or even "maneuver through traffic." In this fashion, a series of modular units can be assembled into the larger-scale solution to the initial problem (Figure 8.13).

This reliance on subroutines can lead to great efficiency. The modular units are often well practiced, and this allows the problem solver to focus attention on the larger-scale plan, rather than worrying about the details of how the plan is to be implemented. In fact, this is one of the reasons why problems that seem impossible for the novice are absurdly easy for the expert: Even when the expert is facing a novel problem, she is likely to rely on a number of familiar subroutines that are already available as "chunks" in memory. Thus, the expert taxi driver gives little thought to maneuvering through traffic and so can focus his thoughts on the more general task of navigation. The novice driver must focus on the maneuvering, and, preoccupied with this, may miss his exit.

*8.12 **Matchstick problem*** *Assemble all six matches to form four equilateral triangles, each side of which is equal to the length of one match. (For the solution, see p. 320.)*

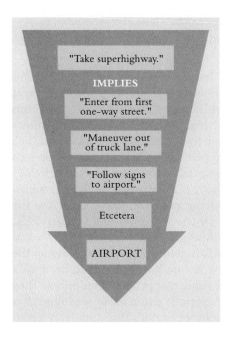

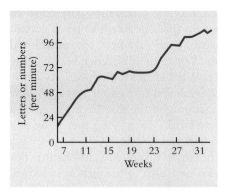

8.14 An apprentice telegrapher's learning curve *The curve plots the number of letters or digits the operator could receive per minute against weeks of practice. Note the plateau in the learning curve. The curve stays level from weeks 16 to 23 and then starts to rise again. According to Bryan and Harter, the new rise indicates the use of larger chunks. (After Bryan and Harter, 1899)*

8.13 Hierarchical organization of a plan *Plans have components that have still lower-level subcomponents, as here illustrated by the taxi driver's task.*

SKILLS AS THE DEVELOPMENT OF SUBROUTINES

These suggestions imply that subroutines play an important role in the development of skill, and the evidence indicates that this is correct, both for mental skills, such as reading or doing arithmetic, and for skills involving the perceptual and motor systems, such as typing or playing tennis.

The role of subroutines is well illustrated by one of the earliest studies in this area, a study focusing on how telegraph operators mastered their trade—learning to send and receive Morse code messages at a high rate. The student operators were apprentices at a telegraph company, and their on-the-job learning was charted over a period of about forty weeks. Figure 8.14 plots one student's performance, and the pattern of improvement is clearly uneven. Following an initial rise, this learning curve flattens into a plateau, so that there is little visible improvement from week 16 to week 23. But then the curve rises again until it reaches another plateau (Bryan and Harter, 1897).

These plateaus actually represent crucial periods in the learning process. During the first fifteen weeks, the apprentice was focusing on the individual letters being sent or received. This is an inefficient way to perform the task, since it takes no advantage of the patterns and redundancies within the language (for example, the fact that *q* is almost invariably followed by *u* or that *st* is generally followed by either a vowel or an *r*). But no matter how helpful these patterns might be, they are inaccessible to the novice: He is so busy deciphering each letter that there is no time left over for thinking about anything else—such as spelling patterns or word sequences. Of course, the student does improve in recognizing individual letters—this is what's happening across the first dozen weeks of practice. Eventually, though, the limitations of this strategy become apparent, and the operator hits a temporary ceiling—he has become as fast as he can be with this inefficient letter-by-letter strategy. (In Figure 8.14, this has happened by week 15 or so.)

As practice continues, letter recognition becomes more and more automatic, freeing the student (at last!) to devote some attention to the larger units—the syllables or even whole words. This allows him to start using the patterns within the message, so that actual perception can be supplemented to some extent by inference; in some cases, the operator may even be able to anticipate the message before it arrives. It is this which leads to the improved performance visible in Figure 8.14 starting in week 23.

Similar effects have been observed in the acquisition of many other skills, including both physical skills and mental ones. In all cases, the pattern is the same: Early on, the lower-level aspects of the task consume our attention. With practice, these same aspects become automatic and can largely be taken for granted. They become, in other words, subroutines within the larger task, and this frees us to contemplate the larger-scale aspects of the situation, rather than fretting about the details.

EXPERTS

These ideas about skill improvement can be developed still further to describe the extreme levels of skill that make someone an expert in a particular domain. Of course, experts have several different advantages when compared to those of more modest skill. For one, experts simply know more in their domain of expertise. In addition, an expert's knowledge is heavily cross-referenced, so that each bit of information has associations with many other bits, making the knowledge easily accessed when needed (Bédard and Chi, 1992). Crucially, though, and consistent with our previous discussion, experts also have a different sort of knowledge than novices do, knowledge focused on higher-order patterns. As a consequence, experts can, in effect, think in larger units, tackling problems in big steps rather than small ones.

Consider studies of chess players (de Groot, 1965; Chase and Simon, 1973a, b). In one study, players at different levels of expertise (including two former world champions) were posed various chess problems and asked to select the best move. All of the masters chose continuations that would have won the game, while few of the other players did. Why? Many theorists believe that the reason lies in the way the players organized the problem. The chess masters structured the chess position in terms of broad strategic concepts (e.g., *a king-side attack with pawns*) from which many of the appropriate moves follow naturally. In effect, the masters have a "chess vocabulary" in which these complex concepts are stored as single memory chucks, each with an associated set of subroutines for how one should respond to that pattern. Some estimate, in fact, that the masters may have as many as 50,000 of these chunks in their memories, each representing a strategic pattern (Chase and Simon, 1973a).

These chunks can be detected in many ways, including the pattern of a player's eye movements as she inspects the board, and also in the way that players remember a game. For example, players of different ranks were shown chess positions for five seconds each and then asked to reproduce the positions a few minutes later. Grandmasters and masters did so with hardly an error; lesser players performed much worse (see Figure 8.15). This is not because the chess masters had better visual memory. When presented with bizarre positions, unlikely ever to arise in the course of a game, they recalled them no better than novices did, and in some cases, they remembered these bizarre patterns *less* accurately than did novices (Gobet and Simon, 1996a, b). The superiority of the masters, therefore, was in their conceptual organization of chess, not in their memory for patterns as such.

We should say again that these chess masters, like experts in general, have other advantages in addition to their huge vocabulary of chess chunks. For example, they are also better in evaluating chess positions and look further ahead in their mental calculations (Charness, 1981; Holding and Reynolds, 1982; Holding, 1985). But chunks, and their associated subroutines, clearly play a major role in this mental skill, just as they do in telegraphy, typing, and tennis (e.g., Allard, Graham, and Paarsalu, 1980).

8.15 Memory for chess positions in masters and average players *(A) An actual chess position that was presented for five seconds after which the positions of the pieces had to be reconstructed. Typical performances by masters and average players are shown in (B) and (C) respectively, with errors indicated in red. (After Hearst, 1972)*

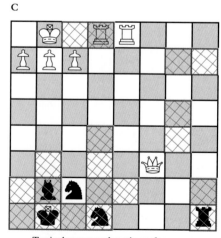

A

Actual position

B

Typical master player's performance

C

Typical average player's performance

A	B
ZYP	RED
QLEKF	BLACK
SUWRG	YELLOW
XCIDB	BLUE
WOPR	RED
ZYP	GREEN
QLEKF	YELLOW
XCIDB	BLACK
SUWRG	BLUE
WOPR	BLACK
SUWRG	RED
ZYP	YELLOW
XCIDB	GREEN
QLEKF	BLUE
WOPR	GREEN
QLEKF	BLUE
WOPR	RED
ZYP	YELLOW
XCIDB	BLACK
SWRG	GREEN

8.16 The Stroop effect The two lists, A and B, are printed in four colors—red, green, blue, and yellow. To observe the Stroop effect, name the colors (aloud) in which each of the nonsense syllables in list A is printed as fast as you can, continuing downward. Then do the same for list B, calling out the colors in which each of the words of the list is printed, again going from top to bottom. This will very probably be easier for list A than for list B, a demonstration of the Stroop effect.

ANAGRAM

PROBLEM

SOLVE

INSIGHT

SOLUTION

Solution to anagrams (Figure 8.10, p. 313)

AUTOMATICITY

The reliance on familiar routines has many advantages. As we have discussed, it allows the problem solver to focus on the more strategic aspects of a problem, rather than on the details. The vocabulary of patterns supplied by memory can also serve to organize the problem from the very start, highlighting useful subgoals. Thus, novices tend to focus on the surface form of a physics problem and so might group together, say, all the problems involving springs or all the problems involving inclined planes. Experts, in contrast, instantly perceive the deeper structure of each problem, and so they group the problems, not according to surface features, but according to the physical principles relevant to each problem's solution. Here, too, the initial perception—in terms of higher-order patterns—calls attention to the strategies needed for solving the problem (Chi, Feltovich, and Glaser, 1981).

This reliance on routine can become so well practiced, so familiar, that the routine is executed without much thought. The routine, in other words, becomes *automatic* and so is performed with minimal attention. Often this is just what one wants, but in some circumstances this **automaticity** can create its own problems: Automatic actions, once set in motion, are difficult to turn off or modify.

A striking example of this is known as the **Stroop effect,** named after its discoverer (Stroop, 1935). To demonstrate this effect, research participants are asked to name the colors in which groups of letters are printed (Figure 8.16). If the letters are random sequences (*fwis, sgbr*) or irrelevant words (*chair, tape*), this task is rather easy. If, however, the letters form color names (*yellow, red*), the task becomes much harder. Thus, a participant might see *red* printed in green ink, *blue* in brown ink, and so on. His task, of course, is simply to name the ink color, and so he should say "green, brown," etc. But in this setting, the participant can't help reading the words, and this produces a strong competing response: He is likely to respond very slowly, because while trying to name the ink colors, he is fighting the tendency to read the words themselves aloud.

OBSTACLES TO PROBLEM SOLVING

So far, we have discussed only the general structure of problem solving—its constant orientation toward the goal, its hierarchical nature, its reliance on memory patterns and subroutines. But no matter how hard we try, some problems—whether an infuriating crossword puzzle or a demoralizing job dispute—seem downright intractable. Can our knowledge about how problem solving works help us in approaching these complex problems?

We have already mentioned one crucial factor: Problem solvers, be they novices or experts, bring certain assumptions and habits with them whenever they approach a problem. Some of these assumptions, whether those of expert or novice, are sensible and productive. For instance, a taxi driver—even a beginner—does not waste time wondering whether a magic carpet might be the fastest transport to the airport; and even a novice cook realizes that pickles are an unpalatable topping for the morning's pancakes. But sometimes these background assumptions are wrong or at least inappropriate to the present situation. In this case, the would-be problem solver may end up a victim of his own often unnoticed assumptions, misled by a powerful **mental set.**

A well-known study illustrates this point and shows how people can become fixated on one approach to a task and correspondingly unable to think of the task in any other way. The participants in this study were told that they had three jars, *A, B,* and *C.* Jar A held exactly 21 quarts; jar *B* held exactly 127

TABLE 8.1 THE THREE-CONTAINER PROBLEM

Desired quantity of water (quarts)	Volume of empty jar (quarts)		
	A	*B*	*C*
99	14	163	25
5	18	43	10
21	9	42	6
31	20	59	4

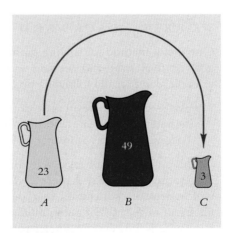

8.17   The standard method for solving the three-container problem   *(After Luchins, 1942)*

quarts; jar *C* held exactly 3 quarts. The participants' job was to use these three jars to obtain exactly 100 quarts from a well.

Participants required a few minutes to solve this problem, but they generally did solve it: The solution is to fill *B* (127 quarts) completely and then pour out enough water from *B* to fill *A*. Now 106 quarts remain in *B* (127 − 21). Next, pour enough water out of *B*, to fill up *C* (3 quarts), leaving 103 quarts in *B*. Finally, dump out *C* and fill it again from *B*, leaving the desired amount—100 quarts—in *B* (Figure 8.17).

Participants then did several more problems, all of the same type. The numerical values differed in each problem (Table 8.1), but in each case, the solution could be obtained by the same sequence of steps: Fill *B*, pour from it into *A*, then pour from *B* into *C*, empty out *C*, and pour again from *B* into *C*. In each case, in other words, the desired amount could be reached by the arithmetical sequence of $B - A - 2C$.

After five such problems, the participants were given two critical tests. The first was a problem that required them to obtain 20 quarts, given jars whose volumes were 23, 49, and 3 quarts. The participants cheerfully solved this problem, using the same sequence—49 − 23 − (2 × 3). They reliably failed to notice that there is a simpler method available for this problem, one that requires only a single step (Figure 8.18).

The participants were next asked to obtain 25 quarts, given jars of 28, 76, and 3 quarts. Note that here the only method that will work is the direct one, that is, 28 − 3 = 25 (Figure 8.19). But the mental set was so powerful that many failed

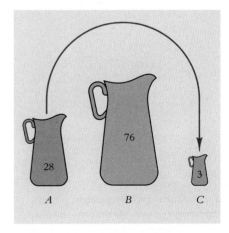

8.18   A simpler method for solving certain three-container problems   *(After Luchins, 1942)*

8.19   A case where only the simple method works   *(After Luchins, 1942)*

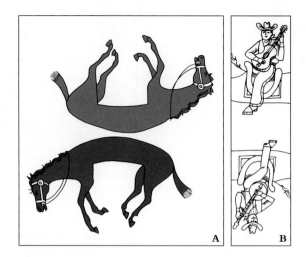

8.20 Horse-and-rider problem *The task is to place* B *on* A *in such a way that the riders are properly astride the horses. (After Scheerer, Goldstein, and Boring, 1941; for solution, see p. 325.)*

to solve the problem altogether. They tried the old procedure, but this did not lead them to the goal $(76 - 28 - [2 \times 3] \neq 25)$, and they could not hit on an adequate alternative! The set had made them so rigid that they became mentally blind (Luchins, 1942).

Other kinds of problems produce similar effects. In many of these there is no need to induce the misleading set by instructions or prior practice; instead, it is engendered by the perceptual arrangement of the problem itself. Examples of such perceptually induced sets are the nine-dot problem (Figure 8.11) and the horse-and-rider problem (Figure 8.20).

OVERCOMING OBSTACLES TO SOLUTION

We should emphasize again that mental sets are generally good things, allowing the problem solver to focus on sensible lines of approach, avoiding unproductive tangents. However, these same sets can cause difficulties, leading us to ask: How can these sets be overcome? Similarly, we have emphasized the importance of subgoals and familiar routines, but what can we do if we fail to perceive the subgoals, or are unfamiliar with the relevant routine?

WORKING BACKWARD

One useful method for solving problems is to work backward, starting with the goal or final state and seeking a path back toward the starting point. For example, consider the following problem:

> Water lilies double in area every twenty-four hours. On the first day of summer, there is one water lily on a lake. It takes sixty days for the lake to become covered with water lilies. On what day is the lake half covered?

This problem can be tackled in this fashion: On day 1, there is one lily; on day 2, there are two; on day 3, there are four; and so on. With sufficient patience, this will lead to the conclusion that, on day 60, there will be 580 million billion lilies; half of this is 290 million billion, which would have been reached on day 59. There is, however, a simpler path, one that skips all the calculations: If the lake is fully covered on day 60, it must be half covered on the day before, since lilies double in area every day, which means that the answer is day 59 (after Sternberg and Davidson, 1983; see Figure 8.21).

8.21 The water-lily problem *Water lilies double in area every twenty-four hours. On the first day of summer, there is one water lily as in* A. *On the sixtieth day, the lake is all covered, as in* B. *On what day is the lake half-covered?*

FINDING AN APPROPRIATE ANALOGY

Another suggestion for solving difficult problems is to work by analogy, since many problems are similar to each other. A school counselor is likely to find that the problem he hears about today reminds him of one he heard a few months back, and his experience with the first can help with the second. Similarly, the scientist seeking to understand some new phenomenon often benefits from thinking back to other, similar, phenomena. In fact, analogies have often played an important role in the history of science, with scientists expanding their knowledge of gases by comparing the molecules to billiard balls or enlarging their understanding of the heart by comparing it to a pump, and the like (Gentner and Jeziorski, 1989).

The benefits of analogy are also evident in the laboratory. In one study, research participants were given this problem, devised by Duncker (1945):

> Suppose a patient has an inoperable stomach tumor. There are certain rays that can destroy this tumor if their intensity is great enough. At this intensity, however, the rays will also destroy the healthy tissue that surrounds the tumor (e.g., the stomach walls, the abdominal muscles, and so on). How can the tumor be destroyed without damaging the healthy tissue through which the rays must travel on their way?

This problem is quite difficult, and in this experiment, 90 percent of the participants failed to solve it. A second group, however, did much better: Before tackling the tumor problem, they read a story about a general who hoped to capture a fortress. He needed a large force of soldiers for this, but all of the roads leading to the fortress were planted with mines. Small groups of soldiers could travel the roads safely, but the mines would be detonated by a larger group. How, therefore, could the general move all the soldiers he'd need toward the fortress? by dividing his army into small groups and sending each group via a different road. When he gave the signal, all the groups marched toward the fortress, where they converged and attacked successfully.

The fortress story is similar in its structure to the tumor problem. In both cases, the solution is to divide the "conquering" force so that it enters from several different directions. Thus, to destroy the tumor, several weak rays can be sent through the body, each from a different angle. The rays converge at the tumor, inflicting their combined effects just as desired (Figure 8.22).

With no hints, instructions, or analogous cases, 90 percent of the participants failed to solve the tumor problem. However, if they were given the fortress story to read and told that it would help them, most (about 80 percent) did solve it. Obviously, the analogy was massively helpful. But it's not enough merely to know about the fortress story; participants also had to realize that the story is pertinent to the task at hand. And, surprisingly, they often failed to make this discovery: In another condition, participants read the fortress story but weren't given any indication that this story was relevant to their task. In this condition, only 30 percent solved the tumor problem (Gick and Holyoak, 1980, 1983).

Given how beneficial analogies can be, is there anything we can do to encourage their use? Evidence suggests that people are more likely to use analogies if they are encouraged to focus on the underlying dynamic of the analogies (e.g., the fact that the fortress problem involves converging forces) rather than their more superficial features (e.g., the fact that the problem involves mines). This calls attention to the features shared by the problems, helping people to see the relevance of the analogies and helping them to map one problem onto another (Needham and Begg, 1991; Cummins, 1992).

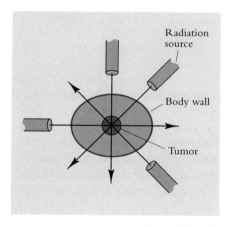

8.22 Solution to the ray-tumor problem *Several weak rays are sent from various points outside so that they meet at the tumor site. There the radiation of the rays will be intense, for all the effects will summate at this point. But since they are individually weak, the rays will not damage the healthy tissue that surrounds the tumor. (After Duncker, 1945)*

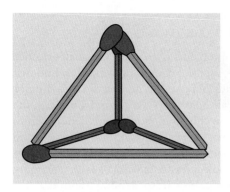

Solution to the matchstick problem *To arrange six matches (see Figure 8.12, p. 313) into four equilateral triangles, the matches have to be assembled into a three-dimensional pyramid. Most participants implicitly assume the matches must lie flat. (After Scheerer, 1963)*

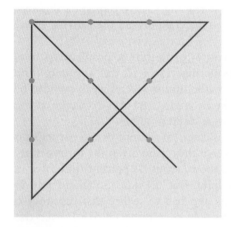

Solution to the nine-dot problem *The problem (see Figure 8.11, p. 313) is solved by going outside of the square frame into which the dots are perceptually grouped. The lines have to be extended beyond the dots as shown. Most participants fail to hit on this solution because of a perceptual set imposed by the square arrangement.*

RESTRUCTURING

Whether a problem is solved or not also depends on how the problem is interpreted or defined. We have already seen this in our discussion of analogies: Understanding a problem in terms of its surface elements may inhibit analogy use, whereas focusing on the problem's underlying dynamic may promote it. But there are other ways in which a problem's interpretation proves even more important.

For example, some problems initially seem quite difficult. Some time later, however, the problem solver discovers an alternative way to conceptualize the problem, breaking the mental set that inhibited her, and soon after, comes up with the answer. Sometimes, this ***restructuring*** of a problem may be quite sudden, experienced as a flash of insight, with an accompanying exclamation of "Aha!" (You may have experienced something similar when you finally solved the nine-dot or matchstick problem, Figures 8.11 and 8.12.)

It should be said, though, that these flashes of insight are sometimes false alarms, because our new interpretation or new approach may lead to yet another dead end (Metcalfe, 1986; Metcalfe and Weibe, 1987). Perhaps, then, the "Aha" experience should be understood simply as "I've discovered a new approach!" Whether this approach will turn out to be productive can only be decided after the fact. One way or another, though, these changes in the way a problem is defined are often essential for breaking out of an unproductive set and moving toward one that may lead to a solution.

CREATIVE THINKING

The restructuring of a problem also plays an important role in those special discoveries we consider creative. In general, scholars call the solution to a problem creative if that solution is both new and valuable or useful. Creativity is of course evident in the scientific discoveries of Marie Curie, the artistic innovations of Martha Graham, or the literary achievements of Toni Morrison. But creativity is also visible—albeit on a modest scale—in many ordinary achievements, ranging from a new conversational ploy to an improved recipe to a novel argument in a term paper.

What leads to these creative achievements? Many factors contribute, but one pattern figures prominently in reports by the creators themselves when they describe how their insights or discoveries arose. In case after case, these accounts indicate that critical insights arrive rather abruptly, typically at unexpected times and places. Often, the thinker has been working steadily on the problem for some time but making relatively little progress. She then sets the problem aside in order to rest or to engage in some other activity. It is during this other activity that the insight emerges—not while at the writer's desk or the composer's piano, but while riding in a carriage (Beethoven, Darwin), while stepping onto a bus (the great mathematician Poincaré), or in the most celebrated case of all, while sitting in a bathtub (Archimedes; see Figure 8.23).

This pattern has often been attributed to a process of ***incubation*** (Wallas, 1926). The idea here is that the thinker believes she has set the problem aside but is actually continuing to think about it unconsciously. Some authors have suggested that this unconscious incubation is actually more creative and less constrained than conscious thought, and this is why solutions to vexing problems so often appear during periods when, on the surface, the thinker is paying attention to some altogether different matter.

Many researchers, however, are skeptical about these claims. One reason is that time away from a problem does not reliably promote its solution. In some stud-

THE PROCESS OF THINKING: SOLVING PROBLEMS

8.23 Archimedes in his bathtub *A sixteenth-century engraving celebrating a great example of creative restructuring. The Greek scientist Archimedes (287–212 B.C.) tried to determine whether the king's crown was made of solid gold or had been adulterated with silver. Archimedes knew the weight of gold and silver per unit volume but did not know how to measure the volume of a complicated object such as a crown. One day, in his bath, he noticed how the water level rose as he immersed his body. Here was the solution: The crown's volume can be determined by the water it displaces. Carried away by his sudden insight, he jumped out of his bath and ran naked through the streets of Syracuse, shouting "Eureka! I have found it!" (Engraving by Walter H. Ryff, courtesy of The Granger Collection)*

ies it does; in other studies it does not. Of course, everyday reports of creativity do emphasize these unexpected insights, but it is conceivable that this simply reflects a bias in reporting: A sudden inspiration while sitting in a bathtub is surprising and worth mentioning to one's friends; progress while working steadily along at one's desk may not be. As a result, the former—even if rare—becomes part of our cultural lore, whereas the latter, perhaps more common, does not.

Even when time away from a problem *is* beneficial, incubation may not be the reason. As an alternative, time away from a problem may simply allow fatigue and frustration to dissipate, and this by itself may be helpful. In addition, the time away may allow the problem solver to shake off unproductive mental sets (Wickelgren, 1974; Smith and Blakenship, 1989; Anderson, 1990). With the passage of time, the thinker can forget, or lose interest in, those lines of attack that initially seemed attractive. Moreover, a drastic change of retrieval cues (the woods or the bathtub) will make the reinstatement of this earlier frame of mind less likely. This obviously increases the likelihood that a different, and possibly more productive, set will be selected. Of course, the chances of this occurring are greater if one is totally familiar with all the ins and outs of the problem, and especially if one has the talents of a Beethoven or an Archimedes. Unfortunately, just taking a bath is not enough.

RESTRUCTURING AND HUMOR

Restructuring is, as we have seen, crucial for insightful problem solving. But the same process also plays a role in a very different context: humor. Indeed, problem solving and humor have several things in common. For example, jokes typically require some insight, since a joke won't strike us as funny unless we get the point. Conversely, insights sometimes have a comical aspect, especially when one recognizes how absurdly simple a problem's solution really is.

In addition, both insight and humor often involve a dramatic shift from one cognitive organization to another (e.g., Suls, 1972, 1983; see Figure 8.24). In a joke, an expectation is created during the joke's setup, only to be dashed by the punch line. This is why so many jokes involve a set of three (three sheep, three lawyers, or some such). The first in the trio establishes the precedent. The

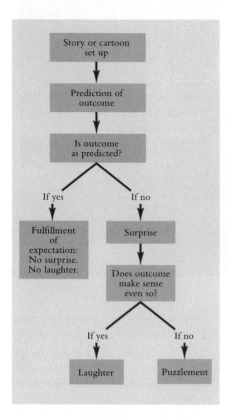

8.24 A cognitive analysis of the appreciation of humor *The joke or cartoon sets up an expectation. The experience of humor arises (1) if this expectation is not fulfilled and (2) if the outcome nevertheless makes sense. (After Suls, 1972)*

second shows that the pattern is continuing. And the third unexpectedly alters the pattern, but in a fashion that makes perfect sense (H. Gleitman, 1990).

As an example, consider the story about a doctor, a lawyer, and an engineer—all of whom are scheduled for execution on a guillotine. As they step up to the scaffold, each is given a choice of lying face up or face down. The doctor goes first, and believing that one should confront one's fate directly, he opts to lie face up. The blade drops, but then screeches to a stop just a foot above the doctor's throat. Amid the gasps of the crowd, the doctor is released.

The lawyer goes next. She is sure that legal precedent would lead to her own release were the blade to stop for her just as it had for the doctor, so she also lies face up. Again the blade stops short, and the lawyer is released.

Now it's the engineer's turn. He figures that his best bet is to go with whatever worked before. So he lies face up and sees the blade overhead. But then, just before the blade drops, he turns to the executioner and says, "Wait! I think I see what your problem is up there."

The ending to this story is unexpected but nonetheless makes perfect sense. The engineer can't resist solving an engineering problem, even if it kills him. And both elements are crucial: If the ending were entirely predictable (the blade simply stops again), there would be no joke. If the ending made no sense (". . . just before the blade drops, he turns to the executioner and says, 'Can I have a blindfold?'"), the result would be puzzlement, not humor. Thus, the punch line works only if the comical ending can be fit into a framework that makes sense of the entire narrative.

Other jokes exploit the same principles, but without the "rule of three." Consider the story about a mountain climber who slipped over a precipice, barely catching hold of a long rope and with a thousand-foot drop gaping below. There was no one with him, and he knew he couldn't hold on very long. In his fear and despair, he looked up to the heavens and shouted: "Is there anyone up there who can help me?" After a long pause, a deep voice was heard from above: "You will be saved if you show your faith by letting go of the rope." The mountain climber looked down at the abyss beneath him, and then looked up again and cried: "Is there anyone *else* up there who can help me?"

Here, the joke sets up a puzzle—what will the mountain climber do now? His response is unexpected. He both has faith and he doesn't. Not content with hearing from one deity, he wants a better bargain from another.

While cognitive restructuring is an important (and perhaps necessary) condition for the production of humor, it is clearly not a sufficient one. In some cases, the "solution" to the "puzzle" posed by the joke is funny because it is simultaneously sensible and absurd. In other cases, the humor arises because elements that had seemed quite unambiguous turn out to be open to an alternative interpretation. This is true in most puns and also true in cases like this one:

Lady Bracknell:	. . . Now to minor matters. Are your parents living?
Jack:	I have lost both my parents.
Lady Bracknell:	To lose one parent, Mr. Worthing, may be regarded as a misfortune; to lose both looks like carelessness.

(Wilde, *The Importance of Being Earnest*, Act I)

In still other cases, the unexpected-but-sensible ending also provides a relatively harmless outlet for wishes that can't be indulged directly, as in sarcastic wit or "dirty" jokes. In these cases, though, it is crucial that the point of the joke be emotionally acceptable to the listener. Jokes about Hitler's extermination camps or about rape are appalling to everyone. We can get away with jokes about the assassination of Julius Caesar, but joking about a contemporary assassination would be unpardonable.

ARTIFICIAL INTELLIGENCE: PROBLEM SOLVING BY COMPUTER

Our discussion so far has left many loose ends. We have suggested, for example, that thinking is organized, but how exactly does this organization come to be? We have emphasized the role of mental sets, but how does the problem solver search for an appropriate set? These and other questions demand a much more precise level of theorizing, but what form should these theories take, and how should the theories be tested?

One line of attack on these issues comes from attempts to program computers so that they simulate human thinking—an enterprise striving for the creation of *artificial intelligence.* The impetus for this work stems from the belief, held by many psychologists, that humans and computers are similar in at least one important regard—they are both information-processing systems. We have already discussed the information-processing approach in our discussions of perception and memory. When, for example, we talk of items that are temporarily activated in working memory, recoded, stored, and later retrieved, we are describing a system in which information is systematically converted from one form into another. In an analogous way, what we call *thinking* may be the systematic manipulation of conceptual chunks by our brains.

Of course, computers and brains are also different in important ways, including the fact that they employ very different physical machinery—semiconductors on the one side, neurons on the other. But this does not imply that they must operate differently. After all, an abacus and a calculator are physically different, but the rules of arithmetic describe the functioning of both. Similarly, for some purposes it may not matter that digital computers are built of inorganic molecules while nervous systems are built of organic ones. Both can nonetheless be understood as information processors, and so the study of one may help us in understanding the other.

ALGORITHMS AND HEURISTICS

Some of the classic work in the attempt to create artificial intelligence was done by Allen Newell and Nobel laureate Herbert Simon, who programmed their computers to play chess, to discover and prove theorems in symbolic logic, and

Computer-generated art *Computers are used to assist in many human endeavors. (A) In 1979, this computer design was generated from a graphic program that incorporates various geometrical algorithms. (Courtesy of Lifesmith Classic Fractals) (B) Twenty years later, Aaron, a program that generates art based on parameters entered by the user, produced this portrait. (Copyright Becky Cohen)*

"This one writes some fine lyrics, and the other one has done some beautiful music, but they just don't seem to hit it off as collaborators." (© 1978 by Sidney Harris—American Scientist Magazine)

to solve word problems. Newell and Simon based many aspects of their programming on work in which research participants were simply asked to think out loud as they tried to solve various problems. These think-out-loud procedures reveal a number of the strategies that people use, and Newell and Simon translated these strategies into computer programs. With this done, the computer performed fairly well—easily solving puzzles that the human subjects found easy and having difficulty with the puzzles that the humans found hard (Newell and Simon, 1972).

In describing research participants' strategies and in writing their programs, Newell and Simon found it useful to distinguish two kinds of strategies, *algorithms* and *heuristics.* Algorithms are procedures in which all of the operations required to achieve the solution are specified step-by-step. If a problem has a solution, an algorithm guarantees that this solution will be found (even though, in some cases, the solution may be very long in coming). For example, consider a person working on a crossword puzzle and trying to find a synonym for *sharp-tongued* that will fit into this frame: _c_ _bi_. An algorithm for finding this word does exist: Every possible combination of letters could be inserted into the four empty spaces and then each combination checked against an unabridged dictionary. This procedure is certain to produce *acerbic,* but it should appeal to few puzzle solvers, for it would require the inspection of nearly 460,000 possibilities.

For many purposes, then, algorithms are much too slow, requiring more time (or effort) than a problem deserves. This is why problem solvers often rely instead on heuristics. These are shortcuts that help us come up with a solution quickly. They usually work (unlike algorithms, which always work) but are sometimes responsible for errors. In a crossword puzzle, for example, heuristics might draw attention to common spelling patterns (such as, if the second letter is *c,* the first must be *s* or a vowel). This is efficient, because it saves us from considering utterly bizarre letter combinations, but it is also somewhat risky, since the solution might just be an uncommon word with an odd spelling.

As another example, take physicians, who reach their diagnoses by first considering the most likely candidates and then testing those. To be sure, this means they will occasionally fail to consider the correct hypothesis, but this danger seems inevitable: If they looked at *every* possibility before moving forward, the diagnosis might come too late to be of any use. Evidence suggests that the use of heuristics is, in truth, extremely common. And wisely so, for life is short and human capacity is limited.

Heuristics take many different forms, and in fact, several of the strategies we have already discussed are heuristics, including working backward when trying to solve a problem or seeking an appropriate analogy. These strategies are by no means guaranteed to work, but they often do, and they tend to be more efficient than an algorithmic approach.

POSSIBLE LIMITATIONS OF ARTIFICIAL INTELLIGENCE

Computer simulation has added a new and exciting dimension to the study of cognitive processes. But research in this arena has also provoked controversy. It is clear that currently available computer programs are quite limited in what they can do. What is not clear is how we should interpret these limits: Will researchers eventually be able to make computers as clever as we are? Or are there genuine limits on what computers can do, or perhaps just on what *digital* computers, or *symbol-processing* computers can do? Psychologists, philosophers, and computer scientists are energetically pursuing answers to these questions. Let's look briefly at some of the obstacles they face.

Well-defined versus ill-defined problems In a well-defined problem, one knows from the start what moves or operations are permitted, and there is also a clear-cut way to evaluate any proposed solution. In playing chess, one simply asks: Is the opposing king checkmated? In solving anagrams, one asks: Do the re-arranged letters form a sequence that appears in the dictionary? In fixing a car engine, one asks: Will the car start now?

In contrast, many problems people face in life are ill-defined. Consider, for example, the problem of writing an excellent short story. Obviously, the "solution" to this problem will involve words on paper, but beyond this, it is difficult to specify what other features the story must have. Likewise for painting a beautiful picture or planning a good vacation or attracting the attention of someone you like.

In cases like these, the critical first step is often to sharpen the definition of the problem in some way—in essence to turn an ill-defined problem into a well-defined one. Similarly, in tackling an ill-defined problem, it often helps to seek reasonable subgoals. By reaching these subgoals, one by one, the problem solver gradually moves toward an overall solution. This implies that a great deal of problem solving depends on a process of defining and redefining ill-defined problems, and so far, this process lies beyond the reach of computer programs. Computer programs do well with well-defined problems but are stymied when confronted by the sort of problem that humans resolve every day.

The lack of common sense Many researchers feel that a crucial difference between human and artificial intelligence lies in the fact that humans have common sense, while computers do not. Consider a simple example: Let's assume that you build a computer program to perform the functions of a college registrar, such as keeping records of enrollments and grades. In fact, you might expect the program to do a better job than a person would—it would never lose an entry or misfile it. Now let's suppose that you ask this computer a simple question: "How many psychology majors passed Math 101 last semester?" The computer will search its memory and may come up with the answer "None." This is a troubling response and might lead you to wonder whether psychology majors have some special disability. But if you understand the limitations of most computer programs, you will ask the computer a further question: "How many psychology majors enrolled in Math 101 last semester?" When the computer comes up with the answer "None," you breathe a sigh of relief. But despite your relief, you also worry deeply about the computer's competence (Joshi, 1983; also see Sperber and Wilson, 1986).

Of course, a computer programmer might try to codify the commonsense knowledge relevant to this case, and all other cases, and to store this knowledge in the computer. However, the prospects for such an endeavor are dim at this point. A major reason is that applying this commonsense knowledge to a particular case often depends on understanding a person's intentions, goals, and values, and for the moment we know rather little about how to give this sort of understanding to a computer. This is roughly what went wrong with our computerized registrar, which failed to realize how its literal answer would be misunderstood. Similarly, consider a computer program called MYCIN that is designed to assist doctors in treating infectious diseases. This program recommends against the administration of a certain antibiotic to children under the age of eight but fails to realize that this is because the antibiotic stains developing teeth. A human physician would obviously decide that these cosmetic side effects should be ignored if the disease is severe enough. However, this is precisely the sort of value-based consideration that computers are so far unable to make.

Current computers, in short, can answer questions but cannot understand why the questions were asked. They can follow rules but are not adequately

Solution to horse-and-rider problem
Solving the horse-and-rider puzzle (see Figure 8.20, p. 318) requires a change of perceptual set. Part A must be rotated 90 degrees so that the two old nags are in the vertical position. One can now see that the head of each (vertical) can join (horizontally) with the hindquarters of the other. The final step is to slide B over the middle of A, and the problem is solved. (After Scheerer, Goldstein, and Boring, 1941)

Expert systems *World chess champion Garry Kasparov contemplates his next move against IBM's Deep Blue. The final score of the 1997 match: three tied games, one game to Kasparov, two games to Deep Blue. (AP Photo/Adam Nadel)*

sensitive to the circumstances that might demand an exception to these rules. In this regard human intelligence is different from artificial intelligence, for human thinking involves a heady mixture of exactness and inexactness, of algorithmic and heuristic procedures that computers have not yet achieved and, some would argue, never will. We must be careful, however, in evaluating this (or any) claim about the state of the art in artificial intelligence. Research in this domain is clearly in its infancy, and new programming techniques and new computer architectures are constantly being invented. Thus, we must simply wait to see what computerized intelligence will be capable of in the future.

EXPERT SYSTEMS

As an illustration of these issues, consider a corner of artificial intelligence research in which there has been enormous progress—the development of ***expert systems.*** These are programs, like MYCIN, designed to solve problems in a subfield of some highly specialized arena. Such programs go way beyond a mere compendium of information. MYCIN, for example, is not just a stored table that lists drugs to combat this or the other microorganism. Instead, it can diagnose, suggest therapies, and estimate their effectiveness. The physician feeds information about the patient's symptoms and the results of various tests into the computer. The computer then consults its memory for lists of potentially useful drugs and chooses among them by following various decision rules (which consider the patient's age, other medications, side effects, and so on). If asked, it will indicate how it arrived at its decision. If appropriately instructed, it will modify its rules; for example, it may add a note that one antibiotic ought not to be administered to a patient with a certain allergy (Shortliffe et al., 1973; Duda and Shortliffe, 1983; Buchanan and Shortliffe, 1985).

A number of studies have assessed the effectiveness of MYCIN by comparing is recommendations with those offered by human experts. The results indicate that the program performs at or near the level of expert physicians, at least in narrowly defined problem areas. Since MYCIN can be continually updated and improved, it is possible that it may outperform most physicians before long. Whether patients will take to MYCIN's bedside manner is another question. (And some physicians have reservations about MYCIN; see Teach and Shortliffe, 1985.)

Are MYCIN and other expert systems intelligent? The answer is a clear no. MYCIN, for example, "knows" only about infectious diseases. If it is asked about a broken bone or a psychiatric condition, it will be utterly lost. As we noted above, MYCIN is also unable to use common sense to overrule one of its own recommendations. MYCIN, therefore, may become a valuable assistant for physicians, but it is not a model of the human intellect, for it simulates only a few human mental operations. Like the other expert systems being developed, MYCIN is meant to aid human intelligence, not replace it.

THE PROCESS OF THINKING: REASONING AND DECISION MAKING

In problem solving, a goal is set, but the means of reaching that goal must be discovered. And as we've seen, the goals that constitute the problem can vary widely. Some are mechanical (e.g., fixing a bicycle), others are numerical (e.g., solving the water jar problem), still others are social (e.g., looking for a graceful way to decline an invitation). But one further form of problem solving is of special interest. This is *reasoning*, in which the goal is to determine what conclusions can be drawn from certain premises.

How do people reason? For many years, scholars assumed that people used processes similar to the formal laws of logic. Thus, George Boole (the nineteenth-century mathematician who invented the Boolean logic underlying many computer operations) wrote an important treatise on the laws of logic, entitled "An Investigation into the Laws of Thought." Today, however, this assumption is widely questioned. Perhaps the laws of logic tell us how people *should* think, but they probably do not correspond to how people really *do* think.

DEDUCTIVE REASONING

In *deductive reasoning,* the reasoner tries to determine whether certain conclusions can be drawn—that is, *deduced*—from a set of initial assertions or *premises.* According to logicians, the validity of the deduction depends on a small number of rules, framed in terms of certain logical relationships, such as *and, or, not,* and the like. But do humans follow these rules?

A classical example of deduction involves the analysis of *syllogisms,* an enterprise that goes back to Aristotle. Each syllogism contains two premises and a conclusion, and the question is whether the conclusion follows logically from the premises (see Figure 8.25). Two examples of such syllogisms (one valid, one invalid) are:

> All *A* are *B*.
> All *B* are *C*.
> Therefore, all *A* are *C*. (valid)

> All *A* are *B*.
> Some *B* are *C*.
> Therefore, all *A* are *C*. (invalid)

Here are the same syllogisms but framed in concrete terms:

> All artwork is beautiful.
> All beautiful things should be cherished.
> Therefore, all artwork should be cherished. (valid)

And:

> All artwork is beautiful.
> Some beautiful things are costly.
> Therefore, all artwork is costly. (invalid)

Notice that the validity of these (or any) syllogisms depends only on whether the conclusion *follows logically* from the premises. The truth of the premises, and the plausibility of the conclusion, are irrelevant to whether the syllogism itself is logical. Thus, the following syllogism, while absurd, is logically valid:

> All artwork is made out of beans.
> All items made out of beans can be turned into clocks.
> Therefore, all artwork can be turned into clocks. (valid)

8.25 Syllogistic argument Insisting upon the execution of the Cheshire Cat, the King of Hearts argued that anything that has a head can be beheaded, including the Cheshire Cat, which at this stage of the story consists of nothing but a head. (Lewis Carroll, Alice in Wonderland, p. 55)

Deductive reasoning. (© *Sidney Harris*)

Until the nineteenth century, most philosophers were convinced that the ability to evaluate syllogisms was an essential aspect of human rationality. Under the circumstances, it was a bit disheartening when experimental psychologists demonstrated that participants make an enormous number of errors in evaluating syllogisms. To be sure, performance varies in response to several factors, and some syllogisms are easier than others. (The valid syllogism just quoted happens to be one of the easier ones; the invalid syllogism, above, happens to be one of the more difficult ones.) Participants are also more accurate if the syllogism is set in concrete terms, rather than in terms of abstract symbols. Nonetheless, across all the syllogisms, mistakes are frequent, with error rates sometimes as high as 70 or 80 percent (Gilhooly, 1988).

Moreover, participants' errors are not the result of mere carelessness. Instead, when solving syllogisms, they rely on systematic strategies, which often lead them astray. For example, participants are more likely to judge a conclusion to be valid if the conclusion strikes them as plausible—quite independent of whether the conclusion follows logically from the stated premises. Thus, they are more likely to endorse the conclusion "All artwork should be cherished" in our earlier example, than they are to endorse the conclusion "All artwork can be turned into clocks." Both of these conclusions are warranted by their premises, but the first is plausible, and thus it is more likely to be accepted as valid.

In some ways, this is a sensible strategy: Participants are doing their best to assess the syllogisms' conclusions based on all they know. At the same time, however, this strategy implies a profound misunderstanding of the rules of logic. A syllogism really doesn't tell us that the conclusion is *true.* Instead, it simply tells us that the conclusion does (or does not) follow from the stated premises. The strategy used by many people implies that they don't understand this. Their strategy leads them to endorse conclusions they accept, even if the premises offered don't support those conclusions, and to reject conclusions they don't endorse, even if those conclusions follow from the premises supplied.

INDUCTIVE REASONING

In deductive reasoning, we reason from the general to the particular. We start with a general rule ("All people are mortal") and ask how it applies to a particular case ("Pat Smith is a person"). But much of the reasoning we engage in is **inductive,** in which this process is reversed. Here we reason from the particular to the general. We consider a number of different instances and try to determine—that is, *induce*—what general rule covers them all.

Induction is at the heart of the scientific enterprise, because the object of science is to determine what common principles underlie seemingly disparate events. To do this, scientists formulate *hypotheses*—tentative assertions about the regularities of the world—and then seek to test them. But hypotheses are also developed by nonscientists, as they seek to understand (and thus to predict or maybe even influence) a pattern of events. We observe the behavior of a moody friend and seek hypotheses for his moodiness. We can't get the car to start and seek hypotheses about what might be wrong. The hypotheses we come up with may not be correct, but they nonetheless constitute our attempts to comprehend an individual case by subsuming it under a more general rule.

FREQUENCY JUDGMENTS

How do we form hypotheses—about the behavior of a friend, the misbehavior of an automobile, or the likely future actions of a politician? In many cases, we are strongly influenced by the pattern of past evidence: How often has the politician kept his promises? How frequently has lack of sleep been the source of a friend's bad moods? How often has the car's performance been improved by pumping the gas pedal? How often has pumping the gas *failed* to work?

Questions like these often provide the basis for our hypotheses: We ask ourselves how frequently an event has occurred, as a way of determining how likely that event will be in the future. In this fashion, hypotheses—both in the scientific world and in our day-to-day lives—depend on *frequency estimates*—estimates of how often we've encountered an event or an object.

Evidence suggests that we often make frequency estimates by means of a simple strategy: We try to think of specific cases relevant to our judgment—examples of politicians keeping their word or of friends feeling awful after a sleepless night. If these examples come easily to mind, we conclude that the circumstance is a common one; if the examples come to mind slowly, or only with great effort, we conclude that the circumstance is rare. This strategy is referred to as the *availability heuristic,* because the judgment uses availability as the basis for assessing frequency.

This heuristic often serves us well: Are most of your close friends male or female? If the first six friends who come to mind are all men, or if they are four women and two men, you will draw the obvious conclusion and probably be correct. In other circumstances, though, this strategy can lead to error. In one study, research participants were asked this question: Considering all the words in the language, does R occur more frequently in the first position of the word (*rose, robot, rocket*) or in the third position (*care, strive, tarp*)? Over two-thirds of the participants said that R is more common in the first position, but in fact the reverse is true, and by a wide margin.

The reason for this error is availability. The participants made their judgments by trying to think of words in which R is the first letter, and these came easily to mind. They next tried to think of words in which it is the third, and these came to mind only with some effort. This difference in ease of retrieval merely shows that our memorial dictionary, like a printed one, is organized according to the starting sound of each word, and this makes it easy to search for words with a particular starting letter. Participants' judgments plainly reflect what's available to them, even when, as in this case, what's available is at odds with the actual frequencies (Tversky and Kahneman, 1973).

Deciding that more words start with R than have it as their third letter seems harmless enough, especially when weighed against the fact that the availability heuristic does, as we have noted, help us come up with the correct answer more often than not. Unfortunately, though, the same strategy can also yield errors of a more serious sort. What are the chances that the stock market will go up tomorrow or that a certain psychiatric patient will commit suicide? The stockbrokers and psychiatrists who make these judgments regularly base their decisions on an estimate of probabilities: In the past, has the market generally gone up after a performance like today's? In the past, have patients with these symptoms generally been dangerous to themselves? These estimates, too, are likely to be based on the availability heuristic, and so (for example) the psychiatrist's judgment may be poor if she vividly remembers a particular patient's repeated bluffs about suicide. This easily available recollection may bias the psychiatrist's frequency judgment, leading to inadequate precautions in the present case.

A different example comes from the public's perception of crime rates. Throughout the 1990s, crime rates have actually declined in many American cities, but *fear* of crime has nonetheless been increasing. This is probably due to the fact that, even though the actual number of crimes has dropped, media coverage of crimes has increased. As a result, memories of crimes are more available to people, leading to an increased estimate of frequency and, in turn, to increased fear.

"There it comes again."
Induction *(Illustration by Henry Gleitman)*

The same pattern is also evident in studies in which people have been asked which is the more common—death by homicide or death by stroke? death from car crashes or death from stomach cancer? People generally identify the first cause in each pair as the more common, although the opposite is the case. (Death by stroke is ten times more likely than death by homicide.) Estimates are, in these cases, clearly influenced by the media: Murders and car crashes make front page stories and so are commonly encountered and easily remembered. This provides an availability advantage that, in turn, biases people's estimates (Slovic, Fischoff, and Lichtenstein, 1982).

EXTRAPOLATING FROM AVAILABLE OBSERVATIONS

The availability heuristic is used in a wide range of settings, including cases in which we are trying to make judgments of considerable importance. It is troubling, therefore, that this generally helpful strategy can, on occasion, lead to error. The same can be said for another common strategy, one that we employ when seeking to generalize from the information we have gathered.

Many of the categories we encounter are uniform in important ways: People don't vary much in their number of fingers or their number of ears. Birds uniformly share the property of having feathers, and hotel rooms all share the property of having beds. This uniformity may seem trivial, but it actually plays an important role: It allows us to extrapolate from our experiences, so that we know what to expect the next time we see a bird or enter a hotel room.

Such extrapolation based on assumed uniformity is generally sensible, but we overuse this strategy, extrapolating from our experiences even when it is clear we should not. In other words, we fall prey to the ***representativeness heuristic***— the strategy of assuming that each case is representative of its class. Reliance on this heuristic is evident whenever someone offers or is persuaded by a "man who" or "woman who" argument: "What do you mean that cigarettes cause cancer? I have an aunt who smokes cigarettes, and she's perfectly healthy at age eighty-two!" Such arguments are often presented in debates, and even on editorial pages, and take their force from our extraordinary willingness to generalize from a single case. We act as though the speaker's aunt is representative of all cigarette smokers, even though there is ample reason to suspect she is not.

In the laboratory, research participants extrapolate from a single case even when they are explicitly warned that the case is in no way typical. In one study, participants watched a videotaped inteview with a prison guard. Some had been told in advance that the guard was quite atypical, chosen for the interview because of his extreme views. Others were not given this warning. After watching the videotape, participants were asked their views about the prison system, and their views were plainly influenced by the interview they saw: Having heard an interview with a harsh, unsympathetic guard, participants were inclined to believe that, in general, prison guards are severe and inhumane. Remarkably, though, participants who had been told clearly that the guard was atypical were just as willing to draw this conclusion: Their use of the representativeness heuristic in this case seems to have overruled the warning (Kahneman and Tversky, 1972, 1973; Hamill, Wilson, and Nisbett, 1980; Nisbett and Ross, 1980).

It is easy to be impressed *and* dismayed by the errors caused by these heuristics. We should therefore emphasize that in general these heuristics serve us well. If a category is frequent in the world, then examples of that category will generally be easily available to us. Therefore, frequency judgments based on availability will often be correct. Likewise, many of the categories we encounter are uniform in important regards and so extrapolations based on assumed representativeness will often be warranted. In addition, both of these strategies are quick and easy to use, so if they do sometimes lead to error, this may be balanced by the efficiency they afford.

In addition, it is important to note that we don't always rely on these strategies in making our judgments. In some settings, we do seem to realize that a member of a particular category is atypical, and so we hesitate to draw conclusions about the entire category based on observations of just a few instances. In other settings, we seem alert to the fact that a large sample of data is more informative than a small sample. Several hypotheses have been offered for why we sometimes are sensitive to these factors and sometimes not, but at the moment, there is no consensus on these points (Nisbett et al., 1983; Gigerenzer and Hoffrage, 1995; Kahneman and Tversky, 1996).

CONFIRMATION BIAS

The fact remains, however, that we do use these heuristics in many circumstances, and in many cases, they lead us into error. One might hope, though, that these errors will soon be corrected as more information becomes available. Thus, we might initially be led to a false belief by a "man who" story, but as we gain experience, as we encounter more and more evidence that doesn't fit this belief, we will be led to revise our view. In other words, hearing about one eighty-two-year-old cigarette-smoking aunt might convince us that smoking is not hazardous, but then hearing about other (more typical) smoking victims will set us straight.

However, a different pattern works against such self-correction. This pattern, called **confirmation bias,** actually takes several different forms. First, when people are given an opportunity to seek out new information, they tend to seek information that will confirm their beliefs, rather than information that might challenge their views. Second, if people are given evidence that is consistent with their beliefs *and* information that is inconsistent, they tend to take the former seriously and discount the latter: We are impressed by evidence that supports our views, and such evidence strengthens our commitment to our beliefs;

The confirmation bias in science   Galileo *vainly trying to persuade a group of university professors to look through his telescope. (From a National Theatre production of* Galileo *by Bertolt Brecht; photograph by Zoe Dominic)*

evidence that counts against our views, in contrast, is greeted with skepticism—subjected to hard criticism, reinterpreted, or in some cases, ignored outright.

Why, for example, do people often harbor erroneous beliefs about their likelihood of winning while gambling? The evidence suggests that gamblers remember their *wins* quite vividly, using those memories to bolster the belief that they have a surefire strategy. Gamblers also remember their *losses* but reinterpret these as near wins, or as chance events (". . . it was just bad luck that I got a two of clubs instead of an ace of hearts!"). In this way, confirming evidence is remembered and disconfirming evidence is discounted, leaving the gamblers' erroneous beliefs intact (Gilovich, 1991).

A different example comes from an experiment in which research participants were given a number series, such as "3, 4, 5." They were told that this series followed a rule, and their task was to figure out the rule. In truth, the rule was exceedingly simple—"any three numbers in increasing order of magnitude"—but participants found inferring the rule quite difficult, usually because they insisted on proposing more complex rules. But the real point lies in how participants went about their task: As soon as they had developed a hypothesis about the rule, they generated a series of numbers that would fit this hypothesis—that is, they generated a *confirming* example—and then asked the experimenter if this example fit the actual rule. In other words, they sought to confirm their hypothesis; they rarely generated a series that was inconsistent with their hypothesis, and, thus, which could potentially be used to disconfirm it (Wason, 1960, 1968; Wason and Johnson-Laird, 1972).

Confirmation bias can be a genuine obstacle to understanding, for, in many ways, disconfirmations are more helpful in the search for truth than confirmations. One disconfirmation shows that a hypothesis is false, but countless confirmations cannot really prove that it is true. Nonetheless, confirmation bias is a powerful phenomenon, often evident in the laboratory, but also found in the real-world behavior of scientists (Mitroff, 1974; Mahoney, 1976; Mahoney and DeMonbreun, 1981).

What accounts for confirmation bias? One idea is that humans have a powerful tendency to seek order in the universe. We try to understand what we see and hear, and to impose some organization on it. The organization may not be valid, but it is often better than none at all, for without some such organization we would be overwhelmed by an overload of information. But the benefits provided by an organization do not come free, for our confirmation bias makes it quite difficult for us to escape a false belief once it is acquired.

THE EFFECT OF EDUCATION

We have discussed several patterns of thinking that are useful but that can, on some occasions, lead to error, and this leads us to ask whether anything can be done to improve the quality of people's reasoning so that errors can be avoided. In fact, the evidence provides grounds for optimism: Training in the elementary principles of statistics seems to make many of these errors less likely, so that after training, students are more alert both to the problems of drawing a conclusion from a small sample and to the possibility of bias within a sample. The benefits of training can also be derived from courses—such as those in psychology—that provide numerous examples of how sample size and sample bias affect any attempt to draw conclusions from evidence (Fong et al., 1986; Lehman et al., 1988; Lehman and Nisbett, 1990; Fong and Nisbett, 1991).

These educational experiences provide students with new knowledge and new strategies, and these improve their ability to think about evidence. Just as important, though, this education seems to build on intuitions that students already possess. What are these intuitions? Students certainly don't need a statistics course to teach them, for example, that accidents sometimes happen. (Sometimes, just by chance, a tossed coin will come up heads four times in a row.) Likewise, they don't need a course to tell them that accidents don't keep happening. (If the same coin comes up heads thirty times in a row, they'll start to suspect a trick!)

These intuitions about accidents are widely shared and, in many circumstances, do help students to think sensibly about sample size: If an astrologer correctly predicts the score of tomorrow's football game, they might not be impressed—perhaps it was just a lucky prediction. (Accidents do happen.) But if the astrologer were able to predict game after game after game, this would be remarkable, and probably not attributable to luck. (Accidents don't keep happening.)

In many circumstances, though, students fail to see the connection between these sensible intuitions and the case under consideration, and this leaves them vulnerable, for example, to "man who" arguments, that is, arguments resting on a very small sample—just one observation. This vulnerability is decreased, however, by some statistical training: After training, students seem able to apply their statistical intuitions to a broader set of cases, and, as a result, the training increases the likelihood that they will reason correctly about evidence, accidents, and sampling whenever they confront a new problem—in the laboratory or in their lives (Nisbett et al., 1983; Fong and Nisbett, 1991).

DECISION MAKING

Induction and deduction both allow us to form new judgments and to form new beliefs. However, we want to do more than this; we also want to put our beliefs into action. In some cases, doing so is a simple matter of marching forward toward one clear goal. In many other cases, though, we have more than one path available to us, and we must choose which one to take. How do we make these choices? This question is illuminated by research on decision making.

FRAMING EFFECTS

Two factors are obviously relevant to any decision. First, we should consider the possible outcomes of the decision and choose the most desirable one: Would you rather have 10 dollars or 100 dollars? Would you rather pay 5 dollars or 10 dollars to see the same movie? In each case, we effortlessly choose the option with the greatest benefit (100 dollars) or the lowest cost (the 5 dollar movie). Second, we should consider the risks: Would you rather buy a lottery ticket with one chance in a hundred of winning, or a lottery ticket for the same prize with one chance in a thousand of winning? If one of your friends liked a movie and another didn't, would you want to go see it? What if five of your friends had seen the movie and all liked it, would you want to see it then? In these cases, we are attracted by the options that give us the greatest likelihood of achieving those things we value (increasing our odds of winning the lottery or seeing a movie we'll enjoy).

Our decisions are clearly influenced by both of these factors—the attractiveness of the outcome and the likelihood of achieving that outcome. But our evaluation of these factors can be heavily influenced by tiny changes in how a question is phrased or how our options are described. These changes in the *framing* of a decision can in many cases reverse our decisions, turning a strong preference in one direction into an equally strong preference in the opposite direction. Take, for example, the following problem:

Imagine that the United States is preparing for the outbreak of an unusual disease, which is expected to kill 600 people. Two alternative programs to combat the disease have been proposed. Assume that the exact scientific estimate of the consequences of the two programs is as follows:

If Program *A* is adopted, 200 of these people will be saved.
If Program *B* is adopted, there is a one-third probability that 600 people will be saved and a two-thirds probability that no people will be saved.

Which of the two programs would you favor?

Given these alternatives, a clear majority—72 percent—opted for Program *A*. Apparently, a sure gain was preferable to the possibility of a larger gain, if that possibility were accompanied by the further possibility of no gain. This decision, by itself, is entirely defensible. However, consider what happens when participants are given the same problem but with a different formulation of their options. Participants were again told that if no action is taken, the disease will kill 600. They are then asked to choose between the following options:

If Program *A* is adopted, 400 people will die.
If Program *B* is adopted, there is a one-third probability that nobody will die and a two-thirds probability that 600 people will die.

Given this formulation, a huge majority—78 percent—chose Program *B*. To them the certain death of 400 people was less acceptable than a two-thirds probability that all 600 people would die (Tversky and Kahneman, 1981). Notice, though, that these two problems are identical—200 saved out of 600 is the same as 400 dead out of 600, and so on. The only difference between the problems lies in how the alternatives are phrased, but this shift in framing has a large impact, turning a majority vote for *A* into an equally strong majority for *B* (Kahneman and Tversky, 1984).

Similar framing effects are easy to observe in other settings, including cases outside of the laboratory. In general, people make choices that will minimize or avoid losses—that is, they show a pattern called **loss aversion.** If, therefore, a problem is framed in terms of losses, people are put off by this, and, if they can, they'll choose to gamble in hopes of diminishing the loss (thus, they choose Program *B* when the problem is phrased negatively, in terms of people dying). Conversely, people hold tight to what they have, and so, once they have a gain, they'll take no chances with it; they are, in this situation, **risk averse** and will scrupulously avoid gambling.

Loss aversion is a strong and sensible inclination, and so is people's hesitancy to risk what they already have. Unfortunately, though, these inclinations leave people open to self-contradiction: If the problem is framed positively, they make one choice; if it is framed negatively, they make the other choice. Thus, physicians are more willing to endorse a program of treatment that has a 50 percent success rate than they are to endorse a program with a 50 percent failure rate— they are put off by the emphasis on the negative outcome. Similarly, people generally refuse to play a fair game of "heads, you get a dollar; tails, I get a dollar." In this case, they are more impressed by the potential loss than they are by the potential gain, so the game seems unattractive. Likewise, research participants make one choice in the problem shown in the top half of Figure 8.26 and the opposite choice in the problem shown in the bottom half of the figure—again, they will gamble in hopes of avoiding a loss but will hold tight to retain a gain.

ARE PEOPLE REALLY IRRATIONAL?

We have now considered an extensive (and perhaps dismaying) list of slips, errors, and inconsistencies in human thinking. How is this possible? Could

"But we just don't have the technology to carry it out." (© 1976 by Sidney Harris—American Scientist *Magazine*)

8.26 Framing effects *The outcomes of these two choices are identical. In both cases, option* a *leaves you with $400, while option* b *leaves you with a 50–50 chance between getting $300 and getting $500. Despite this fact, 72 percent of research participants selected option* a *in choice 1, and 64 percent selected option* b *in choice 2. Once again, the way the outcomes were framed reversed the choices the participants made. (From Tversky and Kahneman, 1987).*

---

1. Assume yourself richer by $300 than you are today. You have to choose between:
   a. a sure gain of $100, and
   b. a 50 percent chance to gain $200 and a 50 percent chance to gain nothing.

2. Assume yourself richer by $500 than you are today. You have to choose between:
   a. a sure loss of $100, and
   b. a 50 percent chance to lose nothing and a 50 percent chance to lose $200.

---

humans really be this prone to error? If so, then how has humanity managed to achieve what it has in mathematics, philosophy, and science? We have already considered some responses to these questions: Our strategies for reasoning and judgment, even though open to error, do reach sensible conclusions more often than not. In addition, we can, with training, be led to better reasoning strategies. A single course in statistics, it seems, can improve one's ability to think about a range of day-to-day judgments. Further courses in scientific method or in logic can magnify these effects (Lehman et al., 1988; Lehman and Nisbett, 1990).

In addition, it is important to remember that the great intellectual achievements of humanity grow out of collective efforts. Each discovery builds on the work of many prior generations, and our forebears have bequeathed to us a powerful set of intellectual tools, including techniques of formal data gathering and analysis. This machinery can supplement each individual's own limited capacities in order to diminish error. Moreover, most discoveries depend on a community of researchers all working on related projects. Errors committed by the majority may still be detected by a minority, and this may be enough to keep us all on track. Similarly, an individual scientist may well be biased toward confirmation and so may not seek evidence that could disprove her hypothesis. But other scientists may prefer different hypotheses and so will be quite glad to disprove the first researcher's claims. This adversarial relation is an important part of scholarly research and serves us well, rooting out error and rendering confirmation bias—a powerful force for the individual—irrelevant for the community.

Still, research on thinking and decision making may yet force us to rethink certain key issues about humanity, our intellectual prowess, and, indeed, the nature of rationality. On the surface, rationality might seem to mean avoiding error, but perhaps it is actually rational to *tolerate* some error if the alternative is spending vastly too much time on each judgment encountered. Better to be right most of the time than to spend life paralyzed in thought. Likewise, rationality might seem to entail avoiding self-contradiction. But perhaps other forces outweigh the need for self-consistency. Perhaps the avoidance of loss, for example, is so powerful a consideration that it is rational to accept some contradiction rather than occasionally losing our shirts.

THE THINKING BRAIN

In this chapter, we have covered a number of topics—the mental representation of knowledge, problem solving, induction and deduction, and decision making. It is important to emphasize, however, that the study of these topics is not unique to psychology. Philosophers have much to say about the nature of knowledge, logicians about deduction, economists about decision making. And while psychologists are deeply interested in processes of thought, neuroscientists are focusing on the neural processes that make thought possible. It is therefore fitting that these various topics are often studied from a multidisciplinary perspective, under the rubric of *cognitive science*.

We close this chapter with two illustrations of the power of this multidisciplinary approach to the study of knowledge, its acquisition, and its use. First, we consider briefly the biological basis for some of the processes described in this chapter and, second, we turn to the relation between cognition and consciousness.

LOCALIZATION OF THOUGHT

In important ways, the processes of thought depend on the entire brain. A person couldn't think without the many midbrain and hindbrain structures that maintain life while the process of thought is going on. But many sites within the forebrain are more directly involved. If a person is thinking about visually presented materials, then sites relevant to the visual system, mostly in the occipital lobe, will be heavily activated; if a person is shifting attention from one aspect of a visual scene to another, this shift in attention to a large extent involves sites in the parietal cortex. If a person is engaged in linguistic tasks, then brain areas crucial for language use—including Broca's area (in the left frontal lobe) and Wernicke's area (near the juncture between the temporal and parietal lobes)—will be heavily involved. (See Chapter 2 for further discussion of all these anatomical regions.)

In addition to these many other brain sites, evidence also indicates that the prefrontal cortex (the brain tissue just behind the forehead) plays a crucial role in many aspects of thought. Chapter 2 presented some of the evidence for this claim: Patients with damage in the prefrontal area often show profound deficits in strategy formation and are particularly unable to deal with novel situations— that is, situations requiring the design and initiation of some new plan or response. These patients often show a pattern known as **perseveration**—they *persevere* in producing the same response over and over and over, even though they remember perfectly well that the task requires them to change their response (e.g., Bianchi, 1922; Milner, 1963; Luria, 1966; Diamond and Goldman-Rakic, 1989).

The role of the prefrontal cortex is also highlighted by studies of the neural basis of working memory. Recall that working memory is best understood as a process or activity, not as a passive repository for remembered material. In Chapter 7, we described working memory as the "workbench" on which various items of experience are sorted, manipulated, and organized. Clearly, there is an intimate tie between working memory and thought—working memory holds the materials one is currently thinking about. And working memory, it seems, depends heavily on the prefrontal cortex.

Evidence for this claim comes from studies of both humans and nonhuman animals (generally monkeys). These studies show that areas of the prefrontal cortex are strongly activated whenever the research participant must think about a stimulus seen just moments earlier, remember a sequence of letters, or make judgments about words ("Is this the name of a vegetable?"). But while there is a consensus that prefrontal areas are crucial for all these tasks, there is enormous debate over how the prefrontal areas are themselves organized. Some researchers claim that portions of the prefrontal cortex are specialized for different types of materials, with one portion dealing with spatial position, another dealing with details of an object's appearance. Other researchers claim that some portions of the prefrontal cortex are pivotal in the retrieval of information from long-term storage, whereas other portions are crucial for the design and coordination of new actions. How these disagreements will be resolved remains to be seen. A conclusion awaits the arrival of new data and, conceivably, new techniques for studying and localizing brain activity (Cohen et al., 1997; Courtney et al., 1997; Rao et al., 1997; Wickelgren, 1997).

COGNITION AND CONSCIOUSNESS

The nervous system provides the substrate for all aspects of thought, so it seems inevitable that we would turn to the study of the nervous system as a source of insight into the nature of these mental processes. But there is also another point of contact among the various areas of cognition, namely, *consciousness*. We don't merely gain the knowledge that the apple is red; instead, we experience redness. When we form a mental image of a red apple, our experience resembles the one we had when examining an actual apple. We don't merely remember the past; instead, we are aware of trying to remember something and then aware of our own recollection.

When scientific psychology first started out, late in the nineteenth century, these observations, and the study of consciousness in general, were central concerns of the newly created field. The early psychologists did their best to describe and analyze their conscious experiences, but since different psychologists came up with very different descriptions, they were led to different, sometimes contradictory, claims. Moreover, there was no way to resolve these disputes. In general, researchers iron out their disagreements by examining each other's data and by considering each other's evidence. But there is no way to do this in the study of consciousness. There is no way for one researcher to share another's experience, and so no way to find out, for example, whether their experiences are the same or different. As a result, psychologists early in the twentieth century concluded that consciousness could not be studied scientifically and, for many years, abandoned the study of consciousness to philosophers.

As the previous chapters have suggested, however, psychologists are now ready to join forces with their colleagues in philosophy to tackle the issue of consciousness once again. To be sure, there are many questions about consciousness that we still can't answer: What exactly is consciousness? How is it possible for a biological mechanism, namely the human brain, to be conscious at all? Are other organisms conscious in the same sense we are? Could computers be conscious? These questions remain the subject of debate, and, generally speaking, philosophers still have more to say on such matters than psychologists do (see, for example, Dennett, 1991; Rosenthal, 1993; Flanagan, 1994; Chalmers, 1996; Block et al., 1997; Searle et al., 1997).

Even so, psychologists have made progress in this arena. Ironically, much of this progress has come not from examining consciousness itself, but by studying what happens when consciousness is absent. By describing what can be done without consciousness, psychologists have gained important clues about just what it is that consciousness contributes to our mental functioning.

MENTAL PROCESSES THAT GO ON BELOW THE SURFACE

People can perform many mental functions—even complex ones—without being conscious that they do so. They can perceive, remember, and reason with no awareness of what they are doing and with no conscious supervision of these complex activities. In that sense, much of what we do we do unconsciously.

Before proceeding, however, we should say a bit about the word *unconscious*. The popular understanding of this term was shaped mightily by the ideas of

Nonconsciousness *Some hints of what consciousness is about come from studies of mental processes that go on in the absence of consciousness. (Figure 14, 1982, by Alfredo Castañeda; courtesy of Mary-Anne Martin/Fine Art, New York).*

Sigmund Freud. Freud believed that certain ideas or memories were "repressed"—that is, actively kept out of consciousness—because they were threatening or anxiety provoking (see Chapter 17). These painful or threatening ideas, however, continued to exist in the mind, or so Freud claimed, and resided in what he called the unconscious.

The mechanisms we will discuss here, however, are of a different sort. Much as one rides in a car without a moment's awareness of the engine's functioning, thought can proceed without any awareness of the vast and intricate mental machinery that makes thought possible. The workings of this machinery, therefore, are simply nonconscious—outside our awareness. In contrast to the Freudian conception, these unconscious contents are in no sense threatening, nor are they actively suppressed. Thus, most psychologists today conceive of the relationship between the conscious and unconscious mental processes—between thoughts of which we are aware and the supporting cognitive activity that proceeds outside our awareness—in a fashion dramatically different than Freud did.

Perception without awareness When we look at the world we see familiar objects—a chair, a dog, a friend, and so on. We respond appropriately to them all: We don't sit on the dog, throw a bone to the friend, or ask the chair how it's doing. Obviously, therefore, each stimulus triggers the relevant memories and knowledge. But we are generally unaware of the steps involved in these achievements. Without our conscious supervision, we separate figure from ground and compute distances in order to achieve constancy (Chapter 6), and we search through memory for pertinent information (Chapter 7). All we are aware of is the product of these operations—the world as it is consciously perceived.

A related point is made by the striking phenomenon of **blindsight,** a pattern observed in some patients who suffer from damage to the occipital cortex (the region of the cortex to which the pathway from the eye and thalamus project;

see Chapter 2). Damage within this area produces blindness in the corresponding part of the visual field so complete that patients report seeing nothing in that part of space, even when exposed to flashes of very bright light.

But this reported blindness is misleading. In some experiments, researchers present stimuli to the patients' affected field and ask them to *guess* what the stimuli are—*X*s or *O*s, circles or squares. The patients complain that this task is absurd: They are blind, so how could they guess? If the investigators persist, however, the patients will venture a guess, and these guesses are surprisingly accurate. It would appear, then, that these patients can see (or, more precisely, can perceive some aspects of the visual world), even though they have no conscious experience of seeing (Weiskrantz, 1986; Rodman, Gross, and Albright, 1989; Cowey and Stoerig, 1992). There has been much discussion of the neural connections that make this possible, but whatever its neurological base, this phenomenon makes it clear that perception can take place without our being aware of it. Perceiving, it seems, does not require conscious supervision, nor does it necessarily yield a conscious experience.

Memory and understanding without awareness   What holds for perception, holds for other cognitive processes as well. We've already seen, for example, that we often rely on *inferences* to fill in gaps in our recollection (see Chapter 7). Usually, these inferences occur unwittingly, and this is one of the reasons why it is difficult to distinguish between those elements of a recollection that are truly based on what we experienced in an earlier episode and those elements that are based on our reconstruction or surmise. This same lack of awareness crops up whenever we listen and understand. Here, too, we routinely consult our memories without any awareness that we are doing so.

Consider the sentence:

Susan put the vase down too firmly on the table and it broke.

In this sentence, what does "it" refer to? The sentence is actually ambiguous, but most of us see only one meaning: "It" has to be the vase, not the table. To draw this conclusion, we rely on our knowledge that vases are often fragile, whereas tables generally are not. Hence, we interpret the sentence in a fashion guided by our knowledge, knowledge supplied to us, obviously, by memory. However, we are not conscious of the fact we are here relying on memory; indeed, we are typically unaware that the sentence was ambiguous in the first place. Instead, we are again conscious only of the product of these operations—our understanding of the sentence's meaning.

Similar claims can be made for all the sentences we hear or read: To understand them, we must construct their meaning from pieces we retrieve from memory, and we do so without awareness. In fact, it is crucial that these memory consultations go on underground: If we consciously registered every ambiguity we encountered and paused to search our memories, seeking the best resolution of each, we would probably never get to the end of any paragraph.

Action without awareness   People can evidently perceive, retrieve memories, use memories, and make judgments—all without conscious awareness. They can also *act* without awareness. For example, we all know how to tie our shoes, but most of us have forgotten the exact sequence of steps needed to accomplish this feat. We intend to tie our shoes and, before we know it, the task is done. We tie our shoes, it seems, without being aware that we're doing so.

More complex tasks can also be done in this unconscious fashion, so that many of our actions are performed on "autopilot." In most cases, this results from extended practice with the task, and this invites us to ask how practice creates this automaticity. One proposal is that, with practice, fewer decisions are required as one steps through a complex task. The well-practiced shoe tier doesn't have to choose what to do next after the first loop is formed. Instead, she can simply draw on the memory of what she has done many times before. A complete subroutine has been stored in memory, encapsulating all of the steps of the procedure, and so once the routine is launched, no decisions are needed—she simply repeats the familiar steps. (For theoretical proposals on how such subroutines are formed, see Logan, 1988; Logan et al., 1996; Boronat and Logan, 1997; Shiffrin, 1997.)

WHAT IS CONSCIOUSNESS GOOD FOR?

Overall, then, it is clear that much of our mental life goes on behind the scenes, out of sight. We seem to be largely unaware of the processes by means of which we perceive, remember, and think. What we are aware of instead are the products that emerge from these processes (Nisbett and Wilson, 1977). But if all this can be accomplished *without* awareness, then what is consciousness good for?

Nonconscious processing is fast and efficient—whether it involves shoelace tying, receiving telegraphic messages, or drawing a conclusion from evidence. Some of this efficiency, we have suggested, derives from the fact that automatized actions rely on familiar routines, allowing us to run off an already-encoded sequence of steps, rather than attending to each new decision. But this efficiency comes at a price: As we described earlier in the chapter, automatized actions are often relatively inflexible. By relying on familiar routines, we ensure that we will approach the task on this occasion just as we approached it on previous occasions.

This leads to an obvious suggestion: Perhaps we need consciousness in order to break away from automaticity, to pay attention to our performance on precisely those tasks on which we must preserve flexibility. For these, we must remain mindful of what we are doing, so that we can choose, step-by-step, how our actions will unfold. Consciousness, in other words, plays its role whenever we must avoid becoming victims of habit and whenever we have reason to give up the efficiency afforded us by nonconscious processing.

Some tasks, by their nature, require a succession of conscious decisions. For these, conscious processing may be mandatory. Other tasks require some degree of fine tuning to make our actions appropriate to the present decision. To take an ordinary example, if we simply relied on habit, we might find ourselves habitually telling the same joke over and over, each time we had an opportunity. Unfortunately, this might lead to our telling the joke a second or a third time to the exact same audience. To avoid this embarrassment, we need to rise above our habits to remember, and reflect on, when we last told the joke and to whom (see Jacoby et al., 1989).

The data we have reviewed also suggest another role for conscious experience: Blindsight patients apparently can perceive some aspects of their world, but they nonetheless do not take action based on what they see—they don't reach for desirable targets, don't duck to avoid bumping into things. Similarly, amnesic patients clearly retain many aspects of their past, but they also take no action based on what they remember and will not, for example, respond to an investigator's direct questions about their memories (Graf, Mandler, and Haden, 1982, provides a particularly clear case of this pattern).

How should we think about these observations? Perhaps our conscious experience plays a role in determining our willingness to act. We decide that a memory is a memory, and not a chance association, because of how we experience that memory, and so we take action based on that memory. Likewise, we decide that a perception is genuine, and not a fleeting impression, because of the conscious experience of that perception. Without this experience, we might gain the information contained within the perception but be incapable of acting on this information.

These last points clearly rest on conjectures, and, so far, research has provided only the earliest of steps on our path toward understanding consciousness. But we should not be surprised by this, since the mysteries surrounding consciousness have, after all, perplexed some of the greatest minds in human history. Even so, we are making progress in this arena, and psychologists and neuroscientists are increasingly turning their attention to these issues. It seems plausible, therefore, that research will continue to provide crucial clues about one of the greatest puzzles of all time.

TAKING STOCK

In looking back over the three domains of cognition—perception, memory, and thinking—we must remember that there are no clear boundaries demarcating these three domains. In describing perception, we often cross over the border into memory. For the way we perceive familiar objects is based in part on how we perceived them in the past. But perception also shades into thinking. We look at an ambiguous picture and eventually solve the perceptual puzzle as we recognize in it the image of a dalmation dappled by sunlight.

Nor is it clear where memory leaves off and thinking begins. Much of remembering seems like problem solving. We try to recall to whom we lent a certain book, conclude that it has to be Jane, for we know no one else who is interested in the book's topic, and then suddenly have a vivid recollection of the particular occasion on which she borrowed it (and the way she swore that she'd return it right away). But if remembering is sometimes much like thinking, thinking can hardly proceed without reference to the storehouse of memory. Whatever we think about—which route to take on a vacation trip, how to fill out a tax form—requires retrieval of items from various memory systems.

All of this shows that there are no exact boundaries separating perception, memory, and thinking. These areas are not sharply separated intellectual domains but are simply designations for somewhat different aspects of the general process of cognition. We will now turn to the one aspect of cognition that we have thus far discussed only in passing—language. It, too, is intertwined with the other domains of cognition, but unlike perception, memory, and thinking, which are found in many animals, language seems unique to human beings.

SUMMARY

1. All thought draws on knowledge we already possess. The components of knowledge can be regarded as *mental representations,* which are either *analogical* or *symbolic.* Analogical representations capture some of the actual characteristics of what they represent (e.g., a mouse and a picture of a mouse), while symbolic representations bear no such relationship to what they represent (e.g., a mouse and the word *mouse*).

2. An important example of analogical representation in thinking is provided by *mental images.* With the possible exception of *eidetic imagery,* visual memories are not a simple reembodiment of stored visual perceptions. But they have some picturelike attributes as shown by studies of *mental rotation* and *image scanning. Spatial thinking* is both symbolic and analogical as shown by studies on *mental maps.*

3.   The elements of symbolic thought are *concepts* and *propositions.* Many of these are stored in *generic memory,* where they constitute the "database" for our thoughts. Unlike *episodic memory,* which concerns memory for particular events in one's life, generic memory concerns items of knowledge as such.

4.   An important component of generic memory is *semantic memory,* whose organization has been described by various *network models.* Semantic memory has been studied by various techniques for assessing *memory search,* including memory activation. An early hypothesis held that this network is hierarchical. Later proposals feature networks that are not hierarchical, but instead are based on *semantic distance.* Such network hypotheses receive support from studies of *semantic priming.* The last decade has seen the development of a new group of network models based on *parallel distributed processing (PDP)* in which the relevant symbolic representations correspond to the state of the network as a whole.

5.   Problem solving is a *directed activity* in which all steps are considered as they fit into the overall structure set up by the task. This structure is typically hierarchical, with *goals, subgoals,* and so on.

6.   Increasing competence at any directed activity goes with an increase in the degree to which the *subroutines* of this activity have become chunked and *automatized.* In learning to send and receive Morse code, as in the attainment of many skills, *learning curves* exhibit plateaus followed by increments, suggesting the acquisition of progressively larger units. Similar chunking seems to occur in many forms of mental activity, including problem solving, and differentiates masters and beginners in many endeavors, such as playing chess.

7.   Problem solving is not always successful. One reason may be a strong, interfering *mental set.* Investigators of thinking have come up with a few suggestions for overcoming obstacles to problem solving. One is *working backward* from the goal; another is trying to find an *analogy.* Sometimes the solution involves a radical *restructuring* by means of which a misleading set is overcome. Such restructurings may be an important feature of much creative thinking. Accounts by prominent writers, composers, and scientists suggest that restructuring often occurs after a period of *incubation.* Restructuring may also play a role in humor, which often occurs when an unexpected cognitive organization turns out to make sense after all.

8.   An influential approach to problem solving comes from work on *artificial intelligence* in which computer scientists try to simulate certain aspects of human thinking. A number of strategies for solving problems have been incorporated into computer programs, including *algorithms* and *heuristics.* Some further extensions feature the use of *expert systems.* Among the limitations of current attempts to bring artificial intelligence programs up to the level of human intelligence is the difficulty in dealing with *ill-defined problems* and the lack of *common sense* knowledge about many aspects of the worlds, together with an understanding of what is relevant to the problem at hand.

9.   Studies of *deductive reasoning* show that people are prone to various errors in thinking. Errors of reasoning in dealing with *syllogisms* are often caused by concentrating on the plausibility of the *conclusion* rather than focusing on whether the conclusion follows from the *premises.*

10.   In deductive reasoning, the thinker tries to deduce a particular conclusion from a premise or set of premises. In *inductive reasoning,* the direction is reversed, for here the thinker tries to induce a general rule from particular instances. An initial, tentatively held induction is a *hypothesis.*

11.   Inductions often involve the estimation of frequencies and then extrapolations from these estimates. For these steps, people often make use of heuristics, cognitive rules of thumb that often serve us well enough but that may also lead to serious errors. One such rule of thumb is the *availability heuristic:* estimating the frequency of an event by how readily examples of such an event comes to mind. Another rule of thumb is the *representativeness heuristic:* assuming that a case is representative of its class. A number of studies have pointed to another problem—a powerful *confirmation bias* that makes participants seek evidence that will confirm their hypotheses rather than look for evidence that would show their hypotheses to be false.

12.   Most people have sensible intuitions about the role of sample size. These intuitions often lead people to realize that a small sample should not be trusted (its pattern might be the result of accident) and that a larger sample is more likely to be informative (since, with a larger sample, the likelihood of an accidental pattern is smaller). However, they often fail to apply these statistical intuitions. Courses in statistics and courses in psychology seem to diminish such errors.

13.   In decision making, people are not only sensitive to the benefit or loss and risk associated with each option. They are also sensitive to the way the options are *framed*. If an option is framed as a gain, they will avoid risk, holding tightly to what they have. If the same option is framed as a loss, they will take risks in hopes of diminishing the loss.

14.   Thinking can be localized in many different parts of the brain. The occipital cortex is active when people are thinking about visual events or forming a mental image. Broca's and Wernicke's areas are active when people are thinking about linguistic materials. The prefrontal cortex is active in many aspects of thought and may provide the neural basis for working memory.

15.   In recent years, psychologists have paid increasing attention to the problem of *consciousness.* Most of the progress in this area has come from studying psychological processes that operate when consciousness is absent. One example is *blindsight,* which occurs in people who have lost some portion of their visual cortex but can nevertheless perform many visual discriminations without being conscious that they can do so. Similar *nonconscious processing* occurs during innumerable occasions of everyday life when people retrieve memories without realizing they are doing so. Yet another everyday occurrence of nonconscious processing is the performance of automatized tasks. These phenomena suggest that consciousness functions as a monitor that lets us rise above habit and routine and allows us to tune our actions more appropriately to the specific circumstances.

CHAPTER 9

LANGUAGE

H uman societies differ enormously in their social forms and physical artifacts. But in all communities and all times, human societies have shared one prominent feature: All human societies have, and use, language. This essential connection, between having language and being human, is one reason why those interested in the nature of human minds have always been particularly intrigued with language.

To philosophers such as Descartes, language was the function that most clearly distinguished beasts from humans and was "the sole sign and only certain mark of thought hidden and wrapped up in the body." All humans have language, Descartes maintained, while no other animals have anything of the sort. But this claim comes up against an immediate objection: There are about 4,000 languages now in use on earth (Comrie, 1987). Each of these languages is obviously different from the others, for the users of one cannot understand the users of another. What do we mean, then, in claiming that all humans have language? Different humans speak different languages—be it French or Chinese or Hindi. In what sense, then, is "language" shared by all in our species?

The answer lies in the fact that human languages are much more alike than they seem to be at first glance. For example, all languages use sentences to organize ideas. In all languages, some sequences of words form an acceptable sentence, whereas other sequences of words do not. In all languages, assertions made about one topic can also be made about another topic. (For example, if a speaker understands the sentence, "Mark is tall," she will also understand the sentences "Susan is tall" and "The tree is tall.") These and many other properties are shared by all human languages but are found in none of the communication systems used by nonhumans. There are, then, important senses in which all human languages are alike. In much of this chapter, we will draw our language examples from English, but it is important to keep in mind that what we say about English generally goes for the other human languages as well.

MAJOR PROPERTIES OF HUMAN LANGUAGE

There are five properties of all human languages that psychology must describe: Language is *creative* (or *novel*), it is highly *structured* (or *patterned*), it is *meaningful,* it is *referential* (that is, it refers to and describes things and events in the real world), and it is *interpersonal* or *communicative* (involving the thoughts of more than one person at a time).

The biblical account of the origin of different languages *According to the Bible, all people once spoke a common language. But they built a tall structure, the Tower of Babel, and tried to reach the heavens. To punish them for their pride and folly, God made them unable to understand each other, each group speaking a different language. (*Tower of Babel *by Jan Brueghel, the Elder, 1568–1625; courtesy of Kunsthistorisches Museum, Vienna)*

LANGUAGE IS CREATIVE

At first glance, language might seem to be based merely on a set of associations, learned through memorization and practice. We observed our mothers, in the presence of a rabbit, saying "Look—there's a rabbit!" Because of this experience, we acquired the same habit, and so when we see a rabbit, we utter the same words.

But this view of language is hard to maintain, for speakers can both utter and understand a great many sentences that they have never uttered or heard before. In addition to "There's a rabbit," each of us can also say and understand:

That's a rabbit over there.

A rabbit is what I see over there.

Obviously, that's a rabbit.

Well bless my soul, if that isn't a rabbit!

And so on, with hundreds of other examples. And, of course, we can talk about many objects and creatures other than rabbits, including aardvarks and Afghans, apples and armies, proceeding all the way to zebras and Zyzzogetons. Since each of us has a vast number of sentences in our repertoire, it is unlikely that we memorized each of these, associating each one with the setting appropriate for its use.

In fact, a good estimate of the number of reasonably short (twenty words or fewer) English sentences is 10^{30}. If a learner memorized one hundred of these every minute, day after day, week after week, he would need a billion trillion years to learn just 1 percent of this huge set (Bloomfield, 1933; Chomsky, 1959).

We can understand virtually any sentence in this set of 10^{30}. Yet in our lifetimes, we've only had the opportunity to encounter a minute fraction of this set. Plainly, we can use and understand sentences we've never encountered before. Of course, some sentences are used over and over. ("How are you?" "What's new?" "Have a nice day!") But all the rest of them are likely to be novel—new to the person who says them and to his listeners as well.

To cope with this novelty, language use must be creative. We each have a limited—though large—number of words in our vocabulary, but we can use these to utter a virtually unlimited number of new sentences. We can do so because our language system allows us to combine the old words in new ways.

A number of other behavior patterns have a similar potential for systematic and novel use. Consider arithmetic. Surely we don't know the sum of, say 5,384 and 9,253 offhand. But we can readily calculate it, for we know a set of laws— the rules or principles of arithmetic. Similarly, we can drive cars to destinations where we have never traveled before, solve chess problems we have never previously encountered, and blush at embarrassments we have never experienced before. Thus, many behavioral systems have the unbounded character that we have just shown for language.

LANGUAGE IS STRUCTURED

We can and do invent new sentences all the time, but there are restrictions governing this creativity. This is evident in the fact that there are many strings of English words that—accidents aside—we would never utter. For example, we would not say "Is rabbit a that" or "A rabbit that's." These strings are incompatible with certain principles of language structure, principles that govern the ways in which words can be combined to make up new sentences. Generally, we do not know these principles consciously, but even so they govern our use of language, allowing us to compose a vast range of new sentences, but blocking us from uttering an equally vast range of nonsentences.

The rules governing actual language use (sometimes called **descriptive rules**) have to be distinguished from certain **prescriptive rules** handed down from various authorities about how they think we *ought* to speak or write. Prescriptive rules are the so-called rules of grammar that many of us learned painfully at school in the fourth grade (and thankfully forgot in the fifth), such as "Never say *ain't*" or "A sentence cannot end with a preposition." These recipes for speech and writing often do not conform to the actual facts about natural talking and understanding. For example, most of us have no qualms about ending sentences with a preposition (as in "Who did you give the packages to?") or even two prepositions ("What in the world are you up to?"). Indeed, in some cases, the "proper" formulation sounds quite unnatural to most language users (as in the case of Winston Churchill's often-quoted spoof of the preposition rule: "This is the kind of language up with which I will not put!").

In this chapter, our focus will be on the **structural principles** that every normal speaker honors without effort and without instruction. Why do we say "the rabbit" rather than "rabbit the"? Why do we say "I wonder where she is" and not "I wonder where is she"? Every language has these regularities, and these are fundamental to understanding language as a universal human skill.

LANGUAGE IS MEANINGFUL

Each word in a language expresses a meaningful idea about some thing (e.g., *camera* or *rabbit*), action (*run* or *rotate*), abstraction (*justice* or *fun*), quality (*red* or *altruistic*), and so on. The purpose of language is to express all these meanings to others. Therefore, we have no choice but to learn the vocabulary of our language—a vocabulary we share with all the other users of the same language.

The power of an "H"   A scene from the stage version of My Fair Lady *in which the cockney flower girl, Eliza (Julie Andrews), is taught by Henry Higgins (Rex Harrison) to pronounce an "H" the way the British upper classes do. She thus becomes a lady. This shows that following prescriptive rules can sometimes confer important social advantages. (Labov, 1970; photograph by Leonard McCombe/LIFE Magazine, © Time Warner, Inc.)*

But meanings are not conveyed just by individual words. Instead, people speak in whole sentences, and the grammatical relations within the sentences are crucial for meaning. "Dogs bite cats" means something different from "Cats bite dogs." Thus, part of meaning is derived, not just from individual words, but from the particular ways they are organized into sentences.

LANGUAGE IS REFERENTIAL

Language users must also know what the words and sentences refer to in the world. If a child said "That's a shoe" (a sentence whose grammar is impeccable and whose meaning is transparent) but did so while pointing to a rhinoceros, we would not think she had learned English very well. This is the problem of *reference:* how to use language to describe the world of real things and events—saying *shoe* to make reference to a shoe, but saying *rhinoceros* to refer to a rhinoceros.

The problem of reference is surprisingly complex in part because there are no simple relationships between the things we hear or say and the stimuli that surround us. The word *lemon* does, of course, refer to lemons, but one does not have to cry out "lemon!" every time one sees this fruit. And often one uses this term even when no lemons are in view. Moreover, there are many different ways to refer to this same fruit (one might say "yellow citrus fruit" instead of "lemon"). This flexibility obviously contributes to the expressive power of the language, but it also adds to the burden of anyone seeking to learn a language or the burden of any investigator seeking to understand the capacities that make human language possible.

LANGUAGE IS INTERPERSONAL

Many aspects of language production and language comprehension take place within a single human mind. But language use is a process that goes beyond the individual, for it is a social activity in which the thoughts of one mind are conveyed to another. To accomplish these social ends, each speaker must know not only the sounds, words, and sentences of his language, but also certain principles of conversation. These principles govern the way in which language is used under varying circumstances.

Suppose, for example, that one sees a lion in the parlor and wants to tell a companion about this. It is not enough that both parties speak English. One has to estimate the listener's capacities, motivations, and relations to oneself in order to speak appropriately. If the companion is a sharpshooter with a revolver, one might say:

Quick, shoot! There is a lion in the parlor.

But if the companion is an artist, one might say:

Quick, draw! Lion of a gorgeous shade of ochre in the parlor.

To a biologist, one might say:

Quick, look! Member of the genus Panthera *in the parlor.*

And to an enemy:

Lovely morning, isn't it? See you later.

Clearly, what one says about a situation is not just a description of that situation, but depends upon one's knowledge, beliefs, and wishes about the listener.

Adam gives names to the animals *The belief that knowledge of word meanings sets humans above animals goes back to antiquity. An example is the biblical tale illustrated in this painting by William Blake, which shows Adam assigning names to the animals. According to some ancient legends, this act established Adam's intellectual superiority over all creation, including even the angels. In one such tale, the angels were unable to call the animals by name, but Adam could: "'Oh Lord of the world! The proper name for this animal is ox, for this one horse, for this one lion, for this one camel!' And so he called all in turn, suiting the name to the peculiarity of the animal" (Ginzberg, 1909, vol. 1, p. 62). Notice that Adam thinks that words sound like what they mean. (William Blake's* Adam Naming the Beasts; *Stirling Maxwell Collection, Pollok House, Glasgow Museums & Art Galleries)*

The stimulus-free property of language use
How many sentences can you think of to de-
scribe this painting? (Henri Rousseau's The
Sleeping Gypsy, *1897, oil on canvas, 5'1" ×*
6'7". Collection, The Museum of Modern
Art, New York. Gift of Mrs. Simon Guggen-
heim)

To communicate successfully, then, one must build a mental picture of the other person to whom speech is addressed (Austin, 1962; Clark and Clark, 1977; Clark, 1978; Prince, 1981; Schiffrin, 1988).

The same problem arises for the listener. To determine the sense of what one has heard, one must make an estimate of the speaker and the circumstances of her utterances. Suppose, for example, the listener hears the question "Could you pass the salt?" If listener and speaker are in the midst of a conversation about arm strength, then a simple "yes" would be an appropriate response. More often, though, this same response would be considered obnoxious. In most settings, the listener understands the question to be just a polite way of requesting the salt, and so the answer should be, "Sure—here you are," accompanied by the relevant action (Searle, 1969; Clark, 1979; Sperber and Wilson, 1986).

In sum, the actual speech acts that pass between people are merely hints about the thoughts that are being conveyed. Talking would take just about forever if speakers literally had to say all, only, and exactly what they meant. Rather, the communicating pair takes the utterance and its context as the basis for making a series of complicated inferences about the meaning and intent of the conversation. A listener who fails to make these inferences is taken as an incompetent at best and a bore (or boor) at worst. A person who blandly answers "Yes" when you say "Could you tell me the time?" has failed to obey the principles of conversation that make communication possible (Grice, 1968; for overviews, see Leech, 1983; Horn, 1987).

THE BASIC UNITS OF LANGUAGE

We have mentioned that language is structured. In fact, languages consist of a hierarchy of structures—with some rules governing the way sounds are combined to form words, other rules governing the way words are combined to form phrases, and still other rules governing the way phrases are combined to form sentences. We will use this hierarchy to organize much of our discussion in this

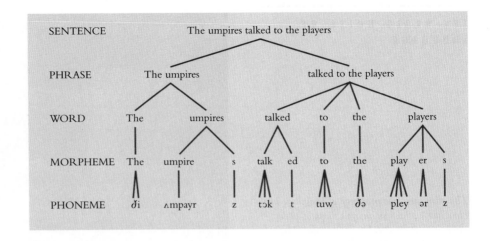

9.1   The hierarchy of linguistic units
Language is hierarchical, with sentences at the top. Sentences are composed of phrases, which in turn are composed of words. Words are made up of morphemes, the smallest units of language that carry meaning. The units of sound that compose morphemes are phonemes, and the symbols represent the actual vocal sounds produced.

chapter, beginning by describing the basic building blocks of language. (See Figure 9.1, which illustrates the hierarchy of linguistic structures.)

PHONEMES

To speak, we force a column of air up from the lungs and out through the mouth, while simultaneously moving the various parts of the vocal apparatus from one position to another (see Figure 9.2). Each of these movements shapes the column of moving air and thus changes the sound produced (MacNeilage, 1972). Many of these differences among speech sounds are ignored by the listener. Consider the word *bus,* which can be pronounced with more or less of a hiss in the *s.* This difference is irrelevant to the listener, who interprets what was heard to mean "a large vehicle" in either case. But some sound distinctions do matter, for they signal differences in meaning. Thus, neither *butt* nor *fuss* will be taken to mean "a large vehicle." This suggests that the distinctions among *s, f,* and *t* sounds are relevant to speech perception, while the difference in hiss magnitude is not.

The words *bus* and *fuss* differ in their initial phoneme but then are identical in their second and third phonemes. **Phonemes** are the basic perceptual units of which speech is composed (Liberman, 1970).

UNDERSTANDING UNFAMILIAR SPEECH

The human speech apparatus can produce hundreds of different speech sounds clearly and reliably. But no language uses all of these sounds. English uses about forty different phonemes.★ Other languages select their own sets. For instance, German uses certain guttural sounds that are never heard in English, and French uses some vowels that are different from the English ones.

Once children have learned the sounds used in their native tongue, they usually become quite rigid in their phonemic ways: It becomes difficult for them to utter sounds not used in their native language or to distinguish these foreign sounds from each other (Werker, 1995). This is one reason why foreign speech often sounds like a vague and undifferentiated muddle, rather than like a sequence of separable sounds.

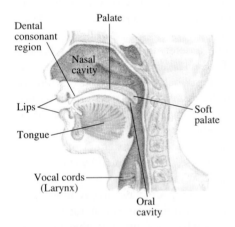

Palate
Dental consonant region
Nasal cavity
Lips
Soft palate
Tongue
Vocal cords (Larynx)
Oral cavity

9.2   The human vocal tract   *Speech is produced by air flow from the lungs that passes through the larynx (popularly called the voice box) containing the vocal cords and from there through the oral and nasal cavities, which together make up the vocal tract. Different vowels are created by movements of the lips and tongue, which change the size and shape of the vocal cavity. Consonants are produced by various articulatory movements that temporarily obstruct the air flow through the vocal tract. For some consonants the air flow is stopped completely. Examples are p, where the stoppage is produced by bringing both lips together, and t, where it is produced by bringing the tip of the tongue to the back of the upper teeth. Some other consonants are created by blocking the air flow only partially, for example th (as in thick), which is produced by bringing the tip of the tongue close to the upper teeth but without actually touching them. (After Lieberman, 1975)*

★ The English alphabet provides only twenty-six symbols (letters) to write these forty phonemes, so it often uses the same symbol for more than one. Thus, the letter *O* stands for two different sounds in *hot* and *cold,* an "ah" sound and an "oh" sound. This fact contributes to the difficulty of learning how to read English.

Another difficulty in understanding unfamiliar speech has to do with the sheer rate at which the speech sounds are produced. Adults can understand speech at the rate of 250 words per minute (Foulke and Sticht, 1969); this converts to about 16 phonemes per second. These phonemes are usually fired off in a continuous stream, with no gaps or silences in between to mark the boundaries of each speech unit. Indeed, the production of one phoneme often overlaps with the production of the next, so that, for example, the speaker begins to pronounce the vowel before finishing the preceding consonant. This is true for successive phonemes within a single word and also for successive words within a phrase, so that sometimes it is hard to know whether one is hearing "a gray tabby" or "a great abbey." Part of the listener's task, therefore, is to **parse** the stream of speech sounds into its appropriate units, a process that is guided by knowledge of the vocabulary and structure of the language being spoken. (We also met the problem of parsing in Chapter 6.)

COMBINING PHONEMES

In all human languages, the relatively small stock of phonemes is combined and recombined to create an impressively large number of words (at least 75,000, for most college students). But the phonemes are not combined in a helter-skelter fashion; this is one of the many ways in which languages are structured. As an illustration, consider the task of an advertising executive who wishes to find a name for a new breakfast food. Will any new arrangement of phonemes do? The answer is no. To begin with, some sequences (gogrps? fpibs?) would be hard to pronounce. But even among phoneme sequences that can be pronounced, some seem somehow un-Englishlike. Consider the following possibilities: Pritos, Glitos, and Tlitos. They can all be pronounced, but one seems wrong: Tlitos. English speakers sense intuitively that English words never start with *tl,* even though this sequence is perfectly acceptable in the middle of a word (as in *motley* or *battling*). So the new breakfast food will be marketed as tasty, crunchy Pritos or Glitos. Either of these two names will do, but Tlitos is out of the question. The restriction against *tl*-beginnings is not a restriction on what human tongues and ears can do. For instance, one Northwest Indian language is named Tlingit, obviously by people who are perfectly willing to have words begin with *tl*. This shows that the restriction is a structural principle of English specifically. Few of us are conscious of this principle, but we have learned it and similar principles exceedingly well, for we honor them in our actual language use (Chomsky and Halle, 1968).

Another structural rule governs the formation of the English plural. If one listens carefully, one can hear that the plural of *buck* or *kit* is pronounced with an *s* sound, but the plural of *bug* or *kid* is pronounced with a *z* sound (although spelled with an *s*). This pronunciation of the plural is governed by the features of the consonant preceding the final *s;* the relevant rule is unconsciously honored by all speakers of English and is learned, without instruction or guidance, by every English-speaking child, usually by the age of three (Berko, 1958).

MORPHEMES AND WORDS

At the next level of the linguistic hierarchy (see Figure 9.1), fixed sequences of phonemes are joined into morphemes. The **morphemes** are the smallest language units that carry bits of meaning. Like phonemes, the morphemes of a language can be combined only in certain ways. Some words consist of a single morpheme, such as *and, run,* or *strange.* But many morphemes cannot stand alone and must be joined with others to make up a complex word. Examples are *er* (meaning "one who") and *s* (meaning "more than one"). When these are joined with the morpheme *strange* (meaning "alien" or "odd") into the complex word *strangers* (*strange* + *er* + *s*), the meaning becomes correspondingly complex ("ones who are odd or alien"). Each of these morphemes has a fixed position within the word. Thus *er* has to follow *strange* and precede *s;* other orders (such as *erstranges* or *strangeser*) are not allowed (Aranoff, 1976).

The morphemes such as *strange* that carry the main burden of meaning are called **content morphemes.** The morphemes that add details to the meaning but also serve various grammatical purposes (such as the suffix *er* or the connecting word *and*) are called **function morphemes.**

The average speaker of English has acquired about 80,000 morphemes by adulthood (Miller and Gildea, 1987), knows the meaning of each, and how they are positioned within words. If we counted vocabulary by words rather than by morphemes, normal people would be credited with several hundred thousand of these, for then *strange, stranger, strangers,* etc., would each count as a separate item.

PHRASES AND SENTENCES

The system of words in a language is very rich and allows us to express an enormous variety of meanings with great precision. Nevertheless, we cannot memorize a new word for each of the hundreds of millions of thoughts that we want to express. Therefore, we combine our limited—though large—stock of words into whole sentences. We may remark either "The lion kicked the gnu" or "The gnu kicked the lion." Both these sequences of words are meaningful, but there is a difference in the meaning that is of some importance—at least to the lion and the gnu.

Just as a morpheme is an organized grouping of phonemes and a word is an organized grouping of morphemes, so a **phrase** is an organized grouping of words. The phrases are the building blocks of which sentences are composed. Consider the sentence

The French bottle smells.

This sentence is **ambiguous:** It can be understood in two ways depending on how the words are grouped into phrases; either

(The French bottle) (smells).

or *(The French) (bottle) (smells).*

Thus by the choice of phrasing (that is, word grouping), the word *bottle* comes out a noun in the first interpretation, so that sentence is telling us something about French bottles. But *bottle* comes out a verb in the next interpretation, in which case the sentence is telling us about what the French put into bottles—namely, smells (that is, perfumes). For another example, see Figure 9.3.

The phrase is thus the unit that organizes words into meaningful groupings within the sentence. Just as for phoneme sequences and morpheme sequences, some phrase sequences (like those we just considered) are acceptable, while others are outlawed: for example, *(The French) (smells) (bottle).*

THE MEANING OF WORDS

What exactly do we know when we know a word's meaning? This turns out to be a surprisingly knotty question. Investigators interested in this problem of **semantics** have been able to give only partial answers (see Putnam,

9.3 How phrase structure can affect meaning   *On being asked what a Mock Turtle is, the Queen tells Alice "It's the thing Mock Turtle Soup is made from." Needless to say, this is a misanalysis of the phrase* mock turtle soup *as* (mock turtle) (soup). *It ought to be organized as* (mock) (turtle soup)—*a soup that is not really made out of turtles (and is in fact usually made out of veal). (Lewis Carroll,* Alice in Wonderland, *1969, p. 73.)*

1975; Fodor, 1983, 1988; Partee, 1996). Let us begin by eliminating some of the answers that appear to be false.

MEANING AS REFERENCE

One approach to the topic of meaning equates a word's (or phrase's) meaning with its **reference.** According to this position, the meaning of a word or phrase is whatever it refers to in the world. On this view, words function just like proper names: The name *George Washington* can be understood as the label for a particular person, the name *Athens* the label for a city in Greece. In the same fashion, the **reference theory of meaning** claims that *cherry* is simply the label for a particular kind of fruit and *locomotive* the label for a particular kind of vehicle. Knowing these words, therefore, is simply a matter of knowing what in the world it is that is being labeled.

But this suggestion soon runs into difficulties. Most of us know the word *unicorn,* and we easily understand the phrase *The Crown Prince of South Dakota.* But these expressions have no real-world referents at all. Similarly, one cannot point to a referent for abstractions like *infinity* or *historical inevitability.* But these terms are far from meaningless. Apparently, a word or phrase can have meaning without referring to something concrete.

Another problem with meaning as reference was noted by the German philosopher, Gottlob Frege. He noted that the expression *the morning star* has one meaning (the last star visible in the eastern sky as dawn breaks), and the expression *the evening star* has quite a different meaning (the first star visible in the western sky as the sun sets). Yet both of these expressions refer to one and the same object in the sky (the planet Venus). Thus, two expressions can have different meanings yet refer to the same thing (Frege, 1892). As another example, it seems clear that the phrase *creature with a heart* means something different from the phrase *creature with a kidney.* Yet in the biology of our planet, it turns out that the creatures referred to by the first phrase are identical to the creatures referred to by the second. (That is, all creatures with hearts also have kidneys, and vice versa.) It follows that there is a distinction between the meaning of a word or phrase and the things that this word or phrase refers to in the world. The meaning of a word is the idea or concept that it expresses. The referents of the word are all those things in the real (or imaginary) world that fall under that concept.

THE DEFINITIONAL THEORY OF MEANING

We have just concluded that the meaning of a word is a concept (or **category**). Some words describe concepts that refer to only one thing or creature in the real or imaginary world, such as *Madonna* or *Pinocchio,* while other words such as *dog* or *unicorn* are more general, describing categories that have many referents. But is the meaning of a word always just a simple concept, irreducible to simpler elements? Most theories of word meaning assert that only a relative handful of the words in a language describe elementary, "simple" concepts. The rest are labels for bundles of concepts. Thus, the words *feathers, flies, animal, wings* might describe simple concepts, but all of these ideas are bundled together in the (relatively) complex word *bird.* One approach of this kind is the **definitional theory of meaning.** It holds that meanings are analyzable into a set of subcomponents, organized in our minds much as they are in standard dictionaries. This approach starts out with the fact that there are various meaning relationships among different words and phrases. Some words are similar in meaning *(wicked-evil);* others are opposites *(wicked-good);* still others seem virtually unrelated *(wicked-ultramarine).* According to the definitional proposal, these relationships can be explained by assuming that words are **bundles of semantic**

Is this the entry for bird in your mental dictionary? "bird . . . n. . . . [ME, fr. OE bridd] . . . **2:** *Any of a class (Aves) of warm-blooded vertebrates distinguished by having the body more or less completely covered with feathers and the forelimbs modified as wings. . . .*

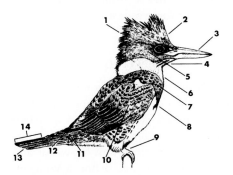

"bird 2 (kingfisher): 1 *crest,* 2 *crown,* 3 *bill,* 4 *throat,* 5 *auricular region,* 6 *breast,* 7 *scapulars,* 8 *abdomen,* 9 *tarsus,* 10 *upper wing coverts,* 11 *primaries,* 12 *secondaries,* 13 *rectrix,* 14 *tail"* (Merriam-Webster's Collegiate Dictionary, Tenth Edition)

features (Katz and Fodor, 1963; Katz, 1972). As an example, take the word *bachelor*. This word clearly has something in common with *uncle, brother, gander,* and *stallion*. As speakers of English, we know that all of these words carry the notion *male*. This point is forcefully made by considering various sentences that most English speakers will regard as odd (or, to use the technical term, *anomalous*). Thus, the sentence *My _____ is pregnant* sounds very peculiar if the missing word is any of the members of the bachelor-related group listed below:

	uncle	
	brother	
My	gander	is pregnant.
	stallion	
	bachelor	

Further thought shows that *bachelor,* for example, contains additional features, such as *unmarried* and *adult*. This explains why the following sentences would also be anomalous in meaning:

My sister is married to a bachelor.

I met a two-year-old bachelor yesterday.

On this view, therefore, the full meaning of *bachelor* might be composed of this set of semantic features: *never married, human, adult,* and *male*. The meaning of *stallion* would bundle together these features: *adult, male,* and *horse*. It is these features that constitute the definition of each word, and according to this theory, we carry such definitions in our heads for each of the words in our vocabulary.

THE PROTOTYPE THEORY OF MEANING

The definitional theory faces a problem, for some members of a meaning category appear to exemplify that category better than others do. Thus, a German shepherd seems to be a more doglike dog than a Pekinese, and an armchair seems to be a better example of the concept of *furniture* than a reading lamp. This seems to be at odds with the analysis we have described thus far, whose aim was to specify the necessary and sufficient attributes that define a concept. When a dictionary says that a bachelor is "an adult human male who has never been married," it claims to have said it all. Whatever fits under the umbrella of this definitional feature list is a bachelor. Whatever does not, is not. But if so, how can one bachelor be more bachelorlike (or one dog more doglike) than another?

The question is whether the semantic categories described by words are really as all-or-none as the definitional theory would have it. Several investigators have made a strong case for an alternative view, called the **theory of prototypes** (Rosch, 1973b; Rosch and Mervis, 1975; Smith and Medin, 1981).

The facts that the prototype theory tries to account for can easily be illustrated. Consider the category *bird*. Are there features that characterize all birds and that only characterize birds? One might think that *able to fly* is a feature of all birds, but it is not. (Ostriches cannot fly.) Instead, one might think that *has feathers* is a feature of all birds, but again it is not. (If one plucked all the feathers from a robin, it would be a naked robin, an abused robin, but it would still be a robin, wouldn't it?) And of course, there are many things that fly that are not birds (airplanes, helicopters). There are also some things that have feathers that are not birds (some hats, quill pens, down comforters). Therefore, we cannot assert that being a bird is simply a matter of having the relevant features; some birds don't have the "birdy" features, and some nonbirds do.

Can a white rose be red? *The Queen had ordered the gardeners to plant a red rose bush, but they planted a white one by mistake. They're now trying to repair their error by painting the white roses red. On the definitional theory of meaning, this seems reasonable enough. For the expressions* red rose bush *and* white rose bush *differ by only a single feature—red versus white. But if so, why are they so terrified that the Queen will discover what they did? (From Lewis Carroll,* Alice in Wonderland, *1971, p. 62)*

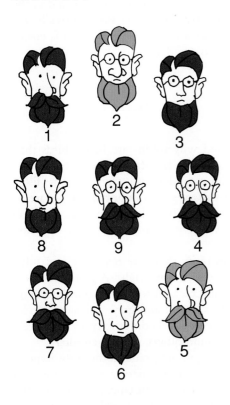

9.4 The Smith brothers and their family resemblance *The Smith brothers are related through family resemblance, though no two brothers share all features. The one who has the greatest number of the family attributes is the most prototypical. In the example, it is Brother 9 who has all the family features: brown hair, large ears, large nose, moustache, and eyeglasses. (Courtesy of Sharon Armstrong)*

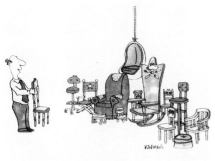

"Attention, everyone! I'd like to introduce the newest member of our family." (Drawing by Kaufman; © 1977 The New Yorker Magazine, Inc.)

Perhaps, then, there are no *necessary* features for being a bird (features that one must have in order to be a bird), and no *sufficient* features (features only found on birds), with the consequence that, if one has these features, one must be a bird. But if not, then the definitonal theory is not correct.

According to the prototype theory, the meaning of many words is described as a whole set of features, no one of which is individually either necessary or sufficient. The concept is then held together by what some philosophers call a **family resemblance structure** (Wittgenstein, 1953). Consider the way members of a family resemble each other. Joe may look like his father to the extent that he has his eyes; he may look like his mother by virtue of his prominent chin. His sister Sue may look like her father to the extent that she has his nose, and she may smile just like her mother. But Joe and Sue may have no feature in common (he has his grandfather's nose and she has Aunt Fanny's eyes), and so the two of them do not look alike at all. Even so, they are both easily recognized as members of the family, for they each bear some resemblance to their parents (see Figure 9.4).

In general, a family resemblance is based on a set of attributes. Probably no single member of the family has all of these attributes. Nor will any two members of a family have all the same ones (except for identical twins). But all will have at least some, and these will identify them as members of the family. Of course, some individuals will have many of the family features and so will sometimes be called "true Johnsons" or "prototypical Smiths." They are the family members most readily identified as being in the family and the best examples to point to as typical.

Many investigators believe that the same pattern holds for many of our common concepts, such as *bird, chair*, and so forth. We have already noted that some members of a category seem more prototypical than others, so that a German shepherd seems more doglike than a Pekinese. This is presumably because the shepherd has many of the features associated with the "dog family," while the Pekinese has few. Similarly, we have discussed the difficulties of finding necessary and sufficient conditions for concepts such as *bird;* this too is compatible with the family-resemblance idea, because, as we mentioned, it is entirely possible that no features will be shared by all members of a family and reasonably likely that no features will be unique to that family.

How is knowledge about a family resemblance structure represented in the mind? According to many investigators, most prominently Eleanor Rosch, each of us carries in memory a mental **prototype** for each of our concepts—a prototypical bird, a prototypical chair, and so on (Rosch, 1973b; Rosch and Mervis, 1975; Smith and Medin, 1981). These prototypes are generally derived from our experiences, so that each prototype provides something like a mental average of all the examples of the concept the person has encountered. In the case of birds, people in our culture have presumably seen far more robins than penguins. As a result, something that resembles a robin will be stored in their memory system and will then be associated with the word *bird*. When the person later sees a new object, she will judge it to be a bird to the extent that it resembles the prototype in some way. A sparrow resembles it in many ways and so is judged to be a "good" bird; a penguin resembles it just a little and hence is a marginal bird; a rowboat resembles it not at all and hence is judged to be no bird.

We have already mentioned some of the evidence consistent with this view— the fact that some category members are reliably judged to be better members than others; also the difficulty in specifying necessary and sufficient conditions for a category. Other evidence comes from numerous laboratory studies. For example, when people are asked to come up with examples of some category, they generally produce instances that are close to the presumed prototype (e.g., robin rather than ostrich). This most likely reflects the fact that their memory search begins with the prototype and then works outward from there. A related result concerns the time required to verify category membership. Study participants respond more quickly to the sentence *A robin is a bird* than to *An ostrich is a bird*. This is perfectly sensible: A robin resembles the bird prototype and so the similarity is readily discerned, allowing a fast "true" response. For an ostrich, one must spend a moment searching for the birdy features, so verification is correspondingly slower (Rosch et al., 1976; Rosch, 1978; for a related discussion, see Chapter 8, pp. 309–10).

COMBINING DEFINITIONAL AND PROTOTYPE THEORIES

The prototype view helps us to understand why robins are better birds than ostriches. But the definitional theory explains why an ostrich is nevertheless recognized as a bird. The prototype view helps us understand why a trout is "fishier" than a sea horse, but the definitional theory seems important if we are to explain why a sea horse is far fishier than a whale (which, of course, is not a fish at all). Perhaps we can combine both views of meaning rather than choosing between them.

Consider the word *grandmother.* For this term, there are necessary and sufficient features, so here the definitional theory seems just right: A grandmother is a female parent of a parent. But there may also be a prototype: A grandmotherly grandmother is a person who bakes cookies, is old and gray, and has a kindly twinkle in her eye. When we say that someone is grandmotherly, we are surely referring to the prototypical attributes of grandmothers, not to genealogy.

In many circumstances, we are likely to rely on our grandmother prototype—for picking a grandmother out of a crowd, for predicting what someone's grandmother will be like, and so on. But in other circumstances, we rely on the definition: If we know some kindly lady who is gray and twinkly but never had a child, we may think of her as grandmotherly but not as a grandmother (Lakoff and Johnson, 1980; Landau, 1982).

It appears, therefore, that people have two partly independent mental representations of *grandmother,* and the same is probably true for most other words as well. They know about prototypical attributes associated with the term and probably store a list (or perhaps a picture) of such attributes as a handy way of picking out likely grandmother candidates. But they also store defining grandmother features (e.g., mother of a parent). These definitional features determine the limits of the term *grandmother* and tell one how to use the prototype appropriately (Miller and Johnson-Laird, 1976; Smith and Medin, 1981; Armstrong, Gleitman, and Gleitman, 1983).

Prototypes   *Members of the bird category. (A) A prototypical bird—the robin. (B) An atypical bird—the ostrich. (C) An exceedingly atypical bird—the penguin. (Photographs by Tim Wright, Alissa Crandall, Wolfgang Kaehler, all courtesy of Corbis)*

9.5 What makes someone a bachelor?
The term bachelor *usually has a clear defini-*
tion: A bachelor is an unmarried adult male.
However, this noun can be understood only in
the context of certain expectations about mar-
riage and marriageable age. As you answer the
questions here, what is it that guides your judg-
ment? (After Fillmore, 1982)

1. Alfred is an unmarried adult male, but he has been living with his girl-
friend for the last twenty-three years. Their relationship is happy and stable. Is
Alfred a bachelor?

2. Bernard is an unmarried adult male, and he does not have a partner.
Bernard is a monk living in a monastery. Is Bernard a bachelor?

3. Charles is a married adult male, but he has not seen his wife for many
years. Charles is earnestly dating, hoping to find a new partner. Is Charles a
bachelor?

4. Donald is a married adult male, but he lives in a culture that encourages
men to take two wives. Donald is earnestly dating, hoping to find a new partner. Is Donald a bachelor?

One further complication: For many terms, even this two-part representation
(prototype plus definition) is not enough. Imagine trying to explain the word
commute to a Bedouin living in the desert. One would first need to explain what
it means to live in one fixed place, then what it means to have an activity called
work that was distinct from the other activities in life, and what it means to have
a workplace to which one must travel. The term *commute,* in other words, can be
understood only with reference to a particular way of life. Similarly, *picnic* is a
term that makes sense only in contrast to how (and where) one ordinarily dines.
Bachelor, too, is a term whose meaning is specific to a particular social system
(Figure 9.5). These examples suggest that many words can be understood only
in the context of other concepts and in terms of a web of beliefs specifying how
these concepts are interrelated (for fuller discussion of this idea, see Reisberg,
1997).

Organizing Words Into Meaningful Sentences

Adults have a vocabulary containing tens of thousands of words, allowing
them to express an enormous variety of meanings. The real power of the
language, though, comes from the fact that we are able to combine these words
into phrases and sentences to express hundreds of millions of different thoughts,
whether we are seeking to describe a particularly beautiful sunset, to ask for a
raise, or to comment on three of the spotted ostriches on Joe Smith's farm.

The basic sentences we use introduce some topic (the **subject** of the sentence)
and then make some comment, or offer some information, about that topic (the
predicate of the sentence). Thus, when we say "The girl hit the ball," we introduce the girl as the topic, and then we *propose* or *predicate* of the girl that she hit
the ball. This is why sentence meanings are often called **propositions:** "The girl
hit the ball" proposes (of the girl) that she hit the ball.

In effect, a proposition describes a miniature drama in which the verb is the
action and the nouns are the performers, each playing a different role. In our
proposition about girl-hitting-ball, the girl is the *doer,* the ball is the *done to,* and
hit is the *action* itself. The job of a listener, then, is to determine which actors are
portraying the various roles in the drama and what the plot (the action) is
(Healy and Miller, 1970). This would be much easier if all sentences were
expressed in a standard sequence of doer, action, done-to. But, of course, sentences can take many other forms ("The ball was hit by the girl"; "what happened to the ball was that the girl hit it"). Thus, the listener's task—discovering

Noam Chomsky

exactly who did what to whom—can become quite complex (Harris, 1952; Chomsky, 1957).

As an added complexity, there are also many kinds of propositions. For example, in sentences about sneezing, there need only be the subject of the sentence and the verb itself (e.g., "John sneezes"). But when we talk of hitting, we need to describe two entities in addition to the verb: who does the hitting and who (or what) gets hit. Correspondingly, sentences with *hit* will have two noun entities in addition to the verb (e.g., "The *girl* hit the *ball*"). For acts of giving, which describe the transfer of objects from one person or place to another, we generally express three entities: the giver, the given, and the getter (e.g., "The *girl* gives a *bone* to the *dog*"). Finally, some verbs such as *think* can express a relation between some entity and a whole proposition (rather than just a relation between two entities). We express this by putting a proposition—essentially, a little sentence—after the verb (e.g., "*John* thinks that *Mary is a mongoose*"). In these ways, then, sentences are a reflection of the variety of ways in which people conceptualize events, scenes, and relations (Fillmore, 1968; Bresnan, 1982; Jackendoff, 1987, 1990; Rappaport and Levin, 1988; Grimshaw, 1990; Fisher, Gleitman, and Gleitman, 1991).

PHRASE STRUCTURE

As we have noted, the number of sentences one can create by combining words in different ways is virtually unlimited. But there are also many combinations of words that we would not utter. One might think that the distinction between acceptable sentences ("The boy ran") and unacceptable ones ("Ran boy the") is a matter of meaning—a sentence must be meaningful in order to be acceptable. But this is plainly false. Some nonsentences have meaning ("Me Tarzan; you Jane"). And many grammatical sentences are entirely uninterpretable: "Colorless green ideas sleep furiously." This sentence makes no sense because abstract ideas have no color and green things are not colorless. But it seems well formed in a way that the following word string does not: "Sleep green furiously ideas colorless."

Thus, it is not meaning that distinguishes sentences from nonsentences. Instead, a series of formal rules seems to govern this distinction. These rules, specifying how words and phrases can be combined, are referred to as the rules of **syntax** (from the Greek, "arranging together"). The study of syntax has been one of the principal concerns of linguists and psycholinguists over the last few decades, with much of the discussion organized around the ideas of Noam Chomsky (Chomsky, 1975, 1980, 1986; Sells, 1985; Radford, 1988).

A grammar lesson at the Mad Hatter's Tea Party The meanings of words change in different linguistic constructions, so grammatical patterns are of great importance for communication.
March Hare: "You should say what you mean."
Alice: "I do—at least I mean what I say—that's the same thing, you know."
Hatter: "Not the same thing a bit! Why, you might just as well say that 'I see what I eat' is the same thing as 'I eat what I see'!"
March Hare: "You might just as well say that 'I like what I get' is the same thing as 'I get what I like.'"
(From Lewis Carroll, Alice in Wonderland, 1971.)

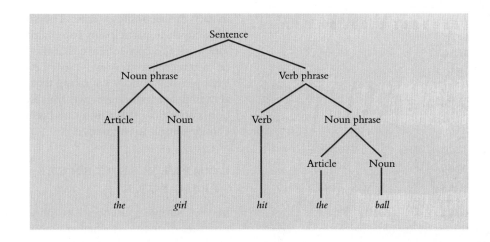

9.6 The structure of the sentence "The girl hit the ball" *This tree is called a phrase-structure description, for it shows how the sentence can be analyzed into phrase units. Notice particularly that there are two noun phrases in this sentence: One noun phrase ("the ball") is part of the verb phrase ("hit the ball"); the other noun phrase ("the girl") is not part of the verb phrase. A description of this kind also shows the word class types (e.g., article, noun, verb) of which each phrase consists. Finally, it shows the words of the sentence. Reading these (the bottom row in the tree) from left to right, we get the actual sequence of words in the sentence being described. Thus (in its bottom row), the tree describes the actual words that speakers say and listeners hear.*

The rules of syntax specify which elements must be included within a sentence and in what order these elements may appear. These rules also specify how the words group together. Consider again the simple sentence "The girl hit the ball." It seems naturally organized into two parts—a noun phrase (*the girl*) and a verb phrase (*hit the ball*). Linguists depict this partitioning of the sentence by means of a tree diagram, so called because of its branching appearance:

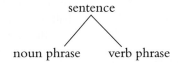

This notation is a useful way of showing that sentences can be thought of as a hierarchy of structures (Figure 9.1, p. 350). Each sentence can be broken down into phrases, and these into smaller phrases, which can in turn be broken down into words. The descending branches of the tree correspond to the smaller and smaller units of sentence structure. The whole tree structure is called a ***phrase structure description*** of the sentence. Figure 9.6 shows the phrase structure of the sentence "The girl hit the ball." At the very top of the tree this description asserts that the example is a sentence; at the bottom it is a string of words; and in between it is a sequence of phrases, subphrases, and word-class names (e.g., noun and verb).

The importance of phrase structure can be demonstrated in many ways. First, these structures capture the fact that there are natural groupings for the words within a sentence. This is reflected in the fact that even children can analyze sentences into the constituents defined by this structure (Read and Schreiber, 1982). Second, these structures also capture some important facts about how words can be combined and recombined. If, for example, a sentence calls for a noun phrase in a particular position, then any noun phrase will do, no matter what words it contains. Replacing one noun phrase with another will, of course, change what the sentence means, but it will not change the sentence's grammatical form or its grammatical acceptability. In this fashion, the phrase structure identifies units that can be swapped around like self-contained modules.

The role of phrase structure is also evident in many aspects of how we perceive, produce, or remember sentences. For example, one investigator asked subjects to memorize strings of nonsense words. Some of the strings had no structure at all, such as: "Yig wur vum rix hum im jag miv." Other strings, however, also included various function morphemes, providing a structure: "The yigs wur vumly rixing hum im jagest miv." One might think that sequences of the second type would be harder than the first to memorize, for they are longer. But

359

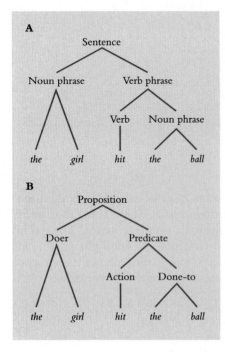

9.7 **_From structure to meaning_** *(A) The structure of the sentence "The girl hit the ball" (simplified); (B) The drama of who-did-what-to-whom as reconstructed by the listener from the structure in (A).*

in fact the opposite is true. The function morphemes in the second version allowed study participants to organize the sequence in terms of a phrase structure, with the consequence that the structured sequences were appreciably easier to remember (Epstein, 1961; Levelt, 1970). This is obviously related to the examples of memory chunking that we discussed in Chapter 7: Memory is reliably improved whenever we are able to organize individual pieces of information, combining them into one higher-level unit that can then be treated as just a single chunk to memorize.

COMPLEX SENTENCES AND UNDERLYING STRUCTURE

In very simple sentences, the phrase structure also reflects the propositional structure of who did what to whom. ("The girl hit the ball"; "The cow kicked the horse"; "The speech stunned the crowd"; see Figure 9.7). But the sentences we encounter every day are usually much more complicated than these examples. Many factors contribute to this complexity. Sometimes, we phrase our sentences in a fashion that allows us to emphasize aspects of the scene other than the doer ("It was *the ball* that she hit"). And often we wish to do more than describe some state of affairs in the world. For example, we may wish to express our attitudes toward these states of affairs ("*I was delighted that* the girl hit the ball"), or we may wish to relate one proposition to another and so will utter two or more of them in the same sentence ("The girl *who ate the hamburger* hit the ball").

This added complexity of meaning obviously adds complexity to the sentence structures themselves. Now the done-to may be mentioned before the doer; many words may intervene between the doer and the action (Figure 9.8). Yet the listener manages to recover the sentence's meaning, still grasping the basic sentence drama of who did what to whom, no matter how this scenario is hidden and disguised in the complex sentence.

To achieve this understanding, listeners seem to think about the sentence in two different ways. The first is the **surface structure** of the sentence—the string of words actually uttered, organized into its various parts (as depicted in Figure 9.6). The second is the **underlying structure** of the sentence—a structure that directly reflects the meaning of the sentence.

9.8 **_The structure of the sentence "The ball was hit by the girl"_** *Notice that the phrase-structure descriptions in Figures 9.6 and 9.8 look quite different: The words in the bottom row are arranged in different ways. Thus the two trees succeed in describing the fact that the active sentence and the passive sentence sound quite different even though they have quite a few words in common.*

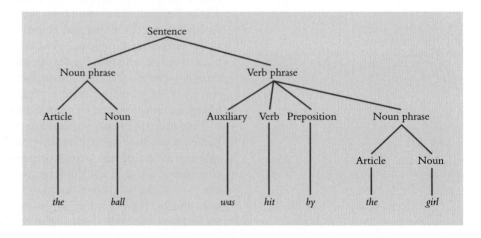

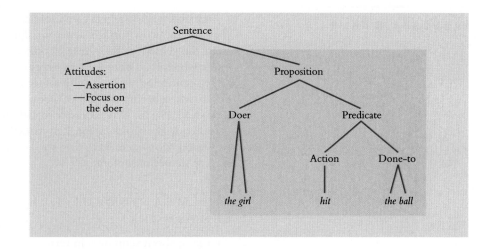

9.9 Underlying structure of "The girl hit the ball" Notice that the actual English sentence "The girl hit the ball" looks exactly like the proposition "The girl hit the ball" as it appears in this underlying structure. But as the diagram shows, the real sentence is something more than the proposition: It is an assertion of the truth of the proposition. In informal wording, when a person says, "The girl hit the ball," he really means, "I assert that it is true that the girl hit the ball." The tree diagram here describes both aspects of the thought: its proposition and the attitude about it.

We have already mentioned one aspect of the underlying structure, namely, the proposition, or basic thought, that the sentence is about (as depicted in Figure 9.9). The proposition is the same in all the different sentences below, for they are all about the idea *girl-hitting-ball:*

1. *The girl hit the ball.*

2. *The girl did not hit the ball.*

3. *The ball was hit by the girl.*

4. *Wasn't the ball hit by the girl?*

Because all these sentences contain the same proposition, they are related in meaning—they are about the same doer, act, and done-to. But clearly they are not identical in meaning. What differs is the stance, or **attitude,** the speaker is adopting toward the proposition. Sentence 1 asserts the truth of the proposition about *girl-hitting-ball,* sentence 2 denies it, sentence 3 asserts it but shifts the main focus of attention onto the ball rather than the girl, and sentence 4 is a complex case of this focus shift along with attitudes of both questioning and denial.

A sentence's underlying structure reflects both the expressed proposition and the attitude (Figure 9.10). And as with surface structure, the organization of the underlying structure can be described in terms of a phrase structure tree. This is because the meaning of the sentence (just as with the sentence's outward form) is naturally organized in terms of phrases that act as coherent wholes.

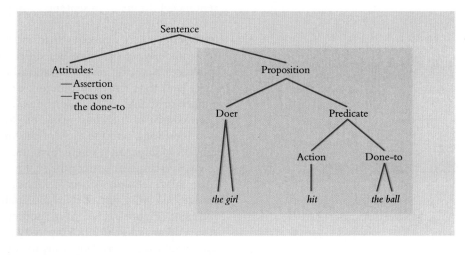

9.10 Underlying structure of the passive sentence "The ball was hit by the girl" The similarity of meaning of this sentence to the one shown in Figure 9.9 is that both have the same proposition. The difference is that their list of attitudes is partly different.

361

In many ways, listeners care more about a sentence's underlying structure than they do about its surface structure. This is reflected in what people remember from the sentences they hear. People are often quite poor at remembering the exact words that were used to express an idea, the sequence in which the ideas were mentioned, or even who said what in a conversation. They are much better at remembering the gist of a conversation or the general plot of a story they have read (Sachs, 1967; Bransford, 1979). This is not surprising: We generally care about the point a speaker made, not the exact way that the point was expressed. Consistent with this, we are more likely to recall propositions than the surface shapes of sentences.

THE MEANINGFUL RELATIONS AMONG SENTENCES

Thinking about sentences in terms of their underlying structure makes it easy to describe many of the relationships of meaning among different sentences.

Paraphrases and opposites   As we have already seen, if two sentences have the same proposition in their underlying structure, then they will be closely related in meaning. But the precise nature of this relation depends on the sentence's attitudes as well. If the only difference between two sentences is in the focus from which the action is regarded, then the two sentences are **paraphrases**—their meanings are essentially equivalent. Thus

1. *Wellington defeated Napoleon.*

and

2. *Napoleon was defeated by Wellington.*

differ in what they emphasize, but they nonetheless express the same idea.

Some differences in sentence attitude, on the other hand, alter the meaning radically, as in the case of assertion versus denial. The sentence

3. *Wellington did not defeat Napoleon.*

obviously does not mean the same as sentence 1. This is not to say, however, that sentences 1 and 3 are unrelated in meaning, for they both take a stand (to be sure, an opposing stand) on the same proposition. They are related in a different way than sentence 1 is related to

4. *Wellington ate hard-boiled eggs.*

Sentence 3 differs from sentence 1 in that it has a negative sentence attitude, but sentence 4 differs from sentence 1 in propositional content.

Ambiguity   Two sentences that are paraphrases have the same proposition in their underlying structure but differ in their surface structures. Other pairs of sentences have the reverse relationship: They have different underlying structures (and thus represent different propositions) but nonetheless have the same surface structure. In this case, the two sentences will look identical, because they both consist of the same string of words. But this single word string will have two meanings, one for each of the underlying structures. As a result, the sentence is **ambiguous,** a single form that can be interpreted in two ways.

As an example, consider the sentence "Smoking volcanoes can be dangerous." One interpretation of this sentence is obvious, namely, that a volcano with smoke billowing out of it is potentially hazardous, since it might erupt at any moment (Figure 9.11A). But another interpretation is possible: One can envision a deranged giant smoking away on a volcano, with effects the surgeon general would regard as dangerous to his health (Figure 9.11B). Related examples

A

SURFACE: *Smoking volcanoes can be dangerous*

UNDERLYING PROPOSITIONS: *Volcanoes smoke. This can be dangerous.*

B

SURFACE: *Smoking volcanoes can be dangerous*

UNDERLYING PROPOSITIONS: *Someone smokes volcanoes. This can be dangerous.*

9.11   Ambiguity of underlying structure

are easy to find. ("The mayor asked the police to stop drinking in public places"; "She was watching the birds in her pajamas.")

In these cases, the ambiguity begins with two different ways of understanding an individual word within the sentence but ends up affecting the sentence's underlying structure—that is, in how one should understand the meaningful relationships among the sentence's parts. Ambiguity exists at every level of the linguistic hierarchy. Sometimes there is more than one way to interpret the sounds we hear—ambiguity at the level of the phonemes (one might hear "the sky" as "this guy"). There is also ambiguity in word meanings. Thus, "He was impressed by the racer's pants" might be a comment on clothing or on respiration. "Someone stepped on his trunk" will give rise to different ideas, depending on whether *trunk* refers to a traveler's suitcase, the main stem of a tree, or an elephant's proboscis. Finally, there can also be ambiguity in surface structure, that is, in how words are grouped into phrases. The double meaning of our old friend "The French bottle smells" was a case of this kind. So is "We sell oil to people in quart containers."

"Boy, he must think we're pretty stupid to fall for that again." (Courtesy of Leigh Rubin, Creators Syndicate, Inc. © 1990 Leigh Rubin)

COMPREHENSION

Given all this ambiguity, how do we ever manage to understand the speech we hear or the sentences we read? How do we get beyond the surface forms in order to recover each sentence's underlying structure? In some ways, the difficulty here resembles the problem we confronted in our discussion of visual perception (see Chapter 6): The perceiver has to determine the real size of an object (that is, a property of the distal stimulus) given its retinal image (the proximal stimulus). This retinal size changes whenever the distance between the observer and the target object changes. Nonetheless, the observer can perceive the object's actual (unchanging) size, for she has a number of cues informing her about her distance from the distal object. Given these cues, the observer can now reconstruct the actual size of the object (see Figure 9.12).

Something analogous happens with language. Here, the listener needs to determine the underlying structure of a sentence, given the linguistic "proximal stimulus," namely, the surface structure. But here, too, there are cues helping the listener to recover the underlying form. One important category of cues is the

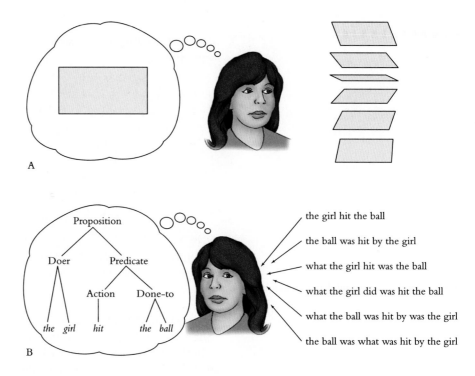

9.12   An analogy between linguistic paraphrase and perceptual constancy   *Linguistic paraphrase is in some ways similar to perceptual constancies of the kind we discussed in Chapter 6. For in both cases, we interpret superficially different patterns of stimulation as roughly equivalent. (A) Shape constancy. When we look at a tabletop, the image that actually falls on our eye is a trapezoid whose exact shape depends on our orientation to the table. But shape constancy allows us to perceive the unchanging rectangular shape that gives rise to these images. (B) Paraphrase. The ear literally hears a variety of surface sentences, but the linguistic system interprets them all as containing the same proposition.*

appearance of certain function words, such as *by* or *who* or *that*. Thus, for example, the pattern *verb*, followed by *-en*, followed by *by*, is a good hint that we are dealing with a passive surface structure ("He was taken by . . ."; "The lecture was given by . . ."; and so on). Similarly, other function words (such as *who* or *or*) are a good cue that there is more than one proposition in the sentence being heard (Kimball, 1973).

THE SENTENCE ANALYZING MACHINERY

Just how do we use these cues to reconstruct the underlying structure from the surface form? According to several psycholinguists, our **sentence analyzing machinery** (let us call it—or him or her—SAM) relies on a few rather general strategies, two of which are discussed below. (For general descriptions of sentence processing and comprehension, see Frazier and Fodor, 1978; Cairns, 1984; Joshi, 1991; Trueswell and Tanenhaus, 1994).

THE SIMPLEST FORM: DOER, ACT, DONE-TO

Several demonstrations have shown that SAM starts out with a strong bias about what kind of sentence it is about to hear: In general, it starts with the assumption that the sentence will first mention the doer, then the act, and then the done-to. In grammatical terminology, SAM starts with the assumption that the sentence will be in this sequence: subject, verb, object.

This strategy is entirely sensible, for in ordinary speech the active form of sentences (e.g., "John hits Fred") is much more frequent than the passive ("Fred is hit by John"). But infrequent or not, passive sentences do occur, and for these SAM's initial strategy fails. SAM recognizes its error as soon as it arrives at the words *is* and *by*. Having found these clues, it revises its first guess and reassigns the first noun phrase as done-to, rather than doer.

9.13   Deciding who is doer and who is done-to   *Subjects were presented with sentences such as "The cat chases the dog" and "The dog is chased by the cat." They were then shown either (A) or (B) and had to decide whether the sentence described the picture. Reaction times were faster for active than for passive sentences. (Slobin, 1966)*

These steps—starting with one hypothesis, then replacing it with another—take some effort, and this can be detected in studies of reaction time. One investigator had study participants listen to sentences such as "The dog is chasing the cat" and "The cat is chased by the dog." Immediately afterward, the participants were shown one of two pictures—a dog chasing a cat or a cat chasing a dog. Their job was to decide whether the sentence did or did not describe the picture. The participants reached the decision more quickly when the sentence was in the active rather than the passive form (Slobin, 1966; see Figure 9.13).

SAM's preference for doer, act, done-to sentences also creates difficulty in other settings. Consider what happens when one proposition occurs smack in the middle of another, e.g., "The girl who ate a hamburger hit the ball." Here, the proposition "The girl hit the ball" is interrupted by another proposition ("who ate a hamburger"). What is the effect of this interruption? In this sort of complex sentence, SAM assumes that the first noun phrase ("the girl") is the subject of the underlying proposition (the doer), in line with SAM's usual bias. But SAM next hopes to hear a verb to which it can assign the role of action. In this sentence, though, the next word is *who*, surely not a verb. This causes SAM to do a kind of mental double take, pausing to analyze the interrupting proposition ("who ate a hamburger") before returning to finish the main sentence ("The girl . . . hit the ball").

This mental double take is once again reflected in reaction time: Careful measurement shows that these **embedded sentences** do require more time and effort than sentences like "The girl ate a hamburger, and the girl hit the ball," which present the propositions one at a time, each in SAM's preferred order of doer, act, done-to (Bever, 1970; Wanner and Maratsos, 1978; Wanner, 1988).

A further, more general point also emerges from these studies: Often the interpretation of words early in the sentence depends on words arriving later. Does the initial noun phrase name the doer or the done-to? Sometimes SAM can't tell until a few words later on, when the verb arrives. If SAM were cautious, it would wait until all the words had arrived and only then begin interpreting the entire sequence. But this is not what it seems to do. Instead, it commits itself early on to a hypothesis about the sentence's structure. If that hypothesis turns out to be correct, all is fine. If the hypothesis is mistaken (if, for example, the sentence turns out to be passive or to contain an embedded phrase), it lets go of its initial assumption and goes hunting for an alternative.

FUNCTION WORDS THAT SIGNAL PROPOSITION BOUNDARIES

Given the variety of sentence forms we encounter, the strategy just described might seem risky. Better to wait a bit, so that more information will be available to guide sentence interpretation. A premature hypothesis about the sentence's structure might easily put SAM on the wrong track. For example, hasty parsing commitments often fool readers into thinking that *Fat people eat accumulates* is about fat people; instead, it is about the fat that people eat, something that becomes clear only when we read the last word (*accumulates*).

In fact, though, many factors help to keep SAM on the right track. And if the analysis does get off track, the cues usually ensure that this will be quickly detected and corrected. For example, in the sentence "The girl who ate a hamburger hit the ball," the boundary between the two propositions is signaled by the word *who*. **Function words** like this play an important role in revealing the structure of the sentence and, thus, in guiding the process of sentence analysis.

Of course, English often allows us to omit these function words in quick speech. For instance, we can say either "She loved the dinner that George cooked" or "She loved the dinner George cooked," leaving out the word *that*. The second sentence can be said more quickly (it is, after all, slightly shorter),

Interpreting the sentence "*The horse raced past the barn fell.*"

but if the listener relies on these function words, then leaving them out will make it a bit more difficult to understand. And it is: Sentence analysis takes longer when the clue provided by the function word is removed (Bever, 1970).

PUSHING SAM BEYOND ITS CAPABILITIES: A LINGUISTIC ILLUSION

Our reliance on these function words can also be illustrated in another way—sometimes, when these clues are absent, our analysis of a sentence fails altogether. Here is one such case:

The horse raced past the barn fell.

If you are like most English readers, your first impression will be that this is a totally ungrammatical sentence, one that has an "extra" verb (*fell*) that just does not fit. Yet this sentence, while awkward, is both grammatical and meaningful. The trick is to notice that it is just a short form of

The horse that was raced past the barn fell.★

To understand why *The horse raced past the barn fell* is so difficult, consider how SAM would proceed through this sentence. In general, SAM expects a sentence to express a single proposition in the sequence of doer, act, done-to. It expects that the first noun in the sentence will name the sentence's subject, the doer of the action, and that this will be followed by a verb identifying the main action of the sentence. In addition, the analyzer starts with the hypothesis that the verb will be in the active voice, not the passive. These are, overall, fine strategies, and they serve the analyzer well most of the time. And the strategies appear to be working here, at least initially. *The horse* names the doer of action. *Raced* appears to be the main action. *Past the barn* simply names where the action took place. All is well, encouraging SAM to stick with its initial hypothesis. But then the last word arrives, *fell,* and it is utterly incompatible with the sentence as analyzed so far. To accommodate this verb, SAM must give up every one of its standard assumptions: The sentence does not express a single proposition; it expresses two propositions, with one embedded within the other. *Raced* is not the main action, *fell* is. *Raced* is in the passive voice, not active (*The horse was raced past the barn*).

In short, this sentence leads the analyzer down a garden path: Everything appears to fit the standard pattern but, in the end, doesn't. (In fact, sentences such as this one are actually called *garden-path sentences.*) And, of course, to add insult to injury, this particular sentence also leaves out the clues that might have

---

★ If the sentence still seems hard to understand, try comparing it to these sentences: "The horse taken past the barn fell," and "The horse who was taken past the barn fell." These sentences are easier to understand because the form of the word *take* (*taken,* a so-called passive participle) could never be the main verb of the sentence. In contrast, *race* happens to have the same form for both past tense *(raced)* and passive participle (again, *raced*), much to the confusion of all!

warned SAM that it was on the wrong track: The sentence omits the function words and says *raced past the barn* rather than *that was raced past the barn*. This is perfectly permissible, but as we have seen, such omissions generally make sentences harder to understand. In the case of "The horse raced . . . ," these omissions virtually guarantee that SAM will be led astray.

With all of these features—embedded proposition, passive voice, omitted function words—it is no surprise that garden-path sentences can overwhelm SAM. Let us emphasize, though, that SAM's strategies ordinarily work quite well. It's usually safe to assume a single-proposition sentence in the active voice. Such assumptions allow SAM to begin each sentence with a plausible working hypothesis about that sentence's structure, and this generally allows it to move swiftly and efficiently forward. These are, in short, good strategies, even if they can occasionally be foiled by a suitably constructed sentence.

THE INTERACTION BETWEEN SYNTAX AND OTHER CUES

Garden-path effects from which readers and listeners just can't recover, like our *horse raced* example, are really very rare. They are useful for seeing inside the mental apparatus under very extreme circumstances, just as visual illusions and ambiguities (also rare) can help us inspect the workings of the machinery that ordinarily lets us perceive the world so efficiently. But garden-path effects of a much more temporary sort, and from which the listener or reader almost immediately recovers, are common indeed and, thus, are important for understanding the act of comprehension: They show us the cases where understanding is just a bit hard. The example we are now going to look at will show that, while SAM is very sensitive to syntax, it is also very sensitive to the meanings of the individual words as they reach the ear (or eye, in reading).

Most of us recall the experience of getting partway through reading a sentence, realizing that we have misgrouped the words, and then rapidly going back to the beginning of the sentence and rereading it correctly. To understand how sentence processing works, investigators ask participants to read sentences and then take measurements of their *regressive eye movements* to discover just where SAM has such temporary processing difficulties. Findings from this kind of study indicate that SAM makes guesses based on plausibility or sensibleness depending on the particular words in sequence. Consider this sentence fragment:

> *The detective examined . . .*

We know that detectives often examine things (like evidence, footprints, etc.), so SAM quickly commits to thinking that *the detective* is the subject and that *examined* is a main verb in the active voice. The detective examined *something*. But when subjects now read the end of the sentence

> *. . . by the reporter revealed the truth about the CIA.*

they are slightly flummoxed. Their eyes whip back to the beginning of the sentence, and they reread it, correctly this time, with *examined* as a passive verb. So it is the reporter who examined something, namely, the detective (and the detective revealed the truth). In contrast, if the sentence begins

> *The document examined . . .*

there are no regressive eye movements, i.e., no garden path. Why? Because no sensible reader would think, even for a few milliseconds, that the sentence was going to be about documents examining something. *The document* is not a good or sensible subject for a verb like *examined* and so the reader is expecting this word to be passive in the first place. He never wanders down the garden path. This example tells us that SAM does not blindly parse sentences syntactically without paying attention to their emerging meaning. Sensibly enough, SAM attends to **semantics** as well, using the particular words as they occur as information for discovering what the sentence is about (Trueswell, Tanenhaus, and Garnsey, 1994).

Similarly, we have noted that active sentences are generally understood more quickly than passive sentences. Thus, it takes more time to understand the second (passive) sentence in the following pair than it does to understand the first (active) one:

> *The cow was kicking the horse.*

> *The horse was kicked by the cow.*

But in some cases semantic cues override this bias. Thus, subjects are equally fast with these two sentences:

> *The cow was kicking the fence.*

> *The fence was kicked by the cow.*

In this case, there's no risk of confusion about who did what: Cows are capable of kicking fences, but fences are not capable of kicking cows. Thus, there is no ambiguity here about the underlying proposition, and as a result, listeners understand the passive sentence just as rapidly as they do the active form (Slobin, 1966; see Figure 9.14).

THE EXTRALINGUISTIC CONTEXT

It's rare that we encounter a single, isolated sentence. Instead, sentences are uttered, and understood, in some context. Perhaps the context is provided by an ongoing conversation or by the rest of the novel or the psychology textbook in which the sentence appears. In any case, the context provides important aids for sentence understanding. Thus, the garden-path problem is much less likely to occur in the following context:

Jacob: Which horse fell?
Sol: The horse raced past the barn fell.

In addition, while we are able to talk about ancient history, far-away places, and circumstances that are entirely imaginary, much of our conversation is focused on more immediate concerns, so the listener can often see what we are referring to and can witness the actions we are describing. To see the importance of these **extralinguistic factors**—that is, factors outside of the language itself—consider the following sentence:

> *Put the apple on the towel into the box.*

9.14 Semantic cues to propositional thought *The passive sentence "The flowers are watered by the girl" takes no longer to understand than the active sentence "The girl waters the flowers," since its meaning will surely be understood as pictured in (A) rather than in (B).*

A

B

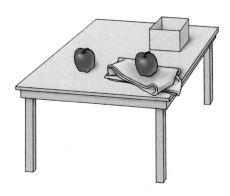

9.15 *"Put the apple on the towel into the box."* *Without any supporting context, a listener might initially interpret this sentence as an instruction to put the apple onto the towel. As a result, the listener will do a double take when the sentence's final three words arrive. But within the context of the illustration the listener immediately detects that "the apple" is an ambiguous phrase—which apple is referred to? The listener therefore counts on the speaker to indicate which apple is to be moved and interprets "on the towel" appropriately.*

For many people, this sentence causes a temporary false interpretation. Early on, it seems to be an instruction to put an apple onto a towel; this understanding must be abandoned, though, when the words *into the box* arrive. Now listeners realize that the box is the apple's destination; *on the towel* is simply a specification of which apple is to be moved. (Which apple should be put into the box? The one that is on the towel.) In short, this is another example of a garden-path sentence—initially inviting one analysis, but eventually demanding another.

This confusion would be avoided, however, if this sentence were uttered in the appropriate setting. Imagine that two apples are in view, one on a towel, and one not (Figure 9.15). In this context, a listener would immediately see the possibility for confusion: Which apple is being referred to? Therefore, the listener would expect the speaker to specify which apple is to be moved. When the phrase *on the towel* is uttered, then, the listener immediately and quite naturally understands it (correctly) as that needed specification. Hence, there would be no confusion and no garden path to be led down.

As we have seen, there are linguistically unambiguous ways to express this message, such as "Put the apple that is on the towel into the box." But now we see also that extralinguistic information is often as useful to SAM as clear syntax (Eberhard et al., 1995; Tanenhaus and Spivey-Knowlton, 1996).

CONVERSATIONAL COOPERATION

The previous section rested on the assumption that conversations go forward in a spirit of cooperation. In a situation like the one shown in Figure 9.15, a speaker would realize that an instruction to put the apple somewhere is ambiguous. Which apple is being referred to? The speaker would quite naturally add the specification *on the towel,* indicating which apple was the one to be relocated.

Symmetrically, the listener counts on the fact that the speaker is trying to be clear. If the listener perceives the possibility for confusion, then she counts on the speaker to clear up that confusion and so interprets the speaker's utterances accordingly. Thus, the listener knows an elaboration of *the apple* is needed and counts on the speaker to provide one.

Much evidence indicates that this sort of communicative cooperation is crucial for conversation. The speaker does not spell out every detail—if he did, the conversation would be hopelessly slow and intolerably boring. But he must spell out enough detail to avoid confusing the listener. To balance these twin concerns for brevity and clarity, the speaker must adjust each utterance in accord with what the listener already does or doesn't know (Clark, 1996).

In the same fashion, the listener also plays an active role: She knows that the speaker won't spell out every premise or every assumption, so she understands that she must fill in the gaps, making reasonable inferences about those details left unspoken.

How should we think about this pattern of conversational cooperation? One description comes from the philosopher H. P. Grice, who argued that conversation is governed by a small number of rules or **maxims** (Grice, 1975). One of these (unspoken) maxims requires the conversational partners to be *relevant*—that is, to say things that are to the point. Such a rule helps us to understand the following conversational exchange:

Brian: Where's the roast beef?
Fernanda: I don't know, but the dog sure looks happy.

Fernanda's remark seems off the track, but, if we assume the Gricean maxim of relevancy, we are led to seek the connection between her comment and Brian's question. This search for relevance leads to the inference that the dog may have stolen the roast beef. A different example concerns the maxim of *quantity*: Conversational partners understand that they should say neither more than is necessary, nor less. This maxim is in play in this bit of dialog:

> Tony: How did you like the dancers?
> Maria: Some of them were good.

Here, Maria is implying that some of the dancers were *not* good; we understand "some" to mean "some but not all." Of course, this interpretation is not logically demanded by Maria's remark. (If she thought that all were good, then she could truthfully say that some were good!) Nonetheless, we draw this conclusion about Maria's intention, because we tacitly assume that if she thought that *all* the dancers were good, she would say so. Otherwise, she would be violating the maxim of quantity.

These maxims, and the general dynamic of a conversation, allow speakers to leave an enormous amount unsaid. Consider this bit of conversation (after Pinker, 1994):

> Woman: I'm leaving you.
> Man (angrily):   Who is he?!?

We can easily provide the soap-opera script behind this exchange, highlighting the richness of interpretation often required for understanding everyday conversation. (For further discussion of the listener's or reader's role in understanding connected discourse, see Sperber and Wilson, 1986; Graesser, Millis, and Zwaan, 1997.)

Of course, neither the speaker nor the listener can read the other's thoughts, so conversational errors do happen: The speaker sometimes says too much (and is boring) or too little (and is obscure). The listener sometimes makes the wrong inference and ends up on the wrong track altogether. But these errors are usually detected and repaired quickly because the conversational participants send each other a variety of signals—both verbal (e.g., intonation) and nonverbal (e.g., a furrowed brow)—indicating when they are confused and, in many cases, what assumptions they have made and what interpretations they have reached. But note that this flow of signals only works for the actual participants in the conversation. If a bystander is eavesdropping on a conversation, or if a reader is reading a transcript of the same conversation, there is no way for them to signal their misunderstandings and confusion. As a result, comprehension errors are more likely for the bystander or reader than they are for the actual participants in the conversation (Schober and Clark, 1989; for other examinations of conversational cooperation, see Clark and Wilkes-Gibbs, 1986; Garrod and Doherty, 1994; Brennan and Clark, 1996).

INTERACTION AMONG VARIOUS FACTORS

It appears from our discussion that the process of language comprehension is marvelously complex, influenced by syntax, semantics, the extralinguistic context, and inferential activity, all guided by a spirit of cooperation. But how are all these factors integrated? One hypothesis is that the listener first uses the syntax of a sentence to uncover its structure; this leads to an initial hypothesis about the sentence, which is then checked against other sources of information. The alternative hypothesis is that all of these sources of information interact from the very start, so that SAM is simultaneously influenced by syntax, semantics, and the context in which the sentence was uttered.

This issue has been a matter of considerable debate, but evidence is accumulating to support the position that these factors interact from the start. However, this is likely to remain an area of controversy for at least some time (see, for example, Marslen-Wilson, 1975; Crain and Fodor, 1985; Crain and Steedman, 1985; Stowe, 1987; Carlson and Tanenhaus, 1988; MacDonald, Pearlmutter, and Seidenberg, 1994; Carpenter, Miyake, and Just, 1995; Hess, Foss, and Carroll, 1995; Trueswell and Tanenhaus, 1991).

No matter how this debate is resolved, it is clear that these many factors ensure that the listener is not drowned in confusion by the pervasive ambiguity of word, phrase, and sentence structure. Still, our sensitivity to all of these factors makes it all the more remarkable that sentence comprehension is in general so effortless and so swift.

THE GROWTH OF LANGUAGE IN THE CHILD

We have emphasized the richness of language, the diversity of its forms, and the complexity of its structure. In this light it is remarkable that virtually every human child manages to learn this complicated system of communication. Whether they are particularly intelligent or quite dull, motivated or apathetic, encouraged by their parents or ignored, children learn to speak the language of their environment. And the learning process is quite rapid: Children usually don't speak at all until sometime after their first birthday, but they are sophisticated language users by the time they are three years old. How is this rapid, reliable learning possible?

IS LANGUAGE LEARNING THE ACQUISITION OF A SKILL?

One obvious account of language learning appeals to imitation. Children hear others speaking, copy them, and so end up speaking the same language as the others in their environment. And in some ways this must be correct: Young children exposed to English end up saying *dog,* and not *perro* or *chien,* to refer to the relevant four-legged creature. So in this sense, children surely imitate the other speakers around them.

But a great deal of a child's language learning cannot be explained in terms of simple imitation. A child may imitate adults in using *dog* to refer to the family's pet poodle, but she also goes well beyond this imitation, using the same word to refer to the bulldog next door and the Irish setter on the next block. Also, children produce many forms that are never produced by mature speakers. For example, they often say things like, "I goed to school yesterday" or "I saw two mouses." For these utterances, we certainly need some account other than imitation.

Another popular hypothesis about language learning is that it is based on explicit **correction** or **reinforcement** by parents. According to this view, grammatical mistakes are immediately pointed out to the young learner, who subsequently avoids them—"Don't say, 'goed,' Hank. Say 'went.'" But this hypothesis is false (Morgan and Travis, 1989). In actual practice, mistakes in grammar and pronunciation generally go unremarked, as in the following exchange:

Two-year-old: Mamma isn't boy, he a girl.
Mother: That's right.

Parents do correct their children's speech, but what they usually correct are errors of fact, not errors of grammar (Brown and Hanlon, 1970). This is perfectly reasonable, since parents are out to create socialized and rational beings, not little grammarians. But this fact undercuts the claim that we can understand the child's language learning in terms of parental instruction.

Other evidence on this point comes from studies of a child who, for neurological reasons, was entirely unable to speak (Pinker, 1995; Stromswold, 1995). This child obviously never had the opportunity to make errors (and thus be corrected) or to form sentences correctly (and thus to be encouraged). Nonetheless, this child was able to understand complicated sentences perfectly well and could judge accurately whether a particular sentence was well formed (grammatical) or not. Plainly, then, neither imitation nor correction (nor some combination of the two) can fully explain the development of language.

How then are we to explain the growth of speech and comprehension? We will begin by tracing the child's progress during the first few years of life.

THE SOCIAL ORIGINS OF SPEECH PRODUCTION

Infants begin to vocalize from the first moments of life. They cry, coo, and babble. They make sounds such as "ga" and "bagoo" that sound very much like words. By the age of about three months, the babbling sounds made by children exposed to different languages can be told apart, showing that language learning is already underway. Deaf children living in an environment in which sign language is used also babble with their hands, producing gestures that look very much like the gestures of sign language (Petitto and Marentette, 1991).

Prelinguistic children also have nonverbal ways of making contact with the minds, emotions, and social behaviors of others. Quite early in life, babies begin to exchange looks, caresses, and sounds with caregivers (Collis, 1975; Fernald, 1992; L. Bloom, 1993). Several investigators have suggested that these are precursors and organizers of the language development to follow. The idea is that this gesture-and-babble interaction helps children to become linguistically socialized, to realize, for instance, that each participant in a conversation takes a turn and responds to the other (Bruner, 1974/1975; Tomasello and Ferrar, 1986).

Thus, language knowledge is essentially social and interpersonal from the beginning (Fernald, 1992). The infant must learn how to direct the caregiver's attention to objects of interest and must also learn to attend to what the caregiver is focusing on. More broadly, in order to speak to another, the infant must gain the idea that the other person lives in the same, mutually perceived world (Bates, 1976; Lifter and L. Bloom, 1989; Baldwin, 1991; Mandler, 1992).

Social origins of speech   (Photograph by Erika Stone, 1989)

DISCOVERING THE FORMS OF LANGUAGE

Most infants don't produce any language until they are a year old or so. But language sensitivity begins much earlier. Indeed, one remarkable study shows that, by the fourth day of life, infants are more attentive to their caregiver's language than they are to a foreign language (Mehler et al., 1988).

THE RUDIMENTS OF PHONEME DISCRIMINATION

We have discussed the fact that each language employs a small number of phonemes. These are the building blocks out of which all the words in that lan-

A

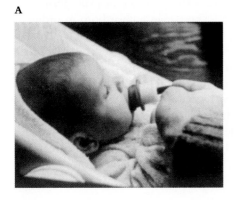

B

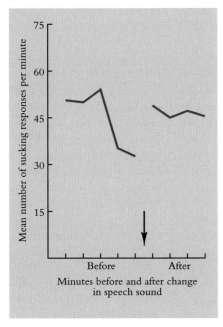

9.16 Sucking rate and speech perception in the infant (A) An infant sucks to hear "ba" or "ga." (Photograph courtesy of Philip Morse, Boston University) (B) The graph shows the sucking rate of four-month-olds to "ba" or "ga." The infants soon become habituated, and the sucking rate drops. When a new stimulus is substituted ("ga" for "ba" and "ba" for "ga"), the infant dishabituates and sucks quickly once again. Similar results have been obtained for one-month-olds. The point of the shift is indicated by the arrow. (From Eimas et al., 1971)

guage are composed. But different languages employ different phonemes. Thus, in English there is a crucial difference between *l* and *r* (as in *lob* vs. *rob*). Physically, these sounds are quite similar, but each of them falls within a different phoneme in English, and English speakers have no trouble perceiving the distinction. In contrast, this distinction has no linguistic significance in Japanese, where *l* and *r* sounds fall within the same phoneme. In consequence, Japanese speakers can neither produce nor perceive a distinction between them.

Initially, infants respond to just about all sound distinctions made in any language—and so Japanese babies can hear the *l* vs. *r* difference as easily as American babies. However, these perceptual abilities erode if they are not exercised, and so infants lose the ability to make distinctions that are not used in their language community. Thus, Japanese infants gradually stop distinguishing between *l* and *r*. Symmetrically, American infants soon cease to distinguish between two different *k* sounds that are perceptually distinct to Arabic speakers (see Figure 9.16; Jusczyk, 1985; Werker, 1991, 1995).

How quickly does this erosion of distinctions take place? If tested at one or two months of age, infants of any nationality respond to just about every contrast that occurs in any human language. By six months of age, some alteration in phonetic sensitivities can be observed (Kuhl et al., 1992), and by twelve months of age, infants' sensitivity to foreign contrasts has diminished significantly (Werker and Tees, 1984).

It seems, then, that infants are prepared by nature to learn any language on earth. This shouldn't be surprising, since infants are not born with a passport that tells them what language they are going to hear. But the diminished sensitivities of twelve-month-olds suggest that babies soon recalibrate their perceptions, concentrating selectively on the distinctions that matter in their own linguistic community (Kemler-Nelson et al., 1989).

THE RUDIMENTS OF THE SENTENCE UNIT: "MOTHERESE"

We have seen that a crucial characteristic of language is that it includes syntax—general principles for combining the finite stock of words into infinitely many sentences. To discover the principles of syntax, infants first must recognize what a sentence is—where one ends and the next one begins. This task may be eased somewhat by the manner in which people talk to infants. This special way of speaking is employed almost universally by adults when they talk to babies and has come to be called, somewhat whimsically, ***Motherese*** (Newport, Gleitman, and Gleitman, 1977). Of course, "Motherese" is something of a misnomer, for this style of speaking is adopted by fathers as well as mothers and by strangers as well as relatives when they are talking to an infant (Fernald et al., 1989). It is characterized by a special tone of voice, with high pitch, slow rate, and exaggerated intonations (Fernald and Kuhl, 1987).

There is good evidence that infants prefer Motherese to adult-to-adult speech, even though they as yet understand neither. Two investigators conditioned four-month-old babies to turn their heads to the left or right so they could listen to speech sounds that came out of two loudspeakers. When the baby turned his head toward the loudspeaker on the right, he heard Motherese (produced not by his own, but by another child's mother). When he turned to the left, he heard adult-to-adult talk. The infants soon began to turn their heads to the right, indicating a preference for Motherese despite the unfamiliarity of the speaker's voice (Fernald and Simon, 1984).

Motherese has several properties that may help the infant in learning language. The slow speed of Motherese will, by itself, make it easier for the infant to follow, and eventually understand, the sound stream. In addition, Motherese clearly marks the boundaries between sentences (Morgan, 1986; Kemler-Nelson et al., 1989; Fisher and Tokura, 1996). In general, several sound cues mark sentence boundaries in spoken language. One cue involves changes of pitch: For most English speakers, the pitch tends to start high at the beginnings of sentences and to fall at their ends. Another cue is the presence of brief periods of silence that often occur between sentences. These cues appear both in ordinary adult-to-adult speech and in Motherese, but they are much more reliably used and also more easily detectable in Motherese. (Try speaking to a baby, and notice the exaggerated changes in pitch that you spontaneously use.)

This remarkable coadjustment between adult and child—the caregiver finding it irresistible to speak in a special way to the infant and the infant finding that style of speech bewitching to listen to—is a first hint of how our species is biologically adapted for the task of learning language. Indeed, such early observers as Charles Darwin (1877) had already noticed these protolinguistic interactions between mothers and their infants, and he called Motherese "the sweet music of the species."

THE ONE-WORD SPEAKER

Children begin to understand a few words that their caregivers say as early as five to eight months of age. For example, some six-month-olds will regularly glance up at the ceiling light in response to hearing their mother say "light." Actual talking begins sometime between about ten and twenty months of age. Almost invariably, children's first utterances are one word long. Some first words refer to simple interactions with adults, such as *hi* and *peekaboo*. Others are names, such as *Mama* and *Fido*. Most of the rest are simple nouns, such as *duck* and *spoon,* with a smattering of action verbs such as *give* and *push.* And as every parent soon discovers, one of the earliest words learned is a resounding *No!* (Caselli et al., 1995; Gentner, 1982; Huttenlocher, Smiley, and Charney, 1983; Dromi, 1987).

Missing almost altogether are the function words and suffixes, such as *the, and,* and *-ed.* These are among the most frequent items the child hears, but even so they are rarely uttered by beginners. This may be, in part, simply because these function words are difficult to perceive, since they are usually not stressed in the caregiver's speech and are uttered in a relatively low pitch (Cutler, 1994; Kelly and Martin, 1994; Gerken, 1996). In addition, the young child has little need to utter these words: Since the child is only saying one word at a time, there is no need to utter morphemes whose central role is to organize groups of words into sentence form (Gerken, Landau, and Remez, 1990).

WORD MEANING AT THE ONE-WORD STAGE

It is hard to find out precisely what young children mean by the words they say. A child who sees a white rabbit hopping by and says "bunny" might mean the same thing an adult would. But it's also possible that the child's word is intended to mean "animal," or "jumping thing," or "white," or a dozen other options.

The same ambiguity actually makes it difficult for children themselves to discover what a word means. Let's imagine that the helpful mother points out a rabbit to her child and clearly pronounces the word *rabbit.* The child still has a big job to do. He has to make up his mind whether the word refers to the object (that is, the rabbit) or to one of the object's properties (so that the mother's utterance might mean *white* or *furry*), or to one of its parts (so that perhaps the mother means *leg* or *tail*), or even to one of its actions (*jumps? runs by?*; see Figure 9.17).

One might expect that, because of these ambiguities, young children would

Learning language requires a receptive human mind Ginger gets plenty of linguistic stimulation but is prepared by nature only to be man's best friend. (This FAR SIDE cartoon by Gary Larson is reprinted by permission of Chronicle Features, San Francisco, California.)

9.17 Symmetrical problems for child learners and investigators of child language *(A) The child's helpful mother points out a rabbit, saying "rabbit." The child sees a rabbit but also sees an animal, an ear, and the ground beneath the rabbit. Which one does the mother mean by the word* rabbit? *(B) The mother's (and the investigator's) problem in understanding young children's speech is much the same. The child may say "rabbit" when she observes a rabbit, but for all the mother knows the child may have made an error in learning and thus may mean something different by this word.*

often be confused about what a word means. Yet, in fact, children seem to be impressively accurate in their understanding of word meaning. In some cases, they do undergeneralize the meaning of a word: They might know that *house* refers to small toy buildings but not that it also refers to large real buildings. In other cases, they overgeneralize. They may think that the word *daddy* refers to any man, not just their own father. Even in these cases, though, the child's understanding is approximately correct, even if too broad or too narrow. Children virtually never make larger-scale errors. Note, for example, that a child always observes the ground whenever she hears the word "rabbit." (This is simply because rabbits can't fly, and so are reliably found near the ground.) But no child mistakenly learns that "rabbit" means *ground*.

And the errors that do occur are short-lived. Overgeneralization and undergeneralization are both common for the first seventy-five or so words the child utters but very rare thereafter (Rescorla, 1980). By the time the child has a one-hundred-word vocabulary, he is almost always correct in using words to refer to the right things. We shall return later to how the child manages this—how he manages to get these word meanings right despite the ambiguity we have already highlighted.

Now, let's consider how these word meanings are represented and organized in the mind of the child. Some investigators believe that children focus on an object's function, and so they use words to classify things together that act alike in their world. In the mind of the child, therefore, a ball is essentially something that one throws and bounces in the playground (Nelson, 1973). Other investigators argue for a featural approach. They believe that children use words to designate things that look alike, that share certain perceptual features. According to this view, the child uses the word *ball* to refer to something round, and so the word may be overgeneralized to include faces or even the moon (Clark, 1973). Still others believe that early word meanings are based on prototypes. In their view, children call things *ball* to the extent that they resemble a particular ball that serves as the model (prototype) for the entire concept (Anglin, 1975; de Villiers, 1980; Keil and Batterman, 1984). Of course, these primitive meanings will change and develop as the child acquires more and more information (Chi,

375

9.18 Set-up for the selective looking experiment *The child sits on the mother's lap and listens to a taped sentence, while two video screens show two cartoon characters performing different actions. A hidden observer notes which screen the child is looking at. The mother wears a visor that covers her eyes to make sure she does not see which screen shows which action and thereby give inadvertent clues to the child. (Adapted from Roberta Golinkoff)*

Glazer, and Rees, 1982) and reorganizes the categories of her physical and mental world (Carey, 1985; for overviews of word-meaning acquisition, see Clark, 1993; Markman and Woodward, in press).

PROPOSITIONAL MEANING AT THE ONE-WORD STAGE

There is another question about children's first words: When a child sees a dog and shouts out "Doggie!" are these one-word utterances merely acts of naming or are they actually attempts at sentences? That is, do children have the proposition "There's a doggie!" in mind when they say "Doggie!"?

Many investigators of child language believe that young children do have full propositions in mind, even when they are speaking only one word at a time. Thus, a child might say "eat" but intend something like "I want to eat," or the child might say "cookie" but intend "Give me the cookie" (Shipley, Smith, and Gleitman, 1969; Bretherton, 1988).

One basis for this belief is that one-word speakers fill out their speech with accompanying gestures (Greenfield and Smith, 1976). A child who says "rabbit" might also reach toward a rabbit at the same time, so the meaning "Give me that rabbit" or "I want that rabbit" comes across to the watching, listening adult. Moreover, one-word speakers differentiate their requests, comments, and demands by intonation: Their pitch goes up when they request information and down when they make a demand (Gallagan, 1987).

Stronger evidence comes from experiments in which children as young as sixteen months (who themselves speak only one word at a time) look at brief movies that depict different events. The toddlers sit on their mothers' laps and can see two video screens, one to their left and one to their right (Figure 9.18). On the screen to the left, Big Bird is tickling Cookie Monster, and on the screen to the right, Cookie Monster is tickling Big Bird (Figure 9.19). Half the children hear a voice saying "Oh look! Big Bird is tickling Cookie Monster." The other children hear the reverse sentence ("Oh look! Cookie Monster is tickling Big Bird"). Hidden observers now record which screen the children turn their attention to. The finding is that the toddlers look primarily at the screen that matches the sentence they heard. To achieve this, the children must understand the syntax of the test sentences, and to be more precise, they must understand the logic of who did what to whom. This is despite the fact that these children themselves speak only in single-word utterances (Hirsh-Pasek et al., 1985; Gleitman, 1990; Naigles, 1990).

9.19 Stimuli for the selective looking experiment *One screen shows Big Bird tickling Cookie Monster, the other shows Cookie Monster tickling Big Bird.*

A    **B**    **C**

The ambiguities of two-word speech The two-word utterances of young children, while systematic and meaningful, can be quite ambiguous. The three panels from the children's story *Higgledy Piggledy Pop*, by Maurice Sendak, show why one young child might want to learn more about adult syntax. (A) An adventurous dog takes a job as nurse to Baby. The dog must get Baby to eat, or it will be fed to the lion down in the basement. Here Baby refuses the food, saying "No eat!" (I will not eat). (B) Here, the dog eats up the food Baby has refused. Baby finds this objectionable and so cries out "No eat!" (Don't eat my porridge!). (C) Baby has angrily pushed the button so the dog-nurse will fall down to the waiting lion, but Baby has accidentally fallen also. To avoid being eaten by the lion, Baby cries out "No eat!" (Don't eat me up!). (From Maurice Sendak, 1979)

THE TWO-WORD (TELEGRAPHIC) SPEAKER

Many drastic changes take place beginning at about the second birthday (Brown, 1973; Braine, 1976). The child's vocabulary grows to many hundreds of words. Soon she begins to put words together into primitive sentences, and then we are aware most poignantly that another human mind is among us.

SYNTAX AND PROPOSITIONAL MEANING IN TWO-WORD SPEECH

We can clearly recognize propositional ideas in the two-year-old's sentences, but these sentences hardly sound like adult speech. Generally, each sentence is only two words long, and each of its components is a content word. The function morphemes are still largely missing, and so these sentences sound like the short ones that people used when sending telegrams: "Throw ball!" "Daddy shoe," "No eat!" (Brown and Bellugi, 1964).

These sentences show some organization, however, despite their simplicity. From the earliest moments of "telegraphic speech," the words seem to be serially ordered according to their propositional roles (Braine, 1963; Bloom, 1970; de Villiers and de Villiers, 1973). Thus, young English speakers will put the doer of the action first and then the verb, and so they say "Mommy throw!" if they want the mother to throw the ball. They put the done-to last, after the verb, so they will say "Throw ball!" in approximately the same circumstances.

Two-year-olds' correct use of word order to express different sentence meanings is consistent with the comprehension that they showed even earlier (in understanding who did what to whom in the Cookie Monster and Big Bird videos). But this leads to a question: Why don't these children produce even longer sentences? If the children understand the doer, act, done-to pattern (and plainly they do), why don't they produce three-, four-, and five-word sentences? One reason, as we have already discussed, is that children are slow to learn the function words and so, of course, don't use these in their own speech (Gleitman and Wanner, 1982; Gerken, 1996). Another factor is memory: It's a complicated business to construct a complex sentence, with much information to keep track of. So the child trims the information load by reducing what she says to the bare essentials needed to communicate (L. Bloom, 1970; P. Bloom, 1990).

377

LATER STAGES OF LANGUAGE LEARNING: SYNTAX

Children soon progress beyond the two-word stage, typically by two-and-a-half years or so. Their utterances now become longer (Figure 9.20), and they can say little sentences that contain all three terms of a basic proposition. Function words begin to appear. Their utterances are still short and simple, but—at least initially—they are correctly formed.

Soon, however, a new phenomenon appears. Children start to make certain errors in their word formation and syntax. An example concerns the *-ed* suffix, indicating the past tense. Early on, the child uses this suffix as an adult would, applying it to regular verbs, but not to irregular ones. Thus, the child says "walked" and "talked" when using the past tense of these verbs and also (correctly) uses irregular forms such as "ran," "came," and "ate." By the age of four or five, however, these same children start to produce *overregularization errors,* treating the irregular verbs as though they were regular. Thus, they sometimes say "runned," "comed," "eated" and so on (Ervin, 1964; Marcus et al., 1992; Prasada and Pinker, 1993). And these are not simply errors of carelessness or slips of the tongue, as can be seen in the following exchange:

Child:	My teacher holded the baby rabbits and we patted them.
Mother:	Did you say your teacher held the baby rabbits?
Child:	Yes.
Mother:	What did you say she did?
Child:	She holded the baby rabbits and we patted them.
Mother:	Did you say she held them tightly?
Child:	No, she holded them loosely. (Bellugi, 1971)

This kind of error is important in several ways. First, it offers evidence that children do not learn language solely, or even mostly, by imitation. Few adults would say "holded" or "eated," and the mother in the quoted exchange repeatedly offers the correct form of the verb for imitation. In fact, parents are often aghast at these errors: A half-year earlier, their child was speaking correctly but now is making errors. Apparently, he is regressing! So parents often try to correct these errors, but to no avail: The child holds firm, despite the correction. This provides further evidence that language learning does not rely on parental instruction and guidance.

Second, we need to ask how these errors come to be. What has happened, in the mind of the child, to produce this pattern? Many investigators argue that the young child starts out by memorizing the past tense of each verb—learning that the past tense of *want* is *wanted,* the past tense of *climb* is *climbed,* and so on. But this is a highly inefficient strategy. It's far more efficient to detect the pattern—simply add the *-ed* suffix—and apply it to new cases. Once the child detects this pattern, though, and stops memorizing each case, it's quite easy to get carried away, and so overregularization errors are produced. The errors will drop out only when the child takes the further step of realizing that, while there is a pattern, there are also exceptions to the pattern. (For an alternative view, see Rumelhart and McClelland, 1986; for discussion, see Pinker and Prince, 1988; Pinker, 1995.)

A number of other overregularization errors also occur. Early on, the child uses both regular plurals ("houses," "cats," "toys") and irregular ones ("mice," "feet"). Later, though, the child overregularizes this pattern and says things like "mouses" and "foots." Similarly, the child hears "she isn't" and "you aren't," and

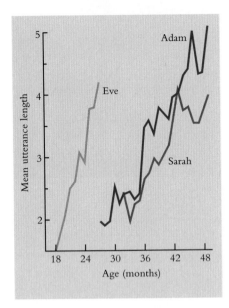

9.20 The average length of the utterances produced by three children *The mean utterance length in three children between one-and-a-half and four years of age. The utterance length is measured in morphemes, where dolls counts as two morphemes (doll + s). Note the variations among the children, who were all within a normal range. (After Brown, Cazden, and Bellugi-Klima, 1969)*

may overregularize to produce the utterance "I amn't." Still another example is the use of nouns as verbs. The child has heard "John bats the ball," where "bat" means *hit with a bat,* so he invents "Don't Woodstock me!" to mean *Don't hit me with a Woodstock toy* (Clark, 1982). A more complicated case is the invention of so-called **causative verbs** (Bowerman, 1982; Pinker, 1989). Children notice that one can say both "The door opened" and also "John opened the door," with the second sentence naming the causal agent. This pattern, too, can be overregularized. The child knows sentences like "I giggled," and she extends the pattern, saying "Daddy giggled me" to mean *Daddy made me giggle.*

FURTHER STAGES OF LANGUAGE LEARNING: WORD MEANING

We have already discussed the fact that children experience remarkably little difficulty in discovering which word stands for which meaning. And they make this discovery over and over at a remarkable pace: Five-year-olds have a vocabulary of ten to fifteen thousand words, whereas at fifteen months they had a vocabulary of zero to about twenty-five words. This means they must be acquiring about ten words a day—every day, every week, every month (Carey, 1978). What makes this rapid learning possible?

CAREGIVER AIDS TO WORD LEARNING

Part of the explanation for this prodigious word learning may come from the way in which caregivers talk to children, for their syntax often contains useful hints about what a word could mean. Let's return to the problem of learning which word means "ear" and which means "rabbit" (see Figure 9.17, p. 375). It turns out that when caregivers refer to the whole rabbit, they use simple sentences ("This is a rabbit") and often point to the rabbit at the same time. But when they want to refer to the ear, they first refer to the whole rabbit and then use such words as *its* in referring to the part: "This is a rabbit; these are its ears" (Shipley, Kuhn, and Madden, 1983).

PERCEPTUAL AND CONCEPTUAL BIASES IN CHILD LEARNERS

Word learning is also heavily influenced by the ways the child is disposed to think about, and categorize, objects and events in the world (Rosch, 1973a; Keil, 1979; Fodor, 1983). This is reflected, for example, in the fact that young children acquire the basic level words (e.g., *dog*) before learning the superordinates *(animal)* or subordinates *(Chihuahua)* (Rosch, 1978). One might think this is just because the basic level words are used most frequently to children. But this does not seem to be the explanation. In some homes, the words *Spot* or *Rex* (specific names) are used much more often than *dog* (a basic level term) for obvious reasons. And it is true that in this case the young learner will use the word *Spot* before she learns to utter *dog.* But she first learns it as a basic level term all the same. This is shown by the fact that she will utter *Spot* to refer to the neighbor's dog as well as her own. She overgeneralizes *Spot* just enough to convert it from a specific name to the basic level of categorization—evidently, the most natural level for carving up experience (Mervis and Crisafi, 1978; Shipley and Kuhn, 1983).

Further evidence comes from experimental attempts to teach new words to children. The method is to point to a new object and label it with a new (nonsense) word. Thus, the experimenter might point toward an object and say

(Photograph by Roberta Intrater, 1980)

"That's a biff." To what new objects will the child apply this new label? He generally won't use *biff* to describe other objects that happen to be made of the same material, nor to name objects of the same color. Instead, he uses *biff* to describe objects having the same shape as the entire original. Apparently, then, he has understood this term as a label for the entire object (Markman and Hutchinson, 1984; Markman, 1989). In the same way, he will still accept an object as being a *biff* if it has the same shape as the original, but a different color or texture. But he won't apply this label if the new object's shape is changed. Evidently, colors and textures are not as salient in the child's perceptual organization as shapes, so the slightest change in the latter will convince the learner that the new item is something wholly different from the one previously called "a biff" (Landau, Smith, and Jones, 1988).

THE CHILD'S PREDISPOSITIONS ABOUT WORD MEANING

Children also seem to have pretty strong ideas about which words pick out which objects. In many contexts, children act as if they believe that no word can have a synonym. Said differently, they seem to assume that any one concept can have only one word that refers to it (Clark, 1987; for an alternative view, see Gathercole, 1987).

Evidence again comes from experiments on new word learning. This time, the investigators showed some preschoolers a picture of a familiar object, one that the children already had a word for (say, a hammer). The investigator said, "This is a picture of a claw," and then asked, "is *this* the claw?" (indicating the whole object) "or is *this* the claw?" (indicating just the claw part). We have already seen that children have an initial bias toward interpreting words as labels for whole objects; this should lead them to interpret *claw* (a label they've not heard before) as another word for *hammer*. But this tendency is overruled in this setting. The children already know the word *hammer*, and so, given their bias against synonyms, they conclude that *claw* must refer to something else—in this case, the part (Markman and Wachtel, 1988; Markman, 1994).

LEARNING SEMANTICS BY PAYING ATTENTION TO SYNTAX

Children also use the structure of the language as a way of guiding their word learning (Brown, 1957; L. Gleitman, 1990; P. Bloom, 1996; L. Gleitman and H. Gleitman, 1996). In one study, three- and four-year-olds were shown a picture in which a pair of hands was performing a kneading sort of motion with a mass of red confetti-like material that was overflowing a low, striped, container (Figure 9.21). Some of the children were asked, "In this picture, can you see sebbing?" These children responded by making the same kneading motions with their hands. Other children were asked, "In this picture, can you see a seb?" In response, the children pointed to the container. Still other children were asked, "Can you see any seb?" These children pointed to the confetti (Brown, 1957; see also Katz, Baker, and MacNamara, 1974; Carey, 1982).

It seems, then, that children proceed in their learning in two directions at once. On the one hand, they use their growing knowledge of word classes within the language to guide their discovery of what a particular new word means. It is almost as if the child were saying to herself, "Since this new word was just used as a noun, it probably describes a thing." And on the other hand, they use their knowledge of individual words to predict how those words can be used. ("Since this Woodstock toy is now an instrument for hitting me on the head, I can use it as a verb"; Pinker, 1984). Using both kinds of evidence, chil-

9.21 Word classes and word meanings
When asked "In this picture can you see any sebbing?" (verb), children pointed to the hands; when asked "Can you see a seb?" they pointed to the blue bowl; and when asked "Can you see any seb?" they pointed to the dark red confetti. (Adapted from Bown, 1957)

dren efficiently "bootstrap" their way into knowledge of tens of thousands of words and the ways these words can be used in sentences (Grimshaw, 1981; Fisher et al., 1994).

THE CAPACITIES NEEDED FOR LANGUAGE LEARNING

We have now said a great deal about the child's progress as language learning proceeds. We have also discussed the kinds of information available to the child in support of this learning. We still need to ask, however, what skills or capacities the young child needs in order to use this information and to make this learning possible.

SENSITIVITY TO PATTERNS

As we have seen again and again, language is structured at many levels. To learn language, one must be alert to the patterns created by this structure—how words are sequenced within sentences, how sounds are sequenced within words, and so on. And many lines of evidence indicate that young children are immensely sensitive to these language patterns.

For example, in one study, eight-month-old infants heard a two-minute tape recording that sounded something like "bidakupadotigolabubidaku." These syllables were spoken in a monotonous tone, with no difference in stress from one syllable to the next and no pauses in between any of the syllables. But there was a pattern: The experimenters had decided in advance to call *bidaku* a "word." Therefore, if the infant heard *bida,* then *ku* was sure to follow (just as, in ordinary circumstances, seeing the letters *lang* makes it highly likely that *uage* is to follow to form the complete word *language*). However, there was no pattern *between* the various "words," so *daku* (the end of the word *bidaku*) would sometimes be followed by *go,* sometimes by *pa,* and so on. (Similarly, if you hear *language,* there's some chance that the next syllable will be *rule,* some chance that it will be *learn-,* and so forth.)

Remarkably, the babies detected this pattern. In a subsequent test, the babies showed no evidence of surprise if they heard the string *bidakubidakubidaku.* From the babies' point of view, these were simply repetitions of a "word" they already knew. However, the babies did show surprise if they were presented with the string *dakupadakupadakupa.* This was not a "word" they had heard before, although of course they had heard these syllables many times. Thus, the babies had learned the "vocabulary" of this made-up language. They had detected the statistical pattern of which syllables followed which, despite their rather brief, entirely passive exposure to these sounds and despite the absence of any supporting cues, such as pauses or shifts in intonation (Saffran, Aslin, and Newport, 1997).

A GENETIC BASIS FOR LANGUAGE?

Without question, the young child's sensitivity to patterns is crucial for language learning. But many investigators argue that this is not enough. In their view, the language patterns are too complex to support the prodigious learning that we observe in children. The child therefore needs some guidance beyond that contained in the stimulus input. Where could that guidance come from? Many scholars who endorse this "poverty of the stimulus" argument are led to the view that language learning must have some genetic basis, that the young child is neurologically "programmed" to learn language. This genetic guidance, then, supplements the information available in the speech the child hears, allowing learning to proceed (Chomsky, 1965; Lenneberg, 1967; Gleitman, 1981; Bickerton, 1984; Pinker, 1994).

This genetically rooted head start could take several different forms. One option is an extreme sensitivity to certain patterns, so that such patterns will be detected even if the evidence for the patterns in the language the child hears is quite weak. Another option is that the child, seeking to understand language, may be inclined toward some sorts of beliefs about how the language is structured and relatively blind toward other possibilities. This might be sufficient to keep the child on the right track, only considering the appropriate hypotheses about language (Wexler and Cullicover, 1980; Roeper and Williams, 1987; Pierce, 1992).

However this neurological program unfolds, the program must not specify any particular language, since, of course, the child's genetic material has no way of knowing whether she'll grow up in the United States, speaking English, or in Australia, speaking Walbiri. Therefore, the neurological program must be appropriate for all languages, so that she is, in effect, ready to learn *any* of them. To make this possible, what the neurological program specifies must be a **universal structure** shared by all languages.

Of course, each language differs from all the others, but these differences involve only a few details, or **parameters,** which define the relatively minor variations on this universal structure. The idea is that innate mechanisms swiftly guide the child toward the universal language structure. What he must learn more laboriously, though, is how to set the parameters in order to learn the language spoken in his own environment (Wexler and Manzini, 1987; Crain and Nakayama, 1986; Figure 9.22).

BIOLOGICAL ADAPTATIONS

This hypothesis—about an innate universal structure for all languages—remains controversial. Nonetheless, a variety of arguments favor it. For example, many features of syntax do indeed seem to be universal (shared by all languages). In addition, many aspects of language learning are difficult to explain if we consider only the language that the child hears. In other words, the child seems to end up knowing things about the language that go well beyond the "linguistic data" that she receives. This suggests that she must have some head start in learning language—some knowledge not dependent on the linguistic input. (For discussion of these points, see Chomsky, 1981; P. Bloom, 1994; Pinker, 1994; Gleitman and Newport, 1995.)

In addition, there is no question that humans are in many ways biologically adapted for language. As we discussed in Chapter 2, several regions of the brain

9.22 The parameter setting theory of language learning (A) Children hearing English and children hearing Spanish both come from nature's factory with the switch set to allow subject omission (SO). (B) The English speaker eventually resets his switch to disallow this (No SO); the Spanish speaker does not.

A

B

seem to be specialized for language use; this is reflected, for example, in the fact that damage to these areas produces disruption of language (aphasia) but seems to have little or no impact on other, nonlinguistic mental functioning. Interestingly, in deaf individuals these same brain areas seem crucial for learning and using sign language, indicating that these brain areas are truly in the business of supporting language, whether that language is verbal or gestural.

And it is not just the brain that is specialized for language. Consider the arrangement of human teeth, with adjacent teeth approximately the same height and with the spaces in between the teeth quite narrow. This configuration makes it easy for us to control air flow in and out of the mouth, with obvious advantages for the production of speech. But it creates problems for many aspects of biting and chewing (which is why most other animals have a rather different dental arrangement). It seems, then, that natural selection favored the configuration that's good for speaking over the configuration that's good for eating—a clear indication of the biological basis for human speech.

Similarly, most mammals can manage the trick of eating and breathing at the same time. (This is handy if you want to sniff the air for predators while you're munching.) Human infants can do this as well (and so babies can breathe and nurse simultaneously). However, adults cannot do this, thanks to the shape of the adult human larynx.

The adult human larynx not only blocks us from breathing while eating, it also dramatically increases the risk of death by choking since it's all too easy for humans to end up with food going down the larynx rather than the esophagus. But the arrangement allows us considerable control over the flow of air through the vocal tract, which is crucial for the production of speech (Lieberman, 1984).

It seems certain that our biological makeup is in many ways specifically adapted for the use of language, and this obviously makes it more plausible that our brains are also specifically prepared for language learning. This returns us, of course, to the suggestion that there may well be a genetically rooted universal structure for languages, with all humans programmed in a fashion that inclines us toward learning this structure. Some of the most remarkable evidence for this claim, however, comes from language learning in circumstances rather different from the ordinary progress we have been describing so far.

LANGUAGE LEARNING IN CHANGED ENVIRONMENTS

Thus far, our focus has been on language development as it proceeds normally. Under these conditions, language seems to emerge in much the same way in virtually all children. They progress from babbling to one-word speech, advance to the two-word telegraphic stage, and eventually graduate to complex sentence forms and meanings. This progression can be observed in children in Peking, learning to speak Chinese, as well as in children in Athens, learning to speak Greek. This uniformity—from one child to the next, from one language to the next—is certainly consistent with the claim that language development is rooted in our shared biological heritage.

But is this pattern truly universal? What happens when children grow up in environments radically different from those in which language growth usually proceeds? Examining these cases may help us to understand the biological roots of human language and will also allow us to ask which aspects of the early environment are essential for language learning.

 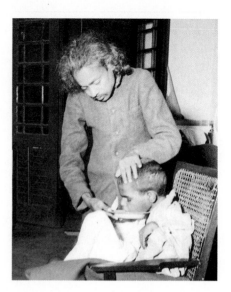

9.23 A modern wild boy *Ramu, a young boy discovered in India in 1976, appears to have been reared by wolves. He was deformed, apparently from lying in cramped positions, as in a den. He could not walk, and drank by lapping with his tongue. His favorite food was raw meat, which he seemed to be able to smell at a distance. After he was found, he lived at the home for destitute children run by Mother Theresa in Lucknow, Utter Pradesh. He learned to bathe and dress himself but never learned to speak. He continued to prefer raw meat and would often sneak out to prey upon fowl in the neighbor's chicken coop. Ramu died at the age of about ten in February 1985.* (New York Times, *Feb. 24, 1985; photographs courtesy Wide World Photos)*

WILD CHILDREN

In 1920, Indian villagers discovered a wolf mother in her den together with four cubs. Two were baby wolves, but the other two were human children, subsequently named Kamala and Amala. No one knows how they got there or why the wolf adopted them.★ Brown (1958) tells us what these children were like:

> Kamala was about eight years old and Amala was only one and one-half. They were thoroughly wolfish in appearance and behavior: Hard callus had developed on their knees and palms from going on all fours. Their teeth were sharp edged. They moved their nostrils sniffing food. Eating and drinking were accomplished by lowering their mouths to the plate. They ate raw meat. . . . At night they prowled and sometimes howled. They shunned other children but followed the dog and cat. They slept rolled up together on the floor. . . . Amala died within a year but Kamala lived to be eighteen. . . . In time, Kamala learned to walk erect, to wear clothing, and even to speak a few words. (p. 100)

The outcome was much the same for the thirty or so other wild children about whom we have reports. When found, they were all shockingly animal-like. None of them could be rehabilitated so as to use language at all normally, though some, including Kamala, learned to speak a few words (Figure 9.23).

ISOLATED CHILDREN

A number of other children have been raised by humans but under conditions that were hideously inhumane, for their parents were either vicious or deranged. Sometimes, such parents will deprive a baby of all human contact.

★ There has always been some controversy attached to these reports (e.g., Ogburn and Bose, 1959; but see Candland, 1993). One concern is that Amala and Kamala may have been retarded and for this reason were abandoned. Thus, the pattern of their development may be due to retardation and not to isolation from other humans. Given this ambiguity, it is important to emphasize that our claims about language acquisition rest on a broad pattern of data and not just on the reports about wolf children.

For example, "Isabelle" (a code name used to protect the child's privacy) was hidden away, apparently from early infancy, and given only the minimal attention necessary to sustain her life. No one spoke to her (the mother was deaf and also emotionally indifferent).

At the age of six, Isabelle was discovered by other adults and brought into a normal environment. Of course, she had no language, and her cognitive development was below that of a normal two-year-old. But within a year, she learned to speak, her tested intelligence was normal, and she took her place in an ordinary school (Davis, 1947; Brown, 1958). Thus, Isabelle at seven years, with one year of language practice, spoke about as well as her peers in the second grade, all of whom had had seven years of practice.

But rehabilitation from isolation is not always so successful. "Genie," discovered in California about twenty years ago, was fourteen years old when she was found. Since about twenty months, apparently, she had lived tied to a chair; she was frequently beaten and never spoken to but sometimes barked at, for her father said she was no more than a dog. Once discovered, Genie was brought into foster care and taught by psychologists and linguists (Fromkin et al., 1974). But Genie did not become a normal language user. She says many words and puts them together into meaningful propositions as young children do, such as "No more take wax" and "Another house have dog." Thus, she has learned certain basics of language. Indeed, her semantic sophistication—what she means by what she says—is far beyond young children. Yet even after years of instruction, Genie has not learned the function words that appear in mature English sentences, nor does she combine propositions together in elaborate sentences (Curtiss, 1977).

Why did Genie not progress to full language learning? The best guess is that the crucial factor is the age at which language learning began. Genie was discovered after she had reached puberty, while Isabelle was only six when she was discovered. As we shall see later, there is some reason to believe that there is a critical period for language learning. If the person has passed this period, language learning proceeds with greater difficulty.

LANGUAGE WITHOUT SOUND

The work on wild and isolated children argues that—to no one's surprise—a child will learn language only if she has some contact with, and some interaction with, other humans. But what aspects of this contact are crucial? An obvious hypothesis is that the child must hear the speech of others to detect the patterns and learn the rules. However, this hypothesis is false.

Deaf people do not hear others speaking; they are never exposed to ordinary (auditory) conversation. Yet they do learn a language, one that involves a complex system of gestures. In the United States, the deaf usually learn *American Sign Language* (or *ASL*), but other sign languages also exist. Plainly, language can exist in the absence of sound.

Are these gestural systems genuine languages? One indication that they are is that these systems are not derived by translation from the spoken languages around them but are independently created within and by communities of deaf individuals (Klima et al., 1979; Senghas, 1995). Further evidence comes from comparing ASL to the structure and development of spoken languages. ASL has hand shapes and positions of which each word is composed, much like the tongue and lip shapes that allow us to fashion the phonemes of spoken language (Stokoe, 1960). It has morphemes and grammatical principles for combining

A

B

C

9.24   Some common signs in ASL   (A) The sign for tree. One difference between ASL and spoken language is that many of the signed words physically resemble their meanings. This is so for tree, in which the upright forearm stands for the trunk and the outstretched fingers for the branches. But in many cases, such a resemblance is not present. Consider (B), which is the modern sign for help, whose relation to its meaning seems as arbitrary as that between most spoken words and their meanings. Even so, such a relation was once present, as shown in (C), a nineteenth-century sign for help. At that time, the sign was not arbitrary; it consisted of a gesture by the right hand to support the left elbow, as if helping an elderly person cross a street. (B) grew out of (C) by a progressive series of simplifications in which signs tend to move to the body's midline and use shorter, fewer, and more stylized movements. All that remains of (C) is an upward motion of the right palm. (Frishberg, 1975; photographs of and by Ted Supalla)

words into sentences that are similar to those of spoken language (Supalla, 1986; see Figure 9.24).

Finally, babies born to deaf users of ASL (whether or not the babies themselves are deaf) pick up the system from these caregivers through informal interaction rather than by explicit instruction, just as we learn our spoken language (Newport and Ashbrook, 1977).★ And they go through the same steps on the way to adult knowledge as do hearing children learning English. Given all of these considerations (and some others), it is hard to avoid the conclusion that ASL and other gestural systems are true languages (Supalla and Newport, 1978; Klima et al., 1979; Newport, 1984, 1990).

Thus, language does not depend on the auditory-vocal channel. When the usual modes of communication are denied to humans of normal mentality, they come up with an alternative that reproduces the same contents and structures as other language systems. It appears that language is an irrepressible human trait: Deny it to the mouth and it will dart out through the fingers.

LANGUAGE WITHOUT A MODEL

Let us revise our hypothesis: In order to learn language, one needs some exposure to language. This requires contact with other humans, but it does not require *auditory* contact: Being able to *see* the gestures of others is enough to enable one to detect the patterns and thus to learn the rules and semantic content of the system.

But is this entirely correct? What if children of normal mentality were raised in a loving and supportive environment but not exposed to language? Researchers found six children who were in exactly this sort of situation (Feldman, Goldin-Meadow, and Gleitman, 1978; Goldin-Meadow and Feldman, 1977). These children were deaf, so they were unable to learn spoken language. Their parents were hearing and did not know ASL. They had decided not to allow their children to learn a gestural language. This is because they shared the belief (held by some educators) that deaf children should focus their efforts on learning spoken language through special training in lip reading and vocalization. This training often proceeds slowly at first, so for some time these children

---

★ In fact, the expert sign-language translators seen on television are usually hearing children of deaf parents. They grow up in a bilingual environment, with ASL learned from their parents and English learned by contact with hearing children and adults, so they achieve perfect knowledge of both and thus are the best translators.

A

B

9.25 Self-made signs in a deaf boy never exposed to sign language A two-sign sequence. (A) The first sign means "eat" or "food." Immediately before, the boy had pointed to a grape. (B) The second sign means "give." The total sequence means "give me the food." (Goldin-Meadow, 1982; drawing courtesy Noel Yovovich)

did not have access to spoken English.★ Not yet able to read lips, unable to hear, and without exposure to a gestural language, these children were essentially without any linguistic input.

Without any access to language, these children did something remarkable: They invented a language of their own. For a start, the children invented a sizable number of gestures that were easily understood by others. For example, the children would flutter their fingers in a downward motion to express snow, twist their fingers to express a twist-top bottle, and so on (Figure 9.25; for earlier, related, observations, see Tervoort, 1961; Fant, 1972). But in addition, this spontaneously invented "language" showed many parallels to ordinary language learning: These children began to gesture one sign at a time at approximately the same age that hearing children begin to speak one word at a time—despite the fact that, unlike hearing children, these deaf children were actually inventing their own words. At two and three years of age, the children went on to two- and three-word sentences, just as hearing children do. And in these basic sentences, the deaf children placed the individual gestures in a serial order, according to semantic role—again, just as hearing children do. Thus, just like hearing children, the deaf children, with their invented language, had ways of distinguishing "chicken eat" from "eat chicken."

While the inventiveness of these deaf children is remarkable, we should not lose sight of the potential difficulties of their circumstances. First, we do not know the long-term cognitive effects of these children's isolation from a formal language system; this is a matter of some controversy. Second, children in these circumstances really have no one to converse with in their small gestural language, for the parents are committed not to signing with them, in the belief that this will motivate the children later on to learn to lip read and vocalize.

However, more recent evidence has come to light that is very informative and optimistic for how far children can go with invented languages in a context where these become the medium of social interchange. In Nicaragua, until about the early 1980s, deaf children from rural areas were widely scattered and usually knew no others who were deaf. Based on the findings just mentioned, it was not surprising to discover that all these deaf individuals developed home-made gestural systems to communicate with the hearing people around them, each system varying from the others in idiosyncratic ways. (These systems are actually called "home sign" by the deaf community; Coppola et al., 1998.) In the early 1980s, a school was created just for deaf children in Nicaragua, and they are bussed daily from all over the countryside to attend it. Just as in the American case, the school authorities have tried to teach these children to lip read and vocalize. But on the bus and in the lunchroom, and literally behind the teachers' backs, these children (aged four to fourteen in the initial group) began to gesture to each other. Bit by bit their different home signs converged on conventions that they all used, and the system grew more and more elaborate. The emerging gestural language of this school has now been observed over two "generations" of youngsters, for new four-year-olds arrive in this environment every year. These new members not only learn the system, but elaborate it and improve upon it, with the effect that in the space of twenty years a language system of considerable complexity and semantic sophistication has literally been invented by these children (Senghas, et al., 1997).

★ The degree of success with lip-reading and vocalization of English, as well as reading acquisition, by deaf children is variable, with the level attained closely related to the degree of deafness. Even the slightest hearing capability helps enormously. But there is growing evidence that the most natural alternative for profoundly deaf children is to learn and use ASL, for in this manual-visual medium they have no language handicap at all.

Perhaps it is true that Rome wasn't built in a day, but for all we know maybe Latin was! In sum, if children are denied access to a human language, they go to the trouble to invent one for themselves.

CHILDREN DEPRIVED OF ACCESS TO SOME OF THE MEANINGS

The extraordinarily robust nature of language development is also apparent when considering language learning in the absence of vision. Imagine a child who hears, "Look! There's a huge dog!" or "Do you see that man playing the guitar?" Surely, the child will find it easier to grasp the meaning of these phrases if he can observe the dog or the guitar player, using the perceptual experience to help decode the linguistic input.

This would seem to suggest that language learning would proceed slowly or be somehow limited in a blind child. A blind child would seem to be cut off from many of the learning opportunities available to the sighted child, with fewer chances to observe the referents of words or to observe the action being discussed. Remarkably, though, the evidence shows that blind children learn language as rapidly and as well as sighted children. One particularly striking example is vision-related words like *look* and *see*, which blind children use as early (two years of age) and as systematically as sighted children. Of course, there are differences in how blind and sighted children understand these words. A young sighted listener asked to "Look up!" will tilt her eyes upward (even if her vision is blocked by a blindfold). For this child, *look* clearly refers to vision (Figure 9.26A). A congenitally blind child, when told to "Look up!" produces a different—but entirely sensible—response. Keeping her head immobile, the blind youngster reaches upward and searches the space above her body with her hands (Figure 9.26B). Thus, each of these children understands *look* differently. But both children realize that the term is an instruction to search a bit of the world by use of the sense organs (Landau and L. Gleitman, 1985; see also Urwin, 1983; Mulford, 1986; Bigelow, 1987).

Once again we see that language emerges in all of its complexity and on schedule despite a dramatic shift away from the standard circumstances of language learning. This provides further support for the claim that language principles are truly part of our nature, allowing language learning to go forward normally even with enormous variation in how and what the child experiences.

At the same time, though, we must strike a cautionary note. It is true that the language forms and word meanings observed with blind children are strikingly similar to those of sighted children. But it is also true that these blind children manifest many problems in understanding the conversations going on around them, and this can create significant frustration in blind toddlers, sometimes leading to severe behavioral problems. This is not surprising. Imagine what it would be like if all your companions were involved in face-to-face conversation, but you were connected to them only by telephone. Like blind children, you would experience confusion about what was being discussed, have trouble identifying the referents of pronouns, and so forth (Landau and L. Gleitman, 1985).

We are left with a two-part conclusion. On the one hand, the blind child's success in learning language stands as testimony to the biological basis of human communication. Prepared as we are to learn language, the learning can proceed despite significant sensory deprivation. On the other hand, experience does play a pivotal role in language learning, and so sensory deprivation (especially early in life) does have a significant impact on the interpersonal use of language in the first few years of life. Even so, anyone who knows a blind adult can attest to the fact that these problems, too, are soon solved.

A

B

9.26   The meaning of "look"   *(A) A blindfolded, sighted three-year-old tilts her head upward in response to "Look up!" for to her the word* look *means "perceive by eye." (B) A congenitally blind three-year-old raises her arms upward in response to "Look up!" for to her the word* look *means "perceive by hand." (Drawings by Robert Thacker)*

THE CASE OF HELEN KELLER

The most dramatic and compelling picture of children cut off from contact with a language community comes to us from the case of Helen Keller (1880–1968). At eighteen months, she was a bright toddler, learning her first few words. But she then suffered a devastating illness (never adequately diagnosed) that left her both deaf and blind. Thus Helen, unlike the congenitally deaf and blind children we have discussed (who never experienced hearing or seeing), was aware of suffering a catastrophic loss. She later wrote (speaking of herself in the third person):

> With appalling suddenness she [Helen] moved from light to darkness and became a phantom. . . . Helplessly the family witnessed the baffled intelligence as Phantom's hand stretched out to feel the shapes which she could reach but which meant nothing to her. . . . Nothing was part of anything, and there blazed up in her frequent fierce anger. . . . I remember tears rolling down her cheeks but not the grief. There were no words for that emotion or any other, and consequently they did not register. (Keller, 1955)

Helen thus suffered the double affliction of sudden darkness and silence, and lived the next five years of her life in many ways isolated from the world of other people. But in the end, she entered Radcliffe, studied algebra, Greek, and literature, wrote classic and elegantly crafted books on her life and experiences, became an illustrious educator, and was personally close to many of the important people of her time, including Mark Twain, Eleanor Roosevelt, and Alexander Graham Bell (Lash, 1980).

Helen Keller gave the credit for this triumphant return to life to her great teacher, Anne Sullivan. Sullivan, herself half-blind and raised in appalling conditions in a "poor house," had acquired a partial manual communication system. It was through this medium that she began to unlock the stifled mind of Helen: She finger-spelled onto her eager pupil's palm. Helen reported her awakening in this famous passage (in which Anne Sullivan is holding one of Helen's hands under a waterspout):

> . . . as the cool stream gushed over one hand, she [Anne Sullivan] spelled into the other the word water. . . . I stood still, my whole attention fixed upon the motions of her fingers. . . . Suddenly I felt a misty consciousness as of something forgotten—a thrill of returning thought; and somehow the mystery of language was revealed to me. . . . Everything had a name, and each name gave birth to a new thought. As we returned to the house every object which I touched seemed to quiver with life. (Quoted in Lash, 1980)

As Anne Sullivan wrote, "She has learned that the manual alphabet is the key to everything she wants to know." Almost immediately, Helen was learning six new words a day. Eventually (though in the face of significant struggles because of the poor materials available for deaf and blind children in these early days), Helen read raised letters and Braille, and went on to achieve a state of literacy and creativity with language that would put most of us to shame.

What can we learn from Helen Keller's case? It is not as though this child was completely unable to communicate or think before the arrival of Sullivan in her life. In Helen's biography, she underestimated her own status at that time, remembering herself as merely "a wild and destructive little animal." But Anne Sullivan saw something else. Like the deaf children we have described in the previous section, Helen had spontaneously invented many gestures to describe her wants and needs. For instance, "a desire for ice cream was shown by turning the freezer and a little shiver; . . . knotting hair on the back of her head symbol-

Helen Keller and her teacher Anne Sullivan (Photograph courtesy of the Perkins School for the Blind)

Helen Keller conversing with Eleanor Roosevelt Helen understood speech by noting the movements of the lips and the vibration of the vocal cords. (Photograph by Larry Morris/New York Times; courtesy of the Perkins School for the Blind)

ized her mother.... If she wanted bread and butter, she imitated the motions of cutting ... and spreading." Sullivan recognized at least sixty such spontaneous "descriptive gestures" when she first met Helen (Lash, 1980).

So Helen's case is consistent with that of the deaf children we discussed earlier. Isolated from language forms, a human infant begins to invent her own. But Helen's case also reveals the crushing limitations of such a homemade language system for communicating with the surrounding community, which neither knows this idiosyncratic system nor understands its significance. Anne Sullivan, an incredibly sophisticated and talented teacher, differed from the loving but bewildered parents by capitalizing on the homemade signs in her first communicative contact with Helen. She wrote that "I use complete sentences ... and fill out the meaning with gestures and her [Helen's] descriptive signs" (Lash, 1980). Anne Sullivan also knew that language learning has to be natural and communicative, and will not succeed by memorizing word lists out of context as had been common in the education of sensorily deprived children at that time. Thus, she signed into Helen's palm "as we talk into the baby's ear." She wrote that the drill methods of her predecessors

> seem to be built up on the supposition that every child is a kind of idiot who must be taught to think.... Let him come and go freely, let him touch real things and combine his impressions for himself.... (Lash, 1980)

Thus, we see that Sullivan's success depended not only on exploiting the child's natural disposition to organize language according to deep-seated principles of form and meaning, but on introducing language in the context of its equally deep-seated functions for communicating about things, events, and feelings with others (see Bates and MacWhinney, 1982).

We should also note one other resemblance between Helen's case and that of the other children we have discussed. Unlike Genie who was first exposed to English during adolescence and who failed to learn anything but rudimentary basics, Helen received language stimulation quite early in life. As in the case of Isabelle, her rehabilitation began at about age six and was richly successful. The medium of transmission Sullivan used to teach Helen Keller—signing onto the palm or cheek—is still employed today with great success for children who are both deaf and blind (C. Chomsky, 1984).

LANGUAGE LEARNING WITH CHANGED ENDOWMENTS

Clearly, language learning can proceed despite severe environmental deprivations. This supports the contention that the mental machinery for language is innate, running its course undeflected by any but the most radical environmental stresses (such as that suffered by Genie). But what happens if the nature of the learners themselves is changed? Since language learning and use are determined by brain function, changing that brain should have strong effects (Lenneberg, 1967; Menyuk, 1977; L. Gleitman, 1986).

There are many indications that the nature and state of the brain have massive consequences for language functioning. We have already mentioned the evidence of aphasia, in which damage in the brain's left hemisphere has a devastating and highly specific impact on language use. If the damage is in one location (Broca's area), the victim loses use of the function words; if the damage is to another part (Wernicke's area), the loss is to the content words (Figure 9.27).

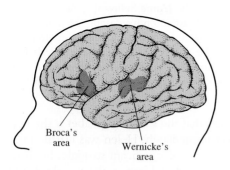

9.27 The language areas of the brain Certain areas of the cerebral cortex (in most individuals, in the left hemisphere) are devoted to language functions. These include Broca's area, where damage produces deficits in speech production, especially of function words (expressive aphasia), and Wernicke's area, where damage leads to deficits in comprehension of word meanings (receptive aphasia). For more details, see Chapter 2. (After Geschwind, 1972)

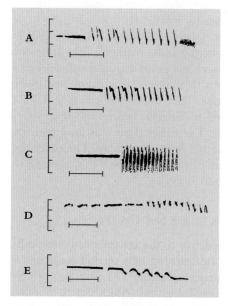

9.28 Critical period in the development of bird song *(A) A graphic presentation of the song of an adult, male white-crowned sparrow. The figure, a sound spectrogram, plots the frequency region of the bird's vocal output over time. Frequency is indicated on the vertical axis, in steps of 2,000 hertz. The horizontal time marker indicates half a second. The figure shows that the normal song begins with a whistle or two, continues with a series of trills, and ends with a vibrato. (B) The song of a bird raised in acoustic isolation but exposed to four minutes of normal song between the ages of 35 and 56 days. His adult song was almost normal. (C) The song of an isolated bird exposed to normal song between days 50 and 71. The adult song of this bird has some crude similarities to normal white-crowned sparrow song. There is a whistle followed by trills, but the details are very different. (D) and (E) show the songs of birds whose exposure to normal song occurred very early in life (days 3 to 7) or very late (after 300 days of age) respectively. Training at either of these times had no effect. (After Marler, 1970)*

Further evidence comes from individuals with an apparently inherited syndrome known as *specific language impairment.* Individuals with this syndrome are generally slow to learn language and throughout their lives have difficulty in understanding and producing many sentences. Yet these individuals seem normal on most other measures, including measurements of intelligence (Tallal, Ross, and Curtiss, 1989; Gopnik and Crago, 1993; Pinker, 1994).

We can also find cases with the reverse pattern—severe disruption of all mental capacities *except* language. Individuals with Williams syndrome are severely mentally retarded (with IQ scores of 60 or lower; see Chapter 15) but still capable of fluent and articulate language (Bellugi, et al., 1991; Pinker, 1995).

Clearly, then, differences in mental endowment can severely affect language learning and language use. If the portions of the brain implicated in language learning are damaged, then language use is disrupted (or, in some cases, devastated), even though other intellectual capacities seem still to function normally. But what about other, less dramatic changes? Can they, too, affect language learning? We now turn to aging to determine what effects that ubiquitous process has on language acquisition.

THE CRITICAL PERIOD HYPOTHESIS

The human brain continues to grow and develop in the years after birth, reaching its mature state more or less at the age of puberty. If language is indeed rooted in brain function, then we might expect language learning to be influenced by these maturational changes. Is it?

According to the *critical period hypothesis,* the brain of the young child is particularly well suited to the task of language learning. As the brain matures, this critical period draws to a close, so that later learning (both of a first language and of later languages) becomes more difficult (Lenneberg, 1967).

Critical periods do seem to govern some aspects of learning in many species. One example is the attachment of the young of various animals to their mothers, which generally can be formed only in early childhood (see Chapter 14). Another example is bird song. Male birds of many species have a song that is characteristic of their own kind. They learn this song by listening to adult males of their own species. But this exposure will only be effective if it occurs at a certain period in the bird's life. To take a concrete case, baby white-crowned sparrows will learn their species' song in all its glory, complete with trills and grace notes, only if they hear this music (sung, of course, by an adult white-crowned sparrow) sometime between the seventh and sixtieth day of their life. If they do not hear the song during this period, but instead hear it sometime during the next month, they acquire only the basics of the song, without the full elaborations heard in normal adults (see Figure 9.28). If the exposure comes still later, it has no effect at all. The bird will never sing normally (Marler, 1970).

Do human languages work in the same way? Are adults less able to learn language because they have passed out of some critical period? Much of the evidence has traditionally come from studies of second-language acquisition, for the obvious reason that it is hard (though not impossible) to find adults who have not been exposed to a first language early in life.

SECOND LANGUAGE LEARNING

In the initial stages of learning a second language, adults appear to be much more efficient than children (Snow and Hoefnagel-Hohle, 1978). The adult will venture halting but comprehensible sentences soon after arrival in the new language community. In contrast, children fluent in one language seem to be filled

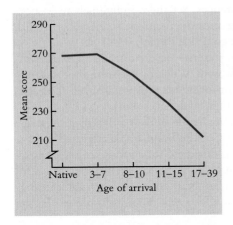

9.29 Critical period for second-language learning *Relation between age of arrival in the United States by 46 Korean and Chinese individuals, and their score (out of 276 test items) on a test of English grammar conducted five years later. (After Johnson and Newport, 1989)*

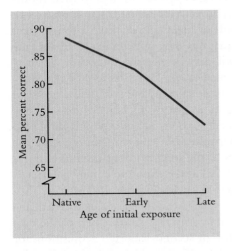

9.30 Critical period for first-language learning *Relation between time of first exposure to ASL by deaf individuals and their score on a test of ASL, conducted thirty or more years later. (After Newport, 1990)*

with confusion and astonishment when they suddenly hear a second language that they cannot understand at all; often they stop talking altogether for some weeks. But in the long run the outcome is just the reverse. After one to two years, very small children speak the new language fluently and soon sound just like natives. This is much less common in adults.

This point has been documented in many studies. In one investigation, the subjects were native Chinese and Korean speakers who came to the United States (and became immersed in the English-language community) at varying ages. The subjects were tested only after they had been in the United States for at least five years, so they had had ample exposure to English. And all of them were students and faculty members at a large midwestern university, so they shared some social background (and presumably were all motivated to learn the new language so as to succeed in their university roles).

In the test procedure, half of the sentences the subjects heard were grossly ungrammatical (e.g., "The farmer bought two pig at the market"; "The little boy is speak to a policeman"). The other half were the grammatical counterparts of these same sentences. The subjects' task was to indicate which sentences were grammatical in English and which were not. The results are shown in Figure 9.29. The learners who had been exposed to English before age seven performed just like native speakers of English. Thereafter there was an increasing decrement in performance as a function of age at first exposure. The older the subjects when they first came to the United States, the less well they seemed to have acquired English (Johnson and Newport, 1989).

LATE EXPOSURE TO A FIRST LANGUAGE

The results just described certainly lend credence to the critical period hypothesis. But these results obviously focus on the learning of a second language. Is this same pattern observed with first-language learning? The best line of evidence comes from work on American Sign Language (ASL), which is often learned late in life. As we discussed earlier, many congenitally deaf children have hearing parents who choose not to allow their offspring access to ASL. Such children's first exposure to ASL may, therefore, be quite late in life, when they eventually establish contact with the deaf community. These people are thus essentially learning a first language at an unusually late point in maturational time.

How does this late start influence language learning? In one study, all of the participants had used ASL as their sole means of communication for at least thirty years, guaranteeing that they were as expert in the language as they would ever become. Some of these participants had been exposed to ASL from birth (because their parents were deaf signers). Others had learned ASL between the ages of four and six years of age. A third group was composed of participants who had first come into contact with ASL after the age of twelve.

Not surprisingly, all of these signers were quite fluent in ASL, thanks to thirty-plus years of practice. But even so, the age of first exposure had a strong effect (Figure 9.30). Those who had learned ASL from birth used and understood all of its elaborations. Those whose first exposure had come after four years of age showed subtle deficits. Those whose exposure began in adolescence or adulthood had much greater deficits, and their use of function items was sporadic, irregular, and often incorrect (Newport, 1990).

One might debate whether these results indicate a clear-cut critical period for language learning: The late learners still learned the language reasonably well. But the results also leave no doubt that language learning is influenced by the learner's age. When exposure is late, there are significant deficits in learning that can be observed even after many years of practice and use.

LANGUAGE IN NONHUMANS

Let us pause to take stock. Human language learning appears to be characterized by a number of universals, generalizations that hold for all children learning all languages. Some of these universals concern the sequence and timing of various milestones in the child's acquisition of language. Others concern the form of language itself, with all languages seeming to share a single universal structure. In addition, children seem able to learn this structure even when the language information they are given is quite sparse. Many scholars believe that this is the situation of every child (we earlier referred to this as the "poverty of the stimulus" argument), but it is certainly the situation of every congenitally blind child and every linguistically isolated deaf child. And, of course, it is the situation of every child who is exposed to *no* language, so that she must, in essence, invent language on her own.

All of these indications push us toward the claim that language learning must have a biological basis, providing the child with a crucial head start in the acquisition of language. This claim is bolstered by the observation that the human brain (and mouth and throat) is plainly specialized for language. Moreover, some forms of brain damage can disrupt language learning while sparing other functions. So in an important sense, we are biologically a linguistic species.

And, finally, we have seen that language learning seems age dependent. The advantages adults may have as students are more than offset by the fact that children's brains are in the appropriate state of readiness for learning language. Hence, the learning of language is one task at which children are unmistakably better than adults.

Clearly, the human biological endowment plays an important role in language learning. Does this imply that other creatures, without this same endowment, will be unable to learn language, or to learn it as humans do? As we will see, the evidence indicates that even our nearest animal relative, the chimpanzee, cannot come close to attaining human language, even with the best of good will and the most strenuous educational procedures. At the same time, though, there is considerable overlap between our biological endowments and those of other primates. For this reason, we should not be too surprised if some rudiments of language can be made to grow in them. If so, they may offer insight into the origins of our own communicative organization.

THE MEDIUM OF TRANSMISSION FOR CHIMPANZEE COMMUNICATION

Chimpanzee vocal tracts differ from our own, so they cannot literally speak as we do (Hayes, 1952). Several investigators have tried to overcome this obstacle by using communication media of other sorts, including artificial systems in which bits of colored plastic, or symbols on a computer screen, stand for words (Premack, 1976; Rumbaugh, 1977). Others have used gesture (Gardner and Gardner, 1969, 1975, 1978; Terrace et al., 1979).

Chimpanzees using these systems can acquire a substantial number of "words." Consider Washoe, a chimpanzee introduced to words at about age one and treated just like a human child, with naps, diapers, and baths. She was taught signs by having her hands physically molded into the desired position; other

A

B

Chimpanzees signing   *A young chimpanzee making the sign for (A) hug and (B) apple. (Terrace, 1979; photographs courtesy of Herbert Terrace)*

signs were learned by imitation (Fouts, 1972). After four years, she had learned about 130 signs for objects (*banana, hand*), actions (*bite, tickle*), and action modifiers (*enough, more*). This is impressive, but cannot compare with the progress of a human child, who learns about 10,000 words in this period (for discussion, see Savage-Rumbaugh et al., 1980).

Also of considerable interest is the finding that some of the chimpanzees use their new acquisitions in naturalistic interactions with their trainers, not just in laboratory tests. Moreover, Washoe appears to have taught some of her human signs to an adopted chimpanzee baby (Fouts, Hirsch, and Fouts, 1982), a possible case of cultural transmission by another species.

SYNTAX

Learning words is an important part of language, but it is only part. Can chimpanzees learn more than this? Can they organize their signs for *Mama, tickle,* and *Washoe* so as to say either *Mama tickles Washoe* or *Washoe tickles Mama?* Some believe that Washoe does have some such ability. As evidence, they point to the fact that, on many occasions, Washoe has produced apparently novel sequences of signs. For instance, she once signed *listen eat* on hearing an alarm clock that signals mealtime, and she signed *water bird* upon seeing a duck.

A number of critics, however, feel that such observations prove little. Take the sequence *water bird.* On the face of it, this seems a remarkable construction, presumably meaning something like *bird that lives in water.* But is this interpretation justified, or did Washoe merely produce an accidental succession of two signs: water (perhaps water was seen just before) and bird (because of the duck)? Put differently, we have no way of knowing whether Washoe intended to relate these words in any way or whether she intended anything by the sequence itself: *water-bird,* as opposed to *bird-water.* (In English, the first of these means "a bird that lives in water"; the second means "water for a bird." Does Washoe mean one of these, rather than the other?) With no way to answer these questions, it is hard to justify any conclusions about Washoe's achievement.

IS IT LANGUAGE?

Efforts to teach language to apes are continuing, and investigators are exploring other teaching techniques as well as other species. For example, some have argued that the bonobo, or pygmy chimpanzee, is a much better prospect for learning language than its full relative, the common chimpanzee (Savage-Rumbaugh et al., 1986; Savage-Rumbaugh, 1987). Thus, it remains to be seen just how much chimpanzees (or any other ape) can accomplish.

For now, though, the evidence allows us to conclude only that chimpanzees can learn words, and that they do show some evidence of propositional thought (e.g., Premack, 1976). There is little satisfactory evidence that they can create (or understand) the sorts of syntactic structures that humans use routinely. Thus, while the debate continues, it seems that only humans are entitled to the label "linguistic creature." Humans learn language in virtually any circumstance, from the most nurturant to the most horribly abusive. Our nearest primate cousins, in contrast, do not approach the competence of an ordinary three-year-old, even if those primates are provided with the utmost in social and linguistic support. (For discussion of some of these issues, see Seidenberg and Petitto, 1979; Van Cantfort and Rimpau, 1982; Pinker, 1994.)

Lewis Carroll's poignant tale of how an animal's mind would be different if it had language *Alice came to a forest where nothing had a name. She met a fawn that walked trustingly by her side: "So they walked together through the wood, Alice with her arms clasped lovingly around the soft neck of the Fawn, till they came out into another open field [where things had names]. And here the Fawn gave a sudden bound into the air, and shook itself free of Alice's arm. 'I'm a Fawn!' it cried out in a voice of delight. "And dear me! You're a human child!' A sudden look of alarm came into his beautiful brown eyes, and in another moment it had darted away at full speed."* (Carroll, Through the Looking Glass, 1901.)

LANGUAGE AND THOUGHT

We have argued that the nature of language learning and the nature of language itself are very much conditioned by the biology of the human brain. In a sense, language takes the form it does because our brains (and our minds) are structured in a certain way. But what about the reverse: Is it possible that the language we speak shapes the way we think? We have mentioned several times that all human languages are similar in important ways, but these languages also differ from each other in their vocabulary and in their syntax. Do these differences between languages lead to corresponding differences in the ways speakers of those languages think?

One frequently mentioned example concerns the number of terms for *snow* in Eskimo languages such as Aleut. This number is sometimes purported to be as large as three hundred, with different terms for naming types of snow such as *powder, slush, ice,* and so forth. The further claim is then made that speakers of such languages are influenced by this extravagance of vocabulary and so end up able to make much finer distinctions among snow types than are speakers of other languages.

But this example is flawed in several ways. The initial claim about vocabulary size is actually false; English turns out to have more snow-related terms than does Aleut (Pinker, 1995)! But even if it were true that Aleut had more words for snow, would that explain why Aleut speakers are more sensitive to

395

snow distinctions (if they are) than, say, English-speaking residents of South Carolina? A plausible alternative is that the Eskimos' day-to-day activities create a functional need for these discriminations, and this leads both to the larger vocabulary and to the greater skill in picking out different types of snow. On this view, language does not shape perception. On the contrary, language and perception are both shaped by environment and culture.

WHORF'S CLAIMS

The *snow* example is, for reasons just discussed, entirely unpersuasive. But might other examples support the claim that language influences thought? Some of the early evidence was offered by the anthropologist Benjamin Whorf, a strong proponent of the view that language categories force us into certain modes of thought. Whorf actually worked as a fire inspector, and he noticed that careless workers sometimes threw their cigarette butts into oil drums that were labeled "empty"—with disastrous consequences, for these drums often still contained flammable vapors. Whorf asserted that the reason the workers did so was that English had only one word for "empty." If English had two words, one for "void of liquid" and the other for "void of everything," the workers would have been more sensitive to the distinction and so would not have had to call the fire inspector so often (Whorf, 1956; for an earlier version of Whorf's claim, see Humboldt, 1836).

But is this likely? Were the workers confused by what comes down to English using a single sound "empty" for two different concepts? Or was it the *appearance* of emptiness—the invisibility of the vapors—that made the trouble? Whorf's interpretation of the evidence in this case is implausible, since we know that languages often use a single sound to express different concepts with no resulting confusion. In English, we use the sound "bat" to refer both to certain small mammals and to a piece of equipment used in baseball, but despite this homonymy, English speakers show no tendency to confuse these two ideas. Similarly for sides of rivers and financial institutions (banks), and for tree stems, elephant proboscises, and certain storage lockers (trunks). It seems that concepts are easily kept distinct even if the language misleadingly labels them with the same sound—in flat contradiction to Whorf's claim.

Whorf also argued for a deeper influence of language on thought. For example, he argued that languages differ in how they mark the tense of a verb, and this, he claimed, has profound consequences for how we think about the passage of time and the relationships among past, present, and future. In the same vein, he argued that a distinction between objects and events is not inevitable. Instead, we partition reality into these categories only because our language distinguishes between nouns and verbs. If this difference were not in our language, we would think of reality very differently.

But on these points, too, Whorf's evidence is quite weak. He tried to show, for example, that Hopi speakers think about time differently from English speakers, but his only evidence came from the ways that the Hopi expressed themselves when talking about different kinds of events. Such evidence is without value: Perhaps the Hopi think in just the same ways that English speakers do but express these thoughts differently because their language differs from English. In this case, the evidence indicates only that the way one expresses oneself is influenced by one's language—a conclusion that seems both unsurprising and not very interesting. (For more on the difficulties inherent in Whorf's claims, see Boyer, 1996; Clark, 1996; Kay, 1996.)

EXPERIMENTAL STUDIES OF LANGUAGE'S INFLUENCE ON THOUGHT

While Whorf's own evidence in unpersuasive, other tests of his conception are more compelling. Overall, these tests provide little support for Whorf's claims. But as we will see, they do suggest that language influences thought in ways rather different from those envisioned by Whorf.

COLOR TERMS AND PARSING THE WORLD

Some languages have a rich and subtle vocabulary for discriminating colors (*puce, mauve, teal*), while other languages have only a few color terms. As an extreme case, the Dani people (of New Guinea) have only two terms for color, one meaning (roughly) "dark" and the other meaning "light." However, the Dani seem to perceive color in exactly the same way that English speakers do: Colors that seem similar to each other to American viewers also seem similar to the Dani. American and Dani observers also agree about which colors are particularly good examples of their categories—which shade of red in a group of reds is a particularly good example of redness, which shade of blue within a group of blues is exemplary of blueness, and so on (Brown and Lenneberg, 1954; Berlin and Key, 1969; Rosch, 1977; Heider, 1972).

Other studies—examining the perception of shapes, for example, or facial expressions—have had similar outcomes (Rosch, 1977), and this has led many investigators to conclude that all peoples, whatever the language they speak, perceive the world in essentially the same ways.

THE LANGUAGE OF SPATIAL POSITION

Another area in which we can examine the interaction of language and thought is in descriptions of space, since there are considerable differences in how languages describe spatial position. For instance, English speakers would say that "the fruit is in the bowl" and also that "the floppy disk is in the computer," using the same preposition (*in*) in both cases. Korean speakers would use two different words in these cases, with one word conveying the idea of fitting in loosely (as "the fruit is *in* the bowl") and the other describing things that fit in tightly ("the disk is *in* the computer"). As another example, English distinguishes between vertical contact (*on*) and vertical noncontact (*above*), while both Japanese and Korean use a single word to convey both *on* and *above*.

Despite these linguistic differences, Japanese, Korean, and English speakers all seem to think about spatial position in the same way. In one study, participants were shown pictures of objects located at various positions with respect to a reference object. A short time later, they were shown another picture and asked if it depicted the same scene or a slightly different one. In some cases, this new picture was altered slightly, but preserved the relationship (of *on* or *above*) shown in the original picture. (The first picture, for example, might have shown a cup on a table; the second, a cup still on a table but shifted slightly to the right.) In other cases, the new picture depicted a change in this relationship (with the original picture showing the cup on the table and the test picture showing the cup above the table).

If English sensitizes us to the contrast between *on* and *above*, then English speakers should detect alterations that change these relationships more easily than Koreans or Japanese do. But the data show no such effect, and the memory performance of all groups was the same (Munnich and Landau, 1998; also see Hayward and Tarr, 1995; Li et al., 1997).

As a different example, speakers of Tzeltal (a Mayan language) seem to have no terms for "to the left of" or "to the right of," expressions that are obviously available (and often used) in English. Similarly, speakers of Guugu Yimithirr (a language spoken in Northern Queensland, Australia) do not speak of things being "behind" another object or "to the left of" another object. Instead, they seem always to specify locations in absolute terms, as in "to the north of" or "to the east of" (Levinson, 1996; also Haviland, 1996).★

Do speakers of Guugu Yimithirr or Tzeltal think about space differently than English speakers do? Some evidence suggests that they do: In one study the native Australians seemed to regard two layouts as similar only if they were aligned in the same way relative to compass directions (Levinson, 1996). Likewise, there is some suggestion that the Tzeltal do not distinguish between mirror images (Levinson, 1996; also see Bowerman, 1996). But other investigators argue that these results reflect only the specific conditions of testing, and also the way that the rural preliterate Tzeltal understood the experimenter's instructions. To evaluate this suggestion, one investigator created test conditions for English speakers like those under which the Tzeltal group had been studied—for example, providing strong landmarks visible to the north and south of the testing area. Under these conditions, American college students exhibited a more absolute strategy rather than their more customary relative strategy (Li, 1998). This clearly suggests that the Tzeltal data reflect only the manner in which the Tzeltal were tested and not some profound effect produced by the Tzeltal language.

LANGUAGE DOES GUIDE THOUGHT

In an important way, the language we use *does* guide our thought. If a speaker says, "I saw a dog," this will lead the listener to a different idea than if the speaker had said, "I saw a cat." Indeed, the very purpose of communication is to affect thought in this way, by conveying the thoughts of one person to another.

Language also influences our thinking in other ways. For example, linguistic descriptions often provide a convenient way of coding, or chunking, information, with important consequences for memory (Chapter 7). The way information is framed in language can also influence our decisions, so that a patient is more likely to choose a medical treatment if told it has a 50 percent chance of success than if told it has a 50 percent chance of failure (Chapter 8). Finally, language can influence our attitudes (Chapter 11), a fact well known to advertisers and propagandists.

In these examples, the choice of words affects our thinking. But the mere fact of verbalizing our thoughts can also have an influence. In several studies, participants were explicitly asked to put their thoughts into words—in some cases, to explain why they made a particular choice, in others, to explain their strategies in solving a problem. In many such cases, the participants did not have the vocabulary they needed to express their thoughts adequately, and so their verbalizations did not do justice to their thought processes. In their subsequent thinking, though, they seemed to recall their own inadequate descriptions of their thought processes rather than the thought processes themselves, and in some cases this actually disrupted their performance (Wilson and Schooler, 1991; Schooler et al., 1993; Fallshore and Schooler, 1995; Dodson et al., 1997).

Yet another example of the effect of language on thought involves the impact of gendered pronouns. In many contexts, the masculine *he* (or *his* or *him*) is used generically to indicate a person of either gender. The evidence suggests, howev-

★ By *absolute,* we mean that these descriptions are not relative to the speaker's or listener's position. Imagine that your textbook is currently in front of you on the desk and also to the north of you. If you turn around, the textbook is now behind you, but it is still to the north of you. It is in this sense that the distinction between *front* and *behind* is relative (relative to your position) but the designation *north* is absolute.

er, that this pronoun is *not* interpreted generically. Instead, the generic *he* tends to suggest a male referent to most readers (MacKay, 1980; Martyna, 1980; Crawford and English, 1984).

In addition, the choice of pronouns may also influence how a passage is remembered later on. In one study, men and women were asked to read an essay on psychology as a profession. Half of the participants read an essay entitled "The Psychologist and His Work," which consistently used masculine pronouns to refer to psychologists in general. The remaining participants read an essay entitled "Psychologists and Their Work," which used both feminine and masculine pronouns ("He or she may do research").

Forty-eight hours later, male participants were better able to recall the essay if they had read the version using masculine pronouns only. Female participants showed better recall if they had read the essay that used both masculine and feminine pronouns (Crawford and English, 1984). Presumably, this reflects the fact that people often have better memory for materials directly pertinent to their interests and their lives, and it would appear that the choice of pronouns influenced whether the participants perceived this essay as pertinent or not.

These many cases remind us that, in important ways, language does influence thought, by drawing attention to some points and away from others, by highlighting certain themes, by framing issues in a certain way. Let us emphasize, though, that these functions are a far cry from the claims offered by Whorf a half-century ago. Whorf's argument was that language shapes what we *can* think, so that there are literally some ideas, for example, that a native Hopi speaker can contemplate but that a native French speaker cannot. In the same way, Whorf contended that, having learned to speak one language, our thought would then forever be governed by the categories and syntax of that initial language experience.

As we have seen, there is no compelling evidence in favor of these stronger claims. When put to a direct test (as, for example, in the case of color perception), there seems to be no relationship between our language and how we perceive the world—our perceptions are not influenced by the perceptual labels provided by our language. In addition, it is important to bear in mind that many aspects of thought seem independent of language, and in these cases, there is no reason at all to expect that language will influence thought. The fact that there are such nonlinguistic forms of thought is supported by evidence that infants who know no language seem able to think relatively complex thoughts (Chapter 13) and by evidence that some of our adult thought takes the form of nonlinguistic mental images (Chapter 7). Moreover, creatures such as digger wasps and migrating birds are able to find their way from place to place across great distances without the benefit of words like *north* and *left*.

Finally, throughout this chapter, we have emphasized the rather impressive sameness of languages—in the processes of language acquisiton, in the hierarchical structure of languages, in many aspects of syntax. This linguistic sameness, in turn, is the reflection of sameness of mentality across the human species. Language influences us and guides us, and surely this is no surprise: This is one of the essential functions of communication. But the suggestion that language governs how we think, or what we can think, is currently without factual basis.

SUMMARY

1. Language has five major properties. It is *creative:* All normal humans can say and understand sentences they have never heard before. It is *structured:* Only certain arrangements of linguistic elements (phonemes, words, and so forth) are allowed. It is *meaningful:* Each word or combination of words expresses a meaningful idea (or concept). It is *refer-*

ential: It relates to things, scenes, and events in the extralinguistic world. It is *interpersonal:* It enables us to communicate with other people.

2. Languages are organized as a hierarchy of structures. The lowest-level units are *phonemes,* the sound elements of language. Each language uses certain phonemes and has specific arrangements of the phonemes it uses. Each language also has *morphemes,* which are the smallest language units that carry bits of meaning. There are *content morphemes,* which carry the bulk of meaning, and *function morphemes,* which determine the structure of the sentence.

3. Word and phrase meaning is not identical to word and phrase reference, for some expressions can refer to the same thing and yet have different meanings. The *definitional theory of meaning* holds that each word describes a bundle of more elementary *semantic features.* Each word is "defined" as some small set of features that together pick out that word from all other words in the language. The *prototype theory of meaning* responds to the fact that it is hard to find necessary and sufficient definitions for all words. Another theory of word meaning combines the definitional and prototype theories. The definitional part picks out properties that a concept must have. The prototype part concerns the most typical properties, the ones that most members of the concept share.

4. The power of language comes from our ability to express *propositions,* which consist of a *subject,* or topic, and a *predicate,* what is said about the subject or topic. Propositions express the miniature drama of doer, action, done-to. The rules of *syntax* specify acceptable combinations of words and phrases, including the elements required and the order in which those elements must appear. Linguists use tree diagrams to show the relations among the phrases and words that make up the full sentences.

5. Sentences have both a *surface structure,* which describes their structural parts (the phrases and words) and the order in which these are uttered in speech, and an *underlying structure,* which describes their meaning. The underlying structure consists of the sentence as interpreted into a *proposition* containing doer, act, and done-to, and various *attitudes* to this proposition, such as negation or questioning.

6. Sentence relations can be described according to various properties of surface and underlying structure. Two sentences that are the same in underlying structure but different in surface structure are *paraphrases.* Two sentences that are the same in surface structure but different in underlying structure are *ambiguous.*

7. Listeners hear only surface structure but to comprehend must recover the underlying structure. The psychological machinery that accomplishes comprehension is called the *Sentence Analyzing Machinery,* or *SAM.* SAM begins with the assumption that the sentence will be in the sequence *subject, verb, object;* if the sentence is not in this form, comprehension is often slower and, in some cases, may fail altogether. But SAM also relies on several other cues, and these generally keep SAM on the right track. Function words, for example, are used as cues to sentence structure, signaling the start of an embedded phrase. Semantic cues also provide important information about who did what to whom.

8. Comprehension is also aided by several aspects of the *context* in which the utterance is encountered. The extralinguistic context can provide important cues about a sentence's structure and the meaning of its phrases.

9. Sentence comprehension is also facilitated by the fact that conversations are usually conducted in a spirit of *cooperation,* with speaker and listener each sensitive to what the other knows and what the other needs to know. This cooperation is in part guided by a set of *conversational maxims,* including a maxim of *relevance* and a maxim of *quantity.*

10. Language learning is more than skill acquisition, for the learning cannot be fully described as a habit acquired through imitation and reinforcement. The proof is that children come to know more than they ever could have heard.

11. Infants are responsive to linguistic stimulation almost from birth. For instance, they have been shown to be responsive to differences among just about all the phonemes used in the various languages of the world. Learning a specific language's phoneme

structure involves learning not to notice those distinctions absent from one's native language. Infants are especially responsive to a form of speech known as *Motherese*—talk used by caregivers—which is characterized by large pitch changes and by pauses at phrase boundaries.

12.   Most infants begin talking in one-word sentences early in the second year of life and rapidly acquire a large vocabulary. They seem to have propositional ideas in mind and some appreciation of syntactic structure, even at this early stage.

13.   At about two years of age, children begin using rudimentary two-word or telegraphic sentences that contain content words but typically omit function morphemes and words. These first sentences may be short, in part, because of the difficulty of planning complex sentences. Still, these short sentences have a good deal of structure.

14.   By the age of four or so, children start to produce *overregularization errors,* including utterances such as "I runned," or "She has two feets." These utterances provide a clear indication that language is not learned by imitation (since no adult produces utterances like these). Instead, these errors indicate that children learn about the patterns of language and then overgeneralize them.

15.   Children learn new words at an extraordinary pace—five to ten words a day, every day, for several years. They tend to learn basic-level words before learning superordinates or subordinates. Their word learning is facilitated by several predispositions, including a general assumption that words name entire objects and an assumption that each concept has only one word that refers to it. Children are also guided by syntax, using sentence structure as an important clue about word meaning.

16.   Children are enormously sensitive to patterns, and this facilitates their language learning. In addition, many investigators have argued that all human languages share a *universal structure* and that *innate mechanisms* guide the child toward this structure.

17.   Many facts indicate that language and language learning are rooted in human biology. The shape of the human mouth and throat are well suited to language production, although this shape may interfere with other functions. The human brain also contains areas specifically dedicated to language, as can be seen in cases of aphasia resulting from brain damage.

18.   Language learning takes place successfully in many radically different environments. It fails only if children are removed from all human company or violently isolated and abused. Even if one is deaf, one learns a language. In this case, the language will be a signed (visual-manual) language rather than a spoken (auditory-vocal) one.

19.   Children isolated from opportunities to learn the language around them invent it for themselves. An example is deaf children not exposed to signed languages who invent gestures for words and combine these into propositions.

20.   When the brain is unusual or deficient, radical changes in language learning are seen. An important case of a "changed brain" that learns a language is that of a second-language learner who is older than the usual first-language learner. The less mature brain and the mature brain appear to have different capacities. The older the second-language learner, the less likely she is to acquire the new language adequately.

21.   Because experimental evidence makes it clear that language learning is based on special properties of the young human brain, we should not expect to find that human language can be fully or even adequately learned by other higher animals such as chimpanzees. Nevertheless, chimpanzees have been shown to have some word-learning capacities, though nowhere near as good as those of a two-and-a-half-year-old human. And there is little credible evidence that chimpanzees can acquire even rudimentary syntactic principles.

22.   Whorf claimed that how we think about the world is derived from the way our language is structured. This position remains popular, but the evidence for Whorf's claims is weak. Language does influence us in many ways, but probably does not shape our basic perception or understanding of the world.

PART THREE

SOCIAL BEHAVIOR

CHAPTER **10**

THE BIOLOGICAL BASIS OF SOCIAL BEHAVIOR

In the preceding chapters, we asked what organisms do, what they want, and what they know. In pursuing these questions, we have largely considered the organism as an isolated individual abstracted from the social world in which it lives. But many aspects of behavior are impossible to describe by considering a single organism. Courtship, sex, parental care, competition, and cooperation cannot take place in a vacuum. They are not merely actions; they are interactions in which each participant's behavior affects, and is affected by, the behavior of others.

In humans, the role of social factors is crucial, and most of our motives—whether the desire for love and esteem, the drives to achieve, to dominate or cooperate, and, in some cases, unhappily, to inflict pain—are social. Even motives that seem asocial, such as hunger, thirst, and temperature maintenance, are enormously affected by long-standing social practices and traditions. Thus, we eat food that is produced by a complex agricultural technology based on millennia of human discovery, and we eat it delicately, many of us with knife and fork, according to the etiquette of a long-dead king.

The study of social behavior is the study of lives inextricably intertwined with those of others both living and dead. It is the study which proves that, to quote John Donne's famous sermon, "no man is an island complete unto himself."

classic question posed by philosophers is, "What in human nature is fixed, and what is changeable (and improveable)?" Are greed, competition, and hate (or for that matter, charity, cooperation, and love) unalterable components of the human makeup, or can these qualities be instilled or nullified by proper training? We can gain important insights into these questions by considering some of the biological roots of our social behavior.

THE SOCIAL NATURE OF HUMANS AND ANIMALS

Are human beings so built that social interaction is an intrinsic part of their makeup? Or are they essentially solitary creatures who turn to others only to exploit them for their own selfish purposes? The English social philosopher Thomas Hobbes (1588–1679) argued for the latter view. As he saw it, humans are self-centered brutes who, left to their own devices, seek their own gain regardless of the cost to others. Except for the civilizing constraints imposed by

Thomas Hobbes *(Painting by John Michael
Wright; courtesy of The Granger Collection)*

Charles Darwin *(Painting by J. Collier;
courtesy of The National Portrait Gallery,
London)*

society, people would inevitably be in an eternal "war of all against all." According to Hobbes, this frightening "state of nature" is approximated during times of anarchy and civil war. These were conditions Hobbes knew all too well, for he lived during a time of violent upheavals in England when Stuart royalists battled Cromwell's Puritans, when commoners beheaded their king in a public square, and when pillaging, burning, and looting were commonplace. Hobbes argued that in such a state of nature, humans are a sorry lot. There are "no Arts; no Letters; no Society; and which is worst of all, continual fear, and danger of violent death; And the life of man solitary, poore, nasty, brutish, and short" (Hobbes, 1651, p. 186). Hobbes argued that as a result, people had no choice but to protect themselves against their own ugly natures. They did so by entering into a social contract to form a collective commonwealth, the State.

Hobbes's psychological starting points are simple enough: People are by nature asocial and destructively rapacious. Society is a means to chain the brute within, providing stern prohibitions against our species' ugly impulses and rules by which we can live together civilly. Given this position, the various social motives that bind us to others, motives such as love and loyalty, must be imposed through culture and convention. These motives must be learned, because on this view they could not possibly be part of our intrinsic makeup.

NATURAL SELECTION AND SURVIVAL

During the nineteenth century, Hobbes's doctrine of inherent human aggression and depravity was garbed in the mantle of science. The Industrial Revolution seemed to give ample proof that life was indeed a Hobbesian battle of each against all, whether in the marketplace, in the sweatshops, or in the far-off colonies. Ruthless competition among people was regarded as just one facet of the more general struggle for existence waged among all living things. This harsh view of nature had gained great impetus at the start of the nineteenth century when Thomas Malthus announced his famous law of population growth. According to Malthus, human and animal populations grow by geometrical progression (for example, 1, 2, 4, 8, 16, . . .) while the food supply grows arithmetically (for example, 1, 2, 3, 4, 5, . . .). As a result, Malthus said, scarcity is inevitable and the battle for such meager resources continual (Malthus, 1798).

After Charles Darwin (1809–1882) read Malthus's essay, he began to formulate the explanatory principle he had been seeking to account for the evolution of living things. He, as many others before him, believed that all present-day plants and animals (including humans) were descended from prior forms. The evidence came from various sources, such as the fossil record that showed the gradual transformation from long-extinct to existing species.

But what had produced these evolutionary changes? Within each species there are variations from one individual to the next, and in many cases, these variations give an individual an important advantage in the struggle for survival and reproduction. Many of these variations are a function of the animal's genetic makeup and thus are bequeathed to its descendants. But will an individual animal have descendants? That depends on how it fares in the struggle for existence. As a matter of fact, most organisms don't live long enough to reproduce. Only a few seedlings grow up to be trees; only a few tadpoles achieve froghood. But certain characteristics may make survival a bit more likely. The faster horse is more likely to escape predators than its slower fellow, and it is thus more likely to reproduce and leave offspring who inherit its swiftness. The horse's swiftness does not guarantee survival and reproduction; it only increases their likelihood.

Genetic survival *The peacock's long tail feathers are a cumbersome burden that may decrease his chances of escaping predators and, thus, his own personal survival. But this cost is more than offset by his increased chances of attracting a sexual partner, thereby assuring survival of his genes. (Photograph © Norbert Wu/Allstock/PNI)*

A woven nest *Many animals have genetically determined behavior patterns characteristic of their species. An example is nest weaving in the thick-billed African weaverbird. (Photo courtesy of Brian M. Rogers/Biofotos)*

Furthermore, unlike his predecessors, Darwin began to realize that evolution did not imply progress in which descendants would be "better" than their ancestors. This was true precisely because the world was ever-changing—with continents drifting, whole mountain ranges continually forming and receding, lakes filling and drying up, and the entire Earth undergoing periodic climatic upheavals. Such enviromental instability means that those traits—whether swiftness, or ferocity, or cunning—that are selected for in one generation may not be the most favorable in the next. Nor are current creatures more "perfect" or "advanced" than their ancestors, only more suited to the current, impermanent set of conditions (Darwin, 1872a).

PERSONAL AND GENETIC SURVIVAL

This process of **natural selection** leads to the "survival of the fittest" in a given environment. But just what does it mean to be fit? Our earlier example of fitness involved attributes that make immediate survival more likely: A faster horse is better able to escape predators. But *personal survival* as such is not what the evolutionary game is about. The trick is to have reproductive success—to have offspring who will pass one's genes along. A horse that manages to outlive all its competitors but leaves no offspring has not flourished in the evolutionary sense. Personal survival is a prerequisite for *genetic survival,* but it alone is not enough.

Seen in this light, it's clear that fitness is determined by all characteristics that enhance reproductive success, whether or not these characteristics contribute to the individual's own personal survival. Consider the magnificent tail feathers of the peacock. His long, cumbersome tail may actually diminish his chances of escaping predators, but it contributes greatly to his evolutionary fitness even so. The peacock has to compete with his fellow males for access to the peahen; the larger and more magnificent his tail, the more likely it is that she will respond to his sexual overtures. From an evolutionary point of view, the potential gain in this case evidently offsets the possible loss; as a result, long tail feathers eventually flourished in the males.

Much the same holds for many other characteristics that are of advantage in sexual competition. This is especially so among males (for reasons we'll discuss later). Some of these characteristics are rather general, such as stature, strength, and aggressiveness. Others, such as the brightly colored plumage of many male birds and the large antlers of the stag, are more specialized. But whatever the particulars of a given attribute, its contribution to the animal's fitness is the extent to which it leads to reproductive success.

INHERITED PREDISPOSITIONS TO BEHAVIOR

Many of the characteristics that promote survival and reproduction involve bodily structures such as the horse's hooves or the stag's antlers. But Darwin and his successors pointed out that natural selection may also involve behavior. Squirrels bury nuts, and beavers construct dams; these behavior patterns are characteristic of the species and depend on the animals' **genes,** the basic units of heredity. Whether these genes will proliferate depends upon the extent to which the behavior they give rise to has **adaptive value**—that is, contributes to survival and subsequent reproduction. A squirrel who has a genetic predisposition to bury nuts in autumn is presumably more likely to survive the winter than one who doesn't. As a result, it is more likely to have offspring who will inherit the gene or genes that somehow predispose it toward nut burying. The end product— assuming some constancy in the squirrels' environment—is an increase in the number of nut-burying squirrels.

407

Granted that behavior can change as a consequence of natural selection, what kind of behavior is most likely to result? And, most important to us, what kind of built-in predispositions are most likely to characterize humankind? Many nineteenth-century thinkers answered in Hobbesian terms. They reasoned that people were animals and that, in the bitter struggle for existence, all animals are shameless egoists by sheer necessity. At bottom, they claimed, all animals are, and necessarily must be, solitary and selfish, and human beings are no exception. To the extent that humans act sociably and on occasion even unselfishly—mating, rearing children, living and working with others—they do so only to satisfy some self-centered motive such as lust or hunger.

On the face of it, this Hobbesian view seems to fit evolutionary doctrine. But on closer examination, Darwinian theory does not imply anything of the sort. It holds that there is "survival of the fittest," but "fittest" only means most likely to have viable offspring; it says nothing about being solitary or selfish. To the contrary, Darwin himself supposed that certain social instincts would enhance surivial and reproduction, and would thus flourish with any natural selection. We now know that something of this sort is true, for animals as well as human beings. As we shall see, there is considerable evidence that, Hobbes notwithstanding, humans and animals are by nature social rather than asocial and that much of their social behavior grows out of innate predispositions rather than running counter to them.

BUILT-IN SOCIAL BEHAVIORS

Most systematic studies that take this view of social behavior have been conducted within the domain of *ethology,* the scientific enterprise whose purview is the study of animal behavior under natural conditions. Led by the Europeans Konrad Lorenz (1903–1989) and Niko Tinbergen (1907–1988), both Nobel laureates, ethologists have analyzed many behavior patterns that are built-in and emerge without any relevant prior experience. These behavior patterns are often *species specific.* Many are social; they dictate the way in which creatures interact with others of their own kind. The situations in which these behaviors occur include securing and defending territory, competing for and consorting with mates, and nurturing and protecting the young.

FIXED-ACTION PATTERNS

The early ethologists believed that many kinds of social behavior are based on genetically programmed *fixed-action patterns,* which in turn are elicited by genetically programmed *releasing stimuli.* An example of such a fixed-action pattern is the begging response of newly hatched herring gulls. They beg for food by pecking at the tips of their parents' beaks. The parent will then regurgitate some food from its crop and feed it to the young. But what is the critical stimulus that instigates the chick's begging pecks? To find out, Tinbergen offered newly hatched gull chicks various cardboard models of gull heads and observed which ones they pecked at the most. The most successful model was one that was long and thin and had a red patch at its tip (see Figure 10.1). These are the very characteristics of an adult herring gull's beak, but the newly hatched chick had never encountered a parent's beak before. Tinbergen concluded that the chick was innately programmed to respond to certain stimulus features so as to recognize the parent's beak at the very first sight (Tinbergen, 1951).

Succeeding studies suggest that the relation between releasing stimuli and fixed-action patterns is not quite so fixed. Right after hatching, the herring gull

Konrad Lorenz *(Photograph by Nina Leen)*

Niko Tinbergen *(Photograph by Nina Leen)*

A

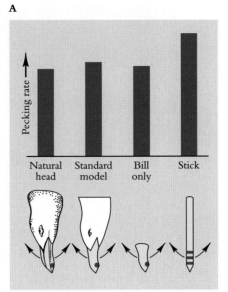

B

10.1 Stimulus releasers for pecking *(A) The figure indicates the pecking rate of a herring gull chick when presented with various models. As the figure shows, a flat cardboard model is more effective than a real head, and a disembodied bill works almost as well. (Adapted from Keeton and Gould, 1993) (B) Best of all was a stick with spots on it moving back and forth horizontally, which the gull chick pecks at while ignoring a full representation of the parent's head. (Photograph courtesy of John Sparks, BBC [Natural History])*

chicks peck at any red spot that moves horizontally across their field of vision, whether it is attached to a gull's head or not. But after two days in the nest with their parents, they peck only when confronted with a proper herring gull's beak. This suggests that the chick's genetic programming provides not only a crude first outline, but also a bit of flexibility that allows the chick's own experience to refine and build upon this outline (Hailman, 1967).

In many species, the releasing stimuli for an animal's behavior are produced by another animal's behavior. What matters then is not just what some other animal looks like (e.g., the red spot on the gull parent's beak) but also what it does. An important example of such behaviorally produced stimulus releasers are ***displays.*** Displays produce an appropriate reaction in other animals and are thus the basis of a simple but effective, innate communication system. The gull chick's begging peck is a signal whose meaning is genetically given to both chick and parent: "Feed me! Feed me now!" (Tinbergen, 1951).

AGGRESSION

Many of the biologically based social tendencies in behavior are much too complex to be described as fixed-action patterns. One of the most important of these is ***aggression.*** Many observers believe that understanding the biological underpinnings of human aggression is necessary if we are ever to live at peace. But studying these underpinnings is difficult, because the manifestations of human aggression are so transformed by cultural rules and traditions. As in many other cases, we can take advantage of the ***comparative method,*** studying nonhumans as well as humans to find commonalities that may reflect some shared biological heritage.

*10.2 Defending the nest A royal tern
attacks an egret that has come too close to its
nest. (Photograph © M. P. Kahl)*

CONFLICT BETWEEN SPECIES:
PREDATION AND DEFENSE

On the face of it, hunting and killing for food might seem the height of
aggression, but nothing could be further from the truth. For predation is
usually a quite dispassionate affair. When an owl kills a mouse, it has slaughtered
for food rather than murdered in hatred. As Lorenz points out, the predator
about to pounce upon its prey does not look angry; the dog who is on the verge
of catching a rabbit never growls, nor does it have its ears laid back (Lorenz,
1966). Neurological evidence leads to a similar conclusion. Rat stalking (predatory attack) and arched-back hissing (aggression or self-defense) in cats are
elicited by the stimulation of two different areas of a cat's hypothalamus (Wasman and Flynn, 1962). Predatory attack is an outgrowth of the hunger motive
and not of aggression: The hypothalamic site whose stimulation gives rise to rat
stalking also elicits eating (Hutchinson and Renfrew, 1966).

Less dispassionate is the cooperative defense lodged by prey animals against
predators (see Figure 10.2). Flocks of birds sometimes mob an intruding cat or
hawk. A colony of lovebird parrots will fly en masse upon a would-be attacker,
flapping their wings furiously and uttering loud, shrill squeaks. In the face of this
orchestrated commotion, the predator often withdraws to look for a less troublesome meal (Dilger, 1962).

Aside from these defensive behaviors, aggression is the exception rather than

*Aggressive encounter between male
bighorn rams (Courtesy of Stouffer Productions, Animals Animals)*

the rule between members of different species. In an aquarium filled with tropical fish, like attacks like but leaves unlike alone. Vicious fights between unrelated species such as tigers and pythons have been photographed for wildlife films, but they are rare; the animals involved are either half-starved or goaded into the unnatural contest by having their escape routes blocked (Lorenz, 1966). Indeed, being cornered leaves destructive fighting as the last resort, and in this circumstance even normally reticent creatures may then become desperate fighters (see Enquist and Leimar, 1990).

CONFLICT BETWEEN LIKE AND LIKE

There is probably no animal species that has forsworn aggression altogether; fighting has been observed in virtually all. Fish chase and nip each other; lizards lunge and push; birds attack with wing, beak, and claw; deer lock antlers; and rats adopt a boxing stance and eye each other warily until one finally pounces upon the other (see Figure 10.3).

Among most vertebrates, the male is generally the more physically aggressive sex. In some mammals, this difference in combativeness is apparent even in childhood play. Young male rhesus monkeys, for instance, engage in more vigorous rough-and-tumble tusslings than do their sisters (Harlow, 1962). But the omnipresence of male-male jousting may have diverted investigators from examining those circumstances in which females are aggressive, such as in defending their home territory, choosing males for mating, or protecting their young.

Aggression seems partially to be influenced by hormones, particularly by the sex hormone *testosterone*. High testosterone levels in the bloodstream accompany increased male aggressiveness; decreased levels with less. This generalization seems to apply over a wide range of species, including fish, lizards, turtles, birds, rats and mice, monkeys, and humans (Davis, 1964; Siegel and Demetrikopoulos, 1993). It would be inaccurate, however, to say that testosterone *produces* aggression, because in fact it can be both a cause and an effect. Thus, testosterone administered externally can increase subsequent aggressiveness, but successful aggressive encounters can cause increased secretion of testosterone (Dabbs, 1992; Rosenzweig et al., 1996).

Females secrete testosterone, too, but in much smaller amounts than males. Nonetheless, it is known that especially violent female criminals have elevated testosterone levels (Dabbs et al., 1988) and that girls with adrenal gland tumors that result in abnormally high testosterone levels tend to prefer rough-and-tumble play and other stereotypically boyish pursuits (Berenbaum and Snyder, 1995; and see Chapter 14).

Finally, there is increasing evidence that certain brain pathways involving serotonin are also involved in aggression and dominance. Low serotonin levels are generally associated with greater impulsive aggression in monkeys (Higley, Suomi, and Linnoila, 1990) and, in humans, with interpersonal assaults, self-injurious behavior, and even violent suicides (New et al., 1997; Rosenzweig et al., 1996). But research in monkeys shows that higher serotonin levels are also associated with the individual's place in the group's dominance hierarchy (Brammer, Raleigh, and McGuire, 1994; Shively, Fontenot, and Kaplan, 1995). Furthermore, levels of serotonin in the same animal can also rise or fall depending on its position in the hierarchy, and drug-induced serotonin increases can raise an animal's status (Raleigh et al., 1991; Raleigh et al., 1992). Thus, it may be that serotonin inhibits impulsive aggression while enhancing the wider range of strategic "social skills" necessary to achieve and maintain dominance.

A

B

10.3 Aggressive fighting *Male rats generally fight in fairly stereotypical ways, including (A) a "boxing" position that often escalates into (B) a leaping, biting attack. (From Barnett, 1963)*

411

SECURING RESOURCES

What do animals fight about? Their struggles are generally about a scarce resource, whether it be a food source, a water hole, or even a mate. To secure such resources, many animals stake out a claim to a particular *territory,* which they then defend as their exclusive preserve.

As an example, consider male songbirds. In the spring, they endlessly patrol their little fiefdoms and furiously repel all male intruders who violate their borders. Contrary to the poet's fancy, the male bird who bursts into full-throated song is not giving vent to inexpressible joy, pouring out his "full heart in profuse strains of unpremeditated art" (Shelley, 1821). Instead, his message is prosaic and double-edged. It is a warning to other males: "Don't trespass!" And it is an invitation to unattached females, who on their fly-bys are appraising his song for tips to his vigor and thus his mateworthiness: "Am fit, have territory, will share."

As already noted, one biological benefit of territoriality is that it helps to secure an adequate supply of resources for the next generation. The songbird who sets territorial boundaries and reliably dispatches his rivals will probably leave more offspring than the one who doesn't, for his progeny will have a better start in life: A well-chosen, defendable territory more or less guarantees an adequate food supply and shelter (Krebs, Davies, and Parr, 1993).

Territoriality also helps to keep aggressiveness within bounds. Good fences make good neighbors, at least in the sense that they keep the antagonists out of each others' hair (or fins or feathers). One mechanism that accomplishes this is rather simple. Once a territory is established, its owner has a kind of home-court advantage in further disputes (Krebs, 1982). On his home ground he is courageous; if he ventures beyond it, he becomes timid and is readily repulsed. As a result, there may be occasional border skirmishes but few actual conflicts. This behavior pattern is used by circus trainers who make sure that they enter the training ring first and that the animals come in later. As a result, the ring becomes the trainer's territory, and even the great cats are more readily subdued (Hediger, 1968).

CONSTRAINTS ON AGGRESSION

Naturally, a certain amount of aggressiveness may increase one's evolutionary fitness. For example, a more aggressive songbird will probably secure a larger and more desirable territory. But aggression also has serious biological costs. Combat is dangerous and can lead to death or serious injury. In addition, it distracts the animal from other vital pursuits. The male who is continually fighting with his sexual rivals will have little time (let alone energy) left to gather food or to mate with the female after his competitors have fled (Enquist and Leimar, 1990).

Thus, natural selection favors aggression only within limits. One of those limits to which animals seem keenly attuned is the strength of the enemy. If the enemy seems much stronger (or more agile, or better armed or armored) than oneself, the best bet is to proclaim a cease-fire or to concede defeat quickly, or better yet, never to start the battle at all. An example is provided by red deer stags who compete with each other for females. In the autumn, stags who hold a harem are challenged by other stags. In the first stage of this contest, the harem owner and the challenger roar at each other, sometimes for days on end. If the harem owner's roar is longer and louder, the intruder will generally back off—a reasonable decision, since a stronger roar is most likely produced by a stronger stag (Clutton-Brock et al., 1979). Similar strategies for avoiding the costs of a bloody defeat are found in many species whose males engage in highly ritualized jousts but rarely inflict serious wounds (see Figure 10.4).

Red deer stag roaring *(Photograph © Manfred Danegger)*

10.4   Ritualized fighting   *Two South African wildebeest males in a harmless ritualized duel along an invisible but mutually defined border between their territories. (Photograph by Hans Reinhard, © Bruce Coleman, Inc., 1988)*

The red stag's roar also exemplifies the blustering diplomacy many animals resort to before declaring war. Like the red stag, male chimpanzees also try to intimidate each other, by staring, raising an arm, or uttering fearsome shouts. Throughout the entire animal kingdom, animals first try to get their way by threat or bluff rather than by actual fighting. This holds for creatures as large as elephants and as fierce as tigers. Animals engage in such ***threat displays*** because they are a much less costly method for achieving one's aim than actual combat (see Figure 10.5).

In some cases, serious fighting will occur even so, for animals no less than human soldiers may miscalculate their chances of victory. But some ways of limiting the cost of defeat still remain. In wolves, the loser may admit defeat by adopting a special submissive gesture, such as begging like a puppy or rolling on his back. This is an ***appeasement display*** that is functionally equivalent to our

A   B

10.5   Threat displays   *(A) Some species threaten by making themselves appear larger and more impressive. (Photograph by Rod Williams, © Bruce Coleman, Inc., 1991) (B) Other species threaten by shouting at the top of their lungs, like howler monkeys, who scream at each other for hours on end. (Photograph © Ferrero)*

Appeasement displays in humans *A Yanamamo Indian youngster smiles appeasingly at another boy who threatens him. (Photograph © I. Eibl-Eibesfeldt, Forschungsstelle f. Humanethologie)*

10.6 Dominance hierarchies *(A) The two baboons at the right jointly threaten the larger baboon on the left who could defeat either of them alone but won't risk fighting them both. (Courtesy of L. T. Nash, Arizona State University) (B) A dominant male baboon with a harem of females and young. (Courtesy of Bruce Coleman)*

white flag of surrender. The victorious wolf generally accepts the loser's submission, and all fighting stops (Lorenz, 1966). The adaptive value of such submissive signals is clear enough. They allow today's loser to withdraw from the field of battle so that he can come back in a year or two when he is older and wiser, and when he may very well win a rematch. The evolutionary rule is simple enough: If you lose and run away, you may live to fight (and mate) another day.

DOMINANCE AND SUBMISSION

Aggression is also shaped and channeled by a group's ***dominance hierarchies.*** In baboons, for example, the dominant male has usually achieved his status through victory in several aggressive encounters. So individual lower-ranking baboons generally step aside to let the ***alpha male*** pass, and nervously scatter if he merely stares at them.

In the early days of ethology, many investigators believed that once a hierarchy was formed, it was fairly stable. As a result, everyone knew his or her place, thus minimizing combat and friction for the good of all (e.g., Lorenz, 1966). But this view has been seriously challenged, because internal friction is actually quite common. Subordinate males continually form coalitions for the express purpose of deposing the alpha male (Packer, 1977; de Waal, 1982). This leaves an alpha male to spend much of his life in efforts to maintain his place at the top—harassing his subordinates, approaching them until they back away, staring at them until they look down, and if necessary, attacking them with teeth and nails. In these endeavors, the alpha male often depends on alliances with other males, who will join him to repel his rivals and who in turn are supported by him in their aggressive encounters (Walters and Seyfarth, 1986; see Figure 10.6A).

Why do animals spend so much time achieving and maintaining dominance? The answer is that rank has considerable privileges. The alpha male has first choice of sleeping site, enjoys easier access to food, and has priority in mating (see Figure 10.6B). Such perquisites undoubtedly make life more pleasant for the alpha male than for his less fortunate fellows. But even more important may be the long-run evolutionary value of rank, for in terms of genetic survival, the higher-ranking animal is more fit: Since he has easier access to females, he will presumably leave more offspring (Smith, 1981; Silk, 1986).

While dominant males often do sire more offspring, the difference in reproductive success isn't great, especially for primates (see, for example, Bercovitch, 1991). One reason is that subordinate males devise all kinds of crafty ways to "beat the system." Sometimes, they sneak into mating areas and impregnate females on the run, or they form temporary coalitions to repel an alpha male who is consorting with a receptive female. A longer-term strategy exhibited by

A

B

A   B

10.7 Personal space *(A) Relatively even spacing in ring-billed gulls (Photograph by Allan D. Cruikshank © 1978/Photo Researchers) (B) Some ethologists believe that the maintenance of personal space in humans is a related phenomenon. Vacationers at a beach on the Baltic Sea in Germany keep a precise distance between each couple or family unit. (Photograph by J. Messerschmidt/Bruce Coleman)*

some primates is to "befriend" a female, interacting with and protecting her young. These acts of ingratiation—done mostly when the alpha males are away—can be effective in swaying the female away from the alpha male the next time she is sexually receptive (Keddy Hector, Seyfarth, and Raleigh, 1989; Keddy Hector and Raleigh, 1992).

What about females? To be sure, the males' aggressive encounters are quite obvious, as they fight and strut and bellow. But in many primate societies, females compete no less than males. Their hierarchies are often more stable than those of males, however, and they handle threats to dominance subtly rather than confrontationally. Moreover, female rank has important long-term consequences, for mothers tend to bequeath their social rank to their offspring, especially to their daughters (Hrdy and Williams, 1983; Walters and Seyfarth, 1986; Cheney and Seyfarth, 1990).

TERRITORIALITY IN HUMANS AND HUMAN CULTURE

At least on the surface, there are parallels between these observations about animals and the behavior of humans. For example, consider territoriality. At home, family members each have their private preserves—their own rooms or corners, their places at the dinner table, and so on. In more public places, territorial claims are more temporary, such as a seat on a train, whose possession we mark with a coat or a book if we have to leave for a while.

The power of human territorial behavior is illustrated by the phenomenon of **personal space,** the physical zone surrounding us whose intrusion we guard against (Figure 10.7). On many New York subways, passengers sit on long benches. Except during rush hour, they will carefully choose their seats so as to leave the greatest possible distance between themselves and their nearest neighbor.

In one study, personal space was deliberately violated. Experimenters went to a library and casually sat next to a person studying there, even though a more distant chair was available. After some fidgeting, the "victim" tried to move away. If this was impossible, books and rulers were neatly arranged so as to create a physical boundary (Felipe and Sommer, 1966).

A desire to maintain some minimal personal space is probably universal, but the physical dimensions of this space depend upon various social factors. By and large, appropriate personal distance increases with age and socioeconomic status (Collier, 1985). It is also affected by the standards of a particular culture. In North America, acquaintances stand two to three feet apart during a conversation; if one moves closer, the other feels crowded or pushed into unwanted intimacy. For Latin Americans, the acceptable distance is much less. Under the circumstances, misunderstanding is almost inevitable. The North American regards the Latin American as overly intrusive; the Latin American in turn feels that the North American is unfriendly and cold (Hall, 1966).

Do these observations truly parallel the evidence from other species? Do humans respond to some sort of built-in, mandatory territorial imperative in the same way that a songbird identifies and defends its turf? The human case and the songbird's (or the wolf's, or the baboon's) do show many parallels, but they also show important points of contrast. One key difference lies in *plasticity,* or susceptibility to change. Territoriality in most nonhuman species is universal for that species, with little evidence that experience affects it. But in humans, territoriality is far from universal and is heavily influenced by learning. This is evident in the fact that human territoriality takes many different forms. In some societies, individuals own certain spaces; in other societies, ownership is communal, rather than private. Within a society, some individuals fiercely protect their real estate, while others seem indifferent to the exclusiveness of their surroundings. These differences are difficult to reconcile with claims of a biologically rooted territorial imperative and call our attention, instead, to the role of cultural values and of learning in shaping how and to what extent humans are territorial.

MATING

Aggression, it seems, is found in a great many species, with many detailed parallels among species. Moreover, many of the properties of aggression are easy to understand in an evolutionary context. All of this suggests that, in important ways, the aggression we observe has biological roots. At the same time, however, aggression in some species—and certainly in humans—is strongly controlled and modified by learning, especially during childhood, and by the situations in which the aggression emerges.

There is yet another force that is just as basic and deeply rooted in the biological makeup of animals and humans. The poets call it love; the biologists, sexual reproduction.

WHY SEX?

In many simple organisms, reproduction is asexual: Thus, amoebas multiply by a process of simple cell division. This form of procreation works well enough; amoebas and other asexual creatures flourish quite nicely. Why, then, do many plants and the vast majority of animal species reproduce sexually? The answer lies in the fact that sexual reproduction assures genetic variability.

Amoebas reproduce through *fission.* One amoeba splits into two to create genetically identical replicas of itself, and so every amoeba ends up virtually identical to every other amoeba. As a result, there is little difference in genetic quality from one amoeba to the next. But as we have seen, such differences are the basis for natural selection: Individuals with better-suited traits are more likely to have offspring and so are more likely to pass on their genes. But since the two amoebas that result from fission are no different in their adaptation to the environment, natural selection has no differences to choose between. This reduces the amoeba's flexibility in adapting to any environmental change or challenge.

10.8 Advertising one's sex *The comb and wattle of this barred rock rooster proclaim that he is a male. (Photograph by Garry D. McMichael, 1987/Photo Researchers)*

A male widow bird in flight *(Photograph courtesy of John Wightman/Ardea London Ltd.)*

Things are quite different in sexual reproduction. Here, specialized cells, **sperm** and **ovum,** must join to form a fertilized egg, or **zygote,** which will then become a new individual. This procedure amounts to a kind of genetic lottery. To begin with, each parent donates only half the genetic material, and within some limits, mere chance determines which genes are contained in any one sperm or ovum. Chance enters again to determine which sperm will join with which ovum. As a result, there will be inevitable differences among the offspring. Now natural selection can come into play, perhaps favoring the offspring with the sharper teeth or the more sexually attractive display or the greater resistance to the current crop of viruses or bacteria, any of which may give the organism a better chance of survival and thus spread the genes that produced the attribute.

Playing this genetic lottery has its costs, because the safest bet for a flourishing organism is simply to clone itself rather than mixing just half its genes with those of another organism that may not fare so well. Moreover, finding a mate and mating itself take time and resources that could well be spent making more clones. Why is it, then, that so many organisms have settled on this reproductive strategy?

The question has long puzzled biologists (see Williams, 1966, 1975), and as yet there is no certain answer (e.g., Muller, 1964; Bernstein, Hopf, and Michod, 1988). One plausible hypothesis concerns germs. On this view, plants and animals are in a perpetual arms race with **pathogens**—fungi, bacteria, and viruses—that seek to infect and exploit them as hosts. With every generation, those pathogens that are most dangerous to hosts will survive and reproduce, but at the same time, those hosts that are most resistant to the pathogens will survive and reproduce themselves. The only way for hosts to survive these canny pathogens over multiple generations is to keep outwitting them by changing their genes and thus their defenses. The gene shuffling of sexual reproduction may be simply a holding action through which creatures preserve their current levels of adaptation against ever changing pathogens (Van Valen, 1973; Hamilton and Zuk, 1982).

SEXUAL CHOICE

For sexual reproduction to occur, sperm and ovum have to meet in the appointed manner, at the proper time and place. Many structures and behavior patterns have evolved to accomplish these ends. Our first concern is with those that underlie sexual choice—the determination of who mates with whom.

ADVERTISING FOR A MATE

One of the first jobs of a would-be sexual partner is to proclaim his or her sex. Many animals have anatomical structures whose function is precisely that—for example, the magnificent tail feathers of the peacock or the comb and wattle of the rooster (see Figure 10.8). These structures are often crucial to mating. In one species of widow birds, the males have long tail feathers—up to twenty inches long. To study the importance of this trait, investigators cut the tails on some males and placed feather extensions on others. After a suitable period, the investigators counted the number of nests in each bird's territory. The males whose tails were cosmetically extended had more nests than did the unaltered males, who in turn had more nests than their unfortunate fellows whose tails had been shortened (Andersson, 1982).

In humans, structural displays of sex differences are less pronounced, but they are present nonetheless. A possible example is the female breast, whose adipose tissue does not really increase the infant's milk supply. According to some ethologists, the breast evolved as we began to walk erect and lost our reliance upon smell, a sense that provides the primary information about sexual readiness in many mammals. Under the circumstances, there had to be other ways of displaying one's sex. The prominent breasts of the human female may be one such announcement (Morris, 1967).

COURTSHIP RITUALS

Advertising one's intentions In many animals, patterns of sexual displays, called **courtship rituals,** provide an important means of advertising one's reproductive intentions. Some of these rituals are mainly a means to exhibit the structural sex differences, as in the peacock spreading his tail feathers. Others are much more elaborate. Thus, penguins bow deeply to each other while rocking from side to side, and certain grebes stage an elaborate aquatic ballet by exchanging gifts of seaweed (Figure 10.9).

In some species, courtship rituals may also involve alternating bouts of approach and withdrawal, of coy retreat and seductive flirtation. What accounts for these apparent oscillations between yes and no? Each animal has reason to approach the other, but each also has reason to fear the other: Is the approach amorous or aggressive? This tension between attraction and threat must be resolved, and the alternating approaches and withdrawals presumably serve this purpose.

Indicating one's species According to some ethologists courtship rituals have a further function. They not only increase the likelihood that "boy meets girl"; they also virtually guarantee that the two will be of the same species. This is because these rituals are highly species specific, as in the case of the gift-exchanging grebes. In effect, they are a code whereby both members of the pair inform the other that they belong, say, to the species *Anas platyrhynochos*, rather than to *Bucephala clangula,* or *Tachyeres patachonicus,* or some other duck species that no self-respecting *Anas platyrhynochos* would ever want to mate with. The effect of such species-specific courtship rituals is that they make it more likely that the mating will produce fertile offspring. For contrary to popular view, dif-

10.9 Courtship rituals *(A) The male bower bird tries to entice the female into an elaborate bower decorated with berries, shells, or whatever else may be available, such as colored clothespins. (Photograph by Phillip Green) (B) Grebes engage in a complex aquatic ballet. (Photograph by Bob and Clara Calhoun/Bruce Coleman) (C) The male tern courts by feeding the female. (Photograph by Jeff Foott/Bruce Coleman)*

A

B

C

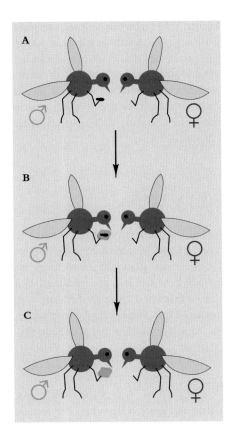

A

B

C

10.10 The evolution of courtship in dancing flies *(A) In some species, the male catches a prey animal and gives it to the female to eat during copulation; this keeps her busy, so she is less likely to eat him. (B) In other species, the male first wraps the prey in a balloon of secreted silk. This keeps the female even busier, since she has to unwrap the prey. (C) Finally, in the dancing fly, the male gives the female a ball of silk without anything in it. (After Klopfer, 1974)*

ferent species can interbreed if they are related closely enough. But the offspring of such unnatural unions are often infertile; an example is the mule, the result of crossing a horse with a donkey. Species-specific courtship rituals probably evolved to avoid such reproductive dead ends.

The evolutionary origin of courtship rituals We can offer plausible explanations for *why* courtship rituals evolved. But explaining *how* they came to be is more difficult. Since displays leave no fossils, there is no direct method for reconstructing their biological origins. We can gain some insights into the issue, however, by comparing displays in related species. By noting their similarities and differences, the ethologist tries to reconstruct the evolutionary steps in their history, much as a comparative anatomist charts the family tree of fins, wings, and forelegs.

An example of how this comparative method works is an analysis of an odd courtship ritual in a predatory insect, the dancing fly (Kessel, 1955). At mating time, the male dancing fly secretes a little ball of silk which he brings to the female. She plays with this silk ball while the male mounts her and copulates. How did this ritual arise? The courtship patterns in a number of related species give a clue. Most flies of related species manage with a minimum of precopulatory fuss; the trouble is that the female may decide to eat the male rather than mate with him. However, if she is already eating a small prey animal, the male is safe. Some species have evolved a behavior pattern that capitalizes on this fact. The male catches a small insect and brings it to the female for her to eat while he mates with her. In still other species, the male first wraps the prey in a large silk balloon. This increases his margin of safety, for the female is kept busy unwrapping her present. The dancing fly's ritual is probably the last step in this evolutionary sequence. The male dancing fly wastes no time or energy in catching a prey animal but simply brings an empty ball of silk—all wrapping and no present. Copulation can now proceed unimpeded since the female is safely occupied. The dancing fly is perhaps the first creature in evolutionary history to realize that it is the thought and not the gift that counts (Figure 10.10).

WHO MAKES THE CHOICE?

The preceding discussions have centered on various factors that bring male and female together. But interestingly, the two don't seem to have an equal voice in the ultimate decision. In most species, it is the female who makes the final choice of whether or not to mate. The biological reason is simple—the female shoulders the major costs of reproduction. If she is a bird, she supplies not only the ovum but also the food supply for the developing embryo. If she is a mammal, she carries the embryo within her body and later provides it with milk. In either case, her biological burden is vastly greater than the male's. If a doe's offspring fails to survive, she has lost a whole breeding season. In comparison, the stag's loss is minimal—a few minutes of his time and some easily replaced sperm. No wonder, then, that females are choosy in picking their mates. For the female, reproduction is a serious business with heavy biological costs (Trivers, 1972).

There are a few interesting exceptions. One is the sea horse, whose young are

Courtship among hanging flies *The male offers a gift of food (a dead fly in this case) and mates with the female while she is consuming it. (Courtesy R. Thornhill, University of New Mexico)*

419

carried in a brood pouch by the male (see Figure 10.11). In this animal, the male exhibits greater sexual discrimination than the female. A similar effect is found in the phalarope, an arctic seabird whose eggs are hatched and whose chicks are fed by the male. Here, a greater part of the biological burden falls on the male, and we should expect a corresponding increase in his sexual choosiness. This is just what happens. Among the phalaropes, the female does the wooing. She is brightly plumaged and aggressively pursues the careful, dull-colored male (Williams, 1966).

10.11 Male sea horse "giving birth" *(Photograph © Rudie H. Kuiter, Oxford Scientific Films)*

REPRODUCTION AND TIMING

Once male and female have met, courted, and determined each other to be a suitable mate, the next step is to arrange for the union of their respective sperm and ova. In terrestrial mammals, the male generally introduces his sperm cells into the genital tract of the female, where the ova are fertilized. But the sperm has to encounter a ready ovum, and a fertilized egg can develop only if it is provided with the appropriate conditions. Thus, timing is of the essence; in mammals (and in birds), it depends upon a complex hormonal feedback system between the brain and the reproductive organs.

ANIMAL SEXUALITY AND HORMONES

Hormonal cycles   Except for the primates, mammals mate only when the female is in heat, or *estrus.* The female rat goes through a fifteen-hour estrus period every four days. At all other times, she will resolutely reject any male's advances. If he nuzzles her or tries to mount, she will kick and bite him. But during estrus, the female responds quite differently to the male's approach. She first retreats in small hops, then stops to look back, and wiggles her ears (McClintock and Adler, 1978). Eventually, she stands still, her back arched, her tail held to the side—a willing sexual partner.

What brings about this change in the female's behavior? The mechanism is an interlocking system of hormonal and neurological controls that involves the pituitary gland, the hypothalamus, and the ovaries. There are three phases: During the first, follicles (ova-containing sacs) in the ovary mature under the influence of pituitary secretions. The follicles produce the sex hormone *estrogen.* As the concentration of estrogen in the bloodstream rises, the hypothalamus responds by directing the pituitary to change its secretions. In consequence, follicle growth is accelerated until the follicle ruptures and releases the mature ovum.

This triggers the second phase during which the animal is in estrus. Estrogen production peaks and stimulates certain structures in the hypothalamus, which make the animal sexually receptive.

The third phase is dominated by the action of another sex hormone, *progesterone,* which is produced by the ruptured follicle. Its secretion leads to a thickening of the uterine lining, a first step in preparing the uterus to receive the embryo. If the ovum is fertilized, there are further steps in preparing the uterus. If it is not, the thickened uterine walls are reabsorbed and another cycle begins. In humans and some primates, too much extra tissue is laid on to be easily reabsorbed; the thickened uterine lining is therefore sloughed off as *menstrual flow* (Figure 10.12).

Hormonal changes and behavior   These and other hormonal changes affect behavior dramatically. When female rats have their ovaries removed, they soon lose all

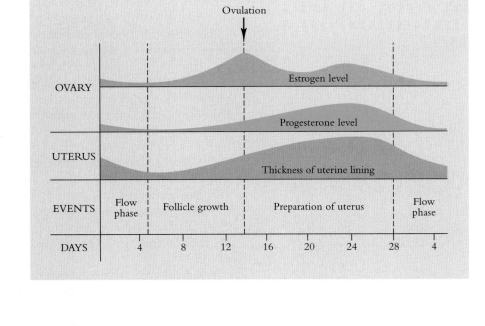

10.12   The main stages of the human menstrual cycle   *The figure shows estrogen and progesterone levels and thickness of the uterine lining during the human menstrual cycle. The cycle begins with the growth of a follicle, continues through ovulation and a maximum estrogen level, is followed by a phase during which the uterus becomes prepared to receive the embryo, and ends with a flow phase during which the thickened uterus lining is sloughed off. (After Keeton, 1980)*

10.13   Estrogen and sexual behavior   *The effect of estrogen injections on the sexual responsiveness of female rats was measured by the number of male attempts at mounting that were accepted by the female. The females' ovaries had been removed, so they could not produce estrogen themselves. The hormone was injected daily in the doses shown above. Sexual behavior was measured eight days after hormone treatment began. (After Bermant and Davidson, 1974)*

sexual interest and capacity, as do male rats when castrated. But sexual behavior is quickly restored in the male by appropriate injections of ***testosterone*** and in the female mainly by estrogen (the female also needs, and secretes, a small amount of testosterone).

Many investigators believe that the behavioral effects of hormones are mediated by receptors in the hypothalamus, which monitors the levels of many different chemicals circulating in the blood (Chapter 3). This hypothesis has been tested by injecting tiny quantities of various hormones into different regions of the hypothalamus. Such studies reveal, for example, that a spayed female cat will go into estrus when estrogen is implanted (Harris and Michael, 1964), and that castrated males will resume sexual behavior after doses of the appropriate male hormones (Davidson, 1969; McEwen et al., 1982; Feder, 1984).

Hormones affect behavior, but the effect can also be the other way around. What an animal experiences and what it does can substantially affect it hormonally. In some animals, the female's courtship behavior can trigger the release of testosterone in courting males. In animals such as rodents, the female's sexual receptivity is triggered by pheromones contained in the male's urine (see Chapter 5). In some cases, copulation itself produces reproductive readiness. For example, the female rat secretes some progesterone during the normal cycle but not enough to permit the implantation of the fertilized ovum in the uterus. The critical dose is secreted only as a reflex response to sexual stimulation. This leaves the sexually aroused male rat with two reproductive functions: supplying sperm and providing the mechanical stimulation necessary for hormonal secretion. Should he ejaculate too quickly and thus leave the female inadequately stimulated, all is lost, for no pregnancy results (Adler, 1979; Rosenzweig et al., 1996).

HUMAN SEXUALITY AND HORMONES

Compared to other animals, humans are much less automatic in their sexual activities, much more varied, and much more affected by prior experience. This difference is especially marked when we consider the effects of hormones. In rats and cats, sexual behavior is highly dependent upon hormone levels; castrated males and spayed females stop copulating a few months after the removal of their gonads (Figure 10.13). In humans, on the other hand, sexual activity may persist for years, even decades, after castration or ovariectomy, provided that the operation was performed after puberty (Bermant and Davidson, 1974).

The liberation from hormonal control is especially clear in human females. To be sure, women are subject to a physiological cycle, but this has relatively little impact on sexual behavior, at least when compared to the profound effects seen in animals. The female rat or cat is chained to an estrus cycle that makes her receptive during only one period; there are no such fetters on the human female, who may initiate or refuse sexual behavior at any time during her cycle.

Although we humans are not entirely at the mercy of our hormones, they still have their effects. Testosterone injections into men—or women—with abnormally low hormone levels will generally increase their sex drive (Davidson, 1986; Rosenzweig et al., 1996). An important demonstration concerns the effects of testosterone administration on gay men. The testosterone-injected gay male becomes more sexually active, but contrary to a common misconception, these injections have no impact on his sexual orientation—the renewed sexual desire is directed toward other men just as before (Kinsey, Pomeroy, and Martin, 1948).

Another demonstration of hormonal effects comes from studies of the menstrual cycle. While women can respond sexually at virtually all points of their cycle, there are still some variations within that period. Sexual desire and activity tend to be highest during the middle of the cycle, when ovulation occurs (Hamburg, Moos, and Yalom, 1968; Bancroft, 1986). But these effects are not very pronounced; they probably represent vestiges of an estrus cycle, left behind by waves of evolutionary change.

EVOLUTION AND MATING SYSTEMS

In many species, the male and female part company after successful copulation and may very well never meet again. But before moving on, males often try to insure that copulation will be successful, that it is *their* sperm, and not the sperm of a competitor, that fertilizes the ova of the receptive female. One way they do this is by **mate guarding,** hovering near females with whom they've mated to keep them from mating with others. Another strategy, used by members of species in which females mate promiscuously, such as chimpanzees, is for males to compete with each other to generate the biggest ejaculation and the most sperm (Alcock, 1993; Eberhard, 1996). The reason for the evolution of such behavior is clear—mate guarding and other behavior to insure successful fertilization increase the chances of reproductive success.

MATING SYSTEMS IN ANIMALS

In many species, though, the partners do remain together, for a breeding season or even longer. In those cases, their arrangement often involves **polygamy**—several members of one sex mating with one individual of the other. And if polygamous, the arrangement either involves **polygyny,** with several females mating with one male, or, more rarely, **polyandry,** with several males mating with one female. Still other animals demonstrate **monogamy,** with a reproductive partnership based on a more or less permanent tie between one male and one female.

What accounts for the different mating systems found among members of the animal kingdom? A clue comes from a difference in the patterns found in mammals and birds. Some 90 percent of all birds are monogamous: They mate and stay together throughout a breeding season. In contrast, more than 90 percent of all mammals are polygynous, with one male mating with a number of females. What explains this diversity?

Birds as monogamous *Birds tend to mate and stay together during a mating season as both parents are needed for successful incubation of their young. Here, a black-bowed albatross male courts a female on the nest that will serve as home for their offspring. (Photograph by Robert W. Hernandez/The National Audubon Society Collection/Photo Researchers)*

A B

10.14 Sexual dimorphism *Polygynous species tend to be dimorphic. (A) A Hooker's sea lion bull with his harem. Note the bull's markedly larger size. (Photograph by Francisco J. Erize/Bruce Coleman Ltd.) (B) In Titi monkeys, which are monogamous, males and females are very similar in size and form. (Photograph © Jim Clare, Partridge Films/Oxford Scientific Films)*

Evolutionary biologists seek the answer through a kind of evolutionary economics: The patterns that evolved maximize each individual's reproductive success. Consider the reproductive problem faced by birds. In many species, successful incubation requires both parents: one to sit on the eggs, the other to forage for food to nourish the bird that's sitting. After hatching, finding food for a nestful of hungry chicks may still require the full-time efforts of both birds. Under the circumstances, monogamy makes reproductive sense for both: The father has to help the mother after she lays her eggs or else no chicks—and therefore, none of his genes—will survive.

The situation is quite different for most mammals. Here, there is no issue of tending the nest, because there is no nest. Instead, the fetus grows within the mother's uterus, allowing her to continue foraging for food during the offspring's gestation. Then, after birth, only the mother can secrete the milk needed to feed the young. Thus, strictly speaking, the father is unnecessary after conception. The young will survive under the mother's care alone, and the male's genes will be carried into the next generation nonetheless.

How should a male behave in these circumstances? Recall that, in evolutionary terms, a successful organism is one that perpetuates its genes through successive generations. The most successful organism, therefore, is the one that has the greatest number of thriving offspring. If the young can survive without his parental care, then the male can maximize his reproductive success by mating with as many females as possible. To accomplish this, he has to become attractive to females (by developing the most impressive antlers or whatever), and he has to win at competitive displays with many other males, all of whom have the identical goal. The end result is polygyny, with a number of females mating with one successful male.

The fact that females in polygynous mating systems select males based on physical vitality creates an interesting anatomical consequence. Almost invariably, polygyny is accompanied by *sexual dimorphism,* a pronounced difference in the size or bodily structures of the two sexes. In fact, the more polygynous the species, the more dimorphic it tends to be, with the males larger and often more ornamented than the females, as shown by the peacock's tail, the stag's antlers, and the male elephant seal's disproportionate size (Figure 10.14A). Polyandrous species, such as the spotted sandpiper bird, also show sexual dimorphism, but here the females are bigger, more aggressive, and more territorial (Oring, 1985). In monogamous species, such as the gibbon, there is no such sexual dimorphism (Figure 10.14B).

4 2 3

The reason for sexual dimorphism is clear. But why would a species need to have some of its members advertise their sex in such a flamboyant way? Why might male widow birds or peacocks grow such extravagant tails? The reason seems to be that the anatomical structures proclaiming one's sex are also good indicators of a potential mate's vitality and, hence, the quality of his or her genes. Large tails, bright colors, or a shiny coat are metabolically expensive to grow and maintain, and they rapidly lose their luster if the individual is ill or undernourished. Thus, these structures provide a generally accurate indicator of whether an individual is healthy and strong—exactly the traits of interest to another individual searching for an appropriate mate (Darwin, 1871; Fisher, 1930; Zahavi, 1975, 1991; Anderssen, 1994).

MATING PATTERNS IN HUMANS

A number of authors have tried to explain human mating behavior in similar evolutionary terms. One focus of this analysis concerns how we humans choose our mates.

Mate selection   What determines who is a more desirable sexual or marital partner? Everyday observation suggests that in our society men and women choose on the basis of somewhat different criteria, and these observations have been confirmed by a number of systematic surveys conducted by David Buss and his coworkers. Their results indicate that in general, the physical attractiveness of the partner seems more important to men than to women. It also appears that men generally prefer younger women, whereas women prefer older men. Yet another difference concerns the social and financial status of the partner, which seems to matter much more to women than it does to men. The data also indicate that these male-female differences are not unique to our own society, but are found throughout the world, in countries as diverse as China, India, France, Nigeria, and Iran (Buss and Barnes, 1986; Buss, 1989, 1992). Quite interestingly, though, the two sexes agree on one point: Across cultures, both men and women value kindness and intelligence in their prospective mates (Buss, 1992).

These results are open to many interpretations. In Buss's view, the best explanation is evolutionary. He argues that our male ancestors preferred attractive women because they were using attractiveness as a means of judging health and thus fertility. And younger mates were preferred because they have more reproductive years ahead of them than would an older mate. The female's preference for wealthy, high-status males, in turn, was based on the potential benefits these resources brought to their offspring. According to this view, such preferences reveal innate mate preference mechanisms that are built into the nervous system, formed as a result of natural selection (Buss, 1992).

But Buss's findings can also be interpreted in other ways. A plausible alternative is that females prefer wealthy, high-status males for current economic reasons, not hardwired biological ones. This contrast between economic and biological factors is important, since economic factors are far more open to change—from one generation to the next or from one culture to the next. In addition, it is quite clear that mate preferences have changed somewhat over the years, so that, for example, women considered highly attractive two hundred years ago would be considered less so today (see Chapter 3). These and other changes make it clear that mate preferences, even if biologically rooted, are open to alteration through learning.

Mating systems   Another issue concerns human mating patterns. Are we biologically inclined toward monogamous relationships? Evolutionary theorists start out with the observation that humans are somewhat dimorphic: On average, the

Polygynous tendencies in humans The archetype of the philandering male is Don Juan, played here by John Barrymore. (From the 1926 film Don Juan, with Mary Astor; courtesy of the Motion Picture and Television Photo Archive)

human male is about 10 percent larger than the female. Recall that, generally, sexual dimorphism is found in polygamous animals but is small or nonexistent in monogamous ones. This suggests that humans would have a tendency toward polygamy and, since we are mammals, that we would incline toward polygyny. As it turns out, most cultures do allow polygyny; only 16 percent of those studied require monogamous marital arrangements, with just one spouse to each partner (Ford and Beach, 1951).★

Within our own culture, there is some suggestion that men have a greater desire for a variety of sexual partners than women (Symons, 1979), and evolutionary theorists believe that these differences are ultimately rooted in our biological nature. In their view, men want greater sexual variety because for them it is reproductively adaptive: The more women they mate with, the more children they father. In contrast, women are much more cautious in evaluating potential sexual partners and more interested in a stable, familial relationship. For reasons we have discussed, this is a good reproductive strategy for women: With their much greater parental investment in each offspring, women have a great stake in finding the best possible father for their young. To be sure, these built-in patterns are less relevant in a modern world in which birth control has, for many cultures, managed to uncouple sex from reproduction. But according to the evolutionary argument, the preferences we observe are remnants of our biological past, still influential even though their current adaptive value may be nil.

But this evolutionary account has been severely challenged. Many critics argue that differences in sexual attitudes reflect cultural values rather than biological predispositions. In their opinion, the male's preference for polygyny is a natural outgrowth of social conditions in which men are dominant and women are considered property (see Gilmore, 1990). As to the differences in men's and women's desire for sexual variety, they regard it as a product of early social training: Boys are taught that many sexual conquests are a proof of "manliness," while girls are taught to value home and family and to seek a single partner.

As one rebuttal to this cultural critique, some writers point to the different sexual practices of gay men and lesbians (Symons, 1979). It turns out that gay men are much more interested in sexual variety than are lesbians. Until ten or fifteen years ago, before the advent of the AIDS crisis, the sexual relations of gay men tended to be briefer and more casual, and to involve many more partners than did those of lesbians (Schäfer, 1977). Such findings were interpreted by some as evidence for a biological rather than a cultural interpretation of mating patterns: Although gay men and lesbians do not conform to cultural norms about sexual orientation, in the end, men remain men (with all of their biologically driven habits) and women remain women. But of course another interpretation is also possible: The culture may have taught gay men (no less than their heterosexual brothers) that being manly means having a lot of sexual experiences and may have taught lesbians (no less than their heterosexual sisters) that a woman should be faithful to just one partner (Gagnon and Simon, 1973). It would seem, therefore, that the available evidence does not sustain strong conclusions about the biological rootedness of polygyny in human mating.

Appropriateness of the evolutionary account What should we make of all these arguments? There is no doubt that we can often gain insights into behavior by taking an evolutionary perspective and asking how that behavior originated. But we need to be cautious in interpreting these evolutionary arguments. As one

★ Note that this 16 percent figure applies to 185 different cultures, indicating that 30 of these cultures were monogamous. Of course, the percentage would be much higher if it were based on individuals rather than cultures, since the monogamous modern cultures (including our own) are much more populous than most of the cultures described in the anthropological literature.

concern, they often rest on comparisons among different species, and this may in some cases be problematic. For example, terms such as *monogamy* have quite a different meaning when applied to geese rather than humans. When applied to geese, the term describes the fact that two parents stay together for one breeding season to hatch and raise their young; when applied to humans, the term describes an arrangement that may only make sense in the context of a network of social, legal, and religious norms.

Nor does saying that a behavior pattern is universal, adaptive, or evolutionarily "reasonable" imply that it is genetically programmed. Many universal traits that were, and still are, adaptive—for example, making and wearing clothes—are acquired by each generation through learning, not through their DNA. Moreover, traits that are clearly part of our genetic inheritance—for example, speech—are nonetheless dramatically shaped by culture.

To put this in different terms, it may well be that natural selection has shaped many of our impulses and desires, but these in turn have shaped the culture in which humans live and mate and bring up their children. Since this is so, it is mere speculation to assert that the reproductive economics that underlie promiscuous sex in chimpanzees, or harem formation in elephant seals, are at bottom the same as those that account for some human sexual behavior and that such behavior is an immutable part of our human nature (Kitcher, 1985).

Orangutan mother and child *(Photograph © Zefa Germany / The Stock Market, 1994)*

PARENTING

There is another bond whose biological foundations are just as basic as those between males and females—the relation between mother and child, and in many animals, the relation between father and child as well. While most fish and reptiles lay eggs by the hundreds and then abandon them, most birds and mammals, in contrast, have fewer offspring but display a strong parental attachment to them, which makes it more likely that these offspring will survive. They feed them, clean them, shelter them, and protect them, trying in all these ways to ensure that most of their brood survive to the point of self-sufficiency and reproductive readiness. While under this parental umbrella, the young can grow and, along the way, acquire some of the skills that will help them survive. This period of juvenile dependency is longest in animals that live by their wits, such as monkeys and apes, and it is longest of all in humans.

THE INFANT'S ATTACHMENT TO THE MOTHER

In most birds and mammals, the young become strongly attached to their mother. Ducklings follow the mother duck, lambs the mother ewe, and infant monkeys cling tightly to the mother monkey's belly. In each case, separation from the mother leads to considerable stress: The young animals give piteous distress calls, and quack, bleat, or cry continuously until the mother returns. The biological function of this attachment is a simple matter of personal survival, and this holds for humans as well as other animals, for there is little doubt that in our early evolutionary history a motherless infant would probably have died an early death—from exposure, starvation, or predation.

The mechanisms that lead to this attachment will be discussed later (see Chapter 14). For now, we will only say that the infant's attachment to the mother goes far beyond the biological functions, the alleviation of hunger, thirst, and pain. This is reflected in the fact that infants—be they birds, monkeys, or humans—show great distress when they are separated from their mother, even when they are perfectly well fed and housed.

THE MOTHER'S ATTACHMENT TO THE INFANT

As we noted above, the biological function of the mother-child bond for the infant is personal survival. For the mother, the biological function is again a matter of survival, but for her, the survival is genetic rather than personal, for unless her young survive to reproduce, her genes will perish. But what are the mechanisms that produce the mother's attachment (and in many species, the father's attachment, too)?

Robins and gibbons behave like proper parents: They care for their young and protect them. But they surely don't do this because they realize that their failure to act in this way would lead to genetic extinction. Instead, it seems likely that one outcome of natural selection is an innate predisposition toward parental behavior.

In many species, the young seem to have a set of built-in responses that elicit caretaking from the parents. We've already considered one example, pecking at the parent's beak in the young herring gull (see pp. 408–9). In many other species, the baby birds open their mouths as wide as they can as soon as the parent arrives at the nest. This gaping response is their means of begging for food (see Figure 10.15), and the parents respond appropriately. In fact, some species of birds have special anatomical features that draw attention to these signals, essentially guaranteeing a proper parental reaction. An example is the cedar waxwing, whose bright red mouth lining evidently provides a further signal to the parent: "I'm young, hungry, and a cedar waxwing!"

Child care among humans takes much longer than it does among herring gulls and cedar waxwings, and the caretaking required is more varied and complex, but it, too, has biological foundations. The mother-child relation grows out of a number of built-in reaction patterns, of child to mother and mother to

10.15 Gaping in young birds (A) The gaping response of the young yellow warbler serves as a built-in signal that elicits the parents' feeding behavior. (Photograph by John Shaw/Bruce Coleman) (B) Cuckoos are parasites that lay their eggs in other birds' nests. The photograph shows a young cuckoo being fed by its foster parent, a reed warbler. The young cuckoo, at about twenty-four hours old, instinctively ejects any eggs or young of its host from the nest, so that it is the sole occupant. Its large orange-red gaping mouth provides a powerful stimulus for feeding. The unwitting warbler will continue to feed the cuckoo even when it has grown to several times the foster parent's size. (Courtesy of Ian Wyllie, Monks Wood Experiment Station)

A

B

A

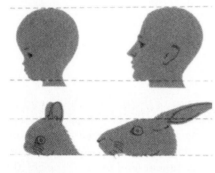

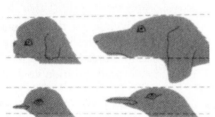

B

10.16   The stimulus features of "babyness"   *"Cute" characteristics of the baby schema are common to humans and a number of animals. (A) These include a rounded head shape, protruding forehead, and large eyes below the middle of the head. (After Lorenz, 1943) (B) The Disney character Mickey Mouse became "cuter" over the years by subscribing more and more to the baby schema, with his eyes and head becoming larger. (© Walt Disney Productions)*

child. For example, human parents use a special sing-song pitch when they talk to their infants; this so-called **Motherese** occurs across cultures and may represent a biologically determined communication style, triggered whenever an adult interacts with a small and dependent creature (Newport, Gleitman, and Gleitman, 1977; and see Chapter 9). Motherese serves several important purposes. Among them, it helps the child learn language and keeps the infant's attention focused on the social interaction; it may also help communicate aspects of the adult's intentions toward the child (Fernald, 1992).

The human infant begins life with several competencies relevant to social interaction, including reflexes that help him find the mother's nipple and suck at it once it is found. He also has an essentially innate signal system through which he tells the mother that he is in distress: He cries. Similar distress calls are found in many animals, for when the young chirp, bleat, mew, or cry, the mother immediately runs to their aid and comforts them.

According to ethologists, natural selection has further equipped the infant with a set of stimulus features that function as innate releasers of parental, and especially maternal, feelings. The cues that define "babyness" include a large, protruding forehead, large eyes, an upturned nose, chubby cheeks, and so on. Endowed with these distinctive properties, the baby looks cute and cuddly to adult humans, something to be picked up, fussed over, and taken care of. The case is similar for the young of various animals who share aspects of the same babyness schema. In all cases, some argue, these stimulus characteristics help ensure that adults will react to the infant in just the right protective, nurturing fashion (Lorenz, 1950). These same tendencies, though, are open to exploitation, and thus many commercial enterprises have devoted themselves to the deliberate manufacture of cuteness. Dolls and Walt Disney creatures are designed to be babied by children, while certain lap dogs are especially bred to be babied by adults (Figure 10.16; see Fridlund and MacDonald, 1998).

Nature has provided the infant with yet another trick to disarm even the stoniest of parental hearts: the smile. In some fashion, smiling may begin within the first month; it is often considered a built-in signal by which humans tell each other "I wish you well. Be good to me." There is reason to believe that both the giving of this signal (smiling) and the response to it are innate. Infants who are born blind smile under conditions that also produce smiling in sighted children, as when they hear their mother's voice. They obviously could not have learned this response by imitation.

COMMUNICATION

Babies smile at their caregivers and cry when they are in distress. Dogs flatten their ears against their heads to signal impending aggression and roll onto their backs to signal submission. In these (and many other) cases, creatures signal their expectations and their intentions to each other, and this in turn has important consequences for the behavior of other individuals. What are the roots of this sort of signaling?

EXPRESSIVE MOVEMENTS: DISPLAYS

Displays represent the mode of communication through which animals inform each other of what they are most likely to do in the immediate future. The crab waves its claws, and the wolf bares its fangs; these threat messages may save both sender and receiver from bodily harm if the message is heeded (Krebs and Dawkins, 1984).

How do ethologists determine what message is conveyed by a given display? Since the sender is tyically an animal, they cannot ask it directly. They can try, however, to infer the message by noting the correlation between a given display and the animal's behavior just before and after the display's occurrence. For example, if a certain posture is generally followed by attack, then it is usually called a threat display; if it is usually followed by mating, it is probably a courtship signal, and so on.

But ethologists have discovered that displays can carry many kinds of information and not just about intentions. Some displays serve to identify characteristics of the displayer, such as its species, age, sex, or whether it is available to breed. Other displays indicate association and are issued only around family or troop members. Still other displays are like homing beacons that simply say, "I'm here!" (Smith, 1977).

Do humans convey information through displays? The answer is yes. Our dis-

A

B

The evolutionary origin of the human smile One theory holds that the human smile grew out of the fear grin. This is an appeasement display found in monkeys and other primates, which usually signifies submission but may also indicate reassurance when directed by a dominant animal to a subordinate (van Hooff, 1972). (A) The fear grin in a young chimpanzee. (Photograph © Tom McHugh/Photo Researchers, Inc., 1978) (B) A smile in an infant (Photograph © Luis Castaneda/The Image Bank)

plays are our various expressions, mostly conveyed by the face. Like many of the animal displays we have discussed, our expressions tell others something about our needs and intentions. But what exactly do they mean, how universal are they, and how rooted are they in biology? These questions have received much attention and will be explored in Chapter 11.

THE DIFFERENCE BETWEEN DISPLAY AND LANGUAGE

With the much richer communication system provided by language, displays have assumed secondary status among humans. While both are used to affect the behavior of others, human language does so with a great deal more versatility.

For one thing, language is by far the more complex and flexible of the two communicative systems. Consider the relative size of the two "vocabularies." Most mammals have some twenty to forty distinguishable display signals (Smith, 1977). This contrasts with an estimated vocabulary size of at least 50,000 words for the average human adult. The contrast is even sharper when we compare the way in which these items can be combined. Human language is based on a creative principle: Given the rules for putting words together (syntax), the speaker can construct any number of new messages that she has never heard before (see Chapter 9). Not so for animal displays. Each seal, robin, and rhesus monkey can send only the messages that were sent by previous seals, robins, and rhesus monkeys. There is little room for originality in the system of display.

Language is also more flexible in the kind of messages it can convey. For the most part, displays are a way of telling a fellow creature what one is, what one is about to do, or what one wants the other to do. In effect, they are statements about the sender's social motives at a particular time and place. Given the goals of displays, we can understand why the relative poverty of the system is no barrier to communication. There is no need for a large vocabulary or a creative combinatorial system because there is a limit to the number of things an animal wants to do to (or with) another of its own kind: flee, attack, feed or be fed by, groom or be groomed by, copulate, and a few others.★ In contrast, human language must precisely describe the world at large and, thus, must be flexible enough to cover a nearly unlimited number of topics. For this, a creative system is absolutely crucial. The variety of possible events and relationships in the world is infinite, and only a system that is capable of an infinite number of utterances can do justice to this variety (see Chapter 9).

(Photograph by Benny Ortiz)

SOCIAL COGNITON

Human social life is massively influenced by what we desire from and of other people, be they friends or enemies, strangers or lovers, parents or children. But our social lives are no less governed by what we know and think about the people around us. We will return to this topic of *social cognition* in Chapter 11. But some studies indicate that there are many counterparts of such social cognition in the animal world.

★ This statement must be qualified somewhat, for some primates have displays that signal different kinds of predators. Thus, vervet monkeys have different alarm calls for eagles, leopards, and pythons (Seyfarth, Cheney, and Marler, 1980; Cheney and Wrangham, 1986). But while this adds some measure of complexity, animal displays can't begin to compare to the richness of human language.

Dorothy Cheney and Robert Seyfarth in the field *(Photograph by Bob Peck, Academy of Natural Sciences, Philadelphia)*

Understanding kinship relationships in primates *This group of female vervet monkeys is looking at the mother of an infant who just sounded an alarm call. Apparently, they know who in their group is related to whom. (Photograph courtesy of Dorothy Cheney)*

AUDIENCE EFFECTS

Animal displays are often significantly influenced by whether there is an audience, and if so, who comprises it. These **audience effects** suggest that many animal displays are emitted not automatically but strategically. One series of studies, led by biologist Peter Marler, explored the foods calls of domestic chickens. These calls, emitted mostly by roosters, were previously considered to be signs of arousal in the presence of food. It turns out, however, that roosters do not emit so-called food calls whenever food is present. Rather, they emit these calls preferentially in the presence of hens, especially strange hens; they emit fewer food calls when alone and the fewest in the presence of another rooster (Gyger and Marler, 1988). Roosters have also been shown to emit false food calls (that is, calling when food was absent) to attract hens at a distance (Karakashian, Gyger, and Marler, 1988).

SOCIAL COGNITION IN PRIMATES

Not suprisingly, more sophisticated versions of social cognition have been observed in primates. Consider the vervet, a small monkey that lives in groups of some fifteen animals or so and that makes its home primarily in the savanna woodlands of Africa. Because staying with one's troop is essential for food and safety, the ability to distinguish among other vervets is crucial. Indeed, vervet monkeys can recognize other vervets in their troop by sight and sound. A demonstration comes from some field studies performed by Dorothy Cheney and Robert Seyfarth in which they set up camp near several vervet groups in Southern Kenya, tape recorded the calls of many of the vervets, and then played these tapes back to the vervets at strategic times. On one occasion, they broadcast the distress cry of a juvenile to its mother and two other nearby females who also had offspring in the group. At the time of the playback, all of the offspring were out of sight. The mother looked in the direction of the (hidden) loudspeaker and approached it, suggesting that she recognized her screaming youngster's voice. The other two females neither looked at the loudspeaker, nor at each other, but instead looked at the mother, as if to say: "It's *your* kid. So what are *you* going to do about it?" (Cheney and Seyfarth, 1982).

DO MONKEY HAVE A THEORY OF MIND?

Evidence of this sort suggests that monkeys have a considerable degree of knowledge of the kinship and relationships in their group (e.g., Dasser, 1988). Further studies suggest that they also know a great deal about the dominance relationships in their group—who's up, who's down, and who's in between. As a result, they can pretty well predict who's likely to chase or cuff them and who is not, and they can then behave according to these beliefs. But do monkeys think that other monkeys also have thoughts and beliefs? To ask this question is to ask whether these animals have what has often been called a **theory of mind,** that is, whether they attribute states of mind such as beliefs and desires to others (Premack, 1978, 1988; Fodor, 1992).* One way of determining whether they do is to see whether they can use deliberate deception to induce a false belief in another individual. While we saw that roosters sometimes emit ersatz food calls to lure hens, there is little evidence that their behavior is self-conscious. There is a suggestion that some monkeys and apes, on the other hand, are intelligent enough (not to speak of immoral enough) to deceive intentionally.

---

* We will later encounter that same question raised about children below four or four-and-a-half years of age (see Chapter 13).

Some evidence comes from a laboratory study in which a chimpanzee saw a desirable piece of fruit being placed in one of two containers while the other was left empty. Unfortunately, the containers were too far removed to be reached through the bars of the cage. As a result, the apes had to rely on the aid of an attendant who stood outside the cage in easy reach of the containers. The trouble was that this attendant had not been there when the food was placed, so that he didn't know which of the two containers held the food. Thus, there was only one way by which the chimpanzees could get the food: They somehow had to inform the attendant—by looking at the correct container or by pointing with hand or foot—which of the two containers was the correct one.

After a while, the animals learned to do this rather well, but then the experimenter introduced an unkind complication. He now used two attendants, one "good," the other "bad." The good one was all a chimpanzee could possibly ask for: Whenever he found food in a container, he gave it to the ape. The bad attendant was a self-seeking egotist: Whenever he found food in a container, he ate it himself. This eventually led the chimpanzees to develop a different strategy. They now gave proper signals to the good but not to the bad attendant. One of four chimpanzees went further and actively misled the bad attendant by pointing to the *incorrect* container with her foot (Woodruff and Premack, 1979; for some complicating evidence, see Premack, 1988). To the extent that these animals could deliberately deceive another individual, they demonstrated that they believed others have beliefs and that these beliefs may be (and in the case of the bad attendant, *should* be) different from their own. It is perhaps ironic that a certain level of what might seem like immorality requires a fairly high degree of intellectual comprehension: Adam and Eve could not lie until after they had eaten from the tree of knowledge.

Such findings suggest that chimpanzees (and perhaps monkeys, too) have some understanding of the fact that other creatures have their own minds, their own beliefs, and their own knowledge. But there is little doubt that this chimpanzoid understanding doesn't begin to approach the complexities of our own adult conceptions of how other people think, feel, and believe. Our own human social interactions depend not just on what we think and believe about other people, but also on what we think and believe *they* think and believe about *us.* Such mutual cognitions are a commonplace of everyday life (e.g., "I think most of my acquaintances like me, and they probably think I like them too, but Joe and Jane seem to feel otherwise, and I don't really know why . . ." and so on). To us, the fact that others have thoughts and wishes and beliefs is an axiom. As will become apparent in the next chapter, it is an axiom from which most of our social behavior flows directly.

ALTRUISM AND SELF-SACRIFICE

As we have seen, animals fight and compete with each other, mate, reproduce, and communicate. Some even make judgments about what their fellows think and use that information to their own advantage. In all these cases, each animal seems only to be striving to further its own ends, its own needs. But in some circumstances, animals stray from this apparently selfish pattern and behave as if they were unselfish altruists.

It is, of course, well known that many animals go to considerable lengths to defend their offspring. Various birds, for example, have evolved the strategy of feigning injury in order to draw a predator away from their nests (see Figure 10.17). The bird drags one wing or paddles in circles in order to appear vulnerable to the predator. Then, when the predator turns to approach this seemingly

10.17 A misleading display *In feigning injury, the killdeer, a small American bird, runs and flies erratically from predators that approach its nest, often flopping about as if it has a broken wing. (Photograph by Wayne Lankinen/Bruce Coleman)*

10.18 Alarm call *Ground squirrels give alarm calls when they sense a nearby predator. Such alarm calls are more likely to be given by females than males. The females usually have close relatives living nearby. As a result, their alarm call is more likely to benefit genetically related rather than unrelated individuals, which suggests that it is based on kin selection. (Photograph by Georg D. Lepp/Bio-Tec Images)*

easy target, the bird moves a little farther away. This process continues, as the bird continues the pretense, and thus lures the predator farther and farther from the nest.

On the face of it, such acts appear heroically unselfish, for the parents court the danger that the predator will seize them. But speaking biologically, in an important way this strategy is self-serving and not at all altruistic (Wilson, 1975). To see this, imagine that the mother bird played it safe and flew off, rather than putting herself at risk to protect her young. This mother is likely to survive, but from an evolutionary perspective what counts is not her *personal* survival but her *genetic* survival. And her genes are more likely to perish if she flies off to safety, leaving the predator to eat her chicks: She will have fewer offspring to whom she has passed on her genes, including the very gene or genes that predispose her toward maternal indifference.

While the self-centered mother, concerned with her personal survival, will contribute few offspring to the next generation, the protective mother will contribute many offspring, even if she does not survive to see those offspring to maturity. Thus, the genes that contribute to the protective act will end up in more members of the next generation than will those that promoted the self-centered behavior. Eventually, the genes contributing to the selfish act will be extinguished, so that only the genes favoring protection will be left.

ALTRUISM IN ANIMALS

Seen in this light, parental self-sacrifice can easily be understood in evolutionary terms. A similar analysis can be applied to altruistic acts that benefit individuals other than one's own children.★ A case in point are the **alarm calls** given by many species at the approach of a predator (see Figure 10.18). When a robin sees a hawk overhead, for example, it gives an alarm call, a special cry that alerts all members of the flock and impels them to seek cover. All robins emit this call when in danger, and they do so even if raised in complete isolation from their fellows. And there is no doubt that this alarm call benefits all robins who hear it. They crouch low and hide, so their chances of escape are enhanced. But the bird who sounds the alarm may not reap these rewards—that bird is busy crying out rather than hiding. In fact, the alarm call actually places the calling bird in greater danger by revealing its location to the hawk. Why, therefore, does the robin play the hero instead of quietly stealing away and leaving its fellows to their fate? There are several possible factors, each of which may play a role.

Enlightened self-interest One possibility is that this act of avian heroism is not as unselfish as it seems, for it may well increase the caller's own chance of personal survival in the long run. If a particular robin spies a hawk and remains quiet, there is a greater chance that some bird in the flock will be captured, most likely some bird other than itself. But what about tomorrow? A hawk who has seized prey in a particular location will probably soon return to the very same place in search of another meal. And this meal may be the very same robin who originally minded its own business and stayed uninvolved (Trivers, 1971).

Kin selection There is another alternative. Let us assume that our heroic robin is unlucky, is seized by the hawk, and dies a martyr's death. While this act may have caused the robin to perish as an individual, it may well have served to preserve some of that bird's genes. This may be true even if none of the birds in the flock

★ In fact, modern biological usage reserves *altruism* for just those cases in which the good deed benefits neither the doers nor their own offspring.

are the hero's own offspring. They may be relatives who carry some of its genes, brothers and sisters who share half of the same genes, or nieces and nephews who share one-fourth. If so, the alarm call may have saved several relatives who carry the alarm-calling genes and who will pass them on to future generations of robins. From an evolutionary standpoint, the alarm call had survival value—if not for the alarm caller or its offspring, then for the alarm-calling genes (Hamilton, 1964; Maynard-Smith, 1965).

According to this view, altruistic behavior will evolve if it promotes the survival of the individual's kin. This **kin-selection hypothesis** predicts that unselfish behavior should be more common among relatives than among unrelated individuals, and there is some evidence that this is indeed the case. Certain deer snort loudly when alarmed, which alerts other deer nearby. This behavior is much more likely among groups of does, who tend to be related, than among groups of bucks, who are less likely to be related. Similar behavior is seen in roosters, who emit alarm calls preferentially, sounding more alarms in the presence of their mate or another hen (Marler, Duffy, and Pickert, 1986a, b). While the roosters may not be genetically related to either, protecting their mates makes good evolutionary sense, as does protecting prospective mates. Results supporting the kin-selection hypothesis have been obtained for various other species as well (Hirth and McCullough, 1977; Sherman, 1977).

Reciprocal altruism   There is yet another possible mechanism that might lead to biologically unselfish acts—**reciprocal altruism.** Some animals—and we may well be among them—may follow a built-in Golden Rule: Do unto others as you would have them do unto you (or unto your genes). If one individual helps another, and that other later reciprocates, the ultimate result is a benefit to both. For example, male baboons sometimes help each other in aggressive encounters, and the one who received help on one occasion is more likely to come to the other's assistance later (Packer, 1977; but see Bercovitch, 1988).

Grooming may be another example of such reciprocity. Monkeys and apes sit in pairs while one meticulously picks vermin out of the other's fur (Figure 10.19). We can certainly see that the animal being groomed benefits. It gets cleaned in areas that may be hard to reach. And it may also find being groomed relaxing—the animal version of a back rub. But it's not clear what the animal doing the gooming gets out of it.

Still, the animal being groomed and the animal doing the grooming both seem to enjoy the process far more than is required for personal hygiene. In fact, grooming is one of their ways of cementing a social bond. It occurs most commonly among kin (mothers and children, brothers and sisters, cousins, and so on), although it may also occur among unrelated animals. But whether they are kin or unrelated, animals who groom most often are also the most closely bonded by other measures of primate togetherness: They sit together, forage for food together, and form coalitions against common antagonists (Walters and Seyfarth, 1986; Boyd and Silk, 1997).

Such social bonds may underlie reciprocal altruism, for reciprocity presupposes the relatively stable groups such bonds promote; it also requires that individuals recognize one another and that there are some safeguards against cheating—accepting help without reciprocating. One such safeguard might be a link between a disposition toward altruism and a disposition to punish cheaters (Trivers, 1971). And a built-in predisposition toward reciprocity may well be one of the biological foundations of altruism in some animals (and perhaps ourselves as well). If the original unselfish act doesn't exact too great a cost—in energy expended or in danger incurred—then its eventual reciprocation will yield a net benefit to both parties.

10.19 Grooming in baboons *(Photograph by P. Craig-Cooper, Nature Photographers Ltd.)*

Braving death for an ideal During the Civil War, a vastly outnumbered group of black Union soldiers attacked an impregnable fortress held by Confederate forces and suffered enormous casualties. They were willing to die for the abolition of slavery. From the 1989 film Glory, directed by Edward Zwick. (Photograph courtesy of Photofest)

Altruism The grave site of Shannon Wright, the Arkansas teacher who gave her life attempting to protect her students from gunfire during a schoolyard attack by two fellow students. (Photograph by J. Pat Carter/Associated Press AP)

ALTRUISM IN HUMANS

There is little doubt that humans are capable of considerable self-sacrifice. Soldiers volunteer for suicide missions, and religious martyrs burn at the stake. We can also catalog (and celebrate) the many lesser acts of altruism—sharing food and money, offering help to the ill or homeless, and the like. Can these human acts be understood in the same biological terms that apply to the alarm calls of birds and hygiene habits of monkeys?

The evolutionary view According to biologist Edward O. Wilson, the answer is yes. Wilson argues that there are certain common themes that can be identified in all human social systems, and he regards these as grounded in our genetic heritage. The most important themes, he claims, revolve around the issue of kinship, because kinship is, on Wilson's view, largely a matter of shared genes. For example, Wilson and other evolutionary theorists suggest that, by and large, we will be most altruistic to our closest relatives. As with the robin, the individual hero may die, but its genes will survive (Wilson, 1975, 1978).

For evolutionary theorists, this position is supported by the fact that kinship is of considerable importance in just about all human societies, as attested to by the elaborate terms used to describe the precise nature of kinship relations: brother, sister, uncle, aunt, cousin, second cousin once removed, and so on. Perhaps more persuasive is the fact that, in our culture, the likelihood that one person will make a sacrifice for another is, as predicted, greater if the two are genetically related. In one study, a fairly large sample of American women was asked who had helped them on occasions when they required assistance (money, emotional support, and so on). The results showed that they were three times more likely to have been helped by their parents, siblings, or children (who share half their genes) than by half-siblings, aunts, uncles, nieces, nephews, and grandchildren or grandparents (who share only a quarter of their genes). This is not to say that genetically unrelated friends (let alone husbands) did not provide help, for indeed they did. But according to the authors, help among friends was probably based on reciprocal altruism. If a participant's friend gave her money (or time or emotional support), there was a mutual expectation that the assistance would be reciprocated at some later time. Among kin, such expectation of later repayment was less common (Essock-Vitale and McGuire, 1985).

Some theorists have expanded this kinship-selection argument even further. As they see it, kinship selection underlies a human tendency toward **tribalism**—putting the welfare of one's own group ahead of others. Our own resources may be limited, but even so we will often share them with our kin. But for the same reasons we are more likely to engage in conflict with those who are not our immediate kin, and by extension, outside our tribe.

This perspective puts human nature in an unflattering light. Acts that seem altruistic turn out to be self-serving (at least genetically so). Kinship altruism may prompt us to help brothers, sisters, and cousins, but it may turn us against all others of our kind. And reciprocal altruism may impel us to be generous, but only in so far as today's generosity is likely to be repaid tomorrow.

Some problems of fact and theory: Biology or culture? This evolutionary analysis of human altruism is highly controversial. Part of the controversy concerns the basic facts themselves. For example, studies of different cultures show that the degree to which relatives help each other is not a simple function of their genetic closeness. The likelihood of helping often depends, instead, on whether individuals *regard* themselves as close, rather than on whether they are, in fact, re-

Human martyrdom *In their darkest hour, Joan of Arc, an unlettered peasant, arose to lead the French against the British during the Hundred Years' War. After several brilliant successes, she was finally captured and burned at the stake by the British. Can we really attribute the actions of a Joan of Arc to kin selection or reciprocal altruism? (From the 1957 film* Saint Joan, *directed by Otto Preminger and starring Jean Seberg; photo courtesy of Photofest)*

lated genetically. Evidence comes from the study of several cultures in which newly married couples live in the household of the groom's father and eventually create an extended family with many brothers, sisters, uncles, and aunts. A young boy in this family will get to know his paternal uncles—they will live in the same hut or one nearby. But he won't have much to do with his maternal uncles; they stayed behind in his maternal grandfather's household. Genetically, he is of course equally close to both, but when questioned about whom he is more likely to help or be helped by, he immediately names his paternal uncles, whom he has known and lived with all his life (Sahlins, 1976).

Critics of the evolutionary perspective hold that these and similar findings show that human social behavior depends crucially on culture rather than genetics. To understand human altruism, they argue, we must understand it in social terms. The boy who feels closer to his paternal uncle is responding to kinship as his culture describes it, rather than as something defined by his genes. The same holds for self-sacrifice. The ancient Romans fell on their swords when defeated, not to save their brothers' genes, but to save their honor. The early Christians defied death because of a religious belief rather than to maintain a particular gene pool. We cannot comprehend the ancient Romans without considering their concept of honor, nor can we explain the martyrdom of the early Christians without reference to their belief in the hereafter.

To sum up, Wilson and other evolutionary theorists have argued that human social behaviors such as altruism and self-sacrifice are fundamentally biological adaptations that guarantee the survival of the most reproductively fit—in principle no different from the social patterns found in primates and other nonhumans. The critics of this view do not deny the powerful influence of biology on human behavior. But they insist that human social behavior is so thoroughly infused by culture—by moral and religious beliefs, by customs, by art—that comparisons with nonhuman behavior are just analogies rather than reflections of biological imperatives. This issue is still being hotly debated in the fields of psychology, biology, and anthropology, and we cannot solve it here. But we will return to it when we discuss altruistic behavior as it is studied by modern social psychologists (see Chapter 12).

Some problems of ethics   There is a final issue that concerns some of the ethical implications of the evolutionary position. Suppose the assertions about humans are true—that men are biologically predisposed toward philandering and women toward coyness, and that all of us are genetically biased toward hostile tribalism. All of these suppositions are vehemently disputed (see, for example, Lewontin, Rose, and Kamin, 1984; Kitcher, 1985, 1987). But for the sake of argument, let's assume for the moment that they are true. What then? Does this mean that these (supposed) biological facts justify sexism or support a blind hostility toward everyone who is different from ourselves? The answer is an emphatic *no.* If the facts are as some evolutionary biologists claim they are (and we have repeatedly said that this is debatable), then philandering may be a biological predisposition in males and may be in that sense natural. But what is natural isn't necessarily good. A preference for sweets is biologically built-in and has a perfectly understandable evolutionary function, for what's sweet is generally also nutritious. But in these days of junk food, most of us learn to curb our natural appetite for sweets or suffer various unpleasant consequences. The same surely holds for whatever callous and self-seeking built-in tendencies we may have but that as civilized men and women we must morally deplore.

This point is recognized by a number of biologists. Sarah Hrdy, an authority on primate behavior, stated it succinctly by quoting the character played by Katharine Hepburn in the film *The African Queen:* "Nature, Mr. Allnutt, is what we were put on this earth to rise above!" (Hrdy, 1988, p. 126).

ETHOLOGY AND HUMAN NATURE

Over three hundred years have passed since Hobbes described the "war of all against all," which he regarded as the natural state of all humankind. We are still far from having a definite description of our basic social nature. But at least we know that Hobbes's solutions are wrong or oversimplified. Humans are not built so as to be solitary. Other people are a necessary aspect of our lives, and a tendency to interact with others is built into us from the very outset. What holds for humans holds for most animals as well. The robin is programmed to deal with other robins, the baboon with other baboons. Some of these interactions are peaceful, while others are quarrelsome. What matters is that there is always some interaction between like and like. This social intercourse is an essential aspect of each creature's existence, as shown by an elaborate repertoire of built-in social reactions that govern reproduction, care of offspring, and intraspecies competition at virtually all levels of the animal kingdom. No person is an island complete unto herself; neither is any other animal.

SUMMARY

1. Thomas Hobbes believed that humans are inherently asocial and self-centered. An alternative position, championed by Charles Darwin among others, is that both humans and animals have built-in social dispositions. The study of such innate bases of social reactions has largely focused on animal behavior and has been undertaken within the domain of *ethology.* Evolutionary theorists have tried to explain the emergence of social behavior in both animals and humans within the framework of natural selection.

2. Most animals exhibit various *species-specific* behaviors, which were once thought to be based on *fixed-action patterns* triggered by *releasing stimuli.* An example is the begging response of newly hatched herring gulls. Many of these species-specific reactions are *displays,* which serve as communicative signals.

3. One realm of social behavior that has important biological roots is *aggression,* a term generally reserved for conflict between members of the same species. To secure a supply of resources for themselves and their descendants, many animals (usually the males) stake out a *territory,* which they then defend. Various methods have evolved to keep aggression within bounds, including territoriality, which separates potential combatants spatially, and *dominance hierarchies,* which separate them in social status. Further constraints on aggression are enacted via *threat* and *appeasement displays.*

4. While there are certain parallels between aggression among animals and among humans—for example, between territoriality and *personal space*—human aggression depends in great part on learning and culture.

5. Compared to *asexual reproduction* (through fission), *sexual reproduction* is a costly biological option. Its benefits, and the reasons it evolved, probably involve the ability to defend against pathogens.

6. Built-in predispositions figure heavily in various aspects of sexual reproduction. Displays advertise the animal's sex, its readiness to mate, and its species. Examples are seen in *courtship rituals,* which are highly species specific and tend to prevent animals from breeding with members of other species. In most species, reproduction and parenting require greater investment on the part of females, who are understandably choosier than males in courtship and mating.

7. Sexual behavior is partially controlled by several sex hormones. In mammals, sex hormones such as *testosterone* (in males) and *estrogen* (in females) stimulate cells in the hypothalamus that trigger sexual activity. Many female animals only mate when they are in *estrus,* the time during which the ovum is ready for fertilization. The estrus cycle depends on the interplay of estrogen, which stimulates the development of the ovum and makes the animal sexually receptive, and *progesterone,* another female hormone that prepares the uterus to receive the embryo.

8. In humans, sexual behavior is more flexible and less dependent on hormonal conditions than it is in animals. Human females have *menstrual cycles* rather than estrus cycles. Thus, although women are only fertile near the time of ovulation, they are capable of sexual behavior at any time in their menstrual cycle.

9. Animals have evolved a number of different mating systems. In some, the pattern is *monogamy,* with a more or less permanent tie between one male and one female. In others, the pattern is *polygamy,* in which several individuals of one sex mate with just one member of the other sex. The most common polygamous pattern is *polygyny,* with one male mating with several females. In a very few others, it is *polyandry,* with one female mating with several males. According to evolutionary theorists, mating systems evolve to maximize each participant's reproductive success. Thus, birds tend to be monogamous, while mammals are likely to be polygynous. Polygamy is generally accompanied by *sexual dimorphism,* a pronounced anatomical difference in the size or bodily structures of the two sexes.

10. The majority of human cultures practice polygyny, and evidence from our own culture suggests that men have a greater desire for sexual variety than do women. These differences may be rooted in our biological nature, or they may be the product of early social training, which in turn is an outgrowth of cultural and economic conditions.

11. In birds and mammals innate factors are important determinants of another bond, that between parents—primarily mothers—and offspring. Parental reactions are elicited, at least in part, by various stimulus releasers produced by the young, such as *distress calls* and the human infant's smile.

12. The key to most animal social behavior is communication by means of displays. Since displays communicate an animal's present motives, they are often described as *expressive movements.* Displays are found in humans as well as animals. The major example is facial expressions.

13. While both display repertories and human language are communication systems, they differ in some important regards. Display systems have a much smaller vocabulary, have no system for rearranging the individual signals to communicate novel ideas, and only convey something about the sender's present intentions. Human languages, in contrast, have a large vocabulary, have some syntactic system for rearranging words to form an infinite number of sentences, and can convey messages on just about anything in the world.

14. Animals, especially monkeys and apes, seem to possess *social cognition.* These animals have a considerable knowledge of the kinship and dominance relations in their

SUMMARY

group and may have some primitive version of a *theory of mind* that allows them to attribute beliefs and desires to others.

15. Some inherited behavior patterns, such as the *alarm calls* of certain birds, seem to be biologically unselfish, since they don't directly contribute to the survival of the individuals or their offspring. The survival value of these behaviors often depends on *kin selection,* for such acts may save a number of relatives who carry the caller's genes. Another mechanism that may lead to biologically unselfish acts is *reciprocal altruism.* Some authors have tried to explain human altruism in similar evolutionary terms, emphasizing the relation between kin selection and *tribalism.* This attempt, like other attempts by evolutionary theorists to interpret human social patterns based on analogies to animal behavior, is controversial.

CHAPTER 11

SOCIAL COGNITION AND EMOTION

I n the preceding chapter, we considered the biological bases of social behavior. Toward that end, we turned to the animal kingdom and examined social interactions among robins and grebes, chimpanzees and vervets. None of these animals lives in total isolation and their interactions tell us something about the biological foundations upon which all social life rests, whether in animals or ourselves. Both animals and humans compete in aggressive encounters, court and mate, and provide for their young. But these similarities aside, enormous differences remain. While the social behavior of animals is relatively rigid and inflexible, that of humans is greatly affected by learning—based on personal experience as well as the experience of previous generations. And our social interactions are vastly more complex than those of any other animal.

In part, this is simply because human social behavior occurs within an elaborate web of cultural patterns. Unlike grebes or vervets, we attend school, vote, buy stock, go to church, and join protest demonstrations. These and countless other actions only make sense because of a whole set of institutions around which most of our social life is organized.

Our distinctive cognitive capabilities are also important, for most of our social interactions depend on how we understand the situation in which they occur. The world we live in is built upon an intricate network of interlocking social cognitions, and it is one in which we take for granted that others have desires and beliefs, and know that they regard us as having desires and beliefs. This cognitive mutuality can become mind-bogglingly complex as in the calculations of a poker player musing about an opponent: "I think that he thinks that I think that he's bluffing." As we've seen, something of that sort also goes on in nonhumans, especially among the primates. But their level of social cognition can't begin to compare to the richness and subtlety of our own. Even a chimp's theory of mind is at best a pale reflection of a human's.

The contrast between human and animal social behavior becomes even clearer when we turn away from primates to other animals, such as birds. Take the herring gull, which pecks at its neighbor when it comes too close. This is sometimes regarded as analogous to our desire for personal space, and in some ways it may be. But the differences between their actions and ours are no less striking than the similarities. Consider personal space on a passenger train. Suppose you are sitting alone and a stranger approaches and sits next to you. Your reaction depends upon your interpretation of her action. Is it an attempt to start a conversation, an unwelcome intrusion, or a flirtation? Or is it simply a response to the fact that all other seats in the car happen to be taken? The point is that humans don't respond to other people's actions automatically; they respond to those actions as they interpret them. The herring gull has no such problems with ambiguity; any other gull that invades its personal space has to be repelled and that is that.★

The purpose of this chapter is to give some sense of the complexity of social cognition in humans. We will organize our account around one of the central questions of modern social psychology: How do individuals interpret social events and how do their interpretations affect their actions?

★ In actual fact, things aren't quite this simple even in birds, for their reactions also depend on various contextual factors (Smith, 1977). But there is no doubt that these modifying factors are much less complex and flexible than they are in humans.

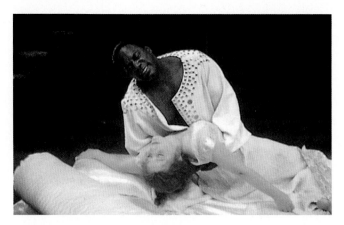

We react to any situation as we understand it to be *The misunderstandings that may occur can form the plot of tragedy as well as comedy. In Shakespeare's* Othello, *the hero strangles his wife because he wrongly believes she committed adultery. In the movie* Tootsie, *the hero disguises himself as a woman with resulting complications in his social relations. (Left: from a production of* Othello *at the 1987 Stratford Festival in Ontario, Canada, with Howard Rollins and Wenna Shaw; photograph by Michael Cooper. Right: from the 1982 film* Tootsie, *with Dustin Hoffman and Jessica Lange; courtesy of Photofest)*

An individual's response to a social situation depends upon what he understands that situation to be. Romeo killed himself in front of Juliet's tomb because he thought that Juliet was dead; had he known that she was only drugged, the play would have had a happy ending. This simple point forms the basis for much of modern social psychology. But many modern social psychologists make an important further assertion: The way we interpret and try to comprehend such social events—that is, the nature of *social cognition*—is in principle no different from the way we interpret and try to comprehend any event whatsoever, whether social or not.

THE INTERPERSONAL NATURE OF BELIEF

Seen in this light, many facets of social psychology are simply an aspect of the psychology of thinking and cognition in general. But over and above this, social cognition has certain features that make it uniquely social. For there is no doubt that much of what we know, we know because of others. The primary medium of this cognitive interdependence is, of course, human language, which allows us to share our discoveries and pass them on to the next generation. As a result, we look at the world not just through our own eyes but also through the eyes of others, and we form our beliefs on the basis of what we've heard them say or what they've written. In fact, our very notion of physical reality is at least in part a matter of mutual agreement. This point was made very dramatically in a classic study performed by Solomon Asch (Asch, 1956).

In Asch's experiment, nine or ten participants were brought together in a laboratory room and shown pairs of cards placed a few feet in front of them. On one card was a black line, say, 8 inches long. On the other card were three lines of varying lengths, say 6¼, 8, and 6¾ inches (Figure 11.1). The participants were asked to make a simple perceptual judgment. They had to indicate which of the three lines on the one card was equal in length to the one line on the other card. The experimenter told them that this procedure was only a minor prelude to another study and so asked them, in the interest of saving time, to indicate their judgments by calling out the appropriate number.

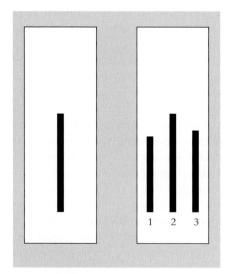

11.1 The stimulus cards in Asch's social pressure experiment *The cards are drawn to scale. (Asch, 1956)*

Solomon E. Asch (1907–1997) *(Courtesy of Swarthmore College)*

The participant in a social pressure experiment *(A) The true participant (center) listens to the instructions. (B) On hearing the unanimous verdict of the others, he leans forward to look at the cards more carefully.*
(C) After twelve such trials, he explains that "he has to call them as he sees them."
(Photographs by William Vandivert)

Considering the sizable differences among the stimuli, the task was absurdly simple, except for one thing: There was actually only one real participant. All of the others were the experimenter's secret confederates, and they had arranged their seating order so that most of them would call out their judgments before the real participant's turn came around.

In the first few trials, these confederates each called out the correct response. But, after these initial trials, the confederates shifted strategy and unanimously rendered *false* judgments on most of the trials thereafter. For example, they might declare that a 6¼-inch line equaled an 8-inch line and likewise for the subsequent trials. What would the real participant do now?

Asch found that the chances were less than one in four that the participant would be fully independent and would stick to her guns on all trials on which the group disagreed with her. Most participants yielded to the group on at least some occasions, in fine disregard of the evidence of their senses—a result with rather uncomfortable implications for the democratic process. When interviewed after the experiment, most of the yielding participants made it clear that the group didn't really affect how they saw the lines. No matter what everyone else said, the 8-inch line still looked longer than the 6¼-inch line. But the participants wondered whether they were right, became worried about their vision and sanity, and were exceedingly embarrassed at expressing their deviance in public (Asch, 1952, 1956; Asch and Gleitman, 1953).

For our present purposes, our primary concern is not so much with what the participants did, but rather with how they felt. In this regard, most of them were alike. Some yielded and some were independent, but assuming they did not suspect a trick (and few of them did), they were generally very much disturbed. Why all the furor? The answer is that Asch's procedure had violated a basic premise of the participants' existence: However people may differ, they all share the same physical reality. Under the circumstances, it is small wonder that the participants in Asch's studies were deeply alarmed by a discrepancy they had never previously encountered. (Needless to say, the whole experiment was carefully explained to them immediately afterward.)

What accounts for the assumption of a socially shared reality? We can only speculate. One possibility is that the notion that others perceive more or less the same world that we do is a built-in facet of the human animal. Another is that this notion is part and parcel of a more general consistency that provides the criterion for what we mean when we say that an object is "real." For example, when something is real, the senses provide consistent information about it. Macbeth sees a dagger but cannot touch it and therefore regards it as "a dagger of the mind, a false creation proceeding from the heat-oppressed brain." Another criterion is consistency across time. Real objects provide what one philosopher called "the permanent possibility of sensation" (J. S. Mill, 1865). You may look away from a tree, but it is still there when your gaze returns to it a moment later. At least in principle, the general notion of a fixed reality that is "out there" and independent of our momentary point of view is a rock-bottom concept that we all accept. If it is

A

B

C

The interpersonal nature of reality *A scene from the 1998 film* The Truman Show, *with Jim Carrey. In this movie, a baby is adopted by a media corporation, is raised by actors, and—unbeknownst to him—has his entire life broadcast on television. (Photograph © Paramount Pictures Corp.; courtesy of the Kobal Collection)*

challenged, we become deeply disturbed. It may be that the definition of reality—perhaps from the very outset—includes not only agreement among different perceptions and memories within one person but also agreement with the perceptions and memories of others. As a result, the belief that others see, feel, and hear pretty much as we do becomes a cognitive axiom of our everyday experience. When this axiom is violated, as it is in Asch's experiment, a vital prop is knocked out from under us, a prop so basic we never even realized it was there.

SOCIAL COMPARISON

The Asch study shows what happens when the clear evidence of one's senses is contradicted by the verdict of a unanimous group. But suppose that our own perception does not provide a clear-cut answer. This will happen,

Social comparison *The two museum visitors don't seem quite sure what to make of Marisol's sculpture* The Family *and compare reactions. (Photograph by Burt Glinn/© 1964 Magnum Photos)*

for example, if the lines differ by only a small amount. If left to our own devices, we will try to obtain some further sensory evidence. We may look at the lines once more but from a different angle or try to measure them with a ruler. But if we can't do that, then it's only reasonable to listen to what others have to say. Their judgments can then be used in lieu of further information provided by our own eyes or hands. If the others now disagree with us, we may well change our own answer on their say-so. Several studies have shown that this is precisely what occurs in an Asch-type experiment in which the discrimination is fairly difficult. There is more yielding and very little emotional disturbance (Crutchfield, 1955; for further discussion of conformity effects, see Chapter 12).

This general line of reasoning may explain why people seek the opinion of others whenever they are confronted by a situation that they do not fully understand. To evaluate the situation, they need more information. If they cannot get it first hand, they will try to compare their own reactions to those of others (Festinger, 1954; Suls and Miller, 1977). The need for such *social comparison* is especially pronounced when the evaluations pertain to social issues, such as the qualifications of a political candidate or the pros and cons of sex education in public schools.

COGNITIVE PROCESSES AND BELIEF

The preceding discussion showed that people try to make sense of the world they encounter. But how? In effect, they do this by looking for some consistency among their own experiences and memories, and then by turning to other people for comparison and confirmation. If everything checks out, then all is well and good. But what if there is some incongruity? The Asch study showed what happens when there is a serious incongruity between one's own experiences (and the beliefs based upon them) and those reported by others. But suppose the incongruity is among one's own experiences, beliefs, or actions. Many social psychologists believe that this will trigger some tendency to restore *cognitive consistency*—to reinterpret the situation so as to minimize whatever inconsistency there may be.

What kinds of mechanisms might explain this general tendency to reinterpret aspects of our experience so that they fit together sensibly? A very influential approach was developed by Leon Festinger, who proposed that any perceived inconsistency among various aspects of knowledge, feelings, and behavior sets up an unpleasant internal state that he called *cognitive dissonance,* which people try to reduce whenever possible (Festinger, 1957).

One of the earliest examples is provided by a study of a religious sect that was awaiting the end of the world. The founder of the sect announced that she had

received a message from the "Guardians" from outer space. On a certain day, there would be an enormous flood. Only the true believers would be saved, and they would be picked up at midnight of the appointed day in flying saucers. (Technology has advanced considerably since the days of Noah's ark.) On doomsday, the members of the sect huddled together, awaiting the predicted cataclysm. The arrival time of the flying saucers came and went; tension mounted. Finally, the leader of the sect received another message: To reward the faithful, the world was saved. Joy broke out, and the believers became more faithful than ever (Festinger, Riecken, and Schachter, 1956).

Given the failure of the clear-cut prophecy, one might have expected the very opposite. A disconfirmation of a predicted event should presumably lead one to abandon the beliefs that produced the prediction. But cognitive dissonance theory says otherwise. By abandoning the belief that there are Guardians, the person who had once held this belief would have to accept a painful dissonance between his present skepticism and his past beliefs and actions. His prior faith would now appear extremely foolish. Some members of the sect went to such lengths as giving up their jobs or spending their savings; such acts would lose all meaning in retrospect without the belief in the Guardians. Under the circumstances, the dissonance was intolerable. It was reduced by a belief in the new message, which bolstered the original belief. Since other members of the sect stood fast along with them, their conviction was strengthened all the more. They could now think of themselves not as fools, but as loyal, steadfast members of a courageous little band whose faith had saved the Earth.

ATTITUDES

Many social beliefs are accompanied by strong feelings. Take the conviction that abortion is murder—one wholly different from the many beliefs we hold that are completely unencumbered by emotion, such as our nonchalant assurance that the sum of the angles of a triangle is 180 degrees. Emotionally tinged social views of the former kind are generally called **attitudes.** Since various people often have different attitudes, they tend to interpret many social situations differently; the same crowd may look like a group of peaceful demonstrators to one observer and a rioting mob to another.

Attitudes   *Attitudes are a combination of beliefs, feelings, and evaluations, coupled with some predisposition to act accordingly. (Left: photograph by Sylvia Johnson/Woodfin Camp, 1989. Right: photograph by Susan McElhinney, 1980/Woodfin Camp)*

As modern social psychologists use the term, an attitude is a rather stable set of mental views and assessments about some idea, object, or person (Eagly and Chaiken, 1993). Examples are attitudes toward nuclear power, abortion, the legalization of marijuana, bilingual education, or bottle-feeding infants. Every attitude is a combination of beliefs, feelings, and evaluations and some predisposition to act accordingly. Thus, people who differ in their attitudes toward nuclear power will probably have different beliefs on the subject (e.g., nuclear power plants are—or are not—unsafe) and will evaluate the topic differently (from extreme pro to extreme con); these differences will also make them more likely to take some actions rather than others (e.g., to support or to protest the construction of a new nuclear power plant).

ATTITUDES AND BEHAVIOR

Attitudes can be measured in a number of ways. The most widely used methods involve some form of self-report. For example, participants might be given an **attitude questionnaire** with items that relate to the matter at hand. Thus, in a questionnaire on nuclear power and related issues, participants might be given a statement such as: "Accidental explosions in nuclear plants pose some danger, but this risk is relatively small compared to the economic and social benefits of cheap and abundant energy." They would then be asked to select a number between, say, +10 and −10 to indicate the extent of their agreement or disagreement. The sum of a person's responses to a number of statements that all tap the same concerns will then provide a quantitative expression of that person's attitude. (For some complications associated with this means of assessing attitudes, see Cacioppo and Berntson, 1994; Thompson et al., 1995.)

Our definition of *attitude* included a predisposition to act in accordance with our beliefs, feelings, and evaluations. So attitudes as measured by self-report seem as if they should predict what people will actually do. Do they? This question has led to controversy, for some early reports suggested that the relationship is much weaker than one might think. During the 1930s when there was considerable prejudice against Asians, Richard LaPiere traveled throughout the United States with a Chinese couple and stopped at over fifty hotels and motels and at nearly two hundred restaurants. All but one hotel gave them accommodations, and no restaurant refused them service. Later on, the very same establishments received a letter that asked whether they would house or serve Chinese persons. Ninety-two percent of the replies were "No" (LaPiere, 1934). It appeared that there was a major inconsistency between people's attitudes as verbally expressed and their actual behavior.

The results of this and related studies led some social psychologists to doubt whether the attitude concept is particularly useful. If attitudes don't predict behavior, what is the point of studying them in the first place (Wicker, 1969)? But upon further analysis, this pessimism proved unwarranted. Later studies showed that under many circumstances attitudes do indeed predict what people will do. Thus, voter preferences as expressed in preelection interviews are a pretty good predictor of later behavior in the voting booth: In one study, 85 percent of the people interviewed voted in line with their previously expressed preference. For the most part, those who shifted had initial preferences that were rather weak (Kelley and Mirer, 1974).

It appears that attitudes often do predict behavior. But if so, how can we explain the fact that they don't always do so? One possible factor concerns situational pressures. Thus, just about everybody stops at a red light, regardless of whether they are bold or shy; and just about everybody is solemn at a funeral,

A

B

Attempts at persuasive communication
Two advertising messages that try to change consumer attitudes toward various products. The advertisement in (A) links love with an expensive gift. (Courtesy of DeBeers) The ad in (B) asserts that a certain bread will appeal to any ethnic group. (Best Foods Baking Group)

regardless of whether they are sociable or withdrawn (see Chapter 16 for further discussion). In these cases, it is the situation, and not someone's character, that determines behavior. The same also holds for attitudes—these too can be overruled by situational pressures. LaPiere's Chinese couple consisted of two young students who were attractive and well-groomed and who were accompanied by a Caucasian professor. Here, the situational pressures probably made refusal difficult and embarrassing.

An even more important factor is how specifically the attitude is defined. The less specific one's definition, the less likely it is to predict a particular bit of behavior. One study analyzed the relation between general attitudes toward environmentalism and a particular act: volunteering for various activities of the Sierra Club. The investigators found no relation. But when they tested the specific attitude toward the Sierra Club as such, they found a substantial correlation between attitude and action; those who had stated strongly positive views toward the club were much more likely to volunteer (Weigel, Vernon, and Tognacci, 1974). In a similar vein are the results of a study on women's attitudes toward birth control. Positive attitudes toward birth control in general showed only a negligible correlation with the use of oral contraceptives during a two-year period. But attitudes toward using birth control pills in particular correlated quite well with their actual use during this period (Davidson and Jaccard, 1979).

Also important is the *strength* of the attitude: Is this an issue the person feels strongly about or not? As expected, people are more likely to behave in a fashion consistent with their strong attitudes than with their weak ones (Bassili, 1993, 1995; Kraus, 1995).

ATTITUDE CHANGE

In modern society, many of our attitudes and beliefs are under continual assault. Hundreds of commercials urge us to buy one product rather than another, political candidates clamor for our vote, and any number of organizations exhort us to fight for or against gun control, or legalized abortion, or environmental protection, and so on. When we add these mass-market appeals to the numerous private attempts at persuasion undertaken by our friends and relatives (let alone our dating partners), it is hardly surprising that attitudes sometimes do change. Social psychologists have spent a great deal of effort trying to understand how such attitudinal changes come about.

PERSUASIVE COMMUNICATIONS

A number of investigators have studied the effectiveness of **persuasive communications.** These are messages that openly try to convince us to stop smoking, to outlaw abortion, to favor capital punishment, or—on a humbler level—to choose one brand of toothpaste over another. Among the factors that determine whether a given message has its desired effect are—not surprisingly—the person who sends the message and the message itself (Cialdini, Petty, and Cacioppo, 1981; McGuire, 1985).

The message source One factor that determines whether someone will change your mind on a given issue is who that someone is. To begin with, there is the element of *credibility.* Naturally, communications have more of an effect if they are attributed to someone who is an acknowledged expert than to someone who is not. Thus, a recommendation that antihistamines should be sold over the counter was more effective when ascribed to the *New England Journal of Medicine* than to a popular mass circulation magazine; a positive review of an obscure modern poem was more likely to lead to upward reevaluations of that poem if the review was attributed to T. S. Eliot rather than to another student (Hovland and Weiss, 1952; Aronson, Turner, and Carlsmith, 1963).

Credibility is important, but so is *trustworthiness*. For the would-be persuader will have a much harder time if we believe that she has something to gain from persuading us. A number of studies have shown that communicators are more effective when they argue for a position that seems to be against their own self-interest. In one study, students were shown statements that argued either for or against the strengthening of law enforcement agencies; the statements were attributed either to a prosecuting attorney or to a criminal. Statements in favor of stronger law enforcement had more effect when they were thought to be made by the criminal rather than by the prosecutor; the reverse was true for statements in favor of weaker law enforcement (Walster, Aronson, and Abrahams, 1966). When a used-car salesman tells you not to buy a car from his lot, you are likely to believe him. (Unless you believe that the other lot he recommends belongs to his brother-in-law.)

The message However important the messenger, the message she delivers is more important. What are the factors that determine whether the message will change attitudes? According to Petty and Cacioppo there are two routes to persuasion. One is what they call the **central route to persuasion** in which we follow the message with some care and mentally elaborate its arguments with yet further arguments and counterarguments of our own. We take this route if the issue is one that matters to us and if we're not diverted by other concerns. Here, content and information are what matter, and strong arguments will indeed be more effective in changing our minds than weak ones. But the situation is quite different if the message comes by way of what Petty and Cacioppo call the **peripheral route to persuasion.** We'll be induced to take this route if we don't care much about the issue, or if the message isn't clearly heard because of background noise, or if we are otherwise distracted. In such circumstances, content and arguments matter little. What counts instead is how or by whom or in what surroundings the message is presented (Petty and Cacioppo, 1985; Petty et al., 1997; for a closely related view, see Chaiken et al., 1989; Eagly and Chaiken, 1993). Similarly, we might be more inclined to be persuaded by the good looks of an attractive spokesperson if we're not paying much attention to the content of the message itself (Shavitt et al., 1994).

The central route to persuasion involves reasoned thought. But just what is the peripheral route? According to some authors, it often represents a kind of mental shortcut. After all, there are only so many things we can pay attention to, and so we use some rules of thumb, or **heuristics,** to help us decide whether to accept or reject the message (Eagly and Chaiken, 1984; Chaiken, 1987). Such heuristics may include some reliance on the nature of the speaker (e.g., his apparent expertise, or likability, or good looks) and also some features of the arguments being presented, such as their sheer length or number, regardless of how good they are. Such heuristics in reacting to persuasive communications are reminiscent of heuristics in decision making; both are mental shortcuts we resort to because our cognitive capacity is limited (see Chapter 8 for a further discussion of heuristics).

In addition to heuristics, the peripheral route to persuasion may also involve other mechanisms. For example, some authors have suggested that processes akin to classical conditioning are sometimes involved, such that a message or product becomes associated in the minds of the audience with some other object or outcome (see Chapter 4; Cacioppo et al., 1993). In other cases, persuasion may involve priming effects that stimulate implicit memories as described in Chapter 7 (Greenwald and Banaji, 1995).

Another attempt to persuade *An American advertisement from around 1900. (Frontispiece from* The Wonderful World of American Advertising, 1865–1900 *by Leonard de Vries and Ilonka van Amstel, Chicago: Follett, 1972)*

Justification of effort *Newly accepted members of a group tend to value their group membership even more if their initiation was especially harsh, as in the case of soldiers who have gone through boot camp. (Courtesy of the U.S. Army)*

COGNITIVE DISSONANCE AND ATTITUDE CHANGE

We've already seen that attitudes can affect behavior. But the relation can also go the other way. In some situations, what an individual does will lead to a change in her attitudes. According to some social psychologists, this effect is produced by a tendency to reduce cognitive dissonance analogous to that which we've considered in the context of a change in beliefs. Suppose there is some inconsistency between a person's attitudes and her behavior. How can she reconcile the inconsistency? She can't change her behavior, for that's done and gone. All she can do is adjust her present attitude.

Justification of effort An illustration of this kind of readjustment comes from retrospective explanations of prior efforts. People often make considerable sacrifices to attain a goal—backbreaking exertion to scale a mountain, years and years of study to become a cardiologist. Was it worth it? According to dissonance theory, the goal will be esteemed more highly the harder it was to attain. If it were not, there would be cognitive dissonance. Support comes from common observation of the effects of harsh initiation rites, such as fraternity hazing. After the ordeal is passed, the initiates seem to value their newfound membership all the more. Similar effects have been obtained in the laboratory. Participants admitted to a discussion group after going through an unpleasant screening test put a higher value on their new membership than participants who did not undergo such a screening (Aronson and Mills, 1959; Gerard and Mathewson, 1966).

Forced compliance A related result is the effect of ***forced compliance.**★ The basic idea is simple. Suppose someone agrees to give a speech in support of a view that is contrary to his own position, as in the case of a bartender arguing for prohibition. Will his public act change his private views? The answer seems to depend on why he agreed to make the speech in the first place. If he was bribed with a large sum, there will be little effect. As he looks back upon his public denunciation of alcohol, he knows why he did what he did—$1,000 in cold cash is justification enough. But suppose he gave the speech with lesser urging and received only a trifling sum. If we later ask what he thinks about prohibition, we will find that he has begun to believe his own speech. According to Festinger, the reason is the need to reduce cognitive dissonance. If the bartender asks himself why he took a public stand so contrary to his own attitudes, he can find no adequate justification; the few dollars he received are not enough. To reduce the dissonance, the compliant bartender does the only thing he can: He decides that what he said wasn't really all that different from what he believes.

A number of studies have demonstrated such forced compliance in the laboratory. In a classic experiment, participants were asked to perform several extremely boring tasks, such as packing spools into a tray and then unpacking them, and turning one screw after another for a quarter turn. When they were finished, they were induced to tell the next participant that the tasks were really very interesting. They were paid either $1 or $20 for lying in this way. When later asked how enjoyable they had found the tasks, the well-paid participants said that they were boring, while the poorly paid participants said that they were fairly interesting. This result is rather remarkable. One might have guessed that the well-paid liar would have been more persuaded by his own arguments

★ The term *forced compliance* was coined to describe the phenomenon when it was first demonstrated experimentally (Festinger and Carlsmith, 1959). It is a bit of a misnomer, however, since the participant is not really forced to lie about his attitudes but is instead persuaded or coaxed. Modern social psychologists prefer the more accurate—if clumsier—designation *counterattitudinal advocacy.*

than the poorly paid one. But contrary to this initial intuition—and in line with dissonance theory—the exact opposite was the case (Festinger and Carlsmith, 1959). A number of other studies have performed variants on the original experiment with essentially the same results (e.g., Rosenfeld, Giacalone, and Tedeschi, 1984; for a discussion of why some individuals are more likely than others to show these effects, see Cialdini et al., 1995).

DISSONANCE RECONSIDERED

The reevaluation of prior decisions and the effect of forced compliance seem to be ways of reducing dissonance. But just what is the dissonance that is being reduced? One might regard dissonance as essentially equivalent to a logical inconsistency, like the inconsistency between the belief that the Earth revolves around the Sun and the belief that the Earth is at the center of the solar system. There is little doubt that cognitions are often adjusted to become consistent in just this sense. A person who hears the mumbled sentence "The woman shaved himself" is likely to hear it as "The man shaved himself" or "The woman shaved herself," so that noun and pronoun agree. The question is whether all cases of dissonance reduction boil down to an analogous tendency to keep cognitions logically consistent. The answer seems to be no, for the evidence suggests that dissonance reduction is not always a cognitive matter. A number of studies indicate that we often try to reduce the dissonance between our acts and beliefs for more emotional reasons. One such factor is an effort to maintain a ***favorable self-picture*** (Aronson, 1969; Steele and Liu, 1983; Cooper and Fazio, 1984; Elliot and Devine, 1994).

Consider the retrospective reevaluation of whether some achievement was worth its cost. People who have made a great sacrifice to attain some goal will value it more than those who achieved the goal with little effort. One hypothesis is that this dissonance reduction is produced by a tendency toward logical consistency—the worth of the goal has to match its cost, just as the noun must fit its pronoun. But there is a noncognitive reason that is just as plausible. An individual who goes through a difficult initiation rite to join a club and later discovers that the club is rather dull might well feel like a fool. To maintain a favorable self-picture, she adjusts her attitude to fit her own acts and overvalues her group membership.

Similar considerations apply to the effect of forced compliance. Someone who has argued for a position he doesn't hold will change his attitude to fit his arguments (assuming he wasn't paid too much for presenting them). One interpretation of this effect is that it was an attempt to reduce a cognitive inconsistency. But the critical factor may have been emotional—a sense of guilt at having persuaded someone to spend an unpleasant hour at a boring task. If we can manage to change our own views just a bit (which is easier if we weren't paid too much for lying), we may salve our conscience. This guilt (and the consequent need to assuage it) will only arise, however, if we believe that our arguments convinced the poor fellow we lied to. And this guilt is likely to be much less if we don't much like that fellow; if so, we might well think that he had it coming. In one study, these predictions were upheld. There was no change of attitude (that is, no dissonance reduction) unless the participant believed that he had managed to convince the person he had lied to and did not dislike him (Cooper, Zanna, and Goethals, 1974).*

---

* Seen in this light, dissonance reduction may be essentially equivalent to what Sigmund Freud called *rationalization* (see Chapter 17).

451

Attitude stability   Attitudes are generally resistant to change. One reason is that people typically stay in the same social environment, keeping company with others whose views of the world are essentially the same. (Photographs from left to right by Paul Fusco/Magnum Photos, Inc.; Rex Features; James Foote/Photo Researchers Inc.)

ATTITUDE STABILITY

We've seen that attitudes can be changed by certain forms of persuasion (if the source is credible and trustworthy and if the message is appropriate) and by tendencies toward cognitive consistency (especially with regard to acts we've already performed). But on balance, the overall picture is one of attitude stability rather than of attitude change. Attitudes can be altered, but it takes some doing. By and large, there seems to be a tendency to hold on to the attitudes one already has.

Why should this be so? One reason for attitude stability is that people generally stay in the same social and economic environment. Their families, their friends and fellow workers, their social and economic situations tend to remain much the same over the years. Top-level executives know other top executives, and trade union members know other union members. On any one day, they may read or hear a speech that advocates a position contrary to their own, and they may even be affected by it. But on that evening and the day after, they will be back in the same old setting and will encounter the same old views that they held before. Under the circumstances, it is hardly surprising that attitude stability is more common than attitude change. To be sure, there are striking events that may transform our attitudes completely—not just our own, but also those of everyone around us. An example is the news of the sneak attack on Pearl Harbor on December 7, 1941. Without a doubt, this led to an instant and radical change in Americans' attitudes toward Japan. But by their very nature, such events—and the extreme changes in attitudes they produce—are rare.

Radical attitude change produced by striking events   Occasionally a rare and momentous event changes attitudes. An example is the opening of the Berlin Wall in the winter of 1989, which signaled the end of the Cold War. (Photograph by Michael Probst, UPI/Bettman Newsphotos)

PERCEIVING OTHERS

Thus far our discussion of how people interpret the social world has focused on the ways they try to harmonize various events with their beliefs and attitudes. A similar approach has been applied to find out how we form impressions of other people and how we try to understand why they do what they do.

FORMING IMPRESSIONS

In the course of ordinary life we encounter many other people. The vast majority of them play the role of anonymous extras in each of our private dramas, especially in big cities where we briefly cross the paths of countless strangers about whom we will know nothing. But a sizable number of other people do impinge upon us, as bit players (a traffic cop we ask for directions), supporting cast (a casual acquaintance), and costars (friends, lovers, bosses, enemies). These we cannot help but evaluate and try to understand, as they, in their turn, evaluate and try to understand us. Much of the plot of our own dramas (and of theirs) depends upon the outcome of these mutual social attempts at understanding. How are they achieved?

Perceiving the characteristics of another person is in some ways analogous to perceiving certain stable attributes of a physical object, such as its shape or size. In our previous discussion of visual perception, we saw that to do this the observer must abstract the crucial relationships within the stimulus input so that she can see the form of the object—say, a catlike shape (see Chapter 6). She must also disregard various transient aspects of the situation, such as illumination, distance, and angle of regard, in order to perceive the stable characteristics of the object—its reflectance, size, and shape. By doing all this, the observer attains perceptual constancy and can answer such life-and-death questions as whether she is dealing with a kitten nearby or a tiger far away.

Something analogous occurs when we perceive—or more accurately, *infer*—such attributes of a person as his violent temper or warmth. In effect, we are making a judgment as to what the person is "really" like, a judgment that is some steps removed from the particulars of this moment and this occasion. Thus, the personal attributes (often called **traits**) that we infer are assumed to be invariant properties that will characterize the individual's behavior in a range of different situations. If we decide, for example, that a person is irascible, we don't mean that he will appear angry every time we meet him, nor that he will utter an impolite expletive when someone deliberately steps on his toe. Instead, we mean that he will generally be short-tempered over a wide range of circumstances. To put it another way, the attempt to understand what another person is like boils down to an effort to note the *consistencies* in what he does over time and under different circumstances (see Chapter 16). The question, then, is how this consistency is abstracted from the few bits of behavior of the other person that we can actually observe.

IMPRESSIONS OF OTHERS AS PATTERNS

Several theorists assume that the processes we use to try to understand another person are in many ways analogous to the ways we perceive the various attributes of physical objects. Consider visual form. This is a perceptual whole that depends upon the relation among the elements of which the form is composed; thus, a triangle can be composed of dots or crosses and still be perceived as the same triangle (see Chapter 6). According to Solomon Asch, a similar principle describes our conceptions of other people. In his view, these conceptions of others are not a simple aggregate of the attributes we perceive them to have. Instead, they form an organized whole whose elements are interpreted in relation to the overall pattern (Asch, 1952).

CENTRAL TRAITS

To test his hypothesis, Asch performed several studies of how people form impressions of others. His gave participants a list of attributes that they were told described a single person. Their task was to write a short sketch of the person so characterized and to rate this person on a checklist of antonyms (generous versus ungenerous, good natured versus irritable). In one study, some participants were given a list of seven traits: *intelligent, skillful, industrious, warm, determined, practical, cautious.* Other participants received the same list except that *cold* was substituted for *warm.* The resulting sketches were quite different. The warm person was seen as "driven by the desire to accomplish something that would be of benefit," while the cold person was described as "snobbish, . . . calculating and unsympathetic." The checklist results were in the same direction. The warm person was seen as generous, happy, and good-natured. The cold person was characterized by the appropriate antonyms (Asch, 1946).

According to Asch, the warm/cold trait acted as a focus around which the total impression of the person was organized. To use his term, it was a **central trait** that determined the perception of the whole. Other traits seemed to be of lesser importance. For example, it made little difference whether the list of traits included *polite* or *blunt.*★

FIRST IMPRESSIONS

New items of information are often incorporated into patterns of organization that are already there. A familiar example is the effect of *mental set.* If someone expects to be shown the name of an animal, then a brief presentation of D_CK will be perceived as DUCK rather than as DOCK (see Chapters 6 and 8). Our everyday experience suggests that a similar phenomenon occurs in person perception. Our first impression of someone often determines how we interpret what we find out about her later on.

This point has been illustrated by Asch in another version of his experiment with personal trait lists. One group of participants was told to describe their impressions of a person who is intelligent, industrious, impulsive, critical, stubborn, and envious. Another group of participants received the exact same list, but in the reverse order (that is, envious, stubborn . . . and so on). The results indicate that it pays to put one's best foot forward. If the list began on a positive note, it set up a favorable evaluative tone that seemed to override the later negative attributes; the opposite effect occurred when the unfavorable traits came first (Asch, 1946). According to Asch, the later attributes in the list take on different shades of meaning depending upon the context provided by the traits encountered earlier in the sequence. While similar **primacy effects** have been obtained by many other investigators (e.g., Luchins, 1957; Anderson, 1965), their interpretation is still a matter of debate (see Ostrom, 1977; Schneider, Hastorf, and Ellsworth, 1979).

Primacy effects can be considerable, but they can be overcome. We sometimes do change our minds and come to respect or even love a person whom we detested on first meeting. The primacy effect only means that such alterations in judgment encounter a certain inertia. In old Hollywood movies, the fact that the hero and heroine took an instant dislike to each other was a tip-off to the audience that they would clinch by the final frame. But in real life, first impressions generally make more of a difference. If nothing else, they often preclude the chance of a later reevaluation.

First impressions *First impressions can be overcome, especially on screen and stage. A famous example is Shakespeare's* Much Ado about Nothing, *whose Beatrice and Benedick begin the play by bickering with each other and end it in each other's arms. (From the 1993 film directed by Kenneth Branagh, with Emma Thompson and Kenneth Branagh; photograph by Clive Coote)*

★ The question of why and when some traits are central and others not has received considerable attention. According to Julius Wishner, the effect is partially dependent on the observer's beliefs about which traits go with others (Wishner, 1960; Schneider, 1973).

IMPRESSIONS OF OTHERS AS COGNITIVE CONSTRUCTIONS

Asch tried to understand impression formation by an analogy to theories of perceptual patterning. A number of more recent authors have championed a view that is in many ways like Asch's approach, but they appeal to concepts derived from modern theories of memory and thinking rather than from principles of visual perception. In their view, our impressions of others are cognitive constructions based on various *schemas*—sets of organized expectations about the way different behaviors hang together. If we believe that someone is outgoing and gregarious, we will also expect him to be relatively talkative. He may or may not be, but the pattern we perceive is partially imposed by our schema of what an outgoing and gregarious person is like. Such schemas about persons are sometimes called *implicit theories of personality* (Bruner and Tagiuri, 1954; Schneider, 1973).

A demonstration of how such cognitive constructions operate used participants who read several lists of attributes. One described a person said to be an extrovert, another a person who was an introvert. On a later recognition test, participants falsely recognized adjectives that had not been on the original list if they fit with the appropriate label. Thus, terms such as *spirited* and *boisterous* that had not been presented previously were misremembered as being part of the original list that described the extrovert; terms such as *shy* and *reserved* were falsely remembered as part of the list that described the introvert (Cantor and Mischel, 1979).

Phenomena of this kind suggest that the processes of social cognition, that is, the ways we gain knowledge of social events, are much like those of cognition in general. Suppose we briefly looked into a tool chest and were then shown a set of objects and asked which of them we had seen. We'd surely be more likely to misremember having seen a hammer than a baby bottle, assuming neither was actually in the chest (see Chapter 7). Our cognitive schema of a tool chest includes a hammer, just as our schema of an extrovert includes the attribute *boisterous*.

THE PROS AND CONS OF TAKING MENTAL SHORTCUTS

Cognitive constructions such as schemas are mental shortcuts that confer obvious benefits. They allow us to circumvent our limited cognitive capacity so that we can cope with a complex world in which there is so much more to see, remember, and think about than we could possibly manage.

What holds for cognition in general also holds for social cognition. We are often forced to make judgments about people, but we rarely have the luxury of assembling all the necessary information that would allow us to make a sure and reasoned decision. As a result, we fill in the gaps by referring to broad schemas. Without such schemas, we would be unable to make any sense of our social world at all. Suppose we hear a man and a woman shout at one another but are too far away from them to make out what they're saying. If we know that the two are in the middle of a rocky love affair, we refer to our lover's quarrel schema and make one interpretation. If we know that the man is the woman's landlord and that she has refused to pay her rent because he hasn't fixed the faulty plumbing, we refer to our stingy landlord schema and make another interpretation.

Group stereotypes and illusory correlation Given our limited cognitive capacity, schematic thinking provides us with a valuable mental tool that ordinarily works reasonably well. But the uncritical use of this tool can lead to errors with serious social consequences. This is particularly clear in the case of social

455

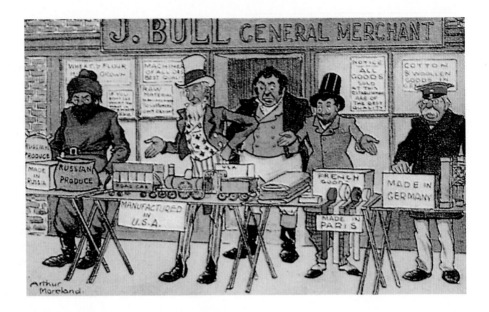

Stereotypes *A British poster circa 1900, protesting competition from foreign goods on the home market in a cartoon featuring national stereotypes.*

stereotypes, when schemas are simplified and applied to whole groups. Such stereotypes are categories we use to simplify the complex world we live in, so that we talk about Greeks, Jews, or African Americans (or student radicals, upwardly mobile yuppies, or little old ladies in tennis shoes) as if they were all alike.

The schema approach cannot explain how particular stereotypes come about, but it has some suggestions for how they are perpetuated. One possible factor is ***illusory correlation.*** Many characteristics of the world are correlated—clouds and rainfall, accidents and sirens, and so on; they go together more often than would occur by chance alone. But some of the correlations we perceive are illusory, a creation of our minds rather than a real relationship in the world outside. Such illusory correlations come about because certain co-occurrences are more readily noted and remembered than are others. One reason may be because they are the ones that are expected. Let's assume that we hold the stereotyped view that the English are reserved. Suppose we now meet two English women: Ms. Parker, who is reserved, and Ms. Brown, who is outgoing and boisterous. Other things being equal, we are more likely to recall that Ms. Parker is English than that Ms. Brown is, for Ms. Parker fits our schema while Ms. Brown doesn't. As a result, we may continue to see a correlation where actually there is none (or overestimate a correlation that is in fact quite low).

Some evidence for this idea comes from a study in which participants were presented with statements that described members of different occupational groups, for example, "Doug, an accountant, is timid and thoughtful" or "Nancy, a waitress, is busy and talkative." Some of the characteristics were judged to fit the stereotype (e.g., accountant-perfectionist; flight attendant-attractive; salesman-enthusiastic), while others did not. But the sentences were so constructed that each occupation was systematically paired with each kind of adjective, so that in fact no correlation was encountered. The participants were later asked to estimate how often each adjective described each occupational group in the sentences they had just read. Their estimates indicated that they believed that accountants were more often described as timid than were waitresses, flight attendants more often as attractive than librarians, and so on—a good example of an illusory correlation, suggesting how stereotypes can be maintained even in the face of contradictory evidence (Hamilton and Rose, 1980).

Group stereotypes and in-group favoritism Although illusory correlation can account for some group stereotypes, it has trouble accounting for why the stereotypes are so often derogatory (Sabini, 1995). One clue may lie in our tendency to look more positively on *our* group, the **in-group,** with the others, the **out-groups,** suffering by comparison. This favoritism seems to be in large part inadvertent. This was shown in a study in which participants were repeatedly exposed to pairings of pronouns with nonsense syllables. Some of the pronouns were self-referential (*we, us,* or *ours*) while the remainder referred to others (*they, them, theirs*). Participants were then asked to rate the pleasantness of each nonsense syllable. Those syllables that had been paired with the self-referential pronouns were rated more pleasant (Perdue et al., 1990). Numerous other findings show that we quickly endorse and remember positive information about our own group and negative information about other groups, especially if that information matches preexisting group stereotypes (Fiske, 1998). (We discuss a related phenomenon, our *self-serving bias,* in a later section.)

"They're all alike"   Much stereotyping also relies on what's called the **out-group homogeneity effect,** which describes how we perceive "us" (the in-group) versus "them" (the out-group). Take the assertions "All Jews are alike" or "All Gentiles are alike." The first is almost invariably made by a Gentile, the second by a Jew. The same holds for assertions such as "All women are alike," "All men are alike," "All blacks are alike," and "All whites are alike." Members of a group tend to see members of other groups as more alike than members of their own.

While the out-group homogeneity effect is only too well known in the real social world, it can also be created in the laboratory. In one demonstration, participants from two New Jersey universities (Rutgers and Princeton) watched a videotape of a student who was waiting in an anteroom before participating in an experiment. The video showed him as he made a rather humdrum choice: to remain alone while waiting or to join a group of other students who were also waiting their turn. The participants' task was to guess how many other students would choose similarly (Quattrone and Jones, 1980).

Here was the trick: Some of the participants from Rutgers were told that the student on the tape came from Princeton, while the rest were told that he, like they, was from Rutgers (and similarly for Princetonians). The results were clear. If, say, the Rutgers students believed that the student on the tape was also from Rutgers, they didn't consider the videotaped choice at all representative—they thought that their fellow Rutgers students would make each choice about 50 percent of the time. On the other hand, if those same Rutgers students thought the student on the tape was from Princeton, then they concluded that whatever decision he made was more likely to characterize Princetonians as a whole. The equivalent result—students at Rutgers are alike, but those from Princeton differ—was found for Princetonians.

IMPRESSION MANAGEMENT

Thus far, we have talked about impression formation as it appears from the perspective of the person who tries to form that impression. We've seen that this process of impression formation is in some ways analogous to the perception of the physical environment, where we try to abstract some intrinsic attributes of a distal object from the abundance of potentially distorting proximal stimulus features in which it appears.

But these analogies can be pushed too far, for social perception is a more complex phenomenon. It is a two-way process in which all participants are potential stimuli as well as observers, the seen as well as the seeing. And most important, each participant knows this and knows that the others know it too. As a result, perceiving people is very different from perceiving a physical object like a rock. In perceiving people, we must be flexible enough to go beyond our ready-made conceptions or first impressions. A rock doesn't know that we are

"I have the impression that they're not very substantial people." (© *The New Yorker Collection 1939, 1967 Chas. Addams from Cartoonbank.com. All rights reserved.)*

looking at it, and it surely isn't trying to make a particular impression. But people often are.

People are constantly working at ***impression management***, a term coined by the sociologist Erving Goffman (Goffman, 1959; see also Schlenker, 1980). As Goffman saw it, much of social interaction is like a theatrical performance in which the actors are "putting on a front." Some "play hard to get," others wear elaborately contrived "casual looks," still others try to appear "above it all." Many of these impressions go along with social or professional roles. The medical student soon discovers that there is more to becoming a doctor than acquiring certain skills. He must also learn how to instill confidence, must develop a proper bedside manner. The audience for whom such productions are staged often includes the actors themselves. The would-be healer gradually comes to believe his own role, as one patient after another greets him as "Doctor" and treats his pronouncements with solemn reverence.

Goffman pointed out that many of these social performances are jointly produced. To begin with, the actor is often supported by a team. The doctor's image is maintained not only by her own behavior but by that of various aides, nurses, and patients as well. Further support comes from the audience itself. We often go to considerable lengths to preserve another person's self-presentation, to allow her to "save face." If we want to break off an encounter at a party, we pretend that we are going to the bar for another drink. The other person may very well know that we have no intention of returning, and we may know that she knows, but this doesn't matter. Both participants tactfully play along. This kind of tact can reach consummate heights as in the case of the legendary English butler who accidentally surprised a lady in her bath and hurriedly mumbled, "I beg your pardon, Sir."

In addition, we all have a repertoire of social maneuvers that we employ in order to put ourselves in the best possible light (Leary and Kowalski, 1990; Schlenker and Weigold, 1992). Many of these maneuvers provide cover for us, protecting us if we run into an awkward situation. For example, participants in one study were asked to present material that was likely to be offensive to their audience (e.g., an argument opposing affirmative action, delivered to an African American). These participants insulated themselves from this potential awkwardness by employing a number of distancing behaviors, including verbal disclaimers and a number of nonverbal displays—rolling their eyes to express sarcasm or grimacing to convey disgust (Fleming and Rudman, 1993).

Similarly, if we *anticipate* an upcoming failure or embarrassment, we often take steps to protect ourselves in advance. One such strategy is known as ***self-handicapping,*** in which one arranges for a visible and nonthreatening obstacle to one's own performance. This way, if failure occurs, it will be attributed to the obstacle and not one's own limitations (Jones and Berglas, 1978; Higgins et al., 1990). Thus, if Sam is afraid of failing next week's biology exam, he might spend more time than usual watching television. Then, if he fails the exam, it will look like he didn't study hard enough rather than that he's stupid.

EMBARRASSMENT

In obvious ways, the maneuvers we have just described are attempts at avoiding embarrassment. But what exactly are the conditions that produce this unpleasant experience? They prove to be complex and varied (Miller, 1996). One factor may be a public failure, a loss of esteem in the eyes of others that produces a loss of esteem in our own eyes (Modigliani, 1971). But that can't be the whole story. First, we can become embarrassed without a loss of esteem, as when our friends ask the waiters to sing "Happy Birthday" to us in a crowded restaurant. Second, we are sometimes embarrassed even when our own self-picture is not involved. An example is ***empathetic embarrassment,*** becoming embarrassed for another person (see Miller, 1987). This might happen when we see a friend in an amateur theatrical performance who suddenly can't remember her lines and stands frozen on the stage for what seems an eternity. Of course, she is horribly embarrassed; truth be known, she wants to sink through the floor. But the fact is that we are also embarrassed and that we, too, want to sink through the floor.

How can we explain the experience of embarrassment? According to one account, it is partially caused by the disruption of a social interaction that no one knows how to repair (Parrott, Sabini, and Silver, 1988). As Goffman points out, all social intercourse is based on various prescribed scripts that provide a general frame within which each participant plays his part. If that script is completely disrupted—as for example, when an actor forgets his lines and can't ad lib—the performance comes to a sudden stop. It's this awkward, "what do we do next?" disruption that leads to embarrassment.

Suppose Joe asks Mary for a date and she declines. If she answers with a flat no, then their interaction has run into an abrupt dead-end; Joe has few options for continuing the conversation gracefully. As a result, he will be embarrassed. He'll be much less embarrassed if she says, "I'd love to go out with you, but I'm afraid I'm involved with someone else." Even if Joe knows that this excuse is untrue, he can at least say, "Okay, well thanks anyway," or "I'm sorry, I didn't know." In this case, the social interaction can still proceed, and Joe can withdraw with a modicum of grace. The show must go on, both on stage and in life, for it's too embarrassing if it does not.

ATTRIBUTION

As we previously noted, the attempt to understand what another person is like is really an attempt to find the pattern, the consistency, in what she does. An important step toward that end is to infer what caused her behavior on any particular occasion—for the meaning of any given act depends upon the cause. But what cause do we see in what the other person does? Consider a football player who violently bumps an opponent in the course of the game. If the bumping

Situation versus disposition? *In ice hockey, it's not always clear whether a player who skates into another at full speed is deliberately trying to hurt him. The usual attribution is that he is, resulting in one of the many fights that characterize hockey. (Courtesy AP/Wide World Photos)*

"I've heard that outside working hours he's really a rather decent sort." (© The New Yorker Collection 1975 Chas. Addams from Cartoonbank.com. All rights reserved.)

occurred while the play was in progress, not much is revealed about the bumper's personality; he was behaving according to the rules of the game. But if the bump occurred some seconds after the official blew his whistle and the play was over, the situation is different. Now the act is more revealing and may be attributed to a grudge or a nasty disposition. The bumpee will conclude that the bumper's action was internally caused and will then self-righteously become a bumper when his own turn comes.

ATTRIBUTION AS A RATIONAL PROCESS

Social psychologists refer to this interpretive process as *causal attribution*—the process by which one decides what cause a behavior should be attributed to. The study of how these attributions are formed is one of social psychology's central concerns (e.g., Heider, 1958; Kelley, 1967; Jones and Nisbett, 1972; Kelley and Michela, 1980). According to Harold Kelley, one of the first investigators in this area, the process through which such decisions are reached is analogous to the way in which a scientist tracks down the cause of a physical event (Kelley, 1967). An effect (such as an increase in gas pressure) is attributed to a particular condition (such as a rise in temperature) if the effect occurs when the condition is present but does not occur when that condition is absent. Kelley believed that when people try to explain the behavior of others, they implicitly operate according to a similar principle.

To answer the question "Why did he bump me?" the aggrieved player has to consider the circumstances under which bumping is known to occur. Does it generally occur in circumstances just like now? Would most other football players do the same under much the same circumstances? If the answer to these and similar questions is yes, the act will probably be attributed to situational factors: essentially external causes, such as the social pressures of team play. But if the answer is no, the act will be attributed to some dispositional quality: something internal to the actor that is characteristic of him. He is a dirty player who took a cheap shot (Heider, 1958; Kelley, 1967).

As used in this context, the term *dispositional quality* refers to any underlying attribute that characterizes a given individual and makes her more disposed than others to engage in a particular bit of behavior. One kind of dispositional quality is the presence or absence of some ability. (For example, one might fall because one is clumsy.) A different kind is a general personality trait. (For example, one might leave a very small tip because one is stingy.) Attributions of this sort place causal responsibility for an act on the actor and not on the situation.

ERRORS IN THE ATTRIBUTION PROCESS

Kelley's analysis indicates that the rational way of trying to explain another person's behavior is to consider that behavior in the context of the total situation. Perhaps the behavior is determined by the person, and perhaps it is determined by the setting. Unless one pays attention to both elements, one may fail to understand why the action occurred and what it means. But this is not always done. For there are a number of biases that lead to errors in the attribution process.

One error concerns the relative weights we give to situational and dispositional factors. While we do consider situational factors in judging the behavior of others, the evidence shows that we do so rather less than we should. Thus, there seems to be a strong bias toward attributing behavior to dispositional qualities, while simultaneously underrating the power of the external situation. This bias is so pervasive that it has been called the *fundamental attribution error* (Ross, 1977). Thus, the person on welfare is often judged to be lazy (a dispositional attribute) when he may really be unable to find work (a situational attribute). Much the same holds for our interpretation of public affairs. We look for heroes and scapegoats, and tend to praise or blame political leaders for acts over which in fact they had little control.

This underemphasis on situational factors is illustrated in an experimental study in which college students were asked to participate in a simulated TV quiz show. Students were run in pairs and drew cards to decide who would be the "quiz master" and who the contestant. The quiz master had to make up questions, drawn from any area in which she had some expertise; the contestant had to try to answer them. Some of the questions were quite difficult (e.g., "What do the initials W. H. in W. H. Auden's name stand for?"). Under the circumstances, it's hardly surprising that the contestants' average score was only 4 correct answers out of 10.

The entire procedure was witnessed by other students who served as observers. When later asked to rate the two participants, the observers judged the quiz masters to be considerably more knowledgeable than the contestants. After all, the quiz masters seemed to have a wealth of factual knowledge, allowing them to generate these challenging questions. The contestants, on the other hand, failed to answer these questions. Obviously, therefore, they didn't know facts that the quiz masters did, and so the contestants must be less knowledgeable.

But, of course, this comparison was rigged, for the quiz masters could choose any question, any topic, that they wished. Hence, if a quiz master had some obscure knowledge on just one topic, he could focus all his questions on that topic, avoiding the fact that he had little knowledge in other domains. The contestants, on the other hand, were at the mercy of whatever questions their quiz masters posed. And, in fact, it would have been an impressive coincidence if the special area of expertise selected by the quiz master was also an area of expertise for the contestant. No wonder, then, that the contestants did so poorly.

This is, in short, a situation plainly set up to favor the quiz master, and so any interpretation of the quiz master's "superiority" needs to take this situational advantage into account. But the observers consistently failed to do this. They knew that the roles in this setting—who was quiz master, who was contestant—had been determined by chance, for they witnessed the entire procedure. But

Attribution People sometimes confuse the actor with his role, as in the case of Boris Karloff who often portrayed monsters such as Frankenstein's but who in real life was a gentle and cultured person. (Photographs courtesy of the Kobal Collection)

even so, they couldn't help regarding the quiz masters as more knowledgeable than the contestants—a tribute to the power of the fundamental attribution error (Ross, Amabile, and Steinmetz, 1977).★

THE ACTOR-OBSERVER BIAS

The tendency to underrate the importance of situational factors occurs primarily when we try to understand the behavior of others. The results are quite different when we ourselves are the actors rather than the observers. If someone else trips, we think she's careless or clumsy. But when we ourselves trip, we say the floor is slippery. If someone else does poorly on a test, we're astonished by her ignorance. But if the poor grade is our own, we conclude that the test must have been either too hard or unfair.

These contrasts illustrate the *actor-observer difference* in attribution: When we are the observers, our attributions tend to emphasize dispositional factors; this is the pattern that defines the fundamental attribution error. But when we are the actors, the causes seem less in us and more in the external situation (Jones and Nisbett, 1972).

A cognitive interpretation: Different information One interpretation of the actor-observer difference is simply that we know ourselves better than we know anyone else. Let's say that on one evening you undertip a waiter in a restaurant. Does this imply that you are a stingy person? You might be certain that you are not, for you have other relevant knowledge about yourself. You might know, for example, that, on other evenings, in other restaurants, you've tipped properly, and perhaps even generously. Thus, you have reason to believe you are not stingy in general; if you've undertipped this evening, this must have been caused by the situation—perhaps the waiter was rude, or you suddenly discovered that you didn't bring enough cash.

Things are obviously different for someone observing you. This observer hasn't seen you in many other situations, and so this one instance of undertipping weighs heavily and can't be discounted. This observer has no basis for concluding that this is an unusual act and may well conclude that it's typical. As a result, the causal attribution will emphasize dispositional factors (your stinginess) rather than the situation.

The suggestion, then, is that the actor-observer difference is a simple consequence of how much we know about ourselves, relative to how much others know about us. Some evidence in line with this hypothesis comes from a study which shows that the tendency to make dispositional attributions is somewhat less when the person we're describing is a close friend rather than a mere acquaintance (Nisbett et al., 1973). As predicted, more knowledge about a person leads to more attention to the situation.

A similar account may explain the out-group homogeneity effect we discussed earlier: the tendency to see members of another group as more alike than members of one's own. Almost without exception, we know more about the members of our own group—including our differences from each other—than about members of the out-group. To the extent that we lack such detailed information about them, they seem all the same.

A perceptual interpretation: Different perspective There is another factor that contributes to the difference between actors and observers—the two have different

★ The actual details of the experimental procedure were somewhat more complex (among other things, because they involved the use of confederates), but they are irrelevant to the present discussion.

11.2 *The actor-observer difference A schematic figure of a study on the effect of visual perspective on the actor-observer difference. Two actors (actually confederates) were engaged in a conversation and observed from three vantage points: from behind Actor A, from behind Actor B, and from midway between them. The results showed that the observer who watched from behind Actor A believed that B controlled the conversation, while the observer behind Actor B thought the reverse. The observer who watched from midway between the two believed that both were equally influential. (After Taylor and Fiske, 1975)*

physical perspectives (see Figure 11.2). To the observer, what stands out perceptually is the actor and her actions. The situation that elicits these actions is seen much less clearly, in part because the stimuli to which the actor responds are not as readily visible from the observer's vantage point. The reverse holds for the actor. She is not focused on her own behavior. One reason is that she cannot see her own actions very clearly (some, such as her own facial expressions, are literally invisible to her). What she attends to is the situation around her—the place, the people, and how she interprets them all. If we assume that whatever serves as the main center of attention (the figure rather than the ground) is more likely to be seen as the cause for whatever happens, then the differences in attribution follow: dispositional for the observer (who thus commits the fundamental attribution error), situational for the actor (Heider, 1958).

Some evidence for this position comes from a study in which two strangers met and engaged in a conversation that was videotaped. When later played back, only one of the two participants was shown (on the pretense that one of the cameras had malfunctioned while the sound was unaffected). As a result, one of the participants saw just what he had seen before: his fellow conversationalist. But the other saw something different: himself. When asked to describe his own behavior, the participant who saw the videotape of his partner gave the usual pattern of attribution—he said that his own actions were caused by the situation. The results were different for the participant who saw himself. The reversed perspective led to a reversal of the usual actor-observer difference. Having watched himself, he described his own behavior in dispositional terms (Storms, 1973).

THE SELF-SERVING BIAS

The two accounts of the actor-observer bias we've just discussed—different information and perspectives—are essentially cognitive; they argue that the bias results from limitations on what the individual can see, remember, and understand. But there is another interpretation that argues for additional motivational factors. For our thoughts are all too often colored by our desires.

The best evidence comes from work on the *self-serving attributional bias,* which shows that people often deny responsibility for failures and take credit for successes, attributing the first to situational and the second to dispositional factors. The tennis player explains a loss by complaining that her serve was off and that the sun was in her eyes, but she takes a win as proof of her ability and

Self-serving bias *The self-serving bias can extend to others we see as members of our group, as shown by the different points awarded to a diver at a swim meet by two coaches from opposing teams. Which of the two judges do you think is the diver's own coach? (Courtesy of Reuter's/Bettman Newsphotos)*

stamina. The student who fails says that the exam was unfair and happened to cover just those parts of the course that she hadn't studied for, but she believes that a good grade is a tribute to her talent and hard work.

This self-serving pattern has been documented very often (Bradley, 1978). In most studies, participants were asked to perform various tasks and were then given fake information on whether they had achieved some criterion of success. In some, these tasks involved sensory or perceptual discriminations (e.g., Luginbhul, Crowe, and Kahan, 1975; Stevens and Jones, 1976); in others, they consisted of various tests that were said to measure social sensitivity (Miller, 1976; Sicoly and Ross, 1977); in yet others, they were competitive games played against fictitious opponents (Snyder, Stephan, and Rosenfield, 1976). The overall pattern of results was always the same: By and large, the participants attributed their successes to internal factors (they were pretty good at such tasks, and they worked hard) and their failures to external factors (the task was too difficult, and they were unlucky).

What holds in the laboratory holds in the real world as well. This is especially true for the world of competitive sports. One study found evidence in the sports pages. The investigators analyzed the postgame comments of college and professional football and baseball players and coaches following important games. Eighty percent of the statements made by the winners were internal attributions: "Our team was great," "Our star player did it all," and so on. In contrast, the losers were less likely to give internal attributions (only 53 percent) and often explained the outcomes by referring to external, situational factors: "I think we hit the ball all right. But I think we're unlucky" (Lau and Russell, 1980, p. 32).

It's worth noting that these self-serving biases apply not just to our own failures or successes but extend to the perception of other people and groups that we regard as in some ways our own: our friends, family members, social and political groups, and even hometown sports teams. Happily married couples are even more prone to a spouse-serving attributional basis than to a self-serving one: The spouse's successes reflect on his or her talents and character; the failures are caused by temporary external circumstances (Hall and Taylor, 1976; Holtzworth-Munroe and Jacobson, 1985). The same holds for people's favorite political candidate. Thus, if a candidate does poorly in a debate, her advocates will argue that she had an off day but that she will be sure to win a rematch, while her opponents will insist that it only proves their own favorite is the superior candidate (Winkler and Taylor, 1979).

The above-average effect An interesting example of the self-serving bias is the **above-average effect.** When people are asked to compare themselves to all others on various favorable characteristics, the vast majority judge themselves to be above average—in stark defiance of all statistical logic (see Harter, 1990). Thus, in 1976–77 the College Board asked one million high-school students to rate themselves against their peers on leadership ability: Seventy percent said they were above average, while only two percent felt they were below. Even more impressive, *all* the students claimed they were above average in their ability to get along with others; 60 percent thought they were in the top 10 percent on this dimension. Similarly for athletic ability, which led to an equally illogical 60 percent above and 6 percent below. Similar findings have been obtained in people's judgments of talents ranging from managerial skills to driving ability (see Dunning, Meyerowitz, and Holzberg, 1989). And it's not just high-school students who show these effects: One study of university professors found that 94 percent believed they were better at their jobs than their colleagues.

What's going on here? Part of the cause lies in the way we search our memories, in order to decide whether we have been good leaders or bad, good drivers or poor ones. Evidence suggests that this memory search is often selective, showcasing the occasions in the past in which we've behaved well and neglecting the occasions in which we've done badly. This is probably because each of us starts with the hypothesis that we have in fact behaved well; we then search our memories for prior episodes that would confirm this obviously self-serving hypothesis (Kunda, 1990; Kunda et al., 1993; for more on this sort of confirmation bias, see Chapter 8).

In addition, people seem to capitalize on the fact that the meanings of these traits—effective leader, good at getting along with others—are often ambiguous. This allows each of us to interpret a trait, and thus to interpret the evidence, in a fashion that puts us in the best possible light. Take driving ability. Suppose Henry is a slow, careful driver: He will tend to think that he's better than average precisely because he's slow and careful. But suppose Jane, on the other hand, is a fast driver who prides herself on her ability to whiz through traffic and hang tight on hairpin turns: She will also think that she's better than average because of the way she's defined driving skill. As a result, both Henry and Jane (and indeed most drivers) end up considering themselves above average. By appropriately redefining *success* or *excellence,* we can each conclude that we are the ones who are successful (Dunning et al., 1989; Dunning and Cohen, 1992).

This analysis implies that the above-average effect will occur more strongly with traits (like *driving ability*) that are, in fact, ambiguous. The evidence bears this out: A strong effect is obtained for traits like *sophisticated,* which allow a multitude of interpretations, but the effect is much diminished for reasonably well-defined traits, such as *well read* (Dunning, Meyerowitz, and Holzberg, 1989).

Interpreting the self-serving bias What accounts for the self-serving bias? The most obvious hypothesis is that it is just another case of impression management. The experimenter asks a participant why he thinks he succeeded or failed. The participant doesn't want to lose face in public and therefore explains his performance to put himself in the best possible light, regardless of what he may actually think. In effect, he is trying to delude the experimenter rather than himself.

While such maneuvers probably play a role, they cannot account for the entire effect. For self-serving biases occur even when participants experience failure but don't think the experimenter knows about it. Under these conditions, their public image is not threatened, so they have no reason to protect it. But they show a self-serving bias even so. Presumably, they are trying to protect the picture they hold of themselves, now deluding themselves instead of—or in addition to—others (Greenberg, Pyszczynski, and Solomon, 1982; Schlenker, Hallam, and McCown, 1983).

(Photograph by Suzanne Szasz)

PERCEIVING ONESELF

We have discussed some of the ways in which we see various qualities in others, as well as some of the ways in which we come to see such qualities in ourselves. We all have a conception of our own selves, what we are really like and why we do what we do—"I am a certain kind of person with such and such capacities, beliefs, and attitudes"—even if we sometimes sugar-coat those capacities with a layer of self-serving bias. But how do such self-concepts arise in the first place?

THE SELF-CONCEPT

One crucial element is some reference to other people. It is obvious that there can be no full-fledged "I" without a "you" or a "they," for the self-concept is undoubtedly social. According to many authors, the child begins to see herself through the eyes of the important figures in her world and, thus, acquires the idea that she is a person—albeit at first a very little person—just as they are (Mead, 1934). As the social interactions become more complex, more and more details are added to the self-picture. In effect, the child sees herself through the mirror of the opinions and expectations of those others—mother, father, siblings, friends—who matter to her. Her later behavior cannot help but be shaped by this early "looking-glass self" (Cooley, 1902). Examples of such effects include the roles in which society casts children from the moment of birth, roles defined by race, gender, ethnicity, and so on. (For different theoretical approaches to the development of the self-concept, see Chapters 13 and 14; and see Chapter 17 for a sociocultural perspective on personality and conceptions of the self.)

SELF-PERCEPTION AND ATTRIBUTION

According to this looking-glass theory, we learn who we are by finding out through others—by noting how they treat us, how they react to us, and what they expect from us. But isn't there a more direct method? Can't we discover who we are and what we feel simply by observing ourselves?

According to some authors, the answer is no. In their view, our conceptions of self are attained through an attributional process no different from the one we use to form conceptions of other people. The advocates of this self-perception theory maintain that, contrary to commonsense belief, we do not know our own selves directly (Bem, 1972). In their view, self-knowledge can only be achieved indirectly, through the same attempts to find consistencies, discount irrelevancies, and interpret observations that help us to understand other people.

One line of evidence concerns the relation between attitude and behavior. Common sense argues that attitudes cause behavior, that our own actions stem from our feelings and our beliefs. To some extent, this is undoubtedly true. Those in favor of a strong military are unlikely to join a rally demanding cuts in the defense budget. But under some circumstances, the cause-and-effect relation is reversed. For as already noted in our discussion of cognitive dissonance, sometimes our feelings or beliefs are the result of our actions.

A demonstration comes from the **foot-in-the-door technique,** originally perfected by traveling salesmen. In one study, suburban homeowners were asked to comply with an innocuous request, to put a three-inch square sign advocating auto safety in a window of their homes. Two weeks later, another experimenter came to visit those homeowners who had agreed to display the small sign. This time they were asked to grant a much greater request, to permit the installation of an enormous billboard on their front lawns, proclaiming "Drive Carefully" in huge letters while obstructing most of the house. The results showed that agreement depended upon prior agreement. Once having complied with the first, small request, the homeowners were much more likely to give in to the greater one (Freedman and Fraser, 1966).

One interpretation of this and similar findings is a change in self-perception (Snyder and Cunningham, 1975). Having agreed to put up the small sign, the homeowners now thought of themselves as active citizens involved in a public

Self-perception and attribution In the movie Donnie Brasco, an undercover FBI agent infiltrates the mob. As his involvement deepens, he grows uncertain of his own allegiances. (Al Pacino and Johnny Depp in the 1997 film; photograph courtesy of Photofest)

The foot-in-the-door effect and the environment *The foot-in-the-door effect can start at an early age. The photo shows young children induced to do their bit for conservation. Whether the cans they collect now make much of a difference matters less than that these acts are likely to lead to greater efforts in the future, as the children come to think of themselves as environmentalists. (Photograph by S. C. Delaney/EPA)*

issue. Since no one forced them to put up the sign, they attributed their action to their own convictions. Given that they now thought of themselves as active, convinced, and involved, they were ready to play the part on a larger scale. Fortunately for their less-involved neighbors, the billboard was in fact never installed—after all, the request was only part of an experiment. But in real life we may not be let off so easily. The foot-in-the-door approach is a common device for persuading the initially uncommitted; it can be used to peddle encyclopedias or harden political convictions. Extremist political movements generally do not demand violent actions from newcomers. They begin with small requests like signing a petition or giving a distinctive salute. But these may lead to a changed self-perception that ultimately may ready the person for more drastic acts.★

This line of argument may have some bearing on our understanding of how social systems function. The social world casts people in different roles that prescribe particular sets of behaviors; representatives of labor and management will obviously take different positions at the bargaining table. But the roles determine attitudes as well as behavior. If one acts like a union representative, one starts to feel like one. The same holds for the corporate executive. This point has been verified in a study of factory workers both before and after they were elected union steward or promoted to foreman. As one might have expected, the newly elected union stewards became more prounion; the newly promoted foremen became more promanagement (Lieberman, 1956).

CULTURE AND SOCIAL COGNITION

Many of the social phenomena we have reviewed—the ways we make social comparisons, tend to conform, and attempt to explain the behavior of ourselves and others—have been presumed to reflect very basic properties of our social cognition. But the results of some studies suggest that these phenomena are by no means universal and depend, instead, in important ways on the norms, values, and teachings of one's culture.

Many authors believe that the most relevant distinction between current cultures and ethnic subgroups lies in whether they are *collectivist* or *individualist* (Triandis, 1989, 1994). Collectivist societies include many of the societies of Latin America, and most of the cultures of Asia and Africa. Individualist societies include the dominant cultures of the United States, western Europe, Canada, and Australia. These kinds of societies exhibit profound differences in whether people are considered fundamentally *in*dependent or *inter*dependent (Fiske et al., 1998).

In collectivist societies, people are considered to be fundamentally interdependent, and the emphasis is on obligations within one's family and immediate community. These primary groups determine what is expected and what is frowned upon, and provide the major motives and rewards; any efforts to individuate or stand out from one's social group are considered disruptions of the group's harmony.

In individualist societies, on the other hand, people are viewed as independent,

★ These phenomena are very reminiscent of the effects of forced compliance and justification of effort we discussed previously in the context of dissonance reduction. Under the circumstances, it may not be surprising that some authors have suggested that such effects are best explained by self-perception theory rather than by a tendency to reduce cognitive dissonance. The resulting controversy between adherents of the dissonance position and of the self-perception approach is beyond the scope of this book (Bem, 1967, 1972).

separable entities whose actions are driven by internal needs, desires, emotions, and so on. In these societies, the emphasis is on the ways a person can stand out through achieving private goals. There are still obligations, of course, to family and to community, but individuals have some leeway in how (or whether) they fulfill these obligations. Thus, one's important life choices—of occupation, friends, and spouse—are much less affected by the wishes of family and neighbors, for the ultimate goal is to be true to oneself, and not to conform.

Thus, students from individualist California are more likely to agree with statements that emphasize self-reliance, such as "Only those who depend on themselves get ahead in life," than are students from collectivist Hong Kong or Costa Rica. In contrast, students from Hong Kong and Costa Rica will be more likely to agree with statements that affirm a concern for one's family and close friends, such as "I would help within my means if a relative told me he (she) is in financial difficulty" and "I like to live close to my friends" (Triandis et al., 1988).

The collectivism-individualism difference offers a fresh perspective on many of the social psychological phenomena we have reviewed, with much of the relevant evidence coming from studies that have used participants from diverse cultures; here, we summarize some of the main results of such *cross-cultural studies.*

CONFORMITY

Asch's studies of conformity and most others like it (see also the Milgram studies of obedience in Chapter 12) were conducted on participants from an individualistic society, the United States. Many of these participants did conform but experienced enormous discomfort as a result, plainly suffering from the contrast between their own perceptions and the perceptions of others. The pattern is different in collectivist cultures. Here, individuals are much less distressed about conforming even when it means being wrong. Over two dozen Asch-type conformity studies have now been conducted in collectivist cultures, and they support such a conclusion (Smith and Bond, 1993).

ATTRIBUTIONS ABOUT CAUSES OF BEHAVIOR

We have noted the many studies which demonstrate that participants tend to explain others' behavior in terms of internal dispositions rather than properties of the situation. But these explanations presume that people are independent and driven internally, a view much more typical in individualist than collectivist societies. We should expect, then, that situational explanations would be more prominent among members of collectivist cultures. Supportive evidence comes from a study in which participants were asked to explain the actions of the main characters in brief stories. Some of the participants were American adults, others Hindu adults from India. The results showed that Americans explained behavior chiefly in terms of personal qualities by a ratio of three to one. Indian participants, on the other hand, were twice as likely to explain the behavior in terms of social roles and other situational factors. For example, one of the stories described a driver and passenger going to work on a motorcycle. The cycle took a spill in which the passenger, but not the driver, was injured. Following the accident, the driver dropped the injured passenger off at the hospital, and proceeded to work. Overall, the Americans typically labeled the driver "obviously irresponsible" or "in a state of shock," whereas the Indians typically explained that it was the driver's duty to be at work or that the passenger's injury must not have looked serious (Miller, 1984; see also Smith and Bond, 1993; Fiske et al., 1998).

Another study examined Chinese and American newspaper accounts of two murders that occurred in the United States. The American accounts were prominently about personal qualities: The murderer was mentally unstable, or had a "very bad temper" or a "psychological problem." In the Chinese accounts, the murders were blamed on the availability of guns, or social isolation, or interpersonal rivalry (Morris and Peng, 1994).

Cross-cultural investigators are quick to point out, however, that using dispositional rather than situational factors to explain behavior (and vice versa) are cultural tendencies, not absolutes. Indeed, even the most collectivist cultures retain the notion of personal traits and dispositions, just as the most individualist cultures retain the notion that situations can explain behavior. The cultural differences may lie instead in the extent to which each member of the culture pays attention to the situations in which behavior occurs. For members of collectivist cultures, people's actions occur in an interlocking social matrix, where the actions of any one may be explained by the actions of all the others (that is, in terms of the situation). But for members of individualist cultures, actions tend to be seen as an outgrowth of an individual's dispositions, so there is little need to look further (Fiske et al., 1998).

IN-GROUPS AND OUT-GROUPS

Collectivists and individualists (that is, members of collectivist and individualist societies) tend to differ in some further ways. Consider group pressure. On the face of it one might expect collectivists to agree or conform with a group's judgments or actions more often than do individualists. But it turns out that this depends on the nature of the group. Collectivists are more likely to agree or conform with members of their in-group, a group to which they are tied by traditional bonds—their family (including second cousins and great-aunts and so on),★ classmates, close friends, and fellow workers. But in contrast, they are less affected than individualists by members of the out-group, with whom they share no such bonds.

A related phenomenon is the permanence of an individual's social bonds. Collectivists belong to relatively few in-groups, but their bonds to those are strong and long lasting. It's no accident that in Japan (a collectivist society) workers tend to remain in whatever organization they started out with, wearing their company's colors and singing company songs, such as "A bright heart overflowing with life links together Matsushita Electric" (Weisz, Rothbaum, and Blackburn, 1984).

In contrast, members of individualist cultures belong to a whole set of overlapping in-groups, but their relation to these groups is more fragile and less enduring. In part, this is a consequence of their different values. To the individualist, what matters most is the freedom to pursue personal goals and preferences. As these change, so do social relationships. As a result, individualists generally make friends more easily than collectivists do, but their friendships tend to be impermanent and to lack intimacy. Freedom is precious, but for some individualists the price is loneliness.

★ Of course, individualists and collectivists both have families to which they have strong ties. But in a collectivist society, the family is normally greatly extended. Typical individualists, on the other hand, take family to mean the *nuclear* family: two parents and their children. Individualists often feel deep affection for their parents, but they don't feel obliged to live with them or close to them after they've started their own families.

ABOVE-AVERAGE EFFECT

Recall that, illogically, about 70 percent of American college students consider themselves above average in their leadership ability as well as on a host of other traits. For the above-average effect to occur, most of the students must have been motivated to see themselves as better than their peers, signifying not only a standing apart from one's group but a self-serving standing *over* it.

Why should deciding that we are somehow superior to our reference group make us feel better? Such a question is rarely asked by members of individualist cultures, who are thoroughly accustomed to the premium those cultures place on self-aggrandizement. But for members of collectivist cultures, self-aggrandizement brings disharmony, and this is too great a price to pay. Evidence for this conclusion comes from a study in which both American and Japanese college students were asked to rank their abilities in areas ranging from math and memory to warmheartedness and athletic ability. The American students showed the usual result: On average, 70 percent rated themselves above average on each trait. But among the Japanese students, only 50 percent rated themselves above average, indicating no self-serving bias, and perhaps pointing instead to a self-harmonizing one (Takata, 1987; Markus and Kitayama, 1991).

We end this discussion of the sociocultural perspective on social cognition with two points. First, it is important to realize that terms that describe a culture don't necessarily apply to all of its members. They designate what is typical or average. There are surely some students from Hong Kong who would marry against their parents' wishes and some from California who would not. But the average student from Hong Kong will be more likely to behave along collectivist lines than the average student from California.

Second, fully considering culture is relatively new to social psychology (see Fiske et al., 1998). Already, findings that were considered fundamental and reliable within social psychology have been shown to be highly dependent on culture. But it is still too early to conclude that our social cognition and its operation are merely the constructions of society. Are there universal aspects of our social cognition that reflect innate predispositions guiding how we think about ourselves and others? Discovering which aspects are part of our human heritage and which we owe to our particular culture is the promise of the sociocultural perspective.

EMOTION

Our discussion of cultural differences raises many questions, including whether there are some aspects of our inner lives shared by all cultures, uniting us as a species. One plausible candidate is *emotion*.

But what is emotion? This question was raised by the psychologist William James in 1884, and it has haunted psychology ever since. We say that we feel love, joy, satisfaction, grief, jealousy, or anger. But what does it mean to say we *feel* or have *feelings*? Do people the world over feel the same things? And do they act the same ways, and make the same facial expressions, when they have these feelings? These are some of the central questions pursued by those researching emotion.

EMOTIONAL EXPERIENCE: INTERPRETATIONS OF INTERNAL STATES

In one of Gilbert and Sullivan's operettas, a character notes that the uninitiated may mistake love for indigestion. While this is probably an overstatement, something of the sort may be valid for all of us. We often have to interpret our internal states to decide whether panting and a knot in our stomach mean fear (say, of an impending examination) or breathless anticipation (say, of a lovers' meeting). According to some psychologists, such interpretive processes are involved whenever we experience an emotion (Schachter and Singer, 1962; Mandler, 1975, 1984). To put their views in perspective, we will begin with a discussion of an earlier theory of emotion.

THE JAMES-LANGE THEORY

Some aspects of emotion, such as our gestures and expressions, are public and can readily be studied. Our physiological responses can also be studied using electronic monitors. But what about the way our emotions are experienced subjectively, the way we feel "inside"?

Many nineteenth-century psychologists tried to catalog various emotional experiences much as they had classified the different sensations provided by the senses (such as *red, sour, A-flat*). But their efforts were not very successful. People simply reported too many emotional experiences, and the classifications that were proposed did not seem to do justice to the richness of these subjective feelings. In addition, there were disagreements about the precise meaning of emotional terms. How does *sadness* differ from *weariness* or *dejection*? Different people reported different shades of meaning, and there seemed to be little hope of agreement as long as the description was confined to the subjective experience alone (which, of course, is private by definition).

A different approach to the problem was proposed by William James. To James, the crucial facet of emotion was that it is an aspect of what a person *does*. In fear, we run; in grief, we weep. The commonsense interpretation is that the behavior is caused by the emotion. James stood common sense on its head and maintained that the causal relation is reversed; we are afraid because we run:

> Common-sense says, we lose our fortune, are sorry and weep; we meet a bear, are frightened and run; we are insulted by a rival, are angry and strike. The hypothesis here ... is that we feel sorry because we cry, angry because we strike, afraid because we tremble.... Without the bodily states following on the perception, the latter would be purely cognitive in form, pale, colorless, destitute of emotional warmth. We might then see the bear, and judge it best to run, receive the insult and deem it right to strike, but we should not actually feel afraid or angry. (James, 1890, v. 2, p. 449)

This is the core of what is now known as the **James-Lange theory of emotions.** (Carl Lange was a European contemporary of James who offered a similar account.) In effect, the theory asserts that the subjective experience of emotion is neither more nor less than the awareness of our own bodily changes in the presence of certain arousing stimuli. These bodily changes might consist of skeletal movements (running) and visceral reactions (pounding heartbeat), although later adherents of the James-Lange theory emphasized the visceral responses and the activity of the autonomic nervous system that underlies them (Figure 11.3).

Some research supports the relationship between the skeletal muscles and

The misattribution of one's own inner state *According to one of the characters in Gilbert and Sullivan's operetta* Patience, *"There is a transcendentality of delirium—an acute accentuation of the supremest ecstasy—which the earthy might easily mistake for indigestion." (From a production by the New York Gilbert and Sullivan Players; photograph by Lee Snider, 1987)*

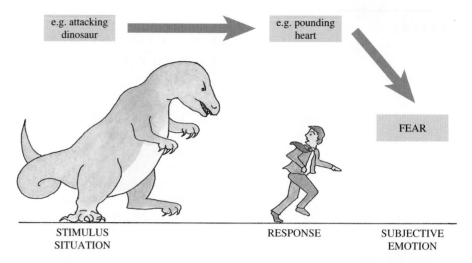

| STIMULUS SITUATION | RESPONSE | SUBJECTIVE EMOTION |

11.3   The sequence of events as conceived by the James-Lange theory of emotions   *According to the James-Lange theory, the subjectively experienced emotion is simply our awareness of our own response to the anger- or fear-arousing situation. We see a dangerous object (an attacking dinosaur will do as well as any other); this triggers a bodily response (running, pounding heart), and the awareness of this response is the emotion (here, fear).*

emotion, leading several researchers to propose that specific muscular movements *can* account for our emotional experience. This notion would not be at all far-fetched to actors schooled in the "method" of Konstantin Stanislavski, who encouraged his students to get "into role" by adopting the postures, gestures, and facial expressions of the character (Stanislavski, 1936). That posture may influence emotional experience was shown in one investigation in which participants took several achievement tests and then received the results while sitting either in a slump or in an upright posture. All participants were told that their performance was far above average, but those who heard the news while sitting upright reported feeling prouder than those who heard it while slumping (Stepper and Strack, 1993; see also Duclos et al., 1989; we discuss whether facial movements influence emotional experience in a later section).

Still, the James-Lange theory has been the focus of considerable controversy. One major attack on the theory was presented by Walter B. Cannon, the pioneer in the study of the physiology of homeostasis (Chapter 3). Cannon pointed out that the nervous and glandular secretions that comprise our sympathetic reactions are too slow to account for the quickness of our emotional reactions. Moreover, he contended that our sympathetic reactions to arousing stimuli are too diffuse and general to account for the wide range of human emotional experience. Take the relation between rage and fear. These two emotions appear to be accompanied by just about the same autonomic discharge, he claimed, and yet we are easily able to distinguish between these two experiences. Therefore, Cannon concluded, the James-Lange theory must be wrong (Cannon, 1927).

Cannon's argument also seemed to gain support from early studies in which participants received injections of epinephrine, triggering broad sympathetic activation with all its consequences—nervousness, palpitations, flushing, tremors, and sweaty palms. According to the James-Lange theory, these should be among the internally produced stimuli that give rise to the intense emotions of fear and rage. But in fact the participants did not experience these emotions. Some simply reported the physical symptoms. Others said they felt "as if" they were angry or afraid, a kind of "cold emotion," not the real thing (Maranon, 1924; Landis and Hunt, 1932). Apparently, the visceral reactions induced by epinephrine are by themselves not sufficient for emotional experience.

More recent evidence suggests, however, that autonomic activity may not be as broad and diffuse as Cannon contended. Some studies of autonomic activity show clear differences in the autonomic patterns that accompany such emotions as anger and fear (e.g., Ax, 1953; Funkenstein, 1956; Schwartz, Weinberger, and Singer, 1981; Ekman, Levenson, and Friesen, 1983; Sinha and Parsons, 1996). And people across cultures report bodily sensations that differ depending on the emotion: People generally report a quickened heart beat and tense muscles when both angry and fearful, and they feel hot or flushed strictly when angry, but when afraid they feel cold and clammy (Mesquita and Frijda, 1992).

However, not all emotions are so easy to distinguish through bodily responses. This, combined with Cannon's other argument regarding the speed of our sympathetic reactions, leaves most contemporary investigators convinced that there is little support for the contention that our behavior alone can account for our emotional experience.

THE ATTRIBUTION-OF-AROUSAL THEORY

In contrast to the James-Lange theory, which emphasizes the role of feedback from the musculature and the autonomic nervous system, an alternative account focuses on cognitive factors. After all, emotional experiences are usually initiated by external events—a letter with tragic news, a loved one's return, a job failure. Events such as these bring grief, joy, dejection, or humiliation, but before they can possibly affect us emotionally they must be appraised and understood. Is the dog friendly or hostile? Is the friend's action generous or indifferent? In each case, our emotional reaction to the situation depends on some cognitive interpretation that in turn depends on what we see, what we know, and what we expect (Arnold, 1970).

Proponents of a theory set forth by Stanley Schachter and Jerome Singer combine a cognitive approach with bodily feedback to explain emotion. According to Schachter and Singer's *attribution-of-arousal theory* (sometimes called *cognitive arousal theory*) various stimuli may trigger a general state of autonomic arousal, but this arousal will provide only the raw materials for an emotional experience (see Figure 11.4). This state of undifferentiated

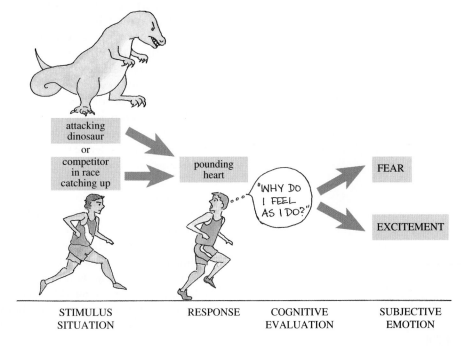

11.4 The sequence of events as conceived by Schachter and Singer's attribution-of-arousal theory of emotions *According to Schachter and Singer, subjectively experienced emotion is the result of an evaluation process in which the participant interprets his own bodily reactions in the light of the total situation. Any number of external stimuli (ranging from attacking dinosaurs to competition in a race) may lead to the same general bodily reaction pattern—running and increased heart rate. The subjective emotion depends upon what the participant attributes these bodily responses to. If he attributes them to a danger signal (the dinosaur), he will feel fear. If he attributes them to the race, he will feel excitement.*

| STIMULUS SITUATION | RESPONSE | COGNITIVE EVALUATION | SUBJECTIVE EMOTION |

473

excitement is shaped into a specific emotional experience by cognitive appraisal and interpretation.

A person's heart beats rapidly and her hands tremble—is it fear, rage, joyful anticipation, or a touch of the flu? If the individual has just been insulted, she will interpret her internal reactions as anger and will feel and act accordingly. If she is confronted by William James's bear, she will attribute her visceral excitement to the bear and experience fear. If she is at home in bed, she will probably assume that she is sick. In short, according to the attribution-of-arousal theory, emotional experience is produced, not by autonomic arousal as such, but rather by the interpretation of this arousal in light of the total situation as the person understands it (Schachter and Singer, 1962; Schachter, 1964; Mandler, 1984, 1998).

The misattribution of arousal To test this general conception, Schachter and Singer performed a now classic experiment in which participants were autonomically aroused but did not know what caused their arousal. The participants were injected with a drug that they believed to be a vitamin supplement but that was really epinephrine. Some participants were informed of the drug's real effects, while others were misinformed. They were told only that the drug might have some side effects, such as numbness or itching. After the drug had been administered, the participants sat in the waiting room for what they thought was to be a test of vision.

In fact, the main experiment was conducted in this waiting room with a confederate posing as another participant while the experimenter watched through a one-way screen. One condition was set up to produce anger: The confederate was sullen and irritable and eventually stormed out of the room. Another condition provided a context for euphoria: The confederate was ebullient and frivolous; he threw paper planes out of the window, played with a hula hoop, and tried to engage the participant in an improvised basketball game with paper balls. Following their stay in the waiting room, the participants were asked to rate their emotions (Schachter and Singer, 1962).

Schachter and Singer reasoned that those participants who had been correctly informed about the physiological consequences of the injection would show less of an emotional response than those who had been misinformed. The informed participants would (correctly) attribute their tremors and palpitations to the drug rather than to the external situation. In contrast, the misinformed participants had to assume that their internal reactions were caused by something outside—the elation of the euphoric confederate or the sullenness of the angry one. Given this external attribution, their emotional state would be in line with the environmental context—euphoric or angry as the case might be. The results were more or less as predicted. The misinformed participants in the euphoria situation described themselves as more joyful than their correctly informed counterparts and were somewhat more likely than those counterparts to join in the confederate's mad antics. Roughly analogous results were obtained in the anger situation.

Carry-over of arousal Some related effects result from a kind of spillover of arousal. Autonomic arousal usually takes a while to subside; as a result, some bodily aftereffects of fear or anger or even physical exercise remain for quite a bit longer than we might expect. Such aftereffects may lead to **excitation transfer** (Zillman, 1983). In one study, some participants first engaged in a bout of strenuous physical activity on an exercise bicycle. A few minutes after they finished pedaling, they were angered by a confederate in an adjacent room who administered a number of mild electric shocks as a way of signaling disagreement on

Excitation transfer *There is some evidence that the arousal immediately following intense exercise can lead to a misattribution of one's own reaction to emotion-producing stimuli. Whether competitive athletes accustomed to strenuous exercise are subject to this effect is an open question. (Photograph by Michael Nichols/Magnum)*

various attitudes they discussed over an intercom. When subsequently given a chance to retaliate, they were more aggressive (that is, administered more severe shocks) than controls who were tested after their heart rate and blood pressure returned to base levels. (Needless to say, no retaliatory shocks were really delivered.) A similar effect was found for sexual excitement in response to erotic films; here, too, arousal was enhanced by preceding physical exercise (Zillman, Katcher, and Milavsky, 1972; Cantor, Zillman, and Bryant, 1975).

The explanation readily follows from Schachter and Singer's theoretical position. Some residual bodily aftereffects of the previous physical exercise are still present even though the participant doesn't know it. She is still aroused but doesn't know why. As a result, she misattributes her arousal to the situation in which she currently finds herself and in so doing amplifies her own emotions. If provoked, she becomes even angrier; if sexually aroused, she becomes more aroused still (Valins, 1966).

The role of the amygdala in emotional appraisal   The Schachter and Singer study has provoked considerable criticism and, like many claims about emotion, remains controversial (Marshall and Zimbardo, 1979; Maslach, 1979; Schacter and Singer, 1979; Reisenzein, 1983). Nonetheless, their theory reminds us that our conception of emotion must include at least two elements—the bodily arousal itself and the cognitive appraisal of the circumstances attending that arousal. In fact, some recent studies of the brain suggest that, while all levels of the brain, from the hindbrain to the neocortex, appear to be involved in emotion, a single structure—the **amygdala**—is largely responsible for integrating arousal with appraisal. The amygdala is well situated in the temporal lobe to perform this integrative role, receiving input from diverse areas of the brain, including sensory areas of the cortex and relay centers for sensory information in the thalamus (see Figure 2.13, p. 27).

Studies with humans and other animals support the contention that the amygdala plays a central role in stimulus appraisal, tagging stimuli with their emotional or motivational significance. For example, monkeys who had their amygdalas removed could recognize objects normally but could not distinguish what they were for: They would try to eat a block of wood or to touch a lighted match (Kluver and Bucy, 1937).

The loss of emotional meaning is particularly apparent in fear. Most animals will show a fear response—for example, cringing or freezing, and increased respiration and blood pressure—when they encounter a stimulus that has previously been associated with electric shock or some other aversive stimulus (see Chapter 4). But this process of fear conditioning is severely disrupted in animals with lesions in the amygdala, even though these animals seem to have a normal capacity for other sorts of learning (Davis, 1992, 1997; LeDoux, 1994). Similarly, patients with damage to the amygdala do not acquire conditioned fear responses, even though they can (calmly) recall which visual or auditory stimuli were paired with the unconditioned stimulus (Bechara et al., 1995).

Still further evidence for the amygdala's role comes from humans suffering from **complex partial seizure disorder**, or **CPSD** (sometimes called *temporal lobe epilepsy*). CPSD is a kind of epilepsy that seems to make the neurons within the amygdala hyperactive, leading sufferers to attach inappropriate emotional and motivational significance to objects, places, and events. For example, a seizure that occurs while the patient is at home may render that setting completely unfamiliar; conversely, a seizure might make a totally unfamiliar setting feel homey. In some cases, these effects persist between seizures, leaving the CPSD sufferer to attach emotional significance to nearly everything (Mullan and Penfield, 1959; Devinsky, Hafler, and Victor, 1982; Devinsky and Bear, 1984).

The face and emotion   *A grieving Cypriot woman. (Photo by Constantine Manos/ Magnum)*

All of these findings support the claim that the amygdala is essential in identifying the emotional significance of a stimulus, with important consequences for our subsequent reactions to that stimulus.

EMOTIONAL BEHAVIOR: FACIAL EXPRESSIONS

Up until now we have discussed emotional experience and what may account for it. But humans have a sizable repertory of expressions associated with emotion, many of them conveyed by the face. Our expressions—our smiles, frowns, laughs, gapes, grimaces, snarls, and winks—are intimately tied to our social lives, and these facial expressions have been of special concern to psychologists studying emotion.

THE UNIVERSALITY THESIS

Much of our current interest in facial expressions is due to Charles Darwin (Darwin, 1872b), who hypothesized that humans possess a set of universal facial expressions that are vestiges of basic adaptive patterns shown by our evolutionary forerunners. For example, our "anger" face, often expressed by lowered brows, widened eyes, and open mouth with exposed teeth, reflects the facial movements our ancestors would have made when biting an opponent. Similarly, our "disgust" face, often manifested as a wrinkled nose and protruded lower lip and tongue, reflects how our ancestors rejected odors or spit out foods. (For elaborations, see Ekman, 1980, 1984; Tomkins, 1963; Izard, 1977; Fridlund, 1994.)

In arguing that these facial expressions are part of our primate heritage, Darwin noted their similarities to many of the displays made by monkeys and apes, and believed that the expressions would be identical, reflecting identical emotions, among humans worldwide, even "those who have associated but little with Europeans" (Darwin, 1872b, p. 15). To support this ***universality thesis,*** Darwin conducted one of the first cross-cultural studies, sending questionnaires to his colleagues in Europe as well as missionaries and other contacts in the Far East. In their answers to his questions, Darwin's respondents provided many cases that suggested the universality of facial expressions. But Darwin's evidence was anecdotal, and only in the 1960s did psychologists begin to test the universality thesis across cultures using more rigorous experimental methods.

Cross-cultural studies of facial expression   About one dozen cross-cultural studies of facial expressions have been conducted, and of these, three have used the participants most crucial for testing the universality thesis: members of relatively isolated, non-Western cultures (see descriptions in Izard, 1971; Ekman, 1973; Ekman and Oster, 1979; Fridlund, Ekman, and Oster, 1983; Russell, 1994).

In one of these studies, American actors posed in photographs designed to convey emotions such as happiness, sadness, anger, and fear. The pictures were then shown to members of different cultures, both literate (Swedes, Japanese, Kenyans) and nonliterate (members of an isolated New Guinea tribe barely advanced beyond Stone Age culture), and they were asked to pick the matching emotion label. In other cases, the procedure was reversed. For example, the New Guinea tribesmen were asked to portray the facial expressions appropriate to various prototypical situations such as happiness at the return of a friend, grief at the death of a child, and anger at the start of a fight (see Figure 11.5). Photographs

A

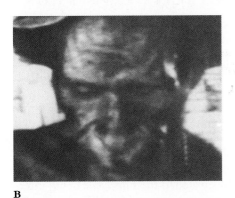

B

C

D

11.5 Attempts to portray emotion by New Guinea tribesman *Acting out expressions appropriate to various situations: (A) "Your friend has come and you are happy"; (B) "Your child has died"; (C) "You are angry and about to fight"; (D) You see a dead pig that has been lying there for a long time." (© Paul Ekman, 1971)*

of their performances were then shown to American college students who were asked to judge which situation the tribesmen had been asked to convey (Ekman and Friesen, 1971).

When given photographs of facial expressions and asked to supply the appropriate emotion term, participants worldwide—even those in relatively isolated cultures—do reasonably well (Russell, 1994; see Figure 11.6). The same is true if participants are asked to describe an emotionally tinged situation that might have elicited the expression shown in the photo. But their success depends in part on the particular facial expression they are shown. Smiles—which are generally matched with "happy" terms and situations—produce much greater consistency in identification than all the other expressions (Russell, 1994; and see discussions by Ekman, 1994; Izard, 1994; and Russell, 1995).

The greater-than-chance worldwide performance in matching facial expressions to the appropriate situations or emotion terms was seized upon by advocates as proving the universality thesis. But critics have indicated several problems with these studies (Fridlund, 1994; Russell, 1994). One problem is that even in the critical New Guinea studies only the most Westernized participants were tested. As it turns out, the degree of success at labeling the faces or supplying appropriate stories depends on the participants' exposure to Western culture:

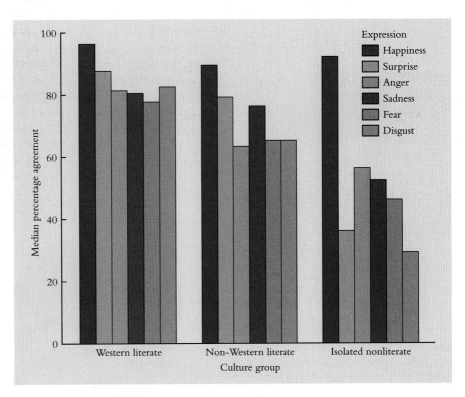

11.6 Success at matching facial expressions to labels for six emotions *The graph shows results for literate Westerners (twenty studies), and non-Westerners who were either literate (eleven studies) or relatively isolated and nonliterate (three studies). (From Russell and Fernandez-Dols, 1997, p. 15).*

The more exposure (either through personal contact or through the media), the higher the success rate.

In short, the data are suggestive of universality in facial expressions but inconclusive, so debate about this claim continues. Are similar facial expressions in similar situations observed among peoples who have truly had no contact with Western culture? We will probably never be able to answer this question, considering how fully Western culture has penetrated the four corners of the globe. And the best test of the universality thesis—the examination of the *spontaneous* expressions of people worldwide in emotional situations—has never been conducted or even approximated (Russell, 1994).

CULTURAL VARIATIONS IN FACIAL EXPRESSIONS

Even if some facial expressions do turn out to be universal, it is clear that the public use of facial expressions is affected by culture. According to some accounts, Melanese chieftains frown fiercely when greeting each other at a festive occasion, and Samurai mothers are said to have smiled upon hearing that their sons had fallen in battle (Klineberg, 1940).

A similar cultural difference was observed in studies in which American and Japanese participants were presented with a harrowing documentary film of a primitive puberty rite. As they watched the film, their facial expressions were recorded with a hidden camera. The results showed that when alone, and when interviewed directly after the film, the facial reactions were virtually identical (see Figure 11.7). But when the participants watched the film *while* being interviewed by a white-coated experimenter, the results were quite different. In this context, the Japanese looked more polite and smiled more than did the Americans (Ekman, 1972, 1977; Friesen, 1972; for further discussion, see Fridlund, 1990, 1994).

One explanation for these departures from universality is obvious: We can easily put on an expression to signify an emotion different from the one we are experiencing. We can smile politely at a joke we really don't find amusing, and we can pretend to be unruffled when we don't want to let on that we are intimidated. Hamlet was surely not the first to note that one may smile and smile and be a villain. But this kind of witting and deliberate duplicity is probably not what accounts for the Japanese-American differences. Instead, they may reflect **cultural display rules,** learned but deeply ingrained conventions—often obeyed without awareness—that govern what facial expressions may or may not be

A **B**

11.7 Culture and spontaneous facial expressions   (A) A Japanese and (B) an American student watched a film that depicted a rather gruesome scene. The photograph shows their expressions when they were alone. Under these conditions, their facial expressions were virtually identical. But when they watched while being interviewed by another person, the Japanese smiled more than the Americans. (From Ekman and Friesen, 1975)

shown in what contexts (Ekman, 1985; Ekman and Friesen, 1986; Ekman, Friesen, and O'Sullivan, 1988). Certainly, the fact that the Japanese may have indicated politeness toward the investigator rather than revulsion toward the film is consistent with the primacy accorded interpersonal harmony in Japanese culture (Markus and Kitayama, 1994).

FACIAL EXPRESSIONS AND THE JAMES-LANGE THEORY

The foregoing discussion has treated our facial expressions as indications of our emotional states. But recall that in the James-Lange theory our bodily changes—including our muscular actions—give rise to our emotional experience. A study cited above suggested that posture might affect emotional response (Stepper and Strack, 1993). Might our facial expressions not only reflect our emotional state, but also help to produce it? Such is the claim of advocates for what has been termed the *facial feedback hypothesis* (Tourangeau and Ellsworth, 1979; and see Tomkins, 1962, 1963). The problem is that research to evaluate this hypothesis is quite difficult to undertake. The usual approach is to ask participants to sustain certain facial movements while engaging them in some other task and then asking them to report their emotional experience during the task. The reported emotional experience of these participants is then compared to that of controls who do not receive the facial-movement instructions. The daunting task for experimenters is findings ways to keep participants from guessing from their facial expressions how they think they *should* react emotionally. Perhaps the most imaginative attempt had participants view cartoons while holding a felt-tip pen either with clenched teeth (producing a smile) or with pursed lips (producing a pucker). Those who puckered rated the cartoons less amusing than those who smiled (Strack, Martin, and Stepper, 1988). Despite this positive outcome, studies of the facial feedback hypothesis show conflicting results, and the hypothesis remains controversial (see Tourangeau and Ellsworth, 1979; Winton, 1986; Adelmann and Zajonc, 1989; Izard, 1990; Fridlund, 1994).

FACIAL EXPRESSIONS AS COMMUNICATIONS

So far we have treated facial expressions as though they were the natural and spontaneous outcome (and, perhaps, a determinant) of an underlying emotional state. Of course, that is not to say that we can't hide or fake an emotional reaction, but, in general, when we are happy, we smile; when sad, we cry. But there is an alternative view. Recall that Darwin proposed a connection between our facial expressions and the displays of our primate relatives. Similarly, some researchers contend that our facial expressions are primarily *communicative displays* that are not so much a revelation of an inner state as they are a message to others about actions we may take or wish others to take. Just as the monkey's fear grin signals submission (Van Hooff, 1972), adherents of the communicative display position argue that the pouty face signals that we want to be comforted or embraced, the angry face that we want others to take us seriously, obey us, or back off, and so forth. The smile doesn't necessarily mean that we are happy, but rather that we want to play or be friends (e.g., Patterson, 1983; Mandler, 1984, 1997; Fridlund, 1991a, 1994).

Advocates of the communicative view offer several lines of evidence. First, it's simply not true that facial expressions are the inevitable and natural result of someone's feeling a particular emotion. This is illustrated, for example, by a study of gold medalists at the 1992 Olympic Games. The medalists were observed as they waited behind the podium for their medals, then while they

11.8 Facial expressions do not necessarily indicate our emotions *Olympic athletes rate standing on the podium in their medals as among the very happiest moments in their lives. Yet few smile—until they shake the presenter's hand. (Morocco's Khalid Skah, gold medalist in the 10,000-meter race at the 1992 Olympics; photograph by Eric Risberg/AP)*

received them from the presenters, and finally, while they stood and faced the flag and listened to the national anthem. Nearly all gold medalists report their mood during the entire awards ceremony as unambiguously, deliriously happy. But even so, they rarely smiled while waiting to receive the medals or while facing the flag and listening to the anthem. Other expressions and facial movements predominated (Fernandez-Dols and Ruiz-Belda, 1995; see Figure 11.8). Only when they received their medal did they smile.

This finding is consistent with other evidence that facial expressions occur mostly when we are in the presence of others and especially when we make eye contact with them. In one study, bowlers were observed when they made spares or strikes. The bowlers didn't smile at the moment of their success. Their smiles came later—when they turned around in the lane and met the gaze of their friends (Kraut and Johnston, 1979). What holds for adult bowlers also holds for ten-month-old infants playing with toys while their mothers watch on the sidelines. They smile most often when they turn to watch their mothers watching them (Jones, Collins, and Raag, 1991; for data on preschoolers, see Schneider and Josephs, 1991).

A possible objection to this position is that we sometimes make faces when we are alone. But we also talk in private, and the instances in which we do so may be the very same ones that lead to private faces. When we talk to or make faces at ourselves, we act as if we are both the sender and the recipient of the message (e.g., when scolding ourselves) or as if we are interacting with others who are present only in our imagination (Fridlund, 1991, 1994; Chovil, 1991).

The power of such implicit interactions was demonstrated by a study in which participants viewed amusing videotapes in one of four contexts: while sitting with a friend, while believing that a friend was also watching in an adjacent room, while believing that a friend was in an adjacent room but taking a test, and while alone. Compared to solitary viewing, participants smiled much more when they viewed the videotape with a friend, but they smiled just as much when they merely believed that the friend was viewing the tape (Fridlund, 1991). Such *audience effects* have been demonstrated for many different facial expressions and in many different situations (Chovil, 1991; Wagner and Smith, 1991; Hess, Banse, and Kappas, 1995; Jakobs, Fischer, and Manstead, 1997; but see Jakobs, Manstead, and Fischer, 1996; and see Chapter 10 for discussion of audience effects in nonhumans).

Of course, considering facial expressions as signals or solicitations does not exclude a role for emotion. In part, facial expressions may signify what is going on inside; in part, they may be messages we send to others. Perhaps our emotional state primes us to make expressions, while the momentary social context determines which expressions we make and when we make them. For now, both perspectives offer valuable insights into what our facial expressions mean.

ARE THERE BASIC, UNIVERSAL EMOTIONS?

Much of our discussion so far has focused on a relatively narrow set of emotions—fear and anger, happiness and sadness. This reflects a belief on the part of many investigators that these are among the *basic emotions*—coherent patterns of feelings, internal physiological changes, outward expressions, and behavior (such as approach or avoidance) that are hardwired, adaptive, automatic, and the result of natural selection (e.g., Izard, 1991, 1994; Ekman, 1992).

Other investigators, however, question this premise. For one thing, the number of emotions held to be "basic" varies from one theorist to another (Ortony and Turner, 1990). One account lists only two, pain and pleasure (Mowrer, 1960); another lists six: surprise, anger, sadness, disgust, fear, and contempt (Ekman, 1984); others list from eight to eighteen and may include emotions like shame, guilt, arrogance, and indifference (e.g., Izard, 1971, 1991; Plutchik, 1980; Frijda, 1986). And one critic noted that lust, by any reasoning, should be a—perhaps *the*—basic emotion, yet it is found on no such list (Mandler, 1997).

Nor is there any consensus on what would make an emotion "basic." On one account, an emotion is basic if it can be linked to an identifiable facial expression (Ekman, 1984). A second account stipulates that a basic emotion must have its own hardwired neural circuitry (e.g., Izard, 1977). The difficulty with these two accounts is that their criteria yield different lists. As we saw in Chapter 3, the states of hunger and thirst have their own dedicated neural circuitry and might therefore be considered emotions, but they have no associated facial expressions. In contrast, many consider sadness to have an identifiable facial expression, yet there is little evidence for any neural circuitry dedicated to this emotion.

In a third approach, what makes an emotion basic is that it cannot be reduced to any combination of other emotions. This approach, reminiscent of that used to establish color primaries, has the advantage of clarifying the complexity of our emotional lives. For example, we can distinguish among resignation, regret, grief, and despair as well as satisfaction, jubilation, rapture, and serenity. Are these two groups of emotions simply shades of sadness and happiness, respectively? Some theorists have suggested so. In one theory, jealousy is not basic because it can be regarded as a mix of fear and anger; nor is anxiety, because it reflects a complex interaction of fear, guilt, sadness, and shame (Izard, 1991).

Although this account is plausible, it is difficult to prove. The example of jealousy shows why: If we are jealous of another's success, we very well may be both angry about it and fearful of what that success may mean for us. But it is equally true that, if we are accosted by a stranger, we may be both fearful that he will hurt us and angry that he has intruded upon us in the first place. In this case, we are again both angry and afraid, but surely not jealous. Explaining why fear and anger might produce jealousy in the first instance but not in the second is likely to be quite complex, and this complexity suggests why the evidence that some emotions are actually composites of other, more basic ones is weak at best (Ortony and Turner, 1990).

Anger at moral transgression *Waiting in line to avoid righteous anger. (© The New Yorker Collection 1960, 1988 Chas. Addams from Cartoonbank. com. All rights reserved.)*

COMPLEX EMOTIONS

Another approach to understanding the full range of human emotions is more cognitive. Adherents of this position contend that some emotions can be distinguished by the level of symbolic processing they require. Embarrassment, for example, seems to require knowledge of both one's social role and one's social standing. Further examples are such emotional experiences as pity, anger, guilt, and regret, all of which depend on a complex appraisal of why we or someone else failed or succeeded in some endeavor, an analysis that even the cleverest chimpanzee would find impossible.

PITY, ANGER, AND GUILT

Consider the emotions of pity, anger, and guilt. Each of them is aroused by some misfortune. According to Bernard Weiner, which particular emotion is felt depends on our perception of how this misfortune came about. If we hear that Mary failed an important exam because she went to a party the night before, we feel a bit angry (all the more so, if we really like her, wanted her to do well, and

Anger as a social emotion *A four-year-old in self-righteous anger at a playmate who is using one of her toys and won't relinquish it. (Photograph by Suzanne Szasz)*

perhaps even helped her study for the exam). But if she failed the exam because she had been ill all semester, we're more likely to pity her. In the first case, we feel that the failure was Mary's own fault, in the second, that she failed but couldn't help it (Weiner, 1982).

In these examples, the emotion is provoked by another person who performed (or did not perform) the act that led to the unfortunate outcome. But a similar analysis applies when the emotional target is oneself. Here, too, what matters is whether one could or could not control the outcome. If it was controllable, we feel guilt (which in a sense is anger directed at oneself). If it was not controllable, we feel self-pity.

Still further complexities are introduced by the fact that, in humans, certain emotions—such as righteous anger and guilt—involve an appreciation of a moral order. Consider anger. Imagine that you are waiting in line to buy a pair of World Series tickets. By the time you reach the ticket office you find out that there are no more tickets left; the person just in front of you bought the very last pair. Do you get angry at him? You may get angry about your bad luck and curse the fates, but you won't get angry at him. You somehow recognize that his position in the line gave him the right to the tickets. The situation would be very different if he had pushed himself ahead of you. In that case you would become fiercely angry, because you would perceive his act as a moral transgression (Averill, 1978; Sabini and Silver, 1982).

Of course, anger also has a biological basis, perhaps similar to the aggression one sees in nonhumans (Chapter 10). But for humans, anger is often much more than this. We've seen that it can involve the appreciation of another person's intentions and capacities. Beyond that, it also involves some sense of moral rights and transgressions. At this point, it is not *rage,* but *outrage.* Given all that, it clearly transcends its biological roots.

REGRET

Yet another complex emotion is regret, a reaction produced by comparing the outcomes of whatever one did with what one might have done. It is the emotion of the might have been.

We've all had the experience of almost achieving some desired goal but just missing out. Somehow such near-misses are much more painful than attempts that don't come close at all. The person who gets a lottery ticket that differs from the winning number by just one digit feels much worse than the one whose number is way off the mark. The same holds for the golfer whose putt rims the hole but doesn't drop in, or the actor who *almost* landed the lead role. This general phenomenon has been documented in a number of studies in which participants were presented with various scenarios and had to indicate their reactions. One example concerns a missed plane:

> Mr. Crane and Mr. Tees were scheduled to leave the airport on different flights, at the same time. They traveled from town in the same limousine, were caught in a traffic jam, and arrived at the airport thirty minutes after the scheduled departure time of their flights.
>
> Mr. Crane is told that his plane left on time. Mr. Tees is told that his flight was delayed, and left five minutes ago.
>
> Who is more upset? (Kahneman and Tversky, 1982, p. 203)

It is no surprise that the virtually unanimous answer was Mr. Tees, who suffered the near miss. But why should this be so, considering that the objective situation of the two men was identical, since they both missed their planes? Kahneman and Tversky believe the near miss is more upsetting because it is much easier to imagine that one might have arrived five minutes earlier than half an hour earlier. If only the limousine had made just one more traffic light, if only the baggage had been unloaded a bit more quickly, if only. . . .

A number of further findings represent variations on the same general theme. In one study, participants read about two people who died of exposure after surviving a plane crash in a remote area. One victim, they learned, made it to within a quarter mile of safety; the other came within seventy-five miles. They were then asked to determine how much the victims' families should be compensated. The participants recommended a considerably higher sum for the family of the victim who came quite close than for the family of the victim who perished farther away. They evidently felt that the fate of the first victim, the one who came so close, was worse (more "unfair" so to speak) than that of the second. In their imaginary reconstructions, they found it easier to construct a mental simulation for undoing the first victim's fate than for undoing the second's—if he'd only known how close he was, if he'd just been able to take a few more steps. . . .

Regret *The sadness of "It might have been."* *(© The New Yorker Collection 1956, 1984 Chas. Addams from Cartoonbank.com. All rights reserved.)*

A similar account may explain why misfortunes that are caused by some exceptional departure from routine seem especially regrettable. That someone died on the *Titanic* is terrible enough, but it appears even more terrible if he only got his ticket because of a last-minute cancellation by a passenger who suddenly fell ill. It's apparently easier to create a mental script for undoing an unusual circumstance than to imagine how more usual patterns of events can be altered (Kahneman and Miller, 1986; also see Gilovich and Medvec, 1995).

CULTURE AND EMOTION

The pattern of these complex emotions undermines the claim that they are somehow the result of mixing together a number of more basic emotions. This in turn weakens the suggestion that there are, in fact, some emotions that are truly "basic." Similar conclusions emerge when we consider another source of evidence—how emotions are experienced by members of other cultures.

Basic emotions are generally assumed to be closely tied to our biology—rooted in our evolutionary past and shaped by hard-wired patterns in our nervous system. If so, then basic emotions are a trait of our species and should be found in all cultures. We have already considered the cross-cultural universality of facial expressions, but what about the emotions themselves?

It is notable that the common lists of "basic" emotions used in cross-cultural research were all constructed by Westerners, because, in fact, cultures differ widely in their **emotion lexicons**—the vocabularies available to describe emotions. Obviously, the words used by different peoples to denote emotions may tell us little about their inner, emotional lives. But if certain emotions are truly basic and universal, then one might expect all cultures to share roughly the same categorization of emotions.

Instead, across cultures one finds no common list of basic emotions. Some cultures appear to have no words for emotions that many Westerners consider basic; thus, the people who live on the western Pacific Island of Ifaluk lack a word for surprise, and the Tahitians lack a word for sadness. Other cultures have words that describe common emotions for which we have no special terms. Thus, the Ifaluk often feel an emotion they call *fago,* which involves a complex mixture of compassion, love, and sadness experienced in relationships in which one person is dependent on the other (Lutz, 1986, 1988). And the Japanese report a common emotion called *amae,* which is a desire to be dependent and cared for (Doi, 1973; Morsbach and Tyler, 1986). The German language reserves the word *Schadenfreude* for the special pleasure derived from another's misfortune.

But putting these issues of vocabulary aside, how are the emotions *felt* by members of various cultures? Some evidence suggests commonality. We have already mentioned the common reports of bodily reactions while experiencing anger and fear. It also seems that certain events lead to pretty much the same emotions the world over; examples are bereavement and the anticipation of physical danger (Mesquita and Frijda, 1992; Frijda and Mesquita, 1994). Furthermore, the ways that people appraise emotional situations are similar across many cultures (Ellsworth, 1994; Scherer, 1997). Thus, Westerners can likely sympathize with the feelings of people who experience *fago* or *amae* or *Schadenfreude* and may sometimes experience such feelings themselves, even if they don't have a name for them.

But there may also be important differences in how people in various cultures experience emotion. Recall, for example, the contrast between individualist and collectivist cultures in both the social roles of their members and in how their members explain the behavior of others. Given these dramatic differences, some observers question whether emotional experience could ever be identical across cultures, especially for complex emotions that require so much symbolic processing. For example, can we feel Western-style guilt if we believe that the situation determined our actions? Can we feel Eastern-style shame if we believe that we are ultimately beholden to no one? Acquiescence, obligation, self-criticism, and submersion of the self within the group are intimately associated with "good" feelings in collectivist cultures and "bad" feelings in individualist ones (Markus and Kitayama, 1994; Kitayama, Markus, and Matsumoto, 1995). And given the difference between individualist and collectivist cultures in attributions about behavior, members of individualist cultures may be more likely to "look inside" and attend to their physiological reactions when they are emotional, whereas members of collectivist cultures may tend to "look outside" and attend to their ongoing social relations (Paez and Vergara, 1995). These contrasts raise the possibility that, in diverse cultures, emotions may not only have different names, but may *feel* different as well (see Schweder, 1994). On this issue, the jury is still out.

EMOTION AND THE THEATER

There is a certain emotional experience that is in some ways quite unlike those we encounter in everyday life—the emotion we feel when watching a play or a movie. Is it a real emotion? Sometimes it seems to be. Some plays or movies can obviously move us to tears. As children, we weep when Bambi's mother is killed; as adults, at Juliet's death. In retrospect, we may insist that while watching the play or the movie, we were really "into it" and had come to accept the characters' joys and sorrows as though they were real. But did we truly?

Consider a great performance of *Oedipus Rex*, climaxed by the awesome scene in which Oedipus blinds himself. We may say that while watching the play we believed that what happened on stage was reality. In fact, we did no such thing. If we had, we would have experienced horror instead of tragic awe; we would have rushed for help, perhaps shouting, "Is there an ophthalmologist in the house?" In fact, we never believe that the stage Oedipus is real; at best, we are willing to suspend our disbelief, as the poet Coleridge so aptly put it. But in the fringes of our consciousness we retain the knowledge that we

Children at a Punch-and-Judy show The younger child, upset over the fate of one of the puppets, is reassured by her older brother. (Photograph by Suzanne Szasz)

are sitting a comfortable theater seat. We may suspend disbelief, but this does not mean that we believe.

The emotions we experience in the theater cannot be identical to those we have in the real world. But then, what are they? When we witness certain events in real life—a tearful reunion, a fistfight, a funeral—we experience real emotions. When analogous events occur on stage or on the screen, they trigger a similar arousal. But the cognitive context is quite different, for we still know that we are sitting in a darkened theater. The experience is analogous to that "cold fear" produced by injecting epinephrine, that "as if" emotion that occurs in participants who cannot attribute their arousal to any external cause.

The special esthetic flavor of the theatrical experience probably depends upon just this "as if." This quality requires a delicate balance between disbelief and belief, between too little arousal and too much. On the one hand, there must be some sense of being "into it," or we will remain cold and dispassionate, like the bored usher who has seen the same show over and over again. On the other hand, too much arousal will also defeat the esthetic goal, for the "as if" feeling will then be lost altogether. A theatrically naive audience may believe that what happens on stage is the real thing, as in children's theater, where the four- and five-year-olds shout fearful warnings at Snow White when the evil old witch approaches. Their seven-year-old cousins are less naive and thus more capable of enjoying a genuine dramatic experience. They feel aroused and excited, but they can reassure their young friends with an air of theaterwise sophistication, "Don't worry—it's not really real."

When a performance threatens to become too real, sophisticated adults may protect themselves by laughing nervously and thus breaking the spell altogether. This reaction to the loss of "psychical distance" (Bullough, 1912) is sometimes seen in theaters in the round, where the audience surrounds the playing area and those in the front row can almost touch the actors. If the play is a blood-and-guts melodrama, in-the-round staging may become too close for comfort. Suppose there is a well-acted scene in which a man almost murders his wife with an ax. The members of the audience directly adjacent to the two actors are very likely to avert their heads. The scene has become too real and the emotion too genuine. The audience responds by breaking contact.

The "as if" experience may also be an important ingredient in the emotion the actor feels as she plays her part. Many dramatic critics have asked the question, "What does the actor feel when portraying the jealousy of Othello or the anger, pride, disillusionment, and sorrow of Nora in *A Doll's House*?" According

Emotion and the actor *A scene from Arthur Miller's* The Crucible, *in which John Proctor confronts Abigail Williams after she accused his wife of witchcraft. John and Abigail are no doubt in a turbulent emotional episode. But were the actors who portrayed them? (Daniel Day-Lewis and Winona Ryder in the 1996 film; photograph courtesy of Photofest)*

to some schools of acting (such as the famous Actors' Studio of New York, which teaches Stanislavski's "method"), the actor's job is to bring emotional reality to her role. In practice, the actor accomplishes this by vividly recalling some emotion-filled fragments of her own life that are appropriate to her present role. The result is often a scene of genuine dramatic truth, felt by both actor and audience.

Admirable as this may be, is it real in the sense in which everyday emotion is real? Again, the answer is almost surely no. No sane actor who ever played Othello really wanted to strangle the actress who portrayed Desdemona. Yet there is nevertheless this "as if" experience, a state of arousal perceived and interpreted within a cognitive context that includes both the situation of the character and that of the actor who plays the character (H. Gleitman, 1990).

The "as if" experience may be an important ingredient in the appreciation of several art forms. In theater, it is our simultaneous awareness of events that may move us deeply and yet that we know to be unreal. In the visual arts it is the simultaneous awareness of a scene or object that looks lifelike but that is nonetheless seen to be a flat, painted canvas (see Chapter 6).

TAKING STOCK

On looking back, we should note that many of the phenomena we've considered in this chapter may involve the operation of either (or both) cognition and motivation, or to use two old-fashioned terms, reason and passion. Consider the effect of forced compliance: Is it caused by a force toward cognitive consistency (that is, dissonance reduction) or by an attempt to minimize guilt? Or take the actor-observer bias in attribution: Is it produced by such cognitive factors as differential information and distinct perspectives or by the self-serving bias? Finally, consider emotion: Here, if anywhere, motivational factors should be paramount, but we saw that even here—the very stronghold of passion—cognitive processes operate jointly with motivational ones to determine what we experience.

Both reason and passion determine what we think, and feel, and do. As we try to make sense of our social world, we try to be rational, but our otherwise useful cognitive strategies often lead us to rely on various mental shortcuts and schemas that may result in errors and biases. Since we are people with motives, and passions, and a need to maintain self-esteem, we are sometimes wishful thinkers rather than rational ones.

SUMMARY

1. Social behavior depends in part on how people interpret the situations they encounter. The processes that lead to such interpretations are in many ways similar to those that underlie our cognitive processes in general.

2. Our conception of what is real is heavily affected by confirmation from others, as shown by Asch's study on the effects of group pressure and by the need for *social comparison,* especially in ambiguous situations.

3. To make sense of the world, people look for *cognitive consistency.* According to *cognitive dissonance theory,* they will do what they can to reduce any inconsistency (disso-

nance) they perceive by reinterpreting information to fit with their knowledge, feelings, and behavior.

4.   The interpretation of the situations people encounter is affected by their *attitudes,* which vary from one person to another. Attitudes are rather stable mental positions held toward some idea, object, or person, which combine beliefs, feelings, evaluations, and predispositions toward action.

5.   Social psychologists have studied a number of approaches to changing attitudes. One concerns the effectiveness of persuasive communications. This depends in part on various characteristics of the message's source, including that source's trustworthiness and credibility. It also depends on characteristics of the message itself. Some contend that strong arguments will be more likely to change attitudes if the message comes in through the *central route* than if it enters through the *peripheral route,* where there is more reliance on rough-and-ready heuristics.

6.   Another approach asserts that attitude change is often produced by an attempt to reduce *cognitive dissonance.* There is some evidence, however, that the dissonance reduction effects observed in *justification-of-effort* and *forced-compliance studies* are a way of protecting the individual's *favorable self-picture* rather than a means to remove logical inconsistency.

7.   While these various means for changing attitudes have some effect, attitudes tend to remain rather stable, in part because of cognitive consistency, which on the whole is a force for keeping things the way they are, and in part because people tend to stay in the same social and economic environment.

8.   The way we perceive others is in some ways similar to the way we perceive and think of inanimate objects or events. Some theorists believe that impressions of others can be regarded as patterns whose elements are interpreted in terms of the whole, thus accounting for the role of *central traits* and of *primacy effects* in impression formation. More recent theorists emphasize the role of social cognition, which leads to the formation of *schemas* and *implicit theories of personality.*

9.   Our perception of people is further complicated by the fact that they know they are being perceived, which may lead to attempts at *impression management.* Failures at impression management may lead to embarrassment. This can be caused by loss of self-esteem and also by the disruption of a social interaction that no one knows how to repair, as in *empathetic embarrassment.*

10.   Attribution theory tries to explain how we infer the causes of another person's behavior, attributing them either to *situational factors* or to *dispositional qualities.* In part, this process is quite rational and depends on the conditions in which the behavior in question is seen to occur. But it can also lead to various errors. In judging others, we tend to make the *fundamental attribution error,* overestimating the role of dispositional qualities and underestimating that of situational factors. This attribution bias is reversed when we ourselves are the actors rather than the observers. Reasons for the *actor-observer difference* include the fact that we know ourselves better than anyone else and that actors and observers have different perspectives. An additional reason is the *self-serving bias,* which tends to make people deny responsibility for their failures while taking credit for their successes; it is probably also responsible for the *above-average effect.*

11.   According to self-perception theory, similar attribution processes determine how we perceive ourselves. In line with this theory is evidence that people realign their self-perceptions to fit their behavior, as shown in studies using the *foot-in-the-door technique.*

12.   *Cross-cultural research* suggests that many sociopsychological phenomena such as the distress experienced with conformity, the fundamental attributional error, the self-serving bias, and the above-average effect may be especially pronounced in, or even the result of, the individualistic values of Western cultures. These effects tend to be reduced or nonexistent in collectivist cultures.

13.   An influential attempt to explain what gives rise to emotion is Schachter and Singer's *attribution-of-arousal theory,* which is a successor of the *James-Lange theory of emotions.* According to the James-Lange theory, our subjective experience of emotion is sim-

SUMMARY

ply an awareness of our own bodily changes (both autonomic and skeletal) in the presence of certain arousing stimuli. In contrast, proponents of the attribution-of-arousal theory argue that the emotion we feel is an interpretation of bodily responses and especially of our own autonomic arousal in light of the situation to which we attribute it. *Misattribution effects* of autonomic arousal occur when the situation is inaccurately credited with the arousal; carry-over of arousal can also occur, as in *excitation transfer.*

14.   All levels of the brain, from the hindbrain to the neocortex, appear to be involved in emotion, but one region has received particular attention—the *amygdala*, which lies within the temporal lobe, and plays an important role in tagging stimuli with emotional significance.

15.   Charles Darwin offered the *universality thesis* of facial expressions—that facial expressions are shared by all humans and used to express the same emotions—which has been supported by some cross-cultural studies, although the evidence is not conclusive. Learned *display rules* may also determine which expressions are appropriate in a given culture.

16.   Some theorists hearken back to the James-Lange theory and suggest that facial expressions not only reflect our emotional state but also help to produce it. Since studies of this *facial feedback theory* offer conflicting results, the theory remains controversial. An alternative view proposes that facial expressions are primarily *communicative displays,* as shown by the fact that they occur primarily when we are in the presence of others or when we think about others.

17.   Many theorists contend that several *basic emotions* underlie the wide range of emotions that humans are able to experience and that the *complex emotions* we feel are composites of the basic emotions. Others question the existence of basic emotions, pointing to the fact that lists of so-called basic emotions vary from researcher to researcher and that supporters do not agree on what makes an emotion "basic." Critics also point out that the composite approach to complex emotions doesn't work because it can't explain why a combination of certain emotions does not always yield the same complex response. An alternative explanation of complex emotions takes a more cognitive approach, contending that complex emotions are those that require a high level of symbolic processing. Some depend on the judgments that a bad outcome was controllable (anger) or that it was not (pity). Others depend on the construction of cognitive scenarios that involve what might have been (regret). Still others depend on an "as if" experience, such as the emotion we feel while watching a theatrical performance.

CHAPTER **12**

S O C I A L
I N T E R A C T I O N

I n the previous chapter, we discussed the ways in which we try to understand our social world. Our primary emphasis was on social cognition: our attitudes and how they are changed, our impressions of people, our interpretation of why they do what they do, and finally, the way that we ourselves interpret our own actions and experiences. In this chapter, our focus will be on action, or more precisely, *interaction*, as we ask how people deal with each other, influence each other, and act in groups.

We will consider four major kinds of interaction: Some are *one on one,* as when two friends have dinner or a customer tries to bargain with a used-car salesman; some are *many on one,* where many people act upon one individual, as when teenagers pressure one of their peers to wear the same clothes as all the rest; some are *one on many,* where one person influences many others, as in various forms of leadership; some are interactions that can be described as *many on many,* as in riots or panics when many people affect many others and are in turn affected by them.

RELATING TO OTHERS: ONE-ON-ONE INTERACTIONS

How do people interact one on one? To a large extent, the answer depends on the relationship they have with one another. We deal one way with strangers, another with people we know and like, and yet another with those we know but don't like. Still, according to many social scientists, there are some common threads that run through most of our relationships, no matter how tenuous or strong.

SOCIAL EXCHANGE AND RECIPROCITY

A number of theorists believe that one common principle that underlies the way people deal with others is **social exchange.** According to this view, each partner in a relationship gives something to the other and expects to receive something in return. Just what is exchanged depends on the relationship. If the relationship is primarily economic, as between buyers and sellers or employees and employers, the exchange will involve goods or labor for money. If it is between friends, lovers, or family members, the exchange will involve valued intangibles such as esteem, loyalty, and affection. According to social exchange theory, all (or at least, most) human relationships are **exchange relationships,** which have this underlying give-and-take quality. If one partner gives and receives nothing in return, the relationship will disintegrate sooner or later (Kelley and Thibaut, 1978).

Social exchange *The process of social exchange is most obvious when it is economic.*

The social exchange perspective is essentially economic and thus quite appropriate to the realm of material transactions. In the marketplace, money provides a common standard by which the value of commodities can be assessed. As a result, the value of what is given and received can be compared. This comparison is much harder (if not impossible) to make when the exchange involves such "commodities" as praise or loyalty, let alone love.

In fact, some social psychologists have identified what they call ***communal relationships,*** which do not seem to operate according to rules of exchange. In such relationships, the "self" is expanded to include the "other," so that "we" becomes the operative unit, and the other's gains are seen as one's own. Such communal relationships are most commonly observed among romantic partners and close family members (Clark and Mills, 1979, 1993; Borden and Levinger, 1991; Mills and Clark, 1994).

Whether the social exchange approach applies to all social interactions is therefore a matter of debate, but that it applies to some is indubitable. One important indication is the operation of the ***reciprocity principle.*** This is a basic rule that affects many aspects of social behavior. We feel that we somehow must repay whatever we have been given: a favor for a favor, a gift for a gift, a smile for a smile. As one author points out, this sense of social indebtedness is so deeply ingrained that it has been built into the vocabulary of several languages: Thus, *much obliged* is a virtual synonym for *thank you* (Cialdini, 1984).

RECIPROCITY AND PERSUASION

According to Robert Cialdini, the reciprocity principle can become a powerful tool of persuasion (Cialdini, 1984, 1993). Cialdini points out that accepting a favor necessarily leads to a sense of indebtedness. We feel that we must repay a donor, even if we never wanted his gift in the first place. As a result, we are sometimes manipulated into compliance—saying yes or buying some merchandise or making a donation—despite the fact that we never really wanted to. As an example, Cialdini describes the techniques the Hare Krishna Society used to employ in soliciting donations. Members of this sect would approach airport travelers and press a flower into their hands. Travelers would typically want to return the unwanted gift, but the Krishna members would not take the flower back, insisting sweetly that "It is our gift to you." The members' next step would be to request a donation to the society. Many travelers felt that under the circumstances they had no choice. Since they took the gift (no matter how unwillingly), they believed that they had to reciprocate. Their only defense—and many travelers resorted to it—was to beware of Krishnas bearing gifts!

The reciprocal-concession effect Still another kind of behavior often affected by the reciprocity rule is bargaining. The seller states her price. The potential buyer says no. Now the seller makes a concession by offering the item (the house, the car, or whatever) at a lower price. This very concession exerts a pressure on the buyer to increase her offer; since the seller offered a concession, the buyer feels that she ought to give a little on her side too.

The reciprocal-concession effect has been the subject of several investigations. In one study, an experimenter approached people walking on a university campus and first made a very large request. He asked them to work as unpaid volunteer counselors in a juvenile detention center for two hours a week over a two-year period. Not a single person agreed. The experimenter then made a much smaller request: that they accompany a group of boys or girls from the juvenile detention center on a single two-hour trip to the zoo. When this smaller request came on the heels of the large request that had been refused, 50 percent of those asked consented. In contrast, only 17 percent acceded to the smaller request

Homogamy American Gothic *by Grant Wood, 1930 (Photograph © 1992 The Art Institute of Chicago, all rights reserved)*

magnets do, for the evidence suggests that, in general, people tend to like others who are similar to themselves. For example, elementary school students prefer other children who perform about as well as they do in academics, sports, and music (Tesser, Campbell, and Smith, 1984), and best friends in high school resemble each other in age, race, year in school, and high-school grades (Kandel, 1978).

Whether similarity of personality characteristics such as sociability and extroversion play a similar role in determining attraction is still unclear. But there is no doubt that attributes such as race, ethnic origin, social and educational level, family background, income, and religion do affect marital choice. This also holds for such behavioral patterns as the degree of gregariousness and drinking and smoking habits. One widely cited study showed that engaged couples in the United States are generally similar along all of these dimensions (Burgess and Wallin, 1943). The authors interpreted these findings as evidence for **homogamy**—a powerful tendency for like to select like.

Another study showed that homogamy also plays a role in determining a couple's stability: Couples who remained together after two-and-a-half years were more similar than those who had broken up (Hill, Rubin, and Peplau, 1976). And married couples tend to be similar on nearly all personality dimensions (Caspi and Herbener, 1990). However, this association may in part be a function of the longevity of the relationship, given that couples may become more alike over time by virtue of their continual interaction; indeed, some evidence suggests that they grow more similar in their verbal skills, degree of open-mindedness, and even their physical appearance (Zajonc et al., 1987; Gruber-Baldini, Schaie, and Willis, 1995).

Is homogamy really produced by the effect of similarity on mutual liking? Or is it just a by-product of proximity, of the fact that "few of us have an opportunity to meet, interact with, become attracted to, and marry a person markedly dissimilar from ourselves"? (Berscheid and Walster, 1978, p. 87). The answer is uncertain, but, in either case, the end product is the same: Like pairs with like, and few heiresses ever marry the butler except in the movies. We're not really surprised to discover that when a princess kisses a frog he turns into a prince. But we would be surprised to see the frog turn into a peasant, and then see the princess marry him anyway.

PHYSICAL ATTRACTIVENESS

There is little doubt that for a given time and culture there is considerable agreement as to how physically attractive a particular man or woman is. Nor is there any doubt that this factor is overwhelmingly important in determining a person's appeal—or at least his or her initial appeal—to most members of the opposite sex. The vast sums of money spent on cosmetics, fashion, health and beauty magazines, diets, and various forms of plastic surgery are one kind of testimony; our everyday experience is another. Under the circumstances, one may wonder whether there is any need to document the point experimentally, but in any case, such documentation does exist.

In one study, freshmen were randomly paired at a dance and later asked how much they liked their partner and whether they might want to go out with him or her. The main factor that determined each person's desirability as a future date was his or her physical attractiveness (Walster et al., 1966). Similar results were found in a study of the clients of a commercial video-dating service, who selected partners after consulting files that included a photograph, background information, and detailed information about interests, hobbies, and personal ideals. When it came to the actual choice, the primary determinant was the photograph: Both male and female clients selected on the basis of physical attractiveness (Green, Buchanan, and Heuer, 1984).

501

Physically attractive individuals also benefit from the common belief that what is beautiful is good, because people tend to associate physical attractiveness with a variety of positive personality traits, including dominance, good social skills, intelligence, happiness, and good mental health (see Dion, Berscheid, and and Walster, 1972). And there is an element of truth to this stereotype: physically attractive people actually are more popular and sexually experienced, less socially anxious and lonely, but at least they are not more intelligent (Eagly et al., 1991; Feingold, 1992; Jackson, Hunter, and Hodge, 1995).

Matching for attractiveness   Physical attractiveness is clearly a very desirable quality. But if we all set our sights on only those at the very top of this dimension, the world would soon be depopulated—there are simply not enough movie stars to go around. Since world population continues to rise, we must assume that people behave in a more sensible fashion. They may covet the most attractive of all possible mates, but they seek partners whose physical attractiveness is comparable to their own; they also seem to have a fairly reasonable perception of their own social desirability (which is determined in part by their own physical appeal). For while trying to get the most desirable partner, they also try to avoid rejection. This **matching hypothesis** predicts a strong correlation between the physical attractiveness of the two partners (Berscheid et al., 1971). This hypothesis is well supported by everyday observations ("They make such a fine couple!") and has been repeatedly documented in various empirical observations (Berscheid and Walster, 1974; White, 1980; Feingold, 1988).

What underlies physical attractiveness?   Our discussion has assumed that physical attractiveness is a given and that people pretty much agree on who is and who is not attractive. But why should this be? Why should one set of particular features, one set of bodily proportions, represent the apex of attractiveness for so many people in our time and culture? As yet we don't know.

So far we are only beginning to discover just what it is that constitutes physical attractiveness in our own culture. According to one study, American college men judge photographs of women (whether white, black, or Asian) as more attractive if their faces have certain features that tend to be found in children, such as relatively large, round, and widely separated eyes, a short nose, and a small chin. One might interpret this by claiming that perceived youthfulness is attractive because it is a sign of fertility. The trouble is that there are a number of other features

Attractiveness   *People ornament themselves in virtually every culture but choose different ways of doing so. (A) Masai man wearing ceremonial body paint (Photograph by Yann Arthus-Bertrand/© Corbis), (B) Karen (Myanmar) woman wearing brass neck coils to elongate her neck (Photograph by Kevin R. Morris/© Corbis)*

A   B

Attractiveness in our own society *Jennifer Lopez and George Clooney in a scene from* Out of Sight. *(Photograph by Merrick Morton, © 1998 Universal City Studios)*

judged to be attractive that are associated with maturity rather than immaturity, for example, wide cheekbones and narrow cheeks (Cunningham, 1986).

Another evolutionary prediction is that people should find symmetry in bodily features attractive, because even subtle asymmetries in potential mates—which may indicate malformation or disease—might reveal poor genetic quality. Consistent with such a prediction, symmetrical faces are perceived as somewhat more attractive (Grammer and Thornhill, 1994). Furthermore, subtle asymmetries in other parts of the body (for example, in the size of the hands or the feet) are associated with fewer sexual partners and later onset of sexual behavior (Thornhill and Gangestad, 1994). That people seem to be affected by such subtle asymmetries is notable, but people with asymmetrical features needn't worry, because the preference for symmetry is only a tendency. Nor is it clear whether this preference for symmetry constitutes an adaptation for mate selection or whether it merely reflects a general aesthetic preference for balance.

In any case, it is clear that the standards of attractiveness of face or body are not the same at different times and in different places. To be sure, some similarities do exist. Signs of ill health and deformity (which might suggest a poor genetic bet) are considered unattractive in all cultures. The same holds for signs of advancing age (which generally signal lower fertility, especially in women). In addition, all cultures want men to look like men and women to look like women, although the specific cues that inform this judgment vary widely. Beyond this, however, the differences—from one culture to the next and from one individual to the next—probably outweigh the similarities.

LOVE

Attraction tends to bring people closer together. If they are close enough, their relation may be that of love. According to some authorities, psychologists might have been "wise to have abdicated responsibility for analysis of this term and left it to poets" (Reber, 1985, p. 409). But wise or not, in recent years psychologists have tried to say some things about this strange state of mind that has puzzled both sages and poets throughout the ages.

Psychologists have tried to distinguish between different kinds of love. Some of the resulting classification systems are rather complex. One such scheme tries to analyze love relationships according to the presence or absence of three main

Revisiting Figure 12.4 *The familiarity-leads-to-liking hypothesis would predict a preference for the left panel—a retouched photograph of the Mona Lisa (see p. 500). The panel on the right is a mirror image of that photograph, which is presumably the less familiar of the two.*

components: intimacy, passion, and commitment (Sternberg, 1986, 1988). Whether we're at the stage at which we can really make the fine distinctions such systems propose is debatable. But most psychologists would agree that there are at least two crude categories. One is romantic—or passionate—love, the kind of love that one "falls into," that one is "in." The other is companionate love, a less violent state that emphasizes companionship, mutual trust, and care.

ROMANTIC LOVE

Romantic love has been described as essentially passionate: "a wildly emotional state [in which] tender and sexual feelings, elation and pain, anxiety and relief, altruism and jealousy coexist in a confusion of feelings" (Berscheid and Walster, 1978). The extent to which the lovers feel that they are in the grip of an emotion they can't control is indicated by the very language in which they describe their love: They "fall in love," "are swept off their feet," and "can't stop themselves." Surprisingly, men tend to fall in love more often and more quickly than women do, and women tend to fall out of love more easily than men do (Hill, Rubin, and Peplau, 1976).

The tumultuous emotions of romantic love are sharply focused on the beloved, who is almost always seen through a rosy glow. The lover constantly thinks about the beloved and continually wants to be in his or her company, sometimes to the point of near obsession. Given this giddy mixture of erotic, irrational, obsessive passions and idealized fantasy, it's understandable why Shakespeare felt that lovers have much in common with both madmen and poets. They are a bit mad because their emotions are so turbulent and their thoughts and actions so obsessive; they are a bit poetic because they don't see their beloved as he or she really is but as an idealized fabrication of their own desires and imaginings.

Romantic love *The blindness of romantic love is epitomized by Titania, Queen of the Fairies, in Shakespeare's* A Midsummer Night's Dream. *Titania is made to fall in love with Bottom whose head had been turned into that of an ass. (*Titania Awakes, Surrounded by Attendant Fairies, Clinging Rapturously to Bottom, Still Wearing the Ass's Head, *1793/94, by Henry Fuseli; Kunsthaus, Zurich (Switzerland), Society of Zurich Friends of Art;* © *1994 Kunsthaus Zurich. All rights reserved.)*

Romantic love and theories of emotions A number of investigators have argued that if romantic love is an emotion, then theories such as Schachter and Singer's attribution-of-arousal theory (see Chapter 11) should apply to it just as they do to fear, anger, and euphoria. According to some authors, the attribution-of-arousal theory does hold for romantic love (Walster and Berscheid, 1974; Walster and Walster, 1978).

According to Schachter and Singer, emotions have two components. One is a state of physiological arousal. The other is the appropriate cognitive context in the light of which that arousal is interpreted. Let's begin with the context for romantic love. This includes our various ideas of what love and falling in love are all about. Our notions of romantic love—that one must find one's "soul mate" and that no one else will do, that it can occur at "first sight," that one is often "helpless in the throes of love," that the beloved is a paragon of all possible virtues, and so on and so on—are at least in part cultural inventions. They were fashioned by a historical heritage that goes back to Greek and Roman times (with tales of lovers hit by Cupid's arrows), were revived during the Middle Ages (with knights in armor slaying dragons to win a lady's favor), and were finally mass-produced by the Hollywood entertainment machine (with a final fade-out in which boy and girl embrace to live happily ever after).★ This complex set of ideas about what love is, together with an appropriate potential love object—attractive, of the right age, more or less available, and so on—constitute the context that may lead us to interpret physiological arousal as love.

★ While various Hindu myths and Chinese love songs make it clear that romantic love is found in other times and places than our own, it's unlikely that any other cultural epoch has taken it quite as seriously as ours does; thus, love as a precondition for marriage is a relatively new and Western concept (e.g., De Rougemont, 1940; Hunt, 1959; Grant, 1976).

Rocky course of romantic love *Parental opposition tends to intensify Romeo and Juliet's passion. Pictured here is the balcony scene from Prokofiev's ballet,* Romeo and Juliet. *(From a 1990 performance by American Ballet Theater; photograph by Martha Swope)*

What leads to the relevant bodily arousal? One obvious source is erotic excitement, although other forms of stimulation may have the same effect. We previously saw that physiological arousal produced by sheer physical exertion can induce excitation transfer and enhance sexual feelings (see Chapter 11). In a similar vein, fear, pain, and anxiety may heighten general arousal and thus lend fuel to romantic passion. In a widely cited experiment, investigators compared the reactions of young men who crossed a long, narrow, wobbly suspension bridge, precariously suspended over a shallow rapids 230 feet below. The men were approached by an attractive young woman who asked them to fill out a questionnaire and who gave them her telephone number so they could call her later if they wanted to know more about the project. Some of these young men were approached while they were on the bridge itself. Others were approached after they had already crossed the bridge, and were back on safe and solid ground. Some of the men did indeed call the young woman later (ostensibly to discuss the experiment, but really to ask her for a date). But the likelihood of their doing so depended on whether they were approached on the bridge or later, after they had crossed it. If they filled out the questionnaire while crossing the bridge—at which point they might well have felt some fear and excitement—the chances were approximately one in three that the men would call. If they met the young woman when they were back on safe ground, the chances of their calling were very much reduced (Dutton and Aron, 1974; but see also Kenrick and Cialdini, 1977; Kenrick, Cialdini, and Linder, 1979).

The rocky course of romantic love This general approach may help us understand why romantic love seems to thrive on obstacles. Shakespeare tells us that the "course of true love never did run smoothly" but if it had, the resulting love might have been lacking in ardor. The fervor of a wartime romance or an illicit affair is probably fed in part by danger and frustration, and many a lover's passion becomes all the more intense for being unrequited. In all these cases, there is increased arousal, whether through fear, frustration, or anxiety. This arousal continues to be interpreted as love, a cognitive appraisal that fits in perfectly with our ideas about romantic love, for these include both agony and rapture.

Romance and the knightly quest for adventure *A painting based on a sixteenth-century Italian epic celebrating the heroic deed of Roger, a valorous knight doing battle with a sea monster to rescue the virtuous Angelica.* (Roger and Angelique, *by Jean-Auguste-Dominique Ingres, 1819; © Photo Réunion des Musées Nationaux)*

An interesting demonstration of this phenomenon is the ***Romeo-and-Juliet effect*** (named after Shakespeare's doomed couple whose parents violently opposed their love). This describes the fact that parental opposition tends to intensify a couple's romantic passion rather than to diminish it. In one study, couples were asked whether their parents interfered with their relationship. The greater this interference, the more deeply the couples felt in love (Driscoll, Davis, and Lipitz, 1972). The moral is that if parents want to break up a romance, their best bet is to ignore it. If the feuding Montagues and Capulets had simply looked the other way, Romeo and Juliet might well have become bored with each other by the end of the second act.

A related characteristic of romantic love is that it has some of the qualities of an adventure (Simmel, 1911; Sabini, 1995). Initially, the word *romance* described a tale written in medieval French (a language derived from Latin, or "Roman") about the wondrous feats of knights in armor who fought dragons and monsters and undertook quests to win some lady's love. In time, the word's meaning centered on the knight-meets-lady aspect of these stories and became more or less synonymous with "love affair." Some of its original sense still inheres in the way the term *romantic* is used today, for it often suggests some of the quality of fanciful adventure that the medieval romances described.

COMPANIONATE LOVE

It's widely agreed that romantic love tends to be a short-lived bloom. That wild and tumultuous state, with its intense emotional ups and downs, with its obsessions, fantasies, and idealizations, rarely if ever lasts forever. Eventually, there are no further surprises and no further obstacles except those posed by the inevitable problems of ordinary life. The adventure is over, and romantic love ebbs. Sometimes it turns into indifference or active dislike. But sometimes—and hopefully more often—it is transformed into a related but gentler state—***companionate love.*** This is sometimes defined as the "affection we feel for those with whom our lives are deeply intertwined" (Hatfield and Walster, 1981, p. 124). In companionate love, the similarity of outlook, mutual concern, and trust that develop through day-to-day living become more important than the fantasies and idealization of romantic love, as the two partners try to live as happily ever after as it is possible to do in the real world. This is not to say that the earlier passion doesn't flare up occasionally. It may. But it no longer has the obsessive quality that it once had, where the lover is unable to think of anything but the beloved (Neimeyer, 1984; Hatfield, 1988; Caspi and Herbener, 1990).

Companionate love *When passion and obsession ebb, the trust and affection of companionate love, as shown here, may follow. (Photograph © Sonlight/Stock South/PNI)*

SOCIAL INFLUENCE: MANY-ON-ONE INTERACTIONS

Up to now, our discussion has focused on one-on-one interactions, some between comparative strangers, others between friends and lovers. In such interactions, other people often affect what we do, as in the case of a salesman trying to sell a car to a potential customer or a would-be lover trying to persuade his beloved to reciprocate his affections. But there are instances in which the interaction is more complex and in which the social effects come from many people simultaneously.

Such situations are usually discussed under the general heading of ***social influence.*** In these cases, the interaction is of the form of many on one: The influence of many others converges upon one individual. In some cases, the influence

Social facilitation *Audiences generally enhance the performance of an accomplished professional. But the effect on novices is not always beneficial. (Photograph by Gale Zucker/Stock, Boston)*

of others may make us tailor our behavior to conform to theirs. In others, it will make us obey them and comply with their orders. And in still other cases, the others exert their influence upon us in an even simpler way—by their mere presence as an audience.

SOCIAL FACILITATION: SOCIAL INFLUENCE BY THE PRESENCE OF OTHERS

It has long been known that the presence of other people has an effect on us. One example is laughter: Every comedian knows that laughter is contagious; each guffaw triggers another and then another, a fact that led to the use of canned TV laughter on the theory that if the viewers at home hear the (dubbed) laughs of others, they will laugh along (Wilson, 1985). Similar effects have been demonstrated by many investigators who compared people on various tasks that they performed either alone or in the presence of others. The initial results suggested that the social effect is always beneficial. When with others who are engaged in the same task, people race bicycles faster, learn simple mazes more quickly, and perform more multiplication problems in the same period of time. Such effects have been grouped under the general heading *social facilitation* (Allport, 1920).

Other studies, however, have indicated that the presence of others can sometimes hinder rather than help. While college students are faster at solving simple mazes when working with others, they are considerably slower when the mazes are more complex (Hunt and Hillery, 1973; Zajonc, 1965, 1980). An audience can evidently inhibit as well as facilitate. How can such divergent results be reconciled?

According to Robert Zajonc, the explanation is that the presence of others leads to a state of increased drive or arousal. Such an increase would resolve the apparent contradiction if we assume that it strengthens the tendency to perform highly dominant responses—the ones that seem to come automatically. Thus, the presence of others improves performance when the dominant response is also the correct one, as in performing simple motor skills or learning simple mazes. But when the task gets harder, as in the case of complex mazes, then the dominant response is often incorrect. As a result, performance gets worse when others watch, for in that case the dominant response (enhanced by increased arousal) inhibits the less dominant but correct reaction.★

As an example from ordinary life consider an accomplished actor. Such a person generally thrives on the attention of the audience—the bigger the audience, the happier she is. For her, the dominant responses are precisely those demanded by her role; she knows her part and how to make the most of it, and so the audience brings her performance to even greater heights. But the situation is very different for an unpracticed amateur who is still stumbling over her lines and unsure of her part. Her dominant responses are inappropriate to what she ought to be doing, and so she coughs, gives embarrassed smiles, and takes a few undecided half steps. She becomes aroused by the audience, but this arousal makes her performance even worse than it would be otherwise (Zajonc, 1965, 1980). Supporting evidence comes from observations of pool players in a college union

---

★ This hypothesis goes back to some earlier findings on people who seem to be more anxious (and thus presumably more driven and aroused) than average. Such people do better than less anxious people when faced with relatively simple tasks and worse when faced with more complex ones (Spence and Spence, 1966).

Conformity *(Photograph by G. Frank Radway)*

building. When good players were watched by an audience of four others, their accuracy rose from 71 to 80 percent. But when poor players were observed, their accuracy became even worse than it was before, dropping from 35 to 25 percent (Michaels et al., 1982).

Zajonc's general hypothesis may well be right, but there is still the question of why the presence of others should affect arousal. Some authors suggest that it triggers concern at being evaluated and perhaps embarrassed (e.g., Cottrell et al., 1968; Bond, 1982; Geen, 1991); others propose that it leads to distraction and conflict about whether to pay attention to the audience or the task, a situation that people then must try hard to overcome (Sanders, 1981; Baron, 1986).

While such factors almost certainly play a role, they are probably not the only ones, for similar results have been obtained with lower animals. In one study, cockroaches learned to escape from a bright light by running down a simple alley or by learning a maze. Some performed alone; others were run in pairs. When on the runway, the animals performed better in pairs than alone—for this simple task, the dominant response was appropriate. The reverse was true for the maze—for this more complex task, the dominant response was incorrect and inappropriate (Zajonc, Heingertner, and Herman, 1969). The close parallel between these findings and those obtained with humans has led some authors to suggest that some of the factors that underlie social facilitation may be the same across species, although such cross-species factors are surely more primitive than, say, evaluation anxiety. (It is hard to believe that a cockroach is seriously concerned about what another cockroach thinks about it.) Zajonc suggests that this common factor is an increased alertness in the presence of another member of one's own species; such alertness increases arousal, which in turn augments the strength of dominant responses, with resulting enhancement or impairment of performance (Zajonc, 1980).

CONFORMITY

Social facilitation (and inhibition) may well be the simplest form of social influence. It shows that our behavior is affected by the mere presence of others just about regardless of what they do. But in other forms of social influence, what others do matters very much indeed. An important example is ***conformity*** in which we go along with other people. In the last chapter, we saw that people may go along with a group even when the group is patently wrong—collectivists, with little distress if the group they're going along with is their in-group, individualists with a great deal of stress indeed. So the participants in Asch's experiment who yielded to the majority in judging line length were quite distressed but went along with the group nevertheless (Asch, 1952, 1955, 1956; see Chapter 11).

THE CAUSES OF CONFORMITY

Why do people in individualistic cultures conform? The evidence suggests that there are two main reasons: One is that they want to be right; another is that they want to be liked (or at least that they don't want to appear foolish).

One basis for following others is that we ourselves aren't sure what is right. In such cases, the group exerts influence because it provides information that we believe we ourselves don't have. This holds for information about any difficult judgment, whether it is sensory, social, or moral. If we are nearsighted and aren't wearing glasses, we'll ask others to read distant street signs; if we are unsure of what to wear (or what to say, or whom to vote for), we will watch what others

NURIT KARLIN

"Twenty-two is out of step. Pass it on." (© 1974 Saturday Review, *cartoon by Nurit Karlin)*

do to figure out how we ourselves should act. Thus, if people are made to believe that they are more competent and knowledgeable in some area than others are (for example, in seeing hidden figures), they are less likely to conform (e.g., Wiesenthal et al., 1976; Campbell, Tesser, and Fairey, 1986).

Another reason for going along with the crowd is not so much cognitive as motivational. For we sometimes conform even if we believe that we are right and the others are wrong. Consider the original Asch study in which a unanimous majority made a grossly incorrect judgment. The participant saw the world as it is but had every reason to believe that the others saw it differently. If she now said what she believed, she couldn't help but be embarrassed; after all, the others would probably think that she was a fool and would then laugh at her.★ Under the circumstances, the participant would prefer to disguise what she really believed and go along. That something of this sort is going on was shown in another variant of the Asch experiment in which the participant came in while the experiment was already in progress. The experimenter told her that since she arrived late, it would be simpler for her to write her answers down in private rather than to announce them out loud. Under these circumstances, there was little yielding. The lines being judged were of the original unambiguous sort (e.g., 8 inches vs. 6¼ inches in height), so that there was no informational pressure toward conformity. And since the judgments were made in private, there was no (or little) motivational pressure either. As a result, there was a great deal of independence (Asch, 1952).

MAJORITIES AND MINORITIES

A unanimous majority evidently exerts a powerful effect on a solitary individual that makes him want to conform. What happens when the individual is no longer alone?

The ally effect To answer this question, Asch varied his experiment by having one of the confederates act as the participant's ally; all of the other confederates gave wrong answers while the ally's judgments were correct. Under these conditions, the participant yielded very rarely and was not particularly upset.

The moral seems simple enough: One person who believes as we do can sustain us against all others. But on closer examination, things are not quite as

---

★ This suspicion is by no means unjustified. In yet another variation of the Asch experiment, one confederate gave false responses when run with a group of sixteen real participants who of course gave the correct answer. Under these circumstances, the group found the confederate's behavior ludicrous and laughed aloud at him (Asch, 1952).

The ally effect *Not being alone sustains one against a majority but also in other struggles, such as against evil witches and all-powerful wizards. (From the 1939 movie,* The Wizard of Oz, *with Judy Garland, Ray Bolger, Jack Haley, and Bert Lahr; courtesy of The Kobal Collection)*

The effect of a consistent minority *A steadfast minority can gradually create genuine changes in what people think and feel as in the case of the American civil rights movement. A scene from the 1965 march from Selma to Montgomery. (Photograph by Dan Budnick/Woodfin Camp)*

simple as that. For in another variation, the confederate again deviated from the majority but not by giving the correct answer. On the contrary, she gave an answer that was even further from the truth than was the group's. Thus, on a trial in which the correct answer was 6¼ inches and the group answer was 6¾ inches, the confederate's answer might be 8 inches. This response was obviously not arrayed on the side of the participant (or of the truth), but it helped to liberate the participant even so. She now yielded very much less than when confronted by a unanimous majority. What evidently mattered was the group's unanimity; once this was broken, the participant felt that she could speak up without fear of embarrassment (Asch, 1952). Similar studies have been performed in other laboratories with essentially similar results (Allen and Levine, 1971; Allen, 1975; Nemeth and Chiles, 1988).

Even if we can't find a supporter, the next best thing is to find someone else who also opposes the majority, even if for different reasons than our own. Thus, totalitarian systems have good reason to stifle dissent of any kind. The moment one voice is raised in dissent, the unanimity is broken and others may (and often do) find the courage to express their own dissent, whatever its form.

The role of a consistent minority Some authors believe that the impact of a minority may go beyond its role in breaking up unanimity. In their view, consistent minorities sometimes have yet another and distinctly different effect, that of introducing novel solutions and perspectives (Nemeth, 1992). History shows us that small minorities often create social innovations. They begin by challenging an established majority, as did early advocates of civil rights for American minorities. They often prevail in part because their members seem utterly unanimous in their determination and their confidence. As time goes on, these minorities tend to convert many of their erstwhile opponents. In this regard, their influence is rather different from that exerted by a majority. While a majority tends to produce overt conformity, its effect is essentially superficial; it changes what people do or say rather than what they think. In contrast, the effect of a unanimous and steadfast minority, while slower and less dramatic, may eventually affect more than overt behavior. It may lead to genuine change in what people think and feel (Maass and Clark, 1984; Moscovici, 1985).

BLIND OBEDIENCE

There is another way of influencing the behavior of others that is much more direct than any we've considered thus far. It is by getting people to obey what we command them to do. Of particular interest is the case of blind obedience to orders that violate one's own conscience, actions in which the individual subordinates his own appraisal of the situation to that of some authority. On the face of it, obedience might appear to differ from the forms of social influence we have considered thus far because commands are usually delivered one to one: The student obeys the teacher, the automobile driver obeys the police officer. But at bottom, the interaction is not truly one on one, because the teacher and the police officer speak with the authority of the whole society behind them when they order us to hand in our homework or to pull over to the roadside. To the extent that this is so, obedience and conformity (and social facilitation and inhibition) are all instances of social influence.

A certain degree of obedience is a necessary ingredient of social life. In any society, whether industrial or agrarian, some individuals have authority over others, at least within a limited sphere. Obedience is particularly relevant as societies get more complex, where the spheres within which authority can be exerted become much more differentiated. Teachers assign homework, doctors prescribe medications, and police officers stop automobiles. The pupils, patients, and motorists generally obey. Their obedience is based on an implicit recognition that those who issued the orders were operating within their legitimate domains of authority. If these domains are overstepped, obedience is unlikely. Police officers can't order motorists to recite lists of irregular French verbs or to take two aspirin and go to bed.

Some tendency to obey authority is thus a vital cement that holds society together; without it, there would be chaos. But the atrocities of this century—the Nazi death camps, the Soviet "purges," the Cambodian massacres, the so-called ethnic cleansing in Bosnia—give terrible proof that this disposition to obedience can also become a corrosive poison that destroys our sense of humanity. Such atrocities could not have been committed without the obedience of tens or hundreds of thousands and the acquiescence of many more. How could such obedience have come about?

Psychologists who try to answer this question have adopted two different approaches. One focuses on the personality structure of the blindly obedient individual, suggesting that her acts are essentially irrational and stem from primitive, emotional sources. The other approach emphasizes the social situation in which the obedient person finds herself; it proposes that some aspects of her behavior can be explained in cognitive terms, by asking how she interprets the situation. In short, these two approaches to obedience hearken back to the two approaches toward attribution that we encountered in Chapter 11; the first is *dispositional,* the second, *situational.*

OBEDIENCE AND PERSONALITY STRUCTURE

An influential version of the person-centered, or dispositional, hypothesis was proposed shortly after World War II by a group of investigators who believed they had discovered a personality type that is predisposed toward totalitarian dogma and is thus ready to obey unquestioningly. Such *authoritarian personalities* are prejudiced against various minority groups and also hold certain sentiments about authority, including submission to those above, harshness to those below, and a general belief in the importance of power and dominance. These authoritarian attitudes are shown by a tendency to agree emphatically with

Obedience *The commandant of a concentration camp in Germany stands amid some of his prisoners who were burned or shot as the American army approached the camp during the last days of World War II. Most Nazis who held such positions insisted that they were "just following orders." (Courtesy of United Press International)*

statements such as: "Obedience and respect for authority are the most important virtues children should learn," "Most of our social problems would be solved if we could somehow get rid of the immoral, the crooked, and feeble-minded people," and "People can be divided into two distinct classes: the weak and the strong" (Adorno et al., 1950).

According to the investigators, this constellation of attitudes was an expression of underlying personality patterns formed in childhood. They found that people who scored high on minority prejudice and authoritarianism described their childhoods as dominated by stern and harshly punitive fathers who insisted on absolute obedience. According to the investigators, the children reared in this manner felt hostility toward their domineering fathers but couldn't express it, so they developed what psychoanalysts call a "reaction formation" (see Chapter 17). They adopted obedience and submission to authority as exalted virtues, redirecting their anger and resentment toward their fathers at safer targets, such as minority groups. As a result, they saw the outside world as populated by a horde of dangerous enemies—African Americans, Hispanics, Asians, Jews, foreigners, Bolsheviks, and so on—who had to be crushed before they themselves were crushed.

The initial work on the authoritarian personality has been the subject of considerable criticism (for review, see Snyder and Ickes, 1985). Some critics focused on the fact that the sample on which the conclusions were based was limited to white middle-class Californians, others on the fact that the information about the participants' childhoods was drawn largely from their own recollections, and so on. But while the original claims of the investigators may have been too extravagant, their studies did focus on an important set of relationships between social and political attitudes (Brown, 1965; Fiske, 1998). Minority prejudice probably does tend to go together with authoritarian sentiments, and people with such sentiments do show a number of political characteristics that might be expected: They tend to be more obedient to authority, vote for conservative and law-and-order candidates, and accept the attitudes of those in power (Elms and Milgram, 1966; Izzett, 1971; Poley, 1974). In addition, there is some evidence that these authoritarian attitudes are often accompanied by certain ways of remembering and idealizing one's parents and a belief in stern childhood discipline. But whether this constellation of attitudes is caused by childhood experiences and emotions is still very much debatable. There is also evidence that authoritarianism is more pronounced among people with less education (Christie, 1954). As one writer put it in the sixties, "Authoritarianism may be the worldview of the uneducated in Western industrialized societies" (Brown, 1965, p. 523). Not surprisingly, perhaps, working-class parents are more likely to stress obedience to authority much more strongly than are middle-class parents, since they themselves are more subject to the authority of a boss or a supervisor (Kelly, 1969; Hess, 1970; see Chapter 14).

OBEDIENCE AND THE SITUATION

Can the person-centered hypothesis explain the atrocities of recent times? Are those who obey the order to massacre countless innocents sick individuals completely different from the rest of us? Some of them probably are (Dicks, 1972). But the frightening fact is that many seem to be cast from a much more ordinary mold; what is horrifying about them is what they do and not who they are. In a well-known account of the trial of Adolf Eichmann, the man who supervised the deportation of six million Jews to the Nazi gas chambers, the author comments on the grotesque "banality of evil": "The trouble with Eichmann was precisely that so many were like him, and that the many were neither perverted nor sadistic, that they were, and still are, terribly and terrifyingly normal" (Arendt, 1965, p. 276).

It appears that obedience to inhuman orders is in part a function of the total situation in which a person finds himself. Under some social systems—Hitler's Germany, Stalin's Russia, Pol Pot's Cambodia—the conditions for compliance or tacit acceptance are so powerful that an outsider might well pause to wonder whether "there but for the grace of God go I."

The Milgram studies The importance of situational factors in producing obedience is highlighted by the results of what may be the best known study in modern social psychology, conducted by Stanley Milgram (1963). The participants in Milgram's study were drawn from a broad spectrum of socioeconomic and educational levels; they were recruited by a local newspaper ad offering $4.50 per hour to persons willing to participate in a study of memory. They arrived at the laboratory where a white-coated experimenter told them that the study in which they were to take part concerned the effect of punishment on human learning.

The participants were run in pairs and drew lots to determine who would be the "teacher" and who the "learner." The task of the learner was to master a list of associations. The task of the teacher was to present the stimuli, to record the learner's answers, and—most important—to administer punishment whenever the learner responded incorrectly. The learner was conducted to a cubicle where the experimenter strapped him in a chair, to "prevent excess movement," and attached the shock electrodes to his wrist—all in full view of the teacher. After the learner was securely strapped in place, the teacher was brought back to the main experimental room and seated in front of an imposing-looking shock generator. The generator had 30 lever switches with labeled shock intensities, ranging from 15 volts to 450 volts in 15-volt increments. Below each of the levers there were also verbal descriptions ranging from "Slight Shock" to "Danger: Severe Shock." The labels below the last two levers were even more ominous; they were devoid of any verbal designation and were simply marked "XXX" (Figure 12.5).

The teacher presented the items that had to be memorized. She was instructed to move on to the next item on the list whenever the learner responded correctly but to administer a shock whenever an error was made. She was told to increase the level of punishment with each succeeding error, beginning with 15 volts and going up by one step for each error thereafter until 450 volts was reached. To get an idea what the learner experienced, the teacher first submitted to a sample shock of 45 volts, the third of the 30-step punishment series, which gave an unpleasant jolt. During the experiment, all communications between teacher and learner were conducted over an intercom, since the learner was out of sight, strapped to a chair in the experimental cubicle.

Needless to say, the shock generator never delivered any shocks (except for the initial sample) and the lot drawing was rigged so that the learner was always a confederate, played by a mild-mannered, middle-aged actor. The point of the experiment was simply to determine how far the *teacher* would go in obeying the experimenter's instructions. Since the learner made a fair number of errors, the shock level of the prescribed punishment kept on rising. By the time 120 volts was reached, the victim shouted that the shocks were becoming too painful. At 150 volts he demanded that he be let out of the experiment. At 180 volts, he cried out that he could no longer stand the pain. At 300 volts, he

A

B

C

D

12.5 The obedience experiment *(A) The "shock generator" used in the experiment. (B) The learner is strapped into his chair and electrodes are attached to his wrist. (C) The teacher receives a sample shock. (D) The teacher breaks off the experiment. (© 1965 by Stanley Milgram. From the film* Obedience, *distributed by Penn State Audio-Visual Services.)*

screamed that he would give no further answers and insisted that he be freed. On the next few shocks there were agonized screams. After 330 volts, there was silence.

The learner's responses were of course predetermined. But the real participants—the teachers—did not know that, so they had to decide what to do. When the victim cried out in pain or refused to go on, participants usually turned to the experimenter for instructions. In response, the experimenter told the participants that the experiment had to go on, indicated that he took full responsibility, and pointed out that "the shocks may be painful but there is no permanent tissue damage."

How far do participants go in obeying the experimenter? The results were astounding: About 65 percent of the participants in Milgram's study—both men and women—continued to obey the experimenter to the bitter end. This proportion was unaffected even when the learner mentioned that he suffered from a mild heart condition. This isn't to say that the obedient participants had no moral qualms—quite the contrary. Many of them were seriously upset. They bit their lips, twisted their hands, sweated profusely—but obeyed even so. Similar results were obtained when the study was repeated with participants from other countries—Australia, Germany, and Jordan (Kilham and Mann, 1974; Mantell and Panzarella, 1976; Shanab and Yahya, 1977).

Is there a parallel between obedience in these artificial laboratory situations and obedience in the all-too-real nightmares of Nazi Germany or Khmer Rouge Cambodia? In some ways, there is no comparison, given the enormous disparities in scope and degree. But Milgram believed that some of the underlying psychological processes may be the same in both cases.

Being another person's agent   In Milgram's view, one of the crucial factors is the fact that all of us are brought up in a world in which there is a continual stress on obedience to legitimate authority, first within the family, then in school, and still later within the institutional settings of the adult world. As a result, we all become well practiced in adopting the attitude of an agent who performs an action that is initiated by someone else. The responsibility belongs to that someone else and not to us. The good child does what she is told; the good employee may raise a question but will accept the boss's final decision; the good soldier is not even allowed to question why. All of them come to feel that they are just an agent who executes another's will: the hammer that struck a nail, not the carpenter who wielded it.

The feeling that one is a mere instrument with little or no sense of personal responsibility can be increased yet further. One means is by increasing the psychological distance between one's own actions and their end result. This phenomenon was studied in Milgram's laboratory. In one variation, two teachers were used. One was a confederate who was responsible for administering the shocks; the other was the real participant who was asked to perform such subsidiary tasks as reading the stimuli over a microphone and recording the learner's responses. In this new role, the participant was still essential to the smooth functioning of the experimental procedure. If he stopped, the victim would receive no further shocks. Even so, the participant might be expected to feel further removed from the ultimate consequence of the procedure, like a minor cog in a bureaucratic machine. After all, he didn't do the actual shocking! Under these conditions, over 90 percent of the participants went all the way (Milgram, 1963, 1965; see also Kilham and Mann, 1974).

If obedience is increased by decreasing the participant's sense of personal responsibility, does the opposite hold as well? To answer this question, Milgram decreased the psychological distance between what the participant did and its effect upon the victim. Rather than being out of sight in an experimental cubi-

12.6 Obedient teacher pressing the learner's hand upon the shock electrode *(© 1965 by Stanley Milgram. From the film* Obedience, *distributed by Penn State Audio-Visual Services.)*

cle, the victim was now seated directly adjacent to the participant who was told to administer the shock in a brutally direct manner. She had to press the victim's hand upon a shock electrode, holding it down by force if necessary. (Her own hand was insulated by a sheet of plastic to "protect" it from the shock; see Figure 12.6). Now compliance dropped considerably, in analogy to the fact that it is easier to drop bombs on an unseen enemy than to plunge a knife into her body when she looks you in the eye. But even so, 30 percent of the participants still reacted with perfect obedience. (For further discussion of this and related issues, see Miller, 1986.)

Cognitive reinterpretations   In addition to emphasizing his role as a mere instrument, the obedient person develops an elaborate set of further cognitive devices to reinterpret the situation and his own part in it. One of the most common approaches is to put on psychic blinders and to try to shut out the awareness that the victim is a living, suffering fellow being. According to one of Milgram's participants, "You really begin to forget that there's a guy out there, even though you can hear him. For a long time I just concentrated on pressing the switches and reading the words" (Milgram, 1974, p. 38). This dehumanization of the victim is a counterpart to the obedient person's self-picture as an agent of another's will, someone "who has a job to do" and who does it whether he likes it or not. The obedient person sees himself as an instrument; by the same token, he sees the victim as an object. In his eyes, both have become dehumanized (Bernard, Ottenberg, and Redl, 1965).

The dehumanization of the opponent is a common theme in war and mass atrocity. Victims are rarely described as people, but only as bodies, objects, numbers. The process of dehumanization is propped up by euphemisms and bureaucratic jargon. The Nazis used terms such as *final solution* (for the mass murder of six million people) and *special treatment* (for death by gassing); the nuclear age contributed *fallout problem* and *preemptive attack*; the Gulf War gave us *collateral damages* (for civilian deaths); and the war in Bosnia-Herzegovina added *ethnic cleansing*—all dry, official phrases that are admirably suited to keep thoughts of blood and human suffering at a reasonably safe distance.

By dehumanizing the victim, moral qualms are pushed into the background. For all except the most brutalized, though, these qualms can't be banished forever. To justify continued obedience, such queasy feelings remain suppressed only by invoking some higher, overriding moral ideology. In Milgram's study, the participants convinced themselves that science had to be served regardless of the victim's cries. In a related kind of self-justification, the fault is projected on the victims; they are considered to be subhuman, dirty, evil, and only have themselves to blame. In Nazi Germany, the goal was to cleanse humanity by ridding it of Gypsy and Jewish "vermin."

The slippery slope   The cognitive reorientation by which a person no longer feels responsible for her own acts is not achieved in an instant. Usually, inculcation is gradual. The initial act of obedience is relatively mild and does not seriously clash with the person's own moral outlook; each successive step seems only slightly different from the one before. This, of course, was the pattern in Milgram's study, which created a slippery slope that participants slid down unawares. A similar program of progressive escalation was evidently used in the indoctrination of death-camp guards. The same is true for the military training of soldiers everywhere. Draftees go through "basic training," in part to learn various military skills, but much more importantly, to acquire the habit of instant obedience. Raw recruits are rarely asked to point their guns at another person and shoot. It's not only that they don't know how; it's that most of them probably wouldn't do it.

515

Milgram's study, the person, and the situation   Modern social psychologists generally interpret Milgram's results as a pointed reminder that the situation in which people find themselves is a powerful determinant of what they do, perhaps more important than the sort of people they are. Everyone knows that this is true for many situations of everyday life; virtually everybody stops at a red light, regardless of any quirks in their personalities. But that a situation such as Milgram's would lead two-thirds of his participants to impose serious pain and harm on another person was a sobering surprise. Before Milgram published his results, he described his study to several groups of experts, including a group of forty psychiatrists. All of them predicted that he would encounter a great deal of defiance. In their view, only a pathological fringe of at most 2 percent of the participants would go to the maximum shock intensity. As we now know, their predictions were far off the mark. In effect, the experts' judgments provide yet another example of the *fundamental attribution error*—the belief that what people do is largely caused by who they are and to a much lesser extent by the situation in which they find themselves (see Chapter 11).

Clearly, Milgram's results highlight the role of the situation in determining what people do. They argue against an extreme version of the person-centered (or dispositional) view, such as that expressed by the investigators who studied authoritarianism (see pp. 511–12). But this shouldn't blind us to the fact that personal factors also matter. The fact that two-thirds of Milgram's participants obeyed to the bitter end is surprising and deeply disturbing. But it's no less true that another third did *not* obey.

SOCIAL IMPACT THEORY

The preceding discussion dealt with several different forms of social influence, including social facilitation and inhibition, conformity, and obedience. According to Bibb Latané's ***social impact theory*** (Latané, 1981, 1997), all of these forms of social influence can be understood by thinking of the individual as exposed to a field of social forces that converge upon him much as a number of light bulbs cast light upon a target surface (see Figure 12.7). How much light

12.7   *Convergence of social forces*
(Freely adapted from Latané, 1981)

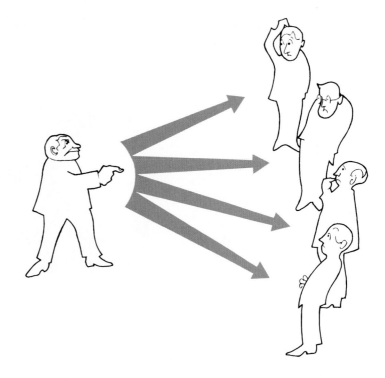

12.8 Diffusion of social impact *(Freely adapted from Latané, 1981)*

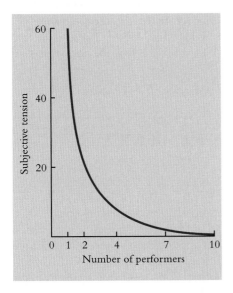

12.9 Diffusion of social impact and performance anxiety *Ratings of nervousness obtained prior to a college talent show from persons who performed alone or with two, four, seven, or ten others. (After Jackson and Latané, 1981)*

will be cast depends on their number, the strength of each bulb, and how close the bulbs are to the target. According to Latané, the impact of social forces converging on one individual works in a similar manner. The total impact will depend on the number of people who affect the target individual, how strong (in age, status, or power) each of these people is and how close they are to him in space or time.

Evidence for the role of strength comes from work on stage fright: Performers are more anxious when anticipating playing before audiences of higher than of lower status (Latané and Harkins, 1976). There is also evidence for the role of immediacy: Performing for a live audience produces more stage fright than performing for an audience watching the performance on a video monitor in another room (Borden, 1980). Evidence for the effect of number is even more convincing, for in virtually all many-on-one situations, the influence the many exert on the one goes up as their number increases. The larger the unanimous majority, the greater the conformity; the larger the audience, the greater the stage fright; the larger the crowd looking up at the sky, the greater the number of others who look up too. Each additional individual increases the social impact, though with diminishing returns: Adding one person to a group of two will produce a much greater increase in social impact than adding one to a group of eight.

Thus far, we've only considered cases where the social influence exerted by several different sources converges upon a single target individual. In such cases, the impact goes up with their number (though, to be sure, with diminishing returns). What happens when that influence is spread out over more than one target? According to Latané, the impact, which will now be divided over all the targets, is diffused: The more targets there are, the less the social impact will be for any one of them (see Figure 12.8; adapted from Latané, 1981). Again, evidence comes from a study of stage fright in participants at a college talent show. The acts at the show had from one to ten performers. The stage fright exhibited by these performers depended on the number of coperformers in the act: the greater their number, the less stage fright any one member of the act felt (Jackson and Latané, 1981; see Figure 12.9).

A similar dilution of social impact is relevant to the bystander effect, which

Social loafing   *In a tug-of-war, everyone seems to pull as hard as he can, but the total force exerted by the group tends to be less than would be the sum of the members' solo efforts. (Photograph © Aneal Vohra)*

we discussed in another context (see pp. 495–97). The likelihood that any one person will provide help in an emergency decreases as the number of bystanders increases. Here, diffusion of social impact is partially produced by the diffusion of responsibility, for the obligation to help is spread out over all the onlookers, and each can ask, "Why me? Why not the others?"

A final example of diffusion of social impact comes from a phenomenon called *social loafing.* This describes the fact that when individuals work as a group on a common task, all doing the same thing, they often generate less total effort than they would if they each worked alone (Karau and Williams, 1995). An example is pulling at a rope. In one study, one man working alone pulled with an average force of 139 pounds, while groups of eight pulling together averaged 546 pounds—only about 68 pounds per person. In another study, students were asked to clap and cheer as loudly as they could, sometimes alone, sometimes in groups of two, four, or six. Here, too, the results showed social loafing: Each person cheered and clapped less vigorously the greater the number of others she was with (Latané, Williams, and Harkins, 1979). There is an old adage: "Many hands make light the work." The trouble is that they don't make it as light as they should.

LEADERSHIP: ONE-ON-MANY INTERACTIONS

The preceding section dealt with interactions that are many-on-one, such as those in which groups exert influence on an individual and produce conformity and compliance. We will now turn the tables and look at the reverse condition, the effect of one on many, wherein one individual exerts influence on a number—sometimes a very large number—of others. The most important example of such one-on-many interactions is leadership.

Leadership occurs in a multitude of social contexts, including politics, the military, business and commerce, academia, sports, social clubs, and even the family. The ways this leadership may be exercised are even more varied (Hollander, 1985; Bass, 1990). One difference concerns the size of the group being led, which may be as large as the People's Republic of China or as small as a kids' club.

Another concerns the leader's authority: Is that leader the ultimate authority, or does that person report to another higher up? A further difference is whether the leader tries to influence her followers directly or whether she exerts her influence through a special group of loyal subordinates. Considering these many differences, is there anything one can say about leadership in general?

GREAT PERSON OR SOCIAL FORCES

From one perspective, history is essentially created by exceptional individuals, who, for better or worse, determine the course of human events. In the nineteenth century, the proponents of this great-person theory often cited the case of Napoléon Bonaparte. According to the Scottish essayist Thomas Carlyle, Napoléon was a political and military genius whose brilliant mind and unyielding will overcame all opposition for over two decades (Carlyle, 1841).

But from another perspective, the success or failure of individuals like Napoléon is determined by the situations in which they find themselves. Thus, to the great Russian novelist Leo Tolstoy, Napoléon's initial successes were caused by circumstance: the ineptitude of the opposing generals, the zeal of the French soldiers, the huge armies under his command. And when he finally failed, it was not because his genius deserted him but because of the ferocious Russian winter, the long supply lines, and so on (Tolstoy, 1868). The same controversy has emerged in the discussion of many other historical events. Would there have been a Bolshevik Revolution if Vladimir Lenin had remained in exile from Russia? Would voting rights for American women have been sanctioned as early without the efforts of Susan B. Anthony? Would the apartheid government of South Africa have fallen when it did without the efforts of Nelson Mandela? The same issue applies to intellectual and cultural leadership. Would natural selection have prevailed in nineteenth-century biology without Darwin? The two poles of the argument have surfaced again and again, one stressing the genius of the leader, the other the historical situation (Hook, 1955; Jennings, 1972; Burns, 1978; Weisberg, 1986).

Leadership—person or situation? *(A) Some historians focus on the personality of the individual leader. To them, Napoléon was a military and political genius who shaped history. (B) Others see the leader in the context of the total situation in which he finds himself. To them, instead of history being made by Napoléon, Napoléon was the creation of history.* (Napoléon on the Battlefield of Eylau, February 9, 1807, *1808, by Jean-Antoine Gros, Louvre, Paris)*

A

B

This debate among historians has its counterpart in an issue we considered in our discussion of obedience above and in our previous discussion of attribution in Chapter 11: Do we (and should we) attribute a person's actions to his dispositional qualities or to the situation? To be sure, most behaviors studied in the social psychologist's laboratory don't have the momentous quality of those performed by history's leaders; answering a quiz master's questions (see pp. 461–62) is hardly on a par with fighting the Battle of Waterloo or extending voting rights to 50 percent of the adult population.

But the underlying questions are quite similar. Do we attribute the participant's poorer performance to something in her (she is not as smart and knows less) or to something in the situation (she is not the one who picked the questions)? Similarly for issues in history: Do we attribute Napoléon's defeat to something in him (e.g., his genius finally flagged) or to something in the situation (e.g., the fact that the combined armies of England, Russia, and Prussia were too powerful)?

Put another way, the question is whether all—or most—successful leaders share any personal characteristics. The great-person theory would predict that they do, that a Napoléon or a Susan B. Anthony or a Nelson Mandela would in all likelihood have achieved leadership even if they'd never entered the military, compaigned for women's rights, or joined the African National Congress. What evidence can social psychology offer?

LEADERSHIP IN THE LABORATORY

To determine whether there are, in fact, such leadership qualities, social psychologists have tried to relate various personal characteristics of group members to whether they are perceived as leaders and whether they are effective in this role. Leadership *perception* and *performance* have been assessed in many ways, including ratings by subordinates, peers, and supervisors. They have also been assessed by a number of laboratory studies in which small groups of four to six are given some joint task that has to be solved by discussion. Thus, participants may be told that they are explorers stranded 200 miles from their base. To get back to base, they have to jettison some of their equipment (tent, tools, etc.). Each member first tells the others which item he would jettison first, which second, and so on. Then the group comes up with a consensus list. To assess leadership perception, each member is rated by all others on the degree to which he influenced the group. To assess leadership performance, each member's initial list is compared with the group's consensus list, and the extent to which a member's list resembles the final list is the index of his effectiveness as a leader (Cammalleri et al., 1973; Bottger, 1984).

The next step is to see whether leadership perception and performance are related to any other personal characteristics. The verdict to date seems to be that there are, indeed, such relationships, although they are not as powerful as the great-person theory might lead one to suspect. Thus, people who are seen as leaders tend to be more intelligent, more outgoing, and more dominant than those who are not regarded as leaders (e.g., Kenny and Zaccaro, 1983; Lord, deVader, and Alliger, 1986), but only somewhat. For overall, the role of the situation the leader confronts seems to be at least as important as her own personal characteristics (Bass, 1981; Hollander, 1985).

What are the characteristics of the situation that make a leader effective? Relatively favorable situations are those in which the leader has considerable authority, the task to be performed is clear cut, and the group members get along with each other and with the leader. To the extent that any of these conditions do not apply, the situation is unfavorable. It seems, then, that both the personal characteristics of would-be leaders and the situations they confront determine how effective they will be.

But there is a complication: The person who becomes an effective leader of one group will not necessarily become the leader of another. This is especially true if the two groups have different missions. On reflection, this is pretty much what one might expect. The qualities that make for leadership on a corporate board of directors are surely different from those that make for leadership in a seminary, Scout troop, or research laboratory. And all differ from those that make for leadership in a political movement, the military, or a street gang. (For a more detailed proposal on the proper match-up between leaders and situations, see Fiedler, 1978.)

How does any of this research relate to the broad questions raised by speculative historians? Would the Nazi movement have risen to power in Germany without Adolf Hitler? Would the theory of natural selection have triumphed without Darwin? Social psychology obviously cannot answer momentous questions of this sort. Even to try would be exceedingly presumptuous. For surely such issues require the combined efforts of all the social sciences—anthropology, economics, history, political science, social psychology, sociology—and even then, there may very well be no answers. For history—like life itself—has no control groups. It is a science that can only predict the past.

CROWD BEHAVIOR: MANY-ON-MANY INTERACTIONS

In this chapter we've considered three broad classes of social interaction. The first class involved one-on-one interactions between two persons who might be relative strangers, friends, or lovers. In the second group, the interactions were of many on one, cases of social influence in which the impact of a number of others converged on an individual to produce social facilitation or inhibition,

A

B

Deindividuation *(A) Some deindividua-tion effects are harmless. (Photograph © 1983 by Michael Sheil/Black Star) (B) Others rep-resent a menace to a humane, democratic soci-ety. (Photograph © Detroit Free Press, 1988, Pauline Lubens/Black Star)*

conformity or obedience. In the third, we looked at the effects of one on many, in which one person influenced or led a group of others. We now turn to a fourth class of social interactions in which the relation is many on many. These are group interactions in which a number of people interact with a number of others simultaneously. An important example is crowd behavior.★ Certainly, under some circumstances people in crowds behave differently from the way they do when alone. In a riot or lynch mob, they express aggression with a viciousness that would be inconceivable if they acted in isolation. In a tightly packed auditorium, they become fearful and frantic when someone shouts "Fire." In a crowd that gathers to watch some disturbed person on a ledge atop a tall building, they often taunt the would-be suicide, urging him to jump.

What does the crowd do to its members to make them act so differently from their everyday selves? In analogy with the attempt to explain blind obedience, we can distinguish between two contrasting views. One focuses on emotional factors and holds that the crowd incites its members to lose their individuality and become essentially irrational. Another position stresses cognitive aspects. It holds that a crowd's behavior reflects its members' cognitive appraisals of the total situation, appraisals that are not so irrational as they seem.

THE EMPHASIS ON THE IRRATIONAL: DEINDIVIDUATION

An early exponent of the role of irrational factors was Gustav Le Bon (1841–1931), a French writer of conservative leanings whose disdain for the masses was reflected in his theory of crowd behavior. According to Le Bon, people in a crowd become wild, stupid, and irrational, giving vent to primitive impulses that are normally suppressed. Their emotion spreads by a sort of conta-gion and rises to an ever-higher pitch as more and more crowd members become affected. Thus, fear becomes terror, hostility turns into murderous rage, and the crowd member becomes a savage barbarian—"a grain of sand among other grains of sand, which the wind stirs up at will"(Le Bon, 1895).

A number of social psychologists have tried to translate some of these ideas into modern terms. To them, the key to crowd behavior is ***deindividuation,*** a state in which an individual in a group loses awareness of herself as a separate individual. This state is more likely to occur when there is a high level of arousal and anonymity. Deindividuation tends to disinhibit impulsive actions that are normally under restraint. Just what the impulses are that are disinhibited by deindividuation depends on the group and the situation. In a carnival, the (masked) revelers may join in wild orgies; in a lynch mob, the group members will torture and kill (Festinger, Pepitone, and Newcomb, 1952; Zimbardo, 1969; Diener, 1979).

To study deindividuation experimentally, one investigation focused on the effect of anonymity in children who were trick-or-treating on Halloween. Some came alone; others came in groups. Some were asked for their names by the adults in the homes they visited; others were not. All children were then given an opportunity to steal pennies or candy when the adult left the room on some pretext. The children were much more likely to steal if they came in groups and were anonymous. Thus, an increase in wrongdoing may have occurred because

---

★ The many-on-one versus many-on-many distinction is not hard and fast. Fundamentally, most many-on-many interactions are probably composed of a large number of many-on-one interac-tions, as each member in a panicky crowd or a rioting mob is influenced by the collective force of the mass of others.

anonymity made the children less aware of themselves as separate individuals—
that is, made them deindividuated—with a resulting disinhibition of petty thiev-
ery. But there may have been a simpler and perfectly rational reason: Being
anonymous, the children were less afraid of being caught (Diener et al., 1976).

COGNITIVE FACTORS AND THE PANICKY CROWD

Is crowd behavior really as irrational as the deindividuation approach suggests? Our primary focus will be on panics. Panics prove that people in
groups sometimes act in ways that have disastrous consequences that none of
them foresaw or desired. This shows that crowd behavior can be profoundly
maladaptive, but does it prove that the individual members of the crowd acted
irrationally? Several social psychologists have argued that it does not (Brown,
1965). They point out that in certain situations, such as fires in crowded audito-
riums, the optimum solution for all participants (that is, escape for all) can only
come about if they all trust one another to behave cooperatively (that is, not to
run for the exits). If this trust is lacking, each individual will do the next best
thing given his goals and his expectations of what others will do. He will run to
the exit because he is sure that everyone else will do the same, hoping that if he
runs quickly enough he will get there before them. The trouble is that all others
make the same assumption that he does, and so they will all arrive more or less
together, jam the exit, and perish.

According to this cognitive interpretation, intense fear as such will not produce crowd panic, contrary to Le Bon's assertion. What matters are people's
beliefs about escape routes. If they think that the routes for escape (the theater
exits) are open and readily accessible, they will not stampede. Nor will panic
develop if all escape routes are thought to be completely blocked, as in a mine
collapse or a submarine explosion. Such disasters may lead to terror or apathetic
collapse, but there will be none of the chaos that characterizes a panicky crowd.
For panic to occur, the exits from danger must be seen to be limited or closing.
In that case, each individual may well think that she can escape only if she rushes ahead of the others. If everyone thinks this way, panic may ensue (Smelser,
1963).

THE PRISONER'S DILEMMA

Roger Brown believes that some facets of escape panic can be understood in
terms of a problem taken from the mathematical theory of games (Brown,
1965). It is generally known as the *prisoner's dilemma* (Luce and Raiffa, 1957).
Consider the hypothetical problem of two men arrested on suspicion of bank
robbery. The district attorney needs a confession to guarantee conviction. She
hits on a diabolical plan. She talks to each prisoner separately and offers each a
simple choice—confess or stay silent. But she tells each man that the consequences will depend not just on what he does, but also on his partner's choice. If
both confess, she will recommend an intermediate sentence of, say, eight years in
prison for each. If neither confesses, she will be unable to prosecute them for
robbery, but she will charge them with a lesser crime such as illegal possession of
a gun and both will get one year in jail. But suppose one confesses and the other
does not. In this case the two men will be dealt with very differently. The one
who confesses will be treated with extra leniency for turning state's evidence; he
will receive a suspended sentence and won't go to jail at all. But the one who
remains silent will feel the full force of the law. The D.A. will recommend the
maximum penalty of twenty years.

523

TABLE 12.1 PAYOFF MATRIX FOR THE PRISONER'S DILEMMA

		Prisoner B:	
		Stays silent	Confesses
Prisoner A:	Stays silent	1 year for A 1 year for B	20 years for A No jail for B
	Confesses	No jail for A 20 years for B	8 years for A 8 years for B

As the situation is set up, there are four possible combinations of what the prisoners may do. Both may remain silent; Prisoner A may confess while B does not; B may confess while A does not; or both may confess. Each of the four sets of decisions has a different consequence, or payoff, for each of the two prisoners. The four sets of decisions and the payoffs associated with each yield a payoff matrix as shown in Table 12.1.

Given this payoff matrix, what can the prisoners do? If both remain silent, the consequence is reasonably good for each of them. But how can either be sure that his partner won't double-cross him? If A remains silent while B tells all, B is even better off than he would be if both kept quiet; he stays out of jail entirely, while poor, silent A gets twenty years. Can A take the chance that B will not confess? Conversely, can B take this chance on A? The best bet is that each of them will decide that it's too risky to trust the other, for they both know that the other will be mightily tempted to squeal. As a result, neither takes the chance, and so they both defect from the common good and confess. The D.A. gets her conviction, and both men get eight years.

In a sense, the prisoners' behavior is maladaptive, for the outcome is far from optimal for each. But this doesn't mean that either of the two men behaved irrationally—on the contrary. Paradoxically enough, each picked the most rational course of action considering that he couldn't be sure how his partner would decide. Each individual acted rationally; the ironic upshot was an unsatisfactory outcome for both. In the best of all possible worlds they would have been able to trust each other, would have remained silent, and been in jail for a much shorter period. (But in the best of all possible worlds they wouldn't have robbed the bank in the first place.)

THE PRISONER'S DILEMMA AND PANIC

The underlying logic of the prisoner's dilemma applies to various social interactions whose payoff matrix is formally analogous. Brown has shown how it pertains to panic. In such cases there are more than two participants, but the essential ingredients are much the same. Each individual in the burning auditorium has two choices—he can wait his turn to get to the exit, or he can rush ahead. What are the probable outcomes? As in the case of the prisoners, they partially depend upon what others in the auditorium (especially those nearby) will do. If the individual rushes to the exit and everyone else does too, they will all probably suffer severe injuries and run some risk of death. If he takes his turn and others decorously do the same, the outcome is better; they will probably all escape, though they may suffer some minor injuries. The best outcome for the individual is produced if he ruthlessly pushes himself ahead while the others continue to file out slowly. In this case he will surely escape without a blister, but the chances for the others to escape are lessened. Suppose the situation is reversed so

Panic *In June of 1985, a riot broke out at a soccer match in Brussels resulting in the collapse of a stadium wall that killed 38 spectators and injured more than 200 others. The photo gives a glimpse of the resulting panic. (Photograph by Eamonn McCabe,* The Observer)

TABLE 12.2 PAYOFF MATRIX FOR AN INDIVIDUAL AND OTHERS IN A BURNING AUDITORIUM

		Others (O):	
		Take turns	Rush ahead
Individual (I):	Takes turn	Minor injuries for *I* Minor injuries for *O*	Increased chance of death for *I* No injuries for *O*
	Rushes ahead	No injuries for *I* Increased chance of death for *O*	Severe injuries for *I* Severe injuries for *O*

that the individual waits his turn while everyone near him runs ahead? Now the others may very well get out without injury while he himself may die. These sets of decisions and their associated outcomes represent just another version of the prisoner's dilemma, and they are shown in the payoff matrix of Table 12.2.

Given the payoff matrix of Table 12.2, most people will probably opt to rush ahead rather than wait their turn. As in the case of the two prisoners, this solution is grossly maladaptive, but from the point of view of each separate individual it is, sadly enough, quite rational. We again face the peculiar irony of the prisoner's dilemma. As Brown notes, "This irony about escape behavior . . . is always worked over by newspaper editorialists after panic occurs. 'If only everyone had stayed calm and taken his turn, then . . .' " (Brown, 1965, p. 741).

Brown's model of panic applies only if certain qualifications are met. As already noted, the danger must seem serious and the escape routes must appear inadequate. Another factor is the strength of social inhibitions. Most of us have been socialized to act with some respect for others; pushing ahead is socially disapproved and would therefore contribute a negative value to the relevant cells in the payoff matrix. The weight of this factor depends on the situation. If the fire seems minor, the embarrassment at behaving discourteously (or acting like a coward) might outweigh the fear of being the last to escape. If so, the payoff matrix will not be that of the prisoner's dilemma, and no panic will ensue.

SOCIAL DILEMMAS

In the classic prisoner's dilemma only two criminals are involved in the choice. But as the panic scenario illustrates, the dilemma can be expanded to include any number of individuals, each of whom has to decide whether to cooperate or to defect. Thus, the prisoner's dilemma and its payoff structure can be applied to many serious social and economic issues (Dawes, 1980).

Consider the social dilemma posed by industrial pollution. Suppose ten companies make various plastic toys and in the process create toxic wastes. Antipollution devices can be installed to remove the toxins, but they are expensive. What will the companies do? If all ten toy manufacturers make the same environmentally sound choice, none will have a price advantage, and air and water quality will remain the same. If they all attempt to look out for themselves alone and omit antipollution devices, none still will have a price advantage but the environment will be terribly degraded. If the other nine toy manufacturers can be counted on to make the environmentally sound choice, one toy producer could omit the antipollution devices, undercut the competition on price, and only degrade air and water quality slightly. But if all but one of the other

Social dilemmas *A roadside dump in Edgerton, Kansas. (Photograph © Dave Gleiter/FPG International)*

manufacturers choose to ignore environmental degradation, that one high-minded toy producer will probably be driven out of business.

In the modern world we face social dilemmas in many areas, including industrial pollution, deforestation, and the depletion of energy reserves. Is there anything we can do to encourage individuals to make the socially beneficial decision? We can skew the payoff matrix to create a bias (see Chapter 5). This is largely what our district attorney did to encourage the prisoners to throw loyalty to the wind. In the case of social dilemmas we can skew the payoff matrix by imposing penalties such as taxes or fines on individuals or companies that pollute, or we can enhance the appeal of altruistic behavior through education. Many of the social scientists who have studied social dilemmas suggest what may be the most effective strategies for their amelioration: teaching the ultimate benefits of cooperation, ensuring open communication among individuals, and increasing our trust that others won't exploit us (e.g., Orbell, van de Kragt, and Dawes, 1988; Rapoport, 1988; Kerr and Kaufmann-Gilliland, 1994). Whether such methods will be sufficient to save Earth from the follies of its inhabitants is another question (Dawes, 1980).

SOME FINAL COMMENTS

In this and the preceding chapter we asked how the individual interprets the social world in which she lives and how she interacts with the other people in it. This led to a survey of many topics, including the way we perceive the motives and acts of others as well as those of our own selves, how we interact with others, how we conform and obey, and how we behave in crowds.

COMMON THEMES

Can we isolate some major threads that run through the many theories, phenomena, and experimental demonstrations we've examined thus far? One theme that has arisen several times is that of reason versus passion.* We've repeatedly noted the fact that social behavior is affected by both cognitive and motivational factors. In our discussion of social cognition this point came up in relation to the self-serving bias, as well as the attribution-of-arousal theory of emotional experience. We encountered it again when dealing with social interaction. A case in point is conformity, which may be produced because the person thinks that others know more than he or because he is embarrassed or ashamed to disagree with them. It arose once more in terms of crowd behavior, which may be produced by the disinhibition of various impulses or by the cognitive factors that underlie the prisoner's dilemma. Reason and passion are the twin engines of human behavior, all the more so if that behavior is social.

Another theme that comes up again and again is whether events are driven by individuals or by the situations in which individuals find themselves. We discussed this distinction in the context of social cognition: In studies on attribu-

---

* While items are often stated as polar opposites, in actuality there are no genuine either-or dualities in psychology. We are swayed in our judgments neither by reason nor by passion alone. The same holds for the nature-nurture distinction: Both nature and nurture exert a powerful influence.

tion the question is whether someone performs a certain action because of something in her (a dispositional attribute) or because of something in the situation. The same distinction comes up repeatedly when dealing with social interaction. The two contending hypotheses in studies of blind obedience were that it stems from a certain personality pattern (e.g., the authoritarian personality) or that it is produced by the situation (as the Milgram experiment demonstrated). Another example is leadership, where we encountered the same polarity under the heading of the great-person versus social-forces theories. In all these cases we saw a widespread tendency to overrate the role played by personal characteristics and to underrate those played by situational factors.

Both the person and the situation evidently enter into the equation. But we must not conclude that this equation is a simple sum of the two, for the real relation between person and situation is always an interaction. The particular traits of an individual may be relevant in one situation and not in another. The stubborn eloquence and force of will of Winston Churchill made him the undisputed leader of an embattled Britain during World War II. But in the years before that war when many Britons longed for peace at any price, these qualities made him an unpopular member of his own party.

THE GENERALITY OF SOCIAL PSYCHOLOGY

Social psychology has clearly contributed to our understanding of social behavior. But how broadly applicable is this understanding? Does it bring us closer to an understanding of basic human nature, or is it necessarily limited to our own time and place?

Some authors argue that the discoveries of modern social psychology are limited to our social and cultural circumstances and cannot be generalized beyond them. Perhaps consistency, attribution of motives, self-perception, obedience, diffusion of responsibility, and so on are patterns of behavior that are specific to twentieth-century industrialized society, in particular, to that of modern North American society. If so, they may not describe how people act and think in other places and at other times (Gergen, 1973; Jahoda, 1979; Kitayama and Markus, 1994; Fiske et al., 1998). In this chapter and in Chapter 11, we have reviewed some of the areas in which this cultural critique has had particular force.

The culture-specific critique may be a valuable corrective to the notion that a genuine science of the psychology of social behavior can be developed in isolation from other social disciplines such as anthropology, sociology, economics, political science, and history. To understand the social situation the individual confronts, one has to refer to many cultural (or sociological or historical or political or economic) factors that transcend the individual (Pepitone, 1976; Price-Williams, 1985). We will return to this issue when we discuss the topic of personality, where we will consider different concepts of the self as they affect various aspects of cognition, emotion, and behavior (see Chapter 17).

Nevertheless, there are good reasons to believe that human social nature is much more stable than the culture-specific critique assumes it to be. Such diverse political theorists as Aristotle, Hobbes, and Confucius are still read despite the fact that they lived many centuries ago and under very different political systems than our own; they wrote about human social behavior that we can recognize even today. History provides many other examples of enduring social reactions. There are records of panics in Roman amphitheaters when the stands collapsed and of riots during sporting events in Byzantium. And the Great Wall of China, the pyramids of South and Central America, and the cathedrals of Europe all

Electioneering in Pompeii *Electoral inscriptions on the outer walls of houses in Pompeii. (From* The Buried Cities of Pompeii and Herculaneum; *photograph by Carlo Bevilacqua, © 1978 Instituto Geografico De Agostini; courtesy of the New York Public Library)*

527

testify to the ability of large groups of people to work together and to take direction from a leader. The cast and costumes differ, but the basic plots remain much the same. Some of the ancients even used certain of our modern propaganda devices. When the city of Pompeii was destroyed by a volcano in 79 A.D., it was evidently in the midst of a municipal election. Modern archeologists have found some of the election slogans on the excavated walls: "Vote for Vatius, all the whoremasters vote for him" and "Vote for Vatius, all the wife-beaters vote for him." While the techniques of the anti-Vatius faction may be a bit crude for our modern taste, they certainly prove that the psychology of the smear campaign has a venerable history (Raven and Rubin, 1976).

Phenomena of this sort suggest that there are some invariant properties of human social behavior that have genuine generality.

SUMMARY

1. Social interactions can be classified as those that are *one on one* (our relations with both strangers and people to whom we are close), those that are *many on one* (including various manifestations of social influence), those that are *one on many* (including leadership), and those that are *many on many* (including crowd behavior).

2. According to some theorists, all one-on-one interactions are *exchange relationships.* Evidence comes from the operation of the *reciprocity rule,* which applies not only to material things, such as food and gifts, but also to intangibles such as self-disclosure. Other theorists contend that not all relationships are based on reciprocity and suggest that in *communal relationships,* found often between romantic partners and close family members, the identities of the individuals merge so that the other's gains and losses are felt as one's own.

3. In investigating altruism, social psychologists have found that people often fail to help others in an emergency. One reason is the *bystander effect:* The greater the number of people who are present, the less likely that any one of them will provide help, in part because of *pluralistic ignorance,* in part because of *diffusion of responsibility.*

4. Social psychologists have studied some of the factors that attract people to each other. They include *proximity, similarity,* and *physical attractiveness.* There is evidence in favor of the *matching hypothesis,* which predicts a strong correlation between the physical attractiveness of the two partners.

5. Love is an especially close relation between two partners. Some authors distinguish between *romantic love,* in which the emotions are turbulent and intense, and *companionate love,* which is more stable and long lasting.

6. A number of many-on-one situations involve social influence. In some cases, all that matters is the mere presence of others, which produces *social facilitation* and *inhibition.* Another case of social influence is *conformity.* One reason for conformity is informational: We may believe that the group has knowledge we don't possess. Another reason is motivational: We go along because we want to be liked. A dissenting minority often leads to a massive reduction in the force toward conformity and may produce genuine changes in what people think and feel.

7. Still another form of social influence is obedience. Blind obedience has sometimes been ascribed to dispositional qualities within the person, as in studies on the *authoritarian personality.* But situational factors may be even more important, as shown by *Milgram's obedience studies.* His findings suggest that obedience depends on the psychological distance between one's own actions and their end result. When this distance is increased—by decreasing one's sense of responsibility, by dehumanization, and by means of various cognitive reinterpretations—obedience increases as well.

8. According to social impact theory, various phenomena of social influence can be understood by thinking of the individual as the target in a field of social forces. Social influences increase with the social forces that converge upon one individual. The greater the number, importance, or closeness of others, the greater the social force on the targeted individual. When the social impact is diffused over several other targets, as in the *bystander effect* and *social loafing,* the social influence diminishes.

9. An important example of one-on-many interactions is leadership. A major question in contemporary social psychology is what used to be called the *great-person versus social-forces controversy:* Does successful leadership depend on the special qualities of the leader or on the situation? The answer is that it is generally an interaction between the two.

10. In many-on-many interactions, a number of people interact with a number of others simultaneously. An example is crowd behavior, as in panics or riots. According to one account, the behavior of such crowds is essentially irrational and is based on *deindividuation.* According to another interpretation, it is not as irrational as it appears at first. The *prisoner's dilemma* shows that under certain conditions there can be collective irrationality even though all of the participants behave rationally as individuals. This has been applied to behavior in panics and to social dilemmas.

PART FOUR

DEVELOPMENT

CHAPTER 3

PHYSICAL AND COGNITIVE DEVELOPMENT

Thus far, we've considered two different kinds of psychological explanation. The first is concerned with mechanism—it tries to understand how something works. The second approach focuses on function—it tries to explain what something is for. But there is yet another approach to explanation in psychology that focuses on development. This approach deals with questions of history and trajectory—it asks how a given state of affairs came into being and how it is likely to progress.

In the next two chapters, we will consider this developmental perspective on psychological phenomena. We will ask how we come to reason and think, feel and act as we now do; how it is that we are no longer children, but for better or worse have become adults in mind as well as in body.

T he early part of the nineteenth century was a time of dramatic upheaval. The French Revolution and the birth of the United States a few decades earlier had ushered in a period of continued political unrest. The Industrial Revolution was transforming the social and economic structure of Europe and North America. In the eyes of many, it was a time of extraordinary progress (Bury, 1932). It is perhaps no surprise, therefore, that the scientists of the time became interested in development wherever they saw it. There were heated debates over the history of the planet, how it changed from molten rock into its modern form. Darwin was charting the evolution of the planet's many creatures. And, at the same time, there was increasing concern with the life history of individual organisms, starting from their embryonic beginnings and continuing as they developed toward maturity.

All animals develop, and so do we. It doesn't matter whether we are considering Mother Theresa or Attila the Hun, Marie Curie or John D. Rockefeller—all started life as infants; all learned to walk and to talk; all gained the basic intellectual and social skills we associate with being human. How did this development unfold? This question lies in the province of developmental psychology.

WHAT IS DEVELOPMENT?

Humans (and most other creatures) develop in a variety of ways over their lives. Some changes involve *physical development*, the maturation of various bodily structures; others involve *motor development*, the progressive attainment of various motor skills. Still other changes involve *cognitive development*, the growth of the child's intellectual functioning, and *social development*, changes in the ways the child perceives and deals with others. But these various forms of development all share some common features: differentiation, growth, and orderly progression.

DEVELOPMENT AS DIFFERENTIATION

The concept of differentiation grows out of some early discoveries in embryology, the study of an organism's development before birth. In the nineteenth century, the German biologist Karl Ernst von Baer (1792–1876) pointed out that most embryological development involves a progressive change from the general to the particular, from the simple to the complex—in short, *differentiation.*

Others before von Baer had noted that the embryos of very different species seem quite similar at early stages of development; only later do the dissimilarities among organisms emerge (Figure 13.1). Thus, a young chick embryo looks much like the embryo of any other vertebrate at a similar stage of development. As development proceeds, however, specialized features begin to emerge, and the chick embryo begins to look, first, like a bird, then like some kind of fowl, and still later like a chicken (Gould, 1977).

Von Baer's differentiation principle was initially regarded solely as a description of anatomical development. But a number of psychologists soon suggested that a similar principle applies to the development of behavior. Consider the development of grasping movements in human infants. When reaching for a small block, they initially curl their entire hand around the block; still later, they oppose the thumb to all four fingers. By the time they are one year old, they can victoriously coordinate hand, thumb, and one or two fingers to pick up the block with an elegant pincer movement (although such ultimate triumphs of manual differentiation as picking up a tea cup while holding the little finger extended will probably have to wait until they are old enough to read a book on etiquette) (Halverson, 1931; see Figure 13.2). Here, too, there is a pattern of differentiation, with an initially crude motion (the infant uses the same hand shape for grasping or for swatting) eventually replaced by a refined and specialized movement.

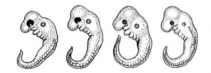

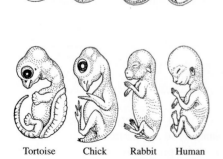

DEVELOPMENT AS GROWTH

One of the most obvious characteristics of development is growth. Organisms grow as they change from a fertilized egg to a fetus, and, of course, they continue to grow after birth, both in physical dimensions (e.g., height) and psychological ones (e.g., vocabulary size).

Tortoise Chick Rabbit Human

13.1 Differentiation during embryonic development *The figure shows three stages in the embryonic development of four different vertebrates—tortoise, chick, rabbit, and human. At the first stage, all of the embryos are very similar to each other. As development proceeds, they diverge more and more. By the third stage, each embryo has taken on some of the distinctive characteristics of its own species. (From Keeton and Gould, 1993. Redrawn from Romanes, 1882)*

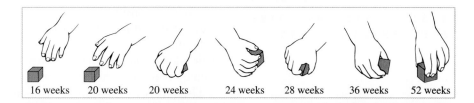

16 weeks   20 weeks   20 weeks   24 weeks   28 weeks   36 weeks   52 weeks

13.2   The development of manual skills
The diagram shows the progressive differentiation in the infant's use of the hand when holding an object. At sixteen weeks of age, he reaches for the object but can't hold on to it. At twenty weeks, he grasps it using the hand as a whole, with no differentiated use of the fingers. Between twenty-four and thirty-six weeks, the fingers and thumb become differentiated in use, but the four fingers operate more or less as a whole. By fifty-two weeks of age, hand, thumb, and fingers are successfully differentiated to produce precise and effective pincer movements. (Adapted from Liebert, Polous, and Strauss, 1974) Photos illustrate the same point at twenty-three, twenty-eight, and fifty-eight weeks. (Photographs by Kathy Hirsh-Pasek)

23 weeks   *28 weeks*   *58 weeks*

GROWTH BEFORE BIRTH

Each human existence begins at conception when a sperm and egg cell unite to form the fertilized egg. This egg divides and redivides repeatedly, producing a cellular mass that attaches itself to the wall of the uterus. Two weeks after conception the mass of cells (now called an ***embryo***) begins to differentiate into separate cell layers. After two more weeks, the embryo is a fifth of an inch long and looks like a tiny worm. A month later (two months after conception) the mass of cells is about one inch in length and is now called a ***fetus.*** In the next month, the fetus grows to about three inches in length and begins to resemble a miniature baby, with some functioning organ systems and a number of early reflexes, including sucking movements when the lips are touched. In another four months (that is, seven months after conception), the fetus has grown to sixteen inches, has a fully developed reflex pattern, can cry, breathe, swallow, and has a good chance of survival if it should be delivered at this time.

GROWTH AFTER BIRTH

Nine months after conception the human fetus leaves the uterus to enter the outer world. But is it really ready to do so? A newborn calf can walk at birth, and it can manage pretty well on its own shortly thereafter. The human infant, in contrast, is extraordinarily helpless and utterly dependent on others, and remains so for many months.

The immaturity of the human infant can be documented in many different ways. Consider the nervous system: The infant's neurons begin to mature in the later stages of prenatal growth, and their axons and dendrites form increasingly complex interconnections with other nerve cells (Schacher, 1981). But the brain is far from mature at birth: Figure 13.3 shows sections of the human cortex in a newborn, a three-month-old, and a fifteen-month-old child (Conel, 1939, 1947, 1955). As the figure clearly shows, there is tremendous growth across this period in the number of neural interconnections. If one simply counts the number of synapses per cortical neuron, this number is ten times greater—that is, there are ten times as many connections—for a one-year-old than it is for a newborn (Huttenlocher, 1979).

A   B   C

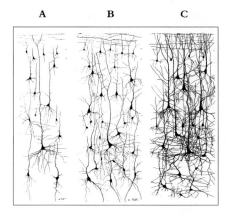

13.3   Growth of neural interconnections
Sections of the human cortex in (A) a newborn, (B) a three-month-old, and (C) a fifteen-month-old. (Conel, 1939, 1947, 1955)

535

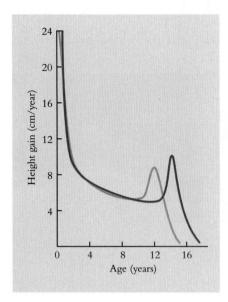

13.4 Physical growth *Height gains for British boys (dark red) and girls (blue) from birth until nineteen years of age. Physical growth continues for almost twenty years after birth with a special spurt at adolescence. (From Tanner, 1970)*

Capacity for learning *Learning from culture is not accomplished overnight. A ten-month-old baby is trying to master the intricacies of eating with a spoon. (Photograph courtesy of Kathy Hirsh-Pasek)*

Likewise, consider brain size. In most mammals, the newborn's brain is nearly adult sized, and just about fully formed. But not so in primates and most especially not so in humans. Human newborns have achieved only 23 percent of their adult cranial capacity at birth and have still only reached 75 percent of it even by two-and-a-half years of age (Catel, 1953, cited in Gould, 1977).

The growth of the child in brain size and complexity continues for many years. So, too, does her physical growth. In fact, physical growth continues for almost two decades after birth. This growth isn't continuous; rather, it comes in spurts. These periods of accelerated growth each last only a few months and occur throughout childhood, with children growing faster overall in the spring than in the winter (Ramsey, Bock, and Gasser, 1995; Giani, Filosa, and Causa, 1996; Thalange et al., 1996). The most dramatic growth spurt, though, occurs during adolescence with the onset of puberty (see Figure 13.4).

The child's brain also grows in fits and starts, with the spurts beginning around ages two, six, ten, and fourteen, and continuing for about two years each (Epstein, 1978). Each of these spurts leaves the brain up to 10 percent heavier than it was when the spurt began.

What happens during these growth spurts? The answer is complex. Although the newborn has all the neurons it will ever have, these neurons continue to establish new functional connections and withdraw malfunctioning or unneeded ones (see Chapter 2). At first, the formation of new connections outpaces the disconnections, and so the number of synapses appears to reach a maximum when the child is around two years old. But after the age of two, the pruning of synapses exceeds the formation of new ones, ultimately leaving the adult with only half the number of synapses the child had at two. And what explains the brain's weight gain with each growth spurt? In part, the gain is due to the growth of glial cells, some of which are responsible for the myelin sheaths that surround the axons that must travel long distances in the brain and spinal cord (see Chapter 2). Such myelination begins just after birth and lasts through puberty and perhaps beyond (Kolb and Whishaw, 1996).

THE SLOW PACE OF HUMAN GROWTH

Compared to any other organism, human development is amazingly slow, and one might think that this would be a great disadvantage for our species. After all, human parents are burdened with years of childcare and must devote a great quantity of resources to raising their children. This stands in marked contrast to, say, lions, whose male cubs are chased off from the pride when they are two to three years old.

Actually, many authors believe that the slow pace of human development is not a disadvantage at all. The immaturity of the human infant, and the slow pace of development, do make an extended period of dependency inevitable, and, in some ways, this is inconvenient (for child and parent alike). But this long period of dependency is tailor-made for a creature whose major specialization is its capacity for learning and whose basic invention is culture—the ways of coping with the world that each generation hands on to the next. Human infants, in other words, have a great deal to learn and a huge capacity for learning. Under these circumstances, there's much to be gained by a decade (or two) of living at home.

THE NEWBORN'S EQUIPMENT

We have emphasized the immaturity of human infants, but it is also true that newborns arrive in the world with some very important capacities. In Chapter 9, we considered their biologically given predisposition for language learning.

What other skills do infants bring with them into the world? We begin with their motor and sensory capacities.

The infant's response capacities   Initially, infants have little ability to control their motor apparatus. They thrash around in an uncoordinated manner and can't even hold up their heads. But they also have a number of important reflexes that help them through this period of helplessness. An example is the **grasp reflex**— when an object touches an infant's palm, he closes his fist tightly around it. If the object is lifted up, the infant hangs on and is lifted up along with it, supporting his whole weight for a minute or more. Reflexes of this sort are sometimes regarded as a primitive heritage from our primate ancestors whose infants had to cling to their mothers' furry bodies.

Other infantile reflexes pertain to feeding. An example is the **rooting reflex.** When her cheek is lightly touched, a baby's head turns toward the source of stimulation, her mouth opens, and her head continues to turn until the stimulus (usually a finger or nipple) is in her mouth. When this point is reached, sucking begins.

Many infantile reflexes disappear after a few months. In some cases, the reflex is replaced by a more directed response. Thus, infants stop reflexive grasping when they are about three or four months old, but this doesn't mean that they will never again grasp objects in their hands. Of course they will. But when they do (at about five months of age), they do so because they want to—their grasp has become voluntary rather than reflexive. Such voluntary actions have to wait until various parts of the cerebral cortex have matured sufficiently to make them possible. But until this point, the infantile reflexes serve as a temporary substitute.

A vital reflex in the newborn   The sucking reflex is initiated when an appropriate object is inserted three or four centimeters into the mouth. (Photograph by Kenneth Garrett 1984/Woodfin Camp)

The infant's sensory capacities   While newborns' motor capacities are initially very limited, their sensory channels function nicely from the start. They can discriminate between tones of different pitch and loudness and, as it turns out, also show an early preference for their mother's voice in comparison to that of a strange female (DeCasper and Fifer, 1980; Aslin, 1987). Newborns also can see: They are quite near-sighted and unable to focus on objects farther off than about four feet, but they can readily discriminate brightness and color, and they can follow a moving stimulus with their eyes (Bornstein, 1985; Aslin, 1987). In addition, they can touch, smell, and taste (Crook, 1987).

All in all, infants seem well equipped to sense the world they enter. But are they able to interpret what they see, hear, or touch? This is a disputed issue to which we will return in a later section. For now we merely note that young infants are quite competent to receive sensory inputs. Whether they have some built-in knowledge of what these inputs might signify (as nativists would argue) or have to acquire this knowledge by relating various sensory inputs to each other (as empiricists would have it) is another matter.

DEVELOPMENT AS ORDERLY PROGRESSION

In prenatal growth some events invariably come before others, as though there were a fixed sequence of steps through which development must proceed. Many developmental psychologists argue that there is a similar fixed sequence for psychological development after birth.

In motor development, for example, there is a regular sequence of achievements that begins with holding the head erect, followed by rolling over, then crawling, sitting up, standing up, taking a step or two, and finally walking, first

A

FETAL POSITION
0 month

CHIN UP
1 month

CHEST UP
2 months

REACH AND MISS
3 months

SIT WITH SUPPORT
4 months

SIT ON LAP
GRASP OBJECT
5 months

SIT ON HIGH CHAIR
GRASP DANGLING OBJECT
6 months

SIT ALONE
7 months

STAND WITH HELP
8 months

CREEP
10 months

WALK WHEN LED
11 months

PULL TO STAND
BY FURNITURE
12 months

CLIMB STAIR STEPS
13 months

STAND ALONE
14 months

WALK ALONE
15 months

13.5   The development of locomotion   *(A) The average age at which babies master locomotor skills, from holding their chins up to walking alone. These ages vary considerably. (From Shirley, 1961) (B) A pictorial record of these milestones in the life of one child. (Photographs courtesy of Kathy Hirsh-Pasek)*

B

2 days

2 months

6 months

shakily and then with increasing confidence. There is a good deal of variability in the age at which a given baby masters each of these skills, but the sequence itself rarely varies. No baby can walk before he can sit. (The average age at which children reach each of these milestones of motor development is shown in Figure 13.5.)

Similar progressions are found in aspects of intellectual development. Consider the acquisition of language. Initially the baby coos, then she babbles, then she utters her first word or two. Next she develops a small vocabulary but is limited to one-word utterances. Two-word sentences follow, and so on (see Chapter 9). As with motor development, there is a good deal of variability among infants in the timing of these achievements. Some begin to talk by ten months, others as

8 months

10 months

10 months

14 months

TABLE 13.1 CHARACTERISTIC LINGUISTIC ACHIEVEMENTS IN THE FIRST 30 MONTHS	
Age	*Linguistic achievement*
3 months	cooing
4 months	babbling
10 months	first word
18 months	about 20 words; one-word utterances
24 months	about 250 words; two-word utterances
30 months	about 500 words; three-plus utterances

SOURCE: From Lenneberg, 1967, pp. 128–30.

late as twenty. But little depends on this timing. The best evidence indicates, for example, that the age of initial language onset is no predictor of later linguistic competence. Whether early or late, though, the sequence of development is the same for all children, be they hearing children learning English or Arabic or deaf children learning a sign language (see Table 13.1). Here, as in so many other areas, development proceeds by an orderly sequence of steps, whether in the growth of minds or bodies.

THE PHYSICAL BASIS OF DEVELOPMENT

What produces the many changes that constitute development? One important factor is the genetic blueprint that each organism inherits; another factor is its environment—both before and after it is born.

THE MECHANISM OF GENETIC TRANSMISSION

An organism's genetic makeup is encoded in the *genes,* the units of hereditary transmission. These genes provide a set of instructions that determine growth and steer the organism's development from fertilized cell to mature animal or plant. The genes are stored within the *chromosomes* in the cell's nucleus, with each chromosome holding a thousand or more of these genetic commands. In organisms that reproduce sexually, the chromosomes come in pairs; one member of each pair is contributed by the mother, the other by the father (see Figure 13.6).

SEX DETERMINATION

The genetic commands that determine whether a given animal will be male or female are inscribed in a pair of sex chromosomes. In males, one of the members of this pair is called an **X chromosome;** the other is somewhat smaller and is called a **Y chromosome.** In females, both members of the pair are X chromosomes.

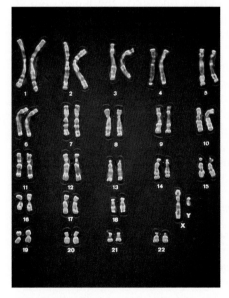

13.6   The human chromosome pairs
The figure shows the twenty-three pairs of chromosomes in a human male. The twenty-third pair determines the individual's sex. In males, one member of this pair is an X chromosome, the other a Y chromosome. In females, both are X chromosomes. (Photograph courtesy of M. M. Grumbach)

539

Which sex the child will be depends mostly on the father. The mother has only X chromosomes to contribute, and so every egg cell contains an X chromosome. Sperms cells contain either an X chromosome or a Y chromosome. Depending upon which of the two kinds joins up with the egg cell, the resulting fertilized egg (or zygote) will end up with an XX pair (and thus develop into a female) or an XY pair (a male).

DOMINANT AND RECESSIVE GENES

Chromosomes, we have noted, come in pairs, and the same is true for genes. Each gene occupies a specific position within its chromosome, and so, for each gene, there is a partner gene, located at the corresponding position on the other member of the chromosomal pair. The two genes in each pair—one contributed by each parent—may or may not be identical. Consider eye color. If both genes in the pair specify the same eye color (both coding for blue or both for brown), the eye color will follow suit. But suppose they are different. In humans, the gene for brown eyes is **dominant;** it will exert its effect regardless of whether the other member of the gene pair calls for brown or blue eyes. In contrast, the gene for blue eyes is **recessive.** This recessive gene will lead to blue eyes only if the gene in the corresponding locus of the paired chromosome also calls for blue eyes. Or, to put this differently, the baby's eyes will be blue only if both parents contributed a genetic instruction for blue; if either parent contributed an instruction for brown, the eyes will be brown.

Many other human traits are also based on a single gene pair, with one trait dominant and the others recessive. The list includes dark hair, dimples, and thick lips (all dominant); baldness, red hair, and straight nose (all recessive). A single gene pair also determines red-green color blindness or susceptibility to poison ivy (both recessive). Much more seriously, a single gene pair also determines whether a child will be born with hemophilia (in which the blood clots so slowly that a person may bleed to death from a minor injury). But hemophilia is a recessive trait and so will be manifested only if both parents transmit the relevant gene.

In fact, many disorders, not just hemophilia, are associated with recessive traits, and this may partially account for the widespread cultural prohibition against incest. A recessive trait, by definition, will only be manifested if both parents transmit the recessive gene, and this requires, of course, that both parents carry the recessive gene. This genetic similarity between the parents is obviously more likely if the parents are closely related, and this is why the offspring of related parents run a greater risk of serious genetic defects.

POLYGENIC INHERITANCE

So far, we have considered only those characteristics governed by a single gene pair. More typically, though, an organism's attributes are influenced by many gene pairs—a pattern known as **polygenic inheritance.** Thus, one gene pair might influence an early stage of development for a particular attribute, while a different pair influences an intermediate stage, and still another pair influences a later stage. Alternatively, the various gene pairs influencing a trait might all be active simultaneously, with each pair controlling some aspect of the body's inner workings, but with all the pairs collectively shaping the manifested trait.

In all cases, though, it is worth emphasizing that the genes do not directly control the observable traits. In truth, there is no gene that literally governs eye color, and certainly no gene that literally governs height or intelligence. Instead, what each gene truly controls is the production of a specific protein or enzyme;

Genetic effects on behavior *(© The New Yorker Collection 1989 Shanahan from The Cartoon Bank. All rights reserved.)*

these then regulate a specific biochemical sequence within the developing organism. It is this sequence that eventually leads (or in some cases, fails to lead) to the organism's manifest traits.

Notice, therefore, that the link between the genetic blueprint (the *genotype*) and the organism's actual characteristics (the *phenotype*) is indirect. Genes control biochemical processes within the body, and these processes eventually lead to the characteristics we observe in an individual. But many other factors also influence these same biochemical processes, and so many other forces shape the complex developmental sequence. Thus, genetic influences on development are profoundly important, but it is meaningless to speak of a characteristic as being entirely determined by the genes. Instead, genes are simply one factor within the set of factors that determine each aspect of the developing organism. (We will return to these issues, and the role of genetic factors in development, in Chapter 15.)

ENVIRONMENTS AT DIFFERENT POINTS IN DEVELOPMENT

Clearly, development involves both heredity and environment. But the relation between the two is subtler than may be apparent at first, for what is meant by environment changes continually as development proceeds.

THE ENVIRONMENT BEFORE BIRTH

Early embryonic development   Some of the cells in the embryo will eventually become part of the organism's brain; others will become part of the skin or part of the foot. But every cell in the embryo has the same genes, and so presumably all receive the same genetic instructions. How, therefore, does each cell manage to develop appropriately?

In part, the fate of each cell is determined by its cellular neighbors—the cells that are adjacent to it and form its physical environment. Evidence comes from studies of salamander embryos. At an early stage of their development, salamanders have an outer layer of tissue that gradually differentiates: Cells in this layer will become teeth if they make contact with certain other cells in the embryo's mouth region. Without this contact, cells in this layer instead become skin. Proof for this claim comes from studies in which parts of the embryo's outer cell layer were surgically rearranged. Had these cells stayed in their initial position, they would have developed into the skin on the salamander's flank. Transplanted into the embryo's mouth region, these cells became teeth (Spemann, 1967).

In another study, the experimenters performed a similar surgery, but the cells they transplanted into the salamander's mouth region were taken from another species—they were taken from the flank of a frog embryo. The results illustrate the crucial importance of both genetics and environment: The newly transplanted cells did become part of the salamander's mouth, in strict obedience to their new environment. But they became horny jaws rather than teeth—the mouth appendages of a frog rather than of a salamander—in appropriate homage to their genetic heritage. Thus, the environment determined whether these cells became the skin of a frog's sides or the horny jaw of its mouth, but, no matter what the environment, the cells could never escape their essential froghood (Spemann, 1967).

Studies such as these make it clear that both heredity and environment are effective from the very start of life. The two interact to determine the further course of development.

5 4 1

The development of sexual structures   In an early stage of embryonic development, each cell's environment consists of its cellular neighbors. Somewhat later, development is affected by another kind of environment—the organism's own bodily fluids, especially its blood. Moreover, the bloodstream of mammalian embryos is intimately connected to the mother's blood supply, and so this too becomes part of the embryo's environment.

An example of the influence exerted through the bloodstream is the development of sexual structures and behavior. What determines whether an individual is biologically male or female? We earlier suggested that this is a matter of genetics—you are male if you are chromosomally XY and female if you are XX. But the full story is more complicated than that. At about six weeks of age, the human embryo has primordial **gonads** that as yet give no indication of the baby's sex. A week or so later, the chromosomes initiate the differentiation of ovaries and testes (see Figure 13.7). In a genetic male, the XY chromosome pair leads to the formation of testes. Once formed, these produce **androgens,** the male sex hormones, and it is the presence of these hormones in the bloodstream that leads to the differentiation of the external genitals.

The pattern is different for females. The formation of the female's external genitals depends on hormones only indirectly. As long as no androgens circulate in the bloodstream, the fetus will develop the appropriate female organs. Thus, the basic genetic plan for humans, shared by both sexes, seems to call for the building of a female.★ If it is left undisturbed (that is, if no androgens are present), the plan runs its course. To build a male, the developmental path has to be diverted by the appropriate hormones. It would seem that biologically—if not biblically—speaking, Adam was created from Eve (Money and Ehrhardt, 1972; Money, 1980).

Thus, the chromosome pairs define an individual's genetic sex. But the way in which that sex is actually shaped depends on the organism's internal environment—the presence or absence of male hormones in its bloodstream.

THE ENVIRONMENT AFTER BIRTH

After birth, the range of environmental events affecting development broadens appreciably, and now includes many aspects of the surrounding physical, social, and cognitive worlds. We will have much more to say about specific environmental influences later in this chapter, but for now let us simply note the rich diversity of this set of influences. They include the nutrients (and toxins) that enter the child; the behavior of other people, which the child observes, learns from, and sometimes imitates; the explicit instructions that the child receives from others; and the feedback the child receives, after trying this or that behavior and observing its consequences. These factors are, to no one's surprise, all enormously important in guiding the child's learning and development.

Which aspects of the environment are critical, though, depends in part on the child's age. As an example, imagine a three-month-old who hears an older sibling shout "Surprise!" as the parents put some new toy into the baby's crib. In all likelihood, the baby will cry in fear, for all he hears is a loud noise. At three years of age, the same shout will probably produce joyous squeals of anticipation, for now the sound has meaning and that meaning is vastly more important than its acoustic intensity.

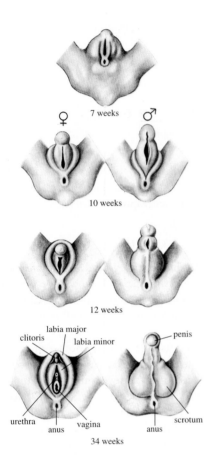

13.7   The development of external genitals in the human fetus   *At seven weeks, the genitalia of human male and female fetuses are virtually indistinguishable. Some differentiation is seen at ten weeks and becomes increasingly pronounced in the weeks thereafter. At thirty-four weeks, the distinctive characteristics of the different genitalia are fully apparent. (From Keeton and Gould, 1993)*

★ In birds, the basic plan is male, with females the result of special hormonal intervention (Shepherd, 1994).

The creation of Eve *According to the Bible, Eve was created after Adam. But biologically, the order is reversed. (Panel from the Sistine Chapel ceiling, by Michelangelo, 1508–1512. Courtesy of Scala/Art Resource)*

SENSITIVE PERIODS

We have just noted that a child's reaction to an event (or any other environmental influence) depends on her age. Some developmental theorists, however, believe this idea should be framed in much stronger terms: They argue that there are ***critical periods*** in development during which certain events will have an enormous impact; these same events will have much less impact if they arrive either earlier or later.

The hypothesis of critical periods was derived from embryological development. Take the differentiation of organ tissue. We previously saw that at a very early stage, parts of a salamander embryo's outer tissue may become skin or teeth, depending upon the cells they are adjacent to. If transplanted at this time, they will take the shape appropriate to their new surroundings. But at a later time, this plasticity is gone. If the cells destined to be teeth are transplanted at this point, they still become teeth. For these cells, the critical period has passed, and the path of development is already set (Spemann, 1967).

Many psychologists believe that similar critical periods exist for key developments after birth, but the boundaries of these periods are not as rigidly fixed as are the critical periods in embryological development. As a result, these windows of opportunity are often called ***sensitive periods,*** to indicate that this is a time in which the organism is especially sensitive to a particular influence. An example is the attachment of the young of many species to their mother, an attachment that is much more readily formed at an early age (see Chapter 14). In humans, a related example is the acquisition of language, which as we've seen is also easier at younger ages (see Chapter 9).

ENVIRONMENT AND MATURATION

As noted earlier, development is typically orderly and progressive. Infants sit up before they can walk and babble before they can talk. What accounts for this schedule of early developmental achievements?

13.8 Learning, maturation, and walking
*A Shoshone infant strapped into a cradle.
Swaddling has little effect on the child's ability
to walk later on. (Shoshone Indian Reservation, Wyoming; photograph by Victor Englebert/Photo Researchers)*

The benefits of starting young *Tiger
Woods may be a good example of someone on
whom early practice conferred a lifelong advantage. He first held a golf club at age two, became devoted to the sport and practiced incessantly; in 1997, when he was only
twenty-one, he won the Masters, a major tournament, by twelve strokes, setting the new
tournament record of eighteen under par.*

Some theorists argue that many of the infant's early achievements (especially in motor and sensory development) are produced by **maturation**—the unfolding of behavior patterns that are genetically programmed into the species. Maturation is dependent on the environment in a very general way (there must, for example, be an adequate supply of nutrients and an absence of toxins). But maturation is not dependent on any specific experience or any particular instruction from the outside. Thus, maturation will go forward in almost any environment.

Theorists who emphasize the importance of maturation believe that the sequence of behavioral milestones in the infant is analogous to the orderly progression that characterizes physical growth. Each behavioral achievement—sitting, crawling, and then walking—takes place when growth in the infant's brain and muscles makes it possible, all at the appropriate point in the developmental schedule.

MATURATION AND PRACTICE

Are these achievements truly dependent solely on maturation? To find out, a number of investigators have compared infant-rearing practices in different cultures. In some societies—for example, that of the Hopi and Navaho—infants are swaddled and bound to a cradle or carrying board, with their activity severely inhibited for much of the first year of life (see Figure 13.8). Despite some initial reports to the contrary (Dennis, 1940), the evidence suggests that these early restrictions do postpone the occurrence of later motor milestones (Brazelton, 1972). In contrast, other cultures provide their children with systematic practice in various motor activities, which seems to lead to some developmental acceleration (Super, 1976).

Let us note, though, that the effects of immobilization are slight, as are the effects of special practice. In either case, the child does learn to walk, and the developmental sequence from that point forward is the same for those infants regardless of when they began walking.

In line with this conclusion are studies in which infants within a single culture are given special practice in such basic activities as walking or climbing stairs. Infants who receive this practice do start walking or stair climbing a little earlier than their untrained comrades. A few months later, though, this advantage vanishes: Once the untrained infants mature a bit and practice a little on their own, they attain exactly the same level of locomotor proficiency as the group that received the training (Gesell and Thompson, 1929; McGraw, 1935; for a broader perspective on locomotion, see Bertenthal, Campos, and Kermoian, 1994). Thus, an account based on maturation does seem promising: The speed of development (at least for activities basic to the species) can be altered somewhat by experience, but the sequence (and quality) of development goes forward normally in almost any circumstances.

Let us emphasize, however, that a different verdict holds for skills that are specific to a particular culture or subgroup, such as swimming, climbing trees, playing tennis, or throwing a boomerang. Here, early experience does seem to have lasting effects, and practice in these activities at a young age may create a lifelong advantage. This may be because such skills are more easily acquired at an early age (as is the case in learning a language, see Chapter 9). It may also be that starting early provides the necessary motivation for the grueling efforts required for eventual mastery.

SPECIFIC VERSUS NON-SPECIFIC EXPERIENCE

Maturation proceeds no matter what the specific experiences of the developing child. But maturation is dependent on experience in a broader sense. For exam-

13.9 Effects of environmental enrichment *After eighty days in the enriched environment of this rat playground, the animals had 23 percent more neural interconnections than control animals. (Photograph courtesy of Dr. Mark Rosenzweig)*

ple, the maturation of the visual system is strongly shaped by genetic factors and will unfold on its preset schedule no matter what the organism sees or looks at. Nonetheless, experience does play a crucial role: Animals reared in total darkness in early life will not develop certain structures of the visual system and will not be able to see properly when they are later exposed to light (Gottlieb, 1976). Thus, no *specific experience* is required for visual development, but *some experience* is needed.

Similarly, just as sensory deprivation can retard maturation, environmental enrichment can help it along. In one study, rat pups were placed in either an impoverished or an enriched environment right after they were weaned. The animals in the impoverished environment were individually housed in a standard laboratory cage with continual access to a water bottle and food. In contrast, animals in the enriched environment were housed in groups of about twelve in a large cage that was a veritable rats' playground: It contained a variety of objects that served as toys that the rats could climb on, walk across, and run in and out of and that were changed daily to provide additional opportunities for informal learning (Rosenzweig and Bennett, 1972; Renner and Rosenzweig, 1987; see Figure 13.9).

After eighty days of exposure to these different environments, the brains of the animals were examined. The results showed that the brains of the environmentally enriched rats were heavier than those of the environmentally impoverished rats. The two groups of rats had the same number of neurons in their brains; what differed was the number of neural interconnections. In one study, the enriched animals were estimated to have about 9,400 synapses per neuron, while the impoverished animals only had about 7,600 (Turner and Greenough, 1985). The increase in the number and complexity of synaptic junctions produced by exposure to a varied environment may well be the biological basis on which later behavioral development depends (Schapiro and Vukovich, 1976).

PIAGET'S THEORY OF COGNITIVE DEVELOPMENT

Thus far, our discussion of development has focused on physical growth and changes in motor behavior. But children grow in mind as well as body—in what they know, how they think about it, and in the fact that they can tell it to others (sometimes interminably so). This intellectual growth from infancy to adulthood is generally called **cognitive development.**

Children as miniature adults *Children dressed as did the adults of their time and class as shown in this 1786 Dutch painting. (Helena van der Schalke, by G. ter Borch, Courtesy of the Rijksmuseum, Amsterdam)*

For most of this century, the study of cognitive development has been focused on theoretical claims developed by the Swiss psychologist Jean Piaget (1896–1980), and we will organize our discussion around Piaget's work. Piaget was the first to develop methods for studying the ways infants and children see and understand the world, the first to suggest that these ways are profoundly different from those of adults, and the first to offer a systematic theoretical account of the process of mental growth from infancy to adulthood. As we will see, Piaget's formulations have aroused considerable controversy: Many of his empirical claims have been disputed, and most of his theoretical proposals have come under serious attack. But even so, we cannot begin the study of cognitive development without first considering Piaget's views, since these have shaped the way all subsequent investigators have approached the subject.

Piaget believed that mental growth involves major qualitative changes. This hypothesis is relatively recent. According to the eighteenth-century empiricists, the child's mental machinery is fundamentally the same as the adult's, the only difference being that the child has fewer associations. Nativists also minimized the distinction between the child's mind and the adult's, for they viewed the basic categories of time, space, number, and causality as being part of the native mental equipment that all humans have at birth. Thus, both empiricists and nativists regarded the child as much like an adult; the first saw her as an adult in training, the second as an adult in miniature. In contrast, Piaget claimed that there were profound differences between child and adult, and he tried to chart the often large changes that he believed were taking place as the child grows intellectually.

Piaget's original training was as a biologist, which may be one of the reasons why his conception of intellectual development bears such a resemblance to the way an embryologist thinks of the development of anatomical structures. The human fetus doesn't just get larger between, say, two and seven months; its whole structure changes drastically. Piaget argued that mental development is characterized by similar changes. In the early stages of development, he argued, the child's perception and thinking are governed by the here and now of the immediate, concrete present. The main thrust of development, therefore, is an emancipation from this pattern, as the child develops the capacity to think about the world in increasingly symbolic and abstract terms.

Piaget proposed that there are four main stages of intellectual growth. They are the period of ***sensory-motor intelligence*** (from birth to about two years), the ***preoperational period*** (two to seven years), the period of ***concrete operations*** (seven to eleven years), and the period of ***formal operations*** (eleven years and on). The age ranges are very approximate, however, and successive stages are often thought to overlap and blend into one another.★

SENSORY-MOTOR INTELLIGENCE

According to Piaget, the child's mental life during the first few months consists of nothing but a succession of transient, disconnected sensory impressions and motor reactions. There is no distinction between stable objects and fleeting events, and no differentiation between the "me" and the "not me." The critical achievement of the first two years is the development of these distinctions.

★ These stages roughly correspond to the categories employed by modern developmental psychologists, regardless of their stand on Piaget's theory: infancy (from birth to about two-and-a-half years), early childhood (two-and-a-half to six years), middle childhood (six to eleven years), and adolescence and beyond (twelve years and up).

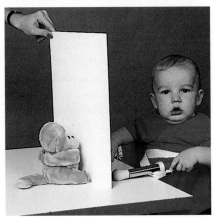

13.10   Object permanence   (A) A six-month-old looks intently at a toy. (B) But when the toy is hidden from view, the infant does not search for it. According to Piaget, this is because the infant does not as yet have the concept of object permanence. (Photographs by Doug Goodman 1986/Monkmeyer)

OBJECT PERMANENCE

Consider an infant holding a rattle. At the moment, the infant might be looking at the rattle, but this *looking at* is not part of the rattle's identity. If the infant looked away, the rattle would still exist. Likewise, the infant is now holding the rattle, but this too is incidental; the rattle's continued existence is in no way dependent on its being held.

According to Piaget, infants understand none of this. For infants, the only world that exists is the world of their own sensations. Therefore, infants are aware of looking at the rattle but have no conception of the rattle itself existing as a permanent, independent object. If infants look away from a rattle (and thus stop seeing it), then the rattle ceases to exist. It's not just "out of sight, out of mind." More strongly, it's "out of sight, out of existence." In this way, Piaget claims, infants lack a sense of **object permanence**—the understanding that objects exist independent of our momentary sensory or motoric interactions with them.

What led Piaget to this view? He observed that infants typically look at a new toy with evident delight, but if the toy disappears from view, they show little concern (see Figure 13.10). At a slightly later age, infants might show some signs of distress when the toy disappears but still make no effort to retrieve it. This is true even if it seems perfectly obvious where the toy is located. For example, an experimenter might drape a light cloth over the toy, while an infant is watching. In this situation, the toy is still easily within reach and its shape is still (roughly) visible through the folds of the cloth. The child watched it being covered just moments earlier. But still the infant makes no effort to retrieve it. According to Piaget, this is because the toy, no longer visible, has ceased to exist in the mind of that child.

At about eight months of age, infants do start to search for toys that have been hidden or that have fallen out of their cribs. Apparently, an eight-month-old knows that objects endure even when they are out of view. But the child's searching for the toy shows a peculiar limitation, and this indicated to Piaget that the child still lacks a mature concept of object permanence.

Consider a nine-month-old who sees an experimenter hide a toy monkey under a cover located, say, to the child's right. The child will happily push the cover off and snatch up the monkey. The experimenter now repeats the process a few times, always hiding the monkey in the same place, under the same cover to the child's right. Again and again the child pulls the cover off and retrieves the monkey. But now the experimenter introduces a slight change in the procedure. Very slowly and in full view of the child, she now hides the toy in a different place, say, under a cover to the child's left. The child watches her every movement with grave attention—and then does exactly what he did before. He searches under the cover on the right, even though he saw the experimenter hide the toy in another place just a moment earlier.

This phenomenon is often called the ***A-not-B effect,*** where *A* designates the place where the object was first hidden and *B* the place where it was hidden last. Why does this peculiar error occur? According to Piaget, the nine-month-old still has not grasped the fact that an object's existence is entirely independent of his own actions. Thus, the child believes that his reaching toward place *A* (where he found the toy previously) is as much a part of the monkey as the monkey's tail. In effect, the child isn't really searching for a monkey; he is searching for the-monkey-that-I-find-on-the-right. No wonder, then, that the child continues searching on the right (Piaget, 1952; Flavell, 1985; Harris, 1987).

According to Piaget, the notion that objects exist on their own and continue to exist even if they are not seen, heard, felt, or reached for is a major accomplishment of the sensory-motor period. This notion emerges as infants gradually correlate their various sensory experiences with their motor reactions. Eventually, they coordinate the information provided by the different modalities—of vision, hearing, touch, and bodily movement—into one spatial framework in which all of the world's objects—themselves included—exist. What makes this possible is their increasingly sophisticated **schemas.**

SENSORY-MOTOR SCHEMAS

Newborns start life with a rather limited repertoire of built-in reactions, such as sucking, swallowing, and, after a few days, certain orienting responses such as head and eye movements. In Piaget's view, these action patterns provide the first mental categories, or schemas, through which infants organize the world that impinges upon them: The world is understood, in effect, as consisting of the suckables, the swallowables, and so on.

At first, these various schemas operate in isolation. A one-month-old infant will look at an object if it's placed in front of his eyes and will grasp it if it's pressed into his palm. But he is as yet unable to grasp whatever he's looking at or to look at whatever he's grasping. The coordination of these patterns is not complete until he's about five months of age.

How is this integration achieved? According to Piaget, the answer lies in the two processes that in his view are responsible for all of cognitive development: **assimilation** and **accommodation.** In assimilation, children use the mental schemas they have to interpret (and act upon) the environment: Objects in the environment are *assimilated* into the schema. But the schemas also change as the child gains experience in interacting with the world; the schemas *accommodate* to the environment.

For example, the schema for sucking initially applies only to the nipple. But with time, infants start to suck other objects, such as a rattle. Piaget would say that by doing this they have assimilated the rattle into their sucking schema. The rattle is now understood and dealt with as a suckable. But the process does not stop there. After all, rattles are not the same as nipples; while both are suckable, they are not suckable in quite the same way. This necessarily leads to new discriminations. As a result, the sucking schema adjusts to (that is, accommodates) the new object to which it is applied. This process continues, with further assimilations followed by yet further accommodations, so that the schemas gradually become more and more differentiated. At the same time, the increasing skill acquired with each schema allows the infants to use more than one schema at a time—reaching while looking, grasping while sucking—and this allows them to coordinate these individual actions into one unified exploratory schema (Piaget, 1952).

BEGINNINGS OF REPRESENTATIONAL THOUGHT

According to Piaget, the last phase of the sensory-motor period (about eighteen to twenty-four months) marks a momentous change in intellectual development. Children begin to conceive of objects and events that are not immediately present. These early mental representations may be internalized actions (one anticipates throwing an object that's not currently in view), or images (one remembers what the object looked like), or even words. But in any case this ability to represent objects in one's mind is a crucial step on the path toward abstract symbolic thought.

This capacity for mental representation grows out of the achievements we have already discussed. In order to attain a full concept of object permanence, for example, the child must be able to think about (*represent*) an object in a fashion that is emancipated from the immediate here and now of sensorimotor experi-

Assimilation and accommodation *The three-month-old has assimilated the rattle into her sucking schema and has accommodated the schema so that it now includes the rattle as a suckable object. (Photograph by Steve Skloot/ Photo Researchers)*

Jean Piaget *(Photograph by Yves De-Braine, Black Star)*

ence. The child must be able to think about an object seen earlier, even if it is not visible at the moment. Thus, the achievement of object permanence must go hand in hand with the capacity for mental representation.

This capacity can be demonstrated in the child in various ways. At eighteen months or so, children actively search for absent toys and are surprised (and sometimes outraged) if they don't find them under the sofa cover where they saw the experimenter hide them; it is reasonable to infer that they have some internal representation of the sought for object. Even more persuasive are examples of **deferred imitation** in which children imitate actions that occurred some time past, such as a playmate's temper tantrum observed a day ago. This, too, requires the ability to hold in one's mind some representation of the act observed earlier—an ability, Piaget argued, that is pivotal in launching the next major stage of intellectual growth.

THE PREOPERATIONAL PERIOD

Given the capacity for representational thought, two-year-olds have taken a gigantic step forward. A year ago, they could interact with the environment only through direct sensory or motor contact; now they can carry the whole world in their heads. But their mental world is still a far cry from the world of adults. Two-year-olds have learned how to represent the world mentally but have not yet learned how to interrelate these representations in a coherent way. The achievement of the next five years, therefore, is the emergence of a reasonably well-ordered world of ideas. In Piaget's view, this requires a new and more sophisticated set of schemas that he called **operations**. These allow the internal manipulation of ideas according to a stable set of rules. In his view, genuine operations do not appear until about seven or so, hence the term **preoperational** for the period from two to about seven years.

FAILURE OF CONSERVATION

Conservation of quantity and number A revealing example of preoperational thought is the fact that young children fail to conserve quantity. This failure can be demonstrated in many ways; one procedure uses two identical glasses, *A* and *B,* which stand side by side and are filled with the same amount of colored liquid. A child is asked whether there is more orangeade in one glass or the other, and the experimenter obligingly adds a drop here, a drop there until the participant is completely satisfied that there is "the same to drink in this glass as in that." Four-year-olds can easily make this judgment.

The next step involves a new glass, *C,* which is taller but also narrower than *A* and *B* (see Figure 13.11). While the child is watching, the experimenter pours

13.11   Conservation of liquid quantity
Patrick, aged four years, three months, is asked by the experimenter, "Do we both have the same amount of juice to drink?" Patrick says yes. (B) The experimenter pours the juice from one of the beakers into a new, wider beaker. When now asked, "Which glass has more juice?" Patrick points to the thinner one. (Photographs by Chris Massey)

A

B

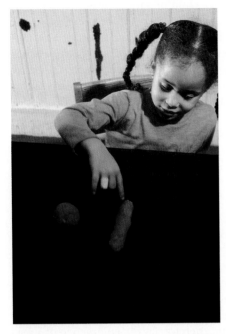

13.12 Conservation of mass quantity
In parallel to the failure to conserve liquid quantity is the preschooler's failure to conserve mass. Jennifer, aged four years and four months, is shown two clay balls which she adjusts until she is satisfied that there is the same amount of clay in both. The experimenter takes one of the balls and rolls it into a "hot dog." When now asked which is more, Jennifer points to the hot dog. (Photograph by Ed Boswell)

the entire contents of glass *A* into glass *C*. She now points to *B* and *C*, and asks, "Is there more orangeade in this glass or in that or are they the same?" For an adult, the question is almost too simple to merit an answer. The amounts are obviously identical, since *A* was completely emptied into *C*, and *A* and *B* were set to equality at the outset. But four- or five-year-olds don't see this. They insist that there is more orangeade in *C*. When asked for their reason, they explain that the liquid comes to a much higher level in *C*. They seem to think that the orangeade has somehow increased in quantity as it was transferred from one glass to another. They are too impressed by the visible changes in appearance that accompany each transfer (the changing liquid levels) to realize as yet that there is an underlying constancy (the quantity of liquid).

By the time children are about seven years old, they respond much like adults. They hardly look at the two glasses, for their judgment needs little empirical support. "It's the same. It seems as if there's more because it's thinner, but it's the same." The experimenter may continue with other glasses of different sizes and shapes but the judgment remains what it was: "It's still the same because it always comes from the same glass." To justify their answer, the children point to the fact that they could always pour the liquid back into the original glass (that is, *A*), and thus obtain the same levels. They have obviously understood that the various transformations in the liquid's appearance are reversible. For every transformation that changes the way the liquid looks, there is another that restores its original appearance. Given this insight, children at this age recognize that there is an underlying attribute of reality, the quantity of liquid, that remains constant (is conserved) despite the various perceptual changes. (For comparable results with malleable solids like clay, see Figure 13.12.)

A related phenomenon is conservation of number. The child is first shown a row of six evenly spaced bottles, each of which has a glass standing next to it. The child agrees that there are as many bottles as there are glasses. The experimenter now rearranges the six glasses by setting them out into a much longer row while leaving the six bottles as they were. Here the turning point comes a bit earlier, at about five or six. Up to that age, children generally assert that there are more glasses because "they're more spread out" (see Figure 13.13). From about six on, there is conservation; the child has no doubt that there are just as many bottles in the tightly spaced row as there are glasses in the spread-out line. If asked to justify this response, the child again emphasizes reversibility: Just as liquid can be poured back into the shorter glass, restoring the earlier situation, the child knows that the long line of glasses can be reassembled into a compact row.

Attending to several factors simultaneously Why do preschool children fail to conserve? According to Piaget, part of the problem is their inability to interrelate the different dimensions of a situation. Consider conservation of liquid quantity.

13.13 Conservation of number *(A) The experimenter points to two rows of checkers, one hers, the other Tyler's. She asks, "Do I have as many checkers as you?" and Tyler (aged four years, five months) nods. (B) One row of checkers is spread out and the experimenter says, "Now, do we still have the same?" Tyler says no and points to the spread-out row, which she says has more. (Photographs by Chris Massey)*

A

B

To conserve, the children must first comprehend that there are two relevant factors: the height of the liquid column and the width of the glass. They must then appreciate that an increase in the column's height is accompanied by a decrease in its width. Thus, the children must be able to attend to both dimensions concurrently and relate the dimensions to each other. This is the capacity that they lack, since it requires a higher-order schema that reorganizes initially discrete perceptual experiences into one conceptual unit.

In Piaget's view, children gain this capacity only when they begin to focus on the *transformations* from one experience into another, rather than on the individual experiences themselves. Children see that these transformations are effected by actions that are reversible, such as pouring the contents of one glass into another and then back again. This reversible action eventually becomes internalized, so that they can *think about* the liquid being poured back and forth with no overt action. The result of this reversible mental operation is conservation of quantity (Piaget, 1952).

In summary, preoperational children are the prisoners of their own immediate perceptual experiences and tend to take appearance for reality. When a seven-year-old watches a magician, he can easily distinguish between his perception and his knowledge. He sees the rabbits coming out of the hat, but he knows that they couldn't possibly do so. His four-year-old sister has no such sophistication. She is delighted to see rabbits anytime and anywhere, and if they want to come out of a hat, why shouldn't they?

EGOCENTRISM

Preoperational children are similarly limited in how they understand the social world: Here, too, the children focus on one dimension at a time and are locked into their own perspective on a situation. They do not understand another person's point of view and don't even recognize that another person's point of view may be different from their own.

Piaget used the term *egocentrism* to describe this characteristic of preoperational thought. As Piaget used the term, it does not imply selfishness. Instead, the children simply haven't yet grasped that there are other selves, with their own needs, their own beliefs, and their own perspectives.

An interesting demonstration of egocentrism involves a literal interpretation of "point of view." If two adults stand at opposite corners of a building, each knows that the other sees a different wall. But according to Piaget, preoperational children don't understand this. In one study, children were shown a three-dimensional model of a mountain scene. While a child viewed the scene from one position, a small teddy bear was placed at various other locations around the model. The child's job was to decide what the teddy bear saw from its vantage point (see Figure 13.14). To answer, the child had to choose one of several drawings that depicted different views of the mountain scene. Up to four years of age, children didn't even understand the question. From four to seven years old, their response was fairly consistent—they chose the drawing that showed what they themselves saw, regardless of where the teddy bear was placed (Piaget and Inhelder, 1956).

13.14   The three-mountain test of egocentrism   *The child is asked to indicate what the doll sees. The results suggest that the child thinks the doll sees the scene just as she does, including the little house, which is of course obstructed from the doll's vantage point. (After Piaget and Inhelder, 1967)*

CONCRETE AND FORMAL OPERATIONS

By the age of three or four (early in the preoperational period), children have learned how to represent the world mentally. By age seven or so, they have learned how to interrelate these representations. They now grasp the fact that changes in one aspect of a situation are compensated for by changes in some other aspect. They are able to transform their own mental representations in a variety of ways and thus understand what would happen if the water were poured back into its original glass and how a setting would look if viewed from another angle.

But according to Piaget, children's intellectual capacities are still limited in an important way: They have gained skill in a variety of mental operations, but they apply these operations only to relations between concrete events (hence, the term *concrete operations*). Thus, children are able to think about a wide range of concrete cases, but lack skill in thinking abstractly.

For example, eight- and nine-year-olds can easily see that 4 is an even number and 4 + 1 is odd. Similarly, they understand that 6 is even, while 6 + 1 is odd, and likewise for 8 and 8 + 1. But the same children fail to see the inevitability of this pattern; they fail to see that the addition of 1 to any even number must always produce a number that is odd. According to Piaget, the comprehension of this abstract and formal relationship requires *formal operations*, operations of a higher order, which emerge at about eleven or twelve years of age.

An illustration of the role of formal operations comes from a study in which children were shown how to construct a pendulum by hanging an object from a string. They were also shown how to vary the length of the string, the weight of the suspended object, and the initial force that set the pendulum in motion. With this backdrop, the children were now asked to discover what makes a pendulum go fast or go slow.

To solve this problem efficiently, one needs to think abstractly about the various dimensions involved (the weight of the object, the length of the string). One is then likely to realize that it would be good to vary just one of these dimensions at a time, while holding the others constant. In this fashion, one can ask how (or whether) each factor influences the pendulum's swing.

Children older than eleven employed this efficient strategy, planning and executing an appropriate series of tests. Children younger than eleven used a much less sophisticated approach and typically varied several factors each time they tried a new test. These children would also draw conclusions from their tests that were plainly not justified: Thus, if they used a heavy pendulum in one of their tests and observed the pendulum swinging particularly quickly, they might conclude that the weight of the pendulum was crucial in determining the pendulum's swing, failing to realize that some other factor present in the same test (e.g., the pendulum's length) might instead be the key. As a result of all this, the problem was vastly more difficult for the children younger than eleven than it was for their older comrades (Inhelder and Piaget, 1958).

Once children have entered the period of formal operations, therefore, their ability to reason and solve problems takes a large step forward. Their thought can now embrace the possible as well as the real; they can now entertain hypothetical possibilities and can deal with what might be no less than what is.

WHAT IS THE COGNITIVE STARTING POINT?

The account offered by Piaget—children's initial achievement of sensorimotor intelligence and then their progress through preoperational thought, concrete operations, and, finally, formal operations—has been enormously influential. Piaget's theories have shaped the ways in which psychologists, educators, and even parents conceptualize children's intellectual growth. The phenomena discovered by Piaget are quite striking and reliable, and provide key insights into children's intellectual capacities and, sometimes, their intellectual limitations.

At the same time, though, Piaget's claims have not gone unchallenged. We now turn, therefore, to some of the responses to Piaget's claims.

SPACE AND OBJECTS IN INFANCY

One critical challenge to Piaget's work concerns his views of very young infants. To be more precise, many investigators have argued that Piaget—who in this regard was much like the early British empiricists—seriously underestimated the intellectual capacities of infants. Their minds, they claim, are not a mere jumble of sensory impressions and motor reactions. Instead, infants begin life with primitive concepts of space, objects, number, and even the existence of other minds. These are, of course, the same concepts that adults use to organize their world, and so the suggestion is that the infants' world may be less different from the adults' than Piaget claimed.

THE VISUAL CLIFF

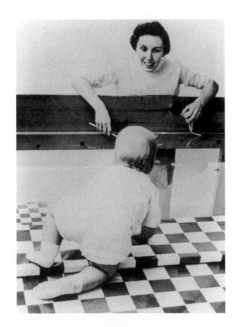

The visual cliff *Eleanor Gibson is testing an infant on the visual cliff apparatus she developed with Richard Walk. On one side of a centerboard, tiling rests right under a sheet of glass; on the other side, the tiling is several feet below. Despite tactile cues suggesting the firmness of the glass, an infant placed in the centerboard will not venture across the side with the drop-off, even when summoned by her mother.*

One demonstration of the infants' perceptual capacities is a classic study by Richard Walk and Eleanor Gibson. They noted that crawling infants are surprisingly successful in avoiding the precipices of everyday life (Walk and Gibson, 1961). To investigate this skill, Walk and Gibson used an apparatus known as the *visual cliff*—a large glass table, about three feet above the floor, divided in half by a wooden center board. On one side of the board, a checkerboard pattern is attached directly to the underside of the glass; on the other side, the same pattern is placed on the floor. This appears to adults as a sudden drop-off in the middle of the table; the clear glass provides a "safety net" but does not alter the visual depth cues. But will six-month-old infants respond to these cues? The babies were placed on the center board, and their mothers called and beckoned to them. When the mother beckoned from the shallow side, the baby usually crawled quickly to her. But only a very few infants ventured forth when called from across the apparent precipice.

It seems, then, that infants as young as six months old can utilize perceptual cues in order to perceive depth, and they use this information to guide their locomotion.

THE EFFECT OF OCCLUSION

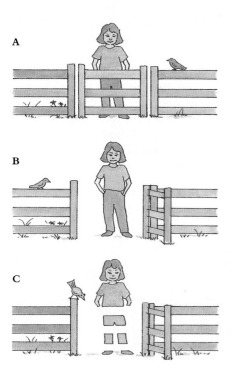

A

B

C

What about even younger infants? Consider Figure 13.15A, which shows an object partially *occluding* (hiding from view) another object behind it. When adults encounter this sight, they will surely perceive it as a child behind a gate. They are completely certain that when the gate is opened, they will see a whole child (Figure 13.15B) and would be utterly astounded if the opened gate revealed a child with gaps in her body (Figure 13.15C).

This ability to perceive partially occluded objects as they really are is continually called upon in our everyday life. Most of the things we see are partially concealed by other objects in front of them, but we perceive a world of complete objects rather than one of disjointed fragments (see Chapter 6).

13.15 *The perceptual effect of occlusion* *(A) A child occluded by a gate is perceived as a whole person behind a gate, so that she will look like (B) when the gate is opened, rather than being perceived as (C), a child with gaps in her body.*

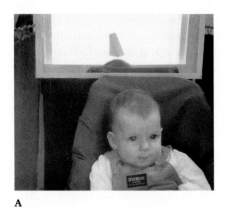

A

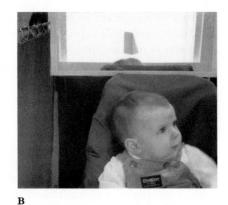

B

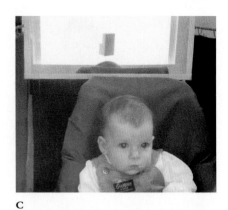

C

13.16   The habituation procedure
(A) A four-month-old's face, looking at a small slowly rotating pyramid in front of her (the pyramid can be seen in the mirror that is behind the infant and above her head). (B) Habituation: The infant becomes increasingly bored and looks away. (C) Dishabituation: The infant sees a new object (the rotating cube shown in the mirror) and looks again. This dishabituation effect provides evidence that the infant perceives a difference between the first and the second stimulus (that is, the pyramid and the cube). (Photographs courtesy of Phillip Kellman)

Do infants perceive partially hidden objects in the same way? If so, this would be evidence that their perceptual experience is organized to some extent and not as fragmented as Piaget had proposed. More, this would indicate that infants understand that the physical world contains unitary objects whose parts stay connected regardless of whether the object is entirely visible or not. It would also imply that infants are equipped with some (primitive) understanding of what an object is, again contrary to Piaget's claims.

To pursue these questions, many experiments employ a **habituation procedure** (Figure 13.16). In one such study, infants were shown a rod that moved back and forth behind a solid block that occluded the rod's central portion (Figure 13.17A). This display was kept in view, with the rod continuing to move back and forth, until the infants became bored with it (that is, *habituated*) and ceased looking at the display. The investigators then presented the infants with either of two test displays. One was an unbroken rod that moved back and forth (Figure 13.17B). The other consisted of two aligned rod pieces that moved back and forth in unison (Figure 13.17C).

If these infants had perceived the original stimulus as a complete, unitary rod, then Figure 13.17B would show them nothing new, whereas Figure 13.17C would show them something novel. This pattern would be reversed if the infants had perceived only the pieces of the original stimulus. In this case, Figure 13.17C would show them nothing new and Figure 13.17B would be the novel display.

Since these infants had already become habituated to (bored with) the original stimulus, a novel stimulus should attract their attention and hold it longer. Thus, we can measure how long the infants looked at the display to find out which the infants consider novel; and once we know what the infants consider novel, then we will know how they perceived the original display.

The evidence in this study is clear: The four-month-old infants spent more

13.17   The perceptual effect of occlusion in early infancy   *Four-month-olds were shown a rod that moved back and forth behind an occluding block as shown in (A). After they became habituated to this display and stopped looking at it, they were shown two new displays, neither of which was occluded. In (B) the rod that moved back and forth was unbroken. In (C) it was made of two aligned rod pieces that moved back and forth together. The infants spent much more time looking at (C) than at (B). (After Kellman and Spelke, 1983)*

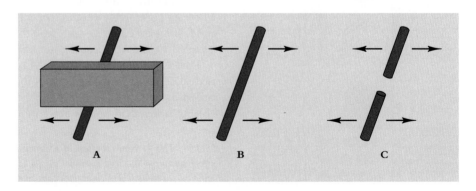

A   **B**   **C**

time looking at the broken rod than at the complete rod. Apparently, they found the broken rod more novel, which tells us that they had perceived the original stimulus as *not* broken. Instead, they had perceived the parts of the rod in the original stimulus as being connected to each other (just as adults would). This suggests that some notion of a real physical object exists even at four months of age (Kellman and Spelke, 1983; Kellman, Spelke, and Short, 1986).

KNOWING ABOUT OBJECTS

How much do infants understand about the objects in the world around them? Do they have any knowledge about the physical properties shared by all solid objects? Do they understand, for example, that two objects can't occupy the same space at the same time?

To answer this question, four-and-a-half-month-olds were shown a miniature stage in the middle of which was a medium-sized box. In front of the box was a screen that was hinged on a rod attached to the stage floor. Initially, that screen was laid flat so that the box behind it was clearly visible, but the screen was then rotated upward like a drawbridge, hiding the box from view (Figure 13.18A). There were two conditions. In one condition, the screen rotated backward until it reached the box, stopped, and then rotated forward again, returning to its initial position (Figure 13.18B). In the other condition, the screen rotated backward until it reached the occluded box and then kept on going as though the box were no longer there. Once it finished the full 180 degree arc, it reversed direction and swiveled all the way forward, at which point the box was revealed again (the box being surreptitiously removed and replaced as required; see Figure 13.18C; Baillargeon, Spelke, and Wasserman, 1985; Baillargeon, 1987).

To adults, the first of these conditions makes perfect physical sense: Since two objects can't occupy the same space at the same time, the screen necessarily stops when it encounters the box. But the second event is radically different: The box seems to be blocking the screen's path, as the screen rotates backward. Therefore, the screen should not be able to rotate all the way back. When the screen does rotate all the way, it appears to have passed through the box—a physical impossibility.

Do infants react to these events in the same way? The answer seems to be yes. The four-month-olds evidently found the second condition more surprising (and, presumably, more puzzling) than the first condition, just as adults would. This was revealed by the fact that they spent much more time looking at the stage in the second condition than they did in the first. This strongly indicates that these young infants had some notion of object permanence, for they evidently continued to believe in the box's existence (and its ability to block the motion of other objects) even when it was entirely hidden from view. In addition, this finding suggests that young infants do have some notion of the principles that govern objects in space; they evidently know that two objects (here, the screen and the box) can't occupy the same space at the same time.

OBJECT PERMANENCE AND THE SEARCH PROCESS

All in all, there is reason to believe that, Piaget and the empiricists to the contrary, infants come remarkably well-equipped to see the world as it really is. But if so, how can we explain the findings that led Piaget to argue for the lack of object permanence in infancy, such as infants' persistent failure in retrieving objects that are out of sight? Most modern investigators feel that there is no real inconsistency here. They hold that infants do believe that objects continue to

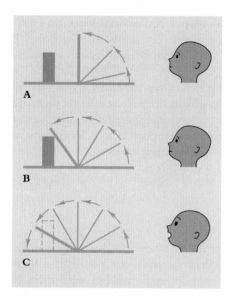

13.18 Knowing about objects *A four-and-a-half-month-old infant is looking at a stage on which he sees an upright box. In front of the box is a screen that initially lies flat and then starts to rotate upward (A). In the first condition (B), the screen stops rotating as soon as it hits the box. In the second condition (C), when the screen is at a point high enough to hide the box, the box is surreptitiously removed and the screen continues to rotate backward. The infant seems to find this quite surprising as shown by the fact that he continues to look at the stage much longer than he did in the first condition. (After Baillargeon, 1987)*

exist, even when hidden from view, but, at the same time, that infants are exceedingly inept in *searching for* these objects.

For example, consider the *A-not-B* effect. As we have discussed, this refers to the infant's tendency to search at a place where he previously found a toy rather than at a place where he has just seen a toy hidden. What accounts for this effect? If the infant has just reached toward *A* several times, then the reaching-toward-*A* response is well primed. To reach toward *B*, therefore, the infant must override this newly acquired habit, and that is the problem. The infant does know where the toy is, but he is unable to inhibit the momentarily potent reach-toward-*A* response. In line with this hypothesis is the fact that many infants *look at B* at the same time that they reach for *A*, as if they knew where the object was but couldn't tell their arms what they had learned with their eyes (see Figure 13.19; Baillargeon and Graber, 1987).

Some investigators believe that the ability to override a dominant action depends on the maturation of a certain region in the prefrontal cortex, a region just in front of the motor projection area. Evidence comes from work on monkeys with lesions in this area; they show a pattern very similar to the *A-not-B* error shown by human infants (Diamond, 1988, 1989; Diamond and Goldman-Rakic, 1989).

Thus, there is good reason to believe that Piaget was mistaken about infants' understanding of object permanence. Young infants do understand that there are objects out in the world and that these objects (and their parts) continue to exist even when out of view. What infants do not have is much of an idea of how to deal with those objects—for example, how to find them when they are hidden.

NUMBER IN INFANCY

Infants also have unexpected competence in other domains. For example, Piaget argued that children younger than six years old have little understanding of number. After all, children do not conserve number until then. In failing to conserve, children might say that a row of four buttons, all spread out, has more buttons in it than a row of four bunched closely together. This certainly sounds like they have failed to grasp the concept of numbers.

But more recent experiments have shown that children much younger than six do have some numerical ability. In one study, infants only six months old were shown a series of slides that displayed different sets of objects. The specific items shown varied from one slide to the next, but each slide contained exactly three objects. One slide, for example, might show a comb, a fork, and a sponge; another might show a bottle, a brush, and a toy drum; and so on. Each slide also differed in the spatial arrangement of the items. They might be set up with two on top and one below, or in a vertical column, or with one above and two below, and so on.

With all these variables, would the infants be able to detect the one property shared by all the slides—the fact that all contained three items? To find out, the

A

B

C

13.19   A dissociation between what the infant knows and what the infant does
(A) A seven-month-old looks at a toy that has just been placed in B, one of the two wells. (B) He continues to look at well B after both wells are covered. (C) When finally allowed to reach for the toy, he uncovers well A in which he found the toy on a previous trial rather than well B in which he saw the toy being placed. In this particular sequence, he actually still looks at B while uncovering A, suggesting a dissociation between what the infant knows and what he does. (Courtesy Adele Diamond)

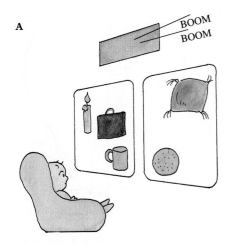

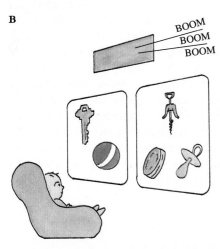

13.20 *Some rudiments of number in six-month-olds* *Six-month-olds were shown two panels that contained either two or three simple objects. Concurrently, a drum was sounded over a loudspeaker, producing rhythmic booms either in twos ("boom, boom") or in threes ("boom, boom, boom"). (A) When the drum was sounded "boom, boom," the baby looked at the panel that contained two items. (B) When the drum was sounded "boom, boom, boom," the baby looked at the panel that contained three items. This result suggests that the baby has some rudimentary concept of twoness and threeness, a concept that holds whether the items "counted" are visual objects or sounds. (Starkey, Spelke, and Gelman, 1983)*

experimenters used the habituation technique: They presented these sets of threes until the infants became bored and stopped looking. Then they presented a series of new slides in which some of the slides showed two items, while others continued to show three. The results were clear: The infants spent more time looking at the slides that displayed two items rather than three. Evidently, the infants were able to step back from all the particulars of the various slides and detect the one abstract property that all the slides had in common. In this regard, at least, the infants had grasped the concept of "threeness" (Starkey, Spelke, and Gelman, 1983, 1990; for related evidence, see Figure 13.20).

Further studies indicate that these young infants even grasp the rudiments of certain arithmetical relations. For example, infants evidently can perceive numerical equivalence (at least with sets of up to four or five; e.g., Treiber and Wilcox, 1984). They also have the rudiments of addition: In one study five-month-olds were shown a toy mouse on a small stage. After the infants had looked at this scene for a while, a screen came up from the floor and hid the mouse from view. The infants then saw the experimenter's hand appear from the side, holding another mouse and placing it behind the screen. The final step was the test: The screen was lowered to reveal either one mouse or two. If the infants had some primitive understanding of the meaning of addition, they should have expected to see two mice and be surprised to see only one. In fact, this surprise is just what happened. The infants continued to look at the single mouse as if wondering why the other one wasn't there. Analogous results were found in a pint-sized subtraction task in which the experimenter presented two mice at first and then took one away. Here, the infants looked longer when they saw two mice as if surprised that none had been removed (Wynn, 1992).

SOCIAL COGNITION IN INFANCY: THE EXISTENCE OF OTHER MINDS

The social world provides yet another domain in which infants are surprisingly competent. It is certainly true that much of what we know about other individuals is acquired through learning. But there is reason to believe that this learning builds upon a substantial substructure that is innately given.

To begin with, infants come into the world with a built-in predisposition to look at human faces. One group of investigators studied babies immediately (that is, nine minutes) after they were born. The experimenter held each baby in his lap and moved several patterns in front of their eyes. The infants turned their heads and looked longer at the pattern if it was of a schematic rather than a scrambled face. Further studies suggest that this very early face recognition process is based on a subcortical mechanism that drops out within a month or two and is then replaced by more sophisticated recognition machinery that comes into its own as the visual cortex matures (Goren, Sarty, and Wu, 1975; Johnson, 1993; see Figure 13.21).

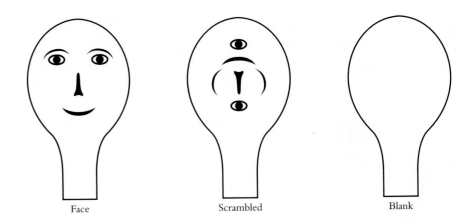

Face Scrambled Blank

13.21 Rudimentary face recognition in newborns *Newborn babies look longer at a pattern showing a schematic face than at a scrambled or a blank pattern. (From Johnson and Morton, 1991)*

In addition, infants seem to recognize rather early that others live in the same physical world that they do, and so can see more or less what they see, hear what they hear, and so on. Evidence comes from work on shared attention. Thus, nine-month-olds will tend to look in the direction of their mothers' gaze (Scaife and Bruner, 1975). And soon this capacity expands: In one study, infants between twelve and eighteen months old were held in their mothers' laps while the mothers looked at a particular toy in a particular position. But while the mothers looked toward the toy, the children were held with their heads facing their mothers, so that they could not see the target of the mothers' gaze. All they could see were their mothers' eyes. Evidently, that was enough—as soon as the mothers' hold was released the infants squirmed around and looked at just the toy the mothers had looked at a moment before (Butterworth and Cochran, 1980; Butterworth and Jarrett, 1991).

COGNITIVE DEVELOPMENT IN PRESCHOOLERS

It seems clear, then, that infants know more, and have more capacities, than Piaget realized. But what about the process of development from then on? Central to Piaget's conception is the idea that cognitive development goes through several qualitatively distinct stages. Is this view correct? No one doubts that there is mental growth and that children change in the way they think as they get older. But is this growth best described as a progression through successive stages?

THE MEANING OF MENTAL STAGE

What does it mean to say that development proceeds through stages? Piaget used the term *stage* in the same way that the term is used in embryology. Embryological stages tend to be discrete rather than continuous. The difference between a tadpole and a frog, for example, is not just a matter of "more this" or "less that." Instead, there is a qualitative difference between the two, with different breathing mechanisms, different food needs, and so on. To be sure, the change from one to the other takes a while, but by the time the creature is a frog, its tadpole days are emphatically over.

Piaget's claim was that the same discreteness characterizes cognitive development. According to this view, the cognitive capacities that mark one period of development are totally absent at prior periods. But is this correct? Consider conservation of quantity or number. According to the stage hypothesis, the capacity to conserve should be totally absent at an early age—say, five years old and younger—and then emerge virtually full blown when the curtain finally opens on the next act of the developmental drama—namely, the period of concrete operations.

Many modern investigators disagree with this claim, for they deny that cognitive development is essentially all-or-none. As they see it, cognitive achievements such as conservation have primitive precursors that appear several years earlier than the Piagetian calendar would predict. If we identify these precursors, and then chart the course of their development, we will see that children's growth is more gradual than Piaget envisioned. As a result, the contrast between six-year-olds and four-year-olds, or between ten-year-olds and five-year-olds, may be less dramatic than Piaget believed (Gelman, 1978; Gelman and Baillargeon, 1983).

As illustrations, we will consider two areas of cognitive growth during the preschool period—number and social cognition—from the perspective of some of these modern investigators.

NUMERICAL SKILLS IN PRESCHOOLERS

We've seen that infants can abstract the properties of twoness and threeness. This provides the initial basis for the development of numerical abilities (Gelman and Gallistel, 1978; Gelman, 1982). But what happens in the years following infancy?

COUNTING

Consider counting. Some precursors of this skill appear as early as two-and-a-half. At this age, children may not know the conventional sequence of number terms, but they have grasped the idea of what the counting process is all about. Thus, one two-year-old consistently counted "one, two, six," and another used "one, thirteen, nineteen." But what is important is that they used these series consistently and realized that each of these number tags has to be applied to just one object in the to-be-counted set. They also realized that the tags must always be used in the same order and that the last number applied is the number of items in the set. Thus, the child who counted "one, thirteen, nineteen," confidently asserted that there were thirteen items when he counted a two-item set, and nineteen items when he counted a three-item set. This child is obviously not using the adult's terms but surely does seem to have mastered some of the key ideas on which counting rests (Gelman and Gallistel, 1978).

NUMERICAL REASONING

A child who can count (even if rather idiosyncratically) has taken a big step. But there is more to numerical understanding than counting. The child must also grasp some principles of numerical reasoning. She must understand that adding an item increases the total number of items in the set that is being counted, that subtracting one decreases it, and that adding one and then subtracting one leaves everything unchanged. The comprehension of these basic numerical truths will not suffice to make the child a mathematician, but they are basic to all further advances in the numerical domain.

Preschoolers gradually acquire these conceptual basics. When comparing two sets of items, three- and four-year-olds can correctly point to the one that is smaller or larger if the number of items are small enough (Gelman and Gallistel, 1978; Gelman, 1982).

But if preschool children have these skills, then why do they fail the Piagetian tests for conservation of number? We have already described the standard Piagetian finding: When preschoolers are asked to compare two rows that each contain, say, four toy ducks, they often say that the longer row contains more ducks, in an apparent confusion of length and number. How can we reconcile this with the demonstrations of the preschooler's numerical competence?

Some studies suggest that the problem lies in how the children were questioned in Piaget's studies. In these procedures, the child is typically questioned twice. First, the two rows of items are presented in an evenly spaced manner, so that both rows are the same length. When asked, "Which row has more or do they both have the same?" the child quickly answers "The same!" Now the experimenter changes the length of one of the rows—perhaps spreading the items out a bit more or pushing them more closely together—and asks again: "Which row has more or do they both have the same?"

Why is the same question being asked again? From the point of view of the child, this may imply that the experimenter didn't like his first answer and so, as adults often do, is providing him the opportunity to try again. This would obviously suggest to the child that his first answer must have been wrong, and so he changes it.

Of course, this misinterpretation is possible only because the child is not totally sure of his answer. Hence, he is easily swayed by this subtle hint from the experimenter. However, if the number of items in the row is small enough, the child won't be confused and so will resist the hint. And with small numbers of items, children do show evidence of conserving at appreciably younger ages (Siegal, 1991).

Thus, here as in other cognitive realms, the achievements of later periods are built upon foundations established much earlier. If we look carefully enough, we see that the accomplishments of the concrete-operational period do not come out of the blue but have preludes in much earlier childhood years. It may well be true that there are milestones of intellectual growth that, as Piaget had argued, must be passed in an orderly sequence. But there is more continuity in development than Piaget asserted, with no neat demarcations between stages and no sharp transitions. The stages of cognitive development are not as all-or-none as the changes from tadpole to frog (let alone from frog to prince).

SOCIAL COGNITION IN PRESCHOOLERS: DEVELOPING A THEORY OF MIND

Similar conclusions emerge when we consider other aspects of development, including the development of a young child's understanding of the social world. Here, too, Piaget emphasized the limitations of preschoolers, arguing that such children are still dominated by egocentrism and thus unable to appreciate the difference between another's point of view and their own. More recent evidence, however, makes it clear that even very young children have some understanding of the social world, so that, once again, we find more continuity in development than Piaget envisioned.

Much of the recent discussion has focused on what some theorists call the

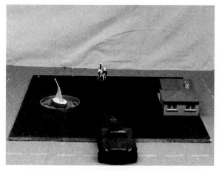

A

B

C

13.22 A simplified test of egocentrism
Poor performance on Piaget's test of egocentrism may have resulted from the fact that the spatial layout of his three-mountain task is unduly complicated. In a later study, three- and four-year-olds were shown various three-dimensional displays such as (A) and (B), as well as a three-mountain scene (C). Grover, a doll, was shown to drive a toy car around each layout. When he stopped the car, the child was asked to turn an identical display on another table until "you are looking at it the same way Grover is." The children did quite well with all displays except (C), the three-mountain scene. This one probably caused trouble because the children couldn't distinguish the mountains as readily as they could distinguish the toy objects in (A) and (B). (Borke, 1975; photograph courtesy of H. Borke)

child's **theory of mind.** In general, this term refers to the set of interrelated concepts and beliefs that we employ whenever we try to make sense of our own behavior or that of other individuals (Premack and Woodruff, 1978; Wellman, 1990; Leslie, 1992; Fodor, 1992).★

An adult's theory of mind has many elements: Each of us knows that other people have beliefs, that their beliefs may be true or false, and that their beliefs may differ from our own, which may also be true or false. We know that other people have desires and that these desires may also differ from our own. We also know that other people sometimes know things that we do not and that we sometimes know things that they do not.

We usually don't give much thought to our theory of mind, but, nonetheless, it is an essential resource for us all, providing a crucial knowledge base that we rely on in all of our day-to-day social functioning. Our theory of mind helps us to understand the behavior of other people and allows us (within certain limits) to predict how people will behave in the future. Without a theory of mind, we would be bewildered by much of the social action going on around us and incapable of acting appropriately in most social situations.

EGOCENTRISM REVISITED

The theory of mind that each of us holds is not explicitly stated, but it functions just like a scientist's theory does—allowing us to make sense of certain types of evidence and to predict new observations in the appropriate domain. But what about children? Do they have a theory of mind? Do they have any understanding of the actions (or thoughts) of other individuals?

If tested in the right way, even very young children reveal some of this understanding. To take a simple example, children in one study were asked to show a photograph to their mother, who was seated opposite them. The two-and-a-half and three-year-olds all turned the picture so that it faced the mother, which implies that they had some conception of the difference between one person's angle of regard and another's. If they were totally egocentric, they would have shown their mothers the back of the picture, while continuing to look at it from the front (Lempers, Flavell, and Flavell, 1977; see also Figure 13.22).

Similarly, two- and three-year-olds can hide things (to be sure, quite ineptly), and they try to help someone see a small picture by bringing it closer to his eyes

★ As Premack and Woodruff, who coined the phrase, use the term, "an individual has a theory of mind if he imputes mental states to himself and others" (Premack and Woodruff, 1978). They make a good case that chimpanzees have such a theory of mind (though, to be sure, a rather primitive one), and there is some suggestion that monkeys also have some limited capacity to attribute beliefs and desires to other monkeys (Premack and Woodruff, 1978; Cheney and Seyfarth, 1990; see Chapter 10).

(Lempers, Flavell, and Flavell, 1977; Flavell, Shipstead, and Croft, 1978). These observations provide further evidence that children are not hopelessly egocentric; instead, they have some understanding of the perception and vantage point of other individuals.

These same children also know something about the motivations and desires of other people—again contrary to the claim of egocentrism. If two-year-old Mario is told that Lisa wants a cookie, then he will correctly predict that Lisa will look for a cookie and that she will be happy if she finds one. These are hardly earth-shaking insights into Lisa's actions, but they do indicate that the toddler is beginning to understand why other people do the things they do and feel the things they feel.

TRUE AND FALSE BELIEFS

The child's task becomes a bit more difficult when it comes to beliefs. Suppose you tell three-year-old Alicia that Johnny wants to play with his puppy. You also tell her that Johnny thinks the puppy is under the piano. If Alicia is now asked where Johnny will look, she'll sensibly say that he'll look under the piano (Wellman and Bartsch, 1988). It appears, therefore, that a three-year-old (just like an adult) understands that a person's actions depend not just on what she sees and desires, but also on what she believes.

But does the three-year-old truly understand the concept of belief? Does he understand, for example, that beliefs can be true or false or that different people can have different beliefs? According to several authors, the three-year-old does not understand these things and won't until he is about four or four-and-a-half. On this view, then, there is something seriously lacking in the three-year-old's theory of mind.

Evidence for this comes from studies using false-belief tests (Dennett, 1978; Wimmer and Perner, 1983). In a typical study of this kind, a child and a teddy bear sit in front of two boxes, one red and the other green. The experimenter opens the red box and puts some candy in it. She then opens the green box and shows the child—and the teddy—that this box is empty. The teddy bear is now taken out of the room (to play for a while) and the experimenter and the child move the candy from the red box into the green one. Next comes the crucial step: The teddy bear is brought back into the room, and the child is asked: "Where will the teddy look for the candy?" Virtually all three-year-olds and some four-year-olds will answer "In the green box." If you ask them why, they will answer, "Because that's where it is."

It would appear, then, that these children do not really understand the nature of belief. They seem to assume that their beliefs are inevitably shared by others, and likewise, they seem not to appreciate that others might have beliefs that are false. However, by age four-and-a-half or so, children get the idea. Now if they're asked, "Where will the teddy look for the candy?" they'll answer: "He'll look in the red box because that's where he thinks the candy is" (Wimmer and Perner, 1983; Wellman, 1990; see Figure 13.23).

OTHER DOMAINS OF COMPETENCE

Apparently, young children do know something about the beliefs and desires of other individuals. But is it sensible to speak of a three- or four-year-old as having

A

B

C

13.23 The false-belief test (A) The child watches as the experimenter makes the puppet "hide" the ball in the oatmeal container. (B) While the puppet is gone, the experimenter and the child move the ball to the box. (C) When the child is now asked, "Where does the puppet think the ball is?" she points to the box. (Photographs by Kimberly Canidy)

a *theory of mind*? Many authors believe it is: A scientist uses a theory to account for evidence and to predict new findings. The child's theory does the same. In a scientist's theory, the various specific claims are all interrelated, and this, too, is a trait of the child's theory of mind: The child cannot understand how belief influences action unless she also understands what belief is; she cannot truly understand what a belief is without realizing that false beliefs are possible; and so on. Finally, the scientist's theory has a specific domain of application: Einstein's theory of relativity tells us a great deal about space and time but tells us nothing about how to make a really good pizza. Likewise for the child's theory: A theory of mind helps the child understand the behavior of others but is of little use in helping her solve an arithmetic problem or find her way through the mall.

These parallels seem to justify using the term "theory" when describing the child's theory of mind. But, in addition, the notion of a theory's limited domain invites a question: Do young children have other theories that help them make sense of other aspects of their experience? The evidence suggests that they do. For example, children seem to have a set of interrelated beliefs about biological functioning that provide the basis for their thinking about sickness and health, birth and death (Wellman and Gelman, 1992). These same beliefs also guide children's thinking about more mundane topics, such as parental instructions concerning good nutrition ("Eat your spinach").

SEQUENCE OR STAGES?

What can we conclude about Piaget's stages of mental development? The evidence as a whole suggests that the mental growth of children does not proceed as neatly as a simple stage theory might lead one to expect (Flavell, 1985). Does this mean that Piaget's cognitive milestones have no psychological reality? Certainly not. Consider the difference between a preschool child and a seven-year-old. The younger child can tell the difference between two and three mice regardless of how they are spaced on the table and in this fashion seems to be conserving number. But he hasn't yet grasped the underlying idea—that number and spatial arrangement are entirely independent of each other and that this is so for *all* numbers and for *all* spatial arrangements. As a result, the preschooler will fail a slightly more difficult test for conservation of number, in which he must recognize that two rows of, say, nine buttons each contain the same number of buttons, regardless of how the rows are expanded or compressed.

The seven-year-old, in contrast, has no such problem. She can count higher, but that's not the issue. She knows that there is no need to count, because she is confidently aware of the fact that a change in the buttons' arrangement will not change their number. As a result, she can conserve number in general.

What holds for conservation of number, holds for many other intellectual achievements. Most of them have precursors, often at much earlier ages than Piaget supposed. But these precursors usually represent isolated pockets of knowledge that can't be applied very widely. The seven- or eight-year-old's understanding of physical, numerical, and social reality is thus considerably more general than the younger child's, so much so that it seems qualitatively different from what went on before. By simplifying the task in various ways, experimenters can induce preschoolers to perform creditably. But by the time the child is seven or eight years old, no such simplification is necessary. A seven- or eight-year-old conserves with barely a glance at the containers in which the liquid is sloshed around. He knows that the liquid quantity is unaffected no matter how the containers are shaped.

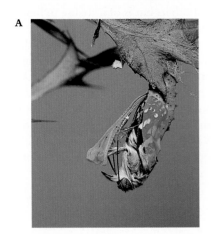

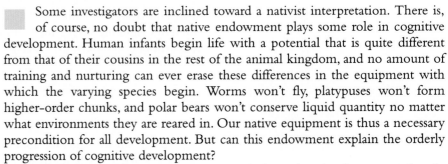

THE CAUSES OF COGNITIVE GROWTH

We've described cognitive development as it proceeds from early infancy into the school years. But what explains these changes? As so often in the field of cognition, the attempts to come up with an adequate explanation have fluctuated between the two poles of the nature-nurture controversy.

THE NATIVIST APPROACH: MATURATION

Some investigators are inclined toward a nativist interpretation. There is, of course, no doubt that native endowment plays some role in cognitive development. Human infants begin life with a potential that is quite different from that of their cousins in the rest of the animal kingdom, and no amount of training and nurturing can ever erase these differences in the equipment with which the varying species begin. Worms won't fly, platypuses won't form higher-order chunks, and polar bears won't conserve liquid quantity no matter what environments they are reared in. Our native equipment is thus a necessary precondition for all development. But can this endowment explain the orderly progression of cognitive development?

Some theorists believe that it can. They believe that development is largely driven by some form of physical maturation, a pre-programmed process of growth based on changes in underlying neural structures that are relatively independent of environmental conditions.

Could cognitive development be a matter of maturation (in part or in whole) in the sense in which walking is (Figure 13.24)? As we've seen, there is a tenfold increase in the number of synaptic connections in the cortex between birth and twelve months of age, with further changes in brain size that last well into the school years (see pp. 535–36). If the brain gets more complex, wouldn't cognition follow suit (Siegler, 1989)?

This view is buttressed by the fact that, at least in broad outline, mental growth seems rather similar in children of different cultures and nationalities. Thus, Arab, Indian, Somali, and British children pass the various developmental milestones at somewhat different ages, but they all pass these landmarks in the same order and make the same errors at comparable ages (Hyde, 1959). This is reminiscent of physical maturation. Different butterflies may emerge from their chrysalis at slightly different times, but none is a butterfly first and a chrysalis second. The timing of the transitions may well be affected by environmental conditions: in humans, by culture; in butterflies, by temperature. But according to the maturational hypothesis, the order of the stages is predetermined by the genetic code.

13.24 Development as maturation? *(A) Emerging from its chrysalis for a butterfly and (B) walking for a child are largely matters of maturation. (C) Is the cognitive growth that underlies a seven-and-a-half-year-old's success in a Piagetian conservation task to be understood in similar terms? (A: photograph © Frederic B. Siskind; B: photograph by Ray Ellis/Photo Researchers; C: photograph by Chris Massey)*

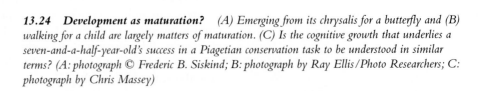

COGNITIVE DEVELOPMENT AS LEARNING

The simplest alternative to a maturational approach is one that emphasizes learning. But how should we think about this learning? One option was suggested early on by the British empiricist John Locke (see Chapter 5). He argued that each human mind begins as a blank tablet, a *tabula rasa*, upon which experience gradually leaves its mark. The modern heirs to this position are the students of Pavlov and of Skinner, who argue that children's progress can be understood in terms of the conditioning processes we discussed in Chapter 4.

Piaget argued, however, that simple learning theories of this kind will not do. As one concern, these theories imply that children's development is driven largely by external events—by the specific experiences and learning opportunities afforded each child. And, of course, these experiences and opportunities will differ somewhat from one child to the next, especially if the children are growing up in different cultures or different environments. But as we've just noted, the pattern of mental growth is quite similar for all children, at least in broad outline, no matter where they grow up.

Piaget also offered another objection to these simple learning theories: According to such theories, learning is the acquisition of relatively specific skills that could in principle be mastered at any age. But this is precisely what Piaget denied. According to Piaget, four-year-olds cannot possibly be taught how to use a measuring cup correctly, no matter how attractive the reinforcements or how many the number of trials. He argued that four-year-olds lack the prerequisite concepts of number and quantity (which they cannot attain before the concrete-operational level), so that any attempt to teach them would be as fruitless as trying to build the third story of a house without a second story underneath it. Children will learn each skill, in other words, only when they are intellectually ready to learn the skill. Thus, on Piaget's view, learning is not something impressed on children from the outside; instead, it is something achieved by children, and so very much dependent on what they have mastered up to that point.

Who is right? Can intellectual skills be mastered at any age, as an empiricist would argue? Or are skills gained only when children are ready, as Piaget would have it? In an attempt to find out, many investigators have tried to teach intellectual skills to relatively young children, asking whether the children can master these skills ahead of the Piagetian schedule. The results are generally more favorable to Piaget's position than to that of the empiricists. For example, the early investigators concluded that specific training has little impact. In some cases, young children were trained to conserve, but later checks revealed that the children had not really understood the underlying principles of conservation and quickly reverted to their previous, nonconserving ways (e.g., Smedslund, 1961). This is certainly consistent with Piaget's claim: children learn when they are ready to learn.

Some later studies have shown more substantial gains from training (e.g., Botvin and Murray, 1975; Murrary, 1978). However, there is reason to believe that the children who benefited from training already had most of the necessary conceptual ingredients in place, prior to the experimental procedure. If so, then the training really didn't teach them anything new; it only helped to uncover what was already there (Gold, 1978; Gelman and Baillargeon, 1983).

Related findings come from a study conducted in a Mexican village whose inhabitants made pottery and whose children participated in this activity from early on. When tested for conservation of mass, these children turned out to be more advanced than their North American counterparts (or those studied by

Piaget in Switzerland). Having spent much of their lives working at a potter's wheel, they were more likely to know that the amount of clay is the same whether it is rolled into a ball or stretched into a long, thin sausage (Price-Williams, Gordon, and Ramirez, 1969). But these effects of pottery making were relatively specific. They led to an advance on tests of conservation of mass but to little else. (For further discussion, see Greenfield, 1976; Price-Williams, 1981; Rogoff, Gauvain, and Ellis, 1984.)

All in all, the developmental pattern described by Piaget seems quite robust. Children's progress can be accelerated slightly through appropriate training or exposure, but only slightly. Children can acquire precursors for skills at an earlier age, but these are only precursors and usually applicable only to a limited range of circumstances. Thus, it does appear that children must be ready for each step forward before learning is truly possible.

PIAGET'S APPROACH: ASSIMILATION AND ACCOMMODATION

If we cannot understand children's development in terms of simple learning mechanisms, then how should we think about development? As we have discussed, Piaget's view was that children's mental progress is propelled by the twin engines of assimilation and accommodation. At any one stage, the environment children face is interpreted in terms of the mental schemas they have at that time—the environment is assimilated to the schemas. But these schemas cannot help but change as children continue to interact with the world around them—the schemas accommodate to the environment. In these terms, children are intellectually ready for some new learning only if they have the relevant schemas; otherwise, new experiences cannot be assimilated. And children must be actively involved in the learning; otherwise there will be no accommodation and, hence, no mental growth.

This conception emphasizes the fact that organism and environment interact in producing mental growth: We cannot understand development unless we understand both the nature of children's experience and the resources they bring to it. At the same time, however, this conception plainly leaves a great deal unsaid. In particular, Piaget offered no mechanism whereby schemas are changed through accommodation. If schemas adjust in light of experience, what is the nature of the adjustment? What mechanisms cause this adjustment to occur? Thus, Piaget's proposal still leaves us with the unanswered question of why children go from one stage of thought to another. This has led many investigators to seek an alternative conception of children's intellectual growth.

THE INFORMATION-PROCESSING APPROACH

In Chapters 7 and 8, we discussed adult thinking and reasoning in terms of certain cognitive resources: the adult's ability to pay attention, her capacity for remembering (both in the long term and in the short), and so on. In general, we used the *information-processing approach* to conceptualize adult intellectual functioning. Perhaps it would be useful to conceptualize the child's intellectual functioning in the same way.

As we discussed in earlier chapters, a person has to acquire, retrieve, or transform information whenever he perceives, remembers, or thinks. If adults think differently (and with greater success) than children, this is presumably because they process information differently. Let us examine this approach, beginning with the development of memory.

THE CHILD AS A LIMITED MENTAL PROCESSOR

Memory in infancy   How well, and for how long, can infants remember? In one series of experiments, a string was loosely tied to the leg of a three-month-old; whenever the infant kicked, this tugged on the string, and set off the movement of an overhead mobile. The infant quickly learned this contingency and happily kicked at every opportunity. Two weeks later, the infant returned to the laboratory, and the mere sight of the mobile was enough to make him kick his feet. Even after two months, the infant still remembered this earlier experience, especially if the experimenter provided a small reminder, by jiggling the mobile just a bit (Rovee-Collier and Hayne, 1987; Rovee-Collier, 1990; Rovee-Collier and Gerhardstein, 1997).

Such findings show that infants can retain experiences over time. The remembering may be of a primitive sort, resembling what we called implicit memory in Chapter 7. But however primitive, it serves as the foundation for the later memorial feats of the adult.

Memory in early childhood   By the time the child gets to be a toddler, her memory prowess is much increased but still limited in comparison to an adult's. For example, the capacity of the child's working memory seems relatively small. Often, this capacity is measured with a memory-span task, which determines how many items the participant can reproduce after just one presentation. This number is roughly one item at eighteen months, three at three-and-a-half years, and four at four-and-a-half years, compared to a span of seven (plus or minus two) in adulthood (see Figure 13.25).

The child's limitations are also evident in describing remembered events. By age four or so, children seem reasonably competent in remembering their experiences, but they generally do a poor job in reporting what they remember. Many children of this age are unable to formulate a clear narrative, and they often fail to grasp what their listeners need to know in order to understand the earlier episode. As a result, one often gains little information by merely asking a four-year-old, "What happened in school today?" or "Tell me about your class trip last month." To learn what the child knows, a questioner needs to ask more specific, focused questions: "Did you see any elephants at the zoo?" or "Did you have a hot dog for lunch?" Note, though, that these more detailed questions make it all too easy for an adult questioner to shape the child's report, inadvertently leading the child to report on, and perhaps "remember," events that never occurred. Thus, considerable care is needed to obtain a full and accurate memory report from a young child (Ceci, Toglia, and Ross, 1987; Ceci and Bruck, 1995; for more on the effects of leading questions, see Chapter 7).

THE CHILD AS NOVICE

The increase in the child's working-memory span is probably a matter of maturation: As children's brains grow, so does their memory capacity. But the inability of children to report what they remember comes largely from the fact that they know relatively little about the world. For children, everything is new, and so they have no way of knowing which aspects of an event are quite common and which unusual, which are interesting and which perfectly ordinary. As a result, they know neither what to focus on as an event unfolds, nor what's worth describing when the time comes to recall.

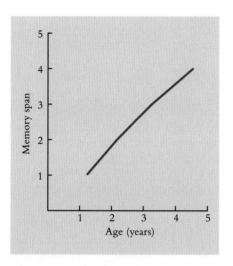

13.25   Memory span in young children (After Case, 1978)

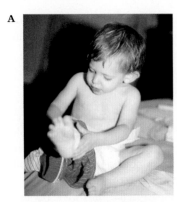

From apprentice to master *(A) At two, getting the right body part through the right hole of a shirt is still a major problem. (B) Only six months later, dressing is well on the way to becoming automatic, (C) though complete mastery is not quite there yet. (Photographs courtesy of Kathy Hirsh-Pasek)*

In short, children suffer simply from inexperience. Adults are guided by their experience in many aspects of day-to-day functioning. Children, in contrast, cannot rely on this guide, with important consequences for their intellectual performance.

But suppose we could find a group of children who are experienced in a particular domain. There are, after all, nine-year-old *Star Wars* experts and eight-year-olds who are fascinated by horses and who therefore have learned a great deal about horses. In such domains of expertise, do these children benefit from their experience, reasoning and remembering just like adults?

One investigator studied the ability of ten-year-old chess experts, recruited from local chess clubs, to remember chess positions. Just like adult chess experts, these children had excellent memories for chess positions, out-performing adults who happened to be chess novices. Clearly, what mattered here was experience and expertise in the specific domain and not overall level of cognitive development (Chi, 1978; Chi, Glaser, and Farr, 1988; for more on the memory-effects of expertise, see Chapter 8).

THE CHILD AS A POOR STRATEGIST

Strategies for remembering   It seems, then, that one important factor in intellectual development is the accumulation of knowledge, with this knowledge then serving as a guide to further intellectual functioning. Still another factor is the acquisition of strategies that can broadly improve both reasoning and memory.

For example, when adults are presented with a series of items and told to repeat them a moment later, they do their best to keep them in mind. They rehearse, perhaps by repeating the items mentally, perhaps by organizing them in various ways. What about young children? By age three or so, children do show signs of deliberate memory strategies, but the strategies are relatively primitive. In one study, three-year-olds watched while an experimenter placed a toy dog in one of two containers. The experimenter told the children that he'd leave the room for a little while, but that they should tell him where the dog was hidden as soon as he came back. During the interval, some children kept looking at the hiding place and nodding "yes"; others kept their eyes on the wrong container while shaking their heads "no"; yet others kept their hands on the correct container. They all had found a way of building a bridge between past and present by performing an overt action—keeping the toy dog in their minds by marking its location with their bodies (Wellman, Ritter, and Flavell, 1975).

Keeping one's hand on the to-be-remembered object may be a forerunner of rehearsal, but it's a far cry from the real thing. Genuine rehearsal does not occur spontaneously until around age five or six. One experiment used participants of five, seven, and ten years of age. The stimuli were pictures of seven familiar objects (e.g., a pipe, a flag, an owl). The experimenter slowly pointed at three of them in turn. The children's job was to point at the same three pictures in the same order after a fifteen-second interval. During this interval their eyes were covered (by a specially designed space helmet), so they couldn't bridge the interval by looking at the pictures or by surreptitiously pointing at them.

Not surprisingly, the older children did better on the recall test than the younger ones did (Figure 13.26). And, without question, part of their advantage derived from using memory strategies: One of the experimenters was a trained lip reader who observed that almost all of the ten-year-olds silently mouthed the

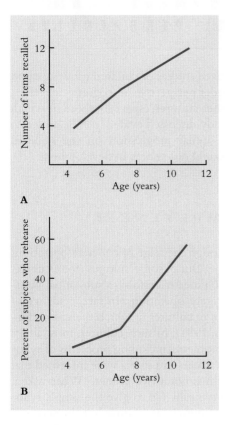

A

B

13.26 Strategies for memorizing in children (A) Nursery-school children, first-graders, and fifth-graders were shown a number of pictures and were asked to try to remember them. The figure shows recall as a function of age. (B) While the participants watched the stimuli, the experimenters observed them for signs of rehearsal—naming the pictures, moving their lips while watching, and so on. The figure shows the proportion of all children who rehearsed. In the older children, there was quite a bit of rehearsal, but there was very little for the first-graders and virtually none for the nursery-school children. Absence of rehearsal has also been found for retarded participants. (Data from Appel et al., 1972)

names of the to-be-remembered pictures—that is, they used rehearsal—during the retention interval, compared to only 10 percent of the five-year-olds. The older children remembered more than the younger ones, not because they had more memory "space," but because they used their memories more effectively (Flavell, Beach, and Chinsky, 1966).

METACOGNITION

In several studies young nonrehearsers were trained to rehearse, and they easily mastered (and benefited from) the use of this simple strategy. But when later presented with another memory task, most of these participants abandoned the rehearsal method they had just been taught. This was especially likely if the new task was somewhat different from the old. A child taught to remember a set of names by reciting it aloud probably won't apply the same strategy to a shopping list (Flavell, 1970, 1977).

What these children seem to lack, therefore, is a master plan for dealing with memory tasks in general, a strategy for using strategies. To put this more broadly, the children seem to lack an understanding of their own mental processes and with it an understanding of when a strategy would be useful and, likewise, which strategies should be applied to which tasks. Their shortcoming, therefore, lies in their ***metacognition***—their thinking about their own mental functioning.

Human adults know that rehearsal is useful, know that it helps to pay attention when trying to learn, and can even assess the state of their own knowledge: Have they studied a to-be-remembered item sufficiently? Or is further study still needed? Likewise, adults have a fairly realistic idea of what they can and cannot recall: If briefly shown pictures of four common objects, adults will (correctly) predict that they will be able to recall them after one presentation. If shown ten pictures, they will predict (again correctly) that this set exceeds their capacity. In children, all of these metacognitive skills are less well developed. Thus, for example, first- and second-graders are much less realistic in predicting their own memory performance (Yussen and Levy, 1975).

Metacognition is not limited to memory. Adults also know a great deal, for example, about their own perception—they recognize the role of perspective, know the difference between reality and illusion, and become artists and art connoisseurs (Flavell, Flavell, and Green, 1983). Adults also have metacognitive understanding about language, so that they can do more than talk and understand—they can also play with language, as in puns or poems, recognize that some sentences are ill-formed, and become poets or linguists (Gleitman, Gleitman, and Shipley, 1972). Adults also manifest metacognition in thinking and problem solving. Of course, they think and solve problems, but they can do more—they can use general strategies for reaching solutions, know when they need more information, recognize a paradox, and become scientists or logicians. In all of these domains, the young child is rather limited, and so this is an arena of enormous growth across the first decade or so of life. The importance of this growth cannot be overstated, since it may well be that these metacognitive processes are one of the distinguishing hallmarks of adult human intelligence (Gleitman, 1985).

The child as expert *Ten-year-old chess champion Etienne Bacrot plays an adult opponent. To make the competition a bit more even, she wears a blindfold. (Photograph by Benainous, © Gamma)*

Polynesian navigators The seafarers of the Caroline Islands in the Pacific Ocean guide their sailing canoes over hundreds of miles of open ocean without benefit of compass or Western navigational mathematics. Instead, they rely on an elaborate navigational method that is based on a knowledge of star positions, ocean swells and currents, and the behavior of birds, and is carefully handed on from generation to generation. The figure shows a master navigator (A) guiding a boat, (B) teaching the star positions to students of all ages. (Reproduced from S. D. Thomas, The Last Navigator, *New York: Holt, 1987. By permission of the publisher)*

COGNITIVE DEVELOPMENT FROM A CROSS-CULTURAL PERSPECTIVE

Throughout this chapter, we have emphasized studies of children growing up in the Western world. But we can gain a broader perspective on cognitive development by asking how people develop in other cultures, especially those in which there is no formal schooling. We have already discussed evidence indicating that children from different cultures show a similar progression on the standard Piagetian tasks. But there are also cross-cultural differences in development.

DIFFERENCES IN COMPETENCE?

In the west, most adolescents pass through the stage of concrete operations and into the stage of formal operations. But in some cultures (for example, that of Australian aborigines and of New Guinea tribesfolk), a substantial number of adults fail the standard tests of concrete operations. In fact, evidence of formal operations using standard tests is rare in cultures in which there is no formal schooling (Cole, 1975; Price-Williams, 1981). In such cultures, most adults seem unable to deal with certain abstract problems, including problems of syllogistic reasoning. Thus, unschooled Kpelle farmers in Liberia were informed that "All Kpelle men are rice farmers. Mr. Smith is not a rice farmer." When asked, "Is Mr. Smith a Kpelle man?" they would typically fail to give the simple syllogistic "No." Instead, they would be noncommittal: "If I know him in person, I can answer that question, but since I do not know him in person, I cannot answer that question" (Scribner, 1975, p. 175).

However, these same preliterate peoples do seem capable of complex, sophisticated reasoning within the context of their own lives. One example is provided by Polynesian sailors who reveal extraordinary skills of mental calculation in navigating their boats from one island to the next (Gladwin, 1970). Another comes from the !Kung San hunter-gatherers of the Kalahari desert, who perform remarkable feats of inference while hunting game: weighing the chances of tracking down a wounded giraffe against the cost of a drawn-out search, searching for clues in the pattern of crushed grasses, judging whether blood fell on a twig before or after the twig was bent, and evaluating the various interpretations to decide on a course of action (Blurton-Jones and Konner, 1976).

How could someone be capable of these impressive feats of reasoning, yet do so poorly on standard cognitive tests? One possibility is that the non-Western participants don't understand the standard testing procedures and, in particular, don't understand what kind of answer the experimenter wants. As an example, consider a study in which the participants were Russian farmers, some of whom had a few years of schooling while others had none. All of the participants were shown sets of four pictures. In each set, three pictures showed members of a well-defined category, such as tools (e.g., a saw, an ax, and a shovel). The fourth picture showed an item that did not belong in that category, but was functionally related to two of the other items (e.g., a piece of wood).

When asked to pick out the three pictures that belonged together, the schooled farmers behaved much as Western participants do. They chose according to the abstract semantic category and grouped all the tools together. The unschooled farmers behaved differently. They chose on the basis of which objects would be used together. Thus, they selected the ax, the piece of wood, and the saw; in their view, these three sensibly went together, since the tree must be felled, and then sawed into pieces (Luria, 1971).

In a sense, these unschooled farmers are employing a relatively concrete mode of classification; one could therefore interpret this as further evidence for the lack of abstract thought in the unschooled. But one could also interpret these data rather differently: Perhaps these participants understood perfectly well that three of the objects were tools, while one was not. But perhaps they thought that grouping by function was more useful than grouping by category. And, after all, either grouping provides a perfectly legitimate answer to the experimenter's vague question about which objects "belong together."

Consistent with this suggestion, one investigator found that when unschooled Kpelle participants were asked to sort objects (including tools and foods) into groups, they arranged them by function—a knife with an orange, a hoe with a potato, and so on. Asked why they sorted the objects as they did, they replied: "That is the way a wise man would do it." When the experimenter asked "How would a fool do it?" he received the response that he had originally looked for— food in one pile and tools in another (Glick, 1975). Thus, the participants obviously were capable of grouping by categories; this simply wasn't the grouping scheme that they deemed most useful.

Clearly, we need to be cautious in interpreting cross-cultural differences in cognition. If non-Westerners act differently, is this because they lack competence or because they approach the task differently than Westerners?

EFFECTS OF SCHOOLING

Cross-cultural studies have uncovered one factor, however, that does seem to shape and guide thought: There seem to be genuine differences in the way schooled and unschooled peoples think.

We've already cited evidence indicating that many cross-cultural differences in cognitive performance can at least partly be attributed to differences in formal schooling. Other studies indicate that schooled West African children are more likely to conserve than unschooled ones (Greenfield, 1966) and that schooled children in such diverse places as Morocco, Yucatan, and Liberia do better on various tests of free recall than their unschooled counterparts (Cole et al., 1971; Wagner, 1974, 1978).

Why does schooling make a difference? First, schooled people are more likely to understand just what an experimenter has in mind. (For example, they are used to being asked a question by someone who already knows the answer but wants to find out whether they do.) But another reason is more far reaching. Western schools teach their students concepts and techniques of considerable power: In studying mathematics or science, for example, children acquire skills that can be applied to many problems, in many domains. Many aspects of schooling also encourage children to focus on what various situations have in common, and this leads them to operate at a more abstract level in thinking about the day-to-day world. All of this provides children with a powerful set of intellectual tools, applicable to an enormously broad range of settings.

But we should maintain a balanced perspective here: The skills engendered by Western schooling are exactly the skills needed to succeed in most Western cultures. These same skills would be less valuable in other cultural settings. Formal schooling would not help children survive in the !Kung culture; courses in calculus and logic would be of little use in hunting giraffes (Scribner and Cole, 1973). Thus, if schooling seems to provide children with special advantages, let us remember that this is a judgment offered by Westerners, based on tests devised by Westerners.

571

TAKING STOCK

Having reviewed the various lines of evidence, we conclude that cognitive development is the joint outcome of both maturational and environmental factors. Certain aspects of cognitive growth do seem to be driven largely by maturation: Examples are the sensory-motor achievements of the first two years and the acquisition of language. These earlier achievements will unfold in a broad range of environments (though, if the environment is hostile enough, they may be impaired). The situation is different for various aspects of cognitive development that typically occur later and involve broadly generalizable, abstract skills, especially those that are often identified with Piaget's formal operations. For these, environmental and cultural conditions are of paramount importance. Conditions in our own culture (especially the provision of formal schooling) help children develop higher-order concepts that can serve as a foundation for yet higher ones. These allow children to acquire increasingly effective strategies for learning and thinking, strategies that become ever more widely applicable (and thus more abstract) as they grow up.

SUMMARY

1. Embryological development involves progressive anatomical *differentiation*. According to many theorists, differentiation also occurs in the development of behavior. An example is the development of grasping during the infant's first year.

2. Development can be considered a process of growth. After conception, the fertilized egg divides, redivides, and differentiates. In the process, it becomes an *embryo*, and then, two months later, a *fetus*. At birth, the infant comes equipped with a set of early reflexes and good sensory capacities. However, human newborns are further removed from adulthood than are the newborns of most other animal species. This leads to a long period of dependency, which may be one of the factors that led to the development of human culture.

3. A general characteristic of development is that it is progressive. An example is motor development in which such steps as creeping, crawling, and walking occur in much the same sequence for all babies.

4. The changes that constitute development are produced by the interaction of genetic endowment and environmental factors. In humans, the genetic commands are contained in twenty-three pairs of *chromosomes*. One of these pairs determines the sex of the organism. If female, it is an XX pair; if male, an XY pair. Every chromosome contains thousands of *genes*, some *dominant* and some *recessive*.

5. What is meant by the term *environment* changes as development proceeds. In early embryonic development, the environment of a given cell is the other cells with which it makes contact. Somewhat later, the embryonic environment includes hormonal conditions. An example is the formation of external genitals, which differentiate into those of a male in the presence of *androgens*, but remain those of a female when androgens are absent. That the same physical environment exerts different effects at different ages is shown by *sensitive periods*.

6. Some aspects of the orderly progression of development are determined by *maturation*, which is genetically programmed and independent of specific environmental conditions. An example is walking. This and other early sensory and motor achievements

seem to be relatively unaffected by specific practice. On the other hand, more general kinds of experience, such as sensory deprivation and sensory enrichment, seem to exert important effects.

7. All humans go through a process of *cognitive development*. According to Jean Piaget, they do so by passing through the same sequence of developmental stages.

8. In Piaget's account, the first stage is the period of *sensory-motor intelligence*, which lasts until about two years of age. During this period, the infant develops the concept of *object permanence*, builds up coordinated sensory-motor *schemas*, becomes capable of *deferred imitation*, and acquires increasingly complex mental representations.

9. The next period lasts till about six or seven. It is the *preoperational period* during which children are capable of representational thought but lack mental *operations* that order and organize these thoughts. Characteristic deficits include an inability to conserve number and quantity, and *egocentrism*, an inability to take another person's perspective.

10. At about seven, children begin to acquire a system of mental operations that allows them to manipulate mental representations with consequent success in conservation tasks and similar tests. But until they are about eleven, they are still in the period of *concrete operations*, which lacks an element of abstractness. After eleven, they enter the period of *formal operations*. As a result, they can consider hypothetical possibilities and are capable of scientific thought.

11. One critical challenge to Piaget's views concerns his beliefs of what is present by the time of birth. A number of critics deny that the infant's mind is the mere jumble of unrelated sensory impressions and motor reactions that Piaget declared it to be, for they believe that some of the major categories by which adults organize the world—such as the concepts of space, objects, number, and the existence of other minds—have primitive precursors in early life.

12. Studies of visual perception in infancy using the *habituation procedure* suggest that humans come equipped with some built-in notions of space and objects. Infants show appropriate reactions to perceptual occlusion and have some notions of the principles that govern objects in space. Piaget to the contrary, they have object permanence. But while they believe that objects exist, they are quite inept in searching for them.

13. Further studies show that infants can perceive numerical equivalence if the number of objects in the set is small enough and also that they have some rudiments of numerical reasoning.

14. Other criticisms suggest that Piaget also underestimated the preschoolers' capacity for social cognition. Three- and four-year-olds show less egocentrism than Piaget would have predicted and have the rudiments of a *theory of mind*. But they have difficulties on false-belief tests until they're about four-and-a-half years of age.

15. Trying to explain cognitive growth has turned out to be even more difficult and controversial than trying to describe it. The nativist approach assumes that development is largely driven by maturation. Empiricists assume that the answer is learning. Piaget himself rejected both empiricist and nativist extremes, arguing that development involves *assimilation* and *accommodation,* a constant interchange between organism and environment, as the environment is assimilated to the child's current schema and the schema in turn accommodates itself to aspects of the environment. A current approach sees cognitive development as a change in *information processing* and argues that increased mental growth is based in part on the acquisition of new knowledge, and also various strategies for thinking and remembering that depend on the development of *metacognition*.

16. Studies of cognitive development in non-Western cultures, especially those in which there is no formal schooling, have provided another perspective on theories of cognitive development. While some unschooled people do poorly on standard cognitive tasks, this may be because these participants don't adequately assess these tasks, in part, because they don't know what kind of answer the experimenter is looking for. This is especially likely given the remarkable intellectual feats of these people in the context of their own everyday lives, as shown by the navigational skills of Polynesian sailors and the abilities of !Kung hunters to track game.

CHAPTER 14

SOCIAL DEVELOPMENT

I n the preceding chapter we discussed physical and cognitive development: the ways in which we progress from embryos to full-grown adults, from faltering toddlers to agile adolescents, from babbling babes to articulate adults. But humans don't just grow bigger and smarter; they also develop in their relations with other people. They learn to behave in socially acceptable ways. They learn to perceive the nuances in another's behavior and to communicate their own needs and wishes. They learn to be good friends to allies and to deal warily with adversaries. Finding out how they learn to do all this is the task of psychologists who study *social development.*

Physical, cognitive, and social development are all areas in which our abilities expand on the human journey from birth to senescence. Physically, we grow in sheer size and strength, letting us move more freely within our environment. Cognitively, we learn to inhabit not only the physical world but also the world of concepts and ideas.

Socially, our horizons expand just as much. In the first weeks of life, our social world is limited to just one person, usually the mother. But in time, this social sphere enlarges to include both parents, then the rest of the family, then young peers in the neighborhood, nursery, and school. With the onset of adolescence, a small number of special friends assume more and more importance as sexuality blossoms. Before long, many of us become parents and start the reproductive cycle all over again. Of course, social development continues even at this point, as we move into midlife and then old age, at each stage growing and changing in important ways.

Alongside these overt changes are many adjustments that are not immediately visible but that are crucial nonetheless. As we mature, we come in contact with the system of social rules through which we are linked, not just to our own family circle, but to a larger social universe. A major concern of this chapter is to chart the course of this social expansion through which babes in arms become citizens of the world.

ATTACHMENT

The course of social development begins with the very first human bond—that between infants and their primary caregiver, usually the mother.★ This bond— the attachment of infants to the person who takes care of them—is sometimes said to lay the foundations for all later relationships. What is the nature of this attachment?

Infants want to be near their mothers, and when distressed, they are comfort-

★ Since the primary caregiver is typically the child's mother (she almost always was in earlier eras), we will refer to the child's caregiver by that traditional term. Of course, the actual caregiver may well be another person, such as the father or a nanny; moreover, many children have multiple caregivers, as when mother and father are joint and equally involved caregivers.

Attachment *(Mother and Child, c. 1890, by Mary Cassatt; Courtesy of Wichita Art Museum, Wichita, Kansas; the Roland P. Murdock Collection)*

Free-floating anxiety *(Photograph by Suzanne Szasz)*

ed by their mother's face, voice, and touch. In this regard, human children have much in common with the young of many other species. Rhesus monkey infants cling to their mother's body, chicks follow the hen, and lambs run after the ewe. As the young mature, they venture farther from the mother, gaining courage for ever more distant forays. But for quite a while, the mother continues to provide a secure home base, a safe retreat from unmanageable threats.

THE ROOTS OF ATTACHMENT

What accounts for the infant's attachment to the mother? Until some forty years ago, it was widely believed that the love for the mother was a direct consequence of the fact that she provided the means to satisfy basic biological needs—she provided food, warmth, physical protection, and relief from pain. The most influential version of this approach was probably that of Sigmund Freud, who believed that the terror of infants at their mother's absence is based on the expectation that they would go unfed (Chapter 17). Because mothers were seen primarily as being a food repository (whether through breast or bottle), Freud's view became known as the ***cupboard theory*** of mother love (Bowlby, 1969, 1973).

BOWLBY'S THEORY OF ATTACHMENT

The cupboard theory has been criticized on several grounds, one being the fact that babies often show great interest in people other than those who feed them. For example, infants seem to enjoy being cuddled, smiled at, and played with, and there is not one shred of evidence to indicate that babies enjoy peek-a-boo, say, only because it is associated with food.

Concerns such as these led British psychiatrist John Bowlby to argue that infants find this social interaction intrinsically rewarding. For Bowlby, infants don't form attachments because they are seeking food or warmth. Instead, they are born with social needs, inborn tendencies to seek direct contact with an adult (usually the mother).

In many ways, this social contact is pleasing for infants. They enjoy interacting with their mother and quickly learn to recognize and prefer their mother's voice and even her smell (MacFarlane, 1975; DeCasper and Fifer, 1980). When contented, they peacefully gaze, gurgle, and, by about six weeks of age, produce a full-blown social smile. Mothers and other important adults happily reciprocate; when babies smile, adults smile back. As infants get older and acquire some locomotor control, they will do whatever they can to be in the adults' company—smiling beseechingly toward their mother and father, reaching for them, and crawling toward them (Campos et al., 1983).

For Bowlby, however, such behavior is motivated not only by the pleasures of contact but also by a built-in fear of the unknown and unfamiliar, which drives the young of most mammals and birds to huddle with a very familiar object, most likely the ever-present mother. And the mother is not merely familiar. She also possesses certain stimulus properties that are critically important for the young of her species: If she is a duck, she quacks; if she is a rhesus monkey, she is furry.

Bowlby suggests that a built-in fear of the unfamiliar has a simple survival

14.1   The need for contact comfort   *A frightened rhesus monkey baby clings to its terry-cloth mother for comfort. (Photograph by Martin Rogers/Stock, Boston)*

14.2   Contact comfort in humans   *(Photograph by Suzanne Szasz)*

value. Infants who lack it will stray from their mothers and will be more likely to get lost and perish. In particular, they may fall victim to predators, who tend to attack weak animals that are separated from their flock.

Of course, the infants of most species can't identify likely predators, so their built-in fear is initially quite general. In the absence of the mother, therefore, even mild external threats become overwhelming for the child; this heightened need for reassurance may lead to desperate whining and clinging in the dark or during a thunderstorm.

So powerful is this need to cling to the parents that it may occur even when the fearful stimulus comes from the parents themselves. Children who are severely punished by their parents may become even more clinging and dependent on them. The parents caused the fear, but they are the ones who are approached for reassurance. This is analogous to dogs who lick the hand that whipped them. The whipping led to fear and pain, but whom can dogs approach for solace but their masters? Similar phenomena may be observed in the Stockholm Syndrome in which hostages grow fond of and even romantically attached to their captors, and in domestic abuse, where victims often defend their partners, refusing to press charges or testify against them (Auerbach et al., 1994; Graham, Rawlings, and Rigsby, 1994).

THE ESSENCE OF MOTHERING: COMFORT NOT CUPBOARDS

According to Bowlby, fear of the unfamiliar is what produces attachment. Of course, the mother provides food and warmth, but for purposes of attachment what really matters is the sense of safety, comfort, and refuge the mother provides.

Independent evidence consistent with Bowlby's view comes from some landmark studies conducted by Harry Harlow (1905–1981). Harlow raised newborn rhesus monkeys without their mothers. Each rhesus infant lived alone in a cage that contained two stationary figures. One of these models was built of wire; the other was made of soft terry cloth. The wire figure was equipped with a nipple that yielded milk, but no similar provision was made for the terry-cloth model. Even so, the monkey infants spent much more time on the terry-cloth "mother" than on the wire figure. This was especially clear when the infants were frightened. When faced with a mechanical toy that approached with clanking noises, they invariably rushed to the terry-cloth mother and clung to her tightly. The terry-cloth figure could be clung to and provided what Harlow called "contact comfort" (Figure 14.1).

Notably, the infants never sought similar solace from the wire mothers, even though these were their source of food (Harlow, 1958), results that stand in complete opposition to the cupboard theory.

This suggests that the monkey infant loves its mother (whether real or terry cloth), not because she feeds it, but because she provides "comfort." Rhesus infants in the wild grasp and cling to their mother's fur at any threat; presumably, in Harlow's laboratory the terry cloth felt more furlike than did the wire.

Whether contact comfort is equally important to human infants is unclear, but very likely it plays some role. Frightened young humans run to their mothers and hug them closely just as rhesus infants do (Figure 14.2). Human infants even have the same grasping and clinging reflexes shown by rhesus infants, although human mothers don't have the fur that permits easy clinging. Children also like stuffed, cuddly toys such as teddy bears, and they clasp these toys tightly when they feel threatened. Could these toys be the human analog to the terry-cloth mother? Perhaps they are, but—contrary to the cupboard theory—not because they are a surrogate breast or bottle.

14.3 Imprinting in ducklings *Imprinted ducklings following Konrad Lorenz. (Courtesy of Nina Leen)*

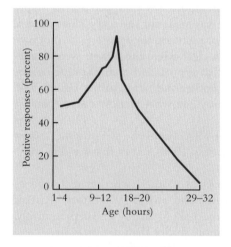

14.4 Imprinting and the sensitive period *The curve shows the relation between imprinting and the age at which a duckling was exposed to a male moving model. The imprinting score represents the percentage of trials on which the duckling followed the model on a later test. (After Hess, 1958)*

IMPRINTING AND ATTACHMENT

Infant monkeys seem biologically programmed to seek familiar objects. Similar patterns can be observed in many other species. For example, consider the phenomenon of *imprinting* in birds, which was studied extensively by the European ethologist Konrad Lorenz. Imprinting is a kind of learning that occurs very early in life and provides the basis for the bird's attachment to its mother.

For example, as soon as a duckling can walk (about twelve hours after hatching), it will approach and follow virtually any moving stimulus. If the duckling follows this moving object for about ten minutes, an attachment is formed. The bird has now imprinted on this object and, from this point forward, will continue to follow it, will show distress if separated from it, and will seek proximity to it in times of fear or stress.

In nature, the first moving stimulus the duckling sees is generally the duckling's mother. Hence, the duckling forms an attachment to the mother, as it should. But attachments can be formed to other objects, sometimes through accidental exposure and sometimes through an experimenter's manipulations. (The situation is much like a fairy-tale enchantment: "You will fall deeply in love," the witch said, "with the first person you see tomorrow." If the person being enchanted is lucky, it will be the handsome prince who appears first thing. But sometimes fate is less kind.)

In some studies, ducklings have been exposed to a moving toy duck on wheels or to a rectangle sliding back and forth behind a glass window, or even to Konrad Lorenz's booted legs (Figure 14.3). In each case, the result is the same. The duckling becomes imprinted on the toy or the rectangle or on Lorenz; it follows these objects as if following its mother, uttering plaintive distress calls whenever the attachment object is not nearby (Hess, 1959, 1973).

Imprinting occurs most readily during a specific period in the animal's life. In ducklings, this period lasts for about two days, with a maximum sensitivity at about fifteen hours after hatching (Hess, 1959). Subsequent to this period, imprinting is difficult to achieve (see Figure 14.4). For many years, this period of time was referred to as the *critical period* for imprinting. Contemporary investigators, however, prefer the term *sensitive period* to highlight the fact that imprinting is still possible after this period has ended, even though it is far less likely. (See Chapters 9 and 13 for other examples of critical or sensitive periods.)

Why is imprinting limited in this way? One hypothesis is that there is a decline in the plasticity of some part of the young bird's brain—a decline that is somehow tied to a physiological clock (Gottlieb, 1961). Another possible explanation why ducklings do not easily imprint after the sensitive period is because, by then, they have become thoroughly afraid of all new objects. When exposed to the wooden duck, the bird flees instead of following. Having lived for several days, it has learned something about what is familiar, and it can therefore recognize—and fear—what is strange. Some evidence for this position comes from the fact that older ducklings can imprint on new objects if they are forced to remain in their presence for a while. One group of investigators exposed five-day-old ducklings to a moving rectangle. The ducklings initially tried to flee and huddled in a corner. After a while, though, their fear diminished. At this point, they began to follow the rectangle and gave distress calls when it was withdrawn. They had imprinted on the rectangle even though they were long past the sensitive period (Hoffman, 1978; for still another interpretation, see Bateson, 1984).

Do humans show imprinting? Based on animal findings such as Lorenz's, some investigators questioned whether human infants have a sensitive period just after birth during which they form their attachments to their mothers (Klaus et al., 1970; Klaus and Kennell, 1976). If so, then the hospital practice of separating newborns from their mothers and moving them to a separate nursery (once done routinely but now reserved for premature and other high-risk babies) would be detrimental. However, this concern appears not to be well founded: Studies comparing infants who had after-birth contact with their mothers to those who did not (usually due to medical complications in either mother or baby) show little evidence for such a sensitive period. Instead, normal attachments form as soon as circumstances allow (Eyer, 1992). ★

PATTERNS OF ATTACHMENT

Attachment to the mother is seen in two ways: Being with her brings contentment, and separation from her evokes distress. During the first few months of life, infants will accept substitute mothers, perhaps because they have not yet clearly differentiated their own mothers from other people. But from about six to eight months of age, infants learn who "mother" is, and they now cry and fuss when she departs. The age at which children begin to protest this separation—that is, the age at which children start to show *separation anxiety*—is pretty much the same for African bushmen in Botswana, U.S. city dwellers, Indians in a Guatemalan village, and members of an Israeli kibbutz (Kagan, 1976).

ASSESSING ATTACHMENT

This reaction to separation provides a means for examining the attachment infants have to their mothers. A widely used procedure is the Strange Situation devised by Mary Ainsworth and her colleagues for children of about one year of age (Figure 14.5). A child is first brought into an unfamiliar room that

14.5 A diagrammatic sketch of the Strange Situation M *indicates the mother, and* S *the stranger. (Adapted from Ainsworth et al., 1978)*

★ Moreover, when infants must spend their initial days with a nurse, or in an incubator, they do not form a lasting attachment to either. Instead, they form a more normal attachment to their mother some days later. Clearly, the pattern of imprint-to-object-of-first-exposure, so common in many other species, is not found in humans.

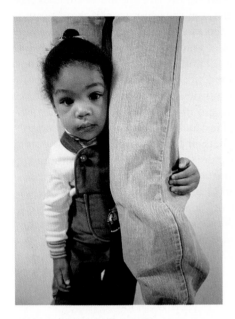

(Photograph by J. Blyenberg/Leo de Wys)

contains many toys and then allowed to explore and play with the mother present. After a while, a stranger enters, talks to the mother, and then approaches the child. The next step is a brief separation—the mother leaves the child alone with the stranger. After a few minutes, though, a reunion follows—the mother returns and the stranger leaves (Ainsworth and Bell, 1970; Ainsworth et al., 1978).

According to Ainsworth and her colleagues, the behavior of one-year-olds in this situation falls into one of three major categories. The children described as "securely attached" explore, play with the toys, and even make wary overtures to the stranger, so long as the mother is present. They show some distress when the mother leaves, but greet her return with great enthusiasm. The remaining children show behavior patterns that Ainsworth and her colleagues regard as signs of insecure attachment. Some of these children are described as "anxious/resistant." They don't explore even in the mother's presence, become upset and panicky when she leaves, and act ambivalent during the reunion, running to her to be picked up and then angrily struggling to get down. Other children show a pattern called "anxious/avoidant." They are distant and aloof from the very outset, show little distress when the mother leaves, and ignore her when she returns.

Just how many children are securely or insecurely attached? The answer appears to depend on the culture. In Ainsworth's studies, which used middle-class children from the United States, a clear majority of the one-year-olds (about 65 percent) were securely attached. However, among Israeli children reared on a kibbutz (a collective farm in which child rearing is communal), only about 37 percent showed secure attachments (Sagi et al., 1985).

STABILITY OF ATTACHMENT

Ainsworth and others believe that behavior in the Strange Situation reflects characteristics that are fairly stable, at least for the first few years of life. They suggest that we can use the children's behavior in this situation as a basis for predicting how the children will act in other settings and at other times. And, in fact, children rated as securely attached at fifteen months of age are likely to be more outgoing, popular, and well-adjusted in nursery school at age three-and-a-half (Waters, Wippman, and Sroufe, 1979). According to Ainsworth and her colleagues, such correlations show that the Strange Situation provides a good index of the quality of the early mother-child relationship, which then provides the foundation for later social and emotional adjustment. Some theorists even suggest that this early pattern of attachment predicts the pattern of romantic relationships in adolescence and adulthood (Hazan and Shaver, 1987; Rothbard and Shaver, 1994).

However, other investigators interpret the data differently. If behavior in the Strange Situation is correlated with subsequent behavior, perhaps this merely reflects the relative constancy of the child's physical and emotional health, family members, nutrition, and so on: If the child is healthy at age one, for example, that is a decent predictor that the child will continue to be healthy at age three or four. If so, then the benefits of this health will be visible both in early and in later tests—hence, the child will appear secure in the Strange Situation and will appear well adjusted in nursery school. Thus, both assessments of social behavior (early attachment and later adjustment) are effects deriving from a single underlying cause. This is different from the Ainsworth claim, in which early adjustment is seen as the cause of later adjustment.

Some relevant evidence for this possibility comes from studies of securely attached infants (at age one or so) who subsequently endured a period of severe family stress, such as serious illness in the family, marital conflict, or unemployment of a parent. In one study of ten disadvantaged infants observed at twelve months, over one-third showed a change to less secure attachment six months later, and the infants most likely to show the changed pattern were those whose mothers reported the most domestic stress (Vaughn et al., 1979). In this setting, therefore, attachment status was not a stable feature of the child but instead responded in obvious ways to changes in the child's life circumstances.

If attachment status is generally stable, this may also reflect a constancy in the mother's behavior, rather than some form of constancy in the child. A mother who was gentle and loving when her child was fifteen months old probably remained gentle and loving during the next two years; likewise for the mother who was short-tempered and rejecting. And, not surprisingly, these differences have a direct impact on the child: Studies show, for example, that mothers of securely attached children are more involved, expressive, and responsive when compared to mothers of insecurely attached children (Lamb et al., 1985; Isabella, 1993).

Still another factor to consider is a child's own temperament—whether she is constitutionally irritable or sociable. This temperament may underlie both her early attachment behavior and her later adjustment. If so, the correlation may be due more to the child herself than to other factors we have mentioned (Kagan, 1984).

Cause and effect in attachment and adjustment   These comments all serve to highlight a crucial point: Cause-and-effect relations in child development are enormously difficult to disentangle. It is often easy to observe correlations—for example, the fact that the children who show the most stable attachments at one age are also the best adjusted at a later age. The trick comes in interpreting this correlation: What is causing what? We illustrate some of the possibilities just discussed in Figure 14.6. Since each of these possibilities is consistent with the correlation, we cannot use the correlation itself as a means of choosing among these different hypotheses.

There are various ways in which investigators have tried to address these ambiguities. Some of the techniques are statistical, some involve experimental manipulation of the key variables. But research in this domain is also limited by obvious ethical constraints: There are powerful ethical reasons why we must not try to manipulate the mother's parenting style, the child's health, or the family

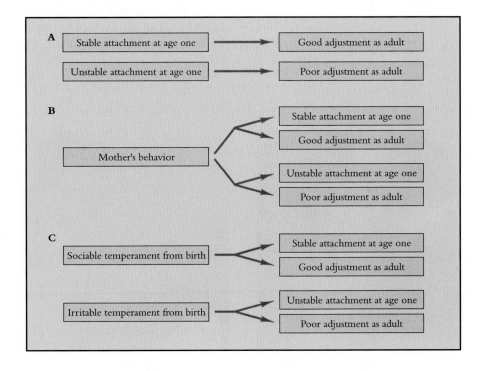

14.6   Ambiguity in interpreting developmental correlations   *Studies demonstrate a correlation between the stability of attachment at age one, and the quality of adjustment as an adult. (Infants who show stable attachment are likely to be well adjusted years later; infants who show unstable attachment are likely to be poorly adjusted years later.) But what is the cause and effect relationship linking these observations? Panels A, B, and C show three different possibilities, all of which could lead to the observed correlation.*

environment, even if these manipulations would provide us with clean scientific data. As a result, direct tests of developmental hypotheses are often difficult to arrange.

ATTACHMENT TO THE FATHER

Thus far, we've concentrated entirely on the child's attachment to the mother. This is no accident, since in most of the world's cultures—whether agrarian or technological—young children spend the vast majority of their time with their mothers (Lamb, 1987, 1997).

Are fathers left out in the cold? Not at all. Studies using the Strange Situation with fathers as well as mothers have found similar signs of distress when the father left and clinging and touching when he returned (see Figure 14.7). Moreover, infants develop attachments to their fathers and their mothers at about the same time (Pipp, Easterbrooks, and Brown, 1993). It thus appears that young children become strongly attached, and attached early on, to both parental figures.

But if attachments to both parents are deep and formed early, they nonetheless differ in kind. The chief difference, observed across numerous studies, is in playing versus caring. Fathers are more likely than mothers to play with their children. And fathers tend to be physical and vigorous in their play, lifting or bouncing their children or tossing them in the air. In contrast to such roughhousing, mothers generally play more quietly with their children, telling them stories or reciting nursery rhymes, and providing hugs and caresses rather than tumbles and bounces. The children act accordingly, tending to run to the mother for care and comfort but to the father for active play. This difference in the response to the two parents begins in early infancy, when there are more smiles for the mother and more giggles for the father. By the time the children are toddlers, two out of three pick the father as the one they want to play with. Although there are obvious exceptions, the overall pattern is clear: Mother is security and comfort; father is fun (Clarke-Stewart, 1978; Parke, 1981; Lamb, 1997).

What accounts for these differences in interaction with mothers and fathers? Certainly, social and economic circumstances play a role. In most cultures, fathers tend to be the breadwinners in the household and are correspondingly less involved in actual caregiving. Thus, while mothers tend to care for the children throughout the day, fathers condense their caregiving into episodes of concentrated, intense play (Roopnarine, Johnson, and Hooper, 1994)

14.7 Stranger anxiety *An eleven-month-old taken from his father's lap by a stranger. (Photographs by Stephanie Arch, courtesy of Kathy Hirsh-Pasek)*

A

B

C

(Photograph courtesy of Photo Researchers, Inc.)

But this difference in typical patterns of parental care may not be the whole story. Evidence comes from a comparison of fathers who were the infants' secondary caregivers (the usual role in our culture) and fathers who were the primary caregivers. The behavior of these two groups of fathers was quite similar. Both groups engaged in much more physical play with the infants than the mothers did (Field, 1978). This suggests that the fathers' behavior does not merely reflect social circumstances. Instead, their behavior may also be based on deeply embedded cultural gender roles or perhaps on a strong, innate predisposition. After all, rough-and-tumble play is much more common in male than in female primates, whether monkeys, apes, or humans (see Chapter 10).

EARLY MATERNAL SEPARATION AND DAY CARE

A number of authors believe that early separation from the mother may lead to lasting psychological damage. Thus, John Bowlby, in keeping with the views already described, asserts that any disturbance of a child's initial attachment to the mother will render that child less secure in later life. In this view, separation is psychologically dangerous, and the continuity of a child's first attachment relationship plays an important role in shaping his ultimate mental health (Bowlby, 1973).

This position has been widely accepted and influential in the United States, with various social consequences. It has made many women uneasy about leaving their children with another caretaker—an issue of some concern for any mother employed outside the home. It has also affected legal policies in cases of child placement, with the courts biased toward keeping children in homes (in which they had presumably formed attachments) despite evidence of neglect or abuse (Maccoby, 1980).

But Bowlby's views have become more controversial in recent years, and this controversy obviously has enormous importance, given current social and economic conditions in the United States. With over 60 percent of mothers now employed outside the home and a growing number of single-parent households (U.S. Department of Labor, 1995), family life in the United States today is not that depicted by Norman Rockwell or *Little House on the Prairie*. Increasingly, child care is provided in out-of-home day-care centers, with the staff in these centers sometimes spending more time with the child than do members of the child's own family (Hofferth, 1996). What are the consequences of this for the psychological welfare of our children?

Some evidence does suggest that this increase in nonmaternal child care is indeed problematic: A few studies, for example, have examined children who spent extensive amounts of time in the care of others (more than twenty hours per week) during their first year of life. These children are more likely to show insecure patterns of attachment in the Strange Situation and are less likely to comply with adults' requests or instructions (Barglow, Vaughn, and Molitor, 1987; Belsky, 1988; Belsky and Braungart, 1991).

Do these results condemn day care? Some authors don't think so. They argue that the added insecurity is minimal and that certain kinds of behavior in the test situation have been misinterpreted. Thus, the "noncompliance" observed in these studies may not indicate rebelliousness or disobedience; instead, it may indicate that the day-care children had become more independent and self-reliant. And, in fact, other evidence indicates that day-care children often outstrip their non–day-care peers on measures of sociability, persistence, and achievement (Clarke-Stewart, 1989, 1993). Perhaps this is unsurprising, if we

Attachment and day care *While some contend that any early separation from the primary caregiver may adversely affect the child, others contend that it's not the fact of day care that's important so much as it is the quality of day care. (Photograph © Stephen Shames/ Matrix; The Caring Center, West Philadelphia)*

bear in mind that a day-care child lives in a world filled with social interactions with agemates. Perhaps this enriched social experience provides benefits that compensate for any disadvantages that might result from diminished contact with one's own family.

Our best estimate, overall, is that when the day care is of reasonable quality, children do not seem to suffer (Howes and Hamilton, 1993; NICHD Early Child Care Research Network, 1997). When the quality of care is poor, however, the picture may be different. For example, one study indicated that infants enrolled in poor day-care centers end up inattentive and unsociable in preschool, compared to children who spent the same amount of time in good day-care centers (Howes, 1990). In a similar study, four-year-olds who attended higher quality day-care centers showed better social and emotional development at age eight than children who had attended poorer quality centers, even when factors such as social class and income were equated (Vandell, Henderson, and Wilson, 1988).

What defines a good quality day-care center or a bad one? The relevant factors include the adult-child ratio; the manner in which the teachers are selected, trained, and paid; the rate of staff turnover; and the quality of the physical facilities. Tragically, by these criteria, most day-care centers in the United States—86 percent in one major U.S. survey—qualify as poor or mediocre, with only 14 percent qualifying as good (Cost, Quality, and Outcomes Study Team, 1995). Additionally, day care is poorest for those children who are most vulnerable—infants and toddlers, especially those from low-income families who may only be able to afford the least-expensive care (Helburn and Howes, 1996).

DISRUPTED ATTACHMENT: DOMESTIC CONFLICT AND DIVORCE

Day care outside the home involves one sort of early separation routinely experienced by young children. A different, and often more distressing, form of separation is endured by children whose parents divorce—a situation faced by up to 30 percent of children in the United States (Furstenberg and Cherlin, 1991). When there is sole custody by one parent, the children often lose or suffer reduced contact with the other parent; in shared custody, there is diminished contact with both. In addition, children of divorced parents often must change residences, schools, and churches or synagogues, and break contact with many peers and adult figures in the process. Parents (usually mothers) who were able to stay at home with their children before the divorce often need to join the workforce after the divorce to support themselves (especially when money for child support from the other parent is insufficient or delinquent). As a result, children previously raised at home, with full-time parenting, may now find themselves in some sort of institutional child care. And, of course, many of these children must endure considerable domestic strife before the divorce, as well as an atmosphere filled with anger, guilt, and recrimination during the divorce itself (Buchanan, Maccoby, and Dornbusch, 1996).

There is some evidence that children of divorced parents may suffer a variety of emotional difficulties in later years. They may show conduct problems, may become depressed and withdrawn, and are less likely to finish high school (Hetherington, Stanley-Hagen, and Anderson, 1989; Forgatch, Patterson, and Ray, 1996).

Of course, it may well be that it is not the divorce itself that produces these unhappy consequences. Instead, these consequences may be the result of living in the stressful home environment that existed prior to the divorce—for example, living with parents who fight constantly. Consistent with this suggestion, retrospective studies of children whose parents divorced show that the children manifested many of the same problems before the divorce as they did after (Cherlin et al., 1991).

WHEN THERE IS NO ATTACHMENT AT ALL

We have seen that deleterious effects on children tend to occur with the impoverished attachments associated with poor day care and the disrupted attachments of acrimonious divorce. But what happens when no attachment is formed at all? The results are apparently drastic.

MOTHERLESS MONKEYS

We previously considered some of Harlow's experiments with rhesus monkeys and, in particular, the fate of monkeys raised with substitute mothers made of terry cloth. But suppose the monkey infants were reared without any contact at all? In one study, the infants were isolated for periods that ranged from three months to one year. During this time, they lived in an empty steel chamber and saw no living creature.

After their period of solitary confinement, the animals' reactions were observed in various test situations. A three-month isolation had comparatively little effect. But longer periods led to dramatic disturbances. The animals huddled in a corner of the cage, clasped themselves, and rocked back and forth. When they were brought together with normally reared agemates, the results were unambiguous. There was none of the active chasing and playful romping that is characteristic of monkeys at that age. Instead, the monkeys reared in isolation simply withdrew, huddled, rocked, and bit themselves (Figure 14.8).

This social inadequacy persisted into adolescence and adulthood. One manifestation was a remarkable incompetence in sexual and parental matters. Formerly isolated males were utterly inept at courtship and mating: If they approached other animals at all, they would, in Harlow's words, "grasp other monkeys of either sex by the head and throat aimlessly, a semi-erotic exercise without amorous achievements" (Harlow, 1962). Formerly isolated females were no better off and resisted the sexual overtures of normal males. Some of them were eventually impregnated but in many cases by artificial means. When these

14.8 Motherless monkeys *(A) A monkey reared in isolation, huddling in terror in a corner of its cage. (B) An isolated monkey biting itself at the approach of a stranger. (Courtesy of Harry Harlow, University of Wisconsin Primate Laboratory)*

A   B

motherless monkeys became monkey mothers themselves, they seemed to have no trace of love for their offspring. In a few cases, they actually abused their offspring in horrible ways, chewing off its toes or fingers, or worse (Figure 14.9). The early social deprivation experienced by these animals had evidently wreaked havoc on their subsequent social and emotional development (Suomi and Harlow, 1971; Harlow and Harlow, 1972; Harlow and Novak, 1973).

HUMANS REARED IN INADEQUATE INSTITUTIONS

Can we generalize from monkey infants to human children? There is reason to suspect that we can, for just like monkeys, human infants reared under conditions of isolation suffer in both their social and their emotional development.

Some of the evidence comes from studies of infants who were reared in orphanages that supplied adequate nutrition and bodily care but provided rather little in the way of sensory and social stimulation. In one such institution the infants were kept in separate cubicles for the first eight months or so as a precaution against infectious disease. Their brief contacts with adults were restricted to the times when they were fed or diapered. Feeding took place in the crib with a propped-up bottle. There was little social give and take, little talk, little play, and little chance that the busy attendant would respond to any one baby's cry (Goldfarb, 1955; Provence and Lipton, 1962; Dennis, 1973).

When these infants were compared to others who were raised normally, there were no differences for the first three or four months. Thereafter, the two groups diverged markedly. The understimulated infants showed serious impairments in their social development. Some were insatiable in their demands for love and attention. But the majority went in the opposite direction and became extremely apathetic in their reactions to people. They rarely tried to approach adults, either to hug and caress them or to get reassurance when in distress. A few others were reminiscent of Harlow's monkeys; they sat in a corner of their cribs, withdrawn and expressionless, and rocked back and forth.

These ill effects of early isolation can be long lasting. For example, a number of studies have shown that many of these orphanage children (although by no means all) have a number of intellectual deficits, for example in language and in abstract thinking, that persist into adolescence and beyond. There are also long-term social and emotional effects, including heightened physical aggression, delinquency, and indifference to others (Yarrow, 1961).

These problems do not arise merely because the child was in an orphanage; instead, what is critical is the quality of the orphanage (a point that parallels the findings on out-of-the-home child care): When children are raised in orphan-

14.9 Motherless monkeys as mothers *Female monkeys raised in isolation may become mothers by artificial impregnation. They usually ignore their infants. Sometimes, as shown here, they abuse them. (Courtesy of Harry Harlow, University of Wisconsin Primate Laboratory)*

ages of adequate quality, they seem to emerge without serious harm. For example, one study examined children who were raised in decent quality orphanages until they were two years old or older. When assessed at age four or eight, after they were adopted or placed in foster homes, these children had better emotional and social adjustment than those who had been returned to their biological parents (Tizard and Hodges, 1978).

ARE THE EFFECTS OF EARLY SOCIAL DEPRIVATION REVERSIBLE?

It's clear that serious social deprivation in early life has unfortunate effects. But is that because the experience occurred early in life? In other words, is early life a particularly formative period for human development? And are the effects of unfortunate early experiences irreversible? According to Freud—and many others—the answer to these questions is yes. To Freud there was no question that "the events of [the child's] first years are of paramount importance for his whole subsequent life." This position is in some ways analogous to the Calvinist doctrine of predestination. According to John Calvin, each person is predestined to be blessed or damned before ever being born. To Freud, the die is cast by the age of five or six.

UNDOING THE PAST IN ANIMALS

Some further evidence suggests that the dead hand of the past is not quite as unyielding as Freud had supposed. For one thing, many of the effects of early isolation in monkeys turn out to be substantially reversible. In one study, young rhesus monkeys were rehabilitated for social life after six months of isolation. They were placed together with carefully chosen monkey "therapists," monkeys who had been reared normally and were three months younger than their "patients." The therapist monkeys were thus too young to display physical aggression but old enough to seek and initiate social contact.

When first introduced to these younger monkeys, the previously isolated monkeys withdrew and huddled in a corner. But they hadn't counted on the persistence of their little therapists who followed them and clung to them. After a while, the isolates clung back, and within a few weeks, patients and therapists were playing vigorously with each other (Figure 14.10). Six months later, the patients seemed to have recovered.

Later studies showed that this kind of therapy was beneficial even for monkeys isolated for an entire year. After the therapy, the treated ex-isolates were admittedly less resilient, appearing more susceptible to stress than control animals. But they usually played and fought and copulated in much the manner of normal monkeys, and were often indistinguishable from them (Suomi and Harlow, 1972; Novak and Harlow, 1975; Suomi, 1989).

A related finding concerns formerly isolated females who later became mothers. As we saw, these motherless females were abject failures at the business of mothering. But while they ignored, rejected, or abused their first-borns, they were perfectly maternal to their second offspring—so much so, that they, too, were virtually indistinguishable from normal rhesus monkeys. What could account for this discrepancy? One guess is that the first-borns served as "therapists" who helped their mothers become accustomed to another animal, especially an infant. This helped the mothers later, when dealing with succeeding offspring. Unfortunately, the therapy was evidently not sufficient to protect the little therapists themselves (Seay, Alexander, and Harlow, 1964).

A

B

14.10 Therapy to undo the effects of early isolation *(A) A young, would-be therapist tenaciously clings to an unwilling isolate. (B) Some weeks later, there are strong signs of recovery as both patient and therapist engage in vigorous play. (Courtesy of Harry Harlow, University of Wisconsin Primate Laboratory)*

UNDOING THE PAST IN HUMANS

With appropriate intervention, the past can evidently be overcome in animals, at least to some extent. Is the same true for humans? In a few instances, isolated or horribly neglected children have been studied after they were rescued and placed in more benign care. The outcomes are quite variable and depend upon the case: Some children improve substantially, while others remain severely socially and intellectually impaired (Cole and Cole, 1996).

Although early deprivation usually results in some liability, the results of one study give some grounds for optimism. The participants were children at an over-crowded orphanage. There were few staff members and little individual attention. After about one-and-a-half years, some of the children were transferred out of the orphanage to an institution for mentally retarded women. Ironically, this institution provided the necessary means for emotional and intellectual rehabilitation. There was a richer and more stimulating environment, but most important, there were many more caregivers. Each of the transferred children was "adopted" by one adult—either an institutionalized woman or an attendant—who became especially attached to the child. This new emotional relationship led to improvements in many spheres of behavior. While the intelligence-test scores of the children who remained in the orphanage dropped during the succeeding years, those of the transferred children rose considerably. Similarly for their social adjustment: When they reached their thirties, the transferred participants had reached an educational and occupational level that was about average for the country at the time. In contrast, half of the participants who remained behind never finished the third grade (Skeels, 1966).

REASSESSING THE ROLE OF EARLY EXPERIENCE

In light of all this, we must evidently reassess the once-common view that early social experience is all important. Early experience certainly provides a vital foundation upon which further social relationships are built. But experiences in infancy or childhood do not affect adult behavior directly. What happens instead is that each step in a sequence of social developments paves the way for the next. In monkeys, the mother's presence during the first six months allays the infants' fears of approaching other monkeys. As a result, they can play with their age-mates and enter the social apprenticeship of childhood and adolescence. In interacting with their peers, they gradually acquire the social skills of adult monkeyhood. They can chase and be chased, can cope with aggression, and when necessary, inhibit their own. These skills allow both sexes to mate when they reach maturity and also enable them to respond appropriately to their own off-spring. Given this step-by-step progression, the motherless infants can be substantially redeemed by introducing them to the subsequent peer stage by an unusual and special means—the unthreatening young therapists.

Something of a similar nature probably holds for human social development as well. The early years are crucial in the sense that certain social patterns are much more likely to be acquired then, such as the capacity to form attachments to other people. These early attachments are a likely prerequisite for the formation of later ones. Children who have never been loved by their parents will be frightened by their peers and hampered in their further social development. But while the earlier attachments (to mother and father) lay the foundation for later ones (to friends, lovers, and their own children), the two are nevertheless quite different. As a result, there may be ways—as with Harlow's monkey therapists—of acquiring the social tools for dealing with their later lives that circumvent the handicaps of their early childhood. For while the past affects the present, it does not determine it.

To sum up, the easiest way of getting to the second floor of a house is by way of the first floor. But in a pinch one can always bring a ladder and climb in through a second-floor window.

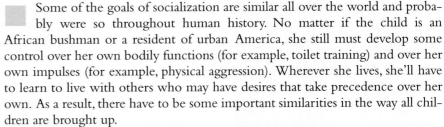

CHILDHOOD SOCIALIZATION

Infants' attachment to their caregivers marks their entrance into the social world. But infants—and later, children—still have much to learn about this world: how to behave and how not to behave; how to understand the intentions of others and how to convey their own intentions. Children learn all these things through *socialization,* the process by which they acquire the patterns of thought and behavior that characterize the society in which they are born.

CULTURAL VALUES AND CHILD REARING

Socialization *Most authors agree that parents exert some effect on the personality development of their children. What is at issue is what effects they have and how they achieve them. (Photographs courtesy of George Gleitman)*

Some of the goals of socialization are similar all over the world and probably were so throughout human history. No matter if the child is an African bushman or a resident of urban America, she still must develop some control over her own bodily functions (for example, toilet training) and over her own impulses (for example, physical aggression). Wherever she lives, she'll have to learn to live with others who may have desires that take precedence over her own. As a result, there have to be some important similarities in the way all children are brought up.

But human societies are diverse, and so the specific dos and don'ts of socialization depend on whether the child is to become a member of a band of nomadic herders, a rural village, or a tribe of Polynesian fishermen. Each of these societies will try to instill different characteristics in its young members-to-be. This point is especially clear when we consider the economy on which the society is based. Cultures that make their living through agriculture or animal husbandry tend to stress compliance, conformity, and responsibility as they raise their children. These attributes fit the adult role that the child must eventually assume—the patient, cooperative life of a farmer who must plow his soil or milk his cows at specified times so as to protect and augment the family's (or the village's) food supply. In contrast, hunting and fishing societies emphasize self-reliance and initiative—reasonable values for people who have to wrest their food from nature in day-to-day individual encounters (Barry, Child, and Bacon, 1959).

Similar differences emerge even within a society. For example, in Western society, working-class parents tend to stress the importance of controls from the outside, emphasizing the role of obedience to authority. Middle-class parents try to instill control from within, stressing the importance of self-control. These differences make sense if we consider the world in which these parents live and work. By and large, members of the working class are in occupations in which their work is closely supervised—a boss or a supervisor tells them what to do and how to do it. In contrast, the work of the middle class is less supervised and more self-directed. Thus, parents try to make their children behave at home as they themselves do in the work place—working-class children are required to become obedient and to follow orders, middle-class children to become their own boss. A further result fits in neatly: The more closely supervised the father is at work, the more likely he is to use physical punishment in disciplining his children—external control in one of its more extreme versions (Kohn, 1969; Hess, 1970).

MECHANISMS OF SOCIALIZATION

We've asked about the goals of socialization. But what about the means whereby these goals are achieved? Some theorists stress the role of reward and the fear of punishment. Others point to the importance of imitation. Still others argue for the importance of the child's growing understanding of what she's supposed to do and why. The best guess is that all three of these mechanisms contribute to the child's socialization.

REINFORCEMENT THEORY

According to both operant conditioning and psychoanalytic theory (see Chapters 4 and 17), children are socialized by a calculus of pain and pleasure. They will continue to do (or wish or think or remember) whatever previously brought them gratification and will refrain from whatever led to punishment and anxiety.

Modeling in real life (Photograph © Spencer Grant/Stock Boston)

Social learning theory There is no doubt that reward and punishment do play a large part in socialization. But for many psychologists, a theory based exclusively on these mechanisms cannot do justice to the socialization process. They note that we are animals with a culture, which makes us altogether unlike any of the animals studied in the learning laboratory. Thorndike's cats had to discover how to get out of the puzzle box by themselves (see Chapter 4): No other cat told them how to do it; no other cat could. But over the course of a lifetime, human beings learn a multitude of solutions that were discovered by those who came before them. They do not have to invent clothes, spoken language, or the alphabet; they do not have to discover fire or the wheel or even how to eat baby food with a spoon. Other people show them.

These observations have led some psychologists to endorse a view known as *social learning theory.* According to this conception, *observational learning* is one of the most powerful mechanisms of socialization. Children observe another person who serves as a model and then imitate what the model does, thus learning how to do something they didn't know before (Figure 14.11). Children see adults hammer nails into boards and try to duplicate the same feat (with any luck, not into either their finger or the new furniture).

Many cultures explicitly encourage such imitative patterns as a way of inducting the child into adult ways. In one Central American society, young girls are presented with miniature replicas of a water jar, a broom, and a grinding stone. They observe how their mothers use the real objects and through constant imitation acquire the relevant skills themselves (Bandura and Walters, 1963). The modern West has a similar practice: Toy stores are full of kid-sized tools and kid-sized vacuum cleaners, cooking sets, and dolls that need feeding and diaper changing.

We should note, though, that learning via imitation can be quite complicated. In some cases, much of the learning seems to occur quite a bit before the first performance ever takes place (learning without performance; see Chapter 4). In other cases, the learning can occur without either the learner, or the person imitated, receiving a reward (learning without reinforcement). Even with these (and other) complexities, however, imitation is quite common for our species and for

14.11   Learning by imitation   *Performing a traditional tea ceremony is learned by imitating an accomplished model. (Photograph by Michael Heron/Woodfin Camp)*

Imitating an absent model   *The child may dress up to feel like an adult out of a desire for competence and mastery of the universe. (Photograph by Erika Stone)*

a few other species as well. Very young human infants, for example, can imitate the facial expressions of the people they view; some studies have documented this skill in newborns (Meltzoff and Moore, 1977). Of course, as the child grows and matures, the capacity for imitation grows as well.

COGNITIVE DEVELOPMENTAL THEORY

A different perspective on socialization is offered by the **cognitive approach,** which emphasizes the role of understanding in interpersonal conduct and thought. In this view, children have some understanding of their own actions; they know that some things are "bad" and others "good," and also why these things are considered so. Hand in hand with this, they have some comprehension of how they should relate to others (and why), and as their mental development unfolds, so does their comprehension.

Like social learning theorists, cognitive theorists perceive a crucial role for observational learning. However, the cognitive theorists emphasize the intellectual operations needed to make this learning possible. In important ways, therefore, they view social development as dependent on cognitive development. (For more on children's cognitive development, see Chapter 13.) Consistent with this emphasis, we have already noted that even simple imitation requires considerable cognitive complexity. To see this, suppose a child imitates his father pulling up his trousers. In order to pull up his own pants, the boy must physically transpose the various steps: The father is facing one way, the child another way. These absolute positions, however, must be ignored; what matters instead are the relative positions. ("My foot, in relation to my trousers, must be in the same position as my father's foot, in relation to his trousers.") Similarly, the child must ignore many peripheral details ("My father is standing on the rug; I'm on the bare floor") but must be alert to other details ("My father started with his zipper unzipped and so must I"). Given all these complexities, it is no wonder that children are able to imitate more accurately as they get older (Yando, Seitz, and Zigler, 1978).

Children's imitation of an adult model is not blind and irrational. Novice mountain climbers who follow a guide are not like sheep that run after a leader;

Lessons in social behavior *Not all parent-child interactions are sweetness and light. (Photograph © Nancy Richmond/The Image Works)*

they follow because they know that the guide will bring them safely up and down the slope. Children who imitate are no less rational, for they proceed from the perfectly reasonable premise that, by and large, adults know more than they do (Kohlberg, 1969).

THE FIRST AGENTS OF SOCIALIZATION: THE PARENTS

Thus far, we have looked at socialization from the standpoint of the children who are being socialized, and we have considered how they learn the lessons that society tries to teach them—whether by reinforcement, by modeling, by understanding, or by all three. We now shift our focus to those who serve as society's first teachers: children's parents. Do different ways in which they rear their children produce differences in their children's behavior? If so, how lasting are the effects?

FEEDING AND TOILET TRAINING

To answer questions of this sort, one must first decide which particular aspects of the parents' behavior one wants to pinpoint. Until forty or so years ago, developmental psychologists interested in these general issues concerned themselves with aspects of child rearing that had been identified as crucial by Sigmund Freud and his followers, such as breast feeding and toilet training. Does breast feeding produce happier (or unhappier) infants? What about early weaning or early toilet training? As it turns out, the answer is that these child-rearing particulars have little or no effect on the long-term social, emotional, or intellectual development of the child (Orlansky, 1949; Zigler and Child, 1969; Zigler, Lamb, and Child, 1982).

DIFFERENT PARENTING STYLES

Other developmental psychologists have taken a different approach. Instead of concentrating on specific child-rearing practices, they have turned their attention to the general home atmosphere in which children are raised (Baumrind, 1967, 1971; Maccoby and Martin, 1983).

In a number of studies, parents were asked to describe how they dealt with their children and were also observed with them in various situations. Several patterns of child rearing emerged. One is the ***autocratic pattern*** in which the parents abide by strict standards about how children should and shouldn't speak and act, and attempt to mold their children's behavior accordingly. Such parents set down firm rules and greet any infractions with stern and sometimes severe punishment (sometimes including spanking). Autocratic parents do not believe it necessary to explain the rules to their children but expect their children to submit to them by virtue of parental authority: "It's because I say so, that's why."

At the opposite extreme is the ***permissive pattern*** in which children encounter few do's and don'ts. The parents try not to assert their authority, impose few restrictions and controls, tend not to have set schedules (for, say, bedtime or watching TV), and rarely use punishment. They also make few demands on their children—such as putting toys away, doing schoolwork, or helping with chores.

Autocratic parents brandish parental power; permissive parents abdicate it. But there is a third approach that is in some ways in between. It is called the authoritative-reciprocal pattern because the parents both exercise their power and accept the reciprocal obligation to respond to their children's points of view and their children's reasonable demands. Such parents set rules of conduct for their children and enforce the rules when they have to. They are fairly demanding, assign duties, and expect their children to behave in a mature fashion. They spend a good deal of time teaching their children how to perform appropriately, but also encourage independence and allow a good deal of verbal give and take. Unlike the permissive parents, they govern; but unlike the autocratic ones, they try to govern with the consent of the governed.

These parenting styles were formulated from observations of mostly middle-class children in the United States. But they may not fit all cultures. For example, in Chinese families children are expected to act very obediently, but such obedience is encouraged through parental warmth, trust, and close involvement rather than through bullying or emotionally distant rule enforcement (Chao, 1994).

Are there any differences among children raised in these different styles? One investigator observed U.S. preschoolers in various settings. She found that children raised autocratically were more withdrawn, lacked independence, and were more angry and defiant (especially the boys). Interestingly enough, children at the opposite end of the spectrum had similar characteristics. Thus, children whose parents were permissive were not particularly independent, and (if boys) they were more prone to anger. In addition, they seemed very immature and lacked social responsibility. In contrast, the children raised in the authoritative-reciprocal mode were more independent, competent, and socially responsible.

There is also evidence that the parental pattern children experienced when they were three or four is related to the way they behave in later years. When observed at the age of eight or nine, children whose parents had been judged to be either autocratic or permissive five years earlier seemed to be relatively low in intellectual self-reliance and originality. Once again, the children raised in the authoritative-reciprocal style fared best. They were more self-reliant when faced by intellectual challenges, strove for achievement, and were socially more self-confident and at ease (Baumrind, 1977). More recent studies have shown that the benefits of the authoritative-reciprocal style extend into the high-school years, where this parental pattern is associated with better grades as well as better social adjustment (Dornbusch et al., 1987; Steinberg, Elman, and Mounts, 1989).

But should we conclude that these various differences in behavior and school achievement are the result of parenting style? Again, we confront the same cause-and-effect ambiguity that we faced with attachment styles. It may be that autocratic parenting produces sullen, defiant children, but it is equally possible that parents faced with sullen, defiant children must resort to autocratic parenting as their only recourse. Similarly, parents of good-natured, peaceable children may find that permissive parenting works fine, while parents of independent, responsible children may develop more peerlike, reciprocal relations early on with their children. This theme has larger implications, as we will discuss next.

"They never pushed me. If I wanted to retrieve, shake hands, or roll over, it was entirely up to me." (© *The New Yorker Collection 1971 Frascino from Cartoonbank.com. All rights reserved.*)

THE CHILD'S EFFECT ON THE PARENTS

Our asking whether parenting styles are a cause or consequence of children's behavior reflects the increasing awareness that socialization is a two-way street. For children are more than a lump of psychological clay that is shaped by various social influences. Instead, they actively participate in their own rearing. Their own behavior affects that of their parents, whose behavior in turn

593

affects them. To the extent that this is true, the parents don't just socialize their children. They are also socialized by them (Bell, 1968; Bell and Harper, 1977).

One of the main reasons why socialization works in both directions is that—as many parents will testify—infants differ from each other from the day they are born. For example, we mentioned earlier that there are differences in temperament from one child to the next and that these may be genetically programmed (see Chapter 16) or the result of prenatal environment. Thus, one infant may be relatively placid and passive from the very start; another may be more active and assertive. These differences persist over at least the first two years of life and may last much beyond.

Parents respond quite differently to infants of different temperament. As a consequence, there will be a correlation between the parents' behavior and their children's, but this is not because the parents are shaping their children's behavior; instead, the opposite is the case (Thomas, Chess, and Birch, 1970; Osofsky and Danzger, 1974; Olweus, 1980; see Figure 14.6).

Temperament is one variable that has this effect; another is ability. For example, a child who learns to crawl, walk, speak, or read precociously will be treated differently than a child who does not. The more general point, however, is simply that children help to make their own environments. To the extent that children differ in either temperament or ability (or in any of several other ways), their parents, siblings, and eventually their peers cannot help but treat them differently (Scarr and McCartney, 1983).

These observations underscore the difficulties in interpreting correlations between children's personalities and the way they were reared. As an example, consider the effect of spanking. There is some evidence to suggest that parents who spank their children have children who tend to be especially aggressive (Feshbach, 1970; Parke and Slaby, 1983). If this relationship is genuine, how should we interpret it? One possibility is that their children are simply learning through imitation: "To get what you want, hit other people—Mommy and Daddy do." But there is an alternative. Some children may be more aggressive to begin with, and they are the ones who are more likely to be spanked.

We have posed this issue as an either-or choice: Either the child's personality determines the parent's behavior or the other way around. But, in truth, both of these effects may be operating simultaneously. The parents' behavior affects the children, and the children's behavior also affects the parents—a positive feedback loop in which all parties in the family act as both cause and effect. Thus, more aggressive children will probably be punished more severely, which will lead to more aggression in the child, which will then provoke yet further parental countermeasures. Conversely, parental warmth and firmness may lead to loving and respectful children, which may in turn encourage warmth and firmness.

THE DEVELOPMENT OF MORALITY

Initially, the social world of children is largely confined to the family, and their first lessons in social behavior are taught in the family context—pick up your toys, don't push your baby brother, use your fork not your fingers—all circumscribed commands that apply to a very narrow social setting. But their social sphere soon grows to include young peers: at home, in kindergarten or day care, still later in school. These peers become increasingly important, and their

Internalization *A four-year-old reproaches her doll: "Bad girl! Didn't I tell you to keep out of the dirt?" In imitating how her mother scolds her, the child is taking the first steps toward internalizing the mother's prohibitions. (Photograph by Suzanne Szasz)*

approval is then sought as eagerly as that of the parents (and by adolescence, often more eagerly).

As children's social universe expands, so does the set of the commands and admonitions they are expected to obey. While the first rules came directly from their parents, the rules later encountered come from people they have never met and probably never will. These are the rules of the society at large, and among the most important are those of moral conduct.

NOT DOING WRONG

All societies have prohibitions that its members must obey. In many cases, these prohibitions are enforced by a watchful authority, and so children rarely steal from the cookie jar when their parents are present, just as adults rarely steal automobiles when the police are watching. But civil societies require that their citizens resist temptation even when they are not being watched, and so one aim of socialization is to inculcate moral values that are abided by not only to avoid punishment, but also because people believe that they are right.

INTERNALIZATION AND SELF-PUNISHMENT

What leads to the internalization of right and wrong? Freud believed that internalization is produced by self-punishment in the form of guilt and anxiety. A child kicks her little brother, and her parents punish her. As a result, the forbidden act becomes associated with anxiety, and so to avoid this anxiety, the child avoids repeating the act. Indeed, to avoid the anxiety, the child must avoid even *wanting* to repeat the forbidden act. She has internalized the sanction, and so she is her own monitor and her own enforcer. It doesn't matter, therefore, that the external authorities that once punished her childhood transgressions have long stopped watching the cookie jar. Instead, the authorities now inhabit her mind, where she can no longer hide from them.

INTERNALIZATION AND MINIMAL SUFFICIENCY

If conscience is in this fashion a vestige of past punishments, one might predict that the nature or degree of internalization should be related to the manner of childrearing. Imagine, for example, a pair of parents who rely on powerful sanctions in disciplining their children—strong punishments or harsh withdrawals of privileges. In this case, the anxiety associated with these punishments should be strong and, on the account just sketched, should lead to a strongly established internal sense of right and wrong.

This prediction turns out not only to be false but exactly backward. A number of studies suggest instead that prohibitions are less effectively internalized by children whose parents relied primarily on power in its various forms to discipline their children. The children of power-asserting (autocratic) parents were more likely to cheat for a prize when they thought no one was looking, and they were less likely to feel guilt about their misdeeds or to confess them when confronted. In contrast, prohibitions are most internalized by children whose parents took them aside to explain just how they had misbehaved and why they should behave differently (Hoffman, 1970).

One proposal to explain these and other facts uses the *principle of minimal sufficiency.* This principle states that children will internalize a certain way of acting if there is just enough pressure to get them to behave in this new way, but

Minimal sufficiency *If the older sister's scolding is of minimal sufficiency, it may lead to internalization. (Photograph by Roberta Intrater)*

not enough so that they feel they were forced to do so. This principle seems to fit a number of experimental findings. An example is a study in which children were kept from playing with a particularly attractive toy. For some children, the prohibition was backed with a mild threat (e.g., "I will be a little bit annoyed with you"); for others, the threat was severe (e.g., "I will be very upset and very angry with you"). When later tested in a different situation in which they thought they were unobserved, the mildly threatened children resisted temptation more than the severely threatened ones. Punishment led to internalization, but only if the punishment was relatively mild.

The same principle may help account for some of the effects of child rearing we discussed above. Children of authoritative-reciprocal parents are more likely to internalize their parents' standards than are the children of autocratic or permissive parents. From the standpoint of the minimal sufficiency hypothesis, autocratic parents too coercively induce their children to behave appropriately, leaving their children outwardly compliant but inwardly unchanged (or even defiant). Permissive parents apply no force at all, so their children never change their behavior in the first place—they won't even comply outwardly, let alone internalize. But authoritative-reciprocal parents somehow manage to strike the proper balance. They are just forceful enough to get their children to change their behavior but mild enough so that the children come to believe that they behaved morally of their own free will (Lepper, 1983).★

DOING GOOD

So far our discussion of moral action has dealt with the inhibition of forbidden acts. But moral action pertains to do's no less than to don'ts, to doing good as well as to committing no evil. In a previous chapter, we considered the fact that humans are capable of positive moral actions that require personal sacrifice (see Chapter 10). We now ask how this capacity develops in children.

We are still far from an answer. A number of studies show that even very young children try to help and comfort others, and occasionally share with them (Rheingold, Hay, and West, 1976; Radke-Yarrow, Zahn-Waxler, and Chapman, 1983). The question is why. According to a Hobbesian view of human nature, such apparently altruistic acts are actually quite selfish. Parents and teachers constantly hector children about the importance of sharing, so perhaps children share their toys in order to obtain or maintain their approval. In the same fashion, perhaps children learn to share and to help others in order to preserve the esteem and support of their friends.

EMPATHY

But is such a cynical position justified? Some findings argue against the Hobbesian position that humans are by nature self-centered, indicating instead that we often show ***empathy***—a direct emotional response to another person's circumstances even when we stand to gain nothing from such a reaction. We see a stranger writhe in pain in a hospital bed, and we ourselves experience vicarious distress (Aronfreed, 1968; see also Chapter 12). This sort of empathic response is

---

★ This is reminiscent of the effects of forced compliance on attitudes. As we saw in Chapter 11, participants who are pressured into performing some action that runs counter to their own attitudes will tend to change their attitude if the pressure (the threat or the bribe) is relatively small, but will not change the attitude if the pressure is large (Festinger and Carlsmith, 1959; Aronson and Carlsmith, 1963).

quite common: It is found in most people and is triggered by a wide range of situations.

Simple precursors to these empathic reactions can even be found in very young infants, in the first two or three days of life. On hearing another newborn's cry, for example, one-day-old infants cry, too, and their hearts beat faster (Simner, 1971; Sagi and Hoffman, 1976). Such infants are less likely to cry in response to nonhuman noises of comparable loudness, including a computer simulation of another infant's crying.

What accounts for such empathic reactions at this tender age? According to one hypothesis, infants' cries are initially triggered by their own pain or discomfort, which makes them associate the sound of crying with the feeling of distress. Hearing another infant's cries would then remind them of distress, leading to empathic crying. Alternatively, some empathic reactions may be innate, a position that is by no means implausible given the facts on built-in alarm and distress reactions in many animals (see Chapter 10). As yet it is too early to choose between these two views. But whichever turns out to be correct, it is clear that some forerunner of what may later become a feeling for others is found at the very start of life.

FROM EMPATHIC DISTRESS TO UNSELFISH ACTION

But *empathy* just means feeling for another, not necessarily helping the other. Helping someone requires more than just feeling; it requires action and knowing how to help. And learning what constitutes help is also part of socialization.

Consider a two-year-old boy who sees an adult in pain—say, his mother has cut her finger. In all likelihood, the child will feel empathy and become distressed himself. But what will his empathic distress make him do? A number of anecdotes suggest that he will give his mother whatever he finds most comforting himself—for example, his teddy bear. While appreciating his kindly sentiments, the mother would probably have preferred a Band-Aid. But the child is as yet too young to take Mommy's perspective and doesn't realize that his mother's needs are not the same as his own (Hoffman, 1977a, 1979, 1984).★

As we develop, we become more able to discern what other people are likely to feel in a given situation and how to help if help is needed. But even that is not enough to ensure that we will act, because helping is only one means of allaying one's own empathic distress. A more direct but callous method is simply to look away. This often occurs in urban environments, where passers-by grow inured to sights of the homeless and impoverished. It can also occur in war and other situations wherein both adults and children "harden their hearts" to the suffering of others (see Chapter 12).

Thus, empathy does not guarantee altruism. In fact, there may be some circumstances in which empathic distress interferes with appropriate action. Effective soldiers must not experience the enemy's wounds, nor should dentists feel their patients' pain. This point was made in a study of nursing staff on a hospital ward for the severely ill. Those nurses who appeared to experience the greatest degree of empathy for their patients were the least effective. The reason was simple: They couldn't bear their patients' pain, and so they tried to have as little contact with them as possible (Stotland et al., 1978).

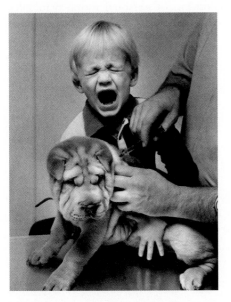

Feeling distress at the distress of another
The young boy cries as the veterinarian gives an injection to his puppy. (Photograph by Janet Kelly/Reading Eagle-Times, © Reading Eagle Company)

★ Some authors make a distinction between *empathic distress* in which the primary focus is on the unpleasant feelings the victim's plight arouses in us and *sympathetic distress* in which there is a desire to help the other person—not merely to relieve one's own empathic distress but to relieve the victim's. According to this view, empathic distress is a more primitive forerunner of sympathetic distress, which does not occur until children are about two years old (Hoffman, 1984).

MORAL REASONING

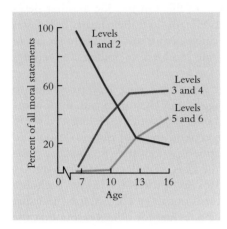

14.12   Level of moral reasoning as a function of age   *With increasing age, the level of moral reasoning changes. In this figure, the percent of all moral judgments made by children at various ages falls into one of three general categories defined by Kohlberg. At seven, virtually all moral judgments are in terms of avoiding punishment or gaining reward (Kohlberg's levels 1 and 2). At ten, about half the judgments are based on criteria of social approval and disapproval or of a rigid code of laws (Kohlberg's levels 3 and 4). From thirteen on, some of the children refer to more abstract rules—a generally agreed-upon social contract or a set of abstract ethical principles (Kohlberg's levels 5 and 6). (After Kohlberg, 1963)*

Up to now, our focus has been on the development of moral behavior. What about the development of moral thought? How do children develop a sense of right and wrong, and how does their conception of right and wrong change as they grow up?

KOHLBERG'S STAGES OF MORAL REASONING

An influential account of moral development was devised by Lawrence Kohlberg. His basic method was to confront participants with stories that pose moral dilemmas. An example is a story about a man whose wife will die unless treated with a very expensive drug, a drug that costs $2,000. The husband scraped together all the money he could, but it was not enough. He promised to pay the balance later, but the pharmacist still refused to give him the drug. In desperation, the husband broke into the pharmacy and stole the drug. The participants were asked whether the husband's act was right or wrong and why (Kohlberg, 1969).

Kohlberg analyzed the participants' answers and concluded that moral reasoning develops in a series of stages. The progression, roughly speaking, begins with a primitive morality guided by fear of punishment or desire for gain ("If you let your wife die, you'll get in trouble"). This stage is superseded by one in which right or wrong are defined by convention and by what people will say ("Your family will think you're inhuman if you don't help your wife"). Finally, moral development culminates with the internalization of personal moral principles ("If you didn't steal the drug, you wouldn't have lived up to your own standards of conscience").

People advance from stage to stage as they age, but only a few attain Kohlberg's highest level (Kurtines and Gewirtz, 1995). Considering that this final stage characterizes such individuals as Mahatma Gandhi and Mother Teresa, the failure of Kohlberg's participants (and no doubt, most of us) to attain it is probably not too surprising (Figure 14.12; Table 14.1).

TABLE 14.1 KOHLBERG'S STAGES OF MORAL REASONING	
Stage of moral reasoning	*Moral behavior is that which:*
Preconventional morality	
Level 1	Avoids punishment
Level 2	Gains reward
Conventional morality	
Level 3	Gains approval and avoids disapproval of others
Level 4	Is defined by rigid codes of "law and order"
Postconventional morality	
Level 5	Is defined by a "social contract" generally agreed upon for the public good
Level 6	Is based on abstract ethical principles that determine one's own moral code

SOURCE: Adapted from Kohlberg, 1969.

THE DEVELOPMENT OF MORALITY

Moral reasoning in men and women
The belief that men and women focus on different aspects of morality has ancient roots. A classical example is Sophocles's tragedy Antigone, *which revolves around the irreconcilable conflict between Antigone, who insists on burying a slain brother, and her uncle Creon, the king, who issues a decree forbidding anyone from doing so on pain of death. To Antigone, the ultimate moral obligation is to the family; to Creon, it is to the state and its laws. (From a 1982 production at the New York Shakespeare Festival, with F. Murray Abraham and Lisa Banes; photograph by Martha Swope)*

IS KOHLBERG'S FRAMEWORK UNIVERSAL?

There are many questions to be asked about Kohlberg's framework. For one thing, Kohlberg intended his conception to describe all people—both men and women, and people in all cultures. Does it?

Moral reasoning in men and women An influential discussion by Carol Gilligan suggests that it may not. In her view, men tend to see morality as a matter of justice, ultimately based on abstract, rational principles by which all individuals will end up being treated fairly. As one eleven-year-old boy put it in describing the moral dilemmas posed by Kohlberg: "It's sort of like a math problem with humans." Women, in contrast, see morality more in terms of compassion, human relationships, and special responsibilities to those with whom one is intimately connected (Gilligan, 1982, 1986).

Gilligan's view certainly does not imply that one gender is more or less moral than the other. In fact, studies of moral reasoning reveal no reliable sex differences on Kohlberg's test; of 108 studies, only 8 showed a superiority of males over females, while 4 or 5 went in the opposite direction (Brabeck, 1983; Walker, 1984, 1995; but see Baumrind, 1986, Walker, 1989).

Even with these demonstrations of gender equality, the possibility remains that men and women do emphasize different values in their moral reasoning—an abstract conception of justice on the one side, and principles of compassion and human responsibility on the other. That such a difference in emphases exists is suggested by various findings, including the fact that girls seem to place a greater value on going out of one's way to help other people and show more emotional empathy than do boys (Hoffman, 1977b). Just why women emphasize the perspective of care rather than that of abstract justice is still unsettled. The best guess is that it is a result of gendered patterns of socialization that stress different values for boys and girls (Hoffman, 1984).

Is either perspective preferable to the other? Virtually everyone agrees that the answer is no, that an appropriate conception of morality must include both justice and compassion. As Kohlberg points out, both of these orientations are built into the New Testament's Golden Rule. That rule is formulated in two ways. One insists on justice: "Do unto others as you would have them do unto you." The other urges care and compassion: "Love thy neighbor as thyself" (Kohlberg and Candee, 1984).

Moral reasoning in other cultures Moral perspectives and values may also differ from one cultural group to the next. A number of studies have shown that when members of less technological societies are asked to reason about moral dilemmas, they generally attain comparatively low scores on Kohlberg's scale. They justify acts on the basis of concrete issues, such as what neighbors will say or concern over one's wife, rather than on more abstract conceptions of justice and morality (Kohlberg, 1969; Tietjen and Walker, 1985; Walker and Moran, 1991). How should we interpret this evidence? Does it mean that the inhabitants of, say, a small Turkish village are less moral than the residents of Paris or New York City? A more plausible interpretation is that Turkish villagers spend their lives in a small community in continual face-to-face encounters with all the community's members. Under the circumstances, the most likely outcome is a more concrete morality that gives the greatest weight to care, responsibility, and loyalty (Simpson, 1974; Kaminsky, 1984).

Two points follow from this. First, our moral principles are, in important ways, shaped by the communities (and families) in which we live, emphasizing once again the importance of experience and socialization in shaping who we are. Second, Kohlberg's "higher" levels of morality may not reflect a "better" or "more sophisticated" morality. Instead, the moral principles guiding each individual need to be understood in the broader context of who that individual is and where he or she lives.

MORAL REASONING AND MORAL CONDUCT

Kohlberg's test focuses on moral reasoning—how do people think about (and talk about) a situation involving some moral dilemma? But we also care about moral behavior—whether they do the right thing at the right time. Can we predict how people will act if we know how they reason on the Kohlberg test?

To some extent, we can make such predictions. A number of studies have found that delinquents show lower scores on Kohlberg's tests than do nondelinquents of the same age and IQ. Other studies suggest that individuals at higher, principled levels of moral reasoning are less likely to cheat in an ambiguous situation and are more likely to remain intransigent in the face of other people's views.

But other results suggest that the relation between moral reasoning and moral conduct is far from perfect (Blasi, 1980; Rest, 1983; Gibbs et al., 1986): Often, people with high scores on Kohlberg's tests fail to do the right thing, whereas people with lower scores often behave in a fashion that seems moral and deeply honorable. Thus, Kohlberg's stages do seem to tell us more about what people will say than what they will do. It appears that being able to espouse moral principles doesn't mean abiding by them (for discussion, see Blasi, 1984; Kohlberg, Levine, and Hewer, 1984; Rest, 1984).

Moreover, Kohlberg's stages don't just indicate what an individual's moral principles are. They also signify that person's ability to describe these principles and to reason on the basis of them. Kohlberg has indeed shown that this ability increases with age and mental development. But this is not particularly unexpected. After all, the same holds for the ability to describe and reason about various other rules of mental life—for example, those that pertain to space, to number, and to language. Seen in this light, what is really surprising is that Kohlberg's stages correlate with behavior as well as they do. One reason why they don't correlate any better may be that they have less to do with the development of morality than with the development of something we might call "metamorality"—in analogy with metacognitive processes: the ability to reflect on moral rules, regardless of whether one lives by them (see Chapter 13).

THE DEVELOPMENT OF SEX AND GENDER

We have been considering the process of social development as one of growth and expansion, and socialization as the effort to fit the developing person to her culture. But like physical and cognitive development, social development has a flip side—that of *differentiation*. Even as she becomes socialized, the child becomes increasingly aware of the fact that people differ from each other and from herself. This awareness leads the child to a clearer conception of her own "self" and her own personality—what she is really like, in her own eyes and in others' eyes as well.

Seen in this light, social development goes hand in hand with the development of a sense of personal identity. And one of the most important elements of

Social learning of gender roles *(Photograph by David Turnley/© Corbis)*

Gender-role stereotypes *Once parents and others recognize an infant's sex, they will treat the child differently. Notice the difference in the cards sent to parents congratulating them on the birth of a son or daughter. (© Hallmark Cards, Inc.)*

this is **sexual identity**—the sense of being male or female and all that goes with it. Biologically, sexual identity seems simple enough. It may refer to **genetic sex**—possessing XX or XY chromosome pairs. Or it may refer to **morphological** (that is, structural) **sex**—the possession of a clitoris, vagina, and ovaries or penis, scrotum, and testes.

But what does sexual identity mean psychologically? It refers to three issues. One is **gender role**—a whole host of behavior patterns that a given culture deems appropriate for each sex. Fundamental to gender roles is a second issue, that of **gender identity**—our inner sense that we are male or female. A third issue is **sexual orientation**—the inclination toward a sexual partner of the same or opposite sex. Gender identity, gender role, and sexual orientation are among the most important determinants of a person's social existence.★ How do they come about?

GENDER ROLES

Gender roles pervade all of social life. The induction into one or the other of these roles begins with the first question typically asked when a human being enters the world: "Is it a boy or a girl?" As soon as the answer is supplied—which now, due to fetal ultrasound, may be months before birth—the process of gender typing begins, and the infant is ushered onto one of two quite different social trajectories. Many of the patterns of gender typing have probably changed in the wake of modern feminism, but powerful differences in child rearing persist. In our culture, infants are still dressed in either pink or blue; children play with either dolls or trucks.

And children can easily observe gender roles in the adult world, providing further clues about how boys and girls are "supposed" to act. While these gender roles are beginning to blur a bit, children are still likely to observe that adult women (like Mom) often work at home as unpaid housekeepers, cooks, and child-care workers, while adult men (like Dad) go off to a workplace and earn a paycheck. If both parents work outside the home, children may well observe that men and women generally have different kinds of jobs: Mom is unlikely to be a truck driver or Dad, a secretary. And children are also likely to realize that men's jobs are more highly valued by society than are women's—truck drivers generally earn more than secretaries do.

Children may observe, too, that society has different expectations about how the two sexes should act. Men are generally expected to be tougher and more aggressive, more restrained emotionally, and more interested in things than in people. In contrast, women are expected to be submissive, more emotionally expressive, and more interested in people than in things.

There is no doubt that these gender-role stereotypes shape the world that children perceive and also how others interact with them. For example, parents talk to their male and female children differently (Lamb, 1997). They also play with their children differently, with rough-and-tumble play far more common

★ It has become customary to distinguish between *sex* and *gender*. *Sex* generally refers to aspects of male-female differences that pertain to reproductive functions (for example, having ovaries versus testes, vagina versus penis) or genetically related factors (for example, differences in height or muscular strength). It is also used to designate erotic feelings, inclinations, or practices (for example, heterosexuality and homosexuality). *Gender*, on the other hand, refers to social or psychological aspects of being seen as a man or woman or regarding oneself to be so. Thus, it is one thing to be male and another to be a man; one thing to be female, another to be a woman (Stoller, 1968). A special note about the term *sex difference*: This term is used here strictly to designate male-female differences, with no presuppositions about whether they have biological or cultural origins.

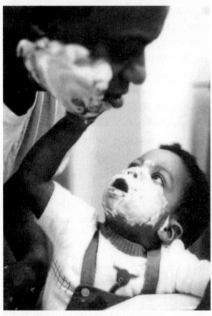

Male and female models *(Top: photograph by Suzanne Szasz. Bottom: photograph by Burk Uzzle/Woodfin Camp)*

with boys (O'Brien and Nagle, 1987). This difference in styles of play was demonstrated in a study in which mothers of young infants were asked to participate in an experiment on how children play. They were then introduced to a six-month-old baby, little "Joey" or "Janie," and asked to play with him or her for a few minutes. In fact, the six-month-old was a baby actor who was dressed up as a boy or girl regardless of the child's actual sex. The results showed that the participants' behavior depended on whether they thought they were playing with "Joey" or "Janie." To "Joey" they offered toys such as a hammer or a rattle, while "Janie" was invariably given a doll. In addition, the participants physically touched and handled "Joey" and "Janie" differently. In dealing with "Joey," they often bounced "him" about, thus stimulating the whole body. In contrast, their response to "Janie" was gentler and less vigorous (Smith and Lloyd, 1978).

Children soon behave as adults expect them to. Starting at about age one-and-a-half, they begin to show gender-typed differences. By three years of age, they prefer different toys and play mainly with peers of their own sex (Huston, 1983). As they grow older, they learn more about male and female stereotypes. In one study, both male and female children had to decide whether certain characteristics were more likely in a man or a woman. Over 90 percent of a group of U.S. eleven-year-olds thought that the adjectives weak, emotional, appreciative, gentle, soft-hearted, affected, talkative, fickle, and mild probably described a woman, while the adjectives strong, aggressive, disorderly, cruel, coarse, adventurous, independent, ambitious, and dominant probably described a man. Boys and girls endorsed just about the same gender-role stereotypes (Best et al., 1977).

Many of these stereotypes are reinforced by parents and peers. When young children play with toys that are deemed inappropriate—as when a boy plays with a dollhouse, or a girl with a toy electric drill—their parents are likely to express disapproval (Fagot, 1995). This is especially so for fathers, who sternly object to any such behaviors in their sons. By and large, girls are allowed more latitude in such matters. A girl can be a "tomboy" and get away with it; a boy who is a "sissy" is laughed at or taunted (Langlois and Downs, 1980).

SEX DIFFERENCES IN GENDER ROLES

What accounts for the difference in current gender roles? We will consider both constitutional and social factors in an attempt to understand how biology and society conspire to make boys into men and girls into women.

It's self-evident that gender roles are influenced by anatomical and physiological differences. Some of these differences pertain in obvious ways to reproduction, but there are also differences between the sexes in average size, strength, and physical endurance. On many dimensions, girls mature more quickly than boys, as evidenced by a host of measures that includes speaking, toilet training, developing fine motor skills (such as drawing), getting permanent teeth, reaching puberty, and attaining one's adult body size; boys excel only in basic activity level and at skills requiring power and force (Martin et al., 1984; Eaton and Yu, 1989; Tanner, 1990). There are also certain *sexually dimorphic* areas of the brain—that is, areas that reliably differ in men and women (Allen et al., 1989). These areas, many of which lie in and around the hypothalamus, seem involved in sexual behavior and, as we shall see, sexual orientation.

But what about psychological differences? There is no doubt that such differences do exist and that some of them fit cultural stereotypes. The question is whether any of these differences—in physical aggression, independence, emotional expressiveness, social sensitivity, and so on—are biologically programmed or whether, instead, these differences are merely the consequence of socially transmitted cultural norms.

Before proceeding, two cautions: The first is that any psychological difference between the sexes is one of averages. The average three-year-old girl seems to be more dependent than her male counterpart; she is more likely to ask for help, to cling, and to seek affection (Emmerich, 1966). But this doesn't mean that this generalization applies to every boy and girl, because there are certainly many three-year-old girls who are less dependent, or more physically aggressive, than many three-year-old boys. Thus, we must be careful not to overinterpret the evidence. There is variability within virtually any group, and so findings that describe an entire group should not be used to characterize each individual within the group.

The second caution is about interpretation. No trait—whether an individual's hair color or his level of physical aggression—is shaped directly and entirely by biology. Biology and environment interact in rich and complex ways, so that traits that are genetically programmed can often be altered by environmental variation, and traits apparently shaped by culture often depend on some sort of biological support. Hand in hand with this, if we find that a trait is shaped by biology, this does not mean that the trait is fixed and immutable. After all, the color of one's hair is strongly governed by genetic factors, but can also be altered by exposure to the sun or by appropriately chosen chemicals. The same is true for almost any other trait one can name. (We return to this issue in Chapter 15.)

AGGRESSION

If there is one sex difference that seems biologically predisposed, it is **physical aggression.** Males are on average more active and physically more assertive than females. This difference is apparent from the very start; male infants are more irritable and physically active than female infants, and mothers even report that their boys were more active than their girls *in utero.* At age two or three, boys are much more likely to engage in rough-and-tumble play and mock fighting than are girls (a difference also seen in apes and monkeys; see Figure 14.13). By four or five, they are more ready to exchange insults and to greet aggression with bodily retaliation than are girls (Legault and Strayer, 1990; Crick and Grotpeter, 1995).

The sex difference in physical aggression continues into adulthood. Acts of violence are relatively rare among both sexes, but they are much more common among men than women. Adolescent males are arrested for violent crimes five times more often than are adolescent females (Johnson, 1979). A similar pattern holds in such widely different cultural settings as Ethiopia, India, Kenya, Mexico, Okinawa, and Switzerland (Maccoby and Jacklin, 1974, 1980; Whiting and Whiting, 1975; Parke and Slaby, 1983).

But how should we think about the sex difference in physical aggression? This difference is found early in life, is observed in many different cultures, and is also seen in our primate relatives. All of this suggests a biological predisposition—all the more so given that aggressiveness is enhanced by the administration of male sex hormones (see Chapter 10).

Even if boys are constitutionally predisposed toward physical aggression, cultural influences seem to maintain and even magnify it. Boys are encouraged to be tough and are given toy swords and guns, while girls are expected to be well behaved and receive cooking sets and Barbie dolls. Parents will generally allow and even foster a degree of physical aggressiveness in a boy that they would never countenance in a girl. Thus, fathers often encourage their sons to fight back when another boy attacks them (Sears, Maccoby, and Levin, 1957).

This process continues in adolescence, where aggressive behavior in boys is tolerated or indulgently winked at, while the same behavior in girls is discour-

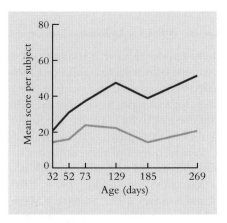

14.13   The development of rough-and-tumble play in male and female rhesus monkeys *Roughhouse play in two male and two female rhesus monkeys during the first year of life. The scores are based on both frequency and vigor of this activity, in which monkeys wrestle, roll, or sham bite—all presumably in play, since no one ever gets hurt. Roughhouse play is considerably more pronounced in males (dark red) than in females (blue), a difference that increases during the first year of life. (After Harlow, 1962)*

aged in favor of a more sociable, approval-seeking pattern. The scales are tipped still further by the way in which the two sexes are usually portrayed by the media, with strong, silent heroes and charming, adoring heroines. Thus, while males and females may start life with different biological dispositions toward physical aggression, by the time they are adults society has exaggerated this initial difference appreciably (Parke and Slaby, 1983).

We must repeat that these differences all involve *physical* aggression. This is not because girls are less aggressive overall; rather, it is because girls are less likely to be aggressive in physical ways. They tend to engage, instead, in **relational aggression,** which is focused on altering social alliances. Relational aggression can take many forms—disdainfully pretending not to know another person, befriending someone else as revenge against another, contemptuously excluding someone from one's group ("I'm not your friend"), or trying to harm another's friendships ("Kristen thinks you're dumb") (Feshbach, 1969; Lagerspetz, Bjorkquist, and Peltoneu, 1988; Crick and Grotpeter, 1995; Crick, Casas, and Mosher, 1997; Galen and Underwood, 1997; but see Tomada and Schneider, 1997).

PATTERNS OF INTELLECTUAL APTITUDES

There is another psychological difference between the sexes that is often said to be based on biological givens—a different pattern of intellectual abilities. Overall, there seems to be no intelligence difference between men and women: Studies comparing males' and females' IQ scores, for example, have reported only small differences, and the direction of the differences (which sex has the higher scores) has varied from study to study (Held et al., 1993; Lynn, 1994). But the sexes do differ on more specific tests. On average, boys and men do better on some tests of spatial and mathematical ability (Figure 14.14), whereas girls and women do better on many verbal tasks (Maccoby and Jacklin, 1974, 1980; Hines, 1990; Halpern, 1992, 1997; Masters and Sanders, 1993; Stanley, 1993)—although the size of the difference on verbal tasks is contested and, according to some authors, has significantly decreased (Hyde and Linn, 1988; Halpern, 1992).

This sex difference can also be documented in school performance, especially if we focus on just those children who do particularly well or particularly poorly. For example, a large-scale, thirty-two-year retrospective study looked at children who had scored in the top 10 percent on various tests and found that three times as many boys as girls scored in the top 10 percent of math (and science) tests but twice as many girls as boys excelled on writing tests (Hedges and Nowell, 1995).

The difference between boys' and girls' school performance in mathematics is especially striking, and a number of authors believe that this difference is ultimately produced by a difference in certain spatial abilities. An example is the ability to visualize objects in space. This ability is often assessed by asking participants to imagine a three-dimensional object rotated to a new position and then obtaining their judgments about the object's shape. (See Chapter 8 for further discussion of this mental rotation task.) This is a task on which men reliably outperform women, and since a number of branches of mathematics seem to rely on such visualization, it does not seem far-fetched to assume that the sex difference in this ability underlies those in quantitative aptitude and achievement (Burnett, Lane, and Dratt, 1979; Hunt, 1985a; Halpern, 1992). But women shouldn't be counted out in the visuospatial realm either, because on certain tasks that require memory for shapes and perceptual speed (for example, quickly matching shapes to numbers), women excel reliably (Kolb and Whishaw, 1996).

What accounts for these sex differences in cognitive aptitudes? In part, they may simply reflect a difference in the way boys and girls are brought up. Boys are often encouraged to pursue certain paths and girls others, so it would be no surprise if members of each sex ended up more skilled in the kinds of tasks for

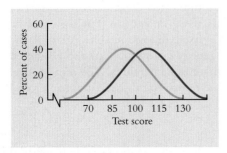

14.14   Sex differences in spatial ability
Results on a spatial-mathematical test, which included questions such as "How many times between three and four o'clock do the hands of a clock make a straight line?" The curve plots the percentage of participants who receive a particular score (with men in dark red and women in blue). As the curve shows, the men perform better than the women, though the two curves overlap considerably. (Data from Very, 1967, with test scores adjusted by a method called "normalization")

which they had more experience or received special encouragement. But various lines of evidence suggest that this may only be part of the story. An example is a study of SAT scores in 40,000 adolescents. The investigators found the usual sex differences on spatial and mathematical tasks, even when they limited their comparison to boys and girls who had taken the exact same high-school math courses and had expressed the same degree of interest in mathematics (Benbow and Stanley, 1983; Benbow, 1988).

Other investigators have searched for a biological basis for the male-female differences in cognitive performance and have generally focused on the differences in the brains of males and females. Indeed, post-mortem studies of individuals with aphasia and studies of conscious participants using both PET scans and functional MRI (Chapter 2) have revealed considerable differences between the brains of males and females, including regions that play an essential role when participants are engaged in verbal and visuospatial tasks (Shaywitz et al., 1995; Kolb and Whishaw, 1996). What accounts for these differences? Various hypotheses have been advanced, including direct genetic programming (McGee, 1979) and the quicker maturation of females' brains (Waber, 1977, 1979; Boles, 1980; Kolb and Whishaw, 1996).

Testosterone and spatial abilities   One current hypothesis about the sex difference in visuospatial abilities focuses on the influence of testosterone. Males who produce abnormally low levels of testosterone show impairments in visuospatial abilities (Hier and Crowley, 1982), while older males (aged 60–75), whose testosterone levels fall with age, show dramatic improvements in spatial cognition after receiving testosterone supplements (Janowsky, Oviatt, and Orwoll, 1994). And girls born with adrenal gland tumors that secrete abnormally high levels of testosterone show enhanced spatial abilities as well (Resnick et al., 1986).

How might testosterone influence spatial abilities? Animal studies indicate that sex hormones, especially testosterone—prenatally and throughout life—have a profound effect on the development and functioning of the hippocampus, an area of the "old cortex" associated with spatial memory in birds and mammals (see Chapters 2 and 4); (Sherry, Jacobs, and Gaulin, 1992; Maren, De Oca, and Fanselow, 1994; Weekes, 1994; Petersen and Sherry, 1996; McEwen et al., 1997).

But why might testosterone have come to affect the hippocampus? An evolutionary perspective may help here: Males of many species forage farther from home than do females, who must remain close to the nest. Therefore, the males are the ones who need the greater navigational skills—lest they leave home and not be able to find their way back! It makes some sense, therefore, that males would develop more neural machinery—that is, a bigger hippocampus—to support navigation. One way to ensure this development in males is to link hippocampal development to testosterone—just the pattern that seems to occur (Sherry et al., 1992).

Culture and cognitive abilities   Just as with physical aggression, however, we must not overstate the power of these biological effects. As one consideration, there is obviously enormous variability from one male to the next and from one female to the next. Therefore, the sexes may differ *on average,* but it is relatively easy to find males with verbal skills greater than those possessed by many females and to find females with spatial skills much better than those of most males.

In addition, there is no question that culture also plays a large role in creating and sustaining these cognitive differences. In American society, for example, girls are generally expected to do better in English than in math. This belief is shared by teachers, parents, and the pupils themselves, and all conspire to make it come

Social factors and sex differences   *Social effects augment constitutional differences. (Photograph © Yvonne Hemsey, The Gamma Liaison Network)*

true. Thus, even those girls who could do well on spatial and mathematical tests may nonetheless fail—perhaps because they receive no encouragement in mathematics or perhaps because they are told directly that they should spend their efforts elsewhere.

These societal influences can take many forms, but, crucially, these influences include expectations that are often shared by the students themselves. They often endorse the widespread sentiment that math-related careers are a male province and that the women who succeed in them are somehow unfeminine. One review quotes a female mathematics professor's description of this stereotype:

> Many people on hearing the words "female mathematician" conjure up an image of a six-foot, gray-haired, tweed-suited, oxford-clad woman. This image, of course, doesn't attract the young woman who is continually bombarded with messages, both direct and indirect, to be beautiful, "feminine" and catch a man. (Quoted in Halpern, 1992, p. 216)

A four-year-old and her doll Is she trying to conform to her gender identity or simply acting like a parent? (Photograph by Erika Stone)

GENDER IDENTITY

In discussing some of the obvious differences in boys' and girls' gender roles, we have assumed that children all have a fixed gender identity—that they *know* they're boys or girls and that their parents, peers, doctors, and teachers all share this knowledge. Indeed, by about the age of three, most children can report accurately who is male and who is female, and they also know in which category they themselves belong (Fagot, Leinbach, and Hagen, 1986). But initially their classifications are somewhat flexible. For example, when shown a picture of a girl, even four-year-olds say that she could be a boy if she wanted to or if she wore a boy's haircut or wore a boy's clothes (Marcus and Overton, 1978; and see Kohlberg, 1966).

Nor is anatomy taken into account. For example, when presented with dolls that have either male or female genitals and also varying hair length and asked to tell which are the boys and which the girls, preschoolers generally decide on the basis of hair length (McConaghy, 1979; but see Bem, 1989). It takes children until the age of five or so to achieve the concept of **gender constancy**—the recognition that being male or female is irrevocable and not dependent upon what one wears or does.

But how does gender identity come about? Some investigators believe that the knowledge that one is male or female is fundamental and emerges from the basic wiring of the child's nervous system. Other investigators suggest that the caretakers' knowledge that a child is male or female leads them to socialize the child as one or the other, with the child inferring his or her own gender identity from how he or she is treated. As yet, there is no clear answer.

INTERSEXUALITY AND SEX REASSIGNMENT

Of course, all this assumes that the child *is* actually either a boy or a girl. The situation isn't so simple for **intersexuals,** children who are not clearly either. Studies of these individuals have provided great insights about the influence of biology and culture on gender identity and gender roles.

Intersexuality has various causes. Some cases result from sex chromosomes that depart from the usual XX or XY complements. Others are due to drugs taken during pregnancy or specific hormonal or genetic disorders. When all causes are considered, one or two of every one hundred births may be intersexed (Fausto-Sterling, 1993).

Intersexuality also varies considerably in its manifestations. One kind of intersexuality is *true hermaphroditism,* which occurs when an individual has functioning reproductive tissue from both sexes, such as a testicle on one side and an ovary on the other (Simpson, 1976).

In contrast with true hermaphroditism is *pseudohermaphroditism.* Individuals born with this disorder (perhaps one in two thousand births) have external genitals, and sometimes internal organs, that are anatomically ambiguous—that is, not clearly male or female (Fausto-Sterling, 1993).

Ambiguous genitalia and sex reassignment   In cases of intersexuality, parents and physicians sometimes decide to use plastic surgery to make the external genitalia unambiguous and then give the child a lengthy course of hormone therapy, often with the view that an ambiguously sexed child will become a socially dysfunctional adult. The child's sex is then officially reassigned both in medical records and legal documents, and the child is reared accordingly.

Because of the difficulty of constructing functioning male organs, and the core belief that no male could ever grow up well adjusted without a normal penis, the surgical rule for most cases has been "when in doubt, make it female." The end result in these cases is a person who looks female and can participate sexually as a female (the remnant of the penis becomes the clitoris, and the scrotum is fashioned to make a vagina). But since the newly constructed female has had a great deal of sensitive sexual tissue removed, she is likely to have reduced sexual feeling; and since she lacks ovaries and a uterus, she cannot have children. These facts make it easy to understand why some intersexed individuals regard this outcome as a very bad bargain, considering the reassignment to be mutilation rather than treatment (Diamond, 1997).

The effects of reassignment   It is also unclear how well surgical reassignment works to make the person identify with the new sex. Early studies were optimistic and suggested that if the reassignment occurred early enough—according to some investigators, the upper limit was eighteen months, for others, three or four years—the child would adjust well, becoming a he or a she, in part because of other people's expectations (Money and Ehrhardt, 1972).

One influential case study involved "John," born in 1963 as a genetic XY male with normal genitals, but whose penis was burned beyond repair during minor surgery. The doctors urged the parents to allow sex reassignment, and at the age of seventeen months, John had "corrective" surgery. John became "Joan," and Joan's parents, doctors, and teachers all accepted the child as a girl, giving her a life of dolls, dresses, and "girl things." The first assessment of Joan's case considered the reassignment a success (Money and Ehrhardt, 1972), and the story was widely reported in texts and the mass media as showing the power of socialization over biology in determining gender identity and gender roles.

But Joan's life was far from happy. Her mother reports that from the start Joan tore off her dresses, preferred climbing trees to playing house, and, when her brother refused to share his toys, saved her allowance to buy her own toy truck. As she neared puberty, Joan was given the female sex hormone estrogen to help her appear more feminine, but she nonetheless came to believe that she was a boy and kept trying to urinate standing up. By age fourteen, Joan was depressed and suicidal. She finally revealed her suspicions to her endocrinologist, and—without being apprised of her unique history—she agreed to plastic surgery to construct a penis, along with treatments of male hormones. Only after the surgery did her (now his) father finally reveal—to an upset and bewildered John—the original accident and surgery.

John became an attractive male, interested romantically in women, and despite a penis that was only partly functional, he married at the age of twenty-five and adopted his wife's children from her previous marriage. Today, he is happy overall and reasonably well adjusted but bitter about what happened to him and concerned that no one else be treated similarly (Diamond and Sigmundson, 1997).

How typical is John/Joan's case? For one thing, John's fetal development had been normal—his brain and body had been fully masculinized during development. So in some respects the John/Joan case is quite atypical: Those reassigned are generally pseudohermaphrodites, not those who developed normally. Since comprehensive follow-up studies of reassignment are generally lacking, however, evaluating how often sex reassignment works and what factors lead to successful outcomes is extremely difficult.

But one thing John/Joan's case makes clear is that constitutional factors play a crucial role. Additional evidence on this point comes from a series of studies of girls who were exposed as fetuses to an abnormally high level of androgens, which tends to masculinize both their brains and their bodies. At birth, many of these girls were pseudohermaphrodites, with ambiguous external genitals. After appropriate plastic surgery they were raised as females. But follow-up studies showed that the excess androgen during pregnancy had some long-term psychological effects. When compared to a control group, the androgenized girls were much more likely to be tomboys during childhood: They chose trucks over dolls, loved to participate in energetic team sports, preferred slacks to dresses, and had little interest in jewelry or perfume. As adolescents, they looked forward to a future in which marriage and maternity were subordinated to a career (Money and Ehrhardt, 1972; Money, 1980; Ehrhardt, 1984; Hines and Kaufmann, 1996). They also had higher rates of lesbianism and lesbian sexual fantasies (Dittmann, Kappes, and Kappes, 1992).

The guevedoces syndrome: A critical period for gender identity?   While it is clear that sex reassignment is a procedure with mixed results, until fairly recently, most practitioners agreed that to have any chance of success the reassignment had to occur early in the child's life. Failure was certain, they argued, if it occurred after the child was four or five years old. This in turn led to the belief that there is a critical period for the establishment of gender identity (e.g., Money and Ehrhardt, 1972).

This view has been called into question by the discovery of a number of male children with a rare genetic disorder, called ***guevedoces syndrome,*** in three rural villages in the Dominican Republic. In the fetal stage, these children are relatively insensitive to many of the effects of androgens. As a result, their external genitals at birth look much like a female's, and so they often are thought to be girls and raised as such. But puberty, with its sudden upsurge in male hormone levels, brings a dramatic change. The misidentified "girls" develop male genitals, their voices deepen, and their torsos become muscular (although they never develop beards).

If sex reassignment after age four or five is as difficult as it has been said to be, the result in these cases—with reassignment at puberty (around age eleven or twelve)—ought to be a psychological catastrophe. But in fact, the majority of these adolescents come to adopt their new male identity with relatively little difficulty. They change their name and take up male occupations. While they are initially anxious about sex, they ultimately seem to adjust and form normal relationships. Thus, fifteen out of sixteen men with this syndrome eventually married or lived in common-law relationships (Imperato-McGinley et al., 1974, 1979).

It's hard to know how this surprising finding should be interpreted. It turns out that those with this syndrome lack a hormone responsible for masculinizing the body, but not the hormones for masculinizing the brain—that is, developing a brain with the structures and functions common to males. It also seems pertinent that these changes are accepted by the community and are common enough so that the villagers have coined a name for individuals with this condition: *guevedoces* (which, roughly translated means "testes at age twelve"). Such factors set these cases apart from the more common cases of surgical reassignment of sex among pseudohermaphrodites, so we should refrain from drawing conclusions too quickly about one based on the other. Nonetheless, the *guevedoces* syndrome is an argument against the ironclad view that gender identity cannot change after the age of five.

SEXUAL ORIENTATION

The majority of men and women are **heterosexual;** they exclusively seek a partner of the opposite sex. But for a significant minority, the sexual orientation is otherwise. Some of these individuals experience erotic and romantic feelings exclusively toward members of their own sex; such people are **homosexual.** Others experience such feelings for both their own and the opposite sex; such people are **bisexual.**

Importantly, though, virtually all gay and bisexual men think of themselves as men and are so regarded by others; the analogous point holds for lesbians (Marmor, 1975).★ Their gender identity is thus not in question. This clearly illustrates the fact that sexual orientation, gender identity, and gender role are in principle independent.

THE PREVALENCE OF HETEROSEXUALITY AND HOMOSEXUALITY

Perhaps the most comprehensive study of sexual patterns among Americans was an anonymous survey conducted in the 1940s by a research team led by biologist Alfred Kinsey. Kinsey and his associates found that 4 percent of American men are exclusively homosexual during their lifetime (Kinsey, Pomeroy, and Martin, 1948). The comparable prevalence of exclusive homosexuality among women seems to be lower—about 2 percent (Kinsey et al., 1953).

A substantially larger group is predominantly homosexual but has also had some heterosexual experience. According to Kinsey's data, this category includes about 13 percent of American men and 7 percent of women.

Some believe that these estimates are too high, arguing that Kinsey's criteria for homosexual experience were not sufficiently stringent and his survey sample not adequately representative (Reisman and Eichel, 1990; Hamer et al., 1993a, b). But more recent surveys of both men and women basically confirm Kinsey's estimates, both in the United States and in other Western cultures (e.g., ACSF Investigators, 1992; Johnson et al., 1992). These studies also indicate that despite the sexual revolution of the 1960s and the increasing social acceptance of gays and lesbians, the prevalence of homosexuality has remained about the same since Kinsey's first survey roughly fifty years ago (Pillard, 1996).

★ A small percentage of individuals forms the exception to this rule. Transsexuals are genetically and physiologically entirely male or female but believe that they were born the wrong sex; complete surgical and hormonal sex reassignment is the usual treatment. Transsexuals should not be confused with transvestites, individuals who enjoy dressing like the opposite sex. Transvestites are typically heterosexual males.

Homosexual behavior in antiquity
Among the ancient Greeks homosexual relations between men were widely practiced and accepted, as the mural from the Tomb of the Diver (c. 480 B.C.–470 B.C.), found in what was a Greek settlement in southern Italy, suggests. (Courtesy of National Archaeological Museum, Paestum, Italy)

Thus, a substantial number of men and women are erotically and romantically oriented toward partners of their own sex. And this orientation persists despite the fact that, while our society is changing, the combined forces of parenting, peers, religion, and the mass media still typically endorse heterosexuality and stigmatize homosexuality. We should mention, however, that this cultural taboo against homosexual behavior is by no means universal. According to one cross-cultural survey, two-thirds of the world's societies regard homosexuality as normal and acceptable, at least for some people or for some age groups (Ford and Beach, 1951). In certain historical periods, the practice was glorified and extolled, as in classical Greece where Pericles, the great Athenian statesman, was regarded as rather odd because he was not attracted to beautiful boys.

It is also important to realize that much of the sexual behavior of gays and lesbians revolves around feelings of romance and love just as does that of heterosexual people. In other words, dating and love and (often) long-lasting relationships occur within the homosexual community in a manner virtually identical to that observed in the heterosexual community. The only difference, of course, is the obvious one—the gender of the romantic "other." These facts plainly contradict the widely held belief that a homosexual orientation leads only to brief, romantically shallow, and furtive liaisons, especially among gay men. While this may be true for some subgroups, it does not describe the majority of the gay and lesbian population. To the contrary, many gays and lesbians form lasting bonds and become couples, despite the fact that our culture rarely offers any recognized route for such relationships (Mattison and McWhirter, 1987; Green and Clunis, 1988).

BISEXUALITY: DUAL ATTRACTION

The statistics from Kinsey's study cited above focused exclusively on those whose sexual orientation was solely toward the same sex or toward the opposite sex. But one need not be categorically heterosexual or homosexual. As Kinsey and others discovered, a sizable number of people do not fit easily or exclusively into either of these two categories. Many individuals are predominantly but not exclusively homosexual; likewise, some individuals are predominantly but not exclusively heterosexual. Exceptions to the either/or pattern are people with a bisexual orientation.

Bisexuality has many forms, and for that reason an exact definition is elusive (Hansen and Evans, 1985). Some bisexuals actively seek out romantic and sexual relationships with members of both sexes. Others are romantically attracted to one sex but sexually attracted to the other. Still others live mostly heterosexual lives—and may identify themselves as heterosexual, or "straight,"—but seek out occasional, sometimes furtive, same-sex contacts. Even so, bisexuals are probably not more promiscuous than heterosexuals, and many recognize their attractions to both sexes but choose to live monogamously with either same-sex or opposite-sex partners. But overall, bisexuals attest that, in finding and building a relationship, whether a prospective partner is male or female doesn't have the overriding importance it does for either heterosexual or homosexual individuals.

How many people are bisexual? Good estimates are scarce, not only because of the ambiguity of the term, but also because bisexuals are especially reluctant to disclose their orientation (Weinberg, Williams, and Pryor, 1994). Additionally, with few exceptions (which we note below), research on sexual orientation has lumped bisexual with homosexual individuals (Chung and Katayama, 1996). Generally, however, investigators agree that bisexuality is probably rarer than homosexuality, and more common in women than in men (Hamer, 1994; Pattatucci and Hamer, 1995; Pillard, 1996).

DETERMINANTS OF SEXUAL ORIENTATION: ENVIRONMENTAL FACTORS?

Experience in early life   Some of the attempts to explain what causes homosexuality focus on the role of early childhood experience. According to Freud, for example, homosexuality for many men is a response to fears aroused during the Oedipal conflict. The little boy is too terrified to compete with his father for his mother's affections, and his terror generalizes to other women. He, therefore, tries to ingratiate himself with his father by identifying with the mother instead (after all, Father loves her).

There is very little evidence to support Freud's theory. In one study, about 1,000 gays and lesbians provided various items of information about their life histories. There was some difference in how gay people and heterosexuals viewed their parents. Compared to heterosexual controls, gay people had a less satisfactory relationship with their parents, especially with those of their own sex. But on closer analysis, it turned out that these familial relationships did not have much of an effect on the development of sexual orientation. If gay men don't get along too well with their fathers (although in fact many of them do), this is probably because the fathers can't accept various aspects of their sons' sexual orientation. If so, the unsatisfactory father-son relationship is a result of the son's sexual orientation, not its cause. Something of the same sort applies to the mother-daughter relationship in lesbians. Such findings give little support to the psychoanalytic framework with its emphasis on the crucial role of the early family constellation (Bell, Weinberg, and Hammersmith, 1981).

Experience in later childhood or adolescence   Further evidence undermines the widely held stereotype that homosexuality is produced when a boy is "seduced" by an older man or a girl by an older woman. The main predictor of eventual homosexuality is the way people *felt* about sexuality in childhood and early adolescence rather than what they *did*. Homosexual feelings and erotic fantasies usually preceded any actual homosexual encounters people might have had (Bell, Weinberg, and Hammersmith, 1981). Many individuals report that "I've been that way all my life" (Saghir and Robins, 1973), and just as future heterosexuals imagine star-struck romances with members of the opposite sex, so do those who will become homosexual imagine same-sex love and romance. Same-sex desires and the corresponding fantasies usually emerge before biological puberty, sometimes as early as age three or four (Green 1979; Zuger, 1984; Hamer et al., 1993).

But perhaps the most decisive evidence against the idea that early sexual experience determines sexual orientation comes from other cultures. In a number of cultures, there are socially prescribed periods of homosexual behavior, usually between boys and older men, which begin in childhood and last through adolescence. Despite this intensive homosexual experience, which occurs amid the boys' puberty and sexual awakening, at adulthood most of the young men show the expected heterosexual orientation and pursue marriage and fatherhood (Stoller and Herdt, 1985; Herdt, 1990).★

★ One recent theory about early environment and sexual orientation relies on the principle of *heterogamy,* that is, the idea that opposites attract. In this theory, males typically become romantically and sexually attracted to females, and females to males, because they seek union with their gender opposites (Bell, 1983). According to this view, early childhood experiences with same-sex peers build a sense of familiarity with one's own gender, and a distant, apprehensive fascination with the opposite sex. At puberty, this apprehension becomes eroticized as lust, and "exotic" becomes "erotic" (Bem, 1996). Homosexuality should be more likely, then, among boys who have typically female interests and with girls who have typically male interests. This view receives some support from findings

DETERMINANTS OF SEXUAL ORIENTATION: BIOLOGICAL FACTORS?

None of the theories we have looked at so far—all emphasizing childhood experience—seems to provide the answer to what determines sexual orientation. As an alternative, a number of investigators have looked to biology.

Genetics and inheritance patterns   One line of research using twin studies considers genetic dispositions: Recall that identical twins share all their DNA, while fraternal twins (like other siblings) share only half their genetic material. Given this information, it is striking that, if a man's identical twin is gay, then the chances that he will also be gay are 52 percent; if the gay twin is fraternal, the chances drop to 22 percent (Bailey and Pillard, 1991). Likewise, a woman's chance of having a homosexual orientation is 48 percent if she has a lesbian identical twin, whereas if her gay twin is fraternal, the chances drop to 16 percent (Bailey et al., 1993). Clearly, then, the greater the similarity in genetic makeup, the greater the likelihood of having the same sexual orientation. The obvious implication is that one's genotype carries a predisposition toward homosexuality.

Further genetic evidence comes from a team of researchers led by geneticist Dean Hamer (Hamer et al., 1993). They have obtained results suggesting that the homosexual orientation in males might largely be attributed to a gene or genes in a specific area of the X chromosome. These results are preliminary, but even if they hold up, the question remains of just what the X-linked genes do to produce the homosexual orientation. One possibility is that these genes code for an individual's hormonal makeup, and it is this hormonal pattern that governs sexual orientation. A different possibility is that these genes directly govern the development of certain structures in the brain. Each of these topics has received the attention of investigators.

Hormones in adulthood   A number of early investigators proposed that male heterosexuality is governed by the levels of certain androgens in the bloodstream. If these levels were too low, homosexuality would result. But their results on this issue were quite inconsistent. Some authors found that androgen levels tend to be lower in gay men than in heterosexuals; others found no such difference (e.g., Kolodny et al., 1971; Brodie et al., 1974).

In addition, many studies have shown that administration of androgens to gay men enhances their sexual vigor but does not change its direction—their renewed interest is still toward same-sex partners (see Chapter 10; Kinsey, Pomeroy, and Martin, 1948). This and other evidence makes it clear that male homosexuality is not caused by an insufficiency of male hormones. It seems reasonable to assume that the same is true for lesbians, with no straightforward link between hormone levels and orientation. (For another discussion of the relation between homosexual orientation and neuroendocrine effects, see Gladue, Green, and Hellman, 1984.)

Hormones in the prenatal environment   A different hypothesis maintains that hormones are indeed critical to sexual orientation but that their influence is exerted not during adulthood, but in the months prior to birth (Ellis and Ames, 1987). According to this view, certain neural circuits in and around the hypothalamus become sexually differentiated between the second and fifth months of preg-

---

that children who share more interests early on with members of the opposite sex are more likely to become gay, lesbian, or bisexual (Green, 1987). But it cannot explain those children who conform fully to gender stereotypes and yet become homosexual, or those who do not conform but nevertheless become heterosexual. Nor can it explain how children in large families, who grow up quite familiar with both sexes and find neither "exotic," still become overwhelmingly heterosexual.

nancy, with the nature of this differentiation governed by the hormones circulating in the fetal bloodstream. Ordinarily, these hormones ensure that a male fetus will have a masculinized brain and a female fetus will have a feminized brain. But if the normal hormonal condition is disrupted, then this brain development will be atypical or incomplete.

What can cause this sort of hormonal disruption? There are several possibilities, including unusual stress during pregnancy and various genetically produced effects. One such effect has already been mentioned: prenatal overexposure of females to testosterone. As we discussed above, such exposure not only produces a pronounced tomboy pattern in childhood, it also has lasting effects, producing higher rates of lesbian behavior and lesbian sexual fantasies (Dittmann, Kappes, and Kappes, 1992).

Differences in brain structure   A number of investigators have reported differences in brain structure between individuals with heterosexual and homosexual orientations. One study by Simon Le Vay examined a sexually dimorphic area in the anterior hypothalamus that affects sexual behavior in animals; this structure had previously been found to be twice as large in the brains of men as in those of women (LeVay, 1991; Allen et al., 1989). When Le Vay looked at the brains of gay men, he found that this area of the hypothalamus was about the size typical for heterosexual women and therefore only half that typical for heterosexual men.

At present, the reasons for the brain differences are unknown; they might be genetic, hormonal, or both. Nor is it known what role these structures play in the development of sexual orientation. Indeed, there may be no such role. It is possible that these brain differences are associated with sexual orientation but in no way a cause of it—they may have developed secondarily as a function of other differences. The jury is still out.

TWO SIDES OF THE COIN

So what leads to homosexuality? A biological, perhaps genetically based predisposition is very likely a major factor in determining the direction of the child's emerging sexual desire. But cultural conditions undoubtedly contribute heavily in shaping how children see themselves as they grow up. As yet there is no clear answer to this question. It may well be that the question simply represents the other side of the question, "What leads to heterosexuality?" This second question is rarely asked because most people take the heterosexual orientation for granted. Yet if we knew how to explain the origin of heterosexuality, we would be much closer to understanding how homosexuality comes about as well.

Stating the two questions in this parallel form may help us see another point. People sometimes ask whether gay men and lesbians can somehow be transformed into heterosexual men and women. The answer is that such a transformation is extremely difficult if not impossible. Nor do most gay men and lesbians wish for such a change. Like heterosexuality, homosexuality is much more than a sexual preference that can be done or undone at will. It represents a fundamental part of an individual's makeup, a makeup that is essential to defining who the person is.

Whatever the causes of a homosexual or bisexual orientation, one thing is clear: Such an orientation is not a psychological disorder or defect. It is only abnormal in the sense of being the orientation of a minority, say, of some 10 percent or so of the population, but so is left-handedness. Gays and lesbians are neither better nor worse than heterosexuals. While their number includes great artists (e.g., Leonardo da Vinci), writers (e.g., Gertrude Stein), and warriors (e.g., Alexander the Great), the great majority are ordinary people whose names will not be recorded in history books. The same no doubt holds for left-handers—and for heterosexuals.

A lesbian couple   (© Deborah Davis/Pho-toEdit/PNI)

Erik Erikson *A pioneer in the study of development after childhood. (© 1990 Olive Pierce/Black Star)*

DEVELOPMENT AFTER CHILDHOOD

Thus far, our focus in describing human development has been on infancy and childhood. This emphasis reflects the orientation of the major figures in the history of the field. For example, Piaget focused most of his research on the child's mental growth from birth until the achievement of formal operations, roughly at age eleven. Freud's focus was even more restricted; to him, the most important events of social development took place before the age of five or six. Both Freud and Piaget, in common with most developmental psychologists, understood the term *development* just as it is generally used in biology: the processes by which the newly formed organism changes until it reaches maturity.

In recent years, however, a number of authors have argued that this interpretation of *development* is too narrow. In their view, there is no reason to assume that the human personality stops developing after childhood, for humans continue to change as they pass through the life cycle. The problems faced by adolescents are not the same as those of young adults about to get married or become parents, let alone those of the middle aged at the peak of parenthood or their careers, or of the elderly at the sunset of their lives. And just as the problems change, so do the strategies, responses, and resources used in dealing with these problems. It thus seems reasonable to ask how individuals continue to develop, in adolescence and throughout the life span (Baltes, Reese, and Lipsitt, 1980).

As an initial question, we might ask: What are the stages of development after childhood? On this issue, many investigators have been strongly influenced by the psychoanalyst Erik Erikson's "eight ages of man" (see Table 14.2). Accord-

TABLE 14.2 ERIKSON'S EIGHT AGES OF MAN

Approximate age	*Developmental task of that stage*	*Psychosocial crisis of that stage*
0–1 ½ years	Attachment to mother, which lays foundation for later trust in others	Trust versus mistrust
1 ½–3 years	Gaining some basic control of self and environment (e.g., toilet training, exploration)	Autonomy versus shame and doubt
3–6 years	Becoming purposeful and directive	Initiative versus guilt
6 years–puberty	Developing social, physical, and school skills	Competence versus inferiority
Adolescence	Making transition from childhood to adulthood; developing a sense of identity	Identity versus role confusion
Early adulthood	Establishing intimate bonds of love and friendship	Intimacy versus isolation
Middle age	Fulfilling life goals that involve family, career, and society; developing concerns that embrace future generations	Productivity versus stagnation
Later years	Looking back over one's life and accepting its meaning	Integrity versus despair

SOURCE: Based on Erikson, 1963.

ing to Erikson, all human beings endure a series of major crises as they go through the life cycle. At each stage, there is a critical confrontation between the self the individual has achieved thus far and the various demands posed by social and personal settings. The first few of these occur in early childhood and roughly correspond to stages identified within Freud's theory (see Chapter 17). These are followed by adolescence, early adulthood, middle age, and the final years (Erikson, 1963). These crises (and their resolution) define Erikson's "eight ages."

This developmental scheme has influenced many investigators of adult development. We will continue to refer to Erikson's organization as we briefly discuss some issues in the study of adolescence and adulthood.

ADOLESCENCE

The term *adolescence* is derived from the Latin for "growing up." It is a period of transition in which children become adults. There are biological changes: a physical growth spurt, a change in bodily proportions, and the attainment of sexual maturity (see Figure 14.15). These changes in children's bodies contribute in important ways to social and economic changes: from dependence on one's family to a legally and morally sanctioned independence. And, of course, there are the numerous psychological changes as well. These include the progressive maturing of sexual attitudes and behaviors that will ultimately allow adolescents to form romantic attachments and possibly start their own families. At the same time, adolescents are also acquiring many social skills that will eventually enable them to become well-socialized adults. In effect, adolescence for humans is simply a protracted form of what in many animals is rather abrupt—the transition point at which pups or fledglings must leave or are ejected from the nest to make their own way.

THE NATURE OF THE TRANSITION

Compared to other animals, humans attain adult status rather late in their development, and the transition from childhood to adulthood is itself stretched out over several years. This is, as we mentioned in Chapter 13, an important difference between ourselves and our animal cousins, for it provides time for each generation to learn from the one before. When is this period over?

If we only consider biology, girls can reach their physical adulthood by age fifteen or so and boys by age seventeen. By this age, physical growth is pretty much complete. But society usually defines different boundaries for the beginning of adulthood. As an example, a study of New England families shows that the age at which sons become autonomous has changed over the course of generations. The sons of the first settlers stayed on their parents' farms until their late twenties before they married and became economically independent. As farmland became scarcer and other opportunities opened in the surrounding villages and towns, the sons left home, learned a trade, married, and became autonomous at a younger age (Greven, 1970). But with the onset of mass education in the mid-nineteenth century, this pattern was reversed again. Instead of leaving to become an apprentice or take a job, more and more youths continued to live with their families and remained in school through their late teens. This allowed them to acquire the skills required for membership in a complex, technological society, but it postponed their social and economic independence and their full entry into the adult world (Elder, 1980).

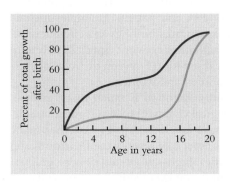

14.15 The growth spurt at adolescence
The figure shows the percentage of total growth after birth attained between the ages 0 and 20 years for overall height (dark red) and size of genital and reproductive organs (blue) averaged for males and females. (After Tanner, 1970)

14.16 Initiation rites *These rites signify induction into adulthood, as in (A) a bar mitzvah (photograph by David Reed/Corbis), or (B) an Apache girl sits on a ceremonial rug during a puberty rite. (Photograph © Bill Gillette/Stock Boston)*

A

B

Culture evidently has an important say in the when and how of the transition period. It also sets up special occasions that mark the end of this transition period or that highlight certain points along the way. These ***initiation rites*** and ***rites of passage*** are found in many human societies (Figure 14.16). In some preliterate cultures, these rites can be violent, prolonged, and painful. Examples include certain puberty rites for boys that involve ceremonial beatings and circumcision. According to some anthropologists, these initiation rites are especially severe in cultures that try to emphasize the dramatic distinction between the roles of children and adults, as well as between those of men and women.

In our own society, the transition to full adulthood is much more gradual, with milestones that refer not just to biological changes but also to various educational and vocational attainments. We have not one initiation rite but many (none of which would ever be regarded as especially severe): confirmations and bar (or bas) mitzvahs, "sweet sixteen" parties, high-school and college graduations, and so on. Each of these marks an important event, but each represents just one more step on a protracted road to adulthood (Burton and Whiting, 1961; Muuss, 1970).

Cultural factors also determine the time at which other benchmarks of development are reached. An example is the average age at which virginity is lost, which has steadily decreased in our own society during the past few decades, reflecting a change in sexual mores for both men and women. This change is undoubtedly caused by many factors, not the least of which is the existence of increasingly effective methods of birth control that allow the separation of the emotional and recreational aspects of sexuality from its reproductive function.

IS ADOLESCENCE ALWAYS TURBULENT?

Traditionally, adolescence has been considered a period of great emotional stress. This notion goes back to the romantic movement of the early nineteenth century, when major writers such as the German poet Johann Wolfgang von Goethe (1749–1832) wrote influential works that featured youths in desperate conflict with a cynical, adult world, that drove them to despair, suicide, or violent rebellion. This view was later endorsed by a number of psychological theorists, including Sigmund Freud and many of his followers. To Freud, adolescence was necessarily a period of conflict, since this is the time when the sexual urges repressed by the close of the Oedipal period resurge, only to clash violently with one's unconscious prohibitions. Further conflicts center on struggles with the older generation, especially the same-sex parent, that were repressed in childhood but now come to the fore (see Chapter 17).

Certainly the universal neuroendocrine events of puberty force adolescents to come to terms with a new, more adultlike physical appearance. This change can itself cause others to treat them more as adults and to expect adult behavior in return. One consequence may be strain at adjusting to these new reactions and expectations.

But some researchers contend that the turbulence of adolescence is by no means inevitable. Whether there is marked emotional disturbance depends, they argue, on the way the culture handles the transition. Some evidence for this view comes from studies of preliterate cultures in which the shift from childhood to adulthood is gradual. Among the Arapesh of New Guinea, the young increasingly participate in adult activities as they get older. Given the somewhat simpler social and economic structure of Arapesh life, the change seems less drastic (Mead, 1939). Still, the Arapesh have many of the same concerns as members of contemporary technological societies. One influential observer reports that the Arapesh place a premium on female virginity, discourage premarital sex and homosexuality, and demonstrate relatively high rates of adolescent rape (Freeman, 1983).

A gentle adolescent transition may be difficult enough to achieve among even the Arapesh, but it is especially so in our technological societies. Because of the complexities of our modern world, adult routines are often very different from childhood routines, with no easily located way stations in between. Accordingly, one might expect a fair level of disturbance during adolescence in our own society. And, indeed, such emotional disturbance is a theme often sounded by the mass media and much twentieth-century American literature (for example, J. D. Salinger's *Catcher in the Rye*). But in fact, a number of studies suggest that such turbulence is by no means universal among modern American adolescents. Several investigators find that for many adolescents "development . . . is slow, gradual, and unremarkable" (Josselson, 1980, p. 189). What probably matters is the particular social and psychological setting, which surely differs from individual to individual in a complex society such as ours.

TRYING TO FIND A PERSONAL IDENTITY

Adolescence may not necessarily be a time of troubles. Even so, it does pose a number of serious challenges for adolescents as they prepare to become autonomous individuals. A number of writers have tried to understand some characteristic adolescent behavior patterns in light of this ultimate goal.

Establishing a separate world Unlike fledgling birds, adolescents in our society remain in the nest for quite a while after they can fly (or more aptly, after they get their driver's licenses). Thus, living in the world of their parents, adolescents are likely to seek special means of identifying themselves as separate and different from their parents. As one means to this end, many adolescents form small cliques that become like second families, identify themselves as part of a crowd (such as the "brains," "jocks," or "nerds" in a school), and adopt all kinds of external trappings of what's "cool," "rad," or "in," such as adopting new clothing, hair styles, and speech idioms (Figure 14.17; Dunphy, 1963; Brown, 1990). These often change with bewildering rapidity, as yesterday's adolescent fads diffuse into the broader social world and become today's adult fashions (witness the music of the Beatles, once considered subversive but now played as background music in shopping malls). When this happens, new adolescent fads quickly spring up to maintain the differentiation (Douvan and Adelson, 1958).

The identity crisis of adolescence According to Erikson, differentiating themselves from the adult world is only part of what adolescents really want to achieve. Their major goal throughout adolescence is to discover who and what they

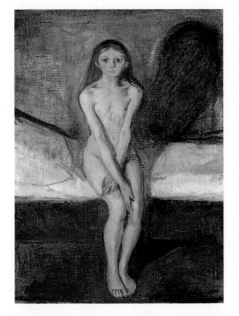

Puberty by Edward Munch, 1895 (Copyright © The Munch Museum/The Munch-Ellingsen Group/ARS, 1994)

A

B

C

14.17 Adolescent fads *New adolescent fads spring up to maintain the differentiation between the adolescents' own world and that of the adults around them. They then disappear rather quickly to be replaced by yet newer fads. These photos show some such fads prominent at various times: (A) seventies—streaking (photograph by T. Lowell/Black Star), (B) eighties—punk fashions (photograph © Spencer Grant/The Picture Cube), (C) nineties—rap singers' styles (Photograph © Timothy Ross/The Image Bank).*

really are, as they go through what he calls an ***identity crisis.*** In our complex culture, there are many social roles, and adolescence is a time to try them on to see which one fits best—which vocation, which ideology, which group membership. The primary question adolescents ask themselves is, "Who am I?" and to answer it, they strike a succession of postures, in part for the benefit of others, who then serve as a mirror in which they see themselves. Each role, each human relationship, each worldview is adopted totally, uncompromisingly, and sometimes defiantly, but only for awhile. Like costumes, they are tried on for size, and when adolescents find that some fit, they retain them as part of their adult identity (Erikson, 1963).

ADULTHOOD

Erikson describes a number of stages of personality development after adolescence. In young adulthood, healthy individuals must develop a capacity for closeness and intimacy through love or else suffer from a personal isolation that permits only shallow human relationships. Those in early middle age must develop a sense of personal creativity toward the wider world, toward others, toward their trade or profession, and toward their communities. And near the end of life, the elderly must come to terms with their own lives, accepting them with a sense of integrity rather than despair. Erikson eloquently sums up this final reckoning: "It is the acceptance of one's own and only life cycle as something that had to be and that, by necessity, permitted of no substitutes. . . . Healthy children will not fear life if their elders have integrity enough not to fear death" (Erikson, 1963, pp. 268–69).

RECENT ATTEMPTS TO FIND COMMON STAGES

Erikson's developmental scheme is a literary and moving account of the human odyssey through life, but is it accurate? Are the crises he listed universal and as he described them? A number of modern investigators have studied adults at various stages of their lives to find out what, if any, patterns characterize a given time of life. By and large, most of them have described a number of developmental periods that resemble some of Erikson's "ages of man" (Gould, 1978; Levinson, 1978).

A stage of adult development that has received considerable attention from both Erikson and later authors is the *midlife transition* (which sometimes amounts to the "midlife crisis"), in which individuals reappraise what they have done with their lives thus far and may reevaluate their marriage and career. It is a period when individuals begin to see physical changes that show that the summer of

DEVELOPMENT AFTER CHILDHOOD

(Photograph © David Young Wolff/ PhotoEdit/PNI)

life is over and its autumn has begun, a recognition that may occur earlier in women than in men (in part, because of the psychological and physiological impact of menopause). There is a shift in the way one thinks about time, from "How long have I lived?" to "How much time do I have left?" Some investigators point out that the middle aged are in the middle in more than one sense as they observe their children grow up and their own parents age and die:

> It is as if there are two mirrors before me, each held at a partial angle. I see part of myself in my mother who is growing old, and part of her in me. In the other mirror I see part of myself in my daughter.... (Neugarten and Datan, quoted in Colarusso and Nemiroff, 1981, p. 124)

HOW UNIVERSAL ARE THE STAGES OF ADULT DEVELOPMENT?

The results obtained by various investigators of adult development are consistent enough to suggest that the stages and transitions they describe apply fairly widely to people in our time and place. But are they universal? When we considered various stage theories of child development, we asked whether these stages occur in all cultures. The same question can be asked about adult development. Is there a midlife transition among the Arapesh? Do Eskimo villagers of fifty agonizingly reappraise what they've done with their lives? If the answer is no, then we have to ask ourselves what the various stages described by Erikson and other students of the adult life span really are.

Thus far there is little concrete evidence one way or the other, so we can only guess. Certain adult milestones are clearly biological. In all cultures, humans reach puberty, mate, have children, go through female menopause or male climacteric, endure the discomfitures and diseases of old age, and finally die. But the kinds of crises that confront persons at different points of the life cycle surely depend on the society in which they live.

An example of the effect of social conditions on adult crises is the transition into old age. Over a century ago in the United States, different generations often lived close together as part of an extended family, and there was much less segregation by age. Nursing homes and retirement communities were unheard of. Older people contributed to the family even when they were too old to work outside the home by caring for the children, helping with the housekeeping, and so on. Older people were also sought out for advice on matters of child rearing and housekeeping. But today, the elderly have no such recognized family role.

(Photograph © Rosanne Olson/Allstock/PNI)

619

The ages of man   Jacob Blessing the
Sons of Joseph *by Rembrandt, 1656 (Copyright by Staatliche Museem Kassel; photograph by M. Busing)*

They usually live apart, are effectively segregated from the rest of society, are excluded from the workforce, and have lost their role as esteemed advisers. Given these changes, it follows that the transition into senescence is quite different from what it was 150 years ago. People still age as they did then—although many more people than ever now live into their seventies, eighties, and even nineties—but they view aging differently and face different life circumstances (Hareven, 1978).

Facts of this sort suggest that the stages of adult development vary in their specifics. But has Erikson still provided some truths that transcend our own time and place? Perhaps the best suggestion comes from a lecture by Erikson in which he tried to define adulthood:

> . . . In youth you find out what you care to do and who you care to be. . . . In young adulthood you learn whom you care to be with. . . . In adulthood, however, you learn what and whom you can take care of. . . . (Erikson, 1974, p. 124)

Seen in this light, the later phases of the life cycle are a final expansion in which our concern turns from ourselves to others and from the present to the future. This may or may not be a good description of what genuine adulthood is. But it seems like an admirable prescription for what it ought to be.

SUMMARY

1. The *social development* of infants begins with their first human bond—their *attachment* to their mothers, fathers, or other caregivers. Studies of infant humans and monkeys indicate that this attachment is not caused by the fact that the mother feeds them, but

SUMMARY

rather because she feels so comforting. Separations from the mother generally lead to *separation anxiety*.

2.   Developmental psychologists have tried to assess the quality of the child's attachment to the mother by observing the behavior of infants and young children in the Strange Situation. There is some evidence that the quality of attachment at about fifteen months of age predicts behavior two years later, but there is controversy as to whether this reflects a long-term effect of the early mother-child relationship or is based on other factors, such as persistent patterns in the mother-child relationship or some continuity of childhood temperament.

3.   Some theorists have proposed that the attachment to the mother can only be formed during a *sensitive period* in early life. In part, this position derives from work on *imprinting* in birds. According to this view, if such an early attachment is not formed, later social development may be seriously impaired, as indicated by studies of motherless monkeys and children reared in deprived orphanages. But there is little evidence of imprinting in humans, and later work on monkey isolates and adopted children suggests that impairments from early deprivation can often be ameliorated.

4.   The process of *socialization* continues with child rearing by the parents. Some important differences in the way children are reared depend on the dominant values of their culture. Modern attempts to explain the mechanisms that underlie socialization include *social learning theory*, which emphasizes modeling, and *cognitive developmental theory*, which emphasizes the role of understanding.

5.   Freud notwithstanding, the evidence indicates that different modes of weaning or toilet training have little or no long-term effects. What seems to matter instead is the general home atmosphere, as shown by the effects of *autocratic, permissive,* and *authoritative-reciprocal patterns* of child rearing. On the other hand, how the parents treat the child is partially determined by the child's own characteristics, as suggested by studies on infant temperament.

6.   One aspect of moral conduct concerns the *internalization* of prohibitions. According to some theorists, punishment is more likely to lead to such internalization if the threatened punishment fits the *principle of minimal sufficiency*. Another aspect of moral conduct involves altruistic acts. Studies of *empathy* and *empathic distress* suggest that some precursors of altruism may be present in early infancy.

7.   The study of *moral reasoning* has been strongly affected by Kohlberg's analysis of progressive stages in moral reasoning. According to a later critique by Carol Gilligan, there are some important sex differences in moral orientation, with men emphasizing justice and women stressing human relationships and compassion. Related differences have been found between different cultural groups.

8.   Both socialization and constitutional factors play roles in determining various senses of being male or female, including *gender role, gender identity,* and *sexual orientation.*

9.   Certain psychological differences between the sexes may be biologically rooted. One is *physical aggression,* which tends to be more pronounced in males. Another is *relational aggression,* the manipulation of social alliances, which may be more pronounced in females. Still another is a male advantage on spatial tests of mental ability. To whatever extent such differences are biologically based, they are undoubtedly maintained or magnified by socially imposed gender roles.

10.   The causes of *sexual orientation* are not yet clear. There is little evidence to support the view that sexual orientation is determined either by a particular pattern of relations with parents in early childhood or by childhood sexual experiences. Current evidence points to such determinants as differences in brain structure and a genetic link. But whatever are the ultimate influences, sexual orientation is fairly stable and can be changed only with great difficulty, if at all.

11.   Development continues after childhood. Some theorists, notably Erik Erikson, have tried to map later stages of development. One such stage is *adolescence,* which marks the transition into adulthood.

PART FIVE

INDIVIDUAL DIFFERENCES

CHAPTER 15

INTELLIGENCE: ITS NATURE AND MEASUREMENT

People differ from one another. They vary in height, weight, and strength, eye color and hair color. They also vary along many psychological dimensions. They may be proud or humble, adventurous or timid, intelligent or dull—the list of psychological distinctions is very large.

Thus far, these differences from one individual to the next have not been our main concern. Our emphasis has, instead, been on the attempt to find general psychological laws—whether in physiological function, memory, or social behavior—laws that apply to all people. To be sure, we have occasionally dealt with individual differences, but our focus was not on these differences as such; rather, it was on what they could tell us about people in general—how color blindness could help to explain the underlying mechanisms of color vision or how variations in child rearing might help us understand some aspects of socialization.

In essence, then, our concern has been with the nature of humankind and not with the traits of particular men and women. It's time, though, to change this emphasis and to consider individual differences as a topic in its own right. We will start, in this chapter, with one regard in which humans differ: their intelligence. In subsequent chapters, we will turn to a discussion of personality traits and then to the more extreme variation that carries us outside the range of the "normal" and into the domain of mental disease.

In twentieth-century society, especially in the United States, there is a flourishing enterprise of mental testing or psychological assessment. This enterprise has produced a huge number of psychological tests, allowing us to measure many different characteristics, including those that pertain to intellectual aptitude. This interest in individual differences is fueled by several factors, but one large influence derives from the social climate of the last century. After all, in a caste society (for example), if a child's parents were farmers, then the child would grow up to be a farmer. If born to royalty, then the child would be royalty. In this setting, there was no need for vocational counselors or personnel managers, since there was no issue of *choice* for each individual's career. In this setting, there would be no point in administering mental tests to assist in educational selection or job placement.

In our society, in contrast, there is a good deal of mobility across a highly diverse set of socioeconomic niches. This creates a real need for the systematic assessment of human characteristics, as employers seek an appropriate person to occupy each niche and employees look for the niche that best suits them.

Mental tests were, from their beginning, designed to fill this pragmatic need. They were devised as instruments to help in educational and occupational selection and for use in various forms of personal guidance and diagnosis. As a result, questions about mental testing are obviously linked to a number of social and political issues. Who will get a good job? Who will receive the benefits of the finest-quality education? Should disadvantaged students be denied college admission because of low Scholastic Aptitude Test (SAT) scores? It is hardly surprising that these questions, especially when they concern intelligence testing, are debated in an emotionally charged atmosphere.

Any intelligent discussion of these questions must be well informed by the relevant scientific underpinnings: an understanding of what the tests measure, how they measure it, and why we should (or shouldn't) take these tests seriously. We will try to answer these questions in this chapter, providing the background against which the political and social issues must be evaluated.

MENTAL TESTS

Some mental tests are used to assess *achievement:* They measure what an individual has learned, what skills she has mastered. They are designed to indicate the test taker's current status: The results will change only when she learns more or gains new skills.

Other tests are used to assess *aptitude:* They are designed to predict what an individual will be able to do, given the proper training and the right motivation. An example is a test of mechanical aptitude devised to determine the likelihood that an individual will do well as an engineer after an appropriate education. The Scholastic Aptitude Test (SAT), as the name implies, is an aptitude test designed to predict how well students will do in educational settings after high school. Most scholars also consider intelligence tests measures of aptitude, although critics of intelligence testing regard such tests as measures of achievement, not measures of potential.

Still other tests have other purposes. Neuropsychological tests, for example, are diagnostic tools for assessing certain learning disabilities as well as the effects of brain damage. Personality tests assess an individual's behavioral dispositions, whether the test taker is outgoing or withdrawn, confident or insecure, even-tempered or moody, and so on.

Before looking at any of these tests, though, we need to explain the reasoning underlying the construction and use of all such tests.

THE STUDY OF VARIATION

To understand the study of individual differences, and the tests used to assess these differences, we need to understand a bit about measurement, and also the ways in which psychologists summarize measurements, using the concepts and the vocabulary of statistics.★ In fact, the study of how individuals differ from one another has grown up in close association with the development of statistical methods, with these methods serving as powerful tools for interpreting and theorizing about these differences.

Two hundred years ago, the term **statistics** meant little more than the systematic collection of various state records (*state*-istics), such as birth and death rates. In poring over such figures, the Belgian scientist Adolphe Quetelet (1796–

★ For a fuller description of these and other statistical matters that will be referred to in this chapter, see Appendix 2, "Statistics: The Collection, Organization, and Interpretation of Data."

TABLE 15.1 HEIGHTS (IN INCHES) FOR A GROUP OF FIFTY WOMEN			
Name	Height (in inches)	Name	Height (in inches)
Ann	54.00	Tracey	65.50
Michelle	55.50	Jenny	65.75
Abigail	57.00	Rachel	66.00
Patricia	57.50	Brianna	66.25
Marie	58.25	Amanda	66.75
Erica	58.50	Enriqueta	67.00
Kathryn	59.25	Gretchen	67.00
Angela	60.25	Jeanette	67.25
Allison	60.50	Jessica	67.75
Dina	60.75	Elena	68.00
Jane	61.00	Lynn	68.25
Kelly	61.00	Anna	69.50
Joanna	61.25	Sylvia	69.50
Gena	62.50	Kristina	69.75
Sarah	62.75	Kirsten	70.00
Ingrid	63.00	Chris	70.75
Heather	63.50	Alicia	71.25
Lynn	63.75	Laura	71.50
Deborah	64.00	Eve	71.50
Caitlin	64.00	Jennifer	72.25
Alisha	64.50	Britney	73.50
Elizabeth	64.75	Susan	74.75
Melanie	65.00	Carolyn	76.00
Muriel	65.00	Miriam	77.50
Lois	65.25	Chelsea	79.00

TABLE 15.2 FREQUENCY DISTRIBUTION OF HEIGHTS IN TABLE 15.1	
Category	Number of cases
0–54.00	1
54.25–56.00	1
56.25–58.00	2
58.25–60.00	3
60.25–62.00	6
62.25–64.00	7
64.25–66.00	8
66.25–68.00	7
68.25–70.00	5
70.25–72.00	4
72.25–74.00	2
74.25–76.00	2
76.25–78.00	1
78.25–80.00	1

1874) began to see patterns in these numbers, and this led him to chart the *frequency distribution* of various observations—that is, how often individual cases fall into different categories, with those categories systematically subdividing the full range of measurements.

For example, Table 15.1 merely lists the (fictional) heights of fifty women. In this format, it's difficult to see any pattern at all. Once we summarize these data in terms of a *frequency distribution* (Table 15.2) and then put this frequency distribution into graphic form (Figure 15.1), the pattern becomes easily visible: The women in this particular group range in height from 54 inches to 79 inches, but most have heights close to 65 inches. Eight women are exactly this height, and as we move further and further from this middle value, the number of women at each height interval gradually drops.

THE NORMAL CURVE

Quetelet made graphs of frequency distributions for many human attributes—height, weight, waist size, and so on—and he realized that, if the sample was large enough, then most of these distributions were bell shaped, like the curve in Figure 15.1. To describe such bell-shaped curves, it's usually sufficient to specify just two things: First, where is the curve's center? This gives us a measure of the "average case"—in Figure 15.1, the average height for women in this group. The most common way of determining this average is to add up all the scores and then divide the sum by the number of scores; this process yields the **mean**. But there are other ways of determining the average as well. For example, it is sometimes convenient to refer to the **median** score, which is the score that separates the top 50 percent of the scores from the bottom 50 percent. (In Figure 15.1, the mean and the median are the same, but often this is not the case.)

A second important aspect of a bell-shaped curve is its **variability**. How much do the individual cases differ from one to the next? A highly variable group will have a frequency distribution that is wide and relatively flat, like the one shown

15.1 Graphic display of a frequency distribution *This figure shows the data from Table 15.2 in graphic form. In this format, the pattern is easily visible: Most women in this sample have heights close to 65 inches. Values further and further from this middle value are less and less frequent. Each dot represents the frequency of each height (i.e., a row in Table 15.2).*

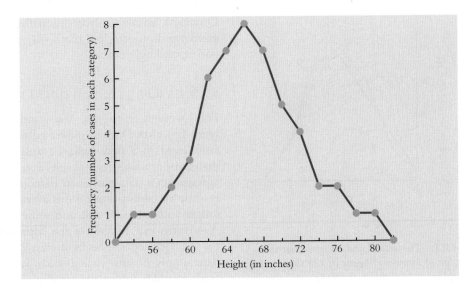

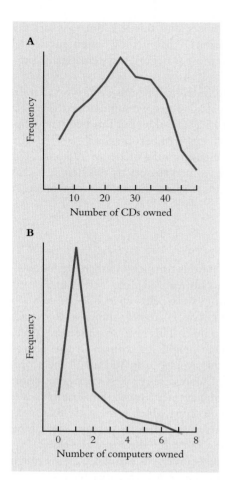

15.2 Frequency distributions with high variability or low (A) People vary enormously in how many CDs they own, ranging from those who own only one or two to those who own hundreds. The frequency distribution (showing fictional data) reflects this high degree of variability. (B) There is relatively little variability in how many computers a family owns. Many families own one computer; some own none; a few own two or three. The (fictional) frequency distribution reflects this narrow variability.

in Figure 15.2A; a group with little variability will be narrow and steep, like the one shown in Figure 15.2B.

Highly variable or not, these curves all have the same bell shape, a shape closely resembling what mathematicians call a **normal curve.** In general, normal curves describe the frequency pattern that emerges when an event is being influenced by random accidents. For example, suppose that someone threw six coins in the air and counted how many of the coins landed heads up. Now suppose that this person had the patience to repeat this procedure a thousand times. How often, in these thousand tosses, would the coins fall with all six heads up? How often with five or four or three? So long as the coins are fair, it's a matter of pure chance how each coin will land, so the number of heads or tails that come up in each toss will also be a matter of chance. Still, a pattern emerges. Figure 15.3 shows what happens if six coins are actually thrown over and over. With each throw, the distribution approaches that of the normal curve.

Quetelet realized that the distributions of many human characteristics—height, weight, chest or shoe size—resemble that of the normal curve. Since the normal curve is the pattern of chance events, perhaps the distributions of these human characteristics are also the product of chance events. More precisely, Quetelet proposed that nature aims at an ideal value for each of these attributes, but a host of little accidents pull most of us away from this ideal. Sometimes the accidents cause us to fall short of the ideal—perhaps a child happened to catch the flu when he was four years old, and this interrupted a growth spurt so that he ended up, as an adult, a few millimeters shorter than he otherwise might have been. Sometimes the accidents cause us to overshoot: Perhaps the child happened to like vegetables when he was nine, and this led him to ingest more of these vitamin-rich foods, adding a millimeter or two. These and many other accidents accumulate, some adding height, some subtracting it, and in the end produce a distribution just like the distribution of heads shown in Figure 15.3. For most people, this mix of height-promoting or height-detracting accidents more or less balance each other, leaving the individual with a height close to Quetelet's "ideal." Only occasionally will height-promoting or height-detracting accidents dominate, and that's why extremely tall or extremely short people are correspondingly rare.

VARIABILITY AND DARWIN

For Quetelet, variability was something unfortunate—a departure from the ideal. But after Darwin published the *Origin of Species*, variability was suddenly considered in a new light, because, for Darwin, variability provided the raw material on which natural selection could work. Suppose, for example, that the average finch on a particular island has a long and narrow beak. However, there is some variability around this average, so a few finches will have beaks that are longer and narrower still, and some will have beaks that are shorter and wider. As it turns out, finches of the latter sort are particularly successful in cracking hard-shelled seeds. This by itself might convey no advantage if there is an abundant supply of soft-shelled seeds. In this case, the ability to crack hard-shelled seeds would be of little value. But circumstances can change (perhaps because of

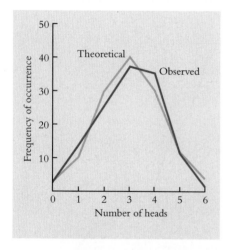

15.3 Theoretical and observed distribution of number of heads in 128 throws of 6 coins (After Anastasi, 1958)

15.4 Evolution of the honeycreeper
These related species of Hawaiian honeycreepers display dramatic differences in beak size and shape. Like the finches that provided an important impetus to Darwin's theory of natural selection, these honeycreepers are thought to have evolved from a common ancestor. (Courtesy of H. Douglas Pratt)

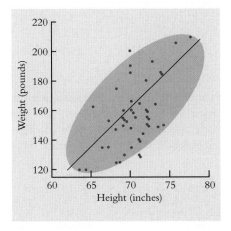

15.5 Correlation *A scatter diagram of the heights and weights of fifty male undergraduates. Note that the points fall within an ellipse, which indicates that the data are correlated. The correlation for these data was +.70.*

a shift in the climate), and a day might arrive in which soft-shelled seeds become rare and hard-shelled seeds become the main foodstuff in this habitat. In this case, the short-beaked finches would find themselves at a reproductive advantage. They would gain more food, and so outlive and outbreed their long-beaked comrades. Eventually, the long-beaked finches would all die off, so that only short-beaked finches (and their offspring) remained.

Seen in this light, variability should not be lamented as though it reflected some sort of corruption of an ideal. Instead, it is the very stuff of which natural selection is made, giving it something to select *from* (Figure 15.4). Without variability, there can be no natural selection.

In addition, the *sources* of variability in the Darwinian scheme are very different than they are in Quetelet's view. For Darwin, natural selection functions because short-beaked finches have short-beaked offspring. It is in this fashion that survival advantages for one generation could shape the characteristics of subsequent generations. Therefore, having a short beak was not the consequence of some number of accidents occurring during the organism's lifetime. Instead, there was a systematic source for this attribute and, presumably, for other attributes as well.

CORRELATION

Could this line of reasoning be applied to variations in human characteristics? Are these characteristics transmitted from one generation to the next, much as beak length is? Several of the techniques for pursuing this sort of question were developed by Darwin's contemporaries.

Francis Galton (1822–1911), a half-cousin of Darwin's, spent much of his life trying to prove that heredity plays a crucial role in many human characteristics—including both physical and mental traits. Galton pursued these issues in a number of ways, but one important part of his research called for the assessment of similarity among relatives. If an individual is tall, how likely is it that her siblings are also tall? If someone is smart or friendly, how likely is it that her children will share these traits?

Galton knew from the start that children tend to be like their parents to some extent and that there is some resemblance among siblings. To examine these relationships in detail, however, he needed some means of measuring this relationship, so that he could determine when the relationship was strong and when weak.

What Galton was seeking was a measure of **covariation** or **correlation.** To see how these measures work, consider the relationship between height and weight. If we know how tall someone is, does this give us any information about what his weight is likely to be? Data for fifty undergraduate men are graphed in Figure 15.5, a **scatter diagram.** Each point in this diagram represents one person, with his height determining the horizontal position of the point and his weight determining the vertical position.

The pattern in this scatter diagram—an ellipse running from the lower left to the upper right of the graph—suggests that these two measurements are related: Taller people (points to the right on the scatter diagram) also tend to weigh more (points higher up on the figure). But the relationship is not perfect. If it were, all the points would fall on the diagonal line. Nonetheless, the overall pattern of the scatter diagram does indicate a relationship: If we know someone's height, we can make a reasonable prediction about what that person's weight is likely to be, and if we know the weight, we can predict the height.

Figure 15.6 shows a different scatter diagram, this time examining the relationship between students' heights and their SAT scores. Again, each point on the scatter diagram represents one person, with height determining the point's

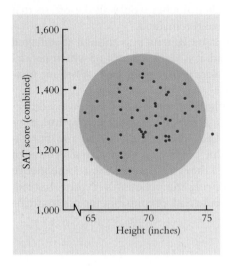

15.6 A correlation of zero *A scatter diagram of Scholastic Aptitude Test scores and the heights of fifty undergraduate males. Not surprisingly, there was no relation, as shown by the fact that the points fall within a circle. The correlation was +.05, which for all essential purposes is equivalent to zero.*

Francis Galton *A pioneer in the study of individual differences. (Courtesy of National Library of Medicine)*

horizontal position and SAT score determining its vertical position. Here there is no relationship: The dots do not cluster to form an elliptical pattern; instead, they are more or less evenly dispersed, and so we can readily find tall people with both high and low SAT scores, short people with both high and low scores.

Galton and his students developed a mathematical expression that summarized these sorts of relationships. This measure is called the **correlation coefficient,** symbolized by the letter **r,** and it can take any value between +1.00 and −1.00. When r = + 1.00 or −1.00, the correlation is perfect. For the data depicted graphically in Figure 15.5, which shows the relationship between height and weight, r = +.70. This is a strongly positive correlation, but it's also considerably less than r = +1.00. In other words, the correlation between height and weight is not perfect. For the data used to draw Figure 15.6, showing the relationship between height and SAT score, r = +.05, close to zero, reflecting the fact that there is no relationship here.

When r is *positive,* higher scores on one measure (say, height) are associated with higher measures on the other (say, weight). When it's *negative,* higher scores on one measure are associated with lower scores on the other. For example, consider the correlation between an individual's verbal SAT score and the time needed for that same individual to read *Hamlet:* Students with higher scores generally need less time, so as the SAT verbal score goes up, reading time goes down and vice versa. We should emphasize, though, that the strength of a correlation is reflected by its absolute value—its value regardless of sign: r = −.70 is just as strong as r = +.70.

As we saw in Chapter 14, correlations provide a useful measure of the degree to which two variables are related, but they also have an important limitation: They cannot, by themselves, tell us whether there is any *causal* relationship between the variables. Sometimes there is: There is a negative correlation between the number of cigarettes smoked per day and life expectancy (the more cigarettes smoked, the shorter the life expectancy), and the causal link here is well known. But often this is not the case. For example, there is also a negative correlation between life expectancy and the number of ashtrays an individual owns, but this is not because owning ashtrays is bad for your health. Instead, owning ashtrays is itself correlated with cigarette smoking (positively: the more ashtrays, the more cigarettes smoked), and smoking is the health risk.

EVALUATING MENTAL TESTS

The notions of variability and correlation are important in evaluating the tests psychologists have designed to assess individual differences. How can we determine whether a given test adequately assesses the traits on which people differ? Do tests of artistic aptitude or intelligence, say, actually measure what they are designed to measure?

RELIABILITY

One criterion of a test's adequacy is its **reliability**—that is, the consistency with which it measures what it measures. Consider a bathroom scale. Imagine that you step onto the scale, and it shows your weight to be 135 pounds. You step off the scale, surprised by the good news. But then you ask: Could this be? What about the large pizza you had yesterday? You step back onto the scale, and it reports your weight as 125 pounds. Puzzled by this change, you step off the scale and quickly back on, and now the scale says you weigh 140 pounds. You would surely conclude that it's time to buy a new scale—this one is not reliable.

This example also suggests that one way to assess reliability is by administering the test more than once. The correlation between scores would seem to be a good index of the test's reliability. However, this **test-retest method** is not always suitable. Sometimes the quality to be assessed is itself not stable. The bathroom scale might not register the same weight before and after Thanksgiving dinner, but that wouldn't be the scale's fault. The same might be true of a test to assess mood: the score on the test taken today might not correlate with the score if the test was taken yesterday. But that may not mean a problem with the test, since people's moods change from one day to the next. Tests of knowledge face a similar problem; test takers may well learn more between the test and the retest, reducing the correlation between their two scores.

One solution to this problem is to assess reliability on a single occasion by dividing a test into parts—say, the even-numbered questions versus the odd-numbered ones. If the test consistently measures the same trait, then the test taker's score on one half of the test should correlate with her score on the other half of the test.

Most psychological tests now in use have **reliability coefficients** (that is, test-retest correlations or correlations between the test's halves) in the .90s or in the high .80s. These are high values (recall that $r = +1.00$ or -1.00 is a perfect correlation), but reliability is crucial if we hope to interpret these tests as revealing stable and enduring characteristics of the individual.

VALIDITY

Even more critical than reliability is a test's **validity,** defined simply as the extent to which the test measures what it is supposed to measure. Imagine a psychology professor who assigns final grades in a course based largely on penmanship on exams. This assessment procedure might be reliable (assuming the professor is consistent in his assessment of handwriting), but it is surely not valid, since handwriting has little to do with mastery of a course's content.

Predictive validity   How can we assess a test's validity? One approach is to consider the test's **predictive validity,** that is, its ability to predict future performance. If a test claims, for example, to measure scholastic aptitude, then we'd probably expect that students who do well on the test will do well in school later on. Similarly, a test of vocational aptitude ought to predict how well people do on the job. One index of a test's validity, therefore, is its ability to make these predictions. This is usually measured by the correlation between the initial test score and some appropriate criterion.

As it turns out, tests of scholastic aptitude can be used to predict subsequent academic performance, so that there is a correlation of about $+.50$ between a high-school student's SAT scores and her grade-point average in college, a year or two later. Similarly, tests of vocational aptitude can be used to predict subsequent job performance, with correlations in the same range.

Such correlations are strong enough to indicate that these tests have predictive validity. But their predictions are far from perfect (i.e., the correlation is well below 1.00). This is hardly surprising, since (as just one concern) it is obvious that school grades depend on many factors in addition to ability (for example, motivation). In fact, given this concern, we should perhaps be impressed by the high validity scores actually observed for these aptitude measures.

Construct validity   Another (related) way to assess whether a test measures what it claims to measure is to examine its **construct validity** (Cronbach and Meehl, 1955). This is the extent to which performance on the test fits into a theoretical scheme—or *construct*—about the attribute the test is seeking to measure. For example, present-day chemical tests of pregnancy have both construct and predictive validity. They have construct validity because modern medical science knows enough about the hormonal changes during pregnancy to understand *why* the chemical reacts as it does. In other words, there is a well-articulated theoretical framework giving us good reason to believe that these tests do, in fact, assess factors diagnostic of a pregnancy. It's no surprise, therefore, that these tests also have predictive validity, for they correlate almost perfectly with the visible manifestations of pregnancy that appear some time later.

STANDARDIZATION

Suppose we learn that a student's verbal aptitude score is 130. By itself, this number tells us very little, even if we also have reason to believe that this aptitude test is both reliable and valid. To interpret this score, we need to know more about the scores obtained by other people who took the same test. These other scores provide the **norms** against which our student's test results can be evaluated. If we knew, for example, that an average performance on this test was 82, then 130 is impressive indeed. If we instead knew that the average test score is 200 or more, then 130 looks very different.

To obtain these norms, a test is first administered to a large sample of the population on which the test is to be used. This initial group is the **standardization sample.** Of course, this sample must be chosen with care: In interpreting an adult's score, it may be of little use to know how children generally perform on the test, in interpreting an American's score, it may (for many tests, and for many purposes) not be relevant to know how a group of Ghanaians did, and so on.

INTELLIGENCE TESTING

Now that we have the relevant concepts in place, we can turn, at last, to the actual enterprise of mental testing. Our focus here will be on the testing of intelligence.

The first question we need to ask is, What is *intelligence?* We all have some notion of what this term refers to, and our vocabularies are filled with words that describe different levels and types of intellectual functioning—*smart, bright,* and *clever; dull, slow,* and *dim-witted.* But it is difficult to specify exactly what these terms mean, and attempts at specification often lead to disagreements.

Even experts disagree on exactly how *intelligence* should be defined (Sternberg and Determan, 1986). Some researchers emphasize the capacity for abstract thinking. Others focus on the ability to acquire new abilities or new knowledge. Still others highlight the ability to adapt to new situations. No single definition of intelligence has been accepted by all. Remarkably, though, this has not been an obstacle to progress in intelligence testing, and so even without an agreed-upon definition, we do have intelligence tests. These tests were developed to fill certain practical needs, and as we will see, for many purposes these tests work quite well.

MEASURING INTELLIGENCE

While people plainly disagree about the definition of intelligence, there is a reasonable consensus on the sorts of tasks that require intelligence. For example, it seems obvious that little intelligence is needed to dig a hole with a shovel—Einstein would have been no better at this task (and might have been worse) than someone with far less intellectual prowess. Alternatively, intelligence does seem necessary for learning calculus—for this complex task, someone like Einstein has a considerable advantage.

A century ago, these relatively straightforward intuitions served as the basis for intelligence testing. We can find out how smart someone is by looking at their performance on tasks that seem, on the face of things, to require intelligence.

TESTING INTELLIGENCE IN CHILDREN

In 1904, the French minister of public instruction appointed a committee with the task of identifying children who were performing badly in school and, crucially, children who would benefit from remedial education. The committee concluded that they needed an objective diagnostic test to assess each child, and much of what we know about the measurement of intelligence grows out of their pioneering work.

One member of this committee, Alfred Binet (1857–1911), played a pivotal role. His project was, from the start, entirely pragmatic in its goals and quite optimistic in its tone, as he sought both to identify the weaker students and then to improve their performance through special training. As his work developed, Binet prescribed courses in "mental orthopedics" for students with low scores, and, in one book, his chapter on the "training of intelligence" began with the ambitious phrase: "After the illness, the remedy."

Intelligence as a general cognitive capacity Binet and his collaborator, Théophile Simon, believed that intelligence was a general attribute, manifesting itself in many different spheres of cognitive functioning. This led them to construct a test that included many subtasks varying in both content and difficulty: copying a drawing, repeating a string of digits, understanding a story, and so on. Their idea was that a person might do well on one or two of these tasks just by luck or by virtue of some specific prior experience. However, a truly intelligent person would be able to perform well on virtually any task and certainly on all of the tasks in this array. Therefore, intelligence could be measured by a composite score assessing how an individual did on all the tasks in this set. Moreover, the diversity of the tasks would ensure that the test was not measuring some specialized talent but was instead a measure of ability in general. As Binet (1911, p. 329) put it, "it matters very little what the tests are so long as they are numerous."

Binet found that this composite measure did correlate reasonably well with a child's school grades and also with the teacher's evaluation of the child's intelligence. Thus, the test had predictive validity.

The intelligence quotient, IQ Binet also believed that intelligence grew as the child grew, and this provided the basis for the test's scoring system. Binet and Simon first gave their test to children of varying ages, in order to find out which items were passed by the average six-year-old, which by the average seven-year-old, and so on. They were then able to compare each individual's scores to these age-based norms. Can a child handle all the test items passed by the average eight-year-old but not those passed by a nine-year-old? If so, then the child's **mental age** (usually abbreviated **MA**) is eight. Can the child handle items passed by the average nine-year-old but not those passed by an older child? If so, the child's MA is nine.★

The child's MA, assessed in this fashion, can then be compared to his actual

Alfred Binet *(Courtesy of National Library of Medicine)*

★ Appropriate scoring adjustments were made when the performance pattern did not work out quite as neatly; for example, if a child passed all items at the seven-year-old level, and 75 percent of those at the eight-year-old level, then her MA would be seven years and nine months.

A boy taking the Bayley Scales developmental test. (Laura Dwight/Corbis)

chronological age (**CA**). To the extent that his MA exceeds his CA, we regard the child as "bright" or advanced. To the extent that his MA is lower than his CA, the child is regarded as "slow." Typically, MA is divided by CA, and the resulting quotient is then multiplied by 100 to get rid of decimal points. Thus,

$$IQ = MA/CA \times 100.$$

If a child's MA is the same as her CA, then her IQ is 100: Her score matches the average score of other children her age; she is of average intelligence. By the same token, if her IQ is greater than 100, then her intelligence is above average; if it is below 100, then her intelligence is below average.

However, there is an obvious problem with this calculation: Obviously the child eventually reaches his full level of adult intelligence, and his MA reaches its peak. Consistent with this idea, the top rung of Binet's mental age ladder was sixteen. (In later revisions of the test, the maximum age was higher, but the point remains: Eventually, one reaches the maximum.) But his CA continues to rise. So if the MA of a forty-eight-year-old is 16—the maximum score—his IQ would be $16/48 \times 100 = 33$, a score that indicates severe mental retardation.

To address this problem, IQ is currently calculated not by comparing an individual's score to her chronological age, but by comparing her score to the norm for her agemates. There are several ways to make this comparison, but one commonly used measure is the *deviation IQ.* On this measure, an IQ of 100 still indicates average intelligence, an IQ of 85 indicates that the individual scored better than only 16 percent of her agemates, an IQ of 115—that she scored better than 84 percent. An IQ of 70 or lower locates an individual in the bottom 2 percent of the scores for that age group; an IQ of 130 or higher locates the individual in the top 2 percent of the scores for that age.

TESTING INTELLIGENCE IN ADULTS

The Binet test was originally meant for children, but demand soon arose for the assessment of adults' intelligence. This led to the development of a test standardized on an adult population—the Wechsler Adult Intelligence Scale, or WAIS

(Wechsler, 1958). This scale was divided into various verbal and performance subtests. The verbal tests include items that assess general knowledge, vocabulary, comprehension, and arithmetic skills. The performance test includes tasks that require the test taker to assemble the cut-up parts of a familiar object to form the appropriate whole, to complete an incomplete drawing, and to rearrange a series of pictures so that they are in the proper sequence (Figure 15.7).

The revised version of the WAIS (the WAIS-R) is widely used but has the disadvantage that it can be administered to only one person at a time. Other tests,

15.7   Test items similar to some in the Wechsler Adult Intelligence Scale   (A) Verbal tests. These include tests of information, comprehension, and arithmetic. (B) Picture completion. The task is to note the missing part. (C) Block design. The materials consist of four blocks, which are all dark green on some sides, all light green on other sides, and half dark green and half light green on the rest of the sides. The test taker is shown a pattern and has to arrange the four blocks to produce this design. (D) Object assembly. The task is to arrange the cut-up pieces to form a familiar object. (Courtesy of The Psychological Corporation)

COMPREHENSION
1. Why should we obey traffic laws and speed limits?
2. Why are antitrust laws necessary?
3. Why should we lock the doors and take the keys to our car when leaving the car parked?
4. What does this saying mean: "Kill two birds with one stone."

INFORMATION
1. Who wrote *Huckleberry Finn?*
2. Where is Finland?
3. At what temperature does paper burn?
4. What is entomology?

ARITHMETIC
1. How many 15¢ stamps can you buy for a dollar?
2. How many hours will it take a cyclist to travel 60 miles if he is going 12 miles an hour?

A. Verbal tests
3. A man bought a used stereo system for ³/₄ of what it cost new. He paid $225 for it. How much did it cost new?
4. Six men can finish a job in ten days. How many men will be needed to finish the job in two and a half days?

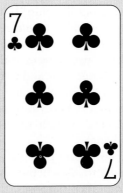

B. Picture completion

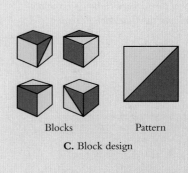

Blocks   Pattern

C. Block design

D. Object assembly

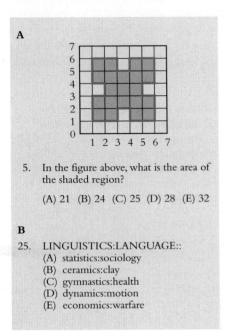

A

5. In the figure above, what is the area of the shaded region?

   (A) 21 (B) 24 (C) 25 (D) 28 (E) 32

B

25. LINGUISTICS:LANGUAGE::
    (A) statistics:sociology
    (B) ceramics:clay
    (C) gymnastics:health
    (D) dynamics:motion
    (E) economics:warfare

15.8   Two items from the Scholastic Aptitude Test (SAT) 1: Reasoning Test *(Courtesy of the College Entrance Examination Board and the Educational Testing Service)*

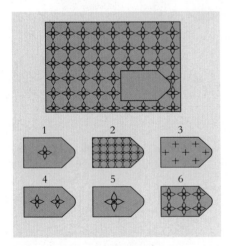

15.9   A sample item from the Progressive Matrices Test *The task is to select the alternative that fits into the empty slot above. (Courtesy of H. K. Lewis).*

developed to assess cognitive and academic aptitude, use a paper-and-pencil multiple-choice format that allows the simultaneous testing of large groups of people. Some examples are the SAT, taken by most college applicants, and the Graduate Record Examination (GRE), a more difficult version of the SAT designed for applicants to graduate schools (Figure 15.8). A test that emphasizes nonverbal intellectual ability is the Progressive Matrices Test (Figure 15.9).

SOME NEW DEVELOPMENTS IN INTELLIGENCE TESTING

A new test for children   In recent years, a new test for children has come to prominence, the Kaufman Assessment Battery for Children (K-ABC). Like virtually all intelligence tests, this is an outgrowth of those devised by Binet and Wechsler. However, the construction of this test and the selection of its subtests has been heavily influenced by recent research seeking to understand intelligence within the conceptual framework of information processing (see pp. 644–49 and Chapters 8 and 13). In addition, this test gives particular attention to the assessment of handicapped children and is also appropriate for cultural and linguistic minorities. Toward that end, it includes a nonverbal scale with questions that are presented in pantomime and have to be answered with various gestures. Because of these features, it's not surprising that scores on this test seem less affected by sociocultural conditions than those on the Stanford-Binet or on Wechsler's scales for children (Anastasi, 1984, 1985; Coffman, 1985; Kaufman, Kamphaus, and Kaufman, 1985; Page, 1985; see pp. 652–53 for discussion of the sociocultural conditions that can affect test results).

A neuropsychological test   In a standard intelligence test, the test taker is asked questions like this: "If it takes two bricklayers six days to build a wall, how many days would it take three bricklayers?" This question is designed to assess arithmetic skills, but, of course, an incorrect response might signify many things other than a weakness in arithmetic. That's because this question also requires that the examinee hear and understand the question correctly (speech comprehension), keep the problem and the numbers in mind long enough to solve it (working memory), know how to set up the problem (mathematical reasoning), and do it quickly enough to give the answer in the allotted time (speed of problem solving).

For many purposes, we are willing to lump these various skills together in order to ask whether the individual has the package of skills needed for this task. For other purposes, though, we want a more fine-grained assessment. This would be useful, for example, in trying to pinpoint cognitive impairments stemming from a learning disability, aging, or brain injury (Heilman and Valenstein, 1979; Lezak, 1983; Orsini, Van Gorp, and Boone, 1988). For these purposes, we need a more specialized test, known as a ***neuropsychological assessment.***

This assessment is often based on an extension of the WAIS-R in which each of the standard subtests is followed by a succession of more specialized tasks, allowing the neuropsychologist to discover exactly why the examinee's performance has faltered (Kaplan et al., 1991). In the arithmetic subtest, for example, all of the standard questions are asked and the answers scored in just the usual way. But then the examinee is asked to attempt to answer the missed questions again. This time the questions are presented in written form, with no time limit. If the examinee still can't answer the question, he is asked to work out the solution on paper, in order to lighten the memory load. If he still can't solve the problem, further steps are taken to determine whether the difficulty is in mathematical reasoning, in ignorance of the multiplication tables, and so on.

The participant tries to match his blocks to the pattern on the pad. (© Dan McCoy/Rainbow/PNI)

Similar methods have been used to construct tests designed to assess verbal learning, abstraction, visuospatial perception, and motor functioning (Delis et al., 1988, 1990).

AN AREA OF APPLICATION: MENTAL RETARDATION

Are any of these tests valid? Do they actually measure intelligence? One way to answer this is by looking at the tests' effectiveness in predicting school success. As we have mentioned, the tests' predictive validity is reasonably good, with correlations of around +.50 between test scores and subsequent measures of academic performance (for example, grade-point average). Another criterion grows out of Binet's original goal, which was to design an instrument for the detection of students in need of remedial education. How well did he and his followers succeed in this pursuit?

On the whole, intelligence tests perform this function rather well, and so they serve, for example, as an important first step toward the diagnosis of mental retardation. Generally, someone is said to be retarded if she has an IQ of 70 or lower, and by this criterion, about 2.5 percent of the population of the United States would be counted as retarded (Grossman, 1983). Of course, test performance is not the only criterion to be used in assessing retardation. Equally important is the ability to learn, the ability to cope with the demands of society, and the ability to take care of oneself. An individual with these capacities might not be classified as retarded, even though he has an IQ below 70; similarly, an individual without these skills might be considered retarded, even though he has an IQ above 70. As one author notes, "Individuals with IQs of 60 have been known to make satisfactory adjustments to the demands of daily living, while some with IQs close to 100 may require special care and guidance" (Anastasi, 1988, p. 285).

Recognizing that the diagnosis of retardation does not depend solely on IQ test scores is all the more important when diagnosing a child from a disadvantaged ethnic or racial minority, or from a different linguistic background. In these cases, there is a serious danger of misclassification, especially since (until recently) most intelligence tests used norms based entirely on white, English-speaking standardization groups.

To avoid misclassification, clinicians now recommend the use of assessment programs that include information about a child's social adjustment and sociocultural background. These assessments also evaluate the child's test performance against norms taken from his own subgroup, so that he is compared with other children who share his background (Mercer, 1973). Some other tests, such as the K–ABC, are especially useful in this context, since they include nonverbal scales deliberately designed to minimize sociocultural biases.

This shift in assessment strategy may explain in part why the number of children classified as retarded has been declining in recent years (MacMillan, 1988, 1989). It may also have reduced the number of children tainted by the stigma of the label "retarded." Further, it may have channeled more children into appropriate remedial programs, especially since many of those previously categorized as retarded are now recognized as having a learning disability. At the same time, however, the strong inclination not to identify children as retarded may have ended up depriving them of needed services. Therefore, the significance of this trend is difficult to assess (Zigler and Hodapp, 1991).

CLASSIFYING RETARDATION

Despite these complexities, IQ is still an important element in determining retardation. It can also be used to classify four degrees of retardation: mild (IQ between 55 and 69), moderate (40 to 54), severe (25 to 39), and profound (below 25). The more severe the retardation, the less frequently it occurs: In 100 retarded persons, one would expect the degree of retardation to be mild in 90, moderate in 6, severe in 3, and profound in 1 of the cases (Robinson and Robinson, 1970).

Table 15.3 presents a description of the general level of intellectual functioning at various ages in each of these four categories. Among other things, the table shows that mentally retarded persons do not have to be excluded from useful participation in society. This is especially true for those whose degree of

TABLE 15.3 CHARACTERISTICS OF THE MENTALLY RETARDED*			
Degree of retardation	*IQ range*	*Level of functioning at school age (6–20 years)*	*Level of functioning in adulthood (21 years and over)*
Mild	50–55 to approx. 70	Can learn academic skills up to approximately sixth-grade level by late teens; can be guided toward social conformity.	Can usually achieve social and vocational skills adequate to maintain self-support, but may need guidance and assistance when under unusual social or economic stress.
Moderate	35–40 to 50–55	Can profit from training in social and occupational skills; unlikely to progress beyond second-grade level in academic subjects; may learn to travel alone in familiar places.	May achieve self-maintenance in unskilled or semiskilled work under sheltered conditions; needs supervision and guidance when under mild social or economic stress.
Severe	20–25 to 35–40	Can talk or learn to communicate; can be trained in elemental health habits; profits from systematic habit training.	May contribute partially to self-maintenance under complete supervision; can develop self-protection skills at a minimum useful level in controlled environment.
Profound	below 20–25	Some motor development present; may respond to minimal or limited training in self-help.	Some motor and speech development; may achieve very limited self-care; needs nursing care.

retardation is mild, and they account for 90 percent of all the cases. If provided with appropriate training, such people can ultimately achieve an acceptable level of adjustment in adult life (Tyler, 1965).

THE CAUSES OF RETARDATION

What causes retardation? In some cases, retardation can be traced to a specific genetic disorder, as, for example, in Down's syndrome or a pattern known as fragile-X syndrome (so-called because it involves damage to the X chromosome). In other cases, retardation arises because of a problem that affected the developing fetus—for example, alcohol in the mother's bloodstream or certain diseases during pregnancy, such as rubella. Still other cases are the result of problems related to birth itself, including premature birth or temporary oxygen deprivation to the fetus. And yet other cases arise from conditions subsequent to birth, such as meningitis or head injury.

This is obviously a diverse set of factors, and, in fact, some have estimated that there are over two hundred causes of mental retardation, each with a specific organic basis (Grossman, 1983). What these cases have in common, though, is that they all lead to identifiable problems in the nervous system; they also tend to have other symptoms associated with them, and these symptoms play an important role in the diagnosis of individual cases.

All of these various causes, however, account for only the minority of retarded individuals. For the remaining cases (50–75 percent), the causes of the retardation are unknown but probably involve many factors. Some of these factors are again genetic, reflecting the combined effect of hundreds of different genes. Other factors operate after birth, including impoverished environmental conditions (Edgerton, 1979). For example, severe malnutrition during early life (a condition all too common in poor or underdeveloped countries) can by itself produce retardation, although some controversy remains about exactly how this retardation emerges and whether the damage can be reversed or reduced (Birch et al., 1971; Stoch et al., 1982; Brown and Pollitt, 1996).

Thus, we can distinguish, roughly, between cases of retardation that involve a single cause and identifiable damage to the nervous system and those that involve a complex set of causes and more diffuse damage (Zigler, 1967; Zigler and Hodapp, 1991). The former category tends to involve more severe retardation but is also much less frequent. The latter category is generally more frequent but involves only mild retardation. Some have proposed that cases in this second group do not constitute a separate diagnostic category, distinguishable from ordinary (nonretarded) individuals. Instead, they may simply represent the lower reaches of a naturally occurring variation in intelligence.

WHAT IS INTELLIGENCE? THE PSYCHOMETRIC APPROACH

Intelligence tests do appear to have validity: They aid in the diagnosis of retardation; and they allow us to assess the severity of retardation. They predict school performance fairly well, and are also a reasonable predictor of several other variables, including (in some circumstances) the quality of one's job performance (Neisser et al., 1996).

But let's be careful in interpreting these findings. Noting that IQ is an effective predictor of job performance, for example, might lead us to assume that it's above-average intelligence that enables people to perform effectively in the workplace. But other interpretations are also possible: Individuals with high IQ scores might stay in school longer, perhaps because they do better initially and so receive more encouragement from parents or teachers. The extra years of schooling then provide these individuals with skills that improve their on-the-job performance. In short, the chain of events might not be

$$\text{intelligence} \longrightarrow \text{better performance}$$

but instead

$$\text{intelligence} \longrightarrow \text{encouragement} \longrightarrow \text{more school} \longrightarrow \text{more skills}$$
$$\longrightarrow \text{better performance.}$$

One way or the other, though, the fact remains that IQ scores do predict other variables of considerable interest, and this gives us reason to believe that the tests are valid. In addition, the tests also seem to distinguish among people in ways that correspond with our intuitions about intelligence: People who seem smart to us do tend to score well on such tests; those who seem less intelligent generally do poorly.

In addition, the test results are impressively reliable—that is, stable from one occasion to the next. IQ scores obtained at age eighteen, for example, are correlated .89 with scores obtained at age twelve, and .77 with those obtained at age six (Moffitt et al., 1993). Some studies have even documented correlations between IQ scores obtained at age four or six and various measures of infant behavior, taken in the first half-year of life (Bornstein, 1989; McCall and Corriger, 1993).

But what exactly are these tests measuring? As we discussed above, there is no consensus on the definition of *intelligence*. But in the absence of such a consensus, perhaps we can scrutinize the test data themselves in an attempt to discover the regularities associated with success on IQ tests. Can we discern a "profile" of people who do well on the tests? people who do poorly? This is the essence of the ***psychometric*** (literally, "mind-measuring") ***approach*** to intelligence: One begins with the pattern of the measurements and, from this pattern, seeks to build a theory of what intelligence is.

THE STRUCTURE OF MENTAL ABILITIES

To understand the psychometric approach, consider how it addresses a crucial question about intelligence: Is intelligence a unitary ability or are there different types and qualities of intelligence? In other words, does intelligence provide an advantage on virtually any intellectual task or might someone be smart in some ways (and do better on some tasks) but be perfectly ordinary in other ways and on other tasks?

The psychometric approach tries to answer these questions by starting with people's scores on various tests. These scores presumably reflect each person's underlying abilities—perhaps their intelligence in general (if such a trait exists) or more specific, focused talents. We cannot observe (or measure) these abilities directly, but we can learn a great deal about the abilities by examining the details of the test performance.

To get an intuitive idea of this approach, consider looking at a lake and seeing what appear to be serpentlike parts:

A

The viewer can entertain various hypotheses. One is that all visible parts belong to one huge sea monster. This would be analogous to the hypothesis that there is a unitary intellectual ability, tying together the various test scores:

B

There might also be several such beasts (analogous to a hypothesis of separate mental abilities):

C

Or finally, there might be as many sea animals as there are visible parts (analogous to the hypothesis that every test measures a totally different ability):

D

How can the viewer choose among these alternatives, given that he has no way of peering below the waters? His best bet is to wait and watch how the serpentine parts change over time and space. If he does this, he can find out which parts go together. If all parts move jointly (B), the most reasonable interpretation is that they all belong to one huge sea monster. (For the purposes of our example, we will assume that sea serpents are severely arthritic and so unable to move their body portions separately.) If the first part goes with the second, while the third goes with the fourth (C), there are presumably two smaller creatures. If all parts move separately (D), the best bet is that there are as many sea serpents as there are visible parts.

In effect, our sea-serpent watcher has studied a correlation pattern. Some parts of the sea serpent are directly visible, just as test scores are directly visible. But what is interesting is how these parts (or test scores) are linked to each other, and the links are not visible—they are hidden below the surface. However, we can infer the (invisible) structure by seeing how the visible parts move: If they rise and fall together, we conclude they are linked (different tests all depend on a single ability); if they rise and fall independently, we conclude the opposite— each test depends on a different sort of skill.

SPEARMAN AND THE CONCEPT OF GENERAL INTELLIGENCE

To address the question of whether intelligence is unitary or multiple, let's consider the WAIS-R. This is one of the most widely used intelligence tests. It includes four subtests: information or general knowledge (I), compre-

TABLE 15.4 CORRELATION MATRIX OF FOUR SUBTESTS ON THE WECHSLER ADULT INTELLIGENCE SCALE

	I	C	A	V
I (Information)	—	.70	.66	.81
C (Comprehension)		—	.49	.73
A (Arithmetic)			—	.59
V (Vocabulary)				—

NOTE: The matrix shows the correlation of each subtest with each of the other three. Note that the left-to-right diagonal (which is here indicated by the dashes) can't have any entries because it is made up of the cells that describe the correlation of each subtest with itself. The cells below the dashes are left blank because they would be redundant.

SOURCE: From Wechsler, 1958.

hension (C), arithmetic (A), and vocabulary (V). As it turns out, the scores on these subtests are quite highly correlated with scores on the other subtests. The correlation between I and C is +.70, that between I and A is +.66, and so on. These results are presented in the form of a **correlation matrix** in Table 15.4.

This pattern certainly suggests that some common factor runs through all of these subtests, since individuals who perform well do so across the board; individuals who do poorly are consistent in their poor performance. Perhaps, therefore, these tasks all draw on the same basic skill. Individuals who are well-endowed with this skill do well on all the tests; individuals with less of this skill do poorly across the board.

To assess this pattern, psychologists rely on a statistical technique known as **factor analysis,** developed by Charles Spearman (1863–1945). Factor analysis allows us to extract a measurement of the common factor that seems to be shared among all of these tasks; Spearman argued that this factor is best described as **general intelligence,** or **g.** He proposed that *g* is a mental attribute called upon for any intellectual task, and so individuals with a lot of *g* have an advantage in every intellectual endeavor. If *g* is in short supply, the individual will do poorly on a wide range of tasks.

Spearman realized, though, that this cannot be our entire account of intelligence. If test performance were determined entirely by *g*, then the correlations between any two subtests should be perfect (that is, $r = +1.00$). But the correlations, while strongly positive, fall short of this. Spearman proposed, therefore, that each test depends both on *g* and also on some other ability that is specific to the particular subtest. Thus, performance on an arithmetic subtest depends on *g* and on numerical skills; performance on vocabulary tests depends on *g* and its own specialized skill. People differ from each other both in general intelligence and in these different specialized skills, and this is why the correlations among different subtests are not perfect (Spearman, 1927; for further discussion, see Baron, 1985).

GROUP-FACTOR THEORIES

According to Spearman, there truly is such a thing as intelligence in general, a capacity that gives some individuals an advantage in all of their intellectual endeavors. This claim, however, has been highly controversial. Other researchers have argued that the correlations among subtest scores are better explained by a *set* of underlying mental abilities rather than by a single overarching factor. L. L.

Thurstone (1887–1955), for one, argued that the various subtests assemble themselves into groups, with each group having its own underlying factor, separate from the factors that support the other groups. Thurstone regarded these **group factors** as the primary mental abilities. Some of the more important of these are spatial, numerical, verbal, and reasoning abilities. On this view, we shouldn't speak of intelligence in general, nor should we seek to summarize intelligence with just a single score. Instead, each individual has his or her own profile of primary abilities, and these will determine which tasks the individual will perform well on, and which not.

GENERAL INTELLIGENCE OR GROUP FACTORS?

Is there such a thing as general intelligence? Or is intelligence instead characterized by several more specialized skills, each operating in its own arena? It turns out that both conceptions capture important aspects of the data. Test scores do cluster into groups as Thurstone argued. Tests of spatial ability, for example, are highly correlated, whereas spatial tests correlate less highly with, say, tests of vocabulary. This provides our justification for taking these groups seriously and so distinguishing among the primary mental abilities—each contributing to its own group of tests—rather than lumping all these abilities together.

At the same time, scores on these primary abilities are fairly highly correlated with each other, so that individuals with a great deal of spatial ability, say, also tend to have larger vocabularies, and so on. The fact that the primary abilities rise and fall together provides evidence for g contributing to performance in all of these diverse domains.

But what exactly do these correlations mean? Some researchers argue that g truly does represent an identifiable skill or capacity and have sought to characterize this skill, and to explain how this skill contributes to such a wide range of activities (Jensen, 1980). For example, some have proposed that g is a measure of the neural efficiency of the brain (Eysenck, 1986; Vernon, 1987). But other researchers read the data differently (e.g., Ceci, 1990; Hunt, 1995). They agree that g provides a useful statistical summary of the data but disagree that g is itself a single identifiable capacity.

To understand the argument, consider the relationship between **fluid intelligence** and **crystallized intelligence.** The first of these refers to the ability to deal with new and unusual problems; it is an ability heavily influenced by mental speed and flexibility. The second refers to the individual's repertoire of previously acquired skills and information, a repertoire that's obviously useful for dealing with familiar problems or problems similar to those already encountered (Cattell, 1963, 1971; Horn, 1985).

There is a substantial correlation ($r = +.60$) between an individual's fluid intelligence and her crystallized intelligence. Perhaps, therefore, this is further evidence for g, with fluid and crystallized intelligence merely being different manifestations of this single underlying skill. If an individual is well endowed with this capacity, she will do well both on tests requiring fluid intelligence and on tests requiring crystallized intelligence. If an individual is lacking in this capacity, she will do well on neither.

However, other evidence suggests that fluid and crystallized intelligence are truly different from each other. For example, crystallized intelligence seems to increase with age, so long as the individual remains in an intellectually stimulating environment. Fluid intelligence, on the other hand, reaches its height in early adulthood and declines steadily with age (Horn, 1985; Horn and Noll, 1994). Similarly, alcohol consumption and some forms of brain damage cause more impairment in tasks requiring fluid intelligence than in those dependent on crystallized intelligence (Duncan, 1994; Hunt, 1995).

Notice, therefore, how much depends on one's perspective. For purposes of statistical summary, we can usefully describe an individual's fluid and crystallized intelligence with a single number. This is guaranteed by the fact that these two measures are, as we noted, strongly correlated, and so, if we know either one of these measures, we can predict the other with reasonable accuracy. For the development of theory, however, we cannot collapse fluid and crystallized intelligence into a single theoretical entity. Instead, we should understand them as separate and distinct capacities—each relevant to different tasks and subject to different influences.

This contrast in perspectives can also be used to summarize the broader state of the art in intelligence testing. If our purpose is to summarize the data or to predict performance then there is no question that measures of g are quite useful. These measures provide broad summaries of an individual's abilities, telling us how well that individual will perform in a wide range of intellectual tasks. Of course, we can then supplement this information with measures of the individual's more fine-grained skills; this will tell us still more, but in a narrower, more focused fashion.

If in contrast, our purpose is to define *intelligence,* things remain more uncertain. Some argue that g is actually a measure of an intellectual capacity that all of us have to some degree. Others argue that g is simply a convenient summary of the data and nothing more. On this view, measures of g reflect a complex and diverse set of capacities that we should not, for purposes of theory, be lumping together. The debate between these two positions is likely to continue for some time. In the meantime the practical value of g measures remains strong, at the same time that the theoretical meaning of g remains open.

WHAT IS INTELLIGENCE? THE INFORMATION-PROCESSING APPROACH

The instruments devised by Binet and his successors are of considerable practical importance. They are used in diagnosis, guidance, and selection and thus often have an important impact on individual lives. Moreover, these tests have provided insights into many of the skills that contribute to intelligent performance and so have spurred theory as well.

At the same time, there are many questions that these tests cannot answer. What are the mechanisms that underlie intelligent behavior? Why is it that some individuals fail on a particular problem while others succeed? These are crucial questions if we wish to understand what intelligence is, and how intelligent thinking proceeds. These questions are no less important for practical purposes. If we wish to improve someone's performance, it will obviously be useful first to locate the problem: Why does that individual have difficulties? what strategies, or what information, is the person missing?

For these reasons, many psychologists have turned to a different approach to the study of intelligence, one that is based on an analysis of the cognitive operations needed for intellectual performance, including performance on intelligence tests. The basic idea is to link differences in overall test performance to more fine-grained differences in the way individuals perceive, attend, learn, remember, and think.

SIMPLE COGNITIVE CORRELATES

Some investigators have proposed that large-scale differences in intellectual capacity actually derive from some remarkably low-level cognitive operations. Skill in carrying out these simple operations is far from what we typically think of as intelligence. But these low-level operations are used again and again in intelligent performance, and so they may well be the building blocks of this performance.

Reaction time An idea that goes back to Galton is that differences in mental ability are related to speed of mental processing. As a relatively direct test of this notion, a number of investigators have tried to correlate reaction time with intelligence-test performance. Some studies have measured **simple reaction time,** in which the participant merely responds as quickly as he can when a stimulus appears. Others have measured **choice reaction time** in which the participant must again respond as quickly as possible but now has to choose among several responses, depending on the stimulus presented. In one such setup the participant places his finger in the center of a board that contains eight small light bulbs, each with a button alongside of it (see Figure 15.10). He must press the associated button as quickly as he can after a bulb lights up. In this task, short reaction times are in fact correlated with higher intelligence-test scores. There is also some suggestion that these correlations are weaker for simple reaction time than they are for choice reaction time, and that the correlations go up as the number of choices increases (Jensen, 1987; but see Detterman, 1987).

According to some investigators, these reaction-time measures are a way of getting at rock-bottom differences in neurological functioning, differences that may be the underpinning of Spearman's *g*. (As we noted earlier, some researchers have literally interpreted *g* as a measure of "neural efficiency.") But is this really sensible? Reaction time is affected by many variables, including the ability to understand the experimenter's instructions, the ability to keep one's attention focused, and so on. It's possible, therefore, that short reaction times are simply one more achievement made possible by intelligence, rather than the underlying cause of intelligence (Detterman, 1987; Brody, 1992). In addition, we should note that the correlations between IQ and reaction time are not large—around −.35. (The correlation is negative because higher reaction times go with lower intelligence-test scores.) Therefore, even if reaction time does reflect some basic process underlying mental ability, it can only account for a small portion of the variability in the population.

Verbal ability and lexical access time Perhaps intelligence is not associated with mental speed in general. Perhaps intelligence depends instead on the speed of some specific process or some particular mental event. For example, in order to understand a sentence, one needs to think about the meanings of the individual words within the sentence. Presumably, one retrieves these meanings from some sort of mental dictionary, and this process of looking up each word is swift but not instantaneous (see Chapter 8). Moreover, one must do this look-up again and again, for each of the words encountered. Therefore, being slightly quicker at this task might add up to a considerable benefit, being slightly slower to a considerable cost (Hunt, 1976, 1985b).

One plausible hypothesis, then, is that speed at this mental look-up is an important contributor to performance on tests of verbal intelligence. To test this hypothesis, investigators have used the **lexical decision task,** which was designed to provide a direct measure of how quickly words can be accessed in long-term memory. A participant is presented with strings of letters, such as *bread* or *blead,*

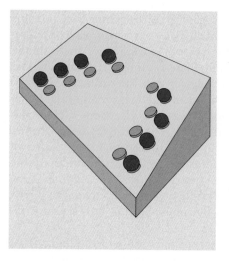

15.10   Choice reaction time as a measure of speed of mental processing *An apparatus for measuring choice reaction time. The participant has to place his finger in the center of a board that contains eight small light bulbs. As soon as he sees one of the bulbs light up, he has to press the button alongside it. (Jensen, 1980)*

645

and asked to decide whether the string is a word or not. Her speed of lexical access is measured by the time it takes her to make this decision.★ Several studies show that these memory look-up times are shorter for people who do well on tests of verbal intelligence, exactly as predicted. The difference is especially marked when the comparison is between normal participants and participants at the lower extremes of the population, such as persons with brain damage (Hunt, 1978). But to a lesser extent, such differences have also been obtained within normal populations, for example, between college students with high and low scores on the verbal portion of the SAT or on tests of reading comprehension (Hunt, Lunneborg, and Lewis, 1975; Jackson and McClelland, 1975, 1979).

COMPLEX COGNITIVE COMPONENTS

Simple cognitive operations such as choice reaction time and memory look-up are clearly correlated with intelligence-test performance, presumably because intelligence depends on the smooth operation of these simple, rock-bottom cognitive processes. But surely there is more to intelligence than this. Consider the performance of a ballet dancer. She can't dance if she can't walk and run and jump, but dancing is more than walking, running, and jumping. It involves the intricate organization of higher-level actions such as pirouettes, combinations of ballet steps, and so on. These cannot be performed without the lower-level operations, but this doesn't mean that the two are identical. Much the same may be true for intelligence. To reason about a problem in arithmetic, one has to recognize the numbers (e.g., 1 means "one"), and one may have to retrieve the multiplication table from memory (e.g., $2 \times 3 = 6$). But recognizing numbers and retrieving the multiplication table are not the same as reasoning arithmetically.

These considerations have led researchers to study some of the higher-level processes that might constitute intelligence, in contrast to the lower-level processes we have considered so far. One such undertaking was Robert Sternberg's analysis of analogical reasoning (Sternberg, 1977). Analogy problems are a staple of many intelligence tests, and since analogy tests are highly correlated with other intelligence subtests, they may provide a particularly good measure of Spearman's g-factor. For example:

Hand is to foot as finger is to (arm, leg, thumb, toe).

Or to give a more difficult item:

Washington is to one as Lincoln is to (five, ten, twenty).

What mental processes, or **cognitive components,** are needed to solve these problems? Sternberg proposed that the problem is solved in separate stages. First, one identifies attributes of each term that might be relevant (e.g., both Washington and Lincoln were presidents; Washington was the first president and Lincoln the sixteenth). After this, one tries to discover relationships between the first and second terms of the analogy (e.g., Washington was the first president, hence Washington-president one) and then between the first and third terms (e.g., Washington-president and Lincoln-president). Finally, one takes the relationships inferred for the Washington-president one pair and tries to apply them to create an appropriate match for Lincoln. For example, applying the relationship

---

★ Strictly speaking, it is the time she takes to make this yes-no decision minus the time it takes her to react to the letter strings when no decision is asked for.

15.11 *Washington is to one as Lincoln is to five*

Washington-president one to Lincoln would yield Lincoln-president sixteen. But this doesn't work, since sixteen is not one of the options available. A different relationship links Washington's portrait to the one-dollar bill, and this does work, since Lincoln's portrait is on the five-dollar bill, and "five" is one of the options (Sternberg, 1977; see Figure 15.11).

Perhaps it is skill in these component stages that characterizes intelligence, so that someone better at the discovery of these relationships, or the application of these relationships to new terms, will perform more effectively on intelligence tests (or any other task requiring intelligence). Results consistent with this suggestion come from a study in which participants were presented with various tests of reasoning (Sternberg and Gardner, 1983). Some of the tests involved analogies, others involved classification tasks (e.g., which pair of words does *Italy* go with, *Germany/France* or *Vietnam/Korea*?). There was a remarkable correspondence between decision times on these tasks and the participants' scores on several psychometric tests of abstract reasoning. The average correlation was −.65, a very encouraging result for the theory of complex cognitive components. (As before, the correlation was negative because higher decision times correspond to lower reasoning scores.)

THE ROLE OF WORKING MEMORY AND ATTENTION

A related proposal focuses on the role of working memory and attention in intelligence (see Chapters 7 and 8). In solving an analogy problem, for example, one must keep track of the various terms and of their attributes. One must also remember which relationships have already been examined (and found unsatisfactory), so that one doesn't keep examining the same relationships over and over. All of this requires memory storage, as well as attention, as one focuses on different aspects of the problem and develops new interpretations of it.

Again, this leads to an obvious proposal: Individuals with ample working memory and attention should perform better on analogy tests and also on a wide range of other tasks. Individuals without these capacities will perform worse. To test this suggestion, researchers have developed *active-span tasks*, procedures designed to assess an individual's ability to store and manipulate different pieces of information simultaneously. One such test is illustrated in Figure 15.12. In this procedure, the participant must first decide whether each equation is true, and then read the word out loud. For the first item, therefore, the subject would say, "true; dog." Then the subject sees another item and another. After a series of these items, a cue appears, and the subject must write down as many of the words as he can recall ("dog, gas, nose . . .").

This seems a peculiar task, but it does require the subject to remember materials while simultaneously working with other materials—exactly the combination we hope to measure. And, as hypothesized, scores on such tasks do correlate with a variety of other intelligence-test scores, including the verbal SAT score, measures of reading comprehension and of reasoning, and some versions of the IQ test (Carpenter, Just, and Shell, 1990; Kyllonen and Cristal, 1990; Engle, Cantor, and Carullo, 1992; Just and Carpenter, 1992).

$$(7 \times 7) + 1 = 50; \text{dog}$$
$$(10/2) + 6 = 10; \text{gas}$$
$$(4 \times 2) + 1 = 9; \text{nose}$$
$$(3/1) + 1 = 4; \text{beat}$$
$$(5/5) + 1 = 2; \text{tree}$$
$$(8 \times 2) - 4 = 13; \text{help}$$
$$(6/2) - 3 = 2; \text{stay}$$

15.12 *Test items for an active-span task* *For each item, the person being tested must say aloud whether the answer to the math problem is true or false and then must read the associated word. For the first item the person would say, "true, dog"; for the second, "false, gas," and so forth. After a series of these items, the person must write down as many of the words as he can ("dog, gas, nose . . ."). The number of words correctly recalled is the person's active span.*

STRATEGIES AND INTELLECTUAL FUNCTIONING

Still another approach to the study of intelligence focuses on the strategies that participants use for solving problems, for learning, and for remembering. We discussed such strategies earlier in our discussion of cognitive development (see Chapter 13). As we saw there, a normal adult can master memory tasks that are generally beyond the reach of a six-year-old, and an important reason for this lies in the strategies the adult uses. Suppose she is asked to memorize unrelated materials, such as the words

tulip plumber tiger sweater lily tailor daisy

raincoat monkey butcher zebra jacket.

An adult will do her best to rehearse this list of items and probably will also try to organize the list in some way. For example, she might try rhythmic grouping by, say, repeating the items in threes: "tulip, plumber, tiger . . . sweater, lily, tailor, . . . daisy, raincoat, monkey. . . . " Or she might try to organize the list of items into categories, thinking first about the flowers, then the occupations, then the animals. Any of these organizational devices will help her in later tests of recall. A six-year-old, in contrast, is unlikely to have such organizational tricks in her repertoire and so will be less successful at such intellectual tasks (Flavell and Wellman, 1977).

The use of such strategies also accounts for some of the intellectual differences among adults, with the best evidence coming from extreme differences in ability, such as the differences between adults who function normally and retarded individuals. The evidence suggests, for example, that retarded examinees attack memory tasks with little or no resort to organization. They are less likely to rehearse, to group items in a list, or to show recall clustering by semantic categories (Brown, 1974; Campione and Brown, 1977; Campione, Brown, and Ferrara, 1982). Strategy use also provides part of the reason why the elderly often have trouble in remembering—they fail to use strategies when they first encounter the to-be-remembered materials and so are at a disadvantage later on, when the time comes to remember this material (Craik and Byrd, 1982; Craik and Jennings, 1992). The same is true for individuals who are depressed; they engage poorly with the to-be-remembered materials during learning, and so have difficulty retrieving them later on.

TRYING TO TEACH THE MISSING STRATEGIES

Is there some way to teach people to use strategies for problem solving and remembering? If the answer is yes, then some aspects of retardation may be remediable. Several studies have shown that memory performance can be improved for mildly retarded participants simply by requiring them to repeat the to-be-remembered items aloud. This induced rehearsal, in some studies, leads to recall performance virtually identical to that of average adults (Brown et al., 1973; for related data showing the benefits of training with the elderly, see Craik and Jennings, 1992). Sadly, though, other studies suggest that these newly acquired strategies are abandoned by the participants shortly after they are taught. Furthermore, the participants regularly fail to transfer the strategies learned in one context to other rather similar contexts (Bilsky, Evans, and Gilbert, 1972; Campione and Brown, 1977; for parallel data with the elderly, see Hertzog, Dixon, and Hultsch, 1990).

Does this mean it's fruitless to teach these strategies to retarded persons? A

number of investigators have shown that the answer is no. The newly taught strategies *will* transfer to new situations if the retarded person is explicitly taught that the strategies are useful in other settings, beyond the initial context of learning. Suppose, for example, he is trained to use a particular mode of rehearsal: grouping the items in a list by threes and repeating them out loud. He will then have to be carefully reminded to use this technique on each trial. He'll also have to be trained to use the same technique with different lists and somewhat different methods of presentation. But if all of this is done, the strategy will be learned and will show a reasonable degree of transfer (Campione, Brown, and Ferrara, 1982). Similar techniques have been employed to help schoolchildren who are not retarded but who are poor at learning from texts (Brown, Campione, and Day, 1981).

Why is it that retarded persons and young children don't generalize strategies without clear and explicit instruction? If retarded individuals learn to remember a set of names by rehearsing them aloud, why don't they apply the same principle to a shopping list? According to several writers, what is lacking is a "master plan" for dealing with memory tasks in general, a strategy for using strategies (Flavell, 1970; see Chapter 13). Adults of normal intelligence adopt this higher-order strategy as a matter of course whenever they try to learn. They know that remembering telephone numbers, or traffic directions, or the months that have thirty days are at bottom similar memory tasks. They also know that trying to learn them means using some aids to learning—rehearsal, semantic grouping, or whatever. But young children and retarded persons lack this general insight. They don't recognize what all memory tasks have in common and what they all require for mastery. Young children will get it in time; retarded persons may never attain it.

WHAT IS INTELLIGENCE? BEYOND IQ

We have now filled in many of the blanks in our portrait of intelligence. We have impressive means of measuring intelligence. We understand many of the elements and processes that make intelligent performance possible. One might well ask, however, what is *left out* of this portrait. Unmistakably, the tests devised by Binet and his successors do tap many aspects of what we ordinarily mean by "intelligence." But surely there are other aspects that we have not yet covered. Consider someone's competence in dealing with the world of practical affairs. Nothing in the intelligence tests will assess someone's common sense, or street smarts, or know how. A related aptitude is social competence: the ability to persuade others and to judge their moods and desires. Shrewd salespeople have this ability as do successful politicians, even if they don't have the most spectacular IQ.

A demonstration of the difference between academic and nonacademic intelligence comes from a study of experienced racetrack handicappers who were asked to predict the outcomes and payoffs in upcoming horse races. This is a tricky mental task that involves highly complex reasoning. Track records, jockeys, track conditions, and so on all have to be remembered and weighed against each other. On the face of it, one might suppose that the ability to perform such mental calculations is just what intelligence tests measure. But the results proved otherwise, for the handicappers' success turned out to be completely unrelated to their IQs (Ceci and Liker, 1986).

649

PRACTICAL INTELLIGENCE

These results with racetrack handicappers, and a variety of other evidence, have persuaded researchers that we need to broaden our conception of intelligence, including some forms of intelligence simply not measured by IQ tests. For example, a number of researchers, particularly Robert Sternberg, have emphasized the importance of *practical intelligence.* We earlier mentioned Sternberg's "componential" approach to intelligence; this approach provides key insights into what Sternberg calls *analytic intelligence,* the sort of intelligence typically measured by intelligence tests. However, other forms of intelligence, Sternberg argues, are just as important, including practical intelligence and *creative intelligence* (Sternberg, 1985).

In one study of practical intelligence, business executives were asked to rate the relative importance of various skills needed to head a company department, such as the ability to delegate authority or to promote communication. It turned out that the skills these executives rated as most important were excellent predictors of business success: Those who had these skills tended to perform particularly well and to earn the highest salaries. Interestingly, there was virtually no correlation between these measures of business success and IQ (Wagner, 1987; Wagner and Sternberg, 1987; Sternberg and Wagner, 1993).

Practical and analytic intelligence differ in many ways. Problems demanding practical intelligence tend to be poorly defined initially and usually require some amount of information gathering before they can be tackled. Problems requiring analytic intelligence typically have none of these properties (Neisser et al., 1996). Sternberg and his collaborators have also argued that practical intelligence relies heavily on what they call *tacit knowledge*—practical know-how that is accumulated from everyday experience (Sternberg et al., 1995). Tacit knowledge and practical intelligence in general tend to be specific to a particular domain. The business executive acquires tacit knowledge that is relevant to running a company but not to navigating a ship or handicapping horses. The highly talented handicapper has no advantage in tasks away from the race track.

THE NOTION OF MULTIPLE INTELLIGENCES

A different attempt to expand the notion of intelligence is Howard Gardner's concept of *multiple intelligences* (Gardner, 1983). Gardner's claims are based, in part, on a consideration of individuals with special talents or special deficits. He notes, for example, that some individuals are exquisitely talented in music, even though they seem quite ordinary in other respects. This suggests to Gardner that musical intelligence is separate and distinct from other forms of intelligence. Similar considerations led him to argue for the existence of six specialized "intelligences": linguistic, logical-mathematical, spatial, musical, bodily-kinesthetic, and personal intelligence.

The first three of these are familiar enough, for they are assessed by most standard intelligence scales (and emerged as primary mental abilities in Thurstone's analyses—see p. 643). Musical ability includes skill in composition and in performance. By bodily-kinesthetic intelligence, Gardner refers to the ability to learn and create complex motor patterns, as in dancers and skilled athletes. By personal intelligence, he refers to the ability to understand oneself and others.

One line of evidence for Gardner's claim comes from studies of brain lesions that devastate some abilities while sparing others. Thus, certain lesions will make

Bodily-kinesthetic intelligence *According to Howard Gardner, the ability to learn complex motor patterns, such as those performed here by the Golden Domes of Russia, is one of several "multiple intelligences" that are largely independent of each other. (Photograph by François Mori/AP)*

15.13 Drawing ability in a retarded savant *A drawing by Nadia, a severely retarded child with remarkable drawing ability. This horse was drawn when she was four years old. (From Selfe, 1977)*

a person unable to recognize drawings (spatial intelligence), while others will make her unable to perform a sequence of movements (bodily-kinesthetic intelligence) or will produce major changes in personality (personal intelligence).

Another argument for Gardner's theory comes from the study of so-called **savants** (formerly, *idiot savants*). These are generally profoundly retarded persons who nonetheless have some single extraordinary talent. Some display unusual artistic talent (see Figure 15.13). Others are "calendar calculators," able to answer immediately (and correctly!) if asked questions such as, "What day of the week was March 17 in the year 1682?" (see Figure 15.14). Still others have unusual mechanical talents or unusual musical skills, for example, effortlessly memorizing lengthy and complex musical works (Hill, 1978).

Gardner's claims are controversial. For example, the number of savants is quite small: perhaps one or two for every thousand institutionalized retarded persons (Hill, 1978). Why are such cases so rare if the various "intelligences" are really as independent as Gardner claims? It is also unclear what to make of the abilities of these savants. The calendar calculators, for example, can do extraordinary things with dates, but they are unable to calculate $8 + 9$ or $7 - 6$. Is it sensible, therefore, to count this as a case of exceptional mathematical intelligence?

15.14 Unusual numerical achievements in an autistic savant *A scene from the 1988 film* Rainman, *which featured an autistic person with extraordinary numerical gifts that enabled him to note the exact number of matches remaining in a matchbox after the box was dropped and some were spilled on the floor, to keep track of all the cards in a casino blackjack game, and so forth. (From* Rainman, *with Dustin Hoffman and Tom Cruise; courtesy of Photofest)*

"Son, your mother is a remarkable woman."

We might, in addition, raise a further concern about Gardner's theory: There is no question that some individuals—whether savants or otherwise—have special talents and that these talents are immensely impressive. However, is it appropriate to think of these talents as forms of intelligence? Or might we be better served by a distinction between intelligence and talent? To put this differently, is being smart a talent in the same sense that being able to play the violin is a talent? The answers to these questions are far from clear, and this makes Gardner's claims difficult to evaluate.

Whatever the ultimate verdict on Gardner's theory, there is no doubt that he has performed a valuable service by drawing attention to a set of abilities that is often ignored and certainly undervalued by our society. Gardner and Sternberg are both surely correct in noting that we tend to focus too much on the skills and capacities that help people succeed in school. Whether or not these other abilities are forms of intelligence, they are still abilities to be highly esteemed and, if at all possible, nurtured and developed.

THE CULTURAL CONTEXT OF INTELLIGENCE

Sternberg's work on practical intelligence and Gardner's on multiple intelligences point up certain limitations of standard intelligence tests. These limitations become more glaring when trying to assess intelligence in members of other cultures. To begin with, many standard intelligence tests emphasize quick and decisive responses. But not all cultures share our Western preoccupation with speed. Indians and Native Americans, for example, place a higher value on being deliberate; in effect, they'd rather be right than quick. In addition, they prefer to qualify, or to say "I don't know" or "I'm not sure," unless they're absolutely certain of their answer. But such deliberations and hedging won't help their test scores; on standard intelligence tests you get more points if you guess (Sinha, 1983; Triandis, 1989).

Further factors have to do with formal Western schooling, which teaches the students the kinds of questions teachers (and tests) tend to ask. We saw previously that the unschooled in Liberia group objects not according to an abstract semantic category (e.g., tools vs. foods), but rather on the basis of the concrete situation in which the objects would be used together (e.g., a knife with an orange; see Chapter 13). A similar concreteness is seen in the response of an

unschooled Russian peasant who was asked: "From Shakhimardan to Vuadil it takes three hours on foot, while to Fergana it is six hours. How much time does it take to go on foot from Vuadil to Fergana?" The reply was: "No, it's six hours from Vuadil to Shakhimardan. You're wrong. . . . It's far and you wouldn't get there in three hours." (Luria, 1976, quoted in Sternberg, 1990, p. 229). If this had been a question on a standard intelligence test, the poor peasant would have scored poorly. But why? He had not gone to school, and thus he didn't know that questions of this sort are simply trying to get at arithmetical reasoning, so that it doesn't matter what the actual distances between the towns really are. It turned out that he was quite able to perform the relevant calculation but couldn't accept the form in which the question was presented.

All of this makes it clear that we have to be very careful in applying intelligence measures. Intelligence tests do capture important aspects of intellectual functioning, but they do not capture all aspects or all mental abilities. These tests may be useful instruments for predicting school success in Western cultures, but they do much less well in other contexts and on other forms of success. In the end, it seems clear that intelligence tests do measure something of considerable interest, but the meaning and utility of these tests must be understood in the appropriate environmental and cultural context. (For further discussion, see Sternberg, 1985, 1990.)

NATURE, NURTURE, AND INTELLIGENCE

We have emphasized a number of complexities and limitations associated with intelligence testing. But the fact remains that intelligence tests do predict success in a number of different contexts (especially in Western cultures), and the test scores are widely used—by educators deciding whom to admit to a program and by employers deciding whom to hire. Perhaps it is no surprise, therefore, that these test scores have been the focus of a fierce debate, with important political and social implications (see Block and Dworkin, 1976; Eysenck vs. Kamin, 1981; Fancher, 1987).

SOME POLITICAL ISSUES

Intelligence testing has been connected to political debate from the very beginning. Recall that Binet intended his test as a means of identifying schoolchildren who would benefit from extra training. In the early years of the twentieth century, however, a number of people—scientists and politicians—put the test to a different use. They noted the fact (still true today) that there was a correlation between IQ and socioeconomic status: Those who are well off tend to have higher IQs than those who are disadvantaged. They concluded that there was little point in trying to educate low-IQ individuals: The correlation seems to suggest that these individuals will never amount to anything, so why waste resources on them? They also argued that the observed differences in intelligence were largely inherited—a view that was certainly comforting to those who benefited from the status quo, since it suggested that they got what they "deserved."

In contrast, advocates for the disadvantaged took a different view. To begin with, they often disparaged the tests themselves, arguing that they were biased to

Anti-immigration sentiment in the
United States *"Immigration Restriction.*
Prop Wanted" A cartoon that appeared in the
January 23, 1903, issue of the Philadelphia
Inquirer *calling for more restrictive immigra-*
tion laws. (Courtesy of the New York Public
Library)

favor some cultures and some intellectual styles over others. In addition, they argued that intellectual aptitudes are much more determined by nurture than nature. In their view, differences in intelligence, especially those between different ethnic and racial groups, are determined predominantly by environmental factors such as early home background and schooling. Seen in this light, the children of the poor obtain lower test scores not because they inherit deficient genes, but because they inherit poverty.

These contrasting views obviously led to different prescriptions for social policy, and for many years, those biased toward the first of these positions—emphasizing heredity—dominated the debate. An example is the rationale behind the United States' immigration policy between the two world wars. The Immigration Act of 1924 set rigid quotas to minimize the influx of what were thought to be biologically "weaker stocks," specifically those from southern and eastern Europe. To "prove" the genetic intellectual inferiority of these immigrants, a congressional committee pointed to the scores of these groups on the army intelligence test, which were indeed substantially below those attained by Americans of northern European ancestry.

In actual fact, these differences were primarily related to the length of time that the immigrants had been in the United States prior to the test. When they first arrived, the immigrants lacked fluency in English as well as knowledge of certain cultural facts important for the tests; it's no surprise, then, that their test scores were low. For those immigrants who were admitted, these factors were gradually erased, and so, after some years of residence in the United States, their scores became indistinguishable from those of native-born Americans. This observation plainly undermines the hypothesis of a hereditary difference in intelligence between, say, northern and eastern Europeans. But the congressional proponents of immigration quotas did not analyze the results so closely. They had their own reasons for restricting immigration, such as fears of competition from cheap labor. The theory that the excluded groups were innately inferior provided a convenient justification for their policies (Kamin, 1974).

A more contemporary example of the relation between psychological theory and social policy is the argument over alleged racial differences in intelligence-test scores. A highly controversial book by Herrnstein and Murray argued that these differences must be taken seriously and are largely attributable to genetic factors. Herrnstein and Murray note a number of policy implications that follow from their view, including a reevaluation of many affirmative action programs and special education programs, such as Head Start, designed to improve the scholastic performance of disadvantaged preschool children (Herrnstein and Murray, 1994).

Herrnstein and Murray's claims have been criticized on many counts. There has been considerable debate, for example, about their interpretation of the test scores and even about whether race is a meaningful biological category. We will return to these points later in the chapter; for now, we simply highlight the fact that these remain questions with profound political importance, making it imperative that we ensure that policy debates are informed by good science.

GENETIC FACTORS

Plainly, people differ from each other in their intelligence and talents. But what causes these differences? Can we separate the contributions of heredity from the contributions of environment? And can we determine the extent to which these differences are permanent and immutable and the extent to which they can be eroded by means of education or enrichment?

GENETIC TRANSMISSION

Before turning to the relationship between intelligence-test performance and genetic endowment, let us review a few points about the transmission of genetic characteristics, some of which were discussed in a previous chapter (see Chapter 13).

Phenotype and genotype   For most purposes, what we care about is an organism's actual structure, its observable traits and its actual behavior. But these traits are not what are specified by the genes. Instead, the genes specify a series of commands that constitute something like an architectural blueprint—a set of plans for how the organism should develop. And, of course, it is easy to find cases in which the observable traits, or **phenotype,** depart from the traits specified in the genes, or **genotype.** Thus, an individual born with blonde hair can't change his genotype, but he can, with a bottle of hair dye, change his phenotype.

The key idea, then, is that the traits one ends up with may be quite different from the traits specified in one's genetic material. In some cases, this is because the genetically specified pattern can be altered after the fact (as hair color can be changed with dye). In other cases, environmental circumstances can block the genetically specified pattern from ever being expressed in the first place. Consider the dark markings on the paws, tail, and ear tips of a Siamese cat. These markings are not present at birth, but they appear gradually as the kitten matures, and the genealogical records kept by cat breeders leave no doubt that these markings in the mature animal are almost entirely determined by heredity. But this does not mean that they emerge independently of the environment. The dark markings will only appear if the kitten's extremities are kept at their normal temperature during the relevant developmental episodes. If the extremities are too warm during early kittenhood (and cat breeders often arrange for this, by such devices as leggings or earmuffs), they will not darken—in apparent defiance of the creature's genotype (Ilyin and Ilyin, 1930). Similar findings have been obtained with some other animals (see Figure 15.15).

Clearly, then, genes do not operate in a vacuum. They are instructions to the developing organism, specifying how and when certain processes should unfold. But these instructions will be followed only within a given range of environmental conditions, so that, in important ways, the expression of the genetic plan depends on an *interaction* between the genotype and the environment. This interaction is especially important during the early stages in the organism's development, since a particular genetic command can only be executed if certain physical characteristics (oxygen concentration, hormone levels, temperature) both inside and outside of the developing body are within a certain range. Thus, it makes no sense to talk about a trait—*any* trait—as being a result of either heredity or environment alone. All traits depend on both. There can be no organism without a genotype, and this genotype cannot express itself independently of the environment.

The inheritance of psychological characteristics   It is obvious that many physical characteristics (e.g., height, eye color) are determined by heredity, but the same is true for many psychological characteristics as well. And here, too, the contrast between genotype and phenotype is crucial. An important illustration involves a severe form of mental retardation associated with **phenylketonuria** or **PKU.** In the United States, about one baby in every fifteen thousand is born with this defect, caused by a problem with a single gene. This gene ordinarily governs the production of an enzyme needed to transform **phenylalanine,** one of the **amino acids** (the building blocks of proteins), into a different amino acid. A defect in this gene, however, leads to a deficiency in the enzyme, and as a result,

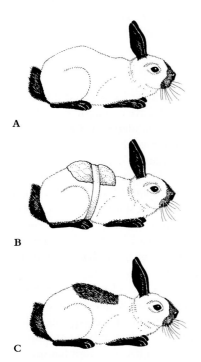

15.15   The effect of temperature on coat color   *Normally only the feet, tail, ears, and nose of the Himalayan rabbit are black (A). But when an ice pack is applied to a region of the back (B), the new fur grown at an artificially low temperature also comes in black (C). (After Winchester, 1977)*

A

B

C

655

phenylalanine is instead converted into a toxic agent that accumulates in the infant's bloodstream and damages her developing nervous system.

Although PKU is unmistakably of genetic origin, it can be dealt with by a simple intervention—a special diet that contains very little phenylalanine. If this diet is introduced at an early enough age, retardation can be minimized or avoided altogether. In this case, the genotype for PKU is present but with no phenotypic expression.

This case underscores an important point: Many people believe that if a trait is inherited, it is unchangeable. After all, one can't change one's genes! The fallacy of this belief, however, lies in conflating phenotype with genotype: We can't change a person's genotype, but we can take steps that will markedly change his phenotype. In the case of PKU, we know how to do this, and so this disorder is not merely treatable; it is entirely avoidable (McClearn and DeFries, 1973).

Polygenic inheritance   Traits governed by a single gene or gene pair are usually all-or-none: One either inherits the genetic code for brown eyes or for producing enough of the enzyme needed to digest phenylalanine or one doesn't. Other traits, such as height and weight, vary in a more continuous fashion. These traits are a matter of degree and are not simply present or absent. Traits like these are governed by **polygenic inheritance,** in which the trait is controlled not by one gene or one gene pair but by many genes. In the case of height, for example, some genes promote processes that lead to increased stature, others promote processes that lead to lesser stature. The individual's overall genetic potential for height (for now, ignoring environmental effects) is determined by the combined action of all these genes. If more and more genes within the individual favor tallness, then the person will probably end up correspondingly tall. As more and more genes favor shortness, the person will probably end up shorter.

GENETICS AND IQ

Clearly height is (to a large extent) determined by genetic factors, and therefore differences in height, from one individual to the next, have a genetic basis. How can we find out whether the same is true for human intelligence? One strategy is to examine the similarities among relatives, an approach that dates back to Galton (e.g., Galton, 1869). For example, the correlation between the IQs of children and the IQs of their parents is about +.47; the correlation between the IQs of siblings is in the same neighborhood (Bouchard and McGue, 1981). Such a correlation might suggest inheritance of mental ability, since family members are highly similar genetically. But parents and children also live in similar social and financial circumstances, and they are likely to receive a similar education. So their similar IQs might be attributable to the effects of their shared environment, rather than their overlapping sets of genes.

A similar ambiguity arises in another connection. IQs tend to be fairly stable over time, so a ten-year-old with an IQ of 130 will probably get a similar score at age fifteen. Supporters of a genetic theory of intelligence have suggested that this relative constancy shows that intelligence tests measure an inborn and unalterable capacity, sometimes called "native intelligence." This argument has sometimes been used to justify such educational practices as early assignment to one or another school track. But, of course, IQ constancy provides no proof at all that intelligence is fixed or inborn. To the extent that this constancy occurs, it only demonstrates that a child tends, over time, to maintain her standing relative to her agemates. This may well be because the child's environment stays pretty much the same as time goes on. If a child is born in a slum, the odds (sadly) are pretty good that she will still be there at fifteen; the same holds if she is born in a palace. Once again, the evidence is inconclusive.

15.16 Identical twins *Identical twins tend to be very much alike in both physical and mental characteristics. The photo shows two such twins, Faye and Kaye Young, who both played professional basketball for the New York Stars. As Faye put it: "We've always participated the same amount of time and done the same things and have progressed the same." (Photograph © Kathryn McLaughlin Abbe and Frances McLaughlin Gill, 1980. From Twins on Twins [New York: Clarkson N. Potter, Inc. 1980], pp. 134–35)*

Apparently, we need better evidence if we are to disentangle the hereditary and environmental contributions to intelligence. In the last few decades, that evidence has become available. We will consider two important sources of this evidence: the study of twins and the study of adopted children.

Twin studies **Identical twins** originate from a single fertilized egg. Early in development, that egg splits into two exact replicas, and these develop into two genetically identical individuals (see Figure 15.16). In contrast, *fraternal twins* arise from two different eggs, each fertilized by a different sperm cell. Therefore, the genetic similarity between fraternal twins is the same as that between ordinary siblings.

It is interesting, therefore, that the IQs of identical twins tend to be highly correlated (+.86); the correlation for fraternal twins is strongly positive, but appreciably lower, around +.60 (Bouchard and McGue, 1981); some further findings on similarity in IQ scores of family members are presented in Table 15.5. On the face of it, this suggests a strong genetic component in the

TABLE 15.5 CORRELATIONS BETWEEN THE IQS OF FAMILY MEMBERS

Identical twins reared together	+.86
Fraternal twins reared together	+.60
Siblings reared together	+.47
Child and biological parent by whom child is reared	+.42
Child and biological mother separated from the child by adoption	+.31
Child and unrelated adoptive mother	+.17

SOURCE: Data on twins, siblings, and children reared with biological parents from Bouchard and McGue, 1981; data on adopted children from Horn, Loehlin, and Willerman, 1979.

determination of IQ. After all, one might argue, a pair of twins (of either type) grows up in a single environment, so that the twins are matched with regard to factors such as nutrition, education, and social setting. Even within these matched environments, though, greater genetic similarity (as in identical twins) leads to greater IQ similarity.

However, we need to be cautious here: Identical twins surely resemble each other genetically more than fraternal twins do. But identical twins may also have more similar environments than fraternal twins, and it may be this greater environmental similarity that leads to their greater IQ similarity. Identical twins obviously look alike, and this may encourage others to treat them the same way. For example, parents and teachers may develop the same expectations for them. In contrast, fraternal twins are neither more nor less similar in appearance than ordinary siblings, and so they may evoke a more differentiated reaction from others—with different expectations, different styles of interaction, and the like. This possibility renders the comparison between identical and fraternal twins ambiguous (Anastasi, 1971; Kamin, 1974).

In a study designed to address this concern, over three hundred twins were classified as identical or fraternal according to two criteria. One was by a comparison of twelve blood-type characteristics, a reliable and objective method for assessing genotype similarity. To be judged identical, the members of a twin pair must correspond on all of the twelve indices. Another criterion involved the twins' own belief that they are identical or fraternal. This belief is presumably based on how similar the twins think they are and how similarly they feel that they are treated. Surprisingly, this subjective judgment often does not correspond to the biological facts as revealed by the blood tests. (If a pair of fraternal twins happen to look alike, they may believe they are identical twins, even though they're not.) This allows us to ask which of the two ways of classifying a twin is a better predictor of similarity in intelligence-test scores—shared genes or shared appearances (and, with that, more closely shared environment). The results are clear cut: When the classification was by blood tests, identicals scored more similarly to each other than did fraternals, echoing the results of many other studies. But when the classification was based on the twins' own judgments, this effect was markedly reduced. This suggests that the greater intellectual similarity of identical twins is not merely an artifact of their highly similar environments. Instead, it is, at least in part, genetically determined (Scarr and Carter-Saltzman, 1979).

Even more persuasive are the results obtained for identical twins reared apart. A research center in Minnesota has studied over fifty such twins who were separated in early life, reared apart during their formative years, and reunited as adults. Aptitude tests showed a correlation for these twins of about +.75, which is not substantially less than the correlation for identical twins reared together (Bouchard et al., 1990; McGue et al., 1993). It appears, then, that identical genotypes lead to highly similar IQs even when the individuals grow up in markedly different environments.

Adopted children   Another line of evidence comes from studies of adopted children. One study was based on three hundred children who were adopted immediately after birth (Horn, Loehlin, and Willerman, 1979, 1982; Horn, 1983). When these children were later tested, the correlation between their IQs and those of their biological mothers (whom they had never seen) was greater than the corresponding correlation between their IQs and those of their adoptive mothers (+.28 versus +.15). Other investigators have shown that this pattern persists into adolescence (Skodak and Skeels, 1949). Thus, genetic relatedness again seems to be influencing IQ similarity, and, in this case, shared genetic material seems to matter more than shared environment.

ENVIRONMENTAL FACTORS

It seems clear, therefore, that genetic relatedness does, to some extent, allow us to predict IQ. But, since genes do not operate in a vacuum, environmental factors are also crucial.

Some of the evidence comes from the same data that demonstrate the importance of heredity: similarities between family members. For example, the IQs of adopted children correlate +.15 with those of their adoptive mothers. While this correlation is fairly low, it still demonstrates that environment exerts some effect. Another argument for the role of environment comes from the fact that the correlation between the IQ scores of fraternal twins seems to be a bit higher than the correlation of scores between ordinary siblings (+.60 versus +.47). This cannot be explained in genetic terms, since, as we noted, the genetic similarity between fraternal twins is the same as that of ordinary siblings. But it can be explained environmentally. If, for example, there were any changes in the family circumstances (changed economic circumstances or an improvement in school district), these changes would hit both twins at the same age.

IMPOVERISHED ENVIRONMENTS

Further evidence for the importance of environmental factors comes from studies of the effects of impoverished environments. For example, researchers studied children who worked on canal boats in England during the 1920s and hardly attended school at all and children who lived in remote regions of the Kentucky mountains. These certainly seem like poor conditions for the development of the intellectual skills tapped by intelligence tests. If so, exposure to these conditions should have a cumulatively adverse effect: The longer the child remains in the environment, the more depressed his IQ should be. This is precisely what was found. There was a sizable negative correlation between IQ and age. The older the child (the longer he had been in the impoverished environment), the lower his IQ (Gordon, 1923; Asher, 1935).

Similar effects have been observed in communities where schools have closed. These closings typically lead to a decline in intelligence-test scores—in one study, a drop of about six points for every year of school missed (Green et al., 1964).

Environmental deprivation *A migratory family from Texas in 1940 living in a trailer in an open field without water or sanitation. The evidence suggests that the longer a child lives under such conditions the lower her IQ will be. (Photograph by Dorothea Lange; courtesy of the National Archives)*

ENRICHED ENVIRONMENTS

Impoverishing the environment is evidently harmful. Enriching it has the opposite effect. An example is a community in East Tennessee that was quite isolated from the U.S. mainstream in 1930 but became less and less so during the following decade, with the introduction of schools, roads, and radios. Between 1930 and 1940, the average IQ of individuals in this community rose by 10 points, from 82 to 92 (Wheeler, 1942).

A related effect, produced by explicit training, has been observed by the Venezuelan Intelligence Project, which provides underprivileged adolescents in Venezuela with extensive, theoretically based training in various thinking skills (Herrnstein et al., 1986). Assessments after training showed substantial benefits on a wide range of tests. A similar benefit was observed for American preschool children in the Carolina Abecedarian Project (Campbell and Ramey, 1994). These programs leave no doubt that suitable enrichment and education can provide substantial improvement in intelligence-test scores.

WORLDWIDE IMPROVEMENT IN IQ SCORES

Another dramatic demonstration of environmental influences comes from the fact that scores on intelligence tests have been gradually increasing over the last few decades, with a gain of approximately three points for every ten years. This pattern is generally known as the *Flynn effect,* after James Flynn, one of the first researchers to document this effect systematically (Flynn, 1984, 1987). This improvement seems to be occurring worldwide, with clear IQ gains documented, for example, in the United States, the Netherlands, France, and Norway, to name just a few.

This effect cannot be explained genetically. While the human genome does change gradually (this is, of course, at the heart of human evolution), it does not change at a pace commensurate with the Flynn effect. So how should the effect be explained? Some have proposed that this worldwide improvement reflects the increasing complexity and sophistication of our shared culture: Each of us is exposed to more information and a wider set of perspectives than were our grandparents, and this may lead to an improvement in intelligence-test scores. A different possibility is that the Flynn effect is attributable to widespread improvements in nutrition (Neisser et al., 1996). Whatever the explanation, though, this effect is a powerful reminder that intelligence can be systematically and considerably improved by suitable environmental conditions.

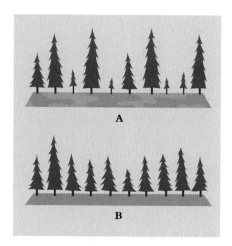

15.17 Heritability *Consider the group of evergreen trees shown in (A). They vary in height, and the degree to which they differ from each other is measured by the variance. What produces this variance? Some is presumably caused by genetic factors. To determine how much, we equalize environmental conditions—the soil, water, light, and so on. We now take a group of seedlings randomly chosen from (A), plant them in this equalized environment, and patiently wait until they reach maturity (B). We note that the size variation in (B) is less than that in (A). This reduction in the variance reflects the fact that environmental conditions are equal for (B), so that one important source of variation has been removed. The remaining variance in (B) is entirely produced by genetic factors. We can now determine the heritability of height for (A). It is the variance in (B) (that is, the variation attributable to genetic factors) divided by the variance in (A) (that is, the total variation in the population).*

HERITABILITY

When we consider the evidence as a whole, we must conclude that both genetic and environmental factors play a role in determining intelligence. What is at issue is the relative weight exerted by each of these factors.

To address this question, we must refer to a technical expression developed by geneticists, the *heritability ratio (H).* For any trait, this ratio begins with an assessment of the total phenotypic variability: How much do individuals differ in their phenotype from each other? We then seek to ask what proportion of this variability can be attributed to genetic variation (Figure 15.17).

Researchers estimate that the value of H for IQ falls between .40 and .70; often a figure of .50 is quoted (Neisser et al., 1996). This can be understood as the assertion that, of the variability we observe in IQ, approximately 50 percent is attributable to variations in genetic material. It is crucial, though, to understand what this means, since there are some widely held misconceptions about heritability. For example, in popular discussions, it is sometimes said that 50 percent of a person's intelligence is determined by heredity and the rest by environment. This is nonsense. Heritability is a measure that applies only to trait variations within a population; it does not apply to individuals. For any given person, both heredity and environment are equally important in determining whatever he or she is.

Moreover, it must be emphasized that heritability is measured for a particular population at a particular point in time—and so heritability estimates can change as circumstances change. For example, consider a case we have already discussed: the mental retardation caused by PKU. Many years ago, we had no way to remedy this condition, and so the heritability was extremely high. The phenotypic variation (whether someone did or did not have this type of retardation) was almost entirely attributable to whether or not they had the relevant genetic pattern. But we now know that a simple environmental manipulation can minimize the impact of PKU, and, as a result, the heritability estimate for PKU is currently quite low. Whether retardation is observed depends largely on the individual's diet, and so most of the phenotypic variation we observe is due to this factor (an aspect of the person's environment) and not his or her genes.

This example reminds us of two crucial points. First, heritability estimates are quite fluid. In the world today, the heritability of intelligence is approximately .50, but this estimate could change dramatically if the environment were to change in some relevant fashion (as it did in the case of PKU). Second, a very high heritability estimate tells us little about the prospects for changing a trait. Even if a trait's heritability is 1.00, we may be able to alter that trait enormously, once a suitable intervention is found.

GROUP DIFFERENCES IN IQ

Thus far, we have focused on intelligence differences within groups and have considered the nature-nurture debate as it pertained to these. But the real fury of the controversy rages over another issue—the differences in average IQ that are found between groups, such as different socioeconomic classes or racial-ethnic groups.

Numerous studies have shown that the average score of American blacks is 10 to 15 IQ points below the average of the American white population (Loehlin, Lindzey, and Spuhler, 1975). The fact that there is such a difference is not in dispute. What is at issue is what this difference means and how it comes about.

Before proceeding, though, we should emphasize that these differences are between *averages*. The scores of European-American test takers vary enormously as do the scores of African-American test takers; indeed, these *within-group* variations are much greater than the *between-group* variations, and as a consequence, there is enormous overlap between the two populations. We therefore learn relatively little about any individual's IQ simply by knowing her group membership. Nonetheless, the average difference between groups remains. How should we think about this difference?

BETWEEN-GROUP DIFFERENCES: ARE THE TESTS CULTURE-FAIR?

Some psychologists have argued that the between-group difference in IQ scores is artificial, a by-product of a cultural bias built into the tests themselves

(Sarason, 1973). According to this view, the intelligence tests were designed to assess the cognitive skills of the European-American middle class. When these tests are administered to another group with different customs or values—such as inner-city African-American children—the pattern of cultural bias underlying the tests makes the yardstick no longer applicable.

Cultural bias can take many forms. Cultural groups differ in the vocabulary that they routinely use, and so if the test is phrased using one group's vocabulary, this can create a testing advantage for that group. Likewise, groups may differ in their day-to-day experience and exposure, so the test will be biased if it relies on experiences common to only one group. In addition, intelligence tests are usually administered in standard English—a familiar dialect for some test takers but not for all. According to some linguists, many American blacks speak a different dialect, sometimes called black English, with a syntax, phonology, and lexicon different from standard English (e.g., Labov, 1970). This may put some African-American test takers at a linguistic disadvantage.

Some versions of the IQ test probably are biased in these regards. However, these forms of bias can be removed by ensuring that the test uses only vocabulary familiar to all test takers or by rephrasing test questions to make them fully accessible. Still, once these and other similar steps are taken, the contrast between the test scores of European Americans and African Americans remains. For example, in one study, the Stanford-Binet test was translated into black English and then administered orally to black children by black examiners. The performance of these children was virtually identical to that of a group tested with the test's regular version (Quay, 1971). Apparently, the contrast between white's and black's test scores cannot be attributed to dialect differences or to these other forms of test bias.

BETWEEN-GROUP DIFFERENCES: HEREDITY OR ENVIRONMENT?

The between-group difference in average IQ is evidently not an artifact of test bias. So what accounts for it? In the thirty years before 1965, the consensus among social scientists in the United States was that the effect resulted from the massively inferior environmental conditions that were (and in many ways, still are) the lot of most blacks—systematic discrimination, poorer living conditions, lower life expectancies, inadequate diets and housing, and inferior schooling. But the issue was reopened in the sixties and early seventies by, among others, Arthur Jensen, who felt that the hypothesis of a genetic contribution to the between-group difference had been dismissed prematurely (Jensen, 1969, 1973, 1985). Similar arguments have been offered more recently by Herrnstein and Murray (1994).

As currently conceived, human racial groups (some authors prefer the term *racial-ethnic groups*) are populations whose members are more likely to mate with other members of the group than they are to mate with outsiders. This restriction on the gene flow between different subgroups may be imposed by geographical barriers, such as oceans or mountains, or by social taboos, such as prohibitions on intermarriage. The restrictions are not complete, but if they last long enough, they may result in a population that differs from other groups in the statistical frequency of various genes. This is undeniable for genes that determine such characteristics as skin color, pattern of hair growth, and various blood types. But does the same hold for behavioral traits like intelligence-test performance? More specifically, is the difference in average black and white IQs partially attributable to different frequencies of IQ-determining genes in the two populations?

Within-group heritability   One of Jensen's arguments was based on the finding that IQ has a substantial within-group heritability. Jensen suggested that, given this fact, it was plausible to suppose that the between-group difference (that is, the difference between the black and white averages) could be interpreted in similar terms.

However, a number of critics disagreed, arguing that the within-group heritability of IQ actually tells us nothing about whether there's a genetic contribution to the difference *between* groups (e.g., Layzer, 1972). To see the point, imagine a bag of grass seed that contains several genetically different varieties. Some of the seeds from this bag are planted in barren soil and given inadequate care. These will grow poorly, but, even so, some will grow better than others. We cannot attribute these differences to environmental factors, since, in this case, all the seeds are growing in the same (barren) environment. Instead, this within-group variation must be attributed entirely to genetic factors, with some seeds genetically better-prepared for these poor conditions.

Other seeds from this same bag are planted in uniformly rich soil and given excellent care. These will grow well, but again, some will grow better than others. In this completely uniform environment, the observed variation can again be attributed entirely to genetic sources, with some seeds more prepared to flourish in this rich environment.

Thus, in both cases the within-group variation is of genetic origin. Nonetheless, the contrast between groups is attributable to environmental factors—the quality of soil, the quality of care (after Lewontin, 1976; see Figure 15.18). The moral is simple: Differences within a group may be produced by very different factors than those producing differences between groups. This holds for plants and the heights they attain at maturity. And it applies just as strongly to human racial-ethnic groups and the average IQ scores of these groups.

Matching for environment   If the black-white difference in IQs is really a result of environmental factors, then the difference should disappear when comparing

15.18   Between-group and within-group differences   *Between-group differences may be caused by very different factors than within-group differences. Here, the between-group difference reflects an environmental factor (soil) while the within-group difference reflects genetic variation (seed).*

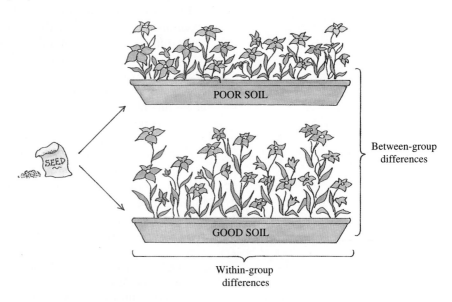

black and white groups that are equated in these regards. It is reasonable to suppose that the relevant factors include socioeconomic variables like education, parents' education, income, occupation, and so on. A number of studies have tried to match black and white children on indices of this kind and then compare the IQ averages of the two matched groups. The general result was that the black-white difference was markedly reduced (Loehlin et al., 1975).

Similarly, one study focused on the out-of-wedlock children fathered by U.S. servicemen stationed in Germany after World War II. Some of these American fathers were black; others were white. But all children grew up in similar environments with white German mothers. When these children were tested with a German version of the IQ test, both groups had about the same average IQ (Eyferth, 1961). This seems to suggest that a matched environment for children of black and white fathers eliminates the group difference, contradicting the genetic claim (but also see Flynn, 1980).

Other investigators have taken a different approach. Rather than trying to match environments, they have asked what happens when the environment is changed. A widely cited example is a study of black children who were adopted at an early age by white middle-class parents, most of whom were college educated (Scarr and Weinberg, 1976). The mean IQ of these children was 110—a value exceeding the national average for black children by about 25 points. (For further discussion, see Scarr and Carter-Saltzman, 1982; Scarr and Weinberg, 1983).

On the face of it, all of these results seem to vindicate the environmentalists' view: Equate the soil, and the two sets of seeds will grow up alike; move the seeds into more nourishing soil, and the plants will flourish all the more. But the hereditarians have a response to these results: Equalizing socioeconomic variables certainly diminishes the black-white difference but does not abolish it (e.g., Loehlin et al., 1975). In their view, this residual difference—after matching for environment—makes a genetic hypothesis even more plausible.

This hereditarian argument might be persuasive if the environments for black and white children could truly be matched. But it seems likely that matching for parental education, income, and occupational level is not enough. Black children, after all, grow up knowing that they're black; white children, that they're white. More, each group is treated differently by the people in their social environment because of the color of their skin. In these ways, their environments and experiences are *not* matched.

Evidence consistent with this idea comes from studies that have used blood-group methods to estimate the degree of African ancestry for each test taker. It turns out that this measure of the genotype is unrelated to IQ, in contradiction to what we might expect on a genetic hypothesis (Loehlin, Vendenberg, and Osborne, 1973; Scarr et al., 1977). What matters instead is the phenotype of having dark skin, as we would expect if the IQ difference is based on cultural or environmental factors.

How could skin color and the social environment influence IQ? Intelligence-test performance (and many aspects of school achievement) depends on a number of factors in addition to intelligence itself: motivation, expectations of success or failure, attitudes about how hard to strive in the face of frustration, and so on. We are only beginning to understand how these factors influence test performance, but they certainly are important ways in which racial groups might differ—especially if one of the groups has been the victim of centuries of slavery and racist oppression. As one recent report put it:

> Only a single generation has passed since the Civil Rights movement opened new doors for African Americans, and many forms of discrimination are still all too familiar in their experience today. Hard enough to bear in its own right, discrimina-

tion is also a sharp reminder of a still more intolerable past. It would be rash indeed to assume that those experiences, and that historical legacy, have no impact on intellectual development. (Neisser et al., 1996, p. 95; for other perspectives on these cultural issues, see Boykin, 1994; Steele and Aronson, 1995)

SOME FINAL THOUGHTS

Undeniably, individuals do differ in their intellectual capacities. As we have seen, though, capacities can be improved in a number of ways—by enhancing nutrition, by enriching the environment, by improving education. Even when a capacity is strongly shaped by genetic factors, environmental interventions can play an important role. The clearest case is PKU—a genetic disorder entirely remediable through appropriate diet. As scientists, we may seek to map and explain the differences that exist. As citizens, however, we should try to maximize the potential of each individual and celebrate the talents—perhaps in academic affairs, perhaps in other realms—that each of us possesses.

In addition, we have now seen that the group differences—for example, that between blacks and whites—must be approached with great caution. At least part of the difference between blacks and whites (and perhaps a large part) is likely to have an environmental origin, reflecting the profound impact of three hundred years of slavery and racist oppression. These environmental conditions, however, are surely mutable, and so there is no reason to regard the black-white difference as inevitable. But even if this difference turns out, to some extent, to be influenced by genetics, what then? Such differences may still be subject to change—again, the example of PKU is pertinent, a genetic disadvantage subject to environmental remediation. Thus, regardless of whether the group difference is genetic or environmental in origin, the conclusion is the same: There is no reason to regard the difference as an enduring one and every reason to seek means of reducing the difference.

Above all, though, we must emphasize the considerable variation within each of these groups. And we should also emphasize that in a democratic society the focus is, and should be, on each individual's merits, abilities, and attributes. A given individual may be a member of a subgroup that, on average, has a particular quality; that individual's subgroup may also have a greater or smaller average gene frequency for this or the other trait. But these facts should have no bearing on how that particular person is judged. When people are assessed according to the average characteristics of the group to which they belong, rather than according to the characteristics they themselves possess, one of the most essential premises of a democratic society is violated.

TAKING STOCK

What has been the upshot of the work on human individual differences in cognitive aptitudes that Francis Galton began over a hundred years ago? One consequence was the development of a whole host of sophisticated techniques for the creation and evaluation of mental tests. Modern intelligence tests document the variability of intellectual skills, and they have found wide (though not always salutary) applications for selection and clinical guidance. People differ in their test performance, and these differences correlate substantially with success in our Western school systems.

There is no denying the practical significance of intelligence tests. But many questions remain about the nature of the differences they reveal. Investigators who take a psychometric perspective ask whether intelligence-test performance is best ascribed to one underlying ability or to several (Spearman's *g* versus Thurstone's group factors). Those influenced by the information-processing approach try to discover the cognitive operations that underlie intellectual ability (or abilities), such as speed of processing and strategies for remembering, learning, or solving problems. Yet other questions are raised by the fact that the term *intelligence* can also refer to mental abilities that only make sense within a given environmental and cultural context.

A rather different question goes back to the nature-nurture controversy we've encountered so often before: Are the differences revealed by intelligence tests produced by heredity or environment? As usual, the answer is both, for humans are shaped both by their genes and their environment, and by the interaction between them. But while there is clear-cut evidence that genetic factors are of considerable importance in determining variation within groups (as shown by the comparison of identical and fraternal twins and adopted children), there is but little evidence for a genetic account of the difference between groups.

So far, our discussion has been concerned with differences between individuals that have to do with abilities, especially cognitive abilities. But people don't just differ in what they can do but also in what they want to do, how they do it, and how they feel about it. Those and many other differences between people—whether they are usually sociable or solitary, pleasant or surly, anxious or self-confident—belong to the topic of human personality and are the subject to which we turn next.

SUMMARY

1. Many physical and psychological characteristics vary from one individual to another. This pattern of variation is often displayed by *frequency distributions.* The scores in a frequency distribution tend to cluster around some average case, usually measured by either the *mean* or the *median.* The graphed frequency distributions of many physical and psychological characteristics have a shape approximating that of the *normal curve,* which describes the pattern of chance events.

2. The extent to which two characteristics vary together is measured by the *correlation coefficient,* or *r.* Perfect correlation is indicated by an *r* of +1.00 or −1.00, no correlation by an *r* of 0.

3. One criterion of a test's adequacy is its *reliability,* the consistency with which it measures what it measures, as given by *test-retest* correlations and similar indices. An even more important criterion is a test's *validity,* the extent to which it measures what it is supposed to measure. *Predictive validity* is assessed by determining the correlation between the test and an appropriate criterion. *Construct validity* is the extent to which performance on a test fits into some relevant theoretical scheme.

4. Alfred Binet, the originator of intelligence tests, was primarily interested in assessing children. His tests measured *mental age,* or *MA.* The standing of a child relative to her agemates was determined by comparing her MA with her *chronological age,* or *CA.* To determine the child's *intelligence quotient,* or *IQ,* MA is divided by CA and multiplied by 100. Modern testers prefer the *deviation IQ,* which is based on a comparison between an individual's score and the norm for her agemates and can be used with both children and adults.

5.   Different intelligence tests have been developed for various uses. Some are meant to test children, others to test adults; some can be administered individually, others in groups. Specialized tests have also been developed as instruments for *neuropsychological assessment.* Intelligence tests can also be used to assess mental retardation, which can vary from mild to profound.

6.   Investigators using the *psychometric approach* try to discover something about the underlying nature of intelligence by studying the pattern of results provided by intelligence tests themselves. One issue is the structure of mental abilities. To determine whether intelligence is one unitary ability or is composed of several unrelated abilities, investigators have looked at the correlations among different subtests. *Factor analysis* of these correlations led to a number of competing theories of mental structure, including Spearman's theory of *general intelligence,* or *g,* and Thurston's *group-factor theory.*

7.   In the information-processing approach, individual differences in intellectual performance are seen as differences in the cognitive processes that underlie remembering, problem solving, and thinking. One line of inquiry tries to relate Spearman's *g* to differences in *reaction time.* Another approach focuses on a subfactor, such as verbal intelligence, and relates it to simple cognitive operations, such as memory look-up times. A third approach emphasizes the more complex *cognitive components* of the tasks posed by standard intelligence tests, as exemplified in studies of analogical reasoning. A fourth line of inquiry investigates the role of working memory and attention. A fifth tries to relate intellectual differences to success or failure in the acquisition and use of various cognitive strategies.

8.   Some investigators have concerned themselves with some aspects of the term *intelligence* that go beyond IQ, such as *practical* and *social intelligence,* and with the cultural spheres in which intelligence is used and assessed. Another related approach has led to the notion of *multiple intelligences,* buttressed by evidence from studies of brain lesions and of retarded *savants.*

9.   Intelligence-test performance seems to be determined by both environmental and genetic factors. Evidence for the role of genetic factors comes from the fact that the correlation between IQs of *identical twins* is higher than that for *fraternal twins* and that this correlation is remarkably high even when identical twins are reared apart. Further evidence for a hereditary contribution comes from adopted children whose IQs correlate more highly with those of their biological than their adoptive parents. Evidence for environmental effects is provided by increases and decreases in the mean IQ of populations whose cultural or educational level has risen or fallen. Environmental effects may also explain a worldwide improvement in IQ scores. A similar point is made by adoption studies that show some correlation in IQ between children and their adoptive parents.

10.   The relative weight of genetic and environmental factors in determining the variation of a given characteristic is given by the *heritability ratio,* or *H.* The value of H depends in part upon the given population, for H only describes the degree to which the variability within this population can be attributed to genetic variance.

11.   In recent years, much interest (and polemic) has focused on IQ differences among racial-ethnic groups. The mean IQ of American blacks is about 10 to 15 points lower than that of American whites. Some authors have argued that this is in part a consequence of a genetic difference between the two groups. Environmentalists reply that the difference is markedly reduced by various environmental changes such as interracial adoption. A similar point is made by the fact that the mean IQs of children of white German mothers fathered by U.S. soldiers after World War II are just about the same whether the fathers were black or white. It is also supported by the fact that IQ is more closely related to the phenotype of dark skin than it is to the genotype.

PERSONALITY I: ASSESSMENT, TRAIT THEORY, AND THE BEHAVIORAL-COGNITIVE APPROACH

I n the preceding chapter, our focus was on differences in intelligence. But people also differ in their nonintellectual attributes. They differ in their desires and feelings (and how they express them). They differ in how they regard and judge themselves and others. And they differ in their outlooks on the world and the future. All of these distinctions fall under the general heading of personality differences.

The fact that personality differences exist is hardly a recent discovery; it was probably known since prehistoric times. Cro-Magnons surely knew that all Cro-Magnons were not the same; they probably liked some, disliked others, and spent some of their time gossiping about the Cro-Magnons in the cave next door. But we do not know whether they did so self-consciously, whether they had any explicit ideas about the ways in which one person is different from another. Such explicit formulations probably came later. In the main, they were the work of various writers who concerned themselves with the representation of character.

An example is a series of sketches entitled "The Characters" that was written in the fourth century B.C. by the Greek philosopher Theophrastus (ca. 370–287 B.C.). "The Characters" featured such diverse types as the Coward, the Flatterer, the Boor, and so on. At least some of his types are as recognizable today as they were in ancient Greece:

> The Garrulous man is one who will sit down close beside somebody he does not know, and begin with a eulogy of his own life, and then relate a dream he had the night before, and after that tell dish by dish what he had for supper. As he warms to his work he will remark that we are by no means the men we were, and the price of wheat has gone down, and there's a ship of strangers in town. . . . Next he will surmise that the crops would be all the better for some more rain, and tell him what he's going to grow on his farm next year, adding that it's difficult to make both ends meet . . . and "I vomited yesterday" and "What day is it today?" . . . And if you let him go on, he will never stop. . . . (Edmonds, *The Characters of Theophrastus,* 1929, pp. 48–49)

Even more influential than Theophrastus's literary efforts were those of the playwrights. The very origin of the word *personality* suggests a possible relationship between the dramatic rendering of character and the psychologists' attempts to describe and understand it. The word comes from *persona,* the mask that Greek and Roman actors wore to indicate the character that they played (Allport, 1937; and see Monte, 1995).

In their comic drama, the Greeks and the Romans tended to think of people as types, a tradition that has continued in various forms to the present day. Their comedy created a large cast of stock characters: the handsome hero, the pretty young maiden, the restless wife, her jealous husband, the angry old man, the sly servant, the panderer, the kind-hearted prostitute, the boastful soldier, the pedant, and so on. Many of these types were resurrected in later times and other countries. An example is the comic theater of Renaissance Italy, the commedia dell' arte, which boasted a large stable of such stock characters, each invariably played by the same actor and always with a mask that indicated who he was. While modern movie and television actors usually don't wear masks (Batman is

669

Masks used by actors in Roman comic drama *(Capitolone Museums, Rome; courtesy of Scala/Art Resource)*

A

B

Characters in sixteenth- and seventeenth-century Italy's commedia dell' arte
(A) Pantalone, the rich, stingy, old merchant, who is invariably deceived by his servants, his children, and his young wife. (B) Pulcinella, a sly and boisterous comic. (Courtesy of Casa Goldoni, Venezia; photographs by Paul Smit, Imago)

one exception), they often represent stock characters even so. The hero and villain of the Western and the busybody and conniving schemer of the television soap opera are only a few of such instantly recognizable types.

Over the ages, there have been many discussions of the appropriate conception of these dramatic and literary characters. One such discussion concerned the use of type characters in drama and literature. Some critics argued that such characterizations are necessarily flat and two-dimensional and could not possibly do justice to an individual; in reality, even the most passionate lover is not just passionate, for she surely has other attributes as well. They therefore felt that drama and literature should avoid all such stock characters and instead only present fully rounded, complex characters (such as Hamlet) who are essentially like no one else. Such rounded characters are as difficult to describe perfectly as a person in real life and are therefore capable of surprising us (Forster, 1927). But other critics disagreed and felt that while simplified types could not possibly do full justice to any individual, they accomplished another and equally important aim: They showed what all people of a certain kind have in common rather than what distinguishes them as individuals (Johnson, 1765).

Other arguments concerned the relative importance of internal versus external forces in determining what a character does. Some critics insisted that all dramatic action ultimately springs from within and grows out of the character's essential nature, while others disagreed and pointed to the role of the external situation, as in the case of realistic modern dramas (such as *Death of a Salesman*) whose heroes do what they do because their social or economic situation forces them to. Yet another issue concerns the character's self-knowledge. Do his actions spring from goals of which he is aware, or is he reacting to unconscious forces that he himself does not recognize (Bentley, 1983)?

These arguments among different schools of drama and literature are mirrored in current debates among proponents of different psychological theories of personality. As we will see, the drama of types is a distant cousin of modern **trait theory,** which holds that personality is best understood by the description and analysis of underlying personality traits.

The insistence that a character's action is prompted by external circumstances is related to some formulations of the **behavioral-cognitive approach,** which defines personality differences by the ways various people act and think about their actions, and insists that these acts and thoughts are largely produced by the situation that the individuals face now or have faced on previous occasions.

The belief that characters may act because of unconscious impulses is of course a dominant view of **psychodynamic theory,** which argues that the crucial aspects of personality stem from deeply buried, unconscious conflicts and desires (see Chapter 17).

The insistence that characters be rounded and to some extent unpredictable would be congenial to a **humanistic approach** to personality, which maintains that what is most important about people is how they achieve selfhood and actualize their human potential (see Chapter 17).

Finally, the formative effects of culture, so important in the understanding of social cognition and emotion (Chapter 11), are the focus of the **sociocultural approach,** which attempts to discern what is universal in human personality and what is culture specific (Chapter 17).

We will refer back to some of the issues raised by the representation of dramatic character in both this and the following chapter, because they will provide us with a useful metaphorical framework within which to approach our present topic.

METHODS OF ASSESSMENT

There is an implicit assumption that underlies Theophrastus's sketches or, for that matter, any drama that uses character types. This assumption is shared by most authors who concern themselves with personality: The personality patterns they ascribe to their characters are assumed to be essentially consistent from one time to the next and from one situation to another. The hero is generally heroic, the villain villainous, and the garrulous man talkative regardless of who is listening. The traits by which modern students of personality describe people are subtler than those that define the stock characters of the classical or Renaissance stage, but for many investigators the key postulate of this trait theory still exists. They assume that certain traits can characterize a person's behavior in a variety of situations. This is just another way of saying that knowledge of an individual's personality traits will permit us to predict what she is likely to do, even in situations in which we have never observed her (Allport, 1937).

Personality tests were devised in an attempt to supply the information that would make such prediction possible. In a way, they are analogous to an audition; the director asks an actor to try out for a part by reading a page or two from a scene. Such an audition is a test that tries to determine (by no means perfectly) whether this actor can play a certain part. In contrast, a personality test tries to determine (again, far from perfectly) whether a person *is* that part.

Character types in the Nō drama of Japan
In the traditional Nō drama of Japan, character is indicated by a mask. The mask shown in the figure is that of a mystical old man with godlike powers. Before donning the mask, the actor who performs this part must go through various rituals of purification, because after he puts it on, the actor "becomes" the god. (Photograph by George Dineen/Photo Researchers)

STRUCTURED PERSONALITY TESTS

As in the case of intelligence measurement, the impetus for the development of personality tests came from the world of practical affairs. The first personality test was designed to identify emotionally disturbed U.S. Army recruits during World War I. This test was an "adjustment inventory" consisting of a list of questions that dealt with various symptoms or problem areas (for instance, "Do you daydream frequently?" and "Do you wet your bed?"). If the recruit reported many such symptoms, he was singled out for further psychiatric examination (Cronbach, 1970a). Such tests, because they ask specific questions and require specific answers, are called *structured personality tests* (or sometimes, *objective* personality tests).

The parallel between tests of intelligence and those of personality ends when we turn to the question of how these tests are validated. Binet and his successors had various criteria of validity: teachers' evaluations, academic performance, and, perhaps most important, chronological age. It turns out that validity criteria are much harder to come by in the field of personality measurement.

THE MMPI: CRITERION GROUPS FROM THE CLINIC

To provide an objective validity criterion, some investigators turned to the diagnostic categories developed in clinical practice. Their goal was to construct a test that could assess a person's similarity to the members of a psychiatric criterion group—for example, paranoid patients, depressives, schizophrenics, and so on. The best-known test of this sort is the *Minnesota Multiphasic Personality Inventory,* or *MMPI,* which first appeared in 1940 (see Table 16.1; Hathaway and McKinley, 1940). The original MMPI, together with its new revision the MMPI-2, are widely used in both clinical practice and research (Lanyon and Goldstein, 1982; Butcher et al., 1989; Greene, 1991) and constitute the psychological tests most frequently administered in professional settings (Lubin et al., 1985; Butcher and Rouse, 1996).

Constructing the MMPI   The authors of the MMPI began by compiling a large set of test items taken from previously published objective tests (often called *personality inventories*), from psychiatric examination forms, and from their own clinical hunches. The intent from the outset was to make the test multiphasic, that is, diagnostic of a number of different kinds of psychopathology. The test was then administered to several patient groups who had already been diagnosed as having this or that mental disorder, as well as to a group of nonpatients. The next step was to eliminate all items that did not discriminate between the patients and the nonpatient controls and to retain those items that did. The result was the MMPI—an inventory of 566 items the responses to which are collated and tallied to form 10 major scales. The score on each of these scales indicates how the examinee's answers compare with those of the relevant criterion group (Table 16.1). For example, items on the Pa (Paranoia) scale are the ones that were endorsed by the paranoid patients but not by the nonpatients. Thus, a person's score on this scale reflects how closely she resembles the paranoid patients.

After nearly half a century, the original MMPI was supplanted by the *MMPI-2,* in which the wording of many of the original MMPI questions was updated and a few questions deleted. But it contains the same scales and is scored the same way. The biggest change in the new version is its standardization group. Whereas the nonpatients used to standardize the original MMPI were almost all white, middle-aged Minnesotans (many of whom were family members of the

TABLE 16.1 SOME MMPI SCALES WITH REPRESENTATIVE EXAMPLE ITEMS*

Scale	Criterion group	Example items
Depression	Patients with intense unhappiness and feelings of guilt and hopelessness	"I often feel that life is not worth the trouble."
Paranoia	Patients with unusual degree of suspiciousness, together with feelings of persecution and delusions of grandeur	"Several people are following me everywhere."
Schizophrenia	Patients with a diagnosis of schizophrenia, characterized by bizarre or highly unusual thoughts or behavior, by withdrawal, and in many cases by delusions and hallucinations	"I seem to hear things that other people cannot hear."
Psychopathic deviance	Patients with marked difficulties in social adjustment, with histories of delinquency and other antisocial behavior	"I often was in trouble in school, although I do not understand for what reasons."

* In the example items here shown, the response appropriate to the scale is "true." For many other items, the reverse is true. Thus, answering "false" to the item "I liked school" would contribute to the person's score on the Psychopathic Deviance scale.

patients), the standardization group for the MMPI-2 consisted of 2,600 individuals from diverse areas of the United States selected to be representative of the population in such factors as age, marital status, and ethnicity (Greene, 1991).

Using the MMPI Interpreting an MMPI record is a complicated business. Clinicians don't merely inspect the absolute scores obtained on any one scale. Instead, they consider the various scale values in relation to each other. This is most easily done by inspecting score profiles, which present the scores on every scale in graphic form (Figure 16.1). For example, a clinician may find that a

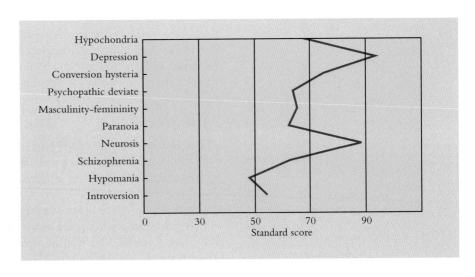

16.1 MMPI profile *The profile is of an adult male seeking help in a community mental health center. The scales are those described in Table 16.1. The scores are based on the performance of the standardization group. Scores above 70 will occur in about 2.5 percent of the cases; scores above 80 in about .1 percent. The profile strongly suggests considerable depression and anxiety. (After Lanyon and Goldstein, 1971)*

673

patient has a high score on the D (Depression) scale, but a low score on the Si (Social Introversion) scale. This might lead the clinician to conclude that the patient is depressed, but his depression is uncomplicated by excessive shame, shyness, or social withdrawal.

Validity scales One trouble with self-administered personality inventories is that participants can easily misrepresent themselves. Some may want to avoid the stigma of a mental-disorder diagnosis and try to "look good" on the test. Others may try to "fake bad" in order to claim disability benefits, obtain desired medications, or attain a paid-for stay in the hospital. To cope with this and related problems, the originators of the MMPI added a set of further items that comprise several so-called validity scales. One is a simple lying scale. It contains items like "I gossip a little at times" and "Once in a while I laugh at a dirty joke. . . ." The assumption is that a person who denies a large number of such statements is either a saint (and few of those take personality tests) or is lying. Another validity scale consists of a number of bizarre statements like "There are persons who are trying to steal my thoughts and ideas" and "My soul sometimes leaves my body." To be sure, some of these statements will be endorsed by severely disturbed psychiatric patients, but even they will only agree with a small proportion of them. As a result, we can be reasonably sure that a person who checks an unusually large number of such items is either careless, has misunderstood the instructions, or is trying to fake mental disorder. If the scores on these and similar validity scales are too high, the test record is considered invalid (see Greene, 1988).

THE CPI: CRITERION GROUPS FROM NORMAL LIFE

While the MMPI can be employed to test normal examinees, it has some limitations when used in this way. The main problem is that the criterion groups that defined the scales were composed of psychiatric patients. This prompted the development of several new inventories constructed according to the same logic that led to the MMPI but with normal rather than with pathological criterion groups. One of the best known of these is the **California Psychological Inventory, or CPI.**

Unlike the MMPI, the CPI's focus is nonclinical and is aimed especially at high-school and college students. It tests for various personality traits such as dominance, sociability, responsibility, a sense of well-being, and so on.

As an example of how scales for these and other traits were derived, consider dominance. High-school and college students were asked to name the most and the least dominant people within their social circles. The people who comprised these two extremes were then used as the criterion groups that defined the dominance-submission dimension. An individual's score on this dimension, therefore, reflects how much she resembles members of these criterion groups. Other traits were defined in a similar manner (Gough, 1975, 1990).

THE VALIDITY OF PERSONALITY INVENTORIES

The originators of the MMPI and the CPI took considerable pains to ground their tests on a solid, empirical foundation. To evaluate the success of their efforts, we must look at the validity of these tests.

Predictive validity The usual way to assess validity is to determine the degree to which a test can predict some real-world events. There is evidence that personality tests do indeed have some **predictive validity.** For instance, among college women during the fifties and sixties, the sociability scale of the CPI correlated somewhat with how often the examinee went out on dates and whether she joined a sorority. Other scales correlate with how examinees are rated by their peers (Hase and Goldberg, 1967).

The trouble is that while personality inventories can predict behavior, their accuracy in doing so is not terribly high. The correlations between test scores and validity criteria are generally in the neighborhood of +.30, indicating a low-to-moderate association (recall that a perfect association between sets of scores produces a correlation of (+/−) 1.00, whereas scores that are totally unrelated produce a correlation of 0). This doesn't compare very well with the validity coefficients of intelligence tests (usually assessed by correlating IQ and academic performance), which are about +.50. The contrast is even sharper if we compare the predictive ability of these personality tests with that of commonsense measures such as relevant past behavior in related situations. The result is simple: In most cases, the best predictor of future performance (for example, of mental disorder or delinquency) is past performance. A dramatic and widely cited example is provided by a study which showed that the thickness of a psychiatric patient's file folder correlates +.61 with the probability of rehospitalization following discharge (Lasky et al., 1959).

Construct validation   The relatively low predictive validity of personality inventories may not be grounds for as much chagrin as one might assume. Personality tests try to measure certain psychological entities, such as traits, that are presumed to explain overt behavior. In effect, the trait—whether sociability, or psychopathic deviance, or whatever—is a theoretical concept devised by the psychologist in an effort to understand not just one set of observations but many. For example, the acts of opening doors for others, giving gifts to friends, handing money to the homeless, giving up one's seat on a train, and smiling to strangers may *all* reasonably be considered aspects of friendliness.

To validate this sort of construct, one has to devise and test hypotheses about the relation between the underlying trait and various behavioral manifestations. This is **construct validation,** an approach we discussed in Chapter 15 in the context of intelligence testing.

Construct validation is often built on a set of diverse relationships between test scores and rather different behavioral manifestations. An example is provided by the Pd (psychopathic deviance) scale of the MMPI, a scale originally based on those items that differentiated a group of delinquents from other groups (see Table 16.1). Not too surprisingly, normal (that is, nondelinquent) high-school students who are regarded as "least responsible" by their classmates have much higher Pd scores than students rated as "most responsible." A related fact is that high Pd scores are characteristic of school dropouts. Another set of findings shows that high Pd scorers tend to be relatively aggressive and are unlikely to be considered good natured. Rather further afield is the finding that hunters who have carelessly shot someone in a hunting accident have higher Pd scores than other hunters. Even more remote is the fact that high Pd scores are also characteristic of professional actors and psychologists.

On the face of it, many of these findings seem unrelated, but they do fit together if understood as different manifestations of the same underlying personality trait—psychopathic deviance. In its extreme form, this trait is characterized by shallow social and emotional ties, a disregard of social mores and conventions, a failure to consider potential dangers and to worry about the consequences of one's own actions—in short, an attitude that says, "I just don't give a damn" (Cronbach and Meehl, 1955). In a less extreme form, this trait amounts to an ability to view and interact with others strategically and with some degree of detachment. (This is presumably what underlies findings with actors and psychologists.)

The various correlations just described are all fairly small. None of these effects—being rated irresponsible, having hunting accidents, and so on—correlates strongly enough with the Pd scale to provide a decent single criterion for predictive validity. But when these effects are considered together, they form a network of relationships that does seem to give some validity to the underlying construct. Seen in this light, the fact that the individual correlations are not very strong is not surprising. "If they were, we would find the same person dropping out of school, being ill natured, becoming a Broadway actor and shooting a fellow hunter.... Personality structure, even if perfectly measured, represents only a disposition rather than a determining force" (Cronbach, 1970a, p. 555). How that disposition manifests itself depends upon the particular circumstances the person is in.

Barnum effects Discovering whether a personality test predicts some relevant performance, or whether it fits some theoretical construct, is a reasonable criterion for assessing its validity. But there is one criterion that is of little use and that is the person's own acceptance of the test interpretation. For when that interpretation is so broad that it fits just about anyone, many of us will be all too ready to accept it. This phenomenon is called the ***Barnum effect*** after P. T. Barnum of Barnum & Bailey Circus fame, who coined the slogan "There's a sucker born every minute."

An early demonstration of the Barnum effect was performed by Bertram Forer, who got the students in one of his classes to take a personality test (Forer, 1949). This test asked them to list the hobbies, personal characteristics, secret hopes, and ambitions of the person they would like to be. Forer promised that within a week he would give each student a brief description of his or her personality based on the results of the test. True to his word, he returned what appeared to be a personalized interpretation: typed personality sketches with each student's name written at the top. The students were assured that their privacy would be strictly respected, since no one except themselves and Dr. Forer would ever know the contents of the sketches.

After reading the sketches, the students were asked to rate the accuracy of the test in describing their personality, using a scale from 0 (poor) to 5 (perfect). They evidently thought that the test had done a good job, for their average rating was 4.3. There was only one thing wrong: Unbeknownst to the students, Forer had given each of them the identical personality sketch.

So how could nearly all the students have judged the sketch a good description of their own unique personalities? We can understand what happened when we consider the kind of statements that Forer compiled to make up the sketch (see Table 16.2).

As the table shows, the statements that comprised the personality sketch were sufficiently vague to apply to just about all the students. For most of them must surely have felt a desire to be liked by others, or been occasionally insecure, or worried, or concerned about their sexual adjustment, and so on.

Under the circumstances, it's not surprising that the students believed that the test had indeed done a good job.★ Numerous later studies confirmed Forer's general findings (e.g., Snyder, Shenkel, and Lowery, 1977; Dickson and Kelly, 1985). The upshot is clear: The mere fact that people believe that a test interpretation fits them is no guarantee of the test's validity.

"You are trustworthy, loyal, helpful, friendly, courteous, kind, obedient, cheerful, thrifty, brave, clean, reverent."

The Barnum effect *(© The New Yorker Collection 1936, 1964 Chas. Addams from Cartoonbank. com. All rights reserved.)*

★ Interestingly enough, most of the statements in the sketch were taken from a newsstand astrology book. After all, astrologers (and palmists and tea-leaf readers) undoubtedly depended on the Barnum effect for thousands of years before Barnum was born.

TABLE 16.2 PERSONALITY SKETCH LIKELY TO PRODUCE A BARNUM EFFECT

1. You have a great need for other people to like and admire you.
2. You have a tendency to be critical of yourself.
3. You have a great deal of unused capacity, which you have not turned to your advantage.
4. While you have some personality weaknesses, you are generally able to compensate for them.
5. Your sexual adjustment has presented problems for you.
6. Disciplined and self-controlled outside, you tend to be worried and insecure inside.
7. You have found it unwise to be too frank in revealing yourself to others.
8. At times you are extroverted, affable, sociable, while at other times you are introverted, wary, reserved.

SOURCE: Adapted from Forer, 1949.

PROJECTIVE PERSONALITY TESTS

The 1940s and 1950s saw the increasing popularity of a new approach to personality assessment—the use of *projective techniques* (sometimes called *unstructured* personality tests). These tests present the examinee with a relatively unstructured task, such as making up a story to fit a picture, or describing what he sees in an inkblot. In part, this approach was a protest against the highly structured tests of personality discussed above. As we saw, the MMPI and similar tests contain various safeguards to assure that the test taker will not lie to the test administrator. But critics pointed out that these tests give no guarantee that the examinees will not lie to *themselves*. In line with psychoanalytic thinking (of which more later—see Chapter 17), these critics were convinced that the deeper layers of any individual's personality contain repressed wishes and unconscious conflicts that are not accessible by ordinary means. In their view, these deeper layers can't be accessed by means of the direct questioning that characterizes the MMPI, the CPI, and related tests.

But how can one possibly penetrate below the surface to find out what the examinee does not know herself? Exponents of the projective approach argue that the trick is to circumvent the examinee's defenses against threatening impulses and ideas by presenting her with stimuli that are essentially unstructured or ambiguous. In their view, the examinee cannot help but impose a structure of her own when trying to describe such stimuli; they believed that in doing so she would unveil deeper facets of her personality. The test materials are thus considered a kind of screen upon which the examinee "projects" her inner feelings, wishes, conflicts, and ideas.

The number and variety of projective techniques is remarkable. Some require the examinee to give word associations or to complete unfinished sentences, others to draw a person or to copy designs, yet others to state three wishes. We will consider only the two that are used most widely—the *Rorschach inkblot technique* and the *Thematic Apperception Test.*

THE RORSCHACH INKBLOTS

Hermann Rorschach, a Swiss psychiatrist, used the perception of unstructured forms as a diagnostic tool (Rorschach, 1921). He used ten symmetrical inkblots,

Young girl taking a Rorschach test
(Photograph by Mimi Forsyth, Monkmeyer)

some colored and some black and white, and presented them to various groups of psychiatric patients. When the patients were asked what they saw in the inkblots, their responses seemed to differ depending upon the diagnostic group to which they belonged. Rorschach regarded these findings as tentative, but he nevertheless used them to devise a system for scoring and interpretation (Zubin, Eron, and Shumer, 1965).

Administration and scoring   While there are now several different systems for administering, scoring, and interpreting the Rorschach, all share certain overall features (Klopfer et al., 1954; Exner, 1974, 1978, 1993). The examinee is presented with each of ten cards, one at a time, and is asked what he sees, what the blots might be (see Figure 16.2 for an example of a card similar to those used in the test). After all ten cards have been presented, the examiner questions the examinee about each response to find out which part of the blot was used and which of its attributes were most important.

The responses are scored according to various categories, such as the portion of the blot that is used in the response (e.g., the whole blot, a large detail, a small detail), the attributes of the stimulus that are the basis of the response (e.g., form, shading, color), and the content of the response (e.g., human figures, parts of human figures, animals or parts of animals, inanimate objects, blood).

Interpretation   Rorschach experts stipulate that the interpretation of a Rorschach record cannot be performed in a simple cookbook fashion. Instead, one must pay attention to the interrelations among all of the record's features in all their complexity. According to this view, interpretation is a subtle art that requires much talent and even more expertise. Nevertheless, we can at least sketch a few of the major hypotheses about certain Rorschach signs. For example, using the entire inkblot is said to indicate integrative, conceptual thinking, whereas the use of a high proportion of small details suggests compulsive rigidity. A relatively frequent use of the white space (which then serves as figure rather than as ground) is supposed to be a sign of rebelliousness and negativism, and responses that are dominated by color suggest emotionality and impulsivity.

Assessing the validity of Rorschach interpretation is a difficult task (see Exner, 1995), one complicated by major inconsistencies among all the various scoring systems (Kline, 1992). Critics of the Rorschach have noted the absence of any

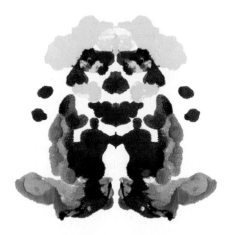

16.2   An inkblot of the type used in the Rorschach test   *Because familiarity with the cards makes it difficult to evaluate a person's first reaction, most psychologists prefer not to print the actual inkblots used in the test. Five of the actual cards are in black and white; five others are colored.*

16.3 A picture of the type used in the TAT

psychological theory that justifies these interpretations (Kline, 1995). We will consider this issue together with similar ones raised by the other major projective technique in current use, the ***Thematic Apperception Test,*** or ***TAT,*** developed by Christiana Morgan and Henry Murray (Morgan and Murray, 1935).

THE THEMATIC APPERCEPTION TEST (TAT)

To Rorschach, the content of the examinee's responses was a secondary concern. What mattered to him was not so much whether an examinee interpreted the inkblot as a giant moth, or a human face, or a splotch of blood, as the features of the card that were used—the whole card or just a part, the form or the color, and so on. In contrast, the originators of the TAT took content as their primary focus, for their emphasis was on the person's major motives and preoccupations, defenses, conflicts, and ways of interpreting the world.

Administration   The TAT test materials consist of thirty pictures of various scenes (Figure 16.3), along with one blank card (which requires the examinee to imagine her own scene). The examinee is asked to tell a story about each picture, to describe what is happening, what led up to the scene, and what the outcome will be.

Interpretation   In clinical practice, TAT interpretation is usually a rather free-wheeling affair. Each story suggests a hypothesis that is then checked and elaborated (or discarded) by looking at the person's later stories. The desired end product is a picture of the person's major motives and conflicts, pieced together by interpreting the TAT stories in the light of all available information, of which the case history is probably the most important.

Some illustrations of this impressionistic and global approach to TAT interpretation are provided by the stories elicited by one of the cards, which shows a boy looking at a violin that lies on a table in front of him. A forty-five-year-old businessman, who was an important executive in his firm and believed to have an even brighter future, gave this story:

> This is a child prodigy dreaming over his violin, thinking more of the music than anything else. But of wonderment that so much music can be in the instrument and in the fingers of his own hand. . . . I would say that possibly he is in reverie about what he can be or what he can do with his music in the times that lie ahead. He is dreaming of concert halls, tours, and . . . the beauty he will be able to express and even now can express with his own talents.

A clerk in the same firm was about the same age but had been in the same position for many years and was regarded as unlikely to advance further. He produced this story:

> . . . This is the son of a very well-known, a very good musician. . . . The father has probably died. The only thing the son has left is this violin which is undoubtedly a very good one. . . . To the son, the violin is the father and the son sits there day-dreaming of the time that he will understand the music and interpret it on the violin that his father had played.

According to the interpreter, the difference in the two stories reflects the difference between the achievements and aspirations of the two men. Both presumably identify with the boy in the picture but in different ways. The successful executive concentrates on the work to be accomplished (the music), visualizes eventual success (the concert halls), and sees himself as part of it (the fingers of his own hand). In contrast, the clerk focuses on the difference between the boy and his successful, deceased father whom he may not be able to emulate (very well-known, very good musician), so that he only daydreams of future success and understanding (Henry, 1973).

Interpretations of this sort are very beguiling. But are the facets of personality suggested by the test interpretation actually there? Are these interpretations equally astute when the examiner does not have the benefit of hindsight, when she does not know the salient facts of the examinee's life history?

VALIDITY OF PROJECTIVE TECHNIQUES

By now, there are over eleven thousand published articles that are explicitly devoted to the Rorschach or the TAT. Considering all this effort, the gain has been disappointing. According to some experts, these techniques have some limited validity; according to others, they have little or none (Holt, 1978; Kleinmuntz, 1982; Rorer, 1990; Kline, 1995).

Validity and the Rorschach Individual Rorschach indices—especially those that don't refer to content—show little or no relation to external validity criteria. In one study of psychiatric patients, over thirty different measures from the Rorschach records (for instance, the number of responses using the whole inkblot, as opposed to those using just a part or a small detail) were studied to see whether there was any relation to later diagnosis. There was none. Similar results apply to nonpsychiatric populations. For example, a preponderance of responses that involve human movement is said to indicate creativity, but a group of eminent artists were no different from ordinary persons in this regard (Zubin, Eron, and Shumer, 1965).

Studies of this kind have sometimes been criticized as too reductionistic, for they focus on single aspects of an examinee's Rorschach record. Wouldn't it be better to use the test as a whole, allow the judge to read the entire record verbatim (or even to administer the test), and then predict the criterion on the basis of this overall, global knowledge? One study that meets these conditions used twelve eminent Rorschach experts who tried to assess the personalities of various patients on the basis of their complete Rorschach records. These Rorschach-based assessments were then compared to the pooled judgment of a number of psychiatrists who had read each patient's case history, obtained in six or so interviews of several hours each. The mean correlation between the Rorschach experts' predictions and the psychiatrists' judgments was +.21. Apparently then, global assessment on the basis of the verbatim record does have some modest validity (Little and Shneidman, 1959).

Some efforts by John Exner suggest that the clinical usefulness of the Rorschach may be increased by using a more rigorous system of administration, scoring, and interpretation (Exner, 1974, 1978, 1995; Exner and Clark, 1978). The system he developed to accomplish this, which includes numerous numerical indices of the examinee's responses to the blots, has led to a considerable improvement in the test's reliability, as shown by a large increase in its test-retest stability. Whether it will also increase the test's diagnostic power (that is, its validity) is as yet unclear.

Validity and the TAT The TAT has fared no better than the Rorschach in studies that assess its ability to predict psychiatric diagnosis. In one such study, the TAT was administered to over a hundred male veterans, some in psychiatric facilities and others in college. The TAT results showed no difference between normals and patients, let alone between different psychiatric groups (Eron, 1950).

While the TAT may have little value as a diagnostic tool for psychiatric classification, the test does seem to have some validity for more limited purposes. A number of studies have shown that the TAT may be a fair indicator of the presence of certain motives, though probably not of all. One group of investigators worked with examinees who had not eaten for various periods of time. When presented with TAT-like pictures, some of which suggested food or eating, hungry examinees came up with more stories whose plots concerned hunger or food seeking than a control group of sated participants (Atkinson and McClelland, 1948). Related findings have been obtained concerning various other motives, including aggression, sexual arousal, the need for achievement, and so on. The success of these efforts represents a kind of construct validation of the TAT as an assessment device for at least some motives.

Projective techniques and utility Given the verdict of these various validation studies, many projective experts have become convinced that their devices are not really tests at all but instead are really adjuncts to a clinical interview (Zubin, Eron, and Shumer, 1965). Rorschach and TAT scores make little sense to a practitioner who has not administered the tests personally or at least read the verbatim records. They are also hard to interpret without a knowledge of the examinee's background and life history, but proponents of these techniques argue that when they are used as part of the total clinical evaluation, they help to provide a richer understanding of the person. When the Rorschach and TAT are used in this manner, they do indeed have some modest predictive validity for diagnosis. But according to some critics, predictive validity is not enough; the real issue is whether these tests have **incremental validity** (Meehl, 1959). The question is how much additional information these techniques provide over and above that contained in case histories and similar data that have to be gathered anyway. To give and score a Rorschach or a TAT is very time consuming and, thus, expensive. To make spending this much time and money worthwhile, these tests ought to provide a reasonable increase in information. But the available evidence suggests they don't. Several studies have shown that when clinical psychologists were asked to make inferences about an examinee's personal characteristics, they were just as accurate with only the case history to go on as they were when also provided with the Rorschach or TAT records (Kostlan, 1954; Winch and More, 1956).

THE TRAIT APPROACH

Personality tests have a very practical purpose: They are meant to aid in diagnosis, counseling, and even job placement. But psychologists who study personality have aims that go beyond such applications, no matter how socially useful those might be. They want to understand the kinds of differences that personality tests uncover, to find a useful framework within which to describe such differences, and to discover how they come about. In their efforts to answer these questions, they appeal to several so-called personality theories.

Most of the theories of personality that have been developed thus far aren't really theories in the conventional sense. They are not specific enough to make the clear-cut predictions that would help us choose among them. What they are instead are different orientations from which the subject of personality is approached. We will begin with the **trait approach,** which is intended to describe differences among individuals using a standard set of attributes.

The Seven Dwarfs as character types
Doc, Sleepy, Grumpy, Dopey, Sneezy, Happy, and Bashful. (From Walt Disney's Snow White; *courtesy of the Kobal Collection)*

A   B

Stock characters in the Hollywood Western (A) The hero (played by William S. Hart) and a woman in distress in Wild Bill Hickok, *and (B) the hero (played by Roy Rogers) and the villain (played by George Hayes) in* Young Buffalo Bill. *(Courtesy of Movie Stills Archives)*

The trait approach is first of all an attempt to be descriptive. It tries to find some way to characterize people by reference to some underlying basic traits. But just which traits are basic? The comic stages of classical and Renaissance days—and modern trait theory—imply not merely that a particular person has a characteristic personality, but that this personality can be categorized along with those of others who are in some ways equivalent. But what are the categories along which people should be grouped? The early playwrights (and many film makers) picked a few attributes that were easy to characterize and caricature— the tight-lipped silence of the Western hero who speaks only with his guns, the chaste innocence of the eternal heroine, the cowardice of the braggart soldier (who in Shakespeare's hands transcends his type and becomes Falstaff). But are these the personality traits that are really primary for the description of human personality?

The trait theorists' search for an answer is a bit like an attempt to find a few general principles that underlie the multitude of masks on, say, an Italian Renaissance stage. At first glance, these masks are very different, as different as the many persons we encounter in real life. Is there a way to classify these masks according to a few basic dimensions? Put another way, can we classify the variations in human personality by reference to a few fundamental traits?

THE SEARCH FOR THE RIGHT TAXONOMY

The question of classification is faced during the early stages of any science. At this point, a major task is the development of a useful *taxonomy.* Consider the early biologists. They recognized that various creatures differ in a multitude of ways—in their size and color, in the absence or the presence of a skeleton, in the number and kind of appendages they have, and so on. The biologists had to decide which of these distinctions provided the most useful categories. The psychologist who studies personality differences faces exactly the same issues. The unabridged English dictionary lists 18,000 words referring to personality traits (Allport and Odbert, 1936). But without some kind of taxonomy, it is difficult to decide which of these words refer to traits that are basic and applicable to all people, in contrast to those that are either variations on the basic traits or mere synonyms.

Transcending type in the modern Western Some modern filmmakers deliberately play on the stock conceptions of earlier days, as in the recent Western Unforgiven, *in which Gene Hackman plays a sadistic sheriff and Clint Eastwood a sympathetic gunman. (Photograph © Warner Bros., Inc.; courtesy of Photofest)*

CLASSIFICATION THROUGH LANGUAGE

One step toward a taxonomy of personality traits grew out of an examination of the language used to describe personality attributes (Allport and Odbert, 1936). Advocates of this procedure argue that the adjectives we use to describe people (e.g., trustworthy, loyal, helpful, friendly, obedient, and so on) embody the accumulated observations of many previous generations. If these terms have remained in the language for decade after decade, this probably reflects the fact that these are useful terms for describing the individuals around us; terms that were superfluous or uninformative have presumably dropped out of common usage. Thus, a systematic sifting of such trait adjectives might give us clues about individual differences whose description has been important enough to withstand the test of time (Goldberg, 1982).

This line of reasoning led to the development of a widely used personality inventory by Raymond Cattell (1957). Cattell's starting point was a set of 4,500 terms taken from the 18,000 trait words in the unabridged dictionary. This list was further reduced by eliminating synonyms, slang, and difficult or uncommon words. Finally, 171 trait names were left. A group of judges was then asked to rate participants using these terms. Their ratings were then subjected to a *factor analysis* using methods similar to those employed in the study of intelligence-test performance—yielding what Cattell thought were some sixteen primary personality dimensions that reasonably encompassed the 171 trait names. Each of these dimensions was defined by a pair of adjectives that describe the opposite poles of the dimension, such as *outgoing* versus *reserved, suspicious* versus *trusting, tense* versus *relaxed, happy-go-lucky* versus *sober,* and so on (Cattell, 1966).

DIMENSIONS OF PERSONALITY: THE BIG FIVE

Later work by other investigators managed to reduce the number of primary dimensions to a smaller set. A widely quoted study by Warren Norman featured five major dimensions of personality, often dubbed the **Big Five:** extroversion (sometimes called *extra*version), neuroticism (sometimes reversed in direction and labeled emotional stability), agreeableness, conscientiousness, and openness to experience (Norman, 1963; see also Goldberg, 1993; Bouchard, 1995).

Norman's analysis, like Cattell's, relies largely on factor analysis. As an example, someone who is described as talkative is very likely to be described as gregarious as well, and not at all likely to be described as secretive or reclusive. Therefore, there is little point in counting these terms as separate traits; instead, we can regard them as reflections of a single trait, with talkative and gregarious indicating the presence of that trait, and secretive and reclusive indicating its absence. In this fashion, we can replace four descriptive terms with just one. Continuing in this way, we can arrive at the five dimensions identified by Norman.

Of course, there are differences between being talkative and being gregarious. This is accommodated by the fact that the model is hierarchical in the sense that several lower-level traits are identified as more specific manifestations of each of the Big Five factors. These specific traits can be regarded as variations on the basic themes identified by the Big Five themselves (see Table 16.3).

The proposal, therefore, is that human personalities can be fully described in terms of five dimensions, just as physical size can be fully described in three (height, depth, and width). This still allows infinite variety in the personalities we will encounter, but each of those personalities can be described in a reasonably

TABLE 16.3 THE "BIG FIVE" TAXONOMY OF PERSONALITY TRAITS

Factor names	Scale dimensions
Extroversion	Talkative/Silent
	Frank, open/Secretive
	Adventurous/Cautious
	Sociable/Reclusive
Agreeableness	Good-natured/Irritable
	Not jealous/Jealous
	Mild, gentle/Headstrong
	Cooperative/Negativistic
Conscientiousness	Fussy, tidy/Careless
	Responsible/Undependable
	Scrupulous/Unscrupulous
	Persevering/Quitting, fickle
Neurotism	Poised/Nervous, tense
	Calm/Anxious
	Composed/Excitable
	Not hypochondriacal/Hypochondriacal
Openness to Experience	Artistically sensitive/Artistically insensitive
	Intellectual/Unreflective, narrow
	Polished, refined/Crude, boorish
	Imaginative/Simple, direct

SOURCE: Adapted from Norman, 1963.

economical way. We'll need the more fine-grained traits (*tidy/careless,* rather than *conscientious*) to characterize these personalities with precision, but even so, the five-dimensional description will tell us a great deal about what any individual is like.

DIMENSIONS OF PERSONALITY: NEUROTICISM/EMOTIONAL STABILITY, AND EXTROVERSION/INTROVERSION

While many later studies have come up with other five-factor descriptions of personality that are quite similar to Norman's (see Brody, 1988; Goldberg, 1990, 1993; John, 1990; Costa and McCrae, 1992a), a number of investigators have suggested that the underlying dimensions may be fewer (e.g., Livneh and Livneh, 1989; Boyle, Stankov, and Cattell, 1995). The most influential alternative is that proposed by Hans Eysenck (1916–1997), who originally tried to encompass the whole spectrum of personality differences in a space defined by just two dimensions: neuroticism versus emotional stability, and extroversion versus introversion. (These obviously correspond to two of Norman's five dimensions.)

Neuroticism is equivalent to emotional instability. It is assessed by affirmative answers to questions like "Do you ever feel just miserable for no good reason at all?" and "Do you often feel disgruntled?" Extroversion and introversion refer to the main direction of a person's energies, toward the outer world of material objects and other people or toward the inner world of one's own thoughts and feelings. The extrovert is sociable, impulsive, and enjoys new experiences, while the introvert tends to be more solitary, cautious, and slow to change. Extroversion is indicated by affirmative answers to questions such as "Do you like to have many social engagements?" and "Would you rate yourself as a happy-go-lucky individual?"

As Eysenck conceived it, neuroticism/emotional stability and extroversion/introversion are independent dimensions. To be sure, introverts and many neurotics have something in common: They are both unsociable and withdrawn. But in Eysenck's view, their lack of sociability has different roots. Healthy introverts are not afraid of social activities: They simply do not like them. In contrast, neurotically shy people keep to themselves because of fear: They want to be with others but are afraid of joining them.

Eysenck's two-dimensional classification defines a conceptual space into which many trait terms can be fitted (see Figure 16.4). To the extent that it or similar systems succeed, they are analogous to the classification schemes that have proved so successful in the field of sensory psychology, such as the color solid, which accommodates all possible colors on the basis of just three dimensions—brightness, hue, and saturation (see Chapter 5).

Eysenck pointed to an interesting relation between his own two-dimensional classification and the venerable four types of temperaments proposed by the ancient Greek physician Hippocrates (ca. 400 B.C.). Hippocrates believed that there are four human temperaments that correspond to four different personality types: sanguine (cheerful and active), melancholic (gloomy), choleric (angry and violent), and phlegmatic (calm and passive). He believed that these temperaments reflected an excess of one of four bodily humors; thus, sanguine people were thought to have relatively more blood, melancholy people to have an excess of black bile, phlegmatic people to have an excess of phlegm, and choleric

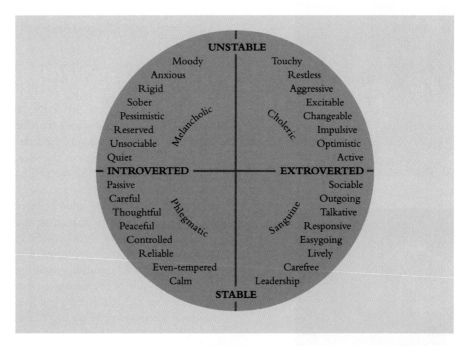

16.4 Eysenck's two-dimensional classification of personality *Two dimensions of personality—neuroticism/emotional stability and extroversion/introversion—define a space into which various trait terms may be fitted. Eysenck pointed out that the four quadrants of this space seem to fit Hippocrates's temperaments: introverted and stable, phlegmatic; introverted and unstable, melancholic; extroverted and stable, sanguine; extroverted and unstable, choleric. (After Eysenck and Rachman, 1965)*

16.5 An early taxonomy of personality   *A medieval illustration of one of the earliest attempts to classify human personality, Hippocrates's four temperaments: sanguine (cheerful and active), melancholic (gloomy), choleric (angry and violent), and phlegmatic (calm and passive). According to Hippocrates, these temperaments reflected an excess of one of four bodily humors; thus, sanguine persons were thought to have relatively more blood. Today, the humor theory is a mere historical curiosity, but some aspects of Hippocrates's classification are still with us. (Courtesy of the Bettmann Archive)*

people an excess of yellow bile (see Figure 16.5). Today the humor theory is a mere historical curiosity, but Hippocrates's four-fold classification is in some ways still with us. For the four quadrants of Eysenck's two-dimensional conception seem to fit Hippocrates's four temperamental types. The category introverted and stable corresponds to phlegmatic, introverted and unstable to melancholic, extroverted and stable to sanguine, and extroverted and unstable to choleric (Eysenck and Rachman, 1965).

BIG FIVE OR BIG THREE?

A later version of Eysenck's system added a third dimension independent of the other two, called **psychoticism**—a characteristic related to aggressive, antisocial, cold, impulsive, and self-centered attributes.★ This new dimension evidently encompasses two more of the Big Five dimensions—agreeableness and conscientiousness—and so the difference between Eysenck's conception and the Big Five is not large. Eysenck believed that the Big Five dimension openness to experience is important but is not a dimension of personality; it is related, instead, to cognitive and educational traits, including intelligence (Eysenck and Eysenck, 1975, 1983; Eysenck, 1992, 1998; for discussion, see Claridge, 1983). This suggestion is consistent with the fact that people's degree of openness to experience is correlated with their scores on several subtests of the Wechsler Adult Intelligence Scale (Costa and McCrae, 1992a).

IS FACTOR ANALYSIS THE PROPER ROAD TO A TAXONOMY?

A number of psychologists have taken issue with factor analytical approaches such as Eysenck's and those that led to the Big Five. Factor analysis provides a powerful way of summarizing a data set, but this means that the results of the analysis depend heavily on the exact contents of that data set. In the cases we have been describing, the factor analysis describes clusters of items (e.g., someone described as jealous is also likely to be described as irritable and not cooperative). But if the items included in the analysis are changed (with some added, and others subtracted), the clusters observed (and thus the resulting factors) may well be different. As a consequence, the critics argue, it is difficult to assert that any single factor analysis allows us to identify the *real* dimensions of personality. (For some further complications, see Boyle, Stankov, and Cattell, 1995.)

This critique of the factor-analytic approach has some merit, but there is no denying the fact that some of the personality dimensions discovered in this manner seem to come up again and again, even if different tests are used. This

---

★ Eysenck uses the term *psychoticism* because he believes that some of the psychiatric disorders that used to be categorized under the broad psychiatric rubric *psychosis* represent the absolute extreme on this axis. The same holds for the term *neurosis*, a term now obsolete in psychiatric diagnosis but still in popular usage, designating an individual plagued by disabling, anxiety-related inner conflicts.

is especially true for the two main pillars of Eysenck's classification system, extroversion/introversion and neuroticism/emotional stability. In fact, there is some evidence that these two dimensions may apply not just to our own culture but to others, since much the same factor pattern was obtained in such diverse societies as Bangladesh, Brazil, Hong Kong, and Japan (Eysenck and Eysenck, 1983; Lynn, 1995; for a further discussion of personality differences and similarities in different cultures, see Chapter 17).

TRAITS VERSUS SITUATIONS: THE CONSISTENCY CONTROVERSY

Different trait theorists may argue about the kind and number of trait dimensions with which to describe personality. Yet on one thing they all agree: There are personality traits that are stable and enduring properties of the individual. Indeed, the entire enterprise of personality testing is based on the presumption that people's personalities are not moving targets but are stable enough to measure.

But this basic credo has come under serious attack. One reason was the predictive validity of personality tests. For while tests such as the MMPI and the CPI predict behavior, they don't predict it all that accurately. Critics of the trait approach suggest that the reason the predictive validity of these tests is low is because what they attempt to measure—a set of stable personality traits—isn't really there. To put it another way, they contend that there is no real consistency in the way people behave at different times and in different situations.

THE ATTACK ON TRAIT THEORY

The challenge to the trait concept was launched over thirty years ago by Walter Mischel, whose survey of the research literature led him to conclude that people behave much less consistently than a trait theory would predict (Mischel, 1968). A classic study concerns honesty in children (Hartshorne and May, 1928). Grade-school children were placed in a variety of settings in which they had the opportunity to lie, cheat, or steal: in athletic events, in the classroom, at home, alone, or with peers. The important finding was that the child who was dishonest in one situation (say, cheating on a test) was not necessarily dishonest in

Traits versus situations Do the fighters punch each other because they want to win the prize money (situation) or because they are angry men (trait)? The blows probably hurt just as much either way. (Stag at Sharkey's. Oil on canvas, 1909, 92 × 122.6 cm. George Bellows, American, 1882–1925. © The Cleveland Museum of Art, 1994, Hinman B. Hurlbut Collection, 1133.22)

another setting (cheating in an athletic contest). There was some consistency, but it was rather unimpressive; a later reanalysis of the results revealed an average correlation of +.30 between honest behavior in one setting and honesty in another (Burton, 1963). The more similar the two settings, the greater were the correlations. Thus, honesty in one classroom situation was more consistent with honesty in another classroom situation than with honesty at home.

Mischel argued that a similar inconsistency across situations exists for many other behavior patterns, such as aggression, dependency, rigidity, and reactions to authority. The correlations among different behavioral measures of what seems to be the same trait are often low—rarely going above +.30 to +.40—and are sometimes nonexistent (Mischel, 1968; Nisbett, 1980). In Mischel's view, this inconsistency also explains why personality tests have unimpressive validity. A personality test taps behavior in one situation, while the criterion by which a test is validated assesses behavior in another context. Since cross-situational consistency tends to be low, so are the measures of test validity.

SITUATIONISM

These results suggest that it is not someone's personality that leads him to act in one way rather than another. For if it were, we would expect some consistency in the person's behavior from one situation to the next (assuming, of course, that someone's personality doesn't change dramatically from moment to moment). But if it is not personality that determines behavior, then what does?

One answer is offered by **situationism,** the notion that human behavior is largely determined by the characteristics of the situation itself rather than by the characteristics of the person. This is doubtless true in some cases. Given a red light, most drivers stop; given a green light, most go—regardless of whether they are friendly or unfriendly, stingy or generous, dominant or submissive, and so on. Situations of this sort produce predictable behavior in virtually all of us. According to situationism, the same principle applies to much or nearly all of human behavior. Consider the enormous effect of social roles, which often define what an actor must do with little regard to who the actor is (see Chapter 11). To predict how someone will act in a courtroom, there is little point in asking whether she is sociable or extravagant with money or whether she gets along with her mother. What we really want to know is the role that she will play—judge, prosecutor, defense attorney, or defendant. Seen in this light, what we do depends not on who we are but on the situation we find ourselves in.

This is not to say that situationists deny the existence of individual differences. They certainly agree that various demographic and socioeconomic factors—such as age and sex, marital status, ethnic background, occupation, and income—are powerful determinants of human behavior. Nor do they dispute the important effect of differences in ability, especially cognitive ability. But as they see it, all of these factors determine the kinds of situations a person is likely to encounter (or to have encountered) and thus to learn from. In their view, it is these situations, rather than their personality traits, that determine what people actually do.

IS CONSISTENCY AN ILLUSION?

If situationism is correct, the underlying consistency of the personalities of our friends and acquaintances (and perhaps our own) is more or less illusory. But if so, how can we explain the fact that most people have been subject to this particular illusion since the days of Greek drama and no doubt much before? According to critics of trait theory, one explanation is that people's personalities *seem* to be stable because we repeatedly see them in the same social settings. But

Consistency as an illusion At a class re- union people may think that their old class- mates haven't changed at all. They really have changed, but they act as they once did because they have returned to the old situation. Here, wearing their original uniforms, are cheerlead- ers from Hot Springs High School's class of 1964, which included President Clinton. (Photograph by Eric Draper/AP)

Consistency over time? *In 1964, director Michael Apted interviewed a group of English seven-year-olds for his film* Seven Up. *He then reinterviewed his subjects at seven-year intervals. (*42 Up *is due out in 1998.) Jackie Bassett, Lynn Johnson, and Susan Davis, pictured above at age seven and below at twenty-one (holding a photo of themselves at fourteen), are among the participants. Some of the interviewees betrayed early promise or rejected the goals they had embraced as children. But does this suggest that consistency of personality is illusory? (Photographs courtesy of Photofest)*

the critics make an even more important point. In their view, personality traits are mental constructions devised by the observer who watches another person's actions and tries to make sense out of them. This constructive process depends on both inference and memory and so is open to the various errors and biases we described in general terms in Chapters 7 and 8, and which arose again in our discussion of person perception in Chapter 11. It's these biases that lead to the belief that there are consistent personality traits (e.g., Shweder, 1975; Nisbett and Ross, 1980; Ross and Nisbett, 1991). On this view, then, personality descriptions are more in the eyes of the beholders than in the people they behold (Cantor and Mischel, 1977, 1979).

IN DEFENSE OF TRAITS

The emphasis on situations provides a useful corrective to those who seek to explain everything people do as a manifestation of their own essential nature. But if pushed to the extreme, this position becomes just as questionable as the one it tried to correct. For in this form, situationism can be interpreted as asserting that personality does not exist at all. Whether any psychologist has actually gone to this extreme is doubtful; certainly Mischel never did (Mischel, 1973, 1979). But the very possibility that someone might climb all the way out on this theoretical limb was enough to produce a spirited counterreaction to Mischel's attack on the trait concept.

Consistency over time The reaction to the situationist position took several forms. Many authors argued that even if there is little personal consistency across situations, there is considerable consistency over time (Block, 1971, 1977). Proof comes from a number of longitudinal studies that show a fair degree of behavioral consistency over sizable stretches of the life span. Thus, in one study, dependability in males as judged in high school correlated quite well with ratings of the same attribute made by different judges some ten or more years later ($r = +.55$; Block, 1971). In another study, male adults were given the same personality inventory at six- and twelve-year intervals. The correlations between their scores on the first and second administration of the inventory (on traits such as dominance, sociability, and emotional stability) ranged from $+.59$ to $+.87$ (Costa, McCrae, and Arenberg, 1980).

Consistency across situations Consistency over time there might be, but what about consistency across situations, which was the major focus of Mischel's critique? According to Seymour Epstein, this cross-situational consistency is much higher than Mischel had supposed. In Epstein's view, studies that seem to show low cross-situational consistency usually employ only a small sample of behaviors. As a result, the assessment of the relevant trait is necessarily unreliable. And if so, the correlation between two (unreliable) measures of this trait cannot help but be low or nonexistent. To determine whether people behave consistently from one situation to another, the behavior in each situation (e.g., cheating in class and cheating on the athletic field) must be measured not just once, but on a number of different occasions.

To buttress his position, Epstein observed participants' moods and behavior over about thirty days. He found that correlations from one day to any other day were very low. He then compared correlations based on the average score on any two days, then on any three days, and so on. As the number of observations increased, the correlations rose from about $+.30$ to $+.80$ (Epstein, 1979, 1980). Thus, to put this in concrete terms: If we know how someone behaved for a single hour, we have little basis for predicting how he will behave during any other hour. But if we know how someone behaved for a whole week, then we can,

689

Consistency across situations? *In some situations, most people behave the same way. In others, people behave differently. A major task of personality psychology is to discover whether they behave consistently across situations. (Left: Photograph by Yogi, Inc./Corbis. Right: Photograph by Roberto Borea/AP)*

with reasonable accuracy, predict what he'll do in a subsequent week. (For further discussion, see Mischel and Peake, 1983; Epstein, 1983.)

The definition of consistency Another issue concerns the definition of cross-situational consistency. Whether such consistency is found may well depend on what behaviors the experimenter defined as equivalent for the purposes of assessing a given trait. Thus, two reactions that are at first glance quite dissimilar may turn out to be manifestations of the same underlying trait when examined more closely. As a result, behavioral inconsistency may often be more apparent than real (e.g., Moskowitz, 1982; Buss and Craik, 1983; Rorer and Widiger, 1983).

Some examples come from the study of development. Consider physical aggression. In males, physical aggression is fairly consistent between childhood and adolescence, but it takes different overt forms at different ages. Young boys pummel each other with their fists; young men rarely do more than shout in anger (Kagan and Moss, 1962). Another example concerns the distinction between the attributes happy-outgoing and somber-reserved. When different judges were asked to assess this trait in people first studied at age six and then again at age fifteen, their ratings were quite similar, yielding correlations of about +.60. This consistency disappeared, however, when the judges were asked to rate overt behavior only. But as the author saw it, this result made sense. The five-year-old who is reserved and somber shows this by a low level of physical activ-

Physical aggression in boys and men
The same trait is often (though not always) expressed differently at different ages. (Left: Photograph by Wayne Miller/Magnum. Right: Photograph by Paul Kennedy/Leo de Wys)

Person-by-situation interaction *Like some other fantasy heroes, Superman is utterly fearless when faced with physical danger but is shy and timid—at least as his alter ego, Clark Kent—when around women. (Photographs Courtesy of Photofest)*

ity. At ten, the same underlying attribute manifests itself as cautiousness and emotional vulnerability. Still later, during adolescence, this basic pattern goes together with a sense of inferiority (Bronson, 1966).

Here, as in so many other aspects of behavior, a superficial difference may mask a deeper commonality. At the surface, the two sentences "Jane eats the apple" and "The apple is eaten by Jane" are obviously different. But at a deeper level, they are in many ways alike and mean much the same thing (Chapter 9).

THE INTERACTION BETWEEN PERSON AND SITUATION

If neither the situation (by itself) nor personality traits (by themselves) determines behavior, what does? The obvious suggestion is that we must consider both together, and, indeed, a number of psychologists contend that the debate between situationists and trait theorists was misguided and simplistic. As originally formulated, the question was whether an individual's actions are better predicted by the situation or by personal characteristics. But there is a third alternative: The critical factor may be the **interaction** between person and situation (e.g., Magnusson and Endler, 1977).

The person-by-situation interaction The term *interaction* is used here in a technical sense. To understand what it means in this context, consider a hypothetical experiment in which we study the reactions of several pairs of individuals to two different situations. The response will be anxiety as indicated by the galvanic skin response (GSR), an index of sympathetic activation in the autonomic nervous system (see Chapter 3). The two situations are waiting to take a test and being threatened with electric shock. Let's call the participants Jane and Tony, Mary and David, and let us assume that the GSR scale runs from 0 (no anxiety) to 12 (maximal anxiety). Two extreme outcomes are displayed in Tables 16.4 and 16.5.

These results seem to be diametrically opposed. Table 16.4 depicts a powerful situational effect. For these two participants, Jane and Tony, the shock is evidently much more frightening than the test. But the participants' personalities seem to exert little influence, since Jane and Tony behave identically. In Table 16.5 we see the reverse. Here, personal differences have a profound effect; David is evidently much more fearful than is Mary. But in this second example, situational differences are insignificant as the two situations provoke essentially the equivalent amount of fear.

These two illustrations fit the extreme positions that ascribe all behavior either to the situation or to personality. But there are also intermediate outcomes

TABLE 16.4 AN EFFECT OF SITUATION

Person	Situation		Average for each person
	Test	Shock	
Jane	3	9	6
Tony	3	9	6
Average for situation	3	9	

TABLE 16.5 AN EFFECT OF PERSONALITY

Person	Situation		Average for each person
	Test	Shock	
Mary	3	3	3
David	9	9	9
Average for situation	6	6	

TABLE 16.6 AN INTERACTION EFFECT

Person	Situation		Average for each person
	Test	Shock	
Donna	9	3	6
Joe	3	9	6
Average for situation	6	6	

in which both factors play a role. Consider the pattern of results shown by yet another pair of participants, Donna and Joe, as shown in Table 16.6.

What is important about the results of Table 16.6 is that they neither exhibit situational effects nor personality effects as such. When we look at the average GSRs, Donna and Joe prove equally fearful. The same holds for the difference between the situations; on average, the test and the threatened shock produce equal GSRs. But there is a new twist that is obscured by the averages. The two situations produce radically different effects in the two persons. Joe is evidently much more afraid of the shock than of the test, while the opposite holds for Donna. In statistical language, a relationship of this kind, in which the effect of one variable (fear-evoking situation) depends upon another variable (personality) is called an *interaction*.

The test-shock experiment described here is a highly simplified version of a large number of studies that have actually been conducted. An example is a study in which participants were asked to describe their usual reaction to various threats (Endler and Hunt, 1969). Some of these perils involved loss of self-esteem (failing an examination), others physical danger (being on a high ledge on a mountain top), still others a threat whose nature was still unclear (getting a police summons). The results showed that both personality and situation affected behavior to some extent. Some people seemed more generally fearful than others, and some situations (being approached by cars racing abreast) evoked more fear than others (sitting in a restaurant).

What is more interesting, though, is that the bulk of these effects were produced by the person-by-situation interaction. In other words, people tend to be frightened (or angered or reassured) by different things. This finding undercuts the usefulness of general traits such as anxiety. To predict behavior more accurately, such traits should be qualified; for example, anxiety in an interpersonal setting, anxiety when facing physical danger, anxiety in the face of the unknown, and so on. By using the person-by-situation interaction, the notion of stable personality differences can be maintained.

But there is a price, for the process of qualification may be endless. Consider anxiety when facing physical dangers. Should this be further qualified so that we separately consider anxiety when facing inanimate nature, anxiety when facing threatening strangers, and anxiety in the presence of animals, with the last of these subdivided into anxiety with cats, anxiety with dogs, anxiety with horses? The end result of such a process can only be an enormous subdivision of ever more finely drawn traits (Cronbach, 1975; Nisbett, 1977).

Reciprocal interaction We've seen that different situations may affect different people differently. But the interaction between person and situation needn't be a one-way street, because in many cases, the relation between situation and person is reciprocal. People often play a major role in choosing the situations they confront—the places they live, the work they do, the friends they associate with. And those choices are partially determined by their personality traits: The extrovert is more likely to seek out a party, while the introvert will find a quiet corner where he can curl up with a book. The situation may (and often does) determine a person's behavior, but the person's traits often determine what situation that person finds himself in (Snyder, 1981; Endler, 1982; Ickes, Snyder, and Garcia, 1997).

Reciprocal effects of this sort pervade social psychology and psychopathology. They are commonplace in the psychiatric clinic where many unhappy individuals don't recognize that the situations that trouble them so greatly are partially of their own creation. Further examples come from developmental psychology, where many investigators point to the fact that children of different temperaments elicit different reactions from their parents (e.g., Scarr and McCartney, 1983; Scarr, 1992; Rowe and Waldron, 1993; see Chapter 14).

CONSISTENCY AS A TRAIT

As we have seen, a major criterion for determining whether traits are present is cross-situational consistency in behavior. But psychologists have also come to realize that consistency itself—the degree to which people do much the same thing in different situations—may vary from person to person. To the extent that this is true, cross-situational consistency may be regarded as a trait in its own right.

Some people are more consistent than others For most of us, what we do is affected by both our personal characteristics and by the demands of the situation. But the extent to which one or the other predominates varies from person to person. It goes without saying that there are some social situations that affect most people equally and allow little room for personal variations. At a funeral, everyone is respectful and generally somber (Price and Bouffard, 1974; Monson, Hesley, and Chernick, 1982). But what about situations that are more ambiguous? Here some people will tend to behave much more consistently than others.

Self-monitoring Some people adjust their behavior to fit the social situation more than do others. One of the factors that determines the extent to which they do this is the degree to which they try to control the impression they make on others, so that they can be the right person in the right place at the right time. The tendency to do this is assessed by the **Self-Monitoring Scale,** developed by Mark Snyder. (For some representative items, see Table 16.7.) High

---

TABLE 16.7 SOME REPRESENTATIVE ITEMS FROM THE SELF-MONITORING SCALE *

1. I can look anyone in the eye and tell a lie with a straight face (if for a right end). (True)
2. In different situations and with different people, I often act like very different persons. (True)
3. I have trouble changing my behavior to suit different people and different situations. (False)
4. I can only argue for ideas which I already believe. (False)

* In the items shown, the key after each question is in the direction of self-monitoring. Thus, high self-monitors would presumably answer "true" to questions 1 and 2, and "false" to questions 3 and 4.

SOURCE: Snyder, 1987.

A   B

The extremes of the self-monitoring scale
(A) Woody Allen as the high self-monitor,
Zelig, the man who can fit in with anybody,
anywhere, anytime. (B) As the hero of most of
his other movies, Woody Allen is the ultimate
low self-monitor, who stays true to himself re-
gardless of the situation. (Pictured with Calvin
Coolidge and Herbert Hoover in Zelig,
1983, courtesy of the Kobal Collection; with
Mira Sorvino in Mighty Aphrodite, *1995*
courtesy of Photofest)

self-monitors care a great deal about how they appear in a social situation. By constantly adjusting to the situation, they are necessarily inconsistent; they'll act like cultured highbrows when with art lovers and boisterous sports fans when in the bleachers with other fans. In effect, they always seem to ask themselves, "How can I be the person this situation calls for?"★ In contrast, low self-monitors are much less interested in how they appear to others. They want to be themselves whatever the social climate in which they find themselves. As a result, their behavior is much more consistent from situation to situation (Snyder, 1987, 1995).

On the face of it, the high self-monitor seems to cut a rather less admirable figure than her low self-monitoring counterpart. But as Snyder points out, whether such value judgments apply depends on the way the self-monitoring pattern fits into the rest of the individual's life. The high self-monitor is probably rather pleasant to be with, and her diplomatic skill and adaptability may well be an asset in dealing with the many roles required in a complex society such as ours. The virtues of the low self-monitor are even more apparent; there's much to be said for the person of integrity who is the same today as she'll be tomorrow and to herself is ever true.

But at the extremes, neither approach is particularly appealing. An extremely high self-monitor may very well be a shallow, unprincipled poseur. And an extremely low self-monitor may manage to turn the virtues of his pattern into vices, given that consistent adherence to principle can become blind and stubborn rigidity. To march to the music of a different drummer is not necessarily admirable. It depends on what the music is (Snyder, 1987, 1995).

PERSON CONSTANCY

In looking back it's worth noting that the trait-situation controversy corresponds to a debate we encountered when discussing social psychology (see Chapters 11 and 12). In the realm of personality, critics of trait theory contend that traits alone do not predict what people will do. Likewise, in the social realm,

★ One might guess that high self-monitoring is just another aspect of extroversion, since the social skills of high self-monitors would seem to be closely related to the lifestyle of extroverts. There is indeed a correlation between the self-monitoring scale and tests of extroversion, but it is very slight. It appears that the two traits are at bottom quite different. High self-monitors can readily be the life of the party, but they will only be so when it seems appropriate. They know when the situation calls for greater decorum, say, at an upper-class tea party or in an art gallery, and then they will be properly reserved. The extrovert is much more likely to be gregarious and outgoing even in such situations (Snyder, 1987).

observers have noted a corresponding tendency to overstate the role of the individual and to underestimate the power of the situation, a pattern that leads to the fundamental attribution error; a similar overemphasis on traits is evident in the commonly held belief that unusual acts (such as blind obedience in the Milgram experiment) reflect unusual personality characteristics (see Chapter 12).

The person-situation debate comes up again and again, and social psychologists—and their like-minded colleagues in the field of personality—have redressed the overemphasis on personality traits by highlighting the crucial and often underrated role of the situation. But what can we then say about the other end of the polarity—the assumption that there *is* an underlying coherence in how an individual acts, thinks, and feels, a personality that plays a role in determining behavior?

The evidence indicates that this assumption—which goes back to the ancient dramatists and before—still stands. We all have an intuitive belief in something like person constancy, a phenomenon analogous to object constancy in perception (see Chapter 6). A chair is perceived as a stable object whose size remains the same whether we are near it or far away and whose shape remains unchanged regardless of our visual orientation. These constancies are not illusions; they reflect a genuine stability in the external world. The stability of persons is in some ways analogous. For we somehow manage to peer through a kaleidoscope of ever-changing situations to perceive an individual's behavioral consistency. The constancy of personality is not as sturdy as that of objects, but it has some reality even so.

To be sure, we sometimes err and see more uniformity and coherence than is actually there, so that we exaggerate person constancy in others and in ourselves (Shweder, 1975; Nisbett and Wilson, 1977; Nisbett, 1980; Kihlstrom and Cantor, 1984). But the fact that there are errors in our perception of persons doesn't mean that their personality is entirely in our own eyes. After all, there are visual illusions, but their existence does not erase the fact that by and large we see the world as it really is. What holds for the world of vision probably holds for person perception as well, and this is probably why trait theory has continued to have so much appeal (Kenrick and Funder, 1988; Funder, 1995). Person constancy is a fact. Jane remains Jane whether she is at home or at the office, whether it is today or yesterday or the day after tomorrow. And at some level she is different from Cathy and Margaret and six billion other humans alive today, for her personality—just like theirs—is unique.

Person constancy and caricature *Most artists have always believed that there is a constancy of behavioral as well as of bodily features, as illustrated in this print by Louis Leopold Boilly, ca. 1825. (Detail from* Thirty-six Faces of Expression, *courtesy Explorer, Paris / SuperStock)*

TRAITS AND BIOLOGY

To the extent that person constancy exists, we are probably justified in holding on to some version of the trait approach. People vary in their characteristic modes of behavior, and their variations can be described and assessed, however imperfectly, by the trait vocabulary. But how do such variations arise?

Thus far, we've talked about traits as if they were merely descriptive labels for broad groups of behavior patterns. But some trait theorists go further. In their view, traits are general predispositions to behave in one way or another that are ultimately rooted in the individual's biological makeup.

PERSONALITY AND TEMPERAMENT

A number of modern investigators believe that personality traits grow out of the individual's ***temperament,*** a characteristic reaction pattern of the individual that is present from a rather early age (Rothbart and Ahadi, 1994). Like Hippocrates who coined the term some 2,500 years ago, they believe that such temperamental patterns are largely genetic and constitutional in origin (though they obviously don't share his archaic ideas that they are the result of four bodily humors). Such characteristic behavior patterns may emerge during the first few months of life. An example comes from a study of 141 children, observed for about a decade following birth:

> Donald exhibited an extremely high activity level almost from birth. At three months . . . he wriggled and moved about a great deal while asleep in his crib. At six months he "swam like a fish" while being bathed. At twelve months he still squirmed constantly while he was being dressed or washed. . . . At two years he was "constantly in motion, jumping and climbing." At three, he would "climb like a monkey and run like an unleashed puppy." . . . By the time he was seven, Donald was encountering difficulty in school because he was unable to sit still long enough to learn anything. . . . (Thomas, Chess, and Birch, 1970, p. 104)

Subsequent investigators have tried to describe temperament within the framework of traditional trait classifications. An example is a temperament scale developed by Buss and Plomin that includes two major dimensions, sociability and emotionality (Buss and Plomin, 1984). According to Buss and Plomin, these two traits are the core components of the main axes of Eysenck's system—extroversion/introversion and neuroticism/emotional stability. They believe that in young children, extroversion is best represented by sociability (which presumably affects the attachment between mother and child, reactions to strangers, and the like), while neuroticism (emotional instability) is mainly represented by a greater tendency to be fearful (anxiety and guilt are reactions that appear in later years). In line with these views, both sociability and emotionality show a fair degree of stability over the first twenty years of life, as demonstrated by correlations of +.48 between fearfulness assessed at age five and again assessed in adulthood, and of +.53 between sociability at age six and at age fifteen (Bronson, 1966, 1967).

PERSONALITY AND THE GENES

Consistencies of this sort suggest the operation of genetic factors. Such hereditary effects are no news to animal breeders. Different strains of dogs show marked differences in temperament produced by centuries of breeding: Basset hounds are calm, and terriers are excitable and aggressive, while spaniels become easily attached to people and are very peaceable (Scott and Fuller, 1965; see Figure 16.6). We wouldn't expect to find such enormous differences in human

16.6   Temperamental differences in breeds of dogs   (A) Basset hounds are calm (Photograph by Wilfong Photographic/ Leo de Wys), (B) terriers are excitable, and (C) spaniels are very sociable and affectionate. (Photographs by H. Reinhard/Bruce Coleman)

A

B

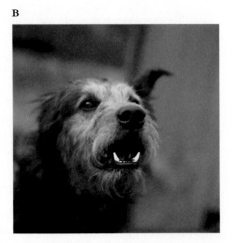

C

temperaments, since there are fortunately no people breeders working to create purebred human strains. But some fairly sizable genetic effects on human personality exist even so.

The evidence comes from some of the same methods that have been used to study hereditary effects in the determination of intelligence—chiefly, studies of twins and adopted children. In just about all cases, identical twins turn out to be more alike than fraternal twins on various personality attributes (e.g., Buss and Plomin, 1984; Zuckerman, 1987). For example, several studies suggest sizable genetic factors underlying the Big Five personality traits (Loehlin, 1992), and one study of 123 pairs of identical twins and 127 pairs of fraternal twins found that estimates of genetic influence for the Big Five traits ranged from 40 to 60 percent (Jang, Livesley, and Vernon, 1996).

In a twin study investigating the traits in Eysenck's system, a personality questionnaire was administered to over 12,000 pairs of twins in Sweden. The results showed average correlations of +.50 between identical twins on scores both of extroversion/introversion and of neuroticism/emotional stability. The corresponding correlations for fraternal twins were +.21 and +.23 (Floderus-Myrhed, Pedersen, and Rasmuson, 1980). Given all these findings, there is a strong suspicion that hereditary factors make a sizable contribution to differences in personality.

A number of investigators thought that such results might help to provide a concrete underpinning for the taxonomy of personality traits. The idea is simple: Those traits that are especially heritable are presumably more basic and should therefore serve as the primary categories for classification. But the facts seemed to prove otherwise. In one study, 1,700 twins of high-school age took the CPI. As expected, the scores of identical twins were more alike than those of the fraternal twins. The trouble was that this difference was just about the same on each of the test's eighteen scales. This suggests that each of these eighteen traits—for example, dominance, sociability, self-acceptance, self-control—are about equally heritable (Loehlin and Nichols, 1976). Much the same is true for responses to questionnaires assessing altruism ("I have donated blood"), empathy ("I like to watch people open presents"), and aggressiveness ("Some people think I have a violent temper"). Identical twins proved to be more alike than fraternal twins and to just about the same extent on each of the scales (Rushton et al., 1986). Such findings suggest that virtually all personality traits may be equally heritable. The only exceptions are characteristics that are generally regarded as attitudes rather than as traits, such as adherence to fundamentalist religious beliefs (Pogue-Geile and Rose, 1985).

But a reassessment of the CPI results of the 1,700 high-school aged twins suggests that the equal heritability of all these traits reflects the fact that all are influenced by Eysenck's two "supertraits"—extroversion/introversion and neuroticism/emotional stability—both of which are substantially heritable (Loehlin, 1982). In fact, heritability is particularly high for the specific traits that are closely related to these supertraits (for example, sociability). For traits that are not tied to these supertraits, such as stereotyped masculinity (e.g., "I like adventure stories better than romantic stories") and persistence (e.g., "I always tried to make the best school grades I could"), the heritability is much lower (Loehlin, 1982).

The point is especially telling given the various kinds of traits for which genetic factors have been found. For example, genetic linkages have been identified for traits such as television watching, traditionalism, and the willingness to divorce (Bouchard et al., 1990; Plomin et al., 1990; McGue and Lykken, 1992). Does this mean that there are genes for each of these? Obviously not, since for one thing, broadcast television didn't exist until fifty years ago. Instead, the genetic influence on each may reflect the operation of more general traits. For example television watching may be associated with extroversion and traditionalism with conscientiousness. In fact, the case of willingness to divorce demonstrates just this point: In a study of adult twins, those twins who divorced were likely to score higher on measures related to extroversion and neuroticism, and lower in impulse control (Jockin, McGue, and Lykken, 1996).

Given this reanalysis, we may have reason to return to the idea of a few basic personality dimensions that have genuine primary status. The most likely candidates seem to be extroversion/introversion and neuroticism/emotional stability. It's too early to judge whether this conception will hold up, but it is worth noting that a number of different approaches to the study of traits—factor analysis of personality inventories, developmental studies of temperament, and research on the hereditary basis of personality traits—all appear to converge toward the same conclusion.

THE INTERACTION BETWEEN GENES AND ENVIRONMENT

We've seen that some traits have a genetic basis. But genes alone cannot account for the variability in personality. Consider extroversion. The correlation between the extroversion scores of identical twins is roughly +.50. If heredity alone accounted for all of the differences in extroversion and if there were no error in measurement, that correlation should be +1.00. The fact that it is not indicates that nongenetic differences also operate to produce differences in personality. But what are the nongenetic, probably environmental differences that have this effect?

Between-family differences One environmental factor concerns **between-family differences,** such as the socioeconomic status of the parents, or the parents' religion, or their attitudes about child rearing: The Smiths live in the city and are very strict, the Browns live in the suburbs and are very permissive, and so on. A recent analysis by Plomin and Daniels suggests that, surprisingly enough, between-family differences of this sort are relatively unimportant in determining such personality traits as extroversion, emotionality, conscientiousness, and the like. Some evidence comes from studies of adoption. If between-family differences in environment played a significant role in determining personality traits,

"Separated at birth, the Mallifert twins meet accidentally." (© The New Yorker Collection 1981 Chas. Addams from Cartoonbank. com. All rights reserved.)

Within-family differences *The fact that children within the same family are often very different is an ancient theme of myth and literature. Among the many examples are the biblical stories of Cain and Abel and of Jacob and Esau, and of the three daughters of Shakespeare's* King Lear, *pictured here in this painting by Edwin Abbey. (Courtesy of Metropolitan Museum of Art; gift of George A. Hearn, 1913 [13.140])*

we would expect a reasonable correlation between the trait scores of adopted children and their adoptive siblings. But the facts say otherwise. In four such studies, the average correlation between adopted children and their adoptive siblings was +.04, that between those children and their adoptive parents was +.05 (Plomin and Daniels, 1987). Likewise, a review of studies of the Big Five traits found that the between-family differences in environment were similarly negligible in their influence (Loehlin, 1992).

Further proof comes from a study conducted at the University of Minnesota, comparing the personality traits of pairs of twins tested as adults. Some of the twins had been reared together; others had been reared apart and had been separated for an average of over thirty years. The results for the twins that were reared together were just as expected. As usual, the median correlation between the scores of identical twins was substantially larger than that between the scores of fraternal twins, with correlations of +.51 and +.23 respectively. But amazingly enough, the results were virtually identical for twins that were reared *apart* and had been separated for many years. Here the median correlations were +.50 and +.21 for identical and fraternal twins respectively. Similar results were found in a study that looked at the twins' vocational interests (Moloney, Bouchard, and Segal, 1991). On the face of it, one might have expected the correlations between the personality traits and vocational interests of the identical twins to be considerably lower, since they were raised in different family environments. The fact that the results were virtually identical is a strong further argument against the importance of between-family environmental factors (Bouchard, 1984; Tellegen et al., 1988; Bouchard et al., 1990).

Within-family differences Between-family environmental differences are evidently less important than one might have thought. But if so, what environmental factors *do* matter? According to Plomin and Daniels, the key is in differences in the environment encountered by different children in the same family. These include various accidents and injuries that befall one child in a family but not another; for example, one sibling may contract pneumonia while another does not. Other differences concern birth order and spacing (that is, the age difference between siblings). Still others concern the fact that parents treat different children differently. Finally, there are differences in friends, teachers, and peer groups; one sibling may be a member of a local Scout troop while another is not, and so on. All of these are differences within the family environment; their sum total accounts for some of the differences that are found among children in the same family.

How do **within-family differences** come about? There are no doubt many reasons, including chance encounters, accidents, changing family fortunes that affect younger and older children differently, and so on. But an important further factor is the reciprocal interaction between a child's genetic makeup and the environment, an interaction we've considered in another context (see pp. 692–93). If two siblings differ genetically, they will necessarily create different environments for themselves. A very sociable, active infant is likely to evoke more social stimulation than one who is passive and somber, and this in turn is likely to reinforce his initial pattern and make him even more sociable. The same holds for emotionality. The very moody child, prone to frequent bursts of temper, may well provoke a host of adverse reactions from his frustrated parents, who will respond with a mixture of guilt, anger, and confusion; here, too, the parents' reaction is likely to reinforce the behavior that evoked their reaction in the first place (Chess, 1987).

In these examples, the child's own behavioral tendencies—many of which are genetically determined—produce changes in her environment. Still further changes are produced at a somewhat later age when children actively seek out an environment that suits them—in the activities they engage in (sports, scholarship, or whatever) and the people they associate with (friends, teachers, and so on). All of these factors will combine to produce a correlation between an individual's genetic predisposition and the environment she comes to inhabit (Scarr and McCartney, 1983; Scarr, 1992).

When between-family environmental differences do matter It appears that, once genetic factors are set aside, the differences between families are of less importance than the differences within families. But this statement requires a number of important qualifications.

To begin with, between-family differences in environment do matter for intelligence. One line of evidence comes from studies of adopted children whose intelligence-test scores correlate about +.20 with those of their adopted parents (Bouchard and McGue, 1981; compare this to the correlations mentioned earlier of about +.05 for personality traits). Further proof comes from studies in which young children have been moved from an economically deprived to a middle-class environment with a resultant increase of 10 to 15 points in IQ (Scarr and Weinberg, 1976; Schiff et al., 1982).

Another qualification concerns the range of possible environments we have considered. All of the evidence we've summarized thus far was based on children of families whose socioeconomic level was working class or above. Within this range, between-family differences don't seem to affect personality traits very much, but this range constitutes a rather limited sample of environments. It tends not to include the environments provided by parents who are unemployed or that of parents who abuse their children or neglect them grossly. Nor does it include families that belong to another culture entirely, such as a family of Masai cattle herders in East Africa or a group of villagers in New Guinea. If the range had been broadened to include all these, between-family environmental differences would almost surely have been more important (Scarr, 1987, 1992).

PERSONALITY AND PHYSIOLOGICAL AROUSAL

To say that personality traits are in part inherited is to say that they have some physical basis, ultimately determined by the genes. But just what is this physical basis? Here the search for an answer has just begun.

Extroversion/introversion An interesting approach comes from attempts to link certain personality traits to aspects of neurophysiological arousal. The pioneer in this area was Hans Eysenck, who tried to relate the extroversion/introversion dimension to many phenomena outside of personality.

Some people seek sensations *(Top: photograph by Phil Schermeister/© Corbis; bottom: photograph © Philippe Blondel, Agence Vandystadt/Photo Researchers, Inc.)*

Others prefer a quieter existence *(Photograph © Jonathan Blair/Corbis)*

As Eysenck conceived it, introversion corresponds to a higher natural level of central nervous system reactivity than does extroversion: In effect, introverts are more reactive to external stimuli than extroverts are. The difference is not a matter of basic alertness, for introverts seem not to differ from extroverts in that area; instead, introverts react more when they *are* alerted (Stelmack, 1990). Thus, introverts have lower pain tolerance (Bartol and Costello, 1976) and when studying prefer a lower noise level and fewer opportunities for socializing (Campbell and Hawley, 1982). In effect, the more sensitive introverts guard themselves against stimulation from the outside, which to them amounts to *over-stimulation*.

In a recent study, these findings were linked directly to cerebral functioning. The investigators measured the electrical reaction to auditory clicks in several areas of the brain stem that are thought to help activate the cortex.★ In line with Eysenck's theory, introverts showed a faster response than extroverts, indicating greater reactivity (Bullock and Gilliland, 1993).

Sensation seeking   A related topic concerns **sensation seeking.** This is the tendency to seek varied and novel experiences, to look for thrills and adventure, and to be highly susceptible to boredom, as shown by affirmative answers to items such as: "I would like to try parachute jumping," "I sometimes like to do crazy things just to see the effect on others," and "I wish I didn't have to waste so much of a day sleeping" (Zuckerman, 1979). While sensation seeking is related to extroversion, it is not identical to it. It encompasses the liveliness and intolerance of boredom that characterize extroversion, but unlike extroversion, it seems to have little to do with sociability (see also Chapter 3).

Marvin Zuckerman, who developed the personality scales that contained these items, has provided convincing evidence of their validity (Zuckerman, 1994a). People who score at the high end of these scales are more likely to participate in risky sports such as sky diving, get more restless in a monotonous, confined situation, are less likely to be afraid of snakes, and are more likely to drive at faster speeds than people at the lower end (Zuckerman, 1983). A final bit of validation comes from a study on streaking, a popular fad of the 1970s whose practitioners took off their clothes and then ran, walked, or bicycled naked through some public area. When students were asked whether they had ever considered streaking (or had in fact streaked), their answer showed a substantial correlation with the sensation-seeking scales (Bacon, 1974, quoted in Zuckerman, 1979).

According to Zuckerman, the biological basis of sensation seeking is similar to that which Eysenck suggested for extroversion. In Zuckerman's view, sensation seekers are people who show greater responses to novelty in certain systems of the brain, specifically those whose neurotransmitter systems contain the enzyme monoamine oxidase (MAO). This includes systems that rely on norepinephrine (NE) and dopamine as their transmitters (Zuckerman, 1987, 1990). One of his lines of evidence comes from a study in which the level of NE in the spinal fluid was correlated with various measures on personality scales. The results showed a negative correlation: The greater the sensation-seeking tendency, the lower the NE level (Zuckerman et al., 1983). This fits in with the general hypothesis: People whose NE level is low are presumably underreactive in their NE systems. In effect, they are underaroused, which makes them seek thrills and take risks to jog their sluggish NE systems into greater activity (Zuckerman, 1994a). Other investigators have focused on dopamine, a transmitter that is chemically related to NE (see Chapters 2 and 3). They found that drug abusers are likely to rate highly as sensation seekers, and they suggest that the

★ The technical term for this reaction is *evoked potential*—an averaged electrical response of a region of the brain evoked by repeated presentations of a stimulus.

biological underpinnings for both involve the dopamine-mediated reward systems of the brain (Bardo, Donohew, and Harrington, 1996; see Chapter 3).

Sensation seeking runs in families, and some researchers suspect a genetic predisposition to it (Koopmans et al., 1995). So it was with considerable excitement that two separate research groups identified a gene that seems to code for one type of dopamine receptor and is associated with sensation seeking (Benjamin et al., 1996; Ebstein et al., 1996; Ebstein et al., 1997). But a recent attempt to substantiate these findings has not proved successful, and so conclusions on this point must remain tentative (Jonsson et al., 1997).

The need for caution   Recent genetic findings have encouraged those who seek a biological basis for personality differences. But the inability of others to substantiate them thus far should temper optimism with a dose of caution. There may be correlations between some personality traits and certain physiological indices of cerebral arousal (though this is still a matter of debate; see Gale, 1983; Gale and Edwards, 1986). But even if these correlations hold up, their eventual interpretation may turn out to be rather different and considerably more complex than those currently offered (Zuckerman, 1990, 1994a, b). So while it is apparent that some facets of our personality have a biological basis, it is as yet unclear just what that biological basis is.

THE BEHAVIORAL-COGNITIVE APPROACH

Trait theory tries to explain the differences in what people do by reference to something that is within them, to stable and perhaps built-in internal predispositions (that is, traits). According to this approach, people do what they do because of who they are: The jovial backslapper is the life of the party because he is an extreme extrovert. But there is an alternative view that takes issue with this position. This is the **behavioral approach** (which, as we'll see, is a view with several variations).

In contrast to trait theorists, adherents of the behavioral approach assert that human actions are determined from without: They are reactions to external forces. In recent times, this has often been called the **behavioral-cognitive approach,** since many recent adherents of the behavioral position assign increasing importance to cognitive factors such as expectations and beliefs.

In part, this position grows out of the situationist critique of trait theory we considered previously, for its proponents hold that people do what they do because of the situation in which they find themselves or in which they have found themselves on previous occasions. The life of the party acts her part precisely because she is at a party, a situation in which she will be reinforced for being outgoing and zany, as she has no doubt been reinforced on many previous occasions. This general view is traditionally associated with **behaviorism,** a very influential theoretical outlook that dominated American psychology for the first half of this century, emphasizing the role of environment and of learning, and insisting that people, no less than animals, must be studied objectively, from the outside (see Chapter 4).

If the trait approach can be likened to dramatic productions with character types who wear one mask that defines them throughout, the behavioral view corresponds to the dramatic approach of a repertory company in which every member takes many parts. Today an actor plays one role, tomorrow he learns to

Is personality coherent?   *Some early versions of the behavioral-cognitive approach argued that the consistency of personality is an illusion. (Pablo Picasso's* Girl before a Mirror. *Boisegeloup, March 1932. Oil on canvas, 64 × 51¼". The Museum of Modern Art, New York. Mrs. Simon Guggenheim Fund. Photograph © 1994 The Museum of Modern Art, New York)*

A **B** **C**

Repertory roles Lawrence Olivier is often regarded as the prototype of the repertory actor who could play any part. He once said that "in finding a character . . . I do it from the outside in," an approach quite different from that of method actors. (A) As Hamlet (from the 1948 film he directed), (B) as Archie Rice, a cheap music hall entertainer (from the 1960 film, The Entertainer*), (C) as the Mahdi, the fanatical leader of a nineteenth-century Sudanese sect (from the 1966 film* Khartoum*). (Courtesy of Photofest)*

play another, all depending upon the play. Nor is the way he plays them determined by anything from inside. Actors of the behavioral, "technical" school don't worry about inner motivations or subtle subtexts. If required to enact an emotion, they pay a great deal of attention to its visible bodily manifestations; they tremble or sway or clench their fists or breathe more rapidly, depending upon the particular emotion they want to enact. For in their view, all that matters is their outward behavior, because that's all the audience ever hears or sees. Here again, they are much like behavior theorists, who believe that the only way to understand people is by studying them objectively, from the outside.

RADICAL BEHAVIORISM

As we mentioned above, behaviorism comes in a number of different forms. The most influential modern exponent of *radical behaviorism* was B. F. Skinner (1904–1990). To him, the subject matter of psychology was overt behavior and nothing else, with little if any reference to inferred, internal processes such as wishes, traits, or expectations. In Skinner' s view, humans—no less than rats and pigeons—behave according to the way they are prompted by the external environment. This environment may be today's—people wear overcoats in the winter and polo shirts in the summer. But more often the relevant environment is yesterday's, when a particular situation led to learning.

In some cases, the relevant learning is by *classical conditioning.* Some hitherto neutral stimulus is paired with some motivationally significant event, and a response is then elicited; a dog salivates when it sees the food dish or a child cries when she sees the nurse who gave her a painful injection. In other cases, the learning is by *operant* (or *instrumental*) *conditioning,* in which the response is controlled by its consequences. If it is reinforced, then it is more likely to be emitted in the future. In all these cases, what matters is the external environment that provides the conditions for learning. (For an overview of conditioning, see Chapter 4.)

Skinner's behaviorism represents a powerful and influential view of human—and, of course, of animal—nature. But can it account for the characteristics that comprise what we call personality? Many behaviorists believe that it can. In their view, to say that people are different is just to say that they behave

differently. Suppose Jason is generally sociable, while Alan is withdrawn, even when the external circumstances are the same. As Skinner saw it, there is little gained by attributing this difference to a difference in the trait of sociability. He would instead assume that there is a difference in the reinforcement histories of these two people. In the past, Jason was probably reinforced for amiable chatting, while Alan was offered little or no encouragement. Seen in this light, the so-called trait of sociability is just another case of operant learning (e.g., Skinner, 1969, 1971).

This line of argument brings up an immediate question. If reinforcement produces the difference between Jason and Alan or Jane and Margaret, why do such differences often persist even when the consequences for the behavior have changed? For persist they do. Jane will continue to smile and chatter even after her dinner party companions have become bored and stopped listening, while Margaret will sit back in a corner despite everyone's best efforts to lure her out. Eventually, no doubt, both women will respond to the changed circumstances, but why does it generally take so long? Felix and Oscar of *The Odd Couple* will stay respectively fussy and sloppy no matter what, and Theophrastus's garrulous man will keep on talking even after every citizen of Athens has repeatedly yawned in his face. How can Skinner (or any other behavior theorist) account for this persistence of characteristic behaviors?

If the relevant behavior was developed by operant conditioning, then according to Skinner, its persistence would be based on **partial reinforcement.** As we saw in Chapter 4, resistance to extinction is markedly increased by partial reinforcement. Rats who are rewarded every time they run down an alley will stop running after a few trials if a reward is no longer obtained. But the situation is quite different when they are rewarded on only some proportion of the trials. Now they'll keep on running even when there is no immediate reward, as if they've learned that if at first you don't succeed, it generally pays to try and try again.

According to Skinner and other behaviorists, what holds for rats holds for people, too. Many behavior patterns persist because they've been rewarded only sometimes. Gamblers keep on pulling slot machine levers because the machine pays off every once in a while, and children continue to throw temper tantrums because their parents did not ignore their tantrums—and thus extinguish the response—every single time. Some people consistently whine and wheedle favors, others bully, and still others sulk. Wheedling worked for the one, bullying for the other, and sulking for the third; not always, but sometimes, and that is precisely why each still persists in the characteristic behavior pattern. Similarly for Jason and Alan, who continue to smile or sit quietly because of previous intermittent reinforcement for these actions.

Learning theorists offer a different explanation for the persistence of classically conditioned reactions that are based on fear. The reason is that avoidance learning is generally difficult to extinguish. Consider a little girl who became intensely afraid of dogs after she was accidentally knocked down by a playful Saint Bernard. Her fear was based on classical conditioning, with the dog as the conditioned stimulus and the pain as the unconditioned stimulus. Her fear generalized, so she avoided all dogs. As a result, she was never exposed to situations in which the presence of a dog was free of unpleasant consequences, so the fear was never extinguished. In effect, the fear was self-perpetuating: It kept her from testing reality, so she could never discover that the fear was now essentially groundless (Mowrer, 1939; see Chapters 4, 18, and 19).

SOCIAL LEARNING THEORY

While impressed with radical behaviorism's successes in the animal laboratory, many authors have had misgivings about its ability to describe, let alone to explain, the more complex aspects of human personality. To be sure, people differ in their behavior—some brag, others sulk, still others tease—but can we define these subtle, interpersonal responses as readily as we can define the response of lever pressing in a rat?

Nor is it clear that outer behavior is all that matters. Personality differences involve not only what people do but also what they think and believe and expect. The fact that Joe believes that women can't be trusted and that Carol expects to fail no matter how hard she tries are important aspects of their personalities. Such facts clearly go beyond the outwardly observable aspects of behavior, and as such they are difficult to describe in the language of radical behaviorism.

Such considerations gradually led to a liberalized behavioral approach to personality, which now accepts terms like *expectation* and *belief* as a matter of course. Those who subscribe to this modified approach are often called **social learning theorists** and include such figures as Albert Bandura and Walter Mischel.

At first glance, one might well think that social learning theorists would downplay the role of personality differences in predicting human behavior. For it was they (most prominently, Walter Mischel) who attacked trait theory by arguing that differences between situations are more important than differences between persons in determining what people do. But by now, virtually everyone—whether trait or social learning theorist—has abandoned the extremes of the trait-situation controversy and agrees that both personality and situation matter, as well as the interaction between the two. Thus, social learning theorists accept the notion of personality differences after all. But how do they express that notion?

In essence, they contend that many of the personal qualities that characterize individuals are essentially cognitive: different ways of seeing the world, thinking about it, and interacting with it, all acquired over the course of an individual's life. Mischel lists some of the cognitive qualities on which people may differ. One concerns the individual's **competencies**—the kinds of things a person can do and understand. Another concerns his **encoding strategies**—the way he tends to interpret situations. A third refers to his **expectancies**—his beliefs about what follows what, what acts will produce what outcomes, what events will lead to what consequences, and so on. A fourth difference concerns his **subjective values**—which outcomes he values. A final difference involves what Mischel calls **self-regulatory systems**—the way he regulates his own behavior by various self-imposed goals and plans (Mischel, 1973, 1984).

CONTROL

We will consider only a few of the cognitive categories along which personalities may differ. Here we'll talk about a certain kind of expectancy: people's beliefs about the control they can exert on the world around them. And just about all of us generally seem to desire control.

In a previous chapter, we saw that animals and babies behave as if they want to

Loss of control *Patients in a Florida nursing home. (Photograph by Michael Heron, 1983/Woodfin Camp)*

have a sense of control over their lives. Babies smile if an overhead mobile turns around because they made it turn; if it turns around regardless of what they do, they stop smiling. Dogs can cope with electric shocks if they can escape them; other dogs who get the same number of shocks no matter what they do will suffer from learned helplessness (see Chapter 4). What holds for animals and babies also holds for human adults. They, too, prefer control.

A widely cited illustration of this common desire for control is a series of studies of elderly people in a nursing home. Patients on one floor of a nursing home were given small houseplants to take care of, and they were also asked to choose the time at which they wanted to participate in some of the nursing home activities (for example, visiting friends, watching television, planning social events). Patients on another floor were also given plants but with the understanding that the plants would be tended by the staff. They also participated in the same activities as the first group of patients, but at times chosen by the staff rather than by them. The results were clear-cut. According to both nurses' and the patients' own reports, the patients who were allowed to exert control were more active and felt better than the patients who lacked this control; this difference was still apparent a year later (Langer and Rodin, 1976; Rodin and Langer, 1977).

EXPLANATORY STYLE

The actual control an individual exercises over vital events in her life is important. But no less important is the extent to which she *believes* that these events are under her control. These beliefs are intimately related to her **explanatory style** (formerly, attributional style), a characteristic pattern of designating the causes of whatever good or bad fortunes may befall her. This style can be measured by a specially constructed **attributional style questionnaire** (**ASQ**) in which a participant is asked to imagine herself in a number of situations (for example, failing a test) and to indicate what would have caused those events if they had happened to her (Peterson et al., 1982; Dykema et al., 1996).

Much of the interest in explanatory style comes from its use in predicting whether a person is likely to suffer from depression, a psychological disorder that can range from a mild case of feeling "blue" to an intense, chronic, and ultimately hospitalizable condition characterized by utter dejection, apathy, hopelessness, and such physical symptoms as loss of appetite and sleeplessness (for details, see Chapter 18). Being prone to depression is correlated with a particular attributional style—a tendency to attribute unfortunate events to causes that are internal, global, and stable. Thus, a person who is prone to depression is likely to attribute life events to causes that refer to something within the person, that will generalize to other situations, and that will continue over time, for example, being unattractive or unintelligent (Peterson and Seligman, 1984; Buchanan and Seligman, 1995).★

According to proponents of this approach, the internal-global-stable explanatory style creates a predisposition that makes the person vulnerable to depression. This vulnerability will then be transformed into the actual disorder by a stressful event (Seligman and Nolen-Hoeksema, 1987; for more on this hypothesis and for a further discussion of this approach to mental disorders, see Chapter 18).

SELF-CONTROL

Expectancies about control represent one category of personality differences that social learning theorists have considered. Another concerns differences in

---

★ This account is a reformulation of an earlier model of depression based on helplessness (e.g., Seligman, 1975).

patterns of self-regulation, especially *self-control.* Control refers to an individual's ability to do what he wants to do, unobstructed by external forces or obstacles. Self-control, in contrast, refers to his ability to overcome *internal* forces and obstacles, the ability to refrain from doing some of the things he wants to do, and likewise the ability to do things he would rather not do in order to get what he really wants at some time in the future.★

An important example of self-control is ***delay of gratification.*** Much of our ordinary life requires us to postpone immediate rewards for the sake of some more important reward in the future. Some of the postponements involve delays of years or even decades, as in the case of a student who takes arduous courses in college in hopes of an exciting career later on or the athlete who spends tiresome hours in the gym in hopes of Olympic gold. Others are reckoned in shorter intervals, such as waiting for a paycheck at the end of the week or waiting one's turn in a cafeteria line. In all these cases, it's hard to imagine any culture that does not require some system of such self-imposed delays, with efforts now often rewarded only at a long delay and with many pleasures available only at a certain time and place. Farmers have to sow before they reap, and most cultures have elaborate rules that prescribe the when and where of sexuality and procreation (e.g., Freud, 1930; Mischel, 1986).

What is often called *will power* is presumably just this ability to forgo some immediate gratification in order to pursue some ultimate goal. According to popular wisdom, some people have this ability to a greater degree than others. But do they really? That is, is this ability consistent over time and across situations?

Delay of gratification in young children   Walter Mischel and his associates studied this ability in young children and showed that it is related to a number of personality attributes in later life (Mischel, 1974, 1984; Mischel, Shoda, and Rodriguez, 1992). Their participants were children between four and five years of age who were shown two treats, one of which they had previously said they preferred to the other (for example, two marshmallows or pretzels versus one). To obtain the more desirable treat, they had to wait for an interval of about fifteen minutes. If they didn't want to wait or grew tired of waiting during the delay interval, they were given the less desirable treat immediately but then had to forgo the more desirable one. The results showed that the length of time the children were able to wait depended on just what happened during that period. If the marshmallows were hidden from view, they waited ten times longer than if they were visible during the waiting period (Mischel, Ebbesen, and Zeiss, 1972).

Further study showed that the mere physical presence or absence of the rewards was not the primary factor. What really mattered was what the children did and thought during the interval. If they looked at the marshmallow, or worse—thought about eating it, they usually succumbed and stopped waiting. But they could delay if they found (or were shown) some way of distracting their attention from the desired treat, for example, by thinking of something fun, such as Mommy pushing them on a swing. They could also delay if they thought about the desired objects in some way other than consuming them, for example, by focusing on the pretzels' shape and color rather than on their crunchy taste. By mentally transforming the goals in this fashion, the children managed ultimately to have their cake (or pretzel) and eat it too. By the time they were seven or eight, some of the children seemed to understand their own cognitive strategies for achieving self-control. One child explained why one mustn't look at the marshmallows: "If she's looking at them all the time, it will make her hungry . . . and she'd want to [stop waiting] . . ." (Mischel and Baker,

Delay of gratification   *(Photograph by George Gleitman)*

★ Some manifestations of self-control involve forgoing a particular gratification altogether for the sake of some other reward or to avoid some aversive state of affairs. An example is quitting smoking.

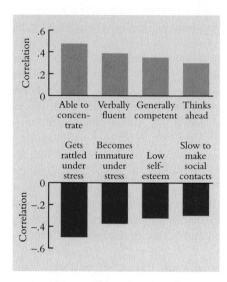

16.7 Childhood delay and adolescent competence *The figure indicates the relation between the ability to delay gratification at age four or five and personality traits at about age sixteen; it depicts correlations between various personality traits of adolescents as rated by their parents and the length of time they delayed gratification as preschoolers. Bars in blue show positive correlations; bars in dark red show negative correlations. (Data from Mischel, 1984)*

1975; Mischel and Moore, 1980; Mischel and Mischel, 1983; Mischel, 1984; Rodriguez, Mischel, and Shoda, 1989).

As Mischel points out, such results suggest that will power is not really the grimly heroic quality it is often said to be. At least in children, the trick is not in bucking up and bearing what's difficult and aversive but in mentally transforming what's unpleasant into what is pleasant while yet sticking to the task at hand (Mischel, 1986; Mischel and Rodriguez, 1993).

Childhood delay and adolescent competence These various findings show that whether a child delays gratification depends on how she construes the situation. But it apparently also depends on some qualities in the child herself. The best evidence comes from follow-up studies that have demonstrated remarkable correlations between children's ability to delay at four years of age and some of their characteristics ten years later. The results show that the ability to tolerate lengthy delay of gratification in early childhood augurs well for later development. It correlates significantly with academic and social competence (as rated by the child's parents) and with general coping ability in adolescence. Thus, participants who delayed longer in early childhood were judged to be more verbally fluent, attentive, self-reliant, able to plan and think ahead, academically competent, and less likely to go to pieces under stress than were participants whose delay times were shorter (Mischel, Shoda, and Peake, 1988; Shoda, Mischel, and Peake, 1990; see Figure 16.7).

Why should a four-year-old's willingness to wait fifteen minutes to get two pretzels rather than one be an indicator of such important personal characteristics as academic and social competence a full decade later? So far, we can only guess. One possibility is that some of the same cognitive characteristics that underlie this deceptively simple waiting task in childhood are similar to those demanded by successful performance in the more serious undertakings of adolescence and adulthood. To succeed in school, the student must be able to subordinate short-term goals to long-term purposes. Much the same is true of his social relations, for the person who is at the mercy of every momentary impulse will probably be unable to keep friendships, sustain commitments, or participate in any kind of team play. In both the academic and social domains, reaching any long-term goal inevitably means some renunciation of lesser goals that beckon in the interim.

If there is some general capacity for delaying gratification, useful for child and adult alike, where does it originate? One possibility is that there is some built-in disposition that underlies both the child's and the adult's behavior. But it may also be that the common personal quality is produced by learning. Some children may acquire certain general cognitive skills (say, keeping their attention on distant goals without getting too frustrated in the process) that they continue to apply to more complex goal-directed efforts as they get older.

SOCIAL LEARNING THEORY AND BEHAVIORISM

Looking back over our discussion, it's clear that social learning theorists have taken a considerable interest in relatively stable and generalized personality traits, as revealed by studies of explanatory style and delay of gratification. But if so, how do they differ from trait theorists? They have also moved further and further away from radical behaviorism, having become increasingly interested in all kinds of cognitive processes, such as expectations, beliefs, and plans, none of which are directly observable from the outside. In what sense do they still regard themselves as behaviorists?

There are two answers. One has to do with the situation. By now, everyone agrees that both traits and situations matter, but even so, social learning theorists, true to their behaviorist lineage, are more likely to stress the role of situational factors (or of a person-situation interaction) than are trait theorists. Thus, Mischel found that delay of gratification is an index of a surprisingly stable personal attribute, but he was quick to point out that this index is strongly affected by the way the situation was set up (was the reward visible?) and how it was construed (did the child think about eating the reward?).

The second answer is even more important. For unlike trait theorists, who are generally inclined to believe that the major personality traits have a built-in, genetic basis, social learning theorists are more likely to assume that these attributes are a result of learning. In this regard, social learning theory still shares the environmentalist bias that is a hallmark of American behaviorism. For both radical behaviorists and their descendants in social learning theory hold to an empiricist worldview that, in its extreme form, asserts that virtually anyone can become anything by proper (or in some cases, improper) training. This view was well-expressed in a widely quoted pronouncement by the founder of American behaviorism, John B. Watson:

> Give me a dozen healthy infants, well-formed, and my own specified world to bring them up in and I'll guarantee to take any one at random and train him to become any type of specialist I might select—doctor, lawyer, artist, merchant-chief, and, yes even beggarman thief, regardless of his talents, penchants, tendencies, abilities, vocations, and race of his ancestors. (Watson, 1925)

This is just another way of committing to the most extreme environmentalist pole of the nature-nurture controversy as it pertains to personality. Put in terms of our theatrical metaphor, it's a way of saying that any actor can take any part at all, put on any mask whatever, as long as she is properly coached.

Needless to say, such an extreme position is no longer held by anyone. As in most other areas of psychology, there is virtually no one who believes that behavior is determined by nature or nurture alone. In this sense, the nature-nurture controversy is resolved. The same holds for the trait-situation controversy. What's left are different biases. For different psychologists will still make different bets about which factors—traits or situations, a built-in genetic disposition or the individual's experiences—are most involved in determining this or another facet of a personality. Trait theorists generally make one bet, and social learning theorists make the other. But biases only play a role when we don't yet know the facts. When these are in—and they are coming in ever more quickly—there will be no more room for betting.

Self-control? (© *The New Yorker Collection 1963 W. Miller from Cartoonbank. com. All rights reserved.*)

TAKING STOCK

In this chapter, we've considered the trait approach, which tries to describe differences in personality in terms of underlying attributes that may well originate in built-in predispositions, and the behavioral-cognitive approach, which focuses on the individual's observable acts and emphasizes the power of both learning and the situation. Both approaches have made important contributions to our understanding, but they are not the only ones. In the next chapter, we will consider three further perspectives from which personality can be viewed: the psychodynamic, the humanistic, and the sociocultural. As we will see, each perspective has its own value. For like a statue, the subject matter of personality can be viewed from several different angles, all of which contribute to our overall appreciation.

SUMMARY

1.   People differ in their predominant desires, in their characteristic feelings, and in their typical modes of expressing these desires and feelings. All of these distinctions fall under the general heading of personality differences. The five main attempts to understand these differences are the *trait approach,* the *behavioral-cognitive approach,* the *psychodynamic approach,* the *humanistic approach,* and the *sociocultural approach* to personality.

2.   One approach to personality assessment is by *structured personality tests,* such as the *Minnesota Multiphasic Personality Inventory,* or *MMPI.* The MMPI assesses traits by means of a number of different scales, each of which measures the extent to which a person's answers approximate those of a particular psychiatric criterion group. In actual practice, MMPI records are interpreted by inspecting the person's score profile, including his response to various *validity scales.* The same is true of its new revision, the MMPI-2. A number of other personality inventories, such as the *California Psychological Inventory,* or *CPI,* were constructed in an analogous manner but using normal rather than pathological criterion groups.

3.   The validity of personality inventories has been evaluated by using indices of *predictive validity.* The results show that while these tests predict, they don't predict very well, for their validity coefficients are relatively low. When the evaluation is based on construct validity, the results look more promising. *Barnum effects* show that the one criterion that is of little use is the person's own acceptance of the test interpretation.

4.   A very different way of assessing personality is by means of projective techniques. Two prominent examples are the *Rorschach inkblot test* and the *Thematic Apperception Test,* or *TAT.* While these tests are often used in clinical practice, they have been criticized because of their relatively low predictive validity and even lower *incremental validity.* Moreover, they are costly to administer, making them not very useful.

5.   *Personality traits* are attributes that define distinctions in people's predominating desires and feelings, and their typical modes of expressing them. The underlying assumption of *trait theory* is that such traits are fundamentally consistent over time and situations.

6.   One of the first tasks of the trait approach is to find an appropriate taxonomy for personality attributes. Many investigators have tried to develop such a taxonomy using *factor analysis.* This method has led to the identification of five major dimensions, often called the *Big Five: extroversion, neuroticism, agreeableness, conscientiousness,* and *openness to experience.* An alternative scheme proposed by Eysenck features two main dimensions—*neuroticism/emotional stability* and *extroversion/introversion.*

7.   The concept of stable personality traits was challenged by critics who argued that people behave much less consistently than a trait theory would lead one to predict. One alternative is *situationism,* which claims that human behavior is largely determined by the situation in which the individual finds herself. Proponents of this view believe that the underlying consistency of human personalities is more or less illusory and that personality traits are mental figments devised by an observer who watches other people's actions and tries to make sense out of them.

8.   While most observers have concluded that there is strong support for behavioral consistency over time, there is still disagreement over the degree to which there is behavioral consistency across situations. Some authors argue that the failure to find *cross-situational consistency* is caused by assessments that are based on too few observations. Others argue that many inconsistencies in behavior are apparent rather than real.

9.   Many commentators argue that behavioral consistencies will show up best if one looks at the *interaction* between person and situation. Such interactions can be reciprocal because people have a hand in creating the situations they face.

SUMMARY

10.   Consistency of behavior can be regarded as a trait in its own right. Some people tend to be more consistent than others. To the extent that people monitor their behavior to fit the social situation, they will behave inconsistently; the tendency to do so is assessed by the *self-monitoring scale.*

11.   While some trait theorists view traits as merely descriptive categories, others see them as predispositions to behave in certain ways that are ultimately rooted in the individual's biological makeup. Some evidence for this view grows out of studies of *temperament,* an individual's characteristic reaction pattern that may be inborn and emerges in infancy.

12.   There is evidence that some personality traits have a genetic basis. Twin studies, for example, show that the correlations on traits such as dominance, sociability, self-acceptance, and self-control are considerably higher in identical than in fraternal twins. Some theorists believe that these effects are based on the high heritability of Eysenck's two supertraits, neuroticism/emotional stability and extroversion/introversion.

13.   Environmental differences also contribute to the variability on traits such as extroversion and neuroticism. But contrary to expectations, what matters are not *between-family differences* (at least for samples that are limited to this culture), but *within-family differences.* Evidence comes from the fact that the correlation between the personality traits of adopted children and their adoptive siblings is essentially zero, and that the correlations between the traits of identical twins reared together are virtually identical to those of identical twins reared apart.

14.   Some investigators have tried to link certain personality traits to aspects of neurophysiological arousal. According to Eysenck, introversion corresponds to a higher level of central nervous system reactivity than does extroversion. As a result, introverts prefer lower levels of physical and social stimulation, while extroverts prefer to enhance their level of stimulation. Much the same may hold for the trait of *sensation seeking,* which is thought to relate to underarousal of certain regions of the brain.

15.   In contrast to trait theory, adherents of the *behavioral-cognitive approach* assert that people do what they do because of the situation that they are in or have been in on previous occasions. The most thoroughgoing version of this approach is the *radical behaviorism* of B. F. Skinner, which focuses on overt behavior and asserts that differences in the ways people act are produced by differences in what they have learned through either classical or operant conditioning. The fact that characteristic behavior patterns persist even when the reinforcements that produced them are no longer there may reflect the effect of partial reinforcement on resistance to extinction.

16.   *Social learning theory* is a somewhat liberalized behavioral approach to personality. Unlike radical behaviorists, social learning theorists, such as Bandura and Mischel, are interested in what people think no less than in what they do, which is why their orientation is sometimes called the *behavioral-cognitive approach.* But like radical behaviorists, they emphasize the role of situational factors in determining behavior. Unlike trait theorists, who tend to believe that major personality traits have a built-in basis, social learning theorists share the radical behaviorists' belief that most such attributes are the result of learning.

17.   Social learning theorists are interested in various cognitive characteristics along which personalities may differ. One of these concerns the beliefs people have about the control they can exert on the world around them. One difference concerns their characteristic *explanatory style*—the causes to which they tend to attribute events that happen to them. Some of the interest in explanatory style comes from its use in predicting depression. Being prone to depression is correlated with a tendency to attribute unfortunate events to internal, global, and stable causes.

18.   While control refers to a person's ability to do what he wants to do, *self-control* refers to his ability to refrain from doing what he wants to do in order to get something he wants even more. There is evidence that four-year-olds who are able to tolerate *delay of gratification* for the sake of a more desirable reward show more social and academic competence in adolescence.

CHAPTER 17

PERSONALITY II: PSYCHODYNAMIC, HUMANISTIC, AND SOCIOCULTURAL APPROACHES

T he preceding chapter described many of the ways in which people differ in their characteristic modes of thought, desires, and behavior—that is, in their distinctive patterns of personality. Trait theorists try to understand these differences by reference to underlying trait dimensions, while adherents of the behavioral-cognitive approach stress the importance of the situation and of learning. We will now consider several alternatives to these approaches that take another tack entirely: the psychodynamic, the humanistic, and the sociocultural.

THE PSYCHODYNAMIC APPROACH: FREUD AND PSYCHOANALYSIS

Adherents of the **psychodynamic approach** do not deny that some people are more sociable than others, that some are more impulsive, or emotionally unstable, or whatever. But they contend that explaining such tendencies as the expression of a personality trait or as the result of simple learned patterns is rather superficial. In their view, what people do and say—and even what they consciously think—is only the tip of the iceberg. As they see it, human acts and thoughts are just the outer expression of a whole host of motives and desires that are often derived from early childhood experiences, that lie buried beneath the surface, that are generally pitted against each other, and that are for the most part unknown to the person himself. They believe that to understand a person is to understand these hidden psychological forces (often called *dynamics*) that make him an individual divided against himself.

We saw previously that the trait approach bears a certain similarity to dramatic forms that employ stock characters, such as the comedies of the classical and Renaissance ages. In such plays, everything was exactly what it appeared to be. Once the character entered, the audience knew what to expect. If the actor wore the mask of the cowardly soldier, he would brag and run away; if he wore the mask of the miserly old man, he would jealously guard his money.

The psychodynamic perspective, in contrast, is related to a more modern approach to drama in which nothing is quite what it seems. In playing a character, actors who follow this approach pay attention to the *subtext*, the unspoken thoughts that go through the character's head while she speaks her lines. And many actors are interested in a still deeper subtext, the thoughts and wishes of which the character is *un*aware. According to the psychodynamic approach, this most basic subtext is the wellspring of all human personality.

Acting with the subtext *Certain modern approaches to acting, such as those developed by New York's Actor's Studio, emphasize the importance of subtexts. The photo shows a scene from the film,* The Godfather, Part II, *featuring Lee Strasberg, the late head of the Actor's Studio, and Al Pacino, one of its illustrious graduates. In the scene, a gangster overlord plans a deadly double-cross of another, while telling him: "You're a wise and considerate young man." (From* The Godfather, Part II, *1974; courtesy of the Kobal Collection)*

The dramatic presentation of inner conflicts *In some cases, an actor plays a character who is not fully aware of her own subtext, so she, like one of Freud's patients, is really lying to herself. An example is Blanche, from Tennessee Williams's play* A Streetcar Named Desire. *She is both sexually attracted to and repelled by her brutal brother-in-law Stanley. (From the stage version of* A Streetcar Named Desire, *1947, with Marlon Brando and Jessica Tandy; photograph courtesy of the Museum of the City of New York)*

THE ORIGINS OF PSYCHOANALYTIC THOUGHT

We will begin our discussion with the views of Sigmund Freud (1856–1939), the founder of **psychoanalysis,** for all current versions of the psychodynamic approach are ultimately derived from his. Initially, our primary emphasis will be on exposition, postponing critical analysis until later.

In some ways, Freud can be regarded as a modern Hobbesian. Hobbes had insisted that at bottom humans are savage brutes whose natural impulses, if left unchecked, would inevitably lead to murder, rape, and pillage (see Chapter 10). To curb this beast within, they entered into a social contract in some distant past and subordinated themselves to a larger social unit, the state. Like Hobbes, Freud regarded the basic human instincts as a seething cauldron of pleasure seeking that blindly strives for gratification regardless of the consequences. This savage, selfish human nature has to be tamed by civilization.

Unlike Hobbes, however, Freud did not believe that the subjugation of the brute in humankind was a onetime event in political history. Rather, he argued that it occurs in every lifetime, for the social contract is renewed in the childhood of every generation. Another difference concerns the nature of the taming process. According to Hobbes, people's baser instincts are curbed by external social sanctions; they want to rob their neighbors but don't do so because they are afraid of the king's men. According to Freud, the restraints of society are internal, incorporated into each person's thoughts during the first few years of childhood. The first curbs on behavior are based on a simple (and quite Hobbesian) fear of direct social consequences—of a scolding or spanking. But eventually the child inhibits his misdeeds because he feels that they are bad and not just because he fears that he will be caught and punished. At this point, the taming force of society has become internalized. The king's men are now within, internalized embodiments of society's dictates whose weapons—the pangs of conscience—are no less powerful for being mental.

According to Freud, the taming process is never fully complete. The forbidden impulses cannot be ruled out of existence. They can be denied for a while, but eventually they will reassert themselves, often along new and devious channels, leading to yet further repressive measures that will probably fail in their

The Dream of Reason Produces Monsters *An engraving by Francisco Goya (1799), which suggests that the same mind that is capable of reason also produces unknown terrors. (Courtesy of the National Library of Medicine)*

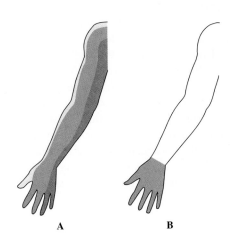

17.1 Glove anesthesia *(A) Areas of the arm's skin that send sensory information to the brain by way of different nerves. (B) A typical region of anesthesia in a patient with hysteria. If there were a nerve injury (in the spinal cord), the anesthesia would extend over the length of the arm, following the nerve distribution shown in (A).*

turn as well. As a result, there is constant conflict between the demands of instinct and the demands of society, but this war goes on underground, within the individual and usually without her own knowledge. As a result, the individual is divided against herself, and her unconscious conflicts express themselves in thoughts and deeds that appear irrational but that make sense if understood in terms of the underground drama.

HYSTERIA AND HYPNOSIS

When Freud began his medical practice, many of his patients suffered from a disorder then called *hysteria* (now called *conversion disorder;* see Chapter 18). The symptoms of hysteria presented an apparently helter-skelter catalogue of physical and mental complaints—total or partial blindness or deafness, paralysis or anesthesia of various parts of the body, uncontrollable trembling or convulsive attacks, and gaps in memory. Except for these symptoms, the patients were in no sense deranged; they were generally lucid and did not have to be institutionalized. Was there any underlying pattern that could make sense of this confusing array of complaints?

The first clue came with the suspicion that hysterical symptoms are *psychogenic,* the results of some unknown psychological cause rather than the product of organic damage to the nervous system. This hypothesis grew out of the work of Jean Charcot (1825–1893), a French neurologist, who noticed that many of the bodily symptoms of hysteria make no anatomical sense. For example, some patients suffered from anesthesia of the hand but retained sensation above the wrist. This *glove anesthesia* (so called because of the shape of the affected region) could not possibly be caused by any nerve injury, since an injury to any of the relevant nerve trunks would also affect a portion of the arm above the wrist (Figure 17.1). This ruled out a simple organic interpretation and suggested that glove anesthesia has some psychological basis instead. While such findings showed that the hysterical symptoms were somehow psychological, they did not mean that the hysterical symptoms were therefore unreal. From the patients' point of view, the symptoms were utterly real. The patients weren't malingering (faking); their symptoms were genuine enough to them and often caused considerable suffering.

In collaboration with another physician, Josef Breuer (1842–1925), Freud came to believe that hysterical symptoms are a disguised means of keeping certain emotionally charged memories under mental lock and key. When such memories are finally recovered, there is *catharsis,* an explosive release of previously dammed-up emotions (Freud and Breuer, 1895). Originally, Freud and Breuer tried to uncover these memories while the patients were in a hypnotic trance, but Freud eventually abandoned this method, in part because not all patients were readily hypnotized. He decided that crucial memories could be recovered even in the normal, waking state through the method of *free association.* The patients are told to say anything that enters their mind, no matter how trivial and unrelated it may seem, or how embarrassing, disagreeable, or indiscreet. Since Freud presumed that all ideas were linked by association, he concluded that the emotionally charged "forgotten" memories would be evoked sooner or later. But a difficulty arose, for it seemed that the patients did not readily comply with Freud's request: There was a *resistance* of which the patient was often unaware.

> The patient attempts to escape . . . by every possible means. First he says nothing comes into his head, then that so much comes into his head that he can't grasp any of it. Then we observe that . . . he is giving in to his critical objections, first to this, then to that; he betrays it by the long pauses which occur in his talk. At last he

admits that he really cannot say something, he is ashamed to. . . . Or else, he has thought of something but it concerns someone else and not himself. . . . Or else, what he has just thought of is really too unimportant, too stupid, and too absurd. . . . So it goes on, with untold variations, to which one continually replies that telling everything really means telling everything. (Freud, 1917, p. 289)

Freud believed that the intensity of resistance was often an important clue to what was really important: When a patient seemed to struggle especially hard to change a topic, to break off a train of thought, he was probably close to the recovery of an emotionally charged memory. Eventually it would come, often to the patient's great surprise. But if this was so, and if the recovery of these memories helped the patient to get better (as both Freud and his patients believed), why then did the patients resist the retrieval of these memories and thus obstruct their own cure? Freud concluded that the resistance was the overt manifestation of some powerful force that opposed the bringing of the critical memories into consciousness. Certain experiences in the patient's life—certain acts, impulses, thoughts, or memories—that were especially painful or anxiety provoking had been forcefully pushed out of consciousness, in Freud's term **repressed,** and the same repressive forces that led to their original expulsion were mobilized to oppose their reentry into consciousness when the patient later talked to the psychoanalyst.

Freud believed that the repressed material is not really eradicated but remains in the unconscious.★ This is not an actual place, but rather a metaphorical expression which only means that the repressed ideas still exert a powerful effect. Again and again, they struggle to reemerge into consciousness, like a jack-in-the-box, whether fueled by the biological urges that gave rise to them in the first place or triggered by associations in the here and now. As these repressed ideas threaten to regain consciousness, they also bring back anxiety and are therefore pushed out once more. The result is a never-ending unconscious conflict.

The task Freud set for himself was the analysis (as he called it, the **psychoanalysis**) of these conflicts, the discovery of their origins, of their effects in the present, of their removal or alleviation. But he soon came to believe that the same mechanisms that produce the symptoms of psychopathology also operate in normal persons, that his discoveries were not just a contribution to psychopathology but laid the foundation for a general theory of human personality. Thus, Freud's psychoanalytic enterprise contained three interlocking parts: a theory of normal personality, a theory of mental disorder, and a set of techniques for alleviating mental suffering. Here, we will take up his theory of personality and, by extension, his theory of mental disorder. His techniques for treating such disorders will be taken up in Chapter 19.

UNCONSCIOUS CONFLICT

Our sketch of Freud's theory of the nature and development of human personality will concentrate on those aspects that represent the highlights of a labyrinthine theoretical formulation that was continually revised and modified over the course of Freud's long career. We will treat separately two aspects

Sigmund Freud *(Courtesy of the National Library of Medicine)*

★ The term *unconscious* as Freud used it is not equivalent to *nonconscious*. Freud employed the term *unconscious* to apply to ideas or memories that in his view are actively kept out of consciousness because they are threatening or anxiety provoking. In contrast, the term *nonconscious* is applied to the many mental processes that go on outside of consciousness, for example, tying one's shoelaces. We are simply not aware of these mental processes in just the sense in which we are usually unaware of our heartbeat (see Chapter 8 and this chapter, pp. 734–35).

THE PSYCHODYNAMIC APPROACH: FREUD AND PSYCHOANALYSIS

Inner conflicts as envisaged by Plato *The Greek philosopher Plato anticipated Freud's tripartite division of the mind by over two thousand years. In one of his dialogues, he likened the soul to a chariot with two horses that often pull in opposed directions. The chariot's driver is Reason, the two horses are Spirit (our nobler emotions) and Appetite. This Renaissance medallion depicts Plato's image of the internal conflict.*

of Freudian theory: First, we will discuss his conception of the separate (and often antagonistic) elements of personality, and the mechanisms of unconscious conflict. Then, we will deal with his theory of the origins of these conflicts in the individual's life history and their relation to the development of sexual identity, gender roles, and morality.

THE ANTAGONISTS OF INNER CONFLICT

Freud's theories concern both the hypothesized forces whose antagonism produces unconscious conflict and the effects produced when these forces clash. But who fights whom in unconscious conflict?

When conflict is external, the antagonists are easily identified: David and Goliath, Dorothy and the Wicked Witch of the West, and so on. But what, according to Freud, are the warring forces when the conflict is inside the individual? In essence, they are different wishes or motives, such as a patient's sexually-tinged desire to be at a dance and her conflicting reactions of guilt at leaving her dying father. One of the tasks Freud set for himself was to classify the tendencies that participate in such conflicts, to see which of them are usually arrayed together and allied in combat. Freud eventually devised a threefold classification of conflicting tendencies within the individual, which he regarded as three more or less distinct subsystems of the human personality: the *id,* the *ego,* and the *superego.* In some of his writings, Freud treated these three mental systems as if they were separate persons inhabiting the mind. But this is only a metaphor that must not be taken literally; id, ego, and superego are just the names he gave to three sets of very different reaction patterns. They are not persons in their own right (Freud, 1923).

The id The id is the most primitive portion of the personality, the portion from which the other two emerge. It consists of all of the basic biological urges: to eat, drink, eliminate, be comfortably warm, and, most of all, to gain sexual pleasure.★ The id is the incarnation of Hobbes's natural brute: It abides entirely by the *pleasure principle*—satisfaction now and not later, regardless of the circumstances and whatever the cost.

The id's blind strivings for pleasure know no distinction between self and world, fantasy and reality, wishing and having. Its insistent urges spill out into reflex motor action, like emptying the bladder when it is full. If that doesn't work, the clamoring for pleasure leads to primitive thoughts of gratification, fantasies of wish fulfillment that cannot be distinguished from reality.

The ego At birth, the infant is all id. But the id's shrill clamors are soon met by harsh reality. Some gratifications come only after delay. The breast or the bottle is not always present; the infant has to cry to get it.

The confrontations between hot desire and cold reality lead to a whole set of new reactions that are meant to reconcile the two. Sometimes the reconciliation is by appropriate action (saying "please"), sometimes by suppression of a forbidden impulse (not touching one's genitals). These various reactions become organized into a new subsystem of the personality—the ego. The ego is derived from the id and is essentially still in its service. But unlike the id, the ego obeys the *reality principle.* It tries to satisfy the id (that is, to gain pleasure), but it does so pragmatically, in accordance with the real world and its real demands. As time proceeds, the opposition between need and reality leads to the emergence of more and more skills and strategies, all directed toward the same end, as well as a

---

★ These urges are sometimes called *instincts,* but that is a misnomer caused by an unfortunate translation of Freud's original term.

whole system of thoughts and memories that develops concurrently. Eventually, this entire system becomes capable of looking at itself and now deserves the name Freud gave it, ego or "self." Until this point, there was no "I" but only a mass of undifferentiated strivings (named after the Latin impersonal pronoun *id*, literally "it").

The superego   The id is not the ego's only master. As the child matures, a new reaction pattern develops from within the ego that acts as a kind of judge that decides whether the ego has been good or bad. This new mental agency is the superego, which represents the internalized rules and admonitions of the parents and, through them, of society. Initially, the ego only has to worry about external reality. It may inhibit some id-inspired action to avert chastisement: You don't steal cookies, because you might be caught and sent to your room. But a little later, the forbidden act is suppressed even when there can never be any real punishment. This change occurs because the child starts to act and think as if he himself were the parent who administers praise and reproof. A three-year-old is sometimes seen to slap his own hand as he is about to play in the mud or commit some other heinous deed; he sometimes mutters some self-righteous pronouncement like "Dirty! Bad!" This is the beginning of the superego, the ego's second master, which praises and punishes just as the parents did. If the ego lives up to the superego's dictates, then pride is the reward. But if one of the superego's rules is broken, the superego metes out punishment just as the parents scolded or spanked or withdrew their love. There is then self-reproach and a feeling of guilt.

The formation of the superego puts the ego in a difficult position, for its two masters often issue conflicting commands. The promptings of the id are all too often in forbidden directions; if the ego gives in, the superego will punish it. What's worse is that both masters are essentially infantile. We have seen that the id's demands are blind and unreasoning, but the superego's strictures are also rooted in childish irrationality. The superego was formed when the child's cognitive abilities were still quite primitive. At that time, it could only internalize what it understood then—blacks and whites, dos and don'ts. As a result, the superego is essentially irrational. It issues absolute imperatives that are not amenable to reason and does so largely unconsciously. If the ego obeys, it must throttle various urges of the id, even if those are merely expressed in a thought or a memory. To accomplish this feat, the ego must resort to repression.

In summary, Freud's threefold division of the personality is just a way of saying that our thoughts and actions are determined by the interplay of three major factors: our biological drives (the id), the commands and prohibitions of society (the superego), and the various ways we have learned to satisfy the former while respecting the latter (the ego). Freud's contribution is his insistence that the conflicts among these three forces are inside the individual, are shaped critically by childhood experiences, and occur without the individual's conscious awareness.

THE MECHANISMS OF UNCONSCIOUS CONFLICT: REPRESSION AND ANXIETY

We now turn to Freud's formulation (here, drastically simplified) of the rules by which these inner wars are waged. In rough outline, conflict begins when id-derived urges and various associated memories are pushed out of consciousness, are repressed. But the forbidden urges refuse to be kept down. They find substitute outlets whose further consequence is a host of additional defenses that are erected to reinforce the original repression, hold off the id-derived flood, and allow the ego to maintain its integrity (Freud, 1917, 1926, 1946).

What underlies repression? Freud came to believe that the crucial factor is intense **anxiety,** an emotional state akin to that which we experience when

A

B

Ego and superego in popular culture   *(A) If Freud were asked to describe Walt Disney's creations in psychoanalytic terms, he would probably describe* Fantasia's *sorcerer's apprentice (a.k.a. Mickey Mouse) as the ego and the sorcerer as the superego. (From* Fantasia, *1940; photograph © The Walt Disney Company) (B) In his film* Pinocchio, *the character of Jiminy Cricket serves as a "kinder, gentler" superego. (From* Pinocchio, *1940; photograph courtesy of Photofest)*

threatened from the outside (see Chapter 3). According to Freud, various forbidden acts become associated with anxiety as the child is scolded or disciplined for performing them. The parents may resort to physical punishment, or they may merely register their disapproval with a frown or reprimand; in either case, the child is threatened with the loss of their love and becomes anxious. The next time he is about to perform the same act—say, touch his penis or pinch his baby brother—he will feel a twinge of anxiety, an internal signal that his parents may castigate or leave him and that he will be abandoned and alone.

Since anxiety is intensely unpleasant, the child will do everything she can to remove it or to ward it off. If the cause of the anxiety is a real-world event or object, the child can simply run away and thus remove herself from it. But how can she cope with a danger that comes from within? As before, she will attempt to flee from whatever evokes the anxiety, but now the flight is from something inside herself. To quell her anxiety, the child must suppress that which triggers it—the forbidden act.

Freud's concept of repression applies to the thought no less than the deed. We can understand that a four-year-old boy who is punished for pinching his baby brother will refrain from such combative acts in the future. But, for Freud, the boy not only stops performing these acts; he may also stop *thinking* about them and even fail to remember doing them! Why might this happen? One answer is that thinking about an act is rather similar to performing it, especially for children, who have limited cognitive abilities and have not as yet fully mastered the distinction between thought and action. Nor do children know that their parents can't really read their minds, that their thoughts are private and thus immune from parental prosecution. The inhibition therefore applies not just to overt action, but to related thoughts, memories, and wishes.

THE MECHANISMS OF UNCONCIOUS CONFLICT: SUPPLEMENTARY DEFENSE MECHANISMS

Repression can be regarded as the primary, initial **mechanism of defense** that protects the individual against anxiety. But repression is often incomplete. Often enough the thoughts and urges that were pushed underground refuse to stay buried and resurge instead. But as they do, so does the anxiety with which they are associated. As a result, various further mechanisms of defense are brought into play to reinforce the original dam against the forbidden impulses.

One such supplementary defense mechanism is **displacement.** When a geyser is dammed up, its waters usually penetrate other cracks and fissures and eventually gush up elsewhere. According to Freud, the same holds for repressed urges, which tend to find new and often disguised outlets. An example is **displaced aggression,** which develops when fear of retaliation blocks the normal direction of discharge. The woman who is berated by her boss may return home and start a fight with her spouse; the child who is disciplined by her parent may vent her anger on her Barbie doll. According to many social psychologists, the same mechanism underlies the persecution of minority groups. They become convenient scapegoats for aggressive impulses fueled by social and economic unrest (Hovland and Sears, 1940).

In displacement, the forbidden impulse is rechanneled into a safer course. Certain other mechanisms of defense are attempts to supplement the original repression by blocking the impulse altogether. An example is **reaction formation** in which the repressed wish is warded off by its diametrical opposite. The young boy who hated his sister and was punished for acts against her may turn his feelings into the very opposite; he now bombards her with exaggerated love and tenderness, a desperate bulwark against aggressive wishes that he cannot accept. But the repressed hostility can still be detected underneath the loving exterior; his love is overly solicitous, and the sister probably feels smothered by it.

In reaction formation, there is an attempt (albeit not terribly successful) to keep the forbidden wishes at bay. Some other mechanisms represent a different line of defense; the repressed thoughts break through but they are reinterpreted and are not recognized for what they are. One example of this is *rationalization,* in which the person interprets some of her own feelings or actions in more acceptable terms. The cruel mother beats her child mercilessly but is sure that she does so "for the child's own good." Countless atrocities have been committed under the same guise of altruism: Heretics have been tortured to save their immortal souls, and cities have been razed to protect the world against barbarism. Rationalization is also employed at a more everyday level, as a defense not only against repressed wishes but against any thought that would make the individual feel unworthy and anxious. An example is the sour-grapes phenomenon. The jilted lover tells her friends that she never really cared for her lost love; eventually she comes to believe this herself.

Another example of a defense mechanism in which cognitive reorganization plays a major role is *projection.* Here, the forbidden urges well up and are recognized as such. But the person does not realize that these wishes are his own; instead, he attributes them to others. "I desire you" becomes "You desire me" (as when rapists say their victims "really wanted it"), and "I hate you" becomes "You hate me"—desperate defenses against repressed sexual or hostile wishes that can no longer be banished from consciousness (Freud, 1911).

In yet another defense mechanism, *isolation* (sometimes called *intellectualization*), the dangerous memories are allowed back into consciousness; what's held back is their relation to the individual's motives and emotions. The memories themselves are retained, but they are isolated (so to speak, compartmentalized) from the feelings that go along with them. This mechanism is sometimes seen in people who have suffered severe distress, such as concentration camp survivors or rape victims, who are able to relate their experiences in precise detail, but whose recollections are devoid of the agony that accompanied them.

UNCONSCIOUS CONFLICT AND THE FORMATION OF PERSONALITY

Freud believed that the unconscious conflicts he uncovered always derived from critical events in the individual's early life. His observations of his patients convinced him that these crucial events are remarkably similar from person to person. He concluded that all human beings go through a largely similar sequence of significant emotional events in their early lives, that some of the most important of these involve sexual urges, and that it is this childhood past that shapes our personality (Freud, 1905).

Stages of psychosexual development   Freud's theory of *psychosexual development* emphasizes different stages, each of which is built upon the achievements of those before. (In this regard it resembles Jean Piaget's theory of cognitive growth, which we took up in Chapter 13.) In Freud's view, the child starts life as a bundle of pleasure-seeking tendencies. Pleasure is obtained by the stimulation of certain zones of the body that are particularly sensitive to touch: the mouth, the anus, and the genitals. Freud called these regions *erogenous zones,* for he believed that the various pleasures associated with each of them have a common element that is sexual.* As the child develops, the relative importance of the

Rationalization   The expression sour grapes *comes from a fable by Aesop, which tells of a fox who desperately desired some grapes that hung overhead. When the fox discovered that the grapes were so high that he could not reach them, he said that he never really wanted them, for they were much too sour. (From* Baby's Own Aesop *by Walter Crane, engraved and colored by Edmund Evans; reproduced from the print collection of The New York Public Library, Astor, Lenox, and Tilden Foundations)*

---

* One of his arguments for regarding oral and anal stimulation in infancy as ultimately sexual was the fact that such stimulation sometimes precedes (or replaces) sexual intercourse in adulthood.

zones shifts. Initially, most of the pleasure seeking is through the mouth (the *oral stage*). As the infant attains bowel control, the emphasis shifts to the anus (the *anal stage*). Still later, there is an increased interest in the pleasure that can be obtained from stimulating the genitals (the *phallic stage*). The culmination of psychosexual development is attained in adult sexuality when pleasure involves not just one's own gratification but also the social and bodily satisfaction brought to another person (the *genital stage*).

How does the child progress from one stage to the next? In part, it is a matter of physical maturation. For example, bowel control is simply impossible at birth, for the infant lacks the necessary neuromuscular readiness. But there is another element. As the child's body matures, there is an inevitable change in what the parents allow, prohibit, or demand. Initially, the child nurses, then she is weaned. Initially, she is diapered, then she is toilet trained. Each change automatically produces some frustration and conflict as former ways of gaining pleasure are supplanted.

Oral and anal characters　According to Freud, many patterns of adult personality can be understood as remnants of reactions at one or another stage of childhood psychosexual development. As Freud saw it, each step in this development will necessarily produce some frustration (say, as in weaning), and these frustrations may have lasting consequences. One reaction to such frustrations is *fixation,* which refers to some degree of lingering attachment to an earlier stage of pleasure seeking even after a new stage has been attained. When fixation occurs, some remnants of the earlier pattern may hang on for a while, such as thumb sucking in weaned infants. The defense mechanism of reaction formation (discussed above), whereby a forbidden impulse that was pushed out of consciousness is replaced by its very opposite, is another mode of response to frustration during development. Thus, during toilet training, the child's forbidden urge—to relax the anal sphincter and defecate whenever he feels like it—leads to anxiety. One means of dealing with the conflict is for the child to do the exact opposite of what he really wants. This reaction formation may manifest itself as constipation.

Eventually, Freud became convinced that what is really important in these stages is not just the particular anatomical region, whether mouth or anus, through which the child gains pleasure at the time. More crucial are certain ways

Hidden meanings　*This painting,* Hide and Seek, *by the Russian émigré artist Pavel Tchelitchew shows different aspects of childhood development as hiding in the branches of a gnarled tree. (* Hide and Seek, *1941–42, oil on canvas, 6′6 ½″ × 7′ ¾″, collection of the Museum of Modern Art; reproduced by permission)*

of relating to other people that are characteristic of a given stage and leave residues in adult behavior. According to one view, the degree to which the early social patterns persist is one important determinant of adult personality (Freud, 1940).

An example is what Freud called the *oral character,* which he believed was grounded in an oral fixation. During the oral stage, the infant feels warm, well-fed, and protected, leading an idyllic existence in which all is given and nothing is asked for in return. According to Freud and his student Karl Abraham, certain adults are oral characters, whose relations to others recapitulate the passive dependency they enjoyed while suckling at the mother's breast (Abraham, 1927).

Freud and Abraham believed that there is also an *anal character,* whose personality derives from severe conflicts during toilet training. These conflicts may lead to various forms of reaction formation in which the child inhibits rather than relaxes her bowels (Freud, 1908; Abraham, 1927). This pattern then broadens and becomes manifest in more symbolic terms. The child becomes compulsively clean and orderly ("I must not soil myself"). Another effect is obstinacy and defiance. The child asserts herself by holding back on the potty ("You can't make me if I don't want to"), a stubbornness that may soon become a more generalized defiant "No." Another characteristic is stinginess. According to Freud, this is a general form of withholding, a refusal to part with what is one's own (that is, one's feces). This refusal also generalizes, and the child becomes obsessed with property rights and jealously hoards her possessions. Freud believed that excessive conflicts during the anal stage may lead to an adult personality that also displays the three symptomatic attributes of the anal character—compulsive orderliness, stubbornness, and stinginess.

The Oedipus complex We now turn to that aspect of the theory of psychosexual development that Freud himself regarded as the most important—the family triangle of love, jealousy, and fear that is at the root of internalized morality and out of which grows the child's identification with the same-sex parent. This is the **Oedipus complex,** named after the mythical king of Thebes who unwittingly committed two awful crimes—killing his father and marrying his mother. According to Freud, an analogous family drama is reenacted in the childhoods of all men and women. Because Freud came to believe that the sequence of steps is somewhat different in the two sexes, we will take them up

Oedipus Rex *From a 1955 production directed by Tyrone Guthrie with Douglas Campbell in the title role, at Stratford, Ontario. (Courtesy Billy Rose Theatre Collection, The New York Public Library at Lincoln Center, Astor, Lenox, and Tilden Collections)*

THE PSYCHODYNAMIC APPROACH: FREUD AND PSYCHOANALYSIS

"Why can't you be more like Oedipus?" (© The New Yorker Collection 1972 Chas. Addams from Cartoonbank.com. All rights reserved.)

separately. We will start with his theory of how genital sexuality emerges in males (Freud, 1905).

At about three or four years of age the ***phallic stage*** begins. The young boy becomes increasingly interested in his penis, which becomes a source of both pride and pleasure. He masturbates and this brings some pleasure, but it is not enough. His urges seek an external object. The inevitable choice is his mother (or some mother substitute). But there is an obstacle—the boy's father. The little boy wants to have his mother all to himself, as a comforter as well as an erotic partner, but this sexual utopia is out of the question. His father is a rival, and he is bigger. The little boy wants his father to go away and not come back—in short, to die.

At this point, a new element enters into the family drama. The little boy begins to fear the father he is jealous of. According to Freud, this is because the boy is sure that the father knows of his son's hostility and that the father will surely answer hate with hate. With childish logic the little boy suspects that his punishment will fit his crime: The same organ by which he sinned will be the one that is made to suffer. The result is ***castration anxiety.*** As a result, the boy tries to push the hostile feelings out of consciousness, but they refuse to stay ignored. They return, and the only defense left is projection: "I hate father" becomes "Father hates me." This naturally increases the boy's fear, which increases his hate, which is again pushed out of consciousness, resurges, and leads to yet further projection. This process snowballs, until the father is finally seen as an overwhelming ogre who threatens to castrate his son.

As the vicious cycle continues, the little boy's anxiety eventually becomes unbearable. At this point, he throws in the towel, renounces his mother as an erotic object, and renounces genital pleasure, at least for a while. Instead, he ***identifies*** with his father. He concludes that by becoming like him, he will eventually enjoy an erotic partnership of the kind his father enjoys now, if not with his mother, then at least with someone much like her. Instead of wanting his mother, the boy's theme becomes, "I want a girl just like the girl who married dear old Dad."

Freud believed that once the tumult of the Oedipal conflict dies down, there is a period of comparative sexual quiescence which lasts from about five to twelve years of age. This is the latency period during which boys play only with boys, devote themselves to athletics, and want to have nothing to do with the opposite sex. Part of the latency period is the acquisition of sexual shame sufficient to withstand the hormonally induced onslaught of sexual urges at puberty. But as hormone levels rise and the sex organs mature, the repressed sexual impulses can no longer be denied. As these impulses surge to the fore, parts of the Oedipal family skeleton come out as well, dragging along many of the fears and conflicts that had been comfortably hidden away for all these years.

According to Freud, this is one of the reasons why adolescence is so often a period of deep emotional turbulence. The boy is now physically mature, and he is strongly attracted to the opposite sex, but this very attraction frightens him, and he doesn't know why. Sexual contact with women arouses the unconscious wishes and fears that pertain to mother and father. In healthy individuals, the Oedipus complex has been resolved well enough so that these fears can be overcome. The boy can eventually accept himself as a man and achieve genital sexuality in which he loves a woman as herself rather than as some shadowy substitute for his mother, and in which his love involves giving as well as taking.★

★ For Freud, a sexual interest in the opposite sex was part of a healthy Oedipal resolution, and homosexual interest indicated a deficient one. As discussed in Chapter 14, contemporary investigators reject Freud's view that homosexuality is a disorder.

The primal couple *Male and female ancestor figures of the Dogon tribe in Mali, western Africa. From the psychoanalytic perspective, they can be regarded as a symbolic representation of the primal couple, the father and mother, whether in Western culture or in other societies. (Photograph © Wettstein and Kauf, Museum Rietberg, Zürich)*

The Electra complex We have traced Freud's account of the male psychosexual odyssey to adult sexuality. What about the female? In Freud's view, she goes through essentially identical oral and anal phases as does the male. And in many ways, the development of her phallic interests (Freud used the same term for both sexes) is symmetrical to the male's. As he focuses his erotic interests on the mother, so she focuses hers on the father. As he resents and eventually comes to fear the father, so she the mother. In short, there is a female version of the Oedipus complex (sometimes called the **Electra complex** after the Greek tragic heroine who goaded her brother into slaying their mother). But there is a theoretical difficulty. How does the little girl get to desire her father in the first place? Her first attachment was to the mother. But if so, what accounts for the little girl's switch of love objects?

To answer this question, Freud elaborated a far-fetched scheme that is widely regarded as one of the weakest aspects of his whole theory. He proposed that the shift of attachment begins as the little girl discovers that she does not have a penis. According to Freud, she regards this lack as a catastrophe, considers herself unworthy, and develops **penis envy.** One consequence is that she withdraws her love from the mother, whom she regards as equally unworthy. The little girl wants a penis, but how can she get one? She turns to her father, who has the desirable organ and who she believes can help her obtain a penis substitute—a child. Fulfilling as childbearing is, it is only a consolation prize that fails to gratify completely, leaving the girl (Freud says) prone for life to depression and masochistic relationships. (Why child equals penis requires even more far-fetched arguments.) From here on, the rest of the process unfolds more or less like its counterpart in the boy: love of father, jealousy of mother, increasing fear of mother, eventual repression of the entire complex, and identification with the mother (Freud, 1925, 1933; LaFarge, 1993).

This theory of female psychosexual development has been widely attacked on both scientific and political grounds. For example, why does the girl want a penis? And if she does, why does she blame her mother for the lack of it? Of course, the fact that the girl envies her little brother's social role in a culture in which men have more power and status is not surprising. But there is no evidence that what she really envies is that particular male organ, and not the role and status that maleness confers in many cultures (Chodorow, 1989).

WINDOWS INTO THE UNCONSCIOUS

Freud arrived at his theory of unconscious conflict by studying the behavior of disturbed individuals, usually hysterics. But he soon concluded that the clash of unconscious forces that he believed resulted in symptoms of mental disorder is also found normal people. Their inner conflicts are under control, with less resulting anxiety and fewer crippling effects, but the conflicts are present nonetheless. We will consider three areas to which Freud appealed as evidence: lapses of memory, slips of the tongue in everyday life, and the content of dreams.

ERRORS OF MEMORY AND SPEECH

Freud continually drew attention to what he called the "psychopathology of everyday life." One kind is illustrated by our momentarily forgetting a name that might call up embarrassing memories or suffering a slip of the tongue that unwittingly reveals an underlying motive (Freud, 1901). Suppressed intentions sometimes emerge to make us become absent minded about things we don't really want to do. Freud cites the example of a friend who wrote a letter that he forgot to send for several days. He finally mailed it, but it was returned by the post office, for there was no address. He addressed it and sent it off again only to have it returned once more because there was no stamp.

This is not to say (though psychoanalytic writers often seem to say it) that all slips of the tongue, misplacements of objects, and lapses of memory are motivated in Freud's sense. The husband who calls a female coworker by his wife's name may not be having unconscious adulterous urges so much as speaking out of habit. And a host who cannot recall a guest's name when introducing him to another guest is unlikely to have some hidden reason for keeping that name out of consciousness. The name is probably forgotten because of simple, and quite unmotivated, memory interference (Baars, 1992; and see Chapter 7).

DREAMS

One of Freud's most influential works was his theory of dreams (Freud, 1900). He argued that dreams have a meaning that can be deciphered if one looks deeply enough. In his view, dreams concern the dreamer's past and present, and they arise from within the unconscious. He saw dreams as somewhat analogous to hysterical symptoms. On the surface, they both appear meaningless and bizarre, but they become comprehensible when understood as veiled expressions of an unconscious clash between competing motives.

Although Freud knew that some dreams were a recounting of life events (what he called the "day residue"), he began with the assumption that many dreams, especially the seemingly indecipherable ones, are at bottom attempts at **wish fulfillment.** While awake, a wish is usually not acted upon right away, for there are considerations of both reality (the ego) and morality (the superego) that must be taken into account: Is it possible? Is it allowed? But during sleep these restraining forces are drastically weakened and the wish then leads to immediate thoughts and images of gratification. In some cases the wish fulfillment is simple and direct. Starving explorers dream of sumptuous meals; people stranded in the desert dream of cool mountain streams. According to a Hungarian proverb quoted by Freud, "Pigs dream of acorns, and geese dream of maize."

Simple wish-fulfillment dreams are comparatively rare. What about the others, the strange and illogical nightly narratives that are far more common? Freud

An artist's dream *A painting that depicts a dream in which an artist is at a friend's house, when the door suddenly opens and a man to whom he was once apprenticed enters, accompanied by a nude woman who was one of his most beautiful models. Freud would probably have noted the Oedipal theme, considering that the dream featured a former mentor and his nude model. (The frontispiece of* Les rêves et les moyens de les diriger, *by Marquis d'Hervey de Saint Denis, 1867)*

Dreams and symbolism *The 1927 German silent film* The Secrets of a Soul *by Georg Pabst tried to depict a case history in psychoanalytic terms. Its subject was a middle-aged man suffering from erectile dysfunction ("impotence"). The film portrays several of the patient's dreams. In this one, he tries to plant a tree, a symbol for impregnating his wife. (Courtesy of the Museum of Modern Art/Film Stills Archive)*

argued that the same principle of attempted wish fulfillment could explain these as well. But here a new process comes into play. The underlying wish touches upon some forbidden matters that are associated with anxiety. As a result, various mechanisms of defense are invoked, and these mechanisms censor any direct expression of the wish. But it is often possible to slip the wish past the censors by expressing it only in symbolic terms. It's for this reason that the dreamer never experiences the underlying *latent dream* that represents her own hidden wishes and concerns. What she experiences instead is the carefully laundered version that emerges after the defense mechanisms have done their work—the *manifest dream.* The end product is reminiscent of hysterical symptoms and various pathologies of everyday life. It represents a compromise between forbidden urges and the repressive forces that keep them subdued. The underlying impulse is censored, but it emerges surreptitiously and in disguise.

In some dreams, the underlying wish finds expression in various displaced forms. There is *symbolism* in which one thing stands for another. Some symbols are widely shared because certain physical, functional, or linguistic similarities are recognized by most people (for example, screwdriver for penis and box for vagina). But there is no simple cipher that can be generally applied. After all, many physical objects are either long and pointed or round and hollow, and so a pat equation with male and female genitals will be of little use. (As Freud himself is supposed to have said to his students, "Sometimes a cigar is just a cigar.") Instead, most symbolic relationships depend upon the dreamer's own life experience and can only be interpreted by noting his free associations to the dream.

PSYCHOANALYTIC THEORY OF MYTHS

Freud and his students contended that just as dreams are a window into the individual's unconscious, so myths, legends, cultural icons, and fairy tales allow us a glimpse into those hidden concerns that are shared by whole cultural groups, if not all of humanity. Indeed, one of Freud's earliest colleagues, the Swiss psychiatrist Carl Jung (1875–1961), argued for a *collective unconscious* consisting of primordial stories and images—he called these *archetypes*—that shape our perceptions and desires just as much as Freud's psychodynamics (Monte, 1995).

THE PSYCHODYNAMIC APPROACH: FREUD AND PSYCHOANALYSIS

Psychoanalysts who have delved into such tales have found, for example, an ample supply of Oedipal themes. There are numerous ogres, dragons, and monsters to be slain before the prize can be won. The villain is often a cruel stepparent, a fairly transparent symbol of Oedipal hostilities.

As an illustration of a psychoanalytic interpretation of a fairy tale, consider "Snow White and the Seven Dwarfs" (Brown, 1940). Snow White is a child princess who is persecuted by her stepmother, the wicked queen. The queen is envious of Snow White's beauty and tries to have her killed. The child escapes and lives with seven dwarfs who work in an underground mine. The queen finally discovers Snow White and persuades her to eat part of a poisoned apple. Snow White falls as if dead. The dwarfs place her in a beautiful casket in which she lies motionless for seven years. At this point, a handsome prince appears, opens the casket with his sword, awakens Snow White from her long sleep, and the two live happily ever after.

According to psychoanalytic authors, this fairy tale is a veiled allegory of the Oedipal sequence. The wicked queen is the mother on whom the child projects her own hate and sexual jealousy. The Oedipal—or more precisely, Electra—conflict is temporarily resolved as the child's erotic urges go underground and remain dormant for the seven years of the latency period, symbolized both by Snow White's long sleep and by the seven dwarfs. At the end of this period, her sexuality is reawakened in adult form by the young prince. (The meaning of the sword is left as an exercise for the reader.)

Is this interpretation valid? It is hard to know by what ground rules validity can be judged. There are undoubtedly many alternative (and perhaps more plausible) interpretations of this fairy tale. The same holds for many other legends that psychoanalysts have tried to squeeze into their scheme. Death and resurrection are old themes in mythology that probably refer to many important natural cycles, such as the daily succession of darkness and light and the yearly alternation of winter's desolation and spring's green rebirth; it's not obvious, therefore, why we should prefer an interpretation of these cycles in terms of psychosexual development. In addition, myths may also embody dim folk memories of long-past wars, dynastic conflicts, ancient religions, and various catastrophes. The psychoanalytic view may throw some light on an aspect of our cultural heritage, but it is just one light among many. (For a critique, see Darnton, 1984.)

A psychoanalytic interpretation of "Little Red Riding Hood"   *"Little Red Riding Hood" is the story of a pretty young girl who is sent on an errand through the forest. Her mother tells her to walk directly, without ever leaving the path. On her trip, she meets a wolf who persuades her to run off the path and pick some beautiful flowers in the forest. According to psychoanalysts, the wolf stands for male sexuality, and Little Red Riding Hood is torn between resisting temptation (staying on the right path) and giving in to it (picking the flowers). (Courtesy of the Granger Collection)*

Hamlet confronting his mother in her bedroom   *A scene from Lawrence Olivier's 1948 film* Hamlet. *Olivier's conception of the role of Hamlet was seriously affected by Ernest Jones's psychoanalytic interpretation of the play. His casting of a young attractive actress, Eileen Herlie, for the part of Hamlet's mother helped to underscore the Oedipal theme. (Courtesy of Universal Pictures)*

PSYCHOANALYSIS AND LITERATURE

Freud's approach to the interpretation of works of art and literature was very similar to the way in which he tried to understand the hidden meanings of dreams and myths. The artistic production reflects the artist's own inner conflicts and has impact on others because it strikes the same unconscious chords in them. Perhaps the most famous example of psychoanalytic literary interpretations is Freud's analysis of Shakespeare's *Hamlet,* later elaborated by his student Ernest Jones (Jones, 1954). The central puzzle of the play is Hamlet's indecisiveness. He waits until the end of the fifth act before he finally avenges his father's death, a delay that causes his own death, as well as the death of virtually everyone else in the play, innocent as well as guilty. To Freud and Jones, the clue to Hamlet's inaction is the Oedipus complex. Hamlet is paralyzed because he must kill a man who did precisely what he himself unconsciously wanted to do, kill his father and marry his mother. According to Freud and Jones, the play grips the audience because it stirs the same latent conflicts in them.

Shakespearean scholars are by no means agreed on the virtues of this interpretation, though some find it interesting. But the issue goes further than that. Suppose we accept the interpretation that Freud and Jones offer. Is this the key to *Hamlet,* which is then shorn of all its mysteries, like a completed crossword puzzle that is discarded once it is solved? The truth is that there is no one key, there is no one meaning of *Hamlet,* for works of art are necessarily ambiguous. As with myths and legends, this or the other interpretation may help explain them, but it does not explain them *away. Hamlet* may be about Oedipal conflicts, but many hack novels have the same theme. What makes the one a great literary treasure while the others are forgotten almost immediately?

These points argue against the overenthusiastic application of psychoanalytic interpretation to literary works. But for good or ill (probably for both), Freud's impact on literature and literary criticism has been enormous. Most literary critics today have at least a passing acquaintance with Freud's basic works, and many major authors have been fundamentally influenced by him (Miller, 1972), though many literature scholars have come to reject Freud's influence (e.g., Crews, 1995). By now, his insights have become part of our culture, and Freudian lore—often vulgarized—has become a staple of our popular literature, our stage, and our screen.

A CRITICAL LOOK AT FREUDIAN THEORY

Thus far, we have presented Freud's views with a minimum of critical comment. (Our discussions of Freud's theory of female psychosexual development and the psychoanalytic approach to myths and literature were exceptions.) We now shift our perspective to consider some of his assertions in the light of current thought and evidence.

TECHNICAL AND CONCEPTUAL ISSUES

By what evidence can one determine whether Freud's assertions are correct? Freud's own evidence was drawn from the analytic couch. He considered his patients' free associations, their resistances, their slips of the tongue, their dreams and then tried to weave them into a coherent pattern that somehow made sense of all the parts. But can one really draw conclusions from this kind of clinical evidence alone? Clinical practitioners cannot be totally objective no matter how hard they try. There are many sources of bias. First, as they listen to a patient, psychotherapists are more likely to hear and remember those themes that fit their own views than those that do not. (This point is especially pertinent to Freud who never took notes during psychoanalytic sessions.) Would a clinician with different biases have remembered the same themes? Second, most patients who enter therapy need help, are anxious to please their therapists, and so may find themselves wanting to provide "evidence" that will confirm their therapists' theories (see Chapter 7).

Nor did the ways that Freud sought to develop psychoanalysis as a profession insure theoretical or therapeutic objectivity. Freud tended to surround himself with colleagues who agreed with his formulations and to dispatch those who did not, and he also built psychoanalytic associations that largely operated outside the more scientific—and skeptical—universities. These factors, many observers argue, soon made psychoanalysis more a religious cult than a science (Sulloway, 1992; Torrey, 1992; Webster, 1995).

Yet another problem is conceptual. Scientific theories lead to certain predictions; if these fail, the theory is refuted. But are Freud's assertions theories in this

A picture of Freud's consultation room
In classical psychoanalysis, the patient reclines on the couch while the analyst sits behind her, out of sight. Freud adopted this method to avoid influencing the patient's flow of associations by his own facial expressions. He also had a personal motive: "I cannot bear to be gazed at for eight hours a day." (Freud, 1913; photograph by Edmund Engelman)

sense? What specific predictions do they lead to? Consider the hypothetical case of a boy raised by a harsh, rejecting mother and a weak, alcoholic father. What will the boy be like as an adult? Will he seek dominating women who will degrade him as his mother did? Will he try to find a warm, comforting wife upon whom he can become dependent and thus make up for the mothering he never had as a child? There is no way of predicting on psychoanalytic grounds. Each outcome makes perfectly good sense—after it has occurred.

Another problem with many psychoanalytic arguments is that the analyst's theory often determines whether a patient's statement should or should not be accepted at face value. Suppose a woman insists that she hates her mother. The analyst will probably believe her. But if she swears that she loves her mother, the analyst may conclude that she, like Shakespeare's lady, "doth protest too much," that her protestations of love mean the exact opposite, and reflect a reaction formation against her "real" feelings of hate. The trouble with this kind of two-way reasoning is that it becomes difficult to find any sort of disproof—no matter what the patient says, it will fit the analyst's interpretation. (For a discussion of this and related issues, see Grünbaum, 1984, 1996.)

Such considerations suggest that if we want to test Freud's assertions, we must look for further evidence and be more rigorous in how we interpret it. We will begin by considering some criticisms from theorists who agreed with Freud's thesis that there is unconscious conflict, but who were skeptical of his particular assertions of what these conflicts are.

BIOLOGY OR CULTURE?

A number of psychoanalytically oriented theorists took strong exception to Freud's insistence that the pattern of unconscious conflicts is biologically based and will therefore be found in essentially the same form in all men and all women.

The emphasis on social factors Since Freud believed that the key to emotional development lay in biology, he assumed that its progression followed a universal course. In his view, all humans pass through oral, anal, and phallic stages and suffer the conflicts appropriate to each stage. This conception has been challenged by various clinical practitioners, many of whom used Freud's own psychoanalytic methods. These critics felt that Freud had overemphasized biological factors at the expense of social ones.

The criticisms took several forms, and some were by Freud's own European associates. For example, Alfred Adler (1870–1937) argued that a well-adjusted life wasn't just a matter of psychic harmony but required involvement in one's social community; Carl Jung, whose theory of the collective unconscious we mentioned earlier, renounced Freud's focus on biology and embraced spirituality as the culmination of human strivings (see Noll, 1995).

Other criticisms came from a group of like-minded psychoanalysts, situated mostly in America, who are often grouped together under the loose label **neo-Freudians,** including Erich Fromm (1900–1980), Karen Horney (1885–1952), and H. S. Sullivan (1892–1949). For these neo-Freudians, the important question was not about psychic conflict, but about how humans relate, or try to relate, to others—whether by dominating, or submitting, or becoming dependent, or whatever. Their description of our inner conflicts is therefore in social terms. For example, if they see a mother who toilet trains her child very severely, they are likely to interpret her behavior as part of an overall pattern whereby she tries to push the child to early achievement; the specific frustrations of the anal stage as such are of lesser concern to them. Similarly for the sexual sphere. According to Freud, much psychological conflict centers on the repression of erotic impulses. According to the neo-Freudian critics, the real difficulty is in the area

Karen Horney *(Photograph courtesy the U.S. National Library of Medicine)*

of interpersonal relationships. Inner conflicts often lead to sexual symptoms, not because sex is a powerful biological motive that is shoved out of consciousness, but rather because it is one of the most sensitive barometers of interpersonal attitudes. The man who can only relate to other people by competing with them may well be unable to find sexual pleasure in his marriage bed, but his sexual dysfunction is an effect of his disturbed social pattern rather than its cause.

The same emphasis on social factors highlights the neo-Freudian explanation of how these conflicts arise in the first place. In contrast to Freud, the neo-Freudians deny that these conflicts are biologically ordained; they contend, rather, that these conflicts depend upon the specific cultural conditions in which the child is reared. According to the neo-Freudians, the conflicts that Freud observed may have characterized his turn-of-the-century, mostly upper-middle-class Viennese patients, but this does not mean that these same patterns will be found in people who live at other times and in other places.

These neo-Freudian criticisms are important for their own sake, but they also highlight the need for objective evaluation of any psychoanalytic interpretation. Freud examined his case studies and saw unconscious conflict growing out of sexual urges. Later analysts examined the same case studies and found a different pattern. Apparently, therefore, the case studies are amenable to more than one interpretation, and it is precisely this ambiguity that makes it impossible to draw strong conclusions from the case studies by themselves. To choose among these interpretations—Freud's, Adler's, Jung's, or a neo-Freudian's—we need some means of *testing* these interpretations. It won't be enough to ask whether the interpretation fits the analyst's view of the patient's thoughts and feelings, since all the interpretations seem to pass this test.

CRITIQUE OF FREUD'S THEORIES OF DEVELOPMENT

Some related criticisms concern Freud's theories of psychosexual development. It's rather ironic that Freud, whose views of childhood development had such a powerful influence on Western thought, never himself studied children. His theories of early development were mostly based on his adult patients' recollections, dreams, and free associations. But by now of course, the study of childhood development is a flourishing enterprise (see Chapters 13 and 14). What light has it shed on the role of early childhood events in producing adult personality?

Oral and anal characters   The verdict on the oral character is simple. There is little or no evidence to support the claim that differences in the way the infant was fed have much of an effect on later personality (assuming adequate nutrition). Later adjustment and development appear to be much the same whether the infant was fed by breast or bottle, or weaned early or late. (For an overview, see Zigler and Child, 1969, 1973.)

Some who study childhood development contend that the concept of the anal character may have more validity. They cite evidence that the critical anal traits—neatness, obstinacy, and frugality—do in fact correlate to a significant extent (Fisher and Greenberg, 1977). In one study, a number of undergraduates were asked to rate their own and their friends' characteristics. Their ratings showed that the three critical traits do indeed form a coherent cluster. Those students who judged themselves (or were judged by others) to be obstinate were also those who tended to be orderly and a bit stingy. More important, the students with these anal characteristics tended to have mothers with similar attributes, as shown by questionnaires administered to the mothers. These results may seem to vindicate Freud's theory, since it appears that anal children have anal mothers. But a further finding runs counter to the theory. The mothers were asked at what age they toilet-trained their children. There was no correlation whatever between this factor and the personality traits that define the anal character (Beloff, 1957).

This result accords with other studies on the effects of toilet training. Some parents begin toilet training when their infant is as young as five months old; others wait until the child is two or even three years old. There are some slight indications that starting later makes the whole process simpler and may minimize certain childhood disorders of elimination such as bedwetting (Brazelton, 1962). But there is little evidence of long-term effects of toilet-training practices, either in our own or other cultures (Orlansky, 1949). For example, there seems to be no relation between the severity of toilet training in different cultures and the degree of hoarding or economic competition (Cohen, 1953). There is thus little evidence for Freud's claim that the toilet is a prep school, whether for banking or industry.

But if so, what can we make of the fact that the three so-called anal traits form a cluster and seem to be transmitted from parent to child? One guess is that they may reflect different aspects of temperament, which may be partly inherited (Torrey, 1992; see Chapter 16). Another is that they may be transmitted as part of a general pattern of middle-class values and attitudes, communicated by the general social atmosphere in which the child is raised and instilled as one facet of what the parents want the child to become. Seen in this light, obstinacy, orderliness, and parsimony may well be a result of the parents pushing their child toward independence and achievement. Either way, such traits are not by-products of getting the child out of diapers.

The universal Oedipus complex   Freud suggested that the "romantic" mother-son-father triangle, which he called the Oedipus complex, was inevitable and universal. This prediction led some anthropologists to conduct studies of other cultures.

The initial evidence seemed to go against such universality. It was collected some seventy years ago by the English anthropologist Bronislaw Malinowski (1884–1942) on the basis of his observations of the Trobriand Islanders of the western Pacific (Malinowski, 1927). The family pattern of the Trobriand Islanders is quite different from our own. Among the Trobrianders, the biological father is not the head of the household. He spends time with his children and plays with them, but he exerts no authority. This role is reserved for the mother's brother, from whom the male children inherit property and status and who acts as disciplinarian to all the children. The Trobriand Islanders thus separate the roles that in Freud's Vienna were played by one and the same person.

According to Freud, this different family pattern should make no difference. There should still be an Oedipus complex in which the father is the hated villain, for after all, it is he who is the little boy's sexual rival. But Malinowski reported a different state of affairs, observing no signs of friction between sons and fathers, though he did observe a fair amount of hostility directed at the maternal uncle. The same held for dreams and folk tales. The Trobriand Islanders, he reported, believe that there are prophetic dreams of death; these generally involve the death of the maternal uncle. Similarly there seemed to be no myths about evil fathers or stepfathers; again, the villain is typically the mother's brother. If we accept Freud's notion that dreams (and myths) involve unconscious wishes and preoccupations, we are forced to conclude that the Trobriand boy hates his uncle, not his father. In sum, the child has fears and fantasies about the authoritarian figure in his life, the man who bosses him around. This is the father in Freud's Austria, but the uncle on the Trobriand Islands. His fears are not about his mother's lover as such, for the Trobriand boy does not hate the father who plays this role. (For some alternative interpretations, see Powell, 1969; Spiro, 1982; Brown, 1991.)

Freud at age sixteen with his mother, Amalie Nathanson Freud   *Freud was his mother's first-born and her favorite, a fact that may have affected his theory of the human family drama. As he put it, "A man who has been the indisputable favorite of his mother keeps for life the feeling of a conqueror, that confidence of success that often induces real success." (E. Jones, 1954, p. 5; photograph courtesy of Mary Evans/Freud copyrights)*

The Nightmare *This painting by Henry Fuseli (painted in 1783 and said to have decorated Freud's office) highlights what seems to be one of the difficulties of Freud's dream theory. If all dreams are wish fulfillments, what accounts for nightmares? According to Freud, they are often dreams in which the latent dream is not sufficiently disguised. The forbidden wish is partially recognized, anxiety breaks through, and the sleeper suffers a nightmare. (Courtesy of The Detroit Institute of Arts)*

FREUD'S THEORIES OF DREAMS, REPRESSION, AND DEFENSE

Thus far, we have looked at critiques that came from those within the psychodynamic fold. They disagreed with Freud's theories about what internal conflicts were about but accepted his notion of unconscious conflict and its effect on mental processes. Other of Freud's critics, though, are skeptical about even these basic ideas, and we next consider two lines of research that bear on their objections. One concerns Freud's theory of dreams; the other his theory of repression and defense.

Freud's theory of dreams   Stated in the most general terms, Freud's theory asserts that dreams tend to reflect the current emotional preoccupations of the dreamer, including those of which he is unaware, and are often portrayed in a condensed and symbolic form. This is probably quite true. Thus, patients who await major surgery reveal their fears in what they dream about during the two or three nights before the operation. Their fears are rarely expressed directly; few, if any, of their dreams are about scalpels or operating rooms. The reference is indirect and symbolic, as in dreams about falling from tall ladders, or standing on a high, swaying bridge, or about a decrepit machine in dire need of repair (Breger, Hunter, and Lane, 1971).

Such evidence indicates that dreams often express whatever motives are currently most important. But Freud's theory went much further than this, for it insisted that the manifest dream represents a wish fulfillment and is a censored and disguised version of the latent dream that lies underneath. This conception of dreams has been much criticized. To begin with, there is considerable doubt that all (or even many) dreams are attempts at wish fulfillments, whether disguised or open. In one study, participants were made extremely thirsty before they went to sleep. Since thirst is hardly a forbidden urge, there is no reason to suppose an internal censorship. However, none of the participants reported dreams of drinking. Since they were so thirsty, why didn't they gratify themselves in their dreams (Dement and Wolpert, 1958)?

Another problem is the fact that the same urge can be freely expressed in some dreams, but heavily disguised in others. Tonight, the sleeper dreams of unabashed sexual intercourse; tomorrow night, she dreams of riding a team of wild horses. For sake of argument, let us agree that riding is a symbol for intercourse. Why should the censor disguise tomorrow what is so freely allowed tonight?

One investigator, C. S. Hall, has come up with a plausible suggestion (Hall, 1953). According to Hall, the dream symbol does not disguise an underlying idea; on the contrary, it *expresses* it. In Hall's view, the dream is a rather concrete mental shorthand that embodies a feeling or emotion. Riding a horse, plowing a field, planting a seed—all of these may be concrete renditions of the idea of sexual intercourse. But they are not meant to hide this idea. Their function is much the same as the cartoonist's picture of Uncle Sam or John Bull. These are representations of the United States and of England, but they are certainly not meant as disguises for them. During sleep, more specifically during the vivid visual dreaming of REM sleep (see Chapter 3), we are incapable of the complexity and abstractness of waking mental life. We are thus reduced to a more concrete and schematic form of thinking. The wishes and fears of our waking life are still present at night, and we dream about them. But the way in which these are now expressed tends to be more primitive, a concrete pictorialization that combines fragments of various waking concerns and serves as a kind of symbolic cartoon.

Such findings do not dispute Freud's belief that dreams involve complex cognitive processes many of which are hidden from view. But they argue against the central tenet of his theory: that they are disguised representations of forbidden urges that are held underground in their threatening, unmasked form.

Studies of anxiety and recall   The concept of repression is the cornerstone of psychoanalytic thought. According to Freud, painful (or anxiety-provoking) material is intolerable to the conscious mind and therefore repressed—not thought about (at least consciously) and not remembered. But whatever Freud claimed, studies seeking to document repression's effects have been largely unsuccessful. Some results supporting Freud's claims turn out to be ambiguous, and many others contradict his claims outright. As a result, most psychologists are now deeply skeptical about the notion of repression.

For example, psychoanalytic theory suggests that motivated forgetting is an important defense against anxiety. One would therefore expect that materials associated with anxiety would be recalled less readily than neutral items, and many results do show this pattern. In one study, the investigator selected a set of words likely to be anxiety provoking for each participant; when these words were later used in a memory task, the participant had more trouble producing these emotional words (Jacobs, 1955; for a review and methodological critique, see Holmes, 1990). Other studies have shown that participants are more likely to recall events that put them in a good light, in comparison to those that are less flattering (Erdelyi and Goldberg, 1979; Kunda, 1990). Clearly, then, self-service plays a role in memory, whether one is remembering an experimenter's stimuli or the events in one's own life.

But do we need to think of these results in Freudian terms? As we saw in Chapter 7, information will become established in memory only if suitably rehearsed; it is plausible that a person simply elects not to mull over unpleasant experiences, making it less likely that these will be remembered later on. Likewise, memory retrieval is a process that requires both effort and strategy (see Chapter 7); for unpleasant memories, someone might choose neither to spend the effort nor to engage an effective strategy. In these ways, we can explain a self-serving bias in memory with no appeal to the sort of imperious censor envisioned by Freud.

In addition, a number of studies have examined how people remember real-life traumatic events, and here, too, the data provide little indication of repression. Some studies do show poor memory for prior traumas—for example, cases in which adult women fail to remember a time when, as children, they had been admitted to a hospital because of abuse (Williams, 1994). But many of these women were infants or toddlers when the abuse occurred, and so their forgetting may be understood in terms of ordinary childhood amnesia, not repression. In addition, many of these women had been abused on many occasions and did remember other incidents of abuse, even while forgetting the hospitalization. This is certainly not the pattern one would expect on Freudian grounds.

Moreover, it is all too easy to find cases in which individuals do remember—in vivid and terrifying detail—the horrible traumas they have endured. A group of children kidnapped on a school bus remembered the terrible episode long afterward; rape victims are typically plagued by too *much* memory of their hideous experience; children who have witnessed violent crimes are often long haunted by nightmares of these events (Terr, 1991, 1994). In all such cases, these deeply painful memories would seem highly eligible for repression, if repression exists. The fact that these memories are *not* repressed creates a serious problem for Freud's conception. (For further discussion, see Schacter, 1996; Shobe and Kihlstrom, 1997; see also Chapter 7.)

A final point: It is worth noting that a number of contemporary psychologists have tried to fit the concept of the unconscious into the framework of modern cognitive psychology. They agree with the psychoanalysts' assertion that much of mental life is affected by processes of which we are not conscious, pointing to such phenomena as blindsight, implicit retrieval, and automaticity as illustrations (see Kihlstrom, 1996a, b, and Chapters 7 and 8). But they strongly dispute Freud's contention that these unconscious processes are defenses against anxiety or that they have the sexual and aggressive quality Freud attributed to them. To quote one author, our modern view of *non*conscious mental life suggests that, while quite extensive, it is often "kinder, gentler, and more rational than the seething unconscious of Freud" (Kihlstrom, 1990).

FREUD'S CONTRIBUTIONS IN RETROSPECT

We have seen that many of Freud's beliefs have not been confirmed. There are good evolutionary grounds to doubt Freud's essentially Hobbesian view of human nature (see Chapter 10). There is little evidence for his general theory of psychosexual development, even less for his male-centered—and some would say misogynistic—conception of feminine psychology (Chodorow, 1989). There is also good reason to believe that he overemphasized biological givens at the expense of cultural factors.

We have also seen that Freud can be criticized not just for what he asserted but for the way he tried to prove his claims. Freud's work was seriously flawed as science. By now, there is general agreement that the psychoanalytic couch is not a source of objective fact and that many of Freud's theoretical proposals are rather vague and metaphorical, so that it is not clear how they can be tested. Freud also seemed vulnerable to confirmation bias (see Chapter 8)—he looked for evidence that would support his theory but shied away from disconfirming data. All in all, this is a formidable set of criticisms. Even so, many psychologists would maintain that, despite these serious (perhaps crippling) flaws, Sigmund Freud must nevertheless be regarded as one of the major figures in psychology.

They want to grant Freud this status for two major reasons. The first concerns a conception of his that still stands, however much it may have to be modified and reinterpreted—the notion that there is some kind of internal conflict of which we are often unaware. Freud was far from the first to recognize that we

Freud looking at a bust of himself sculpted for his seventy-fifth birthday *By O. Nemon*
(Courtesy of Wide World Photos)

are often torn in opposite directions and that we frequently deceive ourselves about what we want (Ellenberger, 1970; Sulloway, 1979). But he was the first for whom this insight was the cornerstone of an entire point of view. Whether his own therapeutic procedure, psychoanalysis, is an appropriate tool to make the unknown known and thus to restore a measure of free choice to the emotionally crippled victims of inner conflict is questionable (see Chapters 7 and 19). Still, Freud's contribution remains, because he saw so clearly that we do not know ourselves, that we are not masters of our own souls. By pointing out how ignorant we are, he set a task for later investigators who may ultimately succeed, so that we may then be able to follow Socrates' deceptively simple prescription for a good life, "Know thyself."

The other major reason why Freud deserves a lasting place among the greats of intellectual history, they argue, is that, while his theoretical conception was seriously flawed, it offered a view of human nature that was virtually all-embracing. It tried to encompass both rational thought and emotional urges. It conceived of psychological ailments as a consequence of the same forces that operate in everyday life. It saw humans as biological organisms as well as social beings, as creatures whose present is rooted in their past. The range of psychological phenomena that Freud encompassed within his theory is staggering—symptoms of mental disorder, personality patterns, social groupings, family relations, humor, slips of the tongue, dreams, artistic productions, aspects of religious thought. Freud's theory has many faults, but this litany highlights some of its virtues: It dealt with matters of genuine human significance; it concerned both human beings and their works; it was an account of the whole of humanity.

Many of Freud's views have now been disconfirmed, but there is no doubt that they have influenced virtually all thinkers in these areas who have come after him. For Freud was one of those rare intellectual figures who cast his shadow over a whole century. And right or wrong, he showed us the kinds of questions we must answer before we can claim to have a full theory of human personality.

THE PSYCHODYNAMIC APPROACH: PERSONALITY DIFFERENCES

While the primary focus of psychodynamic theory (and of Freud's theory in particular) is about human personality in general, it does offer many proposals about the way in which people (especially "normal" people) differ from each other and also how those differences come about. Freud's questionable theory of oral and anal personalities is one example. More recent attempts at theorizing by various neo-Freudians classify and analyze personality differences in terms of the person's dominant patterns of defense. The neo-Freudians, like Freud himself, believe that anxiety is an inevitable part of human existence and that some defenses against anxiety will therefore be found in everyone. What makes people different, they claim, is the pattern of defenses they have erected.

PATTERNS OF CONFLICT

A major figure in the analysis of these patterns of defenses was Karen Horney, who argued that many people in our society suffer from basic anxiety—an "all-pervading feeling of being alone and helpless in a hostile world" (Horney, 1937, p. 89). Horney believed that this anxiety should not be traced to childhood struggles with infantile sexual conflicts. She felt, instead, that its roots are in our culture, which often makes incompatible demands on the individual.

According to Karen Horney, basic anxiety leads some to the frantic pursuit of various goals, sought less for themselves than as a way to deaden this anxiety. They try to assuage their anxiety by seeking love, by seeking prestige or possessions, by withdrawing from any genuine emotional involvements, or by deadening the anxiety with alcohol or drugs (Horney, 1937, 1945, 1950). Such efforts often fail, but they generally persist and harden into enduring patterns of personality. The question is why. Horney's answer is that such pursuits create a self-perpetuating vicious circle.

For example, a vicious circle can develop in an unhealthy search for love. If a man needs a woman's love to deaden his sense of basic anxiety, his demands for affection will be unconditional and excessive. But if so, they can't possibly be fulfilled. The slightest failure to accede to his wishes will be interpreted as a rebuff and rejection. This will increase his feelings of anxiety, which will make him even more desperate for affectionate reassurance, which will further increase the chances of rebuff, and so on. Add the fact that such rebuffs—whether real or imagined—lead to hostility, which he can't possibly acknowledge lest he lose his lover altogether. Add the further fact that since his basic anxiety makes him devalue himself, he may well begin to devalue her. How could she be as wonderful as he thought at first, if she loves him? As Groucho Marx once said, "I wouldn't want to belong to any club that would have me as a member." All of these further factors combine to enhance the love-seeking neurotic's sense of anxiety, which then refuels his desperate need for love and affection.

While vicious circles of this kind are a characteristic of deeply disturbed and unhappy persons, minor versions of such circular mechanisms are found in everyday life. A student has to write an important paper. The paper worries her, so she puts it off. This makes her feel guilty, which makes her more anxious,

Self-destructive behavior *(From B. Kliban,* Luminous animals. *Copyright 1983, B. Kliban, Penguin Books)*

which makes her put it off yet further, and so on (Hall et al., 1985). But as Horney points out, there are occasional "lucky circles." Some fortunate encounters in work or love may reverse the circle by increasing self-confidence, which leads to appropriate further efforts and further successes. But all too often, the person's own conflicts make her unable to recognize whatever luck may come her way. Put another way, such conflicts tend to perpetuate themselves, which is one reason why at least some people try to break the pattern by seeking some form of psychotherapeutic help.

COPING PATTERNS AND MENTAL HEALTH

The patterns we have just described characterize people with emotional conflicts that in some cases are quite serious. But can they help us understand normal people? Contemporary psychodynamically oriented theorists would say that they can. For in their view, unconscious conflict and defense mechanisms are found in the well adjusted as well as in people with disabling mental disorders; what distinguishes the two is the extent to which those conflicts are appropriately resolved.

Several investigators have studied characteristic patterns of defense using normal people. Much of this work was influenced by a movement in psychoanalysis called *ego psychology,* whose initial impetus probably came from Freud's daughter Anna Freud (1895–1982). Its leaders include Heinz Hartmann (1894–1970), as well as Erik Erikson (1902–1994), whose work we encountered in a previous chapter (see Chapter 14). Adherents of this position share the neo-Freudian concern with cultural and interpersonal factors. But they add a further element by stressing the healthy aspects of the self as it tries to cope with the world—to deal with reality as it is rather than to distort it or hide from it. Seen in this light, the ego is not just an arbiter between id and superego, but a clever strategist with intrinsic competencies (Freud, 1946; Hartmann, 1964).★

LONGITUDINAL STUDIES OF COPING PATTERNS

To find out how coping patterns are employed over the course of the life span, a number of investigators have performed longitudinal studies. Such studies, which generally cover a span of twenty to thirty years, represent an arduous undertaking; participants drop out of these studies for any number of reasons, and the investigators who begin them are rarely the ones who finally complete them. In longitudinal studies of personality, the raw material is usually in the form of interview records conducted at different times. These records are later rated for various characteristics, such as certain personality traits or the use of this or another mechanism of defense.

An example of such a longitudinal study is George Vaillant's analysis of the case reports of ninety-four male Harvard College graduates studied at different points in their life span. They were extensively interviewed at age nineteen, and then again at thirty-one, and yet again at forty-seven. Vaillant studied the predominant patterns of defense—that is, ways of coping—each man used at these three ages. He classified these coping patterns according to their level of psychological maturity. At the bottom of the hierarchy were mechanisms that are often found in early childhood and during serious mental disorder, such as denial or

Anna Freud *(Photograph courtesy of the Bettmann Archive)*

★ A more recent and influential version of this ego-oriented approach is self psychology, developed by Heinz Kohut (1913–1981) (Kohut, 1978).

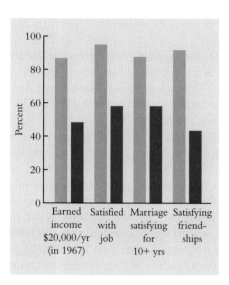

17.2 Maturity of defense mechanisms and life adjustment *Adult success at work and love, as shown by men with predominantly mature (blue) and immature (dark red) adaptive styles. (After Vaillant, 1971)*

gross distortions of external reality. Further up the ladder were patterns often seen in adolescence and in disturbed adults, such as projection, hypochondria, and irrational, emotional outbursts. Still higher were the mechanisms studied by Freud and seen in many adults—repression, isolation, reaction formation, and the like. At the top of the hierarchy were coping patterns that Vaillant considered healthy (in adolescents and adults)—such as humor, suppression (a conscious effort to push anxiety-provoking thoughts out of mind, at least for the time being, as opposed to repression, which is an unconscious process), and altruism (in which one tries to give to others what one might wish to receive oneself).

Vaillant's findings are simple enough. It's not particularly surprising (though it is certainly reassuring) that as the participants grew older, their coping mechanisms generally became more mature. There was growth and change, but there was also continuity; men whose coping patterns were better integrated at nineteen were somewhat more likely to have mature patterns in their forties, which then predicted the results on various objective indices—satisfaction in marriage, rewarding friendships, gratifying jobs, and good physical health (see Figure 17.2). As so often, it is by no means clear just what in those men's lives was cause and what was effect, but regardless of whether the mature coping defenses produced success in marriage and career or vice versa, it is worth knowing that the two tend to be correlated (Vaillant, 1974, 1976, 1977, 1994). This correlation of coping mechanisms with good late-life outcomes isn't restricted to Harvard males; it was also observed in a study of 131 inner-city males interviewed in junior high school and then surveyed thirty years later (Vaillant, Bond, and Vaillant, 1986).

Similar results were obtained in a study by Jack Block that may be one of the most systematic longitudinal studies of personality ever undertaken. Block studied case records of some 250 men and women in junior high school, in senior high school, and in their thirties (Block, 1971). In many ways, the results were similar to Vaillant's. Like Vaillant, Block found a general increase in overall personal adjustment. But he also found continuity in characteristics such as enjoyment of social activities, self-assurance, and desire for achievement. In addition, he found a relation between the participants' adjustment as adults and their family background. By and large, the well-adjusted adults were those who grew up in a (psychologically) benign family atmosphere. Their mothers and fathers were active, self-assured, and warm and took their parenting tasks seriously; they provided firm guidelines but were affectionate in the process. In contrast, the participants judged to be more poorly adjusted as adults came from less favorable family backgrounds. The parents were often at odds with each other, and they were either overinvolved with their child, or rejecting, dictatorial, or indifferent. As Block points out, these early histories differ widely; all they have in common is that they are unfavorable. This is quite different from those of the more well-adjusted participants, which tend to be much more alike. There are more ways to make a machine (or a human body, or a human personality) function badly than to make it work properly. As the Russian novelist Leo Tolstoy put it in *Anna Karenina,* "Happy families are all alike; every unhappy family is unhappy in its own way" (Tolstoy, 1875, p. 1).

Block interprets these correlations in cause-and-effect terms. As he sees it, the parents provided a familial atmosphere that ultimately helped shape their children for good or ill by inducing healthy or unhealthy coping patterns. But as we saw above, this interpretation does not necessarily follow. One possibility is that the correlation was produced by a genetic similarity between child and parents. Another possibility is that the cause-and-effect relation is the reverse of the one proposed by Block: The children's own personalities (in part, perhaps, based on genetic factors) may have influenced the way their parents treated them. No doubt there are other interpretations as well. Our present concern is merely to stress the enormous complexity of the issue. As yet, we have no easy solutions to the question of how any of us came to be the people we now are. (For further discussion, see Chapters 14 and 16.)

COPING AND THE UNCONSCIOUS

On the face of it, the preceding discussion of adaptive patterns may appear rather distant from the orientation of psychodynamic theorists, especially as represented by Freud. After all, Freud emphasized unconscious processes that operated in a murky underground of which we are unaware. In contrast, the coping responses of normal people seem much more ordinary, and they are at least sometimes in plain view. Is there any relation between these two?

Ego-oriented psychoanalysts—and most modern psychologists—would answer yes. For whatever their many differences, the defense mechanisms of the anxiety-ridden adult and the "What, me worry?" shrug of the carefree adult have one thing in common—they are both ways of trying to cope with and adapt to the strains and stresses of existence.

The fact that some of these adaptive reactions are fully conscious while others are not doesn't necessarily mean that there is a sharp break between them. For a number of psychologists have pointed out that what Freud called *unconscious mechanisms* may be regarded as ways of not attending, in line with the "kinder, gentler, and more rational" unconscious we discussed previously (see p. 735; Bowers, 1984; Erdelyi, 1985; Kihlstrom, 1987). The person who is in favor of a particular political candidate is much more likely to attend to arguments on his behalf than to arguments that favor his opponent. The first he will tend to remember; the second he is likely to forget. Similarly, the man who has just suffered a painful divorce may prefer not to think about his ex-wife. When some topic comes up that starts to remind him about her, he will deliberately try to think about something else and may forget what it was that started the new train of thought. This method of turning away from one's own pain may not be as exotic as the complicated repressive maneuvers that Freud thought he saw in his patients, but it belongs to the same family.

Most of us physically avoid some situations we would rather not face; by the same token, some of us mentally avoid (that is, don't attend to) sights or thoughts or memories we find unpleasant or frightening. Seen in this light, the so-called unconscious mechanisms lose some of their mystery. They are just one more way of dealing with the world.

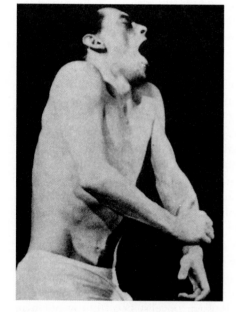

Spontaneity in the theater *Several modern movements emphasize spontaneity and creativity in the theater. An influential example is the theatrical school founded by the Polish director Jerzy Grotowski, who requires his actors to perform in a kind of trance, to give themselves totally in a confrontation with the play and the audience. The photograph is taken from one of his productions,* The Constant Prince, *by Pedro Calderón de la Barca. (Reproduced by permission of Jerzy Grotowski)*

THE HUMANISTIC APPROACH

Some forty years ago, a new perspective on human motivation and personality—the **humanistic approach**—gained prominence. According to its adherents, neither trait theorists, behaviorists, nor psychodynamic theorists have much to say about healthy, striving human beings. In their view, psychoanalysts look at people as if they are all conflict-ridden emotional cripples, behaviorists regard them as if they are dumb animals or unthinking automatons, and trait theorists see them as no more than grab bags of descriptors to file in sterile pigeon holes.

Humanistic psychologists believe that all of these views have lost sight of what is truly human about human beings. Healthy humans want to feel free to choose

Improvisation *Director Mike Leigh relies
on his actors to develop a story through improvisation. Only after many months of rehearsal
was the script for his 1996 film* Secrets and
Lies *finally refined. In that film, a mother
(played by Brenda Blethyn) is reunited with
the daughter she gave up for adoption (Marianne Jean-Baptiste). Did the actors' work in
developing the script make the emotions of
mother and daughter seem more genuine?
(Photograph courtesy of Photofest)*

and determine their own lives rather than to exist as mere pawns either driven
by demons from within or pushed around by stimuli from without. They seek
more than food and sex and safety, strive for more than mere adjustment—they
want to grow, to develop their potential, to become *self-actualized.*

Returning to our theatrical analogy, the humanistic approach can be likened
to certain modern movements in theater that emphasize spontaneity and improvisation. Actors who belong to this school insist that what is most important is
genuine, authentic feeling. At least in principle (though rarely in actual practice), such actors might depart from the playwright's words and the director's
stagings to provide the audience and themselves with a sense of freedom and
spontaneity. To the extent that this occurs, there is no mask left at all; the actor
and the part have become one.

THE MAJOR FEATURES OF THE HUMANISTIC MOVEMENT

According to Abraham Maslow (1908–1970), the humanistic movement
represents a kind of "third force" in American psychology—the other two
being behaviorism and psychoanalysis. For expositional purposes, we will begin
by presenting some of the major features of this movement before discussing
them more critically.

A POSITIVE VIEW OF HUMAN MOTIVATION

A major contrast between humanistic psychologists and the behaviorists and
psychoanalysts that they oppose is in their conception of human motivation.
According to Maslow, behaviorists and psychoanalysts see human beings as
engaged in a never-ending struggle to remove some internal tension or make up
for some deficit. The result is an essentially pessimistic and negative conception
of human nature. Seen in this light, people always want to get away from something (pain, hunger, sexual tension) rather than to gain something positive.

This perspective necessarily leads to an emphasis on the physiological needs—
hunger, thirst, escape from threat, sex. Maslow called these **deficiency needs;** in all
such cases, we experience a lack and want to fill it. According to Maslow, an
analogous deficiency sometimes underlies social needs, such as the desire for
prestige or security; an example is the person who hungers for the admiration of
all around her and feels empty without it.

But as Maslow pointed out, release from pain and tension does not account
for everything we strive for. We sometimes seek things for their own sake, as
positive goals in themselves. There is the joy of solving a puzzle, the exhilaration
of windsurfing or horseback riding, the ecstasy of fulfilled love, the quiet rapture
in the contemplation of great art and music or a beautiful sunrise. All of these
are experiences that human beings seek, and it is these positive, enriching experiences—rather than the filled stomach or the sexual release at orgasm—that
make us most distinctively human. A hungry rat and a sexually aroused monkey
seek food and orgasmic release pretty much as we do, but the joy of Beethoven's
Ninth Symphony is ours alone. Maslow insisted that to understand what is truly
human, psychologists must consider motives that go beyond deficiency needs
(Maslow, 1968).

Thus, Maslow proposed a **hierarchy of needs** in which the lower-order physiological needs are at the bottom, safety needs are further up, the need for attachment and love is still higher, and the desire for esteem is higher yet. At the very

7 4 1

17.3   Maslow's hierarchy of needs   People will strive for higher-order needs (such as esteem or artistic achievement) generally after lower-order needs (hunger, safety) have been satisfied. (After Maslow, 1954)

top of the hierarchy is the striving for self-actualization—the desire to realize oneself to the fullest (of which more later) (see Figure 17.3).

Maslow believed that people will only strive for higher-order needs (say, self-esteem or artistic achievement) when lower-order needs (such as hunger) are satisfied. By and large this is plausible enough; the urge to write poetry generally takes a back seat if one hasn't eaten for days. But as Maslow pointed out, there are exceptions. Some artists starve rather than give up their poetry or their painting, and some martyrs proclaim their faith regardless of pain or suffering. But to the extent that Maslow's assumption holds, the motive at the very top of his hierarchy—that is, the drive toward self-actualization—will become primary only when all other needs beneath are satisfied.

THE SELF IN HUMANISTIC PSYCHOLOGY

Before trying to describe what Maslow and other humanistic psychologists mean by *self-actualization,* we should say a word about the self that is (or is not) being actualized. We've previously encountered some issues related to the self. Social psychologists study it under the headings of self-perception theory and self-presentation (Chapter 11), while Freud and Piaget treat it as a developmental matter, since they believe that the "ego" emerges from an earlier diffuse state in which there is no self at all (Chapter 13). To humanistic psychologists, the self is even more important, for one of their primary concerns is with subjective experience—with what the individual thinks and feels right here and now. According to Carl Rogers (1902–1987), a major figure in the humanistic movement, a crucial facet of this subjective experience is the *self* or *self-concept.* This self-concept develops in early childhood and eventually comes to include one's sense of oneself—the "I"—as an agent who takes (or doesn't take) actions and makes (or doesn't make) decisions. It also includes one's sense of oneself as a kind of object—the "me"—that is seen and thought about, liked or disliked (Rogers, 1959, 1961).

In the course of his work in clinical counseling, Rogers came to feel that an important condition for adult mental health is a solid sense of personal self-worth. Rogers believed that to achieve this the child requires ***unconditional positive regard***—the sense of being accepted and loved without condition or reservation. But such a prescription for child rearing is difficult to follow. For the parents can (and must) disapprove of some of the things the child does; they are unlikely to applaud when little Janie spills ketchup all over the new living room rug, or, worse, when she pummels her brother. They could still show Janie their unconditional positive regard by making it clear that, while they certainly don't love her behavior, they do and will always love *her*. But this is much easier said than done. Most parents probably do set some conditions on their love, no matter how subtly, indicating that they will love her if she'll do well at school, or if she has good manners, or whatever. Rogers believed that the likely upshot is that the child will suppress some aspect of herself in order to feel loved and accepted. And this in turn may lead to a sense of confusion and disquiet, and a doubt of her real self-worth.

SELF-ACTUALIZATION

Given a reasonable sense of self-worth and the satisfaction of the lower-level needs, the stage is set for the motive at the very top of Maslow's hierarchy of needs, the desire for ***self-actualization.*** Maslow and other humanistic psychologists describe this as the desire to realize one's potential, to fulfill oneself, to become what one can become (Maslow, 1968, 1970). But exactly what does this mean?

Maslow gave some examples by presenting case histories of a number of people that he and his collaborators regarded as self-actualized. Some of them were individuals that he had personally interviewed; others were historical figures (for example, Thomas Jefferson and Ludwig van Beethoven) or more recent luminaries (such as Eleanor Roosevelt), whose lives were studied by means of historical or other documents. Unlike most other investigators in the field, Maslow was not interested in these peoples' specific attributes or behavior patterns; all he looked for were some overall patterns that he felt were shared by them all. As Maslow saw it, these self-actualizers had many admirable characteristics. Among other things, they were realistically oriented, accepted themselves and others, were spontaneous, cared more about the problems they were working on than about themselves, had intimate relationships with a few people rather than superficial relationships with many, and had democratic values—all in all, an admirable list of human qualities (Maslow, 1968, 1970).

Self-actualization shown through self-portraits *To actualize one's self may take a whole lifetime. Some great artists have given us a graphic record of the process at different points in their lives, as in these self-portraits by Rembrandt. One was created at the age of thirty-four, when he was very successful and saw himself as a Renaissance gentleman artist and virtuoso. The other was painted at about age sixty, when he tried to reaffirm his identity through his art and portrayed himself as a painter holding the tools of his craft (Wright, 1982). (Left:* Self-Portrait at the Age of Thirty-four; *courtesy of the National Gallery. Right:* Portrait of the Artist; *courtesy of English Heritage, The Iveagh Bequest)*

According to Maslow, another characteristic of self-actualized persons is that they are more likely than other people to have what he called **peak experiences.** Peak experiences are profound and deeply felt moments in a person's life in which there is a "feeling of great ecstasy and awe . . . with the conviction that something extremely important and valuable had happened . . ." (Maslow, 1970, p. 164). Such moments might come while with a lover, or while watching the sea or a sunset, or while listening to music or watching a play. But regardless of when and where they occur, they seem to have some important and lasting effects on the individual, who thereafter is likely to see himself and others in a more spontaneous and healthier way.

GROWTH

What happens to people whose self-regard is so low that the possibility of self-actualization doesn't arise? Rogers believed that new experiences in later life could provide some of the spontaneous warmth and positive regard that was lacking earlier. To that end, his therapy offered the client warmth and showed her that her feelings are accepted and that she is worthy of love (Rogers, 1980; for more details, see Chapter 19). The result of such successful psychotherapy was a person who showed three basic qualities: openness to experience, the ability to live spontaneously and exuberantly, and a trust in one's own judgments and reactions (Rogers, 1964).

Rogers's approach to therapy illustrates that he—and indeed most humanistic psychologists—believed that, given the appropriate conditions, people will grow so as to realize their inherent potential. They further believe that in general this potential is for good rather than for evil. In this regard, their position is the very opposite of that held by such pessimists as Hobbes and Freud, who insisted that humans cannot help but be brutes unless their baser instincts are tamed by civilization. In contrast, Rogers and Maslow felt that humans will only turn sour and ugly if they are somehow twisted and frustrated by social conditions.

According to Rogers, people will attain a healthy sense of self if they are provided with the proper emotional climate. To grow into a healthy rose, the rose seedling needs water, sun, and soil. In the same vein, Rogers believed that to grow into emotionally healthy adulthood, the child needs warmth and acceptance, what he called **empathic understanding** (where someone seems to understand what you feel and, so to speak, to feel it with you), and the presence of another person who is genuine (open, trustworthy, and without a facade).

EVALUATING THE HUMANISTIC APPROACH

In trying to evaluate the humanistic approach to personality, we must begin by asking about its empirical and conceptual foundations.

EMPIRICAL AND CONCEPTUAL DIFFICULTIES

Consider Rogers's account of the origins of the feeling of self-worth. Is it really true that unconditional positive regard and empathic understanding are essential for the development of self-worth? We've previously noted the enormous difficulties in drawing any conclusions about the effects of child rearing on later personality development (see Chapter 14). Under the circumstances, Rogers's description of the parent-child relationships that lead to feelings of adequate or inadequate self-worth seems oversimplified. Nor is his form of psychotherapy a

"I'm quite fulfilled. I always wanted to be a chicken." (© The New Yorker Collection 1989 Joseph Farris from Cartoonbank.com. All rights reserved.)

panacea; instead, it is generally about as effective as most other therapies (see Chapter 19 for discussion).

Similar qualifications apply to a number of other assertions made by the proponents of the humanistic approach. How do we know that self-actualizers are in fact as Maslow described them—for example, realistically oriented, accepting of themselves and others, spontaneous, problem centered, democratic, and so on—or that peak experiences have lasting and often beneficial effects on later life, or that self-actualizers have more peak experiences than other people? As yet, there is no real evidence that would allow us to draw such conclusions.

An even more serious criticism is the fact that many of the core conceptions of the humanistic approach are exceedingly unclear. Just what is meant by *self-actualization,* or by *letting yourself go* and *being yourself,* or by *unconditional positive regard,* or by *peak experience*? Since these terms are only vaguely defined, it is difficult to know how to evaluate any assertions about them.

Consider Maslow's study of self-actualizers. Maslow chose a number of persons as exemplars, including a number of prominent and historical figures. But by what criteria did he select them? Among the historical figures he chose were Thomas Jefferson, Abraham Lincoln (in his later years), and Eleanor Roosevelt. Most of us would agree that these were admirable and creative people, and we can understand what is meant when someone says that they fulfilled their potential and "actualized" themselves. But why can't the same term be applied to many other individuals, some of whom are far from admirable and may be veritable monsters? What about Al Capone, or Jiang Qing (Madame Mao), or even Adolf Hitler? It's very likely that these persons felt that they had become what they were meant to be (at least until Alcatraz, or Mao's death, or the final days in the Berlin bunker). But if so, why shouldn't we regard them as self-actualized? Given their belief that human growth has an inherent tendency toward good rather than evil, Maslow and Rogers would presumably exclude—by definition—such moral monsters. But this line of reasoning can certainly be questioned. The development of personality may be a growth process, but this alone is not enough grounds for optimism. Given soil, sun, and water, a rose seedling will indeed become a rose. But a seedling of another kind may self-actualize and become a full-grown stand of poison ivy.

HUMANISTIC PSYCHOLOGY AS A PROTEST MOVEMENT

It appears that many of the major tenets of the humanistic approach to personality rest on rather shaky foundations. But if so, why should we take it seriously? One answer is that the humanistic approach is best considered as a protest movement (see Monte, 1995). It reacts against both behaviorism and psychoanalysis because it regards them as representatives of a sterile mechanistic view of people as marionettes pushed and pulled by forces from without and within. It reacts against trait psychology because it regards this approach as devoted to an endless cataloguing that reduces humans to mere ciphers. And it reacts against contemporary medicalized views of psychopathology, which it regards as narrow and pessimistic, oriented toward human sickness and deficiency rather than toward health and upward striving.

In some ways, the humanistic approach to personality is reminiscent of some prior movements in the political and literary spheres. Some two hundred years ago, the romantic poets in England and Germany elevated feeling over reason, celebrated individualism and natural man, and deplored the effects of eighteenth-century science and technology. Some, such as William Blake and Samuel Coleridge, sought peak experiences in mystical visions or in opium dreams. Others railed against the cold, mechanical science that had left the universe dessicated

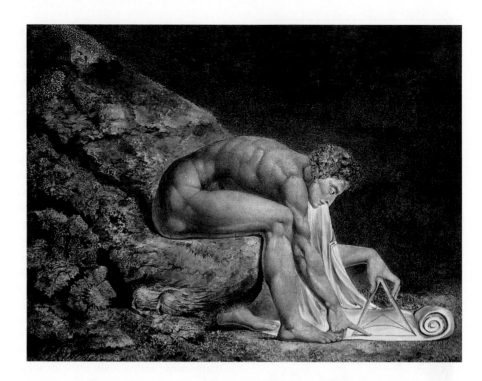

Romanticism in the arts *Just as Keats berates Newton for "destroying all the poetry of the rainbow" through scientific analysis, Blake depicts Newton as a man so focused on his mathematics that he is unaware of the natural world of which he is a part. (Newton, 1795, by William Blake; Tate Gallery, London/Art Resource)*

and barren. An example is John Keats's lament that "Newton has destroyed all the poetry of the rainbow by reducing it to the prismatic colors" (in Abrams, 1953, p. 303). And many of them agreed with the social philosopher Jean-Jacques Rousseau (1712–1778), whose writings helped to shape the French and American Revolutions, that "man is by nature good, and . . . only our institutions have made him bad!" (in Durant and Durant, 1967, p. 19).

The similarity between these sentiments and many of the themes of the humanistic psychologists is clear enough. The romantics protested against what they regarded as a cold, mechanical approach to nature and politics; the humanistic psychologists lodge similar complaints against contemporary approaches to psychology. This is not to say that the humanistic psychologists were directly influ-

The theater of protest *The humanistic approach to personality is reminiscent of protest movements in the literary and political spheres. Examples are various modern dramatic productions that attack contemporary attitudes, as in Peter Weiss's play* Marat/Sade *in which contemporary society is likened to an insane asylum. (From the 1966 film* Marat/Sade, *directed by Peter Brook; courtesy of the Kobal Collection)*

enced by Rousseau or the eighteenth-century romantics, for they almost surely were not. The point is that by now romanticism is a part of our cultural heritage that has provided a general vocabulary for many later protest movements. One example is the student rebellion of the 1960s, fueled in great part by the Vietnam War. Another is the humanistic movement in American psychology.

To be sure, the romantic poets did much more than protest; they also made lasting contributions to literature. And Rousseau influenced the political landscape of Europe for a century after his death. Is there a corresponding positive contribution of humanistic psychology? Some critics contend that apart from Rogers's work on the practice and evaluation of psychotherapy, the humanists' concepts are too vague and their assertions too unproven (and maybe too unproveable) to count as serious scientific accomplishments (e.g., Smith, 1950). Others argue that the humanists often serve as moral advocates rather than dispassionate scientists. They tell us what personality *should* be rather than what it is.

But there is one accomplishment of which we can be sure. The humanistic psychologists remind us of many phenomena that other approaches to the study of personality have largely bypassed. People do strive for more than food and sex or prestige; they read poetry, listen to music, fall in love, have occasional peak experiences, try to actualize themselves. Whether the humanistic psychologists have really helped us to understand these phenomena better than we did before is debatable. But there is no doubt that what they have done is to insist that these phenomena are there, that they constitute a vital aspect of what makes us human, and that they must not be ignored.

THE SOCIOCULTURAL PERSPECTIVE

Whatever their many differences, all of the approaches to personality we've discussed thus far have one thing in common: a focus on the individual. But surely all individuals exist in a social and cultural context that is critical in shaping and defining who they are. Yet by and large personality theorists have ignored that context and focused their efforts almost entirely on the individual, whether by categorizing her (trait theory), by studying how different situations shape her (social learning theory), by trying to uncover her hidden motives (psychodynamic theory), or by celebrating her uniqueness (humanistic psychology). None of these approaches concerns itself particularly with the culture of which the person necessarily is a part. Some modern critics feel that this is a serious lack. They point out that virtually all of the data on which modern personality theory is based come from the study of middle-class western Europeans or North Americans. Can we really be sure that what holds true for these people can be generalized to people in different times, different places, and different cultures?

As we might expect, the answer is both yes and no. For it turns out that in some regards people throughout the world are very different from each other, while in other respects they are much the same.

HUMAN DIVERSITY AND PERSONALITY

Much of the evidence that bears on these matters comes from cultural anthropology, a discipline that studies ways of living that characterize different societies throughout the world. An early pioneer in this enterprise was Franz Boas (1858–1942), who convinced many anthropologists to study the

Margaret Mead in Samoa, 1925 *(Courtesy of the Institute for Intercultural Studies)*

preliterate cultures of the world before they disappeared altogether. Among his students were Ruth Benedict (1887–1948) and Margaret Mead (1901–1978), two of the most influential figures in this area; their work reports an enormous diversity in human character and personality, shaped as they are by drastically different cultural traditions.

Ruth Benedict's *Patterns of Culture* (1934) described personality patterns that she believed characterized three very different preliterate societies. Among the Kwakiutl Indians of the Canadian Northwest, the dominant theme seemed to be rivalry and boastful self-glorification. Among the Pueblo Indians of the American Southwest, the primary theme appeared to be self-control, cooperation, and very little aggression within the community. And among the Dobu Islanders, there was apparently a great deal of mutual enmity and distrust, and a near-universal conviction that everyone practices sorcery against everyone else.

Other accounts pointed to variations in the way gender roles were defined in different cultures. Thus, Margaret Mead compared the personality traits of men and women in three preliterate New Guinea tribes that lived within a hundred-mile radius of one another. Among the Arapesh, she described both men and women as mild, cooperative, and, so to speak, "maternal" in their attitudes toward each other and especially toward children. Among the neighboring Mundugomor, Mead reported that both sexes were ferociously aggressive and quarrelsome. In Mead's account of yet another tribe, the Tchambuli, the usual sex roles seemed reversed: The women were the hale and hearty breadwinners who fished and went to market unadorned; while the women managed such worldly affairs, the men gossiped, adjusted elaborate hairdos, carved and painted, and practiced intricate dance steps (Mead, 1935, 1937).

Of course, neither Benedict nor Mead suggested that every member of a given culture exhibits the pattern they described. Not every Kwakiutl was vehemently boastful; not every Arapesh was gentle and cooperative. What they tried to describe is a typical and common personality pattern that characterizes a given cultural group. And the fact that different cultures could show such different patterns seemed to demonstrate that the ways of modern Western society are not necessarily universal characteristics of human nature.

HUMAN SAMENESS AND UNIVERSAL PATTERNS OF PERSONALITY

The trait approach to personality that we outlined in Chapter 16 used trait dimensions as ways to describe the basic differences among people. But note that this method cannot inform us about the ways in which people are alike. For a number of authors, our common biological heritage implies that, at least in some respects, the personality patterns and emotions of the Kwakiutl, Arapesh, Dobu Islanders, and ourselves must, in fact, be similar, even though the anthropological evidence shows that in many ways we are different. Ironically enough, the differences may provide the key to discovering some universal principles of human nature. That, at least, is the underlying rationale of the ***cross-cultural method.***

In arguing for universals in personality patterns, several anthropologists have criticized Benedict's and Mead's accounts as inaccurate and oversimplified. For example, they take issue with some of Mead's work by pointing out that there are probably some universal sex roles after all; for example, warfare is generally conducted by the men, even among the Tchambuli. They argue that this may very well be due to biological factors, for physical aggression is in part under hormonal control; as testosterone levels rise, both human and nonhuman males become more aggressive (Reinisch, Ziemba-Davis, and Sanders, 1991; Lynn, 1995; and see Chapters 10 and 14).

From this biological standpoint, some aspects of physical aggression are part of our biological nature regardless of the culture to which we belong. What culture does is determine how this physical aggression is channeled and against whom, whether it is valued, and how much of it is allowed. (For recent discussions of Mead's work, see Brady, 1983; Freeman, 1983, 1986; Patience and Smith, 1986; Brown, 1991; Torrey, 1992; and Chapter 14.)

Also, a difference between cultures in the level of certain personality traits does not undermine the universality of those traits. To demonstrate this, let's assume that we could administer personality tests to some of the people studied by Mead and Benedict. Even granting that some of their descriptions may be overdrawn, one would still guess that the average Kwakiutl male would score much higher on such traits as dominance and irritability than his Arapesh counterpart. To that extent, the typical personality patterns of the cultures surely differ. But one thing may still be the same: the *dimensions* along which these personalities vary.

Some relevant evidence comes from translated personality tests administered in such diverse societies as those in Bangladesh, Brazil, Hong Kong, and Japan. When the results were factor analyzed, the pattern that emerged was much the same as that found in the United States and in Britain. This was especially true for Eysenck's two main dimensions of extroversion and neuroticism (see Chapter 16). This is not to say that people in these different cultures are identical on these personality traits, for they certainly do differ. For example, extroversion scores are very much higher in the United States than in Japan. What is the same is the way the responses to the items hang together; as a result, the same dimensions of personality emerge. To use an analogy, people come in different shapes and sizes, but their diversity can nevertheless be described by just a handful of tailor's measurements. To be sure, people in Sweden tend to be taller than people in Japan, but the same measuring tape can be used for them all (Eysenck and Eysenck, 1983; for some qualifications see Bond, 1979; Yang and Bond, 1990).

In some ways, these results are not unexpected. Traits such as extroversion and emotional stability may well be based on built-in characteristics related to temperament, which we know is in part genetically based (see Chapter 16). If so, these trait dimensions should correspond to a broad framework that fits all humankind. What should vary is just where within this framework a particular person falls. And this in part depends on the culture of which an individual is a member.

THE CROSS-CULTURAL METHOD: STUDIES OF THE EFFECTS OF CHILDHOOD

We've repeatedly encountered the notion that what happens in early childhood determines later personality. This view is most prominently associated with Freud, but it is found in the writings of many other authors as well and permeates much of modern American thinking. Those who embrace the cross-cultural method examine this view by studying the relation between a culture's beliefs and practices—family structures, child-rearing patterns, rituals and religious beliefs—and the typical personality characteristics of its members. In effect, they take advantage of cultural differences to ask how—and whether—certain cultural variations, especially in the area of child rearing, shape personality.

We saw an interesting application of the cross-cultural method in Chapter 14, where we discussed the effect of cultural and socioeconomic factors on child rearing. One study demonstrated a relationship between the economy on which a society is based and its methods of child rearing: Cultures that make their living through agriculture tend to stress compliance, conformity, and responsibility in raising their children, whereas hunting and fishing societies tend to stress self-reliance and initiative (Barry, Child, and Bacon, 1959). Other studies demonstrated that some differences in child rearing in our own society may be associated with social class. The evidence suggests that parents encourage their children to behave at home as they themselves do at work. Since members of the working class tend to be more closely supervised than are members of the middle class, working-class parents tend to emphasize control from outside and are more likely to use physical punishment, an extreme version of physical control. Because the work of the middle class tends to be self-directed, they are inclined to encourage self-control in their children as well (Kohn, 1969; Hess, 1970).

COLLECTIVISM AND INDIVIDUALISM

The relations between child-rearing patterns and cultural or socioeconomic factors just described seem clear enough. But does either cause the other? Most likely there is no direct cause-and-effect link. Instead, they are probably both strands in a complex web of patterns of thought and action handed down from one generation to the next. It is this web that constitutes the culture, and according to many anthropologists, its strands cannot be studied in isolation. As they see it, a culture is a kind of social Gestalt, whose parts only make sense by reference to the whole, much as a note takes its character from the melody in which it appears. If so, the best way to compare cultures would be along some dimension that considers the culture as a whole.

As we discussed in Chapter 11, many authors believe that cultures and ethnic subgroups can be distinguished according to their position on the dimension of *collectivism–individualism* (Triandis, 1989, 1994). As well as offering a different perspective on some of the social-psychological studies we reviewed in Chapter 11, differences in the collectivism-individualism dimension help to clarify the notions of individuality and the self as they are conceived by members of Western and non-Western cultures.

INDIVIDUALISM AND SELF-EXPRESSION

Individualism was, and is, a formative concept in Western cultures. Indeed, deindividuation is demonized in individualistic cultures as a cause of riots, orgies, and torture (see Chapter 12). In contrast, members of collectivist cultures regard a deindividuated society as optimal and see *individuation* as the source of mayhem and social turmoil (see Markus and Kitayama, 1994).

Historians point to a number of sources for our modern concept of individualism, especially in America. Some point to special environmental factors, such as the presence of the frontier in eighteenth- and nineteenth-century America (Tocqueville, 1835). Others trace it to the Protestant Reformation, which insisted that each individual has a direct relationship with God (Weber, 1904–5). Still others go further back and see its origin in the Italian Renaissance. In that period artists began the practice of signing their works as if to say "Look here! It's mine!" Until then, painters were craftsmen whose job was simply to paint a pious picture of the Madonna or a good likeness of their patron. But since the Renaissance, the artist's task has changed, for his job now is to make his work different from that of others, to be creative and original, to express himself (Burckhardt, 1860).

John Sabini has argued that Western individualism has much in common with the value we place on artistic creativity. We celebrate personal uniqueness, appreciate sincerity, approve of spontaneity, and applaud individual accomplish-

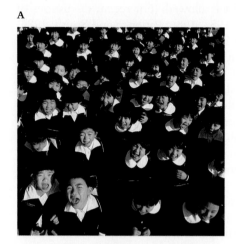

Japanese collectivism versus U.S. individualism (A) Tokyo school children. (Photograph © Yves Gellie/Odyssey Matrix, 1990) (B) Kindergartners from P.S. 75, New York City. (Photograph courtesy of Marian Johnson, 1994)

ment. The unique self is regarded as a thing of value in itself, for we prize self-expression, regardless of what is expressed (Sabini, 1995). In this regard, we are quite different from collectivists. Americans try to excel and are asked to "be the best that you can be." In contrast, collectivists like the Japanese try to become "so identified with their in-group that [their] individuality is not noticed." Where American children are urged to stand out, Japanese children are taught to "stand in" (Barlund, 1975; Weisz, Rothbaum, and Blackburn, 1984).

CULTURAL DIFFERENCES IN THE CONCEPT OF THE SELF

Some authors believe that differences among cultures indicate that our Western conception of the self and human personality has only limited application to cultures other than our own. In their view, many other cultures don't see the individual as we do—as ultimately separate and independent from the social framework in which she lives. They neither see nor value this socially abstracted personal independence but define the self through its interdependence with others (e.g., Markus and Kitayama, 1991, 1994). Richard Shweder and his collaborators have tried to demonstrate this difference by comparing the responses of Western and non-Western participants when asked to describe a close acquaintance. Americans were likely to use abstract trait terms, such as, "She is friendly." In contrast, participants in India were inclined to describe what a person does in a particular social context, as in "She brings cakes to my family on festival days," or "He has trouble giving to his family" (Shweder and Bourne, 1986).

Whether Shweder's findings really prove that different cultures have different conceptions of the self is debatable; the real difference may be in how the participants talk about people rather than in how they think about them (e.g., Sabini, 1995). A more persuasive argument comes from some detailed accounts of life on the Indonesian island of Bali, provided by the anthropologist Clifford Geertz. As Geertz describes it, Bali's culture (at least until about 1950 or so) is at one extreme end of the collectivism-individualism dimension and may well possess a different conception of selfhood (Geertz, 1983).

Consider people's names. In Bali, individuals have personal names (our equivalent of Henry or Lila), but they are rarely used. Instead, they have an elaborate system of other labels. One is a birth-order name (first-child, second-child, and so on) that parents and siblings use to address children and adolescents. Another is a complex naming system based on the name of one's first child (e.g., "Father

A

Individualism versus collectivism in art (A) After the middle ages, artists expressed their own individuality in their works, as in this self-portrait by Albrecht Dürer painted in 1499. (From Alte Pinakothek, Munich. Courtesy of Giraudon/Art Resource, New York) (B) In contrast, medieval painters, print makers, and architects saw themselves primarily as craftsmen who often dedicated themselves to some collective effort and were content to remain anonymous. Their lack of interest in individuality is illustrated in this French woodcut circa 1250, depicting the building of the biblical Tower of Babel, in which all workers look virtually alike. (From The Pierpont Morgan Library, New York; courtesy of The Pierpont Morgan Library/Art Resource, New York) (C) Great medieval cathedrals, like Notre Dame in Paris (shown here), are the result of just such collective efforts. (Photograph © John Heseltine/Corbis)

B

C

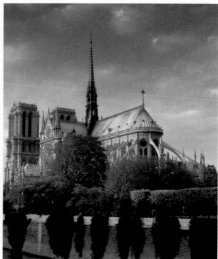

Westernization of non-Western cultures
Solar-powered television in Nigeria. (Photograph © John Chiasson, Liaison International)

of Henry"). When one's first grandchild is born, one's own name changes (e.g., "Grandfather of Ellen"). And if one lives until the first great-grandchild is born, one's name changes again (e.g., "Great-grandfather of Philip"). In addition, there is a complex system of status titles (e.g., high caste, middle caste, and so on) and social role indicators (e.g., elder of such and such a village). There is quite a difference between this and the American "Hi, I'm Joe."

This complex system of names and titles is part and parcel of a pattern of social life ruled by an elaborate system of ritual and etiquette that enters into every sphere of Balinese existence, whether familial, economic, political, or religious. Individuality is suppressed; all that matters is the proper outward form. To quote Geertz:

> . . . Anything idiosyncratic, anything characteristic of the individual merely because he is who he is physically, psychologically, or biographically is muted in favor of his assigned place in the continuing pageant that is Balinese life. . . . Physically men come and go, mere incidents in a happenstance history, of no genuine importance even to themselves. But the masks they wear, the stage they occupy, the parts they play . . . remain, and they comprise not the facade but the substance of things, not least the self. . . . (Geertz, 1983, p. 62)

This description of Balinese life is one of the best expositions of what some authors mean when they argue that modern psychology's notions of personality and the self are a Western invention that may not apply to cultures (or at least to all cultures) other than our own.

How does any of this bear on the various approaches to personality we discussed in this and the preceding chapter? It certainly reminds us that some aspects of these personality theories are bound up with our own individualist Western notions of what a person is. But that is to be expected. All of these theoretical approaches are efforts to understand what makes people different: Trait theory concentrates on differences in largely built-in characteristics, social learning theory focuses on differences in what people have learned, and psychodynamic theory looks at differences in unconscious motivations. The humanistic approach is even more Western in its emphasis, for its focus is on human uniqueness, which it both studies and exalts. It is clear that all of these approaches could only arise in a culture in which people are differentiated over and above their differences in age, gender, race, and religion. In Bali such differences are suppressed; in many other non-Western, collectivist societies they are muted. Under the circumstances, we may have to be cautious about supposing that what makes sense in the West makes sense everywhere.

In closing, let us suppose that the sociocultural critique is valid in all regards (and this is by no means undisputed, e.g., Sabini, 1995). If this were so, then our various personality theories would only make sense for people in Western societies, who believe that there is a separate and separable self to explain. While this would obviously limit their range of application, we shouldn't forget that this range is still very large indeed, encompassing perhaps a billion people. And for better or worse, probably for both, that number may well get larger as much of the world becomes progressively Westernized, watching U.S. television, listening to Western rock music, and wearing Western jeans. Even so, the sociocultural critique has provided a valuable corrective. It reminds us that we are not the only society in an ever-shrinking world and that others have different perspectives, a reminder that is all the more valuable as the United States becomes increasingly aware of its own multicultural nature.

TAKING STOCK

In this and the previous chapter, we considered a number of approaches to personality. One is the trait approach, in which personality is described by reference to a few basic characteristics, many of which have a built-in basis. Another is the behavioral approach, which focuses on the individual's outwardly observable acts and argues that these acts are produced by the situation that the individual faces now or has faced on previous occasions. Yet another is the psychodynamic approach, which centers on submerged feelings, unconscious conflicts, and desires. Still another is the humanistic approach, which asks how people achieve selfhood and realize their potential. And we concluded with a discussion of the sociocultural perspective, which suggests that certain conceptions of human individuality and the self may be a product of our Western culture and may not apply to cultures other than our own.

Today, there are relatively few theorists who would espouse any of these approaches in their most extreme form. By now most adherents of the behavioral approach have shifted to a more cognitive conception of personality, most psychodynamic theorists see unconscious defenses and conscious coping mechanisms as parts of a continuum, virtually everyone grants that what people do depends on both traits and situations, and many theorists recognize that there are both cultural differences and universals.

Even so, some important differences in approach clearly remain. This is probably fortunate. For these different theoretical orientations reflect different perspectives on the same subject matter, and each of these orientations has some utility. Some aspects of personality are clearly built in (trait theory); others are learned (social learning theory); some reflect buried conflicts (psychodynamic theory); others reveal the need for self-actualization (humanistic approach); and yet others may be limited to a particular cultural worldview (the sociocultural perspective). We cannot envisage what a complete theory of personality will look like, but it will surely have to describe all of these aspects of human functioning.

In this regard, the different perspectives on personality are again similar to different approaches to the presentation of character in literature or on the stage. Is the human drama best described by the use of a number of stock types, perhaps designated by a few well-chosen masks, or by well-rounded characters that are like themselves alone and no one else? The answer cannot be a simple yes or no, for people are both similar to and different from each other. Is character best described by classical authors, who stress human reason, or by the romantics, who emphasize feeling? Again there is no simple answer, for both emotion and rationality are part of human nature. Should actors portray the inner life and concentrate on what lies behind the mask, or should they focus on the mask, since that is what the audience sees? Here, too, there is no simple answer, for we all have both an inner and an outer life.

We are similar to others, but we are also different. We—especially those of us in individualist cultures—see ourselves as pulled by outer and inner forces, but we also share the conviction that we are free to make our own choices. We are rational, but we are also impelled by feeling. We are both the masks we wear and something else beneath. We are members of a particular culture, but we are also members of the human race. Each of the approaches to personality—and to dramatic character—focuses on one or another of these aspects of our nature. Each of these aspects exists. And to that extent each of these approaches is valid.

SUMMARY

1. The *psychodynamic approach* to personality is derived from Sigmund Freud's *psychoanalytic theory*. Freud asserted that all people experience *unconscious conflicts* originating in childhood. His theories grew out of studies of a *psychogenic* mental disorder then called *hysteria*. Freud proposed that hysterical symptoms are a means of keeping *repressed* thoughts or wishes unconscious. He believed that the symptoms would be eliminated once the repressed materials were recovered and devised a procedure, *psychoanalysis*, directed toward this end.

2. Freud distinguished three subsystems of the human personality. One is the *id*, a blind striving toward biological satisfaction that follows the *pleasure principle*. The second is the *ego*, a system of reactions that tries to reconcile id-derived needs with the actualities of the world, in accordance with the *reality principle*. A third is the *superego*, which represents the internalized rules of the parents and punishes deviations by feelings of guilt.

3. According to Freud, internal conflict is initially prompted by *anxiety*, which becomes associated with forbidden thoughts and wishes, usually in childhood. To ward off this anxiety, the child resorts to repression and pushes the forbidden materials out of consciousness. Repression is the initial, primary *defense mechanism* against anxiety. But the repressed materials generally surface again, together with their associated anxiety. To push these thoughts and wishes down again, further, supplementary defense mechanisms come into play, including *displacement, reaction formation, rationalization, projection,* and *isolation*.

4. Freud believed that most adult unconscious conflicts are ultimately sexual in nature and refer to events during childhood *psychosexual development*. According to Freud, the child passes through three main stages that are characterized by the *erogenous zones* through which gratification is obtained: *oral, anal,* and *phallic*. In Freud's view, differences in adult personality can be understood as residues of early *fixations* and *reaction formations* that occurred during psychosexual development. An example is the *oral character*, whose nature he believed goes back to a powerful oral fixation. Another example is the *anal character*, whose attributes include compulsive neatness, obstinacy, and stinginess.

5. According to Freud, during the phallic stage, the male child develops the *Oedipus complex*. He directs his sexual urges toward his mother, hates his father as a rival, and comes to dread him as he suffers increasing *castration anxiety*. He finally renounces his sexual urges, *identifies* with his father, and represses all relevant memories. At adolescence, repressed sexual urges surface, are redirected toward adult partners, and the person generally achieves *genital sexuality*. In female children, the *Electra complex* develops, with love toward the father and rivalry toward the mother.

6. Freud tried to apply his theory of unconscious conflict to many areas of everyday life, including slips of the tongue, memory lapses, and dreams. He believed that most dreams are at bottom *wish fulfillments*. Since many of these wishes prompt anxiety, their full expression is censored. The underlying *latent dream* is transformed into the *manifest dream* in which the forbidden urges emerge in a disguised, sometimes symbolic form. A similar approach led to the psychoanalytic interpretation of myths and literature that, in Freud's view, provide a glimpse into the hidden concerns shared by whole groups of people.

7. Some early critiques of Freudian theory came from within the psychoanalytic movement. Among the most influential of these were the *neo-Freudians*, who disputed many of Freud's theories about the nature and origins of unconscious conflict. In particular, they denied the notion of a universal Oedipus complex.

8. Attempts to find evidence for repression and unconscious conflict have not met with unqualified success. While dreams are often relevant to personal preoccupations and may feature symbolism, there is little evidence that they are disguised representations of hidden urges. Laboratory studies of repression suggest that when motivated forgetting occurs, it may be a special case of retrieval failure. There are clearly nonconscious mental activities, but they are not necessarily a defense against anxiety, nor do they have the sexual and aggressive quality that Freud attributed to them, prompting some critics to hypothesize a "kinder, gentler . . . unconscious."

9. Later psychodynamic theorists take a neo-Freudian orientation. In contrast to Freud, they generally focus on interpersonal rather than biological forces in the individual and are generally more interested in the individual's present situation than his childhood past. An example is Karen Horney, who studied the self-perpetuating vicious circles that characterized much psychological conflict. Some modern psychodynamic theorists have studied characteristic patterns of defense and coping in normal persons, which show considerable consistency over an individual's lifetime.

10. Another major orientation to personality is the *humanistic approach*, which maintains that what is most important about people is how they achieve their own selfhood and actualize their human potential. The humanistic approach emphasizes what it considers positive human motives, such as *self-actualization*, and positive personal events, such as *peak experiences*, rather than what it calls *deficiency needs*. According to Abraham Maslow, people only strive for higher-order needs when lower-order needs are satisfied.

11. A major concern of humanistic psychologists is the self. According to Carl Rogers and other humanistic psychologists, its development is essentially based on growth. In their view, given the appropriate conditions, people will grow so as to realize their potential, which is for good rather than evil. Rogers believed that children will only achieve a solid sense of personal self-worth if they have experienced a sense of *unconditional positive regard*. Some defects in a person's self can be healed later in life by providing the individual with important growth experiences she lacked before.

12. A number of authors have argued that much of modern personality theory is based on the study of middle-class western Europeans and North Americans and may not be applicable to cultures other than our own. The *sociocultural approach* is an attempt to provide a corrective. Testimony to the remarkable diversity of human beings has come from the work of *cultural anthropologists* like Ruth Benedict and Margaret Mead. Considerable diversity has been shown in characteristic personality patterns and in gender roles. But as *cross-cultural methods* demonstrate, there is also evidence for some sameness across cultures, including similar personality dimensions.

13. A number of investigators have tried to use the cross-cultural method as a tool to discover the effects of child rearing on adult personality. Evidence suggests that socioeconomic factors affect child-rearing styles in hunting and agricultural societies, and in different socioeconomic classes in our own culture.

14. According to many psychologists and anthropologists, an important psychological dimension along which different cultures can be classified is *collectivism-individualism*. In collectivist societies the emphasis is on the members' interdependence. In individualist societies, including our own, the focus is on the person's private aims and aspirations, and special value is placed on self-expression. Some authors interpret these and other differences as demonstrations that different cultures have different conceptions of the self.

CHAPTER 18

PSYCHOPATHOLOGY

I n the two preceding chapters, we considered normal variations in human personality. We now turn to conditions that are departures from normal functioning. The study of such conditions is the province of *psychopathology* or, as it sometimes is called, *abnormal psychology.* There is considerable debate about how psychopathology should be defined. Some observers believe that what we call "psychopathology" merely reflects everyday behavior that departs far from the norm in either frequency or intensity. In other words, it refers just to a question of statistical deviance. For example, most of us have occasionally heard someone talk to us or call our names, only to discover, when we turned around, that no one was there. In the statistical deviance view, hearing voices once a year might be normal, but hearing them three times a day might be diagnosable.

For other observers, the different kinds of psychopathology are qualitatively different from the norm. The symptoms aren't just more intense or more frequent versions of naturally occurring patterns. Instead, the symptoms are distinct from the normal patterns and thus represent true illnesses, like influenza or cancer. Of course, if we take this view, there are many questions we need to ask: Are these illnesses distinctly mental, with origins that are equally psychological? Or are they fundamentally physical illnesses, originating in the hardware of the brain but whose consequences are mental and behavioral?

As we shall see, there is no one answer to these questions. Nor can we say *in general* whether the symptoms of psychopathology represent a pattern qualitatively distinct from the norm, for the conditions that comprise psychopathology are a mixed lot. Some kinds of psychopathology do seem to reflect real illness, while for others, it is not so clear. In any case, there is little doubt that many of the conditions that come to the attention of the psychopathologist—the psychiatrist, clinical psychologist, social worker, or other mental health specialist— often cause considerable anguish and disability.

DIFFERENT CONCEPTIONS OF MADNESS

Mental disorders existed long before there were mental health professions. One of the earliest known medical documents, the Eber Papyrus (written about 1900 B.C.), refers to mental disorders such as depression (Andreasen and Black, 1996). The Greek hero, Ajax, slew a flock of sheep that he mistook for his enemies; King Saul of Judea alternated between bouts of homicidal frenzy and suicidal depression; and the Babylonian King Nebuchadnezzar walked on all fours in the belief that he was a wolf. Such phenomena were evidently not isolated instances. According to the Bible, young David feigned madness while seeking refuge from his enemies at the court of a Philistine king. This king had obviously encountered

An early example of mental disorder King Nebuchadnezzar as depicted by William Blake (1795). (Courtesy of the Tate Gallery, London)

psychopathology before and upbraided his servants, "Do I lack madmen, that you have brought this fellow to play the madman in my presence?"★

PSYCHOPATHOLOGY AS DEMONIC POSSESSION

What leads to mental disorder? One of the earliest theories held that the afflicted person was possessed by evil spirits. It followed that the cure for such a malady was to drive the devils out, and so one of the earliest approaches was merely to provide them with a physical escape route. According to some anthropologists, this may explain why Stone Age people sometimes cut large holes into their fellows' skulls; many such *trephined* skulls have been found, often with signs that the patient managed to survive the operation. Among some preliterate tribes this practice extended well into the twentieth century (Stewart, 1957; Figure 18.1).

Later treatment regimens attempted to calm the unruly demons by music, to chase them away with prayers or exorcisms, or even to purge them with emetics (potions that induce vomiting) or laxatives. An alternative was to make the evil spirit so uncomfortable in the patient's body that it would be induced to flee. Accordingly, patients were variously chained, starved, flogged, or immersed in icy or boiling water. It is hardly surprising that none of the treatments was particularly effective, and patients were often driven into worse and worse derangement. Excruciating as these treatments were, the patients who received them

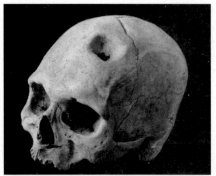

18.1 Trephining *A trephined prehistoric skull found in Peru. The patient apparently survived the operation for a while, for there is some evidence of bone healing. (Courtesy of The American Museum of Natural History)*

★ The terms *madness* and *insanity* are sometimes used colloquially to refer to severe cases of psychopathology. *Madness* is simply archaic and doesn't refer to any particular mental illness. The term *insanity*, however, is current, but it isn't a psychological term. It is a legal term, used to refer to a judgment by a court that one cannot be held responsible for one's actions. Of course, opinions of mental health specialists may contribute to the court's decision, and the defense of "not guilty by reason of insanity" is occasionally used when a criminal defendant was so disabled by mental illness at the time of a crime that the focus in any sentencing is on treatment rather than incarceration (Simon and Aaronson, 1988).

were nonetheless lucky compared to those who were summarily tortured and killed as demonic threats to society.

PSYCHOPATHOLOGY AS A DISEASE

This demonological theory of mental abnormality is largely a thing of the past. Even in its heyday, during the plague-ridden Middle Ages, there was an alternative view that such conditions were actually kinds of diseases (Allderidge, 1979; Neugebauer, 1979). Regrettably, this belief usually did not lead to more humane treatment of the afflicted. The diseased "madmen" were treated with little sympathy. They seemed to have no common bond with the rest of humanity and even less chance of developing one. They were considered nuisances at best and menaces at worst. In either case, the interests of society were deemed best served by "putting them away."

To this end, a number of special hospitals were established throughout Europe. Sadly, until the beginning of the nineteenth century (and in some cases, even later), most of these were hospitals in name only. Their real function was to confine all kinds of social undesirables and isolate them from the rest of humankind. Criminals, beggars, the elderly, epileptics, incurables of all sorts, were institutionalized and treated the same way as the mentally disturbed (Rosen, 1966). And the treatments were barbaric. One author described conditions in the major mental hospital for Parisian women at the end of the eighteenth century: "Madwomen seized by fits of violence are chained like dogs at their cell doors, and separated from keepers and visitors alike by a long corridor protected by an iron grille; through this grille is passed their food and the straw on which they sleep; by means of rakes, part of the filth that surrounds them is cleaned out" (Foucault, 1965, p. 72).

At the time, this treatment seemed only natural. After all, "madmen" were like dangerous animals and had to be caged. But since caged animals are interesting to watch, some of the hospitals took on another function—they became zoos. At London's Bethlehem hospital (known as "Bedlam," as it sounds when pronounced with a Cockney accent), the patients were exhibited to anyone curious enough to pay the required penny per visit. In 1814, there were 96,000 such visits (Figure 18.2).

18.2 The mentally disturbed on exhibit
*An eighteenth-century depiction of a tour of Bethlehem asylum. (*The Madhouse, *1735/1763, William Hogarth; courtesy of the Bettmann Archive)*

A number of reformers gradually succeeded in eliminating the worst of these practices. Historians have given much of the credit to the French physician, Philippe Pinel (1745–1826), who was put in charge of the Parisian hospital system in 1793 when the French Revolution was at its height. Pinel wanted to remove the inmates' chains and fetters (albeit treating inmates from upper-class families preferentially) and give them exercise and fresh air (Figure 18.3), but the government gave its permission only grudgingly. One official argued with Pinel, "Citizen, are you mad yourself that you want to unchain these animals?" (Zilboorg and Henry, 1941, p. 322). This concern about the prospect of the inmates running free is echoed even today; many people attach a severe stigma to mental illness and believe that mental hospitals are a good idea, just so long as neither the hospitals nor the patients come into their neighborhoods.

MENTAL DISORDER AS AN ORGANIC ILLNESS

Pinel and other reformers sounded one clear theme: "Madness" was a disease. This implied that inmates were patients needing treatment rather than animals deserving confinement. But if these patients had a disease (or, rather, diseases, since it was already known that there were several varieties of mental disorder), then what was the cause? Two hundred years after Pinel, we are still searching for the causes of most mental disorders.

At first, the notion of mental disorder as an illness suggested an organic or bodily cause, most likely from within the brain. Proponents of this **somatogenic** hypothesis (from the Greek *soma*, meaning "body") could point to the obvious effects of strokes in impairing speech (see Chapter 2), clear evidence that a disorder in the brain could impair psychological functioning. But the somatogenic position gained its greatest impetus at the end of the nineteenth century, thanks to the discovery of the cause of a once commonplace, severe, and debilitating disorder, **general paresis.** This disorder is characterized by a general decline in physical and psychological functions, culminating in a grossly disturbed gait and marked personality aberrations that may include childish delusions ("I am the King of England") or profound hypochondriacal depressions ("My heart has stopped beating"). Without treatment, the cognitive deterioration progresses, paralysis ensues, and death occurs within a few years (Dale, 1975).

18.3 Pinel ordering the removal of the inmates' fetters *(Copyright Stock Montage, Inc.)*

Mental disorder as seen by an artist   *This painting undoubtedly shows aspects of what Francisco Goya saw when he visited an insane asylum in Spain, but it may also have been affected by the then current views of the classification of mental disorder. Most early descriptions included the raving maniac (here the nude men wrestling in the center), the hopeless melancholic (the despairing figures on the left), and those with grotesque delusions (the men with crowns demanding allegiance from their subjects). (The Insane Asylum, c. 1810, Francisco Goya, Accademia S. Fernando, Madrid; courtesy of Art Resource)*

By the end of the nineteenth century, the conviction had grown that general paresis was a consequence of venereal disease—specifically, of syphilis contracted many years before any symptoms appeared. Experimental proof came in 1897 when the Viennese physician Richard von Krafft-Ebbing inoculated several paretic patients with matter taken from syphilitic sores. None of them developed any of the early symptoms of syphilis, a clear sign that they had contracted the disease previously.★ Once the cause of the disease was known, developing ways to prevent and cure it was just a matter of time. The preferred modern treatment is an antibiotic like penicillin, and such treatment is highly effective if the infection is caught early. While general paresis at one time accounted for more than 10 percent of all admissions to mental hospitals, by 1970, it accounted for less than 1 percent (Dale, 1975).

The discovery of the cause of general paresis was a triumph for the somatogenic view and led many clinicians to believe that all mental disorders would ultimately be shown to have a similar organic basis. Further support for this view came from studies of senility (a group of disorders now known as the *dementias*) in which there is atrophy of cortical cells and from studies of Korsakoff's syndrome, a disease primarily characterized by severe amnesia and resulting from the brain effects of a particular vitamin deficiency. (This dietary deficiency is particularly common in alcoholic individuals, who are often malnourished; for more on this syndrome, see Chapter 7.) Given these late-nineteenth-century discoveries, the question became not whether there was value to the somatogenic view, but whether it could account for *all* mental disorders.

MENTAL DISORDER AS A PSYCHOLOGICAL ILLNESS

The achievements of the somatogenic approach were impressive, but by the end of the nineteenth century it became clear that this approach could not explain the full spectrum of mental disorders. One such exception was then known as **hysteria,** which we already encountered in our discussion of psychoanalysis (see Chapter 17).

★ Modern medical and scientific practitioners are considerably more sensitive than our forebears to the ethical issues raised by this and similar studies. Today, such a procedure would require the patients' informed consent.

The study of hysteria (now called *conversion disorder*) was crucial in leading Freud to develop his theories about psychopathology. For now, we will only repeat the highlights. Patients with hysteria had odd complaints that seemed organic but did not conform to the clinical picture of organic disorders. For example, hysterics would appear with limbs that were "paralyzed." Under hypnosis, however, the patients could move their limbs perfectly well at the hypnotist's suggestion, indicating that the nerves and muscles were fully functional. It seemed logical, then, to suggest that hysteria was a *psychogenic* disorder, that is, a disorder whose origins were psychological rather than organic. But what were these psychological origins? A number of cases studied by French hypnotists of the nineteenth century appeared to originate in traumatic incidents. For example, one patient trapped underneath a derailed railroad car developed hysterical paralysis of his legs. His legs were actually in perfect physical condition, but his belief that they had been crushed ultimately produced his symptoms. Freud's theories borrowed this emphasis on trauma but elaborated on the mechanisms by which he thought the trauma led to the symptoms. For Freud, these mechanisms hinged on repressed wishes from early childhood that threatened to break into consciousness. The anxiety produced by these repressed wishes could only be restrained by drastic defensive maneuvers of which the disabling somatic symptom was one (see Chapter 17).

We will turn to the modern conception of conversion disorder later. For now, the important point is that by 1900, most theorists had become convinced that hysteria was psychogenic. In other words, there were illnesses that did not conform to a strictly somatogenic account.

EVALUATING THE SOMATOGENIC-PSYCHOGENIC DISTINCTION

The distinction between somatogenic and psychogenic disorders is sometimes criticized as artificial. As this argument goes, all behavior and mental activity are products of the nervous system. Thus, all mental diseases must have organic causes and so must ultimately be somatogenic. Labeling certain diseases "psychogenic" merely implies that we have not yet discovered their bodily causes.

Should we accept this logic and discard the distinction? The answer is no. Undoubtedly, all our psychological processes are based in the nervous system. But this doesn't imply that the best way to explain all psychological phenomena is by resort to neurophysiology. For example, consider two people who can speak and see but who are unable to read. One of the two has a brain lesion that produces a severe dyslexia (Chapter 2); the other can't read because he was never taught. One could of course maintain that both conditions are somatogenic. In one case, the organic basis (a brain lesion) is obvious. In the other case, certain brain pathways are missing because the person never learned to read. So while the organic account is useful in the former case, it adds nothing to the latter.

This is not just because our knowledge of the neurological basis of learning is limited. Even with perfect knowledge, explaining illiteracy by describing millions of synaptic connections that were never formed is altogether unwieldy. In addition, notice that the neurological account would, in this case, become a circular argument: Why can't the person read? Because he is missing certain synaptic paths. Which synaptic paths are missing? The ones needed for reading. Thus, the person can't read because he is missing the paths needed for reading—an explanation that is neither deep nor informative. Thus, it seems far better and simpler to say that the person can't read because he never learned.

The same arguments apply to the somatogenic-psychogenic distinction. Calling a disorder "somatogenic" is tantamount to claiming that we can most directly explain the malfunction organically, as with the syphilitic infection in general paresis. Likewise, terming a disorder "psychogenic" does not mean that it occurs independent of the nervous system; it just asserts that the disorder is explained most usefully at the psychological level—in terms of an individual's attitudes, beliefs, memories, expectations, and so on.

THE MODERN CONCEPTION OF MENTAL DISORDER

Whether they are considered somatogenic or psychogenic, there does seem to be a class of conditions we can classify as mental disorders—that is, departures from normal psychological functioning. These are called *mental* disorders, because their primary symptoms are psychological (Wakefield, 1992). But how can we meaningfully define *disorder*? One commonly accepted definition was provided by the American Psychiatric Association in its now standard manual for categorizing such conditions, the **Diagnostic and Statistical Manual for Mental Disorders** (now in its fourth revision and hence known as the **DSM-IV**). As the DSM-IV defines it:

> . . . Each of the mental disorders is conceptualized as a clinically significant behavioral or psychological syndrome or pattern that occurs in a person and that is associated with present distress (a painful symptom) or disability (impairment in one or more important areas of functioning) or with a significantly increased risk of suffering death, pain, disability, or an important loss of freedom. (American Psychiatric Association, 1994, p. xxi)

Notice that this definition makes no reference to normality or abnormality. To see why, consider the Black Death, which wiped out half of all Europeans in the fourteenth century (Zigler, 1991). At that time, having the plague may well have been statistically normal. But this did not change the plague's status as a disease. The same applies to behavior. Certain patterns of behavior may qualify as a mental disorder no matter how common they are.

In practice, however, mental disorder often involves aberrations in how people typically function in a given situation. The disordered person may hear voices, suffer from severe mood swings, or behave in ways that are clearly bizarre.

Psychopathology is not defined by statistical abnormality According to the underlying pathology model, deviation from some statistical norm does not define psychopathology. The Black Death killed half to three-quarters of the population of many European countries during the fourteenth century, but that did not make it any less pathological. (Triumph of Death by Pieter Bruegel the elder, Prado, Madrid; photograph courtesy of Scala/Art Resource)

Thus, deviation from a statistical norm is often found in psychopathology but does not define it.

Notice also that the DSM-IV definition makes no reference to *illness* or *disease*. Rather, mental *disorders* are those mental conditions that render one distressed, disabled, or at increased risk of harm, regardless of whether the condition is clearly a disease (for example, Alzheimer's dementia) or not (for example, a phobia about air travel).

THE UNDERLYING PATHOLOGY MODEL

Many mental health professionals believe that one can understand the various mental disorders using the traditional framework by which we understand most physical disorders, whether tuberculosis, diabetes, or whatever. According to this **underlying pathology model** of disease, various observable signs and symptoms are produced by some underlying cause—the pathology. The goal of the would-be healer, therefore, is to discover (and ultimately to remove) this underlying pathology. After this is done, the signs and symptoms will presumably disappear or at least not progress.

In its most general form, the underlying pathology model makes no initial assumptions about the nature of the pathology underlying a given mental disorder. Whether the pathology turns out to be somatogenic or psychogenic (or perhaps a little of both) is only discoverable through the appropriate research. Nonetheless, it is possible to describe some general subcategories of the underlying pathology model.

VARIATIONS ON THE PATHOLOGY MODEL

There are many approaches within the pathology model. Each amounts to a set of beliefs about how mental disorders should be classified, how they arise, and how they should be treated. As we will see, some of these approaches have been more useful than others, and even the more useful ones seem to apply only to some mental disorders and not to others.

THE BIOMEDICAL MODEL

Some authors endorse the **biomedical model.** This approach emphasizes somatogenic causes of mental disorders, and its practitioners therefore employ forms of therapy that treat the body directly, such as medication or surgery. In addition, this approach usually assumes that would-be healers should be medical doctors such as psychiatrists or neurosurgeons (Siegler and Osmond, 1974).

THE PSYCHODYNAMIC MODEL

Adherents of the **psychodynamic model** believe that mental disorders are the end products of internal psychological conflicts that generally originate in our childhood experiences. In this view, such conflicts hobble our full functioning in adulthood by causing us to distort how we view ourselves and relate to others.

Psychodynamic models come in many varieties. One example is the classical *psychoanalytic model* (Chapter 17), developed by Sigmund Freud and his colleagues, which emphasizes the role of the repression of early sexual and aggressive drives in producing psychopathology. The preferred treatment consists of psychotherapy based on psychoanalytic principles, which allows the patient to gain insight into his conflicts and then resolve them, thus removing the symptoms of the pathology at the roots (see Chapter 19).

Other psychodynamic views derive from Freud but attend more to early family relationships and how the conflicts present in these relationships get replayed in adulthood. Here, the treatment frequently involves a special focus on using the ongoing therapist-patient relationship as a learning lab for recognizing one's habitual (and historic) ways of relating to others and as a training ground for exploring new ones (for example, Luborsky, 1984; and see Grenyer and Luborsky, 1996).

THE LEARNING MODEL

The *learning model* views mental disorders as the result of maladaptive learning. According to some practitioners (usually called *behavior therapists*), these faulty learning patterns are best described using the laws of classical and instrumental conditioning (see Chapter 4). Treatment typically consists first of identifying the situations that elicit or reinforce the problematic responses and then of learning new responses to those situations (see Chapter 19).

A popular current variant on the learning model is the *cognitive-behavioral model,* which regards certain disorders as caused or perpetuated by faulty habits of thought, such as pessimistic or catastrophic thinking. Practitioners of this model, often called *cognitive therapists,* deal with disorders by helping the patient change the ways in which he thinks about himself, his situation, and his future (see Chapter 19).

CLASSIFYING MENTAL DISORDERS

Mental disorders differ. They differ in their manifestations, their severity, their duration, and their prognosis (their outlook for recovery). How should we think about these variations? Is there some way to classify the many forms of mental disorder? To answer these questions, practitioners have tried to set up classificatory schemes analogous to the diagnostic systems used in other branches of medicine. Here, as elsewhere in science, the purpose of the taxonomy is to bring some order into what at first seems a host of diverse phenomena. If the taxonomy is valid, then conditions that have been grouped together will turn out to have the same cause, the same prognosis, and better yet, the same treatment.

The great German psychiatrist Emil Kraepelin (1855–1925) began the practice of systematically diagnosing mental disorders in the same way as physical ones. In psychopathology, as in physical medicine, the diagnostic process begins with a *clinical interview* in which the practitioner asks the patient to describe her problems and concerns, and observes the patient throughout. The first consideration is the patient's set of complaints or *symptoms.* Patients who say, "I hear voices," "I feel nervous all the time," and "I feel hopeless" are providing symptoms. The practitioner then looks for any *signs* that might accompany these symptoms. If the same patients, respectively, turn toward a stapler as though it were speaking, shake visibly, and look teary eyed, these would be signs that parallel the patients' symptoms. Sometimes symptoms do not correspond to signs,

Emil Kraepelin *The major figure in psychiatric classification, Kraepelin distinguished between two groups of severe mental disorders, schizophrenia and manic-depressive psychosis (now called bipolar disorder). (Courtesy of Historical Pictures Service)*

and such discrepancies are also important. In some cases of conversion disorder, for example, a patient might state, "My head hurts so bad it's like a buzz saw running through my brain" but the patient seems to be quite calm and unconcerned while saying it.

In physical medicine, a single symptom like "I always feel tired" or a single sign like a low red blood cell count is rarely sufficient to reach a conclusion about what ails the patient, because feeling tired is a symptom of many disorders and a low red blood cell count is a sign of many others. However, the combination of multiple symptoms and multiple signs may narrow the choices considerably (to disorders like anemia, among others). The same holds for psychopathology, and so the mental health practitioner looks for a pattern of signs and symptoms that tend to go together. These patterns are called *syndromes.* An example is a pattern of signs like disorganized speech, altered gait, and subdued facial expressions, together with symptoms like restlessness, persecutory beliefs, and hallucinations. This syndrome is characteristic of one kind of schizophrenia.

The practitioner also attempts to obtain other information during the interview with the patient and, if possible or necessary, from family and friends. When did the problems start (the illness *onset*)? Has the patient's everyday functioning stayed the same, improved, worsened, or been irregular with good spells and bad spells (the *course* of the illness)? Has anything extraordinary happened recently in the person's life? Has the person been abusing drugs or alcohol? Does the patient have any other medical conditions that might exacerbate or mimic a mental disorder? The clinician will also observe the patient's grooming, mannerisms, speaking style and content, and overall mood, and may ask the patient to engage in brief tasks that assess attention, memory, perception, judgment, and insight. Psychological or neuropsychological testing (see Chapters 2 and 15) can be used to obtain supplementary information about the patient's personality traits or intellectual and cognitive functioning. Finally, laboratory tests such as MRI scans or blood tests can inform the practitioner about relevant aspects of a patient's physical well being—for example, whether the patient has suffered a stroke or taken a cognition-impairing drug (Andreasen and Black, 1996).

The full pattern of the patient's signs and symptoms, taken together with their onset and course, will usually allow the practitioner to render an opinion as to the specific disorder(s), and this opinion is called the patient's *diagnosis.* The diagnosis is not set in stone but serves as the practitioner's best judgment about the patient's current state. A proper diagnosis can imply the outlook for the patient, can suggest the most effective treatments, and can sometimes point to the cause (the disorder's *etiology*).

How many disorders are there? Until about twenty-five years ago, the majority of mental health specialists believed that most mental disorders could be subsumed under three broad supercategories. First were *organic brain syndromes,* such as the dementias or brain damage from chronic alcoholism. Second was *neurosis,* which referred to any disorder that was thought to be characterized by underlying conflict and anxiety. Examples of neuroses were the disorders now called phobias, panic disorder, obsessive-compulsive disorder, and the dissociative disorders. Neurotic patients might be severely distressed or handicapped by their symptoms, but they had not lost contact with reality. In contrast, the third supercategory, *psychosis,* referred to conditions such as schizophrenia and bipolar disorder (formerly called manic-depressive illness), which in their severe forms could render the patients' thoughts, moods, and deeds grossly disturbed and no longer in touch with reality (American Psychiatric Association, 1968).

In recent years, however, this classification scheme has changed considerably. The term *neurosis* is no longer widely used in psychiatric classification. A major reason was the change to more specific diagnoses based on clear, observable criteria, rather than on theory-based inferences about unseen psychological processes (such as "unconscious conflict"). The term *psychosis* is still used but only descriptively; it is applied now to any disorder so severe that the victim loses contact with reality. Terms that were once used in official diagnosis, such as *sociopathy, hysteria,* and *senility,* have been largely abandoned.

This emphasis on observable criteria is central to the DSM-IV. Both it and its immediate predecessors (DSM-III, 1980, and DSM-IIIR, 1987) departed from earlier diagnostic manuals in a number of ways. The most important was a greater stress on the description of disorders rather than on theories about their origin. As a result, many disorders that were traditionally grouped together because they were thought to result from similar psychological processes are now considered separate disorders, because their manifest signs and symptoms are different. An example is provided by the various conditions that were once considered subcategories of neurosis, such as phobias and obsessive-compulsive disorders (see pp. 792–93). Although some critics—mostly adherents of the psychodynamic view—believe that this splintering of the traditional categories is an unfortunate setback, a major consequence of these changes is the substantially increased diagnostic reliability of the new manual (Matarazzo, 1983; American Psychiatric Association, 1994).

An additional consequence of this breakdown of the traditional supercategories is the sheer number of disorders currently recognized. DSM-IV now lists and describes nearly 400 disorders in 17 categories, an enormous range that includes mental retardation, dementias such as Alzheimer's disease, schizophrenia, mood disorders such as bipolar disorder and depression, phobias, conversion disorders, sleep disorders, sexual disorders, and substance abuse, to mention only some of the most prominent.

EXPLAINING DISORDER: DIATHESIS, STRESS, AND PATHOLOGY

Clearly, understanding mental disorder as a kind of pathology requires more than a knowledge of the diagnostic process and all the possible categories. It is also important to know how mental disorders arise and how they can be treated. To understand how these questions might be approached, it is helpful to begin with a bodily illness, such as diabetes, and examine how it is approached and explained. We can then use this example as a basis for describing how mental illnesses might be approached.

In diabetes, the symptoms include fatigue, an increased frequency of urination with enormous thirst, and, in many cases, a voracious appetite. A frequent sign is a high sugar level in the urine. The next step is to look for the pathology underlying this syndrome. The most common kind of diabetes was discovered to be a disorder of carbohydrate metabolism in which the body cannot effectively use insulin produced by the pancreas (see Chapter 3). These pathological conditions represent the immediate or ***proximate*** cause of the syndrome. And in the case of diabetes, this knowledge of the proximate cause led to moderately effective treatments—controlled diet, exercise, and oral or injected insulin supplements (Dolger and Seeman, 1985). But a full understanding of diabetes requires a further step, an inquiry into its more remote or ***ultimate*** causes, those that led to the inefficient use of insulin in the first place.

It turns out that tracing the causal chain that leads to diabetes backward leads to two factors. One is a set of conditions that ***stress*** the body and cause the insulin mechanism to begin malfunctioning. Obesity is one such stressor; some of the infirmities that accompany normal aging can also be stressors. But not all obese or aged individuals become diabetic. These stressors precipitate diabetes

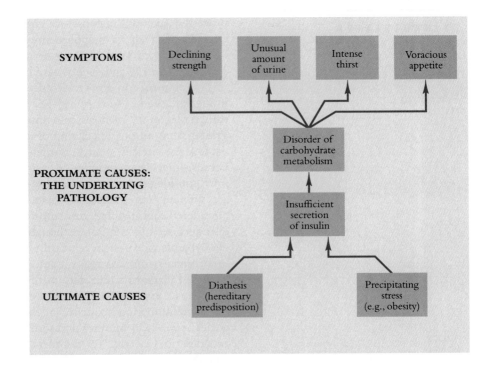

18.4   The pathology model as applied to diabetes

only if the individual has a predisposition (technically, a ***diathesis***) toward the illness. In diabetes, the diathesis is based largely on genetic factors that create a susceptibility to the disease. Other diseases have different sorts of diatheses, such as the mother's illness during pregnancy or the individual's poor nutrition in childhood, which can leave him vulnerable to a different set of stressors and to a different set of diseases. Neither the diathesis nor the stress by itself *causes* the disease. It's the combination of the predisposition plus the precipitating factors that triggers it.

This discussion illustrates the ***diathesis–stress model,*** which applies to many physical diseases and to many mental disorders as well. As with physical diseases, in psychopathology the nature of the diathesis depends on the particular disorder. In schizophrenia, as we'll see, a diathesis may be genetic (see pp. 775–77). For other disorders, it may lie in personal experience, as in acute and posttraumatic stress disorders, which germinate in extraordinary psychological trauma (see pp. 795–96).

Figure 18.4 diagrams our discussion of diabetes, a physical ailment with few direct psychological manifestations. The figure depicts how a disease can be analyzed when it is reasonably well understood. This is the framework we will use when we ask whether a particular mental disorder is an illness and if so, in what sense. The ways that such disorders are treated will be taken up in the next chapter.

SCHIZOPHRENIA

One of the most serious disorders in all of psychopathology is schizophrenia (from the Greek *schizo,* "split," and *phrene,* "mind"), which was first identified as a mental disorder by Kraepelin. The term *schizophrenia* itself was coined by the

Swiss psychiatrist Eugen Bleuler (1857–1939) to designate what he regarded as the main attribute of this disorder—an abnormal disintegration of mental functions (Bleuler, 1911).★

Schizophrenia is quite prevalent, being found worldwide in about 1 percent of humanity (Torrey, 1987). According to one estimate, between 1 and 2 percent of Americans will need treatment for this disorder at some period during their lifetimes, suggesting that in the United States up to 5 million people have schizophrenia (Black and Andreasen, 1994). At any one time, about 400,000 people are hospitalized with this condition. This accounts for about half of all of the beds in the country's mental hospitals (Babigian, 1975).

The diagnosis is usually made not at the first subtle signs of the disorder but much later, when the condition has become so severe that evaluation and diagnosis in a clinic or hospital is required (Babigian, 1975; Goldstein and Tsuang, 1990; Andreasen and Black, 1996). Men are usually diagnosed with schizophrenia in their early twenties, and women in their late twenties; the reasons for the age difference are uncertain (Black and Andreasen, 1994).

Many and perhaps most contemporary investigators believe that schizophrenia is straightforwardly somatogenic. They regard it as a brain disorder with no psychological cause. In short, both ultimate and proximate causes are physiological. Other investigators grant that the brain is affected in schizophrenia (the proximate cause), but they argue that the ultimate cause is to some degree psychological. To evaluate this question of etiology, we now take a close look at schizophrenia.

SIGNS AND SYMPTOMS

Sufferers of schizophrenia experience disruptions in all aspects of their lives, including their cognition, their motives and emotions, and their social relationships. But most patients who are diagnosed as schizophrenic do not exhibit all of these manifestations. Until fairly recently, this led to considerable disagreement in diagnosis, since different clinicians often disagreed about how many symptoms had to be present before the diagnosis of schizophrenia was warranted. This meant that a person diagnosed with schizophrenia by one clinician might well be diagnosed differently by someone else. This changed with the new, more specific criteria for diagnosis introduced by DSM-III and continued in DSM-IV, and now the diagnosis of schizophrenia is rather clear cut.

DISORDERS OF COGNITION

A key sign of schizophrenia is a pervasive thought disturbance. The person with schizophrenia doesn't "think straight"; she cannot maintain one coherent train of thought, but rather skips from one idea to the next. An example is a fragment of a letter written by one of Bleuler's patients:

> I am writing on paper. The pen I am using is from a factory called "Perry & Co." This factory is in England. I assume this. Behind the name of Perry Co., the city of London is inscribed; but not the city. The city of London is in England. I know this from my school-days. Then, I always liked geography. My last teacher in that subject was Professor August A. He was a man with black eyes. I also like black eyes. There

Eugen Bleuler *(Courtesy of National Library of Medicine)*

★ This etymological derivation is responsible for a widespread confusion between schizophrenia and multiple personality ("split personality") disorder, now called dissociative identity disorder. While both are varieties of psychopathology, the two conditions are wholly distinct.

Schizophrenia *The delusional world of some schizophrenia sufferers may resemble the bizarre images created by some surrealist artists. (Frederico Castellión,* The Dark Figure, *1938; courtesy of the Whitney Museum of American Art, New York; photograph by Geoffrey Clements, NY)*

are also blue and gray eyes and other sorts too. I have heard it said that snakes have green eyes. All people have eyes. There are some, too, who are blind. These blind people are led about by a boy. (Bleuler, 1911, p. 17)

This example shows that an individual with schizophrenia may have difficulty in suppressing irrelevant thoughts. Similar problems arise with irrelevant external stimuli. We have seen that in ordinary perception one focuses on some aspects of the world while de-emphasizing others, such as when we pay attention to just our partner's voice in a crowded restaurant (see Chapter 6). But schizophrenia seems to cripple its sufferers on this basic task. They hear (and see and feel) too much, perhaps because they can't exclude what is extraneous (McGhie and Chapman, 1961).

LOSS OF PERSONAL CONTACT

Another common feature of schizophrenia is a withdrawal from other people. In some patients this withdrawal begins quite early, with a history of few friends and little or no adolescent sexual experience. What accounts for this withdrawal is unclear. It may simply be a consequence of the difficulty in filtering out what is irrelevant, so that the individual withdraws to shield himself from overstimulation. Alternatively, the withdrawal may reflect a reduced ability to follow the complex rules that govern everyday social interaction.

Whatever led to it, the schizophrenic's social withdrawal has drastic consequences. The individual starts to develop an inner world that becomes more and more private and less and less in contact with the social world. The withdrawal from others provides fewer opportunities for the *social reality testing* through which one's ideas are validated against those of others. As a result, the schizophrenic's thoughts become ever more idiosyncratic, until the patient may have trouble communicating with others even if she wants to. Others may rebuff her because they can't understand her and think she's "weird." The result is a vicious cycle of rebuffs leading to further withdrawal and still further idiosyncrasy, until the patient can no longer distinguish between her own thoughts and fantasies and the reality shared by all those around her. She has lost touch with the world.

A

B

Paintings by sufferers of schizophrenia
Paintings by schizophrenia sufferers often have an odd, eerie quality. In many cases, the usual artistic conventions are disregarded, and the pictures include written comments, digits, and other idiosyncratic material. (A) Saint-Adolf-Grand-Grand-God-Father (1915), a painting by Adolf W., who was institutionalized in early adulthood and elaborated a fantastic autobiography that featured himself as Saint Adolf II, a young god who travels through space and has many adventures. (B) Guardian Angels by Else B., an institutionalized schizophrenic. In all her works, the legs of angels are painted as though they had fused at the top, to make sure that "nothing happens there." (Prinzhorn, 1972; courtesy of Galerie Rothe Heidelberg)

ELABORATING THE PRIVATE WORLD

In our previous discussion of personality (Chapters 16 and 17), we considered just how much we seek consistency in others and in the world. This is no less true for the sufferer of schizophrenia, who tries to make sense of a world that is increasingly sealed off from the outside. Bleuler believed that this drive for consistency led to what he called **restitutional symptoms,** which include elaborate, and often eccentric, false beliefs (**delusions**) and hearing voices that are not there (**hallucinations**).

Delusions Once having initiated the break with the social world, many schizophrenics develop **ideas of reference.** They begin to believe that external events are somehow specially related to *them*. The patient observes some strangers talking and concludes that they are talking about him; he sees people walk by and decides that they are following him; he sees a television commercial and is sure that it contains a secret message aimed at him. Eventually, he may weave these false ideas, or delusions, into an entire **delusional system** in which he may believe, for example, that agents of the government are talking about him, following him everywhere, and have taken over the media to spread secrets about him. Such delusions are especially common in a subcategory called **paranoid schizophrenia.**

A common symptom of paranoid schizophrenia is a **delusion of persecution.** The patient is sure that "they"—the Martian invaders or the FBI or the members of the American Medical Association or whoever—are actively spying on and plotting against her. This delusion gradually expands as the patient gathers further evidence that convinces her that her family, her ward psychiatrist, and the woman in the bed near the door are all part of the conspiracy.

Hallucinations Delusions are beliefs that result from the misinterpretation of real events. In contrast, **hallucinations** are perceptions that occur in the absence of actual sensory stimulation. These phenomena are fairly common in schizophrenia. Usually they are **auditory hallucinations** in which the patient "hears" voices—of God, the devil, relatives, or neighbors. If the patient can make out what the voices are saying, he will report that they are talking about him, shouting obscenities at him, threatening him, telling him what to do, or making accusations about him.

Some authors believe that such hallucinations reflect an inability to distinguish between experiences that originate from within and those that originate from without—that is, between memories or fantasies on the one hand and actual perceptions on the other. In some auditory hallucinations, for example, the patients may believe they are hearing voices when they are actually just hearing themselves talk (McGuigan, 1966; Green and Preston, 1981).

DISORDERS OF MOTIVATION AND EMOTION

When we examine the schizophrenic individual's motives and feelings, we find similar evidence of disruption and fragmentation. In the early phase of the disorder, there is often a marked emotional overreactivity in which the slightest rejection may trigger an extreme response. Eventually, this sensitivity declines, often too much, to the point that the individual shows virtual indifference to her own fate or that of others. This lack of reactivity is especially pronounced in many long-term schizophrenics, who stare vacantly, their faces expressionless, and answer questions in a flat monotone voice.

18.5 Patient with a diagnosis of catatonic schizophrenia *The patient spent virtually all waking hours in this crouched position.* *(Photograph by Bill Bridges/ Globe Photos)*

In some patients, however, emotional reaction is preserved but the emotion is strikingly inappropriate to the situation. A patient may break into giddy laughter at the news of a brother's death "because she was so pleased at receiving letters with black borders"; another becomes enraged when someone says hello (Bleuler, 1911).

DISORDERS OF BEHAVIOR

Given the disruptions in the schizophrenics' thoughts, motives, and feelings, it is hardly surprising that there is often disruption in normal movements and actions. Some patients—in a subtype of schizophrenia called *catatonic schizophrenia*—exhibit very unusual motor reactions. They can become stuporous, remaining virtually motionless for long periods of time. They may stand or sit "frozen" in some unusual posture and can maintain this position for hours on end (Figure 18.5). Then, with no notice, they can become frenzied, running haphazardly, shouting nonsensically, and acting violently.

In another subtype, *disorganized schizophrenia* (formerly, *hebephrenia*), thought, emotion, and behavior become chaotic. The predominant symptoms are incoherence of speech and marked inappropriateness of behavior and emotion. In many ways, the disorganized schizophrenic is the closest match to the popular stereotype of madness. His speech is often bizarre and babbling, and while he is talking, he giggles, makes silly smiles or odd grimaces, assumes odd postures, and may have sudden fits of laughing and crying. Such patients often deteriorate profoundly, lose all concern over personal appearance, and ignore the most elementary rules of social conduct.

THE SEARCH FOR THE UNDERLYING PATHOLOGY

We have described the various manifestations that define schizophrenia. As with any other disease, the next step is to investigate whether one underlying pathology can explain all of these signs and symptoms. And if a somatogenic disorder is suspected, the search begins for an organic pathology that might produce the disorder.

IS THERE A CENTRAL PSYCHOLOGICAL MALFUNCTION?

One view is that the central malfunction in schizophrenia is psychological. The details of the proposed explanations vary, but most proponents agree that the major deficit of schizophrenic patients is cognitive—an inability to keep their thoughts and actions on track. Normal people perceive other persons, objects, and events without being distracted by extraneous stimuli; they execute plans without interference from irrelevant responses. Not so most schizophrenics, who have considerable difficulty in holding onto one line of thought or action and are forever being lured off the main path (Chapman and Chapman, 1973; Patterson et al., 1986). Certainly this idea of a central cognitive deficit has some appeal, but it presents problems. A major one, which we will discuss in detail later, is that patients with various types of schizophrenia differ so profoundly in their signs and symptoms—some being garrulous and paranoid, others being inactive, "vacant," and mute—that one psychological mechanism seems hard put to account for them all.

By now, most investigators believe that the signs and symptoms of schizophrenia are expressions of a somatogenic pathology. Some have proposed that the cause is a biochemical disorder in certain neurotransmitter systems in the brain; others focus on structural abnormalities in the brains of those who suffer from schizophrenia (Meltzer, 1987).

Malfunctioning neurotransmitters Some investigators believe that the proximate organic pathology underlying schizophrenia involves some malfunction in one or more neurotransmitter systems in the brain. As we discussed in Chapter 2, neurons communicate with one another mainly via chemical secretions called *neurotransmitters.* According to the **dopamine hypothesis,** the proximate organic cause of schizophrenia is an abnormally high level of activity in certain brain circuits sensitive to the neurotransmitter dopamine. The increased activity may result from any of several mechanisms, including an overabundance of dopamine itself, an overabundance or oversensitivity of dopamine receptors, or the abnormal facilitation of dopamine transmission by other transmitters (Van Kammen and Kelley, 1991).

One strong line of evidence for the dopamine hypothesis comes from the effects of a number of medications known as **classical antipsychotics** (sometimes called *major tranquilizers* or *neuroleptics*). Among the most commonly used today are Thorazine and Haldol. These drugs are known to block receptors for dopamine (Figure 18.6). Some kinds of antipsychotics are more effective than others in producing this blockade and, as predicted by the dopamine hypothesis, the stronger the blockade, the more therapeutic the drug (Snyder, 1976).

If a decrease in dopamine activity makes schizophrenics better, an increase should presumably make them worse. This is indeed the case. One group of investigators took patients with schizophrenia who were in a comparatively mild state and injected them with small doses of a drug that temporarily increases dopamine activity. Within a minute, the patients' symptoms became florid. One patient began shredding a pad of paper, announcing that he had been sending and receiving messages from ancient Egypt. Others became catatonic (Davis, 1974). Fortunately, these effects were short-lived, confirming the hypothesis but with no lasting impact on the patients.

Related effects are seen in nonschizophrenic subjects who take overdoses of amphetamines. These are stimulants whose effects include the enhancement of dopamine activity. When taken often enough and in large enough doses, these drugs produce a temporary **amphetamine psychosis** that is in many ways quite similar to paranoid schizophrenia (Angrist et al., 1974). As the dopamine hypothesis would predict, those medications that block dopamine activity at the synapse also reduce the psychotic symptoms that follow chronic amphetamine abuse.

Why should a hyperactive dopamine system produce some of the manifestations of schizophrenia? One possibility is that it leads, in essence, to chronic overstimulation of the brain. When dopamine-releasing neurons in an animal's brain are destroyed, the animal ignores sensory stimuli (Ungerstedt and Ljungberg, 1974). Perhaps the opposite—a diminished ability to ignore—is produced when dopamine tracts are hyperactive. This may cause an inability to shut out sensory messages from the outside or irrelevant thoughts from the inside, leading to that jangling, screeching cognitive overload that some schizophrenics describe in retrospective accounts of their condition.

The dopamine hypothesis has much to recommend it, but in recent years a revision of this theory has been spurred by the development of new **atypical antipsychotics,** such as Clozaril, Risperdal, and Zyprexa (see Chapter 19). In

18.6 *The dopamine-blockade hypothesis of classical antipsychotic action*

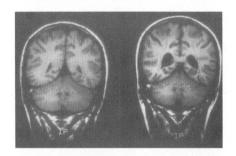

MRI scans of the brains of twins *MRI scans of the brains of two twenty-eight-year-old identical twins. One (right) is hospitalized for schizophrenia; the other (left) is well. The schizophrenic twin has enlarged cerebral ventricles. The fact that just one twin has schizophrenia shows that heredity is not the only factor in producing this disorder; the slightly different prenatal environments of the two twins, as well as birth complications, may be involved. (Courtesy of Drs. E. Fuller Torrey and Daniel R. Weinberger, NIMH Neuroscience Center, Washington, D.C.)*

contrast to classical antipsychotics, these appear to operate by blocking receptors for both dopamine *and* serotonin (though some argue that their greater effectiveness is produced by a selective effect on some group of dopamine receptors). The fact that they work better than the older medications for many patients (especially those with negative symptoms, who are not helped by the classical antipsychotics—see below) seems to imply that schizophrenia, as well as the antipsychotic effects of the atypical antipsychotics—may be best explained not by a simple dopamine hypothesis, but by a ***dopamine–serotonin interaction hypothesis*** (Kapur and Remington, 1996; Megens and Kennis, 1996).

Structural defects   In addition to these physiological accounts of schizophrenia, other researchers have suggested that some schizophrenics may suffer from structural abnormalities in their brains. This suggestion has recently been confirmed by magnetic resonance imaging (MRI; see Chapter 2), which shows that a certain proportion of schizophrenics—males, especially—suffer an enlargement of the ventricles, the fluid-filled cavities in the brain. The ventricles enlarge because, simply put, there is not enough brain to fill the skull. This indicates that in many cases of schizophrenia, there is either a dramatic loss of brain tissue or a deficiency that existed from the start (Andreasen et al., 1986; Meltzer, 1987; Chua and McKenna, 1995; Nopoulos, Flaum, and Andreasen, 1997).

Other structural abnormalities have been reported in other areas of the brain, including parts of the basal ganglia and cerebellum (Heckers, 1997; Jacobsen et al., 1997). But the most persuasive findings involve the frontal and temporal lobes (Black and Andreasen, 1994; Martin and Albers, 1995). When these areas are dissected and examined during autopsy, schizophrenic individuals show various irregularities, for example, cell derangement and missing or abnormally sized neurons. These neuronal defects would obviously affect brain function, and indeed, PET and functional MRI scans of brain metabolism, as well as cerebral blood-flow studies, suggest atypical patterns of functioning in schizophrenics in just these areas (Bloom, 1993; Chua and McKenna, 1995; Carter et al., 1997; Woodruff et al., 1997).

Multiple-syndrome hypotheses   Both the malfunctioning-neurotransmitter and the structural-defect hypotheses face a problem: Each fits some cases of schizophrenia but not all. For example, many schizophrenic patients respond to neurotransmitter-blocking medications, but a number do not. Likewise, a significant number of schizophrenics show signs of cerebral atrophy, but many do not. Investigators have therefore wondered whether "schizophrenia" might better be considered a group of heterogeneous disorders rather than just one. An influential early hypothesis by British psychiatrist Timothy Crow proposed two separate schizophrenia syndromes (Crow, 1982, 1985). Crow's hypothesis began with the distinction between positive and negative symptoms. ***Positive symptoms*** are those that involve what the patients do (and see and think) that normals don't; these include hallucinations, delusions, and bizarre behaviors. In contrast, ***negative symptoms*** are those that involve a lack of normal functioning, such as apathy, poverty of speech, emotional blunting, and the inability to experience pleasure or be sociable.

According to Crow's hypothesis, schizophrenia is really a composite of two underlying pathologies, which he named Type I and Type II. Crow proposed that Type I schizophrenia was caused by a neurotransmitter malfunction (especially dopamine) and produces the positive symptoms. Type II, he suggested, was produced by cerebral damage and atrophy and leads to the negative symptoms. Support for this view comes from the fact that, by and large, patients with mostly positive symptoms tend to respond well to standard antipsychotic medications and show no cerebral damage. The reverse holds for patients with negative symptoms, who are generally not improved by treatment with standard antipsychotics and are more likely to show signs of cerebral damage (Crow, 1980, 1985).

But Crow's hypothesis may not have gone far enough. More recent studies suggest that schizophrenia is best described by three syndromes, not just two. Although Crow's basic positive-negative distinction still holds, there also seems to be a distinction between cases of schizophrenia based on the *kinds* of positive symptoms they show. For example, some schizophrenics show predominantly psychotic symptoms (delusions and hallucinations, typically), whereas others are less psychotic but show more signs of disorganization (inappropriate emotions, incoherent speech, or bizarre behavior).

Distinguishing three syndromes (negative, psychotic, and disorganized) may also help us understand the progress of the illness. Thus, negative symptoms, when they occur, tend to endure, whereas psychotic symptoms tend to decline over time, and disorganized symptoms tend to fluctuate and may even increase over the course of the illness (Andreasen et al., 1995; Arndt et al., 1995; Lieberman, 1995).

Despite some intriguing evidence, these various hypotheses about the underlying organic pathology of schizophrenia are still just hypotheses. All face a number of difficulties. We've already mentioned that the atypical antipsychotics pose a problem for the simple dopamine hypothesis. An additional problem with the dopamine and dopamine-serotonin hypotheses is that, while the antipsychotics block dopamine receptors within a few hours, the onset of therapeutic effects can take weeks (Davis, 1978). Multiple-syndrome hypotheses also have their shortcomings. For one, the negative symptoms do not map onto structural brain damage as clearly as these hypotheses would predict. Another problem concerns the relationships among the syndromes: Do they represent distinct diseases, different degrees of severity of a single disease, or varying sites of brain dysfunction (Andreasen, 1985; Andreasen et al., 1989; Cannon, Mednick, and Parnas, 1990; Zorilla and Cannon, 1995)? As yet, we don't know. But whatever the final verdict, it is very likely that our eventual understanding of schizophrenia will include some reference both to biochemical malfunctions and anatomical abnormality.

ULTIMATE CAUSES OF SCHIZOPHRENIA

We have considered several analyses of the basic pathology in schizophrenia, including hypotheses about an underlying psychological malfunction and some findings that suggest organic defects. These are hypotheses about the proximate causes of the disorder. But what causes these psychological, physiological, or anatomical deficits? This is the question of more ultimate causes. As we saw in our discussion of diabetes, we must consider both the proximate causes (in diabetes, a metabolic malfunction brought on by inefficiency in insulin usage) and the more ultimate ones (genetic factors, environmental effects) if we are to understand a disorder fully. We will follow the same approach in our discussion of schizophrenia.

HEREDITY

First, let us consider the diathesis for this disease. Many researchers believe that it is a hereditary predisposition. To study this issue researchers have used the same means as those used to assess the role of heredity in other human traits, such as intelligence (Chapter 15). They start with family history. For example, the

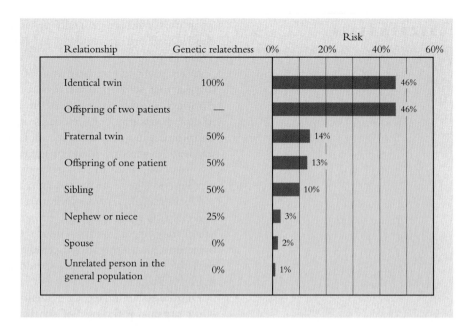

Relationship	Genetic relatedness	Risk
Identical twin	100%	46%
Offspring of two patients	—	46%
Fraternal twin	50%	14%
Offspring of one patient	50%	13%
Sibling	50%	10%
Nephew or niece	25%	3%
Spouse	0%	2%
Unrelated person in the general population	0%	1%

18.7 Genetic factors in schizophrenia
Risk estimates for schizophrenia as a function of relationship to a schizophrenic patient. (From Nicol and Gottesman, 1983)

likelihood that a person who has a schizophrenic sibling is schizophrenic herself or will eventually become so is considerable—about 8 percent, four times greater than the 1 to 2 percent lifetime risk of schizophrenia in the general population (Rosenthal, 1970; Andreasen and Black, 1996).

But as with intelligence, family histories aren't decisive on the nature-nurture issue. (After all, this increased risk among siblings might reflect some factor in the home or family environment.) Better evidence requires techniques that disentangle the contributions of heredity and environment, and often this evidence comes from studies of twins and adopted children. It turns out that if one of a set of twins is schizophrenic, then the other twin is much more likely to be schizophrenic as well. The probability of this event, technically called **concordance,** is 55 percent if the twins are identical, compared to 9 percent if they are fraternal (Gottesman and Shields, 1972, 1982; Gottesman, McGuffin, and Farmer, 1987; Tsuang, Gilbertson, and Faraone, 1991; see Figure 18.7).

Separate evidence comes from adoption studies. Consider a child who is born to a schizophrenic mother but placed in a foster home (with nonschizophrenic foster parents) within a week or so after birth. The odds are about 8 percent that this child will become schizophrenic, the same percentage as for children who remain with the schizophrenic biological parent (Kety, 1983; Kendler and Gruenberg, 1984; Tsuang et al., 1991).

These findings suggest a genetic basis for schizophrenia—or at least a genetic basis for some *vulnerability* to schizophrenia. Some investigators believe that these findings actually indicate that schizophrenia is a **neurodevelopmental disorder** (Waddington et al., 1991). According to this theory, pathological genes produce abnormalities in the brain during fetal development. These abnormalities, in turn, lead to behavioral and cognitive eccentricities that may be the early indicators of schizophrenia. One line of evidence for this view comes from the fact that many cases of schizophrenia *do* show preludes in childhood. Affected children are less active and "cuddly," and show delayed motor behavior; by adolescence, they have a host of subtle cognitive and perceptual deficits (Marcus et al., 1993). Additionally, children who will later develop the negative symptoms of schizophrenia also tend to seek isolation and be passive and socially unresponsive, whereas those who will later develop the positive symptoms tend to be irritable, distractible, and aggressive (Parnas and Jorgensen, 1989; Cannon, Mednick, and Parnas, 1990).

PRENATAL ENVIRONMENT

But a hereditary diathesis cannot tell the whole story, as studies of identical twins show. The concordance for schizophrenia among identical twins is considerable but is much less than 100 percent. Since identical twins have the same genotype, there must be some nongenetic factors that also have a say in determining who becomes schizophrenic and who does not. What are these nongenetic factors?

In recent years, considerable attention has focused on environmental stressors—in the uterus and during delivery—as playing a large role in the development of schizophrenia. It may well be that these prenatal factors are the most important triggers by which the predisposition for schizophrenia progresses to the full-blown disorder.

One important line of evidence comes from obstetric reports on the effects of various complications during pregnancy and birth. Such complications evidently increase the likelihood that a genetic predisposition will eventually be expressed as schizophrenia (Cannon, 1991; Zorilla and Cannon, 1995). Other evidence implicates an infectious agent in some cases of schizophrenia. The influenza virus has attracted special attention based on the finding that when mothers are in the second trimester of pregnancy during influenza epidemics, the children are somewhat more likely to develop schizophrenia (Adams et al., 1993; Mednick, Huttunen, and Macho'n, 1994; Sham et al., 1992).

All of this points to the possibility of a happy conclusion, because in the last few decades, better maternal care, more widespread flu vaccinations, and better delivery procedures have resulted in fewer such risks. The expected (and hopeful) result might be fewer cases of schizophrenia. There indeed is some evidence that the incidence of schizophrenia is on the decline, but it is too soon to be certain (Warner, 1995).

SOCIAL AND PSYCHOLOGICAL ENVIRONMENT

What about stressors later in life? Can these precipitate schizophrenic reactions? Some investigators suggested that psychological stressors might bring out the latent pathology if the person was genetically predisposed. The stronger the predisposition, the less stress would be required to precipitate the full-blown disorder (Meehl, 1962; Gottesman and Shields, 1982). What sources of psychological stress were held responsible? The usual culprits were social class and family of origin.

Social class Early on, epidemiological studies of schizophrenia revealed an undeniable fact. Compared to an individual at the top of the socioeconomic hierarchy, one at the bottom is far more likely to be schizophrenic—nine times as likely, according to one study (Hollingshead and Redlich, 1958). The same point can be made geographically, since the prevalence of schizophrenia is highest in the poorest and most dilapidated areas, and diminishes as one progresses toward higher-income regions (Figure 18.8; and Kohn, 1968). The original interpretation of these findings was that poverty, inferior status, and low occupational rank lead to increased psychological stress, which led vulnerable individuals to become schizophrenic. But most researchers now favor an alternative view, that of **downward drift,** which holds simply that schizophrenics fall to the bottom of the socioeconomic ladder because they cannot hold down a job or sustain a personal relationship.

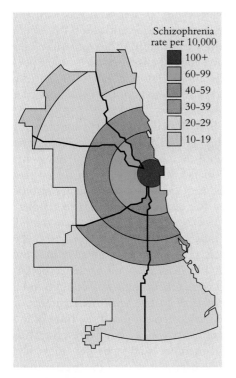

Schizophrenia
rate per 10,000

- 100+
- 60–99
- 40–59
- 30–39
- 20–29
- 10–19

18.8 The prevalence of schizophrenia in different regions of a city *A map of Chicago (1922–1934) represented by a series of concentric zones. The center zone is the business and amusement area, which is without residents except for some transients and vagabonds. Surrounding this center is a slum region inhabited largely by unskilled laborers. Further out are more stable regions: a zone largely populated by skilled workers, followed by zones of middle- and upper-middle-class apartment dwellers, and, furthest out, the upper-middle-class commuters. The map shows clearly that the incidence of schizophrenia increases the closer one gets to the city's center. (After Faris and Dunham, 1939)*

Family environment Some psychodynamically oriented investigators have looked to the personality of the schizophrenic's parents as a precipitating stressor. Schizophrenics' mothers, they argued, were rejecting, cold, dominating, and prudish, while their fathers were detached, humorless, weak, and passive (Arieti, 1959). But even if schizophrenics have less benign family backgrounds than do nonschizophrenics, this is far from proof that the family environment caused or triggered the patient's disorder. As an alternative, it is possible that the family pattern is a *consequence* of the disorder, rather than a cause. Having a family member who suffers from schizophrenia can be tragic for the family. Parents often blame themselves and each other for their disturbed child—and their guilty agony may be redoubled if their therapist is psychogenically inclined and believes the parents *did* precipitate the schizophrenia. Such parents also become frustrated and despondent in their attempts to reach their child (Torrey, 1983).

In one study, investigators observed mothers who had both a schizophrenic and a healthy daughter (Mishler and Waxler, 1968). When observed with the schizophrenic daughter, the mothers seemed unresponsive and aloof. But when observed with the healthy daughter, the mothers behaved more normally. This suggests that their unresponsiveness was not a general characteristic of their personality (and thus perhaps a cause of their child's disorder) but was instead a reaction to the schizophrenic daughter (and thus an effect of the child's disorder upon the mother's behavior).

In addition, schizophrenic children may have difficult parents for another reason: Given the linkage between schizophrenia and genetics, a schizophrenic child is likely to have at least one parent with the same pathological genes that eventuated in schizophrenia in the child. In fact, there is some evidence that even the nonschizophrenic parents and siblings of schizophrenics manifest biological markers for the propensity (Reveley, Reveley, and Clifford, 1982; Holtzman et al., 1988; Tsuang et al., 1991).

Thus, there is no compelling evidence that poor familial relations cause the patient's illness. But the family context surely does matter considerably for how well the schizophrenic person copes with the disorder. The evidence comes from studies of schizophrenic patients who were functioning well enough to be discharged from the hospital and who went back to live with their parents or spouses. These family members had been interviewed earlier, at the time of the patient's initial breakdown, to assess the extent to which they were critical or hostile toward the schizophrenic family member and whether they had expressed these sentiments to the patient. The data showed that the greater these **expressed emotions,** the more likely the patient was to relapse with sufficient severity to warrant readmission to the mental hospital (Hooley, 1985). On reflection, this is hardly surprising. Such reactions by family members are unlikely to ease the patient's adjustment to his illness, and make the hospital look inviting by comparison.

But one encouraging study indicates that such families can change. When family members participated in a program that taught them about schizophrenia and gave them the chance to talk about their own problems, they tended to become less negative toward their schizophrenic member. The result was a lower rate of readmission to the hospital compared to patients whose families did not participate (Leff et al., 1982).

The studies of social class and family environment discussed above were both used to support—at least in part—a psychogenic model of schizophrenia. But in both cases, it now appears that the causal arrow should be reversed. Low socioeconomic status and disturbed family environment have at most a small role in causing schizophrenia, but they are frequently consequences for those afflicted with it.

THE PATHOLOGY MODEL AND SCHIZOPHRENIA

We have considered schizophrenia under the same headings that we used to analyze physical illnesses—the pattern of signs and symptoms, the underlying pathology, the role of ultimate causes such as genetic predisposition and precipitating stressors. What can we conclude? To guide our evaluation, the main factors pertinent to schizophrenia can be diagrammed in a way that is analogous to the way we analyzed diabetes (Figure 18.9).

The schizophrenic syndrome can be understood as the manifestation of a psychological deficit, perhaps a defect in the ability to maintain consistency in one's current thoughts and actions. This psychological malfunction derives from an organic pathology whose exact nature is uncertain but probably involves two sources: a biochemical defect, most likely involving some critical neurotransmitter systems, and anomalous or deficient brain tissue, characterized by cellular derangement or progressive atrophy. One of the more ultimate causes of the disorder is a hereditary diathesis. Another may be a set of environmental stresses, such as problems during pregnancy and delivery, that trigger the pathological process in those with the initial diathesis.

What is the outlook for schizophrenic patients? Although the incidence of the disease may be declining, for those afflicted the prospects are not encouraging. One study tracked down two hundred people who had been diagnosed with schizophrenia some thirty years previously. Of these patients, 20 percent were doing well at the time of this thirty-year follow-up, while 45 percent were incapacitated. Sixty-seven percent had never married, and 58 percent had never worked (Cutting, 1986; Andreasen and Black, 1996).

Clearly schizophrenia is devastating in its overall impact, but we hasten to note that about one in five schizophrenics do well and continue to do well. We can hope that the odds will improve as researchers converge on the etiology of the disease and perfect new treatments. Indeed, some new treatments for schizophrenia give grounds for optimism, as we will discuss in the next chapter.

18.9 The pathology model as applied to schizophrenia *The diagram shows that the causal analysis by which nonbehavioral disorders such as diabetes are described (see pp. 767–68) can be applied to mental disorders such as schizophrenia. The basic logic applies regardless of whether the disorder ultimately turns out to be in part somatogenic or not.*

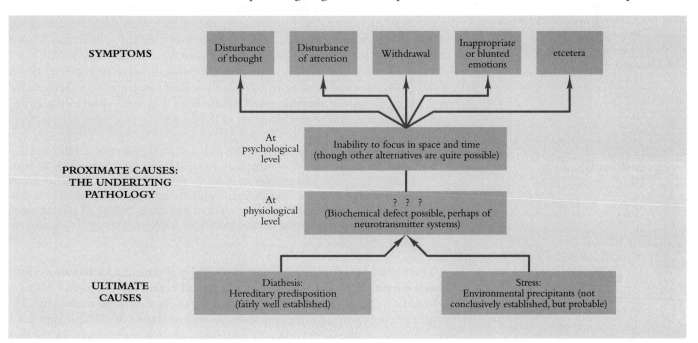

MOOD DISORDERS

In schizophrenia, the primary symptoms involve disorders in thinking. In the **mood disorders,** in contrast, the predominant disturbances lie in mood and motivation. These disorders (which are sometimes called the **affective disorders**) are characterized by emotional and energetic extremes—the maelstrom of mania, the despair of depression, or both.

BIPOLAR AND UNIPOLAR SYNDROMES

An initial distinction is that between **bipolar disorder** (formerly called **manic-depressive illness**) and **major depression.** In bipolar disorder, the patient swings from one energetic and emotional extreme to the other (with normal periods interspersed). These manic and depressive phases may be as short as a few hours or as long as several months or more. Bipolar disorder occurs in about 0.5 to 1 percent of the population and is diagnosed more often in women by a ratio of 3 to 2 (Andreasen and Black, 1996). Much more frequent are cases of **major depression** (sometimes called **unipolar depression,** since the mood extreme is of one kind only). According to several estimates, about 10 percent of all men and 20 percent of all women in the United States will suffer from a major depressive episode (defined as one that lasts for at least two weeks) at some time during their lives (Hirschfeld and Cross, 1981; Weissman and Boyd, 1985).

MANIA

In their milder form, manic states are often hard to distinguish from buoyant spirits. At this point, the person is said to show **hypomania.** She seems to have shifted into high gear: She is infectiously merry, extremely talkative, charming, utterly self-confident, and indefatigable. It is hard to see that something is amiss unless one notices that she jumps from one plan to another, seems unable to sit still for a moment, and quickly shifts from unbounded elation to brittle irritation if she meets even the smallest frustration. Kay Redfield Jamison, a psychologist and expert on bipolar disorder—and a sufferer of it as well—provided a lyrical and frank account of the ecstatic allure of hypomania:

> When you're high it's tremendous. The ideas and feelings are fast and frequent like shooting stars, and you follow them until you find better and brighter ones. Shyness goes, the right words and gestures are suddenly there, the power to captivate others a felt certainty. There are interests found in uninteresting people. Sensuality is pervasive and the desire to seduce and be seduced irresistible. Feelings of ease, intensity, power, well-being, financial omnipotence, and euphoria pervade one's marrow. (Jamison, 1995, p. 67)

These signs become greatly intensified as the hypomania escalates into full-blown **mania.** Now the motor is racing and all brakes are off, and in his perceived invincibility the person will likely quit all his antimanic medication. He may begin to stay up all night, engage in an endless stream of talk that runs from one topic to another and knows no inhibitions of social or personal (or for that matter, sexual) propriety.

PET scan of a rapid-cycling bipolar disorder patient *The top and bottom row are scans obtained on days in which the patient was depressed; the middle row on a day in which he was hypomanic. Reds and yellows indicate a high rate of metabolic activity; blues and greens indicate low rates. (Courtesy Dr. John Mazziotta)*

But the feelings of omnipotence recede as *acute* or *psychotic mania* sets in. Feelings of invincibility are replaced by terror as the patient loses her tenuous grip on reality:

> The fast ideas are too fast, and there are far too many; overwhelming confusion replaces clarity. Memory goes. Humor and absorption on friends' faces are replaced by fear and concern. Everything previously moving with the grain is now against—you are irritable, angry, frightened, uncontrollable, and enmeshed totally in the blackest caves of the mind. (Jamison, 1995)

Patients in the acute manic state may burst into shouts of song, smash furniture out of sheer overabundance of energy, do exercises, sleep only rarely, engage in reckless sexual escapades, spend all their money on gambling, conceive grandiose plans for redirecting the nation's foreign policy or making millions in the stock market, and go on drinking or drug-abuse bouts (nearly 60 percent of people with bipolar disorder are alcohol or drug abusers; Feinman and Dunner, 1996). As Jamison described this chaotic state:

> I kept on with my life at a frightening pace. I worked ridiculously long hours and slept next to not at all. When I went home at night it was a place of increasing chaos: Books, many of them newly purchased, were strewn everywhere. . . . There were hundreds of scraps of paper as well. . . . One scrap contained an incoherent and rambling poem; I found it weeks later, apparently triggered by my spice collection, which, needless to say, had grown by leaps and bounds during my mania. I had titled it, for reasons that I am sure made sense at the time, "God is an Herbivore." (Jamison, 1995, p. 79)

This ceaseless torrent of activity can continue unabated over many days and sleepless nights and will eventually sap the patients' health (and that of those around them) if they are not treated.

DEPRESSION

In many ways, depression is the polar opposite of mania. The patient's mood may be utterly dejected, his outlook hopeless. He has lost interest in other people and believes he is utterly sinful or worthless. In describing the depths of his own depression, the novelist William Styron wrote:

> All sense of hope vanished, along with the idea of a futurity; my brain, in thrall to its outlaw hormones, had become less an organ of thought than an instrument registering, minute by minute, varying degrees of its own suffering. The mornings themselves were becoming bad now as I wandered about lethargic . . . but afternoons were still the worst, when I'd feel the horror, like some poisonous fogbank, roll in upon my mind, forcing me into bed. There I would lie for as long as six hours, stuporous and virtually paralyzed, gazing at the ceiling and waiting for that moment of evening when, mysteriously, the crucifixion would ease up just enough to allow me to force down some food and then, like an automaton, seek an hour or two of sleep again. (Styron, 1990, pp. 58–59)

In many cases, both thought and action slow to a crawl:

> The patient . . . speaks only in response to questions and even then answers in a word, not a sentence. . . . He speaks in such a low tone that one finds oneself moving close to him and speaking more loudly as if he were the one who could not hear. (Cohen, 1975, p. 1019)

About 20 percent of depressions have psychotic features; that is, they are accompanied by delusions or hallucinations. Some of these are variations on the

Depression *In his book,* Darkness Visible, *writer William Styron describes his battles with depression. (Photograph by Rhoda Sydney, Leo de Wys)*

theme of worthlessness: "I must weep myself to death. I cannot live. I cannot die. I have failed so. It would be better if I had not been born. . . . I am the most inferior person in the world. . . . I am subhuman" (Beck, 1967, p. 38). Others concern guilt about some unspeakable, unpardonable sin, and patients report hearing the devil tell them that they will surely burn in hell for eternity (Andreasen and Black, 1996). Whatever the manifestation, depressions with psychotic features are more severe, less responsive to treatment, and more likely to recur (Coryell, 1996). The extreme of depression is a ***depressive stupor*** in which the person may become entirely unresponsive, rock back and forth, urinate or defecate on herself, and mutter incoherently.

Specific cognitive deficits often accompany severe depression, including disrupted attention and short-term memory. Moreover, depressed patients often exhibit various physical manifestations that are called ***vegetative signs.*** These can include a loss of appetite and weight loss, weakness, fatigue, poor bowel functioning, sleep disorders (most often early morning awakenings), and loss of interest in sex. It is as if both bodily and psychic batteries have run down completely.

Vegetative symptoms seem to predominate in the depressions that occur in non-Western cultures, while mood symptoms like feelings of worthlessness and sinfulness are largely confined to Western depressions. The reasons for this difference are unknown, but several hypotheses have been proposed. These include the implicit blame that individualist Western cultures affix on people who are not faring well and the various ways that the cultures understand and cope with death and mourning (Jenkins, Kleinman, and Good, 1991).

DEPRESSION AND SUICIDE

Given the depressed individual's bottomless despair it is not surprising that suicide is a very real risk. Here is Kay Jamison's description of an episode of depression:

> Each day I awoke deeply tired, a feeling as foreign to my natural self as being bored or indifferent to life. Those were next. Then a gray, bleak preoccupation with death, dying, decaying, that everything was born but to die, best to die now and save the pain while waiting. (Jamison, 1995, p. 38)

Both those with major depression and those in a depressive phase of bipolar disorder can become suicidal. Some attempt suicide, and more than a few succeed. The risk of suicide is greater among those with bipolar disorder than among those with major depression. In fact, up to 20 percent of individuals with bipolar disorder commit suicide. As might be expected, people with bipolar disorder rarely commit suicide during manic episodes (Andreasen and Black, 1996). But it may come as a surprise that suicide risk is *also* relatively low for those in the depths of depression. At that point gloom is deepest, but so is inertia, and although the patient may resolve that suicide is his only alternative, he will be unable to complete the act. He will be more likely to follow through on his resolution as he begins to recover from depression and emerge from closely supervised care. Times of greatest risk, therefore, include weekend leaves from the hospital and the period immediately after discharge (Beck, 1967).

The patient may become oddly calm or even cheerful as she contemplates what she is about to do and the relief from suffering she expects it to offer. If her hints about suicide—and most people in that position do relay them—go unheeded, her friends and loved ones may be deceived that she has recovered, when she has only gained solace from the prospect of death.

We hasten to add that those who succeed in committing suicide, whatever the reason, are but a fraction of those who attempt it. Women are three times as like-

Hamlet on depression *Probably no patient in real life has described his preoccupation with death, suicide, and dissolution as eloquently as that greatest depressive in all of English literature, Prince Hamlet:*
"O that this too too sullied flesh would melt,
Thaw, and resolve itself into a dew,
Or that the Everlasting had not fixed
His canon 'gainst self-slaughter. O God, O God,
How weary, stale, flat, and unprofitable
Seem to me all the uses of this world!
Fie on 't, ah fie, fie! 'Tis an unweeded garden
That grows to seed. . . ."
(Hamlet, I: ii, photograph from the 1948 film version of the play starring Sir Laurence Olivier)

ly to attempt suicide as men are, but when men make the attempt, they are much more likely to succeed; in fact, four times as many men as women kill themselves. One reason for the difference is in the choice of methods. Women are more likely than men to cut their wrists or swallow a bottle of sleeping pills, whereas men tend to use methods that are irreversible, such as shooting themselves or jumping off a roof top (Fremouw, Perczel, and Ellis, 1990).

SEASONAL AFFECTIVE DISORDER

Many people who live in cold climates have experienced the phenomenon of "cabin fever," a lethargy that ensues as the days grow short with precious few hours of sunlight. Clinical investigators observed that this phenomenon often reaches serious proportions, with depressions that start in late fall when the days become shorter and then remit—or even switch to mania—when the days lengthen in March or April. Such *seasonal affective disorders* (or *SAD*s) are evidently linked to the amount of sunlight the patients receive (see Figure 18.10). When they travel south in the winter, their depression lifts within a few days; when they travel north, their depression gets worse. And needless to say, SAD is nonexistent in equatorial countries where there are no seasons and all days are equally long. But the relationship between latitude and SADs isn't simple, for not all people living in polar climes develop the disorder. In fact, people indigenous to polar regions seem to have adapted to short days. For example, one investigation found that native Icelanders show much lower than expected rates of seasonal disorders, lower than residents of the northeastern seaboard of the United States (Magnusson and Stefansson, 1993).

Since SADs seems mostly to affect transplants to northern latitudes (or southern latitudes in the southern hemisphere), it was only natural to attempt a treatment using bright artificial lights to replace the sun during one's "dark days." According to several studies, this treatment relieves even severe seasonal depressions within a few days or weeks, but the patient will relapse just as fast if the light therapy is discontinued. As might be expected, one of the first regions in which this therapy was employed was Alaska (Rosenthal et al., 1984; Hellekson, Kline, and Rosenthal, 1986; Lewy et al., 1987; Rosen et al., 1990).

What might account for this effect of light on mood? As yet we don't know. One possibility is that it is connected both with the sleeping-waking cycle and with the pineal gland's secretion of the hormone *melatonin,* both of which are sensitive to daylight. Indeed, there is some evidence that all depression, not just the seasonal variety, may involve a disturbance in sleep rhythms, including an

18.10 Seasonal affective disorder and day length *(A) Percentage of patients with seasonal affective disorder who report being depressed in any given month. (B) Mean minutes of daylight per month. (From Rosenthal et al., 1984)*

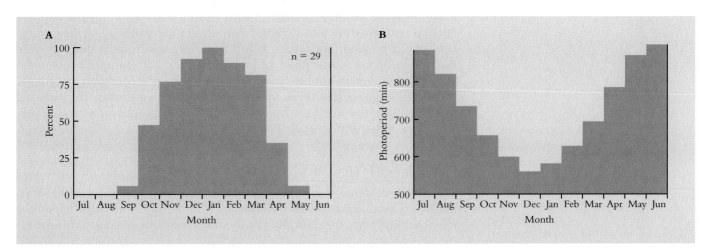

overly quick onset of REM sleep during the night (Wehr and Goodwin, 1981; Nofzinger et al., 1993). The close link between depression and sleep is underscored by the fact that sleep deprivation is a powerful antidepressant, although unfortunately, it works for only a few days (Riemann et al., 1996).

ORGANIC FACTORS

What produces mood disorders, the extremes of bipolar disorder, major depression, and SADs? According to one view, some of these conditions—especially bipolar disorder—are best regarded as organic pathologies.

GENETIC COMPONENTS

It is likely that many mood disorders have important hereditary components. Overall, concordance rates for mood disorders are some four times higher in identical than in fraternal twins (Siever, Davis, and Gorman, 1991; Andreasen and Black, 1996).

Further evidence, specifically for bipolar disorder, comes from detailed genetic linkage studies of extended families with numerous cases of this disorder. In these families, the individuals with bipolar disorder tend also to have a particular enzyme deficiency as well as a type of color blindness. The fact that both of these latter anomalies are due to defective genes on the X-chromosome strongly suggests that the gene(s) causing bipolar disorder may be nearby (Hodgkinson, Mullan, and Gurling, 1990).

What of major depression? It is certainly conceivable that a syndrome like major depression *could* be genetically determined. Such is the implication of studies of a special breed of rat known as the flinders sensitive line (FSL) rat. This rat, originally bred to show an atypical response to one enzyme, shows many of the manifestations of human depression, such as reduced locomotion and body weight, increased REM sleep and altered sleep rhythms, cognitive (learning) difficulties, and special sensitivity to behavioral stress (such as the helplessness tasks we discuss below). FSL rats also act more normally when administered antidepressant medications (Overstreet, 1993)! It is still uncertain whether the physiological alterations produced by breeding in FSL rats resemble those exhibited by humans prone to major depression. Nonetheless, FSL rats provide a promising avenue for understanding how genetics might predispose an individual to depression.

Human adoption and twin studies also indicate that genetics plays a role in major depression, though probably a less powerful one than in bipolar disorder. Such genetic evidence also indicates that, despite the similarity of their symptoms, the depression that occurs with major depression is quite different from that which occurs as one phase of bipolar disorder. For example, people with one of these disorders tend to have relatives with the one condition but not the other. This suggests that there are separate inheritance pathways for each and makes it likely that they are largely separate disorders (Gershon et al., 1985; Torgersen, 1986; Wender et al., 1986).

BIOCHEMICAL HYPOTHESES

The genetic evidence provides a strong argument for the involvement of biological factors in mood disorders. But what are these factors? The major hypothesis is biochemical and applies mainly to major depression. In this view, a biochemi-

Depression and despair *Edward Adamson, a professional artist, founded a studio in a British mental hospital for the use of the institutionalized patients. Many of their works forcefully express these patients' depression and despair, as in the case of this painting entitled* Cri de Coeur *or Cry from the heart. (Cri de Coeur, by Martha Smith; reproduced from Adamson, 1984)*

cal defect leaves some important neurotransmitters in short supply at critical sites in the brain, directly producing depression. Many investigators have singled out the transmitter **serotonin;** others believe that **norepinephrine** is crucial; still others suspect that both are involved (Schildkraut, 1965; Schildkraut, Green, and Mooney, 1985).

It is difficult to measure directly the brain's supply of these neurotransmitters, but investigators can make these measurements indirectly, by assessing the quantity of the by-products left over when these neurotransmitters are metabolized by the body. These by-products can be found in the spinal fluid or the urine; a low level of these by-products indicates a correspondingly low supply of the neurotransmitters from which they are derived. As predicted, the relevant metabolic by-products are in fact lower in at least some depressed patients than in controls.

Confirmation also comes from the effect of various **antidepressant medications.** These medications increase the amounts of norepinephrine and/or serotonin available for synaptic transmission, with the implication that the problem was a shortage of these same chemicals in the first place. Moreover, drugs that decrease the amounts of these neurotransmitters can produce profound depressions (Rosenzweig, Leiman, and Breedlove, 1996).

Despite these supportive lines of evidence, other findings complicate the picture. One problem is the length of time before medications take effect. While the antidepressants lead to an almost immediate increase in the amount of norepinephrine and/or serotonin available, this increase is short-lived; within a few days, the transmitter levels subside to what they were before the medications were first administered. But the drugs only begin to relieve the depression two to three weeks after the drug therapy was started. How, therefore, do these drugs accomplish their mission? Some studies indicate that instead of increasing the supply of the neurotransmitters, the antidepressants make the relevant neurons more sensitive to them (Schildkraut, Green, and Mooney, 1985; Briley and Moret, 1993).

What of bipolar disorder? As in major (unipolar) depression, norepinephrine levels in bipolar patients are below average when the patients are in a depressed phase; they increase when the patients become manic (Muscettola et al., 1984; Schildkraut, Green, and Mooney, 1985). But in bipolar disorder there is something else to explain. In those with the disorder, the switch from mania or hypomania to depression (and vice versa) is often quite rapid and seemingly divorced from external circumstances. This suggests the operation of some internal biological switch. The nature of this switch is uncertain, but some investigators believe that it is related to neuronal membranes that do not adequately dampen fluctuations in the levels of certain neurotransmitters (Meltzer, 1986; Hirschfeld and Goodwin, 1988).

PSYCHOGENIC FACTORS

The organic pathology—whatever it may turn out to be—might account for the extremes of some patients' moods, but what about the other symptoms? Can the organic pathology explain the manic's exuberance and self-glorification or the depressive's despair and self-loathing? How do changes in neurotransmitter levels of norepinephrine or serotonin lead to beliefs that one is omnipotent and righteous or helpless and morally wretched? These symptoms, in the eyes of many investigators, call for psychological, not biochemical, explanations—especially in the case of major depression.

COGNITION AND DEPRESSION: CAUSE OR CONSEQUENCE?

Many theorists regard depression as primarily somatogenic. They argue that mood is biologically set, with the patient's thinking just following from that mood. If a neurotransmitter insufficiency (or some other biochemical state) downgrades his mood such that he feels sluggish and gloomy, he looks for reasons to explain this. Eventually he finds those reasons: The world is no good, and neither is he. The end result is that he produces cognitions to match his mood. (For an analogous approach to the nature of emotions in normal people, see Chapter 11.)

Other theorists, however, believe that this approach to the mood disorders makes cognition too peripheral. For major depression in particular, they insist that the individual's thinking plays a crucial *causal* role.

BECK'S COGNITIVE THEORY OF DEPRESSION

According to a psychogenic, cognitive view of depression, the patient's beliefs that she and the world are hopeless and wretched aren't derived from the patient's mood. Instead, the beliefs come first and produce the depression. This cognitive view underlies a very influential approach to the understanding and treatment of depression developed by psychiatrist Aaron Beck (Beck, 1967, 1976). For Beck, the depression stems from a triad of intensely negative and irrational beliefs that the person holds about herself, her future, and the world around her. The individual believes that she is worthless, that her future is bleak, and that whatever happens around her is sure to turn out for the worst. These beliefs, then, form the core of a **negative cognitive schema** in terms of which the patient interprets whatever happens to her. Facing a minor setback, the depressive makes mountains out of molehills—such as insisting that her car is ruined when she's only scratched a fender. Conversely, after a major accomplishment like winning an award, she makes molehills out of mountains, such as believing that the competition must have been mediocre or the judges incompetent.

Beck contends that these schemas stem from an accumulation of unfortunate experiences earlier in life—perhaps a harshly critical attitude in the home or school, the loss of a parent, rejection by peers, and so on. Regardless of their origins, the negative schemas become self-fulfilling; expecting defeat, the depressed person eventually will be defeated. To overcome depression, therefore, this system of beliefs must be counteracted. For this purpose, Beck developed a psychological treatment called **cognitive therapy** during which the patients confront their defeatist beliefs and replace them with more positive ones (we will discuss this in a later section—see Chapter 19; Beck, 1967; Beck et al., 1979).

LEARNED HELPLESSNESS AND DEPRESSIVE EXPLANATIONS

Beck's cognitive theory grew out of clinical work with depressed patients. A related cognitive account, proposed by Martin Seligman, began instead with studies of animal learning. We first met this line of research in Chapter 4, and it is a line that has led to the **learned helplessness theory** of depression (Seligman, 1975).

Learned helplessness and depression   As we discussed in Chapter 4, learned helplessness was first observed in dogs. The dogs were placed in a shuttle box containing two compartments and had to learn to jump from one compartment to another in order to escape an electric shock. For one group of dogs, this was the first step in the procedure; these animals learned easily how to escape the shock and, after a bit of practice, how to jump early enough so that they avoided the shock altogether. Things were different, though, for a second group of dogs: Before encountering the shuttle box, they had first been exposed to a series of painful shocks about which they could do absolutely nothing. They were, in other words, objectively helpless in this initial situation, and all they could do was endure the shocks. When this second group was then placed in the shuttle box, their performance was drastically different from that of the dogs in the first group. They did not look for some means of escape. Nor did they ever find the correct response—jumping over the hurdle separating the chambers. Instead, they simply gave up; they lay down, whimpered, and passively accepted their fate. Having once been made helpless, they seemed to have learned that they were generally helpless and so, accordingly, did nothing (Seligman, Maier, and Solomon, 1971).

Seligman has argued that this learned helplessness pattern is similar to at least some forms of depression. Like the helpless dogs, depressed patients have given up. They lie passively, unable to take any initiative that might help them cope. And, strikingly, depressed humans and helpless animals even respond to the same medications: The antidepressant medications that alleviate human depression have a similar effect on animals rendered helpless—their helplessness disappears, and the animals behave much like normal (nonhelpless) animals (Porsolt, LePichon, and Jalfre, 1977).

Seligman supposed that what helpless dogs share with depressed people is the expectation that their acts are of no avail. In dogs, the cause is a series of inescapable shocks that the animals can do nothing about. In humans, the precipitating factor may be some personal catastrophe—rejection, bankruptcy, physical disease, the death of a loved one. In both cases, this experience of helplessness may lead to a generalized sense of impotence, a belief that one is a passive victim of circumstances that are overwhelming and uncontrollable.

Explanatory style and depression   The learned helplessness interpretation of depression, however appealing, is incomplete. To begin with, an experience of helplessness doesn't always lead to depression. Not every cancer victim, not every widower, becomes depressed. It appears, therefore, that some factor in addition to the experience of helplessness must be needed. A further problem is the depressive's self-hatred. If he thinks that he is helpless, then why does he blame himself (Abramson and Sackheim, 1977)?

Considerations of this sort led to a revision of the helplessness theory in which what really matters is the individual's **explanatory style** (formerly, *attributional style*), that is, the way she habitually tries to explain events—especially bad events—that happen to her (see also Chapter 16). If something bad happens, does she tend to believe that the event was caused by something she did (an internal explanation) or by something about the world? Does she believe the cause is something that will bring about bad consequences in other settings (a global explanation), or does she believe the bad event is an isolated instance? And does she believe the cause is something that will be lasting (a stable explanation), or something that's merely temporary? If the explanation is internal, global, and stable, then the individual has an explanatory style that will predispose her to depression: When some bad event comes along, she will think about the event in these unfortunate ways, with depression the result (Abramson, Seligman, and Teasdale, 1978).

There is good evidence that this pessimistic explanatory style is indeed characteristic of depressed persons (as shown by results with the Attributional Style Questionnaire described in Chapter 16; Peterson and Seligman, 1984). But which of these is the cause and which is the effect? Critics have pointed out that hopelessness, helplessness, and unmitigated self-blame are among the *symptoms* of the condition we call "depression." To say they are the cause is a bit like saying that sneezing and nose blowing cause colds (Coyne and Gotlib, 1983; Lewinsohn et al., 1985).

Seligman, Beck, and other cognitively inclined theorists have responded to this suggestion with arguments and evidence, claiming that a depressive's cognitive schema, or explanatory style, really do cause the illness. As one crucial line of argument, they provide evidence that these cognitive patterns can be detected in an individual *before* the depression actually begins, making it clear which is cause and which is consequence. Several studies have identified people who are not currently depressed but who exhibit the depressive explanatory style. According to the theory, these are people who are at special risk for depression, and in fact, these people are more likely to become depressed later on, when faced with failure or stress. Thus, college students who showed this style at the start of a semester were more prone to become depressed after learning that they had done badly on an examination; inmates who displayed it at the start of their prison terms were more prone to depression after some months of imprisonment; and pregnant mothers who showed it in their second trimester were more likely to be depressed three months after childbirth (Peterson and Seligman, 1984). Some findings do not fit this pattern, but taken as a whole, there is reason to believe that the cognitive pattern does predate the depression for some individuals, carrying the clear implication that certain habitual ways of interpreting the world can predispose an individual toward depression. (For some contrary evidence, see Lewinsohn et al., 1985.)

SEX DIFFERENCES IN THE PREVALENCE OF MAJOR DEPRESSION

Whatever theory of depression we eventually endorse, one striking fact about major depression needs to be explained. Across most Western cultures, both major depression and bipolar disorder are diagnosed more often in women than in men (twice as often for major depression and, as we mentioned, in a ratio of three to two for bipolar disorder). These differences persist even after accounting for income and socioeconomic level. What accounts for them? We cannot know for certain, but there are several possibilities. In the case of bipolar disorder, the possibility that predisposing genes lie on the X chromosome may explain the sex difference: Women, after all, have two X chromosomes, one from each parent, whereas men have only one X chromosome; this may double the risk for women.

In the case of major depression, several hypotheses have been advanced for the sex difference. One is hormonal. Women may suffer more from depression because they must endure cyclic hormonal changes, such as significant drops in estrogen and progesterone levels during the premenstrual period, the postpartum period, and menopause, that are themselves associated with depressed moods (Seeman, 1997).

Another hypothesis is psychogenic and proposes important differences in how women and men cope with the early stages of depression. In this view, women who are depressed dwell on their despondency: "I try to determine why I'm depressed," "I talk to other people about my feelings," and "I cry to relieve the tension." This way of dealing with one's feelings—which is probably culturally determined—may make an initial depression more likely to escalate and last longer. And what do men do when they are depressed? They try to distract

Sorrow *(Vincent Van Gogh, 1882; courtesy of the Vincent Van Gogh Foundation/ National Museum Vincent Van Gogh, Amsterdam)*

themselves: "I avoid thinking of reasons why I'm depressed," or "I do something physical." Thus, they may "act out" distress rather than manifest it in depression (Nolen-Hoeksema, 1987).

This escapist strategy may allow men to escape depression, but it is hardly trouble free, because a major way that men act out distress is through alcohol and drug consumption; when depressed, they are much more likely to get drunk or get "high" than get therapy. In fact, men are diagnosed as alcoholic four times as often as women (Andreasen and Black, 1996). Might the male-female difference in depression, then, simply reflect the fact that much male depression is masked by drug and alcohol abuse? Such is the implication of a study of the Old Order Amish of Lancaster County, Pennsylvania. The Amish prohibit illegal drugs and alcohol, and the rates of major depression among men and women are equal (Egeland and Hostetter, 1983). The same pattern also occurs among Americans of Jewish heritage, who exhibit very low rates of substance abuse (Levav et al., 1997).

MOOD DISORDERS AND THE DIATHESIS-STRESS CONCEPTION

Major depressions are often preceded by some stressful event, whether it involves marital or professional difficulties, serious physical illness, or a death in the family (Leff, Roatsch, and Bunney, 1970; Paykel, 1982). But it's clear that environmental stress cannot be the whole story. After all, there are, as we've mentioned, many people who suffer major setbacks or losses but who don't fall into a depressive collapse. There must therefore be some diathesis, such that people differ in their vulnerability to mood disorders. This diathesis may be based on biological factors, such as an insufficiency of available serotonin or norepinephrine. But it may also be at least partially based on psychological factors, such as a negative view of oneself or the world, or a depressive explanatory style. In either case, the diathesis makes the individual more vulnerable to later stress.

Seen in this light, psychological and biological factors may be intermingled in depression, so that the distinction between somatogenic and psychogenic origins of this disorder becomes blurred. Negative cognitions and learned helplessness may produce a depletion of norepinephrine and serotonin, and low neurotransmitter levels may help to bring about these negative cognitions. Thus, the causal arrow may point in both directions, with biochemical factors influencing psychological status, and psychological status having an impact on biochemistry. Either way, these factors might create a predisposition for later depression, manifested in both behavior and biochemistry.

ANXIETY DISORDERS

In major depressions, a primary symptom is a profoundly dejected or apathetic mood: The patient feels awful, considers himself wretched, and believes that his prospects are hopeless. In another group of conditions, the *anxiety disorders,* the primary manifestations include the experience of anxiety, as well as behavioral efforts to cope with anxiety: The patient is chronically apprehensive, fears the worst, and must guard vigilantly against anticipated disasters. While such symptoms often cause serious distress and impair the person's functioning, they generally do not become so extreme as to render the person psychotic.★

PHOBIAS

A relatively common anxiety disorder is **phobia,** which is an intense and irrational fear. Unlike, say, a delusion in which a patient believes she is being watched, persecuted, or whatever, the sufferer of a phobia *knows* that her fear is irrational. Phobias can be about objects or situations, and their target can be either general or focal.

SOCIAL PHOBIA

One example of a wide-ranging phobia is **social phobia** in which the problem is fear of embarrassment or humiliation in front of others (Juster and Heimberg, 1995; Rapaport, Paniccia, and Judd, 1995). People with social phobia will desperately try to avoid situations in which they must expose themselves to public scrutiny. They will avoid public speaking or performing because they might falter, will not eat in restaurants for fear they will choke on their food, and won't go to parties or professional meetings because they may stutter and stammer when trying to make small talk. When forced into situations of this sort, they may try to "fortify" themselves with alcohol or drugs, making substance abuse or dependence a constant risk.

SPECIFIC PHOBIAS

Unlike the pervasive fear seen in social phobia, the **specific phobias** concern particular objects or events. During the nineteenth century, some of these irrational fears were cataloged and assigned exotic-sounding Greek or Latin names. Examples are fear of high places (acrophobia), enclosed places (claustrophobia), crowds (ocholophobia), germs (mysophobia), cats (ailurophobia), and even the number 13 (triskaidekophobia)—the list is potentially endless. The crucial point in the definition is that the fear must be irrational, existing out of all proportion to any danger. An African villager who lives in the jungle and is worried about leopards has an understandable fear; a San Francisco apartment dweller incapacitated by a similar fear has a phobia. In most cases, this irrationality is quite apparent to the sufferer, who knows that the fear is groundless but continues to be afraid all the same. Still, these irrational fears can be intense and include heart palpitations, cold sweats, and even fainting. Why can't the phobic person simply avoid the feared object? Certainly, if he is afraid of leopards and snakes, he can generally stay clear of them; if he is terrified of heights, he can quit mountain climbing. For some phobias this may be satisfactory. But for other cases avoidance may be impossible or handicapping, as when an executive must travel to keep her job but has a fear of flying or a student wants to be a physician but faints at the sight of blood. Such phobias can also expand in scope, coming to exert an enormous effect on every aspect of the sufferer's life. The fear of leopards, say, can grow to

---

★ In psychiatric classification systems prior to DSM-III, anxiety disorders were listed under the general rubric *neurosis* because it was believed that these conditions, along with a number of others such as conversion disorders and dissociative states, could all be understood as the manifestation of unconscious defenses against anxiety. Because DSM-III and its successors dropped the emphasis on origins, the anxiety disorders are now grouped purely descriptively, based upon their shared signs and symptoms.

become a fear of the locale where the zoo is located, of all cats and things catlike, of all spotted objects, and so on.

THE CONDITIONING ACCOUNT OF SPECIFIC PHOBIAS

What is the mechanism that creates and maintains the specific phobias? One notion goes back to John Locke, who believed that such fears were produced by the chance association of ideas, as when a child is told stories about goblins that come by night and is forever after terrified of the dark (Locke, 1690). Several modern authors express much the same idea in the language of conditioning theory (Chapter 4). In their view, phobias result from classical conditioning; the conditioned stimulus is the feared object (e.g., cats), and the response is the autonomic upheaval (increased heart rate, cold sweats, and so on) characteristic of fear (Wolpe, 1958).

A number of phobias may indeed develop in just this fashion. Examples include fear of dogs after dog bites, fear of heights after falling off a ladder, and fear of cars or driving after a serious automobile accident (Marks, 1969).

PREPARED LEARNING AND SPECIFIC PHOBIAS

Sufferers of specific phobias are generally afraid of a rather limited class of stimuli, such as snakes, spiders, and heights. Stimuli like automobiles, bathtubs, hammers, and electrical outlets are statistically much more dangerous but rarely become the focus of phobias. These facts seem peculiar if phobias are produced by mere association between a stimulus and some trauma or aversive event. After all, there's little doubt that more people have been hit by an automobile or have slipped in the bathtub than have been bitten by a snake or a spider. So why are there a disproportionate number of snake and spider phobias?

One hypothesis about the specificity of phobias derives from the notion of belongingness that we discussed in Chapter 4. Recall, for example, that rats are very quick to associate tastes with illness, but are unlikely to associate illness with tones or lights. This suggests that from the rat's point of view some stimuli belong together and some don't, so the rat is prepared to learn some associations more readily than others. The same is true for other organisms as well.

This pattern can then be extended to create the **preparedness theory of phobias:** Snakes, spiders, and a small number of other stimuli were ever-present dangers for our primate ancestors, and so natural selection may have favored animals who were innately predisposed (that is, prepared) to learn to fear these stimuli very quickly—after a single trial, even if the gap between the stimulus and its aversive consequence was quite long (Seligman, 1971). (Recall that these attributes—selectivity, one-trial learning, and learning despite a long CS-US interval—are precisely the attributes associated with learned taste aversions and similar phenomena; see Chapter 4.) A few centuries of industrialization, in contrast, haven't given natural selection sufficient time to favor those of us prepared to fear more modern hazards.

Conditioning accounts can explain some phobias, and some aspects of phobias, but certainly not all. This has led many investigators to be skeptical of these accounts, suggesting that relatively few phobias can be understood in these terms. Several considerations support these latter views. First, some specific phobias arise with no identifiable history of traumatic learning. Most snake phobics, for example, have never been bitten by a snake, nor harmed by a snake in any fashion; often, they show fear of the snake the very first time they encounter one. These observations are difficult to reconcile with a conditioning account. Second, not everyone who does have a fearful encounter with a snake or spider

Prepared fears of snakes in monkeys *The sight of the snake in the foreground leads to a characteristic fear grimace in the monkey, accompanied by a quick retreat to the rear of its cage while leaving its food untouched. (Courtesy of Susan Mineka)*

791

or who falls from a height develops a specific phobia. The conditioning theories provide no account of this, and no explanation of why some traumatic encounters lead to phobias, whereas others do not. Third, specific phobias affect females more than males, and because most originate in childhood, it is hard to argue that girls are exposed more than boys to snakes, spiders, and heights.

A final point is that phobias, and phobias of the same type, tend to run in families (Andreasen and Black, 1996). The reason for this is uncertain, but it suggests some possibilities. Parents may genetically transmit either their phobias or a temperament conducive to developing phobias. It may also be that phobias can be transmitted through social learning, such that watching Mommy or Daddy "freak out" over a cockroach may be sufficient to acquire the same reaction.

OBSESSIVE-COMPULSIVE DISORDER

In phobias, anxiety is aroused by external objects or situations. In contrast, anxiety in **obsessive-compulsive disorder** is produced by internal events—persistent thoughts or wishes that intrude into consciousness and cannot be stopped. Obsessions usually involve certain themes, and several studies have found that the most common ones concern dirt and contamination, aggression and violence, religion, sex, bodily functions like elimination, and the need for balance and symmetry. For example, an otherwise loving parent may have recurrent thoughts of strangling his children; a salesperson may worry constantly about whether she might have hit someone with her automobile and not noticed it. A seemingly normal businessman may spend hours each night straightening the paintings on his apartment walls and untangling all the fringe on his carpets.

Obsessive thoughts can produce considerable anxiety, and many **compulsions** may be understood as attempts to *counteract* this anxiety. An obsession with dirt may lead to compulsions like ritualistic cleaning or repeated hand washing (that is, washing one's hands every few minutes, so often that severe skin irritation is likely). An obsession over loss might lead to compulsive counting. In all of these cases, the sufferers know that their behavior is irrational, but they are helpless to stop the thoughts and urges, and are all the more tormented by them. Lady Macbeth knew that "what's done cannot be undone," but she kept washing invisible blood off her hands nonetheless.

Minor and momentary obsessional thoughts and compulsions are commonplace. After all, most people have on occasion checked and rechecked the alarm clock to make certain it is properly set. But in obsessive-compulsive disorder, such thoughts and acts so preoccupy the patient that they become crippling. The example of compulsive hand washing was already mentioned; a compulsive checker may check and recheck the stove to be certain it's turned off and may as a result take hours to leave the house for even a simple errand.

Obsessive-compulsive disorder often begins in childhood, and afflicts as much as 2 to 3 percent of the population sometime in their lives (March, Leonard, and Swedo, 1995). It is also quite serious: If untreated, most cases worsen over time and are accompanied by recurrent bouts of major depression (Barlow, 1988). As with many other disorders, there may be a biological predisposition to develop obsessive-compulsive disorder. To begin with, there seems to be some genetic basis, as shown by the fact that the concordance rate is higher for identical than for fraternal twins (Black and Noyes, 1990; Rasmussen, 1993). And as with major depression, the neurological mechanism apparently involves the neurotransmitter serotonin: Medications that increase serotonin activity in certain

Compulsive hand washing in literature
A scene from the Old Vic's 1956 production of Macbeth *with Coral Browne. It shows Lady Macbeth walking in her sleep and scrubbing imaginary blood off her hands, as she relives the night in which she and her husband murdered the king. (Courtesy of the Performing Arts Research Center, The New York Public Library)*

brain areas reduce obsessive-compulsive manifestations, with portions of the basal ganglia and frontal cortex implicated the most (Zohar et al., 1988; Insel, 1990, 1992; Winslow and Insel, 1990; Swedo et al., 1992; Piccinelli et al., 1995).

GENERALIZED ANXIETY DISORDER

In a phobia, anxiety is aroused by the phobic stimulus. In obsessive-compulsive disorder, the sufferer is besieged and tormented by intrusive, uncontrollable thoughts and urges. In ***generalized anxiety disorder,*** the anxiety is not related to anything in particular; instead, it is all-pervasive, or free floating. Still, it can be just as disabling. Patients with this disorder are visibly worried and fretful. They feel inadequate, are oversensitive, can't concentrate or make decisions, and suffer from insomnia. This state of affairs is generally accompanied by any number of physiological concomitants—rapid heart rate, irregular breathing, excessive sweating, and chronic diarrhea.

Generalized anxiety disorder is probably the most common of the anxiety disorders, occurring in as much as 6 percent of the population in any one year (Weissman, 1985). However, there is uncertainty about its cause and whether there is a genetic predisposition or not. Some theorists believe the disorder is psychogenic. A psychoanalytic interpretation holds that the disorder occurs when unacceptable impulses break into consciousness and create massive anxiety because one's ego defenses are too weak to block them. Conditioning theorists, in contrast, contend that generalized anxiety disorder is much like a phobia. The difference is that anxiety is conditioned to a very broad range of stimuli so that avoidance is virtually impossible (Wolpe, 1958). Both of these interpretations are difficult to evaluate: the psychoanalytic one because it relies on unob-

The Scream *(Edward Munch, 1893; courtesy Nasjonalgalleriet, Oslo)*

servable processes, and the conditioning one because the supposed stimuli are not easily specified.

Other theorists favor a somatogenic interpretation. They believe that the condition is linked to certain abnormalities in the secretion of the neurotransmitter GABA (for gamma aminobutyric acid), which can, among other effects, overactivate the sympathetic branch of the autonomic nervous system. Support comes from findings that the medications that lower anxiety work by locking onto specific receptor sites in the brain where GABA is plentiful (Costa, 1985).

PANIC DISORDER

A related disorder is **panic disorder.** Patients with this disorder don't suffer from the nagging, chronic worries that beset people with generalized anxiety disorder. Instead, their anxiety is intermittent. But when the anxiety strikes, it strikes with a vengeance.

At the heart of panic disorder are **panic attacks,** sudden episodes of terrifying bodily symptoms such as labored breathing, choking, dizziness, tingling in the hands and feet, sweating, trembling, heart palpitations, and chest pain. These bodily sensations are accompanied by feelings of intense apprehension, terror, and a sense of impending doom.

Panic attacks occur in a number of disorders. The snake-phobia sufferer may have one at the sight of a snake; the patient with obsessive-compulsive disorder may experience one if a compulsion goes unperformed for too long. But the hallmark of panic disorder is that the panic attacks seem to come out of the blue. As a result, the patient often has an intense experience of unreality and fears that he is losing control, is going insane, or is about to die. Panic disorder is diagnosed when there are recurrent unexpected attacks and when either behavioral or psychological troubles follow the attacks. Based on that criterion, it is found in about 2 to 3 percent of women and 1 percent of men (Robins et al., 1984; American Psychiatric Association, 1994).

Panic disorders can be frightening enough, but in addition, sufferers often develop a profound fear of *having* panic attacks, especially in places such as shopping malls, where they might be embarrassing, or in circumstances that might prove dangerous, such as while driving. As a result, people with the condition can rarely venture outside their designated "safe" places—their houses or even just their bedrooms. A common result is **agoraphobia,** a fear of being alone and outside the home, especially in a public place.★

What accounts for panic disorder? Most current theories are neurobiological and suggest that the main problem is one of autonomic nervous system overexcitability (Andreasen and Black, 1996). Some authors contend that cognition is also crucial. They believe that panic disorder is produced by a vicious cycle that begins with a misinterpretation of certain bodily reactions. In circumstances that produce fear, the sympathetic nervous system ordinarily produces a number of circulatory and respiratory responses, such as quicker heartbeats and faster and shallower breathing. These are entirely normal, and they act to prepare the person to deal with the threat. But the person with the panic disorder overreacts to her own internal sensations. Because she is not in a threatening situation, she believes that the shortness of breath and quickened heart beat are a sign of an impending heart attack. This makes her more fearful, which intensifies the bodily reactions, which makes her even more fearful, and so on, spiraling upward

★ The term is derived from the Greek word *agora* meaning "marketplace."

The Dead Mother *(Edward Munch, 1899–1900, Courtesy of Eigentum der Kunsthalle, Bremen)*

toward the full-blown attack. This pattern becomes even worse after the patient has her first panic attack, for now every normal anxiety reaction becomes a potential signal of a further panic (Clark, 1986).

REACTIONS TO EXTREME STRESS: ACUTE AND POST-TRAUMATIC STRESS DISORDERS

Human beings sometimes undergo traumatic events that involve the greatest extremes of emotion. For women, the most common such stressor, sad to say, is rape or physical assault. For men, equally sadly, it is combat experience. But other stressors can also carry humans to this extreme—being involved in a serious automobile accident, witnessing a homicide, and other horrors (Wolf and Mosnaim, 1990; Andreasen and Black, 1996).

The psychological effects of such stress have long been known to medics who treated combat soldiers, and these effects reached wide public attention because of their prevalence among Vietnam War veterans (Figley, 1978). Regardless of what the traumatic event was, the reactions are similar. Immediately after the trauma, there is usually a period of numbness during which the sufferer feels wholly estranged, socially unresponsive, and oddly unaffected by the event, a reaction technically known as *dissociation.* During this *acute stress disorder,* there are often recurrent nightmares and waking flashbacks of the traumatic event. These can be so intense and intrusive that the sufferer may momentarily believe that he is back in the situation. Below is a description of the flashbacks experienced by soldiers who served as body handlers:

> . . . A dental X-ray technician reported seeing skulls when he saw the teeth of smiling people. A young lieutenant could not enter a local fast food establishment because the smell of burning food elicited a vomiting response. . . . Soldiers reported

seeing bodies when they closed their eyes. Their dream content consisted of nightmarish horror shows where zombie-like bodies were coming to kill the dreamer. One soldier reported seeing himself in a dream where he searched through human body parts and found his own ID tag. (Garrigan, 1987, p. 8)

For many individuals the reactions to such traumas are enduring, and if they persist one month after the stressor, the diagnosis technically becomes one of **post–traumatic stress disorder (PTSD).** Gradually, the psychological numbness decreases, but other consequences remain. These can include sleep disturbances, outbursts of anger, difficulties in concentration, and exaggerated responses to being startled. Still another effect may be "survival guilt" if friends or relatives were harmed or killed by the same traumatic event (Friedman and Marsella, 1996). The individual with PTSD stays emotionally raw and socially estranged. Drug and alcohol abuse are common among PTSD sufferers, as are bouts of major depression and diminished physical health. If the trauma is severe enough, the manifestations of PTSD may remain for years and even decades, even with the best available treatments (see Zatzick et al., 1997).

Why do some individuals experience a trauma and develop PTSD, while others endure comparable horrors but seem not to suffer permanent harm? Although the evidence is not definitive, studies suggest that early adverse experiences, such as child abuse or neglect, may predispose an individual to PTSD if she is then stressed as an adult (McCranie et al., 1992; Bremner et al., 1993; Zaidi and Foy, 1994). How might these early events create a diathesis for PTSD? Some investigators believe that the predisposition is biochemical and point to findings that sufferers of PTSD show abnormally low levels of the substance known as **cortisol,** which is secreted by the adrenal glands during stress. In their view, the low cortisol levels may be a marker both of early adversity and later vulnerability (Heim et al., 1997; Yehuda, 1997; see Chapter 14).

DISSOCIATIVE DISORDERS

Acute and post-traumatic stress disorders show that people can distance themselves psychologically, or dissociate, from ongoing events. In many cases, people find some means of thinking about the traumatic events that avoids integrating these events with other beliefs and other knowledge. In addition, people often find some alternative perspective for viewing the traumatic events, different from the perspective they ordinarily adopt. They view these events as somehow not real or somehow not truly involving them.

These adjustments are often adaptive, a way of coping with extraordinary events. But such adjustments can also go too far and thus, in their extreme form, are the defining feature of a number of syndromes now called **dissociative disorders.**★ An example is **dissociative amnesia**† in which the individual is suddenly unable to remember some period of his life, or even his entire past, including his

---

★ Some authors suggest that the dissociative disorders are really severe cases of post-traumatic stress disorder or, alternatively, that the dissociations seen in post-traumatic stress disorder imply that it should be reclassified within the dissociative disorders.

† These amnesias are distinct from the pattern sometimes alleged for "repressed" memories. Dissociative amnesias typically lift within a few days, unlike the decades-long memory loss claimed for repressed memory. Dissociative amnesias also tend to involve the loss of an entire period in the person's life, unlike repressed memory, which is generally understood as removing only some (painful) elements from the remembered time, leaving most other memories untouched.

own identity. Such episodes usually last less than one week (Andreasen and Black, 1996). In other cases, the dissociation produces *dissociative fugue* in which the person wanders away from home and then, days or even months thereafter, suddenly realizes that he is in a strange place, doesn't know how he got there, and has total amnesia for the entire period.

Still more drastic are cases of *dissociative identity disorder* (formerly known as multiple personality disorder). Here the dissociation is so massive that it results in two or more distinct personalities. The "auxiliary" personalities, which can number from just a few to several dozen, seem to be built upon a nucleus of memories or fantasies. An example is a shy and inhibited person who has had fantasies of being carefree and outgoing from childhood on. These fantasies eventually take on the characteristics of a separate self. Once formed, the new self may appear quite suddenly, as in the famous case of Eve White, loosely depicted in the movie *The Three Faces of Eve:*

> After a tense moment of silence, her hands dropped. There was a quick, reckless smile and, in a bright voice that sparkled, she said, "Hi there, Doc.". . . There was in the newcomer a childishly daredevil air, an erotically mischievous glance, a face marvelously free from the habitual signs of care, seriousness, and underlying distress, so long familiar in her predecessor. This new and apparently carefree girl spoke casually of Eve White and her problems, always using she or her in every reference, always respecting the strict bounds of a separate identity. When asked her own name she immediately replied, "Oh, I'm Eve Black." (Thigpen and Cleckley, 1957, as described in Coleman, 1972, p. 246)

Some twenty years later, Eve White wrote an autobiography in which she described herself more fully. It turned out that at one time in her life she had as many as twenty-two subpersonalities rather than just three (Sizemore and Huber, 1988). The various personalities seen in such cases are not confined to differences in mood and attitudes. Sometimes the individual segregates different skills to different personalities, such that one plays the piano, while another cooks, and yet a third speaks French. The personalities can know of each other, have amnesia for each other, or exhibit any combination of acquaintanceship.

Until twenty years ago, dissociative identity disorder was considered very rare, with fewer than two hundred cases reported before 1975. Now cases number in the thousands; the large majority are females (Kluft, 1987). The rash of reported cases began with the publication of *Sybil*, a popular book about one case of dissociative identity disorder, subsequently made into a television movie (Schreiber, 1973). The disorder has always been controversial, with critics arguing that the flood of diagnoses reflects a fad among therapists who inadvertently lead their suggestible and therefore fad-prone patients—many of whom know the many books and movies on the subject—to develop the signs and symptoms of dissociative identity disorder (Spanos, 1994). Even the diagnosis of "Sybil" herself has been called into question by an expert therapist who examined her (Borch-Jabobsen, 1997).

The controversy extends to the legal realm, now that defendants in some celebrated criminal cases have claimed that "I didn't do it, my other personality did" (Slovenko, 1995). Although the diagnosis may be faddish and subject to abuse, dissociative identity disorder is nonetheless considered an entirely valid diagnosis for some patients (Gleaves, 1996).

A movie recreation of a case of dissociative identity disorder Joanne Woodward in The Three Faces of Eve *portraying Eve White (above) and Eve Black (below). (Courtesy the Museum of Modern Art/Film Stills Archive)*

FACTORS UNDERLYING DISSOCIATIVE DISORDERS

The mechanisms that underlie the dissociative disorders are still obscure. Some authors suggest that phenomena like the development of auxiliary personalities may represent an attempt to gain attention by using an unusual form of self-dramatization (Ziegler, Imboden, and Rodgers, 1963; Sarbin and Allen, 1968). Others try to understand dissociation in the context of human information processing and stress its similarity to phenomena like encoding specificity and implicit memory (Kihlstrom, 1992; see Chapter 7). In cases of encoding specificity, for example, knowledge acquired in one context may not be recalled if the context changes. Likewise, implicit memories can influence behavior even without any conscious recollection of the relevant events. Both parallel some of the phenomena of dissociation.

There is less debate, however, about the psychological function played by dissociation. On this issue, most authors hold to one or another variant of a view first expressed by Freud. He believed that dissociation was a defense against something too psychologically painful to confront. The acute stress reaction is a case in point. Rape victims sometimes report that, during the event, they felt that they were outside their own bodies watching themselves being raped. Similarly for people who watch their houses burn; they sometimes experience a strange calm and report the feeling that "it's like it's not really happening to me." In obvious ways, these reactions may create a sense of distance from a catastrophe, thus providing a means of diminishing an otherwise intolerable experience, and of keeping it from poisoning other aspects of one's life. Dissociation, then, is a valuable and powerful defense mechanism, but dissociative disorders emerge when dissociation becomes too general or too extreme.

DISSOCIATIVE DISORDERS AND THE DIATHESIS-STRESS CONCEPTION

Consistent with a diathesis-stress conception, people seem to differ in their propensity to dissociate and in the intensity of the circumstances that make them do so. Some of the relevant evidence comes from work on hypnosis, which some investigators regard as a form of guided dissociation (Hilgard, 1986). If this is so, one might suspect that people with dissociative disorders should be more hypnotizable than others, and this indeed turns out to be the case (Ganaway, 1989). This seems to be especially so for patients with dissociative identity disorder. According to one investigator, such patients were unusually adept at self-hypnosis during childhood and created their new personality (and often more than just one) during a self-induced hypnotic trance. Presumably, this allowed these children a form of escape from threatening traumatic events (Bliss, 1980).

The readiness to dissociate represents the predisposition or diathesis toward dissociative disorder. To precipitate a full-fledged disorder, there also has to be some unusual stress. And, in fact, most cases of dissociative amnesia occur after the same kinds of cataclysmic events that may lead to post-traumatic stress disorder. The same holds for dissociative fugues, which can also develop suddenly after personal misfortunes or financial pressures (Andreasen and Black, 1996).

There is reason to believe that the most serious and disabling of the dissociative conditions, dissociative identity disorder, results from the most harrowing stresses in early life. In a large percentage of the case histories, there are terrifying stories of repeated brutal physical and sexual abuse in childhood, often including incest (Putnam et al., 1986). These findings have led many psychotherapists to believe that child abuse, and especially sexual abuse, is a likely antecedent of dissociative identity disorder. But others urge caution in accepting this interpretation. Although one report does show a higher incidence of verified early child abuse (Coons, 1994), nearly all the remaining studies are based on the patients' uncorroborated memories of early childhood, and it is unclear how much faith we can place in these reports (Frankel, 1993; see also Chapter 7 for a broader discussion of why we cannot assume the veracity of these, or any, memories). In addition, individuals who are likely to dissociate also may be more prone to developing false memories. Hence, if dissociative symptoms and memories of childhood abuse go together, this *may* indicate that the incidents of abuse lead to dissociation, or the cause-effect relationship may be the reverse: Dissociation may predispose toward memories of childhood abuse. Because of ambiguities like these, conclusions about early child abuse and dissociative identity disorder cannot yet be drawn with confidence.

SOMATOFORM AND PSYCHO- PHYSIOLOGICAL DISORDERS

Finally, we turn to a set of disorders of a rather different type, disorders in which the predominant symptoms are not mental or emotional, but bodily. We will discuss two categories of such disorders: the somatoform and the psychophysiological.

SOMATOFORM DISORDERS

Some people experience anxiety directly and others dissociate from it. It appears that still others turn it into bodily complaints. At least this is the most common interpretation of the **somatoform disorders** (those disorders that take bodily form). There are several kinds of such disorders, but in each the patient exhibits or describes concerns about his bodily functions in the absence of any known physical illness. The best known of the somatoform disorders is **hypochondriasis** in which the sufferer believes she has a specific disease and goes to doctor after doctor to be evaluated for it. Somewhat similar is the person with **somatization disorder.** She brings to the doctor a host of miscellaneous aches and pains in various bodily systems that do not add up to any known syndrome in physical medicine. And then there is **somatoform pain disorder** in which the sufferer describes chronic pain for which no sufficient physical basis can be found.

The most dramatic of the somatoform disorders is **conversion disorder.**★ This

---

★ The term *conversion* was coined by Freud, who believed that the repressed energies that fueled the patient's unconscious conflict were converted into a somatic symptom much as a steam engine converts thermal energy into mechanical energy. Until recently, this condition was called *conversion hysteria.* The authors of DSM-III dropped the term *hysteria* because of its erroneous implication that conversion disorders were found only in women. (*Hysteria* is derived from the Greek *hystera,* for "womb").

disorder, which we mentioned early in the chapter, represented the first and most dramatic argument for the psychogenic approach to psychopathology and was also the foundation on which psychoanalytic theory was built. According to Freud, people with these disorders resolve some intolerable conflict by developing an hysterical ailment, such as being unable to see or hear or move an arm, even though there is nothing organically wrong (see Chapter 17). The soldier who is terrified of going into battle, for example, may become hysterically paralyzed. This allows him to yield to his impulse of refusing to march. But it also lets him do so without guilt or shame—he is not marching because he *cannot* march.

A century ago, such cases were fairly common, but today they account for a much smaller fraction of mental disorders. How can we explain this change? Some believe that it is due to a less restrictive family atmosphere and more permissive child rearing, especially in the sexual sphere. As a result, there is less repression of sexual and aggressive thoughts and with it a decline in symptoms (Chodoff, 1954). Others suggest that the reason is education: Because of a general increase in medical sophistication among lay persons, there are fewer people who believe that one can suddenly be struck blind or become paralyzed without some other accompanying bodily signs (say, of a stroke). In this era, hysterical blindness or paralysis would be rather transparent psychological defenses and thus much less acceptable to both the patient and those around him. One historian has suggested that disorders such as chronic fatigue syndrome and somatoform pain disorder have become the conversion hysterias of the late twentieth century (Shorter, 1992), serving the same function, but in a more plausible fashion, given our current understanding of medicine. So may be what neurologists term "nonepileptic seizures," those that occur in the absence of the abnormal brain waves that are usually diagnostic of genuine epilepsy. Conversion disorder is the most common explanation for these otherwise puzzling "seizures" (Alper et al., 1995; Bowman and Markand, 1996).

A final problem is inherent in the diagnosis of conversion disorder itself, because it must necessarily be a diagnosis by exclusion. Before conversion can be diagnosed, all conceivable physical conditions must be ruled out. In this regard, diagnoses of conversion disorder may be declining due to medical advances in identifying subtler illnesses that might otherwise have been diagnosed as conversion disorders. Support for this notion comes from follow-up studies of patients whose symptoms were diagnosed as conversions. A fair proportion of these patients were later found to have had organic disorders after all, many of which involved neurological damage (Slater and Glithero, 1965; Watson and Buranen, 1979). And in today's medical malpractice climate, a physician diagnoses conversion disorder at her own risk.

PSYCHOPHYSIOLOGICAL DISORDERS

In a conversion disorder, the primary symptoms seem psychological; there is no actual damage to the body. But other psychological disorders are associated with tissue damage. For example, high blood pressure, migraine headaches, and asthma usually result from organic causes, as in the case of an asthmatic allergic reaction. Yet these same problems can also be precipitated or aggravated by emotional factors. If so, they are called ***psychophysiological disorders*** (or, to use an older term, ***psychosomatic disorders***).*

---

* Notably, DSM-IV does not categorize psychophysiological disorders separately, considering them instead to be regular medical disorders that are exacerbated by psychological factors.

If a patient suffers from a conversion disorder, then the symptoms may disappear after the psychological conflict is resolved. If, for example, the patient suffers from hysterical paralysis of the legs, the fact remains that his locomotor machinery is still intact. But the patient who has hypertension (high blood pressure) because he worries all the time has a genuine bodily disorder, and a dangerous one to boot. His blood pressure will strain his heart and blood vessels just as much as if it resulted from kidney or vascular disease; if it results in a heart attack or a stroke, he will be no less disabled; and if he dies, his death will be no less final.

CORONARY HEART DISEASE

Perhaps the best-documented example of a disorder brought on or aggravated by psychological factors is **coronary heart disease,** a progressive narrowing of the arteries that supply blood to the heart muscles. This may result in severe chest pains (angina), indicating that the muscle tissue of the heart isn't getting enough oxygen to maintain its current workload. It may also result in the death of some portion of the heart muscle (a "heart attack") that received no oxygen at all. There are a number of biological factors that are known to increase the risk of coronary heart disease, such as cholesterol level, obesity, smoking, and gender (men are initially more prone to the disease than women, but women are equally susceptible after menopause). Others factors, such as bacterial infections of the vasculature, are suspected. In addition, researchers have identified certain characteristic behavior patterns that increase risk.

The Type A behavior pattern   One example is the **Type A behavior pattern.** People with this pattern tend to be highly competitive and hard driving, always in a hurry, irritable, impatient, and hostile. In the words of Friedman and Rosenman, the two cardiologists who first described this pattern, such individuals are "aggressively involved in a chronic, incessant struggle to achieve more and more in less and less time, and if required to do so, against the opposing efforts of other things or other persons" (Friedman and Rosenman, 1974, p. 67). In contrast, those with the **Type B behavior pattern** are less hurried and competitive, and more easygoing and friendly than their Type A counterparts. The Type A person runs up escalators, whereas the Type B lets the escalator do the work. In traffic jams, the Type A fumes and curses, while the Type B sits back and enjoys the music on the radio. Needless to say, most people are not extreme A or B types but fall somewhere in between.

One early large-scale study suggested that people with a Type A pattern are more likely to contract coronary heart disease than Type B individuals. Over three thousand men with no sign of coronary heart disease were evaluated to determine their behavior type. The Type A's were twice as likely to become victims as the Type B's (about 5 percent of the Type A's and 2.5 percent of the Type B's). Could this be because Type A's smoked more, or had higher blood pressure, or had higher cholesterol levels? The answer is no, for the relation between behavior pattern and heart disease held up even when these other risk factors were statistically held constant (Rosenman et al., 1975).

Further work showed that the same relation held for women. Overall, women prior to menopause are much less likely to suffer coronary heart disease, for reasons that are still a matter of debate (but women's estrogen levels seem to exert a protective effect). But compared to Type B women, Type A women are more at risk; they are two to three times more likely to suffer a heart attack, and this is regardless of whether or not they hold a job outside the home (Haynes, Feinleib, and Kannel, 1980).

"I don't care if they are moving better over there. This is the fast lane. This is where I live." (© The New Yorker Collection 1983 Handelsman from Cartoonbank.com. All rights reserved.)

The decline of Type A: Is hostility the real culprit? The Type A behavior pattern did seem initially to predict coronary heart disease in a fairly clear way. But later studies showed the picture to be murkier. One concern emerged from a follow-up to the original three-thousand-man study. True, the Type A men were twice as likely to develop coronary heart disease, but after surviving a first heart attack, they went on to live much longer than the Type B's (Ragland and Brand, 1988)! In addition, various investigators found that the different components of the behavior pattern were not as tightly linked to each other as Friedman and Rosenman had thought (Mathews, 1982; Shekelle et al., 1983). Thus, many individuals had some traits of the Type A pattern but not other traits. This made the categorization of these individuals uncertain and the categorization scheme correspondingly more difficult to use.

Some investigators suggested the need for a more fine-grained categorization. They attempted to isolate the different components of the Type A pattern rather than the entire package and questioned whether one or more of the components had special consequences for cardiovascular health. A reasonable amount of evidence now demonstrates that this is so. It appears that the major pathological ingredient is *hostility,* manifested as a combination of continual anger, cynicism, and distrust of other people. This trait is found in some—but by no means all—Type A's (Booth-Kewley and Friedman, 1987; Matthews, 1988; Dembroski et al., 1989; Smith, 1992). Individuals with pronounced hostility are more likely to fall victim to cardiac disease. The other facets of the Type A pattern, such as the sense of hurry and competitiveness, seem to be of lesser importance (Williams, 1987; Krantz et al., 1988; Barefoot et al., 1989).

An as yet unanswered question concerns the mechanism. How does the Type A individual's impatience, her inability to relax, or, most of all, her continual hostility produce the progressive narrowing of her coronary arteries that eventually leads to angina or a heart attack? One hypothesis is that the sympathetic branch of the Type A person's autonomic nervous system is in a continual state of arousal, which leads to an enhanced secretion of epinephrine (adrenaline), norepinephrine, and various steroid hormones produced by the adrenal gland. On a long-term basis, secretion of these substances stimulates the formation of cholesterol deposits on the walls of the coronary arteries, which leads to the progressive narrowing of these blood vessels. If this process continues day in and day out, it is likely to culminate in coronary heart disease (Friedman and Rosenman, 1974).

THE DIATHESIS-STRESS CONCEPT AND PSYCHOPHYSIOLOGICAL DISORDERS

What determines whether an individual under psychological stress develops a psychophysiological disorder? It appears that certain nonpsychological factors—including genetics—make an individual susceptible, and then, given enough emotional stress, the body will cave in at its most vulnerable point. With prolonged stress, then, one individual may develop migraine headaches, while another may develop chronic neck spasms or high blood pressure.

With high blood pressure (or hypertension), this interaction of diathesis and stress is especially clear. Many studies show that elevated blood pressure tends to run in families, in mice as well as people. In humans, a blood-pressure correlation between children and parents is seen even in infancy. Moreover, certain ethnic groups are especially prone to hypertension. Taken together, these lines of evidence suggest that hypertension is partly hereditary, and this suggestion has been confirmed with the identification of certain genes associated with hypertension in both humans and rats (Hiraga et al., 1996; Stec et al., 1996; Schork, 1997). But genetics isn't the whole story, because other nonpsychological risk

TABLE 18.1 A CLASSIFICATION OF SOME MENTAL DISORDERS

		Symptoms	
		Primarily organic	Primarily mental
Presumed underlying disorder	Primarily organic	Diabetes Measles Rickets	General paresis Schizophrenia★ Bipolar disorder★
	Primarily mental	Psycho-physiological disorders	Phobias Dissociative disorders

★Whether the underlying pathology of these disorders is primarily organic or psychogenic is still a matter of debate. In some cases, such as panic disorder, organic and behavioral causes are so intertwined that it's impossible to say which is primary.

factors include cigarette smoking, alcohol, obesity, insufficient exercise, and a diet too high in sodium (Laragh and Brenner, 1995).

Apart from these known organic risks, psychological factors play a considerable role. Numerous studies show that hypertension is associated with both personal and occupational stresses, and with how one copes with such stress (Georgiades et al., 1996; Jorgensen et al., 1996; Schwartz, Pickering, and Landsbergis, 1996). In fact, teaching hypertensive individuals how to manage stress is often valuable in helping them reduce their blood pressures (Blanchard, 1994).

A CATEGORIZING REVIEW

We have now examined many different mental disorders and considered them within the pathology model. This review is summarized in Table 18.1, which classifies disorders both by the nature of their main manifestations and presumed underlying pathologies. As we have emphasized, the main manifestations vary as to whether they are best understood as physiological or psychological, and the same applies to the underlying pathology.

But some diagnostic categories within the DSM–IV don't fit this framework so tidily. These include disorders whose primary manifestation is the deviation from social norms of behavior, which we discuss next.

SOCIAL DEVIANCE

Some conditions are certainly deviant and usually undesirable, such as antisocial personality and alcohol and drug dependence; DSM–IV also includes diagnoses for pedophilia (sexual abuse of children) and pyromania (fire setting). But are these really mental disorders? And is the underlying pathology model the best way to understand them?

Society calls some forms of deviance "disorders" and has set up the mental health system to deal with them. But other forms of deviance are labeled

*18.11   BAD, ILL, and NORMAL, and
their areas of overlap   (After Stone, 1975)*

"criminal," and are considered the bailiwick of the judicial system. In actual fact, these classifications overlap (Figure 18.11). Some kinds of persons can be classified unambiguously: you and I (definitely "normal," or so we hope), a professional criminal ("bad"), and someone with a severe case of schizophrenia ("ill"). Some people, however, occupy a gray area between normality and criminality; an example might be a habitually reckless driver. Others lie between mental disorder and normality, such as a binge drinker. Still others fall vaguely between criminality and mental disorder. They are somehow both "ill" and "bad." We now concern ourselves with the cardinal example of this last category—the remorseless, heart-breaking lawbreakers known as *sociopaths,* or as they are described in DSM-IV, persons with *antisocial personality disorder.*★

THE SOCIOPATH

The clinical picture of the sociopath is of an individual who gets into continual trouble with others and with society. He is grossly selfish, callous, impulsive, and irresponsible. His—or, somewhat less frequently, her—difficulties generally start with truancy from school, runaway episodes, and a wild adolescence marked by belligerence and precocious sexual promiscuity (Robins, 1966). There may also be blatant infractions like fire setting and cruelty to animals. Later on there are various minor scrapes with the law, and these often escalate into increasingly serious legal offenses. Some researchers estimate that up to 75 percent of prisoners are sociopaths (Andreasen and Black, 1996).

But the distinguishing characteristics of sociopaths run deeper, because they lack any genuine feeling of love or loyalty for any person or any group. They also exhibit relatively little guilt or anxiety. As a result, sociopaths are creatures of the present whose primary object is to gratify the impulses they feel now, with little concern for the future and even less remorse about the past.

★ An earlier designation was *psychopath.* Some versions of this term are still in current use. One example is the MMPI *Pd* scale, which attempts to measure psychopathic deviance.

Sociopaths tend to be genuine loners. But they are often quite adept at the machinations and strategies of personal interaction, manifesting a superficial charm and sometimes a greater than average intelligence. In this regard, sociopaths are quite different from ordinary criminals and delinquents. Those individuals also violate society's laws and norms, but unlike sociopaths, they generally have a society of their own, such as a juvenile gang or a crime syndicate, whose code they try to honor and to which they have some sense of loyalty. The sociopath, on the other hand, abides by no code of conduct and readily yields to the desire of the moment (McCord and McCord, 1964). An illustration is the case of a forty-four-year-old man:

> [Roger] was reared in a well-to-do family, the only child of a doting mother. In the past ten years, Roger squandered a substantial inheritance and was beginning to "fall on hard times." Handsome, well-educated and suave in manner, he had always been skillful in charming and exploiting others, especially women. Faced with economic adversity, Roger allied himself with a group of stock promoters involved in selling essentially worthless shares of "sure-bet" Canadian mining stock. This led to other "shady deals"; and in time Roger became a full-fledged "love swindler" who intrigued, lived off, and "borrowed" thousands of dollars from a succession of wealthy and "lonely" mistresses. (Millon, 1969, p. 434)

Sociopaths are not immune to other maladies. Up to one-quarter develop major depressions, and nearly 75 percent are alcoholics or drug abusers. Sociopathy is a lifelong condition, and although the sociopath's crimes and legal entanglements lessen as she ages, her unstable lifestyle, spotty work behavior, and tendency to alcohol and drug abuse persist. About 5 percent of sociopaths commit suicide (Andreasen and Black, 1996).

Some possible causes of sociopathy What accounts for antisocial personality disorder? A central feature may be the sociopath's lack of concern for the consequences of his actions. Sociopaths are comparatively fearless, especially when the danger is far off. One investigator told sociopaths and normals that they would receive a shock at the end of a ten-minute period, and the participants' apprehensiveness was assessed by their galvanic skin response (GSR). As the time grew closer, the control participants grew increasingly nervous. In contrast, the sociopaths showed little anticipatory fear (Lippert and Senter, 1966). If impending pain had just as little import when the sociopath was young, his inadequate socialization becomes partially comprehensible. Whoever tried to teach him the don'ts of childhood found that no deterrents had lasting value (Figure 18.12).

The disquieting fearlessness of sociopaths has been observed by several writers who have noted their "extraordinary poise," their "smooth sense of physical being," and their "relative serenity" under conditions that would produce agitation in most of us (Cleckley, 1976). How does this difference between sociopaths and normals come about? Several investigators believe that there is a difference in some underlying physiological functions. One line of evidence concerns the EEG (electrical recordings from the brain; see Chapter 3). It appears that a fairly high proportion of sociopaths have abnormal EEGs with patterns that resemble those of children. One possible interpretation is that this cortical immaturity of sociopaths is the physiological counterpart of their behavioral and psychological childishness—their desire for instant gratification and their belligerent tantrums when thwarted.

A different hypothesis is that sociopaths are cortically underaroused, as if they were not fully awake under normal conditions. Proponents of this hypothesis argue that because of this underarousal, sociopaths actively seek stimulation—they are easily bored and court thrills and danger to rouse themselves to some

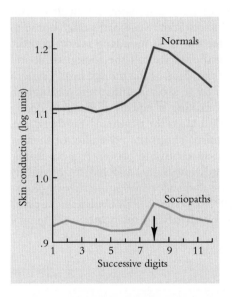

18.12 Anticipation of electric shock in normals and sociopaths *Normals and sociopaths were repeatedly presented with a series of twelve consecutive digits from 1 to 12. Whenever the digit 8 appeared, the subjects suffered an electric shock. To determine whether there were any differences in anticipatory anxiety prior to the advent of shock, the galvanic skin response (GSR) was measured. The results are shown in units of log conductance (a measure of GSR activity) for each of the 12 digits in the series. The sociopaths showed a much lower base-response level. In addition, they showed less anticipatory reaction to the digits just prior to the critical digit. (After Hare, 1965)*

optimal level of stimulation, much like the rest of us might pinch or shake ourselves to keep from dozing off (Quay, 1965; Hare, 1978).★

Both the EEG data and evidence concerning arousal indicate a biological condition underlying sociopathy, and this in turn raises the possibility of a constitutional predisposition toward this disorder. This predisposition may well be genetic, as shown by the fact that identical twins have higher concordance rates for sociopathy than fraternal twins. Early environment also plays a role. There is considerable evidence that sociopaths are more likely to have a sociopathic or alcoholic father than are normals. An additional factor is discipline; inconsistent discipline in childhood or no discipline at all correlates with sociopathy in adulthood (Robins, 1966). Indeed, one theory of psychopathy holds that the primary cause is incompetent parenting leading to poor socialization—although, admittedly, some children may be temperamentally quite difficult to manage (Lykken, 1995).

SOCIOPATHY AND THE DISORDER CONCEPT

We now have some understanding of how sociopathy might arise. But does that justify our calling it a mental disorder? Sociopaths often come to grief, admittedly, but when they do it is for the same mundane reason as ordinary criminals do: They get caught. Why should we call the sociopath ill and the criminal bad? Why should one be the province of the mental health system while the other is the business of the courts? It is often difficult to distinguish sociopathic criminals from ordinary ones, making it equally difficult to determine who should go to prison and who should go for treatment. Furthermore, most mental health practitioners are pessimistic about the possibility of therapy for sociopaths, making moot any treatment alternative to prison. A more insidious problem is that not all psychopathic individuals are "disabled" or obviously disordered. Some may become charismatic and successful politicians, businesspeople, and religious leaders (see Hare, 1993; Lykken, 1995). Under the circumstances, it is not obvious what is gained by classifying sociopathy as a mental disorder.

THE SCOPE OF PSYCHO-PATHOLOGY

Sociopathy is only one of the questionable categories in the psychiatric catalogue. Similar questions can be raised about drug addiction or alcoholism or a number of other deviant or counterproductive patterns of behavior. Are these really mental disorders in the same sense as schizophrenia or obsessive-compulsive disorder? The term "mental disorder" becomes unwieldy when it can be stretched to suit virtually any form of human behavior that causes social harm or personal unhappiness. For example, does the upset caused by losing a spouse merit a clinical diagnosis? How about losing a job? Or the lottery?

Some believe that modern psychopathology is guilty of a sort of imperialism

---

★ This suggests a relation to sensation seeking, which shows a similar pattern (see Chapter 16).

in which it tries to subsume ever more conditions. If this complaint is warranted, this is not solely the fault of an ambitious mental health establishment. Instead, it arises within a society that insists on quick and simple labels, ready diagnoses, and with them, simple solutions. We seem to believe that by designating a problem a mental disorder we have somehow taken a stride toward its solution. But we've really done nothing of the sort. For calling a problem—alcoholism, sexual exhibitionism, drug addiction, or even shoplifting or premenstrual syndrome—a mental disorder does not necessarily make it so. Nor does it mean that we therefore know what to do about it. Moreover, making the term "mental disorder" too inclusive can be dangerous, because a diagnosis can be used not only to label and treat, but also to brand and ostracize.

SUMMARY

1. The field of *psychopathology,* which is sometimes called *abnormal psychology,* deals with a wide assortment of disorders that generally cause considerable anguish and seriously impair the person's functioning.

2. In certain periods in history, mental disorder was seen as a form of demonic possession. In later times, it was regarded as a form of illness. Some of these disorders are *somatogenic,* being the direct consequence of a bodily malfunction. An example is *general paresis,* which was discovered to result from a syphilitic infection contracted years before. Other mental disorders are thought to be *psychogenic,* being better explained using psychological rather than organic causes, a view that seemed to apply to many cases once called *hysteria* (now called *conversion disorder*).

3. A very general conception of psychopathology is provided by the *underlying pathology model,* which makes psychopathology analogous to physical disorders. According to the underlying pathology model, the signs and symptoms of a disorder are thought to result from some underlying and relatively immediate (or proximate) cause—the pathology. Many disorders seem well described by the *diathesis-stress* conception, which proposes the interaction of various predispositions (diatheses) with various precipitants (stressors). As formulated here, the underlying pathology model is largely descriptive and makes no assertion about the nature of the signs and symptoms, their psychogenic or somatogenic causes, or the appropriate modes of treatment. Three subcategories of the underlying pathology model are the *medical model,* the *psychodynamic model,* and the *learning model.*

4. A given disorder has various *signs* and *symptoms* that form a pattern or *syndrome;* these, plus the *course* of the illness, are the bases for diagnosis and classification. The classification system now in use is set out in DSM-IV, the current diagnostic manual for mental disorders.

5. Probably the most serious condition in psychopathology is *schizophrenia.* Its main symptoms are disorders of cognition, social withdrawal, disruption of emotional response, and in many cases, the construction of a private world accompanied by *delusions* and *hallucinations.* Subcategories of schizophrenia used in current classification include the *paranoid, catatonic,* and *disorganized* subtypes.

6. One question about the pathology of schizophrenia is how best to characterize the schizophrenic's underlying *psychological malfunction.* Many authors believe that it is fundamentally a cognitive disorder, based on an inability to keep one's thoughts and actions on track.

7. The search for the biological basis of schizophrenia has focused on two possible kinds of pathology. One involves a malfunctioning of the neurotransmitter *dopamine.* Evidence comes from the therapeutic effect of *classical antipsychotic medications,* which are

known to block dopamine transmission at neuron synapses. An alternative to the dopamine hypothesis is the *dopamine-serotonin interaction hypothesis,* which is supported by the broader effectiveness of *atypical antipsychotics*—medications that block both serotonin and dopamine receptors. Another organic pathology involves an atrophy of brain tissue found in some schizophrenics. Several hypotheses consider schizophrenia to be composed of separate pathologies. According to the *two-syndrome hypothesis,* one type of schizophrenia (Type I) is caused by a neurotransmitter malfunction and produces *positive symptoms,* such as delusions and hallucinations. The second type (called Type II schizophrenia) is caused by cerebral atrophy and leads to *negative symptoms,* such as withdrawal and apathy. Support for this view comes from the fact that patients with mostly positive symptoms respond well to standard antipsychotics and show little cerebral damage, while patients with mostly negative symptoms are not improved by classical antipsychotics and are more likely to show brain damage. More recent studies suggest a *three-syndrome view,* in which schizophrenics with positive symptoms are subdivided into those who are predominantly either psychotic or disorganized.

8.   Researchers of more ultimate causes of schizophrenia now consider it to be a *neurodevelopmental disorder* that includes a genetic factor. The evidence is provided by concordance studies of identical and fraternal twins and by studies of children of schizophrenic mothers adopted shortly after birth. But this genetic factor is only a predisposition; its conversion into the actual schizophrenic disorder depends on some precipitating stress. Many investigators believe that the stressors may occur within the prenatal environment (such as viral infections) or be due to complications during birth. Some investigators had proposed that low socioeconomic class and pathological interactions within the family might constitute environmental stressors that could produce schizophrenia; however, these appear to be consequences of having schizophrenia rather than causes of it.

9.   In another group of conditions, the *mood disorders,* the dominant disturbances are of energy, mood, and motivation, as in the revved-up expansiveness of *hypomania,* the irrational frenzy of *mania,* or the despair and lethargy of *depression.* One form of mood disorder is *bipolar disorder,* with recurrent swings from one extreme to the other. Another is *major depression,* in which the mood extreme is an episode or series of recurrent bouts of depression. Still another is *seasonal affective disorder,* which seems to be related to the amount of light patients are exposed to and is typified by depressions that start in the fall and end in the spring.

10.   According to one view, mood disorders, especially bipolar disorder, are produced by an organic pathology, a belief bolstered by evidence that such conditions have a genetic component. Bipolar disorder may arise from instabilities of neuronal membranes. For major depression, one hypothesis proposes a defect in the supply of certain neurotransmitters, in particular, *serotonin* and *norepinephrine.* Other investigators stress the role of psychogenic factors, such as cognitive outlook. An influential example of such a psychogenic view is the *learned helplessness theory* of depression. Some of its more recent extensions stress the role of *explanatory style* and of *hopelessness.*

11.   Another group of conditions are the *anxiety disorders.* One such disorder is *social phobia,* a general fear of humiliation and avoidance of relevant situations. Another is *specific phobia,* in which there is an intense and irrational fear of some object or situation. According to the *preparedness theory,* specific phobias are based on built-in predispositions to learn to fear certain stimuli that were dangerous to our primate ancestors. In *obsessive-compulsive disorder,* the anxiety is produced by internal wishes or events, such as obsessions that cannot be stopped. In *generalized anxiety disorder* it is all pervasive and free floating. In *panic disorder,* which is often accompanied by *agoraphobia,* there are sudden, intense panic attacks that strike out of the blue. In *acute stress disorder,* there is an immediate reaction to extraordinarily stressful events such as fire, war, rape, and other physical assault. Acute stress disorder usually starts with an initial period of *dissociation,* followed by severe after-effects, including recurrent nightmares, waking flashbacks, and "survival guilt." These effects often persist and after one month are considered *post-traumatic stress disorder (PTSD).* PTSD can last for years, especially after particularly strong trauma, and the sufferer is often left avoidant and socially estranged.

SUMMARY

12. Dissociation is the defining sign of the *dissociative disorders*. Chief among them is *dissociative identity disorder*, which has been somewhat controversially linked to repeated, violent early childhood sexual abuse.

13. Another group are the *somatoform disorders*, characterized by the presence of bodily signs and symptoms that have no apparent organic basis. The somatoform disorders include the classic but now rare disorder that inspired psychoanalysis, *conversion disorder*.

14. In psychophysiological disorders, psychogenic causes have genuine organic consequences. An example is *coronary heart disease*, which was once thought to be related to the impatient, hard-driving, competitive *Type A behavior pattern*. It now appears that the Type A behaviors do not form a consistent pattern and that *hostility* is more predictive of coronary heart disease.

15. The problem of defining psychopathology is acute for conditions such as *antisocial personality disorder* (or *sociopathy*) in which deviance overlaps with mental disorder and criminality. The causes of sociopathy are still unknown; hypotheses include cortical immaturity, a chronic state of underarousal that leads to attempts to seek compensatory stimulation, and a genetic predisposition.

CHAPTER **19**

TREATMENT OF PSYCHOPATHOLOGY

What can be done to help those who suffer from mental disorders? There is no scarcity of therapeutic methods, and each has its own adherents. Some practitioners rely on biological interventions such as medications. Others approach the condition psychologically, through various kinds of psychotherapy. Until recently, the proven benefits of either kind of treatment were relatively modest. Of late, the outlook is more optimistic. There are still no miracle cures, but at least some disorders respond reasonably well to the appropriate treatments.

BIOLOGICAL THERAPIES

One approach to treatment is to make direct changes in various bodily systems. Such *biological therapies* characterize medicine's classical attack on any disease. Once mental disorder was conceived as an illness, it was only natural to try to heal it with the traditional tools of the physician's trade. Until fairly recently, such attempts were largely unsuccessful, with the would-be cures often far worse than the disease. We already mentioned a very early example in Chapter 18: trephining, the removal of pieces of skull bone, a prehistoric practice that persisted into the twentieth century. Other early procedures involved a relentless succession of bloodlettings and purgatives, all intended somehow to restore harmony among the bodily humors. Later developments were hardly milder. For example, Benjamin Rush (1745–1813), one of the signers of the Declaration of Independence and the acknowledged father of American psychiatry, submersed patients in hot or cold water until they were just short of drowning or twirled them on special devices at speeds that rendered them unconscious (Figure 19.1). Such methods were said to reestablish balance between bodily and mental functions. They almost certainly had no such salutary effects, although they were probably welcomed by hospital attendants, since such methods undoubtedly terrified the inmates and thus helped to "keep order" (Mora, 1975).

PHARMACOTHERAPIES

The bleak outlook for such biological therapies did not brighten until the turn of the twentieth century. The first step was the conquest of the global, progressively disabling syndrome of general paresis, accomplished by attacking the syphilitic infection that caused it (see Chapter 18). But the major advances have come only during the last fifty years or so with the discovery and development of a number of *psychotropic drugs,* medications that seem to control, or at least moderate, the manifestations of schizophrenia and the mood and anxiety disorders. These medications have had an enormous impact upon mental health care. They have allowed patients with many disorders to be treated without hospitalization (Olfson and Klerman, 1993).

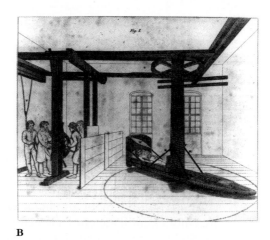

A

B

C

**19.1   Early methods for treating mental
disorder**   *(A) A crib for violent patients.
(Courtesy of Historical Pictures Service)
(B) A centrifugal-force bed. (Courtesy of National Library of Medicine) (C) A swinging
device. (Courtesy of Culver Pictures)*

***Some adverse effects of deinstitutionaliza-
tion***   *Some of the homeless in American
cities are people discharged from mental hospitals who are unable to adjust to the world
outside. (Courtesy of AP/Wide World Photos)*

DRUG TREATMENT OF SCHIZOPHRENIA: ANTIPSYCHOTICS

In the last chapter, we saw that a major argument for a somatogenic theory of
schizophrenia was the effectiveness of certain drugs called ***antipsychotics,*** the
most common of which include Thorazine, Haldol, Clozaril, and Risperdal.
(Here, and in further text discussions, we only give the drug's trade name. Its
technical name, the biochemical family it belongs to, and some related drugs that
have similar effects are shown in Table 19.1.) The ***classical antipsychotics*** (such
as Thorazine and Haldol) reduce the major positive symptoms of schizophrenia
(such as thought disorder and hallucination—see Chapter 18) apparently by
blocking dopamine receptors in certain key brain pathways. But they are ineffective in up to 20 percent of patients with negative symptoms (see Chapter 18).
The ***atypical antipsychotics*** (such as Clozaril and Risperdal) not only reduce the
major positive symptoms; they also reduce the major negative symptoms. Like
the classical antipsychotics, the atypical antipsychotics block the neurotransmission of dopamine. Some authors believe that their enhanced benefits, especially
with negative symptoms, are produced by additional effects on the neurotransmission of serotonin. Others suggests that their advantage is produced by a more
selective effect on some particular group of dopamine neurons rather than on all
(Tandon and Kane, 1993; Wirshing et al., 1995).

It is sometimes said that drugs like Thorazine and Clozaril are not really
antipsychotic agents at all but are only fancy sedatives—"chemical straitjackets"—that merely tranquilize patients. This argument does not square with the
facts. While Thorazine, Clozaril, and similar drugs alleviate schizophrenic symptoms, such powerful sedatives as phenobarbital have no such effect. They put the
patient to sleep, but when he wakes up, his delusions and hallucinations are
unabated. Other evidence suggests that the antipsychotics act specifically on the
signs and symptoms of schizophrenia, with only minor effects on those of other
disorders. For example, they help to clear up the patient's disordered thought but
have little effect on depression or anxiety (Davis, 1985a; Hollister and Csernansky, 1990).

The social reality of treating schizophrenia   Because they allowed many schizophrenic patients to be managed outside of mental hospitals, the classical antipsychotic medications lent impetus to a movement called ***deinstitutionalization,***
which was intended to obtain better and less expensive care for patients in their
own communities—at local community mental health centers rather than at
large, centralized hospitals. In part, this movement worked. Whereas in the 1950s

TABLE 19.1 SOME COMMONLY USED PSY-CHOTROPIC MEDICATIONS

Primary Function	Drug Class	Chemical Name	Trade (Commercial) Name
Antidepressants	MAO inhibitors	Phenelzine Tranylcypromine	Nardil Parnate
	Tricyclics	Clomipramine Imipramine Nortriptyline	Anafranil Tofranil Pamelor
	Selective serotonin reuptake inhibitors	Fluoxetine Paroxetine Sertaline	Prozac Paxil Zoloft
Antipsychotics	Butyrophenones	Haloperidol	Haldol
	Phenothiazines	Chlorpromazine	Thorazine
	Atypical antipsychotics	Clozapine Risperidone Olanzapine	Clozaril Risperdal Zyprexa
Antimanic medications		Carbamazepine Lithium carbonate Sodium valproate	Tegretol Eskalith Depakote
Anxiety-reducing medications (anxiolytics)	Benzodiazepines	Alprazolam Diazepam	Xanax Valium
	Atypical anxiolytics	Buspirone	BuSpar

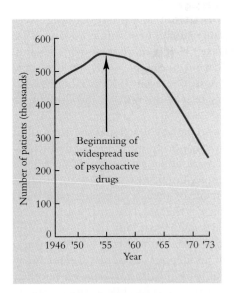

19.2   Number of residents in state and local government mental hospitals in the United States, 1946–1973   *(Based on data from U.S. Public Health Service)*

mental hospitals housed about 600,000 patients, by the 1980s this number had dropped to 125,000. These drugs also made it possible to discharge schizophrenic patients more quickly than ever. According to one estimate, prior to their introduction, two out of three schizophrenic patients spent most of their lives in the state asylum. In the 1980s, their average stay was about two months (Lamb, 1984; Davis, 1985a; see Figure 19.2).

The high hopes created by the classical antipsychotics were soon tempered, because although the medications help to alleviate some of the symptoms of the disorder, they still leave much to be desired as a treatment. As we mentioned, they tend to work well on positive symptoms like delusions and hallucinations but do little for negative symptoms like apathy, emotional blunting, and poor sociability. They also only hold these symptoms in check so long as they are taken; they neither cure the disease nor alter its progress. Finally, they have potent side effects that can include sedation, constipation, dry mouth, blurred vision, difficulty in urination, cardiac irregularities, tremors and muscle spasms, restlessness, a shuffling gait, and a curiously inexpressive, masklike face. Some patients who take them over the long term eventually develop permanent motor disorders (Csernansky and Newcomer, 1995). While the atypical antipsychotics are effective with some of the negative symptoms of schizophrenia, they also have their downside. The usefulness of one of the first of these new medications, Clozaril, was hampered by its high cost (Reid, Pham, and Rago, 1993), and the fact that between 1 and 2 percent of patients taking Clozaril develop a potentially fatal blood disorder, necessistating regular and careful blood testing (Alvir et al., 1993). Investigators therefore moved quickly to seek similar medications that might be as effective but less risky (Meltzer, 1993). One result was the introduction of Risperdal and Zyprexa, which have Clozaril's advantages and are just as costly but do not share its risk (Marder, 1996; Beasley, Tollefson, and Tran, 1997).

One result of all these risks and side effects is that many schizophrenic patients refuse to take their medication reliably, leading to flare-ups of their signs and symptoms and causing repeated hospitalizations—they become "revolving-door patients." Even when they do take their medication regularly, 30 to 50 percent of patients have recurrent outbreaks of the illness and need further hospitalization or a change of dosage or type of medication (Andreasen and Black, 1996). As a consequence, although fewer schizophrenics remain in psychiatric hospitals and do not stay in the hospital as long (Lamb, 1984; Davis, 1985a), the number of times they are readmitted for short stays has increased by 80 percent since the 1960s (Rosenstein, Milazzo-Sayre, and Manderscheid, 1989).

What do schizophrenic patients do when they are discharged from the hospital? Some stay at home with their aging parents. Others live in less than ideal board-and-care homes, while still others become drifters and join the swelling ranks of the homeless. According to one report, some 40 percent of New York City's homeless people suffer persistent mental disorder or have a history of mental illness (Golden, 1990). It is thus clear that while the antipsychotic drugs help to alleviate the symptoms of schizophrenia, they do not provide a cure. Given the current inadequacy—and in many cases, the complete lack—of appropriate community services, this represents, at least for now, a failure to achieve the intentions of deinstitutionalization (Jones, 1983; Lamb, 1984; Westermeyer, 1987).

DRUG TREATMENT OF DEPRESSION: ANTIDEPRESSANTS

Shortly after the introduction of antipsychotics, two major groups of drugs were found that seemed to act specifically on depression. These antidepressants were of two major classes, the ***monoamine oxidase (MAO) inhibitors*** such as Nardil and the ***tricyclic antidepressants*** such as Tofranil (see Table 19.1). Of these, the tricyclics became the most widely used, mostly because patients taking MAO inhibitors must conform to difficult dietary restrictions (Burke and Preskhorn, 1995).

Both Nardil and Tofranil appear to work in part by increasing the amount of norepinephrine and serotonin available for synaptic transmission. (The mechanisms whereby they accomplish this mission are different; for details, see Figure 19.3). These medications are very effective in counteracting depression, producing marked improvement in up to 65 percent of the patients who take them (Hollister and Csernansky, 1990). Not all of the medications work for all patients, however. Some patients may have somewhat different biochemical deficits and thus may do better with Nardil than with Tofranil or vice versa. Furthermore, even within each class of antidepressant, some patients may respond better or have fewer side effects on one medication than on another. There is some evidence that by using blood tests and the like a patient can be matched to the proper antidepressant drug (Maugh, 1981; Davis, 1985b), but the selection of medication is in most cases a matter of clinical judgment.

The use of medication for treating depression changed dramatically in 1988 with the introduction of the first "designer drug" for depression, Prozac

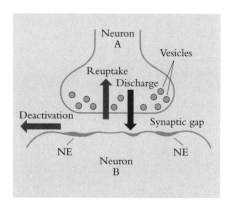

19.3   A schematic presentation of two ways in which a drug may increase the available supply of a neurotransmitter   *A neurotransmitter, norepinephrine (NE), is discharged by Neuron A into the synaptic gap and diffuses across the gap to stimulate Neuron B. The more NE accumulates at the membrane of Neuron B, the more that neuron will fire. NE at the synapse can be diminished through reuptake, in which NE is pumped back into Neuron A, or through deactivation, whereby certain enzymes (such as MAO) break down the neurotransmitter and render it ineffective. Tricyclics (like Tofranil) and MAO inhibitors (like Nardil) increase the amount of available NE (and serotonin) at the synaptic junction but in different ways. Tricyclics interfere with neurotransmitter reuptake; MAO inhibitors prevent MAO from breaking the transmitters down. Second-generation antidepressants like SSRIs (such as Prozac) block reuptake but act selectively upon serotonin neurons.*

(Kramer, 1993). Prozac was engineered in the laboratory to act minimally on norepinephrine and maximally on serotonin, thus marking the introduction of a new class of antidepressants known as *selective serotonin reuptake inhibitors* (*SSRIs;* see Table 19.1). For most patients, Prozac and related drugs reduce the manifestations of depression as quickly and as completely as Nardil or Tofranil, but they have far fewer side effects and are thus safer to prescribe—so safe that most are now prescribed (and perhaps overprescribed) not by psychiatrists but by personal physicians (Olfson and Klerman, 1993). Still, while these antidepressants have been touted by some as panaceas, like all medications they, too, have their side effects, which can include nausea, diarrhea, anxiety, insomnia, and—in upwards of 30 percent of patients—a loss of sexual desire or response (Hollander and McCarley, 1992; Jacobsen, 1992; Montgomery, 1995).

Just as the antipsychotics are not true sedatives, so the antidepressants are not stimulants. Evidence comes from the fact that these drugs do not produce euphoria in normal subjects; they evidently have little effect on mood if there is no depression to begin with (Cole and Davis, 1975). But it is also true that these drugs are more than "just" antidepressants, because they are also quite useful in alleviating the distress of many other conditions, including panic disorder, migraine headache, school phobia, eating disorders like bulimia, and chronic pain (Sheean, 1985; Hollister and Csernansky, 1990; Olfson and Klerman, 1993). Some antidepressants such as the tricyclic Anafranil and several SSRIs are also effective in many cases of obsessive-compulsive disorder (Ananth, 1985; Rapoport 1991; Dominguez, 1992; Heninger, 1995).

DRUG TREATMENT OF BIPOLAR DISORDER: ANTIMANICS

Medications to treat bipolar disorder are called antimanics, even though they can also help forestall the depressive episodes in the disorder. The first medication used specifically for its antimanic action was lithium carbonate (one example is Eskalith; see Table 19.1). Patients who begin taking lithium can generally expect that their manic episodes will subside within five or ten days. Just what accounts for these effects is largely unknown, but according to one hypothesis, lithium carbonate may reregulate neurotransmission by stabilizing the influence of calcium on neuronal membranes (Meltzer, 1986; Wood and Goodwin, 1987).

Despite lithium's effectiveness, it only works in 60 to 80 percent of patients with bipolar disorder (Calabrese and Woyshville, 1995). Taking it is also problematic for many patients, most of whom must endure unpleasant side effects such as weight gain, dry mouth, and tremors. Moreover, lithium is toxic at higher doses, requiring patients to have their blood levels tested frequently and making it a risky treatment for patients who are potentially suicidal and might overdose. Nor can lithium be taken during pregnancy or when the patient has kidney disease.

Fortunately, other drugs are now available that achieve some of lithium's gains but without many of its drawbacks. The two main contenders are Tegretol and Depakote, which were once used strictly as anticonvulsants to treat epilepsy. Like lithium, they also have side effects (some potentially serious), but they are better tolerated by many patients. In most cases, they are just as effective as lithium and may even be superior when the patient's mood cycles are frequent and rapid (Andreasen and Black, 1996; West, McElroy, and Keck, 1996).

DRUG TREATMENT OF ANXIETY: ANXIOLYTICS

When patients suffer from disabling anxiety, they are often treated with medications that are popularly called tranquilizers and technically known as *anxiolytics* (see Table 19.1). The most common kinds of anxiolytics apparently work by increasing neurotransmission at synapses containing the neurotransmitter GABA (Schader and Greenblatt, 1995). Some of these medications, such as Valium and Xanax, are prescribed so often that their names have almost become household words. They are useful as short-term treatments for generalized anxiety disorder, panic disorder, post-traumatic stress disorder, alcohol withdrawal, insomnia, muscle spasms, tension headaches, and various other stress-related disorders. They are rarely used for long-term treatment because, unlike the medications we have reviewed thus far, they are highly addictive and interact dangerously with alcohol. Some newer anxiolytics such as BuSpar are not addictive and have become popular substitutes for the older anxiolytics, especially for patients who are prone to alcohol or drug abuse or will have to take the medications over a long period of time (Schweitzer, Rickels, and Uhlenhuth, 1995; Lydiard, Brawman-Mintzer, and Ballenger, 1996).

EVALUATING A MEDICATION

How can we assess the effectiveness of a medication? We will discuss this issue in detail, because some of the issues raised by drug evaluation methods extend beyond tests of drug therapy. In large part, the same issues apply in evaluating *any* therapeutic procedure, including psychotherapy.

Suppose we want to find out whether a given drug, say Thorazine, reduces the manifestations of schizophrenia. Obviously, we would need to administer Thorazine to a group of schizophrenic patients for some period, assessing how well the patients do before and after receiving the medication. In fact, many studies of treatment effectiveness are of just this kind. But a little reflection shows that relying only on this procedure would be a mistake.

CONTROLLING FOR SPONTANEOUS IMPROVEMENT

One problem with a simple before-and-after assessment is that it ignores the possibility that the patient's condition might have improved without any treatment. Such spontaneous improvements occur in many disorders (though not often in schizophrenia). Moreover, many disorders fluctuate in their severity over time; patients are more likely to seek treatment when they are at their worst, and when they improve, it would be wrong to give automatic credit to the treatment.

Controlling for these factors is a bit complex, though. One has to compare two groups of patients drawn from the same population, one of which received Thorazine for, say, six weeks, while the other group did not receive the drug. Both groups would be assessed at the beginning of the study and after the first group received the treatment (and perhaps at intervals in between). Initially, the groups ought to be equivalent. The question is whether they will be different during or after the treatment.

CONTROLLING FOR PLACEBO EFFECTS

Suppose that after six weeks the patients who were given Thorazine seem to be less bothered by hallucinations and delusions than the untreated controls. This result makes it unlikely that the change in the Thorazine group was due to spontaneous improvement or a natural fluctuation of the illness, since these factors should affect both groups equally. Does this prove that the benefits of treat-

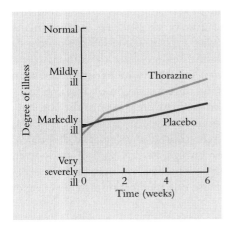

19.4 Controlling for placebo effects
Severity of illness over a six-week period during which patients were treated with either Thorazine or a placebo.

ment were indeed caused by the drug? Unfortunately, no, because we have not yet ruled out the possibility that the result was due to the *placebo effect.*

In medicine, the term *placebo* refers to some inert (that is, medically neutral) substance that is administered to a patient who *believes* that it has therapeutic power. Such placebo effects probably account for many of the cures of ancient physicians, whose medications included such items as crocodile dung, swine teeth, and moss scraped from the skull of a man who died a violent death (Shapiro, 1971). But the placebo effect is by no means a quaint artifact: Numerous modern studies have shown that up to 70 percent of patients suffering from diseases ranging from asthma to coronary heart disease will make some kind of real improvement after taking placebos, be they disguised sugar pills or injections of harmless solutions (Beecher, 1995; Benson and Friedman, 1996).★

Given the power of the placebo effect, how can we be sure that the improvement in the drug-treated group of our example is caused by the properties of the drug itself? Perhaps a sugar pill—or a bit of crocodile dung or a magnet attached to the head or the latest health-food fad—would have done as well. To exclude this possibility, we must administer a placebo to the control patients. They will thus no longer be "untreated." On the contrary, they will receive the same attention from the investigators and the treatment staff, will be told the same things about their treatment, and will be given the same number of pills at the same time as the patients in the true drug group. There will be only one difference between the two groups: The control patients will swallow pills that, unbeknownst to them, contain only inert materials. As a result of this stratagem, we can simultaneously control for two factors, spontaneous improvement and placebo effects. Now that these two factors are controlled, a difference in the way the two groups appear after treatment can finally be attributed to the effect of the drug itself. Figure 19.4 shows the results of such a study, comparing the effects of Thorazine and a placebo after one, three, and six weeks of treatment. As the figure shows, Thorazine was clearly superior. But as the figure also shows, some slight improvement is found in the placebo group as well, highlighting the need for such a control in the evaluation of drug effectiveness.

What explains placebo effects? Some of them may be the result of endorphins, chemicals produced by the brain itself that act like opiates and reduce pain (see Chapter 3). Evidence for this view comes from a study in which pain was reduced by a placebo medication that the patients believed was a pain reliever. But this relief stopped as soon as the patients received a dose of a drug that is known to counteract the effects of any opiate (Levine, Gordon, and Fields, 1979).

CONTROLLING FOR EXPECTATIONS

By definition, a placebo control implies that all of the patients in the group think that they are being treated with the real medicine. But to guarantee this desired state of ignorance, the treating physicians—and the psychologists and social workers and nurses and attendants who may be part of the research staff—must also be kept in the dark about which patients are receiving the medication and which the placebo, because this information may affect their assessment of the patients' progress.

The staff's knowledge can have further effects. Staff members may unwittingly communicate their beliefs and expectations to the patients, perhaps by

---

★ We hasten to add that placebo effects refer to actual healing as a result of placebo administration, not simply the delusion that one is better. Unlike researchers who must try to control for placebo effects in order to ensure that treatments are intrinsically effective, practitioners often discuss how to *maximize* placebo effects so that their patients can benefit as much as possible (Benson and Friedman, 1996).

observing the medicated patients more closely or by being less concerned if a placebo-treated patient fails to take her morning pill. By such signals, the patients may figure out whether the physicians expect them to get better or not, and their progress may be influenced by these expectations. To guard against this, modern medical evaluators use the **double-blind technique.** In this technique, the patients are "blind" as to whether they are in the medication or placebo group, and the same holds for the staff members who work with and evaluate these patients. With both sides kept in the dark, there is no chance for expectations or beliefs to compromise the data. The only ones who know who's in which group are the investigators who are masterminding the study and who have no direct contact with the patients.

There are still problems with using placebos in studies of medication effectiveness, even when the studies are double-blind. First, in many cases it is unethical to give a placebo and thereby withhold an accepted treatment. Second, it is often easy to discern who is taking medication versus placebos, because many medications have characteristic side effects that are hard for either the patient or the treatment staff to ignore. Finally, researchers seldom want to know if a new medication is better than nothing; they want to know whether it's better than the standard treatment. For all of these reasons, the most common research practice is to assess a new medication's incremental effectiveness against the best current treatment. In this kind of study, no one is deprived of an actual treatment, placebo effects are controlled with the current-treatment group, and differences in side effects are less obvious between the groups. In this kind of study, even when patients respond no differently to the new medication than to the accepted one, the results may have an impact, because one medication may be cheaper or safer than the other.

ASSESSING IMPROVEMENT

In even the best-designed investigations of drug effectiveness, success hinges on one question: How do we measure whether the medication works and the patients improve? Typically, *outcome measures* in drug evaluation studies have consisted of patients' opinions about how they feel while taking the medicine and ratings from the treatment staff about how well the patients function while observed in the hospital or clinic. Occasionally, the results from psychological or medical tests also are used as evidence of effectiveness.

These kinds of outcome measures might seem sufficient, but in today's economically pressured medical climate, they are being challenged by critics who wonder whether the treatments are not just effective but *cost-effective*. Does taking the medication shorten costly hospital stays (or visits to expensive psychotherapists)? Will the medication make the patient a more reliable wage earner and reduce the costs (sick leave pay, worker's compensation, Social Security) associated with illness? Will it restore the patient's ability to parent and reduce the costs of children's care? Increasingly, the money spent on treatment is being weighed against the money saved with treatment, and whether a medication "works" is a question whose answer is poised precariously on this balance sheet (Zarkin et al., 1995). The same issue of cost-effectiveness will reemerge in our discussion of psychotherapy.

LIMITATIONS OF PHARMACOTHERAPY

Even excluding the wider issue of cost-effectiveness, medications for mental disorders have their limitations. We have already noted two, that they do not help everyone and that many of them have unpleasant side effects. But how beneficial are these medications? Critics of pharmacotherapy contend that the beneficial results of drug therapy are still quite limited (Fisher and Greenberg, 1989). This is especially so for patients taking the classic antipsychotics and antimanic medications, who must remain on a maintenance dose to minimize their disability but who often quit taking their medicine because they find the side effects so unpleasant.

This criticism is less compelling in the case of antidepressants and anxiolytics, which sometimes do for patients with mood and anxiety disorders what insulin does for patients with diabetes: They don't cure the disease, but they can do a fine job of controlling it.

Whatever these limitations, the modern drug therapies are clearly a major step forward. They have restored some patients to normal functioning. They have allowed others to remain, however imperfectly, in a family or community setting, when they would have otherwise been relegated to long-term hospital stays. No less important is the fact that these medications—particularly the antipsychotics—have completely changed the atmosphere of mental hospitals, especially the remaining large state-run facilities. Until a few decades ago, straitjackets were common, as were feces-smeared and shriek-filled wards; today, such scenes are comparatively rare because the medications can so effectively control the more florid manifestations of mental disorder. As a result, the modern mental hospital can function more as a therapeutic center than a warehouse. It can provide important social and psychological services, including vocational counseling and psychotherapy, all of which would have been unthinkable in the "snake-pit" settings of former times.

PSYCHOSURGERY

Until the advent of the major psychotropic drugs, physicians relied on several other biological therapies, all of which involved drastic assaults on the nervous system. Some of these consisted of *psychosurgery,* or brain surgery, to alter thinking or behavior. In prefrontal lobotomy, for example, the neurological connections between the thalamus and the frontal lobes are severed, in whole or in part. This operation was meant to liberate the patient's thoughts from the pathological influence of his emotions, on the dubious neurological assumption that thought and emotion were localized in the frontal lobes and the thalamus, respectively. Unfortunately, later evaluations often showed that these surgical procedures had deleterious effects on cognitive functions, which led to extreme caution in their application (Robbin, 1958; Maher, 1966; Valenstein, 1986).

In recent years, psychosurgery has reemerged as a useful technique, but the psychosurgery of today has been refined considerably, both in the surgical procedures used and the patients judged suitable for them (Rappaport, 1992). Neurosurgeons now create very precise lesions in very specific brain areas instead of disconnecting or destroying whole lobes or regions. And in the vast majority of cases, such surgery is reserved for those patients who are severely disabled and show no improvement after all other medical or psychotherapeutic alternatives have been exhausted. This surgery-as-last-resort has been used in patients with intractable depression, severe obsessive-compulsive disorder, and chronic pain, and the surgery is often beneficial. There are clearly risks inherent in these surgeries, but the risks may be acceptable compared to the severe level of the patients' ongoing disability (Bridges, 1987; Davies and Weeks, 1993; Hay et al., 1993; Baer et al., 1995).

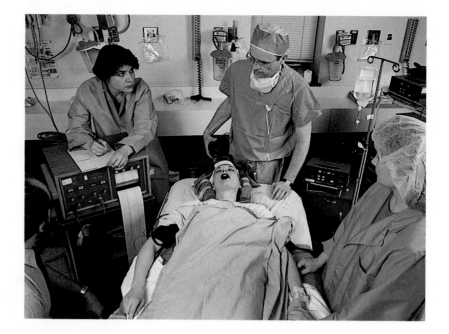

19.5   Patient about to undergo ECT
(Photograph by James D. Wilson/Woodfin Camp)

ELECTROCONVULSIVE THERAPY

Another form of biological therapy is *electroconvulsive therapy (ECT),* sometimes colloquially called "shock treatment." For about half a second a current of moderate intensity is passed between two electrodes attached to the patient's head. The result is a 30- to 60-second convulsive seizure similar to that seen in epilepsy (Figure 19.5), with the usual course of ECT consisting of six to ten treatments over a period of a week or two.

When ECT first came into use, patients were conscious and thrashed about during their convulsions, often suffering serious bruises or bone fractures. Modern ECT actually looks very mild. Patients are given short-acting anesthetics to render them temporarily unconscious and muscle relaxants to reduce the manifestations of the seizure to a few slight twitches (Andreasen and Black, 1996).

ECT was originally meant as a treatment for schizophrenia but was soon established as particularly effective in depression. Here, its efficacy is considerable. It works for as many as 70 to 80 percent of patients who have not responded to any antidepressant medication (Janicak et al., 1985; Andreasen and Black, 1996) or who cannot take such medications because of overdose potential or other medical problems. In addition, ECT seems to act more quickly than antidepressant medications usually do (Weiner, 1984b, 1985). ECT also seems quite effective in treating acute mania as well as various psychotic states associated with drug intoxication (Sackeim, Devanand, and Nobler, 1995).

Despite these advantages, the use of ECT remains controversial and not only because the idea of inducing convulsions seems so medieval. ECT can also produce memory impairment that in some cases lasts for months or even longer (Squire, 1977; Breggin, 1979; for discussion, see Weiner, 1984a, b). Under the circumstances, ECT is generally used only after drug therapy has failed or when there seems to be a serious chance of suicide. In the latter case, the fast-acting quality of ECT may be an overriding advantage (Andreasen and Black, 1996).

What accounts for the therapeutic effects of ECT? As yet, there is no satisfactory explanation. ECT is known to produce widespread effects in many neural pathways and neurotransmitter systems. It also affects gene expression, brain protein synthesis, and the secretion of endocrine hormones. Neuroimaging research is now underway to discover which brain areas are most affected by ECT, and this may shed some light on which of ECT's physiological effects are crucial to its therapeutic effectiveness (Sackeim et al., 1995).

PSYCHOTHERAPY

Biological treatments are but one approach to the treatment of psychopathology. The alternative approach forgoes direct changes to the patient's body and instead relies on psychological means. Such attempts are known collectively as *psychotherapy.*

There are many different kinds, or *modes,* of psychotherapy, and they differ both in how psychopathology is conceived and how the actual therapy is practiced. Some approaches are based on psychoanalysis and so emphasize unconscious conflicts and encourage introspection and insight. Others rely on behavioral findings from animal and human experimentation; these seek to identify maladaptive responses and then promote the learning of new responses. Still others take a cognitive approach, focus on the disabling role of faulty thinking, while teaching more rational thought. A final, humanistic outlook espouses the importance of the concept of free will, views "disorder" as a failure to build a life that is expanding and fulfilling, and assists in discovering personal meaning.

In what follows, we will discuss five common modes of *individual psychotherapy* (therapy conducted with a single patient) that grow out of these approaches: (1) classical psychoanalysis, (2) psychodymanic therapy (a modern offshoot of psychoanalysis), (3) behavior therapy, (4) cognitive therapy, and (5) humanistic therapy. Later we discuss extensions of psychotherapy that treat groups and families.

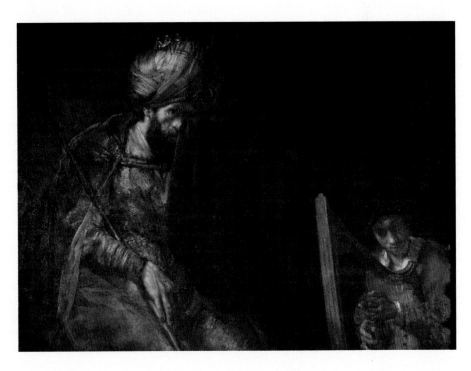

An early attempt at psychotherapy *The biblical King Saul was subject to severe bouts of rage and depression but was apparently calmed by listening to young David playing the harp. (Rembrandt's* David Playing the Harp before Saul; *photograph © Foundation Johan Maurits van Nassau. Courtesy of Mauritshuis, The Hague)*

CLASSICAL PSYCHOANALYSIS

■ **Classical psychoanalysis** is the method Sigmund Freud developed at the turn of the twentieth century, and according to some writers, it is the ancestor of virtually all modern modes of psychotherapy (London, 1964). Freud's basic assumption was that a patient's ills (in Freud's terms, his *neuroses*) stemmed from unconscious defenses against unacceptable urges that date back to early childhood. By adulthood, many of these defenses are relics that, though they protect him from anxiety, also shield him from seeing clearly both the outer world and his own inner world. These defenses become manifest as psychological symptoms, bodily malfunctions, or tendencies to repeat outdated and by now utterly maladaptive patterns of behavior (see Chapter 17).

Freud believed that for the patient to overcome her neurosis, she must lower her mental shield in order to glimpse her buried thoughts and wishes, and gain insight into why she buried them. Only then can she master the internal conflicts that crippled her for so long. Once these conflicts are resolved, her symptoms will presumably wither away by themselves. In effect, Freud's prescription for the neuroses is the triumph of reason over passion: "Where Id was, there shall Ego be."

THE RECOVERY OF UNCONSCIOUS MEMORIES

Psychoanalytic technique originated in Freud's attempts to treat hysteria (now called *conversion disorder*) by helping patients recover emotionally charged memories (see Chapter 17). Freud and his then collaborator, Josef Breuer, initially hypnotized patients to facilitate this recovery. Freud later came to believe that such memories could be exhumed even in the normal waking state by the method of *free association,* in which the patient was instructed to say whatever came into his mind, with the expectation that sooner or later the relevant memory would emerge. The patient's tendency to derail a given train of thought—by changing the topic, forgetting what he was about to say, and so on—was labeled *resistance* to the task. This resistance was believed to indicate that the patient was on the verge of recalling very painful, buried memories and had to work against the forces of repression.

In addition to free association, Freud later asked his patients to tell him their dreams, and he began to interpret nearly any action—whether a slip of the tongue, or the wiggling of a foot on the couch, or a particular choice of words, or whether the patient was late or early for the sessions—as clues to the character of their neurotic conflicts.

In popularized movie or television versions, this dredging up of forgotten memories is often presented as the essence of psychoanalysis: The distraught heroine finally and tearfully recalls a long-forgotten childhood episode and then suddenly feels a great burden lift from her shoulders. She rises from the couch reborn, ready to face life and love serenely, and lives happily—or at least non-neurotically—ever after. But such dramatic "flights into health" are rare and, in Freud's view, should be distrusted when they do occur. He believed that the patient's awareness of her unconscious conflicts commonly comes bit by bit, as a memory surfaces here, a dream or a slip of the tongue suggests a meaning there, and as the analyst supplies interpretations of the resistances that crop up in the course of therapy. To help the patient see how all of these strands of her mental life are interwoven is one of the analyst's main tasks. And the end result of therapy isn't the achievement of blissful happiness, because human life is rarely euphoric and often strife ridden. Instead, the goal and usual result are more modest: as Freud put it, to "turn neurosis into everyday unhappiness."

EMOTIONAL INSIGHT

Psychoanalysts want their patients to attain insights into their long-lost, repressed motives, but they don't want the insights to be merely intellectual. They want their patients to gain access not just to the repressed thoughts, but also to the feelings that accompany them. Freud was emphatic that recollections without emotions have little therapeutic effect and that genuine self-discovery was only achieved when the patient rid himself of the repressive emotional forces that had kept the insights from him. Without this intense emotional involvement, the psychoanalytic process was more intellectual exercise than therapy (Freud, 1913).

For Freud, the necessary emotional component arose mainly as a function of the ***transference,*** the patient's tendency to respond to the analyst in increasingly personal terms. During therapy, the patient begins to react to the analyst as she had reacted to the major figures in her own life, and she will therefore love or hate the analyst as she loved or hated her mother, father, siblings, and, more recently, her lovers and friends. All of these feelings are "transferred" to the analyst, as a kind of repetition of the unresolved problems of the patient's childhood. Patients show transference reactions when they idealize and idolize their analysts, or fall in love with them, or are terrified or distrustful of them, or want to be their "best" patients, or fear that they are not being "good" patients.

Freud argued that this transference-charged relationship with the analyst can be a powerful therapeutic tool. It lets the analyst hold up a mirror to the patient to show him how he really feels and acts toward the important people in his life. For example, take a person who expresses violent anger at his psychoanalyst and then is immediately seized by unspeakable terror. How would his analyst interpret this? Perhaps the patient had equated the analyst with his own tyrannical father, and having acted with flagrant disrespect, was now expecting some horrible retribution. Needless to say, the analyst will not act like Daddy, but instead might say something mildly reassuring, such as "That was hard to get out, wasn't it?" The analyst might then point out how the patient's traumatic memories of Daddy distort the ongoing therapeutic relationship.

Through many such experiences, the patient's anxieties gradually abate. The determinedly neutral analyst allows herself temporarily to stand in for the significant characters in the patient's early family drama but will not let herself be drawn into the play. She lets the patient say the same old lines and go through the same old motions, but she won't respond to them as the cast of characters from childhood did. Her job is to let the patient see what he is really doing, what is really happening on his private stage. The effect of all this emotional reeducation is to create a new life script with better lines and a happier ending.

A psychoanalytic session   *(Photograph by Will and Demi McIntyre/Science Source/ Photo Researchers)*

PSYCHODYNAMIC THERAPY

Many present-day psychotherapists still use techniques that bear Freud's imprint. A few still practice psychoanalysis just as Freud did, but most practitioners have modified Freud's theories and procedures in various ways. Most of them—known variously as psychoanalytic, ego-analytic, or psychodynamic psychotherapists—subscribe to neo-Freudian views or to related approaches such as ego psychology (see Chapter 17). Like Freud, they believe that what underlies "neurosis" is unconscious conflict, but they differ by emphasizing current interpersonal and cultural factors rather than the psychological traumas of early childhood. If early development is discussed in these modern therapies, it is not to discover decades-past episodes but, instead, to identify how the patterns of interaction in one's childhood influence current choices (Eagle and Wolitsky, 1992; Liff, 1992).

Psychoanalytically oriented therapists have also revised Freud's doctrines about women, such as Freud's belief that women are passive by nature and have underdeveloped superegos that render them less moral (Freud, 1933). Today, such therapists are more likely to consider women different but equivalent to men and recognize that any therapy based on doctrines of sexual inferiority is both intellectually and morally misguided—based on false assumptions and by its very nature oppressive (Strouse, 1974; Auld and Hyman, 1991; Bernstein and Lenhart, 1993).

Revisions in the theory have been accompanied by changes in the actual therapeutic technique. In classical analysis, sessions are scheduled five times a week and may continue for five or more years. Apart from the fact that this restricts the therapy to the affluent few, some critics contend that such long-long-term therapy can easily become a substitute for getting well. Rather than making beneficial changes in her life, the patient becomes concerned only about making progress in therapy and in effect becomes "couch ridden" and even more disabled.

To counter this trend, many psychoanalytically oriented therapists began to schedule fewer sessions per week (Alexander and French, 1946). Others started to condense the whole process into a few months, sometimes by defining therapeutic goals in advance or setting definite time limits (e.g., Malan, 1963; Strupp and Binder, 1984). One casualty of these modifications is that venerable Freudian artifact, the psychoanalytic couch. Many practitioners have dispensed with it in favor of regular chairs and face-to-face interviews, in part because it is feared that patients made to lie prone during the sessions will become overly dependent on the analyst and difficult to wean at the end of the therapy (Gill, 1976, 1994; Liff, 1992).

Other modifications concern the relation between what goes on in the therapist's office and what happens in the patient's "real" life. For Freud, the crucial theater of operations was the analysis itself, and to ensure that the patient's unconscious conflicts could be contained there, the patient's outside life had to remain stable. He therefore insisted that his patients make no major life decisions, such as getting married or divorced or changing careers, while they were in analysis. In contrast, later psychoanalytic psychotherapists came to regard the sessions as a microcosm of the patient's entire life and recommend that the

(Cartoon by Sidney Harris)

patient actively attempt to apply the lessons learned in therapy to his life outside of therapy (Alexander and French, 1946).

BEHAVIOR THERAPY

Not all psychotherapists derive their techniques from psychoanalysis. In fact, two major therapeutic approaches are reactions against psychoanalysis, although for opposite reasons. The first is behavior therapy, which maintains that the theoretical notions underlying psychoanalysis are vague and untestable, while its therapeutic effectiveness is dubious. The second consists of various humanistic therapies, which regard psychoanalysis as too mechanistic in focus and concerned more with basic urges like sex and aggression than with the search for higher truths and meanings. Freud, who had a fine sense of irony, would have been wryly bemused to find himself accused by one faction of being too scientific and by the other of not being scientific enough.

Behavior therapists hold that the various conditions Freud called "neuroses" are simply caused by maladaptive learning; the remedy, therefore, involves new learning, replacing or overriding the old habits. These therapists see themselves as applied scientists whose techniques for reeducating troubled people are adapted from the principles of classical and instrumental conditioning discovered in the laboratories of Pavlov, Thorndike, and Skinner (see Chapter 4). As befits this line of descent, behavior therapists are basically pragmatic. They emphasize overt, observable behavior rather than hypothetical underlying causes such as unconscious thoughts and wishes, which they regard as hard to define and impossible to observe. Their concern is with what a person *does* that is causing her distress. It is these specific behaviors that are the behavior therapist's target for intervention. These behaviors are not regarded as "symptoms" through which one can identify and then cure the underlying illness. Instead, the maladaptive behaviors themselves are the problem, and it is they that must be removed.

Toward this end, behavior therapists employ various techniques for learning and unlearning, relying on deliberate exposure to anxiety-producing stimuli, conditioning of incompatible reactions, or whatever. These treatments do not include any attempt to have the patient gain insight into the origin of these symptoms. As behavioral therapists see it, such insights, however valid, can have no therapeutic value. What is wrong and must be fixed is the patient's behavior in the here and now.

EXPOSURE TECHNIQUES

One set of techniques often used in behavior therapy to treat the specific phobias (see Chapter 18) derives from classical conditioning (Wolpe and Plaud, 1997). Behavior therapists frequently suggest that the irrational fears that characterize these phobias are simply classically conditioned responses, evoked by particular stimuli, such as storms, elevators, or finding a spider in one's bed (see Chapters 4 and 18). Therapy for specific phobias, according to this formulation, consists of attempts to break the connections between the phobic stimuli and the associated fears.

The most obvious way is through *extinction.* Imagine a rat that has been shocked on seeing a flashing light. The rat will gradually become afraid of the light. To extinguish this fear, all we have to do is to present the conditioned stimulus (the light) several times without the unconditioned stimulus (the shock). This is easier said than done, because the rat now avoids the light, running away as soon as it starts flashing. This prevents the rat from "testing reality,"

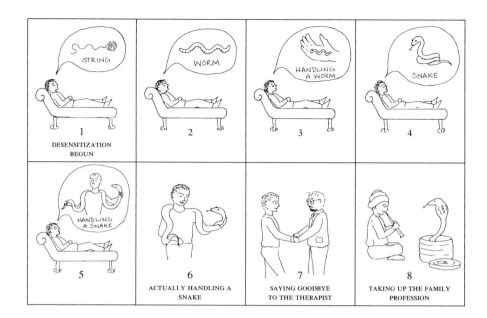

Desensitization *(Courtesy of Henry Gleitman and Mary Bullock)*

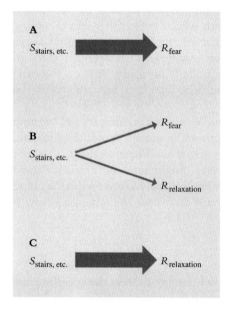

19.6 Systematic desensitization *(A) The state of affairs in phobia. Various stimuli such as flights of stairs arouse fear. (B) These stimuli are conditioned to relaxation. As this connection becomes stronger, the connection between the stimuli and the fear is weakened. (C) The outcome when counterconditioning is complete: Relaxation has completely displaced fear.*

and thus its fear may remain despite the fact that the light no longer signals a shock. What holds for the rat also holds for the person with a phobia. He is afraid of lightning, or enclosed spaces, or spiders, and his fear persists precisely because of his strenuous efforts to avoid these stimuli.

How, then, can we undo the rat's fear or the person's phobia? One way is by getting each to endure the feared stimulus until each perceives that the flashing light or the lightning isn't so threatening. For example, if the rat is forced to remain in the compartment in which it was shocked and repeatedly presented with the flashing light (with no accompanying shock), then its fear of the light will eventually disappear (Baum, 1970). Exactly the same idea underlies what behavior therapists call "exposure techniques."

The most widely used exposure technique is **systematic desensitization,** developed by the psychiatrist Joseph Wolpe. This technique combines the logic just described with one further element: The therapist seeks to extinguish the connection between the phobic stimulus and the fear response; she simultaneously seeks to create a new connection between this stimulus and a different response, one that is incompatible with fear and that will therefore displace it (Wolpe, 1958). The competing response is usually deep muscular relaxation, and the patient is taught a relaxation technique, typically through meditation-like exercises, before the formal therapy begins. Then, once the patient can relax deeply on cue, the goal is to condition this relaxation response to the fear-evoking stimuli (see Figure 19.6).

There is an obvious problem. To establish the desired link between relaxation and the fear-evoking stimulus one must somehow bring this stimulus into the behavior therapist's office. But how can this be done? Some phobias are of heights, others of enclosed spaces, still others of snakes or of meeting strangers. There is no practicable way of physically presenting these stimuli in a clinic room. Wolpe hit on a simple alternative. He asked the patients to imagine these situations as vividly as possible while in deep relaxation. It turned out that such imagined encounters had enough reality for most patients to evoke a reasonable amount of anxiety (Wolpe and Lazarus, 1966).

To ensure that this anxiety is not excessive and counterproductive, Wolpe adopted a policy of deliberate gradualism, in which the therapist sneaks up on the fear response, step by step. He first asks the patient to construct an **anxiety hierarchy** in which feared situations are arranged from least to most anxiety pro-

Behavior therapy in the real world
(A) A person with acrophobia who visits a rooftop in the presence of the therapist. (Photograph © Steve Mellon, 1994) (B) A person with agoraphobia and panic disorder who forces herself to go on a bus ride. (Photograph © Jacques Chenet, all rights reserved; courtesy of Woodfin Camp & Assoc.)

voking. The patient starts out by imagining the first scene in the hierarchy (for example, being on the first floor of the Empire State Building). She imagines this scene while in a state of deep relaxation. She will stay with this scene—imagining and relaxing—until she no longer feels any qualms. After this, the next scene is imagined and thoroughly counterconditioned, and so on, until the patient finally can imagine the most frightening scene of all (leaning over the railing of the observation tower above the 102d floor) and still be able to relax.

According to Wolpe and his followers, this procedure of taking the sting out of imagined horrors carries over almost completely into the real world. But other investigators argue that the transfer into real life is less certain than Wolpe claims and often lags behind the desensitization of the images. A plausible guess is that the shift from image to reality is not automatic but requires some active participation on the part of the patient (Davison, 1968). Toward this end, many patients are given homework assignments that force them to confront progressively more fear-evoking situations in the real world.

These exposure techniques were predicated upon a view that the phobias were classically conditioned responses. This view is problematic, as we discussed in Chapter 18, but the problems with the originating conception do not invalidate the therapies. In fact, exposure techniques are quite effective for specific phobias—suggesting that even if classical conditioning cannot fully explain phobias, it may nonetheless be quite useful in their treatment (Wolpe, 1997).

AVERSION THERAPY

Another behavior therapy technique, ***aversion therapy,*** uses a different strategy: It attempts to eliminate problematic behavior by attaching negative feelings to it. The basic procedure of aversion therapy is very simple and merely involves pairing the stimulus that one wants to render unpleasant with some obnoxious unconditioned stimulus.

One common use is in treating alcoholism. For example, an individual who wants to quit drinking is made nauseous with a special medication. He is then asked to smell, taste, and swallow his favorite alcoholic beverages, all the while desperately wanting to vomit. After a few such exposures, the person will come to associate the nausea with the alcoholic beverage and should, as a result, be far less likely to reach for or accept a drink.

This technique has been applied to behaviors that range from overeating and cigarette smoking to certain sexual deviations such as exhibitionism. But perhaps the most common—and most controversial—use of aversion therapy is with the developmentally disabled and mentally retarded. It is sometimes used with individuals who are sexually disinhibited or frankly aggressive, or who bite themselves or bang their heads repeatedly (Matson and Sevin, 1994). For example, an individual who habitually bangs her head against a brick wall may be given brief electrical shocks every time she performs this self-destructive behavior. In obvious ways, this treatment seems inhumane, but this must be weighed against the likelihood of permanent brain damage if the behavior continues. Even given the benefit to the patient, however, this technique presents moral and legal quandaries (Herr, 1990; Mulick, 1990; Matson and Sevin, 1994).

Still, aversive techniques are undoubtedly effective for reducing destructive or self-destructive behavior among the developmentally disabled (Gerhardt et al., 1991). Several studies have also reported the effectiveness of such techniques in producing abstinence for at least one year in about two-thirds of alcoholic patients studied (Wiens and Menustik, 1983; Elkins, 1991; but also see Wilson, 1991). In these cases, the successful patients seemed to acquire a learned taste aversion so that the actual taste and smell of alcohol becomes repellent (see Chapter 4). For more routine psychotherapeutic concerns, however, there is considerable doubt about the effectiveness of these therapies. The therapy may be effective in controlling the maladaptive response as long as the patient remains in the therapist's office, but this benefit may vanish the moment the patient leaves the office—that is, leaves the context in which the aversive stimuli are administered (Rachman and Teasdale, 1969; Emmelkamp, 1986).

OPERANT TECHNIQUES

A different set of behavioral therapies is derived from the principles of instrumental conditioning and emphasizes the relation between acts and consequences (see Chapter 4). Its theme is the same as that which underlies the entire operant approach—the control of behavior through reinforcement.

An example of this approach is the use of **token economies** in certain hospital psychiatric wards. In these settings, tokens function much as money does in our economy; they can be exchanged for desirable items such as snacks or the opportunity to watch TV. Like money, the tokens must be earned by the patient, perhaps by making his own bed, or being neatly dressed, or performing various ward chores. In this fashion, the patient can be systematically rewarded for producing desirable behaviors and not rewarded for producing undesirable ones.

As in the learning laboratory, the reinforcement contingencies can then be gradually adjusted, using the process known as *shaping* (Chapter 4). Early on, the patient might be reinforced merely for getting out of bed; later on, tokens might be delivered only for getting out of bed and walking to the dining hall. In this fashion, the patient can be led, step by step, to a fuller, more acceptable level of functioning.

The overall effect of this technique seems to be positive. While the patients are certainly not cured, they become less apathetic and the general ward atmosphere is much improved (Ayllon and Azrin, 1968). The problem is that the effects of token economies do not generalize well out of the hospital or even off the ward. Thus, they are probably best seen not as therapy but as ward-management techniques.

But other reinforcement techniques can be useful in individual behavior therapy as part of **contingency management.** In contingency management, the person learns that certain behaviors will be followed by strict consequences (Craighead et al., 1994). For example, a child who is unduly noncompliant can be presented with a menu of "good behaviors" and "bad behaviors," with an associated reward and penalty for each. Being a good listener can earn the child the chance to watch a video, cleaning up her room everyday can get her a dessert after dinner, and so forth, whereas talking back to Mom or making a mess may result in an early bedtime or a time-out in her room. The idea is ultimately not to bribe or coerce the child but to show her that her actions can change how people react to her. Ideally, her changed behavior will result in a more positive social environment that can supplant the "goodies" that initially established her improved behavior.

COGNITIVE THERAPY

Exposure, aversion, and reinforcement therapies focus on fairly obvious observable behaviors and try to modify them using simple classical and operant conditioning techniques. But what treatment is appropriate when the patient's problems do not involve clear-cut responses or easily identifiable problematic behaviors? Suppose a sufferer of obsessive-compulsive disorder is crippled by anxiety because of a constant obsession that he has poisoned his children. He finds temporary piece of mind only by counting his children over and over again, reassuring himself that each is indeed well. The critical features of this case seem to be internal thoughts and feelings rather than public actions or visible reactions. How does a behavior-oriented therapist handle cases such as this?

In these kinds of cases, a number of therapists attempt to confront directly the way the patient thinks. They try to replace the patient's irrational and disabling beliefs and attitudes with a more realistic way of thinking. This general mode of therapy goes under various labels. A relatively recent version is *cognitive therapy*, originally developed by the psychiatrist Aaron Beck as a treatment for depression (Beck, 1967), and eventually applied to disorders ranging from phobias and other anxiety disorders to obesity and chronic pain (Beck, 1976, 1985; Freeman et al., 1989; see Chapter 18 for a discussion of some of Beck's views).

On the face of it, the goal of all these cognitive approaches seems similar to the psychoanalytic quest for emotionally grounded insight. In both, it is the patient's thought patterns that the therapist targets for change. In both, the primary therapeutic interaction involves talk between patient and therapist. Nonetheless, cognitive therapists see themselves as more closely allied with behavior therapists, and their techniques have much in common: Both are extremely directive, with the therapist in many cases explicitly encouraging the patient to think or to act in a different fashion. Both are concerned more about the patient's present life than with her upbringing.

THE MAJOR TECHNIQUES OF COGNITIVE THERAPY

The basic technique of cognitive therapists is to confront patients—actively and often quite directively—with the contradictions inherent in their maladaptive beliefs. Like many modern behavior therapists, a cognitive therapist may also give the patient homework assignments. One such task might be to pinpoint irrational thoughts that come in the form of certain phrases the patient regularly says to herself, such as "it's all my fault," or "if no one loves me, I'm worthless." In this fashion, the therapist hopes to locate the patient's self-defeating mental habits and thereby to discover the roots of the patient's problems. For example, consider a patient who felt a wave of anxiety when he saw an old friend across the street but was clueless as to why he was so anxious. His cognitive therapist was able to clarify the situation, namely that seeing the friend triggered an automatic and irrational thought that led to the anxiety:

> The anxiety seemed incomprehensible until [the patient] "played back" his thoughts: "If I greet Bob, he may not remember me. He may snub me, it has been so long, he may not know who I am. . . ." (Ellis, 1962, quoted in Beck, 1985, p. 1436)

After helping the patient identify the automatic thought, the next task is to reveal its irrationality. After all, Bob may very well remember him. And if he doesn't, it may be because Bob's memory is faulty or because Bob is preoccupied at the moment with his own problems. Here, the cognitive therapist takes the role of a sympathetic Socrates who asks one question after another until the truth is attained. But suppose the patient is right, and Bob never liked him in the first place and might well have snubbed him. Is that the end of the world? Is it really necessary to be liked by everybody? Once these irrational thoughts are exposed, the patient can eventually refrain from thinking them and substitute more rational thoughts. This will lead him both to feel and function better.

Therapy as social education *(© 1950, 1952 United Feature Syndicate Inc.)*

THERAPY AS SOCIAL EDUCATION

Most of the therapeutic techniques we have discussed thus far have goals that are essentially negative—to eliminate irrational fears, suppress unwanted behaviors, and root out illogical beliefs. Yet many therapists, regardless of the mode of therapy they practice, consider such symptom removal to be only part of their job. They believe that the therapist must also help the patient find new and more adaptive behavior patterns to fill the void formerly occupied by the old unhealthy ones. For many patients, this void is all too real, because the psychological difficulties from which they have suffered have prevented them from learning all kinds of complex interpersonal skills that most of us take for granted: establishing and maintaining friendships, flirting with and dating potential romantic partners, seeking advice and mentoring, dealing with interpersonal conflicts, asserting oneself without being unduly aggressive, and so on. These skills must ultimately be learned and honed in the real world, but the therapist can jump-start the process in the office.

A number of techniques have been developed to help the therapist conduct this tutorial in interpersonal relations. One is the use of **graded task assignments** in which the patient is asked to take progressively larger steps in dealing with troublesome real-life social interactions. Another example is **assertiveness training,** which begins with tasks like maintaining eye contact with other people or asking directions from a stranger and extends to complaining to a waiter about an overdone steak (Lazarus, 1971). Another technique is **modeling,** in which the therapist shows the patient some effective ways of handling a particular situation. Yet another is **role playing** in which the patient and therapist act out some scenes, such as a marital confrontation, that are likely to occur.

The use of role playing is illustrated in part of a session with a patient who found it difficult to express affection toward his wife:

> [The therapist] says, "Tom, do you really care for me?"
> Tom says, "I would say to her that I do, but she'd complain."
> Therapist: "Don't tell me what you would do. I'm Jane. Talk to me. Tom, do you really care for me?"
> Tom (turning away, looking slightly disgusted): "Yes."
> Therapist (still as Jane): "You don't say it like you mean it."
> Tom: "Yeah, that's what she says and I usually. . ."
> Therapist (interrupting): "You're again telling me about what you'd say. I'm Jane. Tom, you don't say it like you mean it."
> Tom: "It's very hard for me to answer her when she says that."
> Therapist: "How do you feel when she says it?"
> Tom: "Angry, pushed."
> Therapist: "OK, I'm Jane. Tell me how you feel."
> Tom: "Jane, when you do that it really turns me off. Maybe if you didn't ask me so often I'd be able to say it spontaneously without feeling like a puppet. . . (then, in a tone that indicates he is now talking to the therapist as therapist) Gee, I wonder what would happen if I really said that to her." (Wachtel, 1977, pp. 234–35)

HUMANISTIC THERAPIES

A number of practitioners charge that behavior therapy and, to a lesser extent, psychoanalysis describe human beings too mechanistically and treat them too manipulatively. These **humanistic therapists** try to deal with the individual more holistically and not—so they would claim—as a bundle of conditioned reflexes or a collection of warring, unconscious impulses.

CLIENT-CENTERED THERAPY

One example of a humanistically oriented approach is ***client-centered therapy*** (Rogers, 1951, 1970), which was developed during the early 1940s by psychologist Carl Rogers (1902–1987). Like another prominent humanistic therapist, Abraham Maslow (1908–1970), Rogers believed that personality development is a lifelong, unfolding process and that people have a native impulse toward the full realization of their human potential (Maslow, 1968; see Chapter 17). In this sense, Rogers held that human nature is inherently good. But, alas, such self-actualization is rare, because personality growth is often stunted, leaving many people who dislike themselves, are out of touch with their own feelings, and are unable to reach out to others genuinely. Rogers' remedy was to provide the appropriate psychological soil in which to nurture personal growth—this soil was the therapeutic relationship.★

For Rogers, therapy should be essentially democratic. The Rogerian therapist does not act as an omniscient authority who sagely interprets what the patient says or dreams (as does a psychoanalyst). Nor does she prescribe and shape how the patient should act (as does a behavior therapist). Instead, she tries to help the patient—whom Rogers calls a client—to arrive at his own solutions (Mearns, 1994).

Rogers initially tried to achieve this client-centeredness using a variety of ***nondirective techniques*** (Rogers, 1942). He would never advise or interpret directly but would only try to clarify what the client really felt by echoing or restating what the client herself seemed to say or feel. He soon discovered that he couldn't help but convey some evaluation with even the blandest nod. But more important, Rogers came to believe that successful psychotherapy did not depend upon any particular approach or technique; rather, it required simply that the therapist approach the client as a genuinely involved, participating fellow human. The Rogerian therapist's main job is to let the client know that he understands how the world looks through her eyes; that he can empathize with her wishes and feelings; and, most important of all, that he accepts and values her. In Rogers' view, this therapeutic environment of unconditional acceptance and esteem ultimately helps the client to accept and esteem herself (Rogers, 1961). Perhaps this is just a modern restatement of the old idea that love can redeem us all.

EXISTENTIAL THERAPY

Rogers' approach to therapy was distinctively American in its belief in an almost limitless human capacity for growth and self-improvement. Another humanistic approach to therapy, which originated in Europe, takes a more somber view. This is ***existential therapy,*** a mode of therapy that echoes some of the major themes sounded by a group of philosophers called *existentialists.*

Existential therapists attempt to remedy what they consider the major emotional malady of our times, an inability to endow life with meaning. In their view, this condition stems from the rootless, restless anonymity of twentieth-century Western life but became rife in modern Europe amid the ruins of two bloody world wars and the Nazi terror. It is marked by a sense that one is alienated, lost, and dehumanized; that one is nothing but a cog in a huge, impersonal machine; that one's existence is meaningless. According to existential therapists, this feeling

Existential therapy *(Hand with Re-flecting Sphere, 1935, by M. C. Escher; © M. C. Escher Heirs, courtesy of Cordon Art, Baarn, Holland)*

★ Rogers' humanistic approach has often been attacked by behavior therapists who regard him as antiscientific. Under the circumstances, it is somewhat ironic that Rogers was one of the pioneers of psychotherapy evaluation, the first major figure in the field of psychotherapy who looked for evidence that his techniques were actually having some effect.

that everything is pointless is common to many modern emotional disorders. It is this, rather than the specific manifestations of the disorders—the phobias, the obsessions, and the like—that they want to ameliorate (Ofman, 1985).

In essence, existential therapists try to help people achieve a personal outlook that gives meaning to their lives. How do they do this? It turns out that most existential therapists have no distinctive technique. Some use the couch and ask the patient to free associate; others sit face to face with the patient and engage him in lengthy philosophical discussions. What is distinctive about them is their underlying attitude. They try to make their patients aware of the importance of free choice. They insist that people are persons and not objects, that human acts are not imposed from without but rather spring from within, that there are always choices—even in jail, even in a concentration camp—and that what one *is* is ultimately the result of what one chooses to *do*. The therapist's job is to help the patient realize that the responsibility for finding and making his life's choices is his and his alone. If and when the patient accepts this responsibility, he will no longer be plagued by the vacuum of his own existence but will begin to be "authentic."

Like practitioners of most other schools, existential therapists stress the role of the therapist-patient relationship in effecting therapeutic change. In their view, the key element of this relationship is what they call the *encounter,* in which two individuals interact in the here-and-now without recourse to chitchat or psychological jargon. According to existential therapists, the experience derived from this encounter will ultimately transfer to the way in which the patient sees herself and others (May, 1958).

In the past, what existential therapists attempt to remedy—helping to find meaning in one's existence—was generally considered the province of the clergy and was done within a spiritual framework. As religious values eroded, secular social institutions like existential therapy stepped in and tried to fill the gap. It is no accident that an influential book by a prominent existential therapist bears the title *The Doctor and the Soul* (Frankl, 1966).

SOME COMMON THEMES

Despite the differences in theory and practice that characterize the various forms of psychotherapy, there have been trends toward a rapprochement among the different schools. Some psychoanalytically oriented practitioners have come to use techniques that were formerly the province of behavior therapists, such as modeling and homework assignments (Wachtel, 1977, 1982). From the opposite vantage point, many behavior therapists have come to realize that the client-therapist relationship is a crucial part of treatment, that something like Freud's "transference" comes into play even in mechanistic conditioning therapies such as desensitization (Lazarus, 1971, 1981). The endpoint of this integration is seen in a survey of influential psychotherapists who strongly advocated what they call **technical eclecticism**—basically, doing whatever works—as the trend in therapy (Norcross and Freedheim, 1992). This eclectic orientation dovetails with recent changes in the practice of psychotherapy that were prompted by economic considerations, as we will see below (see pp. 843–44).

Quite apart from this trend toward an eclectic approach to psychotherapy, there are some important underlying themes that run through the beliefs and practices of all the various therapies:

Therapy as socially accepted healing   By and large, psychotherapists operate within a social context that gives them the status of officially designated healers for

Alienation in the modern world *(Government Bureau by George Tooker, 1956, courtesy of the Metropolitan Museum of Art, New York)*

many mental disorders. As a result, the stage is set for patients to glean benefits from psychotherapy that are nonspecific—that is, not due to any specific therapeutic techniques. One is that the patient gains an ally against his problem; this **therapeutic alliance** helps most patients believe that they really can conquer their problems and achieve better lives (Horvath and Luborsky, 1993). In fact, some researchers believe that the therapeutic alliance is the most important single ingredient in the effectiveness of psychotherapy and is indispensable even when medication is the primary treatment (Krupnick et al., 1996). A related benefit is that being in therapy fuels the hope that the patient will finally get better, and this hope can itself promote successes in the outside world. Finally, therapy provides the patient with an intimate, confiding relationship with another person, a kind of secular confessional. This alone may be a boon to some people who have no close bonds to anyone and for whom psychotherapy may amount to "the purchase of friendship" (Schofield, 1964).

Emotional defusing   People usually enter psychotherapy of whatever stripe with many anxieties: "What's wrong with me?" "Am I normal?" These kinds of questions are commonplace. New patients are often worried that their problems are weird or shameful and either too trivial to warrant therapy or so severe that no treatment will work. They may hope for, and dread, the opportunity to reveal things they have kept secret, often for years. All psychotherapists, regardless of their approach, spend a great deal of time in therapy hearing these concerns and secrets, and responding to them in an accepting and nonjudgmental manner. With some reassurance and a little education, patients' anxieties abate as they learn that their problems are understandable, rather common, not shameful, and quite treatable.

Interpersonal learning   All major schools of psychotherapy stress the importance of interpersonal learning and believe that the therapeutic relationship is an important tool for bringing this about. This relationship shows the patient how she generally reacts to others, and it provides a testing ground for trying new and better ways of reacting.

Self-knowledge   Most psychotherapists try to help their patients achieve greater self-knowledge, although the various therapeutic schools differ in what kind of self-knowledge they try to bring about. For psychoanalysts, the crucial emotional insights the patient must acquire refer to his own past; for Rogerians, they concern the client's feelings in the present; for behavior therapists, the relevant self-understanding is the correct identification of the eliciting stimuli or consequences that maintain problematic behavior.

Therapy as an incremental process There is also general agreement that psychotherapy is a gradual affair and that this is so regardless of whether the therapy emphasizes insight, emotion, or overt action. There are few sudden flashes of insight or emotional understanding that change a patient overnight. Instead, each new skill or new-found insight must be laboriously applied in one life situation after another before the patient can call it her own.

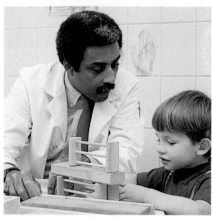

Play therapy, an extension of psychotherapy adapted for children (A) In play therapy, the therapist tries to help the child understand and express his feelings about his parents and other family members through play with various toys. (Photograph by Michael Heron, 1979/Monkmeyer Press) (B) Puppets are sometimes used to act out problems, as in this example of a therapy session with victims of child abuse. (Photograph by Bart Bartholomew, 1984/Black Star)

EXTENSIONS OF PSYCHOTHERAPY

In Freud's time, psychotherapy was still considered a somewhat arcane art, practiced by a few initiates (mostly physicians) and available only to a selected group of well-educated adult patients. Since then, psychotherapy has been extended to cover increasingly broader terrain. The individuals now receiving therapy include children, the developmentally disabled, sociopaths, substance abusers, and sufferers of schizophrenia. Another extension was a shift from the original one therapist–one patient formula to various modes of group therapy that feature all conceivable permutations: one therapist and several patients, several therapists and several patients, several patients and no therapist, and so on.

Treating patients in groups had two initial advantages: More patients could be accommodated by a limited number of therapists, and patients could be provided with care at a lower cost than individual sessions. But it was appealing for other reasons as well. It often allowed therapists to observe and work with problems that emerged more readily in group settings. More profoundly, group treatment also seemed to fill a void, at least temporarily, left by the weakening of family and religious ties of modern urbanized society.

GROUP AND RELATIONSHIP THERAPIES

Shared-problem groups One approach is to organize a group of people all of whom have the same problem. They may all be alcoholics, or abuse victims, or ex-convicts. The members meet, share relevant advice and information, help newcomers along, exhort and support each other in their resolve to overcome their difficulties. The classic example is **Alcoholics Anonymous (AA),** which provides the alcoholic with a sense that he is not alone and helps him weather crises without suffering a relapse. In such we-are-all-in-the-same-boat groups, the primary aim is to manage the problem that all members share. No specific attention is paid to emotional problems that are unique to any one individual.

Therapy groups The rules of the game are very different in groups explicitly organized for the purpose of **group therapy.** Here, a group of selected patients, usually around ten, are treated together under the guidance of a trained therapist. This form of therapy may have some advantages that individual treatment lacks. According to its proponents, in group therapy the therapist does not really treat the members of the group; instead, she helps them to treat each other. The specific techniques of the therapist may vary from psychoanalytically oriented in-

sight therapy to various forms of behavior therapy to Rogerian client-centered approaches.

Whatever techniques the therapist favors, the treatment of each group member really begins as he realizes that he is not all that different from the others. He learns that there are other people who are painfully shy, who have hostile fantasies about their parents, or whatever. Further benefits come from a sense of group belongingness, of support, and of encouragement. But most important of all is the fact that the group provides a ready-made laboratory in interpersonal relations. The patient can discover just what he does that rubs others the wrong way, how he can relate to certain kinds of people more effectively, and so on (Sadock, 1975).

Couples therapy and family therapy   In the therapy groups we've considered thus far, the members are almost always strangers before the sessions begin. This is in marked contrast to what happens in couples and family therapy. Here, the people seeking help know each other very well (sometimes all too well) before they enter therapy.

Couples therapy (including marriage counseling) and family therapy have become major therapeutic movements (Satir, 1967; Minuchin, 1974; Kerr and Bowen, 1988). It is probably no coincidence that this growth has occurred during a time of turmoil in American families, evidenced by spiraling divorce rates and reports of child and spousal abuse, and by the increasing numbers of single-parent households.

Family and couples therapists regard the family as an emotional unit that can influence the onset and continuing manifestation of many mental disorders and social problems. Seen from this perspective, the key to relationship and family distress is not necessarily found in the pathology of any individual spouse or family member. Rather, the interlocking relationships that constitute a family operate in a delicate balance, and any strain will ricochet throughout the family and affect all its members (Dadds, 1995). The situation is rather like the joints of the body: a sprained ankle causes an immediate limp, but the imbalance in posture the sufferer must maintain while healing can cause back strain, headaches, and pain in the *other* leg. Many couples and family therapists feel that their task is like that of the orthopedist who is treating the sprained ankle: They try to restore full function both to the ankle and to all the affected parts as well.

Many therapists prefer to see the members of the couple or family together rather than individually. In such joint sessions, the therapist can act as an

"We're not living happily ever after." (© The New Yorker Collection 1959, 1987 Chas. Addams from The Cartoon Bank. All rights reserved.)

emotional translator who can help the partners or family members to understand each other better. An example is this exchange between therapist (T), husband (H), and wife (W):

H: She never comes up to me and kisses me. I am always the one to make the overtures.

T: [To wife] Is this the way you see yourself behaving with your husband?

W: Yes, I would say he is the demonstrative one. I didn't know he wanted me to make the overtures.

T: Have you told your wife that you would like this from her—more open demonstration of affection?

H: Well, no, you'd think she'd know.

W: No. How would I know? You always said you don't like aggressive women.

H: I don't. I don't like dominating women.

W: Well, I thought you meant women who make the overtures. How am I to know what you want?

T: You'd have a better idea if he had been able to tell you. (From Satir, 1967, pp. 72–73)

Some reviewers believe that this approach can be beneficial, especially when the partners or family members are seen together rather than individually (Gurman and Kniskern, 1981; Hazelrigg, Cooper, and Borduin, 1987). But this conclusion can be questioned on various technical grounds. For example, the superiority of joint to individual therapy may reflect a difference in who chooses what treatment. Perhaps the Smiths who refuse to see a therapist together are more at odds with each other than the Browns who decide to see the therapist jointly. Because of problems like this one, achieving the appropriate controls for outcome evaluation may be even more difficult in this area than in the field of individual therapy.

THE EXPANSION OF THERAPEUTIC GOALS

All of these extensions of psychotherapy have made it available to a much larger number of people. But did all of them really need it? The answer depends on the goals of therapy.

For Freud, the matter was simple. Most of his patients were disabled by terrorizing phobias or all-consuming compulsions and were rendered unable to work and love. Freud wanted to heal these patients so that they could once again live normally. But he never believed that his treatment would automatically produce happiness or fulfillment or the discovery of personal meaning. These the patients had to find for themselves, and they might very well fail to do so even when no longer saddled with undue inner conflict.

Treatment of nondisorders Later therapists broadened the goals of treatment. As we mentioned in the previous chapter, there has been a tendency over the years to group more and more behavior patterns under the broad rubric of "mental disorder" and thus make them fodder for psychotherapy. We have reached the point that people who overspend are called "shopping addicts" and are urged to join a self-help program; women who have had several unrewarding relationships are diagnosed as suffering from an excessive need to love and are referred to groups for "women who love too much," and so on.

The expansion of therapeutic goals is not only confined to getting over problems. Consider humanistic therapists such as Rogers. Rogerian therapists certainly try to remove or alleviate their clients' distress, but their ambitions go further than a cure or the modification of unwanted behavior. They ultimately want to help their clients to "grow" and "realize their human potential." But if this is the goal, then therapy can be appropriate for just about anyone, regardless of whether he suffers from some form of psychopathology (Orne, 1975). After all, who among us can claim to have achieved our full potential?

Treatment of subsyndromal conditions In addition, some observers have suggested that mental health professionals are too conservative in diagnosing even the standard set of disorders (that is, the disorders catalogued in the DSM-IV). They argue that many individuals may have mild versions of mental disorders. As such, these individuals do not meet criteria for formal diagnosis, yet they are still hobbled by "shadow syndromes" (Ratey and Johnson, 1997). For example, take the woman who worries constantly about whether her car's engine is working well and takes her car to the repair shop at least once a week just to make sure that everything is okay. Is she just showing an everyday kind of eccentricity, or is she in fact suffering from a mild form of obsessive-compulsive disorder that should be treated?

One study surveyed over 2,000 individuals for the presence of major depression. Based on their signs and symptoms, these individuals were classified into three groups: normal, diagnosable for major depression, or having subsyndromal depression—that is, they had some of the signs and symptoms of major depression but not enough to be diagnosed as having the disorder. Compared to the normal subjects, both the subsyndromal depressives and the fully diagnosable ones had suffered more financial losses, had poorer health, spent more days in bed because they felt unable to go to work, showed impaired functioning on the job, and reported more stress in the home. On most measures, in fact, the subsyndromal and the major depressives were equally impaired (Judd et al., 1996).

Given such evidence, should those with subsyndromal conditions be treated? Some critics believe that they should, but others argue that this will lead to a "cosmetic psychopharmacology" in which people take medication to adjust their personalities just as they now seek nose jobs, "tummy tucks," and face lifts. Indeed, this view might lead to a world in which nearly any human eccentricity is regarded as problematic and a candidate for treatment, with the term *normal* reserved for the relatively few who are sufficiently bland to survive labeling. Moreover, such indiscriminate diagnosis might also lead people to use their subsyndromal conditions to excuse bad social conduct or poor job performance (see Olson, 1997; Wilson, 1997). There are obvious dangers here, but let us note just as well that diagnostic criteria that are too stringent and rigid may exclude from treatment people who might reasonably benefit from it. Clearly, these issues allow no easy resolution.

CULTURAL COMPETENCE IN PSYCHOTHERAPY

Because the originators of the theories and techniques we have discussed were all Europeans and North Americans, it has been suggested that psychotherapy may ill-serve patients from other cultures. This has led many authors to stress the importance of **cultural competence** in psychotherapy. They argue that the therapist must understand the patient's culture well enough to modify the goals of therapy so as to conform to the values appropriate for that patient.

For example, many Asian cultures place considerable emphasis on formality in all their affairs. Social roles within these cultures are often clearly defined and tend to be structured largely by age and sex, with a father's authority rarely challenged within the family (Sue and Kirk, 1973). Growing up in such a culture may play an important role in shaping the values a patient brings to therapy. A therapist insensitive to these values risks offending the patient and endangering the therapy. Similarly, a therapy that emphasizes individual autonomy over family loyalties might inadvertently run afoul of the patient's cultural traditions and so be counterproductive.

Likewise, therapists who expect their patients to take responsibility for making changes in their lives may be ineffective with clients whose cultural worldview stipulates that important events are due to fate, chance, or powerful others (Pedersen, Fukuyama, and Heath, 1989). And therapies that solely emphasize personal growth and self-exploration may create rather than reduce a patient's problems of daily living, if the individual happens to belong to a group that is regularly discriminated against (Wohl, 1989). Finally, practitioners who consider psychotherapy a secular endeavor would do well to remember that, for non-Western cultures and many Western ones, any kind of healing must fully acknowledge the patient's spirituality.

EVALUATING THERAPEUTIC OUTCOME

We have just surveyed what different kinds of therapists believe and do. But do these practices do any good? Does therapy actually help patients? These questions often arouse indignant protests from therapists, who see the question as akin to asking the clergy to prove its success in saving souls. The members of the clergy believe that their success is self-evident; many therapists believe the same. And these beliefs seem to be shared by patients: Most patients feel utterly certain that they have been helped, and therefore see no point in doubting the obvious (see Seligman, 1995). But testimonials alone are not convincing.★ For one thing, both patients and therapists have a serious stake in believing that psychotherapy works. If it doesn't, the patient has wasted his money, and the therapist has perpetrated a sham (Torrey, 1992; Dawes, 1994). Under the circumstances, neither patient nor therapist may be objective in judging whether there was beneficial change.

Even if change does occur during the weeks (or months) of therapy, what caused it? Our previous explanation of how medications are evaluated should now raise some obvious questions. Was the change produced by the psychotherapy itself, or would it have occurred anyway? People naturally have ups and downs in their lives, and often seek out therapy when they are at their worst. This makes it likely that they will improve somewhat during therapy, thanks simply to the passage of time. And even if we can rule out this concern, other problems remain: If the patient improves, is this attributable to the specific therapeutic intervention? Perhaps, instead, the patient was helped merely by the sense of having an ally during her time of trouble—what we referred to earlier as the therapeutic alliance. Or did the improvement simply come from the decision to turn over a new leaf or from the mere expectation of a cure?

★In the widely touted *Consumer Reports* survey to evaluate whether psychotherapy is beneficial (*Consumer Reports,* 1995), 184,000 of the magazine's readers were asked whether they had received help for a mental health problem since 1991. Those who did were further asked to state the problems for which they sought treatment and to rate their satisfaction with it. Of those who received psychotherapy (2,900, or 1.6 percent of the original sample), 54 percent believed that therapy had helped "a great deal," with 90 percent reporting that it helped at least "somewhat." Despite an enthusiastic commentary by the survey's psychologist consultant (Seligman, 1995; and see description of survey by Kotkin, Daviet, and Gurin, 1996), the survey was roundly criticized as uninterpretable for many of the reasons we discuss in the contexts of evaluating the effectiveness of medication and psychotherapy: no control group, subjective outcome measures, and so on (see Brock et al., 1996; Hollon, 1996; Jacobson and Christenson, 1996).

DOES PSYCHOTHERAPY WORK?

An early impetus for research in this domain came from a sharp attack launched by the late British psychologist Hans Eysenck (1916–1997) (Eysenck, 1961). Eysenck was particularly concerned with the efficacy of psychoanalysis and similar "insight" therapies. To assess these therapies, Eysenck surveyed some two dozen articles that reported the number of "neurotic" patients (mostly, patients with depression or anxiety disorders in today's nomenclature) who improved or failed to improve after psychotherapy. Overall, about 60 percent improved, a result that might be considered fairly encouraging. But Eysenck argued that this was really nothing to cheer about. According to Eysenck's analysis, the spontaneous recovery rate in so-called neurotics—the number of neurotics who got better with no treatment—was, if anything, even higher, about 70 percent. If so, psychotherapy apparently has no curative effects.

In retrospect, it appears that Eysenck's attack was unduly harsh, and today his study is widely discredited (Jacobson and Christenson, 1996). In particular, he evidently overestimated the rate of spontaneous improvement. According to one review, the median rate of patients who get better without therapy is, depending upon the diagnostic composition of the group of patients, around 30 percent. This compares to an average improvement rate of 60 percent for patients who received psychotherapy, a difference that constitutes what the author called "some modest evidence that psychotherapy 'works'" (Bergin, 1971, p. 229; see also Luborsky, Singer, and Luborsky, 1975).

META-ANALYSES OF THERAPY OUTCOME

Several recent analyses of the effectiveness of psychotherapy provide a more optimistic picture. For the most part, they are based on a statistical technique called *meta-analysis,* by means of which the results of many different studies can be combined. In the most comprehensive analysis of this kind, 475 different studies, comprising 25,000 patients in all, were reviewed (Smith, Glass, and Miller, 1980). In each of these studies, patients who received some kind of psychotherapy were compared to a similar group of patients who did not. The studies differed in many respects. One factor that varied was the kind of psychotherapy used, whether psychodynamic, humanistic, behavioral, or cognitive. Another factor that varied was the criterion of improvement. In some cases, the criterion was the level of a symptom: the amount of avoidance that snake phobics eventually showed toward snakes, the number of washing episodes shown by compulsive washers, and so on. In others, it was based on an improvement in functioning, such as a rise in a disturbed student's grade-point average (GPA). In still others, such as studies on depressed patients, it was an improvement in mood, as rated by scales completed by the patient himself or by knowledgeable outsiders such as his spouse and children. Given all these differences among the studies, combining the results seemed problematic, but meta-analysis provided a method.

Consider two hypothetical studies, *A* and *B*. Let's say that Study *A* shows that, after treatment, the average snake phobic can move closer to a snake than the average patient who received no treatment. Let's also assume that Study *B* found that depressed students who received psychotherapy show a greater increase in GPA than do equivalent students in an untreated control group. On the face of it, there's no way to average the results of the two studies, because they are presented using completely different units. In the first case, the average effect of therapy—that is, the difference between the group that received treatment and the one that did not—is measured in feet (how near to the snake the patient will go); in the second, it is counted in GPA points. But here's the trick provided by meta-analysis. Let's suppose we find that in Study *A*, 85 percent of the patients are able to move closer to the snake than the average untreated patient. Let's further suppose that in Study *B*, 75 percent of the students who received psychotherapy earn a GPA higher than the average GPA of the untreated students. Now we can average the scores. To be sure, feet and GPA points are like apples and oranges and cannot be compared. But the percentage relationships—in our case, 85 and 75—are comparable. Since this is so, they can be averaged across different studies.

The conclusion drawn by averaging across the 475 studies reviewed was that the "average person who receives therapy is better off at the end of it than 80 percent of the persons who do not" (Smith, Glass, and Miller, 1980, p. 87). Later analyses used somewhat more stringent criteria in selecting studies for inclusion within the meta-analysis, but these yielded similar results (e.g., Andrews and Harvey, 1981; Shapiro and Shapiro, 1982). Further studies showed that these improvements are still found when patients are studied months or years after treatment (Nicholson and Berman, 1983).

DETERIORATION EFFECTS

Overall, it appears that patients who receive psychotherapy are better off than patients who do not. But this statement applies to averages. When we look at individuals, we find that while psychotherapy has an effect, this effect is not always for the better. A certain proportion of patients seem to get worse. Some evidence that this is so came from an inspection of the variability of post-treatment test scores (for example, self-ratings). After psychotherapy, the scores on such tests are more divergent than the scores of an untreated control group. This suggests that while some patients improve, some others—fortunately, a smaller number, between 5 and 10 percent of patients—become worse (Bergin, 1967; Smith et al., 1980).

Many cases of deterioration in psychotherapy seem to be due to a bad therapist-patient relationship at the outset or to outright incompetence or even pathology in the therapist (Hadley and Strupp, 1976; Smith, Glass, and Miller, 1980). Other cases of deterioration may have a subtler cause. Psychotherapy sometimes disrupts what is stable in the patient's life and provides no substitute (Bergin, 1967; Hadley and Strupp, 1976). Sometimes the original problems worsen, or the patient begins to show new ones. For example, the therapy may lead a patient to regard her marriage as unsatisfactory, but as she takes steps toward separation or divorce she may become severely depressed at the prospect of being alone. Good psychotherapists are alert to such dangers and attempt to avert such deterioration whenever possible.

COMPARING DIFFERENT THERAPIES

Apparently, patients who receive psychotherapy will, on average, be better off than patients who do not. To the extent that this is so, psychotherapy works. But as we've seen, there are many different types of psychotherapy. Do any of them work better than the others? This question is hotly debated among psychotherapists. Psychodynamically oriented therapists tend to believe that their behavioral and cognitive colleagues are doing mere "patch-up" work. Behavioral and cognitive therapists, in turn, believe that their psychoanalytic and existential associates are using unproven techniques based on pseudoscientific theory. Who is right?

"Everyone has won and all must have prizes." (From Lewis Carroll, Alice in Wonderland, *1865/1963*)

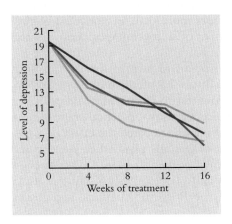

19.7 **The dodo bird verdict** *The figure shows the results of a study of 279 depressed patients receiving either cognitive therapy, interpersonal therapy (Klerman et al., 1984), antidepressant medication (Tofranil), or a placebo. The results after four months show that, while all treated patients were better off than the placebo controls, the particular treatment they received made little difference (Gibbons et al., 1993).*

THE DODO BIRD VERDICT

The answer, which comes from many comparisons of psychotherapeutic outcomes, is unlikely to provide comfort for the adherents of any one school of psychotherapy. Most of these studies suggest that the various psychotherapies are all about equally effective. This view is sometimes called the **dodo bird verdict** after the dodo bird in *Alice in Wonderland* who organized a race among various Wonderland creatures and concluded that "Everyone has won and all must have prizes" (see Figure 19.7; Luborsky, Singer, and Luborsky, 1975). While a few reviewers feel that the behavioral and cognitive therapies have a slight advantage (e.g., Shapiro and Shapiro, 1982), many others judge that the outcome similarities far outweigh the differences (e.g., Sloane et al., 1975; Smith, Glass, and Miller, 1980; Elkin et al., 1989; Shear et al., 1994; Wampold et al., 1997).

PLACEBO EFFECTS

One way to explain equivalence in therapeutic outcome is to propose that psychotherapy simply generates a placebo effect. According to this view, the patients got better because they expected to get better. This is quite analogous to what happens when patients ingest little blue sugar pills in the belief that they are swallowing a potent medicine (see pp. 816–17). We wouldn't expect blue sugar pills to be more helpful than red or green sugar pills; analogously, we shouldn't expect psychodynamic therapies to be more (or less) effective than, say, humanistic therapies. Whether we're dealing with sugar pills or with psychotherapies, in this view all that matters is the patients' belief in the therapy and hope for help through it.

An ingenious demonstration of a placebo effect in psychotherapy was provided in a classic study by Gordon Paul in which students who suffered from severe anxiety during public speaking were given five sessions of a bogus treatment.

Placebos in medieval medicine *Medieval apothecaries prescribed many "medicinal" substances that were of no proven benefit to their patients. They must have had a placebo effect, though, because the patients (that survived) kept coming back. (Courtesy of Österreichische Nationalbibliotek, Vienna)*

During each session, they took what they thought was a potent tranquilizer (it actually was a capsule of sodium bicarbonate) and performed a boring discrimination task. They were told that this task was ordinarily very stressful but would not be so for them because of the "tranquilizer." If repeated often enough, this experience would then inoculate them against anxiety-provoking situations in real life. Needless to say, all of this was a ruse, but the participants accepted it and believed that the treatment would help them. When later tested for speech anxiety, these participants improved considerably more than an untreated control group, providing a powerful demonstration of a psychotherapeutic placebo effect (Paul, 1966).

The mere expectation of getting better seems to help, at least in the short term and in laboratory studies of this type. But is that all there is to psychotherapy? Placebo effects wear thin over the long term: Hope fades and problems often return. Indeed, the bulk of the evidence argues that psychotherapy is more than a placebo. Several meta-analytic studies have compared the effect of placebo treatments (such as Paul's) to the effect of genuine psychotherapies. By and large, genuine psychotherapy led to more improvement than placebo treatments (Smith, Glass, and Miller, 1980; Andrews and Harvey, 1981; Robinson et al., 1990; for a contrary view and discussion, see Prioleau, Murdock, and Brody, 1983).

Thus, placebo effects do occur in psychotherapy, but psychotherapy plainly involves more than placebo effects alone. This is reflected in the fact that genuine psychotherapy produces larger benefits than those produced by the placebo treatments. So we are still left with the problem of explaining the dodo bird effect.

COMMON FACTORS

One explanation centers on the shared themes that underlie many of the beliefs and practices of the various modes of psychotherapy. These include therapeutic efforts to defuse emotional situations, provide interpersonal learning, and offer an empathic relationship with another person (see pp. 832–34). To the extent that these features are indeed beneficial and are common to the various schools, we would expect that they (together with some shared psychological placebo effects) exert similar beneficial effects.

SPECIFIC FACTORS

There may also be some effects that are not so readily detected by the outcome studies (for the most part, meta-analytic) that we've discussed thus far. These studies suggested that all psychotherapies are equally effective, regardless of the banner under which they are practiced. But the real issue may not be which therapy is most effective, but rather which treatment is most effective for which patient under which set of circumstances (Paul, 1967). Meta-analysis may not be the best way to answer this question, for it tends to lump different disorders together. In fact, there may be a more fine-grained pattern in the data, with some therapies superior in some cases and other therapies superior elsewhere; this pattern would probably be missed by the meta-analyses. Indeed, some critics feel that meta-analysis is like combining apples and oranges and coming up with only moderate evidence for fruit.

According to some practitioners, some treatments are more effective for some patients and some conditions than for others. They believe that psychotherapy works best, therefore, if specific therapies are matched to the disorder and the patient (Beutler and Clarkin, 1990; Norcross, 1991; Norcross and Freedheim, 1992). This position is sometimes called *prescriptionism,* for it argues that specific therapies should be prescribed for patients suffering from particular mental disorders just as specific medications are prescribed for particular physical illnesses.

A number of such "prescriptions" are in current use today. For example, it is widely believed that phobias and related anxiety conditions are best treated by any of the behavior therapies that try to eliminate fear, such as systematic desensitization (Emmelkamp, 1986). Panic disorder responds well to cognitive therapy or reflective listening, and such psychotherapy is often accompanied by antidepressant medication to block panic attacks (Clark, 1988; Shear et al., 1994). Schizophrenia responds to the antipsychotics, with medication by Clozaril, Risperdal, or Zyprexa preferable if possible and medically permissible. Depression seems to be effectively treated by antidepressant medications, cognitive therapy, or interpersonal therapy, and ECT tends to work if these do not. Eskalith, Depakote, or Tegretol are the favored medications for bipolar disorder, with psychotherapy of no direct use. These are just a few examples of what amounts to an emerging cookbook of therapeutic prescriptions for mental disorders.

ACCOUNTABILITY FOR PSYCHOTHERAPY

While attacks such as Eysenck's provoked the initial studies of therapeutic effectiveness, a more recent impetus has been the demand for economic accountability. Beginning in the 1970s, private insurance companies that had for years reimbursed patients for both inpatient care and outpatient psychotherapy began to question the costs and benefits of each. As health maintenance organizations (HMOs) began to provide group health care, they too began to require that psychotherapists account for themselves by showing that the time they spent with patients was worth the cost. Finally, tax-funded government programs like Medicare debated whether even to finance psychotherapy (Garfield, 1992).

Did patients do any better with one kind of care than another or with twelve years of therapy rather than twelve weeks? These questions struck at the pocketbook of both patient and practitioner, and they forced drastic changes in the practice of psychotherapy. Instead of justifying psychotherapy based on theories about psychopathology or commentaries about meaning and existence, practitioners suddenly had to show that what they practiced improved patients using the most concrete of dependent variables: How fast could the patient be discharged from therapy? How rapidly could she return to work? How long was the patient able to function without further use of professional services? If the costs of therapy were to be paid or reimbursed by an HMO or private insurer, the insurer began to require that the therapy be the most cost-effective kind. And if a patient was making no progress in therapy, the solution was not to conduct more therapy but to discontinue it entirely.

Similar questions have arisen in legal contexts. Could a therapist be guilty of malpractice for not offering a patient the best treatment or at least a proven treatment? Indeed, this was the question behind a widely cited court case that pitted biological against psychoanalytic approaches to the treatment of depression. The case concerned a patient who was severely depressed and was admitted to a psychoanalytically oriented private hospital where he received no antidepressant medication, only intensive psychoanalytically based psychotherapy. During his hospital stay his condition worsened: He lost forty pounds, and his overall physical condition deteriorated. Even so, the therapy was continued, and the patient's deterioration was interpreted as reflecting the patient's difficulties in "working through his defenses." After seven months, the patient's family became alarmed, removed him from this hospital, and placed him in another in which he was immediately treated with antidepressant medication. He recovered within three months and began initiating the lawsuit against the first hospital (*Osheroff v. Chestnut Lodge*; see Klerman, 1990).

The lawsuit was settled out of court, but the result stirred the medical community to form a set of standards for effective treatment. One of the first such sets concerned the acceptable care for depression. It stipulated that depressed individuals are best treated by a combination of antidepressant medication and psychotherapy. If psychotherapy is attempted alone, it should be only for mild to moderate depressions and only if improvement is seen quickly; otherwise, antidepressant medication must be instituted (American Psychiatric Association, 1993). Standards that were similar, but slightly more sympathetic to psychotherapy, were then adopted as U.S. government health-care guidelines (Depression Guideline Panel, 1993; Persons, Thase, and Crits-Christoph, 1996). These standards will probably come to govern all mental health practitioners, and similar standards of care are expected for other disorders.

Given these legal and economic factors, most psychotherapists today rarely engage patients in long-term insight or humanistic-existential therapy. Instead, they try to provide therapies that have a better-documented chance of working and working quickly. Likewise, the content of psychotherapy today, and not just its theoretical framework, also reflects this pragmatic concern with expense and expediency. Often, therapy consists of brief problem-solving sessions, various psychoeducational interventions such as stress-management classes, and time-limited behavioral therapy (Vandenbos, Cummings, and DeLeon, 1992).

A CENTURY OF THERAPY

Where does all of this leave us? It has been more than a hundred years since Krafft-Ebing's discovery that general paresis is caused by syphilis and since Freud and Breuer's classic studies of hysteria. What can we say today about the treatment of mental disorder?

All in all, there has been considerable progress. Let's begin with psychotherapy. There is little doubt that psychotherapy produces some nonspecific benefits. It helps people by providing someone in whom they can confide, who lends advice about troubling matters, who listens to them, and who instills hope that they will get better. The critic may reply that such gains merely reflect placebo effects and similar matters. According to this view, the benefits are not produced by any specific psychotherapeutic technique but might just as easily have been provided by a wise aunt, the understanding family doctor, or the local clergy.

Even if this were true—and it is certainly not the whole story—it may be irrelevant. Wise aunts are in short supply today; the extended family in which aunts and uncles, nieces, nephews, and grandparents lived nearby is largely a thing of the past. The same is true of the family doctor, who has virtually vanished from the scene, together with his house calls and bedside manner. Nor do many people today have a member of the clergy as a lifelong confidant. All of this suggests that psychotherapy has come to fill a social vacuum. Some of its effect may well be placebo-like, but a placebo is better than nothing. And for the present, the psychotherapeutic professions seem to be the officially designated dispensers of such placebos.

But this is by no means all. Over and above placebo effects, there seem to be some genuine, specific psychotherapeutic benefits that produce improvement, though rarely a complete cure. The specific ingredients that bring these effects about have not been pinpointed, but they probably include emotional defusing, interpersonal learning, and some insight—all acquired within the therapeutic situation and somehow transferred to the patient's life beyond.

How about biological therapies? Here the progress has been dramatic. Antipsychotic drugs control some of the worst manifestations of schizophrenia. The antidepressants and antimanic drugs (and where appropriate, ECT) do the same for the mood swings of depression and mania, as do the anxiolytics for disabling anxiety. These advances are far from what one might wish. The drugs don't begin to effect a cure, and all have side effects. But we've come far from where we started a century ago.

How far is far? As so often, it depends on where we look. If we look back and compare our current practices with those at the time of the American Revolution when Benjamin Rush dunked his patients into ice cold water or whirled them around until they were unconscious, we've come a long way. But if we look ahead to some diagnostic manual of the future in which schizophrenia, mood and anxiety disorders, and all the rest of the current DSM-IV entries have neatly catalogued therapies that are sure to work, we must recognize that we have a much longer way to go. Still, considering our progress over the last hundred years, there is much to celebrate.

SUMMARY

1. *Biological therapies,* especially medications, constitute one major form of treatment of mental disorder. The *classic antipsychotics* like Thorazine and Haldol are helpful in holding in check the major positive symptoms of schizophrenia, and new *atypical antipsychotics* like Clozaril and Risperdal are effective in treating negative as well as positive symptoms. These new atypical antipsychotics can often produce beneficial results in schizophrenics who have not responded to classic antipsychotics.

2. Classic *antidepressants* such as *MAO inhibitors* (like Nardil) and *tricyclics* (like Tofranil) counteract depression, and one particular tricyclic, Anafranil, is effective in

many cases of obsessive-compulsive disorder. These classic antidepressants all have many undesirable side effects, however. *Selective serotonin reuptake inhibitors (SSRIs)* like Prozac were designed to maximize their effects on serotonin neurotransmission. They have fewer side effects and are equally effective for depression and obsessive-compulsive disorder.

3. Lithium carbonate (e.g., Eskalith) is useful in cases of bipolar disorder, especially in forestalling or reducing the intensity of manic episodes. Other *antimanic* medications such as Tegretol and Depakote can control the disorder when lithium doesn't work or the patient cannot take it.

4. The effectiveness of psychotropic medications—as indeed of all therapies—requires careful evaluation that controls for *spontaneous improvement* and *placebo effects,* and that also guards against both the physicians' and the patients' expectations by use of *double-blind techniques.* Studies using appropriate control groups and double-blind techniques have demonstrated that certain psychotropic medications have genuine effects that are quite specific to a particular mental disorder. These medications reduce the signs and symptoms of a disorder but unfortunately do not cure it. Without maintenance doses, some patients discharged from care may relapse.

5. Other biological therapies include *psychosurgery,* a procedure that was once performed rather promiscuously and to the detriment of the recipients but is now conducted much more selectively and precisely. *Electroconvulsive therapy (ECT)* is markedly effective in cases of severe and potentially suicidal depression and for cases of bipolar disorder that resist antimanic medications.

6. Another approach to the treatment of mental disorder, *psychotherapy,* relies on psychological means alone. Much of it is derived from *classical psychoanalysis* but has been expanded and diversified in both its guiding principles and techniques.

7. Psychoanalysts try to help their patients to recover repressed memories and wishes so that they can overcome crippling internal conflicts. Their tools include *free association* and the interpretation of the patient's *resistance* to it. The goal is emotional rather than mere intellectual insight, which is achieved through an analysis of the *transference* relationship between analyst and patient.

8. In *psychodynamic therapy,* therapists follow Freud's basic principles but generally place greater emphasis on current interpersonal and social problems rather than on psychosexual matters in the patient's childhood. They also tend to take a more active role in helping the patient extend the therapeutic experience to the world outside.

9. A different approach is taken by *behavior therapists* whose concern is with unwanted, overt behaviors rather than with hypothetical underlying causes. Many of the behavior therapists' techniques are derived from the principles of classical and instrumental conditioning. Therapies based on classical conditioning include *systematic desensitization,* which tries to countercondition the patient's fear through gradual exposure to the feared object or experience. Another is *aversion therapy* in which undesirable behaviors, thoughts, and desires are coupled with unpleasant stimuli. Therapies based on operant conditioning principles include the use of *token economies* in which patients are systematically reinforced for desirable behaviors, and *contingency management,* in which subjects are appropriately rewarded or punished for good or bad behavior.

10. Some recent offshoots of behavior therapy share its concrete and directive orientation but not its emphasis on conditioning. One example is *cognitive therapy,* which tries to change the way the patient thinks about his situation. Others include various attempts to advance the patient's social education, using techniques such as *graded homework assignments, modeling,* and *role playing.*

11. Another group of practitioners, the *humanistic therapists,* charge that both behavior therapy and psychoanalysis are too mechanistic and manipulative and that they fail to deal with their patients as whole persons. An example of a humanistic approach is Rogers' *client-centered therapy,* which is largely nondirective and is based on the idea that therapy is a process of personal growth. A related approach is *existential therapy,* the goal of which is to help patients recognize the importance of personal responsibility and free choice, and to assist them in imbuing their lives with meaning.

SUMMARY

12. The last few decades have seen an enormous extension of psychotherapy. One extension is of method. An example is *group therapy* in which patients are treated in groups rather than individually. Another example is *couples and family therapy*, whose practitioners believe that family distress is not in the pathology of any one individual but in the relationships within the family system and who therefore try to rectify these faulty relationships. Another extension concerns therapeutic goals. While the original purpose of psychotherapy was to cure pathology, some practitioners gradually broadened this goal to include personal growth and the discovery of meaning in life. Observers also question whether *subsyndromal signs and symptoms* should be identified and treated. Finally, therapists are encouraged to develop *cultural competence,* so that they can adapt their therapies to the specific cultural values and customs that patients bring with them.

13. In recent years, investigators have begun to assess the effectiveness of psychotherapies through a statistical technique called *meta-analysis* by means of which the results of many different studies can be combined. The results of such analyses indicate that the various psychotherapies are more effective than placebo treatments, which in turn are better than no treatment at all. Comparing the effect of different psychotherapies is enormously difficult, but the main finding is that therapies tend to be fairly effective and that they are effective to about the same extent (the *dodo bird verdict*).

14. The dodo bird verdict, however, derives from studies that combine many types of patients and disorders. Work is underway to determine the extent to which therapy can be matched to the patient and the disorder. Practitioners who adopt the *prescriptionist* position believe that in addition to placebo effects and various common factors such as *emotional defusing, interpersonal learning,* and an *empathic relationship* with another person, particular therapies have specific effects on particular conditions.

15. Economic factors and legal issues have forced psychotherapists to reexamine their own efforts and provide only those services that have demonstrated effectiveness. This is leading to the development of generally accepted professional standards of care for specific mental disorders.

EPILOGUE

We have come to the end of our journey. We have traveled through the sprawling fields of psychology, a loosely federated intellectual empire that stretches from the domains of the biological sciences on one border to those of the social sciences on the other. We have gone from one end of psychology to another. What have we learned?

In looking back over our journey, it is clear that very much more is known today about mind and behavior than was known in the days of, say, Thorndike and Köhler, let alone those of Descartes, Locke, and Kant. For by now, psychology has assuredly become a science of considerable accomplishments. But this does not change the fact that what we know today is just a small clearing in a vast jungle of ignorance. As we come to know more, the clearing expands, but so does the circumference that borders on the uncharted wildness.

What can we say? We can point at what we know and congratulate ourselves. Or we can consider what we do not know and bemoan our ignorance. Perhaps a wiser course is one recommended by Sigmund Freud, among others, on thinking about some aspects of human intellectual history (Freud, 1917).

Freud suggested a parallel between the psychological growth of each human child and the intellectual progress of humanity as a whole. As he saw it, the infant is initially possessed by a pervasive sense of his own power and importance. He cries and his parents come to change or feed or rock him, and so he comes to believe that he is the cause of whatever happens around him, the center of a world that revolves around him alone. But this happy delusion of omnipotence cannot last forever. Eventually the growing infant discovers that he is not the hub of the universe. This recognition may come as a cruel blow, but he will ultimately be the better for it. For the child cannot become strong and capable without some awareness that he is not so as yet, without first accepting the fact that he can't have his way just by wishing. His first achievements will be slight—as he lifts his own cup or says his first word—but they are real enough, and they lay the foundation for his later mastery of his environment.

Freud thought that a similar theme underlies the growth of humankind's awareness of the world in which we live. On two crucial occasions in our history, we had to relinquish some cherished beliefs in our own power and importance. With Copernicus, we had to cede our place in the center of the physical universe: The sun doesn't circle us, but we the sun. With Darwin, we had to forfeit our presumption of centrality in the biological sphere: We are not specially created but are descended from other animals. Each of these intellectual revolutions ran into vehement opposition, in large part because each represented a gigantic blow to humanity's self-love and pride. They made us face our own ignorance and insignificance. But however painful it may have been initially, each recognition of our weakness ultimately helped us gain strength, each confession of ignorance eventually led to deeper understanding. The Copernican revolution forced us to admit our minute place in the celestial scheme of things, but this admission was the first step in a journey of ever-increasing physical horizons, a journey which in our own time brought us to the moon. The Darwinian revolution made us aware that we are just one biological species among millions, the product of the same evolutionary process that brought forth sea urchins and penguins. But this awareness opened the way for continually expanding explorations of the biological universe, explorations that have already given us much greater control of our own bodily condition and of the fragile environment in which we and other species exist.

In this century we have had to suffer yet another blow to our self-pride. We learned that we cannot be sure of what goes on in our own minds. Modern psychology, for all its accomplishments, has made it utterly clear that thus far we know even less about our own mental processes and behavior than we know about the physical and biological world around us. Here, too, we have to confess that we are weak and ignorant. We can only hope that this confession will have some of the effects of our previous ones, that here again strength will grow out of weakness and knowledge out of folly and ignorance. If so, we may finally understand why we think and do what we think and do, so that we may ultimately master our inner selves as we have learned to master the world around us.

There are few goals in science that are worthier than this.

APPENDIX **1**

METHODS OF SCIENTIFIC RESEARCH

An enormous body of psychological knowledge has been summarized in this book, and in every chapter, we have included some discussion of how this knowledge was obtained. Our emphasis, though, has been on what psychologists know, rather than how they learned it. In this appendix, we reverse the emphasis, and consider the methods of scientific research more thoroughly. This will allow us to explore why psychologists regard their knowledge as relatively secure—not matters of opinion or conjecture but matters of fact. This discussion will also allow us to highlight how other investigators (including, perhaps, the readers of this book!) will be able to expand this knowledge base in years to come.

The methods of scientific research turn out to have other uses as well. In day-to-day life, we often try to draw conclusions from evidence: A friend is in a foul mood, so we think back over recent events, trying to figure out what caused the mood. A sports commentator offers an explanation for why a particular team is doing so well this year, and we try to evaluate this stand by reviewing what we know about that team. On some mornings the car starts easily, but on other mornings it doesn't, and so we try to figure out what the problem is: Does it start more easily when the weather is warm? when it's parked in a level spot? As we will see, the tools of scientific research can be applied to all of these cases, and, in fact, these intellectual tools can be used to improve the process by which we make these and countless other judgments. There is even reason to believe that an understanding of the methods of research can improve our critical thinking in general (Nisbett, 1993; Kosonen and Winne, 1995; Perkins and Grotzer, 1997; Halpern, 1998).

WHY SCIENCE?

The questions psychologists ask cover a wide range: Why do we do the things we do? Why do we feel the things we feel? How does each of us differ from those around us, and how are we all alike? Questions like these are at the heart of our field's inquiry, but similar questions are asked by many nonpsychologists. Philosophers, novelists, theologians, and sages of all sorts have each offered their own views on these matters. What, then, is distinctive about psychology's answers to these questions? One essential difference lies in psychology's commitment to the scientific method.

It is fascinating to muse about human actions and feelings, relying on personal opinion or common sense. But often we want definitive answers to our questions about behavior, cognition, or emotion. If one form of therapy alleviates depression but another does not, we want to know this, so that we can be sure to use the effective therapy. If human memory is unreliable in some circumstances, then we want to identify those circumstances, so that, for example, we can help the courts in evaluating eyewitness testimony. And, in general, if we hope to

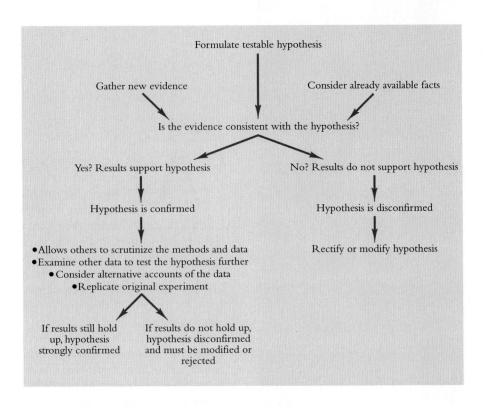

Formulate testable hypothesis

Gather new evidence

Consider already available facts

Is the evidence consistent with the hypothesis?

Yes? Results support hypothesis

No? Results do not support hypothesis

Hypothesis is confirmed

Hypothesis is disconfirmed

- Allows others to scrutinize the methods and data
- Examine other data to test the hypothesis further
- Consider alternative accounts of the data
- Replicate original experiment

Rectify or modify hypothesis

If results still hold up, hypothesis strongly confirmed

If results do not hold up, hypothesis disconfirmed and must be modified or rejected

A.1   The scientific method

build a full understanding of our thoughts, feelings, and actions, then we need to build our understanding on a solid foundation, one that rests on facts, not myths, platitudes, or preconceptions (Sagan, 1996).

The scientific method provides our best path toward achieving these goals, by allowing us to test our ideas objectively and systematically. The methods of science allow us to decide, with a reasonable degree of confidence, whether a particular assertion is correct or not. And with this knowledge, we can develop a set of claims that is genuinely reliable and useful.

The identifying mark of science lies in its method—the process by which ideas are evaluated. Scientists begin by formulating clear, specific questions that can lead to *testable hypotheses*—hypotheses that allow scientists to make specific predictions about what they will find given a particular set of circumstances (see Figure A.1). These predictions are then put to the test. Often this means gathering new data, either by observation or by experiment. Sometimes predictions can be checked by using data already available—perhaps the result of some previous study or the information included in the medical records of U.S. Army recruits or data gathered for the U.S. Census.

But no matter where the data come from, there are strict rules regarding how the data should be gathered, summarized, and evaluated. For example, it's not acceptable for scientists to consider only those facts that favor their hypotheses and ignore those that do not. It's also not acceptable to add new assumptions on the spot to explain away facts that don't support the hypothesis. Scientists should also consider only those facts that were collected in a reliable, objective manner. And, of course, fudging or concocting data for any reason—whether for fame and fortune or because of a sincere belief that claiming a certain result will ultimately benefit society—is anathema to science; it is fraud and grounds for expulsion from the profession.

If the facts are not consistent with the prediction, then the hypothesis is *disconfirmed.* In this case, the scientist is obliged to set the hypothesis aside, turning instead to some new hypothesis. The new hypothesis may be wholly different from the previous one, or it may simply involve some minor adjustment. In either case, the scientist does not continue to endorse a hypothesis that has been tested and found wanting.

If, however, the results are consistent with the prediction, then the hypothesis is **confirmed.**★ But even at this stage, scientists would hesitate to draw firm conclusions from the evidence. The method used to gather the data and the data themselves must first be made accessible to other members of the scientific community; for psychologists, this usually means giving a presentation at a scientific meeting or publishing an article in a professional journal. This allows other investigators to scrutinize the method and the data, to ensure that the hypothesis was evaluated correctly. It also allows others to **replicate** the study—to run the same procedure with a new group of participants. A successful replication (a repetition of the study that yields the same results) assures us that there was nothing peculiar about the initial study and that the study's results are reliable.

Publication of a study also allows other investigators to run alternative experiments in an attempt to challenge the initial findings. Only when the results have been replicated, and survived the challenges, are firm conclusions drawn.

DESIGNING A PERSUASIVE EXPERIMENT

Scientists collect data in many different ways. Sometimes they conduct **experiments,** studies in which they deliberately manipulate the factor they wish to examine, while holding other factors constant. For example, does exercise improve one's mood? To find out, a psychologist might instruct one group of participants to exercise and another group not to, and then compare their moods. In this case, the psychologist has manipulated the presence or absence of exercise. Similarly, is an employer more likely to hire someone who seems very serious during a job interview or someone who seems very cheerful? To find out, a psychologist might have one group of job applicants act serious and another group act cheerful, and then compare their success in getting hired.

FORMULATING A TESTABLE HYPOTHESIS

The design of a persuasive experiment begins with a testable hypothesis. In order for a hypothesis to be testable, the researcher must be able to specify the results that would confirm the hypothesis as well as those that would disconfirm it. If virtually any set of circumstances could count as supporting the hypothesis, then a scientific test is not possible.

For example, imagine an astrologer who, after consulting the stars, announces: "An important public figure will die in the coming year!" This prediction might make for interesting reading in the supermarket checkout line, but it is too

---

★ Note, though, that we say *confirmed,* not *proven.* Sometimes a hypothesis is consistent with an enormous amount of evidence but is challenged when new facts become available. For this reason, scientists never regard a hypothesis as proven correct. A hypothesis that has been confirmed many times, and that has avoided refutation again and again, is considered *strongly confirmed* and highly likely to be true, but it still remains open to refutation if compelling new data come along.

vague to be testable. Who counts as an important public figure? Would the death of Ohio's director of the Department of Motor Vehicles during this time period confirm the hypothesis? How about the death of a once-prominent movie star? Since the astrologer's prediction provides no guidance for making these judgments, we can't tell whether the data would confirm the prediction or not. As a result, a definitive test of this prediction is impossible.

Similarly, consider the superstition that "bad things always come in threes." Chief among the problems here is the unspecified time interval. Three bank robberies occurring within a single week might seem to confirm this claim. But what if two occur within a week and another occurs a month later? What if the third robbery occurs four months later? Would these cases confirm the hypothesis? The hypothesis as stated provides no guidance on these points, so there is no way to determine whether the data support the hypothesis or not. So this hypothesis, too, is untestable.

Of course, we can modify these hypotheses to come up with testable predictions. For example, a testable version of "bad things come in threes" would stipulate precisely what counts as a "bad thing," and also would define "coming in threes." An example might be, "If one Oscar-winning actor dies, then two others will die within that same month, followed by a period of at least one month during which no additional Oscar-winning actors die." Of course, this prediction is far clumsier than the original platitude, but unlike the platitude, it is testable!

THE NEED FOR SYSTEMATIC DATA COLLECTION

In addition to a testable hypothesis, science also requires systematically gathered data. To see why, let's consider an example.

Many companies sell audiotapes that contain subliminal messages embedded in background music. The message might be an instruction to give up smoking or to curb overeating, or it might be a message designed to build self-esteem or overcome shyness. The message is played so softly that you cannot consciously detect it when listening to the tape. Nonetheless, these messages are alleged to provide important benefits—helping you to quit smoking or to stay on a diet, increasing your success in attracting romantic partners, and so on.

Some *anecdotal evidence*—evidence that has been informally collected and reported—suggests that these subliminal messages can be quite effective. Anecdotal evidence can take many forms: "a friend of a friend said . . ." or "in my experience, people . . ." or "a scientist on television said. . . ." But these observations are not scientifically persuasive. For one thing, one might worry about the sincerity of these reports: Is that really a scientist, or just an actor in a white lab coat? More important, these anecdotes do not allow us to evaluate the data. The anecdotes merely provide one person's description of the data, and this leaves us with no way to determine whether the description is accurate and whether the data themselves are reliable and were collected in an appropriate manner. As a result, anecdotal evidence is usually dismissed by scientists, for the same reasons that hearsay evidence is dismissed by judges in the courtroom.

Even if the anecdotal evidence is quite clear, problems remain. Often, this evidence describes just a single case in which subliminal persuasion seemed to have had a powerful effect. In Chapter 8, we call these "man who" (or "woman who"!) stories—"I know a man who tried every other way to give up smoking but finally succeeded by using a subliminal suggestion tape." Such cases, even if well documented, are not persuasive. Perhaps that man is the only one who was helped by such a tape. Or perhaps he would have (at last) given up smoking even without the tape. To evaluate these concerns, scientific studies need data from a broader set of observations.

What if you've heard from several friends who used the subliminal suggestion tapes in their efforts to quit smoking, with some reporting success and others failure? This moves us in the right direction, but here, too, there is a problem: A friend who used the subliminal suggestion tapes and kicked the cigarette habit is likely to be proud of this achievement and announce it publicly. But a friend who tried the tapes and made no progress may be embarrassed by this failure and so report it to no one. This pattern leads to the ***file-drawer problem,*** so-called because studies with encouraging results are often published (or, in less formal settings, simply announced), whereas studies with disappointing results are dumped into a file drawer, never to be seen again. Because of this problem, there's a real chance that informally collected data may be ***biased,*** with the success stories overrepresented in the data and the failures underrepresented.

Even if the file-drawer problem is avoided, yet another difficulty remains: How should one record and evaluate the data? To make good use of your friends' reports, you need some way of tallying the successes and the failures in order to ask which is more likely. How should this tallying be done? You might simply rely on memory, seeking to recall what various friends said about their experiences with the subliminal suggestion tapes. Then you could count up the successes and failures among these remembered cases. But the accuracy of this approach is far from guaranteed: Memory errors are common, and this could compromise your recall of the evidence (see Chapter 7). Memory can also be selective. In Chapter 8 we consider a pattern known as ***confirmation bias,*** which would lead you to recall more of the success stories if you expect that the subliminal tapes are effective, or more of the failures if you expect the opposite. (Chapter 8 also offers several other examples of the strategies and pitfalls of everyday reasoning.)

Of course, memory errors don't happen all the time, and confirmation bias does not always occur. As a result, many of our commonly held beliefs, based on informal data collection, are surely correct. But it is also easy to find cases in which our commonsense assessments of the data are erroneous, and this is why people sometimes end up with peculiar superstitions, unfounded beliefs, and so on (for examples, see Gilovich, 1993; Shermer, 1997). Because of cases like these, scientists are probably justified in viewing informal, memory-based data assessment as risky, and certainly inadequate for the level of certainty that scientists require.

Specifying the Dependent Variable

The problems we've cataloged thus far highlight the need for collecting and recording data in a systematic, objective fashion. This means that one needs to collect *all* the data (to avoid the file-drawer problem) and to record the data faithfully (so that there's no chance of memory error). But how exactly does one do this? Let's pursue this question by continuing with our example. Imagine that an investigator wants to evaluate the subliminal self-help tapes scientifically. She selects for the study a tape that's advertised as "increasing personal attractiveness" and hypothesizes that the tape will have the advertised effect. How should she run the test?

The investigator first needs some way of measuring attractiveness; without this measure, she will have no way of knowing whether the subliminal tapes work or not. This attractiveness measure will provide the experiment's **dependent variable,** *dependent* since the investigator wants to find out if this variable depends on some other factor. The **independent variable,** in contrast, is the variable whose effects she wishes to examine. In this example, the independent variable is using or not using the subliminal self-help tape.

Often, a dependent variable is a quantity that can be assessed directly—percent of correct answers on some test or the number of seconds needed to complete a task. But a quality like attractiveness requires a different sort of yardstick. One option is to use a panel of judges who assess the study's participants on the relevant dimension. The investigator could, for example, videotape the participants during an interview and then show the tape to the judges who would rate each participant's attractiveness on, say, a seven-point scale. Having the judges evaluate all the participants using the same scale would provide a basis for comparison and so for testing the hypothesis.

Why a panel of judges rather than just one judge? For a variable like attractiveness, there is a real possibility that different judges might view things differently. After all, what is attractive to one person may not be attractive to someone else. By using a panel of judges, and then comparing their ratings, the investigator can check on this possibility. If the judges disagree with one another, then no conclusions should be drawn from the study. But if the judges agree to a reasonable extent—that is, if they show adequate **interrater reliability**—then the investigator can be confident that their assessments are not arbitrary or idiosyncratic.

USING A CONTROL GROUP

Using the measurement just described, an investigator might gather data in a straightforward way: He could ask twenty students to listen to the subliminal suggestion tape and then have the judges rate the attractiveness of each student. If all the students turn out to be reasonably attractive, what could he conclude? Perhaps the tapes did help. But perhaps the students were simply attractive to begin with. Or perhaps they appeared attractive due to a boost in self-esteem generated merely by taking part in an experiment. ("Gee, the investigator really cares about me. . . .")

To remove this ambiguity, an investigator needs some basis for comparison in her study. As one option, she might interview and have the judges evaluate each student twice—once before and once after listening to the tape—to determine whether there was any change.

But this procedure still leaves a major problem. The participants might have been uncomfortable during the first interview (before listening to the tape) simply because the setting and procedure were unfamiliar. They might then have been more at ease and confident in the second interview (after listening to the tape) because it was, after all, the second interview. In this case, the experimenter might obtain the predicted result—the participants would seem more attractive after listening to the tape—even if the tape itself had no effect whatsoever.

One solution to this problem would be to have two separate groups of participants. Each group would be interviewed just once—one group after hearing the tape containing the subliminal message, and one group after hearing something else. Here, the first group would be the **experimental group,** because it is with these participants that the investigator introduced the **experimental manipulation** (in our example, listening to the tape with the subliminal message). The second group would be the **control group,** because that group provides the basis for comparison that allows the investigator to assess the effects of the experimental manipulation.

THE PROPER TREATMENT FOR
THE CONTROL GROUP

What should the procedure be for the members of the control group? One possibility is that they would hear no tape at all, whereas those in the experimental group would hear the tape containing the subliminal message embedded in music. In this case, any contrast that the investigator later observes between the two groups might be due to the fact that the experimental group heard the subliminal message, while the control group did not.

But there is also another possibility: Since the subliminal message is embedded in background music, perhaps it is the music, and not the message, that influences the experimental group. (The participants might find it relaxing to spend some quiet minutes listening to music, and so they might appear more attractive later on simply because they were more relaxed.) In this case, it helps to listen to the tape but the result would be the same if there'd been no subliminal message at all.

To avoid this ambiguity, the control group must be matched to the experimental group in all respects except for the experimental manipulation. If the experimental group hears music containing the subliminal message, the control group must hear the identical music without any subliminal message. If ten minutes elapse between hearing the tape and being interviewed for the experimental group, then the same amount of time must elapse for the control group.

PLACEBO EFFECTS AND DEMAND
CHARACTERISTICS

It's also important that the experimenter treat the two groups in precisely the same way. If the experimental group is told that they are participating in an activity that might increase their attractiveness, then the control group should be told the same thing; that way, the two groups will have similar expectations about the procedure. This is crucial, since participants' expectations can have a profound effect on a study's results. In Chapter 19, for example, we discuss the powerful role of *placebo effects,* effects caused by someone's beliefs or expectations about a drug or therapy. Numerous studies have shown that placebo effects can be quite strong, so that patients suffering from a variety of diseases may show marked improvement after taking placebos, be they disguised sugar pills or injections of salt water. Similarly, experimental participants might benefit from listening to the subliminal suggestion tapes simply because they believe the tapes will be effective; in this case, it is their belief about the tape, not the tape itself, that is having an effect.

As a related concern, participants usually want to help the investigator; if they believe that the investigator hopes for a particular result, they will try their best to bring about that result. Similarly, participants are often eager to present themselves in the best possible light, and so they try to perform as well as they can on the experimental task. If, therefore, there are cues in the situation signaling that one response is more desirable than another, participants will respond accordingly.

Psychologists call such cues the *demand characteristics* of an experiment. Sometimes the demand characteristics derive from the way questions are phrased ("You *do* brush your teeth every morning, *don't you?*"). Sometimes they are conveyed more subtly. Perhaps the investigator inadvertently smiles and is more encouraging when the participants answer in one way than when they answer another way, or perhaps the investigator smiles and is encouraging to members of the experimental group but not to members of the control group.

Investigators take several measures to avoid (or control for) all of these effects. First, they phrase questions and instructions to minimize demand, so that no answer or response is identifiable as the preferred or "better" one. In addition, investigators ensure that the members of the experimental and control groups have identical beliefs about the study, by phrasing their instructions in the same way and by treating the two groups in the exact same fashion (except, of course, for the experimental manipulation).

The best way to ensure that the investigator treats both groups identically is to keep him in the dark about which participants are in which group. This is usually accomplished by means of a *double-blind design,* in which neither the investigator nor the study's participants know who is in the experimental group and who is in the control group. In our example, the investigator's assistant might be the one who decides which participants hear the tape with the subliminal message and which hear the tape without the message. This information would then be revealed to the investigator only after the experiment is completed.

The double-blind design helps ensure that the participants in the two groups will have identical expectations about the procedure; it also helps ensure that the experimenter will not treat participants in the two groups differently. As a result, any difference observed between the two groups can be attributed to the one factor that distinguished the groups—the experimental manipulation itself. (For more on double-blind designs, and the design of control groups, see Chapter 19.)

CONFOUNDS

We have highlighted the importance of using well-matched experimental and control groups, to ensure that any contrast between these groups is attributable to the independent variable (in our example, the subliminal message) and not to some other factor. Said differently, it is crucial that an investigator remove any *confounds* from the procedure—uncontrolled factors that could influence the results. For example, if those in the experimental group were interviewed early in the morning and those in the control group were interviewed late in the afternoon, then time of day would be a confound: We would have no way of knowing whether any differences between the groups were due to the experimental manipulation or to the time of day. Similarly, if those in the experimental group received encouraging instructions from the experimenter, whereas those in the control group received discouraging or neutral instructions, then the manner of instruction would be a confound.

In order for an experiment to be considered *internally valid* (that is, successful at measuring what it purports to measure), all confounds must be removed. An experiment is considered internally valid if it accurately reflects the impact of the independent variable and sensibly measures the dependent variable. Ensuring that the experimental and control groups are treated in exactly the same way (except for the experimental manipulation itself) will go a long way toward eliminating confounds that would otherwise invalidate the experiment's result.

AN OVERVIEW OF AN EXPERIMENT'S DESIGN

Our example has now grown somewhat complicated, but the complexities are unavoidable: A scientific experiment will be convincing only if many safeguards ensure that the data provide an unambiguous test of the investigators' hypothesis. The investigator must start with a clear statement of the hypothesis, so that there is no question about what evidence would confirm or disconfirm it. The dependent variables must be well defined, so that the results of the experiment can be measured accurately and reliably. If direct, quantitative measures are available (percent correct in response to some question, response time, change in some biological variable), these should be used. If not, the experimenter can use measures requiring some element of judgment, but this demands further precautions to make certain that the judgments are accurate. (This is why, in our attractiveness example, we relied on a panel of judges, rather than a single judge.)

The experimental and control groups must be matched in all ways except for the experimental manipulation itself. They must receive the same instructions and be treated in the same manner by the investigator. The data themselves must be unambiguous and faithfully recorded, so that there is no issue of misinterpretation or misremembering. And the evaluation of the data must be complete and thorough. For example, *all* the data must be accorded equal weight, including those results that don't fit the experimenter's hypothesis. (See Table A.1.)

All of these safeguards are needed to ensure that our hypothesis receives a definitive test, so that, in the end, we know for certain whether the hypothesis is confirmed or not. And with all these safeguards in place, what about our example? Are tapes containing subliminal suggestions an effective way to give up smoking, or to increase your attractiveness? Several carefully designed studies have examined the effects of these tapes, and the results are clear: Once the investigator controls for placebo effects, the subliminal messages themselves have no effect (Greenwald et al., 1991).

TABLE A.1 SUMMARY OF SUBLIMINAL AUDIOTAPE EXPERIMENT

What is the hypothesis?	A single exposure to a subliminal audiotape will increase an individual's attractiveness.
What would confirm or disconfirm the hypothesis?	If a group exposed to a subliminal tape is then judged to be more attractive than a group not exposed, this would confirm the hypothesis. If there is no difference between the groups following the experimental manipulation, then, this would disconfirm it.
What is the *independent variable*?	The presence or absence of subliminal message.
What is the *dependent variable*?	Attractiveness as measured by judges' ratings on a scale of 1 to 7.
Is the dependent variable measured in an objective and systematic fashion?	No direct objective measure is available, but the use of a panel of judges ensures that the measurement is not idiosyncratic and the use of the scale makes the measurement systematic.
Are the groups matched in all respects other than the experimental manipulation itself (i.e., are the *confounds* removed)?	Yes: Both groups must receive identical instructions and are treated identically by the experimenter. Both groups are tested in the same setting. Both groups hear an audiotape, but with one tape containing the subliminal message and one tape not. The timing is identical for both groups—e.g., duration of the audiotape, interval between the audiotape and the assessment of attractiveness. Ideally, the experiment would be a doubleblind—experimenter, participants, and judges don't know who is in the control group and who is in the experimental group.
Are the data analyzed correctly?	The data should be analyzed using the appropriate statistics—see Appendix 2.

EVALUATING EVIDENCE OUTSIDE OF THE LABORATORY

We have discussed what scientists must do to ensure that an experiment is persuasive, and so to ensure that their conclusions are justified. But it's not only scientists who want to draw conclusions from evidence: Jesse always takes a large dose of vitamin C whenever she feels a cold coming on, and she's noticed that her colds are usually mild and brief. She concludes that the vitamins help her. Sol reads his horoscope in the paper every morning, and he believes that the forecast is usually correct—whenever the stars indicate that he's going to have a day filled with new opportunities, he does! Julie regrets that for months Jacob showed no interest in her. She suspected he was turned off by her shyness, so she tried to act less timid when he was around, and now they're great friends; Julie concludes that her plan was a success. In all of these cases, people are drawing conclusions based on their experiences. Are their conclusions justified?

Notice that Jesse *always* takes Vitamin C. As a result, she has an experimental "group" (herself), which takes vitamin C when coming down with a cold, but no control group (people who take no vitamins). So it is possible that her colds would be just as mild without the vitamins, and so her conclusion (that the vitamin C helps) is unwarranted.

Sol does have a comparison—days with a certain astrological prediction and days without such a prediction. But there's an obvious confound in this comparison: Sol reads his horoscope in the morning paper, and so he starts the day with expectations based on what he read. Perhaps, therefore, he's more likely to *notice* his opportunities if the astrological forecast is good. In this case, the pattern Sol has observed indicates only the power of positive expectations and says nothing about the accuracy of astrology. To see this, let's imagine that the horoscopes were actually generated *randomly:* An upbeat forecast would still lead Sol to a positive attitude, and this attitude would lead him to notice more opportunities. As a result, the randomly generated forecasts would still be associated with Sol detecting more opportunities.

Julie's comparison (act timid versus act bold) also suffers from a confound: Maybe Jacob is just slow in noticing people, so that it wasn't her boldness, but merely the passage of time, that made the difference.

As these examples show, the scientist's concerns apply to commonsense reasoning as well. In the laboratory and in life, control groups are needed if we hope to draw convincing conclusions. In both arenas, we need to rule out confounds if we wish to be certain about the factors leading to a particular outcome. In these ways, the logic of scientific investigation turns out to have a use outside of the laboratory, and, by using this logic, we can avoid drawing unwarranted conclusions. As a result, we can end up with a clearer and more accurate understanding of our personal and social environment.

OBSERVATIONAL STUDIES

So far, our discussion has highlighted experimental studies—studies in which an investigator deliberately manipulates some variable and observes the results. In many cases, however, experiments are either impossible or inappropriate. For example, an investigator might wish to find out whether short people are treated differently than tall people. In this case, physical stature is the independent variable, but obviously the investigator cannot manipulate it. She can't wave a magic wand to make some of her participants tall and some short. Instead, she must use preexisting differences, comparing groups that existed before the investigation was launched.

In the same way, if an investigator wishes to ask at what age children acquire certain social skills, he would presumably want to compare the skills of children at one age with those of children at another age, and perhaps then compare the skills of both groups with those of adults. In this case, age would be the independent variable, and is, of course, something that can easily be assessed (by asking for a birth date) but not something that can be manipulated. Similarly, an investigator might wish to understand how the thought patterns of depressed patients compare with those of the nondepressed. Here, too, we have an independent variable (presence or absence of depression) that cannot be manipulated.

In other cases, an investigator could in principle manipulate the independent variable but must not for ethical reasons. How does physical abuse influence a child's subsequent development? Here, an experiment is possible but ethically repugnant. No investigator would deliberately abuse one group of children, while sparing another group, no matter what scientific questions are at stake.

For these reasons, many questions in psychology cannot be pursued through deliberate experimentation. Nonetheless, we can investigate such questions by exploiting differences that already exist. We can compare short individuals with tall ones, and in this way begin to understand whether society treats these two groups differently. We can compare younger children with older, and depressed individuals with nondepressed. Tragically, many children have previously been physically abused and we can compare them with those who have not, in order to investigate the effects of this abuse.

In all of these cases, investigators rely on *observational studies,* rather than experiments. This terminology reflects the fact that in these studies the investigator observes key factors rather than manipulating them directly.

CORRELATIONAL STUDIES

There are several types of observational studies but for the moment we will focus on *correlational studies* in which the investigator seeks to observe the relationship (or *correlation*) between two variables—the independent variable (height, age, level of depression, and so on) and some dependent variable. As in an experiment, the investigator seeks to determine whether the dependent variable *depends on* the independent variable. Given a child's age, for example, can one estimate the sophistication of her social skills? Given an individual with depression, can one predict the pattern of his thoughts?

THE PROBLEM OF CAUSAL AMBIGUITY

In many ways, correlational studies are similar to the experiments we have been discussing so far. In both cases, the investigator needs to start out with a clearly stated, testable hypothesis. In both cases, the dependent variable must be well defined and reliably measured. In both cases, the data must be systematically recorded, evaluated, and analyzed using appropriate statistics. And in both cases, one needs to be alert to confounds. If the young children are observed in their homes and older children at school, one might wonder whether the observed differences should be attributed to age or to the setting. If short individuals encounter a warm and encouraging interviewer and the tall individuals someone cold and discouraging, this would make the results uninterpretable. As in an experiment, care must be taken to isolate the independent variable.

Ambiguity about the direction of causation   There are many similarities between correlational studies and experiments, but there is also an important difference between the two: In correlational studies, it is often difficult to determine what is causing what. To illustrate this point, let's consider some observations that we discussed more fully in Chapter 14: Many investigators have asked how different patterns of child rearing influence the child's personal, social, and intellectual development. Does punishing a child shape the child's personality and behavior? What effect does the lack of punishment have?

Several studies indicate that more day-to-day aggression is observed among children whose parents regularly use physical punishment than among those whose parents rely on other (nonphysical) forms of discipline (Feshbach, 1970; Parke and Slaby, 1983). This might indicate that physical punishment is a poor child-rearing strategy: It curbs the child's behavior in the short term but has the unhappy consequence of leading to more aggression in the long term. It's also possible, however, that cause and effect are the other way around: It's not the use of physical punishment that causes aggression but the aggression that leads to (causes) the physical punishment. Some children may be more aggressive to begin with, and the parents of these children may quickly discover that severe measures are needed in order to constrain their child's behavior.

This ambiguity in the direction of causality is a common problem in correlational studies. In Chapter 18, for example, we mention the fact that schizophrenia is more prevalent among the poor than among the wealthy. Is this because poverty increases the risk of schizophrenia? Or is it because of downward drift, with schizophrenia leading to poverty? (After all, someone suffering from schizophrenia may have difficulty getting and holding a job, managing expenses, and so on.)

This directional ambiguity makes a correlation difficult to interpret. However, the ambiguity can often be resolved by collecting further data. For example, it's sometimes possible to determine which factor arrived on the scene first. Was the person schizophrenic before she became poor, or was she poor before she became schizophrenic? Here, we exploit the simple fact that causes must precede effects, that something cannot be caused by an event that hasn't yet happened.

The third-variable problem   We have just mentioned some examples in which the direction of causation was unclear: Does schizophrenia lead to poverty or poverty to schizophrenia? Does punishment lead to aggression or aggression to punishment? In other cases, yet another possibility needs to be considered: Perhaps some third factor, different from the dependent and independent variables, is causing both. This is the **third-variable problem.**

For example, students who take Latin in high school often get better than average grades in college. Is there a cause-and-effect relationship here? Does the study of Latin lead to better college performance (see Figure A.2A)? Maybe not. We need to ask who takes Latin in high school (assuming it's taught at all)— generally those students who are academically ambitious, motivated, and able. As a result, these characteristics may lead both to taking Latin *and* to better college grades, as indicated in Figure A.2B. Similarly, Latin is more likely to be offered in larger, better-funded schools, and probably in schools that primarily serve middle- or upper-middle-class students. Perhaps this feature of the schools is the causal agent here (Figure A.2C).

Many correlational studies suffer from the third-variable problem. People who exercise tend to be healthier than people who do not. Is this because exercise promotes good health or because people who exercise are also likely to take

A.2 The third-variable problem *Students who take Latin in high school get better grades on average than do their college classmates who did not take Latin. Is Latin the cause of collegiate success (A) or is there some other underlying factor? (B) Maybe what matters is the type of high-school student who takes Latin. (C) Alternatively, maybe what matters is the type of school where Latin is offered.*

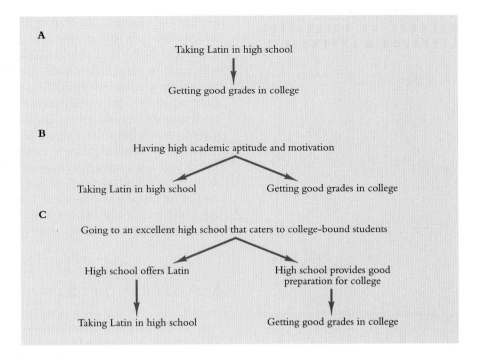

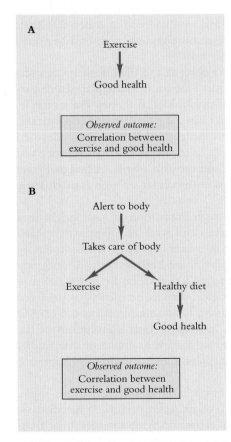

A.3 The relationship between exercise and health *People who exercise tend to be healthier than people who do not. (A) This may be because exercise leads to better health, but (B) there may also be a third variable: Those who exercise are generally likely to take care of their bodies through both exercising and eating a healthy diet, and maybe what matters is the diet.*

better care of themselves? Figure A.3 indicates how either cause might lead to the observed outcome.

The third-variable problem, like the causal ambiguity described in the previous section, makes it difficult to interpret correlational data and leads psychologists to emphasize that *correlation does not imply causation*. Sometimes correlations do reflect causality: Smoking cigarettes is correlated with, and is a cause of, emphysema, lung cancer, and heart disease. But often correlations do not imply causes: The number of ashtrays an individual owns is correlated with that person's health but not because owning ashtrays is hazardous. Similarly, there is a correlation between how many tomatoes a family eats in a month and how late the children in the family go to bed. But this is not because tomato eating keeps kids awake. Instead, tomato eating and late bedtimes are correlated because both are more likely in the summer.

Random-assignment: The essential difference between experimental and correlational designs Correlations cannot by themselves signal a cause-and-effect relationship. To draw a conclusion about cause and effect, we must supplement the correlational result with other data or other arguments. This is the reason why investigators generally prefer experiments over correlational studies.

But this raises a question: How do experiments escape this ambiguity about causality? One answer is that experimental and control groups start out identical to each other and come to differ only after the experimental manipulation is introduced. This makes it clear which came first (the manipulation) and which second (the contrast between the groups). As a result, there can be no ambiguity about the direction of causation.

In addition, the third variable problem does not apply to experimental designs: Since, in a properly controlled experiment, the experimental and control groups start out identical to each other, we don't need to worry about whether some factor besides the independent variable might have influenced the pattern of results.

How do we know that the two groups start out identical to each other? In experiments, participants are assigned randomly to the experimental or control group. Given groups of sufficient size, this *random assignment* makes it extraordinarily unlikely that all the most able participants, say, would end up in one group and all the least able participants in the other or that all the participants who went to good high schools would end up in one group and all the participants from mediocre high schools would end up in the other. In this fashion, random assignment virtually guarantees that the groups are matched at the outset. If they differ at the end of the experiment, it must be because of the experimental manipulations, leaving no doubt about causality.

This is the essential difference between correlational and experimental designs and is also the reason why experiments generally allow investigators to draw stronger conclusions than do correlational studies. Still, since experimental designs are not always possible and since collecting additional data or eliminating the third variable will, in many cases, allow a causal interpretation of correlational data, correlational studies are enormously important and useful for psychologists.

STUDIES OF SINGLE PARTICIPANTS

Both correlational studies and experiments are generally conducted using groups of participants, rather than single individuals, in order that their results might be widely applicable. Under some circumstances, however, psychologists find it useful to study single individuals.

For example, in *case studies,* investigators observe and then describe an individual—one case—in great detail. Historically, case studies have played an enormous role in guiding the development of psychological theory. For example, Sigmund Freud developed most of his ideas based on his detailed observations of individual patients, observations that he reported in books or essays devoted just to one or a few such cases (Chapter 17). Likewise, Jean Piaget's theory was based largely on the study of just three children—his own!—although Piaget and his followers went on test his claims with much larger groups of children (Chapter 13).

In recent years, case studies of patients with brain injuries have taught us a great deal about the functioning of the brain and have also illuminated many central psychological questions. Such is the case of H.M., whose memory deficits resulting from neurosurgery for epilepsy are both severe and intriguing (Chapter 7). H.M. may well be the most studied person in the history of psychology, and the pattern of neuropsychological deficits he shows has provided numerous insights into how normal memory functions. Similarly, the case of Phineas Gage (Chapter 2) was influential in shaping early conceptions of the functions of the brain's frontal lobes. Other important examples of case studies include those of patients with agnosia (Chapters 2 and 6), aphasia (Chapters 2 and 9), and blindsight (Chapter 8).

But case studies have obvious liabilities. For one thing, each patient is unique, with his or her own personality and pattern of aptitudes; each has a specific pattern of brain damage, a specific pattern of signs and symptoms resulting from that damage, and a specific way of attempting to adapt to them. Similar considerations apply to Freud's patients and Piaget's children. Each is unique, with specific traits, skills, and talents. For all these reasons, it is often difficult to know whether the conclusions drawn from a case study can be applied to anyone other than the subject of the original study.

Moreover, many case studies grow out of an extended interaction between the investigator and the participant. Since the published report can represent only a fraction of this long-term observation, questions must be raised about how exactly the data were selected for publication and whether they can be understood outside the context of this ongoing interaction. This is certainly true, for example, of Freud's case studies, as well as with many of the other case studies described by clinical psychologists.

To remedy some of these deficiencies, psychologists have proposed innovative ways of studying single participants systematically, with all the sophistication of standard experimental methods. In such *single-case experiments,* the investigators manipulate the values of some independent variable, just as they would in an experiment with many participants, and then they assess the effects of this variable by recording the participant's responses (Barlow and Hersen, 1984).

For example, consider a school psychologist who must devise a curriculum for a child with a specific learning disability. The psychologist may be able to review previous studies and experiments that suggest the kinds of curricula that tend to benefit children with similar disabilities, but in the end she must develop a curriculum for *that* child with *that* disability. Therefore, the single-case experiment is exactly the right approach.

Let's imagine, for example, that the psychologist has noted that the child is especially distractible and easily frustrated while reading but seems more focused and perseveres longer if soft music is playing in the background. To verify this hypothesis, the psychologist can develop a measure of reading attentiveness (the dependent variable)—perhaps how long the child reads before expressing frustration—and vary the occurrence of soft music (the independent variable). On one day the psychologist would measure attentiveness while the child is reading with music, on the next day while the child is reading without music, and so on for a number of days. After a suitable number of observations, the psychologist can assess the child's average reading attentiveness under each condition. (See Table A.2.)

Single-case experiments are procedurally just as rigorous, and are described just as precisely, as standard group experiments. This rigor reduces the subjectivity that characterizes many case studies and makes replicating the study with other individuals possible. It allows investigators to draw causal inferences. Also, by following up single-case experiments with the proper group experiments, the findings from the single-case can be tested on, and generalized to, a wider population.

THE IMPORTANCE OF MULTIPLE METHODS

We have now discussed several ways in which psychologists gather data—through group experiments and single-subject experiments, correlational studies and case studies. Each of these approaches can be further subdivided by the type of participant: human participants versus animals, adults versus children. A further subdivision might focus on the setting for the study: some studies are conducted in laboratories, while others are conducted in more natural environments, in schools, for example, or the participants' own homes.

A further division involves the type of data collected. Many studies rely on *self-report data,* with participants asked to describe their feelings, thoughts, attitudes or behaviors. Other studies use *behavioral measures,* with no reliance on self-report data. These measures include both what the participants do and also how they do it. (For example, how quickly do they answer the investigator's questions? how accurately do they perform an assigned task? how attractive do they appear to others?) Still other studies rely on *biological assessments,* and these can range from brain imaging to chemical analyses of the participants'

TABLE A.2 SUMMARY OF A SINGLE-CASE EXPERIMENT

What is the hypothesis?	This child will read more attentively and for longer when soft music is playing in the background.
What would confirm or disconfirm the hypothesis?	If the child's reading performance is improved when soft music is playing (compared to a condition with no music), this would confirm the hypothesis. If the child's reading performance is not improved when soft music is playing (compared to a condition with no music), this would disconfirm the hypothesis.
What is the *independent variable*?	The presence or absence of soft music.
What is the *dependent variable*?	How long the child reads before expressing frustration.
Is the dependent variable measured in an objective and systematic fashion?	How long the child reads can be measured directly and objectively; the experimenter would need to define what counts as "expressing frustration." In addition, the number of observations for each condition must be large enough to ensure that the effect is reliable.
Are the conditions matched in all respects other than the experimental manipulation itself (i.e., are the **confounds** removed)?	A double-blind is not possible because the child can easily hear whether the music is present or not. But the experimenter could be blind to condition. In any case, the child must receive identical instructions and be treated identically by the experimenter, regardless of whether soft music is playing. Also, both conditions should be assessed in the same setting; the reading material should be comparable in both conditions—equally interesting, equally difficult, and so on; the timing must be identical for the two conditions—e.g., length of the material, the duration of breaks between sessions, and so on.
Are the data analyzed correctly?	The data should be analyzed using the appropriate statistics—see Appendix 2.

blood, sweat or urine. (Chapter 2 provides a broader description of the biological measurements routinely used by psychologists.)

Each of these research paths has its advantages and its disadvantages. But psychologists often use them all, even when pursuing a single question. For example, our discussion of depression (Chapter 18) draws on experiments and correlational data, self-reported data, behavioral measures, and biological assessments, merging all of these to weave the fabric of what we now know about depression. Similarly, studies of memory (Chapter 7) involve many of these different techniques; indeed, the same could be said for virtually any topic discussed in this book.

In short, the face of modern psychology is characterized by an eclectic mixture of methods, a practice of using any technique we can to answer our questions. Perhaps this is inevitable, since each of the methods has its own strengths and weaknesses. Experiments can address issues of causation, but they are not always feasible or permissible; a partnership between experimental and correlational methods, therefore, can allow us to pursue a wide range of topics, and, in many cases, to disentangle questions about causality. Similar points apply to the partnership between group experiments and case studies, or correlations and single-case experiments. We have, in this appendix, described each of these methods separately, but we emphasize that, in actual practice, these methods are used in close coordination.

GENERALIZING FROM RESEARCH

Thus far, we have considered how a hypothesis should be formulated and how a study should be designed and conducted. In Appendix 2, we will consider what happens next—how we use statistics to analyze the data. Then, once the data are analyzed, the investigator seeks to draw conclusions, usually framed in terms of a confirmation or a disconfirmation of the initial hypothesis.

Almost invariably, though, investigators want to *generalize* from the data. After all, while they have studied just a small number of research participants, they are interested in answering questions that apply to a vast number of people. Likewise, investigators observe research participants for only a brief time but want to understand how people behave (and think and feel) throughout the days of their lives.

Are such generalizations justified? Can we make claims about how people will behave outside of our studies, based on what we observe inside of those studies? This depends on the *external validity* of the study in question. A study is considered externally valid if its participants, stimuli, and procedures adequately reflect the world as it is outside of the investigation. To ensure external validity, the study's participants should be representative of the population to which the results are expected to apply, and the study's stimuli should be representative of the stimuli encountered outside of the laboratory.

SELECTING PARTICIPANTS

Psychologists usually want their conclusions to apply to a particular *population:* all members of a given group—say, all three-year-old boys, all patients suffering from schizophrenia, all U.S. voters, and in some cases, all humans. But they normally can't study all members of the population. As a result, they have to select a *sample,* that is, a subset of the population they are interested in. Their expectation is that the results found in the sample can be generalized to the population from which the sample is drawn.

Generalizations from a sample to a particular population can only be made if the sample is representative of the population to which one wants to generalize. Suppose one does a study on reading skills using college students. Can one generalize the results to adults in general? The answer is no, for college students probably read more, and more difficult materials, than most other adults. As a result, their reading skills may be more sophisticated and are certainly better practiced than those of most non–college students. Under the circumstances, the safest course may be to restrict one's generalizations to the population of college students.

It is easy to find cases in which inadequate sampling led to egregious blunders. The classic example is a 1936 poll that predicted that Franklin D. Roosevelt would lose the presidential election. In fact, he won by a landslide. This massive error was produced by a *biased sample:* All those polled were selected from telephone directories, but in 1936 having a telephone was much more likely among people of higher socioeconomic status. As a result, the sample was not representative of the voting population as a whole. Since socioeconomic level affected voting preference, the poll was externally invalid, and as a result, its prediction was false.

RANDOM AND STRATIFIED SAMPLES

To ensure that one can generalize from one's sample to the population at large, investigators often use a *random sample.* This is a sample in which every member of the population has an equal chance of being picked, as in a jury drawn by lot from all the voters of a given district (assuming that none is disqualified or excuses herself).

But for some purposes, even a random sample may not be good enough. While every member of the population may have an equal chance of being selected, the sample may still turn out to be atypical by chance alone. The danger of this happening diminishes as the size of the sample increases. But if one must be satisfied with a small sample (whether because of lack of time or money), other sampling procedures may be necessary.

Suppose we want to take a poll to determine the attitudes of American voters toward legalized abortion. We can expect people's attitudes to differ depending on their age, sex, and religion. If we need to keep the sample size fairly small, it is important that each subgroup of the population be sampled randomly in proportion to its size. Thus, for example, if 30 percent of the population is below the age of 18 and 70 percent is above that age, the sample should contain the same proportions. This procedure is called *stratified sampling* and is common in studying psychological traits or attitudes that vary greatly among different subgroups of the population.

SAMPLING RESPONSES

The distinction between sample and population not only applies to the research participants. It also applies to their responses. Let's say that an investigator observes his participants on ten occasions. These occasions can then be regarded as a sample of all such occasions, not just the ones actually observed. And here, too, the investigator must ensure that the sample is representative of the broader population. If an investigator wishes, for example, to study physical aggression in children, she must make certain that the children aren't especially tired when she observes them, or inhibited by the school principal's presence, and so on.

EXTERNAL VALIDITY

External validity obviously depends on the details of an investigation— how the participants were selected, how the stimuli or responses were selected, and so on. But external validity also depends on what is being investigated. An investigator interested in the visual system can probably study American college students and draw valid conclusions about how vision works in all humans, whether they are from the United States, Taiwan, or Uganda. This is because the properties of the visual system are rooted in the biology of our species, allowing us to generalize widely. This is obviously different from an example already mentioned—a study of reading skills among college students. In this case, the results of a study of college students might not apply to non–college students, or to people in other cultures.

We should emphasize, though, that questions of external validity must be resolved through research and not based on commonsense assumptions. For example, one might think that the social behavior of college students would be rather different from that of nonstudents or of people in other cultures. Yet research indicates that some of the principles of social behavior are shared across cultures (Chapters 10, 11, and 12). This research has obvious implications for how we think about external validity in social psychological studies—in some regards, it is appropriate to generalize from studies of college students; in other regards, it is not.

As a related point, external validity usually demands that a study use tasks and stimuli that are representative of those we encounter every day. But in some cases, a study may be externally valid even if it employs tasks or stimuli that seem quite unnatural or unrealistic. An important example involves the study of perceptual illusions. We only rarely encounter such illusory figures outside the laboratory, but studies using such stimuli are externally valid nonetheless. Investigators can learn about vision by examining how we perceive these unusual figures because the *processes* we use when perceiving these figures are the same as the processes we use in our everyday perception.

How can we determine whether a study is externally valid? Consider the studies of eyewitness memory that ask how well an observer or victim of a crime will recall that crime. Will he remember the sequence of events or the face of the criminal? Many laboratory experiments have tried to address these questions, but do the principles derived from laboratory studies apply to someone who is angry, afraid, and involved in an event the way an eyewitness is? This is a matter of ongoing debate. One way to resolve the issue is to combine the laboratory studies with case studies of actual eyewitnesses. The case studies are by themselves sometimes difficult to interpret, because (among other concerns) life rarely provides well-designed control groups. But we can nonetheless ask whether the results from a case study are as we would expect, based on the laboratory investigations. If they are, this obviously provides some assurance that our laboratory studies are externally valid. (For discussion of the external validity of eyewitness research, see Loftus, 1983; McCloskey and Egeth, 1983; Ross, Read, and Toglia, 1994; Shobe and Kihlstrom, 1997.)

Questions about external validity are of great importance in all areas of psychology. Are our categories of mental disorder appropriate only in the context of North America and western Europe, or do they apply across cultures (Chapter 18)? Does the pattern of cognitive development seen in healthy, middle-class children describe the cognitive development of children from other socioeconomic groups and other nations (Chapter 14)? Does human reasoning inside the laboratory reflect how people reason in their day-to-day lives (Chapter 8)? Each of these questions is the focus of ongoing research.

RESEARCH ETHICS

The external validity of an investigation depends on the relationship between the study and its real-world context. This, in turn, requires that we study real people and real animals and, of course, both people and other animals have rights that must be protected. Thus, psychological research must be conducted ethically, in a fashion that protects the rights and well-being of the research participants.

Psychologists take the issue of research ethics very seriously, and virtually every institution sponsoring research—every college and university, every funding agency—has special committees charged with the task of protecting human and animal participants. In the United States, psychological research with human participants must also follow the guidelines established by the American Psychological Association (1981, 1982), one of psychology's most prominent professional organizations. Similar guidelines to protect research participants are in place in many other countries. (See Kondro, 1998, for a recent discussion about protection of research participants in Canada.)

If animals are used, the investigator must ensure their health and the adequacy of their housing and nutrition. Human participants must not only be protected physically; their privacy, autonomy, and dignity must be fully respected as well. Accordingly, an investigator must guarantee that the data will be collected either anonymously or confidentially and that participants will not be manipulated in a fashion they might find objectionable. Before the study begins, participants must be fully informed about what their task will involve, must be appraised of any risks, and must have the prerogative to leave the study at any time. The participants cannot be coerced in any way. In short, the investigator must obtain each participant's *informed consent.*

The need to obtain informed consent can produce its own difficulties, however. In many cases, the validity of a study requires that research participants *not* be fully informed about the study's design. For example, the participants in the control group cannot be told they are receiving a placebo, since placebos only work when recipients believe they are getting "real" medicine. In the same way, subliminal suggestion audiotapes are alleged to work through unconscious mechanisms. If so, it may be important that the person hearing the tape not realize exactly what words are spoken on the tape.

Considerations such as these indicate that, in many studies, the need for informed consent can conflict with the procedures needed to ensure the study's validity. In some cases, participants cannot be fully informed; instead, they must be kept in the dark temporarily about some aspects of the procedure or design. In other cases, a study's validity requires that participants be temporarily *misinformed*—systematically deceived about one or another aspect of the procedure.

In general, investigators must do everything they can to minimize the use of deception, just as they must do everything possible to minimize any risks to research participants. Whatever risks remain must be fully justified on scientific grounds. If an experiment involves deception, for example, we need to be certain that the scientific value of the experiment justifies the deception.

At the end of any investigation, it is then crucial that the participants be fully *debriefed.* Any deception or hidden manipulation must be revealed and explained; if the study involved any manipulation of beliefs, mood, or emotion, the investigator must attempt to undo these manipulations. And ideally, participants should end their participation in a study with some understanding of how it, and their participation in it, may be beneficial to psychological knowledge and human welfare.

Decisions about risk or deception are sometimes difficult, and the history of psychology includes many conflicts over the ethical acceptability of psychological studies (e.g., Baumrind, 1964; Savin, 1973; Zimbardo, 1973; Milgram and Murray, 1992; Korn, 1997; Hermann and Yoder, 1998). This is one of the reasons why decisions about ethical acceptability are usually made not by the investigators themselves, but by a multidisciplinary supervisory committee assigned the task of protecting research participants.

In evaluating any investigation, these committees must understand the investigation in the appropriate social context, and their assessments of the procedure's risks must be tied to the values and scientific knowledge prevailing at the time of the investigation. As a result, studies considered ethical at one time would be considered unacceptable today. For example, in 1911, Edouard Claparède examined a patient's memory by abruptly sticking her with a pin on one day and then determining whether she remembered this episode the next day (for a full description of this study, see Reisberg, 1997); this procedure would be considered entirely unethical if conducted today, given the important changes that have taken place in our conception of patients' rights. As a different example, a half-century ago, investigators explored the use of radiation to the throat as a treatment for chronic tonsillitis, but that procedure was abandoned when it was found that it greatly increased the risk of thyroid cancer years later; this is a case in which our assessment of a procedure's risks changed, with a corresponding change in the procedure's ethical status.

In addition, the protection of human and animal rights simply prohibits a number of studies no matter how much might be learned from them. We mentioned earlier the obvious fact that no experimenter would physically abuse research participants to study the effects of this abuse. Likewise, no ethical investigator would expose participants to intense embarrassment or anxiety. Many forms of deception are also considered unacceptable, no matter what the merit of the study. (No investigator, for example, would announce to a participant that his house had just burned down, simply to observe his reaction.)

Throughout this appendix, we have emphasized the power of science. By using scientific methods, psychology has made extraordinary advances and has laid a foundation for still further progress over the next millennium. But we must not lose sight of the fact that our science involves living creatures—including our fellow human beings—who must always be respected and protected. We therefore need a science that is as humane as it is rigorous.

SUMMARY

1. Psychologists use the *scientific method* to ensure that their claims are correct and reliable. This requires a *testable hypothesis,* which allows the researcher to specify the results that would *confirm* or *disconfirm* the hypothesis. If a hypothesis is tested and found to be inconsistent with the results, it is disconfirmed. If the hypothesis is consistent with the results, it is confirmed. But firm conclusions are drawn only after the hypothesis has survived any challenges and the experiment has been *replicated.*

2. Informally collected anecdotal evidence does not allow a persuasive test of a hypothesis because there is no way to evaluate the data described in the anecdote and no way to know if the observation reported is generalizable. The data drawn from a wider set of observations must be systematically collected and tallied to avoid the *file-drawer problem* and *biased* recollection.

3. When designing an experiment, an investigator must specify the *dependent* and *independent variables.* The independent variable is the variable whose nature is changed in accord with the *experimental manipulation.* The dependent variable is what the investigator measures to determine whether the experimental manipulation has had the hypothesized effect.

4. The dependent variable should be clearly defined and easily measured. If a direct quantitative assessment of this variable is not possible, the investigator can use a panel of judges to assess it. So long as the *interrater reliability* of this panel is adequately high, the investigator can be confident that the judges' assessments are not arbitrary.

5. An experimental study generally needs both an *experimental group* and a *control group.* The experimental group is subject to the experimental manipulation; the control group provides a basis for comparison, allowing the investigator to determine whether the independent variable had the hypothesized effect. The control group must be matched to the experimental group in all regards except for the experimental manipulation. This matching includes the makeup of the two groups, the procedures used with the two groups, the instructions they receive, and how they are questioned by the investigator.

6. Investigators attempt to minimize *placebo effects* (effects caused by a participant's beliefs and expectations) and *demand characteristics* (cues signaling the desired response).

This is often accomplished by means of a *double-blind design,* in which neither the investigator nor the study's participants know who is in the experimental group and who is in the control group.

7.   A study is said to be *internally valid* if it successfully evaluates what it purports to evaluate. To ensure validity, all *confounds*—uncontrolled factors that could influence the pattern of results—must be removed.

8.   The scientific method can also be applied to many cases of day-to-day reasoning, leading to a clearer and more accurate understanding of our personal and social environment.

9.   In an *experiment,* the investigator manipulates the independent variable and measures the effect of the manipulation on the dependent variable. In an *observational study,* the dependent and independent variables are observed rather than manipulated.

10.   One type of observational study is a *correlational study,* in which the investigator seeks to observe the ongoing relationship between the dependent and independent variables. Correlational studies differ from experiments in that correlational studies often suffer from *ambiguity* with regard to cause-and-effect relationships. In some cases, the *direction of causation* is ambiguous. In other cases, both the dependent and independent variables might be affected by some third variable, a pattern known as the *third-variable problem.* These ambiguities can often be resolved by collecting further data or by a more fine-grained inspection of the evidence. Experiments are generally not ambiguous with regard to the direction of causation because it is clear that the experimental manipulation preceded the experimental effect. In addition, *random assignment* to groups virtually guarantees that the experimental and control groups are identical at the experiment's start.

11.   *Case studies* and *single-case experiments* involve only single participants. Case studies have allowed investigators to explore particular phenomena in great depth. But they also have serious liabilities: Since each participant is unique, conclusions are not generally applicable and questions about the selection of data and the effect of the relationship between participant and investigator must be raised. An alternative to the case study is the single-case experiment, which uses *replicable procedures* and reduces subjectivity through experimental rigor.

12.   Most psychological investigations employ *multiple methods* (experiments, correlational studies, case studies, and single-case experiments) to overcome the shortcomings of each approach. Investigations of a single topic also generally pool different sorts of data, including *self-reported data, behavioral observations,* and *biological assessments.*

13.   Generalizing from the results of a study is justified only if the study is *externally valid.* This usually requires that the sample of participants be representative of the population. In many studies, this is ensured by use of a random sample; in some cases, *stratified sampling* is also useful. What makes a study externally valid depends on the particular issue being investigated. Questions of external validity must be resolved through research, not based on commonsense assumptions.

14.   *Research ethics* is an extremely important issue, and many precautions must be taken to protect the physical well being of the research participants as well as their privacy, autonomy, and dignity. But these ethical requirements sometimes collide with procedures needed to ensure a study's validity. In such cases, all risks to the participants must be minimized, and those risks that remain must be fully justified on scientific grounds. At the end of the investigation, the participants must be fully *debriefed.*

APPENDIX 2

STATISTICS: THE DESCRIPTION, ORGANIZATION, AND INTERPRETATION OF DATA

I n Appendix 1, we considered how psychologists gather data—how they design a study or an experiment, how they ensure external and internal validity, and so on. But what do they do once the data are gathered? In this appendix, we will focus on the statistical methods investigators use to organize and interpret numerical data.

Let's begin with an example. Suppose some investigators want to find out whether three-year-old boys are more physically aggressive than three-year-old girls. To find out, the investigators will first have to come up with some appropriate measure of physical aggression. They will then have to select the participants for the study. Since the investigators presumably want to say something about three-year-olds in general, not just the particular three-year-olds in their study, they must select their participants appropriately. Even more important, they must select boys and girls who are well matched to each other in all regards except gender, so that the investigators can be reasonably sure that any differences between the two groups are attributable to the difference in sex rather than to other factors (such as intellectual development, social class, and so on).

We discussed in Appendix 1 how investigators design studies and collect data. So we'll start here with what investigators do once their data have been collected. Their first task is to organize these data in a meaningful way. Suppose the study used two groups of 50 boys and 50 girls, each observed on 10 separate occasions. This means that the investigators will end up with at least 1,000 separate numerical entries (say, number of aggressive acts for each child on each occasion), 500 for the boys and 500 for the girls. Something has to be done to reduce this mass of numbers into some manageable form. This is usually accomplished by some process of averaging scores.

The next step involves statistical interpretation. Suppose the investigators find that the average score for physical aggression is greater for the boys than for the girls. (It probably will be.) How should this fact be interpreted? Should it be taken seriously, or might it just be a fluke, some sort of accident? For it is just about certain that the data contain *variability:* The children within each group will not perform identically to each other; furthermore, the same child may very well behave differently on one occasion than on another. As a result, the scores in the two groups will almost surely overlap; that is, some girls will get a higher score for physical aggression than some boys. Could it be that the difference between the groups (that is, the difference between the two averages) is an accidental product of this variability? For example, what if boys and girls are, in fact, rather similar in their levels of aggression, but—just by chance—the study happens to include four or five extremely aggressive boys and a comparable number of extremely unaggressive girls? Could this be the source of the difference between the groups? If so, then another study, which might not include these atypical children, might yield a different result. One of the main reasons for using statistical methods is to deal with questions of this sort, to help us draw useful general conclusions about behavior despite the unavoidable variability.

DESCRIBING THE DATA

In the example above, we assumed that the investigators would be collecting numerical data. We made this assumption because much of the power of statistics results from the fact that numbers can be manipulated using the rules of arithmetic, unlike open-ended responses in an interview, videotapes of social interactions, or lists of words recalled in a memory experiment. As a result, scientists prefer to use numerical response measures whenever possible. Consider our hypothetical study of physical aggression. The investigators who watched the research participants might rate their physical aggression in various situations from 1 to 5, with 1 being "extremely docile" and 5 being "extremely aggressive," or they might count the number of aggressive acts (say, hitting or kicking another child). This operation of assigning numbers to observed events is called *scaling.*

There are several types of scales that will concern us. They differ by the arithmetical operations that can be performed upon them.

CATEGORICAL AND ORDINAL SCALES

Sometimes the scores assigned to individuals are merely *categorical* (also called *nominal*). For example, when respondents to a poll are asked to name the television channel they watch most frequently, they might respond "4," "2," or "13." These numbers serve only to group the responses into categories. They can obviously not be subjected to any arithmetic operations. (If a respondent watches channels 2 and 4 equally often, we can't summarize this by claiming that, on average, she watches channel 3!)

Ordinal scales convey more information, in that the relative magnitude of each number is meaningful—not arbitrary, as in the case of categorical scales. If individuals are asked to list the ten people they most admire, the number 1 can be assigned to the most admired person, 2 to the runner-up, and so on. The smaller the number assigned, the more the person is admired. Notice that no such statement can be made of television channels: Channel 4 is not more anything than channel 2, just different from it.

Scores that are ordinally scaled cannot, however, be added or subtracted. The first two persons on the most-admired list differ in admirability by 1; so do the last two. Yet the individual who has done the ranking may admire the first person far more than the other nine, all of whom might be very similar in admirability. Imagine, for example, a child who, given this task, lists his mother first, followed by the starting lineup of the Chicago Cubs. In this case, the difference between rank 1 and rank 2 is enormous; the difference between rank 2 and rank 3 (or any other pair of adjacent ranks) is appreciably smaller. Or, to put it another way, the difference of eight between person 2 and person 10 probably represents a smaller difference in judged admirability than the difference of one obtained between persons 1 and 2 (at least so the mother hopes).

INTERVAL SCALES

Scales in which equal differences between scores, or intervals, can be treated as equal units are called *interval scales.* Response time is a common psychological variable that is usually treated as an interval scale. In some memory experiments, for example, the participant must respond as quickly as possible to each of several words, some of which she has seen earlier in the experiment; the task is to indicate, by pressing the appropriate button, whether each word had appeared earlier. An unknown, but possibly constant, part of the response time is simply the time required to press the response button; the rest is the time required for making the decision:

$$\text{response time} = \text{decision time} + \text{button-press time} \qquad (1)$$

Suppose that someone requires an average of 2 seconds to respond to nouns, 3 seconds to verbs, and 4 seconds to adjectives. The difference in decision time between verbs and nouns ($3 - 2 = 1$ second) is the same as the difference in decision time between adjectives and verbs ($4 - 3 = 1$ second). We can make this statement—which in turn suggests various hypotheses about the factors that underlie such differences—precisely because response time can be regarded as an interval scale.

RATIO SCALES

Scores based on an interval scale allow subtraction and addition. But they do not allow multiplication and division. Consider the Celsius scale of temperature. The difference between 10 and 20 degrees Celsius is equal to that between 30 and 40 degrees Celsius. But can one say that 20 degrees Celsius is twice as high a temperature as 10 degrees Celsius? The answer is no, for the Celsius scale of temperature is only an interval scale. It is not a *ratio scale,* which allows statements such as 10 feet is one-fifth as long as 50 feet, or 15 pounds is three times as heavy as 5 pounds. To make such statements, one needs a true zero point. Such a ratio scale with a zero point does exist for temperature—the Kelvin absolute temperature scale, whose zero point (*absolute zero* to chemists and physicists) is about −273 degrees Celsius.

Some psychological variables can be described by a ratio scale. For example, it does make sense to say that the rock music emanating from your neighbor's dorm room is four times as loud as your roommate singing in the shower. But there are many psychological variables that cannot be described in ratio terms. Let's go back to response time. This cannot be considered a ratio scale for the decision process. In our previous example we saw that the response time for adjectives was 4 seconds, while that for nouns was 2 seconds. But we cannot say that the 4-second response represents twice as much decision time as the 2-second response, because of the unknown time required to press the response button. Since this time is unknown, we have no zero point.

The fact that very few variables are ratio-scaled does not, of course, prevent people from describing ordinal- or interval-scaled variables in ratio terms. A claim by an advertiser that drug A is "twice as effective" as drug B may mean that A works twice as fast, or for twice as long, or for twice as many people, or requires only half the dose to achieve the same result. A potential consumer needs to know what the advertiser means by *effective* to evaluate the claim. Similarly, a 4-second response time in the word-recognition experiment is certainly twice as long as a 2-second response time; there is no harm in saying so, as long as it is understood that we are not talking about the decision time but only about the *total* response time.

ORGANIZING THE DATA

We have considered the ways in which psychologists describe the data provided by their studies by assigning numbers to them (scaling). Our next task is to see how these data are organized.

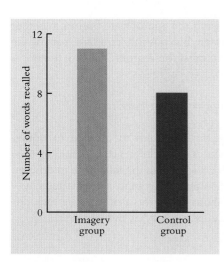

B.1 The results of an experiment on memorizing *Participants in the imagery group, who were asked to form visual images of the words they were to memorize, recalled an average of 11 words. Participants in the control group, who received no special instructions, recalled an average of 8 words.*

TABLE B.1 FREQUENCY DISTRIBUTION	
Score	*Frequency*
11	2
10	0
9	3
8	1
7	1
6	1
5	2

THE FREQUENCY DISTRIBUTION

Suppose that an investigator wanted to determine whether visual imagery aids memory. (See Chapter 7 for some actual research on this topic.) To find out he designed an experiment that required participants to memorize a list of words and later to recall as many of these words as possible. Members of the experimental group were instructed to form visual images connecting each word to the preceding word. Members of the control group were not given any imagery instructions.

The results of this experiment are graphically presented in Figure B.1. The values of the independent variable (in this case, getting imagery instructions) are indicated on the horizontal axis (the x-axis), and the values of the dependent variable (number of words recalled) on the vertical axis (the y-axis).

Of course, the data will not automatically arrange themselves in the form shown in Figure B.1. Instead, the investigator will first be faced with a list of numbers, the scores (number of words recalled correctly) for each participant in a given group. For example, if there were ten people in the control group, their scores (in number of words recalled) might have been

$$8, 11, 6, 7, 5, 9, 5, 9, 9, 11.$$

A first step in organizing the data is to list all the possible scores and the frequencies with which they occurred, as shown in Table B.1. Such an arrangement is called a *frequency distribution* because it shows the frequency with which each number of words was recalled (e.g., how many of the participants recalled 11 words, how many recalled 10 words, and so on).

The frequency distribution can also be expressed graphically. A common means for doing this is a *histogram,* which uses a series of rectangles to depict the frequency distribution (Figure B.2). The values of the dependent variable (the number of words recalled) are shown by the location of each rectangle on the x-axis. The frequency of each score is shown by the height of each rectangle, as measured on the y-axis. This is simple enough for our example, but in practice graphic presentation often requires a further step. The number of possible values the dependent variable can assume is often very large. As a result, exactly equal values rarely occur, as when response times are measured to the nearest millisecond (thousandth of a second). To get around this, the scores are generally grouped by intervals for purposes of graphic display. The histogram might then plot the frequency of all response times between, say, 200 and 225 milliseconds, between 226 and 250 milliseconds, and so on.

B.2 Histogram *In a histogram, a frequency distribution is graphically represented by a series of rectangles. The location of each rectangle on the x-axis indicates a score, while its height shows how often that score occurred.*

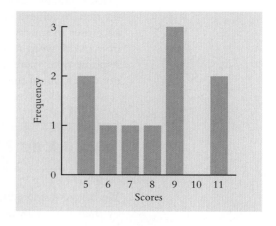

MEASURES OF CENTRAL TENDENCY

For many purposes we want a description of an experiment's result that is even more concise than a frequency distribution. We might, for example, wish to describe how a typical or average participant behaved. This sort of data summary is provided by a *measure of central tendency,* which locates the center of the distribution. Three measures of central tendency are commonly used: the *mode,* the *median,* and the *mean.*

The mode is simply the score that occurs most frequently. In our example, the mode is 9. More people (to be exact, 3) recalled 9 words than recalled any other number of words.

The median is the point that divides the distribution into two equal halves, when the scores are arranged in increasing order. To find the median in our example, we first list the scores:

$$5, 5, 6, 7, 8, 9, 9, 9, 11, 11$$
$$\uparrow$$

Since there are ten scores, the median lies between the fifth and sixth scores, that is, between 8 and 9, as indicated by the arrow. Any score between 8 and 9 would divide the distribution into two equal halves, but it is conventional to choose the number in the center of the interval between them, that is, 8.5. When there is an odd number of scores this problem does not arise, and the middle number is used.

The third measure of central tendency, the mean (M), is the familiar arithmetic average. If N stands for the number of scores, then

$$M = \frac{\text{sum of scores}}{N}$$

$$= \frac{5 + 5 + 6 + 7 + 8 + 9 + 9 + 9 + 11 + 11}{10} = \frac{80}{10} = 8.0$$

Of these three measures, the mode is often the least helpful, because the modes of two samples can differ greatly even if the samples have very similar distributions. If one of the 3 participants who recalled 9 words recalled only 5 instead, the mode would have been 5 rather than 9. But the mode does have its uses. For example, a home builder might decide to include a two-car garage on a new house because 2 is the mode for the number of cars owned by American families; more people will be content with a two-car garage than with any other size.

The median and the mean differ most in the degree to which they are affected by extreme scores. If the highest score in our sample were changed from 11 to 111, the median would be unaffected, whereas the mean would jump from 8.0 to 18.0. Most people would find the median (which remains 8.5) a more compelling "average" than the mean in such a situation, since most of the scores in the distribution are close to the median but are not close to the mean (18.0).

Distributions with extreme values at one end are said to be *skewed.* A classic example is income distribution, since there are only a few very high incomes but many low ones. Suppose we sample ten individuals from a neighborhood and find their yearly incomes (in thousands of dollars) to be:

$$10, 12, 20, 20, 40, 40, 40, 80, 80, 4,000$$

The median income for this sample is 40 ($40,000), since both the fifth and sixth scores are 40. This value reflects the income of the typical individual. The mean income for this sample, however, is (10 + 12 + 20 + 20 + 40 + 40 + 40 + 80 + 80 + 4,000)/10 = 418, or $418,000. A politician who wants to demonstrate that her neighborhood has prospered might—quite honestly—use these data to claim that the average (mean) income is $418,000. If, on the other hand, she wished to plead for financial relief, she might say—with equal honesty—that the average (median) income is only $40,000. There is no single "correct" way to find an "average" in this situation, but it is obviously important to know which average (that is, which measure of central tendency) is being used.

When deviations in either direction from the mean are equally frequent, the distribution is said to be *symmetrical.* In such distributions, the mean and the median are equal. Many psychological variables have symmetrical distributions, but for variables with skewed distributions, like income, measures of central tendency must be chosen with care.

MEASURES OF VARIABILITY

In reducing an entire frequency distribution to an average score, we have discarded a lot of very useful information. Suppose the National Weather Service measures the temperature every day for a year in various cities and constructs a frequency distribution for each city. The mean of this distribution tells us something about the city's climate. That it does not tell us everything is shown by the fact that the mean temperature in both San Francisco and Albuquerque is 56 degrees Fahrenheit. But the climates of the two cities nonetheless differ considerably, as indicated in Table B.2.

The weather displays much more variability in the course of a year in Albuquerque than in San Francisco. A simple measure of variability is the *range,* the highest score minus the lowest. The range of temperatures in San Francisco is 15, while in Albuquerque it is 42.

A shortcoming of the range as a measure of variability is that it reflects the values of only two scores in the entire sample. As an example, consider the following distributions of ages in two college classes:

Distribution *A*: 19, 19, 19, 19, 19, 20, 25

Distribution *B*: 17, 17, 17, 20, 23, 23, 23

Intuitively, distribution *A* has less variability, since all scores but one are very close to the mean. Yet the range of scores is the same (6) in both distributions. The problem arises because the range is determined by only two of the seven scores in each distribution.

TABLE B.2 TEMPERATURE DATA FOR TWO CITIES (DEGREES FAHRENHEIT)

City	Lowest month	Mean	Highest month	Range
Albuquerque, New Mexico	35	56	77	42
San Francisco, California	48	56	63	15

A better measure of variability would incorporate every score in the distribution rather than just two. One might think that the variability could be measured by finding the difference between each score and the mean (M), and then taking the average of these differences:

$$\frac{\text{sum of (score} - M)}{N}$$

This hypothetical measure is unworkable, however, because some of the scores are greater than the mean and some are smaller, so that the numerator is a sum of both positive and negative terms. (In fact, it turns out that the sum of the positive terms equals the sum of the negative terms, so that the expression shown above always equals zero.) The solution to this problem is simply to square all the terms in the numerator, thus making them all positive.★ The resulting measure of variability is called the *variance (V):*

$$V = \frac{\text{sum of (score} - M)^2}{N} \qquad (2)$$

The calculation of the variance for the control group in the word-imagery experiment is shown in Table B.3. As the table shows, the variance is obtained by subtracting the mean (M, which equals 8) from each score, squaring each result, adding all the squared terms, and dividing the resulting sum by the total number of scores (N, which equals 10), yielding a value of 4.4.

Because deviations from the mean are squared, the variance is expressed in units different from the scores themselves. If our dependent variable were a distance, measured in centimeters, the variance would be expressed in square centimeters. As we will see in the next section, it is convenient to have a measure of variability that can be added to or subtracted from the mean; such a measure

---

★ An alternative solution would be to sum the absolute value of these differences, that is, to consider only the magnitude of this difference for each score, not the sign. The resulting statistic, called the average deviation, is little used, however, primarily because absolute values are not easily dealt with in certain mathematical terms that underlie statistical theory. As a result, statisticians prefer to transform negative into positive numbers by squaring them.

TABLE B.3 CALCULATING VARIANCE

Score	Score − mean	(Score − mean)^2
8	$8 - 8 = 0$	$0^2 = 0$
11	$11 - 8 = 3$	$3^2 = 9$
6	$6 - 8 = -2$	$(-2)^2 = 4$
7	$7 - 8 = -1$	$(-1)^2 = 1$
5	$5 - 8 = -3$	$(-3)^2 = 9$
9	$9 - 8 = 1$	$1^2 = 1$
5	$5 - 8 = -3$	$(-3)^2 = 9$
9	$9 - 8 = 1$	$1^2 = 1$
9	$9 - 8 = 1$	$1^2 = 1$
11	$11 - 8 = 3$	$3^2 = 9$
		sum = 44

$$V = \frac{\text{sum of (score} - \text{mean})^2}{N} = \frac{44}{10} = 4.4$$

ought to be expressed in the same units as the original scores. To accomplish this end, we employ another measure of variability, the *standard deviation,* or *SD.* The standard deviation is derived from the variance by taking the square root of the variance. Thus

$$SD = \sqrt{V}$$

In our example, the standard deviation is about 2.1, the square root of the variance which is 4.4.

CONVERTING SCORES TO COMPARE THEM

Suppose a person takes two tests. One measures his memory span—how many digits he can remember after one presentation. The other test measures his running ability—how quickly he can run 100 yards. It turns out that he can remember 8 digits and runs 100 yards in 17 seconds. Is there any way to decide whether he can remember digits as well (or worse or equally well) as he can run 100 yards? On the face of it, the question seems absurd; it seems like comparing apples and oranges. But, in fact, there is a way, for we can ask where each of these two scores is located on the two frequency distributions of other persons (presumably men of the same age) who are given the same two tests.

PERCENTILE RANKS

One way of doing this is by transforming each of the two scores into a *percentile rank.* The percentile rank of a score indicates the percentage of all scores that lie below that given score. Let's assume that 8 digits is the 78th percentile. This means that 78 percent of the relevant comparison group remembers fewer digits. Let's further assume that a score of 17 seconds in the 100-yard dash is the 53rd percentile of the same comparison group. We can now answer the question with which we started. This person can remember digits more effectively than he can run 100 yards. By converting into percentile ranks we have rendered incompatible scores compatible, allowing us to compare the two.

STANDARD SCORES

For many statistical purposes there is an even better method of comparing scores or of interpreting the meaning of individual scores. This is to express them by reference to the mean and standard deviation of the frequency distribution of which they are a part. This is done by converting the individual scores into *standard scores* (often called *z-scores*). The formula for calculating a *z*-score is:

$$z = \frac{(\text{score} - M)}{SD} \tag{3}$$

Suppose you take a test that measures aptitude for accounting and are told your score is 36. In itself, this number cannot help you decide whether to pursue or avoid a career in accounting. To interpret your score you need to know both the average score and how variable the scores are. If the mean is 30, you know you are above average, but how far above average is 6 points? This might be an extreme score or one attained by many, depending on the variability of the distribution.

Let us suppose that the standard deviation of the distribution is 3. Your z-score on the accounting test is (36 − 30)/3 = +2. That is, your score is 2 SDs above the mean.

But how to use this information? Let's say that you are still unsure whether to become an accountant, and so you take a screen test to help you decide whether to become an actor instead. Here, your score is 100. This is a larger number than the 36 you scored on the earlier test, but it may not reveal much acting aptitude. Suppose the mean score on the screen test is 80, and the standard deviation is 20; then your z-score is (100 − 80)/20 = +1. In acting aptitude, you are 1 SD above the mean (that is, z = +1)—above average but not by much. In accounting aptitude, you're 2 SDs above the mean (that is, z = +2), and so the use of z-scores makes your relative abilities clear.

Percentile rank and a z-score give similar information, but one cannot be converted into the other unless we know more about the distribution than just its mean and standard deviation. In many cases this information is available, as we shall now see.

B.3 Normal distribution *Values taken from any normally distributed variable (such as those presented in Table B.4) can be converted to z-scores by the formula z = (score − M)/(SD). The figure shows graphically the proportions that fall between various values of z.*

THE NORMAL DISTRIBUTION

Frequency histograms can have a wide variety of shapes, but many variables that interest psychologists have a **normal distribution** (often called a **normal curve**), which is a symmetrical distribution of the shape shown in Figure B.3. (For more on normal curves, see Chapter 15.) The graph is smooth, unlike the histogram in Figure B.2, because it approximates the distribution of scores from a very large sample. The normal curve is bell shaped, with most of its scores near the mean; the farther a score is from the mean, the less likely it is to occur. Among the many variables whose distributions are approximately normal are IQ, scholastic aptitude test (SAT) scores, and women's heights (see Table B.4).★

These three variables—IQ, SAT score, and height—obviously cannot literally have the same distribution, since their means and standard deviations are different (Table B.4 gives plausible values for them.) In what sense, then, can they all be said to be normally distributed? The answer is that the shape of the distributions for all these variables is the same. For example, an IQ of 115 is 15 points, or 1 SD, above the IQ mean of 100; a height of 165 centimeters is 5 centimeters, or 1 SD, above the height mean of 160 centimeters. Both scores, therefore, have z-scores of 1. And crucially, the percentage of heights between 160 and 165 centimeters is the same as the percentage of IQ scores between 100 and 115, that is, 34 percent. This is the percentage of scores that lie between the mean and 1 SD above the mean for any normally distributed variable.

★ Men's heights are also normally distributed, but the distribution of the heights of *all* adults is not. Such a distribution would have two peaks, one for the modal height of each sex, and would thus be shaped quite differently from the normal curve. Distributions with two modes are called *bimodal.*

TABLE B.4 NORMALLY DISTRIBUTED VARIABLES							
			z-scores				
Variable	Mean	Standard deviation	−2	−1	0	1	2
IQ	100	15	70	85	100	115	130
SAT	500	100	300	400	500	600	700
Height (women)	160 cm	5 cm	150	155	160	165	170

THE PERCENTILE RANK OF A Z-SCORE

When a variable is known to have a normal distribution, a z-score can be converted directly into a percentile rank. A z-score of 1 has a percentile rank of 84, that is, 34 percent of scores lie between the mean and $z = 1$, and (because the distribution is symmetrical) 50 percent of the scores lie below the mean. A z-score of -1 (1 SD below the mean) corresponds, in a normal distribution, to a percentile rank of 16: Only 16 percent of the scores are lower. These relationships are illustrated in Figure B.3.

HOW THE NORMAL CURVE ARISES

Why should variables such as height or IQ (and many others) form distributions that have this particular shape? Mathematicians have shown that whenever a given variable is the sum of many smaller variables, its distribution will be close to that of the normal curve. One example is lifetime earnings—obviously the sum of what one has earned on many prior occasions. A different example is height. Height can be thought of as the sum of the contributions of the many genes and the many environmental factors that influence this trait; it, therefore, satisfies the general condition.

The basic idea is that the many different factors that influence a given measure (such as the genes for height) operate independently. One gene might have the effect of increasing height, another might work to similar effect, while a third might have the opposite effect. But many chance factors determine whether a given individual inherits any one of these genes, or any two, or even all three. In the same way, one environmental circumstance might have the effect of decreasing height (e.g., a virus at a particular age, interrupting what would have otherwise been a strong growth spurt), while another might have the opposite effect. Here, too, chance can enter.

Because of all this, the set of factors influencing a given individual's height is heavily influenced by chance. A good analogy to this situation is a person who tosses a coin repeatedly and counts the number of times the coin comes up heads. In this analogy, a head corresponds to any factor that tends to increase height, a tail to any factor that tends to diminish it. The more often the coin falls heads, the taller the person will be.

What will the distribution of the variable *number of heads* be? Clearly, it depends on the number of tosses. If the coin is tossed only once, then there will be either 0 heads or 1 head, and these are equally likely. The resulting distribution is shown in the top panel of Figure B.4.

If the number of tosses (which we will call N) is 2, then 0, 1, or 2 heads can arise. However, not all these outcomes are equally likely: 0 heads come up only if the sequence tail-tail (TT) occurs; 2 heads only if head-head (HH) occurs; but 1 head results from either HT or TH. The distribution of heads for $N = 2$ is shown in the second panel of Figure B.4. The area above 1 head has been subdivided into two equal parts, one for each possible sequence containing a single head.★

As N increases, the distribution of the number of heads looks more and more like the normal distribution, as the subsequent panels of Figure B.4 show. When

B.4 Histograms showing expected number of heads in tossing a fair coin N times *In successive panels,* N *= 1, 2, 4, and 8. The bottom panel illustrates the case when* N *= 100 and shows a smoothed curve.*

★ The distribution of the number of heads is called the *binomial distribution*, because of its relation to the binomial theorem: the number of head-tail sequences that can lead to k heads is the $(k + 1)$st coefficient of $(a + b)^N$.

N becomes as large as the number of factors that determine height, the distribution of the number of heads is virtually identical to the normal distribution. Similar arguments justify the assumption of normality for many psychological variables.

DESCRIBING THE RELATION BETWEEN TWO VARIABLES: CORRELATION

The basic problem facing psychological investigators is how to account for observed differences in the dependent variable they are studying. Why, for example, do some people have better memories than others? The experimental approach to the problem, described earlier, is to ask whether changes in an independent variable (whether or not imagery instructions are given) produce systematic changes in the dependent variable (memory). Do people using visual imagery as an aid to memorizing recall more words on the average than those who do not? In correlational studies, however, our approach must be different, for in such studies we cannot manipulate the variables. What is often done instead is to observe the relationship between two—sometimes more—variables as they occur naturally, in the hope that differences in one variable correspond to differences in a second. (See Appendix 1 for a detailed discussion of experiments and correlational studies.)

POSITIVE AND NEGATIVE CORRELATION

Imagine that a manager of a taxicab company wants to identify drivers who will earn relatively large amounts of money (for themselves and, of course, for the company). The manager makes the plausible guess that one relevant factor is the driver's knowledge of the local geography, so she devises an appropriate test of street names, routes from place to place, and so on, and administers the test to each driver. The question is whether this test score is related to the driver's job performance as measured by his weekly earnings. To decide, the manager has to find out whether there is a correlation between the test score and the earnings—that is, whether they tend to vary together.

In the taxicab example, the two variables will probably be positively correlated—as the independent variable (test score) increases, the dependent variable (earnings) will generally increase too. But other variables may be negatively correlated—when one increases, the other will tend to decrease. An example is a phenomenon called Zipf's law, which states that words that occur frequently in a language tend to be relatively short. The two variables—word length and word frequency—are negatively correlated, since one variable tends to increase as the other decreases.

Correlational data are often displayed in a *scatter plot* (or *scatter diagram*) in which values of one variable are shown on the x-axis and variables of the other

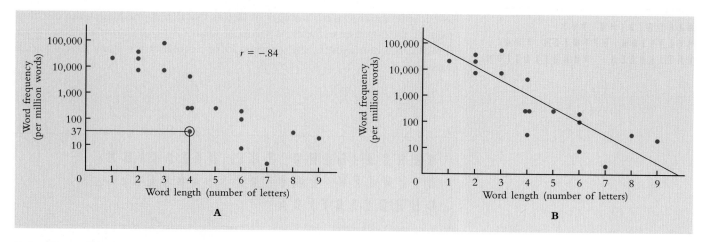

B.5 Scatter plot of a negative correlation between word length and word frequency

on the *y*-axis. Figure B.5A is a scatter plot of word frequency versus word length for the words in this sentence.★ Each word is represented by a single point. An example is provided by the word *plot,* which is four letters long and occurs with a frequency of 37 times per million words of English text (and is represented by the circled dot). The points on the graph display a tendency to decrease on one variable as they increase on the other, although the relation is by no means perfect.

It is helpful to draw a line through the various points in a scatter plot that comes as close as possible to all of them (Figure B.5B). The line is called a ***line of best fit,*** and it indicates the general trend of the data. Here, the line slopes downward because the correlation between the variables is negative.

The three panels of Figure B.6 are scatter plots showing the relations between other pairs of variables. In Figure B.6A hypothetical data from the taxicab example show that there is a positive correlation between test score and earnings (since the line of best fit slopes upward). Test score is not a perfect predictor of on-the-job performance, however, since the points are fairly widely scattered

B.6 Scatter plots of various correlations
(A) The scatter plot and line of best fit show a positive correlation between a taxi-driving test and earnings. (B) A perfect positive correlation. The line of best fit passes through all the points. (C) A correlation of zero. The line of best fit is horizontal.

★ There is no point for the "word" B.5A in this sentence. The frequencies of the other words are taken from H. Kucera and W. N. Francis, *Computational Analysis of Present-Day American English* (Providence, R. I.: Brown University Press, 1967).

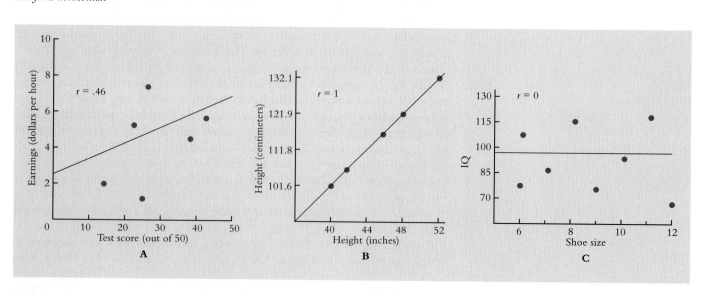

around the line. Points above the line represent individuals who earn more than their test score would lead one to predict; points below the line represent individuals who earn less.

The examples in Figures B.5 and B.6A illustrate moderate correlations; in contrast, panels B and C of Figure B.6 illustrate extreme cases. Figure B.6B shows data from a hypothetical experiment conducted in a fourth-grade class to illustrate the relation between metric and English units of length. The heights of five children are measured twice, once in inches and once in centimeters; each point on the scatter plot gives the two height measurements for one child. All the points in the figure fall on the line of best fit, because height in centimeters always equals 2.54 times height in inches. The two variables, height in centimeters and height in inches, are perfectly correlated—one can be perfectly predicted from the other. Thus, once you know your height in inches, there is no information to be gained by measuring yourself in centimeters.

Figure B.6C presents a relation between IQ and shoe size. These variables are unrelated to each other; people with big feet have neither a higher nor a lower IQ than people with small feet. The line of best fit is therefore horizontal: The best guess of an individual's IQ is the same no matter what his or her shoe size—it is the mean IQ of the population.

THE CORRELATION COEFFICIENT

Correlations are usually described by a *correlation coefficient,* denoted **r**, a number that expresses the strength and the direction of the correlation. For positive correlations, r is positive; for negative correlations, it is negative; for variables that are completely uncorrelated, r equals 0. The largest positive value r can have is +1.00, which represents a perfect correlation (as in Figure B.6B); the largest possible negative value is −1.00, which is also a perfect correlation. The closer the points in a scatter plot come to falling on the line of best fit, the nearer r will be to +1.00 or −1.00 and the more confident we can be in predicting scores on one variable from scores on the other. The values of r for the scatter plots in Figures B.5 and B.6A are given on the figures.

The method for calculating r between two variables, X and Y, is shown in Table B.5 (on the next page). The formula is:

$$r = \frac{\text{sum } (z_x z_y)}{N} \qquad (4)$$

The variable z_x is the z-score corresponding to X; z_y is the z-score corresponding to Y. To find r, each X and Y score must first be converted to a z-score by subtracting the mean and then dividing by the standard deviation. Then the product of z_x and z_y is found for each pair of scores. The average of these products (the sum of the products divided by N, the number of pairs of scores) is r.

INTERPRETING AND MISINTERPRETING CORRELATIONS

It is tempting to assume that if two variables are correlated, then one is the cause of the other. There is, for example, a correlation between how much loud music you listen to as an adolescent and the sensitivity of your hearing in later life. (The correlation is negative—more loud music is associated with less

TABLE B.5 CALCULATION OF THE CORRELATION COEFFICIENT

1. Data (from Figure B.6A).

Test score (X)	Earnings (Y)
45	6
25	2
15	3
40	5
25	6
30	8

2. Find the mean and standard deviation for X and Y.

For X, mean = 30, standard deviation = 10
For Y, mean = 5, standard deviation = 2

3. Convert each X and each Y to a z-score, using $z = \dfrac{(\text{score} - M)}{SD}$

X	Y	z-score for X (z_x)	z-score for Y (z_y)	$z_x z_y$
45	6	1.5	0.5	0.75
25	2	−0.5	−1.5	0.75
15	3	−1.5	−1.0	1.50
40	5	1.0	0.0	0.00
25	6	−0.5	0.5	−0.25
30	8	0.0	1.5	0.00
				2.75

4. Find the product $z_x z_y$ for each pair of scores.

5. $r = \dfrac{\text{sum } (z_x z_y)}{N} = \dfrac{2.75}{6} = .46$

sensitive hearing.) And, in fact, there is a causal connection here, because listening to loud music can damage your hearing. Similarly, there is a correlation between the vividness of your visual imagery while awake and how often you remember your dreams on awakening (Cory et al., 1975). This correlation is positive—greater vividness is associated with more frequent dream recall. And here, too, there may be a causal connection: Vivid waking imagery creates a mental perspective similar to the nighttime experience of dreaming, and this similarity of perspective facilitates recall.

However, as we emphasized in Appendix 1, often a correlation does *not* indicate a cause-and-effect relationship, or, if it does, the direction of causation is ambiguous. For example, consider the negative correlation between obesity and life expectancy: People who are overweight tend to die younger than people who are not overweight. For many years, this was interpreted as a cause-and-effect relationship: being overweight caused early death. Newer evidence, however, suggests that this is incorrect. Instead, it turns out that obesity is often associated with inactivity, and inactivity is what causes the problems. Overweight people who are active actually have lower mortality rates than normal-weight people who are sedentary (Kampert et al., 1996; see Chapter 3).

As we emphasized in Appendix 1, a correlation, by itself, cannot indicate a cause-and-effect relationship. Some correlations do indicate causation, but many do not. As a result, correlational results are important and instructive but must be interpreted with care.

INTERPRETING THE DATA

Any data collected in the real world contain variability, and data in psychology are no exception. In memory experiments, for example, different research participants recall different numbers of items, and the same participant is likely to perform differently if tested again later. But investigators nonetheless hope to draw general conclusions from data despite this variability. Nor is variability necessarily the enemy, because as we shall see, understanding the sources of variability in one's data can provide insights into the factors that influence the data.

ACCOUNTING FOR VARIABILITY

As an example of how variability may be explained, consider a person shooting a pistol at a target. Although she always aims at the bull's-eye, the shots scatter around it (Figure B.7A). Assuming that the mean is the bull's-eye, the variance of these shots is the average squared deviation of the shots from the center. Suppose we find this variance to be 100; we next must explain it.

If the shooting was done outdoors, the wind may have increased the spread; moving the shooter to an indoor shooting range produces the tighter grouping shown in Figure B.7B. The new variance is 80, a reduction of 20 percent. This means that the wind accounts for 20 percent of the original variance.

In addition, some of the initial variance may have resulted from the unsteady hand of the shooter, so we now mount the gun (although still leaving it out-

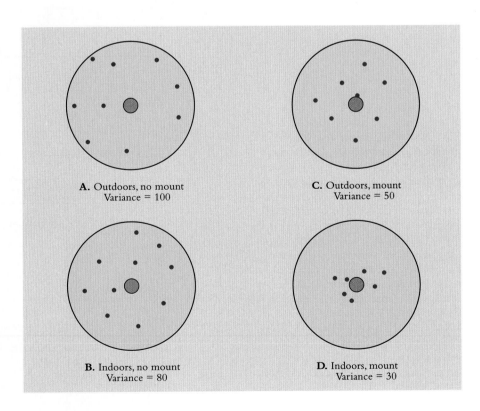

A. Outdoors, no mount
Variance = 100

C. Outdoors, mount
Variance = 50

B. Indoors, no mount
Variance = 80

D. Indoors, mount
Variance = 30

B.7 Results of target shooting under several conditions   In each case, the bull's-eye is the mean, and the variance is the average squared deviation of the shots from the bull's-eye.

doors). This yields a variance of 50 (Figure B.7C), a reduction of 50 percent. So 50 percent of the variance can be attributed to the shaky hand of the shooter. To find out how much of the variance can be explained by both the wind and the shaking, we mount the gun and move it indoors; now we may find a variance of only 30 (Figure B.7D). This means we have explained 70 percent of the variance, leaving 30 percent unaccounted for.★

But not all changes in the situation will reduce the variance. For example, if we find that providing the shooter with earmuffs leaves the variance unchanged, we know that none of the original variance was due to the noise of the pistol.

VARIANCE AND EXPERIMENTS

Figure B.8 shows how this approach can be applied to the experiment on visual imagery described earlier (see p. B4). Figure B.8A shows the distribution of scores for all twenty people in the experiment lumped together; the total variance of this overall distribution is 6.25. But as we saw, the ten members of the experimental group had been instructed to use visual imagery in memorizing, whereas the ten members of the control group were given no special instructions. How much of the overall variance can be explained by the difference in these instructions? In Figure B.8B, the distributions are no longer lumped together. They are instead presented as two separate histograms; the people

★ We are grateful to Paul Rozin for suggesting this example.

B.8 Accounting for variance in an experiment on memorizing (A) The distribution of number of words recalled is shown for all twenty participants lumped together; the variance of this distribution is 6.25. (B) The distributions of the experimental and control groups are displayed separately. The number of words recalled by the group that received imagery instructions is shown in blue; the number recalled by the control group that received no special instructions is shown in dark red. Within each of these groups, the variance is about 4.00. (C) The distribution of words recalled is plotted separately for men and women regardless of how they were instructed. Blue indicates the number of words recalled by women, dark red the number recalled by men. The variance is 6.25.

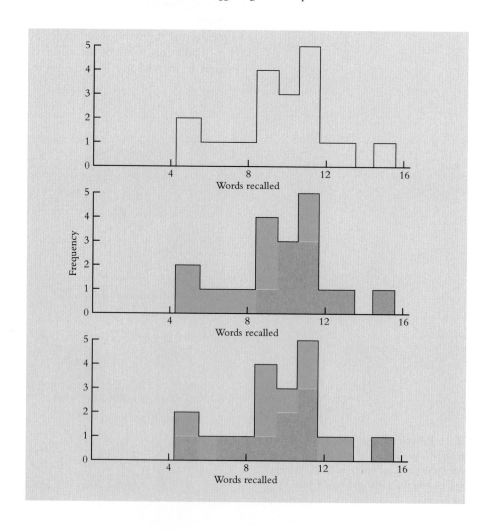

who received imagery instructions are shown in blue, while those who did not are indicated in rust. As the figure shows, there is less variability within either the imagery group or the control group than within the overall distribution that lumped both kinds of participants together. While the variance in the overall distribution is 6.25, the variance within the two subgroups averages to only 4.0. We conclude that the difference between the two sets of instructions accounted for 36 percent of the variance and that 64 percent $(4 \div 6.25)$ still remains unexplained.

Figure B.8C shows a situation in which an independent variable (in this case, sex) accounts for little or none of the variance. In this figure, the participants' scores are again presented as two histograms—separately depicting the scores of the men and the women (regardless of whether they were instructed to use imagery or not). The men's scores are shown in rust, the women's in blue. Now the variance of the two subgroups (that is, men versus women) averages to 6.25, a value identical to that found for the overall distribution. We conclude that the participant's sex accounts for none of the overall variance in recall.

VARIANCE AND CORRELATION

The technique of explaining the variance in one variable by attributing it to the effect of another variable can also be applied to correlational studies. Here, the values of one variable are explained (that is, accounted for) when the values of the other variable are known. Recall the taxicab example, in which a correlation of +.46 was found between taxi drivers' earnings and their scores on an aptitude test. Since the correlation is neither +1.00 nor 0, some but not all of the variance in job performance can be explained by the test scores. The greater the magnitude of r, the more variance is accounted for. The rule is that the proportion of variance that is explained equals r^2. If $r = +.46$, one variable accounts for $(.46)^2 = .21$ (21 percent) of the variance of the other. (Just why this proportion is r^2 is beyond the scope of this discussion.)

To put this another way, suppose all the cab drivers were identical in their performance on the aptitude test, which measured knowledge of local geography. This means that the variance on that variable would be zero. As a result, the variability on the second variable, earnings, would be reduced, and the formula tells us by how much. The original variance on earnings can be determined from the data in Figure B.6A. It is 4. Its correlation with the aptitude test is +.46. If we remove the variance caused by differences in how much the cab drivers know about local geography, the variability on earnings will be $4 - (.46)^2 \times 4 = 3.16$. The drop in the variance from 4 to 3.16 is a reduction of 21 percent. So the aptitude test does help us to predict taxicab earnings, for it accounts for 21 percent of the variance. But a good deal of the variance, 79 percent, is still unexplained.

HYPOTHESIS TESTING

Much behavioral research attempts to answer questions such as: Does the amount of food a person eats depend on the effort required to eat it? Can people learn while they are sleeping? Is drug X more effective than drug Y? Each of these questions suggests an experiment (see Appendix 1 for a discussion of experimental design), and the procedures described in the previous section could be used to discover how much of the variance in the dependent variable could be accounted for by the independent variable. But how can the results of such experiments lead to simple yes-or-no answers to the questions that inspired them?

TESTING HYPOTHESES ABOUT SINGLE SCORES

We will begin by testing a hypothesis about single scores. Consider the problem in identifying people with dyslexia (see Chapter 2). As our first step in identifying such people, we might give each person a test of reading comprehension. If the person's score were unusually low, this might be an indication of dyslexia (although several other tests would be needed to confirm this possibility). The question, though, is how low a score must be before it is "unusually low."

We know from the start that reading scores among nondyslexic readers vary—some read rather well, others read at some middle level, and some read rather poorly. As a result, it's possible that a poor reader isn't dyslexic at all; he's simply at the low end of the normal range for reading skills. How can we evaluate this possibility?

Suppose we tested a large number of nondyslexic readers and found that the average reading score is 50, that the standard deviation of these scores is 10, and that the scores are normally distributed. We now look at the reading score from an individual we're concerned about. Let us say that her score is 40. How likely is it that she has dyslexia? This is equivalent to asking: How *un*likely is a score of 40 within the distribution of scores obtained by the general population (that is, a population of people who we believe are *not* dyslexic)? To answer these questions, we can convert her score to a z-score by computing its distance from the mean and dividing this difference by the standard deviation. The resulting z-score is $(40 - 50)/10$ or -1 SD. Since the distribution is normal, Figure B.3 tells us that 16 percent of the general population would score as low or even lower than this. Under the circumstances, it's plausible that a score of 40 does not indicate dyslexia; this score is common enough even among people without dyslexia. Our conclusion might be different, though, if the score were 30 or below. For then the z-score would be $(30 - 50)/10$ or -2, 2 SDs below the mean for the general population. Only 2 percent of the population obtain scores this low, and so we might now feel more comfortable concluding that a person with this particular score is not drawn from the general population. Instead, we might conclude that this score is drawn from a *different* population—the population of people who do in fact suffer from dyslexia.

In this example we had to decide between two hypotheses about this individual's score. One hypothesis is that the score was drawn from the population of nondyslexic readers. True, the score did seem atypical, but, on this view, this is merely a reflection of the ordinary variability around the mean of the broader population. This is the **null hypothesis,** the hypothesis that there really is no systematic difference between the observation we are interested in and the other observations we have made. The alternative hypothesis is that the null hypothesis is *false* and that the score is far enough away from the other scores for us to conclude that it did not arise by chance and is instead in a different category (in our example, the category of scores obtained by people with dyslexia).

To decide between these two hypotheses, the key observation (in this case, the score of 40) is expressed as a z-score, which in the context of hypothesis testing is called a **critical ratio.** Behavioral scientists generally stipulate a critical ratio of 2 as the cutoff point. If it is 2 or more, they generally reject the null hypothesis and conclude that the test observation *is* systematically different from the control observations. Critical ratios of 2 or more are considered **statistically reliable,** which is just another way of saying that the null hypothesis can be rejected. Critical ratios of less than 2 are considered too small to allow the rejection of the null hypothesis.

This general procedure is not foolproof. It is certainly possible for an individual to have a reading score of 30 (a critical ratio of 2) or lower without being dyslexic. According to Figure B.3, this will happen about 2 percent of the time. Raising the cutoff value to a critical ratio of 3 or 4 would make such errors less common but would not eliminate them entirely; furthermore, raising the critical value might mean failure to detect some individuals with dyslexia. One of the important consequences of the variability in psychological data can be seen here: The investigator who has to decide between two interpretations of the data (the null hypothesis and the alternative hypothesis) cannot be correct all the time.

TESTING HYPOTHESES ABOUT MEANS

In the preceding discussion, our concern was with hypotheses about single scores. We now turn to the more commonly encountered problems in which the hypotheses involve means.

In many experiments, the investigator compares two or more groups—participants tested with or without a drug, with or without imagery instructions, and so on. Suppose we get a difference between the groups. How do we decide whether the difference is genuine rather than due merely to chance?

Let us return to the experiment in which memory for words was tested with and without instructions to imagine the items. To simplify, we will here consider a modified version of the experiment in which the same participants serve in both the imagery and the nonimagery conditions. Each participant memorizes a list of 20 words without instructions, then memorizes a second list of 20 words under instructions to visualize. What we want to know is whether the participants show any improvement with the imagery instructions. There is no separate control group in this experiment. Because each person's score while using imagery can be compared with his score without using imagery, each provides his own control.★

Table B.6 (on the next page) gives data for the ten participants in the experiment. For each one, the table lists the number of words recalled without imagery instructions, the number recalled with such instructions, and the improvement (the difference between the two scores). The mean improvement overall is 3 words, from a mean of 8 words recalled without imagery to a mean of 11 words with imagery. But note that this does not hold for all participants. For example, for Fred and Hortense, the "improvement" is negative: They both do better without imagery instructions. But is there an imagery facilitation effect overall? Put in other words, is the difference between the two conditions statistically reliable?

To show how this question is answered, we will follow much the same logic as that used in the analysis of the dyslexia problem. We have a mean—the average difference score of ten participants. What we must realize is that this mean—3—is really a sample based on the one experiment with the ten participants we have just run. Suppose we had run the experiment again, with another set of ten people, and then suppose we ran it again, and again, and again. Each such repetition of the experiment would yield its own mean. And each of these means would constitute another sample.

★ This sort of design, in which participants serve in more than one condition, is called a *within-subjects design,* in contrast to a *between-subjects design* in which different people serve in the different conditions. Within-subjects designs have certain advantages; among them, we can obviously be certain that the participants in one group are identical to the participants in the other group. But within-subjects designs also introduce their own complications. For example, if the participants serve in one condition first, then in the other condition, then this creates a confound: Any differences observed might be due to the effects of practice, which obviously benefits the second condition. For present purposes, we ignore these complications (and also the steps needed to control for this confound).

TABLE B.6 NUMBER OF ITEMS RECALLED WITH AND WITHOUT IMAGERY INSTRUCTION, FOR TEN PARTICIPANTS

Subject	Score with imagery	Score without imagery	Improvement
Alphonse	11	5	6
Betsy	15	9	6
Cheryl	11	5	6
Davis	9	9	0
Earl	13	6	7
Fred	10	11	−1
Germaine	11	8	3
Hortense	10	11	−1
Imogene	8	7	1
Jerry	12	9	3
Mean	11	8	3

$$\text{Variance of improvement scores} = \frac{\text{sum of (score} - 3)^2}{10} = 8.8$$

$$\text{Standard deviation of improvement scores} = \sqrt{8.8} = 2.97$$

But what is the population from which these samples are drawn? It is the set of all of these means—the average differences between imagery and nonimagery instructions obtained in each of the many repetitions of the experiment we might possibly perform. And the mean of these means—a kind of grand mean—is the mean of the population. Any conclusions we want to draw from our experiment are really assertions about this population mean. If we say that the difference we found is statistically reliable, we are asserting that the population mean is a difference greater than zero (and in the same direction as in the sample). Put another way, we are asserting that the difference we found is not just a fluke but is real and would be obtained again and again if we repeated the experiment, thus rejecting the null hypothesis.

The null hypothesis amounts to the claim that the mean we actually obtained could have been drawn by chance from a distribution of sample means (that is, the many means of the possible repetitions of our experiment) around a population mean of zero. That's because the null hypothesis states that there's no difference between the scores of participants, regardless of whether they are in the experimental or control groups, and so, on this hypothesis, the difference (and thus the population mean) should be zero.

To test this claim, we have to compute a critical ratio that can tell us how far from zero our own mean actually is. Like all critical ratios, this is a z-score that expresses the distance of a score from a mean in units of the standard deviation. Thus,

$$z = \frac{(\text{score} - M)}{\text{SD}}$$

In our present case, the score is our obtained mean (that is, 3); and the mean we'd use in the calculation is the hypothetical population mean of zero (assumed by the null hypothesis). But what is the denominator? It is the standard deviation of the distribution of sample means, the means of the many experiments we might have done.

The standard deviation of such a distribution of sample means is called the *standard error (SE)* of the mean. Its value is determined by two factors: the standard deviation of the sample and the size of that sample. Specifically,

$$SE = \frac{SD}{\sqrt{N-1}} \qquad (5)$$

(It turns out that using _____ for the sample size produces a slightly more accurate estimate of the standard error, for reasons beyond the scope of this discussion.) It is clear that the variability of a mean (and this is what the standard error measures) goes down with increasing sample size. A clue as to why comes from the consideration of the effects of an atypical score. Purely by chance, a sample may include an extreme case. But the larger the size of that sample, the less an extreme case can affect the average. If a sample of three people includes an individual with dwarfism, the average height will be unusually far from the population mean. But in a sample of 3,000, one case of dwarfism will not affect the average very markedly.

We can now conclude our analysis of the results of our memorization experiment. The critical ratio to be evaluated is:

$$\text{Critical ratio} = \frac{\text{obtained sample mean} - \text{population mean}}{SE}$$

Since the population mean is assumed to be zero (by the null hypothesis), this expression becomes:

$$\text{Critical ratio} = \frac{\text{obtained sample mean}}{SE} \qquad (6)$$

This critical ratio expresses the mean difference between the number of words remembered with and without imagery instructions in units of the variability of the sample mean, that is, the standard error.★ To compute the standard error, we first find the standard deviation of the imagery scores; this turns out to be 2.97, as shown in Table B.6. Then equation (5) tells us

$$SE = \frac{SD}{\sqrt{N-1}} = \frac{2.97}{\sqrt{10-1}} = .99$$

The critical ratio is now the obtained mean difference divided by the standard error, or $3/.99 = 3.03$. This is clearly larger than 2.0, so we conclude that the observed difference in memory between the imagery and control conditions probably should not be attributed to chance. Thus, giving visual imagery instructions evidently does improve recall.

CONFIDENCE INTERVALS

In using statistics to test hypotheses, we ask whether a certain sample mean could be drawn by chance from a set of sample means distributed around some

---

★ There are several simplifications in this account. One is that the critical ratio described here does not have an exactly normal distribution. When the sample size is large, this effect is unimportant, but for small samples (like the one in the example) they can be material. To deal with these and related problems, statisticians often use measures that refer to distributions other than the normal one. An example is the *t*-test, a kind of critical ratio based on what is called the *t*-distribution.

assumed population mean. (When testing the null hypothesis, this assumed population mean is zero.) But there is another way of phrasing this question. Can we be reasonably confident that the mean of the population falls within a certain specified interval? If we know the standard error of the mean, the answer is yes. We have already seen that about 2 percent of the scores in a normal distribution are more than 2 SDs above the distribution's mean. Similarly, about 2 percent of the scores have values lower than 2 SDs below the mean. Since this is so, we can conclude that the chances are roughly 96 in 100 that the population mean is within an interval whose largest value is 2 SEs above the sample mean and whose lowest value is 2 SEs below. Because we can be fairly (96 percent) confident that the actual population mean will fall within this specified range, it is often called the ***confidence interval.***

As an example, consider the prediction of elections. During election campaigns, polling organizations report the current standing of various candidates by statements such as the following: "In a poll of 1,000 registered voters, 57 percent favored candidate Smith; the margin of error was 3 percent." This margin of error is the confidence interval around the proportion (that is, ± 3 percent).

To determine this confidence interval, the pollsters compute the standard error of the proportion they found. (In this case, .57.) This standard error is analogous to the standard error of a mean we discussed in the previous section. Given an N of 1,000, this standard error happens to be .015.★ Since 2 × .015 is .03 or 3 percent, the appropriate confidence interval for our example is the interval from 54 to 60 percent. Under the circumstances, candidate Smith can be fairly confident that she has the support of at least 50 percent of the electorate, since 50 percent is well below the poll's confidence interval (see Figure B.9).

★ The standard error of a proportion (e.g., the proportion of polled voters who express pro-X sentiments) is analogous to the standard error of the mean and measures the precision with which our sample proportion estimates the population proportion. The formula for the standard error of a proportion p is:

$$SE_p = \sqrt{\frac{p \times (1 - p)}{N}}$$

In our example, $p = .57$ and $N = 1,000$, so $SE_p = .015$.

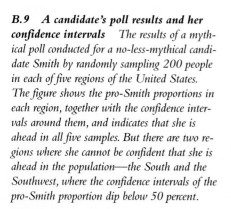

B.9 A candidate's poll results and her confidence intervals *The results of a mythical poll conducted for a no-less-mythical candidate Smith by randomly sampling 200 people in each of five regions of the United States. The figure shows the pro-Smith proportions in each region, together with the confidence intervals around them, and indicates that she is ahead in all five samples. But there are two regions where she cannot be confident that she is ahead in the population—the South and the Southwest, where the confidence intervals of the pro-Smith proportion dip below 50 percent.*

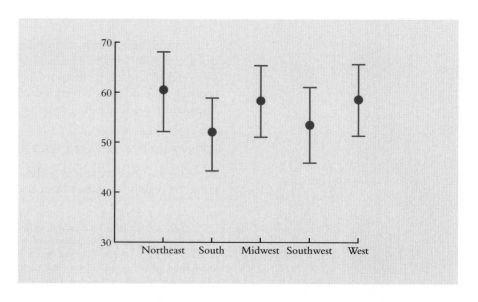

SOME IMPLICATIONS OF STATISTICAL INFERENCE

The methods of testing hypotheses and estimating confidence intervals that we just described are routinely employed in evaluating the results of psychological research. But they have several characteristics that necessarily affect the interpretation of all such results.

THE PROBABILISTIC NATURE OF HYPOTHESIS TESTING AND CONFIDENCE INTERVALS

Since there is always some unexplained variance in any psychological study, there is always some chance that the conclusions based on our sample are wrong as applied to the population. If we use a confidence interval of ± 2 SEs, the chances that the population mean (or proportion, or whatever) falls outside of that interval are less than 4 or 5 in 100. Do we want to be more confident than this? If so, we might use a confidence interval of ± 3 SEs, where the equivalent chance is only 1 in 1,000. The same holds for critical ratios. We can say that a critical ratio of 2 means that a difference is statistically reliable, but that only means that the chances are less than 2 in 100 that the difference as large or larger than this arose by chance. If we want to be even more certain than this, we must insist that the critical ratio be larger—perhaps 3 (a chance factor of 1 in 2,000) or 4 (1 in 20,000), and so on. But the likelihood of these chance occurrences is never zero, and so, as long as there is some unexplained variance, there is some possibility of error.

The probabilistic nature of statistical reasoning has another consequence. Even if we can come to a correct conclusion about the mean of a population (or a proportion, as in polls), we cannot generalize to individuals. Thus, a study which shows that men have higher scores than women on spatial relations tests does not preclude the existence of brilliant female artists or architects. Sample means for the two groups can differ significantly, even though there is considerable overlap in the two distributions of scores.

THE ROLE OF SAMPLE SIZE

A last point concerns the role of sample size in affecting how the results are interpreted. The larger the sample, the smaller the standard error and the smaller the confidence interval around the mean or the proportion. This can have major effects on hypothesis testing.

Suppose that, in the population, a certain independent variable produces a very small difference. As an example, suppose that the population difference between men and women on a certain test of spatial relations is 1 percent. We would probably be unable to reject the null hypothesis (that is, the hypothesis that there is no sex difference on the test) with samples of moderate size. But if the sample size were sufficiently large, we could reject the null hypothesis. For an N of such magnitude would lead to a decrease in the standard errors of the sample means, which in turn would lead to an increase in the critical ratio. Someone who read a report of this experiment would now learn that, by using thousands of participants, we discovered a reliable difference of 1 percent. A fair reaction to this bit of intelligence would be that the null hypothesis can indeed be rejected, but that the psychological significance of this finding is rather slight.

The moral is simple: Statistical reliability does indicate a difference and, moreover, indicates that the difference is unlikely to be a fluke or chance occurrence. But statistical reliability, by itself, does not indicate whether the effect discovered is of psychological significance or of any practical importance.

SUMMARY

1. Statistical methods concern the ways in which investigators describe, organize, and interpret collections of numerical data. A crucial concern of statistical endeavors is to interpret the *variability* that is encountered in all research.

2. An early step in processing numerical data is *scaling,* a procedure for assigning numbers to psychological responses. Scales can be *categorical, ordinal, interval,* or *ratio scales.* These differ in the degree to which they can be subjected to arithmetical operations.

3. An important step in organizing the data is to arrange them in a *frequency distribution,* often displayed in graphic form, as in a *histogram.* Frequency distributions are summarized by a *measure of central tendency.* The common measure of central tendency is the *mean (M),* though sometimes another measure, the *median,* may be preferable, as in cases when the distribution is *skewed.* Important measures of variability are the *variance (V)* and the *standard deviation (SD).*

4. One way of comparing two scores drawn from different distributions is to convert both into *percentile ranks.* Another is to transform them into *z-scores,* which express the distance of a score from its mean in standard deviations. The percentile rank of a *z*-score can be computed if the shape of that score's distribution is known. An important example is the *normal distribution,* graphically displayed by the *normal curve,* which describes the distribution of many psychological variables and is basic to much of statistical reasoning.

5. In observational studies, the relation between variables is often expressed in the form of a *correlation,* which may be positive or negative. It is measured by *r,* the correlation coefficient, a number that can vary from +1.00 to −1.00. Correlations reflect the extent to which two variables vary together, but they do not necessarily indicate that one of them causes the other.

6. A major task of any investigator is to explain the variability of some dependent variable, usually measured by the variance. One means for doing so is to see whether the variance is reduced when a certain independent variable is controlled for. If so, this independent variable is said to account for some of the variability of the dependent variable.

7. One of the main functions of statistical methods is to help test hypotheses about a population given information about the sample. An important example is the difference between mean scores obtained under two different conditions. Here, the investigator has to decide between the *null hypothesis,* which asserts that the difference was obtained by chance, and the *alternative hypothesis,* which asserts that the difference is genuine and exists in the population. The decision is made by dividing the obtained mean difference by the *standard error (SE),* a measure of the variability of that mean difference. If the resulting ratio, called the *critical ratio,* is large enough, the null hypothesis is rejected, the alternative hypothesis is accepted, and the difference is said to be *statistically reliable.* A related way of making statistical decisions is by using a *confidence interval,* or margin of error. This is based on the variability of the scores from a sample and determines the interval within which the population mean or proportion probably falls.

GLOSSARY

ablation The removal of tissue with a vacuum or scalpel, sometimes used as a research technique (allowing investigators to ask how an organism functions in the absence of this tissue).

abnormal psychology *See* psychopathology.

absolute threshold The lowest intensity of some stimulus that produces a response.

accessory structures In sensory processing, the parts of sensory systems that gather external stimulus energies and fashion the proximal stimulus, which the receptors then transduce.

accommodation (1) The process by which the lens is thickened or flattened to focus on an object. (2) In Piaget's theory of development, one of the twin processes that underlies cognitive development. *See* assimilation and accommodation.

accommodative distortion Retrospective alterations of memory to fit a schema. *See also* schema.

acetylcholine A neurotransmitter found in many parts of the nervous system. Among many other functions, it serves as an excitatory transmitter at the synaptic junctions between muscle fibers and motor neurons.

achromatic colors Colors, such as black, white, and the neutral grays, that do not have the property of hue.

acquisition The initial step toward remembering in which new information is taken in.

across-fiber theory The theory that a certain sensory quality is signaled by the pattern of neural activity across a number of different nerve fibers.

action potential A brief change in the electrical potential of an axon, which is the physical basis of the nervous impulse.

activation-synthesis hypothesis An account which holds that dreams may reflect the brain's aroused state during REM sleep, when the cerebral cortex is active but shut off from sensory input. This helps explain the content and often disjointed form of REM dreams.

active memory *See* working memory.

active span tasks Tasks in which research participants are asked to remember materials while simultaneously working on some other task; such tasks are an effective means of measuring working memory's capacity.

activity dependence A property of neuronal plasticity such that changes in a neuron's functioning will occur only if that neuron is active (i.e., firing) at the same time as another neuron.

actor-observer difference The difference in attributions made by actors who describe their own actions and observers who describe another person's. The former emphasizes external, situational causes; the latter, internal, dispositional factors. *See also* attribution theory, fundamental attribution error, self-serving attributional bias.

act-outcome representation A type of association hypothesized by Edward Tolman to be the product of instrumental learning; an organism that has acquired this sort of association has acquired the knowledge that a certain type of act leads to a particular outcome.

acuity The ability to distinguish between separate points projected on the retina. Acuity is greatest in the fovea, where the receptors are closely bunched together.

acute stress disorder A reaction sometimes observed in individuals who have experienced a traumatic event that is characterized by recurrent nightmares and waking flashbacks of the traumatic event.

adaptation The process by which the sensitivity to a particular stimulus declines when it is continually presented.

adaptive value In evolutionary terms, the extent to which an attribute increases the likelihood of viable offspring.

addiction The result of repeated use of some drugs. The consequences are increased tolerance and withdrawal symptoms, which cause addiction to be self-perpetuating.

additive color mixture Mixing colors by stimulating the eye with two or more sets of wavelengths simultaneously (e.g., by focusing filtered light from two projectors on the same spot). *See also* subtractive color mixture.

adequate stimulus An electrical pulse above the threshold, or critical point, that induces an action potential in a neuron.

adipose cells The cells within the body that provide long-term storage of energy resources, usually in the form of fatty acids that can be converted to glucose when needed.

adrenaline *See* epinephrine.

adrenal medulla The inner core of the adrenal gland, which regulates the release of epinephrine (adrenaline) and norepinephrine into the bloodstream.

affective disorders *See* mood disorders.

afferent nerves Nerves that carry messages to the brain.

aftereffect of visual movement An effect observed after one stares at a steadily moving object for a while. If one now looks at a stationary object, it appears to be moving in the direction opposite to the movement observed initially.

agnosia A serious disturbance in the organization of sensory information produced by lesions in certain cortical areas. An example is visual agnosia in which the patient can see but often does not recognize what it is that he sees.

agonists Drugs that enhance the activity of a neurotransmitter, often by increasing the amount of transmitter substance available (e.g., by blocking reuptake or by increasing the availability of precursors).

agoraphobia The fear of being alone and outside of the home, especially in a public place; often observed in those with panic disorder. *See also* phobia.

alarm call Special, genetically programmed cry that impels members of a given species to seek cover. A biological puzzle, since it suggests a form of altruism in which the individual giving the call appears to endanger her own survival. *See also* altruism.

algorithm In computer problem solving, a procedure in which all of the operations are specified step-by-step. *See also* heuristics.

all-or-none law A law that describes the fact that all action potentials have the same amplitude regardless of the stimulus that triggered them.

alpha male The most dominant male in an animal group's dominance hierarchy. *See also* dominance hierarchies.

alpha waves Fairly regular EEG waves, between eight to twelve per second, characteristic of a relaxed, waking state, usually with eyes closed.

alternative hypothesis In statistics, the hypothesis that the null hypothesis is false, that an obtained difference is so far from zero that one has to assume that the mean difference in the population is greater than zero and that the experimental condition has some effect. *See also* null hypothesis.

altruism (1) Acting so as to elevate the interests and welfare of others above one's own. (2) As used by sociobiologists, any behavior pattern that benefits individuals who are not one's own offspring (e.g., an alarm call). Such altruism has biological survival value because the altruist's beneficiaries tend to be close relatives who carry a high proportion of his or her own genes. In cases of reciprocal altruism, altruism is based on the expectation that today's giver will be tomorrow's taker. *See also* alarm call.

Alzheimer's disease A degenerative brain disorder characterized by memory loss followed by increasing disorientation and culminating in total physical and mental helplessness and death. One of the major sites of the destruction is a pathway of acetylcholine-releasing cells leading from the base of the forebrain to the cortex and hippocampus. *See also* acetylcholine.

ambiguity (in sentence meaning) The case in which a sentence (i.e., one surface structure) has two meanings (i.e., two underlying structures). (For example, "These missionaries are ready to eat" overheard in a conversation between two cannibals.)

American Sign Language (ASL) The manual-visual language system of deaf persons in America.

amino acid The building blocks of proteins.

amphetamine psychosis A pattern of symptoms similar to those observed in paranoid schizophrenia, but produced by frequent and large doses of amphetamines.

amphetamines Drugs that increase the availability of dopamine norepinephrine, causing increased arousal and excitement. Large doses may lead to frenetic hyperactivity and delusions. *See also* amphetamine psychosis.

amplitude The height of a wave crest, often used as a measure of intensity of a sound or light wave.

amygdala An almond-shaped structure in the temporal lobe that plays a central role in emotion and in the evaluation of stimuli.

anal character According to Freud, a personality type that derives from serious conflicts during the anal stage and is distinguished by three symptomatic traits: compulsive orderliness, stubbornness, and stinginess. *See also* anal stage.

analgesic A pain reliever.

analogical representation A representation that shares some of the physical characteristics of an object; for example, a picture of a mouse is an analogical representation because it looks like the small rodent it represents.

anal stage In psychoanalytic theory, the stage of psychosexual development during which the focus of pleasure is on activities related to elimination.

analytic intelligence According to some investigators, the type of intelligence typically measured by intelligence tests and crucial for success in academic pursuits.

androgen Any male sex hormone (e.g., testosterone).

angiotensin A substance produced by the kidneys when there is a decrease in the amount of liquid passing through them, activating receptors in the brain that monitor the volume of blood and other fluids in the body.

anomia A difficulty in finding words that is often experienced by people with brain injuries.

anorexia nervosa An eating disorder that primarily afflicts young women and that is characterized by an exaggerated concern with being overweight and by compulsive dieting, sometimes to the point of self-starvation and death. *See also* bulimia.

A-not-B effect The tendency of infants around nine months of age to search for a hidden object by reaching for place *A,* where it was previously hidden, rather than a new place *B,* where it was hidden most recently while the child was watching.

antagonists Drugs that impede the activity of a neurotransmitter, often by decreasing the amount available (e.g., by speeding reuptake and decreasing availability of precursors).

anterograde amnesia A memory deficit suffered after some brain damage. It is an inability to learn and remember any information imparted after the injury, with little effect on memory for information acquired before the injury. *See also* retrograde amnesia.

antidepressant drugs Drugs that alleviate depressive symptoms, presumably because they increase the availability of certain neurotransmitters (especially norepinephrine and serotonin) at synaptic junctions. The three major classes are monoamine oxidase (MAO) inhibitors and tricyclics, and selective serotonin reuptake inhibitors.

antidiuretic hormone (ADH) *See* vasopressin.

antipsychotic drugs *See* atypical antipsychotics, classical antipsychotics.

antisocial personality disorder Also called psychopathy or sociopathy. The term describes persons who get into continual trouble with society, are indifferent to others, are impulsive, and have little concern for the future or remorse about the past.

anxiety A global apprehensiveness related to uncertainty.

anxiety disorders *See* acute stress disorder, dissociative disorders, generalized anxiety disorder, obsessive-compulsive disorder, panic disorder, phobia, post-traumatic stress disorder (PTSD), social phobia, specific phobia.

anxiety hierarchy *See* systematic desensitization.

anxiolytics More commonly known as minor tranquilizers, these drugs are given to patients suffering from disabling anxiety. Most types work by increasing the activity of the neurotransmitter GABA and are highly addictive.

aphagia Refusal to eat (and in an extreme version, to drink) brought about by a lesion of the lateral hypothalamus.

aphasia A disorder of language produced by lesions in certain areas of the cortex. A lesion in Broca's area leads to nonfluent aphasia, one in Wernicke's area to fluent aphasia.

apparent movement The perception of movement produced by stimuli that are stationary but flash on and off at appropriate time intervals.

appeasement display A gesture or pattern of behavior which signals that an organism is conceding defeat in a conflict.

appetitive stimulus In instrumental conditioning, a stimulus that the animal will do everything to attain and nothing to prevent.

apraxia A serious disturbance in the organization of voluntary action produced by lesions in certain cortical areas, often in the frontal lobes.

archetypes According to Carl Jung, the stories and images that constitute our collective unconscious.

artificial intelligence A field that draws on concepts from both cognitive psychology and computer science to develop artificial systems that display some aspects of humanlike intelligence. Examples are computer programs that recognize patterns or solve certain kinds of problems.

assertiveness training A technique sometimes used by therapists to help patients develop skills in interpersonal relations. In this technique, patients are encouraged to state their needs clearly, negotiate confidently, and persevere when thwarted.

assimilation and accommodation In Piaget's theory, the twin processes by means of which cognitive development proceeds. Assimilation is the process whereby the environment is interpreted in terms of the schemas the child has at the time. Accommodation is the way the child changes his schemas as he continues to interact with the environment.

association A linkage between two psychological processes as a result of past experience in which the two have occurred together. A broad term that subsumes conditioning and association of ideas among others.

association areas A name sometimes given to regions of the cortex that are not primary projection areas. They tend to be involved in the integration of sensory information or of motor commands.

associative links Connections in memory that tie one memory, or one concept, to another.

associative retrieval A type of memory retrieval that seems swift and effortless: The sought-after information simply "pops" into mind.

attachment The tendency of the young of many species to stay in close proximity to an adult, usually their mother. *See also* imprinting.

attention A collective label for all the processes by which we perceive selectively.

attitude A fairly stable, evaluative disposition that makes a person think, feel, or behave positively or negatively about some person, group, or social issue.

attribution An interpretive process by which we reach a judgment about the cause(s) of an act or achievement.

attribution theory A theory about the process by which we try to explain a person's behavior, attributing it to situational factors or to inferred dispositional qualities or both. *See also* actor-observer difference, fundamental attribution error, self-serving attributional bias.

attributional style *See* explanatory style.

attribution-of-arousal theory An approach that combines the James-Lange emphasis on bodily feedback with a cognitive approach to emotion. Various stimuli can trigger a general state of arousal, which is then interpreted in light of the subject's present situation and shaped into a specific emotional experience.

atypical antipsychotics Drugs (such as Clozaril, Risperdal, and Zyprexa) that operate by blocking receptors for both dopamine and serotonin; these drugs seem to be effective in treating schizophrenic patients' positive symptoms, such as thought disorders and hallucinations, as well as their negative symptoms, such as apathy and emotional blunting.

audition The sense of hearing.

auditory canal The tube that carries sound from the outer ear to the eardrum.

authoritarian personality A cluster of personal attributes (e.g., submission to persons above and harshness to those below) and social attitudes (e.g., prejudice against minority groups) that is sometimes held to constitute a distinct personality.

authoritative-reciprocal pattern A pattern of child rearing in which parents exercise considerable power but also respond to the child's point of view and reasonable demands. Parents following this pattern set rules of conduct and are fairly demanding but also encourage the child's independence and self-expression.

autocratic pattern A pattern of child rearing in which the parents control the child strictly, setting stern and usually unexplained rules whose infraction leads to severe, often physical, punishment.

automatization A process whereby components of a skilled activity become subsumed under a higher-order organization and are run off automatically.

autonomic nervous system (ANS) A part of the nervous system that controls the internal organs, usually not under voluntary control.

availability heuristic A rule of thumb often used to make probability estimates, which depends on the frequency with which certain events readily come to mind. This can lead to errors, since, for example, very vivid events will be remembered out of proportion to their actual frequency of occurrence.

aversion therapy A form of behavior therapy in which the undesirable response leads to an aversive stimulus (e.g., the patient shocks herself every time she reaches for a cigarette).

aversive stimulus In instrumental conditioning, a stimulus such as an electric shock, which the animal does everything to avoid and nothing to attain.

avoidance learning Instrumental learning in which the response averts an aversive stimulus before it occurs. *See also* escape learning, punishment training.

axon Part of a neuron that transmits impulses to other neurons or effectors.

axon terminals The knoblike swellings on the ends of an axon. The terminals contain the synaptic vesicles that are filled with neurotransmitters.

backward pairing A classical conditioning procedure in which the conditioned stimulus (CS) follows the unconditioned stimulus (US). *See also* forward pairing, simultaneous pairing.

Barnum effect Describes the fact that a description of one's personality will often be uncritically accepted as valid if it is stated in sufficiently general terms.

basal ganglia In the extrapyramidal motor system, a set of subcortical structures in the cerebrum that send messages to the spinal cord through the midbrain to modulate various motor functions.

base rate *See* representativeness heuristic.

basic emotions According to some theorists, a small set of elemental, built-in emotions revealed by distinctinve patterns of physiological reaction and facial expression. *See also* facial feed-back hypothesis.

basilar membrane *See* cochlea.

behavioral-cognitive approach to personality An approach that defines personality differences by the way in which different people act and think about their actions. It tends to emphasize situational determinants and prior learning in trying to explain how such differences come about. *See also* humanistic approach, psychodynamic approach, sociocultural approach, situationism, trait theory.

behavioral contrast A pattern of responding in which an organism seems to evaluate a reward relative to other rewards that are available or that have been available recently. For example, an animal might respond only weakly to a reward of two pellets if it recently received a reward of five pellets for some other response.

behaviorism A theoretical outlook that emphasizes the role of environment and of learning and insists that people must be studied objectively and from the outside.

behavior therapy A general approach to psychological treatment which (1) holds that the disorders to which it addresses itself are produced by maladaptive learning and must be remedied by reeducation, (2) proposes techniques for this reeducation based on principles of learning and conditioning, (3) focuses on the maladaptive behaviors as such rather than on hypothetical unconscious processes of which they may be expressions.

belongingness in learning The fact that the ease with which associations are formed depends upon the items to be associated. This holds for classical conditioning in which some CS-US combinations are more effective than others (e.g., learned taste aversions) and for instrumental conditioning in which some response-reinforcer combinations work more easily than others (e.g., specific defense reactions in avoidance conditioning of species). *See also* biological constraints, equipotentiality.

beta rhythm A rhythmic pattern in the electrical activity of the brain, often observed when one is engaged in active thought.

between-family differences In research on the genetics of behavior, a term often used to refer to the role of environment. It describes environmental differences that apply to entire families, such as differences in socioeconomic status, religion, or child-rearing attitudes. For most personality attributes, these seem to be less important than within-family differences. *See also* within-family differences.

between-group heritability The extent to which variation between groups (as in the difference between the mean IQs of U.S. whites and blacks) is attributable to genetic factors. *See also* heritability ratio (H), within-group heritability.

bidirectional activation models Models of pattern recognition in which elements are activated as well as inhibited from both lower levels (bottom-up processing) and higher levels (top-down processing).

Big Five A nickname often used to refer to Warren Norman's five dimensions of personality: extroversion, neuroticism (or emotional instability), agreeableness, conscientiousness, and openness to experience. These five traits often emerge from factor analyses of trait terms.

binding problem The problem confronted by the brain of recombining the elements of a stimulus, once these elements have been separately analyzed by different neural systems.

binocular disparity An important cue for depth perception. Each eye obtains a different view of an object, the disparity becoming less pronounced the farther the object is from the observer.

biological constraints Principles governing what each species can learn easily and what it cannot learn at all. *See also* belongingness in learning.

biomedical model An approach to mental disorders that emphasizes somatogenic causes.

bipolar cells The intermediate neural cells in the eye that are stimulated by the receptors and excite the ganglion cells.

bipolar disorder A mood disorder in which the patient swings from one emotional extreme to another, experiencing both manic and depressive episodes. Formerly called manic-depressive psychosis.

bisexuality A sexual orientation in which a person has erotic and romantic feelings for both their own and the opposite sex.

blindsight The ability of a person with a lesion in the visual cortex to reach toward or guess at the orientation of objects projected on the part of the visual field that corresponds to this lesion, even though they report that they can see absolutely nothing in that part of their visual field.

blind spot The region of the eye that contains no visual receptors and therefore cannot produce visual sensations.

blocking effect An effect produced when two conditioned stimuli, *A* and *B,* are both presented together with the unconditioned stimulus (US). If stimulus *A* has previously been associated with the unconditioned stimulus while *B* has not, the formation of an association between stimulus *B* and the US will be impaired (that is, blocked).

blood-brain barrier Specialized membranes that surround the blood vessels within the brain and that filter toxins and other harmful chemicals, ensuring brain cells' a relatively pure blood supply.

bottom-up processes *See* top-down processes.

brightness A perceived dimension of visual stimuli—the extent to which they appear light or dark.

brightness contrast The perceiver's tendency to exaggerate the physical difference in the light intensities of two adjacent regions. As a result, a gray patch looks brighter on a black background, darker on a white background.

brightness ratio The ratio between the light reflected by a region and the light reflected by the area that surrounds it. According to one theory, perceived brightness is determined by this ratio.

Broca's area A brain area in the frontal lobe crucial for language production. *See also* aphasia.

bulimia An eating disorder characterized by repeated binge-and-purge bouts. In contrast to anorexics, bulimics tend to be of roughly normal weight. *See also* anorexia nervosa.

bystander effect The phenomenon that underlies many examples of failing to help strangers in distress: The larger the group a person is in (or thinks he is in), the less likely he is to come to a stranger's assistance. One reason is diffusion of responsibility (no one thinks it is *his* responsibility to act).

California Psychological Inventory (CPI) A commonly used personality test, aimed especially at high-school and college students, that tests for traits such as dominance, sociability, responsibility, and so on.

cannula A tiny tube used to inject or withdraw small quantities of brain chemicals.

case study An observational study in which one person is studied intensively. *See also* single-case experiment.

catatonic schizophrenia A subcategory of schizophrenia. Its main symptoms are peculiar motor patterns, such as periods in which the patient is immobile and maintains strange positions for hours on end.

catch trials Trials in a signal detection experiment in which no signal is presented. These trials ensure that the observer is taking the task seriously and truly trying to determine whether a signal is present or not.

catecholamines A family of neurotransmitters that have an activating function, including epinephrine, norepinephrine, and dopamine.

categorical scale A scale that divides responses into categories that are not numerically related. *See also* interval scale, nominal scale, ordinal scale, ratio scale.

catharsis An explosive release of hitherto dammed-up emotions that is sometimes believed to have therapeutic effects.

central fissure   The visible fissure in the brain that separates the frontal and parietal lobes.

central nervous system (CNS)   The brain and spinal cord.

central pattern generators (CPGs)   Circuits in the nervous system that orchestrate lower level reflexes and other neural activities into larger, organized acts. CPGs instigate certain crucial basic actions, such as, chewing, breathing, locomotion, etc.

central route to persuasion   *See* elaboration-likelihood model of persuasion.

central tendency   The tendency of scores in a frequency distribution to cluster around a central value. *See also* measure of central tendency, variability.

central trait   A trait that is associated with many other attributes of the person who is being judged. Warmth and coldness are central because they are important in determining overall impressions.

cerebellum   Two small hemispheres that form part of the hindbrain and control muscular coordination and equilibrium.

cerebral cortex   The outermost layer of the gray matter of the cerebral hemispheres.

cerebral hemispheres   Two hemispherical structures that comprise the major part of the forebrain in mammals and serve as the main coordinating center of the nervous system.

childhood amnesia   The failure to remember the events of our very early childhood. This is sometimes ascribed to massive change in retrieval cues, sometimes to different ways of encoding memories in early childhood.

chlorpromazine   *See* phenothiazines.

choice reaction time   A measure of the speed of mental processing in which the subject has to choose between one of several responses depending upon which stimulus is presented.

cholecystokinin (CCK)   A hormone released by the duodenum that appears to send a "stop eating" message to the brain.

chromatic colors   Colors that have a discernible hue. These are in contrast to the achromatic colors, which include black, the various shades of gray, and white.

chromosomes   Structures in the nucleus of each cell that contain the genes, the units of hereditary transmission. A human cell has forty-six chromosomes, arranged in twenty-three pairs. One of these pairs consists of the sex chromosomes. In males, one member of the pair is an X-chromosome, the other a Y-chromosome. In females, both members are X-chromosomes. *See also* gene, X-chromosome.

chunking   A process of reorganizing (or recoding) materials in memory that permits a number of items to be packed into a larger unit.

circadian rhythm   A rhythm that spans about a twenty-four-hour day, such as that of the sleep-waking cycle. Circadian rhythms in humans originate from a clock circuit in the hypothalamus that is set by information from the optic nerve about whether it is day or night.

classical antipsychotics   Drugs (such as Thorazine and Haldol) that operate by blocking receptors for dopamine; these drugs seem to be effective in treating many schizophrenic patients' positive symptoms, such as thought disorders and hallucinations. Also called major tranquillizers and neuroleptics.

classical conditioning   A form of learning in which a hitherto neutral stimulus, the conditioned stimulus (CS), is paired with an unconditioned stimulus (US) regardless of what the animal does. In effect, what has to be learned is the relation between these two stimuli. *See also* instrumental conditioning.

classical psychoanalysis   The method developed by Sigmund Freud which assumes that a patient's ills stem from unconscious defenses against unacceptable urges that date back to early childhood.

client-centered therapy   A humanistic psychotherapy developed by Carl Rogers. *See also* humanistic therapies.

closure   A factor in visual grouping. The perceptual tendency to fill in gaps in a figure so that it looks complete.

cochlea   A coiled structure in the inner ear that contains the basilar membrane whose deformation by sound-produced pressure stimulates the auditory receptors.

cocktail-party effect   The effect one experiences in settings such as noisy parties, where one tunes in to the voice of the person one is talking to and filters out the other voices as background noise. This phenomenon is often taken as the model for studying selective attention based on listening to speech.

coding   The translation of stimulus information into various dimensions of sensation (e.g., intensity and quality) that are actually experienced.

cognitive-behavioral model   An approach to mental disorders that emphasizes the role of faulty habits of thought, such as pessimistic or catastrophic thinking.

cognitive components   The mental processes needed to solve complex problems. Some theories of intelligence propose that individuals differ in their skill in using these component mental processes.

cognitive consistency   A state in which one's beliefs and preferences are consistent with each other.

cognitive development   Intellectual growth from infancy to adulthood.

cognitive dissonance   An inconsistency among some experiences, beliefs, attitudes, or feelings. According to dissonance theory, this sets up an unpleasant state that people try to reduce by reinterpreting some part of their experiences to make them consistent with the others.

cognitive map   A mental representation of an environment's spatial layout.

cognitive neuropsychology   A field of inquiry in which evidence of damage to certain areas of the brain and corresponding changes in behavior are used to make inferences about underlying psychological functions.

cognitive therapy   An approach to therapy that tries to change some of the patient's habitual modes of thinking about herself, her situation, and her future. It is related to behavioral therapy because it regards such thought patterns as a form of behavior.

collateral sprouts   New branches grown on previously damaged axons, allowing some recovery of function.

collective unconscious   A set of primordial stories and images, hypothesized by Carl Jung to be shared by all of humanity, that underlie and shape our perceptions and desires.

collectivism   A cultural pattern in which people are considered to be fundamentally interdependent and obligations within one's family and immediate community are emphasized. Many of the societies of Latin America, and most of the cultures of Asia and Africa, are collectivist. *See also* individualism.

color circle   A means of representing the visible hues, arranged in a circle according to perceptual similarity.

color disk   A two-dimensional object allowing one to display two of the dimensions of color: saturation and hue. Saturation is represented by radius (with achromatic colors at the center of the disk and fully saturated colors at the periphery), and hue is represented by angular position around the disk.

color solid   A three-dimensional object allowing one to display all three dimensions of color: brightness, saturation, and hue. Brightness is represented by height (with black at the bottom and white at the top), saturation by radius (with achromatic colors at the center of the solid and fully saturated colors at the periphery), and hue by angular position around the solid.

common sense As used in the discussion of artificial intelligence, the term refers to an understanding of what is relevant to a problem.

companionate love A state of emotion (usually contrasted with romantic love) characterized by the affection we feel for those whose lives are deeply intertwined with our own.

comparative method A research method in which one makes systematic comparisons among different species in order to gain insights into the function of a particular structure or behavior, or the evolutionary origins of that structure or behavior.

compensatory reaction An internally produced response through which the body seeks to reduce the effects of some external influence by producing a reaction opposite in its characteristics to those of the external influence. For example, the body produces an increase in pain sensitivity in response to the decrease in pain sensitivity caused by morphine, thereby canceling out morphine's reaction and so producing drug tolerance.

complementary colors Two colors that, when additively mixed with each other in the right proportions, produce the sensation of gray.

complex cells A type of cell in the visual cortex that is sensitive to an input's orientation and so fires at its maximal rate only if the input is tilted appropriately. These cells are often sensitive to the direction of movement of a target.

complex partial seizure disorder (CPSD) A kind of epilepsy that seems to make neurons within the amygdala hyperactive, leading sufferers to attach inappropriate emotional and motivational significance to objects, places, and events.

compulsions *See* obsessive-compulsive disorders.

concept A class or category that subsumes a number of individual instances. An important way of relating concepts is through propositions, which make some assertion that relates a subject (e.g., *chickens*) and a predicate (e.g., *lay eggs*).

concordance The probability that a person who stands in a particular familial relationship to a patient (e.g., an identical twin) has the same disorder as the patient.

concrete operations period In Piaget's theory, the period from ages six or seven to about eleven. At this time, the child has acquired mental operations that allow him to abstract some essential attributes of reality, such as number and substance, but these operations are as yet applicable only to concrete events and cannot be considered entirely in the abstract.

conditioned emotional response (CER) A technique in which a conditioned stimulus evokes fear, which in turn suppresses whatever other activities the animal is currently engaged in. For example, a rat will no longer press a lever for a food reward after several trials involving a light or tone that precedes an electrical shock.

conditioned reflex *See* conditioned response.

conditioned reinforcer An initially neutral stimulus that acquires reinforcing properties through pairing with another stimulus that is already reinforcing.

conditioned response (CR) A response elicited by some initially neutral stimulus, the conditioned stimulus (CS), as a result of pairings between that CS and an unconditioned stimulus (US). This CR is typically not identical with the unconditioned response though it often is similar to it. *See also* conditioned stimulus (CS), unconditioned response (UR), unconditioned stimulus (US).

conditioned stimulus (CS) In classical conditioning, the stimulus which comes to elicit a new response by virtue of pairings with the unconditioned stimulus. *See also* conditioned response (CR), unconditioned response (UR), unconditioned stimulus (US).

cones Visual receptors that respond to greater light intensities and give rise to chromatic (color) sensations.

confabulation Sincere but false recollections, usually produced when one encounters a gap in the memory record and (unwittingly) tries to fill this gap.

confidence interval An interval around a sample mean within which the population mean is likely to fall. In common practice, the largest value of the interval is 2 standard errors above the mean and the smallest value is 2 standard errors below it.

confirmation bias The tendency to seek evidence to support one's hypothesis rather than to look for evidence that will undermine the hypothesis.

conformity The act of going along with what other people think or do. Evidence suggests that there are two main reasons people conform: the desire to be right and the desire to be liked.

confounds Uncontrolled factors in an experiment that could systematically influence the outcome.

conjunction of features In a visual search procedure, a target that is composed of several different features (i.e., a red X as opposed to the feature red or the feature diagonal). Search times required to find these kinds of targets are longer and increase with the number of distractors that are displayed.

connectionist models A model of how information in memory is retrieved that relies on distributed representations. In a distributed representation, a concept is conveyed by a pattern of activation across an entire network, rather than by the activation of a single node. In such models, processing depends on having just the right links between concepts, at just the right strengths.

conservation of number In Piaget's theory, the understanding that the number of objects in a group remains constant despite any changes in their spatial arrangement (e.g., a child at age six realizes that there is the same number of objects in a row of six closely spaced bottles as in a row of six bottles spaced far apart).

conservation of quantity In Piaget's theory, the understanding that the quantity of a substance remains unchanged despite a visible change in appearance (thus in liquid conservation, the realization that the amount of liquid remains the same when poured from a tall, thin beaker into a short, wide jar).

construct validity The extent to which performance on a test fits into a theoretical schema about the attribute the test tries to measure.

content morphemes Morphemes that carry the main burden of meaning (e.g., *strange*). This is in contrast to function morphemes that add details to the meaning but also serve various grammatical purposes (e.g., the suffixes *s* and *er*, the connecting words *and, or, if*, and so on).

contiguity The togetherness in time and space of two events, which is sometimes regarded as the condition that leads to association.

contingency A relation between two events in which one is dependent upon another. If the contingency is greater than zero, then the probability of event *A* will be greater when event *B* is present than when it is absent.

contingency management A form of behavior therapy in which the environment is structured such that certain behaviors are reliably followed by well-defined consequences.

contralateral control The pattern in which movements on the right side of the body are controlled by the left half of the brain, while movements on the left side of the body are controlled by the right half of the brain. Contralateral control is seen in nearly all vertebrate nervous systems.

control group A group to which the experimental manipulation is not applied.

convergence The movement of the eyes as they swivel so that both eyes are pointing toward the same visual target.

conversion disorders Formerly called conversion hysteria. A condition in which there are physical symptoms that seem to have no physical basis. They instead appear to be linked to psychological factors and are often believed to serve as a means of reducing anxiety. *See also* hysteria.

conversion hysteria *See* conversion disorders.

convolutions The wrinkles visible in the cortex that allow the enormous surface area of the human cortex to be stuffed into the relatively small space of the skull.

cornea The eye's transparent outer coating.

corpus callosum A bundle of fibers that connects the two cerebral hemispheres.

correct negative See payoff matrix.

correlation The tendency of two variables to vary together. If one goes up as the other goes up, the correlation is positive; if one goes up as the other goes down, the correlation is negative.

correlational studies Studies in which the investigator is seeking to observe the relationship among variables that were in place prior to the study (as opposed to factors that the investigator creates or manipulates).

correlation coefficient (r) A number that expresses both the size and the direction of a correlation, varying from +1.00 (perfect positive correlation) through 0.00 (absence of any correlation) to −1.00 (perfect negative correlation).

correspondence problem In a moving display, the difficulty in determining which aspects of the display now visible correspond to which aspects of the display visible a moment ago.

cortex *See* cerebral cortex.

counterconditioning A procedure for weakening a classically conditioned response (CR) by connecting the stimuli that presently evoke it to a new response that is incompatible with the CR.

covariation *See* correlation.

cranial nerves The twelve pairs of nerves that enter and exit directly from the hindbrain. These nerves control movements of the head and neck, carry sensations from them including vision, olfaction, and audition, and regulate the various glandular secretions in the head.

creative intelligence The form of intelligence alleged by some authors as essential for devising new ideas or new strategies. Often contrasted with analytic intelligence or practical intelligence.

criterion groups Groups whose test performance sets the validity criterion for certain tests (e.g., the Minnesota Multiphasic Personality Inventory, MMPI, which uses several psychiatric criterion groups to define most of its subscales).

critical period A period in the development of an organism when it is particularly sensitive to certain environmental influences. Outside of this period, the same environmental influences have little effect (e.g., the period during which a duckling can be imprinted). After embryonic development, this phenomenon is rarely all-or-none. As a result, most developmental psychologists prefer the term *sensitive period*.

critical ratio A score, usually a *z*-score, that determines whether an investigator will accept or reject the null hypothesis. If a test score exceeds the critical ratio, the null hypothesis is rejected.

cross-cultural approach *See* sociocultural approach.

cross-cultural method The study of the relation between a culture's beliefs and practices and the typical personality characteristics of its members. *See also* sociocultural approach.

crystallized intelligence The repertoire of information, cognitive skills, and strategies acquired by the application of fluid intelligence to various fields. This is said to increase with age, in some cases into old age. *See also* fluid intelligence.

CT scan (Computerized Tomography) A technique for examining brain structure in living humans by constructing a composite X-ray picture based on views from all different angles. Also called CAT (Computerized Axial Tomography) scan.

cultural anthropology A branch of anthropology that compares the similarities and differences among human cultures.

cultural display rules Learned but deeply ingrained conventions that govern what facial expressions of emotion may or may not be shown in what contexts.

culture fairness of a test The extent to which test performance does not depend upon information or skills provided by one culture but not another.

cupboard theory A hypothesis about the infant's attachment to the primary caregiver; according to this theory, the attachment is motivated largely by the fact that the mother is a source of nourishment (whether through breast or bottle).

curare A drug that completely paralyzes the skeletal musculature but does not affect visceral reactions.

data driven *See* bottom-up.

decay A theory of forgetting in which memory traces erode largely through the passage of time (presumably because of some metabolic events unfolding as time passes).

decibels The logarithmic units used to describe sound intensity (or amplitude).

decision making The process of forming probability estimates of events and using them to choose between different courses of action.

declarative knowledge Knowing "that" (e.g., knowing someone's name) as contrasted with procedural knowledge, which is knowing "how" (e.g., knowing how to ride a bicycle).

deductive reasoning Reasoning in which one tries to determine whether some statement follows logically from certain premises, as in the analysis of syllogisms. This is in contrast with inductive reasoning in which one observes a number of particular instances and tries to determine a general rule that covers them all.

deep processing *See* depth-of-processing approach.

defense mechanism In psychoanalytic theory, a collective term for a number of reactions that try to ward off or lessen anxiety by various unconscious means. *See also* displacement, projection, rationalization, reaction formation, repression.

deferred imitation A pattern of imitation first observed in children late in the second year of life in which the child mimics an action observed some time in the past.

definition (of a word) A set of necessary and sufficient features shared by all members of a category that are the criteria for membership in that category.

definitional theory of meaning The theory that our mental representation of word meaning is made up of a small number of simpler concepts. The representation of *bachelor*, for example, is made up of "adult," "unmarried," and "male."

deindividuation A weakened sense of personal identity in which self-awareness is merged in the collective goals of a group.

deinstitutionalization A movement intended to obtain better and less expensive care for chronically mentally ill patients in their own communities rather than at large, centralized hospitals.

delay of gratification The postponement of immediate satisfaction in order to achieve a more important reward later on, a process that plays an important role in some behavioral-cognitive approaches to personality.

delusion Systematized false beliefs, often of grandeur or persecution.

demand characteristics The cues that tell a research participant what the experimenter expects.

dendrites A typically highly branched part of a neuron that receives impulses from receptors or other neurons and conducts them toward the cell body and axon.

dependent variable *See* experiment.

depolarization A drop of the membrane potential of a neuron from its resting potential. The basis of neural excitation.

depression A state of deep and pervasive dejection and hopelessness, accompanied by apathy and a feeling of personal worthlessness. *See also* major depression.

depth cues Sources of information that signal the distance from the observer to the distal stimulus. Some depth cues are present in a single retinal image (the pictorial cues), some require a comparison of the information received from the two eyes (binocular cues), some involve the pattern of motion in the retinal image (parallax and optic flow), and some arise from the positions of the eyes in viewing (e.g., convergence angle).

depth-of-processing approach An approach to memory that stresses the nature of encoding at the time of acquisition. It argues that deeper levels of processing (for example, attending to a word's meaning) lead to better retention and retrieval than shallower levels of processing (for example, attending to the word's sound). Thus, maintenance rehearsal leads to much poorer retrieval than elaborative rehearsal. *See also* encoding, elaborative rehearsal, maintenance rehearsal.

descriptive rules *See* prescriptive rules.

deviation IQ A measure of intelligence-test performance based on an individual's standing relative to his own age-mates (e.g., an IQ of 100 is average and IQs of 70 and 130 correspond to percentile ranks of 2 and 98 respectively). *See also* Intelligence Quotient.

Diagnostic and Statistical Manual for Mental Disorders *See* DSM.

diathesis *See* diathesis-stress conception.

diathesis-stress conception The belief that many organic and mental disorders arise from an interaction between a diathesis (a predisposition toward an illness) and some form of precipitating environmental stress.

dichotic presentation An experimental procedure in which the participant hears two simultaneous messages, one presented to each ear. Typically, one of these is to be attended to and the other ignored.

difference threshold The amount by which a given stimulus must be increased or decreased so that the research participant can perceive a just-noticeable difference (jnd).

differentiation A progressive change from the general to the particular and from the simpler to the more complex that characterizes embryological development. According to some theorists, the same pattern holds for the development of behavior after birth.

diffusion of responsibility *See* bystander effect.

diminishing returns principle Applied to the perceived value of money, the principle states that the increase in the subjective value produced by every additional dollar decreases the more dollars the person has already.

The same principle applies to the subjective value of other gains and losses. It also applies to the psychological magnitude of sensory qualities, as in the case of Weber's law.

directed thinking Thinking that is aimed at the solution of a problem.

direct perception In Gibson's theory, our ability to perceive information about sizes directly, without any intermediate cognitive steps.

discrimination A process of learning to respond to certain stimuli that are reinforced and not to others that are unreinforced.

discriminative stimuli In instrumental conditioning, the external stimuli that signal a particular relationship between the instrumental response and the reinforcer. For example, a green light is a positive discriminative stimulus when it signals to a pigeon that it will get food if it hops on a treadle; the reverse is true of a red light, or the negative discriminative stimulus, which indicates that this action will not lead to a food reward.

disinhibition An increase of some reaction tendency by the removal of some inhibiting influence upon it (e.g., the increased strength of a frog's spinal reflexes after decapitation).

disorganized type of schizophrenia A subtype of schizophrenia in which the predominant symptoms are extreme incoherence of thought and marked inappropriateness of behavior and affect.

displaced aggression *See* displacement.

displacement In psychoanalytic theory, a redirection of an impulse from a channel that is blocked into another, more available outlet (e.g., displaced aggression, as in a child who hits a sibling when punished by her parents).

display A term used by ethologists to describe genetically preprogrammed responses that serve as stimuli for the reaction of others of the same species, and thus serve as the basis of a communication system (e.g., mating rituals).

display rules A culture's rules about what facial signals may or may not be given and in what contexts.

dispositional quality Any underlying attribute that characterizes a given individual and makes him more disposed than others to engage in a particular behavior (e.g., the presence or absence of some ability or some personality trait).

dissociation (1) A term used for symptoms when a patient is impaired in one function but relatively unaffected in another. (2) In post-traumatic stress disorder (PTSD), the period of numbness immediately after the trauma in which the sufferer feels estranged, socially unresponsive, and oddly unaffected by the traumatizing event.

dissociative amnesia A form of memory loss in which an individual seems unable to remember some period of her life, or even her entire past, including her own identity. This memory loss is often understood as a means of coping with extraordinarily painful events.

dissociative disorders Disorders in which a whole set of mental events is stored out of ordinary consciousness. These include dissociative amnesia, fugue states and, very rarely, cases of dissociative identity disorder.

dissociative fugue A state in which the person wanders away from home, and then, days or even months later, suddenly realizes that he is in a strange place and does not know how he got there; this pattern is often understood as a means of coping with (and escaping from) extraordinarily painful events.

dissociative identity disorder Formerly multiple personality disorder. A dissociative disorder that results in a person developing two or more distinct personalities.

dissonance theory *See* cognitive dissonance.

distal stimulus An object or event outside (e.g., a tree) as contrasted to the proximal stimulus (e.g., the retinal image of the tree), which is the pattern of physical energies that originates from the distal stimulus and impinges on a sense organ.

distance cues *See* depth cues.

distress calls The innate signals through which a human or animal infant indicates its need of aid.

distributed representations A model of cognitive organization, especially semantic memory, in which each concept is represented, not by a designated node or group of nodes, but by a widespread pattern of activation across the entire network. *See also* connectionist models, local representations, network model, node.

doctrine of specific nerve energies The law formulated by Johannes Müller which holds that differences in sensory quality are not caused by differences in the stimuli themselves but by the different nervous structures that these stimuli excite. Thus, stimulating the retina will produce sensations of light, whether the retina is stimulated by a beam of light or pressure to the eyeball.

dodo bird verdict An expression often used to summarize the comparison of the effectiveness of different forms of psychotherapy. According to the dodo bird in *Alice in Wonderland,* "Everyone has won and all must have prizes." Regarding psychotherapy, this statement is understood to mean that all the major forms of psychotherapy are equally effective.

dominance hierarchies A social order developed by animals that live in groups by which certain individuals gain status and exert power over others. *See also* alpha male.

dominant gene *See* gene.

door-in-the-face technique A method for achieving compliance in which a certain request is preceded by a much larger one. The refusal of the first request, and the apparent concession on the part of the requester, makes people more likely to agree to the second demand, feeling that they should now make a concession of their own.

dopamine (DA) A neurotransmitter involved in various brain structures, including those that control motor action.

dopamine hypothesis of schizophrenia Asserts that schizophrenics are oversensitive to the neurotransmitter dopamine. Evidence for this view comes from the fact that the classical antipsychotics, which alleviate positive schizophrenic symptoms, block dopamine transmission. *See also* classical antipsychotics, phenothiazines.

dopamine-serotonin interaction hypothesis Asserts that schizophrenics are oversensitive to both dopamine and serotonin. Evidence for this view comes from the fact that atypical antipsychotics, which relieve both positive and negative symptoms, block receptors for both dopamine and serotonin. *See also* atypical antipsychotics.

double-blind technique A technique for evaluating drug effects independent of the effects produced by the expectations of research participants (placebo effects) and of physicians. This is done by assigning patients to a drug group or a placebo group with both patients and staff members in ignorance of who is assigned to which group. *See also* placebo effect.

drive-reduction theory A theory that claims that all built-in rewards are at bottom reductions of some noxious bodily state. The theory has difficulty in explaining motives in which one seeks stimulation, such as sex and curiosity.

drug tolerance The decrease in responsiveness to a drug developed after repeated use of a drug. Addicts must use increasingly larger doses to obtain the same effect that was produced previously.

DSM-III The diagnostic manual of the American Psychiatric Association adopted in 1980. A major distinction between it and its predecessor is that it categorizes mental disorders by their descriptive characteristics rather than by theories about their underlying cause. Thus, a number of disorders that were formerly grouped together under the general heading "neurosis" (e.g.,

phobias, conversion disorders) are now classified under separate headings. *See also* conversion disorders, neurosis, phobia.

DSM-III-R The diagnostic manual of the American Psychiatric Association adopted in 1987, a relatively minor revision of its predecessor, DSM-III.

DSM-IV The current diagnostic manual of the American Psychiatric Association (adopted in 1994), a substantial revision of its predecessor, DSM-III-R.

dual-center theory A hypothesis about the hypothalamic control of eating. One center (in the lateral hypothalamus) was hypothesized as the "on" center, the initiator of eating; another center (in the ventromedial region) was hypothesized as the "off" center, the terminator of eating. Current evidence indicates, however, that these brain regions, while crucial for eating, are only a part of the circuits controlling eating.

duplex theory of vision The theory that rods and cones handle different aspects of vision. The rods are the receptors for night vision; they operate at low light intensities and lead to achromatic (colorless) sensations. The cones are used in day vision; they respond at higher illumination levels and are responsible for sensations of color.

dyslexia Any difficulty in reading not associated with obvious problems like bad eyesight.

eardrum The taut membrane that transmits vibrations caused by sound waves across the middle ear to the inner ear.

ectotherms Organisms that control their body temperature by using mechanisms that are mostly external (such as choosing a sunny or shady environment). Previously called *cold blooded.*

effectors Organs of action; in humans, muscles and glands.

efferent nerves Nerves that carry messages to the effectors.

ego In Freud's theory, a set of reactions that try to reconcile the id's blind pleasure strivings with the demands of reality. These lead to the emergence of various skills and capacities that eventually become a system that can look at itself—an "I." *See also* id and superego.

egocentrism In Piaget's theory, a characteristic of preoperational children, an inability to see another person's point of view.

ego psychology An approach to psychology that, in addition to the neo-Freudian concern with cultural and interpersonal factors, stresses the healthy aspects of the self as it tries to cope with reality.

eidetic memory A relatively rare kind of memory characterized by relatively long-lasting and detailed images of scenes that can be scanned as if they were physically present.

elaboration-likelihood model of persuasion A theory that asserts that the factors that make for persuasion depend on the extent to which the arguments of the persuasive message are thought about (elaborated). If they are seriously thought about, the central route to persuasion will be used, and attitude change will depend on the nature of the arguments. If they are not seriously considered, the peripheral route to persuasion will be used, and attitude change will depend on more peripheral factors.

elaborative rehearsal Rehearsal in which material is actively reorganized and elaborated while in working memory. In contrast to maintenance rehearsal, this confers considerable benefit. *See also* maintenance rehearsal.

Electra complex *See* Oedipus complex.

electroconvulsive shock treatment (ECT) A somatic treatment, mostly used for cases of severe depression, in which a brief electric current is passed through the brain to produce a convulsive seizure.

electroencephalogram (EEG) A record of the summed activity of cortical cells picked up by wires placed on the skull.

embedded sentence   A sentence structure in which one full sentence is included in the midst of another, as in "The girl who ate the hamburger hit the ball." Here the sentence "[she] ate the hamburger" interrupts the flow of the main sentence, "The girl . . . hit the ball."

embryo   The earliest stage in a developing animal. In humans, up to about eight weeks after conception.

emergency reaction   Intense sympathetic arousal that mobilizes an organism for a crisis.

empathic concern   A feeling of sympathy and concern for the sufferings of another coupled with the desire to relieve this suffering. *See also* vicarious distress.

empathy   A direct emotional response to another person's emotions.

empiricism   A school of thought that holds that all knowledge comes by way of empirical experience, that is, through the senses.

encoding   The process by which information is stored in memory.

encoding specificity principle   The hypothesis that retrieval is most likely if the context at the time of recall approximates that during the original encoding.

endocrine system   The system of ductless glands whose secretions are released directly into the bloodstream and affect organs elsewhere in the body (e.g., adrenal gland).

endorphin   A drug produced within the brain itself whose effects and chemical composition are similar to such pain-relieving opiates as morphine.

endotherms   Organisms that control their body temperature by using mechanisms that are mostly internal or physiological. Previously called *warm blooded*.

epinephrine (adrenaline)   A neurotransmitter released into the bloodstream by the adrenal medulla as part of sympathetic activation (e.g., racing heart).

episodic memory   Memory for particular events in one's own life (e.g., I missed the train this morning). *See also* generic memory.

equipotentiality   The claim (contradicted by much evidence) that organisms can learn to associate any response with any reward or to associate any pair of stimuli.

erogenous zones   In psychoanalytic theory, the mouth, anus, and genitals. These regions are particularly sensitive to touch. According to Freud, the various pleasures associated with each of them have a common element, which is sexual.

escape learning   Instrumental learning in which reinforcement consists of the reduction or cessation of an aversive stimulus (e.g., electric shock). *See also* avoidance learning, punishment training.

estrogen   A female sex hormone that dominates the first half of the female cycle through ovulation.

estrus   In mammals, the period in the cycle when the female is sexually receptive (in heat).

ethology   A branch of zoology concerned with the behavior of animals under natural conditions.

event-related potentials   A pattern of electroencephalogram (EEG) reactions to a particular response, usually averaged together over many trials.

exchange relationship   A hypothesized type of social relationship in which the relationship depends on reciprocity; if goods (or esteem or loyalty) are given by one of the partners in the relationship, then the other must respond in kind.

excitation threshold   The voltage difference between a neuron's interior and exterior that, if exceeded, causes the neuron to fire. This voltage is about -55 millivolts in mammals. If the voltage reaches this threshold (from a "resting" voltage of -70 millivolts), the neuron's membrane destabilizes, leading to an action potential.

excitation transfer effects   The transfer of autonomic arousal from one situation to another, as when strenuous exercise leads to an increased arousal when presented with aggression-arousing or erotic stimuli.

existential therapy   A humanistic therapy that emphasizes people's free will and tries to help them achieve a personal outlook that will give meaning to their lives.

experiment   A study in which the investigator manipulates one (or more than one) variable (the independent variable) to determine its effect on the research participant's response (the dependent variable).

expert systems   Computer problem-solving programs with a very narrow scope that only deal with problems in a limited domain of knowledge (e.g., the diagnosis of infectious diseases).

explanatory style   The characteristic manner in which a person explains good or bad fortunes that befall him. An explanatory style in which bad fortunes are generally attributed to internal, global, and stable causes may create a predisposition that makes a person vulnerable to depression.

explicit memory   Memory retrieval in which there is awareness of remembering at the time of retrieval. *See also* implicit memory.

expressive aphasia   A disorder in which the patient has difficulty with the production of speech. Expressive aphasia is caused by a cortical lesion that damages one's ability to organize the movements necessary for speech production into a unified sequence.

externality hypothesis   The hypothesis that some and perhaps all obese people are relatively unresponsive to their own internal hunger state but are much more susceptible to signals from without.

external validity   The degree to which a study's participants, stimuli, and procedures adequately reflect the world as it actually is.

extinction   In classical conditioning, the weakening of the tendency of the conditioned stimulus (CS) to elicit the conditioned response (CR) by unreinforced presentations of the CS. In instrumental conditioning, a decline in the tendency to perform the instrumental response brought about by unreinforced occurrences of that response.

extralinguistic factors   Factors outside of the language itself that influence (and usually ease) language comprehension. Examples include gestures and the scene that is being discussed.

extrapyramidal system   One of the two cerebral motor control systems; it is older in evolutionary terms, and it controls relatively gross movements of the head, limbs, and trunk.

extroversion/introversion   In Eysenck's system, a trait dimension that refers to the main direction of a person's energies; toward the outer world of objects and other people (extroversion) or toward the inner world of one's own thoughts and feelings (introversion).

facial feedback hypothesis   The hypothesis that sensory feedback from the facial muscles will lead to subjective feelings of emotion that correspond to the particular facial pattern. *See* basic emotions.

factor analysis   A statistical method for studying the interrelations among various tests, the object of which is to discover what the tests have in common and whether these communalities can be ascribed to one or several factors that run through all or some of these tests.

false alarm   *See* payoff matrix.

family resemblance structure Overlap of features among members of a category such that no members of the category have all of the features but all members have some of them.

family therapy A general term for a number of therapies that treat the family or couple, operating on the assumption that the key to family or marital distress is not necessarily in the pathology of any individual family member but is rather in the interrelationships within the family.

feature detectors Neurons in the retina or brain that respond to specific features of the stimulus, such as movement, orientation, and so on.

feature net A model of pattern recognition in which there is a network of detectors, with feature detectors at the bottom.

Fechner's law The assertion that the strength of a sensation is proportional to the logarithm of physical stimulus intensity.

feedback system A system in which some action produces a consequence that affects (feeds back on) the action. In negative feedback, the consequence stops or reverses the action (e.g., thermostat-controlled furnace). In positive feedback, the consequence strengthens the action (e.g., rocket that homes in on airplanes).

fetus The stage in gestation following the embryonic stage. In humans, from about eight weeks until birth.

figure-ground organization The segregation of the visual field into a part (the figure) that stands out against the rest (the ground).

file-drawer problem A tendency for disappointing or negative results not to be reported (and so merely dumped into a file drawer). This tendency can cause a bias in the pattern of evidence available.

final common path The single neural output upon which two groups of nerve fibers converge.

fixation (1) In problem solving, the result of rigid mental sets that makes it difficult for people to approach a problem in new and different ways. (2) In Freud's theory of personality, the lingering attachment to an earlier stage of pleasure seeking, even after a new stage has been attained.

fixed-action patterns Term used by ethologists to describe stereotyped, species-specific behaviors triggered by genetically preprogrammed releasing stimuli.

fixed-interval schedule *See* interval schedule.

fixed-ratio schedule *See* ratio schedule.

flashbulb memories Vivid, detailed memories said to be produced by unexpected and emotionally important events.

flooding A form of behavior therapy based on concepts derived from classical conditioning in which the patient exposes herself to whatever she is afraid of, thus extinguishing her fear. *See also* implosion therapy.

flow chart (1) In computer science, a diagram that shows the step-by-step operation of a computer program. (2) In human cognition, similar diagrams that show the hypothesized flow of information as it is thought to be processed by the human mind.

fluid intelligence The ability, which is said to decline with age, to deal with essentially new problems. *See also* crystallized intelligence.

Flynn effect An effect observed worldwide over the last several decades in which IQ scores seem to be rising.

foot-in-the-door technique A technique of persuasion, initially used by door-to-door salespeople, in which one first obtains a small concession that then makes it easier to persuade the target to make a subsequent, larger concession.

forced compliance effect An individual forced to act or speak publicly in a manner contrary to his own beliefs may change his own views in the direction of the public action. But this will happen only if his reward for the false public pronouncement is relatively small. If the reward is large, there is no dissonance and hence no attitude change. *See also* cognitive dissonance.

forebrain In mammals, the bulk of the brain. Its foremost region includes the cerebral hemispheres; its rear includes the thalamus and hypothalamus.

forgetting curve A curve showing the inverse relationship between memory and the retention interval.

formal operations period In Piaget's theory, the period from about age eleven on, when genuinely abstract mental operations can be undertaken (e.g., the ability to entertain hypothetical possibilities).

forward pairing A classical conditioning procedure in which the conditioned stimulus (CS) precedes the unconditioned stimulus (US). This contrasts with simultaneous pairing, in which CS and US are presented simultaneously, and backward pairing, in which CS follows US. *See also* classical conditioning, conditioned stimulus (CS), unconditioned stimulus (US).

fovea The area of the retina on which an image falls when the viewer is looking directly at the source of the image. Acuity is greater when the image falls on the fovea than it is when it falls on any other portion of the retina.

framing A heuristic that affects the subjective desirability of an event by changing the standard of reference for judging the desirability of that event.

fraternal twins Twins that arise from two different eggs that are (simultaneously) fertilized by different sperm cells. Their genetic similarity is no greater than that between ordinary siblings. *See also* identical twins.

free association Method used in psychoanalytic therapy in which the patient is to say anything that comes to her mind, no matter how apparently trivial, unrelated, or embarrassing.

free recall A test of memory that asks for as many items in a list as a research participant can recall regardless of order.

frequency (1) In sound waves or light waves, the number of wave peaks per second. In sound, frequency governs the perceived pitch of the sound; in light, frequency governs the perceived hue of the light. (2) In statistical analysis, the number of occurrences of a particular observation.

frequency distribution An arrangement in which scores are tabulated by how often they occur.

Freud's theory of dreams A theory that holds that at bottom all dreams are attempts to fulfill a wish. The wish fulfillment is in the latent dream, which represents the sleeper's hidden desires. This latent dream is censored and reinterpreted to avoid anxiety. It reemerges in more acceptable form as the manifest dream, the dream the sleeper remembers upon awakening.

frontal lobe The lobe in each cerebral hemisphere that includes the prefrontal area and the motor projection areas.

function morphemes *See* content morphemes.

function word A word such as *who* or *that* that makes explicit the relationship among various phrases within a sentence.

functional fixedness A set that encourages one to think of objects in terms of their normal function.

functional MRI (fMRI) scan An adaptation of the standard MRI procedures that can measure fast-changing physiology (mostly blood flow and oxygen use) within the brain.

fundamental attribution error The tendency to attribute behaviors to dispositional qualities while underrating the role of the situation. *See also* actor-observer difference, attribution theory, self-serving bias.

GABA (gamma-amino butyric acid) The most widely distributed inhibitory transmitter of the central nervous system.

galvanic skin response (GSR)   A drop in the electrical resistance of the skin, widely used as an index of autonomic reaction.

ganglion   A neural control center that integrates messages from different receptor cells and coordinates the activity of different muscle fibers; plural: *ganglia*.

ganglion cells   In the retina, one of the intermediate links between the receptor cells and the brain. The axons of the ganglion cells converge into a bundle of fibers that leave the eyeball as the optic nerve. *See also* bipolar cells.

gender constancy   The recognition that being male or female is to all intents and purposes irrevocable.

gender identity   The inner sense of being male or female. *See also* gender role, sexual orientation.

gender role   The set of external behavior patterns a given culture deems appropriate for each sex. *See also* gender identity, sexual orientation.

gene   The unit of hereditary transmission, located at a particular place in a given chromosome. Both members of each chromosome pair have corresponding locations at which there are genes that carry instructions about the same characteristic (e.g., eye color). If one member of a gene pair is dominant and the other is recessive, the dominant gene will exert its effect regardless of what the recessive gene calls for. The characteristic called for by the recessive gene will only be expressed if the other member of the gene pair is also recessive. *See also* chromosomes.

general intelligence *(g)*   According to Charles Spearman, a mental attribute that is called upon in any intellectual task a person has to perform.

generalization decrement   In classical conditioning, the weakening of a response to a new stimulus compared to the response elicited by the original conditioned stimulus (CS). The greater the difference between the new stimulus and the original CS, the larger the generalization decrement. In instrumental conditioning, a similar effect occurs when a new discriminative stimulus is presented instead of the original stimulus.

generalization gradient   The curve that shows the relationship between the tendency to respond to a new stimulus and its similarity to the original conditioned stimulus (CS).

generalized anxiety disorder   A mental disorder whose primary characteristic is an all-pervasive, "free-floating" anxiety. A member of the diagnostic category "anxiety disorders," which also includes phobias and obsessive-compulsive disorders. *See also* anxiety disorders.

general paresis   A psychosis characterized by progressive decline in cognitive and motor function culminating in death, reflecting a deteriorating brain condition produced by syphilitic infection.

generic memory   Memory for items of knowledge as such (e.g., The capital of France is Paris), independent of the occasion on which they are learned. *See also* episodic memory.

genetic sex   A designation of an organism's sex based entirely on the genetic pattern, whether XY (male) or XX (female). Often contrasted with morphological sex, which is based on anatomical features.

genital stage   In psychoanalytic theory, the stage of psychosexual development reached in adult sexuality in which sexual pleasure involves not only one's own gratification but also the social and bodily satisfaction brought to another person.

genotype   The genetic blueprint of an organism which may or may not be overtly expressed by its phenotype. *See also* phenotype.

geons   Primitive geometric figures, such as cubes, cylinders, and pyramids, from which all other shapes are created through combination. In many models of pattern recognition, the organism must first determine which geons are present and then determine what the objects are.

Gerstmann syndrome   A syndrome that results from damage to the left parietal lobe which involves a cluster of difficulties, including the inability to form mathematical calculations, the loss of handwriting, and confusion about which direction is left and which is right. *See also* neglect syndrome.

Gestalt   An organized whole such as a visual form or a melody.

Gestalt psychology   A theoretical approach that emphasizes the role of organized wholes (Gestalten) in perception and other psychological processes.

glands   Bodily organs that produce hormones.

glial cell   Cells in the brain that act as guidewires for growing neurons, provide a supportive scaffolding for mature neurons, and form the myelin sheath and blood-brain barrier.

glove anesthesia   A condition sometimes seen in conversion disorders, in which there is an anesthesia of the entire hand with no loss of feeling above the wrist. This symptom makes no organic sense given the anatomical arrangement of the nerve trunks and indicates that the condition has a psychological basis.

glucose   The form of sugar that is the major source of energy for most bodily tissues. If plentiful, much of it is converted into glycogen and stored.

glucose receptors   Receptors in the brain (in the area of the hypothalamus) that detect the amount of glucose in the bloodstream.

glutamate   The most critical neurotransmitter in the retina, it also appears to be important for long-term memory and the perception of pain.

glycogen   A stored form of metabolic energy derived from glucose. To be used, it must first be converted back into glucose.

gonads   The body's primary sexual organs—ovaries in the female, testes in the male.

good continuation   A factor in visual grouping. Contours tend to be seen in such a way that their direction is altered as little as possible.

gray matter   That portion of the brain that appears gray. The color reflects the absence of myelination (which makes the tissue appear white). The gray matter consists of the cell bodies, dendrites, and unmyelinated axons that comprise the nervous system's microcircuitry.

group-factor theory of intelligence   A factor-analytic approach to intelligence-test performance which argues that intelligence is a composite of separate abilities (group factors such as verbal ability, spatial ability, etc.) without a sovereign capacity that enters into each. *See also* factor analysis, general intelligence.

group therapy   Psychotherapy of several persons at one time.

guevedoces syndrome   A genetic disorder in which the external genitals appear to be female, but, at puberty, develop into normal male genitals.

habituation   A decline in the tendency to respond to stimuli that have become familiar. While short-term habituation dissipates in a matter of minutes, long-term habituation may persist for days or weeks.

habituation procedure   A widely used method for studying infant perception. After some exposure to a visual stimulus, an infant becomes habituated and stops looking at it. The extent to which a new stimulus leads to renewed interest and resumption of looking is taken as a measure of the extent to which the infant regards this new stimulus as different from the old one to which he became habituated.

hair cells   The auditory receptors in the cochlea, lodged between the basilar membrane and other membranes above.

hallucination   Perceived experiences that occur in the absence of actual sensory stimulation.

heritability ratio (H)   This refers to the relative importance of heredity and environment in determining the observed variation of a particular trait. More specifically, *H* is the proportion of the variance of the trait in a given population that is attributable to genetic factors.

hermaphrodite A person who possesses portions of both female and male reproductive tissues. *See also* pseudohermaphroditism.

hertz (Hz) A measure of frequency in number of cycles per second.

heterosexuality A sexual orientation leading to a choice of sexual partners of the opposite sex.

heuristics In computer problem solving, a procedure that has often worked in the past and is likely, but not certain, to work again. *See also* algorithm.

hierarchical organization Organization in which narrower categories are subsumed under broader ones, which are subsumed under still broader ones, and so on. Often expressed in the form of a tree diagram.

hierarchy of needs According to Maslow and other adherents of the humanistic approach, human needs are arranged in a hierarchy with physiological needs such as hunger at the bottom, safety needs further up, the need for attachment and love still higher, and the desire for esteem yet higher. At the very top of the hierarchy is the striving for self-actualization. By and large, people will only strive for the higher-order needs when the lower ones are fulfilled. *See also* peak experience, self-actualization.

higher-order conditioning In classical conditioning, a procedure by which a new stimulus comes to elicit the conditioned response (CR) by virtue of being paired with an effective conditioned stimulus (CS) (e.g., first pairings of tone and food, then pairings of bell and tone, until finally the bell elicits salivation by itself).

hindbrain The rearmost portion of the brain just above the spinal cord, which includes the pons, medulla, and cerebellum.

hippocampus A structure in the temporal lobe that is involved in long-term and spatial memory.

histogram A graphic rendering of a frequency distribution which depicts the distribution by a series of contiguous rectangles. *See also* frequency distribution.

hit *See* payoff matrix.

homeostasis The body's tendency to maintain the conditions of its internal environment by various forms of self-regulation.

homogamy The tendency of like to mate with like.

homosexuality A sexual orientation leading to a choice of partners of the same sex.

hormone A chemical released by one of the glands. Hormones travel through the bloodstream and control a number of bodily functions, including metabolic rate, arousal level, sugar output of the liver, and so on.

hue A perceived dimension of visual stimuli whose meaning is close to the term *color* (e.g., red, blue).

humanistic approach to personality Asserts that what is most important about people is how they achieve their selfhood and actualize their potentialities. *See also* behavioral-cognitive approach, psychodynamic approach, situationism, sociocultural approach, trait theory.

humanistic therapies Methods of treatment that emphasize personal growth and self-fulfillment. They try to be relatively nondirective, since their emphasis is on helping the clients achieve the capacity for making their own choices. *See also* nondirective techniques.

Huntington's disease A progressive hereditary disorder that involves degeneration of the basal ganglia and that results in jerky limb movements, facial twitches, and uncontrolled writhing of the body.

hyperphagia Voracious, chronic overeating brought about by a lesion of the ventromedial region of the hypothalamus.

hypnosis A temporary, trancelike state that can be induced in normal persons. During hypnosis, various hypnotic or posthypnotic suggestions sometimes produce effects that resemble some of the symptoms of conversion disorders. *See also* conversion disorders.

hypochondriasis A disorder in which the sufferer believes he has a specific disease and typically goes from doctor to doctor to be evaluated for it.

hypomania A mild manic state in which the individual seems infectiously merry, extremely talkative, charming, and indefatigable.

hypothalamus A small structure at the base of the forebrain that plays a vital role in the control of the autonomic nervous system, of the endocrine system, and of the major biological drives.

hysteria An older term for a group of presumably psychogenic disorders including conversion disorders and dissociative disorders. Since DSM-III, it is no longer used as a diagnostic category, in part because of an erroneous implication that the condition is more prevalent in women (Greek *hystera*—womb). *See also* conversion disorders, dissociative disorders, glove anesthesia.

id In Freud's theory, a term for the most primitive reactions of human personality, consisting of blind strivings for immediate biological satisfaction regardless of cost. *See also* ego and superego.

ideas of reference A characteristic of some mental disorders, notably schizophrenia, in which the patient begins to think that external events are specially related to her personally (e.g., "People walk by and follow me").

identical twins Twins that originate from a single fertilized egg that then splits into two exact replicas that develop into two genetically identical individuals. *See also* fraternal twins.

identification In psychoanalytic theory, a mechanism whereby a child (typically) models himself or herself on the same-sex parent in an effort to become like him or her.

ill-defined problems *See* well-defined problems.

illusory conjunction A pattern of errors found, for example, in visual search tasks, in which observers correctly perceive the features present (redness, greenness, roundness, angularity) but misperceive how these were combined in the display (and so they might see a green O and a red X when, in fact, a green X and red O were presented).

illusory correlation A perception that two facts or observations tend to occur together, even though they do not, such as the erroneous belief that all accountants are introverted.

implicit memory Memory retrieval in which there is no awareness of remembering at the time of retrieval. *See also* explicit memory.

implicit theories of personality Beliefs about the way in which different patterns of behavior of people hang together and why they do so. *See also* illusory correlation.

implosion therapy A form of behavior therapy related to flooding in which the patient exposes himself to whatever he is afraid of in its most extreme form, but does so in imagination rather than in real life (e.g., a person afraid of dogs has to imagine himself surrounded by a dozen snarling Dobermans). *See* flooding.

impossible figure A figure that appears acceptable when looked at locally but poses unresolvable visual contradictions when seen as a whole.

impression management According to Erving Goffman, the characteristic of much social interaction in which people maintain the image that goes along with their social or professional role.

imprinting A learned attachment that is formed at a particular period in life (the critical, or sensitive, period) and is difficult to reverse (e.g., the duckling's acquired tendency to follow whatever moving stimulus it encounters twelve to twenty-four hours after hatching).

incidental learning   Learning without trying to learn (e.g., as in a study in which participants judge a speaker's vocal quality when she recites a list of words and are later asked to produce as many of the words as they can recall). *See also* intentional learning.

incremental validity   The extent to which a test adds to the predictive validity already provided by other measures (e.g., the extent to which a projective technique adds to what is already known through an ordinary interview).

incubation   The hypothetical process of continuing to work on a problem unconsciously after one has ceased to work on that problem consciously. Most contemporary investigators are skeptical about whether such a process truly exists.

independent variable   *See* experiment.

individualism   A cultural pattern in which people are considered to be fundamentally independent and in which the emphasis is on the ways a person can stand out through achieving private goals. Individualists societies include the dominant cultures of the United States, western Europe, Canada, and Australia. *See also* collectivism.

induced motion   Perceived movement of an objectively stationary stimulus that is enclosed by a moving framework.

inductive reasoning   Reasoning in which one observes a number of particular instances and tries to determine a general rule that covers them all.

information processing   A general term for the presumed operations whereby the crude raw materials provided by the senses are refashioned into items of knowledge. Among these operations are perceptual organization, comparison with items stored in memory, and so on.

inner ear   The portion of the ear in which the actual transduction of sound takes place.

insightful learning   Learning by understanding the relations among the components of the problem; often contrasted with "blind trial and error" and documented by wide and appropriate transfer if tested in a new situation.

instrumental conditioning   Also called operant conditioning. A form of learning in which a reinforcer (e.g., food) is given only if the animal performs the instrumental response (e.g., pressing a lever). In effect, what has to be learned is the relationship between the response and the reinforcer. *See also* classical conditioning.

insulin   A hormone with a crucial role in using nutrients. One of its functions is to help promote the conversion of glucose into glycogen.

Intelligence Quotient (IQ)   A ratio measure to indicate whether a child's mental age (MA) is ahead or behind his chronological age (CA); specifically IQ = $100 \times$ MA/CA. *See also* deviation IQ, mental age.

intentional learning   Learning when informed that there will later be a test of learning. *See also* incidental learning.

interference theory of forgetting   The hypothesis that items are forgotten because they are somehow interfered with by other items learned before or after.

intermittent reinforcement   *See* partial reinforcement.

internalization   The process whereby moral codes are adopted by the child so that they control her behavior even when there are no external rewards or punishments.

internal validity   The degree to which a study is successful at measuring what it purports to measure, with all confounds removed and the dependent variable sensibly measured.

interneurons   Neurons that carry information from one neuron to another (rather than to a gland or muscle fiber or from a sensory receptor).

interposition   A monocular depth cue in which objects that are farther away are blocked from view by any other opaque object obstructing their optical path to the eye.

intersexual   A child who is not clearly male or female, in some cases because of genetic factors, in others because of morphology.

interval scale   A scale in which equal differences between scores can be treated as equal so that the scores can be added or subtracted. *See also* categorical scale, nominal scale, ordinal scale, ratio scale.

interval schedule   A reinforcement schedule in which reinforcement is delivered for a first response made after a given interval of time has elapsed. In a fixed-interval schedule, the interval is always the same. In a variable-interval schedule, the interval varies around a specified average.

intracranial recording   The recording of brain activity by monitoring chemical or electrical activity from inside the skull.

intrinsic motivation   Motivation that seems inherent in an activity itself, as when we engage in an activity for its own sake or merely because it is fun.

introversion   *See* extroversion/introversion.

invariant   Some aspect of the proximal stimulus pattern that remains unchanged despite various transformations of the stimulus.

ions   Atoms or molecules that have gained or lost electrons, thus acquiring a positive or negative charge.

iris   The smooth circular muscle in the eye that surrounds the pupil and contracts or dilates under reflex control in order to govern the amount of light entering.

isolation   A mechanism of defense in which anxiety arousing memories are retained but without the emotion that accompanied them.

James-Lange theory of emotions   A theory that asserts that the subjective experience of emotion is the awareness of one's own bodily reactions in the presence of certain arousing stimuli.

just-noticeable difference (jnd)   *See* difference threshold.

kinesthesis   A general term for sensory information generated by receptors in the muscles, tendons, and joints which informs us of our skeletal movement.

kin-selection hypothesis   *See* altruism.

Korsakoff's syndrome   A brain disorder characterized by serious memory disturbances. The most common cause is extreme and chronic alcohol use.

latency   General term for the interval before some reaction occurs. Often *response latency*.

latency period   In psychoanalytic theory, a stage in psychosexual development in which sexuality lies essentially dormant, roughly from ages five to twelve.

latent dream   *See* Freud's theory of dreams.

latent learning   Learning that occurs without being manifested by performance.

lateral fissure   The visible fissure in the brain that separates the frontal lobe from the temporal lobe.

lateral geniculate nucleus   An important way station between the eyeball and the visual cortex in the brain.

lateral hypothalamus   A region of the hypothalamus which is sometimes said to be a "hunger center" and to be in an antagonistic relation to a supposed "satiety center," the ventromedial region of the hypothalamus.

lateral inhibition The tendency of adjacent neural elements of the visual system to inhibit each other; it underlies brightness contrast and the accentuation of contours. *See also* brightness contrast.

lateralization An asymmetry of function of the two cerebral hemispheres. In most right-handers, the left hemisphere is specialized for language functions, while the right hemisphere is better at various visual and spatial tasks.

law of effect A theory that the tendency of a stimulus to evoke a response is strengthened if the response is followed by reward and is weakened if the response is not followed by reward. Applied to instrumental learning, this theory states that as trials proceed, incorrect bonds will weaken while the correct bond will be strengthened.

laws of perceptual organization Max Wertheimer's formulation describing our predisposition to group stimuli based on their proximity, similarity, and good continuation.

learned helplessness A condition created by exposure to inescapable aversive events. This retards or prevents learning in subsequent situations in which escape or avoidance is possible.

learned helplessness theory of depression The theory that depression is analogous to learned helplessness effects produced in the laboratory. *See also* learned helplessness.

learned taste aversion A specialized form of learning in which an organism learns to avoid a taste after just one pairing of that taste with illness. For example, an animal will avoid a food that on an earlier occasion made it sick.

learning curve A curve in which some index of learning (e.g., the number of drops of saliva in Pavlov's classical conditioning experiment) is plotted against trials or sessions.

learning model As defined in the text, a subcategory of the pathology model that (1) views mental disorders as the result of some form of faulty learning, and (2) believes that these should be treated by behavior therapists according to the laws of classical and instrumental conditioning or by cognitive therapists who try to affect faulty modes of thinking. *See also* behavior therapy, cognitive therapy, medical model, pathology model, psychoanalytic model.

learning set The increased ability to solve various problems, especially in discrimination learning, as a result of previous experience with problems of a similar kind.

lens The portion of the eye that bends light rays and thus can focus an image on the retina.

leptin A chemical produced by the adipose cells that seems to signal that plenty of fat is stored and that no more fat is needed. This signal may diminish eating.

lesions The damage incurred by an area of the brain.

lexical access The process of recognizing and understanding a word, which is presumably achieved by making contact with (accessing) the word in the mental lexicon.

lexical decision task A task in which the participant must decide as quickly as possible whether a stimulus *(book, trup, filt)* is or is not a word.

lightness constancy The tendency to perceive the lightness of an object as more or less the same despite the fact that the light reflected from the object changes with the illumination that falls upon it.

limbic system A set of brain structures including the amygdala, hippocampus, cortex, and parts of the thalamus and hypothalamus. It is believed to be involved in the control of emotional behavior and motivation.

line of best fit A line drawn through the points in a scatter diagram. It yields the best prediction of one variable when given the value of the other variable.

lithium carbonate A drug used in the treatment of mania and bipolar disorders.

lobotomy *See* prefrontal lobotomy.

localization of function The process of determining what each region of the brain contributes to which aspects of thinking and behavior.

local representations A model of cognitive organization, especially semantic memory, in which each concept is represented by a single node or, more plausibly, a group of nodes. *See also* distributed representations, node.

lock-and-key model The theory that neurotransmitter molecules will only affect the postsynaptic membrane if their shape fits into that of certain synaptic receptor molecules.

longitudinal fissure The front-to-back cleavage that divides the left and right hemispheres of the brain.

longitudinal study A developmental study in which the same person is tested at various ages.

long-term memory Those parts of the memory system that are currently dormant and inactive, but have enormous storage capacity. *See also* stage theory of memory, working memory.

long-term potentiation (LTP) A form of cellular plasticity in which a postsynaptic neuron becomes more sensitive (potentiated) to the signal received from the presynaptic neuron. This potentiation is usually produced by a rapid and sustained burst of firing by the presynaptic neuron. The potentiation can then spread to other presynaptic neurons provided that they have fired in the past at the same time as the presynaptic cell that produced the potentiation in the first place. *See also* activity dependence.

looming A rapid magnification of a form in the visual field that generally signals impending impact.

loss aversion A widespread pattern, evident in many aspects of decision making, in which people seem particularly sensitive to losses and eager to avoid them. In many cases, this manifests itself as an increased willingness to take risks in hopes of reducing the loss.

luminance ratio The ratio between the light reflected off a figure and that reflected off the background against which the figure is seen. Whatever the illumination, the ratio remains the same.

Mach bands The accentuated edges between two adjacent regions that differ in brightness. This sharpening is maximal at the borders where the distance between the two regions is smallest and the contrast most striking.

magic number According to George Miller, the number (seven plus or minus two) that represents the holding capacity of the working memory system.

magnetic resonance imaging (MRI) *See* MRI.

magno cells Ganglion cells found largely in the periphery of the retina that, because of their sensitivity to brightness changes, are particularly suited to the perception of motion and depth.

maintenance rehearsal Repetition to keep material in working memory for a while. In contrast to elaborative rehearsal, this confers little long-term benefit. *See also* elaborative rehearsal.

major depression A mood disorder in which patients are disabled by guilt or sadness (especially in Western cultures), experience a loss of energy, pleasure and motivation, and disturbances of sleep, diet, and other bodily functions.

major tranquilizers *See* classical antipsychotics.

mania A mood disorder characterized by racing thoughts, pressured speech, irritability or euphoria, and marked impairments in judgment. *See also* bipolar disorder.

manic-depressive psychosis *See* bipolar disorder.

manifest dream *See* Freud's theory of dreams.

MAO inhibitors *See* monoamine oxidase inhibitors.

marital therapy *See* family therapy.

matching hypothesis The hypothesis that persons seek romantic or sexual partners who possess a similar level of physical attractiveness.

matching to sample A procedure in which an organism has to choose which of two alternative stimuli is the same as a third, sample stimulus.

mate guarding A male strategy of insuring paternity by remaining near the female and preventing her from mating with other males.

maturation A genetically programmed growth process that is relatively unaffected by environmental conditions (e.g., flying in sparrows and walking in humans).

maximum-likelihood principle The assertion that we interpret the proximal stimulus pattern as that external stimulus object that most probably produced it.

mean (M) *See* measure of central tendency.

means-end analysis An important strategy for problem solving in which one's current position and resources are continually evaluated with respect to one's goal.

measure of central tendency A single number intended to summarize an entire distribution of experimental results. Three commonly used measures of central tendency are: (1) the mode, or the score that occurs most frequently; (2) the median, or the point that divides the distribution into two equal halves; and (3) the mean, or the arithmetic average.

medial forebrain bundle (MFB) A tract of fibers that runs through the base of the forebrain and parts of the hypothalamus. Electric stimulation of this bundle is usually experienced as rewarding.

median *See* measure of central tendency.

medical model As defined in the text, a subcategory of the pathology model that holds (1) that the underlying pathology is organic and (2) that the treatment should be conducted by physicians. *See also* learning model, pathology model, psychodynamic model.

medulla Part of the hindbrain and the rearmost portion of the brain, just adjacent to the spinal cord. It is involved in the control of respiration, circulation, balance, and protective reflexes such as coughing and sneezing.

melatonin A neurohormone secreted by the pineal gland that is involved in regulating the sleep-waking cycle.

memory reconstruction The automatic filling-in of gaps in memory, typically using general knowledge and expectations (e.g., remembering books on a professor's desk when in fact there were none).

memory search A cognitive process preceding memory retrieval that usually occurs very quickly and outside our awareness.

memory span The number of items that can be recalled after a single presentation. *See also* magic number.

memory trace The physical basis of memory; a change in the nervous system produced by an experience. The exact nature of this change is still uncertain.

menstrual flow The discharge consisting of the sloughed-off uterine lining that was built up in preparation for a fertilized ovum, that signals the onset of menstruation.

menstrual synchrony The phenomenon wherein women who live together tend to develop menstrual cycles that roughly coincide with each other, even though their periods were very different at the outset.

mental age (MA) A score devised by Alfred Binet to represent a child's test performance. A child's MA is assessed by determining what mental tasks he can do sucessfully. If he can perform tasks generally performed well by six-year-olds but not tasks generally performed well by seven-year-olds, his MA is six, and so on.

mental images Analogical representations that reserve some of the characteristic attributes of our senses.

mental representations Internal symbols that stand for something but are not equivalent to it, such as internalized actions, images, or words.

mental retardation Usually defined as an IQ of 70 or below.

mental rotation A task in which participants are presented with a rotated figure and must discern whether the figure is normal or, say, mirror-reversed. Participants apparently must visualize the figure rotated to an upright position before responding.

mental set The predisposition to perceive, remember, or think of one thing rather than another.

meta-analysis A statistical technique for combining the results of many studies even when the studies used different methods to collect the data. This technique has been useful in studies on the outcome of psychotherapy.

metacognition A general term for knowledge about knowledge, as in knowing that we do or don't remember something.

method of loci A mnemonic technique that requires the learner to visualize each of the items she wants to remember in a different spatial location (locus). Recall requires that each location be mentally inspected for the item placed there.

microcircuitry Networks of interneurons within which most of the brain's information processing occurs.

midbrain The portion of the brain between hindbrain and forebrain that is involved in arousal, the sleep-waking cycle, and auditory and visual targeting.

middle ear An antechamber to the inner ear which amplifies the sound-produced vibrations of the eardrum and transfers them to the cochlea. *See also* cochlea.

minimal-sufficiency principle A principle of socialization that holds that children can best internalize ways of acting deemed appropriate if influenced just enough to act as desired, but not enough such that they feel forced to comply.

Minnesota Multiphasic Personality Inventory (MMPI) A structured (objective) test of personality; the most widely used personality test. *See also* criterion groups.

miss *See* payoff matrix.

mnemonics Deliberate strategies for helping memory, many of which use imagery.

mode *See* measure of central tendency.

modeling In psychotherapy, a technique in which the therapist shows the patient some effective ways of handling problematic situations.

monoamine oxidase (MAO) inhibitors The first class of antidepressant medications, such as Nardil and Parnate. They are effective, especially for some kinds of depressions, but they impose difficult dietary restrictions on patients and have been largely superseded by the selective serotonin reuptake inhibitors (SSRIs).

monocular depth cues Features of the visual stimulus (e.g., linear perspective and motion parallax) that indicate depth even when it is viewed with one eye.

monogamy A mating pattern in which a reproductive partnership is based on a special, more or less permanent tie between one male and one female.

mood disorders A group of disorders distinguished primarily by changes in mood and motivation; these include bipolar disorder and major depression. *See also* bipolar disorder, depression, major depression, mania.

morpheme The smallest significant unit of meaning in a language (e.g., the word *boys* has two morphemes, *boy* and *s*).

morphological sex Classification as male or female based on one's sex organs and bodily appearance (e.g., ovaries, vagina, and smooth facial skin versus testes, penis, and facial hair).

Motherese A whimsical term for the singsong speech pattern that mothers and other adults generally employ when talking to infants.

motion detectors Cells in the visual cortex that are sensitive to an image moving across the retina.

motion parallax A depth cue provided by the fact that, as an observer moves, the images cast by nearby objects move more rapidly on the retina than the images cast by objects farther away.

motoneurons Neurons whose cell bodies are in the brain or spinal cord and whose axons terminate on muscle fibers.

motor projection areas *See* primary motor projection area.

MRI (magnetic resonance imaging) A noninvasive neurodiagnostic technique that relies on nuclear magnetic resonance. An MRI scan passes a high frequency alternating magnetic field through the brain to detect the different resonant frequencies of its nuclei. A computer then assembles this information to form a picture of brain structure. *See also* functional MRI (fMRI).

multiple intelligences In Howard Gardner's theory, the six essential, independent mental capacities, some of which are outside the traditional academic notions of intelligence, i.e., linguistic, logical-mathematical, spatial, musical, bodily-kinesthetic, and personal intelligence.

multiple personality disorder *See* dissociative identity disorder.

multiple sclerosis (MS) A progressive neurological disease wherein the immune system mistakenly destroys the myelin sheaths that comprise the brain's white matter, producing manifestations such as numbness, blindness, and paralysis.

myelin sheath The series of fatty wrappers, formed by special glial cells, that surround the axons of those neurons that must communicate over long distances in the nervous system and that allow for fast propagation of action potentials along those axons. *See also* nodes of Ranvier.

naloxone A drug that blocks the pain alleviation ascribed to endorphins and inhibits the effect of morphine and similar opiates by binding to opiate receptors in the brain.

nativism The view that some important aspects of perception and of other cognitive processes are innate.

natural selection The explanatory principle by which Darwin accounted for biological evolution. It refers to the greater number of offspring reaching sexual maturity shown by individual organisms possessing hereditary attributes that are advantageous in a given environment. Continued natural selection over many generations can result in wholesale changes in bodily form and behavior that may result in the development of new species.

negative afterimage In color vision, the persistence of an image that possesses the hue complementary to that of the stimulus (e.g., seeing a yellow afterimage after staring at a blue lamp), resulting from the operation of opponent processes.

negative cognitive schema For Aaron Beck, the core cognitive component of depression, consisting of an individual's automatic negative interpretations concerning himself, his future, and the world. *See also* explanatory style.

negative correlation *See* correlation.

negative feedback *See* feedback system.

negative symptoms of schizophrenia Symptoms that involve deficits in normal functioning, such as apathy, impoverished speech, and emotional blunting. *See also* positive symptoms of schizophrenia.

neglect syndrome The result of certain lesions of the right parietal lobe that leave a patient inattentive to stimuli to her left (e.g., not eating food on the left side of the plate) and result in her ignoring the left side of her body (e.g., putting makeup on only the right side of her face). *See also* Gerstmann syndrome.

neocortex The outermost, convoluted layer of the forebrain, often referred to merely as the *cortex*.

neo-Freudians A group of theorists who accept the psychoanalytic conception of unconscious conflicts but who differ with Freud in ways that can include (1) describing these conflicts in social terms rather than in terms of bodily pleasures or frustrations, (2) maintaining that many of these conflicts arise from specific cultural conditions instead of being biologically preordained.

neophobia Literally "fear of the new," the term is used in the study of food selection to refer to an animal's tendency to refuse unfamiliar foods.

nerve growth factors Neurochemicals that promote the sprouting of new neuronal connections.

nerve impulse *See* action potential.

network model Theories of cognitive organization, especially of semantic memory, which hold that items of information are represented by a system of nodes linked through associative connections. *See also* connectionist model, distributed representations, local representations, node.

neural networks Assemblies of associative elements that use parallel distributed processing and are hypothesized to function like neuronal circuits. *See also* parallel distributed processing.

neural plasticity The capacity for neurons to alter their functioning as a result of experience.

neural plate A small thickening, running the length of the embryo, from which the neural tube and, eventually, the nervous system, develop.

neural tube The tubular structure, formed by the fusion of the edges of the neural plate, from which the central nervous system (forebrain, midbrain, hindbrain, and spinal cord) develops.

neurodevelopmental disorder A disorder that stems from early brain abnormalities. Many researchers believe that schizophrenia is one such disorder and may originate in abnormal fetal brain development.

neuroimaging instruments Electronic devices that permit noninvasive study and depiction of brain structure or function. (*See also* CT scan, MRI scan, fMRI scan, and PET scan).

neuron A nerve cell.

neuropeptide Y (NPY) A chemical found widely in the brain and periphery. In the brain, it acts as a neurotransmitter; when administered at sites in and near the hypothalamus, it is a potent elicitor of eating.

neuropsychological assessment A specialized kind of psychological testing used to pinpoint the pattern of cognitive strengths and impairments that occurs with learning disabilities, aging, brain injuries, or diseases.

neurosis A broad term once used for mental disorders whose primary symptoms are anxiety or what seem to be defenses against anxiety. Since the adoption of DSM-III, the term has been dropped as a broad diagnostic label, and what were once considered the various subcategories of neurosis (e.g., phobia, anxiety, conversion and dissociative disorders) are now classified as separate disorders.

neuroticism A trait dimension that refers to emotional instability and maladjustment.

neurotoxin Any chemical poisonous to neurons.

neurotransmitters Chemicals liberated at the terminals of an axon that cross the synaptic gap and have excitatory or inhibitory effects on the postsynaptic neuron (e.g., norepinephrine, serotonin, GABA).

node A point in a network at which a number of connections converge.

nodes of Ranvier The gaps occurring between the glial-cell wrappers that form the myelin sheath surrounding many kinds of axons. The nodes are crucial to the rapidity at which neural impulses travel along myelinated axons.

nominal scale A scale in which responses are ordered only into different categories. *See also* categorical scale, interval scale, ordinal scale, and ratio scale.

nondirective techniques A set of psychotherapy techniques devised by Carl Rogers. As far as possible, the counselor refrains from offering advice or interpretation but only tries to clarify the patient's own feelings by echoing or restating what he says.

nonfluent aphasia Speech disorder in which the main difficulty is in speech production, often involving damage to Broca's area in the frontal lobe.

nonsense syllable Two consonants with a vowel between that do not form a word. Used to study associations between relatively meaningless items.

noradrenaline *See* norepinephrine.

norepinephrine (NE) The neurotransmitter found in the nerves of the sympathetic branch of the ANS. It is also one of the neurotransmitters involved in various arousal systems in the brain.

normal curve A symmetrical, bell-shaped curve that describes the probability of obtaining various combinations of chance events. It depicts the normal distribution, the frequency distribution of many physical and psychological attributes of humans and animals.

normal distribution A frequency distribution whose graphic representation has a symmetric, bell-shaped form—the normal curve. Its characteristics are often referred to when investigators test statistical hypotheses and make inferences about the population from a given sample.

norms In intelligence testing, the scores taken from a large sample of the population against which an individual's test scores are evaluated.

nucleus accumbens A dopamine-rich area in the forebrain that is critical in the physiology of reward.

null hypothesis The hypothesis that an obtained difference is merely a chance fluctuation from a population in which the true mean difference is zero. *See also* alternative hypothesis.

obesity A condition of marked overweight in animals and humans produced by a large variety of factors including genetic predisposition ("thrifty" genes), metabolic factors (oversecretion of insulin), and behavioral conditions (overeating, insufficient exercise).

object permanence The conviction that an object remains perceptually constant over time and exists even when it is out of sight. According to Piaget, this does not develop until infants are eight months old or more.

objective personality test *See* structured personality test.

observational learning A mechanism of socialization whereby a child observes another person who serves as a model and then proceeds to imitate what that model does.

observational study A study in which the investigator does not manipulate any of the variables but simply observes their relationship as they occur naturally.

obsessions *See* obsessive-compulsive disorder.

obsessive-compulsive disorder A disorder whose symptoms are obsessions (persistent and irrational thoughts or wishes) and compulsions (uncontrollable, repetitive acts), which seem to be defenses against anxiety. A member of a diagnostic category called anxiety disorders, which also includes generalized anxiety disorder and phobias.

occipital lobe The rearmost lobe in each cerebral hemisphere, which includes the primary visual projection area.

occlusion The partial concealment of one object by another object in front of it.

Oedipus complex In psychoanalytic theory, a general term for the cluster of impulses and conflicts that occurs during the phallic phase, at around age five. In boys, a fantasized form of intense, possessive sexual love is directed at the mother, which is soon followed by hatred for and fear of the father. As the fear mounts, the sexual feelings are pushed underground and the boy identifies with the father. An equivalent process in girls is called the Electra complex.

olfaction The sense of smell.

olfactory epithelium The small area at the top of the nasal cavity that contains receptors reactive to airborne chemicals.

one-trial learning In classical conditioning, the establishment of a conditioned response (CR) after only one pairing of conditioned stimulus (CS) and unconditioned stimulus (US).

operant In Skinner's system, an instrumental response. *See also* instrumental conditioning.

operant conditioning *See* instrumental conditioning.

opponent-process theory of color vision A theory of color vision that proposes three pairs of color antagonists: red-green, blue-yellow, and white-black. Excitation of one member of a pair automatically inhibits the other member.

opponent-process theory of motivation A theory that asserts that the nervous system tends to counteract any deviation from the neutral point on the pain-pleasure dimension. If the original stimulus is maintained, there is an attenuation of the emotional state one is in; if it is withdrawn, the opponent process reveals itself, and the emotional state swings sharply in the opposite direction.

optic flow The phenomenon wherein an object's retinal image enlarges as we approach the object and shrinks as we retreat from it. It is used as a depth cue by the visual system.

optic nerve The bundle of fibers that proceeds from each eyeball to the brain, made up of axons whose cell bodies are retinal ganglion cells.

oral character According to Freud, a personality type based on a fixation at the oral stage of development and whose manifestations can include passive dependency or "biting" hostility. *See also* oral stage.

oral stage In psychoanalytic theory, the earliest stage of psychosexual development during which the primary source of bodily pleasure is stimulation of the mouth and lips, as in sucking at the breast.

ordinal scale A scale in which responses are rank-ordered by relative magnitude but in which the intervals between successive ranks are not necessarily equal. *See also* categorical scale, interval scale, nominal scale, and ratio scale.

orexins Hormones synthesized in the lateral hypothalamus that are potent elicitors of eating.

organic brain syndromes Mental disorders that are reliably associated with definitive brain damage (e.g., Alzheimer's disease).

oscilloscope An electronic monitoring device that uses a cathode ray tube (CRT) to display electrical signals such as electrocardiograph signals or action potentials.

osmoreceptors Receptors that help to control water intake by responding to the concentrations of bodily fluids. *See also* volume receptors.

ossicles The three small bones in the ear that transmit vibrations from the eardrum to the oval window.

outcome measures In psychopathology, variables (e.g., mood ratings, work absenteeism) assessed to indicate whether a particular treatment was effective or cost-effective.

outer ear The portion of the structures of the ear that includes the earflap, the auditory canal, and the outer surface of the eardrum.

outgroup A social group with which one does not identify or to which one does not belong.

outgroup homogeneity effect A phenomenon related to stereotyping in which a member of a group (the in-group) tends to view members of another group (the out-group) as more alike (less varied) than are members of his or her own group.

oval window The membrane separating the middle ear from the inner ear.

ovum An egg cell manufactured in an ovary and contributed by the female as part of sexual reproduction.

pain The aversive sensation that usually accompanies tissue damage and alerts the organism to engage in protective or reparative behavior.

paired-associate method A procedure in which research participants learn to provide particular response terms to various stimulus items.

panic attack A sudden episode consisting of terrifying bodily symptoms such as labored breathing, choking, dizziness, tingling in the hands and feet, sweating, trembling, heart palpitations, and chest pain. Panic attacks occur in a number of mental disorders and are common in phobias, panic disorder, and post-traumatic stress disorder (PTSD).

panic disorder An anxiety disorder characterized by repeated or disabling panic attacks. *See also* anxiety disorders, panic attack.

parallel distributed processing (PDP) Models of cognitive processing in which the relevant symbolic representations do not correspond to any one unit of the network but to the state of the network as a whole.

parallel search The simultaneous comparison of a target stimulus to several items in memory. *See also* serial search.

parameter One of the ways that languages can depart from a hypothesized universal linguistic structure (e.g., omission of the subject in certain sentences).

paranoid schizophrenia A subcategory of schizophrenia. Its dominant symptom is a set of delusions that are often elaborately systematized, usually of grandeur or persecution.

paraphrase The relation between two sentences whose meanings (underlying structures) are the same but whose surface structures differ (e.g., "The boy hit the ball"/"The ball was hit by the boy").

parasympathetic system A division of the autonomic nervous system that serves vegetative functions and conserves bodily energies (e.g., slowing heart rate). Its action is often antagonistic to that of the sympathetic system.

parietal lobe The lobe in each cerebral hemisphere that lies between the occipital and frontal lobes, and that includes the primary sensory projection area.

Parkinson's disease A degenerative neurological disorder characterized by various motor difficulties that include tremor, muscular rigidity, and slowed movement. This disease involves degeneration of dopamine-releasing neurons in the basal ganglia of the forebrain, which are crucial for motor control.

parsing The dissection of a complex stimulus into meaningful parts.

partial reinforcement A condition in which repeated responses are reinforced only some of the time.

partial-reinforcement effect The fact that a response is much harder to extinguish if it was acquired during partial rather than continuous reinforcement.

parvo cells Ganglion cells found throughout the retina that, because of their sensitivity to differences in hue, are particularly suited to the perception of color and form.

pathogen Disease-producing microbes, including viruses, fungi, and bacteria, that can trigger the production of fever. In evolutionary terms, defense against pathogens may be the driving force behind sexual reproduction.

pathology model As used in the text, the pathology model describes a general conception of mental disorders which holds that (1) one can generally distinguish signs and symptoms from their underlying causes, and (2) these causes may be regarded as a form of disease. *See also* learning model, medical model, psychoanalytic model.

pattern recognition The process by which the perceptual system matches the form of a figure against the figure as represented in memory.

pattern theory The theory that a stimulus attribute is not coded by being sent along specific sensory fibers, but rather by a specific pattern of firing of all the relevant sensory fibers.

payoff matrix (1) In a signal detection experiment, a table that shows the costs and benefits of each of the four possible outcomes: a hit, reporting the stimulus when it is present; a correct negative, reporting it as absent when it is in fact absent; a miss, failing to report it when it is present; and a false alarm, reporting it as present when it is not.

peak experience As Maslow considered it, a profound and deeply felt moment in a person's life, sometimes said to be more common in self-actualized persons than in others. *See also* hierarchy of needs, self-actualization.

penis envy In psychoanalytic theory, the wish for a penis that normally ensues in females as part of the Elektra complex.

perceived locus of control A person's belief about the source of outcomes that befall her. That perceived source (locus) may be internal (the result of something she did) or external (the result of forces out of her control).

percentile rank The percentage of all the scores in a distribution that lie below a given score.

perceptual adaptation The gradual adjustment to various distortions of the perceptual world.

perceptual constancies Certain constant attributes of a distal object, such as its shape and size, that we are able to perceive despite vagaries of the proximal stimulus.

perceptual hypothesis The perceiver's assumption about what the stimulus is, tested as the perceptual system analyzes the stimulus for appropriate features.

perceptual parsing The process of grouping various visual elements of a scene appropriately, deciding which elements go together and which do not.

period of concrete operations *See* concrete operations period.

period of formal operations *See* formal operations period.

peripheral nervous system   The parts of the nervous system outside the central nervous system, including the cranial and spinal nerves that exit the skull and spinal column, respectively.

peripheral route to persuasion   *See* elaboration-likelihood model of persuasion.

periphery   In vision, the area toward the outside of the retina that has a high concentration of rods, is sensitive to dim light, and is responsible for colorless sensations.

permastore   Near-permanent retention of some kinds of items in memory, mostly involving semantic or general knowledge (e.g., multiplication tables, names of family members).

permissive pattern   A parental style in which parents try not to assert their authority and impose few restrictions or demands on their children.

perseveration   The tendency to repeat the same response inappropriately, typically accompanying the defects in strategy formation often observed with prefrontal lesions.

personal space   The physical region all around us whose intrusion we guard against. This aspect of human behavior has been likened to territoriality in animals.

personality inventories   Paper-and-pencil tests of personality that ask questions about feelings, desires, or customary behavior.

person–by–situation interaction   A view of influences on personality which holds that a person's behavior is the joint outcome of his predispositions and the particular situations he encounters. Thus, some people may on average be equally fearful, but while one is afraid of meeting people but unafraid of large animals, another may be afraid of large animals but be unafraid of meeting people. *See also* reciprocal interaction, situationism.

persuasive communications   Messages that openly try to convince us to act a certain way or to hold a particular belief.

PET (positron emission tomography) scan   A technique for examining brain function by observing the degree of metabolic activity of different regions of the brain.

phallic stage   In psychoanalytic theory, the stage of psychosexual development during which the child begins to regard his or her genitals as a major source of gratification.

phenothiazines   A kind of classical antipsychotic medication, such as Thorazine, that seems to be effective in alleviating the major positive signs and symptoms of schizophrenia.

phenotype   The overt appearance and behavior of an organism, regardless of its genetic blueprint. *See also* genotype.

phenylalanine   An amino acid that cannot be transformed due to an enzyme deficiency in those with phenylketonuria (PKU). In an infant with PKU, phenylalanine is converted into a toxic agent that accumulates in an infant's bloodstream and damages the developing nervous system.

phenylketonuria (PKU)   A condition in which one lacks the gene that enables one to metabolize phenylalanine. If detected early enough, this condition can be treated by means of a special diet. If not detected early, this disorder can cause a severe form of retardation. *See also* phenylalanine.

pheromones   Special chemicals secreted by many animals that trigger particular reactions in members of the same species. Humans seem to have a pheromone that regulates the timing of menstruation in females.

phi phenomenon   *See* apparent movement.

phobia   An anxiety disorder that is characterized by an intense and, at least on the surface, irrational fear. *See also* anxiety disorders, social phobia, specific phobia.

phoneme   The smallest significant unit of sound in a language. In English, it corresponds roughly to a letter of the alphabet (e.g., *apt, tap,* and *pat* are all made up of the same phonemes).

phonology   The rules in a language that govern the sequence in which phonemes can be arranged.

photoreceptor   One of the visual pigment-filled light-sensitive cells at the back of the retina, whether rods or cones.

phrase   A sequence of words within a sentence that functions as a unit.

phrase structure   The organization of sentences into phrases. Surface structure is the phrase organization of sentences as they are spoken or written. Underlying structure is the phrase organization that describes the meaning of parts of the sentence, such as doer, action, and done-to.

phrase structure description   A tree diagram that shows the hierarchical structure of a sentence. The descending branches of the tree correspond to smaller and smaller units of sentence structure.

phrenology   An early nineteenth-century fad that involved palpating bumps and indentations on the head in order to judge the examinee's intellectual and personality traits. A forerunner of modern theories of cerebral localization, phrenology nonetheless had no validity.

pictorial cues   The monocular depth cues (such as, interposition, linear perspective, and relative size) that the eye exploits as an optical consequence of the projection of a three-dimensional world on a flat surface.

piloerection   Erection of the hairs on the surface of the skin, used by furry animals to conserve heat and by some animals (e.g., cats) as a threat display. In humans, piloerection is manifest as "goosebumps," although, since humans lack full body hair, the response is largely vestigial.

pitch   The psychological dimension of sound that corresponds to frequency; as frequency increases, pitch appears to rise.

pituitary gland   An endocrine gland that is actually a functional extension of the hypothalamus. The pituitary gland is often called the master gland because many of its secretions trigger hormone secretions in other glands.

placebo   In medical practice, a term for a chemically inert substance that produces real medical benefits because the patient believes it will help her.

placebo effect   The actual medical or psychological benefits of a treatment administered to a patient who believes it has therapeutic powers even though it actually has none.

place theory   A theory of pitch proposed by Hermann von Helmholtz which states that different regions of the basilar membrane in the cochlea respond to different sound frequencies. The nervous system interprets the excitation from different basilar regions as different pitches.

plasticity   The changeability of a trait or behavior with experience (e.g., eye color shows little plasticity, while hair color shows considerably more).

pleasure center   According to some theorists, a special region of the brain that is triggered whenever any motive is satisfied.

pleasure principle   In Freud's theory, the id's sole law, that of obtaining immediate satisfaction regardless of the circumstances and whatever the cost.

pluralistic ignorance   A situation in which individuals in a group don't know that there are others in the group who share their feelings.

polyandry   A type of polygamous mating system in which one female monopolizes the reproductive efforts of several males.

polygamy   Any mating system, including polyandry and polygymy, in which one member of a sex monopolizes the reproductive efforts of several members of the other sex.

polygenic inheritance Inheritance of an attribute whose expression is controlled not by one but by many gene pairs.

polygraph A device for measuring heart rate, respiration, and galvanic skin response. Sometimes called a "lie detector," the polygraph can only detect signs of physiological stress; whether one is lying is an interpretation made by the polygraph examiner.

polygyny A type of polygamous mating system in which one male monopolizes the reproductive efforts of several females.

pons The topmost portion of the hindbrain just above the medulla and in front of the cerebellum; it is involved in coordinating facial sensations and muscular actions, and in regulating sleep and arousal.

population The entire group of research participants (or test trials) about which the investigator wants to draw conclusions. *See also* sample.

positive correlation *See* correlation.

positive feedback *See* feedback system.

positive reinforcement The process whereby the delivery of a stimulus contingent upon an operant response acts to increase the subsequent probability of that response. It also refers to the procedure in which consequences are arranged to produce increases in operant responding.

positive symptoms of schizophrenia Symptoms that involve behavior or thinking that is either less pronounced or nonexistent in normal individuals, such as hallucinations, delusions, or bizarre behavior. *See also* negative symptoms of schizophrenia.

positron emission tomography scan *See* PET scan.

postsynaptic membrane The membrane of the receiving cell across the synaptic gap that contains specialized receptor sites.

postsynaptic neuron The cell receiving a neural message at the synapse.

post-traumatic stress disorder (PTSD) A chronic, sometimes life-long disorder that has its onset some time after an especially stressful traumatic event. Symptoms include dissociation, recurrent nightmares, flashbacks, and sleep disturbances. *See also* acute stress disorder, anxiety disorders, dissociation.

potentiation In motivation, the tendency to make some behaviors, perceptions, and feelings more probable than others. *See also* long-term potentiation.

practical intelligence The intelligence required to solve everyday problems.

precursor A substance required for the chemical manufacture of a neurotransmitter.

predicate *See* concept.

predictive validity A measure of whether a test assesses what is intended that is based on the correlation between the test score and some external criterion (e.g., a correlation between a scholastic aptitude test score and college grades).

prefrontal area The frontmost portion of the frontal lobes, which is involved in working memory, strategy formation, and response inhibition.

prefrontal lobotomy A neurosurgical treatment that surgically cuts the connections between the prefrontal areas of the frontal lobes and the rest of the brain. Once used widely (and mostly unsuccessfully) for many mental disorders but now performed very rarely.

premise An assumption or stipulation that precedes deductive reasoning.

preoperational period In Piaget's theory, the period from about ages two to six during which children come to represent actions and objects internally but cannot systematically manipulate these representations or relate them to each other. The child is therefore unable to conserve quantity across perceptual transformations and also is unable to take points of view other than his own.

preparedness A built-in predisposition to form certain associations more readily than others.

preparedness theory of phobias The theory that phobias grow out of a built-in predisposition (preparedness) to learn to fear certain stimuli (e.g., snakes and spiders) that may have posed serious dangers to our primate ancestors.

prescriptionism The view that psychotherapeutic treatments for mental disorders may ultimately be like prescriptions for medications: tailored to both the disorder and the individual patient.

prescriptive rules Rules prescribed by "authorities" about how people ought to speak and write that often fail to conform to the facts about how people actually talk and understand. This is in contrast to the structural principles of a language, which describe (rather than prescribe) the principles native speakers of a language actually use when arranging their words into sentences.

presynaptic facilitation A process that underlies many kinds of learning, documented in studies of *Aplysia*. It occurs when learning results in the increased readiness of presynaptic neurons to fire.

presynaptic neuron The cell that shoots a neurotransmitter across the synaptic gap.

primacy effect (1) In free recall, the tendency to recall the first items on a list more readily than those in the middle. (2) In forming an impression of another person, the tendency to give greater weight to attributes noted at the outset than to those noted later. *See also* recency effect.

primary messenger The neurochemicals responsible for neuron-to-neuron communication in chemical synapses, i.e., neurotransmitters. Primary messengers are contrasted with second messengers, those neurochemicals responsible for communication within neurons.

primary motor projection area A strip of cortex located at the back of the frontal lobe just ahead of the primary sensory projection area in the parietal lobe. This region is the primary projection area for muscular movements.

primary projection areas Regions of the cortex that serve as receiving stations for sensory information or as dispatching stations for motor commands.

primary somatosensory projection area A strip of cortex located at the front of the parietal lobe just behind the primary motor area in the frontal lobe. This region is the primary projection area for bodily sensations, including touch, pain, and temperature.

priming effect Phenomenon wherein giving a participant advance knowledge about or exposure to a stimulus can increase the ease of its subsequent recall or recognition.

primitive features Attributes of an object (such as its location, contour, color, and shape) that are first detected separately and then coordinated to enable identification of the object.

prisoner's dilemma A particular arrangement of payoffs in a two-person situation in which each individual has to choose between two alternatives without knowing the other's choice. The payoff structure is arranged such that the optimal strategy for each person depends upon whether she can trust the other or not. If trust is possible, the payoffs for each will be considerably higher than if there is no trust.

proactive inhibition The lessened ability to recall new material because of material learned previously. *See also* retroactive inhibition.

probability of response The likelihood of the occurrence of a response; it is a common measure of response strength in classical and operant conditioning.

procedural knowledge *See* declarative knowledge.

progesterone A female sex hormone that dominates the latter phase of the female cycle during which the uterine walls thicken to receive the embryo.

projection In psychoanalytic theory, a mechanism of defense in which various forbidden thoughts and impulses are attributed to another person rather than the self, thus warding off some anxiety (e.g., "I hate you" becomes "You hate me").

projection areas *See* primary projection areas.

projective techniques Sometimes called *unstructured personality tests.* Methods of assessing personality that use relatively ambiguous stimuli in order to elicit responses that are unguarded and authentic. The most common projective techniques are the TAT and the Rorschach inkblot test. *See also* personality inventories.

propagation The spread of the action potential down an axon, caused by successive destabilizations of the neuronal membrane.

proposition *See* concept.

prosopagnosia The inability to recognize faces, usually produced by lesions in the parietal lobes.

prototype The typical example of a category of (e.g., a robin is a prototypical bird).

prototype theory of meaning The theory that concepts are formed around average exemplars rather than lists of single attributes.

proximal stimulus *See* distal stimulus.

proximate cause The immediate cause in a chain of causation. The proximate cause of a person's death might be a stroke, but *why* he suffered a stroke requires further investigation. *See also* ultimate cause.

proximity (1) In perception, the closeness of two figures. The closer together they are, the more they will tend to be grouped together perceptually; (2) the nearness of people, which is one of the most important determinants of attraction and liking.

pseudohermaphroditism The most common kind of intersexuality, in which individuals have ambiguous genitalia. *See also* intersexual.

psychoanalysis (1) A theory of both normal and abnormal human personality development, formulated by Freud, whose key assertions include unconscious conflict and early psychosexual development. (2) A method of therapy that draws heavily on this theory of personality. Its main aim is to have the patient gain insight into her own, presently unconscious, thoughts and feelings. Therapeutic tools employed toward this end include free association, interpretation, and the appropriate use of the transference relationship between patient and analyst. *See also* free association, transference.

psychoanalytic model As defined in the text, a subcategory of the pathology model which holds (1) that the underlying pathology is a constellation of unconscious conflicts and defenses against anxiety, usually rooted in early childhood, and (2) that treatment should be by some form of psychotherapy based on psychoanalytic principles.

psychodynamic approach to personality An approach to personality originally derived from psychoanalytic theory that asserts that personality differences are based on unconscious (dynamic) conflicts within the individual. *See also* behavioral-cognitive approach, humanistic approach, situationism, sociocultural approach, trait theory.

psychodynamic model An approach to mental disorders which holds that they are the end-products of internal psychological conflicts that generally originate in one's childhood experiences. *See also* learning model, medical model, pathology model.

psychogenic disorders Disorders whose origins are psychological rather than organic (e.g., phobias). *See also* somatogenic mental disorders.

psychogenic symptoms Symptoms believed to result from some psychological cause rather than from actual tissue damage.

psychological intensity The magnitude of a stimulus as it is perceived, not in terms of its physical attributes.

psychometric approach to intelligence An attempt to understand the nature of intelligence by studying the pattern of results obtained on intelligence tests.

psychopathology (1) The study of mental disorders, or (2) mental disorder itself.

psychopathy *See* antisocial personality.

psychophysics An approach to understanding perception that relates the characteristics of physical stimuli to attributes of the sensory experience they produce.

psychophysiological disorders In these disorders (formerly called *psychosomatic*), the primary manifestations involve genuine organic damage, but their onset or severity is heavily influenced by psychological factors (e.g., coronary heart disease).

psychosexual development In psychoanalytic theory, the description of the progressive stages in the way the child gains pleasure as he grows into adulthood, defined by the zone of the body through which maximal pleasure is derived (oral, anal, genital) and by the object toward which this pleasurable feeling is directed (mother, father, adult sexual partner). *See also* anal stage, genital stage, oral stage, phallic stage.

psychosis Loss of contact with reality (most often evidenced as delusions or hallucinations), as can occur in severe cases of many kinds of mental disorders such as mania, major depression, or schizophrenia.

psychosocial crises In Erik Erikson's theory, a series of crises through which all persons must pass as they go through their life cycle (e.g., the identity crisis during which adolescents or young adults try to establish the separation between themselves and their parents).

psychosomatic disorders *See* psychophysiological disorders.

psychosurgery Neurosurgery performed to alleviate manifestations of mental disorders that cannot be brought under control using psychotherapy, medication, or other standard treatments. Psychosurgery can be helpful in severe cases of, for example, obsessive-compulsive disorder.

psychotherapy As used here, a collective term for all forms of treatment that use psychological rather than somatic methods.

psychoticism In Hans Eysenck's personality system, a trait dimension related to aggressiveness, antisocial actions, coldness, impulsivity, and self-centeredness.

punishment training An instrumental training procedure in which a response is suppressed by having its occurrence followed by an aversive event. *See also* avoidance learning, escape learning.

puzzle box An apparatus used by Edward Thorndike to demonstrate trial-and-error learning in cats. Animals were required to perform a simple action in order to escape the puzzle box and obtain food.

pyramidal system One of the two motor systems that originates in the motor cortex of the brain and sends its tracts directly to the motoneurons that activate the muscles. The pyramidal system is more recent in evolutionary terms and orchestrates the body's more precise movements.

pyrogens Chemicals released into the bloodstream at sites of bacterial or viral invasion that stimulate special receptors in the anterior part of the hypothalamus and produce fever, which probably represents the body's effort to kill off the invading pathogens by temporarily overheating.

radical behaviorism An approach usually associated with B. F. Skinner which asserts that the subject matter of psychology is overt behavior, without reference to inferred, internal processes such as wishes, traits, or expectations.

random assignment In experimental design, the random placement of participants in experimental versus control groups in order to insure that all groups are matched at the outset of the experiment.

random sample *See* sample.

range A measure of the variability contained in a set of scores, calculated by subtracting the lowest score from the highest.

rationalization In psychoanalytic theory, a mechanism of defense by means of which unacceptable thoughts or impulses are reinterpreted in more acceptable and, thus, less anxiety-arousing terms (e.g., the jilted lover who convinces herself that she never loved her fiancé anyway).

ratio scale An interval scale in which there is a true zero point, thus allowing statements about proportions (e.g., this sound is twice as loud as the other). *See also* categorical scale, interval scale, nominal scale, ordinal scale.

ratio schedule A reinforcement schedule in which reinforcement is delivered for the first response made after a certain number of responses. In a fixed-ratio schedule, the number of responses required for a reward is always the same. In a variable-ratio schedule, the number of responses required varies irregularly around a specified average.

reaction formation In psychoanalytic theory, a mechanism of defense in which a forbidden impulse is turned into its opposite (e.g., hate toward a sibling becomes exaggerated love).

reaction time The interval between the presentation of a signal and the observer's response to that signal.

reality principle In Freud's theory, the set of rules that govern the ego and that dictate the way in which it tries to satisfy the id by gaining pleasure in accordance with the real world and its demands.

reasoning The determination of the conclusions that can be drawn from certain premises.

recall A task in which some item must be produced from memory. *See also* recognition.

receiver-operating-characteristic curve (ROC curve) A graphical representation of the relationship between stimulus sensitivity and response bias.

recency effect In free recall, the tendency to recall items at the end of the list more readily than those in the middle. *See also* primacy effect (in free recall).

receptive field The retinal area in which visual stimulation affects a particular cell's firing rate.

receptor cells A special type of neuron that can respond to various external energies and transduce (translate) physical stimuli into electrical changes to which other neurons can respond.

receptor molecules The specialized molecules in the postsynaptic membrane that open or close certain ion channels when activated by the correct neurotransmitter.

recessive gene *See* gene.

reciprocal altruism *See* altruism.

reciprocal inhibition The arrangement by which excitation of some neural system is accompanied by inhibition of that system's antagonist (as in antagonistic muscles).

reciprocal interaction The fact that different people seek out different situations. *See also* person-by-situation interaction, situationism.

reciprocity principle A basic rule of many social interactions that decrees that one must repay whatever one has been given.

recoding Changing the form in which information is stored.

recognition A task in which a participant must judge whether he has encountered a stimulus previously. *See also* recall.

reconditioning In classical conditioning, the presentation of further reinforced conditioning trials (i.e., those that include the unconditioned stimulus [US]) after a conditioned response (CR) has been extinguished.

reference The relations between words or sentences and objects or events in the world (e.g., the word *ball* refers to a ball, that spherical object used in games and sports).

reflectance The proportion of light aimed at an object that is reflected by it. An object's reflectance determines whether the object is perceived as light or dark.

reflection The process by which objects give off light from a source of illumination.

reflex A simple, stereotyped reaction in response to some stimulus (e.g., limb flexion in withdrawal from pain).

rehearsal *See* elaborative rehearsal, maintenance rehearsal.

reinforced trial In classical conditioning, a trial on which the conditioned stimulus (CS) is followed by the unconditioned stimulus (US). In instrumental conditioning, a trial in which the instrumental response is followed by reward, cessation of punishment, or some other reinforcer.

reinforcement In classical conditioning, the procedure by which the unconditional stimulus (US) is presented contingent upon the occurrence of the conditioned stimulus (CS). In instrumental conditioning, the procedure by which a sought-after consequence is made contingent upon the occurrence of the instrumental response.

relational aggression A strategy for attaining social advantage by manipulating others' social alliances. Females are apparently more relationally aggressive, whereas males are apparently more physically aggressive.

relative size A monocular depth cue in which far-off objects produce a smaller retinal image than nearby objects of the same size.

releasing stimulus A term used by ethologists to describe a stimulus that is genetically programmed to elicit a fixed-action pattern (e.g., a long, thin, red-tipped beak which elicits a herring gull chick's begging response). *See also* fixed-action patterns.

reliability The degree of consistency with which a test measures a trait or attribute. Assuming that a trait or attribute remains constant, a perfectly reliable test of that measure will produce the same score each time it is given.

reliability coefficient The coefficient used in determining the consistency of mental tests, that is, the repeatability of their results. It is usually derived from test-retest correlations or from correlations between alternative forms of a test. *See also* test-retest method.

REM rebound The tendency to spend more time in REM sleep if deprived of it on previous nights. REM rebound often occurs during withdrawal from medications that suppress REM sleep (e.g., barbiturates or alcohol).

REM sleep The type of sleep characterized by rapid eye movements, an EEG indicative of high cortical arousal, speeded heart rate and respiration, near-paralysis of limb muscles, and recall of highly visual dreams.

repetition priming An increase in the likelihood that an item will be identified, recognized, or recalled caused by recent exposure to that item, which may occur without explicit awareness.

replication A repetition of an experiment that yields the same results.

representational thought In Piaget's theory, thought that is internalized and includes mental representations of prior experiences with objects and events.

representations Cognitions that correspond to (represent) certain events, or relations between events, in the world.

representativeness heuristic A rule of thumb by means of which we estimate the probability that an object (or event) belongs to a certain category based on how prototypical it is of that category, regardless of how common it actually is. *See also* prototype.

repressed memory In psychoanalytic theory, a memory that is so anxiety-laden that it has been pushed out of consciousness where it may fester until it is "recovered." There is little scientific evidence for the existence of recoverable repressed memories.

repression In psychoanalytic theory, a mechanism of defense by means of which thoughts, impulses, or memories that give rise to anxiety are pushed out of consciousness.

resistance In psychoanalysis, a term describing the patient's failure to associate freely and say whatever enters her head.

response amplitude The size of a response, used commonly as a sign of response strength in classical and operant conditioning.

response bias In signal detection experiments, the willingness of the participant to assert that a stimulus has occurred or not occurred, given the costs of false positives or false negatives. *See also* payoff matrix.

response latency The time that elapses between an elicitor and a response (in classical conditioning, between the onset of a conditioned stimulus [CS] and the conditioned response [CR]). As classical conditioning proceeds, response latency usually decreases (i.e., the CR occurs sooner).

response rate The number of responses per unit of time. This is one measure of the strength of an operant response.

response suppression The inhibition of a response by conditioned fear.

response time *See* reaction time.

resting potential The difference in voltage across a neuronal membrane when the neuron is not firing.

restitutional symptoms For Eugen Bleuler, symptoms such as delusions and hallucinations that originated in the schizophrenic patient's attempt to compensate for his increasing isolation from the world

restrained-eating hypothesis The hypothesis that obese persons are oversensitive to external food cues because their conscious restraints on eating have become disinhibited. *See also* externality hypothesis, setpoint hypothesis.

restructuring A reorganization of a problem that can facilitate its solution; a characteristic of creative thought.

retention The survival of a memory over some period of time.

retention intervals In memory experiments, the time that elapses between the original learning and a later test.

retina The tissue-thin structure at the back of the interior of the eye that contains the photoreceptors, several layers of intermediate neurons, and the cell bodies of the axons that form the optic nerve.

retinal image The image of an object that is projected on the retina. Its size increases with the size of that object and decreases with the object's distance from the eye.

retrieval The process of searching for some item in memory and of finding it. If retrieval fails, this may or may not mean that the relevant memory trace is missing. The trace may simply be inaccessible.

retrieval cue A stimulus that helps one to recall a memory.

retrieval failure The inability to access a memory, often due to poor encoding; an alternative to erasure as an explanation for forgetting.

retroactive inhibition The lessened ability to recall old material because of material learned subsequently. *See also* proactive inhibition.

retrograde amnesia A memory deficit, often suffered after a head injury, in which the patient loses memory of some period prior to the injury. *See also* anterograde amnesia.

reuptake A mechanism by which a neurotransmitter is vacuumed back into the presynaptic terminal that released it.

reversible figures Visual patterns that allow parsing such that what is initially figure becomes ground and vice versa (e.g., a drawing that can be seen as either a black picket fence against a white wall or a white picket fence against a black wall).

rhodopsin The photopigment used in the rods within the retina.

risk aversion In decision making, the reluctance to choose an alternative that involves some risk.

rites of passage Ceremonies employed by cultures to mark important developmental transitions (e.g., puberty rites, debutante balls, graduation exercises).

ROC curve *See* receiver-operating-characteristic curve.

rods Photoreceptors in the retina that respond to lower light intensities and give rise to achromatic (colorless) sensations.

role playing In psychotherapy, a technique in which the therapist and patient act out scenes, such as a marital confrontation, that are likely to occur outside the therapeutic situation.

romantic love A state of emotion characterized by idealization of the beloved, turbulent emotions, and obsessive thoughts. *See also* companionate love.

Romeo-and-Juliet effect The intensification of romantic love that can occur with parental opposition.

rooting reflex In the infant, the sucking elicited by stroking applied on or around the lips; aids breast-feeding.

Rorschach inkblot test A projective (unstructured) technique of personality assessment that requires the examinee to look at a series of inkblots and report everything she sees in them.

safety signal A cue which predicts that an aversive stimulus will *not* occur. *See also* contingency.

sample A subset of a population selected by the investigator for study. A random sample is constructed such that each member of the population has an equal chance of being picked. A stratified sample is constructed such that every relevant subgroup of the population is randomly sampled in proportion to its size. *See also* population.

saturation A perceived dimension of visual stimuli that describes the "strength" of a color—the extent to which it appears rich or pale (e.g., light pink vs. hot pink).

savant A mentally retarded person who has some remarkable talent that seems out of keeping with his low level of general intelligence. Previously *idiot savant,* a term now abandoned as derogatory.

scaling A procedure for assigning numbers to a subject's responses. *See also* categorical scale, interval scale, nominal scale, ordinal scale, ratio scale.

scatter plot A graph depicting the relationship between two interval- or ratio-scale variables, with each axis representing one variable; often used to graph correlation data.

schedule of reinforcement The pattern of occasions on which responses are to be reinforced. Commonly, reinforcement is scheduled after a stipulated number of responses occurs or when a response occurs after a preset time interval has elpased. *See also* ratio schedule, interval schedules.

schema (1) In theories of memory and thinking, a term that refers to a general cognitive structure in which information is organized. (2) In Piaget's theory of development, a mental pattern.

schizophrenia A group of severe mental disorders characterized by at least some of the following: marked disturbance of thought, withdrawal, inappropriate or flat emotions, delusions, and hallucinations. *See also* catatonic schizophrenia, disorganized type of schizophrenia, negative symptoms of schizophrenia, paranoid schizophrenia, positive symptoms of schizophrenia.

score profile   *See* test profile.

script   A subcase of a schema that describes a characteristic pattern of behavior in a particular setting, such as a restaurant. *See also* schema.

seasonal affective disorder   A mood disorder that shows reliable fluctuations with the time of year. One example is a depression that ensues in the fall when the days become shorter and ends in the spring when the days lengthen.

secondary memory   *See* long-term memory.

second messengers   Neurochemicals within the neuron that regulate such mechanisms as the creation of receptors sites for specific neurotransmitters and the synthesis of the neuron's own neurotransmitter, thus determining the neuron's overall responsiveness.

second-order conditioning   *See* higher-order conditioning.

selective serotonin reuptake inhibitors (SSRIs)   Medications such as Prozac, Zoloft, and Paxil that increase serotonin turnover in the brain and find wide use as treatments for depression, obsessive-compulsive disorder, panic disorder, and many other disorders.

self-actualization   According to Abraham Maslow and some other adherents of the humanistic approach to personality, the full realization of one's potential. *See also* hierarchy of needs, peak experience.

self-concept   Generally, the sum of one's beliefs about and attitudes toward oneself. For Carl Rogers, the sense of oneself as both agent and object.

self-control   The ability to pursue a goal while adequately managing internal conflicts about it.

self-disclosure   The act of revealing personal information; usually occurs reciprocally and facilitates intimacy.

self-handicapping   A self-protective strategy in which one arranges for an obvious, and nonthreatening obstacle to one's own performance, such that any failure can be attributed to the obstacle and not to one's own limitations.

self-monitoring   The process of making sure that one's own behavior conforms with the demands of the current social situation. At the extremes, high self-monitors are pliant social chameleons, and low self-monitors are rigid and unaccommodating.

self-perception theory   The theory that we know our own attitudes and feelings only indirectly, by observing our own behavior and then performing much the same processes of attribution that we employ when trying to understand others.

self-regulatory systems   For Walter Mischel, ways that individuals regulate their own behavior using self-imposed goals and plans.

self-reported data   Data supplied by the research participant (usually, ratings of attitudes or moods, or tallies of behavior), rather than that collected by the experimenter.

self-serving attributional bias   The tendency, found largely in individualistic cultures, to deny responsibility for failures but take credit for successes. *See also* actor-observer difference, attribution theory, fundamental attribution error.

semantic feature   The smallest significant unit of meaning within a word (e.g., male, human, and adult are semantic features of the word *man*).

semantic memory   The component of generic memory that concerns the meaning of words and concepts.

semantic priming   The enhanced performance on verbal tasks that occurs when the items being considered have similar meanings.

semantics   The organization of meaning in language.

semicircular canals   The three curved tubules found within the inner ear that contain a viscous liquid that is easily perturbed if jostled. The canals provide moment-to-moment information about head movements.

sensation   According to the empiricists, the primitive experiences that emanate from the senses (e.g., greenness, bitterness).

sensation seeking   A predisposition to seek novel experiences, look for thrills and adventure, and be highly susceptible to boredom.

sensitive period   *See* critical period.

sensory adaptation   The decline in sensitivity found in most sensory systems after continuous exposure to the same stimulus.

sensory code   The rule by which the nervous system represents the sensory characteristics of the stimulus. One example is firing frequency which, in touch and vision, encodes increased stimulus intensity.

sensory coding   The process by which the sensory organs translate various stimulus qualities into the dimensions of our sensory experience.

sensory interaction   The increased or decreased sensitivity of the sensory system in response to other ongoing stimulation.

sensory modalities   A technical term for the sensory domains: taste, touch, smell, kinesthesis, vision, and hearing.

sensory-motor intelligence   In Piaget's theory, intelligence during the first two years of life, consisting mainly of sensations and motor impulses, with little in the way of internalized representations.

sensory neurons   Neurons that convey information from sense organs to other portions of the nervous system.

sensory process   According to signal detection theorists, the underlying neural activity in the sensory system upon which all psychological judgments are based. *See also* signal-detection theory.

sensory projection areas   *See* primary projection areas.

sensory quality   A distinguishing attribute of a stimulus (e.g., sound frequency as the determinant of pitch).

sentence analyzing machinery (SAM)   The sequence of strategies that listeners use to comprehend sentences.

separation anxiety   The protest and distress exhibited by a child at the departure of a caretaker.

serial reproduction   An experimental technique in which a drawing is presented to one research participant, who reproduces it from memory for a second participant, whose reproduction is shown to a third, and so on. Each participant's memory distortions become part of the stimulus for the next participant down the line, such that reconstructive alterations accumulate.

serial search   The successive comparison of a target stimulus to different items in memory. *See also* parallel search.

serotonin (5HT)   A neurotransmitter involved in many of the mechanisms of sleep, arousal, aggression, and mood.

servomechanisms   Devices that use negative feedback to maintain a stable state of affairs, such as a heating system that maintains a home at a constant temperature.

set   *See* mental set.

setpoint   A general term for the level at which negative feedback tries to maintain stability. An example is the setting of a thermostat. *See also* setpoint hypothesis.

setpoint hypothesis   The hypothesis that different persons have different setpoints for weight, such that attempts to alter one's weight are physiologically countered and, thus, will ultimately prove ineffectual. *See also* setpoint.

sexual dimorphism The state of affairs, observed in many species, in which the sexes differ in form (such as deer antlers or peacock tail feathers) or size. Sexual dimorphism is minimal among monogamous animals and maximal among polygamous ones.

sexual identity The sense of being male or female and all that goes with it, including issues of gender identity, gender role, and sexual orientation.

sexual orientation A person's predisposition to choose members of the same or the opposite sex as romantic and sexual partners. *See also* bisexuality, heterosexuality, and homosexuality.

shadowing The procedure, often used in dichotic presentations, in which a participant is asked to repeat aloud, word for word, only what she hears through one earphone.

shallow processing The encoding of a stimulus using its superficial characteristics, such as the way a word sounds or the typeface in which it is printed.

shape constancy The tendency to perceive objects as retaining their shapes despite changes in our angle of regard that produce changes in the image projected on the retina.

shaping An instrumental learning procedure in which an animal (or human) learns a rather difficult response through the reinforcement of successive approximations to that response. *See also* successive approximations.

short-term habituation *See* habituation.

short-term memory *See* stage theory of memory.

signal-detection theory The theory that the act of perceiving or not perceiving a stimulus is actually a judgment about whether a momentary sensory experience is due to background noise alone or to the background noise plus a signal. *See also* sensory process.

signs In psychopathology, what the diagnostician observes about a patient's physical or mental condition (e.g., tremor, inattentiveness). *See also* symptoms, syndrome.

similarity In perception, a principle by which we tend to group like figures, especially by color and orientation.

simple cells Neurons in the visual cortex that respond to simple stimulus features such as orientation or position.

simple reaction time A measurement of the speed with which a research participant can respond to a stimulus.

simple reflex A sensorimotor reflex free of modulation by higher-level influences; approximated by Sir Charles Sherrington, who used spinal animals.

simulation heuristic A mental shortcut used in making decisions and evaluating outcomes that employs the imaginary replay of events or situations.

simultaneous color contrast The effect produced by the fact that any region in the visual field tends to induce its complementary color in adjoining areas. For example, a gray patch will tend to look bluish if surrounded by yellow and yellowish if surrounded by blue.

simultaneous pairing A classical conditioning procedure in which the conditioned stimulus (CS) and the unconditioned stimulus (US) are presented at the same time. *See also* backward pairing, forward pairing.

sine waves Waves that correspond to the plot of the trigonometric sine function.

single-case experiment A study in which the investigator manipulates the values of some independent variable, just as she would in an experiment with many participants, and then assesses the effects of this variable by recording the single participant's responses. *See also* case study.

situational factors *See* attribution theory.

situationism The view that human behavior is largely determined by the characteristics of the situation rather than personal predispositions. *See also* behavioral-cognitive approach, humanistic approach, psychodynamic approach, sociocultural approach, trait theory.

size constancy The tendency to perceive objects as retaining their size, despite the increase or decrease in the size of the image projected on the retina caused by moving closer to or farther from the objects.

skeletal musculature The muscles (sometimes called *striated muscles*) that are controlled by parts of the somatic nervous system and that move the face, trunk, and limbs.

skewed A term used to describe distributions of experimental results that are asymmetrical (tending to have outlying values at one end).

sleep paralysis The phenomenon of waking up unable to move for several seconds, due to the persistence of the loss of muscle tone that occurs during REM sleep. While sleep paralysis is sometimes frightening, it is harmless.

slow-wave sleep Type of sleep characterized by slow, rolling eye movements, an EEG indicative of low cortical arousal, slowed heart rate and respiration, and recall of "boring," mostly verbal dreams.

smooth muscles The nonstriated muscles controlled by the autonomic nervous system that constrict the blood vessels to help regulate blood pressure and that line many internal organs such as those that produce peristalsis in the digestive tract.

social cognition The way in which we interpret and try to comprehend social events.

social comparison A process of reducing uncertainty about one's own beliefs and attitudes by comparing them to those of others.

social development A child's growth in his or her relations with other people.

social dilemma A problem similar in structure to the prisoner's dilemma but expanded to include any number of individuals, each of whom has to decide whether to cooperate or act individually. *See also* prisoner's dilemma.

social exchange theory A theory that asserts that each partner in a social relationship gives something to the other and expects to get something in return.

social facilitation The tendency to perform better in the presence of others than when alone. This facilitating effect works primarily for simple or well-practiced tasks.

social impact theory The theory that the influence others exert on an individual increases with their number, their immediacy, and their strength (e.g., status).

social influence A general term for interactions in which an individual's thinking or behavior is affected by the actions of several others.

socialization The process whereby the child acquires the patterns of behavior characteristic of his or her society.

social learning theory A theoretical approach to socialization and personality that is midway between radical behaviorism and cognitive approaches to learning. It stresses learning by observing others who serve as models and who show the child whether a response he already knows should or should not be performed.

social loafing An example of the diffusion of social impact in which people working collectively on a task generate less total effort than they would had they worked alone.

social phobia A fear of embarrassment or humiliation that causes people to avoid situations that might expose them to public scrutiny. *See also* anxiety disorders, phobia, specific phobia.

social reality testing The normal process of validating one's beliefs against others. This process is often disrupted in schizophrenia.

sociocultural approach Within social psychology and personality psychology, the view that many psychological phenomena, some of which have been presumed to be universal, result from or are affected substantially by cultural norms. *See also* behavioral-cognitive approach, humanistic approach, psychodynamic approach, trait theory, situationism.

sociopathy *See* antisocial personality disorder.

somatic nervous system A division of the peripheral nervous system primarily concerned with the control of the skeletal musculature and the transmission of information from the sense organs.

somatic therapies A collective term for any treatment of mental disorders by some organic means, including medication, surgery, and electroconvulsive therapy.

somatization disorder A mental disorder in which the patient reports miscellaneous aches and pains in various bodily systems that do not add up to any known syndrome in physical medicine.

somatoform disorders The generic term for mental disorders in which bodily symptoms predominate despite the absence of any known physical cause; included are conversion disorder, hypochondriasis, somatization disorder, and somatoform pain disorder.

somatoform pain disorder A mental disorder in which the sufferer describes chronic pain for which there is no discernible physical basis.

somatogenic hypothesis The hypothesis that mental disorders result from organic (bodily) causes.

somatogenic mental disorders Mental disorders that have known organic causes. This is the case for some disorders (e.g., general paresis) but almost surely not for all (e.g., phobias). *See also* psychogenic disorders.

somatosensory area *See* primary somatosensory projection area.

sound waves Successive pressure variations in the air that vary in amplitude and wavelength.

source confusion A type of memory error in which information acquired in one context is remembered as having been encountered in another (e.g., a person's recalling that she had chocolate cake on her last birthday when she actually had it two birthdays ago).

source memory The knowledge of the event from which a certain memory derived.

spatial summation The process whereby two or more stimuli that are individually below threshold will elicit a reflex if they occur simultaneously at different points on the body.

spatial thinking The mental computations engaged in when we must locate objects and discern the spatial relationships among them.

Spearman's theory of general intelligence (*g*) Spearman's account, based on factor analytic studies of intelligence-test performance, which proposes one underlying factor, general intelligence (*g*), which is tapped by all subtests, and a large number of specific skills (*s*'s) that are tapped by each subtest. *See also* factor analysis, group-factor theory of intelligence.

species-specific behavior Behavior patterns characteristic of a species that are typically built-in and emerge without any relevant prior experience.

species-specific defense reaction Reactions to threat that are largely innate and found in all members of a species, e.g., flight in birds, "playing dead" in opossums.

specific language impairment An inherited syndrome that impairs language learning and causes lifelong deficits in sentence comprehension and production, despite otherwise normal cognitive functioning.

specific phobia A disabling, irrational fear of certain objects or events such as snakes, heights, or enclosed places. *See also* anxiety disorders, phobia.

specificity theory An approach to sensory experience which asserts that different sensory qualities are signaled by different neurons. These neurons are somehow labeled with their quality, so that whenever they fire, the nervous system interprets their activation as that particular sensory quality.

spectral sensitivity The eye's responsiveness to each of the separate wavelengths that constitute a light stimulus.

spectral sensitivity curve A graphical representation of the eye's spectral sensitivity.

speech plans Coordinated patterns of speech movements, constructed in Broca's area, that are relayed to the primary motor projection area for decoding into discrete muscular movements.

sperm (spermatozoom) A sex cell manufactured in the testes and contributed by the male as part of sexual reproduction.

spinal animal An animal whose spinal cord has been severed in the neck region in order to cut all connections between the body (from the neck down) and the brain, leaving the spinal reflexes free of higher influences.

split brain A condition in which the corpus callosum and some other fibers are cut so that the two cerebral hemispheres are functionally isolated.

spontaneous recovery The reappearance of a previously extinguished response after a time interval in which neither the conditioned stimulus (CS) nor the unconditioned stimulus (US) is presented.

spreading activation model A memory model that assumes that elements in a semantic memory network are more heavily activated the closer they are to each other within the network.

stabilized image technique A procedure that projects a stationary image on the retina even though the eye is moving.

stage theory of memory An approach to memory that proposes several memory stores. One is short-term memory, which holds a small amount of information for fairly short intervals; another is long-term memory, which can hold vast amounts of information for extended periods. According to the theory, information can only be transferred to long-term memory if it has first been in short-term memory.

standard deviation (SD) A measure of the variability of a frequency distribution, calculated as the square root of the variance (V)—$SD = \sqrt{V}$. *See also* variance (V).

standard error of the mean A measure of the variability of the mean whose value depends both on the standard deviation (SD) of the distribution and the number of cases in the sample (N); if SE is the standard error, then $SE = SD/\sqrt{N-1}$.

standardization group The group against which an individual's test score is evaluated.

standard score (*z*-score) A score that is expressed as a deviation from the mean in standard deviations (SDs), which allows a comparison of scores drawn from different distributions; if M is the mean, then $z = (score - M)/SD$.

statistical reliability The degree to which an observed difference in sample means reflects a real difference in population means and is not attributable to chance.

statistics The process of quantitatively describing, analyzing, and making inferences about numerical data.

stereotypes Schemas by which people try to categorize complex groups. Group stereotypes are often negative, especially when applied to minority groups. *See also* out-group homogeneity effect.

stimulant An influence (typically, a drug) that has activating or excitatory effects on brain or bodily functions (e.g., amphetamines, Ritalin, cocaine).

stimulus Anything in the environment that the organism can detect and respond to.

stimulus generalization In classical conditioning, the tendency to respond to stimuli other than the original conditioned stimulus (CS). The greater the similarity between the CS and the new stimulus (CS$^+$), the greater generalization will be. An analogous phenomenon in instrumental conditioning is a response to stimuli other than the original discriminative stimulus.

storage capacity The amount of information that can be retained in memory. *See also* magic number.

strategic retrieval A deliberate effort to recall information by supplying one's own retrieval cues (e.g., "Let's *see*, the last time I remember seeing my wallet was . . .").

stratified sampling An experimental procedure in which each subgroup of the population is sampled in proportion to its size.

stress In psychopathology, the psychological or physical wear-and-tear that, together with a preexisting vulnerability, may lead to mental disorder. *See also* diathesis-stress conception).

stroboscopic movement *See* apparent movement.

Stroop effect A marked decrease in the speed of naming the colors in which various color names (such as green, red, etc.) are printed when the colors and the names are different. An important example of automatization.

structural principles (of language) *See* prescriptive rules.

structured personality test A personality test (e.g., the MMPI or CPI) that asks specific questions and requires specific answers.

subcortical structures Usually the forebrain structures, such as those comprising the limbic system and extrapyramidal motor system, that lie beneath the cortex.

subjective contours Perceived contours that do not exist physically. We tend to complete figures that have gaps in them by perceiving a contour as continuing along its original path.

subjective values The outcomes an individual prefers; in Walter Mischel's view, a determinant of behavior and an important individual difference.

subroutines In a hierarchical organization, lower-level operations that function semiautonomously but are supervised by higher-level ones.

subtractive color mixture Color that results from the subtraction of one set of wavelengths from another set, commonly produced when mixing color pigments or superimposing two colored filters. *See also* additive color mixture.

successive approximations The process of shaping a response by rewarding the steps toward the behavioral goal. *See also* shaping.

superego In Freud's theory, reaction patterns that emerge from within the ego, represent the internalized rules of society, and come to control the ego by punishment with guilt. *See also* ego, id.

surface structure *See* phrase structure.

syllogism A logic problem containing two premises and a conclusion that may or may not follow from them.

symbolic representation A type of mental representation that does not correspond to the physical characteristics of that which it represents. Thus, the word *mouse* does not resemble the small rodent it represents. *See also* analogical representation.

symmetrical distribution A distribution of numerical data in which deviations in either direction from the mean are equally frequent.

sympathetic nervous system The division of the autonomic nervous system that mobilizes the body's energies for physical activity (e.g., increasing heart rate, sweating, and respiration). Its action is typically antagonistic to that of the parasympathetic nervous system.

symptoms In psychopathology, what the patient reports about his physical or mental condition (e.g., nervousness, hearing voices). *See also* signs, syndrome.

synapse The juncture of two neurons, consisting of the presynaptic and postsynaptic membranes, and—in nonelectrical synapses—the synaptic gap between them.

synaptic reuptake *See* reuptake

synaptic vesicles *See* vesicles

syndrome A pattern of signs and symptoms that tend to co-occur.

syntax The system by which words are arranged into meaningful phrases and sentences.

systematic desensitization A behavior therapy that tries to remove anxiety connected to various stimuli by gradually counterconditioning to them a response incompatible with fear, usually muscular relaxation. The stimuli are usually evoked as mental images according to an anxiety hierarchy, whereby relaxation is conditioned to the less frightening stimuli before the more frightening ones.

tacit knowledge Practical "how to" knowledge that is unwittingly accumulated from everyday experience.

tape-recorder theory of memory The erroneous view that the brain contains an indelible record of everything one experiences.

taste buds The receptor organs for taste, located atop the tongue.

taxonomy A classification system.

technical eclecticism In the practice of psychotherapy, the use of whatever techniques work best for particular persons and problems. This approach contrasts with views that therapy should proceed according to a consistent therapeutic orientation (e.g., psychodynamic, behavioral, etc.).

temperament In modern usage, a characteristic level of reactivity and energy, often thought to be constitutional.

temporal contiguity Co-occurrence of stimuli. A condition Pavlov thought would be favorable for forming associations; actually forward pairing is most favorable. *See also* backward pairing, forward pairing, simultaneous pairing.

temporal lobe The lobe of the cortex lying below the temples in each cerebral hemisphere, which includes the primary auditory projection area, Wernicke's area, and subcortically, the amygdala and hippocampus.

temporal summation The process whereby a stimulus that is below threshold will elicit a reflex if the stimulus occurs repeatedly.

territory A term used by ethologists to describe a region a particular animal stakes out as its own. The territory holder is usually a male, but in some species the territory is held by a mating pair or by a group.

testosterone The principal male sex hormone in mammals. *See also* androgen.

test profile A graphical indication of an individual's performance on several components of a test. This is often useful for guidance or clinical evaluation because it indicates that person's pattern of abilities or traits.

test-retest method A way of ascertaining the reliability of a test. It involves administering the same test to the same group of subjects after a certain time lag and assessing the correlation of scores. *See also* reliability coefficient.

texture elements Surface variations that indicate the texture of an object (e.g., pebbles on a trail or blades of grass on a lawn) and whose spacing can be used to judge an object's size or one's distance from the object.

texture gradient A distance cue based on changes in surface texture that depend on how far away the observer is.

thalamus A part of the lower portion of the forebrain that serves as a major relay and integration center for sensory information.

Thematic Apperception Test (TAT) A projective technique in which persons are shown a set of pictures and asked to make up a story about each one.

theory of mind A set of interrelated concepts used to try to make sense of our own mental processes and those of others, including the variability of beliefs and desires.

therapeutic alliance In psychotherapy, the structuring of the patient-therapist relationship such that the patient considers the therapist a sympathetic ally when confronting problems.

thermoreceptors Specialized neurons that respond to the temperature of bodily fluids circulating throughout the brain.

thermoregulation The process by which organisms maintain a constant body temperature. For ectotherms, it is matter of external behavior such as seeking sun or shade, while for endotherms it also involves numerous internal adjustments such as sweating.

third-variable problem The major obstacle to discerning causation from correlation, because two variables may be correlated only because of the operation of a third variable. For example, sales of ice cream are correlated with rates of violent crime, but only because both increase during hot weather and decrease during cold weather.

threat displays In animals, dramatic patterns of behavior (e.g., movements, calls, coloration changes) that indicate the intent to fight if challenged further. Threat displays often allow animals to circumvent actual combat, which is far more costly.

threshold The value a stimulus must reach to produce a response.

tip-of-the-tongue phenomenon The condition in which one remains on the verge of retrieving a word or name but continues to be unsuccessful.

token economy An arrangement for operant behavior modification, usually in institutional settings. Certain responses (e.g., cleaning one's room, talking to others) are reinforced with tokens that can be exchanged for desirable items.

tolerance *See* opponent-process theory of motivation.

top-down processes Processes in form recognition that begin with larger units and then proceed to smaller units (e.g., from phrases to words to letters). This contrasts with bottom-up processes, which start with smaller component parts and gradually build up to the larger units (e.g., from letters to words to phrases). One demonstration of top-down processing is provided by context effects in which knowledge or expectations affect what one sees.

trace consolidation hypothesis The hypothesis that newly acquired memory traces undergo a gradual change that makes them more and more resistant to any disturbance.

trait *See* trait theory.

trait theory The view that differences in personality are best characterized in terms of underlying, possibly innate, attributes (traits) that predispose one toward patterns of thinking and behavior that are essentially consistent over time and across situations. *See also* behavioral-cognitive approach, humanistic approach, psychodynamic approach, situationism, sociocultural approach.

transduction The process by which a receptor reacts to some physical stimulus (e.g., light or pressure) and creates action potentials in another neuron.

transection Surgical cutting of a nerve tract or brain region, performed to isolate functionally the regions on either side.

transference In psychoanalysis, the patient's tendency to react toward her analyst as she did originally toward her own parents (or other people central in her early life).

transfer of training tests Procedures used to ascertain whether skills learned in one setting generalize to other settings.

transposition The phenomenon whereby visual and auditory patterns (i.e., figures and melodies) remain essentially the same even though the parts of which they are composed change.

tree diagram A branched diagram depicting a hierarchical structure.

trephining Drilling or cutting holes in the skull. Purportedly once done by demonologically oriented practitioners to allow the escape of evil spirits that were believed to be causing mental disorders.

trichromatic color vision The principle underlying color vision. Color vision occurs through the operation of three sets of cones, each maximally sensitive to a different wavelength of light.

tricyclic antidepressants (tricyclics) An early class of antidepressant medications that includes Tofranil and Pamelor. Because of unfavorable side effects, they have been largely supplanted by selective serotonin reuptake inhibitors (SSRIs).

true hermaphroditism Rare type of intersexuality in which an individual possesses reproductive tissue of both sexes (e.g., testes and ovaries).

two-syndrome hypothesis of schizophrenia The hypothesis that there may actually be two supercategories of schizophrenia, Type I and Type II. According to the hypothesis, Type I is produced by a malfunction of transmitters, especially dopamine, and produces primarily positive symptoms, while Type II is accompanied by reduced frontal lobe activity and sometimes cerebral atrophy, which lead to negative symptoms.

Type A behavior pattern A constellation of behavior characterized by impatience, competitiveness, and aggressiveness when thwarted. It was believed to be associated with greater incidence of coronary heart disease. *See also* Type B personality.

Type B behavior pattern In contrast to the Type A pattern, Type B's are easygoing, less hurried, less competitive, and friendlier; they are less predisposed to coronary heart disease. *See also* Type A personality.

ultimate cause The remotest cause in a chain of causation; e.g., although a person may have died from a stroke, the ultimate cause might have been his fifty previous years of cigarette smoking, which led to the stroke. *See also* proximate cause.

ultradian rhythm The 90-100 minute biological rhythm that characterizes the alternation of REM and slow-wave periods during sleep and attentiveness while awake. *See also* circadian rhythm.

ultraviolet light Light whose wavelength is too short to lie within the visible spectrum.

unconditional positive regard For Carl Rogers, the belief that one is accepted and loved without reservation; an essential component of psychotherapy.

unconditioned reflex *See* unconditioned response.

unconditioned response (UR) In classical conditioning, the response that is elicited without prior training by the unconditioned stimulus (US). *See also* conditioned response (CR), conditioned stimulus (CS), unconditioned stimulus (US).

unconditioned stimulus (US) In classical conditioning, the stimulus that elicits the unconditioned response (UR) and the presentation of which acts as reinforcement. *See* conditioned response (CR), conditioned stimulus (CS), unconditioned response (UR).

unconscious inference　A process postulated by Hermann von Helmholtz to explain certain perceptual phenomena such as size constancy. An object is perceived to be in the distance and is therefore unconsciously judged to be larger than warranted by its retinal image. *See also* size constancy.

underlying pathology model　An approach to psychopathology which asserts that various overt signs and symptoms are produced by an underlying cause that may be mental or organic or both. The therapist's objective is to discover and remove the underlying pathology, which will then cause the symptoms to disappear.

underlying structure　*See* phrase structure.

unilateral neglect　*See* neglect syndrome.

unipolar depression　*See* major depression.

unique blue　The hue corresponding to a wavelength of 445 nanometers, which is perceived as containing no red or green.

unique green　The hue corresponding to a wavelength of 500 nanometers, which is perceived as containing no blue or yellow.

unique yellow　The hue corresponding to a wavelength of 570 nanometers, which is perceived as containing no red or green.

universality thesis　The hypothesis, originated by Darwin, that facial expressions worldwide look identical, are perceived identically, and express identical emotions.

universal structure　The specific syntactic organization that some observers believe is preprogrammed in human language.

unreinforced trial　In classical conditioning, a trial in which the conditioned stimulus (CS) is presented without the unconditioned stimulus (US).

validity　The extent to which a test measures what it is supposed to measure. *See also* construct validity, incremental validity, predictive validity.

validity coefficient　The correlation between test scores and an independent measure of the trait (for example, scores on a test of "college potential" and the GPAs the test takers earn when they get to college). Such a correlation is obtained in order to evaluate the extent to which a test measures the intended attribute or trait.

variability　The degree to which scores in a frequency distribution depart from the central value. *See also* central tendency, measure of central tendency, standard deviation (SD), variance (V).

variable-interval schedule　*See* interval schedule.

variable-ratio schedule　*See* ratio schedule.

variance (V)　A measure of the variability of a frequency distribution. It is computed by finding the difference between each score and the mean (M), squaring the result, adding all these squared deviations, and dividing the sum by the number of cases. If N is the number of scores, then V = sum of $(\text{score} - M)^2 / N$.

vasoconstriction　The constriction of blood vessels brought on by activation of the sympathetic division of the autonomic nervous system. Vasoconstriction occurs in emergencies, when blood is diverted from the skin and internal organs to the muscles. It is also crucial in mammalian thermoregulation; in response to excessive cold, blood is diverted from the skin to reduce heat loss.

vasodilatation　The dilating of blood vessels brought on by activation of the parasympathetic division of the autonomic nervous system. Vasodilatation is one component of mammalian thermoregulation; in response to excessive heat, warm blood flows to the body's surface and results in heat loss by radiation.

vasopressin (antidiuretic hormone)　A hormone manufactured in the hypothalamus and secreted by the pituitary that elevates blood pressure by producing vasoconstriction and instructs the kidneys to conserve water instead of excreting it.

vegetative signs　Physical manifestations that often accompany major depression, such as loss of appetite and weight loss, weakness, fatigue, poor bowel functioning, sleep disorders (most often early-morning awakenings), and loss of interest in sex.

ventral tegmental area (VTA)　A region in the midbrain containing dopamine-releasing pathways thought to be involved in reward.

ventromedial region of the hypothalamus　*See* lateral hypothalamus.

vesicles　The tiny sacs in the presynaptic neuron that contain neurotransmitters.

vestibular senses　A set of receptors that provide information about the orientation and movements of the head, located in the semicircular canals and the vestibular sacs of the inner ear.

vestibules　Bony cavities on either side of the head that contain the structures of the inner ear.

vicarious distress　The distress produced by witnessing another's suffering. Like empathic concern, it motivates one to help others, but is less reliable. *See also* empathic concern.

vicarious reinforcement　According to social learning theorists, a form of reinforcement that occurs when someone watches a model being rewarded or punished.

visible spectrum　The range of wavelengths to which our visual system can respond, extending from about 400 (the wavelength of the color violet) to 750 nanometers (the wavelength of the color reddish orange).

visual cliff　A device for assessing depth perception, often used with human infants; it consists of a glass surface that extends from a shallow side over an apparently deep side (the cliff).

visual pigments　Light-sensitive chemicals within the rods and cones of the eye.

visual search task　A test in which research participants are briefly presented a display and must indicate whether a certain target is present or absent.

visual segregation　*See* perceptual parsing.

volume receptors　Receptors that help regulate thirst by indicating the total volume of fluids in the body. *See also* osmoreceptors.

vomeronasal organ　A distinct set of receptor cells in the nose that are specialized for the detection of pheromones.

wavelength　The distance between the crests of two successive waves and the major determinant of pitch (for sound) and hue (for light).

Weber fraction　In Weber's law, the fraction given by the change in stimulus intensity (ΔI) divided by the standard intensity (I) required to produce a just-noticeable difference: $\Delta I / I = C$.

Weber's law　The observation that the size of the difference threshold is proportional to the intensity of the standard stimulus.

well-defined problems　Problems for which there is a clear-cut way of deciding whether a proposed solution is correct. This contrasts with ill-defined problems, for which it is unclear what a correct solution might be.

Wernicke's area　A brain area adjacent to the auditory projection area, damage to which leads to deficits in understanding word meaning.

"what" system　The system of visual circuits and pathways leading from the visual cortex to the temporal lobe, especially involved in object identification.

"where" system　The system of visual circuits and pathways leading from the visual cortex to the parietal lobe, especially involved in the spatial localization of objects and in the coordination of movements.

white matter　Whitish appearing patches and paths in the brain composed of myelinated axons.

wish fulfillment in dreams　*See* Freud's theory of dreams.

withdrawal effects   *See* opponent-process theory of motivation.

withdrawal symptoms   A consequence of drug addiction that occurs when the drug is withheld. These effects tend to be the opposite of those produced by the drug itself.

within-family differences   In research on the genetics of behavior, a term often used to refer to the role of environment. It describes differences in the environment (e.g., different schools) of individual family members. For most personality attributes, these seem to be more important than between-family differences. *See also* between-family differences.

within-group heritability   The extent to which variation within groups (e.g., among U.S. whites) is attributable to genetic factors. *See also* between-group heritability, heritability ratio (H).

working memory   A part of the memory system that is currently activated but has relatively little cognitive capacity.

X-chromosome   One of the two sex chromosomes containing the genes that determine whether a given animal will be male or female. In mammalian females, both sex chromosomes are X-chromosomes; in mammalian males, there is one X-chromosome and one Y-chromosome.

Y-chromosome   *See* X-chromosome.

Young-Helmholtz theory   A theory of color vision which holds that each of the three receptor types (short-wave, medium-wave, and long-wave) gives rise to the experience of one basic color (blue, green, or red).

z-score   *See* standard score (*z*-score).

zero stimulus   In signal detection theory, an ideal state in which, in some sensory domain, the participant is perceiving nothing. This state is impossible, because background noise is always present.

Zipf's law   The fact that words that occur frequently in a language tend to be relatively short.

zygote   The fertilized ovum resulting from the union of a sperm and an ovum (egg cell) in sexual reproduction.

REFERENCES

ABRAHAM, K. 1927. The influence of oral eroticism on character formation. In Abraham, K., *Selected papers,* pp. 393–406. London: Hogarth Press.

ABRAMS, M. H. 1953. *The mirror and the lamp: Romantic theory and the critical tradition.* New York: Oxford University Press.

ABRAMSON, L. Y., AND SACKHEIM, H. A. 1977. A paradox in depression: Uncontrollability and self–blame. *Psychological Bulletin* 84:835–51.

ABRAMSON, L. Y.; SELIGMAN, M. E. P.; AND TEASDALE, J. D. 1978. Learned helplessness in humans: Critique and reformulation. *Journal of Abnormal Psychology* 87:49–74.

ACSF INVESTIGATORS. 1992. AIDS and sexual behaviour in France. *Nature* 360:407–409.

ADAMS, W.; KENDELL, R. E.; HARE, E. H.; AND MUNK-JORGENSEN, P. 1993. Epidemiological evidence that maternal influenza contributes to the aetiology of schizophrenia: An analysis of Scottish, English, and Danish data. *British Journal of Psychiatry* 163:522–24.

ADELMANN, P. K., AND ZAJONC, R. B. 1989. Facial efference and the experience of emotion. *Annual Review of Psychology* 40:249–80.

ADLER, N. T. 1979. On the physiological organization of social behavior: Sex and aggression. In Marler, P., and Vandenbergh, J. G. (Eds.), *Handbook of behavioral neurobiology,* vol. 3: *Social behavior and communication,* pp. 29–71. New York: Plenum.

ADOLPH, E. F. 1947. Urges to eat and drink in rats. *American Journal of Physiology* 151:110–25.

ADORNO, T. W.; ADORNO, E. F.-B.; LEVINSON, D. J.; SANFORD, R. N.; in collaboration with ARON, B.; LEVINSON, M. H.; AND MORROW, W. 1950. *The authoritarian personality.* New York: Harper.

AINSWORTH, M. D. S., AND BELL, S. M. 1970. Attachment, exploration, and separation: Illustrated by the behavior of one-year-olds in a strange situation. *Child Development* 41:49–67.

AINSWORTH, M. D. S.; BLEHAR, M. C.; WATERS, E.; AND WALL, S. 1978. *Patterns of attachment.* Hillsdale, N.J.: Erlbaum.

ALBA, J. W., AND HASHER, W. 1983. Is memory schematic? *Psychological Bulletin* 93:203–31.

ALBERT, M. S.; BUTTERS, N.; AND LEVIN, J. 1979. Temporal gradients in the retrograde amnesia of patients with alcoholic Korsakoff's disease. *Archives of Neurology* 36:211–16.

ALCOCK, J. 1993. *Animal behavior: An evolutionary approach,* 5th ed. Sunderland, Mass.: Sinauer.

ALEXANDER, F., AND FRENCH, T. 1946. *Psychoanalytic theory.* New York: Ronald Press.

ALLARD, F.; GRAHAM, S.; AND PAARSALU, M. E. 1980. Perception in sport: Basketball. *Journal of Sport Psychology* 2:14–21.

ALLDERIDGE. P. 1979. Hospitals, mad houses, and asylums: Cycles in the care of the insane. *British Journal of Psychiatry* 134:321–24.

ALLEN, L. S.; HINES, Z. M.; SHRYNE, J. E.; AND GORSKI, R. A. 1989. Two sexually dimorphic cell groups in the human brain. *Journal of Neuroscience* 9:497–506.

ALLEN, V. L. 1975. Social support for non-conformity. In Berkowitz, L. (Ed.), *Advances in experimental social psychology,* vol. 8. New York: Academic Press.

ALLEN, V. L., AND LEVINE, J. M. 1971. Social support and conformity: The role of independent assessment. *Journal of Experimental Social Psychology* 7:48–58.

ALLPORT, F. 1920. The influence of the group upon association and thought. *Journal of Experimental Psychology* 3:159–82.

ALLPORT, G. W. 1937. *Personality: A psychological interpretation.* New York: Henry Holt.

ALLPORT, G. W., AND ODBERT, H. S. 1936. Trait-names: A psychological study. *Psychological Monographs* 47(Whole No. 211).

ALPER, K.; DEVINSKY, O.; PERRINE, K.; VAZQUEZ, B.; AND LUCIANO, D. 1995. Psychiatric classification of nonconversion nonepileptic seizures. *Archives of Neurology* 52:199–201.

ALTMAN, I. 1973. Reciprocity of interpersonal exchange. *Journal for Theory of Social Behavior* 3:249–61.

ALVIR, J. M.; LIEBERMAN, J. A.; SAFFERMAN, A. Z.; SCHWIMMER, J. L.; AND SCHAAF, J. A. 1993. Clozapine induced agranulocytosis—incidence and risk factors in the United States. *New England Journal of Medicine* 32:162–67.

AMATO, P. R. 1983. Helping behavior in urban and rural environments: Field studies based on a taxonomic organization of helping episodes. *Journal of Personality and Social Psychology* 45:571–86.

AMERICAN PSYCHIATRIC ASSOCIATION. 1968. *Diagnostic and statistical manual for mental disorders,* 2nd ed. (DSM-II). Washington, D.C.: American Psychiatric Association.

AMERICAN PSYCHIATRIC ASSOCIATION. 1980. *Diagnostic and statistical manual for mental disorders,* 3rd ed. (DSM-III). Washington, D.C.: American Psychiatric Association.

AMERICAN PSYCHIATRIC ASSOCIATION. 1987. *Diagnostic and statistical manual for mental disorders,* 3rd. ed., rev. (DSM-III-R). Washington, D.C.: American Psychiatric Association.

AMERICAN PSYCHIATRIC ASSOCIATION. 1993. Practice guidelines for major depressive disorder in adults. *American Journal of Psychiatry* 150 (Supplement):1–26.

AMERICAN PSYCHIATRIC ASSOCIATION. 1994. *Diagnostic and statistical manual for mental disorders,* 4th ed. (DSM-IV). Washington, D.C.: American Psychiatric Association.

AMERICAN PSYCHOLOGICAL ASSOCIATION. 1981. Ethical principles of psychologists. *American Psychologist* 36:633–38.

AMERICAN PSYCHOLOGICAL ASSOCIATION. 1982. *Ethical principles in the conduct of research with human participants.* Washington, D. C.: American Psychological Association.

AMOORE, J. E.; JOHNSON, J. W., JR.; AND RUBIN, M. 1964. The stereochemical theory of odor. *Scientific American* 210:42–49.

ANASTASI, A. 1958. *Differential psychology,* 3rd ed. New York: Macmillan.

ANASTASI, A. 1971. More on hereditability: Addendum to the Hebb and Jensen interchange. *American Psychologist* 26:1036–37.

ANASTASI, A. 1984. The K-ABC in historical perspective. *Journal of Special Education* 18:357–66.

ANASTASI, A. 1985. Review of Kaufman's Assessment Battery for Children. *Ninth Mental Measurements Yearbook,* vol. 1, pp. 769–71. Highland Park, N.J.: The Mental Measurements Yearbook.

ANASTASI, A. 1988. *Psychological testing,* 6th ed. New York: Macmillan.

ANATH, J. 1985. Pharmaco-therapy of obsessive-compulsive disorder. In Mavissakalian, M.; Turner, S. M.; and Michelson, L. (Eds.), *Obsessive-compulsive disorder: Psychological and pharmacological treatment,* pp. 167–205. New York: Plenum.

ANDERSON, J. R. 1990. *Cognitive psychology and its implications,* 3rd ed. San Francisco: Freeman.

ANDERSON, N. H. 1965. Averaging versus adding as a stimulus–combination rule in impression formation. *Journal of Experimental Psychology* 70:394–400.

ANDERSSON, M. 1982. Female choice selects for extreme tail length in a widowbird. *Nature* 299:818–20.

ANDERSSON, M. 1994. *Sexual selection.* Princeton: Princeton University Press.

ANDREASEN, N. C. 1985. Positive vs. negative schizophrenia: A critical evaluation. *Schizophrenia Bulletin* 1985:380–89.

ANDREASEN, N. C.; ARNDT, S.; ALLIGER, R.; MILLER, D.; AND FLAUM, M. 1995. Symptoms of schizophrenia. *Archives of General Psychiatry* 52:341–51.

ANDREASEN, N. C., AND BLACK, D. W. 1996. *Introductory textbook of psychiatry,* 2nd ed. Washington, D.C.: American Psychiatric Press.

ANDREASEN, N. C.; FLAUM, M.; SWAYZE, V. W., II; TYRRELL, G.; AND ARNDT, S. 1989. Positive and negative symptoms in schizophrenia. *Archives of General Psychiatry* 47:615–21.

ANDREASEN, N. C.; NASRALLAH, H. A.; DUNN, V.; OLSEN, S. C.; GROVE, W. M.; EHRHARDT, J. C.; COFFMAN, J. A.; AND CROSSETT, I. H. W. 1986. Structural abnormalities in the frontal system in schizophrenia: A magnetic resonance imaging study. *Archives of General Psychiatry* 43:136–44.

ANDRES, R. 1980. Influence of obesity on longevity in the aged. In Borek, C.; Fenoglio, C. M.; and King, D. W. (Eds.), *Aging, cancer, and cell membranes,* pp. 230–46. New York: Thieme-Stratton.

ANDREWS, G., AND HARVEY, R. 1981. Does psychotherapy benefit neurotic patients? A reanalysis of the Smith, Glass, and Miller data. *Archives of General Psychiatry* 38:1203–1208.

ANGLIN, J. M. 1975. The child's first terms of reference. In Ehrlich, S., and Tulving, E. (Eds.), *Bulletin de Psychologie,* special issue on semantic memory.

ANGRIST, B.; SATHANANTHAN, G.; WILK, S.; AND GERSHON, S. 1974. Amphetamine psychosis: Behavioral and biochemical aspects. *Journal of Psychiatric Research* 11:13–24.

ANSTIS, S. M. 1975. What does visual perception tell us about visual coding? In Gazzaniga, M. S., and Blakemore, C. (Eds.), *Handbook of psychobiology.* New York: Academic Press.

APPEL, L. F.; COOPER, R. G.; McCARRELL, N.; SIMS-KNIGHT, J.; YUSSEN, S. R.; AND FLAVELL, J. H. 1972. The development of the distinction between perceiving and memorizing. *Child Development* 43:1365–81.

ARANOFF, M. 1976. *Word-formation in generative grammar* (Linguistic Inquiry Monograph 1). Cambridge, Mass.: MIT Press.

ARBIB, M. A. 1972. *The metaphorical brain.* New York: Wiley.

ARENDT, H. 1965. *Eichmann in Jerusalem: A report on the banality of evil.* New York: Viking Press.

ARIETI, S. 1959. Schizophrenia: The manifest symptomatology, the psychodynamic and formal mechanisms. In Arieti, S. (Ed.), *American handbook of psychiatry,* vol. 1, pp. 455–84. New York: Basic Books.

ARISTOTLE. ca. 330 B.C. On sleep and waking; On dreams; On prophesy in sleep. In *The works of Aristotle,* vol. 3. London: Oxford University Press, 1931.

ARMITAGE, R.; HOFFMANN, R.; AND MOFFITT, A. 1992. Interhemispheric EEG activity in sleep and wakefulness: Individual differences in the basic rest-activity cycle (BRAC). In Antrobus, J. S., and Bertini, M. (Eds.), *The neuropsychology of sleep and dreaming,* pp. 17–45. Hillsdale, N.J.: Erlbaum.

ARMSTRONG, S. L.; GLEITMAN, L. R.; AND GLEITMAN, H. 1983. What some concepts might not be. *Cognition* 13:263–308.

ARNDT, S.; ANDREASEN, N. C.; FLAUM, M.; MILLER, D.; AND NOPOULOS, P. 1995. A longitudinal study of symptom dimensions in schizophrenia. Prediction and patterns of change. *Archives of General Psychiatry* 52:352–60.

ARNOLD, M. B. 1970. Perennial problems in the field of emotion. In Arnold, M. B. (Ed.), *Feelings and emotion: The Loyola symposium.* New York: Academic Press.

ARONFREED, J. 1968. *Conduct and conscience.* New York: Academic Press.

ARONSON, E. 1969. The theory of cognitive dissonance: A current perspective. In Berkowitz, L. (Ed.), *Advances in experimental social psychology,* vol. 4, pp. 1–34. New York: Academic Press.

ARONSON, E., AND CARLSMITH, J. M. 1963. The effect of the severity of threat on the devaluation of forbidden behavior. *Journal of Abnormal and Social Psychology* 66:584–88.

ARONSON, E., AND MILLS, J. 1959. The effect of severity of initiation on liking for a group. *Journal of Abnormal and Social Psychology* 59:177–81.

ARONSON, E.; TURNER, J. A.; AND CARLSMITH, J. M. 1963. Communicator credibility and communication discrepancy as determinants of opinion change. *Journal of Abnormal and Social Psychology* 67:31–36.

ASCH, S. E. 1946. Forming impressions of personality. *Journal of Abnormal and Social Psychology* 41:258–90.

ASCH, S. E. 1952. *Social psychology.* New York: Prentice-Hall.

ASCH, S. E. 1955. Opinions and social pressure. *Scientific American* 193:31–35.

ASCH, S. E. 1956. Studies of independence and conformity: A minority of one against a unanimous majority. *Psychological Monographs* 70 (9, Whole No. 416).

ASCH, S. E., AND GLEITMAN, H. 1953. Yielding to social pressure as a function of public or private commitment. Unpublished manuscript.

ASHER, E. J. 1935. The inadequacy of current intelligence tests for testing Kentucky Mountain children. *Journal of Genetic Psychology* 46:480–86.

ASLIN, R. N. 1987. Visual and auditory development in infancy. In Osofksy, J. D. (Ed.), *Handbook of infant development,* 2nd ed., pp. 5–97. New York: Wiley.

ASTON-JONES, G. 1985. Behavioral functions of locus coeruleus derived from cellular attributes. *Physiological Psychology* 13:118–26.

ATKINSON, J. W., AND McCLELLAND, D. C. 1948. The projective expression of needs. II. The effect of different intensities of the hunger drive on thematic apperception. *Journal of Experimental Psychology* 38:643–58.

ATKINSON, R. C., AND SHIFFRIN, R. M. 1968. Human memory: A proposed system and its control. In Spence, K. W., and Spence, J. T. (Eds.), *The psychology of learning and motivation,* vol. 2, pp. 89–105. New York: Academic Press.

AUERBACH, S. M.; KIESLER, D. J.; STRENTZ, T.; SCHMIDT, J. A.; AND OTHERS. 1994. Interpersonal impacts and adjustment to the stress of simulated captivity: An empirical test of the Stockholm syndrome. *Journal of Social and Clinical Psychology* 13:207–21.

AULD, F., AND HYMAN, M. 1991. *Resolution of inner conflict: An introduction to psychoanalytic therapy.* Washington, D.C.: American Psychiatric Press.

AUSTIN, J. L. 1962. *How to do things with words.* Oxford: Clarendon Press.

AVERILL, J. R. 1978. Anger. In Howe, H., and Dienstbier (Eds.), *Nebraska Symposium on Motivation.* Lincoln: University of Nebraska Press.

AX, A. F. 1953. The physiological differentiation of fear and anger in humans. *Psychosomatic Medicine* 15:433–42.

AXEL, R. 1995. The molecular logic of smell. *Scientific American* (October): 154–59.

AYLLON, T., AND AZRIN, N. H. 1968. *The token economy: A motivational system for therapy and rehabilitation.* New York: Appleton-Century-Crofts.

BAARS, B. J. (ED.). 1992. *Experimental slips and human error: Exploring the architecture of volition.* New York: Plenum.

BABIGIAN, H. M. 1975. Schizophrenia: Epidemiology. In Freedman, A. M.; Kaplan, H. I.; and Saddock, B. J. (Eds.), *Comprehensive textbook of psychiatry–II,* vol. 1, pp. 860–66. Baltimore: Williams & Wilkins.

BADDELEY, A. D. 1976. *The psychology of human memory.* New York: Basic Books.

BADDELEY, A. D. 1978. The trouble with levels: A reexamination of Craik and Lockhart's framework for memory research. *Psychological Review* 85:139–52.

BADDELEY, A. D. 1986. *Working memory.* Oxford: Clarendon Press.

BADDELEY, A. D. 1990. *Human memory: Theory and practice.* Needham Heights, Mass.: Allyn and Bacon.

BAER, L.; RAUCH, S. L.; BALLANTINE, H. T.; MARTUZA, R.; COSGROVE, R.; CASSEM, E.; GIRIUNAS, I.; MANZO, P. A.; DIMINO, C.; AND JENIKE, M. A. 1995. Cingulotomy for intractable obsessive-compulsive disorder. Prospective long-term follow-up of 18 patients. *Archives of General Psychiatry* 52:384–92.

BAHRICK, H. P. 1984. Semantic memory content in permastore: 50 years of memory for Spanish learned in school. *Journal of Experimental Psychology: General* 113:1–29.

BAILEY, J. M., AND PILLARD, R. C. 1991. A genetic study of male sexual orientation. *Archives of General Psychiatry* 48:1089–96.

BAILEY, J. M.; PILLARD, R. C.; NEALE, M. C.; AND AGYEI, Y. 1993. Heritable factors influence sexual orientation in women. *Archives of General Psychiatry* 50:217–23.

BAILLARGEON, R. 1987. Object permanence in 3½- and 4½-month-old infants. *Developmental Psychology* 23:655–664.

BAILLARGEON, R., AND GRABER, M. 1987. Where is the rabbit? 5½-month-old infants' representation of the height of hidden objects. *Cognitive Development* 2:375–92.

BAILLARGEON, R.; SPELKE, E. S.; AND WASSERMAN, S. 1985. Object permanence in five-month-old infants. *Cognition* 20:191–208.

BAKER, T. B., AND TIFFANY, S. T. 1985. Morphine tolerance as habituation. *Psychological Review* 92:78–108.

BALDWIN, D. A. 1991. Infants' contribution to the achievement of joint reference. *Child Development* 62:875–90.

BALOGH, R. D., AND PORTER, R. H. 1986. Olfactory preferences resulting from mere exposure in human neonates. *Infant Behavior and Development* 9:395–401.

BALTES, P. B.; REESE, H. W.; AND LIPSITT, L. P. 1980. Life-span developmental psychology. In Rosenzweig, M. R., and Porter, L. W. (Eds.), *Annual Review of Psychology* 31:65–110.

BANCROFT, J. 1986. The roles of hormones in female sexuality. In Dennerstein and Fraser (Eds.), *Hormones and behavior,* pp. 551–60. Amsterdam: International Society of Psychosomatic Obstetrics and Gynecology, Elsevier.

BANDURA, A., AND WALTERS, R. H. 1963. *Social learning and personality development.* New York: Holt, Rinehart & Winston.

BARBER, T. X. 1969. *Hypnosis: A scientific approach.* New York: Van Nostrand Reinhold.

BARD P., AND RIOCH, D., 1937. A study of four cats deprived of neocortex and additional portions of the forebrain. *Johns Hopkins Hospital Bulletin* 60:73–147.

BARDO, M. T.; DONOHEW, R. L.; AND HARRINGTON, N. G. 1996. Psychobiology of novelty seeking and drug seeking behavior. *Behavioural Brain Research* 77:23–43.

BAREFOOT, J. C.; DODGE, K. A.; PETERSON, B. L.; DAHLSTROM, W. G.; AND WILLIAMS, R. B. 1989. The Cook-Medley Hostility Scale: Item content and ability to predict survival. *Psychosomatic Medicine* 51:46–57.

BARGLOW, P.; VAUGHN, B. E.; AND MOLITOR, N. 1987. Effects of maternal absence due to employment on the quality of infant-mother attachment in a low-risk sample. *Child Development* 58(4):945–54.

BARLOW, D. H. 1988. *Anxiety and its disorders.* New York: Guilford Press.

BARLOW, D. H., AND HERSON, M. 1984. *Single case experimental designs: Strategies for studying behavior change,* 2nd ed. New York: Pergamon Press.

BARLUND, D. C. 1975. *Public and private self in Japan and the United States.* Tokyo: Simul Press.

BARNETT, S. A. 1963. *The rat: A study in behavior.* Chicago: Aldine.

BARNOUW, V. 1963. *Culture and personality.* Homewood, Ill.: Dorsey Press.

BARON, J. 1985. What kinds of intelligence components are fundamental? In Chipman, S. F.; Segal, J. W.; and Glaser, R. (Eds.), *Thinking and learning skills,* vol. 2: *Research and open questions.* Hillsdale, N.J.: Erlbaum.

BARON, R. S. 1986. Distraction-conflict theory: Progress and problems. In Berkowitz, L. (Ed.), *Advances in experimental social psychology,* vol. 20. New York: Academic Press.

BARRY, H., III; CHILD, I. L.; AND BACON, M. K. 1959. Relation of child training to subsistence economy. *American Anthropologist* 61:51–63.

BARTLETT, F. C. 1932. *Remembering: A study in experimental and social psychology.* Cambridge: Cambridge University Press.

BARTOL, C. R., AND COSTELLO, N. 1976. Extraversion as a function of temporal duration of electric shock: An exploratory study. *Perceptual and Motor Skills* 42:1174.

BARTOSHUK, L. 1988. Taste. In Atkinson, R. C.; Herrnstein, R. J.; Lindzey, G.; and Luce, R. D. (Eds.), *Stevens' handbook of experimental psychology,* vol. 1: *Perception and motivation,* rev. ed., pp. 461–502. New York: Wiley.

BASS, B. M. 1981. *Stogdill's handbook of leadership: Theory, research, and managerial applications,* rev. ed. New York: Free Press.

BASS, B. M. 1990. *Bass and Stogdill's handbook of leadership: Theory, research, and managerial applications,* 3rd ed. New York: Free Press.

BASS, E., AND DAVIS, L. 1988. *The courage to heal.* New York: Harper and Row.

BASSILI, J. N. 1993. Response latency versus certainty as indexes of the strength of voting intentions in a CATI survey. *Public Opinion Quarterly* 57(1):54–61.

BASSILI, J. N. 1995. Response latency and the accessibility of voting intentions: What contributes to accessibility and how it affects vote choice. *Personality and Social Psychology Bulletin* 21(7):686–95.

BATES, E. 1976. *Language and context: The acquisition of pragmatics.* New York: Academic Press.

BATES, E., AND MACWHINNEY, B. 1982. Functionalist approaches to grammar. In Wanner, E., and Gleitman, L. (Eds.), *Language acquisition: State of the art.* New York: Cambridge University Press.

BATESON, P. P. G. 1984. The neural basis of imprinting. In Marler, P., and Terrace, H. S. (Eds.), *The biological basis of learning,* pp. 325–39. Dahlem-Konferenzen. Berlin: Springer.

BAUM, W. M. 1970. Extinction of avoidance response following response prevention. *Psychological Bulletin* 74:276–84.

BAUMRIND, D. 1964. Some thoughts on the ethics of research: After reading Milgram's behavioral study of obedience. *American Psychologist* 19:421–23.

BAUMRIND, D. 1967. Child care practices anteceding three patterns of preschool behavior. *Genetic Psychology Monographs* 75:43–88.

BAUMRIND, D. 1971. Current patterns of parental authority. *Genetic Psychology Monographs* 1.

BAUMRIND, D. 1977. Socialization determinants of personal agency. Paper presented at the biennial meetings of the Society for Research in Child Development, New Orleans. Cited in Maccoby, E. E. 1980. *Social development.* New York: Harcourt Brace Jovanovich.

BAUMRIND, D. 1986. Sex differences in moral reasoning: Response to Walker's (1984) conclusion that there are none. *Child Development* 57: 511–21.

BAYER, E. 1929. Beitrage zur Zweikomponententheorie des Hungers. *Zeitschrift der Psychologie* 112:1–54.

BEAR, M. F.; CONNORS, B. W.; AND PARADISO, M. A. 1996. *Neuroscience: Exploring the brain.* Baltimore: Williams & Wilkins.

BEASLEY, C. M.; TOLLEFSON, G. D.; AND TRAN, P. V. 1997. Efficacy of olanzapine: An overview of pivotal clinical trials. *Journal of Clinical Psychiatry* 58 Suppl. 10:7–12.

BECHARA, A.; TRANEL, D.; DAMASIO, H.; ADOLPHS, R.; ROCKLAND, C.; AND DAMASIO, A. 1995. Double dissociation of conditioning and declarative knowledge relative to the amygdala and hippocampus in humans. *Science* 269:1115–18.

BECK, A. T. 1967. *Depression: Causes and treatment.* Philadelphia: University of Pennsylvania Press.

BECK, A. T. 1976. *Cognitive therapy and the emotional disorders.* New York: International Universities Press.

BECK, A. T. 1985. Cognitive therapy. In Kaplan, H. I., and Sadock, J. (Eds.), *Comprehensive textbook of psychiatry,* 4th ed. Baltimore: Williams & Wilkins.

BECK, A.T.; RUSH, A. J.; SHAW, B. F.; AND EMERY, G. 1979. *Cognitive therapy of depression.* New York: Guilford Press.

BECK, J. 1966. Effect of orientation and of shape similarity on perceptual grouping. *Perception and Psychophysics* 1:300–302.

BECK, J. 1982. Textural segmentation. In Beck, J. (Ed.), *Organization and representation in perception,* pp. 285–317. Hillsdale, N.J.: Erlbaum.

BÉDARD, J., AND CHI, M. 1992. Expertise. *Current Directions in Psychological Science* 1:135–39.

BEECHER, H. K. 1955. The powerful placebo. *Journal of the American Medical Association* 159:1602–6.

BEGG, I.; ARMOUR, V.; AND KERR, T. 1985. On believing what we remember. *Canadian Journal of Behavioral Science* 17:199–214.

BÉKÉSY, G. VON. 1957. The ear. *Scientific American* 197:66–78.

BELL, A. P. 1983. Sexual preference: An addendum. In Schwartz, M. F.; Moracsewski, A. S.; and Monteleone, J. A. (Eds.), *Sex and gender: A theological and scientific inquiry,* pp. 235–45. St. Louis: The Pope John Center.

BELL, A. P.; WEINBERG, M. S.; AND HAMMERSMITH, S. K. 1981. *Sexual preference: Its development in men and women.* Bloomington, Ind.: Indiana University Press.

BELL, R. Q. 1968. A reinterpretation of the direction of effects in studies of socialization. *Psychological Review* 75:81–95.

BELL, R. Q., AND HARPER, L.V. 1977. *Child effects on adults.* Hillsdale, N.J.: Erlbaum.

BELLI, R. F. 1989. Influences of misleading postevent information: Misinformation interference and acceptance. *Journal of Experimental Psychology: General* 118:72–85.

BELLI, R.; WINDSCHITL, P.; MCCARTHY, T.; AND WINFREY, S. 1992. Detecting memory impairment with a modified test procedure: Manipulating retention interval with centrally presented event items. *Journal of Experimental Psychology: Learning, Memory and Cognition* 18:356–67.

BELLUGI, U. 1971. Simplification in children's language. In Huxley, R., and Ingram, E. (Eds.), *Language acquisition: Models and methods.* New York: Academic Press.

BELLUGI, U.; MARKS, S.; BIHRLE, A.; AND SABO, H. 1991. Dissociation between language and cognitive function in Williams syndrome. In Bishop, D., and Mogford, K. (Eds.), *Language development in exceptional circumstances.* Hillsdale, N.J.: Lawrence Erlbaum.

BELLUGI, U.; POIZNER, H.; AND KLIMA, E. S. 1983. Brain organization for language: Clues from sign aphasia. *Human Neurobiology* 2:155–71.

BELOFF, H. 1957. The structure and origin of the anal character. *Genetic Psychology Monographs* 55:141–72.

BELSKY, J. 1988. The "effects" of infant day care reconsidered. *Infant Day Care, Early Childhood Research Quarterly* (Special Issue) 3:235–72.

BELSKY, J., AND BRAUNGART, J. M. 1991. Are insecure-avoidant infants with extensive day-care experience less stressed by and more independent in the Strange Situation? *Child Development* 62:657–71.

BEM, D. J. 1967. Self-perception: An alternative interpretation of cognitive dissonance phenomena. *Psychological Review* 74:183–200.

BEM, D. J. 1972. Self-perception theory. In Berkowitz, L. (Ed.), *Advances in experimental social psychology,* vol. 6, pp. 2–62. New York: Academic Press.

BEM, D. J. 1996. Exotic becomes erotic: A developmental theory of sexual orientation. *Psychological Review* 103(2):320–35.

BEM, S. L. 1989. Genital knowledge and gender constancy in preschool children. *Child Development* 60:649–62.

BENBOW, C. P. 1988. Sex differences in mathematical reasoning ability in intellectually talented preadolescents: Their nature, effects, and possible causes. *Behavior and Brain Sciences* 11:169–232.

BENBOW, C. P., AND STANLEY, J. C. 1983. Sex differences in mathematical reasoning: More facts. *Science* 222:1029–31.

BENEDICT, R. 1934. *Patterns of culture.* New York: Houghton Mifflin.

BENJAMIN, J.; LI, L.; PATTERSON, C.; GREENBERG, B. D.; MURPHY, D. L.; AND HAMER, D. H. 1996. Population and familial association between the D4 dopamine receptor gene and measures of Novelty Seeking. *Nature Genetics* 12:81–84.

BENSON, H., AND FRIEDMAN, R. 1996. Harnessing the power of the placebo effect and renaming it "remembered wellness." *Annual Review of Medicine* 47:193–99.

BENTLEY, E. 1983. *The life of the drama.* New York: Atheneum.

BERCOVITCH, F. B. 1988. Coalitions, cooperation and reproductive tactics among adult male baboons. *Animal Behaviour* 36(4):1198–1209.

BERCOVITCH, F. B. 1991. Social stratification, social strategies, and reproductive success in primates. *Ethology and Sociobiology* 12(4):315–33.

BERENBAUM, S. A., AND SNYDER, E. 1995. Early hormonal influences on childhood sex-typed activity and playmate preferences: Implications for the development of sexual orientation. *Developmental Psychology* 31:31–42.

BERGIN, A. E. 1967. An empirical analysis of therapeutic issues. In Arbuckle, D. (Ed.), *Counseling and psychotherapy: An overview,* pp. 175–208. New York: McGraw-Hill.

BERGIN, A. E. 1971. The evaluation of therapeutic outcomes. In Bergin, A. E. and Garfield, S. L. (Eds.), *Handbook of psychotherapy and behavior change: An empirical analysis.* New York: Wiley.

BERKO, J. 1958. The child's learning of English morphology. *Word* 14:150–77.

BERLIN, B., AND KEY, P. 1969. *Basic color terms: Their universality and evolution.* Berkeley and Los Angeles: University of California Press.

BERMANT, G., AND DAVIDSON, J. M. 1974. *Biological bases of sexual behavior.* New York: Harper & Row.

BERNARD, V. W.; OTTENBERG, P.; AND REDL, F. 1965. Dehumanization: A composite psychological defense in relation to modern war. In Schwebel, M. (Ed.), *Behavioral science and human survival,* pp. 64–82. Palo Alto, Calif.: Science and Behavior Books.

BERNSTEIN, A. E., AND LENHART, S. A. 1993. *The psychodynamic treatment of women.* Washington, D.C.: American Psychiatric Press.

BERNSTEIN, H.; HOPF, F. A.; AND MICHOD, R. E. 1988. Is meiotic recombination an adaptation for repairing DNA, producing genetic variation, or both? In Michod, R. E., and Levin, B. R. (Eds.), *The evolution of sex,* pp. 139–60. Sunderland, Mass.: Sinauer.

BERNSTEIN, I. L. 1978. Learned taste aversions in children receiving chemotherapy. *Science* 200:1302–3.

BERSCHEID, E. 1985. Interpersonal attraction. In Lindzey, G, and Aronson, E. (Eds.), *Handbook of social psychology,* vol. 2, pp. 413–84. New York: Academic Press.

BERSCHEID, E.; DION, K.; WALSTER, E.; AND WALSTER, G. W. 1971. Physical attractiveness and dating choice: A test of the matching hypothesis. *Journal of Experimental Social Psychology* 7:173–89.

BERSCHEID, E., AND WALSTER, E. 1974. Physical attractiveness. In Berkowitz, L. (Ed.), *Advances in experimental social psychology,* vol. 7. New York: Academic Press.

BERSCHEID, E., AND WALSTER, E. H. 1978. *Interpersonal attraction,* 2nd ed. Reading, Mass.: Addison-Wesley.

BERTENTHAL, B.; CAMPOS, J. J.; AND KERMOIAN, R. 1994. An epigenetic perspective on the development of self-produced locomotion and its consequences. *Current Directions in Psychological Science* 3:140–45.

BEST, D. L.; WILLIAMS, J. E.; CLOUD, J. M.; DAVIS, S. W.; ROBERTSON, L. S.; EDWARDS, J. R.; GILES, E.; AND FOWLES, J. 1977. Development of sex-trait stereotypes among young children in the United States, England, and Ireland. *Child Development* 48:1375–84.

BEUTLER, L. E., AND CLARKIN, J. 1990. *Systematic treatment selection: Toward targeted treatment interventions.* New York: Brunner-Maazel.

BEVER, T. G. 1970. The cognitive basis for linguistic structures. In Hayes, J. R. (Ed.), *Cognition and the development of language*, pp. 279–362. New York: Wiley.

BIANCHI, L. 1922. *The mechanism of the brain and the function of the frontal lobes.* Edinburgh: Livingstone.

BICKERTON, D. 1984. The language bioprogram hypothesis. *Behavioral and Brain Sciences* 7:173–221.

BIEDERMAN, I. 1987. Recognition-by-components: A theory of human image understanding. *Psychological Review* 94:115–47.

BIEDERMAN, I.; MEZZANOTTE, R. J.; AND RABINOWITZ, J. C. 1982. Scene perception: Detecting and judging objects undergoing relational violations. *Cognitive Psychology* 14:143–77.

BIGELOW, A. 1987. Early words of blind children. *Journal of Child Language* 14(1):1–22.

BILSKY, L.; EVANS, R. A.; AND GILBERT, L. 1972. Generalization of associative clustering tendencies in mentally retarded adolescents: Effects of novel stimuli. *American Journal of Mental Deficiency* 77:77–84.

BIRCH, H. G.; PIÑEIRO, C.; ALCADE, E.; TOCA, T.; AND CRAVIOTA, J. 1971. Relation of kwashiokor in early childhood and intelligence at school age. *Pediatric Research* 5:579–92.

BJORK, R. A. 1970. Positive forgetting: The noninterference of items intentionally forgotten. *Journal of Verbal Learning and Verbal Behavior* 9:255–68.

BJÖRKLUND, A., AND STENEVI, U. 1984. Intracerebral implants: Neuronal replacement and reconstruction of damaged circuitries. *Annual Review of Neuroscience* 7:279–308.

BJÖRKLUND, A.; STENEVI, U.; SCHMIDT, R. H.; DUNNETT, S. B.; AND GAGE, F. H. 1983. Intracerebral grafting of neuronal suspensions I. Introduction and general methods of preparation. *Acta Physiologica Scandinavica* 522(suppl.):1–8.

BLACK, D. W., AND ANDREASEN, N. C. 1994. Schizophrenia, schizophreniform disorder, and delusional paranoid disorder. In Talbott, J. A.; Hales, R. E.; and Yudofsky, S. C. (Eds.), *American Psychiatric Press textbook of psychiatry,* pp. 411–63. Washington, D.C.: American Psychiatric Press.

BLACK, D. W., AND NOYES, R. 1990. Comorbidity in obsessive-compulsive disorder. In Maser, J. D., and Cloninger, C. D. (Eds.), *Comorbidity in anxiety and mood disorders,* pp. 305–16. Washington, D.C.: American Psychiatric Press.

BLAIR, S. N. 1993. Evidence for success of exercise in weight loss and control. *Annals of Internal Medicine* 119:702–6.

BLAKEMORE, C. 1977. *Mechanics of the mind.* New York: Cambridge University Press.

BLANCHARD, E. B. 1994. Behavioral medicine and health psychology. In Bergin, A. E., and Garfield, S. L. (Eds.), *Handbook of psychotherapy and behavior change.* New York: Wiley.

BLASI, A. 1980. Bridging moral cognition and moral action: A critical review of the literature. *Psychological Bulletin* 88:1–45.

BLASI, A. 1984. Moral identity: Its role in moral functioning. In Kurtines, W. M., and Gewirtz, L. (Eds.), *Morality, moral behavior, and moral development,* pp. 128–39. New York: Wiley.

BLASS, E. M., AND EPSTEIN, A. N. 1971. A lateral preoptic osmosensitive zone for thirst in the rat. *Journal of Comparative and Physiological Psychology* 76:378–94.

BLASS, E. M., AND HALL, W. G. 1976. Drinking termination: Interactions among hydrational, orogastric, and behavioral controls in rats. *Psychological Review* 83:356–74.

BLEULER, E. 1911. *Dementia praecox, or the group of schizophrenias.* Zinkin, J., and Lewis, N. D. C., trans. New York: International Universities Press, 1950.

BLISS, E. L. 1980. Multiple personalities: Report of fourteen cases with implications for schizophrenia and hysteria. *Archives of General Psychiatry* 37:1388–97.

BLISS, T. V. P., AND LOMO, T. 1973. Long-term potentiation of synaptic transmission in the dentate area of the anesthetized rabbit following stimulation of the perforant path. *Journal of Physiology* 232:331–56.

BLOCK, J. 1971. *Lives through time.* Berkeley, Calif.: Bancroft Books.

BLOCK, J. 1977. Advancing the psychology of personality: Paradigmatic shift or improving the quality of research. In Magnusson, D., and Endler, N. S. (Eds.), *Personality at the crossroads,* pp. 37–64. New York: Wiley.

BLOCK, N. J., AND DWORKIN, G. 1976. *The IQ controversy: Critical readings.* New York: Pantheon.

BLOCK, N.; FLANAGAN, O.; AND GUZELDERE, G. 1997. *The nature of consciousness: Philosophical debates.* Cambridge: MIT Press.

BLOOM, F. E. 1983. The endorphins: A growing family of pharmacologically pertinent peptides. *Annual Review of Pharmacology and Toxicology* 23:151–70.

BLOOM, F. E. 1993. Advancing a neurodevelopmental origin for schizophrenia. *Archives of General Psychiatry* 50:224–27.

BLOOM, F. E.; LAZERSON, A.; AND HOFSTADTER, L. 1988. *Brain, mind, and behavior.* New York: Freeman.

BLOOM, L. 1970. *Language development: Form and function in emerging grammars.* Cambridge, Mass.: MIT Press.

BLOOM, L. 1993. *The transition from infancy to language: Acquiring the power of expression.* New York: Cambridge University Press.

BLOOM, L., AND MUDD, S. 1991. Depth of processing approach to face recognition: A test of two theories. *Journal of Experimental Psychology: Learning, Memory and Cognition* 17:556–65.

BLOOM, P. 1990. Syntactic distinctions in child language. *Journal of Child Language* 17(2):343–56.

BLOOM, P. 1994. Possible names: The role of syntax-semantics mappings in the acquisition of nominals. In Gleitman, L. R., and Landau, B. (Eds.), *Lexical acquisition, Lingua* (Special Issue) 92:297–329.

BLOOM, P. 1996. Intention, history, and artifact concepts. *Cognition* 60:1–29.

BLOOMFIELD, L. 1933. *Language.* New York: Henry Holt.

BLURTON-JONES, N., AND KONNER, M. J. 1976. !Kung knowledge of animal behavior. In Lee, B., and DeVore, I. (Eds.), *Kalahari hunter-gatherers.* Cambridge, Mass: Harvard University Press.

BODNAR, R. J.; KELLY, D. D.; BRUTUS, M.; AND GLUSMAN, M. 1980. Stress-induced analgesia: Neural and hormonal determinants. *Neuroscience and Biobehavioral Reviews* 4:87–100.

BOGEN, J. E. 1969. The other side of the brain II: An appositional mind. *Bulletin of the Los Angeles Neurological Societies* 34:135–62.

BOGEN, J. E.; FISHER, E. D.; AND VOGEL, P. J. 1965. Cerebral commissurotomy: A second case report. *Journal of the American Medical Association* 194:1328–29.

BOLES, D. B. 1980. X-linkage of spatial ability: A critical review. *Child Development* 51:625–35.

BOLLES, R. C. 1970. Species-specific defense reactions and avoidance learning. *Psychological Review* 77:32–48.

BOLLES, R. C., AND BEECHER, M. D. (EDS.). 1988. *Evolution and learning.* Hillsdale, N.J.: Erlbaum.

BOLLES, R. C., AND FANSELOW, M. S. 1982. Endorphins and behavior. *Annual Review of Psychology* 33:87–102.

BOND, C. F. 1982. Social facilitation: A self-presentational view. *Journal of Personality and Social Psychology* 42:1042–50.

BOND, M. H. 1979. Dimensions of personality used in perceiving peers: Cross-cultural comparisons of Hong Kong, Japanese, American, and Filipino university students. *International Journal of Psychology* 14:47–56.

BOOTH, D. A. 1980. Acquired behavior controlling energy and output. In Stunkard, A. J. (Ed.), *Obesity,* pp. 101–43. Philadelphia: Saunders.

BOOTH-KEWLEY, S., AND FRIEDMAN, H. S. 1987. Psychological predictors of heart disease: A quantitative review. *Psychological Bulletin* 101:343–62.

BORCH-JACOBSEN, M. 1997. Sybil–The making of a disease: An interview with Dr. Herbert Spiegel. *New York Review of Books* 44:60–64.

BORDEN, R. J. 1980. Audience influence. In Paulus, P. B. (Ed.), *Psychology of group influence,* pp. 99–132. Hillsdale, N.J.: Erlbaum.

BORDEN, V. M. H., AND LEVINGER, G. 1991. Interpersonal transformations in intimate relationships. In Jones, W. H., and Perlman, D. (Eds.), *Advances in personal relationships,* vol. 2, pp. 35–56. London: Jessica Kingsley Publishers.

BORG, G.; DIAMANT, H.; STROM, C.; AND ZOTTERMAN, Y. 1967. The relation between neural and perceptual intensity: A comparative study of neural and psychophysical responses to taste stimuli. *Journal of Physiology* 192:13–20.

BORING, E. G. 1964. Size constancy in a picture. *American Journal of Psychology* 77:494–98.

BORING, E. G.; LANGFELD, H. S.; AND WELD, H. P. 1939. *Introduction to psychology.* New York: Wiley.

BORKE, H. 1975. Piaget's mountains revisited: Changes in the egocentric landscape. *Developmental Psychology* 11:240–43.

BORNSTEIN, M. H. 1973. Color vision and color naming: A psychophysiological hypothesis of cultural difference. *Psychological Bulletin* 80:257–85.

BORNSTEIN, M. H. 1989. Information processing (habituation) in infancy and stability in cognitive development. *Human Development* 32(3–4):129–36.

BORONAT, C. B., AND LOGAN, G. D. 1997. The role of attention in automatization: Does attention operate at encoding, or retrieval, or both? *Memory and Cognition* 25:36–46.

BOTHWELL, M. 1995. Functional interactions of neurotrophins and neurotrophin receptors. *Annual Review of Neuroscience* 18:223–53.

BOTTGER, P. C. 1984. Expertise and air time as bases of actual and perceived influence in problem-solving groups. *Journal of Applied Psychology* 69:214–22.

BOTVIN, G. J., AND MURRAY, F. B. 1975. The efficacy of peer modelling and social conflict in the acquisition of conservation. *Child Development* 46:796–97.

BOUCHARD, C.; TREMBLAY, A.; DESPRÈS, J-P.; NADEAU, A.; LUPIEN, P. L.; THÈRIAULT, G.; DUSSAULT, J.; MOORJANI, S.; PINAULT, S. M.; AND FOURNIER, G. 1990. The response to long-term overfeeding in identical twins. *New England Journal of Medicine* 322:1477–82.

BOUCHARD, T. J., JR. 1984. Twins reared apart and together: What they tell us about human diversity. In Fox, S. (Ed.), *The chemical and biological bases of individuality,* pp. 147–84. New York: Plenum.

BOUCHARD, T. J. 1995. Longitudinal studies of personality and intelligence: A behavior genetic and evolutionary perspective. In Saklofske, D. H., and Zeidner, M. (Eds.), *International handbook of personality and intelligence,* pp. 81–106. New York: Plenum.

BOUCHARD, T. J., JR.; LYKKEN, D. T.; MCGUE, M.; SEGAL, N. L.; AND TELLEGEN, A. 1990. Sources of human psychological differences: The Minnesota study of twins reared apart. *Science* 250:223–50.

BOUCHARD, T. J., JR., AND MCGUE, M. 1981. Familial studies of intelligence: A review. *Science* 212:1055–59.

BOWER, G. H. 1970. Analysis of a mnemonic device. *American Scientist* 58:496–510.

BOWER, G. H. 1972. Analysis of a mnemonic device. In Coltheart, M. (Ed.), *Readings in cognitive psychology.* Toronto: Holt, Rinehart & Winston, Inc.

BOWER, G. H.; BLACK, J. B.; AND TURNER, T. J. 1979. Scripts in memory for text. *Cognitive Psychology* 11:177–220.

BOWER, G. H.; MCLEAN, J.; AND MEACHEM, J. 1966. Value of knowing when reinforcement is due. *Journal of Comparative and Physiological Psychology* 62:184–92.

BOWER, T. G. R. 1966. Slant perception and shape constancy in infants. *Science* 151:832–34.

BOWERMAN, M. 1982. Reorganizational processes in language development. In Wanner, E., and Gleitman, L. R. (Eds.), *Language development: State of the art.* New York: Cambridge University Press.

BOWERMAN, M. 1996. Learning how to structure space for language: A crosslinguistic perspective. In Bloom, P.; Peterson, M. A.; Nadel. L.; and Garrett, M. F. (Eds.), *Language and space: Language, speech, and communication,* pp. 385–436. Cambridge, Mass.: MIT Press.

BOWERS, K. S. 1984. On being unconsciously influenced and informed. In Bowers, K. S., and Meichenbaum, D. (Eds.), *The unconscious reconsidered.* New York: Wiley.

BOWLBY, J. 1969. *Attachment and loss,* vol. 1: *Attachment.* New York: Basic Books.

BOWLBY, J. 1973. *Separation and loss.* New York: Basic Books.

BOWMAKER, J. K., AND DARTNALL, H. J. A. 1980. Visual pigments and rods and cones in a human retina. *Journal of Physiology* 298:501–11.

BOWMAN, E. S., AND MARKAND, O. N. 1996. Psychodynamics and psychiatric diagnoses of pseudoseizure subjects. *American Journal of Psychiatry* 153:57–63.

BOYD, R., AND SILK, J. 1997. *How humans evolved.* New York: Norton.

BOYER, P. 1996. Cognitive limits to conceptual relativity: The limiting case of religious ontologies. In Gumperz, J. J., and Levinson, S. C. (Eds.), *Rethinking linguistic relativity. Studies in the social and cultural foundations of language,* pp. 203–31. Cambridge: Cambridge University Press.

BOYKIN, A. W. 1994. Harvesting talent and culture: African-American children and educational reform. In Eiossl, R. (Ed.), *Schools and students at risk.* New York: Teachers College Press.

BOYLE, G. J.; STANKOV, L.; AND CATTELL, R. B. 1995. Measurement and statistical models in the study of personality and intelligence. In Saklofske, D. H., and Zeidner, M. (Eds.), *International handbook of personality and intelligence,* pp. 417–46. New York: Plenum.

BRABECK, M. 1983. Moral judgement: Theory and research on differences between males and females. *Developmental Review* 3:274–91.

BRADLEY, G. W. 1978. Self-serving biases in the attribution process: A reexamination of the fact or fiction question. *Journal of Personality and Social Psychology* 13:420–32.

BRADY, I. 1983. Speaking in the name of the real: Freeman and Mead on Samoa. Special section. *American Anthropologist* 85:908–47.

BRAIN, L. 1965. *Speech disorders: Aphasia, apraxia, and agnosia.* London: Butterworth.

BRAINE, M. D. S. 1963. The ontogeny of English phrase structure: The first phase. *Language* 39:3–13.

BRAINE, M. D. S. 1976. Children's first word combinations. *Monographs of the Society for Research in Child Development* 41(1, Serial No. 164).

BRAMMER, G. L.; RALEIGH, M. J.; AND MCGUIRE, M. T. 1994. Neurotransmitters and social status. In Ellis, L. (Ed.), *Social stratification and socioeconomic inequality,* vol. 2: *Reproductive and interpersonal aspects of dominance and status,* pp. 75–91, Westport, Conn.: Praeger/Greenwood.

BRANSFORD, J. D. 1979. *Human cognition.* Belmont, Calif.: Wadsworth.

BRANSFORD, J. D., AND JOHNSON, M. K. 1972. Contextual prerequisites for understanding. *Journal of Verbal Learning and Verbal Behavior* 11:717–26.

BRAZELTON, T. B. 1962. A child-oriented approach to toilet training. *Pediatrics* 29:121–28.

BRAZELTON, T. B. 1972. Implications of infant development among the Mayan Indians of Mexico. *Human Development* 15:90–111.

BREGER, L.; HUNTER, I.; AND LANE, R. W. 1971. The effect of stress on dreams. *Psychological Issues* 7(3, Monograph 27):1–213.

BREGGIN, P. R. 1979. *Electroshock: Its brain-disabling effects.* New York: Springer.

BRELAND, K., AND BRELAND, M. 1951. A field of applied animal psychology. *American Psychologist* 6:202–4.

BRELAND, K., AND BRELAND, M. 1961. *The misbehavior of organisms.* *American Psychologist* 16:681–84.

BREMNER, J. D.; SOUTHWICK, S. M.; JOHNSON, D. R.; YEHUDA, R.; AND CHARNEY, D. S. 1993. Childhood physical abuse and combat-related posttraumatic stress disorder in Vietnam veterans. *American Journal of Psychiatry* 150:235–39.

BRENNAN, S. E., AND CLARK, H. H. 1996. Conceptual pacts and lexical choice in conversation. *Journal of Experimental Psychology: Learning, Memory, and Cognition* 22: 1482–93.

BRESNAN, J. 1982. *The mental representation of grammatical relations.* Cambridge, Mass.: MIT Press.

BRETHERTON, I. 1988. How to do things with one word: The ontogenesis of intentional message-making in children. In Smith, M. D., and Locke, J. L. (Eds.), *The emergent lexicon: The child's development of a linguistic vocabulary,* pp. 255–57. New York: Academic Press.

BREWER, W. F., AND TREYENS, J. C. 1981. Role of schemata in memory for places. *Cognitive Psychology* 13:207–30.

BRICKMAN, J. C., AND D'AMATO, B. 1975. Exposure effects in a free-choice situation. *Journal of Personality and Social Psychology* 32:415–20.

BRIDGEMAN, B., AND STARK, L. 1991. Ocular proprioception and efference copy in registering visual direction. *Vision Research* 31:1903–13.

BRIDGES, P. 1987. Psychosurgery for resistant depression. In Zohar, J., and Belmaker, R. H. (Eds.), *Treating resistant depression,* pp. 397–411. New York: PMA Publishing.

BRILEY, M., AND MORET, C. 1993. Neurobiological mechanisms involved in antidepressant therapies. *Clinical Neuropharmacology* 16:387–400.

BROADBENT, D. E. 1958. *Perception and communication.* London: Pergamon Press.

BROCK, T. C.; GREEN, M. C.; REICH, D. A.; AND EVANS, L. M. 1996. The *Consumer Reports* study of psychotherapy: Invalid is invalid. *American Psychologist* 51:1083.

BRODIE, H. K. H.; GARTRELL, N.; DOERING, C.; AND RHUE, T. 1974. Plasma testosterone levels in heterosexual and homosexual men. *American Journal of Psychiatry* 131:82–83.

BRODY, N. 1988. *Personality.* New York: Academic Press.

BRODY, N. 1992. *Intelligence,* 2nd ed. New York: Academic Press.

BRONSON, W. C. 1966. Central orientations. A study of behavior organization from childhood to adolescence. *Child Development* 37:125–55.

BRONSON, W. C. 1967. Adult derivatives of emotional expressiveness and reactivity control: Developmental continuities from childhood to adulthood. *Child Development* 38:801–17.

BROWN, A. L. 1974. The role of strategic memory in retardate-memory. In Ellis, N. R. (Ed.), *International review of research in mental retardation,* vol. 7, pp. 55–108. New York: Academic Press.

BROWN, A. L.; CAMPIONE, J. C.; BRAY, N. W.; AND WILCOX, B. L. 1973. Keeping track of changing variables: Effects of rehearsal training and rehearsal prevention in normal and retarded adolescents. *Journal of Experimental Psychology* 101:123–31.

BROWN, A. L.; CAMPIONE, J. C.; AND DAY, J. D. 1981. Learning to learn: On training students to learn from texts. *Educational Researcher* 10:14–21.

BROWN, A. S., AND HALLIDAY, H. E. 1990. Cryptomnesia and source memory difficulties. Southwestern Psychological Association Convention.

BROWN, B. B. 1990. Peer groups and peer cultures. In Feldman, S. S., and Elliott, G. R. (Eds.), *At the threshold: The developing adolescent.* Cambridge, Mass.: Harvard University Press.

BROWN, D. E. 1991. *Human universals.* New York: McGraw-Hill.

BROWN, J. F. 1940. *The psychodynamics of abnormal behavior.* New York: McGraw-Hill.

BROWN, J. L., AND POLLITT, E. 1996. Malnutrition, poverty and intellectual development. *Scientific American* 274(2):38–43.

BROWN, R. 1957. Linguistic determinism and parts of speech. *Journal of Abnormal and Social Psychology* 55:1–5.

BROWN, R. 1958. *Words and things.* New York: Free Press, Macmillan.

BROWN, R. 1965. *Social psychology.* New York: Free Press, Macmillan.

BROWN, R. 1973. *A first language: The early stage.* Cambridge, Mass.: Harvard University Press.

BROWN, R., AND BELLUGI, U. 1964. Three processes in the child's acquisition of syntax. *Harvard Educational Review* 34:133–51.

BROWN, R.; CAZDEN, C.; AND BELLUGI-KLIMA, U. 1969. The child's grammar from 1 to 11. In Hill, J. P. (Ed.), *Minnesota Symposium on Child Psychology,* vol. 2, pp. 28–73. Minneapolis: University of Minnesota Press.

BROWN, R., AND HANLON, C. 1970. Derivational complexity and order of acquisition in child speech. In Hayes, J. R. (Ed.), *Cognition and the development of language,* pp. 11–53. New York: Wiley.

BROWN, R., AND KULIK, J. 1977. Flashbulb memories. *Cognition* 5:73–99.

BROWN, R. W., AND LENNEBERG, E. H. 1954. A study of language and cognition. *Journal of Abnormal and Social Psychology* 49:454–62.

BROWN, R., AND McNEILL, D. 1966. The tip of the tongue phenomenon. *Journal of Verbal Learning and Verbal Behavior* 5:325–27.

BROWNELL, K. D.; GREENWOOD, M. R. C.; STELLAR, E.; AND SHRAGER, E. E. 1986. The effects of repeated cycles of weight loss and regain in rats. *Physiology and Behavior* 38:459–64.

BRUCE, V., AND GREEN, P. 1985. *Visual perception: Physiology, psychology, and ecology.* Hillsdale, N.J.: Erlbaum.

BRUCH, H. 1973. *Eating disorders.* New York: Basic Books.

BRUCH, H. 1978. *The golden cage.* Cambridge, Mass.: Harvard University Press.

BRUNER, J. S. 1974/1975. From communication to language—a psychological perspective. *Cognition* 3:255–78.

BRUNER, J. S., AND TAGIURI, R. 1954. The perception of people. In Lindzey, G. (Ed.), *Handbook of social psychology,* vol. 2. Reading, Mass.: Addison-Wesley.

BRYAN, W. L., AND HARTER, N. 1897. Studies in the physiology and psychology of telegraphic language. *Psychological Review* 4:27–53.

BRYAN, W. L., AND HARTER, N. 1899. Studies on the telegraphic language: The acquisition of a hierarchy of habits. *Psychological Review* 6:345–75.

BUCHANAN, B. G., AND SHORTLIFFE, E. H. (EDS.). 1985. *Rule-based expert systems: The MYCIN experiments of the Stanford Heuristics Programming Project.* Reading, Mass.: Addison-Wesley.

BUCHANAN, C. M.; MACCOBY, E. E.; AND DORNBUSCH, S. M. 1996. *Adolescents after divorce.* Cambridge, Mass.: Harvard University Press.

BUCHANAN, G. M., AND SELIGMAN, M. E. P. (EDS.). 1995. *Explanatory style.* Hillsdale, N.J.: Erlbaum.

BUGELSKI, B. R., AND ALAMPAY, D. A. 1961. The role of frequency in developing perceptual sets. *Canadian Journal of Psychology* 15:205–11.

BULLOCK, W. A., AND GILLILAND, K. 1993. Eysenck's arousal theory of introversion-extraversion: A covergent measures investigation. *Journal of Personality and Social Psychology* 64:113–23.

BULLOUGH, E. 1912. "Psychical distance" as a factor in art and an aesthetic principle. *British Journal of Psychology* 5:87–118.

BURCKHARDT, J. 1860. *The civilization of the Renaissance in Italy.* Oxford: Phaidon Press, 1945.

BURGESS, E. W., AND WALLIN, P. 1943. Homogamy in social characteristics. *American Journal of Sociology* 49:109–24.

BURKE, M. J., AND PRESKHORN, S. H. 1995. Short-term treatment of mood disorders with standard antidepressants. In Bloom, F. E., and Kupfer, D. (Eds.), *Psychopharmacology: The fourth generation of progress,* pp. 1053–65. New York: Raven.

BURNES, J. D., AND MALONE, J. C. 1992. The influence of "preparedness" on autoshaping, schedule performance, and choice. *Journal of the Experimental Analysis of Behavior* 58:399–413.

BURNETT, S. A.; LANE, D. M.; AND DRATT, L. M. 1979. Spatial differences and sex differences in quantitative ability. *Intelligence* 3:345–54.

BURNS, J. M. 1978. *Leadership.* New York: Harper and Row.

BURTON, R. V. 1963. Generality of honesty reconsidered. *Psychological Review* 70:481–99.

BURTON, R. V., AND WHITING, J. W. M. 1961. The absent father and cross-sex identity. *Merrill-Palmer Quarterly* 7:85–95.

BURY, J. B. 1932. *The idea of progress.* New York: Macmillan.

BUSS, A. H., AND PLOMIN, R. 1984. *Temperament: Early developing personality traits.* Hillsdale, N.J.: Erlbaum.

BUSS, D. M. 1989. Sex differences in human mate preferences: Evolutionary hypotheses tested in 37 cultures. *Behavioral and Brain Sciences* 12:1–50.

BUSS, D. M. 1992. Mate preference mechanisms: Consequences for partner choice and intrasexual competition. In Barkow, J. H.; Cosmides, L.; and Tooby, J. (Eds.), *The adapted mind,* pp. 249–66. New York: Oxford University Press.

BUSS, D. M., AND BARNES, M. F. 1986. Preferences in human mate selection. *Journal of Personality and Social Psychology* 50:559–70.

BUSS, D. M., AND CRAIK, K. H. 1983. Dispositional analysis of everyday conduct. *Journal of Personality* 51:393–412.

BUTCHER, J. N.; DAHLSTROM, W. G.; GRAHAM, J. R.; TELLEGEN, A. M.; AND KAEMMER, B. 1989. *MMPI-2: Manual for administration and scoring.* Minneapolis: University of Minnesota Press.

BUTCHER, J. N., AND ROUSE, S. V. 1996. Personality: Individual differences and clinical assessment. *Annual Review of Psychology* 47:87–111.

BUTLER, R. A. 1954. Incentive conditions which influence visual exploration. *Journal of Experimental Psychology* 48:19–23.

BUTTERS, N., AND ALBERT, M. S. 1982. Processes underlying failures to recall remote events. In Cermak, L. S. (Ed.), *Human memory and amnesia,* pp. 257–74. Hillsdale, N.J.: Erlbaum.

BUTTERWORTH, G., AND COCHRAN, E. 1980. Towards a mechanism of joint visual attention in human infancy. *International Journal of Behavioral Development* 3:253–72.

BUTTERWORTH, G., AND JARRETT, N. 1991. What minds have in common is space: Spatial mechanisms serving joint visual attention in infancy. Special issue: Perspectives on the child's theory of mind. *British Journal of Developmental Psychology* 9:55–72.

CACIOPPO, J. T., AND BERNTSON, G. G. 1994. Relationship between attitudes and evaluative space: A critical review, with emphasis on the separability of positive and negative substrates. *Psychological Bulletin* 115(3):401–23.

CACIOPPO, J. T.; CRITES, S. L.; BERNTSON, G. G.; AND COLES, M. G. 1993. If attitudes affect how stimuli are processed, should they not affect the event related brain potential? *Psychological Science* 4(2):108–12.

CAIN, W. S. 1988. Olfaction. In Atkinson, R. C.; Herrnstein, R. J.; Lindzey, G.; and Luce, R. D. (Eds.), *Stevens' handbook of experimental psychology,* vol. 1: *Perception and motivation,* rev. ed., pp. 409–59. New York: Wiley.

CAIRNS, R. B. 1984. Research in language comprehension. In R. C. Naremore (Ed.), *Language science.* San Diego: College-Hill Press.

CALABRESE, J. R., AND WOYSHVILLE, M. J. 1995. Lithium therapy: Limitations and alternatives in the treatment of bipolar disorders. *Annals of Clinical Psychiatry* 7:103–12.

CAMERON, J., AND PIERCE, W. D. 1996. The debate about rewards and intrinsic motivation: Protests and accusations do not alter the results. *Review of Educational Research* 66:39–51.

CAMMALLERI, J. A.; HENDRICK, H. W.; PITTMAN, W. C., JR.; BOUT, H. D.; AND PRATHER, D. C. 1973. Effects of different styles of leadership on group accuracy. *Journal of Applied Psychology* 57:32–37.

CAMPBELL, F. A., AND RAMEY, C. T. 1994. Effects of early intervention on intellectual and academic achievement: A follow up study of children from low income families. *Child Development* 65(2):684–98.

CAMPBELL, J. B., AND HAWLEY, C. W. 1982. Study habits and Eysenck's theory of extraversion-introversion. *Journal of Research in Personality* 16:139–46.

CAMPBELL, J. D.; TESSER, A.; AND FAIREY, P. J. 1986. Conformity and attention to the stimulus: Some temporal and contextual dynamics. *Journal of Personality and Social Psychology* 51:315–24.

CAMPBELL, R., AND CONWAY, M. A. (EDS.). 1995. *Broken memories: Case studies in memory impairment.* Cambridge, Mass.: Blackwell.

CAMPFIELD, L. A., AND ROSENBAUM, M. 1992. Human hunger. Is there a role for blood glucose dynamics? *Appetite* 18:244.

CAMPFIELD, L. A., AND SMITH, F. J. 1990a. Systemic factors in the control of food intake. In Stricker, E. M. (Ed.), *Handbook of behavioral neurobiology,* Vol. 10: *Neurobiology of food and fluid intake,* pp. 183–206. New York: Plenum.

CAMPFIELD, L. A., AND SMITH, F. J. 1990b. Transient declines in blood glucose signal meal initiation. *International Journal of Obesity* 14:15–33.

CAMPIONE, J. C., AND BROWN, A. L. 1977. Memory and metamemory development in educable retarded children. In Kail, R. V., Jr., and Hagen, J. W. (Eds.), *Perspectives on the development of memory and cognition.* Hillsdale, N.J.: Erlbaum.

CAMPIONE, J. C.; BROWN, A. L.; AND FERRARA, R. A. 1982. Mental retardation and intelligence. In Sternberg, R. J. (Ed.), *Handbook of human intelligence,* pp. 392–492. New York: Cambridge University Press.

CAMPOS, J. J.; BARRETT, K. C.; LAMB, M. E.; GOLDSMITH, H. H.; AND STERNBERG, C. 1983. Socioemotional development. In Mussen, P. E. (Ed.), *Carmichael's manual of child psychology,* vol. 2: *Infancy and developmental psychobiology.* Haith, M. M., and Campos, J. J., vol. eds., pp. 783–916. New York: Wiley.

CANDLAND, D. K. 1993. *Feral children and clever animals: Reflections on human nature.* New York: Oxford University Press.

CANNON, T. D. 1991. Genetic and prenatal sources of structural brain abnormalities in schizophrenia. In Mednick, S. A.; Cannon, T. D.; Barr, C. E.; and Lyon, M. (Eds.), *Fetal neural development and adult schizophrenia.* Cambridge: Cambridge University Press.

CANNON, T. D.; MEDNICK, S. A.; AND PARNAS, J. 1990. Antecedents of predominantly negative- and predominantly positive-symptom schizophrenia in a high-risk population. *Archives of General Psychiatry* 47:622–32.

CANNON, W. B. 1927. The James-Lange theory of emotions: A critical examination and an alternative theory. *American Journal of Psychology* 39:106–24.

CANNON, W. B. 1929. *Bodily changes in pain, hunger, fear and rage,* rev. ed. New York: Appleton-Century.

CANNON, W. B. 1932 and 1960 (revised and enlarged). *The wisdom of the body.* New York: Norton.

CANTOR, J. R.; ZILLMAN, D.; AND BRYANT, J. 1975. Enhancement of experienced sexual arousal in response to erotic stimuli through misattribution of unrelated residual excitation. *Journal of Personality and Social Psychology* 32:69–75.

CANTOR, N., AND MISCHEL, W. 1977. Traits as prototypes: Effects on recognition memory. *Journal of Personality and Social Psychology* 35:38–48.

CANTOR, N., AND MISCHEL, W. 1979. Prototypes in person perception. In L. Berkowitz (Ed.), *Advances in experimental social psychology,* vol. 12. New York: Academic Press.

CAREY, S. 1978. The child as word learner. In Halle, M.; Bresnan, J.; and Miller, G. A. (Eds.), *Linguistic theory and psychological reality.* Cambridge, Mass.: MIT Press.

CAREY, S. 1982. Semantic development: State of the art. In Wanner, E., and Gleitman, L. R. (Eds.), *Language acquisition: State of the art.* New York: Cambridge University Press.

CAREY, S. 1985. *Conceptual change in childhood.* Cambridge, Mass.: MIT Press.

CARLSON, G., AND TANENHAUS, M. 1988. Thematic roles and language comprehension. In W. Wilkins (Ed.), *Syntax and semantics,* vol. 21: *Thematic relations.* San Diego: Academic Press.

CARLSON, N. R. 1986. *Physiology of behavior,* 3rd ed. Boston: Allyn and Bacon.

CARLSON, N. R. 1991. *Physiology of behavior.* Boston: Allyn and Bacon.

CARLYLE, T. 1841. *On heroes, hero-worship, and the heroic in history.* Berkeley: University of California Press, 1992.

CARPENTER, P. A.; JUST, M. A.; AND SHELL, P. 1990. What one intelligence test measures. A theoretical account of processing in the Raven Progressive Matrix Test. *Psychological Review* 97 (3):404–31.

CARPENTER, P. A.; MIYAKE, A.; AND JUST. M. A. 1995. Language comprehension: Sentence and discourse processing. *Annual Review of Psychology* 46:91–120.

CARR, D.; BULLEN, B.; KRINAR, G.; ARNOLD, M.; ROSENBLATT, M.; BEITINS, I. Z.; MARTIN, J. B.; AND McARTHUR, J. W. 1981. Physical conditioning facilitates the exercise-induced secretion of betaendorphin and beta-lipopotrin in women. *New England Journal of Medicine* 305:560–63.

CARRINGTON, P. 1972. Dreams and schizophrenia. *Archives of General Psychiatry* 26:343–50.

CARROLL, L. 1865. *Alice in wonderland.* Abridged by Frank, J. and illustrated by Torrey, M. M. New York: Random House, 1969.

CARTER, C. S.; MINTUN, M.; NICHOLS, T.; AND COHEN, J. D. 1997. Anterior cingulate gyrus dysfunction and selective attention deficits in schizophrenia: $^{15}OH_2O$ PET study during single-trial Stroop task performance. *American Journal of Psychiatry* 154:1670–75.

CARTWRIGHT, R. D. 1977. *Night life: Explorations in dreaming.* Englewood Cliffs, N.J.: Prentice-Hall.

CASE, R. 1978. Intellectual development from birth to adulthood: A neo-Piagetian interpretation. In Siegler, R. S. (Ed.), *Children's thinking: What develops?* pp. 37–72. Hillsdale, N.J.: Erlbaum.

CASELLI, M.-C.; BATES, E.; CASADIO, P.; AND FENSON, J. 1995. A cross-linguistic study of early lexical development. *Cognitive Development* 10(2):159–99.

CASPI, A., AND HERBENER, E. 1990. Continuity and change: Assortative marriage and the consistency of personality in adulthood. *Journal of Personality and Social Psychology* 58:250–58.

CATEL, J. 1953. Ein Beitrag zur Frage von Hirnenentwicklung under Menschwerdung. *Klinische Weisschriften* 31:473–75.

CATTELL, R. B. 1957. *Personality and motivation structure and measurement.* New York: Harcourt, Brace and World.

CATTELL, R. B. 1963. Theory of fluid and crystallized intelligence: A critical experiment. *Journal of Educational Psychology* 54:1–22.

CATTELL, R. B. 1966. *The scientific analysis of personality.* Chicago: Aldine.

CATTELL, R. B. 1971. *Abilities: Their structure, growth, and action.* Boston: Houghton Mifflin.

CECI, S. J. 1990. A sideway glance at this thing called LD: A context X process X person framework. In Swanson, H. L., and Keogh, B. K. (Eds.), *Learning disabilities: Theoretical and research issues,* pp. 59–73. Hillsdale, N.J.: Lawrence Erlbaum.

CECI, S., AND BRUCK, M. 1995. *Jeopardy in the courtroom: A scientific analysis of children's testimony.* Washington, D.C.: American Psychological Association.

CECI, S.; HUFFMAN, M.; AND SMITH, E. 1994. Repeatedly thinking about a non-event: Source misattributions among preschoolers. *Consciousness and Cognition* 3:388–407.

CECI, S. J., AND LIKER, J. 1986. Academic and nonacademic intelligence: An experimental separation. In Sternberg, R. J., and Wagner, R. K. (Eds.), *Practical intelligence: Nature and origins of competence in everyday life,* pp. 119–42. New York: Cambridge University Press.

CECI, S. J.; TOGLIA, M. P.; AND ROSS, D. F. (EDS.). 1987. *Children's eyewitness memory.* New York: Springer-Verlag.

CERNOCH, J. M., AND PORTER, R. H. 1985. Recognition of maternal axillary odors by infants. *Child Development* 56:1593–98.

CHAIKEN, S. 1987. The heuristic model of persuasion. In Zanna, M. P.; Olson, J. M.; and Herman, C. P. (Eds.), *Social influence: The Ontario symposium,* vol. 5, pp. 3–40. Hillsdale, N.J.: Erlbaum.

CHAIKEN, S.; LIBERMAN, A.; AND EAGLY, A. H. 1989. Heuristic and systematic information processing within and beyond the persuasion context. In Uleman, J. S., and Bargh, J. A. *Unintended thought,* pp. 212–52. New York: Guilford Press.

CHALMERS, D. 1996. *The conscious mind: In search of a fundamental theory.* New York: Oxford University Press.

CHAMBERS, D., AND REISBERG, D. 1985. Can mental images be ambiguous? *Journal of Experimental Psychology: Human Perception and Performance* 11:317–28.

CHAO, R. K. 1994. Beyond parental control and authoritarian parenting style: Understanding Chinese parenting through the cultural notion of training. *Child Development* 65:1111–19.

CHAPMAN, L. J., AND CHAPMAN, J. P. 1973. *Disordered thought in schizophrenia.* New York: Appleton-Century-Crofts.

CHARNESS, N. 1981. Search in chess: Age and skill differences. *Journal of General Psychology: General* 110:21–38.

CHASE, W. G., AND SIMON, H. A. 1973a. Perception in chess. *Cognitive Psychology* 4:55–81.

CHASE, W. G., AND SIMON, H. A. 1973b. The mind's eye in chess. In Chase, W. G., *Visual information processing.* New York: Academic Press.

CHENEY, D. L., AND SEYFARTH, R. M. 1982. Recognition of individuals within and between groups of free-ranging vervet monkeys. *American Zoologist* 22:519–29.

CHENEY, D. L., AND SEYFARTH, R. M. 1990. *How monkeys see the world.* Chicago: University of Chicago Press.

CHENEY, D. L., AND WRANGHAM, R. W. 1986. Predation. In Smuts, B. B.; Cheney, D. L.; Seyfarth, R. M.; Wrangham, R. W.; and Struhsaker, T. T. (Eds.), *Primate societies.* Chicago: University of Chicago Press.

CHENG, H.; CAO, Y.; AND OLSON, L. 1996. Spinal cord repair of adult paraplegic rats: Partial restoration of hind limb function. *Science* 273:510–13.

CHERLIN, A. J.; FURSTENBERG, F. F.; CHASE-LANSDALE, P. L.; KIERNAN, K. E.; ROBINS, P. K.; MORRISON, D. R.; AND TEITLER, J. O. 1991. Longitudinal studies of effects of divorce on children in Great Britain and the United States. *Science* 252:1386–89.

CHERRY, E. C. 1953. Some experiments upon the recognition of speech, with one and with two ears. *Journal of the Acoustical Society of America* 25:975–79.

CHESS, S. 1987. Let us consider the roles of temperament and of fortuitous events. Peer commentary on Plomin, R., and Daniels, D. 1987. Why are children from the same family so different from one another? *Behavioral and Brain Sciences* 10:38–39.

CHEVRIER, J., AND DELORME, A. 1983. Depth perception in Pandora's box and size illusion: Evolution with age. *Perception* 12:177–85.

CHI, M. T. H. 1978. Knowledge structures and memory development. In Siegler, R. S. (Ed.), *Children's thinking: What develops?* pp. 73–96. Hillsdale, N.J.: Erlbaum.

CHI, M. T. H.; FELTOVICH, P. J.; AND GLASER, R. 1981. Categorization and representation of physics problems by experts and novices. *Cognitive Science* 5:121–52.

CHI, M. T. H.; GLAZER, R.; AND FARR, M. (EDS.). 1988. *The nature of expertise.* Hillsdale, N.J.: Erlbaum.

CHI, M. T. H.; GLAZER, R.; AND REES, E. 1982. Expertise in problem solving. In R. Sternberg (Ed.), *Advances in the psychology of human intelligence,* vol. 1. Hillsdale, N.J.: Erlbaum.

CHODOFF, P. 1954. A reexamination of some aspects of conversion hysteria. *Psychiatry* 17:75–81.

CHODOROW, N. 1989. *Feminism and psychoanalytic theory.* New Haven: Yale University Press.

CHOMSKY, C. 1984. From hand to mouth: A study of speech and language through touch (manuscript, Harvard University).

CHOMSKY, N. 1957 *Syntactic structures.* The Hague: Mouton.

CHOMSKY, N. 1959. Review of B. F. Skinner. Verbal learning. *Language* 35:26–58.

CHOMSKY, N. 1965. *Aspects of the theory of syntax.* Cambridge, Mass.: MIT Press.

CHOMSKY, N. 1975. *Reflections on language.* New York: Pantheon.

CHOMSKY, N. 1980. *Rules and representations.* New York: Columbia University Press.

CHOMSKY, N. 1981. Knowledge of language: Its elements and origins. *Philosophical Transactions of the Royal Society of London* 295(1077, Series B):223–34.

CHOMSKY, N. 1986. *Barriers.* Cambridge Mass.: MIT Press.

CHOMSKY, N., AND HALLE, M. 1968. *The sound patterns of English.* New York: Harper & Row.

CHOVIL, N. 1991. Social determinants of facial displays. *Journal of Nonverbal Behavior* 15(3):141–54.

CHRISTIE, R. 1954. Authoritarianism re-examined. In Christie, R., and Jahoda, M. (Eds.), *Studies in the scope and method of "The authoritarian personality."* New York: Free Press, Macmillan.

CHUA, S. E., AND MCKENNA, P. J. 1995. Schizophrenia: A brain disease? *British Journal of Psychiatry* 166:563–82.

CHUNG, Y. B., AND KATAYAMA, M. 1996. Assessment of sexual orientation in lesbian/gay/bisexual studies. *Journal of Homosexuality* 30:49–62.

CHURCHLAND, P. S., AND SEJNOWSKI, T. J. 1992. *The computational brain.* Cambridge: MIT Press.

CIALDINI, R. B. 1984. *Influence: How and why people agree to do things.* New York: Quill.

CIALDINI, R. B. 1993. *Influence: Science and practice,* 3rd ed. New York: HarperCollins.

CIALDINI, R. B.; PETTY, R. E.; AND CACIOPPO, J. T. 1981. Attitude and attitude change. In Rosenzweig, M. R., and Porter, L. W. (Eds.), *Annual Review of Psychology* 32:357–404.

CIALDINI, R. B.; TROST, M. R.; AND NEWSOM, J. T. 1995. Preference for consistency: The development of a valid measure and the discovery of surprising behavioral implications. *Journal of Personality and Social Psychology* 69(2):318–28.

CIALDINI, R. R.; VINCENT, J. E.; LEWIS, S. K.; CATALAN, J.; WHEELER, D.; AND DARBY, L. 1975. Reciprocal concession procedure for inducing compliance: The door-in-the-face technique. *Journal of Personality and Social Psychology* 31:206–15.

CLARIDGE, D. 1983. The Eysenck psychoticism scale. In Butcher, J. N., and Spielberger, C. (Eds.), *Advances in personality assessment,* vol. 2, pp. 71–114. Hillsdale, N.J.: Erlbaum.

CLARK, D. M. 1986. A cognitive approach to panic. *Behavior Research and Therapy* 24:461–70.

CLARK, D. M. 1988. A cognitive model of panic attacks. In Rachman, S., and Maser, J. D. (Eds.), *Panic: Psychological perspectives.* Hillsdale, N.J.: Erlbaum.

CLARK, E.V. 1973. What's in a word?: On the child's acquisition of semantics in his first language. In Moore, T. E. (Ed.), *Cognitive development and the acquisition of language.* New York: Academic Press.

CLARK, E.V. 1982. The young word-maker: A case study of innovation in the child's lexicon. In Wanner, E., and Gleitman, L. R. (Eds.), *Language acquisition: State of the art.* New York: Cambridge University Press.

CLARK, E.V. 1987. The principle of contrast: A constraint on acquisition. In MacWhinney, B. (Ed.), *Mechanisms of language acquisition.* Hillsdale, N.J.: Erlbaum.

CLARK, E.V. 1993. *The lexicon in acquisition.* New York: Cambridge University Press.

CLARK, H. H. 1978. Inferring what is meant. In Levelt, W., and Flores d'Arcais, G. (Eds.), *Studies in the perception of language.* Chichester Eng.: Wiley.

CLARK, H. H. 1979. Responding to indirect speech acts. *Cognitive Psychology* 11:430–77.

CLARK, H. H. 1996. *Using language.* Cambridge: Cambridge University Press.

CLARK, H. H., AND CLARK, E.V. 1977. *Psychology and language: An introduction to psycholinguistics.* New York: Harcourt Brace Jovanovich.

CLARK, H, H., AND WILKES-GIBBS, D. 1986. Referring as a collaborative process. *Cognition* 22:1–39.

CLARK, M. S., AND MILLS, J. 1979. Interpersonal attraction in exchange and communal relationships. *Journal of Personality and Social Psychology* 37:12–24.

CLARK, M. S., AND MILLS, J. 1993. The difference between communal and exchange relationships: What it is and is not. *Personality and Social Psychology Bulletin* 19:684–91.

CLARKE, A. C. 1952. An examination of the operation of residual propinquity as a factor in mate selection. *American Sociological Review* 27:17–22.

CLARKE-STEWART, A. 1978. And daddy makes three: The father's impact on mother and young child. *Child Development* 49:466–78.

CLARKE-STEWART, A. 1989. Infant day care: Malignant or maligned. *American Psychologist* 44:266–73.

CLARKE-STEWART, A. 1993. *Daycare,* rev. ed. Cambridge, Mass.: Harvard University Press.

CLECKLEY, J. 1976. *The mask of sanity,* 5th ed. St. Louis: Mosby.

CLEMENTE, C. D., AND CHASE, M. H. 1973. Neurological substrates of aggressive behavior. *Annual Review of Physiology* 35:329–56.

CLUTTON-BROCK, T. H., AND ALBON, S. D. 1979. The roaring of red deer and the evolution of honest advertisement. *Behaviour* 69(3–4):145–70.

COBB, S. 1941. *Foundations of neuropsychiatry.* Baltimore: Williams & Wilkins.

COFFMAN, C. E. 1985. *Review of Kaufman's Assessment Battery for Children. Ninth Mental Measurements Yearbook,* vol. 1, pp. 771–73. Highland Park, N.J.: The Mental Measurements Yearbook.

COHEN, D. B., AND WOLFE, G. 1973. Dream recall and repression: Evidence for an alternative hypothesis. *Journal of Consulting and Clinical Psychology* 41:349–55.

COHEN, H. 1972. Active (REM) sleep deprivation. In Chase, M. H. (Ed.), *The sleeping brain: Perspectives in the brain sciences,* vol. 1, pp. 343–47. Los Angeles: Brain Research Institute, University of California.

COHEN, J. D.; PERLSTEIN, W. M.; BRAVER, T. S.; NYSTROM, L. E.; NOLL, D. C.; JONIDES, J.; AND SMITH, E. E. 1997. Temporal dynamics of brain activation during a working memory task. *Nature* 386:604–8.

COHEN, N. J., AND SQUIRE, L. R. 1980. Preserved learning and retention of pattern-analyzing skill in amnesia: Dissociation of knowing how and knowing what. *Science* 210:207–10.

COHEN, R. A. 1975. Manic-depressive illness. In Freedman, A. M.; Kaplan, H. I.; and Sadock, B. J. (Eds.), *Comprehensive textbook of psychiatry–II,* vol. 1, pp. 1012–24. Baltimore: Williams & Wilkins.

COHEN, Y. A. 1953. A study of interpersonal relations in a Jamaican community. Unpublished doctoral dissertation, Yale University.

COLARUSSO, C. A., AND NEMIROFF, R. A. 1981. *Adult development: A new dimension in psychodynamic theory and practice.* New York: Plenum Press.

COLE, J. O., AND DAVIS, J. M. 1975. Antidepressant drugs. In Freedman, A. M.; Kaplan, H. I.; and Sadock, B. J. (Eds.), *Comprehensive textbook of psychiatry,* vol. 2, pp. 1941–56. Baltimore: Williams & Wilkins.

COLE, M. 1975. An ethnographic psychology of cognition. In Brislin, R. W.; Bochner, S.; and Lonner, W. J. (Eds.), *Cross-cultural perspectives on learning.* New York: Wiley.

COLE, M., AND COLE, S. R. 1996. *The development of children,* 3rd ed. New York: Freeman.

COLE, M.; GAY, J.; GLICK, J. A.; AND SHARP, D. W. 1971. *The cultural context of learning and thinking.* New York: Basic Books.

COLEMAN, J. C. 1972. *Abnormal psychology and modern life,* 4th ed. Glenview, Ill.: Scott, Foresman.

COLLIER, G. 1985. *Emotional expression.* Hillsdale, N.J.: Erlbaum.

COLLINS, A. M., AND LOFTUS, E. F. 1975. A spreading activation theory of semantic processing. *Psychological Review* 82:407–28.

COLLINS, A. M., AND QUILLIAN, M. R. 1969. Retrieval time from semantic memory. *Journal of Verbal Learning and Verbal Behavior* 8:240–47.

COLLINS, N. L., AND MILLER, L. C. 1994. Self-disclosure and liking: A meta-analytic review. *Psychological Bulletin* 116:457–75.

COLLIS, G. 1975. The integration of gaze and vocal behavior in the mother-infant dyad. Paper presented at Third International Child Language Symposium, London.

COLWILL, R. M., AND RESCORLA, R. A. 1985. Postconditioning devaluation of a reinforcer affects instrumental responding. *Journal of Experimental Psychology: Animal Behavior Processes* 11:120–32.

COMRIE, B. 1987. Introduction. In Comrie, B. (Ed.), *The world's major languages.* New York: Oxford University Press.

CONEL, J. L. 1939. *The postnatal development of the human cortex,* vol. 1. Cambridge, Mass.: Harvard University Press.

CONEL, J. L. 1947. *The postnatal development of the human cortex,* vol. 3. Cambridge, Mass.: Harvard University Press.

CONEL, J. L. 1955. *The postnatal development of the human cortex,* vol. 5. Cambridge, Mass.: Harvard University Press.

CONRAD, C. 1972. Cognitive economy in semantic memory. *Journal of Experimental Psychology* 92:149–54.

CONSUMER REPORTS. 1995. Mental health: Does therapy work? November, 734–39.

CONWAY, M. A.; COHEN, G.; AND STANHOPE, N. 1991. On the very long-term retention of knowledge acquired through formal education: Twelve years of cognitive psychology. *Journal of Experimental Psychology (General)* 120:395–409.

CONWAY, M.; ANDERSON, S.; LARSEN, S.; DONNELLY, C.; McDANIEL, M.; McCLELLAND, A. G. R.; RAWLES, R.; AND LOGIE, R. 1994. The formation of flashbulb memories. *Memory and Cognition* 22:326–43.

COOLEY, C. H. 1902. *Human nature and the social order.* New York: Scribner's.

COONS, P. M. 1994. Confirmation of childhood abuse in child and adolescent cases of multiple personality disorder and dissociative disorder not otherwise specified. *Journal of Nervous and Mental Disease* 182:461–64.

COOPER, J., AND FAZIO, R. H. 1984. A new look at dissonance theory. In Berkowitz, L. (Ed.), *Advances in experimental social psychology,* vol. 17. New York: Academic Press.

COOPER, J.; ZANNA, M. P.; AND GOETHALS, G. R. 1974. Mistreatment of an esteemed other as a consequence affecting dissonance reduction. *Journal of Experimental Social Psychology* 10:224–33.

COOPER, L. A., AND SHEPARD, R. N. 1973. The time required to prepare for a rotated stimulus. *Memory and Cognition* 1:246–50.

COPPOLA, M.; SENGHAS A.; NEWPORT, E. L.; AND SUPALLA, T. 1998. Evidence for verb agreement in the gesture systems of older Nicaraguan home signers. Boston University Conference on Language Development, Boston, Mass.

COREN, S.; PORAC, C.; AND WARD, L. M. 1978 and 1984. *Sensation and perception,* 1st and 2nd eds. New York: Academic Press.

COREN, S., AND WARD, L. M. 1989. *Sensation and perception,* 3rd ed. San Diego, Calif.: Harcourt Brace Jovanovich.

CORKIN, S. 1965. Tactually-guided maze-learning in man: Effects of unilateral cortical excisions and bilateral hippocampal lesions. *Neuropsychologia* 3:339–51.

CORKIN, S. 1984. Lasting consequences of bilateral medial temporal lobectomy: Clinical course and experimental findings in H.M. *Seminar in Neurology* 4:249–59.

CORNSWEET, T. M. 1970. *Visual perception.* New York: Academic Press.

CORY, T. L.; ORMISTON, D. W.; SIMMEL, E.; AND DAINOFF, M. 1975. Predicting the frequency of dream recall. *Journal of Abnormal Psychology* 84: 261–66.

CORYELL, W. 1996. Psychotic depression. *Journal of Clinical Psychiatry* 57 (suppl.) 3:27–31.

COSMIDES, L., AND TOOBY, J. 1992. Cognitive adaptations for social exchange. In Barkow, J. H.; Cosmides, L.; and Tooby, J. (Eds.), *The adapted mind: Evolutionary psychology and the generation of culture,* pp. 163–228. New York: Oxford University Press.

COST, QUALITY, AND OUTCOMES STUDY TEAM. 1995. *Cost, quality and child outcomes in child care centers, executive summary,* 2nd ed. Denver: Economics Department, University of Colorado at Denver.

COSTA, E. 1985. Benzodiazepine-GABA interactions: A model to investigate the neurobiology of anxiety. In Tuma, A. H., and Maser, J. D. (Eds.), *Anxiety and the anxiety disorders.* Hillsdale, N.J.: Erlbaum.

COSTA, P. T., AND MCCRAE, R. R. 1992. Four ways five factors are basic. *Personality and Individual Differences* 13:653–65.

COSTA, P. T., JR.; MCCRAE, R. R.; AND ARENBERG, D. 1980. Enduring dispositions in adult males. *Journal of Personality and Social Psychology* 38:793–800.

COTTRELL, N. B.; WACK, D. L.; AND SEKERAK, G. J. 1968. Social facilitation of dominant responses by the presence of an audience and the mere presence of others. *Journal of Personality and Social Psychology* 9:245–50.

COURTNEY, S. M.; UNGERLEIDER, L. G.; KEIL, K.; AND HAXBY, J. V. 1997. Transient and sustained activity in a distributed neural system for human working memory. *Nature* 386:608–11.

COUVILLON, P., AND BITTERMAN, M. E. 1980. Some phenomena of associative conditioning in honeybees. *Journal of Comparative and Physiological Psychology* 94:878–85.

COWEY, A., AND STOERIG, P. 1992. Reflections on blindsight. In Milner, A. D., and Rugg, M. D. (Eds.), *The neuropsychology of consciousness,* pp. 11–38. San Diego, Calif.: Academic Press.

COWLES, J. T. 1937. Food-tokens as incentives for learning by chimpanzees. *Comparative Psychology Monographs* 14 (5, Serial No. 71).

COYLE, J. T.; PRICE, D.; AND DELONG, M. R. 1983. Alzheimer's disease: A disorder of cholinergic innervation. *Science* 219:1184–90.

COYNE, J. C., AND GOTLIB, I. H. 1983. The role of cognition in depression: A critical appraisal. *Psychological Bulletin* 94:472–505.

CRAIGHEAD, L. W.; CRAIGHEAD, W. E.; KAZDIN, A. E.; MAHONEY, M. J. (EDS.). 1994. *Cognitive and behavioral interventions: An empirical approach to mental health problems.* Boston: Allyn and Bacon.

CRAIK, F., AND BYRD, M. 1982. Aging and cognitive deficits: The role of attentional resources. In Craik, F., and Trehub, S. (Eds.), *Age and cognitive processes,* pp. 191–221. New York: Plenum.

CRAIK, F., AND JENNINGS, J. M. 1992. Human memory. In Craik, F., and Salthouse, T. (Eds.), *Handbook of aging and cognition,* pp. 51–110. Hillsdale, N.J.: Erlbaum.

CRAIK, F. I. M., AND LOCKHART, R. S. 1972. Levels of processing. A framework for memory research. *Journal of Verbal Learning and Verbal Behavior* 11:671–84.

CRAIK, F. I. M., AND TULVING, E. 1975. Depth of processing and the retention of words in episodic memory. *Journal of Experimental Psychology: General* 104:268–94.

CRAIK, F. I. M., AND WATKINS, M. J. 1973. The role of rehearsal in short-term memory. *Journal of Verbal Learning and Verbal Behavior* 12:599–607.

CRAIN, S., AND FODOR, J. D. 1985. How can grammars help parsers? In Dowty, D.; Kartunnen, L.; and Zwicky, A. (Eds.), *Natural language parsing: Psychological, computational, and theoretical perspectives.* Cambridge: Cambridge University Press.

CRAIN, S., AND NAKAYAMA, M. 1986. Structure dependence in children's language. *Language* 62:522–43.

CRAIN, S., AND STEEDMAN, M. 1985. On not being led up the garden path: The use of context by the psychological syntax parser. In Dowty, D.; Kartunnen, L.; and Zwicky, A. (Eds.), *Natural language parsing.* Cambridge: Cambridge University Press.

CRAWFORD, M., AND ENGLISH, L. 1984. Generic versus specific inclusion of women in language: Effects on recall. *Journal of Psycholinguistic Research* 13(5)373–81.

CRESPI, L. 1942. Quantitative variation in incentive and performance in the white rat. *American Journal of Psychology* 55:467–517.

CREWS, F. 1995. *The memory wars: Freud's legacy in dispute.* New York: New York Review of Books.

CRICK, N. R.; CASAS, J. F.; AND MOSHER, M. 1997. Relational and overt aggression in preschool. *Developmental Psychology* 33:579–88.

CRICK, N. R., AND GROTPETER, N. 1995. Relational aggression, gender and social psychological adjustment. *Child Development* 66:710–22.

CRONBACH, L. J. 1970. *Essentials of psychology testing,* 3rd ed. New York: Harper & Row.

CRONBACH, L. J. 1975. Beyond the two disciplines of scientific psychology. *American Psychologist* 30:116–27.

CRONBACH, L. J., AND MEEHL, P. E. 1955. Construct validity in psychological tests. *Psychological Bulletin* 52:281–302.

CROOK, C. 1987. Taste and olfaction. In Salapateck, P., and Cohen, L. (Eds.), *Handbook of infant perception: From perception to cognition,* vol. 2, pp. 237–64. Orlando, Fla.: Academic Press.

CROW, T. J. 1980. Molecular pathology of schizophrenia: More than one disease process? *British Medical Journal* 280:66–68.

CROW, T. J. 1982. Two dimensions of pathology in schizophrenia: Dopaminergic and non-dopaminergic. *Psychopharmacology Bulletin* 18:22–29.

CROW, T. J. 1985. The two-syndrome concept: Origins and current status. *Schizophrenia Bulletin* 11:471–86.

CROWDER, R. G. 1976. *Principles of learning and memory.* Hillsdale, N.J.: Erlbaum.

CROWDER, R. G. 1982. The demise of short-term memory. *Acta Psychologica* 50:291–323.

CROWDER, R. G. 1985. Basic theoretical concepts in human learning and cognition. In Nillson, L.-G., and Archer, T. (Eds.), *Perspectives on learning and memory.* Hillsdale, N.J.: Erlbaum.

CRUTCHFIELD, R. S. 1955. Conformity and character. *American Psychologist* 10:191–99.

CSERNANSKY, J. G., AND NEWCOMER, J. G. 1995. Maintenance drug treatment for schizophrenia. In Bloom, F. E., and Kupfer, D. (Eds.), *Psychopharmacology: The fourth generation of progress,* pp. 1267–75. New York: Raven.

CUMMINGS, J. L. 1985. *Clinical neuropsychiatry.* Orlando, Fla.: Grune and Stratton.

CUMMINS, D. 1992. Role of analogical reasoning in induction of problem categories. *Journal of Experimental Psychology: Learning, Memory and Cognition* 18:1103–24.

CUNNINGHAM, M. R. 1986. Measuring the physical in physical attraction: Quasi-experiments on the sociobiology of female beauty. *Journal of Personality and Social Psychology* 50:925–35.

CURTISS, S. 1977. *Genie: A linguistic study of a modern-day "wild child."* New York: Academic Press.

CUTLER, A. 1994. Segmentation problems, rhythmic solutions. In Gleitman, L. R., and Landau, B. (Eds.), *Lexical acquisition* (Special Issue) *Lingua* 92:81–104.

CUTTING, J. 1986. Outcome in schizophrenia: Overview. In Kerr, T. A., and Snaith, R. P. (Eds.), *Contemporary issues in schizophrenia,* pp. 436–40. Washington, D.C.: American Psychiatric Press.

DABBS, J. M. 1992. Testosterone measurements in social and clinical psychology. *Journal of Social and Clinical Psychology* 11:302–21.

DABBS, J. M.; RUBACK, R. B.; FRADY, R. L.; HOPPER, C. H.; AND OTHERS. 1988. Saliva testosterone and criminal violence among women. *Personality and Individual Differences* 9:269–75.

DADDS, M. R. 1995. *Families, children, and the development of dysfunction.* Thousand Oaks, Calif.: Sage.

DALE, A. J. D. 1975. Organic brain syndromes associated with infections. In Freedman, A. M.; Kaplan, H. I.; and Sadock, B. J. (Eds.), *Comprehensive textbook of psychiatry—II,* vol. 1, pp. 1121–30. Baltimore: Williams & Wilkins.

DAMASIO, A. R.; TRANEL, D.; AND DAMASIO, H. 1989. Disorders of visual recognition. In Goodglass, H., and Damasio, A. R. (Eds.), *Handbook of neuropsychology,* vol. 2. New York: Elsevier.

DAMASIO, H.; GRABOWSKI, T.; FRANK, R.; GALABURDA, A. M.; AND DAMASIO, A. R. 1994. The return of Phineas Gage: The skull of a famous patient yields clues about the brain. *Science* 264:1102–5.

DARLEY, J. M., AND BATSON, C. D. 1973. "From Jerusalem to Jericho": A study of situational and dispositional variables in helping behavior. *Journal of Personality and Social Psychology* 27:100–108.

DARLEY, J., AND LATANE´, B. 1968. Bystander intervention in emergencies: Diffusion of responsibility. *Journal of Personality and Social Psychology* 10: 202–14.

DARNTON, R. 1984. The meaning of Mother Goose. *New York Review of Books,* February 2: 41–47.

DARWIN, C. 1871. *The descent of man, and selection in relation to sex.* London: Murray.

DARWIN, C. 1872a. *The origin of species.* New York: Macmillan, 6th ed., 1962.

DARWIN, C. 1872b. *The expression of the emotions in man and animals.* London: Appleton.

DARWIN, C. 1877. A biological sketch of a young child. *Kosmos* 1:367–76. Cited in Bornstein, M. H. 1978. Chromatic vision in infancy. In Reese, H., and Lipsitt, L. (Eds.), *Advances in child development and behavior,* vol. 12. New York: Academic Press.

DAVIDSON, A. R., AND JACCARD, J. J. 1979. Variables that moderate the attitude-behavior relation: Results of a longitudinal survey. *Journal of Personality and Social Psychology* 37:1364–76.

DAVIDSON, J. M. 1969. Hormonal control of sexual behavior in adult rats. In Rasp, G. (Ed.), *Advances in bioscience,* vol. 1, pp. 119–69. New York: Pergamon.

DAVIDSON, J. M. 1986. Androgen replacement therapy in a wider context: Clinical and basic aspects. In Dennerstein, L., and Fraser, I. (Eds.), *Hormones and behavior,* pp. 433–40. Amsterdam: International Society of Psychosomatic Obstetrics and Gynecology, Elsevier.

DAVIES, K. G., AND WEEKS, R. D. 1993. Temporal lobectomy for intractable epilepsy: Experience with 58 cases over 21 years. *British Journal of Neurosurgery* 7:23–33.

DAVIS, D. E. 1964. The physiological analysis of aggressive behavior. In Etkin, W. (Ed.), *Social behavior and organization among vertebrates.* Chicago: University of Chicago Press.

DAVIS, J. M. 1974. A two-factor theory of schizophrenia. *Journal of Psychiatric Research* 11:25–30.

DAVIS, J. M. 1978. Dopamine theory of schizophrenia: A two-factor theory. In Wynne, L. C.; Cromwell, R. L.; and Matthysse, S. (Eds.), *The nature of schizophrenia.* New York: Wiley.

DAVIS, J. M. 1985a. Antipsychotic drugs. In Kaplan, H. I., and Sadock, J. (Eds.), *Comprehensive textbook of psychiatry,* 4th ed., pp. 1481–1513. Baltimore: Williams & Wilkins.

DAVIS, J. M. 1985b. Antidepressant drugs. In Kaplan, H. I., and Sadock, J. (Eds.), *Comprehensive textbook of psychiatry,* 4th ed., pp. 1513–37, Baltimore: Williams & Wilkins.

DAVIS, K. 1947. Final note on a case of extreme social isolation. *American Journal of Sociology* 52:432–37.

DAVIS, M. 1992. The role of the amygdala in conditioned fear. In Aggleton, J. P. (Ed.), *The amygdala: Neurobiological aspects of emotion, memory, and mental dysfunction,* pp. 255–306. New York: Wiley Liss.

DAVIS, M. 1997. The neurophysiological basis of acoustic startle modulation: Research on fear motivation and sensory gating. In Lang, P. J.; Simons, R. F.; and Balaban, M. T. (Eds.), *Attention and orienting: Sensory and motivational processes,* pp. 69–96. Mahwah, N.J.: Erlbaum.

DAVISON, G. C. 1968. Systematic desensitization as a counter-conditioning process. *Journal of Abnormal Psychology* 73:84–90.

DAWES, R. M. 1994. *House of cards: Psychology and psychotherapy built on myth.* New York: Free Press.

DAWES, R. W. 1980. Social dilemmas. *Annual Review of Psychology* 31:169–93.

DAY, R. H., AND MCKENZIE, B. E. 1981. Infant perception of the invariant size of approaching and receding objects. *Developmental Psychology* 17:670–77.

DE BENEDITTIS, G.; PANERAI, A. A.; AND VILLAMIRA, M. A. 1989. Effects of hypnotic analgesia and hypnotizability on experimental ischemic pain. *International Journal of Clinical and Experimental Hypnosis* 37:55–69.

DE GROOT, A. D. 1965. *Thought and choice in chess.* The Hague: Mouton.

DE ROUGEMONT, D. 1940. *Love in the western world.* New York: Harcourt Brace Jovanovich.

DE VALOIS, R. L. 1965. Behavioral and electrophysiological studies of primate vision. In Neff, W. D. (Ed.), *Contributions of sensory physiology,* vol. 1. New York: Academic Press.

DE VALOIS, R. L., AND DE VALOIS, K. K. 1975. Neural coding of color. In Carterette, E. C., and Friedman, M. P. (Eds.), *Handbook of perception,* vol. 5, pp. 117–62. New York: Academic Press.

DE VILLIERS, J. G. 1980. The process of rule learning in child speech: A new look. In Nelson, K. (Ed.), *Child language,* vol. 2. New York: Gardner Press.

DE VILLIERS, J. G., AND DE VILLIERS, P. A. 1973. Development of the use of word order in comprehension. *Journal of Psycholinguistic Research* 2:331–41.

DE WAAL, F. 1982. *Chimpanzee politics.* New York: Harper & Row.

DECASPER, A. J., AND FIFER, W. P. 1980. Of human bonding: Newborns prefer their mothers' voices. *Science* 208:1174–76.

DEECKE, L.; SCHEID, P.; AND KORNHUBER, H. H. 1968. Distribution of readiness potential, pre-motion positivity, and motor potential of the human cerebral cortex preceding voluntary finger movements. *Experimental Brain Research* 7:158–68.

DELIS, D. C.; KRAMER, J.; FREELAND, J.; AND KAPLAN, E. 1988. Integrating clinical assessment with cognitive science: Construct validation of the California Verbal Learning Test. *Journal of Consulting and Clinical Psychology* 56:123–30.

DELIS, D. C.; KRAMER, J.; FRIDLUND, A. J.; AND KAPLAN, E. 1990. A cognitive science approach to neuropsychological assessment. In McReynolds, R.; Rosen, J. C.; and Chelune, G. (Eds.), *Advances in psychological measurement,* vol. 7, pp. 101–32. New York: Plenum.

DEMBROSKI, T. M.; MACDOUGALL, J. M.; COSTA, P. T.; AND GRANDITS, G. A. 1989. Components of hostility as predictors of sudden death and myocardial infarction in the Multiple Risk Factor Intervention Trial. *Psychosomatic Medicine* 51:514–22.

DEMENT, W. C. 1974. *Some must watch while some must sleep.* San Francisco: Freeman.

DEMENT, W. C., AND KLEITMAN, N. 1957. The relation of eye movements during sleep to dream activity: An objective method for the study of dreaming. *Journal of Experimental Psychology* 53:339–46.

DEMENT, W. C., AND MITNER, M. M. 1993. It's time to wake up to the importance of sleep disorders (Commentary). *Journal of the American Medical Association* 269:1548–49.

DEMENT, W. C., AND WOLPERT, E. A. 1958. The relationship of eye-movements, body motility, and external stimuli to dream content. *Journal of Experimental Psychology* 55:543–53.

DEMONET, J. F.; WISE, R.; AND FRACKOWIAK, R. S. J. 1993. Language functions explored in normal subjects by positron emission tomography: A critical review. *Human Brain Mapping* 1:39–47.

DENNETT, D. 1978. *Brainstorms: Philosophical essays on mind and psychology.* Montgomery, Vt.: Bradford Books.

DENNET, D. C. 1991. *Consciousness explained.* Boston: Little, Brown.

DENNIS, W. 1940. Does culture appreciably affect patterns of infant behavior? *Journal of Social Psychology* 12:305–17.

DENNIS, W. 1973. *Children of the creche.* New York: Appleton-Century-Crofts.

DEPRESSION GUIDELINE PANEL. 1993. *Clinical Practice Guideline Number 5: Depression in primary care, 2: Treatment of major depression.* AHCPR publication 93–0551. Rockville, Md.: U.S. Dept. of Health and Human Services, Agency for Health Care Policy and Research.

DESCARTES, R. 1662. *Trait de l'homme,* Haldane, E. S., and Ross, G. R. T. (trans.). Cambridge: Cambridge University Press.

DESIMONE, R.; ALBRIGHT, T. D.; GROSS, C. G.; AND BRUCE, C. 1984. Stimulus-selective properties of inferior temporal neurons in the macaque. *Journal of Neuroscience* 4:2051–62.

DETTERMAN, D. K. 1987. What does reaction time tell us about intelligence? In Vernon, P. A. (Ed.), *Speed of information processing and intelligence.* Norwood, N.J.: Ablex.

DEUTSCH, J. A.; PUERTO, A.; AND WANG, M. L. 1978. The stomach signals satiety. *Science* 201:165–67.

DEVANE, W. A.; DYSARZ, F. A.; JOHNSON, M. R.; MELVIN, L. S.; AND HOWLETT, A. C. 1988. Determination and characterization of a cannabinoid receptor in rat brain. *Molecular Pharmacology* 34:605–13.

DEVANE, W. A.; HANUS, L.; BREUER, A.; PERTWEE, R. G.; STEVENSON, L. A.; GRIFFIN, G.; GIBSDON, D.; AND MANDELBAUM, R. 1992. Isolation and structure of a brain constituent that binds the cannabinoid receptor. *Science* 258:1946–49.

DEVINSKY, O., AND BEAR, D. M. 1984. Varieties of aggressive behavior in temporal lobe epilepsy. *American Journal of Psychiatry* 141:651–56.

DEVINSKY, O.; HAFLER, D. A.; AND VICTOR, J. 1982. Embarrassment as the aura of a complex partial seizure. *Neurology* 32:1284–85.

DI VESTA, F.; INGERSOLL, G.; AND SUNSHINE, P. 1971. A factor analysis of imagery tests. *Journal of Verbal Learning and Verbal Behavior* 10:471–79.

DIAMOND, A. 1988. The abilities and neural mechanisms underlying A-not-B performance. *Child Development* 59:523–27.

DIAMOND, A. 1989. Developmental progression in human infants and infant monkeys, and the neural bases of A-not-B and delayed response performance. Paper presented at a meeting on "The development and neural bases of higher cognitive functions," Philadelphia, Pa., May 20–24, 1989.

DIAMOND, A., AND GOLDMAN-RAKIC, P. S. 1989. Comparative development of human infants and rhesus monkeys on Piaget's A-not-B task: Evidence for dependence on dorsolateral prefrontal cortex. *Experimental Brain Research* 74:24–40.

DIAMOND, M. 1997. Sexual identity and sexual orientation in children with traumatized or ambiguous genitalia. *The Journal of Sex Research* 34:199–211.

DIAMOND, M., AND SIGMUNDSON, K. 1997. Sex reassignment at birth: A long-term review and clinical implications. *Archives of Pediatric and Adolescent Medicine* 151:298–304.

DIAMOND, R., AND ROZIN, P. 1984. Activation of existing memories in the amnesic syndrome. *Journal of Abnormal Psychology* 93:98–105.

DICKINSON, A. 1987. Animal conditioning and learning theory. In Eysenck, H. J., and Martin, I. (Eds.), *Theoretical foundations of behavior theory.* New York: Plenum.

DICKS, H. V. 1972. *Licensed mass murder: A sociopsychological study of some S.S. killers.* New York: Basic Books.

DICKSON, D. H., AND KELLY, I. W. 1985. The "Barnum effect" in personality assessment: A review of the literature. *Psychological Reports* 57:367–82.

DIENER, E. 1979. Deindividuation: The absence of self-awareness and self-regulation in group members. In Paulus, P. (Ed.), *The psychology of group influence,* pp. 209–42. Hillsdale, N.J.: Erlbaum.

DIENER, E.; FRASER, S. C.; BEAMAN, A. L.; AND KELEM, Z. R. T. 1976. Effects of deindividuation variables on stealing among Halloween trick-or-treaters. *Journal of Personality and Social Psychology* 5:143–55.

DILGER, W. C. 1962. The behavior of lovebirds. *Scientific American* 206:88–98.

DION, K.; BERSCHEID, E.; AND WALSTER, E. 1972. What is beautiful is good. *Journal of Personality and Social Psychology* 24:285–90.

DITTMAN, R. W.; KAPPES, M. W. E.; AND KAPPES, M. H. 1992. Sexual behavior in adolescent and adult females with congenital adrenal hyperplasia. *Psychoneuroendocrinology* 17:153–70.

DODSON, C. S.; JOHNSON, M. K.; AND SCHOOLER, J. W. 1997. The verbal overshadowing effect: Why descriptions impair face recognition. *Memory and Cognition* 25(2):129–39.

DOI, T. 1973. *The anatomy of dependence.* Tokyo: Kodansha.

DOLGER, H., AND SEEMAN, B. 1985. *How to live with diabetes,* 5th ed. New York: Norton.

DOMINGUEZ, R. A. 1992. Serotonergic antidepressants and their efficacy in obsessive-compulsive disorder. *Journal of Clinical Psychiatry* 53:56–59.

DOMJAN, M. 1980. Ingestional aversion learning: Unique and general processes. *Advances in the Study of Behavior* 11:275–336.

DOMJAN, M. 1983. Biological constraints on instrumental and classical conditioning: Implications for general process theory. In Bower, G. H. (Ed.), *The psychology of learning and motivation,* vol. 17. New York: Academic Press.

DORNBUSCH, S. M.; RITTER, P. L.; LIEDERMAN, P. H.; ROBERTS, D. F.; AND FRALEIGH, M. J. 1987. The relation of parenting style to adolescent school performance. Schools and development. *Child Development* (Special Issue) 58:1244–57.

DOUVAN, E., AND ADELSON, J. 1958. The psychodynamics of social mobility in adolescent boys. *Journal of Abnormal and Social Psychology* 56:31–44.

DRISCOLL, R.; DAVIS, K. E.; AND LIPETZ, M. E. 1972. Parental interference and romantic love: The Romeo and Juliet effect. *Journal of Personality and Social Psychology* 24:1–10.

DROMI, E. 1987. *Early lexical development.* Cambridge: Cambridge University Press.

DUCLOS, S. E.; LAIRD, J. D.; SCHNEIDER, E.; SEXTER, M.; STERN, L.; AND VAN LIGHTEN, O. 1989. Emotion-specific effects of facial expressions and postures on emotional experience. *Journal of Personality and Social Psychology* 57:100–8.

DUDA, R. O., AND SHORTLIFFE, E. H. 1983. Expert systems research. *Science* 220:261–68.

DUNCKER, K. 1929. Über induzierte Bewegung. *Psychologische Forschung* 12:180–259.

DUNCKER, K. 1945. On problem solving. *Psychological Monographs* (Whole No. 270):1–113.

DUNNING, D., AND COHEN, G. L. 1992. Egocentric definitions of traits and abilities in social judgment. *Journal of Personality and Social Psychology* 63:341–55.

DUNNING, D.; MEYEROWITZ, J. A.; AND HOLZBERG, A. D. 1989. Ambiguity and self-evaluation: The role of idiosyncratic trait definitions in self-serving assessments of ability. *Journal of Personality and Social Psychology* 57:1082–90.

DUNPHY, D. C. 1963. The social structure of urban adolescent peer groups. *Sociometry* 26:230–46.

DURANT, W., AND DURANT, A. 1967. *The story of civilization,* part X: *Rousseau and Revolution.* New York: Simon and Schuster.

DUTTON, D. G., AND ARON, A. P. 1974. Some evidence for heightened sexual attraction under conditions of high anxiety. *Journal of Personality and Social Psychology* 30:510–17.

DYER, F. C., AND GOULD, J. L. 1983. Honey bee orientation: A backup system for cloudy days. *Science* 214:1041–42.

DYKEMA, J.; BERGBOWER, K.; DOCTORA, J. D.; AND PETERSON, C. 1996. An attributional style questionnaire for general use. *Journal of Psychoeducational Assessment* 14:100–108.

EAGLE, M. N., AND WOLITSKY, D. L. 1992. Psychoanalytic theories of psychotherapy. In Freedheim, D. K. (Ed.), *History of psychotherapy.* Washington, D.C.: American Psychological Association.

EAGLY, A. H.; ASHMORE, R. D.; MAKHIJANI, M. G.; AND LONGO, L. C. 1991. What is beautiful is good, but . . . : A meta-analytic review of research on the physical attractiveness stereotype. *Psychological Bulletin* 110:109–28.

EAGLY, A. H., AND CHAIKEN, S. 1984. Cognitive theories of persuasion. In Berkowitz, L. (Ed.), *Advances in experimental social psychology,* vol. 17. New York: Academic Press.

EAGLY, A. H., AND CHAIKEN, S. 1993. *The psychology of attitudes.* Fort Worth: Harcourt Brace Jovanovich.

EAGLY, A. H., AND CROWLEY, M. 1986. Gender and helping behavior: A meta-analytic review of the social psychological literature. *Psychological Bulletin* 100:283–308.

EATON, W. O., AND YU, A. P. 1989. Are sex differences in child motor activity a function of sex differences in maturational status? *Child Development* 60:1005–11.

EBBINGHAUS, H. 1885. *Memory.* New York: Teacher's College, Columbia University, 1913. Reprint edition, New York: Dover, 1964.

EBERHARD, K. M.; SPIVEY-KNOWLTON, M. J.; SEDIVY, J. C.; AND TANENHAUS, M. K. 1995. Eye movements as a window into real-time spoken language comprehension in natural contexts. *Journal of Psycholinguistic Research* 24:409–36.

EBERHARD, W. G. 1996. *Female control: Sexual selection by cryptic female choice.* Princeton: Princeton University Press.

EBSTEIN, R. P.; NEMANOV, L.; KLOTZ, I.; GRITSENKO, I.; AND BELMAKER, R. H. 1997. Additional evidence for an association between the dopamine D4 receptor (D4DR) exon III repeat polymorphism and the human personality trait of Novelty Seeking. *Molecular Psychiatry* 2:472–7.

EBSTEIN, R. P.; NOVICK, O.; UMANSKY, R.; PRIEL, B.; OSHER, Y.; BLAINE, D.; BENNETT, E. R.; NEMANOV, L.; KATZ, M.; AND BELMAKER, R. H. 1996. Dopamine D4 receptor (D4DR) exon III polymorphism associated with the human personality trait of Novelty Seeking. *Nature Genetics* 12:78–80.

ECCLES, J. C. 1973. *The understanding of the brain.* New York: McGraw-Hill.

ECCLES, J. C. 1982. The synapse: From electrical to chemical transmission. *Annual Review of Neuroscience* 5:325–39.

EDGERTON, R. B. 1979. *Mental retardation.* Cambridge, Mass.: Harvard University Press.

EDMONDS, J. M., ED. AND TRANS. 1929. *The characters of Theophrastus.* Cambridge, Mass.: Harvard University Press.

EFRON, R. 1990. *The decline and fall of hemispheric specialization.* Hillsdale, N.J.: Erlbaum.

EGELAND, J. A., AND HOSTETTER, A. M. 1983. Amish study, 1: Affective disorders among the Amish. *American Journal of Psychiatry* 140:56–71.

EGETH, H.; JONIDES, J.; AND WALL, S. 1972. Parallel processing of multi-element displays. *Cognitive Psychology* 3:674–98.

EGGER, M. D., AND FLYNN, J. P. 1963. Effect of electrical stimulation of the amygdala on hypothalamically elicited behavior in cats. *Journal of Neurophysiology* 26:705–20.

EHRHARDT, A. A. 1984. Gender differences: A biological perspective. In Dienstbier, R. A., and Sonderegger, T. B. (Eds.), *Nebraska Symposium on Motivation,* pp. 37–58. Lincoln: University of Nebraska.

EICH, J. E. 1980. The cue-dependent nature of state-dependent retrieval. *Memory and Cognition* 8:157–73.

EIKELBOOM, R., AND STEWART, J. 1982. Conditioning of drug-induced physiological responses. *Psychological Review* 89:507–28.

EIMAS, P. D.; SIQUELAND, E. R.; JUSCZYK, P.; AND VIGORITO, J. 1971. Speech perception in infants. *Science* 171:303–6.

EISENBERGER, R., AND CAMERON, J. 1996. Detrimental effects of reward: Reality or myth? *American Psychologist* 51:1153–66.

EKMAN, P. 1972. Universals and cultural differences in facial expressions of emotion. In Cole, J. (Ed.), *Nebraska Symposium on Motivation,* 1971, vol. 19, pp. 207–83. Lincoln: University of Nebraska Press.

EKMAN, P. 1973. Cross-cultural studies of facial expression. In Ekman, P. (Ed.), *Darwin and facial expression,* pp. 169–222. New York: Academic Press.

EKMAN, P. 1977. Biological and cultural contributions to body and facial movement. In Blacking, J. (Ed.), *The anthropology of the body,* A. S. A. Monograph 15. London: Academic Press.

EKMAN, P. 1980. *The face of man: Expression of universal emotions in a New Guinea village.* New York: Garland STPM Press.

EKMAN, P. 1984. Expression and the nature of emotion. In Ekman, P., and Scherer, K. (Eds.), *Approaches to emotion,* pp. 319–43. Hillsdale, N.J.: Erlbaum.

EKMAN, P. 1985. *Telling lies.* New York: Norton.

EKMAN, P. 1992. An argument for basic emotions. *Cognition and Emotion* 6:169–200.

EKMAN, P. 1994. Strong evidence for universals in facial expression: A reply to Russell's mistaken critique. *Psychological Bulletin* 115:268–87.

EKMAN, P., AND FRIESEN, W. V. 1975. *Unmasking the face.* Englewood Cliffs, N.J.: Prentice-Hall.

EKMAN, P., AND FRIESEN, W. V. 1986. A new pan-cultural facial expression of emotion. *Motivation and Emotion* 10:159–68.

EKMAN, P.; FRIESEN, W. V.; AND O'SULLIVAN, M. 1988. Smiles when lying. *Journal of Personality and Social Psychology* 54:414–20.

EKMAN, P.; LEVENSON, R. W.; AND FRIESEN, W. V. 1983. Autonomic nervous system activity distinguishes among emotions. *Science* 221:1208–10.

EKMAN, P., AND OSTER, H. 1979. Facial expression of emotion. *Annual Review of Psychology* 30:527–54.

EKSTRAND, B. R. 1972. To sleep, perchance to dream (about why we forget). In Duncan, C. P.; Sechrest, L.; and Melton, A. W. (Eds.), *Human memory: Festschrift for Benton J. Underwood,* pp. 59–82. New York: Appleton-Century-Crofts.

EKSTRAND, B. R.; BARRETT, T. R.; WEST, J. M.; AND MAIER, W. G. 1977. The effect of sleep on human memory. In Drucker-Colin, R., and McGaugh, J. L. (Eds.), *Neurobiology of sleep and memory.* New York: Academic Press.

ELDER, G. H., JR. 1980. Adolescence in historical perspective. In Adelson, J. (Ed.), *Handbook of adolescent psychology.* New York: Wiley.

ELKIN, I.; SHEA, M. T.; WATKINS, J. T.; IMBER, S. D.; SOTSKY, S. M.; COLLINS, J. S.; GLASS, D. R.; PILKONIS, P. A.; LEBER, W. R.; DOCHERTY, J. P.; FEISTER, S. J.; AND PARLOFF, M. B. 1989. National Institute of Mental Health treatment of depression collaborative research program: General effectiveness of treatments. *Archives of General Psychiatry* 46:971–82.

ELKINS, R. L. 1991. An appraisal of chemical aversion emetic therapy approaches to alcoholism treatment. *Behaviour Research and Therapy* 29:387–413.

ELLENBERGER, H. F. 1970. *The discovery of the unconscious.* New York: Basic Books.

ELLIOT, A. J., AND DEVINE, P. G. 1994. On the motivational nature of cognitive dissonance: Dissonance as psychological discomfort. *Journal of Personality and Social Psychology* 67(3):382–94.

ELLIS, A. 1962. *Reason and emotion in psychotherapy.* Secaucus, N.J.: Lyle Stuart.

ELLIS, L., AND AMES, M. A. 1987. Neurohormonal functioning and sexual orientation: A theory of homosexuality-heterosexuality. *Psychological Bulletin* 101:233–58.

ELLSWORTH, P. C. 1994. Sense, culture, and sensibility. In Kitayama, S., and Markus, H. R. (Eds.), *Emotion and culture,* pp. 23–50. Washington, D.C.: American Psychological Association.

ELMS, A. C., AND MILGRAM, S. 1966. Personality characteristics associated with obedience and defiance toward authoritative command. *Journal of Experimental Research in Personality* 1:282–89.

EMMELKAMP, P. M. G. 1986. Behavior therapy with adults. In Garfield, S. L., and Bergin, A. E. (Eds.), *Handbook of psychotherapy and behavior change,* 3rd ed. New York: Wiley.

EMMERICH, W. 1966. Continuity and stability in early social development, II. Teacher ratings. *Child Development* 37:17–27.

ENDLER, N. S. 1982. Interactionism comes of age. In Zanna, M. P.; Higgins, E. T.; and Herman, C. P. (Eds.), *Consistency in social behavior. The Ontario Symposium,* vol. 2. Hillsdale, N.J.: Erlbaum.

ENDLER, N. S., AND HUNT, J. M. 1969. Generalization of contributions from sources of variance in the S-R inventories of anxiousness. *Journal of Personality* 37:1–24.

ENGLE, R. W.; CANTOR, J.; AND CARULLO, J. J. 1992. Individual differences in working memory and comprehension: A test of four hypotheses. *Journal of Experimental Psychology Learning, Memory, and Cognition* 18(5):972–92.

ENQUIST, M., AND LEIMAR, O. 1990. The evolution of fatal fighting. *Animal Behaviour* 39:1–9.

EPSTEIN, A. N. 1982. Mineralocorticoids and cerebral angiotensin may act together to produce sodium. *Peptides* 3(3)493–94.

EPSTEIN, A. N.; FITZSIMONS, J. T.; AND ROLLS, B. J. 1970. Drinking induced by injection of angiotensin into the brain of the rat. *Journal of Physiology* 210:457–74.

EPSTEIN, H. T. 1978. Growth spurts during brain development: Implications for educational policy and practice. In Chard, J. S., and Mirsky, A. F. (Eds.), *Education and the brain.* Chicago: University of Chicago Press.

EPSTEIN, S. 1979. The stability of behavior: I. On predicting most of the people much of the time. *Journal of Personality and Social Psychology* 37:1097–1126.

EPSTEIN, S. 1980. The stability of behavior. II. Implications for psychological research. *American Psychologist* 35:790–806.

EPSTEIN, S. 1983. The stability of confusion: A reply to Mischel and Peak. *Psychological Review* 90:179–84.

EPSTEIN, W. 1961. The influence of syntactical structure on learning. *American Journal of Psychology* 74:80–85.

ERDELYI, M. H. 1985. *Psychoanalysis: Freud's cognitive psychology.* New York: Freeman.

ERDELYI, M., AND GOLDBERG, B. 1979. Let's not sweep repression under the rug: Toward a cognitive psychology of repression. In Kihlstrom, J. F., and Evans, F. J.(Eds.), *Functional disorders of memory.* Hillsdale, N.J.: Erlbaum.

ERICSSON, K. A.; CHASE, W. G.; AND FALOON, S. 1980. Acquisition of a memory skill. *Science* 208:1181–82.

ERIKSEN, C. W., AND HOFFMAN, J. E. 1972. Temporal and spatial characteristics of selective encoding from multielement displays. *Perception and Psychophysics* 12:201–4.

ERIKSON, E. H. 1963. *Childhood and society.* New York: Norton.

ERIKSON, E. H. 1974. *Dimensions of a new identity: The Jefferson lectures in the humanities.* New York: Norton.

ERON, L. D. 1950. A normative study of the thematic apperception test. *Psychological Monographs* 64 (whole No. 315).

ERVIN, S. 1964. Imitation and structural change in children's language. In Lenneberg, E. H. (Ed.), *New directions in the study of language.* Cambridge, Mass.: MIT Press.

ESSOCK-VITALE, S. M., AND MCGUIRE, M. T. 1985. Women's lives viewed from an evolutionary perspective: II. Patterns of helping. *Ethology and Sociobiology* 6:155–73.

ESTES, W. K., AND SKINNER, B. F. 1941. Some quantitative properties of anxiety. *Journal of Experimental Psychology* 29:390–400.

ETKIN, W. 1964. Reproductive behaviors. In Etkin, W. (Ed.), *Social behavior and organization among vertebrates,* pp. 75–116. Chicago: University of Chicago Press.

EVANS, F. J. 1974. The placebo response in pain reduction. *Advances in neurology,* vol. 4, pp. 289–96. New York: Raven Press.

EXNER, J. E. 1974. *The Rorschach system.* New York: Grune and Stratton.

EXNER, J. E. 1978. *A comprehensive system: Current research and advanced interpretation,* vol. 2. New York: Wiley Interscience.

EXNER, J. E., JR. 1993. *The Rorschach: A comprehensive system,* vol. 1: *Basic foundations,* 3rd ed. New York: Wiley.

EXNER, J. E. (ED.). 1995. *Issues and methods in Rorschach research.* Mahwah, N.J.: Erlbaum.

EXNER, J. E., AND CLARK, B. 1978. The Rorschach. In Wolman, B. B. (Ed.), *Clinical diagnosis of mental disorders.* New York: Plenum.

EYER, D. E. 1992. *Mother-infant bonding: A scientific fiction.* New Haven, Conn.: Yale University Press.

EYFERTH, K. 1961. Leistungen verschiedener Gruppen von Besatzungskindern im Hamburg-Wechsler Intelligenz Test für Kinder (HAWIK). *Archiv für die gesamte Psychologie* 113:222–41.

EYSENCK, H. J. 1961. The effects of psychotherapy. In Eysenck, H. J. (Ed.), *Handbook of abnormal psychology,* pp. 697–725. New York: Basic Books.

EYSENCK, H. J. 1986. Toward a new model of intelligence. *Personality and Individual Differences* 7(5):731–36.

EYSENCK, H. 1992. Four ways five factors are not basic. *Personality and Individual Differences* 13:667–73.

EYSENCK, H. 1998. *Dimensions of personality.* New Brunswick, N.J.: Transaction Publishers.

EYSENCK, H. J., AND EYSENCK, S. B. G. 1975. *Psychoticism as a dimension of personality.* London: Hodder and Stoughton.

EYSENCK, H. J., AND EYSENCK, S. B. G. 1983. Recent advances: The cross-cultural study of personality. In Butcher, J. N., and Spielberger, C. D. (Eds.), *Advances in personality assessment,* vol. 2, pp. 41–72. Hillsdale, N.J.: Erlbaum.

EYSENCK, H. J. VERSUS KAMIN, L. 1981. *The intelligence controversy.* New York: Wiley.

EYSENCK, H. J., AND RACHMAN, S. 1965. *The causes and cures of neurosis.* San Diego, Calif.: Robert E. Knapp.

FAGOT, B. I. 1995. Psychosocial and cognitive determinants of early gender-role development. *Annual Review of Sex Research* 6:1–31.

FAGOT, B. I.; LEINBACH, M. D.; AND HAGEN, R. 1986. Gender labeling and adoption of same-sex behaviors. *Developmental Psychology* 22:440–43.

FALLON, A. E., AND ROZIN, P. 1985. Sex differences in perceptions of desirable body shape. *Journal of Abnormal Psychology* 94:102–5.

FALLSHORE, M., AND SCHOOLER, J. W. 1995. Verbal vulnerability of perceptual expertise. *Journal of Experimental Psychology Learning, Memory, and Cognition* 21(6)1608–23.

FANCHER, R. E. 1987. *The intelligence men: Makers of the IQ controversy.* New York: Norton.

FANT, L. G. 1972. *Ameslan: An introduction to American Sign Language.* Silver Springs, Md.: National Association of the Deaf.

FARAH, M. 1988. Is visual imagery really visual? Overlooked evidence from neuropsychology. *Psychological Review* 95:307–17.

FARAH, M. 1990. *Visual agnosia.* Cambridge, Mass.: MIT Press.

FARAH, M. 1995. Dissociable systems for recognition: A cognitive neuropsychology approach. In Kosslyn, S. M., and Osherson, D. (Eds.), *Visual cognition: An invitation to cognitive science,* 2nd ed. Cambridge: MIT Press.

FARIS, R. E. L., AND DUNHAM, H. W. 1939. *Mental disorders in urban areas.* Chicago: University of Chicago Press.

FAUSTO-STERLING, A. 1993. The five sexes: Why male and female are not enough. *The Sciences* March/April, 20–24.

FEDER, H. H. 1984. Hormones and sexual behavior. *Annual Review of Psychology* 35:165–200.

FEINGOLD, A. 1988. Matching for attractiveness in romantic partners and same-sex friends: A meta-analysis and theoretical critique. *Psychological Bulletin* 104:226–32.

FEINGOLD, A. 1992. Good-looking people are not what we think. *Psychological Bulletin* 111:304–41.

FEINMAN, J. A., AND DUNNER, D. L. 1996. The effect of alcohol and substance abuse on the course of bipolar affective disorder. *Journal of Affective Disorders* 37:43–49.

FELDMAN, H.; GOLDIN-MEADOW, S.; AND GLEITMAN, L. R. 1978. Beyond Herodotus: The creation of language by linguistically deprived deaf children. In Lock, A. (Ed.), *Action, gesture, and symbol: The emergence of language.* London: Academic Press.

FELIPE, N. J., AND SOMMER, R. 1966. Invasions of personal space. *Social Problems* 14:206–14.

FERNALD, A. 1992. Human maternal vocalizations to infants as biologically relevant signals: An evolutionary perspective. In Barkow, J. H.; Cosmides, L.; and Tooby, J. (Eds.), *The adapted mind,* pp. 391–428. New York: Oxford.

FERNALD, A., AND KUHL, P. 1987. Acoustic determinants of infant preference for motherese speech. *Infant Behavior and Development* 10:279–93.

FERNALD, A., AND SIMON, T. 1984. Expanded intonation contours in mothers' speech to newborns. *Developmental Psychology* 20:104–13.

FERNALD, A.; TAESCHNER, T.; DUNN, J.; PAPOUSEK, M.; DE BOYSSON-BARDIES, B.; AND FUKUI, I. 1989. A cross-linguistic study of prosodic modifications in mothers' and fathers' speech to preverbal infants. *Journal of Child Language* 16(3):477–502.

FERNANDEZ-DOLS, J. M., AND RUIZ-BELDA, M.-A. 1995. Are smiles a sign of happiness? Gold medal winners at the Olympic Games. *Journal of Personality and Social Psychology* 69:1113–19.

FERSTER, C. B., AND SKINNER, B. F. 1957. *Schedules of reinforcement.* New York: Appleton-Century-Crofts.

FESHBACH, N. 1969. Sex differences in children's mode of aggressive responses toward outsiders. *Merrill-Palmer Quarterly* 15:249–58.

FESHBACH, S. 1970. Aggression. In Mussen, P. H. (Ed.), *Carmichael's manual of child psychology,* 3rd ed., pp. 159–260. New York: Wiley.

FESTINGER, L. 1954. A theory of social comparison processes. *Human Relations* 7:117–40.

FESTINGER, L. 1957. *A theory of cognitive dissonance.* Evanston, Ill.: Row, Peterson.

FESTINGER, L., AND CARLSMITH, J. M. 1959. Cognitive consequences of forced compliance. *Journal of Abnormal and Social Psychology* 58:203–10.

FESTINGER, L.; PEPITONE, A.; AND NEWCOMB, T. 1952. Some consequences of deindividuation in a group. *Journal of Abnormal and Social Psychology* 47:387–89.

FESTINGER, L.; RIECKEN, H.; AND SCHACHTER, S. 1956. *When prophecy fails.* Minneapolis: University of Minnesota Press.

FIEDLER, F. E. 1978. Recent developments in research on the contingency model. In Berkowitz, L. (Ed.), *Group processes.* New York: Academic Press.

FIELD, T. 1978. Interaction behaviors of primary versus secondary caretaker fathers. *Developmental Psychology* 14:183–84.

FIGLEY, C. R. 1978. Symptoms of delayed combat stress among a college sample of Vietnam veterans. *Military Medicine* 143:107–10.

FILLMORE, C. 1968. The case for case. In Bach, E., and Harms, R. (Eds.), *Universals in linguistic theory.* New York: Holt, Rinehart and Winston.

FILLMORE, C. 1982. Towards a descriptive framework for spatial deixis. In Jarvella, R. J., and Klein, W. (Eds.), *Speech, place, and action: Studies in deixis and related topics.* Chichester, Eng.: Wiley.

FINE, A. 1986. Transplantation in the central nervous system. *Scientific American* August, pp. 52–58.

FINKE, R. 1993. Mental imagery and creative discovery. In Roskos-Ewoldsen, B.; Intons-Peterson, M. J.; and Anderson, R. (Eds.), *Imagery, creativity, and discovery,* pp. 255–85. New York: North-Holland.

FINKE, R. A.; PINKER, S.; AND FARAH, M. J. 1989. Reinterpreting visual patterns in imagery. *Cognitive Science* 13:51–78.

FINKE, R.; WARD, T.; AND SMITH, S. 1992. *Creative cognition: Theory, research and applications.* Cambridge: MIT Press.

FISHER, C., GLEITMAN, H., AND GLEITMAN, L. 1991. On the semantic content of subcategorization frames. *Cognitive Psychology* 23(3):331–92.

FISHER, C.; HALL, G.; RAKOWITZ, S.; AND GLEITMAN, L. R. 1994. When it is better to receive than to give. In Gleitman, L. R., and Landau, B. (Eds.), *Lexical acquisition, Lingua* (Special Issue) 92:333–75.

FISHER, C., AND TOKURA, H. 1996. Prosody in speech to infants: Direct and indirect acoustic cues to syntactic structure. In Morgan, J. L., and Demuth, K. (Eds.), *Signal to syntax: Bootstrapping from speech to grammar in early acquisition,* pp. 343–363. Mahwah, N.J.: Lawrence Erlbaum.

FISHER, R. A. 1930. *The genetical theory of natural selection.* Oxford: Clarendon.

FISHER, R. P., AND CRAIK, F. I. M. 1977. The interaction between encoding and retrieval operations in cued recall. *Journal of Experimental Psychology: Human Learning and Memory* 3:701–11.

FISHER, S., AND GREENBERG, R. P. 1977. *The scientific credibility of Freud's theory and therapy.* New York: Basic Books.

FISHER, S., AND GREENBERG, R. P. (EDS.). 1989. *The limits of biological treatments for psychological distress.* Hillsdale, N.J.: Erlbam.

FISKE, A. P.; KITAYAMA, S.; MARKUS, H. R.; AND NISBETT, R. E. 1998. The cultural matrix of social psychology. In Gilbert, D. T.; Fiske, S. T.; and Lindzey, G. (Eds.), *The handbook of social psychology,* 4th ed., pp. 915–81. New York: McGraw-Hill.

FISKE, S. T. 1998. Stereotyping, prejudice, and discrimination. In Gilbert, D. T.; Fiske, S. T.; and Lindzey, G. (Eds.), *The handbook of social psychology,* 4th ed., pp. 357–411. New York: McGraw-Hill.

FITZGERALD, F. T. 1981. The problem of obesity. *Annual Review of Medicine* 32:221–31.

FITZSIMONS, J. T., AND MOORE-GILLOW, M. J. 1980. Drinking and antidiuresis in response to reductions in venous return in the dog: Neural and endocrine mechanisms. *Journal of Physiology* 307:403–16.

FLANAGAN, O. 1994. *Consciousness reconsidered.* Cambridge, Mass.: Bradford Books.

FLAVELL, J. H. 1970. Developmental studies of mediated memory. In Reese, H. W., and Lipsitt, L. P. (Eds.), *Advances in child development and behavior,* vol. 5. New York: Academic Press.

FLAVELL, J. H. 1977. *Cognitive development.* Englewood Cliffs, N.J.: Prentice-Hall.

FLAVELL, J. H. 1985. *Cognitive development,* 2nd ed. Englewood Cliffs, N.J.: Prentice-Hall.

FLAVELL, J. H.; BEACH, D. H.; AND CHINSKY, J. M. 1966. Spontaneous verbal rehearsal in a memory task as a function of age. *Child Development* 37:283–99.

FLAVELL, J. H.; FLAVELL, E. R.; AND GREEN, F. L. 1983. Development of the appearance-reality distinction. *Cognitive Psychology* 15:95–120.

FLAVELL, J. H.; SHIPSTEAD, S. G.; AND CROFT, K. 1978. Young children's knowledge about visual perception: Hiding objects from others. *Child Development* 49:1208–11.

FLEMING, J. H., AND RUDMAN, L. A. 1993. Between a rock and a hard place: Self concept regulating and communicative properties of distancing behaviors. *Journal of Personality and Social Psychology* 64(1):44–59.

FLAVELL, J. H., AND WELLMAN, H. M. 1977. Metamemory. In Kail, R. V., Jr., and Hagen, J. W. (Eds.), *Perspectives on the development of memory and cognition,* pp. 3–34. Hillsdale, N.J.: Erlbaum.

FLODERUS-MYRHED, B.; PEDERSEN, N.; AND RASMUSON, L. 1980. Assessment of heritability for personality, based on a short form of the Eysenck Personality Inventory: A study of 12,898 twin pairs. *Behavior Genetics* 10:153–62.

FLUOXETINE BULIMIA NERVOSA COLLABORATIVE STUDY GROUP. 1992. Fluoxetine in the treatment of bulimia nervosa: A multicenter, placebo-controlled, double-blind trial. *Archives of General Psychiatry* 49:139–47.

FLYNN, J. R. 1984. The mean IQ of Americans: Massive gains 1932 to 1978. *Psychological Bulletin* 95(1):29–51.

FLYNN, J.; VANEGAS, H.; FOOTE, W.; AND EDWARDS, S. 1970. Neural mechanisms involved in a cat's attack on a rat. In Whalen, R. F.; Thompson, M.; Verzeano, M.; and Weinberger, N. (Eds.), *The neural control of behavior.* New York: Academic Press.

FLYNN, S. 1985. Principled theories of second language acquisition. *Studies in Second Language Acquisition* 7:99–117.

FLYNN, S. 1987. *A parameter-setting model of L2 acquisition: Experimental studies in anaphora.* Dordrecht: Reidel.

FOARD, C. F. 1975. Recall subsequent to tip-of-the-tongue experience. Unpublished first-year graduate research paper, University of Pennsylvania, Philadelphia.

FOCH, T. T., AND MCCLEARN, G. E. 1980. Genetics, body weight, and obesity. In Stunkard, A. J. (Ed.), *Obesity,* pp. 48–71. Philadelphia: Saunders.

FODOR, J. A. 1983. *The modularity of mind.* Cambridge, Mass.: MIT Press, Bradford Books.

FODOR, J. A. 1988. *Psychosemantics.* Cambridge, Mass.: MIT Press.

FODOR, J. A. 1992. A theory of the child's theory of mind. *Cognition* 44:283–96.

FONG, G.; KRANTZ, D.; AND NISBETT, R. 1986. The effects of statistical training on thinking about everyday problems. *Cognitive Psychology* 18:253–92.

FONG, G., AND NISBETT, R. 1991. Immediate and delayed transfer of training effects in statistical reasoning. *Journal of Experimental Psychology: General* 120:34–45.

FORD, C. S., AND BEACH, F. A. 1951. *Patterns of sexual behavior.* New York: Harper & Row.

FORER, B. R. 1949. The fallacy of personal validation: A classroom demonstration of gullibility. *Journal of Abnormal and Social Psychology* 44:118–23.

FORGATCH, M. S.; PATTERSON, G. R.; AND RAY, J. A. 1996. Divorce and boys' adjustment problems: Two paths with a single model. In Hetherington, E. M., and Blechmen, E. A. (Eds.), *Stress, coping, and resiliency in children and families. Family research consortium: Advances in family research,* pp. 67–105. Mahwah, N.J.: Erlbaum.

FORSTER, E. M. 1927. *Aspects of the novel.* New York: Harcourt, Brace, and World.

FOUCAULT, M. 1965. *Madness and civilization.* New York: Random House.

FOULKE, E., AND STICHT, T. G. 1969. Review of research on the intelligibility and compression of accelerated speech. *Psychological Bulletin* 72:50–62.

FOUTS, R. S. 1972. Use of guidance in teaching sign language to a chimpanzee (Pantroglodytes). *Journal of Comparative and Physiological Psychology* 80:515–22.

FOUTS, R. S.; HIRSCH, A. D.; AND FOUTS, D. H. 1982. Cultural transmission of a human language in a chimpanzee mother-infant relationship. In Fitzgerald, H. E.; Mullins, J. A.; and Gage, P. (Eds.), *Child nurturance, vol. 3: Studies of development in nonhuman primates,* pp. 159–69. New York: Plenum.

FRANKEL, F. H. 1993. Adult reconstruction of childhood events in the multiple personality disorder literature. *American Journal of Psychiatry* 150:954–58.

FRANKL, V. E. 1966. *The doctor and the soul.* New York: Knopf.

FRAZIER, L., AND FODOR, J. D. 1978. The sausage machine: A new two-stage parsing model. *Cognition* 6:291–325.

FREED, W. J.; DE MEDICACELLI, L.; AND WYATT, R. J. 1985. Promoting functional plasticity in the damaged nervous system. *Science* 227:1544–52.

FREEDMAN, J. L., AND FRASER, S. C. 1966. Compliance without pressure: The foot-in-the-door technique. *Journal of Personality and Social Psychology* 4:195–202.

FREEMAN, A.; SIMON, K. M.; BEUTLER, L. E.; AND ARKOWITZ, H. (EDS.). 1989. *Comprehensive handbook of cognitive therapy.* New York: Plenum.

FREEMAN, D. 1983. *Margaret Mead and Samoa: The making and unmaking of an anthropological myth.* Cambridge, Mass.: Harvard University Press.

FREEMAN, D. 1986. Rejoinder to Patience and Smith. *American Anthropologist* 88:161–67.

FREGE, G. 1892. On sense and reference. In Geach, P., and Black, M. (Eds.), *Philosophical writings of Gottlob Frege.* Oxford: Oxford University Press, 1952.

FREMOUW, W. J.; PERCZEL, M.; AND ELLIS, T. E. 1990. *Suicide risk: Assessment and response guidelines.* Elmsford, N.Y.: Pergamon.

FREUD, A. 1946. *The ego and the mechanisms of defense.* London: Hogarth Press.

FREUD, S. 1900. The interpretation of dreams. In Strachey, J., trans. and ed., *The complete psychological works,* vols. 4–5. New York: Norton, 1976.

FREUD, S. 1901. *The psychopathology of everyday life.* Translated by Tyson, A. New York: Norton, 1971.

FREUD, S. 1905. Three essays on the theory of sexuality. In Strachey, J., trans. and ed., *The complete psychological works,* vol. 7. New York: Norton, 1976.

FREUD, S. 1908. Character and anal eroticism. In Rieff, P. (Ed.), *Collected papers of Sigmund Freud: Character and culture.* New York: Collier Books, 1963.

FREUD, S. 1911. Psychoanalytic notes upon an autobiographical account of a case of paranoia (dementia paranoides). In Strachey, J., trans. and ed., *The complete psychological works,* vol. 12. New York: Norton, 1976.

FREUD, S. 1913. Further recommendations in the technique of psychoanalysis. In Strachey, J., trans. and ed., *The complete psychological works,* vol. 12. New York: Norton, 1976.

FREUD, S. 1917. *A general introduction to psychoanalysis.* Translated by Riviere, J. New York: Washington Square Press, 1952.

FREUD, S. 1923. *The ego and the id.* Translated by Riviere, J. New York: Norton, 1962.

FREUD, S. 1925. Some psychical consequences of the anatomical distinction between the sexes. In Strachey, J., trans. and ed., *The complete psychological works,* vol. 19. New York: Norton, 1976.

FREUD, S. 1926. *Inhibitions, symptoms, and anxiety.* Translated and revised by Strachey, J. New York: Norton, 1959.

FREUD, S. 1930. *Civilization and its discontents.* Translated by Strachey, J. New York: Norton, 1961.

FREUD, S. 1933a. Femininity. In Strachey, J., trans. and ed., *The complete psychological works,* vol. 22, pp. 112–35. New York: Norton, 1976.

FREUD, S. 1933b. *New introductory lectures on psychoanalysis.* Translated and revised by Strachey, J. New York: Norton, 1965.

FREUD, S. 1940. *An outline of psychoanalysis.* Translated by Strachey, J. New York: Norton, 1970.

FREUD, S., AND BREUER, J. 1895. Studies on hysteria. In Strachey, J., trans. and ed., *The complete psychological works,* vol. 2. New York: Norton, 1976.

FREYD, J. 1996. *Betrayal trauma: The logic of forgetting childhood abuse.* Cambridge, Mass.: Harvard University Press.

FRIDLUND, A. J. 1991. Evolution and facial action in reflex, social motive, and paralanguage. *Biological Psychology* 32(1):3–100.

FRIDLUND, A. J. 1994. *Human facial expression: An evolutionary view.* San Diego: Academic Press.

FRIDLUND, A. J.; EKMAN, P.; AND OSTER, H. 1983. Facial expression of emotion: Review of literature, 1970–1983. In Siegman, A. (Ed.), *Nonverbal behavior and communication.* Hillsdale, N.J.: Erlbaum.

FRIEDMAN, M. I. 1990a. Body fat and the metabolic control of food intake. *International Journal of Obesity* 14:53–67.

FRIEDMAN, M. I. 1990b. Making sense out of calories. In Stricker, E. M. (Ed.), *Handbook of behavioral neurobiology, vol. 10: Neurobiology of food and fluid intake,* pp. 513–29. New York: Plenum.

FRIEDMAN, M. I., AND STRICKER, E. M. 1976. The physiological psychology of hunger: A physiological perspective. *Psychological Review* 83:409–31.

FRIEDMAN, M. J., AND MARSELLA, A. J. 1996. Posttraumatic stress disorder: An overview of the concept. In Marsella, A. J.; Friedman, M. J.; Gerrity, E. T.; and Scurfield, R. M. (Eds.), *Ethnocultural aspects of posttraumatic stress disorder: Issues, research, and clinical applications,* pp. 11–32. Washington, D.C.: American Psychological Association.

FRIEDMAN, M., AND ROSENMAN, R. H. 1974. *Type A behavior.* New York: Knopf.

FRIJDA, N. H., AND MESQUITA, B. 1994. The social roles and functions of emotions. In Kitayama, S., and Markus, H. R. (Eds.), *Emotion and culture,* pp. 51–87. Washington, D.C.: American Psychological Association.

FRISHBERG, N. 1975. Arbitrariness and iconicity: Historical change in American Sign Language. *Language* 51:696–719.

FROMKIN, V.; KRASHEN, S.; CURTISS, S.; RIGLER, D.; AND RIGLER, M. 1974. The development of language in Genie: A case of language acquisition beyond the "critical period." *Brain and Language* 1:81–107.

FUJIMOTO, W. Y.; BERGSTROM, R. W.; BOYKO, E. J.; LEONETTI, D. L.; NEWELL-MORRIS, L. L.; AND WAHL, P. W. 1995. Susceptibility to development of central adiposity among populations. *Obesity Research* 3 (suppl. 2):179S–86S.

FUNDER, D. C. 1995. On the accuracy of personality judgment: A realistic approach. *Psychological Review* 102:652–70.

FUNKENSTEIN, D. H. 1956. Norepinephrine-like and epinephrine-like substances in relation to human behavior. *Journal of Mental Diseases* 124:58–68.

FURSTENBERG, F. F., AND CHERLIN, A. J. 1991. *Divided families: What happens to children when parents part.* Cambridge, Mass.: Harvard University Press.

GAGE, F. H., AND BJÖRKLUND, A. 1986. Cholinergic septal grafts into the hippocampal formation improve spatial learning and memory in aged rats by an atropine-sensitive mechanism. *Journal of Neuroscience* 6:2837–47.

GAGNON, J. H., AND SIMON, W. 1973. *Sexual conduct.* Chicago: Aldine.

GALABURDA, A. M. 1994. Developmental dyslexia and animal studies: At the interface between cognition and neurology. *Cognition* 56:833–39.

GALE, A. 1983. Electroencephalographic studies of extraversion-introversion: A case study in the psychophysiology of individual differences. *Personality and Individual Differences* 4:371–80.

GALE, A., AND EDWARDS, J. A. 1986. Cortical correlates of intelligence. In Gale, A., and Edwards, J. A. (Eds.), *Physiological correlates of human behaviour, vol. 3: Individual differences and psychopathology,* pp. 79–97. Orlando, Fla.: Academic Press.

GALEF, B. G. 1988. Imitation in animals: History, definition, and interpretation of data from the psychological laboratory. In Zentall, T. R., and Galef, B. G. (Eds.), *Social learning: Biological and psychological perspectives.* Hillsdale, N.J.: Erlbaum.

GALEN, B. R., AND UNDERWOOD, M. K. 1997. A developmental investigation of social aggression in children. *Developmental Psychology* 33:589–600.

GALLAGAN, R. 1987. Intonation with single words: Purposive and grammatical use. *Journal of Child Language* 14:1–22.

GALLISTEL, C. R. 1980. *The organization of action.* Hillsdale, N.J.: Erlbaum.

GALLISTEL, C. R. 1990. *The organization of learning.* Cambridge, Mass.: MIT Press (Bradford).

GALLISTEL, C. R. 1994. Space and time. In Mackintosh, N. J. (Ed.), *Animal learning and cognition,* pp. 221–53. New York: Academic Press.

GALLISTEL, C. R.; SHIZGAL, P.; AND YEOMANS, J. 1981. A portrait of the substrate for self-stimulation. *Psychological Review* 88:228–73.

GALLISTEL, R. 1995. Is long-term potentiation a plausible basis for memory? In McGaugh, J. L.; Weinberger, N. M.; and Lynch, G. (Eds.), *Brain and memory: Modulation and mediation of plasticity.* New York: Oxford University Press.

GALTON, F. 1869. *Hereditary genius: An inquiry into its laws and consequences.* London: Macmillan.

GALTON, F. 1883. *Inquiries into human faculty and its development.* London: Macmillan.

GANAWAY, G. K. 1989. Historical versus narrative truth: Clarifying the role of exogenous trauma in the etiology of MPD and its variants. *Dissociation* 2:205–20.

GARCIA, J.; ERVIN, F. R.; AND KOELLING, R. A. 1966. Learning with prolonged delay of reinforcement. *Psychonomic Science* 5:121–22.

GARCIA, J., AND KOELLING, R. A. 1966. The relation of cue to consequence in avoidance learning. *Psychonomic Science* 4:123–24.

GARDNER, H. 1983. *Frames of mind: The theory of multiple intelligences.* New York: Basic Books.

GARDNER, R. A., AND GARDNER, B. T. 1969. Teaching sign language to a chimpanzee. *Science* 165:664–72.

GARDNER, R. A., AND GARDNER, B. T. 1975. Early signs of language in child and chimpanzee. *Science* 187:752–53.

GARDNER, R. A., AND GARDNER, B. T. 1978. Comparative psychology and language acquisition. *Annals of the New York Academy of Science* 309:37–76.

GARFIELD, S. L. 1992. Major issues in psychotherapy research. In Freedheim, D. K. (Ed.), *History of psychotherapy.* Washington, D.C.: American Psychological Association.

GARFINKEL, P. E., AND GARNER, D. M. 1982. *Anorexia nervosa.* New York: Brunner/Mazel.

GARRIGAN, J. L. 1987. Post-traumatic stress disorder in military disaster workers. In *The human response to the Gander military air disaster: A summary report* (Division of Neuropsychiatry Report No. 88–12). Washington, D.C.: Walter Reed Army Institute of Research.

GARROD, S., AND DOHERTY, G. 1994. Conversation, co-ordination and convention: An empirical investigation of how groups establish linguistic conventions. *Cognition* 53(3):181–215.

GATHERCOLE, V. C. 1987. The contrastive hypothesis for the acquisition of word meaning: A reconsideration of the theory. *Journal of Child Language* 14(3):493–532.

GAZZANIGA, M. S. 1967. The split brain in man. *Scientific American* 217:24–29.

GAZZANIGA, M. S. 1983. Right hemisphere language following brain bisection: A 20-year perspective. *American Psychologist* 38:525–37.

GEEN, R. G. 1991. Social motivation. *Annual Review of Psychology* 42:377–99.

GEERTZ, C. 1983. Local knowledge. In *Further essays in interpretive anthropology.* New York: Basic Books.

GEFFEN, G.; BRADSHAW, J. L.; AND WALLACE, G. 1971. Interhemispheric effects on reaction time to verbal and nonverbal visual stimuli. *Journal of Experimental Psychology* 87:415–22.

GELDARD, F. A. 1962. *Fundamentals of psychology.* New York: Wiley.

GELDARD, F. A. 1972. The human senses. New York: Wiley.

GELMAN, R. 1978. Cognitive development. *Annual Review of Psychology* 29:297–332.

GELMAN, R. 1982. Basic numerical abilities. In Sternberg, R. J. (Ed.), *Advances in the psychology of human intelligence,* vol. 1, pp. 181–205. Hillsdale, N.J.: Erlbaum.

GELMAN, R., AND BAILLARGEON, R. 1983. A review of some Piagetian concepts. In Mussen, P. (Ed.), *Carmichael's manual of child psychology,* vol 3: *Cognitive development.* Markman, E. M., and Flavell, J. H., vol. eds., pp. 167–230. New York: Wiley.

GELMAN, R., AND GALLISTEL, R. C. 1978. *The child's understanding of number.* Cambridge, Mass.: Harvard University Press.

GENTNER, D. 1982. Why nouns are learned before verbs: Linguistic relativity versus natural partitioning. In Kuczaj, S. A. II (Ed.), *Language development,* vol II: *Language, thought, and culture,* pp. 301–34. Hillsdale, N.J.: Erlbaum.

GENTNER, D., AND JEZIORSKI, M. 1989. Historical shifts in the use of analogy in science. In Gholson, B.; Shadish, W.; Neimeyer, R.; and Houts, A. (Eds.), *Psychology of science: Contributions to metascience.* Cambridge: Cambridge University Press.

GEORGIADES, A.; LEMNE, C.; DE FAIRE, U.; LINDVALL, K.; AND FREDRIKSON, M. 1996. Stress-induced laboratory blood pressure in relation to ambulatory blood pressure and left ventricular mass among borderline hypertensive and normotensive individuals. *Hypertension* 28:641–46.

GERARD, H. B., AND MATHEWSON, G. C. 1966. The effects of severity of initiation on liking for a group: A replication. *Journal of Experimental Social Psychology* 2:278–87.

GERARD, H. B.; WILHELMY, R. A.; AND CONOLLEY, E. S. 1968. Conformity and group size. *Journal of Personality and Social Psychology* 8:79–82.

GERGEN, K. 1973. Social psychology as history. *Journal of Personality and Social Psychology* 26:309–20.

GERHARDT, P. F.; HOLMES, D. L.; ALESSANDRI, M.; AND GOODMAN, M. 1991. Social policy on the use of aversive interventions: Empirical, ethical, and legal considerations. *Journal of Autism and Developmental Disorders* 21:265–77.

GERKEN, L. 1996. Prosody's role in language acquisition and adult parsing. *Journal of Psycholinguistic Research* 25(2):345–56.

GERKEN, L.; LANDAU, B.; AND REMEZ, R. 1990. Function morphemes in young children's speech perception and production. *Developmental Psychology* 26(2):204–16.

GERSHON, E. S.; NURNBERGER, J. I., JR.; BERRETTINI, W. H.; AND GOLDIN, L. R. 1985. Affective disorders: Genetics. In Kaplan, H. I., and Sadock, J. (Eds.), *Modern synopsis of comprehensive textbook of psychiatry,* 4th ed. Baltimore: Williams & Wilkins.

GESCHWIND, N. 1970. The organization of language and the brain. *Science* 170:940–44.

GESCHWIND, N. 1972. Language and the brain. *Scientific American* 226:76–83.

GESCHWIND, N., AND GALABURDA, A. M. 1985. Cerebral lateralization: Biological mechanisms, associations and pathology. *Archives of Neurology* 42:428–59, 521–54.

GESCHWIND, N., AND LEVITSKY, W. 1968. Human brain: Left-right asymmetries in temporal speech region. *Science* 161(3837):186–87.

GESELL, A. L., AND THOMPSON, H. 1929. Learning and growth in identical twins: An experimental study by the method of co-twin control. *Genetic Psychology Monographs,* vol. 6.

GIANI, U.; FILOSA, A.; AND CAUSA, P. 1996. A non-linear model of growth in the first year of life. *Acta Paediatrica* 85:7–13.

GIBBONS, R. D.; HEDEKER, D.; ELKIN, I.; WATERNAUX, C.; KRAEMER, H. C.; GREENHOUSE, J. B.; SHEA, M. T.; IMBER, S. D.; SOTSKY, S. M.; AND WATKINS, J. T. 1993. Some conceptual and statistical issues in analysis of longitudinal psychiatric data. Application to the NIMH treatment of depression Collaborative Research Program dataset. *Archives of General Psychiatry* 50:739–50.

GIBBS, J. C.; CLARK, P. M.; JOSEPH, J. A.; GREEN, J. L.; GOODRICK, T. S.; AND MAKOWSKI, D. G. 1986. Relations between moral judgment, moral courage, and filed independence. *Child Development* 57:1040–43.

GIBBS, J., AND SMITH, G. P. 1984. The neuroendocrinology of postprandial satiety. In Martini, L., and Ganong, W. F. (Eds.), *Frontiers in neuroendocrinology,* vol. 8. New York: Raven.

GIBBS, W. W. 1996. Gaining on fat. *Scientific American* 275:88–94.

GIBSON, J. J. 1950. *The perception of the visual world.* Boston: Houghton Mifflin.

GIBSON, J. J. 1966. *The senses considered as perceptual systems.* Boston: Houghton Mifflin.

GIBSON, J. J. 1979. *The ecological approach to visual perception.* Boston: Houghton Mifflin.

GICK, M. L., AND HOLYOAK, K. J. 1980. Analogical problem solving. *Cognitive Psychology* 12:306–55.

GICK, M. L., AND HOLYOAK, K. J. 1983. Schema induction and analogical transfer. *Cognitive Psychology* 15:1–38.

GIGERENZER, G., AND HOFFRAGE, U. 1995. How to improve Bayesian reasoning without instruction: Frequency formats. *Psychological Review* 102:684–704.

GILHOOLY, K. 1988. *Thinking: Direct, undirected and creative,* 2nd ed. New York: Academic Press.

GILL, M. M. 1976. Metapsychology is not psychology. In Gill, M. M., and Holzman, P. S. (Eds.), *Psychology versus metapsychology,* pp. 71–105. New York: International Universities Press.

GILL, M. M. 1994. *Psychoanalysis in transition: A personal view.* Hillsdale, N.J.: Analytic Press.

GILLIGAN, C. 1982. *In a different voice: Psychological theory and women's development.* Cambridge, Mass.: Harvard University Press.

GILLIGAN, C. 1986. Profile of Carol Gilligan. In Scarr, S.; Weinberg, R. A.; and Levine, A. 1986. *Understanding development,* pp. 488–91. New York: Harcourt Brace Jovanovich.

GILMORE, D. D. 1990. *Manhood in the making.* New Haven, Conn.: Yale University Press.

GILOVICH, T. 1991. *How we know what isn't so.* New York: Free Press.

GILOVICH, T., AND MEDVEC, V. H. 1995. The experience of regret: What, when, and why. *Psychological Review* 102:379–95.

GINZBERG, L. 1909. *The legends of the Jews,* vol. 1. Translated by Szold, H. Philadelphia: Jewish Publication Society of America.

GLADUE, B. A.; GREEN, R.; AND HELLMAN, R. E. 1984. Neuroendocrine responses to estrogen and sexual orientation. *Science* 225:1496–98.

GLADWIN, T. 1970. *East is a Big Bird.* Cambridge, Mass.: Belknap Press.

GLANZER, M., AND CUNITZ, A. 1966. Two storage mechanisms in free recall. *Journal of Verbal Learning and Verbal Behavior* 5:531–60.

GLEAVES, D. H. 1996. The sociocognitive model of dissociative identity disorder: A reexamination of the evidence. *Psychological Bulletin* 120:42–59.

GLEITMAN, H. 1963. Place-learning. *Scientific American* 209:116–22.

GLEITMAN, H. 1971. Forgetting of long-term memories in animals. In Honig, W. K., and James, P. H. R. (Eds.), *Animal memory,* pp. 2–46. New York: Academic Press.

GLEITMAN, H. 1985. Some trends in the study of cognition. In Koch, S., and Leary, D. E. (Eds.), *A century of psychology as science,* pp. 420–36. New York: McGraw-Hill.

GLEITMAN, H. 1990. Some reflections on drama and the dramatic experience. In Rock, I. (Ed.), *The legacy of Solomon Asch: Essays in cognition and social psychology.* Hillsdale, N.J.: Erlbaum.

GLEITMAN, H., AND JONIDES, J. 1976. The cost of categorization in visual search: Incomplete processing of targets and field items. *Perception and Psychophysics* 20(4):281–88.

GLEITMAN, L. R. 1981. Maturational determinants of language growth. *Cognition* 10:103–14.

GLEITMAN, L. R. 1986. Biological dispositions to learn language. In Demopolous, W., and Marras, A. (Eds.), *Language learning and concept acquisition.* Norwood, N.J.: Ablex.

GLEITMAN, L. R. 1990. Structural sources of verb learning. *Language Acquisition* 1:1–54.

GLEITMAN, L. R.; GLEITMAN, H.; AND SHIPLEY, E. F. 1972. The emergence of the child as grammarian. *Cognition* 1(2):137–64.

GLEITMAN, L. R., AND NEWPORT, E. L. 1995. The invention of language by children: Environmental and biological influences on the acquisition of language. In Gleitman, L. R., and Liberman, M. (Eds.), *Language: An invitation to cognitive science,* 2nd ed., vol. 1, pp. 1–24. Cambridge, Mass.: MIT Press.

GLEITMAN, L. R., AND WANNER, E. 1982. Language acquisition: The state of the art. In Wanner, E., and Gleitman, L. (Eds.), *Language acquisition: The state of the art.* New York: Cambridge University Press.

GLICK, J. 1975. Cognitive development in cross-cultural perspective. In Horowitz, F. G. (Ed.), *Review of child development research,* vol. 4. Chicago: University of Chicago Press.

GLISKY, E.; SCHACTER, D.; AND TULVING, E. 1986. Computer learning by memory impaired patients: Acquisition and retention of complex knowledge. *Neuropsychologia* 24:313–28.

GOBET, F., AND SIMON, H. A. 1996a. Recall of random and distorted chess positions: Implications for the theory of expertise. *Memory and Cognition* 24:493–503.

GOBET, F., AND SIMON, H. A. 1996b. The roles of recognition processes and look-ahead search in time-constrained expert problem solving: Evidence from grand-master-level chess. *Psychological Science* 7:52–55.

GODDEN, D. R., AND BADDELEY, A. D. 1975. Context-dependent memory in two natural environments: On land and underwater. *British Journal of Psychology* 66:325–31.

GOFFMAN, E. 1959. *The presentation of self in everyday life.* Garden City, N.Y.: Anchor Books, Doubleday.

GOLANI, I.; WOLGIN, D. L.; AND TEITELBAUM, P. 1979. A proposed natural geometry of recovery from akinesia in the lateral hypothalamic rat. *Brain Research* 164:237–67.

GOLD, R. 1978. On the meaning of nonconservation. In Lesgold, A. M.; Pellegrino, J. W.; Fokkema, S. D.; and Glaser, R. (Eds.), *Cognitive psychology and instruction.* New York: Plenum.

GOLDBERG, L. R. 1982. From ace to zombie: Some explorations in the language of personality. In Spielberger, C., and Butcher, J. N. (Eds.), *Advances in personality assessment,* vol. 1. Hillsdale, N.J.: Erlbaum.

GOLDBERG, L. R. 1990. An alternative "description of personality": The Big-Five factor structure. *Journal of Personality and Social Psychology* 59:1216–29.

GOLDBERG, L. R. 1993. The structure of phenotypic personality traits. *American Psychologist* 48:26–34.

GOLDEN, T. 1990. Ill, possibly violent, and no place to go. *New York Times,* Monday, April 2, 1990, pp. A1 and B4.

GOLDFARB, W. 1955. Emotional and intellectual consequences of psychological deprivation in infancy: A reevaluation. In Hock, P. H., and Zubin, J. (Eds.), *Psychopathology of childhood.* New York: Grune and Stratton.

GOLDIN-MEADOW, S. 1982. Fragile and resilient properties of language learning. In Wanner, E., and Gleitman, L. R. (Eds.), *Language acquisition: State of the art.* New York: Cambridge University Press.

GOLDIN-MEADOW, S., AND FELDMAN, H. 1977. The development of language-like communication without a language model. *Science* 197:401–403.

GOLDSTEIN, B. 1996. *Sensation and perception,* 4th ed. Pacific Grove, Calif.: Brooks/Cole.

GOLDSTEIN, E. B. 1989. *Sensation and perception,* 3rd ed. Belmont, Calif.: Wadsworth.

GOLDSTEIN, J. M., AND TSUANG, M. T. 1990. Gender and schizophrenia: An introduction and synthesis of findings. *Schizophrenia Bulletin* 16:179–83.

GOMBRICH, E. H. 1961. *Art and illusion.* Princeton, N.J.: Bollingen Series, Princeton University Press.

GOODALE, M. A. 1995. The cortical organization of visual perception and visuomotor control. In Kosslyn, S. M., and Osherson, D. (Eds.), *Visual cognition: An invitation to cognitive science,* 2nd ed. Cambridge: MIT Press.

GOODENOUGH, D. R. 1978. Dream recall: History and current status of the field. In Arkin, A. M.; Antrobus, J. S.; and Ellman, S. J. (Eds.), *The mind in sleep: Psychology and psychophysiology.* Hillsdale, N.J.: Erlbaum.

GOODGLASS, H. 1973. Studies on the grammar of aphasics. In Goodglass, H., and Blumstein, S. (Eds.), *Psycholinguistics and aphasia.* Baltimore: Johns Hopkins University Press.

GORDON H. 1923. Mental and scholastic tests among retarded children. Educational pamphlet, no. 44. London: Board of Education.

GOREN, C. C.; SARTY, M.; AND WU, P. Y. K. 1975. Visual following and pattern discrimination of face-like stimuli by newborn infants. *Pediatrics* 56:544–59.

GOTTESMAN, I. I., AND SHIELDS, J. 1972. *Schizophrenia and genetics: A twin study vantage point*. New York: Academic Press.

GOTTESMAN, I. I., AND SHIELDS, J. 1982. *Schizophrenia: The epigenetic puzzle*. New York: Cambridge University Press.

GOTTESMAN, I. I.; McGUFFIN, P.; AND FARMER, A. 1987. Clinical genetics as clues to the "real" genetics of schizophrenia (a decade of modest gains while playing for time). *Schizophrenia Bulletin* 13:23–47.

GOTTLIEB, G. 1961. Developmental age as a baseline for determination of the critical period for imprinting. *Journal of Comparative and Physiological Psychology* 54:422–27.

GOTTLIEB, G. 1976. The role of experience in the development of behavior and the nervous system. In Gottlieb, G. (Ed.), *Neural and behavioral specificity*, pp. 25–56. New York: Academic Press.

GOUGH, H. G. 1975. *California psychological inventory: Manual*, rev. ed. Palo Alto, Calif.: Consulting Psychologists Press (original edition, 1957).

GOUGH, H. G. 1990. The California Psychological Inventory. In Watkins, C. E., Jr., and Campbell, V. L. (Eds.), *Testing in counseling practice. Vocational*, pp. 37–62. Hillsdale, N.J.: Erlbaum.

GOULD, J. L. 1990. Honey bee cognition. *Cognition* 37:83–103.

GOULD, J., AND GOULD, C. 1988. The insect mind: Physics or metaphysics. In Griffin, R. R. (Ed.), *Animal mind–human mind*. Berlin: Springer Verlag.

GOULD, S. J. 1977. *Ontogeny and phylogeny*. Cambridge, Mass.: Harvard University Press.

GOULD, S. J. 1978, Sociobiology: The art of storytelling. *New Scientist* 80:530–33.

GOULDNER, A. W. 1960. The norm of reciprocity: A preliminary statement. *American Sociological Review* 25:161–79.

GRAESSER, A. C.; MILLIS, K. K.; AND ZWAAN, R. A. 1997. Discourse comprehension. *Annual Review of Psychology* 48:163–89.

GRAF, P., AND MANDLER, G. 1984. Activation makes words more accessible, but not necessarily more retrievable. *Journal of Verbal Learning and Verbal Behavior* 23:553–68.

GRAF, P.; MANDLER, G.; AND HADEN, P. 1982. Simulating amnesic symptoms in normal subjects. *Science* 218:1243–44.

GRAF, P.; MANDLER, G.; AND SQUIRE, L. R. 1984. The information that amnesic patients don't forget. *Journal of Experimental Psychology: Learning, Memory, and Cognition* 10:164–78.

GRAHAM, C. H., AND HSIA, Y. 1954. Luminosity curves for normal and dichromatic subjects including a case of unilateral color blindness. *Science* 120:780.

GRAHAM, D. L. R.; RAWLINGS, E. I.; AND RIGSBY, R. K. 1994. *Loving to survive: Sexual terror, men's violence, and women's lives*. New York: New York University Press.

GRAMMER, K., AND THORNHILL, R. 1994. Human *Homo sapiens* facial attractiveness and sexual selection: The role of symmetry and averageness. *Journal of Comparative Psychology* 108:233–42.

GRANT, V. W. 1976. *Falling in love*. New York: Springer.

GRAY, S. 1977. Social aspects of body image: Perception of normalcy of weight and affect of college undergraduates. *Perceptual and Motor Skills* 45:1035–40.

GREEN, D. M. 1976. *An introduction to hearing*. New York: Academic Press.

GREEN, D. M., AND SWETS, J. A. 1966. *Signal detection theory and psychophysics*. New York: Wiley.

GREEN, G. D., AND CLUNIS, D. M. 1988. Married lesbians. Lesbianism: Affirming Nontraditional Roles. *Women and Therapy* (Special Issue) 8:41–49.

GREEN, P., AND PRESTON, M. 1981. Reinforcement of vocal correlates of auditory hallucinations by auditory feedback: A case study. *British Journal of Psychiatry* 139:204–208.

GREEN, R. 1979. Childhood cross-gender behavior and subsequent sexual preference. *American Journal of Psychiatry* 136:106–8.

GREEN, R. 1987. *The sissy-boy syndrome and the development of homosexuality*. New Haven, Conn.: Yale University Press.

GREEN, R. L.; HOFFMAN, L. T.; MORSE, R.; HAYES, M. E. B.; AND MORGAN, R. F. 1964. The educational status of children in a district without public schools. Cooperatiue Research Project No. 23211. Washington, D.C.: Office of Education. U.S. Department of Health, Education, and Welfare.

GREEN, S. K.; BUCHANAN, D. R.; AND HEUER, S. K. 1984. Winners, losers, and choosers: A field investigation of dating initiation. *Personality and Social Psychology Bulletin* 10:502–11.

GREENBERG, J.; PYSZCZYNSKI, T.; AND SOLOMON, S. 1982. The self-serving attributional bias: Beyond self-presentation. *Journal of Experimental Social Psychology* 18:56–67.

GREENE, R. L. 1988. Assessment of malingering and defensiveness by objective personality inventories. In Rogers, R. (Ed.), *Clinical assessment of malingering and deception*, pp. 123–58. New York: Guilford Press.

GREENE, R. L. 1991. *The MMPI-2/MMPI: An interpretive manual*. Needham Heights, Mass.: Allyn and Bacon.

GREENFIELD, P. M. 1966. On culture and conservation. In Bruner, J. R.; Olver, R. R.; and Greenfield, P. M. (Eds.), *Studies in cognitive growth*. New York: Wiley.

GREENFIELD, P. M. 1976. Cross-cultural research and Piagetian theory: Paradox and progress. In Riegel, K., and Meacham, J. (Eds.), *The developing individual in a changing world*, vol. 1. The Hague: Mouton.

GREENFIELD, P. M., AND SMITH, J. H. 1976. *The structure of communication in early language development*. New York: Academic Press.

GREENWALD, A. G.; AND BANAJI, M. R. 1995. Implicit social cognition: Attitudes, self-esteem, and stereotypes. *Psychological Review* 102(1):4–27.

GREGORY, R. L. 1974. Choosing a paradigm for perception. In Carterette, E. C., and Friedman, M. P. (Eds.), *Handbook of perception*, vol. 1: *Historical and philosophical roots of perception*. New York: Academic Press.

GRENYER, B. F. S., AND LUBORSKY, L. 1996. Dynamic change in psychotherapy: Mastery of interpersonal conflicts. *Journal of Consulting and Clinical Psychology* 64:411–16.

GREVEN, P. J., JR. 1970. *Four generations: Population, land, and family in colonial Andover, Massachusetts*. Ithaca: N.Y.: Cornell University Press.

GREVERT, P., AND GOLDSTEIN, A. 1985. Placebo analgesia, naloxone, and the role of endogenous opioids. In White, L.; Turks, B.; and Schwartz, G. E. (Eds.), *Placebo*, pp. 332–51. New York: Guilford.

GRICE, H. P. 1968. Utterer's meaning, sentence-meaning and word-meaning. *Foundations of Language* 4:225–42.

GRICE, H. P. 1975. Logic and conversation. In Cole, P., and Morgan, J. L. (Eds.), *Syntax and semantics 3: Speech acts*. New York: Academic Press.

GRILL, H. J., AND BERRIDGE, K. C. 1985. Taste reactivity as a measure of the neural control of palatability. *Progress in psychobiology and physiological psychology*, vol. 11, pp. 1–61. New York: Academic Press.

GRILLNER, S., AND WALLÉN, P. 1985. Central pattern generators for locomotion, with special reference to vertebrates. *Annual Review of Neuroscience* 8:233–61.

GRIMSHAW, J. 1981. Form, function, and the language acquisition device. In Baker, C., and McCarthy, J. (Eds.), *The logical problem of language acquisition*. Cambridge, Mass.: MIT Press.

GRIMSHAW, J. 1990. *Argument structure*. Cambridge, Mass.: MIT Press.

GROOP, L. C., AND TUOMI, T. 1997. Non-insulin-dependent diabetes mellitus—a collision between thrifty genes and an affluent society. *Annals of Medicine* 29:37–53.

GROSSMAN, H. J. (ED.). 1983. *Manual on terminology and classification in mental retardation*, rev. ed. Washington, D.C.: American Association for Mental Deficiency.

GROVES, P. M., AND REBEC, G. V. 1988. *Introduction to biological psychology*, 3rd ed. Dubuque, Iowa: W. C. Brown.

GRUBER-BALDINI, A. L.; SCHAIE, K. W.; AND WILLIS, S. L. 1995. Similarity in married couples: A longitudinal study of mental abilities and rigidity-flexibility. *Journal of Personality and Social Psychology* 69:191–203.

GRÜNBAUM, A. 1984. *The foundations of psychoanalysis: A philosophical critique*. Berkeley: University of California Press.

GRÜNBAUM, A. 1996. Is psychoanalysis viable? In O'Donohue, W., and Kitchener, R. F. (Eds.), *The philosophy of psychology*, pp. 281–90. London: Sage.

GURMAN, A. S., AND KNISKERN, D. P. 1981. Family therapy outcome research. In Gurman, A. S., and Kniskern, D. P. (Eds.), *Handbook of family therapy.* New York: Brunner/Mazel.

GUTTMANN, N., AND KALISH, H. I. 1956. Discriminability and stimulus generalization. *Journal of Experimental Psychology* 51:79–88.

GUYTON, A. C. 1981. *Textbook of medical physiology.* Philadelphia: Saunders.

GYGER, M., AND MARLER, P. 1988. Food calling in the domestic fowl, *Gallus gallus:* The role of external referents and deception. *Animal Behaviour* 36:358–65.

HABER, R. N. 1969. Eidetic images. *Scientific American* 220:36–44.

HADLEY, S. W., AND STRUPP, H. H. 1976. Contemporary accounts of negative effects in psychotherapy: An integrated account. *Archives of General Psychiatry* 33:1291–1302.

HAILMAN, J. P. 1967. The ontogeny of an instinct. *Behavior Supplements* 15:1–159.

HALL, C. S. 1953. A cognitive theory of dream symbols. *Journal of General Psychology* 48:169–86.

HALL, C. S. 1966. *The meaning of dreams.* New York: McGraw-Hill.

HALL, C. S.; LINDZEY, G.; LOEHLIN, J. C.; AND MANOSEVITZ, M. 1985. *Introduction to theories of personality.* New York: Wiley.

HALL, C. S., AND VAN DE CASTLE, R. 1966. *The content analysis of dreams.* New York: Appleton-Century-Crofts.

HALL, J. A., AND TAYLOR, S. E. 1976. When love is blind: Maintaining idealized images of one's spouse. *Human Relations* 29:751–61.

HALPERN, D. 1992. *Sex differences in cognitive abilities,* 2nd ed. Hillsdale, N.J.: Erlbaum.

HALPERN, D, F. 1997. Sex differences in intelligence: Implications for education. *American Psychologist* 52:1091–1102.

HALPERN, D. 1998. Teaching critical thinking for transfer across domains. *American Psychologist* 53:449–55.

HALVERSON, H. M. 1931. An experimental study of prehension infants by means of systematic cinema records. *Genetic Psychology Monographs* 47:47–63.

HAMBURG, D. A.; MOOS, R. H.; AND YALOM, I. D. 1968. Studies of distress in the menstrual cycle and the postpartum period. In Michael, R. P. (Ed.), *Endocrinology and human behavior,* pp. 94–116. London: Oxford University Press.

HAMER, D.; HU, S.; MAGNUSON, V.; AND HU, N. 1993a. A linkage between DNA markers on the X-chromosome and male sexual orientation. *Science* 261(5119):321–27.

HAMER, D.; HU, S.; MAGNUSON, V.; AND HU, N. 1993b. Genetics and male sexual orientation (Response). *Science* 261(5126):1259.

HAMILL, R.; WILSON, T. D.; AND NISBETT, R. E. 1980. Insensitivity to sample bias: Generalizing from atypical cases. *Journal of Personality and Social Psychology* 39:578–89.

HAMILTON, D. L., AND ROSE, T. L. 1980. Illusory correlation and the maintenance of stereotypic beliefs. *Journal of Personality and Social Psychology* 39:832–45.

HAMILTON, W. D. 1964. The genetical evolution of social behavior. *Journal of Theoretical Biology* 7:1–51.

HAMILTON, W. D., AND ZUK, M. 1982. Heritable true fitness and bright birds: A role for parasites? *Science* 341:289–90.

HANSEN, C. E., AND EVANS, A. 1985. Bisexuality reconsidered: An idea in pursuit of a definition. In Klein, F., and Wolf, T. J. (Eds.), *Bisexualities: Theory and research,* pp. 1–6. New York: Haworth Press.

HANSEN, J. T., AND SCHULDT, W. J. 1984. Marital self-disclosure and marital satisfaction. *Journal of Marriage and the Family* 46:923–26.

HARE, R. D. 1965. Temporal gradients of fear arousal in psychopaths. *Journal of Abnormal Psychology* 70:422–45.

HARE, R. D. 1978. A research scale for the assessment of psychopathy in criminal populations. *Personality and Individual Differences* 1:111–19.

HARE, R. D. 1993. *Without conscience: The disturbing world of the psychopaths among us.* New York: Pocket Books.

HAREVEN, T. K. 1978. The last stage: Historical adulthood and old age. In Erikson, E. H. (Ed.), *Adulthood,* pp. 201–16. New York: Norton.

HARLOW, H. F. 1950. Learning and satiation of response in intrinsically motivated complex puzzle performance in monkeys. *Journal of Comparative and Physiological Psychology* 43:289–94.

HARLOW, H. F. 1958. The nature of love. *American Psychologist* 13:673–85.

HARLOW, H. F. 1962. The heterosexual affectional system in monkeys. *American Psychologist* 17:1–9.

HARLOW, H. F., AND HARLOW, M. K, 1972. The young monkeys. In *Readings in Psychology Today,* 2nd ed. Albany, N.Y.: Delmar Publishers, CRM Books.

HARLOW, H. F., AND NOVAK, M. A. 1973. Psychopathological perspectives. *Perspectives in Biology and Medicine* 16:461–78.

HARRIS, G. W., AND MICHAEL, R. P. 1964. The activation of sexual behavior by hypothalamic implants of estrogen. *Journal of Physiology* 171:275–301.

HARRIS, P. L. 1987. The development of search. In Salapatek, P., and Cohen, L. (Eds.), *Handbook of infant perception,* pp. 155–208. New York: Academic Press.

HARRIS, ZELIG S. 1952. *Language* 28:474–79.

HARTER, S. 1990. Causes, correlates and the functional role of global self-worth: A life span perspective. In Sternberg, R. J., and Kolligan, J. (Eds.), *Competence considered,* pp. 67–97. New Haven: Yale University Press.

HARTMANN, H. 1964. *Essays on ego psychology: Selected problems in psychoanalytic theory.* New York: International Universities Press.

HARTSHORNE, H., AND MAY, M. A. 1928. *Studies in the nature of character,* vol. 1. New York: Macmillan.

HARVEY, L. O., JR., AND LEIBOWITZ, H. 1967. Effects of exposure duration, cue reduction, and temporary monocularity on size matching at short distances. *Journal of the Optical Society of America* 57:249–53.

HASE, H. D., AND GOLDBERG, L. R. 1967. Comparative validities of different strategies of constructing personality inventory scales. *Psychological Bulletin* 67:231–48.

HATFIELD, E. 1988. Passionate and companionate love. In Sternberg, R. J., and Barnes, M. L. (Eds.), *The psychology of love.* New Haven, Conn.: Yale University Press.

HATHAWAY, S. R., AND McKINLEY, J. C. 1940. A multiphasic personality schedule (Minnesota): I. Construction of the schedule. *Journal of Psychology* 10:249–54.

HAURI, P. 1977. *The sleep disorders.* Kalamazoo, Mich.: Upjohn Pharmaceuticals.

HAURI, P., AND LINDE, S. 1991. *No more sleepless nights.* New York: Wiley.

HAVILAND, J. B. 1996. Projections, transpositions, and relativity. In Gumperz, J. J., and Levinson, S. C. (Eds.), *Rethinking linguistic relativity. Studies in the social and cultural foundations of language,* pp. 271–323. Cambridge: Cambridge University Press.

HAWKES, C. H. 1992. Endorphins: The basis of pleasure? *Journal of Neurology, Neurosurgery and Psychiatry* 55:247–50.

HAY, P.; SACHDEV, P.; CUMMING, S.; SMITH, J. S.; LEE, T.; KITCHENER, P.; AND MATHESON, J. 1993. Treatment of obsessive-compulsive disorder by psychosurgery. *Acta Psychiatrica Scandinavica* 87:197–207.

HAYES, C. 1952. *The ape in our house.* London: Gollacz.

HAYNES, S. G.; FEINLEIB, M.; AND KANNEL, W. B. 1980. The relationship of psychosocial factors to coronary heart disease in the Framingham study: Eight years incidence in coronary heart disease. *American Journal of Epidemiology* 3:37–85.

HAYWARD, W. G., AND TARR, M. J. 1995. Spatial language and spatial representation. *Cognition* 55:39–84.

HAZAN, C., AND SHAVER, P. 1987. Romantic love conceptualized as an attachment process. *Journal of Personality and Social Psychology* 52:511–24.

HAZELRIGG, M. D.; COOPER, H. M.; AND BORDUIN, C. M. 1987. Evaluating the effectiveness of family therapies: An integrative review and analysis. *Psychological Bulletin* 101:428–42.

HEALY, A. F., AND MILLER, G. A. 1970. The verb as the main determinant of sentence meaning. *Psychonomic Science* 20:372.

HEARST, E. 1972. Psychology across the chessboard. In *Readings in Psychology Today,* 2nd ed. Albany, N.Y.: Delmar Publishers, CRM Books.

HECKERS S. 1997. Neuropathology of schizophrenia: Cortex, thalamus, basal ganglia, and neurotransmitter-specific projection systems. *Schizophrenia Bulletin* 23:403–21.

HEDGE, A., AND YOUSIF, Y. H. 1992. Effects of urban size, urgency, and cost of helpfulness: A cross-cultural comparison between the United Kingdom and the Sudan. *Journal of Cross-Cultural Psychology* 23:107–15.

HEDGES, L. V., AND NOWELL, A. 1995. Sex differences in mental test scores, variability, and numbers of high-scoring individuals. *Science* 269:41–45.

HEDIGER, H. 1968. *The psychology and behavior of animals in zoos and circuses.* New York: Dover.

HEIDER, E. R. 1972. Universals in color naming and memory. *Journal of Experimental Psychology* 93:1–20.

HEIDER, F. 1958. *The psychology of interpersonal relationships.* New York: Wiley.

HEILMAN, K. M., AND VALENSTEIN, E. 1979. *Clinical neuropsychology.* New York: Oxford University Press.

HEILMAN, K. M., AND WATSON, R. T. 1977. Mechanisms underlying the unilateral neglect syndrome. In Weinstein, E. A., and Friedland, R. P. (Ed.), *Hemi-inattention and hemisphere specialization.* New York: Raven Press.

HEIM, C.; OWENS, M. J.; PLOTSKY, P. M.; AND NEMEROFF, C. B. 1997. Endocrine factors in the pathophysiology of mental disorders. *Psychopharmacology Bulletin* 33:185–92.

HELBURN, S. W., AND HOWES, C. 1996. Child care cost and quality. *The Future of Children* 6:62–82.

HELD, J. D.; ALDERTON, D. L.; FOLEY, P. P.; AND SEGALL, D. O. 1993. Arithmetic reasoning gender differences: Explanations found in the Armed Services Vocational Aptitude Battery (ASVAB). *Learning and Individual Differences* 5:171–86.

HELLEKSON, C. J.; KLINE, J. A.; AND ROSENTHAL, N. E. 1986. Phototherapy for seasonal affective disorder in Alaska. *American Journal of Psychiatry* 143:1035–37.

HELLER, H. C.; CRANSHAW, L. I.; AND HAMMEL, H. T. 1978. The thermostat of vertebrate animals. *Scientific American* 239:102–13.

HELMHOLTZ, H. 1909. *Wissenschaftliche Abhandlungen,* II, pp. 764–843.

HELMHOLTZ, H. 1910. *Treatise on physiological optics,* vols. 2 and 3. Trans. and ed. from the 3rd German ed. Southall, J. P. Rochester, N.Y.: Optical Society of America.

HENDRY, D. P. (ED.). 1969. *Conditioned reinforcement.* Homeward, Ill.: Dorsey Press.

HENINGER, G. R. 1995. Indoleamines: The role of serotonin in clinical disorders. In Bloom, F. E., and Kupfer, D. (Eds.), *Psychopharmacology: The fourth generation of progress,* pp. 471–82. New York: Raven.

HENRY, W. E. 1973. *The analysis of fantasy.* Huntington, N.Y.: Robert E. Krieger.

HERDT, G. 1990. Developmental discontinuities and sexual orientation across cultures. In McWhirter, D. P.; Sanders, S. A.; and Reinisch, J. M. (Eds.), *Homosexuality/heterosexuality: Concepts of sexual orientation.* New York: Oxford University Press.

HERING, E. 1920. *Outlines of a theory of the light sense,* pp. 150–51. Edited by Hurvich, L. M., and Jameson, D. Cambridge, Mass.: Harvard University Press.

HERMAN, C. P., AND POLIVY, J. 1980. Restrained eating. In Stunkard, A. J. (Ed.), *Obesity,* pp. 208–25. Philadelphia: Saunders.

HERR, S. S. 1990. The law on aversive and nonaversive behavioral intervention. In Harris, S. L., and Handleman, J. S. (Eds.), *Aversive and nonaversive interventions: Controlling life-threatening behavior by the developmentally disabled,* pp. 80–118. New York: Springer.

HERRNSTEIN, R. J. 1979. Acquisition, generalization, and discrimination reversal of a natural concept. *Journal of Experimental Psychology: Animal Behavior Processes* 5:118–29.

HERRNSTEIN, R. J.; LOVELAND, D. H.; AND CABLE, C. 1976. Natural concepts in pigeons. *Journal of Experimental Psychology: Animal Behavior Processes* 2:285–311.

HERRNSTEIN, R. J., AND MURRAY, C. A. 1994. *The bell curve: Intelligence and class structure in American life.* Cambridge, Mass.: Free Press.

HERRNSTEIN, R. J.; NICKERSON, R. S.; DE SANCHEZ, M.; AND SWETS, J. A. 1986. Teaching thinking skills. *American Psychologist* 41:1279–89.

HERTZOG, C.; DIXON, R. A.; AND HULTSCH, D. F. 1990. Relationships between metamemory, memory predictions, and memory task performance in adults. *Psychology and Aging* 5:215–27.

HESS, D. J.; FOSS, D. J.; AND CARROLL, P. 1995. Effects of global and local context on lexical processing during language comprehension. *Journal of Experimental Psychology: General* 124:62–82.

HESS, E. H. 1958. "Imprinting" in animals. *Scientific American* 198:82.

HESS, E. H. 1959. Imprinting. *Science* 130:133–41.

HESS, E. H. 1973. *Imprinting: Early experience and the developmental psychobiology of attachment.* New York: Van Nostrand.

HESS, R. D. 1970. Social class and ethnic influences on socialization. In Mussen, P. H. (Ed.), *Carmichael's manual of child psychology,* 3rd ed., vol. 2, pp. 457–558. New York: Wiley.

HESS, U.; BANSE, R.; AND KAPPAS, A. 1995. The intensity of facial expression is determined by underlying affective state and social situation. *Journal of Personality and Social Psychology* 69:280–88.

HETHERINGTON, E. M.; STANLEY-HAGEN, M.; AND ANDERSON, E. R. 1989. Marital transitions: A child's perspective. *American Psychologist* 41:303–12.

HETHERINGTON, P. A., AND SEIDENBERG, M. S. 1989. Is there "catastrophic interference" in connectionist networks? In *Proceedings of the eleventh annual conference of the Cognitive Science Society,* pp. 26–33. Hillsdale, N.J.: Erlbaum.

HIER, D. B., AND CROWLEY, W. F. 1982. Spatial ability in androgen-deficient men. *New England Journal of Medicine* 306:1202–5.

HIGBEE, K. L., 1977. *Your memory: How it works and how to improve it.* Englewood Cliffs, N.J.: Prentice-Hall.

HIGGINS, R.; SNYDER, C. R.; AND BERGLAS, S. 1990. (Eds.). *Self-handicapping: The paradox that isn't.* New York: Plenum Press.

HIGLEY, J. D.; SUOMI, S. J.; AND LINNOILA, M. 1990. Parallels in aggression and serotonin: Consideration of development, rearing history, and sex differences. In Van Praag, H. M.; Plutchik, R.; and Apter, A. (Eds.), *Violence and suicidality: Perspectives in clinical and psychobiological research,* vol 3: *Clinical and experimental psychiatry,* pp. 245–56. New York: Brunner/Mazel.

HILGARD, E. R. 1977. *Divided consciousness: Multiple controls in human thought and action.* New York: Wiley.

HILGARD, E. R. 1986. *Divided consciousness: Multiple controls in human thought and action,* rev. ed. New York: Wiley.

HILL, A. L. 1978. Savants: Mentally retarded individuals with specific skills. In N. R. Ellis (Ed.), *International review of research in mental retardation,* vol. 9. New York: Academic Press.

HILL, C. T.; RUBIN, L.; AND PEPLAU, L. A. 1976. Breakups before marriage: The end of 103 affairs. *Journal of Social Issues* 32:147–68.

HILTS, P. J. 1995. *Memory's ghost: The strange tale of Mr. M and the nature of memory.* New York: Simon and Schuster.

HINDE, R. A. 1985. Expression and negotiation. In Zivin, G. (Ed.), *The development of expressive behavior,* pp. 103–16. Orlando, Fla.: Academic Press.

HINELINE, P. N., AND RACHLIN, H. 1969. Escape and avoidance of shock by pigeons pecking a key. *Journal of the Experimental Analysis of Behavior* 12:533–38.

HINES, M. 1990. Gonadal hormones and human cognitive development. In Balthazar, J. (Ed.), *Hormones, brains, and behaviors in vertebrates 1. Sexual differentiation neuroanatomical aspects, neurotransmitters, and neuropeptides 1.* Basel: Karger.

HINTZMAN, D. L. 1990. Human learning and memory: Connections and dissociations. *Annual Review of Psychology* 41:109–39.

HIRAGA, H.; OSHIMA, T.; WATANABE, M.; ISHIDA, M.; ISHIDA, T.; SHINGU, T.; KAMBE, M.; MATSUURA, H.; AND KAJIYAMA, G. 1996. Angiotensin I-converting enzyme gene polymorphism and salt sensitivity in essential hypertension. *Hypertension* 27:569–72.

HIRSCHFELD, R. M. A., AND CROSS, C. K. 1981. Epidemiology of affective disorders. *Archives of General Psychiatry* 39:3546.

HIRSCHFELD, R. M., AND GOODWIN, F. K. 1988. Mood disorders. In Talbott, J. A.; Hales, R. E.; and Yudofsky, S. C. (Eds.), *The American Psychiatric Press textbook of psychiatry,* vol. 7. Washington, D.C.: American Psychiatric Press.

HIRSH-PASEK, K., AND GOLINKOFF, R. M. 1991. Language comprehension: A new look at some old themes. In Krasnegor, N.; Rumbaugh, D.; Schiefelbusch, R.; and Studdert-Kennedy, M. (Eds.), *Biological and behavioral determinants of language development.* Hillsdale, N.J.: Erlbaum.

HIRSH-PASEK, K.; GOLINKOFF, R.; FLETCHER; DEGASPE-BEAUBIEN; AND CAULEY. 1985. In the beginning: One-word speakers comprehend word order. Paper presented at Boston Child Language Conference, October, 1985.

HIRTH, D. H., AND MCCULLOUGH, D. R. 1977. Evolution of alarm signals in ungulates with special reference to white-tailed deer. *American Naturalist* 111:31–42.

HOBBES, T. 1651. *Leviathan.* Baltimore: Penguin Books, 1968.

HOBSON, J. A. 1988. *The dreaming brain.* New York: Basic Books.

HOBSON, J. A., AND MCCARLEY, R. W. 1977. The brain as a dream-state generator: An activation-synthesis hypothesis of the dream process. *American Journal of Psychiatry* 134:1335–68.

HOCHBERG, J. E. 1978a. *Perception,* 2nd ed. Englewood Cliffs, N.J.: Prentice-Hall.

HOCHBERG, J. E. 1978b. Art and perception. In Carterette, E. C., and Friedman, M. P. (Eds.), *Handbook of perception,* vol. 10, pp. 225–55. New York: Academic Press.

HOCHBERG, J. E. 1980. Pictorial functions and perceptual structures. In Hagen, M. A. (Ed.), *The perception of pictures,* vol. 2, pp. 47–93. New York: Academic Press.

HOCHBERG, J. 1981. On cognition in perception: Perceptual coupling and unconscious inference. *Cognition* 10:127–34.

HOCHBERG, J. 1988. Visual perception. In Atkinson, R. C.; Herrnstein, R. J.; Lindzey, G.; and Luce, R. D. (Eds.), *Stevens' handbook of experimental psychology,* vol. 1: *Perception and motivation,* rev. ed., pp. 195–276. New York: Wiley.

HODGKIN, A. L., AND HUXLEY, A. F. 1939. Action potentials recorded from inside nerve fiber. *Nature* 144:710–11.

HODGKINSON, S.; MULLAN, M. J.; AND GURLING, H. M. 1990. The role of genetic factors in the etiology of the affective disorders. *Behavior Genetics* 20:235–50.

HOEBEL, B. G., AND TEITELBAUM, P. 1976. Weight regulation in normal and hyperphagic rats. *Journal of Physiological and Comparative Psychology* 61:189–93.

HOFFER, B. J., AND VAN HORNE, C. 1995. Survival of dopaminergic neurons in fetal-tissue grafts (Editorial). *New England Journal of Medicine* 332:1163–64.

HOFFERTH, S. L. 1996. Child care in the United States today. *The Future of Children* 6:41–61.

HOFFMAN, H. S. 1978. Experimental analysis of imprinting and its behavioral effects. *Psychology of Learning and Motivation* 12:137.

HOFFMAN, M. L. 1970. Moral development. In Mussen, P. H., (Ed.), *Carmichael's manual of child psychology,* 3rd. ed., vol. 2, pp. 457–558. New York: Wiley.

HOFFMAN, M. L. 1977a. Empathy, its development and prosocial implications. In Keasey, C. B. (Ed.), *Nebraska Symposium on Motivation* 25:169–217.

HOFFMAN, M. L. 1977b. Sex differences in empathy and related behaviors. *Psychological Bulletin* 84:712–22.

HOFFMAN, M. L. 1979. Development of moral thought, feeling, and behavior. *American Psychologist* 34:295–318.

HOFFMAN, M. L. 1984. Empathy, its limitations, and its role in a comprehensive moral theory. In Kurtines, W. M., and Gewirtz, L. (Eds.), *Morality, moral behavior, and moral development,* pp. 283–302. New York: Wiley.

HOLDING, D. H. 1985. *The psychology of chess skill.* Hillsdale, N.J.: Erlbaum.

HOLDING, D. H., AND REYNOLDS, R. I. 1982. Recall or evaluation of chess positions as determinants of chess skill. *Memory and Cognition* 10:237–42.

HOLLAND, P. 1984. Origins of behavior in Pavlovian conditioning. *Psychology of Learning and Motivation* 18:129–74.

HOLLANDER, E. P. 1985. Leadership and power. In Lindzey, G., and Aronson, E. (Eds.), *Handbook of social psychology,* 3rd ed., vol. 2. New York: Random House.

HOLLANDER, E., AND MCCARLEY, A. 1992. Yohimbine treatment of sexual side effects induced by serotonin reuptake blockers. *Journal of Clinical Psychiatry* 53:197–99.

HOLLINGSHEAD, A. B., AND REDLICH, F. C. 1958. *Social class and mental illness: A community study.* New York: Wiley.

HOLLIS, K. I. 1982. Pavlovian conditioning of signal-centered action patterns and autonomic behavior: A biological analysis of function. In Rosenblatt, J. S.; Hinde, R. A.; Beer, C.; and Busnel, M. (Eds.), *Advances in the study of behavior,* vol. 12, pp. 1–64. New York: Academic Press.

HOLLIS, K. L. 1984. The biological function of Pavlovian conditioning: The best defense is a good offense. *Journal of Experimental Psychology: Animal Learning and Behavior* 10:413–25.

HOLLISTER, L. E., AND CSERNANSKY, J. G. 1990. *Clinical pharmacology of psychotherapeutic drugs,* 3rd. ed. New York: Churchill-Livingstone.

HOLLON, S. D. 1996. The efficacy and effectiveness of psychotherapy relative to medications. *American Psychologist* 51:1025–30.

HOLMES, D. 1990. The evidence for repression: An examination of sixty years of research. In Singer, J. (Ed.), *Repression and dissociation: Implications for personality theory, psychopathology, and health,* pp. 85–102. Chicago: University of Chicago Press.

HOLT, R. R. 1978. *Methods in clinical psychology,* vol. 1: *Projective assessment.* New York: Plenum.

HOLTZMAN, P. S.; KRINGLEN, E.; MALTHYSSE, S.; FLANAGAN, S. D.; LIPTON, R. B.; CRAMER, G.; LEVIN, S.; LANGE, K.; AND LEVY, D. L. 1988. A single dominant gene can account for eye tracking dysfunctions and schizophrenia in offspring of discordant twins. *Archives of General Psychiatry* 45:641–47.

HOLTZWORTH-MUNROE, A., AND JACOBSON, N. S. 1985. Causal attributions of married couples: When do they search for causes? What do they conclude when they do? *Journal of Personality and Social Psychology* 48:1398–1412.

HOLWAY, A. F., AND BORING, E. G. 1947. Determinants of apparent visual size with distance variant. *American Journal of Psychology* 54:21–37.

HOOK, S. 1955. The hero in history. Boston: Beacon Press.

HOOLEY, J. M. 1985. Expressed emotion: A review of the critical literature. *Clinical Psychology Review* 5:119–39.

HORN, J. L. 1985. Remodeling old models of intelligence. In Wolman, B. B. (Ed.), *Handbook of intelligence: Theories, measurements, and applications,* pp. 267–300. New York: Wiley.

HORN, J. L., AND NOLL, J. 1994. A system for understanding cognitive capabilities: A theory and the evidence on which it is based. In Detterman, D. K. (Ed.), *Current topics in human intelligence,* vol. 4: *Theories of intelligence.* Norwood, N.J.: Ablex.

HORN, J. M. 1983. The Texas Adoption Project: Adopted children and their biological and adoptive parents. *Child Development* 54:268–75.

HORN, J. M.; LOEHLIN, J. C.; AND WILLERMAN, L. 1979. Intellectual resemblance among adoptive and biological relatives: The Texas Adoption Project. *Behavior Genetics* 13:459–71.

HORN, J. M.; LOEHLIN, J. C.; AND WILLERMAN, L. 1982. Aspects of the inheritance of intellectual abilities. *Behavior Genetics* 12:479–516.

HORN, L. R. 1987. Pragmatic theory. In Newmeyer, F. J., (Ed.), *Linguistics: The Cambridge survey,* vol. I: *Linguistic theory: Foundations.* New York: Cambridge University Press.

HORNE, J. A. 1988. *Why we sleep: The functions of sleep in humans and other mammals.* New York: Oxford University Press.

HORNEY, K. 1937. *The neurotic personality of our time.* New York: Norton.

HORNEY, K. 1945. *Our inner conflicts.* New York: Norton.

HORNEY, K. 1950. *New ways in psychoanalysis.* New York: Norton.

HORVATH, A. O., AND LUBORSKY, L. 1993. The role of the therapeutic alliance in psychotherapy. *Journal of Consulting and Clinical Psychology* 61:561–73.

HOTHERSALL, D. 1990. *History of psychology,* 2nd ed. New York: McGraw-Hill.

HOVLAND, C. I., AND SEARS, R. 1940. Minor studies in aggression: VI Correlation of lynchings with economic indices. *Journal of Psychology* 8:301–10.

HOVLAND, C. I., AND WEISS, W. 1952. The influence of source credibility on communication effectiveness. *Public Opinion Quarterly* 15:635–50.

HOWE, M. L., AND COURAGE, M. L. 1993. On resolving the enigma of infantile amnesia. *Psychological Bulletin* 113:305–27.

HOWES, C. 1990. Can the age of entry into child care and the quality of child care predict adjustment in kindergarten? *Developmental Psychology* 26:292–303.

HOWES, C., AND HAMILTON, C. E. 1993. Child care for young children. In Spodek, B. (Ed.), *Handbook of research on the education of young children.* New York: Macmillan.

HRDY, S. B. 1988. The primate origins of sexuality. In Smith, M. S.; Hamilton, W. D.; Margulis, L.; Hrdy, S. B.; Raven, P. H.; and Hefner, P. J. (Eds.), *The evolution of sex.* San Francisco: Harper & Row.

HRDY, S. B., AND WILLIAMS, G. C. 1983. Behavioral biology and the double standard. In Wasser, S. K. (Ed.), *The social behavior of female vertebrates,* pp. 3–17. New York: Academic Press.

HUBEL, D. H. 1963. The visual cortex of the brain. *Scientific American* 209:54–62.

HUBEL, D. H., AND WIESEL, T. N. 1959. Receptive fields of single neurons in the cat's visual cortex. *Journal of Physiology* 148:574–91.

HUDSPETH, A. J. 1989. How the ear's works work. *Nature* 341:397–404.

HULL, C. L. 1943. *Principles of behavior.* New York: Appleton-Century-Crofts.

HUMBOLDT, W. VON. 1836. *Über die Verschiedenheit des menschlichen Sprachbaues und ihren Einfluss auf die geistige Entwicklung des Menschengeschlechts.* Berlin: Königliche Akademie der Wissenschaften.

HUMPHREY, G. 1951. *Thinking: An introduction to its experimental psychology.* New York: Wiley.

HUMPHREYS, L. G. 1939. The effect of random alternation of reinforcement on the acquisition and extinction of conditioned eyelid reactions. *Journal of Experimental Psychology* 25:141–58.

HUNT, E. 1976. Varieties of cognitive power. In Resnick, L. B. (Ed.), *The nature of intelligence.* Hillsdale, N.J.: Erlbaum.

HUNT, E. 1978. Mechanics of verbal ability. *Psychological Review* 85:109–30.

HUNT, E. 1985a. The correlates of intelligence. In D. K. Detterman (Ed.), *Current topics in human intelligence,* vol. 1. Norwood, N.J.: Ablex.

HUNT, E. 1985b. Verbal ability. In Sternberg, R. J. (Ed.), *Human abilities: An information processing approach,* pp. 31–58. New York: Freeman.

HUNT, E. 1995. *Will we be smart enough? A cognitive analysis of the coming workforce.* New York: Russell Sage Foundation.

HUNT, E.; LUNNEBORG, C.; AND LEWIS, J. 1975. What does it mean to be high verbal? *Cognitive Psychology* 7:194–227.

HUNT, M. M. 1959. *The natural history of love.* New York: Knopf.

HUNT, P., AND HILLERY, J. M. 1973. Social facilitation in a coaction setting: An examination of the effects over learning trials. *Journal of Experimental Social Psychology* 9:563–71.

HURVICH, L. M. 1981. *Color vision.* Sunderland, Mass.: Sinauer Assoc.

HURVICH, L. M., AND JAMESON, D. 1957. An opponent-process theory of color vision. *Psychological Review* 64:384–404.

HUSTON, A. C. 1983. Sex-typing. In Mussen, P. (Ed.), *Carmichael's manual of child psychology,* vol. 4: *Socialization, personality, and social development,* pp. 387–468. Hetherington, E. M., vol. ed. New York: Wiley.

HUSTON, T. L.; RUGGIERO, M.; CONNER, R.; AND GEIS, G. 1981. Bystander intervention into crime: A study based on naturally occurring episodes. *Social Psychology Quarterly* 44:14–23.

HUTCHINSON, R. R., AND RENFREW, J. W. 1966. Stalking attack and eating behaviors elicited from the same sites in the hypothalamus. *Journal of Comparative and Physiological Psychology* 61:360–67.

HUTTENLOCHER, J.; SMILEY, P.; AND CHARNEY, R. 1983. Emergence of action categories in the child: Evidence from verb meanings. *Psychological Review* 90:72–93.

HUTTENLOCHER, P. R. 1979. Synaptic density in human frontal cortex—developmental changes and effects of aging. *Brain Research* 163:195–205.

HYDE, D. M. 1959. An investigation of Piaget's theories of the development of the concept of number. Unpublished doctoral dissertation. University of London. Quoted in Flavell, J. H., *The developmental psychology of Jean Piaget,* p. 383. New York: Van Nostrand Reinhold.

HYDE, J. S., AND LINN, M. C. 1988. Gender differences in verbal ability: A meta-analysis. *Psychological Bulletin* 104:53–69.

HYMAN, I.; HUSBAND, T.; AND BILLINGS, F. 1995. False memories of childhood experiences. *Applied Cognitive Psychology* 9:181–98.

ICKES, W.; SNYDER, M.; and GARCIA, S. 1997. Personality influences on the choice of situations. In Hogan, R.; Johnson, J. A.; and Briggs, S. R. (Eds.), *Handbook of personality psychology,* pp. 165–95. San Diego: Academic Press.

ILYIN, N. A., AND ILYIN, V. N. 1930. Temperature effects on the color of the Siamese cat. *Journal of Heredity* 21:309–18.

IMPERATO-MCGINLEY, J.; GUERRERO, L.; GAUTIER, T.; AND PETERSON, R. E. 1974. Steroid 5-alpha reductase deficiency in man: An inherited form of male pseudohermaphroditism. *Science* 186:1213–15.

IMPERATO-MCGINLEY, J.; PETERSON, R. E.; GAUTIER, T.; AND STURLA, E. 1979. Androgens and the evolution of male-gender identity among male pseudohermaphrodites with 5-alpha reductase deficiency. *New England Journal of Medicine* 300:1233–37.

INBAU, F. E., AND REID, J. E. 1953. *Truth and deception: The polygraph ("lie detector") technique.* Baltimore: Williams & Wilkins.

INHELDER, B., AND PIAGET, J. 1958. *The growth of logical thinking from childhood to adolescence.* New York: Basic Books.

INSEL, T. R. 1990. New pharmacologic approaches to obsessive compulsive disorder. *Journal of Clinical Psychiatry* (Supplement) 51:47–51.

INSEL, T. R. 1992. Toward a neuroanatomy of obsessive-compulsive disorder. *Archives of General Psychiatry* 49:739–40.

ISABELLA, R. A. 1993. Origins of attachment: Maternal interactive behavior across the first year. *Child Development* 64:605–21.

ISHA, A., AND SAGI, D. 1995. Common mechanisms of visual imagery and perception. *Science* 268:1772–74.

IZARD, C. E. 1971. *The face of emotion.* New York: Appleton-Century-Crofts.

IZARD, C. E. 1977. *Human emotions.* New York: Plenum.

IZARD, C. E. 1990. Facial expressions and the regulation of emotions. *Journal of Personality and Social Psychology* 58:487–98.

IZARD, C. E. 1991. *The psychology of emotions.* New York: Plenum.

IZARD, C. E. 1994. Innate and universal facial expressions: Evidence from developmental cross-cultural research. *Psychological Bulletin* 115:288–99.

IZZETT, R. 1971. Authoritarianism and attitudes toward the Vietnam War as reflected in behavioral and self-report measures. *Journal of Personality and Social Psychology* 17:145–48.

JACKENDOFF, R. 1987. The status of thematic relations in linguistic theory. *Linguistic Inquiry* 18(3):369–411.

JACKENDOFF, R. 1990. *Semantic structures.* Cambridge, Mass.: MIT Press.

JACKSON, J. M., AND LATANÉ, B. 1981. All alone in front of all those people: Stage fright as a function of the number and type of coperformers and audience. *Journal of Personality and Social Psychology* 40:73–85.

JACKSON, L. A.; HUNTER, J. E.; AND HODGE, C. N. 1995. Physical attractiveness and intellectual competence: A meta-analytic review. *Social Psychology Quarterly* 58:108–22.

JACKSON, M., AND MCCLELLAND, J. L. 1975. Sensory and cognitive determinants of reading speed. *Journal of Verbal Learning and Verbal Behavior* 14:565–74.

JACKSON, M. D., AND MCCLELLAND, J. L. 1979. Processing determinants of reading speed. *Journal of Experimental Psychology: Experimental* 108:151–58.

JACOBS, A. 1955. Formation of new associations to words selected on the basis of reaction-time-GSR combinations. *Journal of Abnormal and Social Psychology* 51:371–77.

JACOBS, G. H. 1993. The distribution and nature of colour vision among the mammals. *Biological Reviews of the Cambridge Philosophical Society* 68:413–71.

JACOBSEN, F. M. 1992. Fluoxetine-induced sexual dysfunction and an open trial of yohimbine. *Journal of Clinical Psychiatry* 53:119–22.

JACOBSEN, L. K.; GIEDD, J. N.; BERQUIN, P. C.; KRAIN, A. L.; HAMBURGER, S. D.; KUMRA, S.; AND RAPOPORT, J. L. 1997. Quantitative morphology of the cerebellum and fourth ventricle in childhood-onset schizophrenia. *American Journal of Psychiatry* 154:1663–69.

JACOBSON, N. S., AND CHRISTENSON, A. 1996. Studying the effectiveness of psychotherapy. *American Psychologist* 51:1031–39.

JACOBY, L. L., AND DALLAS, M. 1981. On the relationship between autobiographical memory and perceptual learning. *Journal of Experimental Psychology: General* 3:306–40.

JACOBY, L. L.; KELLEY, C.; BROWN, J.; AND JASECHKO, J. 1989. Becoming famous overnight: Limits on the ability to avoid unconscious influences of the past. *Journal of Personality and Social Psychology: General* 56:326–38.

JACOBY, L. L., AND WITHERSPOON, D. 1982. Remembering without awareness. *Canadian Journal of Psychology* 36:300–24.

JAHODA, G. 1979.; A cross-cultural perspective on experimental social psychology. *Personality and Social Psychology Bulletin* 5:142–48.

JAKOBS, E.; FISCHER, A. H.; AND MANSTEAD, A. S. R. 1997. Emotional experience as a function of social context: The role of the other. *Journal of Nonverbal Behavior* 21:103–30.

JAKOBS, E.; MANSTEAD, A. S. R.; AND FISCHER, A. H. 1996. Social context and the experience of emotion. *Journal of Nonverbal Behavior* 20:123–42.

JAMES, W. 1890. *Principles of psychology.* New York: Henry Holt.

JAMESON, D., AND HURVICH, L. M. 1975. From contrast to assimilation: In art and in the eye. *Leonardo* 8:125–31.

JAMISON, K. R. 1995. Manic-depressive illness and creativity. *Scientific American* 272:62–67.

JANG, K. L.; LIVESLEY, W. J.; AND VERNON, P. A. 1996. Heritability of the big five personality dimensions and their facets: A twin study. *Journal of Personality* 64:577–91.

JANICAK, P. G.; DAVIS, J. M.; GIBBONS, R. D.; ERICKSEN, S.; CHANG, S.; AND GALLAGHER, P. 1985. Efficacy of ECT: A meta-analysis. *American Journal of Psychiatry* 142:297–302.

JANOWSKY, J. S.; OVIATT, S. K.; AND ORWOLL, E. S. 1994. Testosterone influence spatial cognition in men. *Behavioral Neuroscience* 108:325–32.

JENKINS, H. M., AND MOORE, B. R. 1973. The form of the autoshaped response with food or water reinforcers. *Journal of the Experimental Analysis of Behavior* 20:163–81.

JENKINS, J. G., AND DALLENBACH, K. M. 1924. Oblivescence during sleep and waking. *American Journal of Psychology* 35:605–12.

JENKINS, J. H.; KLEINMAN, A.; AND GOOD, B. J. 1991. Cross-cultural studies of depression. In Becker, J., and Kleinman, A. (Eds.), *Psychosocial aspects of depression,* pp. 67–99. Hillsdale, N.J.: Erlbaum.

JENNINGS, E. E. 1972. *An anatomy of leadership: Princes, heroes, and supermen.* New York: McGraw-Hill.

JENSEN, A. R. 1969. How much can we boost I.Q. and scholastic achievement? *Harvard Educational Review* 39:1–123.

JENSEN, A. R. 1973. *Educability and group differences.* New York: Harper & Row.

JENSEN, A. R. 1980. Chronometric analysis of intelligence, *Journal of Social and Biological Structures* 3:103–22.

JENSEN, A. R. 1985. The nature of the black-white difference on various psychometric tests: Spearman's hypothesis. *Behavioral and Brain Sciences* 8:193–263.

JENSEN, A. R. 1987. Individual differences in the Hick paradigm. In Vernon, P. A. (Ed.), *Speed of information processing and intelligence.* Norwood, N.J.: Ablex.

JOCKIN, V.; McGUE, M.; AND LYKKEN, D. T. 1996. Personality and divorce: A genetic analysis. *Journal of Personality and Social Psychology* 71:288–99.

JOHN, O. P. 1990. The "Big Five" taxonomy: Dimensions of personality in the natural language and in questionnaires. In Pervin, L. A. (Ed.), *Handbook of personality: Theory and research,* pp. 676–1000. New York: Guilford Press.

JOHNSON, A. M.; WADSWORTH, J.; WELLINGS, K.; BRADSHAW, S.; AND FIELD, J. 1992. Sexual lifestyles and HIV risk. *Nature* 360:410–12.

JOHNSON, J., AND NEWPORT, E. 1989. Critical period efforts in second-language learning: The influence of maturational state on the acquisition of English as a second language. *Cognitive Psychology* 21:60–99.

JOHNSON, M. H. 1993. Cortical maturation and the development of visual attention in early infancy. In Johnson, M. H. (Ed.), *Brain Development and Cognition.* Cambridge, Mass.: Blackwell.

JOHNSON, M. H., AND MORTON, J. 1991. *Biology and cognitive development: The case of face recognition.* London: Blackwell.

JOHNSON, M. K., AND RAYE, C. L. 1981. Reality monitoring. *Psychological Review* 88:67–85.

JOHNSON, R. E. 1979. *Juvenile delinquency and its origins.* New York: Cambridge University Press.

JOHNSON, S. 1765. Shakespeare criticism. In Danziger, M. K. (Ed.), *Samuel Johnson on literature.* New York: Ungar, 1979.

JONES, E. 1954. *Hamlet and Oedipus.* New York: Doubleday.

JONES, E. E., AND BERGLAS, S. 1978. Control of attributions about the self through self handicapping strategies: The appeal of alcohol and the role of underachievement. *Personality and Social Psychology Bulletin* 4(2):200–206.

JONES, E. E., AND NISBETT, R. E. 1972. The actor and the observer: Divergent perceptions of the cause of behavior. In Jones, E. E.; Karouse, D. E.; Kelley, H. H.; Nisbett, R. E.; Valins, S.; and Weiner, B. (Eds.), *Attribution perceiving the causes of behavior.* Morristown, N.J.: General Learning Press.

JONES, R. E. 1983. Street people and psychiatry: An introduction. *Hospital Community Psychiatry* 34:807–11.

JONES, S.; COLLINS, K.; AND HONG, H. 1991. An audience effect on smile production in 10-month-old infants. *Psychological Science* 2(1):45–49.

JONIDES, J. 1980. Toward a model of the mind's eye's movement. *Canadian Journal of Psychology* 34:103–12.

JONIDES, J. 1983. Further toward a model of the mind's eye's movement. *Bulletin of the Psychonomic Society* 21:247–50.

JONIDES, J., AND BAUM, D. R. 1978. Cognitive maps as revealed by distance estimates. Paper presented at the 18th annual meeting of the Psychonomic Society. Washington, D.C.

JONSSON, E. G.; NOTHEN, M. M.; GUSTAVSSON, J. P.; NEIDT, H.; AND OTHERS. 1997. Lack of evidence for the allelic association between personality traits and the dopamine D-sub-4 receptor gene polymorphisms. *American Journal of Psychiatry* 154:697–99.

JORGENSEN, B. W., AND CERVONE, J. C. 1978. Affect enhancement in the pseudo recognition task. *Personality and Social Psychology Bulletin* 4:285–88.

JORGENSEN, R. S.; JOHNSON, B. T.; KOLODZIEJ, M. E.; SCHREER, G. E. 1996. Elevated blood pressure and personality: A meta-analytic review. *Psychological Bulletin* 120:293–320.

JOSHI, A. K. 1983. Varieties of cooperative responses in question-answer systems. In Keifer, F. (Ed.), *Questions and answers,* pp. 229–40. Amsterdam: D. Reidel Publishing Co.

JOSSELSON, R. 1980. Ego development in adolescence. In Adelson, J. (Ed.), *Handbook of adolescent psychology,* pp. 188–211. New York: Wiley.

JOURARD, S. M. 1964. *The transparent self.* New York: Van Nostrand.

JOUVET, M. 1967. The stages of sleep. *Scientific American* 216:62–72.

JUDD, L. L.; PAULUS, M. P.; WELLS, K. B.; AND RAPAPORT, M. H. 1996. Socioeconomic burden of subsyndromal depressive symptoms and major depression in a sample of the general population. *American Journal of Psychiatry* 153:1411–17.

JULESZ, B. 1978. Perceptual limits of texture discrimination and their implications to figure-ground separation. In Leeuwenberg, E., and Buffart, H. (Eds.), *Formal theories of perception,* pp. 205–16. New York: Wiley.

JULIEN, R. M. 1985. *A primer of drug action,* 4th ed. New York: Freeman.

JUSCZYK, P. 1985. On characterizing the development of speech perception. In Mehler, J., and Fox, R. (Eds.), *Neonate cognition: Beyond the blooming buzzing confusion.* Hillsdale, N.J.: Erlbaum.

JUST, M. A., AND CARPENTER, P. A. 1992. A capacity theory of comprehension: Individual differences in working memory. *Psychological Review* 99(1):122–49.

JUSTER, H. R., AND HEIMBERG, R. G. 1995. Social phobia. Longitudinal course and long-term outcome of cognitive-behavioral treatment. *Psychiatric Clinics of North America* 18:821–42.

KAGAN, J. 1976. Emergent themes in human development. *American Scientist* 64:186–96.

KAGAN, J. 1984. *The nature of the child.* New York: Basic Books.

KAGAN, J., AND MOSS, H. A. 1962. *Birth to maturity: The Fels study of psychological development.* New York: Wiley.

KAHNEMAN, D., AND MILLER, D. T. 1986. Norm theory: Comparing reality to its alternatives. *Psychological Review* 93:136–53.

KAHNEMAN, D., AND TVERSKY, A. 1972. Subjective probability: A judgment of representativeness. *Cognitive Psychology* 3:430–54.

KAHNEMAN, D., AND TVERSKY, A. 1973. On the psychology of prediction. *Psychological Review* 80:237–51.

KAHNEMAN, D., AND TVERSKY, A. 1982. The simulation heuristic. In Kahneman, D.; Slovic, P.; and Tversky, A. (Eds.), *Judgment under uncertainty.* New York: Cambridge University Press.

KAHNEMAN, D., AND TVERSKY, A. 1984. Choices, values and frames. *American Psychologist* 39:341–50.

KAHNEMAN, D., AND TVERSKY, A. 1996. On the reality of cognitive illusions. *Psychological Review* 103:582–91.

KALAT, J. W. 1984. *Biological psychology,* 2nd ed. Belmont, Calif.: Wadsworth.

KAMIN, L. J. 1965. Temporal and intensity characteristics of the conditioned stimulus. In Prokasy, W. F. (Ed.), *Classical conditioning.* New York: Appleton-Century-Crofts.

KAMIN, L. J. 1968. "Attention-like" processes in classical conditioning. In Jones, M. R. (Ed.), *Miami symposium on the prediction of behavior: Aversive stimuli.* Miami: University of Miami Press.

KAMIN, L. J. 1969. Predictability, surprise, attention and conditioning. In Campbell, B. A., and Church, R. M. (Eds.), *Punishment and aversive behavior,* pp. 279–96. New York: Appleton-Century-Crofts.

KAMIN, L. J. 1974. *The science and politics of I.Q.* New York: Wiley.

KAMINSKY, H. 1984. Moral development in historical perspective. In Kurtines, W. M., and Gerwitz, J. L. (Eds.), *Morality, moral behavior, and moral development.* New York: Wiley.

KAMPERT, J. B.; BLAIR, S. N.; BARLOW, C. E.; AND KOHL, H. W. III. 1996. Physical activity, physical fitness, and all-cause and cancer mortality: A prospective study of men and women. *Annals of Epidemiology* 6:452–57.

KANDEL, D. 1978. Similarity in real-life adolescent friendship pairs. *Journal of Personality and Social Psychology* 36:306–12.

KANDEL, E. R. 1979. Small systems of neurons. *Scientific American* 241:66–76.

KANDEL, E. R., AND HAWKINS, R. D. 1992. The biological basis of learning and individuality. *Scientific American* 267:78–87.

KANIZSA, G. 1976. Subjective contours. *Scientific American* 234:48–52.

KAPLAN, E.; FINE, D.; MORRIS, R.; AND DELIS, D. C. 1991. *WAIS-R as a neuropsychological instrument.* San Antonio, Tex.: The Psychological Corporation.

KAPUR, S., AND REMINGTON, G. 1996. Serotonin-dopamine interaction and its relevance to schizophrenia. *American Journal of Psychiatry* 153:466–76.

KARAU, S. J., AND WILLIAMS, K. D. 1995. Social loafing: Research findings, implications, and future directions. *Current Directions in Psychological Science* 4:134–40.

KATZ, B. 1952. The nerve impulse. *Scientific American* 187:55–64.

KATZ, J. J. 1972. *Semantic theory.* New York: Harper & Row.

KATZ, J. J., AND FODOR, J. A. 1963. The structure of a semantic theory. *Language* 39:170–210.

KATZ, N.; BAKER, E.; AND MACNAMARA, J. 1974. What's in a name? A study of how children learn common and proper names. *Child Development* 45:469–73.

KAUFMAN, A. S.; KAMPHAUS; R. W.; AND KAUFMAN, N. L. 1985. The Kaufman Assessment Battery for Children (K–ABC). In Newmark, C. S. (Ed.), *Major psychological assessment instruments.* Boston: Allyn and Bacon.

KAY, P. 1996. Intra-speaker relativity. In Gumperz, J. J., and Levinson, S. C. (Eds.), *Rethinking linguistic relativity. Studies in the social and cultural foundations of language.* Cambridge: Cambridge University Press.

KEDDY HECTOR, A. C., AND RALEIGH, M. J. 1992. The effects of temporary removal of the alpha male on the behavior of subordinate male vervet monkeys. *American Journal of Primatology* 26:77–87.

KEDDY HECTOR, A. C.; SEYFARTH, R. M.; AND RALEIGH, M. J. 1989. Male parental care, female choice and the effect of an audience in vervet monkeys. *Animal Behaviour* 38:262–71.

KEESEY, R. E., AND POWLEY, T. L. 1986. The regulation of body weight. *Annual Review of Psychology* 37:109–34.

KEETON, W. T. 1972 and 1980. *Biological science,* 2nd and 3rd eds. New York: Norton.

KEETON, W. T. AND GOULD, J. L. 1986 and 1993. *Biological science,* 4th and 5th eds. New York: Norton.

KEIL, F. C. 1979. *Semantic and conceptual development: An ontological perspective.* Cambridge, Mass.: Harvard University Press.

KEIL, F. C., AND BATTERMAN, N. 1984. A characteristic-to-defining shift in the development of word meaning. *Journal of Verbal Learning and Verbal Behavior* 23:221–36.

KELLER, H. 1955. *Teacher: Anne Sullivan Macy.* Westport, Conn.: Greenwood Press.

KELLEY, H. H. 1967. Attribution theory in social psychology. In Levine, D. (Ed.), *Nebraska Symposium on Motivation,* pp. 192–238. Lincoln: University of Nebraska Press.

KELLEY, H. H., AND MICHELA, J. L. 1980. Attribution theory and research. *Annual Review of Psychology* 31:457–501.

KELLEY, H., AND THIBAUT, J. W. 1978. *Interpersonal relations: A theory of interdependence.* New York: Wiley-Interscience.

KELLEY, S., AND MIRER, T. W. 1974. The simple act of voting. *American Political Science Review* 68:572–91.

KELLMAN, P. J., AND SHIPLEY, T. F. 1991. A theory of visual interpolation in object perception. *Cognitive Psychology* 23:141–221.

KELLMAN, P. J., AND SPELKE, E. S. 1983. Perception of partially occluded objects in infancy. *Cognitive Psychology* 15:483–524.

KELLMAN, P. J.; SPELKE, E. S.; AND SHORT, K. R. 1986. Infant perception of object unity from translatory motion in depth and vertical translation. *Child Development* 57:72–86.

KELLY, M. H., AND MARTIN, S. 1994. Domain-general abilities applied to domain-specific tasks: Sensitivity to probabilities in perception, cognition, and language. In Gleitman, L. R., and Landau, B. (Eds.), *Lexical acquisition, Lingua* (Special Issue) 92:108–40.

KEMLER-NELSON, D.; JUSCZYK; P.; AND CASSIDY, K. 1989. How the prosodic cues of motherese might assist language learning. *Journal of Child Language* 55–68.

KENDALL-TACKETT, K. A.; WILLIAMS, L. M.; AND FINKELHOR, D. 1993. Impact of sexual abuse on children: A review and synthesis of recent empirical studies. *Psychological Bulletin* 113:164–80.

KENDLER, K. S., AND GRUENBERG, A. M. 1984. An independent analysis of the Danish adoption study of schizophrenia: VI. The relationship between psychiatric disorders as defined by DSM-III in the relatives and adoptees. *Archives of General Psychiatry* 41:555–64.

KENNY, D., AND ZACCARO, S. J. 1983. An estimate of variance due to traits in leadership. *Journal of Applied Psychology* 68:678–85.

KENRICK, D. T., AND CIALDINI, R. B. 1977. Romantic attraction: Misattribution versus reinforcement explanations. *Journal of Personality and Social Psychology* 35:381–91.

KENRICK, D. T.; CIALDINI, R. B.; AND LINDER, D. E. 1979. Misattribution under fear-producing circumstances: Four failures to replicate. *Personality and Social Psychology Bulletin* 5:329–34.

KENRICK, D. T., AND FUNDER, D. C. 1988. Profiting from controversy: Lessons from the person-situation debate. *American Psychologist* 43:23–34.

KERR, M. E., AND BOWEN, M. 1988. *Family evaluation.* New York: Norton.

KERR, N. L., AND KAUFMANN-GILLILAND, C. M. 1994. Communication, commitment, and cooperation. *Journal of Personality and Social Psychology* 66:513–29.

C 5 7

KESSEL, E. L. 1955. The mating activities of balloon flies. *Systematic Zoology* 4:97–104.

KETY, S. S. 1983. Mental illness in the biological and adoptive relatives of schizophrenic adoptees: Findings relevant to genetic and environmental factors in etiology. *Journal of American Psychiatry* 140:720–27.

KHANNA, S. M., AND LEONARD, D. G. B. 1982. Basilar membrane tuning in the cat cochlea. *Science* 215:305–6.

KIHLSTROM, J. F. 1987. *The cognitive unconscious. Science* 237:1445–52.

KIHLSTROM, J. F. 1990. The psychological unconscious. In Pervin, L. A. (Ed.), *Handbook of personality: Theory and research,* pp. 445–64. New York: Guilford Press.

KIHLSTROM, J. F. 1992. Dissociation and dissociations: A comment on consciousness and cognition. *Consciousness and Cognition: An International Journal* 1:47–53.

KIHLSTROM, J. F. 1993. The recovery of memory in the laboratory and the clinic. Paper presented at the 1993 conventions of the Rocky Mountain and the Western Psychological Associations. Phoenix, Arizona.

KIHLSTROM, J. F. 1996a. Perception without awareness of what is perceived, learning without awareness of what is learned. In Velmans, M. (Ed.), *The science of consciousness: Psychological, neuropsychological and clinical reviews,* pp. 23–46. London: Routledge.

KIHLSTROM, J. F. 1996b. Unconscious processes in social interaction. In Hameroff, S. R.; Kaszniak, A. W.; and Scott, A. C. (Eds.), *Toward a science of consciousness: The first Tucson discussions and debates. Complex adaptive systems,* pp. 93–104. Cambridge, Mass.: MIT Press.

KIHLSTROM, J. F., AND CANTOR, N. 1984. Mental representations of the self. In Berkowitz, L. (Ed.), *Advances in experimental social psychology,* vol. 17, pp. 1–47. New York: Academic Press.

KILHAM, W., AND MANN, L. 1974. Level of destructive obedience as a function of transmitter and executant roles in the Milgram obedience paradigm. *Journal of Personality and Social Psychology* 29:696–702.

KIMBALL, J. 1973. Seven principles of surface structure parsing in natural language. *Cognition* 2:15–47.

KIMBLE, G. A. 1961. *Hilgard and Marquis' conditioning and learning.* New York: Appleton-Century-Crofts.

KIMURA, D., AND WATSON, N. 1989. The relation between oral movement and speech. *Brain and Language* 37:565–90.

KING, H. E. 1961. Psychological effects of excitation in the limbic system. In Sheer, D. E. (Ed.), *Electrical stimulation of the brain.* Austin: University of Texas Press.

KINSEY, A. C.; POMEROY, W. B.; AND MARTIN, C. E. 1948. *Sexual behavior in the human male.* Philadelphia: Saunders.

KINSEY, A.; POMEROY, W.; MARTIN, C.; AND GEBHARD, P. 1953. *Sexual behavior in the human female.* Philadelphia: Saunders.

KITAYAMA, S., AND MARKUS, H. R. (EDS.). 1994. *Emotion and culture: Empirical studies of mutual influence.* Washington, D.C.: American Psychological Association.

KITAYAMA, S.; MARKUS, H. R.; AND MATSUMOTO, H. 1995. Culture, self and emotion: A cultural perspective on "self-conscious" emotions. In Tangney, J. P., and Fischer, K. W. (Eds.), *Self-conscious emotions,* pp. 439–87. New York: Guilford.

KITCHER, P. 1985. *Vaulting ambition: Sociobiology and the quest for human nature.* Cambridge, Mass: MIT Press.

KITCHER, P. 1987. Précis of *Vaulting ambition: Sociobiology and the quest for human nature* (and open peer commentary). *Behavioral and Brain Sciences* 10:61–100.

KLAUS, M. H., AND KENNELL, J. H. 1976. *Maternal-infant bonding: The impact of early separation or loss on family development.* St. Louis, Mo.: Mosby.

KLAUS, M. H.; KENNELL, J. H.; PLUMB, N.; AND ZUEHLKE, S. 1970. Human maternal behavior at the first contact with her young. *Pediatrics* 46:187.

KLEINMUNTZ, B. 1982. *Personality and psychological assessment.* New York: St. Martin's Press.

KLEITMAN, N. 1960. Patterns of dreaming. *Scientific American* 203:82–88.

KLERMAN, G. L. 1990. The psychiatric patient's right to effective treatment: Implications of Osheroff v. Chestnut Lodge. *American Journal of Psychiatry* 147:409–18.

KLERMAN, G. L.; WEISSMAN, M. M.; ROUNSAVILLE, B. J.; AND CHEVRON, E. S. 1984. *Interpersonal psychotherapy of depression.* New York: Basic Books.

KLIMA, E.; AND BELLUGI, U.; WITH BATTISON, R.; BOYES-BRAEM, P.; FISCHER, S.; FRISHBERG, N.; LANE, H.; LENTZ, E. M.; NEWKIRK, D.; NEWPORT, E.; PEDERSEN, C.; AND SIPLE, P. 1979. *The signs of language.* Cambridge, Mass.: Harvard University Press.

KLINE, P. 1992. *The handbook of psychological testing.* London: Routledge.

KLINE, P. 1995. A critical review of the measurement of personality and intelligence. In Saklofske, D. H., and Zeidner, M. (Eds.), *International handbook of personality and intelligence,* pp. 505–24. New York: Plenum.

KLINEBERG, O. 1940. *Social psychology.* New York: Henry Holt.

KLOPFER, B.; AINSWORTH, M.; KLOPFER, W. G.; AND HOLT, R. R. 1954. *Developments in the Rorschach technique.* Yonkers, N.Y.: World Book.

KLOPFER, P. H. 1974. *An introduction to animal behavior: Ethology's first century.* Englewood Cliffs, N.J.: Prentice-Hall.

KLUFT, R. P. 1987. An update on multiple-personality disorder. *Journal of Hospital and Community Psychiatry* 38:363–73.

KLUVER, H., AND BUCY, P. C. 1937. "Psychic blindness" and other symptoms following bilateral temporal lobectomy in rhesus monkeys. *American Journal of Physiology* 119:352–53.

KOHLBERG, L. 1963. Development of children's orientations toward a moral order. *Vita Humana* 6:11–36.

KOHLBERG, L. 1966. A cognitive developmental analysis of children's sex-role concepts and attitudes. In Maccoby, E. E. (Ed.), *The development of sex differences,* pp. 82–171. Stanford, Calif.: Stanford University Press.

KOHLBERG, L. 1969. Stage and sequence: The cognitive developmental approach to socialization. In Goslin, D. A. (Ed.), *Handbook of socialization theory of research,* pp. 347–480. Chicago: Rand McNally.

KOHLBERG, L., AND CANDEE, D. 1984. The relationship of moral judgment to moral action. In Kurtines, W. M., and Gewirtz, L. (Eds.), *Morality, moral behavior, and moral development,* pp. 52–73. New York: Wiley.

KOHLBERG, L.; LEVINE, C.; AND HEWER, A. 1984. Synopses and detailed replies to critics. In Kohlberg, L. (Ed.), *The psychology of moral development: The nature and validity of moral stages,* pp. 320–86. San Francisco: Harper & Row.

KÖHLER, W. 1925. *The mentality of apes.* New York: Harcourt Brace and World.

KÖHLER, W. 1947. *Gestalt psychology.* New York: Liveright.

KOHN, A. 1993. *Punished by rewards.* New York: Houghton Mifflin.

KOHN, M. L. 1968. Social class and schizophrenia: A critical review. In Rosenthal, D., and Kety, S. S. (Eds.), *The transmission of schizophrenia,* pp. 155–74. London: Pergamon.

KOHN, M. L. 1969. *Class and conformity: A study in values.* Chicago: University of Chicago Press.

KOHUT, H. 1978. *The psychology of the self: A case book.* New York: International Universities Press.

KOLB, B., AND WHISHAW, I. Q. 1990. *Fundamentals of human neuropsychology,* 3rd ed. New York: Freeman.

KOLB, B., AND WHISHAW, I. Q. 1996. *Fundamentals of human neuropsychology,* 4th ed. New York: Freeman.

KOLODNY, R.; MASTERS, W.; HENDRYX, J.; AND TORO, G. 1971. Plasma testosterone and semen analysis in male homosexuals. *New England Journal of Medicine* 285:1170–74.

KONDRO, W. 1998. New rules on human subjects could end debate in Canada. *Science* 280:1521.

KOOPMANS, J. R.; BOOMSMA, D. I.; HEATH, A. C.; VAN DOORNEN, L. J. P.; AND OTHERS. 1995. A multivariate genetic analysis of sensation seeking. *Behavior Genetics* 25:349–56.

KORDOWER, J. H.; FREEMAN, T. B.; SNOW, B. J.; VINGERHOETS, F. J. G.; MUFSON, E. J.; SANBERG, P. R.; HAUSER, R. A.; SMITH, D. A.; NAUERT, G. M.; PERL, D. P.; AND OLANOW, C. W. 1995. Neuropathological evidence of graft survival and striatal reinnervation after the transplantation of fetal mesencephalic tissue in a patient with Parkinson's disease. *New England Journal of Medicine* 332:1118–24.

KORDOWER, J. H.; WINN, S. R.; LIU, Y. T.; MUFSON, E. J.; SLADEK, J. R., JR.; HAMMANG, J. R.; BAETGE, E. E.; AND EMERICH, D. F. 1994. The aged monkey basal forebrain: Rescue and sprouting of axotomotized basal forebrain neurons after grafts of encapsulated cells secreting human nerve growth factor. *Proceedings of the National Academy of Sciences of the United States* 91: 10898–902.

KORIAT, A., AND LIEBLICH, I. 1974. What does a person in a TOT state know that a person in a "Don't Know" state doesn't know? *Memory and Cognition* 2:647–55.

KORN, J. H. 1997. *Illusions of reality: A history of deception in social psychology.* Albany, N. Y.: State University of New York Press.

KOSONEN, P., AND WINNE, P. H. 1995. Effects of teaching statistical laws on reasoning about everyday problems. *Journal of Educational Psychology* 87:33–56.

KOSSLYN, S. M. 1980. *Image and mind.* Cambridge, Mass.: Harvard University Press.

KOSSLYN, S. M. 1984. *Ghosts in the mind's machine.* New York: Norton.

KOSSLYN, S. M.; BALL, T. M.; AND REISSER, B. J. 1978. Visual images preserve metric spatial information: Evidence from studies of image scanning. *Journal of Experimental Psychology: Human Perception and Performance* 4:1–20.

KOSTLAN, A. 1954. A method for the empirical study of psychodiagnosis. *Journal of Consulting Psychology* 18:83–88.

KOTKIN, M.; DAVIET, C.; AND GURIN, J. 1996. The *Consumer Reports* mental health survey. *American Psychologist* 51:1080–82.

KOULACK, D., AND GOODENOUGH, D. R. 1976. Dream recall and dream recall failure: An arousal-retrieval model. *Psychological Bulletin* 83:975–84.

KRAMER, P. D. 1993. *Listening to Prozac.* New York: Viking.

KRANTZ, D. S.; CONTRADA, R. J.; HILL, D. R.; AND FRIEDLER, E. 1988. Environmental stress and behavioral antecedents of coronary heart disease. *Journal of Consulting and Clinical Psychology* 56:333–41.

KRASNE, F. B., AND GLANZMAN, D. L. 1995. What we can learn from invertebrate learning. *Annual Review of Psychology* 45:585–624.

KRAUS, S. J. 1995. Attitudes and the prediction of behavior: A meta analysis of the empirical literature. *Personality and Social Psychology Bulletin* 21(1):58–75.

KRAUT, R. E., AND JOHNSTON, R. E. 1979. Social and emotional messages of smiling: An ethological approach. *Journal of Personality and Social Psychology* 37(9):1539–53.

KREBS, J. R. 1982. Territorial defence in the great tit (*Parus Major L.*). *Ecology* 52:2–22.

KREBS, J. R.; DAVIES, N. B.; AND PARR, J. 1993. *An introduction to behavioural ecology,* 3rd ed. Oxford: Blackwell.

KREBS, J. R., AND DAWKINS, R. 1984. Animal signals: Mind reading and manipulation. In Krebs, J. R., and Davies, N. B. (Eds.), *Behavioural ecology: An evolutionary approach,* 2nd ed., pp. 380–402. Oxford: Blackwell.

KRECH, D., AND CRUTCHFIELD, R. 1958. *Elements of psychology.* New York: Knopf.

KRIPKE, D. 1982. Ultradian rhythms in behavior and physiology. In Brown, F. M., and Graeber, R. C. (Eds.), *Rhythmic aspects of behavior,* pp. 313–43. Hillsdale, N.J.: Erlbaum.

KRUPNICK, J. L.; SOTSKY, S. M.; SIMMENS, S.; MOYER, J.; ELKIN, I.; WATKINS, J.; AND PILKONIS, P. A. 1996. The role of the therapeutic alliance in psychotherapy and pharmacotherapy outcome: Findings in the National Institute of Mental Health Treatment of Depression Collaborative Research Program. *Journal of Consulting and Clinical Psychology* 64:532–39.

KUBOVY, M. 1986. *The psychology of perspective and Renaissance art.* New York: Cambridge University Press.

KUFFLER, S. W. 1953. Discharge pattern and functional organization of mammalian retina. *Journal of Neurophysiology* 16:37–68.

KUHL, P.; WILLIAMS, K.; LACERDA, F.; STEVENS, K.; AND LINDBLOM, B. 1992. Linguistic experience alters phonetic perception in infants by six months of age. *Science* 255:606–608.

KUNDA, Z. 1990. The case for motivated reasoning. *Psychological Bulletin* 108:480–98.

KUNDA, Z.; FONG, G. T.; SANITIOSO, R.; AND REBER, E. 1993. Directional questions direct self conceptions. *Journal of Experimental Social Psychology* 29(1):63–86.

KUPFER, D. J., AND REYNOLDS, C. F., III. 1997. Management of insomnia. *New England Journal of Medicine* 336:341–46.

KURTINES, W. M., AND GEWIRTZ, J. L. (EDS.). 1995. *Moral development: An introduction.* Boston: Allyn and Bacon.

KUZNICKI, J. T., AND McCUTCHEON, N. B. 1979. Cross enhancement of the sour taste of single human taste papillae. *Journal of Experimental Psychology* 198:68–89.

KYLLONEN, P. C., AND CHRISTAL, R. E. 1990. Reasoning ability is (little more than) working memory capacity? *Intelligence* 14(4):389–433.

LABOV, W. 1970. The logic of nonstandard English. In Williams, F. (Ed.), *Language and poverty: Perspectives on a theme,* pp. 153–89. Chicago: Markham.

LAFARGE, L. 1993. The early determinants of penis envy. In Glick, R. A., and Roose, S. P. (Eds.), *Rage, power, and aggression. The role of affect in motivation, development, and adaptation,* vol. 2, pp. 80–101. New Haven: Yale University Press.

LAGERSPETZ, K. M. J.; BJORKQVIST, K.; AND PELTONUN, T. 1988. Is indirect aggression typical of females? Gender differences in aggressiveness in 11- to 12-year-old girls. *Aggressive Behavior* 14:403–14.

LAKOFF, G., AND JOHNSON, M. 1980. *Metaphors we live by.* Chicago: University of Chicago Press.

LAMB, H. R. 1984. Deinstitutionalization and the homeless mentally ill. *Hospital Community Psychiatry* 35:899–907.

LAMB, M. E. (ED.). 1987. *The father's role: Cross-cultural perspectives.* Hillsdale, N.J.: Erlbaum.

LAMB, M. E. (ED.). 1997. *The role of the father in child development,* 3rd ed. New York: Wiley.

LAMB, M. E.; THOMPSON, R. M.; GARDNER, W.; CHARNOV, E. L.; AND ESTES, D. 1985. *Infant-mother attachment.* Hillsdale, N.J.: Erlbaum.

LANDAU, B. 1982. Will the real grandmother please stand up? The psychological reality of dual meaning representations. *Journal of Psycholinguistic Research* 11:47–62.

LANDAU, B., AND GLEITMAN, L. R. 1985. *Language and experience: Evidence from the blind child.* Cambridge, Mass.: Harvard University Press.

LANDAU, B., AND MUNNICH, E. 1998. The representation of space of spatial language: Challenges for cognitive science. In Olivier, P., and Gapp, K. (Eds.), *Representation and processing of spatial expressions,* pp. 263–72. Mahwah, N.J.: Lawrence Erlbaum.

LANDAU, B.; SMITH, L.; AND JONES, S. 1988. The importance of shape in early lexical learning. *Cognitive Development* 3:299–321.

LANDIS, C., AND HUNT, W. A. 1932. Adrenalin and emotion. *Psychological Review* 39:467–85.

LANGER, E. J., AND RODIN, J. 1976. The effects of choice and enhanced personal responsibility for the aged: A field experiment in an institutional setting. *Journal of Personality and Social Psychology* 34:191–98.

LANGLOIS, J. H., AND DOWNS, A. C. 1980. Mothers, fathers, and peers as socialization agents of sex-typed play behaviors in young children. *Child Development* 51:1237–1347.

LANYON, R. I., AND GOLDSTEIN, L. D. 1971. *Personality assessment.* New York: Wiley.

LANYON, R. I., AND GOLDSTEIN, L. D. 1982. *Personality assessment,* 2nd ed. New York: Wiley.

LaPIERE, R. 1934. Attitudes versus actions. *Social Forces* 13:230–37.

LARAGH, J. H. M., AND BRENNER, B. M. (EDS.). 1995. *Hypertension: Pathophysiology, diagnosis, and management,* 2nd ed. Philadelphia: Lippincott-Raven.

LASH, J. P. 1980. *Helen and Teacher: The story of Helen Keller and Anne Sullivan Macy.* New York: Delacorte Press.

LASKY, J. J.; HOVER, G. L.; SMITH, P. A.; BOSTIAN, D. W.; DUFFENDECK, S. C.; AND NORD, C. L. 1959. Post-hospital adjustment as predicted by psychiatric patients and by their staff. *Journal of Consulting Psychology* 23:213–18.

LASSEN, N. A.; INGVAR, D. H.; AND SKINHOJ, E. 1978. Brain function and blood flow. *Scientific American* 239:62–71.

LATANÉ, B. 1981. The psychology of social impact. *American Psychologist* 36:343–56.

LATANÉ, B. 1997. Dynamic social impact: The societal consequences of human interaction. In McGarty, C., and Haslam, S. A. (Eds.) *The message of social psychology: Perspectives on mind in society*, pp. 200–20. Oxford: Blackwell.

LATANÉ, B., AND HARKINS, S. 1976. Cross-modality matches suggest anticipated stage fright as a multiplicative power function of audience size and status. *Perception and Psychophysics* 20:482–88.

LATANÉ, B., AND NIDA, S. 1981. Group size and helping. *Psychological Bulletin* 89:308–24.

LATANÉ, B.; NIDA, S. A.; AND WILSON, D. W. 1981. The effects of group size on helping behavior. In Rushton, J. P., and Sorrentino, R. M. (Eds.), *Altruism and helping behavior: Social, personality, and developmental perspectives.* Hillsdale, N.J.: Erlbaum.

LATANÉ, B., AND RODIN, J. 1969. A lady in distress: Inhibiting effects of friends and strangers on bystander intervention. *Journal of Experimental Social Psychology* 5:189–202.

LATANÉ, B.; WILLIAMS, K.; AND HARKINS, S. 1979. Many hands make light the work: The causes and consequences of social loafing. *Journal of Personality and Social Psychology* 37:822–32.

LAU, R. R., AND RUSSELL, D. 1980. Attributions in the sports pages. *Journal of Personality and Social Psychology* 39:29–38.

LAYZER, D. 1972. Science or superstition: A physical scientist looks at the I.Q. controversy. *Cognition* 1:265–300.

LAZARUS, A. A. 1971. *Behavior therapy and beyond.* New York: McGraw-Hill.

LAZARUS, A. A. 1981. *The practice of multi-modal therapy.* New York: McGraw-Hill.

LE BON, G. 1895. *The crowd.* New York: Viking Press, 1960.

LEA, S. E. G., AND RYAN, C. M. E. 1990. Unnatural concepts and the theory of concept discrimination in birds. In Commons, M. L.; Herrnstein, R. J.; Kosslyn, S.; and Mumford, D. (Eds.), *Quantitative analysis of behavior*, vol. VIII: *Behavioral approaches to pattern recognition and concept formation*, pp. 165–85. Hillsdale, N.J.: Erlbaum.

LEARY, M. R., AND KOWALSKI, R. M. 1990. Impression management: A literature review and two-component model. *Psychological Bulletin* 107:34–47.

LEASK, J.; HABER, R. N.; AND HABER, R. B. 1969. Eidetic imagery in children: II. Longitudinal and experimental results. *Psychonomic Monograph Supplements* 3(Whole No. 35):25–48.

LEDOUX, J. E. 1994. Emotion, memory, and the brain. *Scientific American* 270:50–57.

LEECH, G. N. 1983. *Principles of pragmatics.* London: Longman.

LEFF, J.; KUIPPERS, L.; BERKOWITZ, R.; EBERLEIN-VRIES, R.; AND STURGEON, D. 1982. A controlled trial of social intervention in the families of schizophrenic persons. *British Journal of Psychiatry* 141:121–34.

LEFF, M. J.; ROATSCH, J. F.; AND BUNNEY, W. E., JR. 1970. Environmental factors preceding the onset of severe depressions. *Psychiatry* 33:298–311.

LEGAULT, F., AND STRAYER, F. F. 1990. The emergence of sex-segregation in preschool peer groups. In Strayer, F. F. (Ed.), *Social interaction and behavioral development during early childhood.* Montreal: La Maison D'Ethologie de Montréal.

LEHMAN, D.; LEMPERT, R. O.; AND NISBETT, R. E. 1988. The effects of graduate training on reasoning: Formal discipline and thinking about everyday-life events. *American Psychologist* 43:431–42.

LEHMAN, D., AND NISBETT, R. 1990. A longitudinal study of the effects of undergraduate education on reasoning. *Developmental Psychology* 26:952–60.

LEIBOWITZ, S. F. 1991. Brain neuropeptide Y: An integrator of endocrine, metabolic and behavioral processes. *Brain Research Bulletin* 27:333–37.

LEMPERS, J. S.; FLAVELL, E. R.; AND FLAVELL, J. H. 1977. The development in very young children of tacit knowledge concerning visual perception. *Genetic Psychology Monographs* 95:3–53.

LENNEBERG, E. H. 1967. *Biological foundations of language.* New York: Wiley.

LEON, M.; COOPERSMITH, R.; BEASLEY, L. J.; AND SULLIVAN, R. M. 1990. Thermal aspects of parenting. In Krasnegor, N. A., and Bridges, R. S. (Eds.), *Mammalian parenting: Biochemical, neurobiological, and behavioral determinants*, pp. 400–15. New York: Oxford University Press.

LEPPER, M. R. 1983. Social control processes, attributions of motivation, and the internalization of social values. In Higgins, E. T.; Ruble, D. N.; and Hartup, W. W. (Eds.), *Social cognition and social behavior: Developmental perspectives.* New York: Cambridge University Press.

LEPPER, M. R.; GREENE, D.; AND NISBETT, R. E. 1973. Undermining children's intrinsic interest with extrinsic rewards: A test of the "overjustification" hypothesis. *Journal of Personality and Social Psychology* 28:129–37.

LEPPER, M. R.; KEAVNYE, M.; AND DRAKE, M. 1996. Intrinsic motivation and extrinsic rewards: A commentary on Cameron and Pierce's meta-analysis. *Review of Educational Research* 66:5–32.

LEROITH, D.; SHILOACH, J.; AND ROTH, J. 1982. Is there an earlier phylogenetic precursor that is common to both the nervous and endocrine systems? *Peptides* 3:211–15.

LESLIE, A. M. 1992. Pretense, autism, and the theory of mind module. *Current Directions in Psychological Science* 1:18–21.

LETTVIN, J. Y.; MATURAN, H. R.; McCULLOCH, W. S.; AND PITTS, W. H. 1959. What the frog's eye tells the frog's brain. *Proceedings of the Institute of Radio Engineers* 47:1940–51.

LEVAV, I.; KOHN, R.; GOLDING, J. M.; AND WEISSMAN, M. M. 1997. Vulnerability of Jews to affective disorders. *American Journal of Psychiatry* 154(7):941–47.

LeVAY, S. 1991. A difference in hypothalamic structure between heterosexual and homosexual men. *Science* 253:1034–37.

LEVELT, W. 1970. A scaling approach to the study of syntactic relations. In Flores d'Arcais, G., and Levelt, W. (Eds.), *Advances in psycholinguistics.* Amsterdam: North-Holland.

LEVINE, J. D.; GORDON, N. C.; AND FIELDS, H. L. 1979. The role of endorphins in placebo analgesia. In Bonica, J. J.; Liebesking, J. C.; and Albe-Fessard, D. (Eds.), *Advances in pain research and therapy*, vol. 3. New York: Raven.

LEVINE, R. V.; MARTINEZ, T. S.; BRASE, G.; AND SORENSON, K. 1994. Helping in 36 U. S. cities. *Journal of Personality and Social Psychology* 67:69–82.

LEVINSON, D. J. 1978. *The seasons of a man's life.* New York: Knopf.

LEVINSON, S. C. 1996. Relativity in spatial conception and description. In Gumperz, J. J., and Levinson, S. C. (Eds.), *Rethinking linguistic relativity: Studies in the social and cultural foundations of language.* Cambridge: Cambridge University Press.

LEVY, J. 1974. Psychobiological implications of bilateral asymmetry. In Dimond, S. J., and Beaumont, J. G. (Eds.), *Hemisphere function in the human brain*, pp. 121–83. New York: Wiley.

LEVY, J. 1979. Personal communication.

LEVY, J. 1983. Language, cognition, and the right hemisphere: A response to Gazzaniga. *American Psychologist* 38:538–41.

LEVY, J. 1985. Right brain, left brain: Facts and fiction. *Psychology Today* 19:38–44.

LEVY, W. B., AND STEWARD, O. 1979. Synapses as associative memory elements in the hippocampal formation. *Brain Research* 175:233–45.

LEWIN, R. 1988. Cloud over Parkinson's therapy. *Science* 240:390–92.

LEWINSOHN, P. M.; HOBERMAN, H.; TERI, L.; AND HAUTZINGER, M. 1985. An integrative theory of depression. In Reiss, S., and Bootzin, R. (Eds.), *Theoretical issues in behavior therapy.* Orlando, Fla.: Academic Press.

LEWIS, E. R.; EVERHART, T. E.; AND SEEVI, Y. Y. 1969. Studying neural organization in aplysia with the scanning electron microscope *Science* 165:1140–43.

LEWONTIN, R. C. 1976. Race and intelligence. In Block, N. J., and Dworkin, G. (Eds.), *The IQ controversy*, pp. 78–92. New York: Pantheon.

LEWONTIN, R. C.; ROSE, S.; AND KAMIN, L. J. 1984. *Not in our genes: Biology, ideology, and human nature.* New York: Random House.

LEWY, A.; SACK, L.; MILLER, S.; AND HOBAN, T. M. 1987. Anti-depressant and circadian-phase shifting effects of light. *Science* 235:352–54.

LEZAK, M. D. 1983. *Neuropsychological assessment*, 2nd. ed. New York: Oxford University Press.

LIBERMAN, A. M. 1970. The grammars of speech and language. *Cognitive Psychology* 1:301–23.

LIEBERMAN, J. A. 1995. Signs and symptoms. Commentary. *Archives of General Psychiatry* 52:361–63.

LIEBERMAN, P. L. 1975. *On the origins of language.* New York: Macmillan.

LIEBERMAN, P. 1984. *The biology and evolution of language.* Cambridge, Mass.: Harvard University Press.

LIEBERMAN, S. 1956. The effects of changes in roles on the attitudes of role occupants. *Human Relations* 9:385–402.

LIEBERT, R. M.; POULOS, R. W.; AND STRAUSS, G. D. 1974. *Developmental psychology.* Englewood Cliffs, N.J.: Prentice-Hall.

LIFF, Z. A. 1992. Psychoanalysis and dynamic techniques. In D. K. Freedheim (Ed.), *History of psychotherapy.* Washington, D.C.: American Psychological Association.

LINDSAY, P. H., AND NORMAN, D. A. 1977. *Human information processing,* 2nd ed. New York: Academic Press.

LIPPERT, W. W., AND SENTER, R. J. 1966. Electrodermal responses in the sociopath. *Psychonomic Science* 4:25–26.

LIPSETT, L. P., AND BEHL, G. 1990. Taste-mediated differences in the sucking behavior of human newborns. In Capaldi, E. D., and Powley, T. L. (Eds.), *Taste, experience, and feeding,* pp. 75–93. Washington, D.C.: American Psychological Association.

LISKE, E., AND DAVIS, W. J. 1984. Sexual behavior of the Chinese praying mantis. *Animal Behavior* 32:916.

LITTLE, K. B., AND SHNEIDMAN, E. S. 1959. Congruencies among interpretations of psychological test and anamnestic data. *Psychological Monographs* 73 (Whole No. 476).

LIVNEH, H., AND LIVNEH, C. 1989. The five-factor model of personality: Is evidence of its cross-measure validity premature? *Personality and Individual Differences* 10:75–80.

LOCKE, J. 1690. *An essay concerning human understanding.* Edited by A. D. Woozley. Cleveland: Meridian Books, 1964.

LOEHLIN, J. C. 1982. Are personality traits differentially heritable. *Behavior Genetics* 12:417–28.

LOEHLIN, J. C. 1992. *Genes and environment in personality development.* Newbury Park, Calif.: Sage.

LOEHLIN, J. C.; LINDZEY, G.; AND SPUHLER, J. N. 1975. *Race difference in intelligence.* San Francisco: Freeman.

LOEHLIN, J. C., AND NICHOLS, R. C. 1976. *Heredity, environment and personality: A study of 850 sets of twins.* Austin: University of Texas Press.

LOEHLIN, J. C.; VANDENBERG, S. G.; AND OSBORNE, R. T. 1973. Blood group genes and Negro-White ability differences. *Behavior Genetics* 3:263–70.

LOEWI, O. 1960. An autobiographical sketch. *Perspectives in Biological Medicine* 4:2–35.

LOFTUS, E. F. 1973. Activation of semantic memory. *American Journal of Psychology* 86:331–37.

LOFTUS, E. F. 1975. Leading questions and the eyewitness report. *Cognitive Psychology* 7:560–72.

LOFTUS, E. F. 1992. When a lie becomes memory's truth: Memory distortion after exposure to misinformation. *Current Directions in Psychological Science* 1:121–23.

LOFTUS, E. F. 1993. The reality of repressed memories. *American Psychologist* 48:518–37.

LOFTUS, E. F. 1997. Creating false memories. *Scientific American* 277(3):70–75.

LOFTUS, E. F., AND LOFTUS, G. R. 1980. On the permanence of stored information in the human brain. *American Psychologist* 35:409–20.

LOFTUS, E. F., AND ZANNI, G. 1975. Eyewitness testimony: The influence of the wording of a question. *Bulletin of the Psychonomic Society* 5:86–88.

LOGAN, G. D. 1988. Toward an instance theory of automatization. *Psychological Review* 95:492–527.

LOGAN, G. D.; TAYLOR, S. E.; AND ETHERTON, J. L. 1996. Attention in the acquisition and expression of automaticity. *Journal of Experimental Psychology: Learning, Memory and Cognition* 22:620–38.

LOGUE, A. W. 1979. Taste aversion and the generality of the laws of learning. *Psychological Bulletin* 86:276–96.

LOGUE, A. W. 1986. *The psychology of eating and drinking.* New York: Freeman.

LONDON, P. 1964. *The modes and morals of psychotherapy.* New York: Holt, Rinehart & Winston.

LONDON, P. 1970. The rescuers: Motivational hypotheses about Christians who saved Jews from the Nazis. In Macauley, J., and Berkowitz, L. (Eds.), *Altruism and helping behavior.* New York: Academic Press.

LORD, R. G.; DEVADER, C. L.; AND ALLIGER, G. M. 1986. A meta-analysis of the relationship between personality traits and leadership perceptions: An application of validity generalization procedures. *Journal of Applied Psychology* 7:401–10.

LORENZ, K. 1950. Part and parcel in animal and human societies. In *Studies in animal and human behavior,* vol. II, pp. 115–95. London: Methuen.

LORENZ, K. Z. 1966. *On aggression.* London: Methuen.

LUBIN, B.; LARSEN, R. M.; MATARAZZO, J. D.; AND SEEVER, M. 1985. Psychological test usage patterns in five professional settings. *American Psychologist* 40:857–61.

LUBORSKY, L. 1984. *Principles of psychoanalytic psychotherapy: A manual for supportive expressive treatment.* New York: Basic Books.

LUBORSKY, L. I.; SINGER, B.; AND LUBORSKY, L. 1975. Comparative studies of psychotherapies. *Archives of General Psychiatry* 20:84–88.

LUCE, R. D., AND RAIFFA, H. 1957. *Games and decisions.* New York: Wiley.

LUCHINS, A. S. 1942. Mechanization in problem-solving: The effect of Einstellung. *Psychological Monographs* 54 (Whole No. 248).

LUCHINS, A. S. 1957. Primacy-recency in impression formation: The effect of Einstellung. In Hovland, C. (Ed.), *The order of presentation in persuasion.* New Haven: Yale University Press.

LUGINBUHL, J. E. R.; CROWE, D. H.; AND KAHAN, J. P. 1975. Causal attributions for success and failure. *Journal of Personality and Social Psychology* 31:86–93.

LURIA, A. R. 1966. *Higher cortical functions in man.* New York: Basic Books.

LURIA, A. R. 1971. *International Journal of Psychology* 6: p. 259 ff. (cited in Scribner, S., and Cole, M. 1973. Cognitive consequences of formal and informal education. *Science* 182:553–59).

LURIA, A. R. 1976. *Cognitive development: Its cultural and social foundations.* Cambridge, Mass.: Harvard University Press.

LUTZ, C. 1986. The domain of emotion words on Ifaluk. In Harr, R. (Ed.), *The social construction of emotions,* pp. 267–88. Oxford, Blackwell.

LUTZ, C. 1988. *Unnatural emotions.* Chicago: University of Chicago Press.

LYDIARD, R. B.; BRAWMAN-MINTZER, O.; AND BALLENGER, J. C. 1996. Recent developments in the psychopharmacology of anxiety disorders. *Journal of Consulting and Clinical Psychology* 64:660–68.

LYKKEN, D. T. 1979. The detection of deception. *Psychological Bulletin* 86:47–53.

LYKKEN, D. T. 1981. The lie detector and the law. *Criminal Defense* 8:19–27.

LYKKEN, D. T. 1995. *The antisocial personalities.* Hillsdale, N.J.: Erlbaum.

LYNN, R. 1994. Sex differences in intelligence and brain size: A paradox resolved. *Personality and Individual Differences* 17(2):257–71.

LYNN, R. 1995. Cross-cultural differences in intelligence and personality. In Saklofske, D. H., and Zeidner, M. (Eds.), *International handbook of personality and intelligence,* pp. 107–21. New York: Plenum.

MAASS, A., AND CLARK, R. D., III. 1984. Hidden impact of minorities: Fifteen years of research on minority influence research. *Psychological Bulletin* 95:428–55.

MACCOBY, E. E. 1980. *Social development.* New York: Harcourt Brace Jovanovich.

MACCOBY, E. E., AND JACKLIN, C. N. 1974. *The psychology of sex differences.* Stanford, Calif.: Stanford University Press.

MACCOBY, E. E., AND JACKLIN, C. N. 1980. Sex differences in aggression: A rejoinder and reprise. *Child Development* 51:964–80.

MACCOBY, E. E., AND MARTIN, J. A. 1983. Socialization in the context of the family: Parent-child interaction. In Mussen, P. H. (Ed.), *Carmichael's manual of child psychology,* vol. 4: *Socialization, personality and social development,* pp. 1–102. Hetherington, M. E., vol. ed. New York: Wiley.

MACDONALD, M. C.; PEARLMUTTER, N. J.; AND SEIDENBERG, M. S. 1994. The lexical nature of syntactic ambiguity resolution. *Psychological Review* 101(4):676–703.

MACFARLANE, A. 1975. Olfaction in the development of social preferences in the human neonate. *Parent-infant interaction.* Amsterdam: CIBA Foundation Symposium.

MACKAY, D. G. 1980. Psychology, prescriptive grammar, and the pronoun problem. *American Psychologist* 35(5):444–49.

MACKENZIE, N. 1965. *Dreams and dreaming.* London: Aldus Books.

MACMILLAN, D. L. 1988. Issues in mild mental retardation. *Education and Training in Mental Retardation* 23(4):273–84.

MACNEILAGE, P. 1972. Speech physiology. In Gilbert, J. (Ed.), *Speech and cortical functioning.* New York: Academic Press.

MACNICHOL, E. F., JR. 1964. Three-pigment color vision: *Scientific American* 211:48–56.

MACNICHOL, E. F., JR. 1986. A unifying presentation of photopigment spectra. *Vision Research* 29:543–46.

MAFFEI, M.; HALAAS, J.; RAVUSSIN, E.; PRATLEY, R. E.; LEE, G. H.; ZHANG, Y.; FEI, H.; KIM, S.; LALLONE, R.; AND RANGANATHAN, S. 1995. Leptin levels in human and rodent: Measurement of plasma leptin and ob RNA in obese and weight-reduced subjects. *Nature Medicine* 1:1155–61.

MAGNUS, O., AND LAMMERS, J. 1956. The amygdaloid-nuclear complex. *Folia Psychiatrica Neurologica et Neurochirurgico Neerlandica* 59:552–82.

MAGNUSSON, A., AND STEFANSSON, J. G. 1993. Prevalence of seasonal affective disorder in Iceland. *Archives of General Psychiatry* 50:941–46.

MAGNUSSON, D., AND ENDLER, N. S. 1977. Interactional psychology: Present status and future prospects. In Magnusson, D., and Endler, N. S. (Eds.), *Personality at the crossroads,* pp. 3–31. New York: Wiley.

MAGOUN, H. W.; HARRISON, F.; BROBECK, J. R.; AND RANSON, S. W. 1938. Activation of heat loss mechanisms by local heating of the brain. *Journal of Neurophysiology* 1:101–14.

MAHER, B. A. 1966. *Principles of psychopathology.* New York: McGraw-Hill.

MAHONEY, M. J. 1976. *Scientist as subject: The psychological imperative.* Cambridge, Mass.: Ballinger.

MAHONEY, M. J., AND DEMONBREUN, B. G. 1981. Problem-solving bias in scientists. In Tweney, R. D.; Doherty, M. E.; and Mynatt, C. R. (Eds.), *On scientific thinking,* pp. 139–44. New York: Columbia University Press.

MAIER, S. F.; SELIGMAN, M. E. P.; AND SOLOMON, R. L. 1969. Pavlovian fear conditioning and learned helplessness: Effects on escape and avoidance behavior of (a) the CS-US contingency and (b) the independence of the US and voluntary responding. In Campbell, B. A., and Church, R. M. (Eds.), *Punishment and aversive behavior,* pp. 299–342. New York: Appleton-Century-Crofts.

MALAN, H. 1963. *A study of brief psychotherapy.* Philadelphia: Lippincott.

MALINOWSKI, B. 1926. *Crime and custom in savage society.* London: Paul, Trench, and Trubner.

MALINOWSKI, B. 1927. *Sex and repression in savage society.* New York: Meridian, 1955.

MALTHUS, T. R. 1798. *An essay on the principle of population.* Flew, A. (Ed.). Harmondsworth, Eng.: Penguin, 1970.

MANDLER, G. 1975. *Mind and emotion.* New York: Wiley.

MANDLER, G. 1984. *Mind and body: Psychology of emotion and stress.* New York: Norton.

MANDLER, G. 1997. *Human nature explored.* New York: Oxford University Press.

MANDLER, G. 1998. Consciousness and mind as philosophical problems and as psychological issues. In Hochberg, J. (Ed.), *Perception and cognition at century's end.* San Diego: Academic Press.

MANDLER, J. M. 1992. How to build a baby: II. Conceptual primitives. *Psychological Review* 99:587–604.

MANFREDI, M.; BINI, G.; CRUCCU, G.; ACCORNERO, N.; BERARDELLI, A.; AND MEDOLAGO, L. 1981. Congenital absence of pain. *Archives of Neurology* 38:507–11.

MANN, F.; BOWSHER, D.; MUMFORD, J.; LIPTON, S.; AND MILES, J. 1973. Treatment of intractable pain by acupuncture. *Lancet* 2:57–60.

MANTELL, D. M., AND PANZARELLA, R. 1976. Obedience and responsibility. *British Journal of Social and Child Psychology* 15:239–45.

MARAÑON, G. 1924. Review of Fr. *Endocrinology* 2:301.

MARCH, J. S.; LEONARD, H. L.; AND SWEDO, S. E. 1995. Obsessive-compulsive disorder. In March, J. S. (Ed.), *Anxiety disorders in children and adolescents,* pp. 251–75. New York: Guilford Press.

MARCUS, D. E., AND OVERTON, W. F. 1978. The development of cognitive gender constancy and sex-role preferences. *Child Development* 49:434–44.

MARCUS, G. F.; PINKER, S.; ULLMAN, M.; HOLLANDER, M.; ROSEN, T. J.; AND XU, F. 1992. Overregularization in language acquisition. *Monographs of the Society for Research in Child Development* 57(4, Serial No. 228).

MARCUS, J.; HANS, S. L.; AUERBACH, J. G.; AND AUERBACH, A. G. 1993. Children at risk for schizophrenia: The Jerusalem Infant Development Study. II. Neurobehavioral deficits at school age. *Archives of General Psychiatry* 50:797–809.

MARDER, S. R. 1996. Clinical experience with risperidone. *Journal of Clinical Psychiatry* 57 (suppl.) 9:57–61.

MAREN, S.; DE OCA, B.; AND FANSELOW, M. S. 1994. Sex differences in hippocampal long-term potentiation LTP and Pavlovian fear conditioning in rats: Positive correlation between LTP and contextual learning. *Brain Research* 661:25–34.

MARKMAN, E. 1989. *Categorization and naming in children: Problems of induction.* Cambridge, Mass.: MIT Press.

MARKMAN, E. M. 1994. Constraints children place on word meanings. In Bloom, P. (Ed.), *Language acquisition: Core readings.* Cambridge, Mass.: MIT Press.

MARKMAN, E. M., AND HUTCHINSON, J. E. 1984. Children's sensitivity to constraints on word meaning: Taxonomic vs. thematic relations. *Cognitive Psychology* 16:1–27.

MARKMAN, E. M., AND WACHTEL, G. A. 1988. Children's use of mutual exclusivity to constrain the meaning of words. *Cognitive Psychology* 20:121–57.

MARKS, D. F. 1983. In defense of imagery questionnaires. *Scandinavian Journal of Psychology* 24:243–46.

MARKS, I. M. 1969. *Fears and phobias.* New York: Academic Press.

MARKUS, H. M., AND KITAYAMA, S. 1994. The cultural construction of self and emotion: Implications for social behavior. In Kitayama, S., and Markus, H. R. (Eds.), *Emotion and culture,* pp. 89–130. Washington, D.C.: American Psychological Association.

MARKUS, H. R., AND KITAYAMA, S. 1991. Culture and the self: Implications for cognition, emotion, and motivation. *Psychological Review* 98:224–53.

MARLER, P. R. 1970. A comparative approach to vocal learning: Song development in white-crowned sparrows. *Journal of Comparative and Physiological Psychology Monographs* 71(No. 2, Part 2):1–25.

MARLER, P. R.; DUFFY, A.; AND PICKERT, R. 1986a. Vocal communication in the domestic chicken: I. Does a sender communicate information about the quality of a food referent to a receiver? *Animal Behaviour* 34:188–93.

MARLER, P. R.; DUFFY, A.; AND PICKERT, R. 1986b. Vocal communication in the domestic chicken: II. Is a sender sensitive to the presence and nature of a receiver? *Animal Behaviour* 34:194–98.

MARMOR, J. 1975. Homosexuality and sexual orientation disturbances. In Freedman, A. M.; Kaplan, H. I.; and Sadock, B. J. (Eds.), *Comprehensive textbook of psychiatry—II,* vol. 2, pp. 1510–19. Baltimore: Williams & Wilkins.

MARSDEN, C. D. 1985. Defects of movement in Parkinson's disease. In Delwaide, P. J., and Agnoli, A. (Eds.), *Clinical neurophysiology in Parkinsonism.* Amsterdam: Elsevier.

MARSHALL, D. A., AND MOULTON, D. G. 1981. Olfactory sensitivity to α—ionine in humans and dogs. *Chemical Senses* 6:53–61.

MARSHALL, G. D., AND ZIMBARDO, P. G. 1979. Affective consequences of inadequately explained physiological arousal. *Journal of Personality and Social Psychology* 37:970–88.

MARSLEN-WILSON, W. 1975. Sentence perception as an interactive parallel process. *Science* 189:226–28.

MARSLEN-WILSON, W. D., AND TEUBER, H. L. 1975. Memory for remote events in anterograde amnesia: Recognition of public figures from news photographs. *Neurobiologia* 13:353–64.

MARTIN, J. A.; KING, D. R.; MACCOBY, E. E.; AND JACKLIN, C. N. 1984. Secular trends and individual differences in toilet-training progress. *Journal of Pediatric Psychology* 9:457–67.

MARTIN, P., AND ALBERS, P. 1995. Cerebellum and schizophrenia: A review. *Schizophrenia Bulletin* 21:241–51.

MARTINEZ, J. L., AND DERRICK, B. E. 1996. Long-term potentiation and learning. *Annual Review of Psychology* 47:173–203.

MARTYNA, W. 1980. Beyond the "he/man" approach: The case for non-sexist language. *Signs* 5(3):482–93.

MASLACH, C. 1979. Negative emotional biasing of unexplained physiological arousal. *Journal of Personality and Social Psychology* 37:953–69.

MASLOW, A. H. 1954. *Motivation and personality.* New York: Harper & Row.

MASLOW, A. H. 1968. *Toward a psychology of being,* 2nd ed. Princeton, N.J.: Van Nostrand.

MASLOW, A. H. 1970. *Motivation and personality,* 2nd ed. New York: Harper.

MASTERS, M. S., AND SANDERS, B. 1993. Is the gender difference in mental rotation disappearing? *Behavior Genetics* 23:337–41.

MATARAZZO, J. D. 1983. The reliability of psychiatric and psychological diagnosis. *Clinical Psychology Review* 3:103–45.

MATHEWS, K. A. 1982. Psychological perspectives on the type A behavior pattern. *Psychological Bulletin* 91:293–323.

MATIN, L.; PICOULT, E.; STEVENS, J.; EDWARDS, M.; AND MACARTHUR, R. 1982. Ocuparalytic illusion: Visual-field dependent spatial mislocations by humans partially paralyzed with curare. *Science* 216:198–80.

MATSON, J. L., AND SEVIN, J. A. 1994. Issues in the use of aversives: Factors associated with behavior modification for autistic and other developmentally disabled people. In Schopler, E., and Mesibov, G. B. (Eds.), *Behavioral issues in autism,* pp. 211–25. New York: Plenum.

MATTHEWS, K. A. 1988. Coronary heart disease and Type A behaviors: Update on and alternative to the Booth-Kewley and Friedman 1987 quantitative review. *Psychological Bulletin* 104:373–80.

MATTISON, A., AND MCWHIRTER, D. 1987. Male couples: The beginning years. Intimate Relationships: Some Social Work Perspectives on Love. *Journal of Social Work and Human Sexuality* (Special Issue) 5:67–78.

MAUGH, T. M. 1981. Biochemical markers identify mental states. *Science* 214:39–41.

MAURICE, D. M. 1998. An ophthalmological explanation of REM sleep. *Experimental Eye Research* 66:139–45.

MAY, R. 1958. Contributions of existential psychotherapy. In May, R.; Angel, E.; and Ellenberger, H. F. (Eds.), *Existence,* pp. 37–91. New York: Basic Books.

MAYER, D. J.; PRICE, D. D.; RAFII, A.; AND BARBER, J. 1976. Acupuncture hypalgesia: Evidence for activation of a central control system as a mechanism of action. In Bonica, J. J., and Albe-Fessard, D. (Eds.), *Advances in pain research and therapy,* vol. 1. New York: Raven Press.

MAYES, A. R. 1988. *Human organic memory disorders.* New York: Cambridge University Press.

MAYEUX, R., AND KANDEL, E. R. 1991. Disorders of language: The aphasias. In Kandel, E. R.; Schwartz, J. H.; and Jessell, T. M. (Eds.), *Principles of neural science,* 3rd ed. New York: Elsevier.

MAYNARD-SMITH, J. 1965. The evolution of alarm calls. *American Naturalist* 100:637–50.

MCBURNEY, D. H.; LEVINE, J. M.; AND CAVANAUGH, P. H. 1977. Psychophysical and social ratings of human body odor. *Personality and Social Psychology Bulletin* 3:135–38.

MCBURNEY, D. H., AND SHICK, T. R. 1971. Taste and water taste of twenty-six compounds for man. *Perception and Psychophysics* 10:249–52.

MCCALL, R. B., AND CARRIGER, M. S. 1993. A meta analysis of infant habituation and recognition memory performance as predictors of later IQ. *Child Development* 64(1):57–79.

MCCLEARN, G. E., AND DEFRIES, J. C. 1973. *Introduction to behavioral genetics.* San Francisco: Freeman.

MCCLELLAND, J. L., AND RUMELHART, D. E. (EDS.) 1986. *Parallel distributed processing: Explorations in the microstructure of cognition,* vol. 2: *Psychological and biological models.* Cambridge, Mass.: MIT Press.

MCCLELLAND, J. L.; RUMELHART, D. E.; AND HINTON, G. E. 1986. The appeal of parallel distributed processing. In Rumelhart, D. E.; McClelland, J. L.; and the PDP Research Group, *Parallel distributed processing,* vol. 1: *Foundations,* pp. 3–44. Cambridge, Mass.: MIT Press.

MCCLINTOCK, M. K. 1971. Menstrual synchrony and suppression. *Nature* 229:244–45.

MCCLINTOCK, M. K., AND ADLER, N. T. 1978. The role of the female during copulation in wild and domestic Norway rats (*Rattus Norvegicus*). *Behaviour* 67:67–96.

MCCLINTOCK, M., AND STERN, K. 1998. Regulation of ovulation by human pheromones. *Nature* 392:177–79.

MCCLOSKEY, M., AND COHEN, N. J. 1989. Catastrophic interference in connectionist networks: The sequential learning problem. In Bower, G. H. (Ed.), *The psychology of learning and motivation,* vol. 23. New York: Academic Press.

MCCLOSKEY, M.; WIBLE, C. G.; AND COHEN, N. J. 1988. Is there a special flashbulb-memory mechanism? *Journal of Experimental Psychology: General* 117:171–81.

MCCONAGHY, M. J. 1979. Gender constancy and the genital basis of gender: Stages in the development of constancy by gender identity. *Child Development* 50:1223–26.

MCCORD, W., AND MCCORD, J. 1964. *The psychopath: An essay on the criminal mind.* New York: Van Nostrand.

MCCRANIE, E. W.; HYER, L. A.; BOUDEWYNS, P. A.; AND WOODS, M. G. 1992. Negative parenting behavior, combat exposure and PTSD symptom severity. Test of a person-event interaction model. *Journal of Nervous and Mental Disease* 180:431–38.

MCEWEN, B. S.; ALVES, S. E.; BULLOCH, K.; AND WEILAND, N. 1997. Ovarian steroids and the brain: Implications for cognition and aging. *Neurology* 48 (suppl. 7):S8–S15.

MCEWEN, B. S.; BIEGON, A.; DAVIS, P. G.; KREY, L. C.; LUINE, V. N.; MCGINNIS, M.; PADEN, C. M.; PARSONS, B.; AND RAINBOW, T. C. 1982. Steroid hormones: Humoral signals which alter brain cell properties and functions. *Recent Progress in Brain Research* 38:41–83.

MCGEE, M. G. 1979. Human spatial abilities: Psychometric studies and environmental, genetic, hormonal and neurological influences. *Psychological Bulletin* 86:889–918.

MCGEOCH, J. A., AND IRION, A. L. 1952. *The psychology of human learning,* 2nd ed. New York: Longmans, Green, and Co.

MCGHIE, A., AND CHAPMAN, J. 1961. Disorders of attention and perception in early schizophrenia. *British Journal of Medical Psychology* 34:103–16.

MCGRATH, M. J., AND COHEN, D. B. 1978. REM sleep facilitation of adaptive waking behavior: A review of the literature. *Psychological Bulletin* 85:24–57.

MCGRAW, M. B. 1935. *Growth: A study of Johnny and Jimmy.* New York: Appleton-Century.

MCGREGOR, G. P.; DESAGA, J. F.; EHLENZ, K.; FISCHER, A.; HEESE, F.; HEGELE, A.; LAMMER, C.; PEISER, C.; AND LANG, R. E. 1996. Radioimmunological measurement of leptin in plasma of obese and diabetic human subjects. *Endocrinology* 137:1501–4.

MCGUE, M.; BOUCHARD, T. J., JR.; IACONO, W. G.; AND LYKKEN, D. T. 1993. Behavioral genetics of cognitive ability: A life span perspective. In Plomin, R., and McClearn, G. E. (Eds.), *Nature, nurture and psychology,* pp. 59–76. Washington, D.C.: American Psychological Association.

MCGUE, M., AND LYKKEN, D. T. 1992. Genetic influence on risk of divorce. *Psychological Science* 3:368–72.

MCGUIGAN, F. J. 1966. Covert oral behavior and auditory hallucinations. *Psychophysiology* 3:421–28.

MCGUIRE, W. J. 1985. The nature of attitude and attitude change. In Lindzey, G., and Aronson, E. (Eds.), *Handbook of social psychology,* 3rd ed., vol. 2. New York: Random House.

MCKENZIE, B. E.; TOOTELL, H. E.; AND DAY, R. H. 1980. Development of size constancy during the 1st year of human infancy. *Developmental Psychology* 16:163–74.

MCNAUGHTON, B. L.; DOUGLAS, R. M.; AND GODDARD, G. V. 1978. Synaptic enhancement in fascia dentata: Cooperativity among coactive afferents. *Brain Research* 157:277–93.

MEAD, G. H. 1934. *Mind, self, and society.* Chicago: University of Chicago Press.

MEAD, M. 1935. *Sex and temperament in three primitive societies.* New York: Morrow.

MEAD, M. 1937. *Cooperation and competition among primitive peoples.* New York: McGraw-Hill.

MEAD, M. 1939. *From the South Seas: Studies of adolescence and sex in primitive societies.* New York: Morrow.

MEARNS, D. 1994. *Developing person-centered counseling.* London: Sage.

MEDDIS, R. 1977. *The sleep instinct.* London: Routledge and Kegan Paul.

MEDDIS, R. 1979. The evolution and function of sleep. In Oakley, D. A., and Plotkin, H. C. (Eds.), *Brain, behavior, and evolution.* London: Methuen.

MEDNICK, S. A.; HUTTUNEN, M. O.; AND MACHO'N, R. A. 1994. Prenatal influenza infections and adult schizophrenia. *Schizophrenia Bulletin* 20:263–67.

MEEHL, P. D. 1962. Schizotaxia, schizotypy, schizophrenia. *American Psychologist* 17:827–38.

MEEHL, P. E. 1959. Some ruminations on the validation of clinical procedures. *Canadian Journal of Psychology* 13:102–28.

MEGENS, A. A., AND KENNIS, L. E. 1996. Risperidone and related 5HT2/D2 antagonists: A new type of antipsychotic agent? *Progress in Medicinal Chemistry* 33:185–232.

MEHLER, J.; JUSCZYK, P.; LAMBERTZ, G.; HALSTED, N.; BERTONCINI, J.; AND AMIEL-TISON, C. 1988. A precursor to language acquisition in young infants. *Cognition* 29:143–78.

MELTZER, H. Y. 1986. Lithium mechanisms in bipolar illness and altered intracellular calcium functions. *Biological Psychiatry* 21:492–510.

MELTZER, H. Y. 1987. Biological studies in schizophrenia. *Schizophrenia Bulletin* 13:77–111.

MELTZOFF, A. N., AND MOORE, M. K. 1977. Imitation of facial and manual gestures by human neonates. *Science* 198:75–78.

MELZACK, R. 1973. *The puzzle of pain.* New York: Basic Books.

MENYUK, P. 1977. *Language and maturation.* Cambridge, Mass.: MIT Press.

MENZEL, E. W. 1973. Chimpanzee spatial memory organization. *Science* 182:943–45.

MENZEL, E. W. 1978. Cognitive maps in chimpanzees. In Hulse, S. H.; Fowler, H.; and Honig, W. K. (Eds.), *Cognitive processes in animal behavior,* pp. 375–422. Hillsdale, N.J.: Erlbaum.

MERCER, J. 1973. *Labeling the mentally retarded.* Berkeley, Calif.: University of California Press.

MERVIS, C. B., AND CRISAFI, M. 1978. Order acquisition of subordinate, basic, and superordinate level categories. *Child Development* 49:988–98.

MESQUITA, B., AND FRIJDA, N. H. 1992. Cultural variations in emotion: A review. *Psychological Bulletin* 112:179–204.

METCALFE, J. 1986. Premonitions of insight predict impending error. *Journal of Experimental Psychology: Learning, Memory and Cognition* 12:623–34.

METCALFE, J., AND WEIBE, D. 1987. Intuition in insight and noninsight problem solving. *Memory and Cognition* 15:238–46.

MEYER, D. E., AND SCHVANEVELDT, R. W. 1971. Facilitation in recognizing pairs of words: Evidence of a dependence between retrieval operations. *Journal of Experimental Psychology* 90:227–34.

MIASKIEWICZ, S. L.; STRICKER, E. M.; AND VERBALIS, J. G. 1989. Neurohypophyseal secretion in response to cholecystokinin but not meal-induced gastric distention in humans. *Journal of Clinical Endocrinology and Metabolism* 68:837–43.

MICHAEL, R. P., AND KEVERNE, E. B. 1968. Pheromones in the communication of sexual status in primates. *Nature* 218:746–49.

MICHAELS, J. W.; BLOMMEL, J. M.; BROCATO, R. M.; LINKOUS, R. A.; AND ROWE, J. S. 1982. Social facilitation and inhibition in a natural setting. *Replications in Social Psychology* 2:21–24.

MILGRAM, S. 1963. Behavioral study of obedience. *Journal of Abnormal and Social Psychology* 67:371–78.

MILGRAM, S. 1965. Some conditions of obedience and disobedience to authority. *Human Relations* 18:57–76.

MILGRAM, S. 1974. *Obedience to authority.* New York: Harper & Row.

MILGRAM, S., AND MURRAY, T. H. 1992. Can deception in research be justified? In Slife, B., and Rubenstein, J. (Eds.), *Taking sides: Clashing views on controversial psychological issues,* 7th ed. Gilford, Conn.: Dushkin Publishing Group.

MILL, J. S. 1865. *An examination of Sir William Hamilton's philosophy.* London: Longman, Green, Longman, Roberts & Green.

MILLER, A. G. 1986. *The obedience experiments: A case study of controversy in social science.* New York: Praeger.

MILLER, D. T. 1976. Ego involvement and attribution for success and failure. *Journal of Personality and Social Psychology* 34:901–6.

MILLER, G. A. 1956. The magical number seven plus or minus two: Some limits in our capacity for processing information. *Psychological Review* 63:81–97.

MILLER, G., AND GILDEA, P. 1987. How children learn words. *Scientific American* 257:94–99.

MILLER, G., AND JOHNSON-LAIRD, P. 1976. *Language and perception.* Cambridge, Mass.: Harvard University Press.

MILLER, J. 1972. *Freud: The man, his world, his influence.* Boston: Little-Brown.

MILLER, J. G. 1984. Culture and the development of everyday social explanation. *Journal of Personality and Social Psychology* 46:961–78.

MILLER, L. C. 1990. Intimacy and liking: Mutual influence and the role of unique relationships. *Journal of Personality and Social Psychology* 59:50–60.

MILLER, L. C., AND KENNY, D. A. 1986. Reciprocity of self-disclosure at the individual and dyadic levels: A social relations analysis. *Journal of Personality and Social Psychology* 50:713–19.

MILLER, N. E.; BAILEY, C. J.; AND STEVENSON, J. A. F. 1950. Decreased "hunger" but increased food intake resulting from hypothalamic lesions. *Science* 112:256–59.

MILLER, R. R.; BARNET, R. C.; AND GRAHAME, N. J. 1995. Assessment of the Rescorla–Wagner model. *Psychological Bulletin* 117:363–87.

MILLER, R. S. 1987. Empathic embarrassment: Situational and personal determinants of reactions to the embarrassment of another. *Journal of Personality and Social Psychology* 53(6):1061–69.

MILLER, R. S. 1996. *Embarrassment.* New York: Guilford Press.

MILLON, T. 1969. *Modern psychopathology.* Philadelphia: Saunders.

MILLS, J., AND CLARK, M. S. 1994. Communal and exchange relationships: Controversies and research. In Erber, R., and Gilmour, R. (Eds.), *Theoretical frameworks for personal relationships,* pp. 29–42. Hillsdale, N.J.: Erlbaum.

MILNER, A. D., AND GOODALE, M. A. 1995. *The visual brain in action.* New York: Oxford University Press.

MILNER, B. 1963. Effects of different brain lesions on card sorting. *Archives of Neuropsychology* 9:90–100.

MILNER, B. 1966. Amnesia following operation on the temporal lobes. In Whitty, C. W. M., and Zangwill, O. L. (Eds.), *Amnesia,* pp. 109–33. London: Butterworth.

MILNER, B.; CORKIN, S.; AND TEUBER, H. L. 1968. Further analysis of the hippocampal syndrome: 14-year follow-up study of H. M. *Neuropsychologia* 6:215–34.

MILNER, B., AND PETRIDES, M. 1984. Behavioural effects of frontal-lobe lesions in man. *Trends in Neurosciences* 7:403–7.

MINUCHIN, S. 1974. *Families and family therapy.* Cambridge, Mass.: Harvard University Press.

MISCHEL, W. 1968. *Personality and assessment.* New York: Wiley.

MISCHEL, W. 1973. Towards a cognitive social learning reconceptualization of personality. *Psychological Review* 80:252–83.

MISCHEL, W. 1974. Processes in delay of gratification. In Berkowitz, L. (Ed.), *Advances in experimental social psychology,* vol. 7. New York: Academic Press.

MISCHEL, W. 1979. On the interface of cognition and personality: Beyond the person-situation debate. *American Psychologist* 34:740–54.

MISCHEL, W. 1984. Convergences and challenges in the search for consistency. *American Psychologist* 39:351–64.

MISCHEL, W. 1986. *Introduction to personality,* 4th ed. New York: Holt, Rinehart & Winston.

MISCHEL, W., AND BAKER, N. 1975. Cognitive appraisals and transformations in delay behavior. *Journal of Personality and Social Psychology* 31:254–61.

MISCHEL, W.; EBBESEN, E. B.; AND ZEISS, A. R. 1972. Cognitive and attentional mechanisms in delay of gratification. *Journal of Personality and Social Psychology* 21:204–18.

MISCHEL, W., AND MISCHEL, H. N. 1983. Development of children's knowledge of self-control strategies. *Child Development* 54:603–19.

MISCHEL, W., AND MOORE, B. 1980. The role of ideation in voluntary delay for symbolically presented awards. *Cognitive Therapy and Research* 4:211–21.

MISCHEL, W., AND PEAKE, P. K. 1983. Some facets of consistency. Replies to Epstein, Funder and Bem. *Psychological Review* 90:394–402.

MISCHEL, W., AND RODRIGUEZ, M. L. 1993. Psychological distance in self-imposed delay of gratification. In Cocking, R. R., and Renninger, K. A. (Eds.), *The development and meaning of psychological distance,* pp. 109–21. Hillsdale, N.J.: Erlbaum.

MISCHEL, W.; SHODA, Y.; AND PEAKE, P. K. 1988. The nature of adolescent competencies predicted by preschool delay of gratification. *Journal of Personality and Social Psychology* 54:687–96.

MISCHEL, W.; SHODA, Y.; AND RODRIGUEZ, M. L. 1992. Delay of gratification in children. In Loewenstein, G., and Elster, J. (Eds), *Choice over time,* pp. 147–64. New York: Russell Sage Foundation.

MISELIS, R. R., AND EPSTEIN, A. N. 1970. Feeding induced by 2-deoxy-D-glucose injections into the lateral ventrical of the rat. *Physiologist* 13:262.

MISHKIN, M., AND APPENZELLER, T. 1987. The anatomy of memory. *Scientific American* 256:80–89.

MISHKIN, M.; UNGERLEIDER, L. G.; AND MACKO, K. 1983. Object vision and spatial vision: Two cortical pathways. *Trends in Neurosciences* 6:414–17.

MISHLER, E. G., AND WAXLER, N. E. 1968. Family interaction and schizophrenia: Alternative frameworks of interpretation. In Rosenthal, D., and Kety, S. S. (Eds.), *The transmission of schizophrenia,* pp. 213–22. New York: Pergamon.

MITA, T. H.; DERMER, M.; AND KNIGHT, J. 1977. Reversed facial images and the mere exposure hypothesis. *Journal of Personality and Social Psychology* 35:597–601.

MITCHELL, D. E.; REARDON, J.; AND MUIR, D. W. 1975. Interocular transfer of the motion after-effect in normal and stereoblind observers. *Experimental Brain Research* 22:163–73.

MITROFF, I. I. 1974. *The subjective side of science.* Amsterdam: Elsevier.

MIYASHITA, Y. 1995. How the brain creates imagery: Projection to primary visual cortex. *Science* 268:1719–20.

MODIGLIANI, A. 1971. Embarrassment, face work and eye contact: Testing a theory of embarrassment. *Journal of Personality and Social Psychology* 17:15–24.

MOFFITT, T. E.; CASPI, A.; HARKNESS, A. R.; AND SILVA, P. A. 1993. The natural history of change in intellectual performance: Who changes? How much? Is it meaningful? *Journal of Child Psychology and Psychiatry and Allied Disciplines* 34(4):455–506.

MOLONEY, D. P.; BOUCHARD, T. J., JR.; AND SEGAL, N. L. 1991. A genetic and environmental analysis of the vocational interests of monozygotic and dizygotic twins reared apart. *Journal of Vocational Behavior* 39:76–109.

MONEY, J. 1980. *Love and love sickness.* Baltimore: Johns Hopkins University Press.

MONEY, J., AND EHRHARDT, A. A. 1972. *Man and woman, boy and girl.* Baltimore: Johns Hopkins University Press.

MONSON, T. C.; HESLEY, J. W.; AND CHERNICK, L. 1982. Specifying when personality traits can and cannot predict behavior: An alternative to abandoning the attempt to predict single-act criteria. *Journal of Personality and Social Psychology* 43:385–99.

MONTE, C. F. 1995. *Beneath the mask,* 5th ed. Fort Worth: Harcourt Brace.

MONTGOMERY, S. A. 1995. Selective serotonin reuptake inhibitors in the acute treatment of depression. In Bloom, F. E., and Kupfer, D. (Eds.), *Psychopharmacology: The fourth generation of progress,* pp. 1043–51. New York: Raven.

MOONEY, C. M. No date. *Closure test* (pamphlet). Montreal: Department of Psychology, McGill University.

MOORE, J. W. 1972. Stimulus control: Studies of auditory generalization in rabbits. In Black, A. H., and Prokasy, W. F. (Eds.), *Classical conditioning II: Current research and theory,* pp. 206–30. New York: Appleton-Century-Crofts.

MORA, F.; ROLLS, E. T.; AND BURTON, M. J. 1976. Modulation during learning of the responses of neurons in the lateral hypothalamus to the sight of food. *Experimental Neurology* 53:508–19.

MORA, G. 1975. Historical and theoretical trends in psychiatry. In Freedman, A. M.; Kaplan, H. I.; and Sadock, B. J. (Eds.), *Comprehensive textbook of psychiatry,* vol. 1, pp. 1–75. Baltimore: Williams & Wilkins.

MORAY, N. 1959. Attention in dichotic listening: Affective cues and the influence of instructions. *Quarterly Journal of Experimental Psychology* 11:56–60.

MORELAND, R. L., AND ZAJONC, R. B. 1982. Exposure effects in person perception: Familiarity, similarity, and attraction. *Journal of Experimental Social Psychology* 18:395–415.

MORET, V.; FORSTER, A.; LAVERRIERE, M.-C.; LAMBERT, H. 1991. Mechanism of analgesia induced by hypnosis and acupuncture: Is there a difference? *Pain* 45:135–40.

MORGAN, C. D., AND MURRAY, H. A. 1935. A method for investigating fantasies: The thematic apperception test. *Archives of Neurological Psychiatry* 34:289–306.

MORGAN, I. G., AND BOELEN, M. K. 1996. A retinal dark-light switch: A review of the evidence. *Visual Neuroscience* 13:399–409.

MORGAN, J. 1986. *From simple input to complex grammar,* Cambridge, Mass.: MIT Press.

MORGAN, J., AND TRAVIS, L. 1989. Limits on negative information in language input. *Journal of Child Language* 16(3):531–52.

MORRIS, D. 1967. *The naked ape.* New York: McGraw-Hill.

MORRIS, M. W., AND PENG, K. 1994. Culture and cause: American and Chinese attributions for social and physical events. *Journal of Personality and Social Psychology* 67:949–71.

MORSBACH, H., AND TYLER, W. J. 1986. In Harr, R. (Ed.), *The social construction of emotions,* pp. 289–307. Oxford: Blackwell.

MORTON, T. U. 1978. Intimacy and reciprocity of exchange: A comparison of spouses and strangers. *Journal of Personality and Social Psychology* 36:72–81.

MOSCOVICI, S. 1985. Social influence and conformity. In Lindzey, G., and Aronson, E. (Ed.), *Handbook of social psychology,* 3rd ed., vol. 2, pp. 347–412. New York: Random House.

MOSCOVITCH, M. 1972. Choice reaction-time study assessing the verbal behavior of the minor hemisphere in normal adults. *Journal of Comparative and Physiological Psychology* 80:66–74.

MOSCOVITCH, M. 1979. Information processing and the cerebral hemispheres. In Gazzaniga, M. S., *Handbook of behavioral neurobiology,* vol. 2, pp. 379–446. New York: Plenum.

MOSCOVITCH, M. 1994. Memory and working-with-memory. Evaluation of a component process model and comparisons with other models. In Schacter, D. L., and Tulving, E. (Eds.), *Memory systems 1994,* pp. 269–310. Cambridge: MIT Press.

MOSCOVITCH, M. 1995. Confabulation. In Schacter, D. L.; Coyle, J. T.; Fischbach, G. D.; Mesulam, M.-M.; and Sullivan, L. E. (Eds.), *Memory distortion: How minds, brains, and societies reconstruct the past,* pp. 226–54. Cambridge, Mass.: Harvard University Press.

MOSCOVITCH, M., AND ROZIN, P. 1989. Disorders of the nervous system and psychopathology. In Rosenhan, D. L., and Seligman, M. E. P. (Eds.), *Abnormal psychology,* 2nd ed., pp. 558–602. New York: Norton.

MOSKOWITZ, D. W. 1982. Coherence and cross-situational generality in personality: A new analysis of old problems. *Journal of Personality and Social Psychology* 43:754–68.

MOWRER, O. H. 1939. A stimulus-response analysis of anxiety and its role as a reinforcing agent. *Psychological Review* 46:553–65.

MOWRER, O. H. 1960. *Learning theory and behavior.* New York: Wiley.

MULFORD, R. 1986. First words of the blind child. In Smith, M., and Locke, J. (Eds.), *The emergent lexicon: The child's development of a linguistic vocabulary.* New York: Academic Press.

MULICK, J. A. 1990. The ideology and science of punishment in mental retardation. *American Journal on Mental Retardation* 95:142–56.

MULLAN, S., AND PENFIELD, W. 1959. Illusions of comparative interpretation and emotion. *Archives of Neurology and Psychiatry* 80:269–84.

MULLER, H. J. 1964. The relation of mutation to recombinational advance. *Mutation Research* 1:2–9.

MURDOCK, B. 1962. The serial position effect of free recall. *Journal of Experimental Psychology* 64:482–88.

MURRAY, F. B. 1978. Teaching strategies and conservation training. In Lesgold, A. M.; Pellegrino, J. W.; Fekkeman, D.; and Glaser, R. (Eds.), *Cognitive psychology and instruction,* vol. 1. New York: Plenum.

MUSCETTOLA, G.; POTTER, W. Z.; PICKAR, D.; AND GOODWIN, F. K. 1984. Urinary 3-methoxy-4-hydroxyphenylglycol and major affective disorders. *Archives of General Psychiatry* 41:337–42.

MUUSS, R. E. 1970. Puberty rites in primitive and modern societies. *Adolescence* 5:109–28.

NADEL, L., AND ZOLA-MORGAN, S. 1984. Infantile amnesia: A neurobiological perspective. In Moscovich, M. (Ed.), *Infant memory,* pp. 145–72. New York: Plenum Press.

NAIGLES, L. 1990. Children use syntax to learn verb meanings. *Journal of Child Language* 17:357–74.

NATHAN, P. W. 1978. Acupuncture analgesia. *Trends in Neurosciences* 1:210–23.

NATIONAL COMMISSION ON SLEEP DISORDERS. 1993. *Wake up America: A national sleep alert.* Washington, D.C.

NATIONAL INSTITUTES OF HEALTH. 1995. Methods of voluntary weight loss and control. Technology Assessment Conference Statement, March 30-April 1, 1992. Washington, D. C.: NIH Office of Medical Applications Research.

NAUTA, W. J. H., AND FEIRTAG, M. 1986. *Fundamental neuroanatomy.* New York: Freeman.

NEEDHAM, D., AND BEGG, I. 1991. Problem-oriented training promotes spontaneous analogical transfer: Memory-oriented training promotes memory for training. *Memory and Cognition* 19:543–57.

NEIMEYER, G. J. 1984. Cognitive complexity and marital satisfaction. *Journal of Social and Clinical Psychology* 2:258–63.

NEISSER, U. 1967. *Cognitive psychology.* New York: Appleton-Century-Crofts.

NEISSER, U. 1982a. *Memory observed.* San Francisco: Freeman.

NEISSER, U. 1982b. On the trail of the tape-recorder fallacy. Paper presented at a symposium on "The influence of hypnosis and related states on memory: Forensic implications" at the meetings of the American Association for the Advancement of Science, Washington, D.C., in January 1982.

NEISSER, U. 1986. Remembering Pearl Harbor: Reply to Thompson and Cowan. *Cognition* 23:285–86.

NEISSER, U. 1989. Domains of memory. In Solomon, P. R.; Goethals, G. R.; Kelley, C. M.; and Stephens, B. R. (Eds.), *Memory: Interdisciplinary approaches,* pp. 67–83. New York: Springer Verlag.

NEISSER, U.; BOODOO, G.; BOUCHARD, T. J., JR.; AND BOYKIN, A. W. 1996. Intelligence: Knowns and unknowns. *American Psychologist* 51(2):77–101.

NELSON, K. 1973. Structure and strategy in learning to talk. *Monographs of the Society for Research in Child Development* 38(1–2, Serial No. 149).

NEMETH, C. J. 1992. Minority dissent as a stimulant to group performance. In Worchel, S.; Wood, W.; and Simpson, J. A. (Eds.), *Group process and productivity,* pp. 95–111. Newbury Park, Calif.: Sage.

NEMETH, C., AND CHILES, C. 1988. Modeling courage: The role of dissent in fostering independence. *European Journal of Social Psychology* 18:275–80.

NEUGEBAUER, R. 1979. Medieval and early modern theories of mental illness. *Archives of General Psychiatry* 36:477–84.

NEW, A. S.; TRESTMAN, R. L.; MITROPOULOU, V.; AND BENISHAY, D. S. 1997. Serotonergic function and self-injurious behavior in personality disorder patients. *Psychiatry Research* 69(1):17–26.

NEWCOMBE, F.; RATCLIFF, G.; AND DAMASIO, H. 1987. Dissociable visual and spatial impairments following right posterior cerebral lesions: Clinical, neuropsychological and anatomical evidence. *Neuropsychologia* 25(1 B):149–61.

NEWELL, A., AND SIMON, H. A. 1972. *Human problem solving.* Englewood Cliffs, N.J.: Prentice-Hall.

NEWPORT, E. L. 1984. Constraints on learning: Studies in the acquisition of American Sign Language. *Papers and Reports on Child Language Development* 23:1–22. Stanford, Calif.: Stanford University Press.

NEWPORT, E. 1990. Maturational constraints on language learning. *Cognitive Science* 14:11–28.

NEWPORT, E. L., AND ASHBROOK, E. F. 1977. The emergence of semantic relations in American Sign Language. *Papers and Reports in Child Language Development* 13.

NEWPORT, E., GLEITMAN, H., AND GLEITMAN, L. 1977. Mother, I'd rather do it myself: Some effects and non-effects of maternal speech style. In Snow, C., and Ferguson, C. (Eds.), *Talking to children: Language input and acquisition.* New York: Cambridge University Press.

NEWSOME, W. T.; SHADLEN, M. N.; ZOHARY, E.; BRITTEN, K. H.; AND MOVSHON, J. A. 1995. Visual motion: Linking neuronal activity to psychophysical performance. In Gazzaniga, M. S. (Ed.), *The cognitive neurosciences,* pp. 401–14. Cambridge, Mass.: MIT Press.

NICHD EARLY CHILD CARE RESEARCH NETWORK. 1997. The effects of infant child care on infant-mother attachment security: Results of the NICHD study of early child care. *Child Development* 68:860–79.

NICHOLSON, R. A., AND BERMAN, J. S. 1983. Is follow-up necessary in evaluating psychotherapy? *Psychological Bulletin* 93:261–78.

NICKERSON, R. A., AND ADAMS, M. J. 1979. Long-term memory for a common object. *Cognitive Psychology* 11:287–307.

NICOL, S. E., AND GOTTESMAN, I. I. 1983. Clues to the genetics and neurobiology of schizophrenia. *American Scientist* 71:398–404.

NISBETT, R. E. 1968. Taste, deprivation, and weight determinants of eating behavior. *Journal of Personality and Social Psychology* 10:107–16.

NISBETT, R. E. 1972. Eating behavior and obesity in man and animals. *Advances in Psychosomatic Medicine* 7:173–93.

NISBETT, R. E. 1977. Interaction versus main effects as goals of personality research. In Magnusson, D., and Endler, L. (Eds.), *Personality at the crossroads: Current issues in interactional psychology,* pp. 235–41. Hillsdale, N.J.: Erlbaum.

NISBETT, R. E. 1980. The trait construct in lay and professional psychology. In Festinger, L. (Ed.), *Retrospections on social psychology,* pp. 109–30. New York: Oxford University Press.

NISBETT, R. E. 1993. *Rules for reasoning.* Hillsdale, N.J.: Erlbaum.

NISBETT, R. E.; CAPUTO, C.; LEGANT, P.; AND MARACEK, J. 1973. Behavior as seen by the actor and as seen by the observer. *Journal of Personality and Social Psychology* 27:154–64.

NISBETT, R. E.; KRANTZ, D. H.; JEPSON, C.; AND KUNDA, Z. 1983. The use of statistical heuristics in everyday inductive reasoning. *Psychological Review* 90:339–63.

NISBETT, R., AND ROSS, L. 1980. *Human inference: Strategies and shortcomings of social judgment.* Englewood Cliffs, N.J.: Prentice-Hall.

NISBETT, R. E., AND WILSON, T. D. 1977. Telling more than we can know: Verbal reports on mental processes. *Psychological Review* 84:231–59.

NOFZINGER, E. A.; BUYSSE, D. J.; REYNOLDS, C. F.; AND KUPFER, D. J. 1993. Sleep disorders related to another mental disorder nonsubstance/primary: A DSM-IV literature review. *Journal of Clinical Psychiatry* 54:244–55.

NOLEN-HOEKSMA, S. 1987. Sex differences in unipolar depression: Evidence and theory. *Psychological Bulletin* 101:259–82.

NOLL, R. 1995. *The Jung cult: Origins of a charismatic movement.* Princeton, N.J.: Princeton University Press.

NOPOULOS, P.; FLAUM, M.; AND ANDREASEN, N. C. 1997. Sex differences and brain morphology in schizophrenia. *American Journal of Psychiatry* 154:1648–54.

NORCROSS, J. C. 1991. Prescriptive matching in psychotherapy: Psychoanalysis for simple phobias? *Psychotherapy* 28:439–43.

NORCROSS, J. C., AND FREEDHEIM, D. K. 1992. Into the future: Retrospect and prospect in psychotherapy. In Freedheim, D. K. (Ed.), *History of psychotherapy*. Washington, D.C.: American Psychological Association.

NORMAN, W. T. 1963. Toward an adequate taxonomy of personality attributes: Replicated factor structure in peer nomination personality ratings. *Journal of Abnormal and Social Psychology* 66:574–83.

NOTTEBOHM, F. 1987. Plasticity in adult avian central nervous system: Possible relations between hormones, learning, and brain repair. In Plum, F. (Ed.), *Higher functions of the nervous system,* section I, vol. 5: *Handbook of physiology*. Washington, D.C.: American Physiological Society.

NOVAK, M. A., AND HARLOW, H. F. 1975. Social recovery of monkeys isolated for the first year of life: I. Rehabilitation and therapy. *Developmental Psychology* 11:453–65.

NOWLIS, G. H., AND FRANK, M. E. 1981. Quality coding in gustatory systems of rats and hamsters. In Norris, D. M. (Ed.), *Perception of behavioral chemicals,* pp. 58–80. Amsterdam: Elsevier.

O'BRIEN, M., AND NAGLE, K. J. 1987. Parents' speech to toddlers: The effect of play context. *Journal of Child Language* 14:269–79.

ODIORNE, J. M. 1957. Color changes. In Brown, M. E. (Ed.), *The physiology of fishes,* vol. 2. New York: Academic Press.

OFMAN, W. V. 1985. Existential psychotherapy. In Kaplan, H. I., and Sadock, J. (Eds.), *Comprehensive textbook of psychiatry,* 4th ed, pp. 1438–43. Baltimore: Williams & Wilkins.

OFSHE, R. 1992. Inadvertent hypnosis during interrogation: False confession due to dissociative state; mis-identified multiple personality and the Satanic Cult Hypothesis. *International Journal of Clinical and Experimental Hypnosis* 40:125–36.

OHANIAN, H. C. 1985 and 1993. *Physics,* 1st and 2nd eds. New York: Norton.

OLDS, J., AND MILNER, P. 1954. Positive reinforcement produced by electrical stimulation of septal areas and other regions of rat brains. *Journal of Comparative and Physiological Psychology* 47:419–27.

OLDS, M. E., AND FOBES, T. 1981. The central basis of motivation: Intracranial self-stimulation. *Annual Review of Psychology* 32:523–74.

OLFSON, M., AND KLERMAN, G. L. 1993. Trends in the prescription of psychotropic medications. The role of physician specialty. *Medical Care* 31:559–64.

OLSON, D. J. 1991. Species differences in spatial memory among Clark's nutcrackers, scrub jays, and pigeons. *Journal of Experimental Psychology: Animal Behavior Processes* 17(4):363–76.

OLSON, G. A.; OLSON, R. D.; AND KASTIN, A. J. 1995. Endogenous opiates: 1994. *Peptides* 16:1517–55.

OLSON, W. K. 1997. *The excuse factory: How employment law is paralyzing the American workplace.* New York: Free Press.

OLTON, D. S. 1978. Characteristics of spatial memory. In Hulse, S. H., Fowler, H., and Honig, W. K. (Eds.), *Cognitive processes in animal behavior,* pp. 341–73. Hillsdale, N.J.: Erlbaum.

OLTON, D. S. 1979. Mazes, maps, and memory. *American Psychologist* 34:583–96.

OLTON, D. S., AND SAMUELSON, R. J. 1976. Remembrance of places passed: Spatial memory in rats. *Journal of Experimental Psychology: Animal Behavior Processes* 2:97–116.

OLWEUS, D. 1980. Familial and temperamental determinants of aggressive behavior in adolescent boys: A causal analysis. *Developmental Psychology* 16:644–66.

ORBELL, J. M.; VAN DE KRAGT, A. J. C.; AND DAWES, R. M. 1988. Explaining discussion-induced cooperation. *Journal of Personality and Social Psychology* 54:811–19.

ORING, L. W. 1985. Avian polyandry. *Current Ornithology* 3:309–51.

ORLANSKY, H. 1949. Infant care and personality. *Psychological Bulletin* 46:1–48.

ORNE, M. T. 1951. The mechanisms of hypnotic age regression: An experimental study. *Journal of Abnormal and Social Psychology* 58:277–99.

ORNE, M. T. 1975. Psychotherapy in contemporary America: Its development and context. In Arieti, S. (Ed.), *American handbook of psychiatry,* 2nd ed., vol. 5, pp. 1–33. New York: Basic Books.

ORNE, M. T. 1979. The use and misuse of hypnosis in court. *The International Journal of Clinical and Experimental Hypnosis* 27:311–41.

ORNE, M. T., AND HAMMER, A. G. 1974. Hypnosis. In *Encyclopaedia Brittannica,* 5th ed., pp. 133–40. Chicago: Encyclopaedia Brittannica.

ORNSTEIN, R. 1977. *The psychology of consciousness,* 2nd ed. New York: Harcourt Brace Jovanovich.

ORSINI, D. L.; VAN GORP, W. G.; AND BOONE, K. B. 1988. *The neuropsychology casebook.* New York: Springer-Verlag.

ORTONY, A., AND TURNER, T. J. 1990. What's basic about basic emotions? *Psychological Review* 97:315–31.

OSOFSKY, J. D., AND DANZGER, B. 1974. Relationships between neo-natal characteristics and mother-infant characteristics. *Developmental Psychology* 10:124–30.

OSTROM, T. M. 1977. Between-theory and within-theory conflict in explaining context effects in impression formation. *Journal of Experimental Social Psychology* 13:492–503.

OVERSTREET, D. H. 1993. The Flinders sensitive line rats: A genetic animal model of depression. *Neuroscience and Biobehavioral Reviews* 17:51–68.

PACKER, C. 1977. Reciprocal altruism in olive baboons. *Nature* 265:441–43.

PAEZ, D., AND VERGARA, A. I. 1995. Culture differences in emotion knowledge. In Russell, J. A.; Fernandez-Dols, J.-M.; Manstead, A. S. R.; and Wellenkamp, J. C. (Eds.), *Everyday conceptions of emotion: An introduction to the psychology, anthropology and linguistics of emotion,* pp. 415–34. Dordrecht, Netherlands: Kluwer Academic Publishers.

PAGE, E. B. 1985. Review of Kaufman's Assessment Battery for Children. *Ninth mental measurements yearbook,* vol. 1., pp. 773–77. Highland Park, N.J.: The Mental Measurements Yearbook.

PAPINI, M. R., AND BITTERMAN, M. E. 1990. The role of contingency in classical conditioning. *Psychological Review* 97:396–403.

PARKE, R. D. 1981. *Fathers.* Cambridge, Mass.: Harvard University Press.

PARKE, R. D., AND SLABY, R. G. 1983. The development of aggression. In Mussen, P. H. (Ed.), *Carmichael's manual of child psychology,* vol. 4: *Socialization, personality and social development,* pp. 547–642. Hetherington, M. E., vol. ed. New York: Wiley.

PARNAS, J., AND JORGENSEN, A. 1989. Premorbid psychopathology in schizophrenia spectrum. *British Journal of Psychiatry* 155:623–27.

PARROTT, W. G.; SABINI, J.; AND SILVER, M. 1988. The roles of self-esteem and social interaction in embarrassment. *Personality and Social Psychology Bulletin* 14:191–202.

PARTEE, B. 1996. The development of formal semantics in linguistic theory. In Lappin, S. (Ed.), *The handbook of contemporary semantic theory,* pp. 11–38. Oxford: Blackwell.

PATIENCE, A., AND SMITH, J. W. 1986. Derek Freeman and Samoa: The making and unmaking of a biobehavioral myth. *American Anthropologist* 88:157–61.

PATTATUCCI, A. M. L., AND HAMER, D. H. 1995. Development and familiarity of sexual orientation in females. *Behavior Genetics* 25:407–20.

PATTERSON, M. L. 1983. *Nonverbal behavior: A functional perspective.* New York: Springer-Verlag.

PATTERSON, T.; SPOHN, H. E.; BOGIA, D. P.; AND HAYES, K. 1986. Thought disorder in schizophrenia: Cognitive and neuroscience approaches. *Schizophrenia Bulletin* 12:460–72.

PAUL, G. L. 1966. *Insight vs. desensitization in psychotherapy: An experiment in anxiety reduction.* Stanford, Calif.: Stanford University Press.

PAUL, G. L. 1967. Insight versus desensitization in psychotherapy two years after termination. *Journal of Consulting Psychology* 31:333–48.

PAVLOV, I. 1927. *Conditioned reflexes.* Oxford: Oxford University Press.

PAVLOV, I. 1928. *Lectures on conditioned reflexes,* vol 1. New York: International Publishers Co., Inc.

PAYKEL, E. S. 1982. Life events and early environment. In Paykel, E. S. (Ed.), *Handbook of affective disorders.* New York: Guilford.

PEDERSEN, P. B.; FUKUYAMA, M.; AND HEATH, A. 1989. Client, counselor, and contextual variables in multicultural counseling. In Pedersen, P. B.; Draguns, J. G.; Lonner, W. J.; and Trimble, J. E. (Eds.), *Counseling across cultures*, pp. 23–52. Honolulu: University of Hawaii.

PELLEYMOUNTER, M. A.; CULLEN, M. J.; BAKER, M. B.; HECHT, R.; WINTERS, D.; BOONE, T.; AND COLLINS, F. 1995. Effects of the obese gene product on body weight regulation in ob/ob mice. *Science* 269:540–43.

PENDERGAST, M. 1995. *Victims of memory: Sex abuse accusations and shattered lives.* Hinesburg, Vt.: Upper Access Inc.

PENFIELD, W. 1975. *The mystery of the mind.* Princeton, N.J.: Princeton University Press.

PENFIELD, W., AND RASMUSSEN, T. 1950. *The cerebral cortex of man.* New York: Macmillan.

PENFIELD, W., AND ROBERTS, L. 1959. *Speech and brain mechanisms.* Princeton, N.J.: Princeton University Press.

PENROSE, L. S., AND PENROSE, R. 1958. Impossible objects: A special type of visual illusion. *British Journal of Psychology* 49:31–33.

PEPITONE, A. 1976. Toward a normative and comparative biocultural social psychology. *Journal of Personality and Social Psychology* 43:641–53.

PERDUE, C. W.; DOVIDIO, J. F.; GURTMAN, M. B.; AND TYLER, R. B. 1990. Us and them: Social categorization and the process of intergroup bias. *Journal of Personality and Social Psychology* 59:475–86.

PERKINS, D. N., AND GROTZER, T. A. 1997. Teaching intelligence. *American Psychologist* 52:1125–33.

PERSONS, J. B.; THASE, M. E.; AND CRITS-CHRISTOPH, P. 1996. The role of psychotherapy in the treatment of depression: Review of two practice guidelines. *Archives of General Psychiatry* 53:283–90.

PETERSEN, K., AND SHERRY, D. F. 1996. No sex differences occur in hippocampus, food-storing, or memory for food caches in black-capped chickadees. *Behavioural Brain Research* 79:15–22.

PETERSON, C., AND SELIGMAN, M. E. P. 1984. Causal explanations as a risk factor for depression: Theory and evidence. *Psychological Review* 91:341–74.

PETERSON, C.; SEMMEL, A.; VON BAEYER, C.; ABRAMSON, L.Y.; METALSKY, G. I.; AND SELIGMAN, M. E. P. 1982. The Attributional Style Questionnaire. *Cognitive Therapy and Research* 6:287–99.

PETERSON, S. E.; FOX, P. T.; POSNER, M. I.; MINTUN, M.; AND RAICHLE, M. E. 1988. Positron emission tomographic studies of the processing of single words. *Journal of Cognitive Neuroscience* 1: 153–70.

PETITTO, L. G., AND MARENTETTE, P. F. 1991. Babbling in the manual mode: Evidence for the ontogeny of language. *Science* 251:1493–96.

PETTY, R. E., AND CACIOPPO, J. T. 1985. The elaboration likelihood model of persuasion. In Berkowitz, L. (Ed.), *Advances in experimental social psychology,* vol. 19. New York: Academic Press.

PETTY, R. E.; WEGENER, D. T.; AND FABRIGAR, L. R. 1997. Attitudes and attitude change. *Annual Review of Psychology* 48:609–47.

PIAGET, J. 1952. *The origins of intelligence in children.* New York: International University Press.

PIAGET, J. 1972. *The child's conception of the world.* Totowa, N.J.: Littlefield, Adams.

PIAGET, J., AND INHELDER, B. 1956. *The child's conception of space.* London: Routledge and Kegan Paul.

PIAGET, J., AND INHELDER, B. 1967. *The child's conception of space.* New York: Norton.

PICCINELLI, M.; PINI, S.; BELLANTUONO, C.; AND WILKINSON, G. 1995. Efficacy of drug treatment in obsessive-compulsive disorder: A meta-analytic review. *British Journal of Psychiatry* 166:424–43.

PIERCE, A. 1992. *Language acquisition and syntactic theory: A comparative analysis of French and English child language.* Dordrecht: Kluwer.

PILIAVIN, J. A., AND CALLERO, P. L. 1991. *Giving blood: The development of an altruistic identity.* Baltimore: Johns Hopkins University Press.

PILLARD, R. C. 1996. Homosexuality from a familial and genetic perspective. In Cabaj, R. P., and Stein, T. S. (Eds.), *Textbook of homosexuality and mental health,* pp. 115–28. Washngton, D.C.: American Psychiatric Press.

PINKER, S. 1984. *Language learnability and language development.* Cambridge, Mass.: Harvard University Press.

PINKER, S. 1989. *Learnability and cognition: The acquisition of argument structure.* Cambridge, Mass.: MIT Press.

PINKER, S. 1994. *The language instinct.* New York: William Morrow.

PINKER, S. 1995. Why the child holded the baby rabbits: A case study in language acquisition. In Gleitman, L. R., and Liberman, M. (Eds.), *Language: An invitation to cognitive science,* 2nd ed., vol. 1, pp. 107–33. Cambridge, Mass.: MIT Press.

PINKER, S., AND PRINCE, A. 1988. On language and connectionism: Analysis of a parallel distributed processing model of language acquisition. *Cognition* 28(1):73–194.

PIPP, S.; EASTERBROOKS, M. A.; AND BROWN, S. R. 1993. Attachment status and complexity of infants' self- and other-knowledge when tested with mother and father. *Social Development* 2:1–114.

PLOMIN, R.; CORLEY, R.; DEFRIES, J. C.; AND FULKER, D. W. 1990. Individual differences in television viewing in early childhood: Nature as well as nurture. *Psychological Science* 1:371–77.

PLOMIN, R., AND DANIELS, D. 1987. Why are children from the same family so different from one another? *Behavioral and Brain Sciences* 10:1–16.

POGUE-GEILE, M. F., AND ROSE, R. J. 1985. Developmental genetic studies of adult personality. *Developmental Psychology* 21:547–57.

POLEY, W. 1974. Dimensionality in the measurement of authoritarian and political attitudes. *Canadian Journal of Behavioral Science* 6:83–94.

POMERANTZ, J. R., AND KUBOVY, M. 1981. Perceptual organization: An overview. In Kubovy, M., and Pomerantz, J. R. (Eds.), *Perceptual organization,* pp. 423–56. Hillsdale, N.J.: Erlbaum.

PORAC, C., AND COREN, S. 1981. *Lateral preferences and human behavior.* New York: Springer-Verlag.

PORSOLT, R. D.; LEPICHON, M.; AND JALFRE, M. 1977. Depression: A new animal model sensitive to antidepressant treatments. *Nature* 266:730–32.

POSNER, M.; SNYDER, C.; AND DAVIDSON, B. 1980. Attention and the detection of signals. *Journal of Experimental Psychology: General* 109:160–74.

POULOS, C. X., AND CAPPELL, H. 1991. Homeostatic theory of drug tolerance: A general model of physiological adaptation. *Psychological Review* 98:390–408.

POWELL, H. A. 1969. Genealogy, residence, and kinship in Kiriwina. *Man* 4:177–202.

PRASADA, S., AND PINKER, S. 1993. Generalizations of regular and irregular morphology. *Language and Cognitive Processes* 8:1–56.

PREMACK, A., AND PREMACK, D. 1983. *The mind of an ape.* New York: Norton.

PREMACK, D. 1965. Reinforcement theory. In Levine, D. (Ed.), *Nebraska Symposium on motivation.* Lincoln: University of Nebraska Press.

PREMACK, D. 1976. *Intelligence in ape and man.* Hillsdale, N.J.: Erlbaum.

PREMACK, D. 1978. On the abstractness of human concepts: Why it would be difficult to talk to a pigeon. In Hulse, S. H.; Fowler, H.; and Honig, W. K. (Eds.), *Cognitive processes in animal behavior.* Hillsdale, N.J.: Erlbaum.

PREMACK, D. 1988. 'Does the chimpanzee have a theory of mind' revisited. In Byrne, R. W., and Whiten, A. (Eds.), *Machiavellian intelligence: Social expertise and the evolution of intellect in monkeys, apes, and humans,* pp. 160–79. Oxford: Oxford University.

PREMACK, D., AND WOODRUFF, G. 1978. Does the chimpanzee have a theory of mind? *Behavioral and Brain Sciences* 4:515–26.

PRICE, R. A., AND GOTTESMAN, I. I. 1991. Body fat in identical twins reared apart: Roles for genes and environment *Behavior Genetics* 21(1):1–7.

PRICE, R. H., AND BOUFFARD, B. L. 1974. Behavioral appropriateness and situational constraint. *Journal of Personality and Social Psychology* 30:579–86.

PRICE-WILLIAMS, D. R. 1981. Concrete and formal operations. In Munroe, R. H.; Munroe, R. L.; and Whiting, B. B. (Eds.), *Handbook of cross-cultural development,* pp. 403–22. New York: Garland.

PRICE-WILLIAMS, D. R. 1985. Cultural psychology. In Lindzey, G., and Aronson, E. (Eds.), *Handbook of social psychology,* vol. 2, pp. 993–1042. New York: Academic Press.

PRICE-WILLIAMS, D.; GORDON, W.; AND RAMIREZ, M. 1969. Skill and conservation: A study of pottery-making children. *Developmental Psychology* 1:769.

PRINCE, E. 1981. Toward a taxonomy of given-new information. In Cole, P. (Ed.), *Syntax and semantics 9 Pragmatics.* New York: Academic Press.

PRINCE, G. 1978. Putting the other half of the brain to work. *Training: The Magazine of Human Resources Development* 15:57–61.

PRINZHORN, H. 1972. *Artistry of the mentally ill.* New York: Springer-Verlag.

PRIOLEAU, L.; MURDOCK, M.; AND BRODY, N. 1983. An analysis of psychotherapy versus placebo studies. *Behavioral and Brain Sciences* 6:275–310.

PRITCHARD, R. M. 1961. Stabilized images on the retina. *Scientific American* 204:72–78.

PROVENCE, S., AND LIPTON, R. C. 1962. *Infants in institutions.* New York: International Universities Press.

PUTNAM, F. W.; GUROFF, J. J.; SILBERMAN, E. K.; BARBAN, L.; AND POST, R. M. 1986. The clinical phenomenology of multiple personality disorder: Review of 100 recent cases. *Journal of Clinical Psychiatry* 47:285–93.

PUTNAM, H. 1975. The meaning of "meaning." In Gunderson, K. (Ed.), *Language, mind, and knowledge.* Minneapolis: University of Minnesota Press.

PUTNAM, K. E. 1979. Hypnosis and distortions in eye witness memory. *International Journal of Clinical and Experimental Hypnosis* 27:437–48.

QUATTRONE, G. A., AND JONES, E. E. 1980. The perception of variability within in groups and out groups: Implications for the law of small numbers. *Journal of Personality and Social Psychology* 38(1):141–52.

QUAY, H. C. 1965. Psychopathic personality as pathological stimulation seeking. *American Journal of Psychiatry* 122:180–83.

QUAY, L. C. 1971. Language, dialect, reinforcement, and the intelligence test performance of Negro children. *Child Development* 42:5–15.

RACHMAN, S. J., AND TEASDALE, J. 1969. Aversion therapy: An appraisal. In Franks, C. M. (Ed.), *Behavior therapy: Appraisal and status,* pp. 279–320. New York: McGraw-Hill.

RADFORD, A. 1988. *Transformational grammar: A first course.* New York: Cambridge University Press.

RADKE-YARROW, M.; ZAHN-WAXLER, C.; AND CHAPMAN, M. 1983. Children's prosocial dispositions and behavior. In Mussen, P. E. (Ed.), *Carmichael's manual of child psychology,* vol. 4: *Socialization, personality, and social development* pp. 469–546. Hetherington, E. M., vol. ed. New York: Wiley.

RAFAL, R. D. 1994. Neglect. *Current Opinion in Neurobiology* 4:231–36.

RAGLAND, D. R., AND BRAND, R. J. 1988. Type A behavior and mortality from coronary heart disease. *New England Journal of Medicine* 318:65–69.

RALEIGH, M. J.; BRAMMER, G. L.; MCGUIRE, M. T.; POLLACK, D. B.; AND OTHERS. 1992. Individual differences in basal cisternal cerebrospinal fluid 5-HIAA and HVA in monkeys: The effects of gender, age, physical characteristics, and matrilineal influences. *Neuropsychopharmacology* 7:295–304.

RALEIGH, M. J.; MCGUIRE, M. T.; BRAMMER, G. L.; POLLACK, D. B.; AND OTHERS. 1991. Serotonergic mechanisms promote dominance acquisition in adult male vervet monkeys. *Brain Research* 559:181–90.

RAMSAY, J. O.; BOCK, R. D.; AND GASSER, T. 1995. Comparison of height acceleration curves in the Fels, Zurich, and Berkeley growth data. *Annals of Human Biology* 22:413–26.

RAMSEY, W.; STICH, S.; AND RUMELHART, D. 1991. *Philosophy and connectionist theory.* Hillsdale, N.J.: Erlbaum Associates.

RAO, S. C.; RAINER, G.; AND MILLER, E. K. 1997. Integration of what and where in the primate prefrontal cortex. *Science* 276:821–24.

RAPAPORT, M. H.; PANICCIA, G.; AND JUDD, L. L. 1995. A review of social phobia. *Psychopharmacology Bulletin* 31:125–29.

RAPOPORT, A. 1988. Experiments with N-person social traps. II. Tragedy of the commons. *Journal of Conflict Resolution* 32:473–99.

RAPOPORT, J. L. 1991. Recent advances in obsessive-compulsive disorder. *Neuropsychopharmacology* 5:1–10.

RAPPAPORT, M., AND LEVIN, B. 1988. What to do with roles. In Wilkins, W. (Ed.), *Syntax and semantics,* vol. 21: *Thematic relations.* San Diego: Academic Press.

RAPPAPORT, Z. H. 1992. Psychosurgery in the modern era: Therapeutic and ethical aspects. *Medicine and Law* 11:449–53.

RASMUSSEN, S. A. 1993. Genetic studies of obsessive-compulsive disorder. *Annals of Clinical Psychiatry* 5:241–47.

RASMUSSEN, T., AND MILNER, B. 1977. The role of early left brain injury in determining lateralization of cerebral speech functions. *Annals of the New York Academy of Sciences* 299:355–69.

RATEY, J., AND JOHNSON, C. 1997. *Shadow syndromes.* New York: Pantheon.

RAVEN, B. H., AND RUBIN, J. Z. 1976. *Social psychology: People in groups.* New York: Wiley.

RAVUSSIN, E. 1994. Effects of a traditional lifestyle on obesity in Pima Indians. *Diabetes Care* 17:1067–74.

RAVUSSIN, E.; PRATLEY, R. E.; MAFFEI, M.; WANG, H.; FRIEDMAN, J. M.; BENNETT, P. H.; AND BOGARDUS, C. 1997. Relatively low plasma leptin concentrations precede weight gain in Pima Indians. *Nature Medicine* 3:238–40.

RAYNER, K. 1978. Eye movements in reading and information processing. *Psychological Bulletin* 85:618–60.

READ, C., AND SCHREIBER, P. 1982. Why short subjects are harder to find than long ones. In Wanner, E., and Gleitman, L. R. (Eds.), *Language acquisition: The state of the art.* New York: Cambridge University Press.

REBER, A. S. 1985. *The Penguin dictionary of psychology.* New York: Viking Penguin.

REBERG, D., AND BLACK, A. H. 1969. Compound testing of individually conditioned stimuli as an index of excitatory and inhibitory properties. *Psychonomic Science* 17:3031.

REED, D. R.; DING, Y.; XU, W.; CATHER, C.; GREEN, E. D.; AND PRICE, R. A. 1996. Extreme obesity may be linked to markers flanking the human OB gene. *Diabetes* 45:691–94.

REID, W. H.; PHAM, V. A.; AND RAGO, W. 1993. Clozapine use by state programs: Public mental-health systems respond to a new medication. *Hospital and Community Psychiatry* 44:739–43.

REINISCH, J. M.; ZIEMBA-XAVIS, M.; AND SANDERS, S. A. 1991. Hormonal contributions to sexually dimorphic behavioral development in humans. *Psychoneuroendocrinology* 16:213–78.

REINITZ, M.; MORRISSEY, J.; AND DEMB, J. 1994. Role of attention in face encoding. *Journal of Experimental Psychology: Learning, Memory and Cognition* 20:161–68.

REIS, H. T., AND WHEELER, L. 1991. Studying social interaction with the Rochester Interaction Record. In Zanna, M. P. (Ed.), *Advances in experimental social psychology,* vol. 24, pp. 269–318. New York: Academic Press.

REISBERG, D. 1996. The non-ambiguity of mental images. In Cornoldi, C.; Logie, R.; Brandimonte, M.; Kaufmann, G.; and Reisberg, D. (Eds.), *Stretching the imagination: Representation and transformation in mental imagery,* pp. 119–72. New York: Oxford University Press.

REISBERG, D. 1997. *Cognition: Exploring the science of the mind.* New York: Norton.

REISBERG, D., AND LEAK, S. 1987. Visual imagery and memory for appearance: Does Clark Gable or George C. Scott have bushier eyebrows? *Canadian Journal of Psychology* 41:521–26.

REISENZEIN, R. 1983. The Schachter theory of emotions: Two decades later. *Psychological Bulletin* 94:239–64.

REISMAN, J. A., AND EICHEL, E. W. 1990. *Kinsey, sex, and fraud.* Lafayette, La.: Huntington House.

RENNER, M. J., AND ROSENZWEIG, M. R. 1987. *Enriched and impoverished environments: Effects on brain and behavior.* New York: Springer.

RESCORLA, R. A. 1966. Predictability and number of pairings in Pavlovian fear conditioning. *Psychonomic Science* 4:383–84.

RESCORLA, R. A. 1967. Pavlovian conditioning and its proper control procedures. *Psychological Review* 74:71–80.

RESCORLA, R. A. 1980. *Pavlovian second-order conditioning.* Hillsdale, N.J.: Erlbaum.

RESCORLA, R. A. 1988. Behavioral studies of Pavlovian conditioning. *Annual Review of Neuroscience* 11:329–52.

RESCORLA, R. A. 1991. Associative relations in instrumental learning: The eighteenth Bartlett Memorial lecture. *Quarterly Journal of Experimental Psychology* 43b:1–23.

RESCORLA, R. A. 1993a. Inhibitory associations between S and R extinction. *Animal Learning and Behavior* 21:327–36.

RESCORLA, R. A. 1993b. Preservation of response-outcome associations through extinction. *Animal Learning and Behavior* 21:238–45.

RESCORLA, R. A., AND HOLLAND, P. C. 1982. Behavioral studies of associative learning in animals. *Annual Reviews of Psychology* 33:265–308.

RESCORLA, R. A., AND WAGNER, A. R. 1972. A theory of Pavlovian conditioning: Variations in the effectiveness of reinforcement and non-reinforcement. In Black, A. H., and Prokasy, W. F. (Eds.), *Classical conditioning II*. New York: Appleton-Century-Crofts.

RESNICK, S. M.; BERENBAUM, S. A.; GOTTESMAN, I. I.; AND BOUCHARD, T. J. 1986. Early hormonal influences on cognitive functioning in congenital adrenal hyperplasia. *Developmental Psychology* 22:191–98.

REST, J. R. 1983. Morality. In Mussen, P. E. (Ed.), *Carmichael's manual of child psychology*, vol. 4: *Socialization, personality, and social development*. Hetherington, E. M., vol. ed. New York: Wiley.

REST, J. R. 1984. The major components of morality. In Kurtines, W. M., and Gewirtz, L. (Eds.), *Morality, moral behavior, and moral development*. New York: Wiley.

REVELEY, A. M.; REVELEY, M. A.; AND CLIFFORD, C. A.; AND OTHERS. 1982. Cerebral ventricular size in twins discordant for schizophrenia. *Lancet* 1:540–41.

REVUSKY, S. H. 1971. The role of interference in association over a delay. In Honig, W. K., and James, H. R. (Eds.), *Animal memory*. New York: Academic Press.

REVUSKY, S. 1977. Learning as a general process with an emphasis on data from feeding experiments. In Milgram, N. W.; Krames, L.; and Alloway, T. H. (Eds.), *Food aversion learning*, pp. 1–51. New York: Plenum.

REVUSKY, S. 1985. The general process approach to animal learning. In Johnston, T. D., and Petrewicz, A. T. (Eds.), *Issues in the ecological study of learning*. Hillsdale, N.J.: Erlbaum.

REYNOLDS, G. S. 1968. *A primer of operant conditioning*. Glenview, Ill.: Scott, Foresman.

RHEINGOLD, H. L.; HAY, D. F.; AND WEST, M. J. 1976. Sharing in the second year of life. *Child Development* 47:1148–58.

RICHARDS, W. 1977. Lessons in constancy from neurophysiology. In Epstein, W. W. (Ed.), *Stability and constancy in visual perception: Mechanisms and processes*, pp. 421–36. New York: Wiley.

RIEMANN, D.; HOHAGEN, F.; KONIG, A.; SCHWARZ, B.; GOMILLE, J.; VODERHOLZER, U.; AND BERGER, M. 1996. Advanced vs. normal sleep timing: Effects on depressed mood after response to sleep deprivation in patients with a major depressive disorder. *Journal of Affective Disorders* 37:121–28.

RIGGS, L. A.; RATLIFF, F.; CORNSWEET, J. C.; AND CORNSWEET, T. N. 1953. The disappearance of steadily fixated visual test objects. *Journal of the Optical Society of America* 43:495–501.

RIPS, L. J.; SHOBEN, E. J.; AND SMITH, E. E. 1973. Semantic distance and the verification of semantic relations. *Journal of Verbal Learning and Verbal Behavior* 12:1–20.

RIPS, L. J.; SMITH, E. E.; AND SHOBEN, E. J. 1978. Semantic composition in sentence verification. *Journal of Verbal Learning and Verbal Behavior* 19:705–21.

ROBBIN, A. A. 1958. A controlled study of the effects of leucotomy. *Journal of Neurology, Neurosurgery and Psychiatry* 21:262–69.

ROBBINS, S. J. 1990. Mechanisms underlying spontaneous recovery in autoshaping. *Journal of Experimental Psychology: Animal Behavior Processes* 16:235–49.

ROBINS, L. N.; HELZER, J. E.; WEISSMAN, M. M.; ORVASCHEL, H.; GRUENBERG, E.; BURKE, J. D.; AND REGIER, D. A. 1984. Lifetime prevalence of specific psychiatric disorders in three sites. *Archives of General Psychiatry* 41:948–58.

ROBINS, L. R. 1966. *Deviant children grown up: A sociological and psychiatric study of sociopathic personality*. Baltimore: Williams & Wilkins.

ROBINSON, H. B., AND ROBINSON, N. M. 1970. Mental retardation. In Mussen, P. H. (Ed.), *Carmichael's manual of child psychology*, vol. 2, pp. 65–66. New York: Wiley.

ROBINSON, L. A.; BERMAN, J. S.; AND NEIMEYER, R. A. 1990. Psychotherapy for the treatment of depression: A comprehensive review of controlled outcome research. *Psychological Bulletin* 108:30–49.

ROCK, I. 1977. In defense of unconscious inference. In Epstein, W. W. (Ed.), *Stability and constancy in visual perception: Mechanisms and processes*, pp. 321–74. New York: Wiley.

ROCK, I. 1983. *The logic of perception*. Cambridge, Mass.: MIT Press.

ROCK, I. 1986. The description and analysis of object and event perception. In Boff, K. R.; Kauffman, L.; and Thomas, J. P. (Eds.), *Handbook of perception and human performance*, vol. 2: *Cognitive processes and performance*, pp. 1–71. New York: Wiley.

RODIN, J. 1980. The externality theory today. In Stunkard, A. J. (Ed.), *Obesity*, pp. 226–39. Philadelphia: Saunders.

RODIN, J. 1981. Current status of the internal-external hypothesis for obesity. What went wrong? *American Psychologist* 36:361–72.

RODIN, J., AND LANGER, E. J. 1977. Long-term effects of a control-relevant intervention with the institutionalized aged. *Journal of Personality and Social Psychology* 35:897–902.

RODMAN, H. R.; GROSS, C. G.; ALBRIGHT, T. D. 1989. Afferent basis of visual response properties in area MT of the macaque. I. Effects of striate cortex removal. *Journal of Neuroscience* 9:2033–50.

RODRIGUEZ, M. L.; MISCHEL, W.; AND SHODA, Y. 1989. Cognitive person variables in the delay of gratification of older children at risk. *Journal of Personality and Social Psychology* 57:358–67.

ROEDER, K. D. 1935. An experimental analysis of the sexual behavior of the praying mantis. *Biological Bulletin* 69:203–20.

ROEDER, L. 1967. *Nerve cells and insect behavior*. Cambridge, Mass.: Harvard University Press.

ROEDIGER, H. L., III. 1980. Memory metaphors in cognitive psychology. *Memory and Cognition* 8:231–46.

ROEDIGER, H. L., III. 1990. Implicit memory: Retention without remembering. *American Psychologist* 45:1043–56.

ROGERS, C. R. 1942. *Counseling and psychotherapy: New concepts in practice*. Boston: Houghton Mifflin.

ROGERS, C. R. 1951 and 1970. *Client-centered therapy: Its current practice, implications, and theory*, 1st and 2nd eds. Boston: Houghton Mifflin.

ROGERS, C. R. 1959. A theory of therapy, personality, and interpersonal relationships as developed in the client-centered framework. In Koch, S. (Ed.), *Psychology: A study of a science*, vol. 3. New York: McGraw-Hill.

ROGERS, C. R. 1961. *On becoming a person: A therapist's view of psychotherapy*. Boston: Houghton Mifflin.

ROGERS, C. R. 1964. The concept of the fully functioning person. *Psychotherapy: Theory, Research, and Practice* 1:17–26.

ROGERS, C. R. 1980. *A way of being*. Boston: Houghton Mifflin.

ROGOFF, B.; GAUVIN, M.; AND ELLIS, S. 1984. Development viewed in its cultural context. In Bornstein, M. H., and Lamb, M. E. (Eds.), *Developmental psychology: An advanced textbook*. Hillsdale, N.J.: Erlbaum.

ROLAND, P. E.; LARSEN, B.; LASSEN, N. A.; AND SKINHØJ, E. 1980. Supplementary motor area and other cortical areas in organization of voluntary movements in man. *Journal of Neurophysiology* 43:539–60.

ROLLS, B. J., AND ROLLS, E. T. 1982. *Thirst*. New York: Cambridge University Press.

ROLLS, E. J. 1978. Neurophysiology of feeding. *Trends in Neurosciences* 1:1–3.

ROMANES, G. J. 1882. *Animal intelligence*. London: Kegan Paul.

ROOPNARINE, J. L.; JOHNSON, J. E.; AND HOOPER, F. H. 1994. *Children's play in diverse cultures*. Albany: SUNY Press.

ROPER, T. J. 1983. Learning as a biological phenomenon. In Halliday, T. R., and Slater, P. J. B. (Eds.), *Genes, development and behavior*, vol. 3: *Animal Behavior*, pp. 178–212. Oxford: Blackwell.

RORER, L. G. 1990. Personality assessment: A conceptual survey. In Pervin, L. A. (Ed.), *Handbook of personality: Theory and research,* pp. 693–722. New York: Guilford Press.

RORER, L. G., AND WIDIGER, T. A. 1983. Personality structure and assessment. In Rosenzweig, M. R., and Porter, L. W. (Eds.), *Annual Review of Psychology* 34:431–63.

RORSCHACH, H. 1921. *Psychodiagnostik.* Berne: Bircher.

ROSCH, E. H. 1973a. Natural categories. *Cognitive Psychology* 4:328–50.

ROSCH, E. H. 1973b. On the internal structure of perceptual and semantic categories. In Moore, T. E. (Ed.), *Cognitive development and the acquisition of language.* New York: Academic Press.

ROSCH, E. 1977. Human categorization. In Warren, N. (Ed.), *Studies in cross-cultural psychology,* pp. 3–49. London: Academic Press.

ROSCH, E. H. 1978. Principles of categorization. In Rosch, E., and Lloyd, B. (Eds.), *Cognition and categorization.* Hillsdale, N.J.: Erlbaum.

ROSCH, E. H., AND MERVIS, C. B. 1975. Family resemblances: Studies in the internal structure of categories. *Cognitive Psychology* 7:573–605.

ROSCH, E. H.; MERVIS, C. B.; GRAY, W. D.; JOHNSON, D. M.; AND BOYES-BRAEM, P. 1976. Basic objects in natural categories. *Cognitive Psychology* 8:382–439.

ROSEN, G. 1966. *Madness in society.* Chicago: University of Chicago Press.

ROSEN, L. N.; TARGUM, S. D.; TERMAN, M.; BRYANT, M. J.; HOFFMAN, H.; KASPER, S. F.; HAMOVIT, J. R.; DOCHERTY, J. P.; WELCH, B.; AND ROSENTHAL, N. E. 1990. Prevalence of seasonal affective disorder at four latitudes. *Psychiatry Research* 31:131–44.

ROSENBLATT, S. I.; ANTROBUS, J. S.; AND ZIMLER, J. P. 1992. The effect of postawakening differences in activation on the REM-NREM report effect and recall of information from films. In Antrobus, J. S., and Bertini, M. (Eds.), *The neuropsychology of sleep and dreaming,* pp. 215–24. Hillsdale, N.J.: Erlbaum.

ROSENFELD, P.; GIACALONE, R. A.; AND TEDESCHI, J. T. 1984. Cognitive dissonance and impression management explanations for effort justification. *Personality and Social Psychology Bulletin* 10:394–401.

ROSENMAN, R. H.; BRAND, R. J.; JENKINS, C. D.; FRIEDMAN, M.; AND STRAUS, R. 1975. Coronary heart disease in the Western Collaborative Group Study: Final follow-up experience of 8 1/2 years. *Journal of the American Medical Association* 233:872–77.

ROSENSTEIN, M. J.; MILAZZO-SAYRE. L. J.; AND MANDERSCHEID, R. W. 1989. Care of persons with schizophrenia: A statistical profile. *Schizophrenia Bulletin* 15:45–58.

ROSENTHAL, A. M. 1964. *Thirty-eight witnesses.* New York: McGraw-Hill.

ROSENTHAL, D. 1970. *Genetic theory and abnormal behavior.* New York: McGraw-Hill.

ROSENTHAL, D. M. 1993. Higher-order thoughts and the appendage theory of consciousness. *Philosophical Psychology* 6:155–66.

ROSENTHAL, N. E.; SACK, D. A.; GILLIN, J. C.; LEWY, A. J.; GOODWIN, F. K.; DAVENPORT, Y.; MUELLER, P. S.; NEWSOME, D. A.; AND WEHR, T. A. 1984. Seasonal affective disorder: A description of the syndrome and preliminary findings with light therapy. *Archives of General Psychiatry* 41:72–80.

ROSENZWEIG, M. R., AND BENNETT. 1972. Cerebral changes in rats exposed individually to an enriched environment. *Journal of Comparative and Physiological Psychology* 80:304–13.

ROSENZWEIG, M. R., AND LEIMAN, A. L. 1982. *Physiological psychology.* New York: Random House.

ROSENZWEIG, M. R., AND LEIMAN, A. L. 1989. *Physiological psychology,* 2nd ed. New York: Random House.

ROSENZWEIG, M. R.; LEIMAN, A. K.; AND BREEDLOVE, S. M. 1996. *Biological psychology.* Sunderland, Mass.: Sinauer.

ROSS, E. D. 1981. The aprosodias: Functional-anatomical organization of the affective components of language in the right hemisphere. *Archives of Neurology* 38:561–69.

ROSS, J., AND LAWRENCE, K. Q. 1968. Some observations on memory artifice. *Psychonomic Science* 13:107–8.

ROSS, L. 1977. The intuitive psychologist and his shortcomings: Distortions in the attribution process. In Berkowitz, L. (Ed.), *Advances in experimental social psychology,* vol. 10. New York: Academic Press.

ROSS, L.; AMABILE, T. M.; AND STEINMETZ, J. L. 1977. Social roles, social control, and biases in social perception processes. *Journal of Experimental Social Psychology* 35:817–29.

ROSS, L., AND NISBETT, R. E. 1991. *The person and the situation.* New York: McGraw-Hill.

ROTHBARD, J. C., AND SHAVER, P. R. 1994. Continuity of attachment across the life span. In Sperling, M. B., and Berman, W. H. (Eds.), *Attachment in adults: Clinical and developmental perspectives,* pp. 31–71. New York: Guilford Press.

ROTHBART, M. K., AND AHADI, S. A. 1994. Temperament and the development of personality. *Journal of Abnormal Psychology* 103:55–66.

ROVEE-COLLIER, C. K. 1990. The "memory system" of prelinguistic infants. In Diamond, A. (Ed.), *The development and neural bases of higher cognitive functions.* New York: The New York Academy of Sciences.

ROVEE-COLLIER, C., AND GERHARDSTEIN, P. 1997. The development of infant memory. In Cowan, N. (Ed.), *The development of memory in childhood: Studies in developmental psychology.* Hove, Eng.: Psychology Press.

ROVEE-COLLIER, C. K., AND HAYNE, H. 1987. Reactivation of infant memory: Implications for cognitive development. In Reese, H. W. (Ed.), *Advances in child development and behavior,* vol. 20. New York: Academic Press.

ROWE, D. C., AND WALDRON, I. D. 1993. The question "how" reconsidered. In Plomin, R., and McClearn, G. E. (Eds.), *Nature, nurture, and psychology,* pp. 355–73. Washington, D.C.: American Psychological Association.

ROZIN, P. 1976c. The selection of foods by rats, humans and other animals. *Advances in the study of behavior,* vol. 6, pp. 21–76. New York: Academic Press.

ROZIN, P. 1982. Human food selection: The interaction of biology, culture, and individual experience. In Barker, L. M. (Ed.), *The psychology of human food selection,* pp. 225–54. Westport, Conn.: AVI Publ. Co.

ROZIN, P., AND KALAT, J. W. 1971. Specific hungers and poison avoidance as adaptive specializations of learning. *Psychological Review* 78:459–86.

ROZIN, P., AND KALAT, J. W. 1972. Learning as a situation-specific adaptation. In Seligman, M. E. P., and Hager, J. L. (Eds.), *Biological boundaries of learning,* pp. 66–96. New York: Appleton-Century-Crofts.

ROZIN, P., AND SCHULL, J. 1988. The adaptive-evolutionary point of view in experimental psychology. In Atkinson, R. C.; Herrnstein, R. J.; Lindzey, G.; and Luce, R. D. (Eds.), *Steven's handbook of experimental psychology,* 2nd ed., vol. 1: *Perception and motivation,* pp. 503–46. New York: Wiley.

RUBIN, Z.; HILL, C. T.; PEPLAU, L. A.; DUNKEL-SCHETTER, C. 1980. Self-disclosure in dating couples: Sex roles and the ethic of openness. *Journal of Marriage and the Family* 42(2):305–17.

RUMBAUGH, D. M. (ED.). 1977. *Language learning by a chimpanzee: The Lana Project.* New York: Academic Press.

RUMELHART, D. E. 1997. The architecture of mind: A connectionist approach. In Haugeland, J. (Ed.), *Mind design 2: Philosophy, psychology, artificial intelligence,* 2nd ed. Cambridge: MIT Press.

RUMELHART, D., AND MCCLELLAND, J. 1986. On learning the past tenses of English verbs. In McClelland, J.; Rumelhart, D.; and the PDP Research Group (Eds.), *Parallel distributed processing: Explorations in the microstructure of cognition,* vol. I. Cambridge, Mass.: MIT Press.

RUSHTON, J. P.; FULKER, D. W.; NEALE, M. C.; NIAS, D. K. B.; AND EYSENCK, H. J. 1986. Altruism and aggression: The heritability of individual differences. *Journal of Personality and Social Psychology* 50:1192–98.

RUSSEK, M. 1971. Hepatic receptors and the neurophysiological mechanisms controlling feeding behavior. In Ehrenpreis, S. (Ed.), *Neurosciences research,* vol. 4. New York: Academic Press.

RUSSELL, J. A. 1994. Is there universal recognition of emotion from facial expressions? A review of the cross-cultural studies. *Psychological Bulletin* 115:102–41.

RUSSELL, J. A. 1995. Facial expressions of emotion: What lies beyond minimal universality? *Psychological Bulletin* 118:379–91.

RUSSELL, J. A., AND FERNANDEZ-DOLS, J. M. (EDS.). 1997. *The psychology of facial expression.* Cambridge: Cambridge University Press.

RUSSELL, M. J. 1976. Human olfactory communication. *Nature* 260:520–22.

RUSSELL, M. J.; SWITZ, G. M.; AND THOMPSON, K. 1980. Olfactory influence on the human menstrual cycle. *Pharmacology, Biochemistry, and Behavior* 13:737–38.

SABINI, J. 1995. *Social psychology,* 2nd ed. New York: Norton.

SABINI, J., AND SILVER, M. 1982. *Moralities of everyday life.* New York: Oxford University Press.

SACHS, J. 1967. Recognition memory for syntactic and semantic aspects of connected discourse. *Perception and Psychophysics* 2:437–42.

SACKEIM, H.; DEVANAND, D. P.; AND NOBLER, M. S. 1995. Electroconvulsive therapy. In Bloom, F. E., and Kupfer, D. (Eds.), *Psychopharmacology: The fourth generation of progress,* pp. 1123–41. New York: Raven.

SACKS, O. 1985. *The man who mistook his wife for a hat.* New York: Harper & Row.

SADLER, H. H.; DAVISON, L.; CARROLL, C.; AND KOUNTZ, S. L. 1971. The living, genetically unrelated, kidney donor. *Seminars in Psychiatry* 3:86–101.

SADOCK, B. J. 1975. Group psychotherapy. In Freedman, A. M.; Kaplan, H. I.; and Sadock, B. J. (Eds.), *Comprehensive textbook of psychiatry,* vol. 2, pp. 1850–76. Baltimore: Williams & Wilkins.

SAFFRAN, J. R.; ASLIN, R. N.; AND NEWPORT, E. L. 1997. Statistical learning by 8-month-old infants. *Science* 274:1926–28.

SAGHIR, M. T., AND ROBINS, E. 1973. *Male and female homosexuality.* Baltimore: Williams & Wilkins.

SAGI, A., AND HOFFMAN, M. L. 1976. Empathic distress in the newborn. *Developmental Psychology* 12:175–76.

SAGI, A.; LAMB, M. E.; LEWKOWICZ, K. S.; SHOHAM, R.; DVIR, R.; AND ESTES, D. 1985. Security of infant-mother, -father, and metaplet attachments among kibbutz reared Israeli children. *Monographs of the Society for Research in Child Development* 50(1–2, Serial No. 209).

SAHLINS, M. 1976. *The use and abuse of biology.* Ann Arbor: University of Michigan Press.

SAKURIAM, T.; AMEMIYA, A.; ISHII, M.; AND OTHERS. 1998. Orexins and orexin receptors: A family of hypothalamic neuropeptides and G protein-coupled receptors that regulate feeding behavior. *Cell* 92: 573–85.

SANDERS, G. S. 1981. Driven by distraction: An integrative review of social facilitation theory and research. *Journal of Experimental Social Psychology* 17:227–51.

SARASON, S. B. 1973. Jewishness, blackness, and the nature nurture controversy. *American Psychologist* 28:926–71.

SARBIN, T. R., AND ALLEN, V. L. 1968. Role theory. In Lindzey, G., and Aronson, E. (Eds.), *The handbook of social psychology,* 2nd ed., vol. 1, pp. 488–567. Reading, Mass.: Addison-Wesley.

SATINOFF, E. 1964. Behavioral thermoregulation in response to local cooling of the rat brain. *American Journal of Physiology* 206:1389–94.

SATINOFF, E. 1978. Neural organization and evolution of thermal regulation in mammals. *Science* 201:16–22.

SATINOFF, E., AND RUTSTEIN, J. 1970. Behavioral thermoregulation in rats with anterior hypothalamic lesions. *Journal of Comparative and Physiological Psychology* 71:77–82.

SATINOFF, E., AND SHAN, S. Y. 1971. Loss of behavioral thermoregulation after anterior hypothalamic lesions in rats. *Journal of Comparative and Physiological Psychology* 77:302–12.

SATIR, V. 1967. *Conjoint family therapy,* rev. ed. Palo Alto, Calif.: Science and Behavior Books.

SAVAGE-RUMBAUGH, E.; McDONALD, D.; SEVCIK, R.; HOPKINS, W.; AND RUPERT, E. 1986. Spontaneous symbol acquisition and communicative use by pygmy chimpanzees. *Journal of Experimental Psychology: General* 115:211–235.

SAVAGE-RUMBAUGH, E.; RUMBAUGH, D.; SMITH, S.; AND LAWSON, J. 1980. Reference: The linguistic essential. *Science* 210:922–25.

SAVAGE-RUMBAUGH, S. 1987. A new look at ape language: Comprehension of vocal speech and syntax. *Nebraska Symposium on Motivation* 35:201–55.

SAVIN, H. B. 1973. Professors and psychological researchers: Conflicting values in conflicting roles. *Cognition* 2:147–49.

SAXE, L.; DOUGHERTY, D.; AND CROSS, T. 1985. The validity of polygraph testing: Scientific analysis and public controversy. *American Psychologist* 40:355–66.

SCAIFE, M., AND BRUNER, J. S. 1975. The capacity for joint visual attention in the infant. *Nature* 253(5489)265–66.

SCARR, S. 1992. Developmental theories for the 1990s: Development and individual differences. *Child Development* 63:1–19.

SCARR, S., AND CARTER-SALTZMAN, L. 1979. Twin method: Defense of a critical assumption. *Behavior Genetics* 9:527–42.

SCARR, S., AND CARTER-SALTZMAN, L. 1982. Genetics and intelligence. In Sternberg, R. J. (Ed.), *Handbook of human intelligence,* pp. 792–896. New York: Cambridge University Press.

SCARR, S., AND McCARTNEY, K. 1983. How people make their own environments: A theory of genotype-environment effects. *Child Development* 54:424–35.

SCARR, S.; PAKSTIS, A. J.; KATZ, S. H.; AND BARKER, W. B. 1977. Absence of a relationship between degree of White ancestry and intellectual skills within a Black population. *Human Genetics* 39:69–86.

SCARR, S., AND WEINBERG, R. A. 1976. IQ test performance of black children adopted by white families. *American Psychologist* 31:726–39.

SCARR, S., AND WEINBERG, R. A. 1983. The Minnesota adoption studies genetic differences and malleability. *Child Development* 54:260–67.

SCHACHER, S. 1981. Determination and differentiation in the development of the nervous system. In Kandel, E. R., and Schwartz, J. H. (Eds.), *Principles of neural science.* New York: Elsevier North Holland.

SCHACHTEL, E. G. 1947. On memory and childhood amnesia. *Psychiatry* 10:1–26.

SCHACHTER, S. 1964. The interaction of cognitive and physiological determinants of emotional state. In Berkowitz, L. (Ed.), *Advances in experimental social psychology,* pp. 49–80. New York: Academic Press.

SCHACHTER, S. 1971. Some extraordinary facts about obese humans and rats. *American Psychologist* 26:129–44.

SCHACHTER, S., AND RODIN, J. 1974. *Obese humans and rats.* Washington, D.C.: Erlbaum-Halstead.

SCHACHTER, S., AND SINGER, J. 1962. Cognitive, social and physiological determinants of emotional state. *Psychological Review* 69:379–99.

SCHACHTER, S., AND SINGER, J. E. 1979. Comments on the Maslach and Marshall-Zimbardo experiments. *Journal of Personality and Social Psychology* 37:989–95.

SCHACTER, D. L. 1987. Implicit memory: History and current status. *Journal of Experimental Psychology: Learning, Memory, and Cognition* 13:501–18.

SCHACTER, D. 1992. Understanding implicit memory. *American Psychologist* 47:559–69.

SCHACTER, D. L. 1996. *Searching for memory: The brain, the mind and the past.* New York: Basic Books.

SCHÄFER, S. 1977. Sociosexual behavior in male and female homosexuals: A study in sex differences. *Archives of Sexual Behavior* 6:355–64.

SCHANK, R. C., AND ABELSON, R. 1977. *Scripts, plans, goals, and understanding.* Hillsdale, N.J.: Erlbaum.

SCHAPIRO, S., AND VUKOVICH, K. R. 1976. Early experience effects on cortical dendrites: A proposed model for development. *Science* 167:292–94.

SCHEERER, M. 1963. Problem solving. *Scientific American* 208:118–28.

SCHEERER, M.; GOLDSTEIN, K.; AND BORING, E. G. 1941. A demonstration of insight: The horse-rider puzzle. *American Journal of Psychology* 54:437–38.

SCHEFF, S. W., AND COTMAN, C. W. 1977. Recovery of spontaneous alternation following lesions of the entorhinal cortex in adult rats: Possible correlation to axon sprouting. *Behavioral Biology* 21:286–93.

SCHERER, K. R. 1997. The role of culture in emotion-antecedent appraisal. *Journal of Personality and Social Psychology* 73:902–22.

SCHIFF, M.; DUYME, M.; DUMARET, A.; AND TOMKIEWICZ, S. 1982. How much could we boost scholastic achievement and IQ scores? A direct answer from a French adoption study. *Cognition* 12:165–96.

SCHIFFMAN, H. R. 1976. *Sensation and perception: An integrated approach.* New York: Wiley.

SCHIFFRIN, D. 1988. Conversational analysis. In Newmeyer, F. (Ed.), *Linguistics: The Cambrige survey,* vol. IV: *The socio-cultural context.* Cambridge: Cambridge University Press.

SCHILDKRAUT, J. J. 1965. The catecholamine hypothesis of affective disorders: A review of supporting evidence. *American Journal of Psychiatry* 122:509–22.

SCHILDKRAUT, J. J.; GREEN, A. I.; AND MOONEY, J. J. 1985. Affective disorders: Biochemical aspects. In Kaplan, H. I., and Sadock, J. (Eds.), *Comprehensive textbook of psychiatry,* 4th ed. Baltimore: Williams & Wilkins.

SCHLENKER, B. R. 1980. *Impression management: The self-concept, social identity and interpersonal relations.* Monterey, Calif.: Brooks/Cole.

SCHLENKER, B. R.; HALLAM, J. R.; AND MCCOWN, N. E. 1983. Motives and social evaluation: Actor-observer differences in the delineation of motives for a beneficial act. *Journal of Experimental Social Psychology* 19:254–73.

SCHLENKER, B. R., AND WEIGOLD, M. F. 1992. Interpersonal processes involving impression regulation and management. *Annual Review of Psychology* 43:133–68.

SCHNEIDER, D. J. 1973. Implicit personality theory: A review. *Psychological Bulletin* 79:294–309.

SCHNEIDER, D. J.; HASTORF, A. H.; AND ELLSWORTH, P. C. 1979. *Person perception,* 2nd ed. Reading, Mass.: Addison-Wesley.

SCHNEIDER, K., AND JOSEPHS, I. 1991. The expressive and communicative functions of preschool children's smiles in an achievement situation. *Journal of Nonverbal Behavior* 15:185–98.

SCHOBER, M. F., AND CLARK, H. H. 1989. Understanding by addressees and overhearers. *Cognitive Psychology* 21:211–32.

SCHOFIELD, W. 1964. *Psychotherapy: The purchase of friendship.* Englewood Cliffs, N.J.: Prentice-Hall.

SCHOOLER, J. W.; OHLSSON, S.; AND BROOKS, K. 1993. Thoughts beyond words: When language overshadows insight. *Journal of Experimental Psychology: General* 122(2):166–83.

SCHORK, N. J. 1997. Genetically complex cardiovascular traits: Origins, problems, and potential solutions. *Hypertension* 29:145–49.

SCHREIBER, F. R. 1973. *Sybil.* New York: Warner Paperback.

SCHWARTZ, B., AND GAMZU, E. 1977. Pavlovian control of operant behavior. In Honig, W. K., and Staddon, J. E. R. (Eds.), *Handbook of operant behavior.* Englewood Cliffs, N.J.: Prentice-Hall.

SCHWARTZ, B., AND ROBBINS, S. 1995. *Psychology of learning and behavior.* New York: Norton.

SCHWARTZ, G. E.; WEINBERGER, D. A.; AND SINGER, J. A. 1981. Cardiovascular differentiation of happiness, sadness, anger, and fear following imagery and exercise. *Psychosomatic Medicine* 43:343–64.

SCHWARTZ, J. E.; PICKERING, T. G.; AND LANDSBERGIS, P. A. 1996. Work-related stress and blood pressure: Current theoretical models and considerations from a behavioral medicine perspective. *Journal of Occupational Health Psychology* 1:287–310.

SCHWEDER, R. A. 1994. "You're not sick, you're just in love": Emotion as an interpretive system. In Ekman, P., and Davidson, R. J. (Eds.), *The nature of emotion,* pp. 32–47. New York: Oxford University Press.

SCHWEITZER, E.; RICKELS, K.; AND UHLENHUTH, E. H. 1995. Issues in the long-term treatment of anxiety disorders. In Bloom, F. E., and Kupfer, D. (Eds.), *Psychopharmacology: The fourth generation of progress,* pp. 1349–59. New York: Raven.

SCOTT, J. P., AND FULLER, J. L. 1965. *Genetics and the social behavior of the dog.* Chicago: University of Chicago Press.

SCRIBNER, S. 1975. Recall of classical syllogisms: A cross-cultural investigation of error on logical problems. In Falmagne, R. J. (Ed.), *Reasoning, representation and process in children and adults,* pp. 153–74. Hillsdale, N.J.: Erlbaum.

SCRIBNER, S., AND COLE, M. 1973. Cognitive consequences of formal and informal education. *Science* 182:553–59.

SEARLE, J. R. 1969. *Speech acts: An essay in the philosophy of language.* New York: Cambridge University Press.

SEARLE, J.; DENNETT, D. C.; AND CHALMERS, D. J. 1997. *The mystery of consciousness.* New York: New York Review of Books.

SEARS, R. R.; MACCOBY, E. E.; AND LEVIN, H. 1957. *Patterns of child rearing.* Evanston, Ill.: Row, Peterson.

SEAY, B.; ALEXANDER, B. K.; AND HARLOW, H. F. 1964. Maternal behavior of socially deprived rhesus monkeys. *Journal of Abnormal and Social Psychology* 69:345–54.

SEEMAN, M. V. 1997. Psychopathology in women and men: Focus on female hormones. *American Journal of Psychiatry* 154:1641–47.

SEIDENBERG, M. S., AND PETITTO, L. A. 1979. Signing behavior in apes: A critical review. *Cognition* 7:177–215.

SELFE, L. 1977. *Nadia: A case of extraordinary drawing ability in an autistic child.* New York: Academic Press.

SELFRIDGE, O. G. 1955. Pattern recognition and modern computers. In *Proceedings of Western Joint Computer Conference.* Los Angeles, Calif.

SELFRIDGE, O. G. 1959. Pandemonium: A paradigm for learning. In Blake, D. V., and Uttley, A. M. (Eds.), *Proceedings of the Symposium on the Mechanisation of Thought Processes.* London: HM Stationary Office.

SELIGMAN, M. E. P. 1970. On the generality of the laws of learning. *Psychological Review* 77:406–18.

SELIGMAN, M. E. P. 1971. Phobias and preparedness. *Behavior Therapy* 2:307–20.

SELIGMAN, M. E. P. 1975. *Helplessness: On depression, development, and death.* San Francisco: Freeman.

SELIGMAN, M. E. P. 1995. The effectiveness of psychotherapy: The *Consumer Reports* study. *American Psychologist* 50:965–74.

SELIGMAN, M. E. P., AND HAGER, J. L. (EDS.). 1972. *Biological boundaries of learning.* New York: Appleton-Century-Crofts.

SELIGMAN, M. E. P.; KLEIN, D. C.; AND MILLER, W. R. 1976. Depression. In Leitenberg, H. (Ed.), *Handbook of behavior modification and behavior therapy.* Englewood Cliffs, N.J.: Prentice-Hall.

SELIGMAN, M. E. P., AND MAIER, S. F. 1967. Failure to escape traumatic shock. *Journal of Experimental Psychology* 74:1–9.

SELIGMAN, M. E. P.; MAIER, S. F.; AND SOLOMON, R. L. 1971. Unpredictable and uncontrollable aversive events. In Brush, F. R. (Ed.), *Aversive conditioning and learning.* New York: Academic Press.

SELIGMAN, M. E. P., AND NOLEN-HOEKSEMA, S. 1987. Explanatory style and depression. In Magnusson, D., and Ohman, A. (Eds.), *Psychopathology: An interactional perspective. Personality, psychopathology, and psychotherapy,* pp. 125–39. Orlando, Fla.: Academic Press.

SELLS, P. 1985. *Lectures on contemporary syntactic theories.* Stanford, Calif.: Center for the Study of Language and Information.

SENDAK, M. 1963. *Where the wild things are.* New York: Harper & Row.

SENDAK, M. 1979. *Higglety pigglety pop! or There must be more to life.* New York: Harper & Row.

SENGHAS, A. 1995. The development of Nicaraguan Sign Language via the language acquisition process. In MacLaughlin, D., and McEwen, S. (Eds.), *Proceedings of the Boston University Conference on Language Development* 19:543–52.

SENGHAS, A.; COPPOLA, M.; NEWPORT, E. L.; AND SUPALLA, T. 1997. Argument structure in Nicaraguan Sign Language: The emergence of grammatical devices. In *Proceedings of the Boston University Conference on Language Development,* 21. Boston: Cascadilla Press.

SEWITCH, D. E. 1987. Slow wave sleep deficiency insomnia: A problem in thermo-regulation at sleep onset. *Psychophysiology* 24:200–215.

SEYFARTH, R.; CHENEY, D.; AND MARLER, P. 1980. Monkey responses to three different alarm calls: Evidence of predator classification and semantic communication. *Science* 21:801–803.

SHADER, R. I., AND GREENBLATT, D. J. 1995. The pharmacotherapy of acute anxiety. In Bloom, F. E., and Kupfer, D. (Eds.), *Psychopharmacology: The fourth generation of progress,* pp. 1341–48. New York: Raven.

SHALTER, M. D. 1984. Predator-prey behavior and habituation. In Peeke, H. V. S., and Petrinovich, L. (Eds.), *Habituation, sensitization and behavior,* pp. 423–58. New York: Academic Press.

SHAM, P. V. C.; O'CALLAGHAN, E.; TAKEI, N.; MURRAY, G. K.; HARE, E. H.; AND MURRAY, R. M. 1992. Schizophrenia following pre-natal exposure to influenza epidemics between 1939 and 1960. *British Journal of Psychiatry* 160:461–66.

SHANAB, M. E., AND YAHYA, K. A. 1977. A behavioral study of obedience in children. *Journal of Personality and Social Psychology* 35:530–36.

SHAPIRO, A. K. 1971. Placebo effects in medicine, psychotherapy, and psychoanalysis. In Bergin, A. E., and Garfield, S. L. (Eds.), *Handbook of psychotherapy and behavior change,* pp. 439–73. New York: Wiley.

SHAPIRO, C. M.; BORTZ, R.; MITCHELL, D.; BARTELL, P.; AND JOOSTE, P. 1981. Slow wave sleep: A recovery period after exercise. *Science* 214:1253–54.

SHAPIRO, D. A., AND SHAPIRO, D. 1982. Meta-analysis of comparative therapy outcome studies: A replication and refinement. *Psychological Bulletin* 92:581–604.

SHAPIRO, P. N., AND PENROD, S. 1986. Meta-analysis of facial identification studies. *Psychological Bulletin* 100:139–56.

SHAVITT, S.; SWAN, S.; LOWREY, T. M.; AND WANKE, M. 1994. The interaction of endorser attractiveness and involvement in persuasion depends on the goal that guides message processing. *Journal of Consumer Psychology* 3(2):137–62.

SHAYWITZ, B. A.; SHAYWITZ, S. E.; PUGH, K. R.; CONSTABLE, R. T.; SKUDLARSKI, P.; FULBRIGHT, R. K.; BRONEN, R. A.; FLETCHER, J. M.; SHAKWEILER, D. P.; KATZ, L.; AND GORE, J. C. 1995. Sex differences in the functional organization of the brain for language. *Nature* 373:607–9.

SHEAR, M. K.; PILKONIS, P. A.; CLOITRE, M.; AND LEON, A. C. 1994. Cognitive behavioral treatment compared with nonprescriptive treatment of panic disorder. *Archives of General Psychiatry* 51:395–401.

SHEEAN, D. 1985. Monoamine oxidase inhibitors and alprazolam in the treatment of panic disorder and agoraphobia. *Psychiatric Clinics of North America* 8:49–82.

SHEFFIELD, F. D., AND ROBY, T. B. 1950. Reward value of a non-nutritive sweet taste. *Journal of Comparative and Physiological Psychology* 43:471–81.

SHEINGOLD, K., AND TENNEY, Y. J. 1982. Memory for a salient childhood event. In Neisser, U. (Ed.), *Memory observed,* pp. 201–12. San Francisco: Freeman.

SHEKELLE, R. B.; HONEY, S. B.; NEATON, J.; BILLINGS, J.; BORLANI, N.; GERACE, T.; JACOBS, D.; LASSER, N.; AND STANDER, J. 1983. Type A behavior pattern and coronary death in MRFIT. *American Heart Association Cardiovascular Disease Newsletter* 33:34.

SHEPARD, R. N., AND COOPER, L. A. 1982. *Mental images and their transformations.* Cambridge, Mass.: MIT Press.

SHEPARD, R. N., AND METZLER, J. 1971. Mental rotation of three-dimensional objects. *Science* 171:701–3.

SHEPHERD, G. M. 1994. Discrimination of molecular signals by the olfactory receptor neuron. *Neuron* 13:771–90.

SHERMAN, P. W. 1977. Nepotism and the evolution of alarm calls. *Science* 197:1246–54.

SHERRICK, C. E., AND CHOLEWIAK, R. W. 1986. Cutaneous sensitivity. In Boff, K. R.; Kaufman, L.; and Thomas, J. P. (Eds.), *Handbook of perception and human performance,* chapter 12. New York: Wiley.

SHERRINGTON, C. S. 1906. *The integrative action of the nervous system,* 2nd ed. New Haven, Conn.: Yale University Press, 1947.

SHERROD, D. 1989. The influence of gender on same-sex friendships. In Hendrick, C. (Ed.), *Close relationships,* vol. 10: *Review of personality and social psychology.* Newbury Park, Calif.: Sage.

SHERRY, D. F.; JACOBS, L. F.; AND GAULIN, S. J. 1992. Spatial memory and adaptive specialization of the hippocampus. *Trends in Neurosciences* 15(8):298–303.

SHETTLEWORTH, S. J. 1972. Constraints on learning. In Lehrman, D. S.; Hinde, R. A.; and Shaw, E. (Eds.), *Advances in the study of behavior,* vol. 4. New York: Academic Press.

SHETTLEWORTH, S. J. 1983. Memory in food-hoarding birds. *Scientific American* 248:102–10.

SHETTLEWORTH, S. J. 1984. Learning and behavioral ecology. In Krebs, J. R., and Davies, N. B. (Eds.), *Behavioral ecology,* 2nd ed., pp. 170–94. Oxford: Blackwell.

SHETTLEWORTH, S. J. 1990. Spatial memory in food-storing birds. *Philosophical Transactions of the Royal Society, Series B* 329:143–51.

SHIFFRIN, R. M. 1997. Attention, automatism, and consciousness. In Cohen, J. D., and Schooler, J. W. (Eds.), *Scientific approaches to consciousness,* pp. 49–64. Mahwah, N.J.: Lawrence Erlbaum Associates.

SHIPLEY, E. F., AND KUHN, I. F. 1983. A constraint on comparisons: Equally detailed alternatives. *Journal of Experimental Child Psychology* 35:195–222.

SHIPLEY, E. F.; KUHN, I. F.; AND MADDEN, E. C. 1983. Mothers' use of superordinate terms. *Journal of Child Language* 10:571–88.

SHIPLEY, E. F.; SMITH, C. S.; AND GLEITMAN, L. R. 1969. A study in the acquisition of language: Free responses to commands. *Language* 45:322–42.

SHIRLEY, M. M. 1961. *The first two years: A study of twenty-five babies.* Minneapolis: University of Minnesota Press.

SHIVELY, C. A.; FONTENOT, M. B.; AND KAPLAN, J. R. 1995. Social status, behavior, and central serotonergic responsivity in female cynomolgus monkeys. *American Journal of Primatology* 37:333–39.

SHOBE, K. K., AND KIHLSTROM, J. F. 1997. Is traumatic memory special? *Current Directions in Psychological Science* 6:70–74.

SHODA, Y.; MISCHEL, W.; AND PEAKE, P. K. 1990. Predicting adolescent cognitive and self-regulatory competencies from preschool delay of gratification: Identifying diagnostic conditions. *Developmental Psychology* 26:978–86.

SHORTER, E. 1992. *From paralysis to fatigue: A history of psychosomatic illness in the modern era.* New York: Macmillan Free Press.

SHORTLIFFE, E. H.; AXLINE, S. G.; BUCHANAN, B. G.; MERIGAN, T. C.; AND COHEN, N. S. 1973. An artificial intelligence program to advise physicians regarding antimicrobial therapy. *Computers and Biomedical Research* 6:544–60.

SHWEDER, R. A. 1975. How relevant is an individual difference theory of personality? *Journal of Personality* 43:455–85.

SHWEDER, R. A., AND BOURNE, E. J. 1986. Does the concept of the person vary cross-culturally? In Shweder, R. A. (Ed.), *Thinking through cultures,* pp. 113–55. Cambridge, Mass.: Harvard University Press, 1991.

SICOLY, F., AND ROSS, M. 1977. Facilitation of ego-biased attributions by means of self-serving observer feedback. *Journal of Personality and Social Psychology* 35:734–41.

SIEGAL, M. 1991. *Knowing children: Experiments in conversation.* Hillsdale, N.J.: Erlbaum.

SIEGEL, A., AND DEMETRIKOPOULOS, M. K. 1993. Hormones and aggression. In Schulkin, J. (Ed.), *Hormonally induced changes in mind and brain*, pp. 99-127. San Diego: Academic Press.

SIEGEL, R. K. 1984. Changing patterns of cocaine use: Longitudinal observations, consequences, and treatment. In Grabowski, J. (Ed.), *Cocaine: Pharmacology, effects, and treatment of abuse*, pp. 92–110. NIDA Research Monograph 50.

SIEGEL, S. 1977. Morphine tolerance acquisition as an associative process. *Journal of Experimental Psychology: Animal Behavior Processes* 3:1–13.

SIEGEL, S. 1979. The role of conditioning in drug tolerance and addiction. In Keehn, J. D. (Ed.), *Psychopathology in animals*. New York: Academic Press.

SIEGEL, S. 1983. Classical conditioning, drug tolerance, and drug dependence. In Israel, Y.; Slower, F. B.; Kalant, H.; Popham, R. E.; Schmidt, W.; and Smart, R. G. (Eds.), *Research advances in alcohol and drug abuse*, vol. 7., pp. 207–46. New York: Plenum.

SIEGEL, S. 1989. Pharmacological conditioning and drug effects. In Goudie, A. J., and Emmett-Oglesby, M. W. (Eds.), *Psychoactive drugs: Tolerance and sensitization*, pp. 115–80. Clifton, N.J.: Humana Press.

SIEGEL, S.; HINSON, R. E.; KRANK, M. D.; AND McCULLY, J. 1982. Heroin "overdose" death: Contribution of drug-associated environmental cues. *Science* 216:436–37.

SIEGLER, M., AND OSMOND, H. 1974. *Models of madness, models of medicine*. New York: Harper & Row.

SIEVER, L. J.; DAVIS, K. L.; AND GORMAN, L. K. 1991. Pathogenesis of mood disorders. In Davis, K.; Klar, H.; and Coyle, J. T. (Eds.), *Foundations of psychiatry*. Philadelphia: Saunders.

SILK, J. B. 1986. Social behavior in evolutionary perspective. In Smuts, B. B.; Cheney, D. L.; Seyfarth, R. M.; Wrangham, R. W.; and Struhsaker, T. T. (Eds.), *Primate societies*. Chicago: University of Chicago Press.

SIMMEL, G. 1911. *On individuality and social form*. Levine, D. N., ed. Chicago, Ill.: University of Chicago Press, 1971.

SIMNER, M. L. 1971. Newborn's response to the cry of another infant. *Developmental Psychology* 5:136–50.

SIMON, R. J., AND AARONSON, D. E. 1988. *The insanity defense: A critical assessment of law and policy in the post-Hinckley era*. New York: Praeger.

SIMPSON, E. L. 1974. Moral development research: A case of scientific cultural bias. *Human Development* 17:81–106.

SIMS, E. A. 1986. Energy balance in human beings: The problems of plenitude. *Vitamins and Hormones: Research and Applications* 43:1–101.

SINHA, D. 1983. Human assessment in the Indian context. In Irvine, S. H., and Berry, J. W. (Eds.), *Human assessment and cultural factors*, pp. 17–34. New York: Plenum.

SINHA, R., AND PARSONS, O. A. 1996. Multivariate response patterning of fear and anger. *Cognition and Emotion* 10:173–98.

SIZEMORE, C. C., AND HUBER, R. J. 1988. The twenty-two faces of Eve. *Individual Psychology: Journal of Adlerian Theory, Research and Practice* 44:53–62.

SKEELS, H. 1966. Adult status of children with contrasting early life experiences. *Monograph of the Society for Research in Child Development* 31 (Serial No. 3).

SKINNER, B. F. 1938. *The behavior of organisms*. New York: Appleton-Century-Crofts.

SKINNER, B. F. 1969. *Contingencies of reinforcement: A theoretical analysis*. New York: Appleton-Century-Crofts.

SKINNER, B. F. 1971. *Beyond freedom and dignity*. New York: Alfred Knopf.

SLATER, A. M.; MATTOCK, A.; AND BROWN, W. 1990. Size constancy at birth: Newborn infants' responses to retinal and real size. *Journal of Experimental Child Psychology* 49:314–22.

SLATER, E., AND GLITHERO, E. 1965. A follow-up of patients diagnosed as suffering from hysteria. *Journal of Psychosomatic Research* 9:9–13.

SLOANE, R. B.; STAPLES, F. R.; CRISTOL, A. H.; YORKSTON, N.J.; AND WHIPPLE, K. 1975. *Psychotherapy vs. behavior therapy*. Cambridge, Mass.: Harvard University Press.

SLOBIN, D. I. 1966. Grammatical transformations and sentence comprehension in childhood and adulthood. *Journal of Verbal Learning and Verbal Behavior* 5:219–27.

SLOVENKO, R. 1995. Multiple personality: Perplexities about the law. *Medicine and Law* 14:623–29.

SLOVIC, P.; FISCHOFF, B.; AND LICHTENSTEIN, S. 1982. Facts versus fears: Understanding perceived risk. In Kahneman, D.; Slovic, P.; and Tversky, A. (Eds.), *Judgment under uncertainty: Heuristics and biases*. New York: Cambridge University Press.

SMEDSLUND, J. 1961. The acquisition of conservation of substance and weight in children. *Scandinavia Journal of Psychology* 2:11–20.

SMELSER, N. J. 1963. *Theory of collective behavior*. New York: Free Press, Macmillan.

SMITH, C. 1985. Sleep states and learning: A review of the animal literature. *Neuroscience and Biobehavioral Reviews* 9:157–68.

SMITH, C. A. 1996. Women, weight and body image. In Chrisler, J. C.; Golden, C.; and Rozee, P. D. (Eds.), *Lectures on the psychology of women*. New York: McGraw Hill.

SMITH, C., AND LLOYD, B. 1978. Maternal behavior and perceived sex of infant: Revisited. *Child Development* 49:1263–65.

SMITH, D. G. 1981. The association between rank and reproductive success of male rhesus monkeys. *American Journal of Primatology* 1:83–90.

SMITH, E. E., AND MEDIN, D. L. 1981. *Categories and concepts*. Cambridge, Mass.: Harvard University Press.

SMITH, M. 1983. Hypnotic memory enhancement of witnesses: Does it work? *Psychological Bulletin* 94:387–407.

SMITH, M. B. 1950. The phenomenological approach in personality theory: Some critical remarks. *Journal of Abnormal and Social Psychology* 45:516–22.

SMITH, M. L.; GLASS, G. V.; AND MILLER, R. L. 1980. *The benefits of psychotherapy*. Baltimore: Johns Hopkins Press.

SMITH, P. B., AND BOND, M. B. 1993. *Social psychology across cultures*. New York: Harvester Wheatsheaf.

SMITH, S. M. 1979. Remembering in and out of context. *Journal of Experimental Psychology: Human Learning and Memory* 5:460–71.

SMITH, S. M., AND BLANKENSHIP, S. E. 1989. Incubation effects. *Bulletin of the Psychonomic Society* 27(4):311–14.

SMITH, T. W. 1992. Hostility and health: Current status of a psychosomatic hypothesis. *Health Psychology* 11:139–50.

SMITH, W. J. 1977. *The behavior of communicating*. Cambridge, Mass.: Harvard University Press.

SNOW, C., AND HOEFNAGEL-HOHLE, M. 1978. The critical period for language acquisition: Evidence from second language learning. *Child Development* 49:1114–28.

SNYDER, C. R.; SHENKEL, R. J.; AND LOWERY, C. R. 1977. Acceptance of personality interpretations: The "Barnum effect" and beyond. *Journal of Consulting and Clinical Psychology* 45:104–14.

SNYDER, M. 1981. On the influence of individuals on situations. In Cantor, N., and Kihlstrom, J. F. (Eds.), *Personality, cognition, and social interaction*. Hillsdale, N.J.: Erlbaum.

SNYDER, M. 1987. *Public appearances/private realities*. New York: Freeman.

SNYDER, M. 1995. Self-monitoring: Public appearances versus private realities. In Brannigan, G. G., and Merrens, M. R. (Eds.), *The social psychologists: Research adventures*, pp. 35–50. New York: McGraw-Hill.

SNYDER, M., AND CUNNINGHAM, M. R. 1975. To comply or not comply: Testing the self-perception explanation of the "foot-in-the-door" phenomenon. *Journal of Personality and Social Psychology* 31:64–67.

SNYDER, M., AND ICKES, W. 1985. Personality and social behavior. In Lindzey, G., and Aronson, E. (Eds.), *Handbook of social psychology*, 3rd ed., vol. 2. New York: Random House.

SNYDER, M., AND OMOTO, A. M. 1992. Volunteerism and society's response to the AIDS epidemic. *Current Directions in Psychological Science* 1:113–16.

SNYDER, M. L.; STEPHAN, W. G.; AND ROSENFIELD, D. 1976. Egotism and attribution. *Journal of Personality and Social Psychology* 33:435–41.

SNYDER, S. H. 1976. The dopamine hypothesis of schizophrenia. *American Journal of Psychiatry* 133:197–202.

SNYDER, S. H., AND CHILDERS, S. R. 1979. Opiate receptors and opioid peptides. *Annual Review of Neuroscience* 2:35–64.

SOLOMON, R. L. 1980. The opponent-process theory of acquired motivation: The costs of pleasure and the benefits of pain. *American Psychologist* 35:691–712.

SOLOMON, R. L., AND CORBIT, J. D. 1974. An opponent-process theory of motivation: I. Temporal dynamics of affect. *Psychological Review* 81: 119–45.

SOLOMON, R. L., AND WYNNE, L. C. 1953. Traumatic avoidance learning: Acquisition in normal dogs. *Psychological Monographs* 67 (Whole No. 354).

SPANOS, N. P. 1994. Multiple identity enactments and multiple personality disorder: A sociocognitive perspective. *Psychological Bulletin* 116:143–65.

SPEARMAN, C. 1927. *The abilities of man.* London: Macmillan.

SPEMANN, H. 1967. *Embryonic development and induction.* New York: Hafner Publishing Company.

SPENCE, J. T., AND SPENCE, K. W. 1966. The motivational components of manifest anxiety: Drive and drive stimuli. In Spielberger, C. D. (Ed.), *Anxiety and behavior.* New York: Academic Press.

SPERBER, D., AND WILSON, D. 1986. *Relevance: Communication and cognition.* Oxford: Blackwell.

SPERLING, G. 1960. The information available in brief visual presentations. *Psychological Monographs* 74 (Whole No. 11).

SPERRY, R. W. 1974. Lateral specialization in the surgically separated hemispheres. In Schmitt, F. O., and Worden, F. G. (Eds.), *The Neuroscience Third Study Program.* Cambridge, Mass.: MIT Press.

SPERRY, R. W. 1982. Some effects of disconnecting the cerebral hemispheres. *Science* 217:1223–26.

SPIES, G. 1965. Food versus intracranial self-stimulation reinforcement in food deprived rats. *Journal of Comparative and Physiological Psychology* 60:153–57.

SPILICH, G. S.; VESONDER, G. T.; CHIESI, H. L.; AND VOSS, J. F. 1979. Text processing of domain-related information for individuals with high and low domain knowledge. *Journal of Verbal Learning and Verbal Behavior* 18:275–90.

SPIRO, M. 1982. *Oedipus in the Trobriands.* Chicago: University of Chicago Press.

SPOONER, A., AND KELLOGG, W. N. 1947. The backward conditioning curve. *American Journal of Psychology* 60:321–34.

SPORER, S. 1991. Deep-deeper-deepest? Encoding strategies and the recognition of human faces. *Journal of Experimental Psychology: Learning, Memory and Cognition* 17:323–33.

SPRINGER, S. P., AND DEUTSCH, G. 1998. *Left brain, right brain: Perspectives from cognitive neuroscience,* 5th ed. New York: Freeman.

SQUIRE, L. R. 1977. ECT and memory loss. *American Journal of Psychiatry* 134:997–1001.

SQUIRE, L. R. 1986. Mechanisms of memory. *Science* 232:1612–19.

SQUIRE, L. R. 1987. *Memory and brain.* New York: Oxford University.

SQUIRE, L. R., AND COHEN, N. J. 1979. Memory and amnesia: Resistance to disruption develops for years after learning. *Behavioral Biology and Neurology* 25:115–25.

SQUIRE, L. R., AND COHEN, N. J. 1982. Remote memory, retrograde amnesia, and the neuropsychology of memory. In Cermak, L. S. (Ed.), *Human memory and amnesia,* pp. 275–304. Hillsdale, N.J.: Erlbaum.

SQUIRE, L. R., AND COHEN, N. J. 1984. Human memory and amnesia. In McGaugh, J.; Lynch, G.; and Weinberger, N. (Eds.), *Neurobiology of learning and memory.* New York: Guilford.

SQUIRE, L. R., AND SHIMAMURA, A. 1996. The neuropsychology of memory dysfunction and its assessment. In Grant, I.; Adams, K. M.; et al. (Eds.), *Neuropsychological assessment of neuropsychiatric disorders,* 2nd ed., pp. 232–62. New York: Oxford University Press.

STACHER, G.; BAUER, H.; AND STEINRINGER, H. 1979. Cholecystokinin decreases appetite and activation evoked by stimuli arising from preparation of a meal in man. *Physiology and Behavior* 23:325–31.

STANISLAVSKI, K. S. 1936. *An actor prepares.* Hapgood, E. R., trans. New York: Theatre Arts.

STANLEY, B. G.; MAGDALIN, W.; AND LEIBOWITZ, S. F. 1989. A critical site for neuropeptide Y-induced eating lies in the caudolateral paraventricular/periformical region of the hypothalamus. *Society for Neuroscience Abstracts* 15:894.

STANLEY, J. 1993. Boys and girls who reason well mathematically. In Beck, G. R., and Ackrill, K. (Eds.), *The origins and development of high ability.* Chichester, Eng.: Wiley.

STARK, L., AND ELLIS, S. 1981. Scanpaths revisited: Cognitive models direct active looking. In Fisher, D.; Monty, R.; and Senders, I. (Eds.), *Eye movements: Cognition and visual perception,* pp. 193–226. Hillsdale, N.J.: Erlbaum.

STARKEY, P.; SPELKE, E. S.; AND GELMAN, R. 1983. Detection of intermodal numerical correspondences by human infants. *Science* 222:179–81.

STARKEY, P.; SPELKE, E. S.; AND GELMAN, R. 1990. Numerical abstraction by human infants. *Cognition* 36:97–127.

STARR, C., AND TAGGART, R. 1989. *Biology: The unity and diversity of life,* 5th ed. Belmont, Calif.: Wadsworth.

STEC, D. E.; DENG A. Y.; RAPP, J. P.; AND ROMAN, R. J. 1996. Cytochrome P4504A genotype cosegregates with hypertension in Dahl S rats. *Hypertension* 27:564–68.

STEELE, C. M., AND ARONSON, J. 1995. Stereotype threat and the intellectual test performance of African Americans. *Journal of Personality and Social Psychology* 69(5):797–811.

STEELE, C. M., AND LIU, T. J. 1983. Dissonance processes as self-affirmation. *Journal of Personality and Social Psychology* 45:5–19.

STEINBERG, L.; ELKMAN, J. D.; AND MOUNTS, N. S. 1989. Authoritative parenting, psychosocial maturity, and academic success among adolescents. *Child Development* 60(6):1424–36.

STEINER, J. E. 1974. The gustafacial response: Observation on normal and anencephalic newborn infants. In Bosma, F. J. (Ed.), *Fourth symposium on oral sensation and perception: Development in the fetus and infant* (DHEW Publication No. NIH 73–546). Washington, D.C.: U.S. Government Printing Office.

STEINER, J. E. 1977. Facial expressions of the neonate infant indicating the hedonics of food-related chemical stimuli. In Weiffenbach, J. M. (Ed.), *Taste and development: The genesis of sweet preference* (DHEW Publication No. NIH 77–1068), pp. 173–88. Washington, D.C.: U.S. Government Printing Office.

STEINMETZ, H.; VOLKMANN, J.; JANCKE, L.; AND FREUND, H. 1991. Anatomical left-right asymmetry of language-relate temporal cortex. *Annals of Neurology* 29:315–19.

STELLAR, J. R., AND STELLAR, E. 1985. *The neurobiology of motivation and reward.* New York: Springer Verlag.

STELMACK, R. M. 1990. Biological bases of extraversion—psychophysiological evidence. *Journal of Personality* 58:293–311.

STEPPER, S., AND STRACK, F. 1993. Proprioceptive determinants of emotional and nonemotional feelings. *Journal of Personality and Social Psychology* 64:211–20.

STERN, J. S.; HIRSCH, J.; BLAIR, S. N.; FOREYT, J. P.; FRANK, A.; KUMANYIKA, S. K.; MADANS, J. H.; MARLATT, G. A.; ST. JEOR, S. T.; AND STUNKARD, A. J. 1995. Weighing the options: Criteria for evaluating weight-management programs. The Committee to Develop Criteria for Evaluating the Outcomes of Approaches to Prevent and Treat Obesity. *Obesity Research* 3:591–604.

STERNBERG, R. J. 1977. *Intelligence, information processing, and analogical reasoning: The componential analysis of human abilities.* Hillsdale, N.J.: Erlbaum.

STERNBERG, R. J. 1985. General intellectual ability. In Sternberg, R. *Human abilities: An information processing approach.* New York: Freeman.

STERNBERG, R. J. 1986. A triangular theory of love. *Psychological Review* 93:119–35.

STERNBERG, R. J. 1988. *The triangle of love: Intimacy, passion, commitment.* New York: Basic Books.

STERNBERG, R. J. 1990. *Metaphors of mind.* New York: Cambridge University Press.

STERNBERG, R. J., AND DAVIDSON, J. E. 1983. Insight in the gifted. *Educational Psychologist* 18:51–57.

STERNBERG, R. J., AND DETTERMAN, D. K. (EDS.). 1986. *What is intelligence? Contemporary viewpoints on its nature and definition.* Norwood, N.J.: Ablex.

STERNBERG, R. J., AND GARDNER, M. K. 1983. Unities in inductive reasoning. *Journal of Experimental Psychology: General* 112:80–116.

STERNBERG, R. J., AND WAGNER, R. K. 1993. The egocentric view of intelligence and job performance is wrong. *Current Directions in Psychological Science* 2:1–5.

STERNBERG, R. J.; WAGNER, R. K.; WILLIAMS, W. M.; AND HORVATH, J. A. 1995. Testing common sense. *American Psychologist* 50:912–27.

STEVENS, A., AND COUPE, P. 1978. Distortions in judged spatial relations. *Cognitive Psychology* 10:422–37.

STEVENS, L., AND JONES, E. E. 1976. Defensive attributions and the Kelley cube. *Journal of Personality and Social Psychology* 34:809–20.

STEVENS, S. S. 1955. The measurement of loudness. *Journal of the Acoustical Society of America* 27:815–19.

STEWART, K. 1951. Dream theory in Malaya. *Complex* 6:21–34.

STEWART, T. D. 1957. Stone age surgery: A general review, with emphasis on the New World. *Annual Review of the Smithsonian Institution.* Washington, D.C.: Smithsonian Institution.

STOCH, M. B.; SMYTHE, P. M.; MOODIE, A. D.; AND BRADSHAW, D. 1982. Psychosocial outcome and CT findings after gross undernourishment during infancy: A 20-year developmental study. *Developmental Medicine and Child Neurology* 24:419–36.

STOKOE, W. C., JR. 1960. Sign language structure: An outline of the visual communication systems. *Studies in Linguistics,* Occasional Papers 8.

STOLLER, R. J. 1968. *Sex and gender: On the development of masculinity and femininity.* New York: Science House.

STOLLER, R. J., AND HERDT, G. H. 1985. Theories of origins of male homosexuality: A cross-cultural look. *Archives of General Psychiatry* 42:399–404.

STORMS, M. D. 1973. Videotape and the attribution process: Reversing actors' and observers' points of view. *Journal of Personality and Social Psychology* 27:165–75.

STOTLAND, E., AND OTHERS. 1978. *Empathy, fantasy and helping.* Beverly Hills, Calif.: Sage.

STOWE, L. 1987. Thematic structures and sentence comprehension. In Carlson, G., and Tanenhaus, M. (Eds.), *Linguistic structure in language processing.* Dordrecht: Reidel.

STRACK, F.; MARTIN, L. L.; AND STEPPER, S. 1988. Inhibiting and facilitating conditions of facial expressions: A non-obtrusive test of the facial feedback hypothesis. *Journal of Personality and Social Psychology* 54:768–77.

STRICKER, E. M., AND ZIGMOND, M. J. 1976. Recovery of function after damage to catecholamine-containing neurons: A neurochemical model for the lateral hypothalamic syndrome. In Sprague, J. M., and Epstein, A. N. (Eds.), *Progress in psychobiology and physiological psychology,* vol. 6, pp. 121–88. New York: Academic Press.

STROMSWOLD, K. 1995. The cognitive and neural bases of language acquisition. Gazzaniga, M. (Ed.), *The cognitive neurosciences.* Cambridge, Mass.: MIT Press.

STROOP, J. R. 1935. Studies of interference in serial verbal reactions. *Journal of Experimental Psychology* 18:643–62.

STROUSE, J. (ED.). 1974. *Women and analysis.* New York: Grossman.

STRUPP, H. H., AND BINDER, J. L. 1984. *Psychotherapy in a new key: A guide to time-limited dynamic psychotherapy.* New York: Basic Books.

STUART, R. B., AND MITCHELL, C. 1980. Self-help groups in the control of body weight. In Stunkard, A. J. (Ed.), *Obesity,* pp. 354–55. Philadelphia: Saunders.

STUNKARD, A. J. 1975. Obesity. In Freedman, A. M.; Kaplan, H. I.; and Sadock, B. J. (Eds.), *Comprehensive textbook of psychiatry–II,* vol. 2, pp. 1648–54. Baltimore: Williams & Wilkins.

STUNKARD, A. 1980. Psychoanalysis and psychotherapy. In Stunkard, A. J. (Ed.), *Obesity,* pp. 355–68. Philadelphia: Saunders.

STYRON, W. 1990. *Darkness visible: A memoir of madness.* New York: Random House.

SUE, D. W., AND KIRK, B. A. 1973. Psychological characteristics of Chinese-American college students. *Journal of Counseling Psychology* 19:142–48.

SULLOWAY, F. J. 1979. *Freud, biologist of the mind: Beyond the psychoanalytic legend.* Cambridge, Mass.: Harvard University Press.

SULLOWAY, F. J. 1992. Reassessing Freud's case histories: The social construction of psychoanalysis. In Gelfand, T., and Kerr, J. (Eds.), *Freud and the history of psychoanalysis,* pp. 153–92. Hillsdale, N.J.: Analytic Press.

SULS, J. M. 1972. A two-stage model for the appreciation of jokes and cartoons: An information processing analysis. In Goldstein, J. H., and McGhee, P. E. (Eds.), *The psychology of humor,* pp. 81–100. New York: Academic Press.

SULS, J. M. 1983. Cognitive processes in humor appreciation. In McGhee, P. E., and Goldstein, J. H. (Eds.), *Handbook of humor research,* vol. 1, pp. 39–58. New York: Springer.

SULS, J. M., AND MILLER, R. L. (EDS.). 1977. *Social comparison processes: Theoretical and empirical perspectives.* New York: Washington Hemisphere Publishing Co.

SUOMI, S. J. 1989. Personal communication.

SUOMI, S. J., AND HARLOW, H. F. 1971. Abnormal social behavior in young monkeys. In Helmuth, J. (Ed.), *Exceptional infant: Studies in abnormalities,* vol. 2, pp. 483–529. New York: Brunner/Mazel.

SUOMI, S., AND HARLOW, H. 1972. Social rehabilitation of isolate-reared monkeys. *Developmental Psychology* 6:487–96.

SUPALLA, I., AND NEWPORT, E. L. 1978. How many seats in a chair? The derivation of nouns and verbs in American Sign Language. In Siple, P. (Ed.), *Understanding language through sign language research.* New York: Academic Press.

SUPER, C. M. 1976. Environmental effects on motor development. *Developmental Medicine and Child Neurology* 18:561–67.

SWEDO, S. E.; PIETRINI, P.; LEONARD, H. L.; SCHAPIRO, M. B.; RETTEW, D. C.; GOLDBERGER, E. L.; RAPOPORT, S. I.; RAPOPORT, J. L.; AND GRADY, C. L. 1992. Cerebral glucose metabolism in childhood-onset obsessive-compulsive disorder. Revisualization during pharmacotherapy. *Archives of General Psychiatry* 49:690–94.

SYMONS, D. 1979. *The evolution of human sexuality.* New York: Oxford University Press.

SYMONS, D. 1993. The stuff that dreams aren't made of: Why wake-state and dream-state sensory experiences differ. *Cognition* 47:181–217.

TAKAHASHI, Y. 1979. Growth hormone secretion related to the sleep waking rhythm. In Drucker-Colín, R.; Shkurovich, M.; and Sterman, M. B. (Eds.), *The functions of sleep.* New York: Academic Press.

TALLAL, P.; ROSS, R.; AND CURTISS, S. 1989. Familiar aggregation in specific language impairment. *Journal of Speech and Hearing Disorders* 54:167–71.

TANDON, R., AND KANE, J. M. 1993. Neuropharmacologic basis for clozapine's unique profile (Letter). *Archives of General Psychiatry* 50:158–59.

TANENHAUS, M. K., AND SPIVEY-KNOWLTON, M. J. 1996. Eye-tracking. *Language and Cognitive Processes* 11:583–88.

TANNER, J. M. 1970. Physical growth. In Mussen, P. H. (Ed.), *Carmichael's manual of child psychology,* 3rd ed., pp. 77–105. New York: Wiley.

TANNER, J. M. 1990. *Fetus into man: Physical growth from conception to maturity,* rev. ed. Cambridge, Mass.: Harvard University Press.

TARPY, R. M. 1997. *Contemporary learning theory and research.* New York: McGraw Hill.

TAYLOR, S. E., AND FISKE, S. T. 1975. Point of view and perceptions of causality. *Journal of Personality and Social Psychology* 32:439–45.

TEACH, R. L., AND SHORTLIFFE, E. H. 1985. An analysis of physicians' attitudes. In Buchanan, B. G., and Shortliffe, E. H. (Eds.), *Rule-based expert systems: The MYCIN experiments of the Stanford Heuristics Programming Project.* Reading, Mass.: Addison-Wesley.

TEITELBAUM, P. 1955. Sensory control of hypothalamic hyperphagia. *Journal of Comparative and Physiological Psychology* 48:156–63.

TEITELBAUM, P. 1961. Disturbances in feeding and drinking behavior after hypothalamic lesions. In Jones, M. R. (Ed.), *Nebraska Symposium on Motivation,* pp. 39–65. Lincoln: University of Nebraska Press.

TEITELBAUM, P., AND EPSTEIN, A. N. 1962. The lateral hypothalamic syndrome: Recovery of feeding and drinking after lateral hypothalamic lesions. *Psychological Review* 69:74–90.

TEITELBAUM, P., AND STELLAR, E. 1954. Recovery from failure to eat produced by hypothalamic lesions. *Science* 120:894–95.

TELLEGEN, A.; LYKKEN, D. T.; BOUCHARD, T. J.; WILCOX, K. J.; SEGAL, N. L.; AND RICH, S. 1988. Personality of twins reared apart and together. *Journal of Personality and Social Psychology* 54:1031–39.

TERMAN, G. W.; SHAVIT, Y.; LEWIS, J. W.; CANNON, J. T.; AND LIEBESKIND, J. C. 1984. Intrinsic mechanisms of pain inhibition: Activation by stress. *Science* 226:1270–77.

TERR, L. C. 1991. Acute responses to external events and posttraumatic stress disorders. In Lewis, M. (Ed.), *Child and adolescent psychiatry: A comprehensive textbook,* pp. 755–63. Baltimore, Md.: Williams & Wilkins.

TERR, L. C. 1994. *Unchained memories: True stories of traumatic memories, lost and found.* New York: Basic.

TERRACE, H. S. 1979. *Nim.* New York: Knopf.

TERVOORT, B. T. 1961. Esoteric symbolism in the communication behavior of young deaf children. *American Annals of the Deaf* 106:436–80.

TESSER, A.; CAMPBELL, J.; AND SMITH, M. 1984. Friendship choice and performance: Self-evaluation maintenance in children. *Journal of Personality and Social Psychology* 46:561–74.

THALANGE, N. K.; FOSTER, P. J.; GILL, M. S.; PRICE, D. A.; AND CLAYTON, P. E. 1996. Model of normal prepubertal growth. *Archives of Disease in Childhood* 75:427–31.

THIGPEN, C. H., AND CLECKLEY, H. M. 1957. *The three faces of Eve.* New York: McGraw-Hill.

THOMAS, A.; CHESS, S.; AND BIRCH, H. G. 1970. The origin of personality. *Scientific American* 223:102–9.

THOMPSON, C. P., AND COWAN, T. 1986. Flashbulb memories: A nicer recollection of a Neisser recollection. *Cognition* 22:199–200.

THOMPSON, M. M.; ZANNA, M. P.; AND GRIFFIN, D. W. 1995. Let's not be indifferent about (attitudinal) ambivalence. In Petty, R. E., and Krosnick, J. A. (Eds.), *Attitude strength: Antecedents and consequences,* vol. 4, pp. 361–86. Mahwah, N.J.: Lawrence Erlbaum.

THOMPSON, R. F. 1973. *Introduction to biopsychology.* San Francisco: Albion Publishing Co.

THOREN, P.; FLORAS, J. S.; HOFFMANN, P.; AND SEALS, D. R. 1990. Endorphins and exercise: Physiological mechanisms and clinical implications. *Medicine and Science in Sports and Exercise* 22:417–28.

THORNDIKE, E. L. 1898. Animal intelligence: An experimental study of the associative processes in animals. *Psychological Monographs* 2 (Whole No. 8).

THORNDIKE, E. L. 1899. The associative processes in animals. *Biological lectures from the Marine Biological Laboratory at Woods Hole.* Boston: Atheneum.

THORNDIKE, E. L. 1911. *Animal intelligence: Experimental studies.* New York: Macmillan.

THORNHILL, R., AND GANGESTAD, S. W. 1994. Human fluctuating asymmetry and sexual behavior. *Psychological Science* 5:297–302.

TIETJEN, A. M., AND WALKER, L. J. 1985. Moral reasoning and leadership among men in a Papua New Guinea society. *Developmental Psychology* 21:982–89.

TINBERGEN, N. 1951. *The study of instinct.* Oxford: Clarendon.

TIZARD, B., AND HODGES, J. 1978. The effect of early institutional rearing on the development of eight-year-old children. *Journal of Child Psychology and Psychiatry* 19:98–118.

TOCQUEVILLE, A. 1835. *Democracy in America.* Mayer, J. P., and Lerner, M. (Eds.), George Lawrence (trans.). New York: Harper and Row, 1966.

TOLMAN, E. C. 1932. *Purposive behavior in animals and men.* New York: Appleton-Century-Crofts.

TOLMAN, E. C. 1948. Cognitive maps in rats and men. *Psychological Review* 55:189–208.

TOLMAN, E. C., AND HONZIK, C. H. 1930. Introduction and removal of reward, and maze performance in rats. *University of California Publications in Psychology* 4:257–75.

TOLSTOY, L. 1868. *War and peace,* second epilogue. Gifford, Henry, ed., Maude, Louise, and Maude, Aylmer, trans. New York: Oxford University Press, 1922.

TOLSTOY, L. 1875. *Anna Karenina.* Garnett, C., trans. New York: Random House, 1939.

TOMADA, G., AND SCHNEIDER, B. H. 1997. Relational aggression, gender, and peer acceptance: Invariance across culture, stability over time, and concordance among informants. *Developmental Psychology* 33:601–9.

TOMASELLO, M., AND FERRAR, M. 1986. Joint attention and early language. *Child Development* 57:1454–63.

TOMASO, E.; BELTRAMO, M.; AND PIOMELLI, D. 1996. Brain cannabinoids in chocolate. *Nature* 382:677–78.

TOMKINS, S. S. 1962. *Affect, imagery, consciousness,* vol. 1: *The positive affects.* New York. Springer.

TOMKINS, S. S. 1963. *Affect, imagery, consciousness,* vol. 2: *The negative affects.* New York: Springer.

TOOBY, J., AND COSMIDES, L. 1996. Friendship and the banker's paradox: Other pathways to the evolution of adaptations for altruism. In Runciman, W. G.; Smith, J. M.; and Dunbar, R. I. M. (Eds.), *Evolution of social behaviour patterns in primates and man. Proceedings of the British Academy* 88:119–43. Oxford: Oxford University Press.

TORGERSEN, S. 1986. Genetic factors in moderately severe and mild affective disorders. *Archives of General Psychiatry* 43:222–26.

TORREY, E. F. 1983. *Surviving schizophrenia: A family manual.* New York: Harper & Row.

TORREY, E. F. 1987. Prevalence studies in schizophrenia. *British Journal of Psychiatry* 150:598–608.

TORREY, E. F. 1992. *Freudian fraud.* New York: HarperPerennial.

TOURANGEAU, R., AND ELLSWORTH, P. C. 1979. The role of facial response in the experience of emotion. *Journal of Personality and Social Psychology* 37:1519–31.

TREIBER, F., AND WILCOX, S. 1984. Discrimination of number by infants. *Infant Behavior and Development* 7:93–100.

TREISMAN, A. M. 1964. Verbal cues, language, and meaning in selective attention. *American Journal of Psychology* 77:206–19.

TREISMAN, A. M. 1986a. Properties, parts, and objects. In Boff, K. R.; Kaufman, L.; and Thomas, J. P. (Eds.), *Handbook of perception and human performance,* vol. II (Chapter 35). New York: Wiley.

TREISMAN, A. M. 1986b. Features and objects in visual processing. *Scientific American* 255:114–25.

TREISMAN, A. M. 1988. Features and objects: The Fourteenth Barlett Memorial Lecture. *Quarterly Journal of Experimental Psychology* 40A:201–37.

TREISMAN, A. M., AND GELADE, G. 1980. A feature-integration theory of attention. *Cognitive Psychology* 12:97–136.

TREISMAN, A. M., AND SCHMIDT, H. 1982. Illusory conjunction in the perception of objects. *Cognitive Psychology* 14:107–41.

TREISMAN, A. M., AND SOUTHER, J. 1985. Search assymetry: A diagnostic for preattentive processing of separable features. *Journal of Experimental Psychology: General* 114:285–310.

TRIANDIS, H. C. 1989. Cross-cultural studies of individualism and collectivism. *Nebraska Symposium on Motivation* 37:41–134. Lincoln: University of Nebraska Press.

TRIANDIS, H. 1994. Major cultural syndromes and emotion. In Kitayama, S., and Markus, H. R. (Eds.), *Emotion and culture,* pp. 285–306. Washington, D.C.: American Psychological Association.

TRIANDIS, H. C.; BONTEMBO, R.; VILLAREAL, M. J.; ASAI, M.; AND LUCA, N. 1988. Individualism and collectivism: Cross-cultural perspectives on self-group relationships. *Journal of Personality and Social Psychology* 54:323–38.

TRIVERS, R. L. 1971. The evolution of reciprocal altruism. *Quarterly Review of Biology* 46:35–57.

TRIVERS, R. L. 1972. Parental investment and sexual selection. In Campbell, B. (Ed.), *Sexual selection and the descent of man,* pp. 139–79. Chicago: Aldine.

TRUESWELL, J. C., AND TANENHAUS, M. K. 1991. Tense, temporal context and syntactic ambiguity resolution. *Language and Cognitive Processes* 6:303–38.

TRUESWELL, J. C., AND TANENHAUS, M. K. 1994. Toward a lexicalist framework of constraint-based syntactic ambiguity resolution. In Clifton, C. Jr., and Frazier, L.(Eds.), *Perspectives on sentence processing,* pp. 155–79. Hillsdale, N.J: Erlbaum.

TRUESWELL, J.; TANENHAUS, M.; AND GARNSEY, S. 1994. Semantic influences on parsing. *Journal of Memory and Language* 33(3):285–318.

TSUANG, M. T.; GILBERTSON, M. W.; AND FARAONE, S. V. 1991. The genetics of schizophrenia. *Schizophrenia Research* 4:157–71.

TULVING, E., AND OSLER, S. 1968. Effectiveness of retrieved cues in memory for words. *Journal of Experimental Psychology* 77:593–606.

TULVING, E.; SCHACTER, D. L.; AND STARK, H. A. 1982. Priming effects in word-fragment completion are independent of recognition memory. *Journal of Experimental Psychology: Learning, Memory, and Cognition* 8:336–42.

TULVING, E.; SCHACTER, D. L.; MCLACHLAN, D. R.; AND MOSCOVITCH, M. 1988. Priming of semantic autobiographical knowledge: A case study of retrograde amnesia. *Brain and Cognition* 8:3–20.

TULVING, E., AND THOMSON, D. M. 1973. Encoding specificity and retrieval processes in episodic memory. *Psychological Review* 80:352–73.

TURNER, A. M., AND GREENOUGH, W. T. 1985. Differential rearing effects on rat visual cortex synapses. I. Synaptic and neuronal density and synapses per neuron. *Brain Research* 329:195–203.

TVERSKY, A., AND KAHNEMAN, D. 1973. Availability: A heuristic for judging frequency and probability. *Cognitive Psychology* 5:207–32.

TVERSKY, A., AND KAHNEMAN, D. 1981. The framing of decisions and the psychology of choice. *Science* 211:453–58.

TVERSKY, A., AND KAHNEMAN, D. 1987. Rational choice and the framing of decisions. In Hogarth, R., and Reder, M. (Eds.), *Rational choice: The contrast between economics and psychology.* Chicago: University of Chicago Press.

TYLER, L. E. 1965. *The psychology of human differences.* New York: Appleton-Century-Crofts.

TZENG, O., AND WANG, W. Y. S. 1984. Search for a common neurocognitive mechanism for language and movements. *American Journal of Physiology* 246:904–11.

U.S. DEPARTMENT OF LABOR. 1995. *Marital and family characteristics of the labor force from the March 1994 Current Population Survey.* Washington, D.C.: Bureau of Labor Statistics.

UNDERWOOD, B. J. 1957. Interference and forgetting. *Psychological Review* 64:49–60.

UNGERLEIDER, L. G., AND HAXBY, J. V. 1994. "What" and "where" in the human brain. *Current Opinions in Neurobiology* 4:157–65.

UNGERLEIDER, L. G., AND MISHKIN, M. 1982. Two cortical visual systems. In Ingle, D. J.; Goodale, M. A.; and Mansfield, R. J. W. (Eds.), *Analysis of visual behavior,* pp. 549–86. Cambridge: MIT Press.

UNGERSTEDT, U., AND LJUNGBERG, T. 1974. Central dopamine neurons and sensory processing. *Journal of Psychiatry Research* 11:149–50.

URWIN, C. 1983. Dialogue and cognitive functioning in the early language development of three blind children. In Mills, A. E. (Ed.), *Language acquisition in the blind child.* London: Croom Helm.

VAILLANT, G. E. 1971. Theoretical hierarchy of adaptive ego mechanisms. *Archives of General Psychiatry* 24:107–18.

VAILLANT, G. E. 1974. Natural history of male psychological health. II. Some antecedents of healthy adult adjustment. *Archives of General Psychiatry* 31:15–22.

VAILLANT, G. E. 1976. Natural history of male psychological health. V: Relation of choice of ego mechanisms of defense to adult adjustment. *Archives of General Psychiatry* 33:535–45.

VAILLANT, G. E. 1977. *Adaptation to life.* Boston: Little, Brown & Co.

VAILLANT, G. E. 1994. "Successful aging" and psychosocial well-being: Evidence from a 45-year study. In Thompson, E. H. (Ed.), *Older men's lives,* vol. 6: *Research on men and masculinities,* pp. 2–41. Thousand Oaks, Calif.: Sage.

VAILLANT, G. E.; BOND, M.; AND VAILLANT, C. O. 1986. An empirically validated hierarchy of defense mechanisms. *Archives of General Psychiatry* 43:786–94.

VALENSTEIN, E. S. 1986. *Great and desperate cures.* New York: Basic Books.

VALENTA, J. G., AND RIGBY, M. K. 1968. Discrimination of the odor of stressed rats. *Science* 161:599–601.

VALINS, S. 1966. Cognitive effects of false heart-rate feedback. *Journal of Personality and Social Psychology* 4:400–408.

VAN CANTFORT, E., AND RIMPAU, J. 1982. Sign language studies with children and chimpanzees. *Sign Language Studies* 34:15–72.

VAN HOOFF, J. A. R. A. M. 1972. A comparative approach to the phylogeny of laughter and smiling. In Hinde, R. A. (Ed.), *Non-verbal communication.* New York: Cambridge University Press.

VAN KAMMEN, D. P., AND KELLEY, M. 1991. Dopamine and norepinephrine activity in schizophrenia: An integrated perspective. *Schizophrenia Research* 4:173–91.

VAN VALEN, L. 1973. A new evolutionary law. *Evolutionary Theory* 1:1–10.

VAN ZOEREN, J. G., AND STRICKER, E. M. 1977. Effects of preoptic, lateral hypothalamic, or dopamine-depleting lesions on behavioral thermoregulations in rats exposed to the cold. *Journal of Comparative and Physiological Psychology* 91:989.

VANDELL, D. L.; HENDERSON, V. K.; AND WILSON, K. S. 1988. A longitudinal study of children with day care experiences of varying quality. *Child Development* 59:1286–92.

VANDENBOS, G. R.; CUMMINGS, N. A.; AND DELEON, P. H. 1992. A century of psychotherapy: Economic and environmental influences. In Freedheim, D. K. (Ed.), *History of psychotherapy.* Washington, D.C.: American Psychological Association.

VAUGHN, B. E.; EGELAND, B. R.; SROUFE, L. A.; AND WATERS, E. 1979. Individual differences in infant-mother attachment at twelve and eighteen months: Stability and change in families under stress. *Child Development* 50:971–75.

VAULTIN, R. G., AND BERKELEY, M. A. 1977. Responses of single cells in cat visual cortex to prolonged stimulus movement: Neural correlates of visual aftereffects. *Journal of Neurophysiology* 40:1051–65.

VERAA, R. P., AND GRAFSTEIN, B. 1981. Cellular mechanisms for recovery from nervous system injury: A conference report. *Experimental Neurology* 71:6–75.

VERNON, P. A. (ED.). 1987. *Speed of information processing and intelligence.* Canada: Ablex Publishing.

VOLPICELLI, J. 1989. Psychoactive substance use disorders. In Rosenhan, D. L., and Seligman, M. E. P. *Abnormal psychology,* 2nd ed. New York: Norton.

WABER, D. P. 1977. Sex differences in mental abilities, hemispheric lateralization, and rate of physical growth at adolescence. *Developmental Psychology* 13:29–38.

WABER, D. P. 1979. Cognitive abilities and sex-related variations in the maturation of cerebral cortical functions. In Wittig, M. A., and Petersen, A. C. (Eds.), *Sex-related differences in cognitive functioning,* pp. 161–89. New York: Academic Press.

WACHTEL, P. L. 1977. *Psychoanalysis and behavior therapy: Toward an integration.* New York: Basic Books.

WACHTEL, P. L. 1982. What can dynamic therapies contribute to behavior therapy? *Behavior Therapy* 13:594–609.

WADDINGTON, J. L.; TORREY, E. F.; CROW, T. J.; AND HIRSCH, S. R. 1991. Schizophrenia, neurodevelopment, and disease. *Archives of General Psychiatry* 48:271–73.

WAGNER, A. R. 1979. Habituation and memory. In Dickinson, A., and Boakes, R. A. (Eds.), *Mechanisms of learning and memory: A memorial to Jerzy Konorski,* pp. 53–82. Hillsdale, N.J.: Erlbaum.

WAGNER, D. A. 1974. The development of short-term and incidental memory: A cross-cultural study. *Child Development* 45:389–96.

WAGNER, D. A. 1978. Memories of Morocco: The influence of age, schooling, and environment on memory. *Cognitive Psychology* 10:1–28.

WAGNER, H. L., AND SMITH, J. 1991. Facial expression in the presence of friends and strangers. *Journal of Nonverbal Behavior* 15:201–14.

WAGNER, R. K. 1987. Tacit knowledge in everyday intelligent behavior. *Journal of Personality and Social Psychology* 52:1236–47.

WAGNER, R. K., AND STERNBERG, R. J. 1987. Tacit knowledge in managerial success. *Journal of Business and Psychology* 1:301–12.

WAID, W. M., AND ORNE, M. T. 1982. The physiological detection of deception. *American Scientist* 70:402–9.

WAKEFIELD, J. C. 1992. The concept of mental disorder: On the boundary between biological facts and social values. *American Psychologist* 47(3): 373–88.

WALD, G. 1950. Eye and camera. *Scientific American* 183:32–41.

WALDFOGEL, S. 1948. The frequency and affective character of childhood memories. *Psychological Monographs* 62 (Whole No. 291).

WALKER, L. J. 1984. Sex differences in the development of moral reasoning: A critical review. *Child Development* 55:677–91.

WALKER, L. J. 1989. Sex differences in the development of moral reasoning: A reply to Baumrind. *Child Development* 57:522–26.

WALKER, L. J. 1995. Sexism in Kohlberg's moral psychology. In Kurtines, W. M., and Gewirtz, J. L. (Eds.), *Moral development: An introduction.* Boston: Allyn and Bacon.

WALKER, L. J., AND MORAN, T. J. 1991. Moral reasoning in a communist Chinese society. *Journal of Moral Education* 20:139–55.

WALL, P. D. 1980. Mechanisms of plasticity of connection following damage of adult mammalian nervous system. In Bach-y-Rita, P. (Ed.), *Recovery of function: Theoretical considerations for brain injury rehabilitation.* Bern: Hans Huber.

WALLACH, H. 1948. Brightness constancy and the nature of achromatic colors. *Journal of Experimental Psychology* 38:310–24.

WALLACH, H. 1976. *On perception.* New York: Quadrangle.

WALLACH, H.; WEISZ, A.; AND ADAMS, P. A. 1956. Circles and derived figures in rotation. *American Journal of Psychology* 69:48–59.

WALLAS, G. 1926. *The art of thought.* New York: Harcourt, Brace.

WALSTER, E.; ARONSON, E.; AND ABRAHAMS, D. 1966. On increasing the persuasiveness of a low prestige communicator. *Journal of Experimental Social Psychology* 2:325–42.

WALSTER, E.; ARONSON, E.; ABRAHAMS, D.; AND ROTTMAN, L. 1966. The importance of physical attractiveness in dating behavior. *Journal of Personality and Social Psychology* 4:508–16.

WALSTER, E., AND BERSCHEID, E. 1974. A little bit about love: A minor essay on a major topic. In Huston, T. L. (Ed.), *Foundations of interpersonal attraction.* New York: Academic Press.

WALTERS, J. R., AND SEYFARTH, R. M. 1986. Conflict and cooperation. In Smuts, B. B.; Cheney, D. L.; Seyfarth, R. M.; Wrangham, R. W.; and Struhsaker, T. T. (Eds.), *Primate societies.* Chicago: University of Chicago Press.

WALSTER (HATFIELD), E., AND WALSTER, G. W. 1978. *A new look at love.* Reading, Mass.: Addison-Wesley.

WAMPOLD, B. E.; MONDIN, G. W.; MOODY, M.; STICH, F.; BENSON, K.; AND AHN, H. 1997. A meta-analysis of outcome studies comparing bona fide psychotherapies: Empirically, "all must have prizes." *Psychological Bulletin* 122:203–16.

WANNER, E. 1988. The parser's architecture. In Kessel, F. (Ed.), *The development of language and of language researchers: Papers presented to Roger Brown.* Hillsdale, N.J.: Erlbaum.

WANNER, E., AND MARATSOS, M. 1978. An ATN approach to comprehension. In Halle, M.; Bresnan, J.; and Miller, G. A. (Eds.), *Linguistic theory and psychological reality.* Cambridge, Mass.: MIT Press.

WAPNER, W. T.; JUDD, T.; AND GARDNER, H. 1978. Visual agnosia in an artist. *Cortex* 14:343–64.

WARNER, R. 1995. Time trends in schizophrenia: Changes in obstetric risk factors with industrialization. *Schizophrenia Bulletin* 21:483–500.

WARREN, R. M. 1970. Perceptual restorations of missing speech sounds. *Science* 167:392–93.

WARRINGTON, E. K., AND WEISKRANTZ, L. 1978. Further analysis of the prior learning effect in amnesic patients. *Neuropsychologia* 16:169–76.

WASMAN, M., AND FLYNN, J. P. 1962. Directed attack elicited from the hypothalamus. *Archives of Neurology* 6:220–27.

WASON, P. C. 1960. On the failure to eliminate hypotheses in a conceptual task. *Quarterly Journal of Experimental Psychology* 12:129–40.

WASON, P. C. 1968. On the failure to eliminate hypotheses—A second look. In Wason, P. C., and Johnson-Laird, P. N. (Eds.), *Thinking and reasoning.* Harmondsworth, Eng.: Penguin Books.

WASON, P. C., AND JOHNSON-LAIRD, P. N. 1972. *Psychology of reasoning.* London: B. T. Batsford, Ltd.

WASSERMAN, E. A.; HUGART, J. A.; AND KIRKPATRICK-STEGER, K. 1995. Pigeons show same-different conceptualization after training with complex visual stimuli. *Journal of Experimental Psychology: Animal Behavior Processes* 21:248–52.

WATERS, E.; WIPPMAN, J.; AND SROUFE, L. A. 1979. Attachment, positive affect, and competence in the peer group: Two studies in construct validation. *Child Development* 50:821–29.

WATKINS, L. R., AND MAYER, D. J. 1982. Organization of endogenous opiate and nonopiate pain control systems. *Science* 216:1185–92.

WATSON, C. G., AND BURANEN, C. 1979. The frequency of conversion reaction. *Journal of Abnormal Psychology* 88:209–11.

WATSON, J. B. 1925. *Behaviorism.* New York: Norton.

WATSON, J. B. 1928. *Psychological care of infant and child.* New York: Norton.

WATSON, J. S. 1967. Memory and "contingency analysis" in infant learning. *Merrill-Palmer Quarterly* 13:55–76.

WAUGH, N. C., AND NORMAN, D. A. 1965. Primary memory. *Psychological Review* 72:89–104.

WEBB, W. B. 1972. Sleep deprivation: Total, partial, and selective. In Chase, M. H. (Ed.), The sleeping brain, pp. 323–62. Los Angeles: Brain Information Service, Brain Research Institute.

WEBB, W. B. 1979. Theories of sleep functions and some clinical implications. In Drucker-Colin, R.; Shkurovich, M.; and Sterman, M. B. (Eds.), *The functions of sleep,* pp. 19–36. New York: Academic Press.

WEBB, W. B. 1982. Some theories about sleep and their clinical implications. *Psychiatric Annals* 11:415–22.

WEBER, M. 1904–1905. *The Protestant ethic and the spirit of capitalism.* Parsons, T. (trans.). New York: Scribner's, 1976.

WEBSTER, R. 1995. *Why Freud was wrong: Sin, science, and psychoanalysis.* New York: Basic Books.

WECHSLER, D. 1958. *The measurement and appraisal of adult intelligence,* 4th ed. Baltimore: Williams & Wilkins.

WEEKES, N. Y. 1994. Sex differences in the brain. In Zaidel, D. W. (Ed.), *Neuropsychology: Handbook of perception and cognition,* 2nd ed., pp. 293–315. San Diego: Academic Press.

WEHR, T. A., AND GOODWIN, F. K. 1981. Biological rhythms and psychiatry. In Arieti, S., and Brodie, H. K. H. (Eds.), *American handbook of psychiatry,* vol. 7, pp. 46–74. New York: Basic Books.

WEIGEL, R. H.; VERNON, D. T. A.; AND TOGNACCI, L. N. 1974. Specificity of the attitude as a determinant of attitude-behavior congruence. *Journal of Personality and Social Psychology* 30:724–28.

WEINBERG, M. S.; WILLIAMS, C. J.; AND PRYOR, D. W. 1994. *Dual attraction: Understanding bisexuality.* New York: Oxford University Press.

WEINER, B. 1982. The emotional consequences of causal attributions. In Clark, M. S., and Fiske, S. T. (Eds.), *Affect and cognition: The 17th annual Carnegie symposium on cognition.* Hillsdale, N.J.: Erlbaum.

WEINER, R. D. 1984a. Does electroconvulsive therapy cause brain damage? (with peer commentary). *Behavioral and Brain Sciences* 7:1–54.

WEINER, R. D. 1984b. Convulsive therapy: 50 years later. *American Journal of Psychiatry* 141:1078–79.

WEINER, R. D. 1985. Convulsive therapies. In Kaplan, H. I., and Sadock, J. (Eds.), *Comprehensive textbook of psychiatry,* 4th ed. Baltimore: Williams & Wilkins.

WEINGARDT, K.; LOFTUS, E.; AND LINDSAY, D. S. 1995. Misinformation revisited: New evidence on the suggestibility of memory. *Memory and Cognition* 23:72–82.

WEINGARTNER, H., AND PARKER, E. S. (EDS.) 1984. *Memory consolidation: Psychobiology of cognition.* Hillsdale, N.J.: Erlbaum.

WEINSTOCK, S. 1954. Resistance to extinction of a running response following partial reinforcement under widely spaced trials. *Journal of Comparative and Physiological Psychology* 47:318–22.

WEISBERG, R. 1986. *Creativity: Genius and other myths.* New York: Freeman.

WEISKRANTZ, L. 1986. *Blindsight: A case study and implications.* Oxford: Clarendon Press.

WEISKRANTZ, L., AND WARRINGTON, E. K. 1979. Conditioning in amnesic patients. *Neuropsychologia* 18:177–84.

WEISS, B., AND LATIES, V. G. 1961. Behavioral thermoregulation. *Science* 133:1338–44.

WEISSMAN, M. 1985. The epidemiology of anxiety disorders: Rates, risks, and familial patterns. In Tuma, A. H., and Maser, J. D. (Eds.), *Anxiety and the anxiety disorders,* pp. 275–96. Hillsdale, N.J.: Erlbaum.

WEISSMAN, M., AND BOYD, J. H. 1985. Affective disorders: Epidemiology. In Kaplan, H. I., and Sadock, J. (Eds.), *Modern synopsis of comprehensive textbook of psychiatry,* 4th ed. Baltimore: Williams & Wilkins.

WEISSTEIN, N., AND WONG, E. 1986. Figure-ground organization and the spatial and temporal responses of the visual system. In Schwab, E. C., and Nusbaum, H. C. (Eds.), *Pattern recognition by humans and machines,* vol. 2. New York: Academic Press.

WEISZ, J. R.; ROTHBAUM, F. M.; AND BLACKBURN, T. C. 1984. Standing out and standing in: The psychology of control in American and Japan. *American Psychologist* 39:955–69.

WELKER, W. I.; JOHNSON, J. I.; AND PUBOLS, B. H. 1964. Some morphological and physiological characteristics of the somatic sensory system in raccoons. *American Zoologist* 4:75–94.

WELLER A.; BLASS, E.; GIBBS, J.; AND SMITH, G. P. 1995. Odor-induced inhibition of intake after pairing of odor and CCK-8 in neonatal rats. *Physiology and Behavior* 57:181–83.

WELLMAN, H. M. 1990. *The child's theory of mind.* Cambridge, Mass.: MIT Press.

WELLMAN, H. M., AND BARTSCH, K. 1988. Young children's reasoning about beliefs. *Cognition* 30:239–77.

WELLMAN, H., AND GELMAN, S. 1992. Cognitive development: Foundational theories of core domains. *Annual Review of Psychology* 43:337–75.

WELLMAN, H. M.; RITTER, K.; AND FLAVELL, J. H. 1975. Deliberate memory behavior in the delayed reactions of very young children. *Developmental Psychology* 11:780–87.

WENDER, P. H.; KETY, S. S.; ROSENTHAL, D.; SCHULSINGER, F.; AND ORTMANN, J. 1986. Psychiatric disorders in the biological relatives of adopted individuals with affective disorders. *Archives of General Psychiatry* 43:923–29.

WERKER, J. 1991. The ontogeny of speech perception. In Mattingly, I. G., and Studdert-Kennedy, M. (Eds.), *Modularity and the motor theory of speech perception: Proceedings of a conference to honor Alvin M. Liberman,* pp. 91–109. Hillsdale, N.J.: Erlbaum.

WERKER, J. F. 1995. Exploring developmental changes in cross-language speech perception. In Gleitman, L. R., and Liberman, M. (Eds.), *An invitation to cognitive science,* vol. 1, pp. 87–106. Cambridge, Mass.: MIT Press.

WERKER, J., AND TEES, R. 1984. Cross-language speech perception: Evidence for perceptual reorganization during the first year of life. *Infant Behavior and Development* 7:49–63.

WERTHEIMER, M. 1912. Experimentelle Studien über das Gesehen von Bewegung. *Zeitschrift fr Psychologie* 61:161–265.

WERTHEIMER, M. 1923. Untersuchungen zur Lehre von der Gestalt, II. *Psychologische Forschung* 4:301–50.

WEST, S. A.; McELROY, S. L.; AND KECK, P. E. 1996. Valproate. In Goodnick, P. J. (Ed.), *Predictors of treatment response in mood disorders.* Washington, D.C.: American Psychiatric Press.

WEST, S. G.; WHITNEY, G.; AND SCHNEDLER, R. 1975. Helping a motorist in distress: The effects of sex, race, and neighborhood. *Journal of Personality and Social Psychology* 31:691–98.

WESTERMEYER, J. 1987. Public health and chronic mental illness. *American Journal of Public Health* 77:667–68.

WETZEL, M., AND STUART, D. G. 1976. Ensemble characteristics of cat locomotion and its neural control. *Progress in Neurobiology* 7:1–98.

WEXLER, K., AND CULICOVER, P. 1980. *Formal principles of language acquisition.* Cambridge, Mass.: MIT Press.

WEXLER, K., AND MANZINI, R. 1987. Parameters and learnability in binding theory. In Roeper, T., and Williams, E. (Eds.), *Parameter setting*. Dordrecht: Reidel.

WHEELER, L. R. 1942. A comparative study of the intelligence of East Tennessee mountain children. *Journal of Educational Psychology* 33:321–34.

WHEELER, L.; REIS, H.; AND BOND, M. H. 1989. Collectivism-individualism in everyday social life: The middle kingdom and the melting pot. *Journal of Personality and Social Psychology* 57:79–86.

WHITE, G. L. 1980. Physical attractiveness and courtship progress. *Journal of Personality and Social Psychology* 39:660–68.

WHITE, S. H., AND PILLEMER, D. B. 1979. Childhood amnesia and the development of a functionally accessible memory system. In Kihlstrom, J. F., and Evans, F. J. (Eds.), *Functional disorders of memory*. Hillsdale, N.J.: Erlbaum.

WHITING, J. W. M., AND WHITING, B. B. 1975. *Children of six cultures: A psychocultural analysis*. Cambridge, Mass.: Harvard University Press.

WHITLOW, J. W., JR., AND WAGNER, A. R. 1984. Memory and habituation. In Peeke, H. V. S., and Petrinovich, L. (Eds.), *Habituation, sensitization, and behavior*, pp. 103–53. New York: Academic Press.

WHORF, B. 1956. *Language, thought, and reality*. Cambridge, Mass.: MIT Press.

WICKELGREN, I. 1997. Getting a grasp on working memory. *Science* 275:1580–82.

WICKELGREN, W. A. 1974. *How to solve problems*. San Francisco: Freeman.

WIENS, A. N., AND MENUSTIK, C. E. 1983. Treatment outcome and patient characteristics in an aversion therapy program for alcoholism. *American Psychologist* 38:1089–96.

WIESENTHAL, D. L.; ENDLER, N. S.; COWARD, T. R.; AND EDWARDS, J. 1976. Reversibility of relative competence as a determinant of conformity across different perceptual tasks. *Representative Research in Social Psychology* 7:319–42.

WILCOXIN, H. C.; DRAGOIN, W. B.; AND KRAL, P. A. 1971. Illness-induced aversions in rat and quail: Relative salience of visual and gustatory cues. *Science* 171:826–28.

WILLIAMS, D. R., AND WILLIAMS, H. 1969. Auto maintenance in the pigeon: Sustained pecking despite contingent non-reinforcement. *Journal of the Experimental Analysis of Behavior* 12:511–20.

WILLIAMS, G. C. 1966. *Adaptation and natural selection*. Princeton, N.J.: Princeton University Press.

WILLIAMS, G. C. 1975. *Sex and evolution*. Princeton: Princeton University Press.

WILLIAMS, H. L.; TEPAS, D. I.; AND MORLOCK, H. C. 1962. Evoked responses to clicks and electroencephalographic stages of sleep in man. *Science* 138:685–86.

WILLIAMS, L. 1994. Recall of childhood trauma: A prospective study of women's memories of child sexual abuse. *Journal of Consulting and Clinical Psychology* 62:1167–76.

WILLIAMS, M. D., AND HOLLAN, J. D. 1982. The process of retrieval from very long-term memory. *Cognitive Science* 5:87–119.

WILLIAMS, R. B. 1987. Psychological factors in coronary artery disease: Epidemiological evidence. *Circulation* 76 (suppl. I):117–23.

WILSON, D. H.; REEVES, A. G.; GAZZANIGA, M. S.; AND CULVER, C. 1977. Cerebral commissurotomy for the control of intractable seizures. *Neurology* 27:708–15.

WILSON, E. O. 1975. *Sociobiology*. Cambridge, Mass.: Harvard University Press.

WILSON, G. 1978. Introversion/extraversion. In London, H., and Exner, J. (Eds.), *Dimensions of personality*. New York: Wiley.

WILSON, G. 1985. *The psychology of the performing arts*. London and Sydney: Croom Helm.

WILSON, G. T. 1980. Behavior modification and the treatment of obesity. In Stunkard, A. J. (Ed.), *Obesity*, pp. 325–44. Philadelphia: Saunders.

WILSON, G. T. 1991. Chemical aversion conditioning in the treatment of alcoholism: Further comments. *Behaviour Research and Therapy* 29:415–19.

WILSON, J. Q. 1997. *Moral judgment: Does the abuse excuse threaten our legal system?* New York: Basic Books.

WILSON, T. D., AND SCHOOLER, J. W. 1991. Thinking too much: Introspection can reduce the quality of preferences and decisions. *Journal of Personality and Social Psychology* 60(2):181–92.

WILTSCHKO, R.; NORH, D.; AND WILTSCHKO, W. 1981. Pigeons with a deficient sun compass use the magnetic compass. *Science* 214:34–45.

WIMMER, H., AND PERNER, J. 1983. Beliefs about beliefs: Representation and constraining function of wrong beliefs in young children's understanding of deception. *Cognition* 13:103–28.

WINCH, R. F., AND MORE, D. M. 1956. Does TAT add information to interviews? Statistical analysis of the increment. *Journal of Clinical Psychology* 12:316–21.

WINKLER, J., AND TAYLOR, S. E. 1979. Preference, expectation, and attributional bias: Two field experiments. *Journal of Applied Social Psychology* 2:183–97.

WINOGRAD, E., AND NEISSER, U. (EDS.). 1993. *Affect and accuracy in recall: Studies of "flashbulb" memories*. New York: Cambridge University Press.

WINSLOW, J. T., AND INSEL, T. R. 1990. Neurobiology of obsessive-compulsive disorder: A possible role for serotonin. *Journal of Clinical Psychiatry* 51(suppl.):27–31.

WINTER, R. 1976. *The smell book: Scents, sex, and society*. Philadelphia: Lippincott.

WINTON, W. M. 1986. The role of facial response in self-reports of emotion: A critique of Laird. *Journal of Personality and Social Psychology* 50:808–12.

WIRSHING, W. C.; MARDER, S. R.; VAN PUTTEN, T.; AND AMES, D. 1995. Acute treatment of schizophrenia. In Bloom, F. E., and Kupfer, D. (Eds.), *Psychopharmacology: The fourth generation of progress*, pp. 1259-66. New York: Raven.

WISE, R. A., AND ROMPRE, P. P. 1989. Brain dopamine and reward. *Annual Review of Psychology* 40:191–226.

WISEMAN, S., AND NEISSER, U. 1974. Perceptual organization as a determinant of visual recognition memory. *American Journal of Psychology* 87:675–81.

WISHNER, J. 1960. Reanalysis of "impressions of personality." *Psychological Review* 67:96–112.

WITTGENSTEIN, L. 1953. *Philosophical investigations*. Anscombe, G. E. M., trans. Oxford: Blackwell.

WOHL, J. 1989. Cross-cultural psychotherapy. In Pedersen, P. B.; Draguns, J. G.; Lonner, W. J.; and Trimble, J. E. (Eds.), *Counseling across cultures*, pp. 79–113. Honolulu: University of Hawaii.

WOLF, M. E., AND MOSNAIM, A. D. 1990. *Post-traumatic stress disorder: Etiology, phenomenology, and treatment*. Washington, D.C.: American Psychiatric Press.

WOLLEN, K. A.; WEBER, A.; AND LOWRY, D. 1972. Bizarreness versus interaction of mental images as determinants of learning. *Cognitive Psychology* 3:518–23.

WOLPE, J. 1958. *Psychotherapy by reciprocal inhibition*. Stanford, Calif.: Stanford University Press.

WOLPE, J., AND LAZARUS, A. A. 1966. *Behavior therapy techniques: A guide to the treatment of neuroses*. Elmsford, N.Y.: Pergamon.

WOLPE, J., AND PLAUD, J. J. 1997. Pavlov's contributions to behavior therapy: The obvious and the not so obvious. *American Psychologist* 52:966–72.

WOLPERT, E. A., AND TROSMAN, H. 1958. Studies in psychophysiology of dreams: I. Experimental evocation of sequential dream episodes. *Archives of Neurology and Psychiatry* 79:603–606.

WOOD, A. J., AND GOODWIN, G. M. 1987. A review of the biochemical and neuropharmacological actions of lithium. *Psychological Medicine* 17:579–600.

WOOD, J. M.; BOOTZIN, R. R.; ROSENHAN, D.; NOLEN-HOEKSEMA, S.; AND JOURDEN, F. 1992. Effects of the 1989 San Francisco earthquake on frequency and content of nightmares. *Journal of Abnormal Psychology* 101:219–24.

WOODRUFF, G, AND PREMACK, D. 1979. Intentional communication in the chimpanzee: The development of deception. *Cognition* 7:333–62.

WOODRUFF, P. W. R.; WRIGHT, I. C.; BULLMORE, E. T.; BRAMMER, M.; HOWARD, R. J.; WILLIAMS, S. C. R.; SHAPLESKE, J.; ROSSELL, S.; DAVID, A. S.; McGUIRE, P. K.; AND MURRAY, R. M. 1997. Auditory hallucinations and the temporal cortical response to speech in schizophrenia: A functional magnetic resonance imaging study. *American Journal of Psychiatry* 154:1676–82.

WOODS, B. T., AND TEUBER, H. L. 1978. Changing patterns of childhood aphasia. *Archives of Neurology* 3:273–80.

WOODS, R. L. 1947. *The world of dreams: An anthology.* New York: Random House.

WRIGHT, C. 1982. *Rembrandt, self-portraits.* New York: Viking.

WYERS, E. J.; PEEKE, H. V. S.; AND HERZ, M. J. 1973. Behavioral habituation in invertebrates. In Peeke, H. V. S., and Herz, M. J. (Eds.), *Habituation,* vol. 1: *Behavioral studies.* New York: Academic Press.

WYNN, K. 1992. Addition and subtraction by human infants. *Nature* 358:749–50.

YAGER, D. D., AND HOY, R. R. 1986. The Cyclopean ear: A new sense for the Praying Mantis. *Science* 231:727–29.

YAGER, D. D., AND MAY, M. L. 1990. Ultrasound-triggered, flight-gated evasive maneuvers in the Praying Mantis *Parasphendale agrionina. Journal of Experimental Biology* 152:41–58.

YANDO, R.; SEITZ, V.; AND ZIGLER, E. 1978. *Imitation: A developmental perspective.* Hillsdale, N.J.: Erlbaum.

YANG, K., AND BOND, M. H. 1990. Exploring implicit personality theories with indigenous or imported constructs: The Chinese case. *Journal of Personality and Social Psychology* 58:1087–95.

YARBUS, A. L. 1967. *Eye movements and vision.* L. A. Riggs, trans. New York: Plenum Press.

YARROW, L. J. 1961. Maternal deprivation: Toward an empirical and conceptual reevaluation. *Psychological Bulletin* 58:459–90.

YEHUDA, R. 1997. Sensitization of the hypothalamic-pituitary-adrenal axis in posttraumatic stress disorder. In Yehuda, R., and McFarlane, A. C. (Eds.), *Psychobiology of posttraumatic stress disorder. Annals of the New York Academy of Sciences* 821:57–75.

YERKES, R. M., AND MARGULIS, S. 1909. Method of Pavlov in animal psychology. *Psychological Bulletin* 6:264.

YOUNG, W. 1996. Spinal cord regeneration. *Science* 273:451.

YUSSEN, S. R., AND LEVY, V. M. 1975. Developmental changes in predicting one's own span of memory. *Journal of Experimental Child Psychology* 19:502–8.

ZAHAVI, A. 1975. Mate selection—a selection for a handicap. *Journal of Theoretical Biology* 53:205–14.

ZAHAVI, A. 1991. On the definition of sexual selection, Fisher's model, and the evolution of waste and of signals in general. *Animal Behaviour* 42:501–3.

ZAIDEL, E. 1976. Auditory vocabulary of the right hemisphere following brain bisection or hemidecortication. *Cortex* 12:191–211.

ZAIDI, L. Y., AND FOY, D. W. 1994. Childhood abuse experiences and combat-related PTSD. *Journal of Traumatic Stress* 7:33–42.

ZAJONC, R. B. 1965. Social facilitation. *Science* 149:269–74.

ZAJONC, R. B. 1968. Attitudinal effects of mere exposure. *Journal of Personality and Social Psychology* 9(monograph suppl.):1–27.

ZAJONC, R. B. 1980. Copresence. In Paulus, P. (Ed.), *The psychology of group influence.* Hillsdale, N.J.: Erlbaum.

ZAJONC, R. B.; ADELMANN, P. K.; MURPHY, S. T.; NIEDENTHAL, P. M. 1987. Convergence in the physical appearance of spouses. *Motivation and Emotion* 11:335–46.

ZAJONC, R. B., HEINGERTNER, A.; AND HERMAN, E. M. 1969. Social enhancement and impairment of performance in the cockroach. *Journal of Personality and Social Psychology* 13:83–92.

ZARAGOZA, M. S., AND MITCHELL, K. J. 1996. Repeated exposure to suggestion and the creation of false memories. *Psychological Science* 7:294–300.

ZARAGOZA, M., AND LANE, S. 1994. Source misattributions and the suggestibility of eyewitness memory. *Journal of Experimental Psychology: Learning, Memory and Cognition* 20:934–45.

ZARKIN, G. A.; GRABOWSKI, H. G.; MAUSKOPF, J.; BANNERMAN, H. A.; AND WEISLER, R. H. 1995. Economic evaluation of drug treatment for psychiatric disorders. In Bloom, F. E., and Kupfer, D. (Eds.), *Psychopharmacology: The fourth generation of progress,* pp. 1897–1905. New York: Raven.

ZATORRE, R. J., AND HALPERN, A. R. 1993. Effect of unilateral temporal lobe excision on perception and imagery of songs. *Neuropsychologia* 31:221–32.

ZATZICK, D. F.; MARMAR, C. R.; WEISS, D. S.; BROWNER, W. S.; METZLER, T. J.; GOLDING, J. M.; STEWART, A.; SCHLENGER, W. E.; AND WELLS, K. B. 1997. Posttraumatic stress disorder and functioning and quality of life outcomes in a nationally representative sample of male Vietnam veterans. *American Journal of Psychiatry* 154:1690–95.

ZENER, K. 1937. The significance of behavior accompanying conditioned salivary secretion for theories of the conditioned response. *American Journal of Psychology* 50:384–403.

ZENTALL, T., AND HOGAN, D. 1974. Abstract concept learning in the pigeon. *Journal of Experimental Psychology* 102:393–98.

ZHOU, W., AND KING, W. M. 1997. Binocular eye movements not coordinated during REM sleep. *Experimental Brian Research* 117:153–60.

ZIEGLER, F. J.; IMBODEN, J. B.; AND RODGERS, D. A. 1963. Contemporary conversion reactions: III. Diagnostic considerations. *Journal of the American Medical Association* 186:307–11.

ZIGLER, E. 1967. Familial mental retardation: A continuing dilemma. *Science* 155:292–98.

ZIGLER, E., AND CHILD, I. L. 1969. Socialization. In Lindzey, G., and Aronson, E. (Eds.), *The handbook of social psychology,* vol. 3, pp. 450–589. Reading, Mass.: Addison-Wesley.

ZIGLER, E. F. AND CHILD, I. L. 1973. *Socialization and personality development.* Reading, Mass.: Addison-Wesley.

ZIGLER, E., AND HODAPP, R. M. 1991. Behavioral functioning in individuals with mental retardation In Rosenzweig, M. R., and Porter, L. W. (Eds.), *Annual review of psychology,* pp. 29–50. Palo Alto, Calif.: Annual Reviews, Inc.

ZIGLER, E. F.; LAMB, M. E.; AND CHILD, I. L. 1982. *Socialization and personality development,* 2nd ed. New York: Oxford University Press.

ZIGLER, P. 1991. *The black death.* Dover, N.H.: Sutton.

ZILBOORG, G., AND HENRY, G. W. 1941. *A history of medical psychology.* New York: Norton.

ZILLMAN, D. 1983. Transfer of excitation in emotional behavior. In Cacioppo, J. T., and Petty, R. E. (Eds.), *Social psychophysiology: A sourcebook,* pp. 215–40. New York: Guilford.

ZILLMAN, D.; KATCHER, A. H.; AND MILAVSKY, B. 1972. Excitation transfer from physical exercise to subsequent aggressive behavior. *Journal of Experimental Social Psychology* 8:247–59.

ZIMBARDO, P. G. 1969. The human choice: Individuation, reason, and order versus deindividuation, impulse and chaos. In Arnold, W. J. and Levine, E. (Eds.), *Nebraska Symposium on Motivation,* pp. 237–308. Lincoln: University of Nebraska Press.

ZOHAR, J.; INSEL, T.; ZOHAR-KADOUCH, R. C.; HILL, J. L.; AND MURPHY, D. 1988. Serotonergic responsivity in obsessive-compulsive disorder. Effects of chronic clomipramine treatment. *Archives of General Psychiatry* 45:167–72.

ZORILLA, L. T. E., AND CANNON, T. D. 1995. Structural brain abnormalities in schizophrenia: Distribution, etiology, and implications. In Mednick, S. A. (Ed.), *Neural development in schizophrenia: Theory and research.* New York: Plenum Press.

ZUBIN, J.; ERON, L. D.; AND SHUMER, F. 1965. *An experimental approach to projective techniques.* New York: Wiley.

ZUCKERMAN, M. 1979. *Sensation seeking: Beyond the optimum level of arousal.* Hillsdale, N.J.: Erlbaum.

ZUCKERMAN, M. 1983. A biological theory of sensation seeking. In Zuckerman, M. (Ed.), *Biological bases of sensation seeking, impulsivity, and anxiety.* Hillsdale, N.J.: Erlbaum.

ZUCKERMAN, M. 1987a. All parents are environmentalists until they have their second child. Peer commentary on Plomin, R., and Daniels, D. Why are children from the same family so different from one another? *Behavioral and Brain Sciences* 10:38–39.

ZUCKERMAN, M. 1987b. A critical look at three arousal constructs in personality theories: Optimal levels of arousal, strength of the nervous system, and sensitivities to signals of reward and punishment. In Strelau, J., and Eysenck, H. J. (Eds.), *Personality dimensions and arousal: Perspectives on individual differences,* pp. 217-30. New York: Plenum.

ZUCKERMAN, M. 1990. The psychophysiology of sensation seeking. Special Issue: Biological foundations of personality: Evolution, behavioral genetics, and psychophysiology. *Journal of Personality* 58:313-45.

ZUCKERMAN, M. 1994a. *Behavioral expressions and biosocial bases of sensation seeking.* New York: Cambridge University Press.

ZUCKERMAN, M. 1994b. Impulsive unsocialized sensation seeking: The biological foundations of a basic dimension of personality. In Bates, J. E., and Wachs, T. D. (Eds.), *Temperament: Individual differences at the interface of biology and behavior,* pp. 219-55. Washington, D.C.: American Psychological Association.

ZUGER, B. 1984. Early effeminate behavior in boys. *Journal of Nervous and Mental Disease* 172:90–96.

ACKNOWLEDGMENTS AND CREDITS

FIGURES

Chapter 1: **1.1** Courtesy of Kaiser Porcelain Ltd. **1.2A,B,C** Bugelski, B. R., and Alampay, D. A., The role of frequency in developing perceptual sets, *Canadian Journal of Psychology* 15 (1961): 205-11. Adapted by permission of the Canadian Psychological Association. **1.3A** Courtesy of Richard D. Walk. **1.3B** Courtesy of William Vandivert. **1.4A** Photograph by Robert Estall/Corbis. **1.4B** Photograph by David Gillison/Peter Arnold, Inc. **1.4C** Photograph by Wolfgang Kaehler/Corbis. **1.5A** Photograph by George H. Harrison/Grant Heilman. **1.5B** Photograph by Peter Hendrie/The Image Bank. **1.6** Collection of Robert H. Helmick; courtesy Brooke Alexander, New York. **1.7 and 1.8** From Dement, W. C., *Some Must Watch While Some Must Sleep.* California: The Portable Stanford, 1972. Copyright © 1972, 1974, 1976 by William C. Dement. **1.9** Courtesy of the Staatlicher Museum für Völkerkunde, Munich. **1.10** Courtesy of The Museum of Modern Art/Film Stills Archive.

Chapter 2: **2.2** Photograph by Cabisco/Visuals Unlimited. **2.3B** Photograph by Dr. John Mazziotta, UCLA School of Medicine/Science Photo Library/Photo Researchers. **2.4A** Courtesy Warren Museum, Harvard Medical School. **2.4B** Damasio, H., Grabowski, T., Frank, R., Galaburda, A. M., & Damasio, A. R. (1994), The return of Phineas Gage: Clues aboutthe brain from the skull of a famous patient, *Science,* 264, © 1994 by the A. A. A. S.; courtesy Hanna Damasio. **2.5** Photograph by Simon Fraser/Science Photo Library/Photo Researchers. **2.6** Photograph © Paul Shambroom. **2.7** NIH/SPL/Photo Researchers. **2.8** Photograph by Dr. John Mazziotta et al./Photo Researchers. **2.9** Reprinted with permission from Dr. Krish Singh, Department of Psychology, University of Liverpool. **2.10** From *Brain: A Scientific American Book,* edited by Scientific American. Copyright © 1979, W. H. Freeman. **2.11A** Photograph by Biophoto Associates/Photo Researchers. **2.11B** From *Biological Science,* Sixth Edition by James Gould and William T. Keeton. Copyright © 1996, 1993, 1986, 1980, 1979, 1978, 1972, 1967 by W. W. Norton & Company, Inc. Reprinted by permission of W. W. Norton & Company, Inc. **2.12 and 2.13** From *Biological Psychology* by Rosenzweig, Leiman, and Breedlove. Copyright © 1996 by Sinauer Associates, Inc. **2.14** Bloom, F. E., Lazerson, A., and Hofstadter, L. *Brain, Mind and Behavior.* New York: Freeman, 1988. Adapted by permission of WNET/Thirteen. **2.16A** The Science Museum/Science & Society Picture Library. **2.16B** Courtesy Alan Gevins, EEG Systems Laboratory, San Francisco. **2.17** Adapted with permission of Macmillan Publishing Co., Inc., from *The Cerebral Cortex of Man* by Wilder Penfield and Theodore Rasmussen. Copyright © 1950 by Macmillan Publishing Co., Inc., renewed 1978 by Theodore Rasmussen. **2.18** Cobb, S., *Foundations of Neuropsychiatry.* Baltimore, Md.: Williams & Wilkins, 1941. © 1941, the Williams & Wilkins Co., Baltimore. Adapted by permission of Lippincott, Williams and Wilkins. **2.19** From *Higher Cortical Functions in Man,* Second Edition by A. R. Luria. Copyright © 1979 by Consultants Bureau Enterprises, Inc. and Basic Books, Inc. Reprinted by permission of Basic Books, a member of Perseus Books, L. L. C. **2.20** *Physiological Psychology,* 2nd ed., by Mark Rosenzweig and Arnold Leiman. Copyright © 1989 by Random House. **2.23** Gazzaniga, M. S., The split brain in man, *Scientific American* 217 (August 1967): 25. Copyright © 1967 by Scientific American, Inc. Drawing by Maura Conron. **2.25** After figure "Space Relations" (p. 354) from *Essentials of Psychological Testing,* 3rd edition, by Lee J. Cronbach. Copyright © 1949 by Harper & Row, Inc. Copyright © 1960, 1970 by Lee J. Cronbach. **2.26** Roeder, K., *Nerve Cells and Insect Behavior.* Cambridge, Mass.: Harvard University Press, 1972, p. 198. **2.27B** Photograph by Manfred Kage/Peter Arnold, Inc. **2.28C** © Guigoz/Dr. A. Privat/Petit Format/Science Source/Photo Researchers. **2.32** From *Biology: The Unity and Diversity of Life,* Fifth Edition, by Cecie Starr and Ralph Taggart, © 1989 by Wadsworth, Inc. Reprinted by permission of the publisher. **2.33** From Eccles, J. C., *The Understanding of the Brain.* Copyright © 1973 the McGraw-Hill Companies. Reproduced with the permission of the McGraw-Hill Companies. **2.37** Drawing by Maura Conron. **2.38** Reprinted with permission from Lewis, E. R., Everhart, T. E., and

Seevi, Y. Y., Studying Neural organization in aplysia with the scanning electron microscope, *Science* 165 (12 September 1969): 1140-1143. Copyright © 1969 American Association for the Advancement of Science. **2.39** Bloom, F. E., Lazerson, A., and Hofstadter, L. *Brain, Mind and Behavior.* New York: Freeman, 1988. Adapted by permission of WNET/Thirteen. **2.40** *Physiological Psychology,* 2nd ed., by Mark Rosenzweig and Arnold Leiman. Copyright © 1989 by Random House. Reprinted by permission of McGraw-Hill. **2.42** Adapted from Björklund, A., Stenevi, U., Schmidt, R. H., Dunnett, S. B., and Gage, F. H., Intracerebral grafting of neuronal suspensions I: Induction and general methods of preparation, *Acta Physiologica Scandinavica* Supplement 522 (1983): 1-7. Reproduced by permission of Acta Physiologica Scandinavica. **2.43** Adapted from Coyle, J. T., Price, D., and Delong, M. R., Alzheimer's disease: A disorder of cholinergic innervation, Science 219 (1983): 1184-90. Copyright 1983 by the American Association for the Advancement of Science. Reproduced by permission of the AAAS and the author. **2.44** Courtesy of Rex Features USA.

Chapter 3: **3.3** Keeton, W. T., and Gould, J. L., *Biological Science,* 4th edition. New York: W. W. Norton & Company, Inc., 1986. Copyright © 1986, 1980, 1979, 1972, 1967 by W. W. Norton & Company, Inc. **3.4** Reprinted with permission from Weiss, B. and Laties, V.G., Behavioral thermoregulation, *Science* 133 (28 April 1961): 1338-44, Figure 1. Copyright © 1961 by the American Association for the Advancement of Science. **3.7B** Courtesy Neal E. Miller, Rockefeller University. **3.8** Photographs courtesy of Jacob Steiner. **3.9A** Laura Riley/Bruce Coleman. **3.9B** Stan Osolinski/Oxford Scientific Films. **3.9C** Helen Williams/Photo Researchers. **3.10** From Bouchard, Tremblay, et.al, The response to long-term overeeding in identical twins. *New England Journal of Medicine* 322: pp. 1477-1482. Copyright © 1990 by the Massachusetts Medical Society. All rights reserved. **3.11** Adapted from Nisbett, R. E., Taste, deprivation and weight determinants of eating behavior, *Journal of Personality and Social Psychology* 10 (1968): 107-16. **3.12** Andres, R., Influence of obesity on longevity in the aged, in Borek, C., Fenoglio, C. M., and King, D. W. (Eds.), *Aging, Cancer, and Cell Membranes,* pp. 230-46. New York: Thieme-Stratton, 1980. **3.13** From *Bodily Changes in Pain, Hunger, Fear and Rage* by W. B. Cannon. **3.14** © Walter Chandoha, 1994. **3.15A** Photograph by Mary Shuford. **3.15B** Inbau, F. E., and Reid, J. E., *The Polygraph ("Lie Detector") Technique,* 2nd ed. Baltimore, Md.: Williams & Wilkins, 1977. © Professor Fred E. Inbau. **3.16B** From *Biological Science,* Sixth Edition by James Gould and William T. Keeton. Copyright © 1996, 1993, 1986, 1980, 1979, 1978, 1972, 1967 by W. W. Norton & Company, Inc. Reprinted by permission of W. W. Norton & Company, Inc. **3.17** Adapted from Bloom, F. E., Lazerson, A., and Hofstadter, L., *Brain, Mind, and Behavior.* New York: Freeman, 1988. Adapted by permission of WNET/Thirteen. **3.18A** Blakemore, C., *Mechanics of the Mind,* p. 42. New York: Cambridge University Press, 1977. Reprinted by permission of the publisher. **3.18B** Photograph © Dan McCoy, 1994/Rainbow/PNI. **3.22** From Dement, W. C., *Some Must Watch While Some Must Sleep.* California: The Portable Stanford, 1972. Copyright © 1972, 1974, 1976 by William C. Dement. **3.23** Adapted from Kleitman, N., Patterns of dreaming, *Scientific American* 203 (November 1960): 82-88. Copyright © 1960 by Scientific American, Inc. All rights reserved. **3.25** Carlson, N. R., *Psychology of Behavior,* 4th ed., p. 295. Boston: Allyn & Bacon, 1991; graph by S. T. Inoueye. **3.26** Photograph courtesy of the University of Wisconsin Primate Laboratory. **3.27** Courtesy of Dr. M. E. Olds. **3.28** Adapted from *Physiological Psychology,* 2nd ed., by Mark Rosenzweig and Arnold Leiman. Copyright © 1989 by Random House.

Chapter 4: **4.4** Pavlov, I. P., *Lectures on Conditioned Reflexes,* vol. I. New York: International Publishers Co., Inc., 1928. **4.5** Stimulus control by Moore, John W. in *Classical Conditioning II: Research and Theory* edited by Black/Prokasy, Copyright © 1972. Reprinted by permission of Prentice-Hall, Inc., Upper Saddle River, N J. **4.11A** Photograph by Mike Salisbury.

4.11B Photograph by Susan M. Hogue. **4.12** From *A Primer of Operant Conditioning* by G. S. Reynolds. (Scott, Foresman & Co.). **4.13A** Photograph courtesy of Animal Behavior Enterprises, Inc. **4.13B** Photograph by Gerald Davis/Contact Press Images. **4.14** Courtesy Yerkes Regional Primate Research Center of Emory University. **4.15, 4.16, 4.17** Ferster, C. B., and Skinner, B. F., *Schedules of Reinforcement*, pp. 56, 399. Englewood Cliffs, N. J.: Prentice-Hall, Inc., 1957. **4.21** Spooner, A., and Kellogg, W. N., The backward conditioning curve, *American Journal of Psychology* 60 (1947): 321-34. Copyright © 1947 by Board of Trustees of the University of Illinois. Used with permission of the publisher, The University of Illinois Press. **4.22** Rescorla, R. A., Predictability and number of pairings in Pavlovian fear conditioning, *Psychonomic Science* 4 (1966): 383-84. **4.23** From *Punishment and Adverse Behavior* by (ed.) Campbell/Church, Copyright © 1969. Adapted by permission of Prentice-Hall, Inc., Upper Saddle River, N J. **4.24** Colwill, R. M., and Rescorla, R. A., Postconditioning devaluation of a reinforcer affects instrumental responding, *Journal of Experimental Psychology: Animal Behavior Processes* 11 (1985): 120-32. **4.25** Drawing by Frank Forney. **4.26** Maier, S. F., Seligman, M. E. P., and Solomon, R. L., Pavlovian fear conditioning and learned helplessness: Effects on escape and avoidance behavior of (a) the CS-US contingency and (b) the independence of the US and voluntary responding, in Campbell, B. A., and Church, R. M. (Eds.), *Punishment and Aversive Behavior*, © 1969, p. 328. **4.27** Photographs by Bruce Moore. **4.30** Olton, D. S., and Samuelson, R. J., Remembrance of places passed: Spatial memory in rats, *Journal of Experimental Psychology: Animal Behavior Processes* 2 (1976): 97-116. **4.34** Figure adapted from *Why Chimps Can Read* by A. J. Premack. Copyright © 1976 by Ann J. Premack. Reprinted by permission of HarperCollins Publishers. Drawing by Maura Conron.

Chapter 5: **5.1** Drawing by Frank Forney. **5.2** *The School of Athens* by Raphael, 1505; Stanza della Segnatura, Vatican; courtesy Scala/Art Resource, New York. **5.5A** From *Elements of Psychology* by David Krech and Richard S. Crutchfield. Copyright © 1958 by David Krech and Richard S. Crutchfield. Reprinted by permission of Alfred A. Knopf, Inc. **5.5B** Adapted from *Biological Psychology*, 2nd ed., by James W. Kalat. © 1984 by Wadsworth, Inc. Reprinted by permission. **5.6** Figure-A cross section through the skin from Carlson, N. R., *Psychology of Behavior* 4/e. Copyright 1986 by Allyn & Bacon. Reprinted/adapted by permission. **5.7** Frank, M., An analysis of hamster afferent taste nerve response functions. *Journal of General Physiology* 61 (1973): 588-618. **5.9** Gibson, James J., *The Senses Considered as Perceptual Systems*, p. 80, Fig. 5.4. Boston: Houghton Mifflin Company, 1966. Reprinted by permission of the publisher. **5.10** Thompson, R. F., *Introduction to Biopsychology*. San Rafael, Calif.: Albion Publishing Company, 1973. **5.12, 5.13A, 5.14A** Lindsay P. H., and Norman, D. A., *Human Information Processing*, 2nd edition, pp. 126, 133, and 136. New York: Academic Press, 1977. Adapted by permission of the author and Harcourt Brace Jovanovich. **5.13** Figure from *Sensation and Perception* by Stanley Coren, Clare Porac, and Lawrence M. Ward. Copyright © 1979 by Harcourt Brace & Company, reproduced by permission of the publisher. **5.14B** Coren, S., and Ward, L. M., *Sensation and Perception*, 3rd ed. San Diego: Harcourt Brace Jovanovich, 1989. Adapted by permission of the author and publisher. **5.15** Wald, G. Eye and Camera. *Scientific American* 183 (August 1950): 33. Illustration by Eric Mose, copyright © 1950 by Eric Mose. Reprinted by permission of the artist. **5.16** Figure from *Sensation and Perception*, Third Edition, by Stanley Coren and Lawrence M. Ward. Copyright © 1989 by Harcourt Brace & Company, reproduced by permission of the publisher. **5.17, 5.18** Cornsweet, T. M., *Visual Perception*. New York: Academic Press, 1970. Adapted by permission of the author and Harcourt Brace Jovanovich. **5.21** Hering, E., *Outlines of a Theory of the Light Sense*, 1920 (translated by Hurvich, L. M., and Jameson, D., 1964), pp. 150-51. Cambridge, Mass.: Harvard University Press, 1964. **5.22A** *Arcturus II* (1966) by Victor Vasarely, Hirshhorn Museum and Sculpture Garden, Smithsonian Institution, gift of Joseph H. Hirshhorn, 1972. **5.23** Coren, S., Porac, C., and Ward, L. M., *Sensation and Perception*, p. 155. New York: Academic Press, 1978. Adapted by permission of the author and Harcourt Brace Jovanovich. Also **5.23** Cornsweet, T. M., *Visual Perception*, p. 276. New York: Academic Press, 1970. Adapted by permission of the author and Harcourt Brace Jovanovich. **5.27** Hurvich, L. M., *Color Vision*. Sunderland, Mass.: Sinauer Associates, 1981. Reproduced by permission of Sinauer Associates. **5.29** Reprinted by permission of Douglas Downing, Seattle Pacific University, Seattle, Washington. **5.30** Courtesy of Munsell Color, 2441 N. Calvert Street, Baltimore, Md., 21218. **5.33** Detail and full use of Georges Seurat's *The Channel of Gravelines* (Petit Fort Philippe), 1890, oil on canvas. © 1994 Indianapolis Museum of Art, gift of Mrs. James W. Fesler in memory of Daniel W. and Elizabeth C. Marmon. **5.39** Hurvich, L. M., and Jameson, D., An opponent-process theory of color vision, *Psychological Review* 64 (1957): 384-404. **5.40** DeValois, R. L., and DeValois, K. K., *Neural Coding of Color*, in Carterette, E. C., and Friedman, M. P., (Eds.), *Handbook of Perception*, vol. 5. New York: Academic Press, 1975. Adapted by permission of the publisher.

5.42 Figure 11.28 from Schiffman, H. *Sensation and Perception* 2/e. Copyright © 1982 by John Wiley & Sons, Inc. Reprinted by permission of John Wiley & Sons, Inc. **5.43** Adapted from Kuffler, S. W., Discharge pattern and functional organization of mammalian retina, *Journal of Neurophysiology* 16 (1953): 37-68. **5.44** Hubel, D. H., The visual cortex of the brain, *Scientific American* 209 (November 1963): 54-58. **5.45** Drawing by Maura Conron.

Chapter 6: **6.1** Julian Hochberg, *Perception*, 2nd ed., 1978, p 56. Copyright © 1978 by Prentice-Hall, Inc., Englewood Cliffs, N.J. **6.3** Wolfgang Kaehler/Corbis. **6.5A** © Stephen J. Krasemann/Allstock. **6.5B** Lee Snider/Corbis. **6.6** Figures 40 and 41 from *The Perception of the Visual World* by James J. Gibson. Copyright © 1978, 1950 by Houghton Mifflin Company. Used with permission. **6.7** Coren, S., and Ward, L. M., *Sensation and Perception*, 3rd ed. San Diego: Harcourt Brace Jovanovich. Adapted by permission of the author and Harcourt Brace Jovanovich. Drawing by Frank Forney. **6.8A** Bruce, V., and Green, P., *Visual Perception: Physiology, Psychology, and Ecology*. Hillsdale, N. J.: Erlbaum, 1985. Reprinted by permission of Lawrence Erlbaum Associates, Inc. **6.8B** Adapted from Figure 56 from *The Perception of the Visual World* by James J. Gibson. Copyright © 1978, 1950 by Houghton Mifflin Company. Used with permission. **6.11** Duncker, K., Uber induzierte Bewegung, *Psychologische Forschung* 12 (1929): 180-259. Adapted by permission of Springer-Verlag, Inc., Heidelberg. **6.12** Drawing by Frank Forney. **6.16** Photograph by Jeffery Grosscup. **6.22** Beck, J., Effect of orientation and shape similarity on perceptual grouping, *Perception and Psychophysics* 1 (1966): 300-302. Reprinted by permission of the Psychonomic Society Publications. **6.24** Figure 10 from *Gestalt Psychology* by Dr. Wolfgang Kohler. Copyright © 1947 by Liveright Publishing Corporation, renewed © 1975 by Lili Kohler. Reprinted by permission of Liveright Publishing Corporation. **6.25A** AP Photo/Ricardo Choy Kifox. **6.25B** Photograph © Michael Fogden/Oxford Scientific Films. **6.26** Kanizsa, G., Subjective Contours, *Scientific American* 234 (1976): 48-52. **6.29** Selfridge, O. G., Pattern recognition and modern computers, in *Proceedings of Western Joint Computer Conference*, Los Angeles, Calif., 1955. **6.31** Biederman, I., Recognition-by-components: A theory of human image understanding, *Psychological Review* 94 (1987):115-47. **6.32** Rubens, A. B., and Benson, D. F., Associative visual agnosia, *Archives of Neurology* 24: 305-16, in Farah, M.J., *Visual Agnosia*, p. 2. Cambridge, Mass.: MIT Press, 1990. **6.33** Photograph by Ronald James. **6.34** Plates 4 & 8 from Closure Test, C. M. Mooney. **6.36** Penrose, L. S., and Penrose, R., Impossible objects: A special type of visual illusion, *British Journal of Psychology* 49 (1958): 31-33. Reprinted by permission of the British Psychological Society. **6.38 and 6.39** From Tarbus et al. *Eye-movements and Vision*. Copyright © 1967, Plenum Publishing Corp. Reprinted with permission of the publisher. **6.41** Gibson, James J., *The Perception of the Visual World*. Copyright 1978, 1950 by Houghton Mifflin Company. Used with permission. **6.44** Photographs by Jeffrey Grosscup. **6.45** Drawing by Maura Conron. **6.47** Courtesy of The Metropolitan Museum of Art. **6.48** *The Annunciation* by Crivelli; courtesy The National Gallery, London. **6.49** *La Cathédrale de Rouen* by Claude Monet (1893), courtesy Le Musée d'Orsay; © photograph R.M.N. **6.50** Pablo Picasso, *Violin and Grapes*. Céret and Sorgues (spring-early fall 1912), oil on canvas, 20 x 24"; collection, The Museum of Modern Art, New York. Mrs. David M. Levy Bequest. **6.51** Georgio de Chirico, *The Enigma of a Day*, 1914. Oil on canvas, 61 $\frac{1}{4}$" x 55", The Museum of Modern Art, New York. James Thrall Soby Bequest.

Chapter 7: **7.1** From *Psychological Review*, Primary memory by N. C. Waugh and D. A. Norman, Vol. 72: pp. 89-108. Copyright © 1965 by American Psychological Association. Reprinted with permission. **7.2** Adapted from Murdock, B., The serial position effect of free recall, *Journal of Experimental Psychology* 64 (1962): 482-88. **7.3** Glanzer, M., and Cunitz, A., Two storage mechanisms in free recall, *Journal of Verbal Learning and Verbal Behavior* 5 (1966): 351-60. Adapted by permission of the author and Academic Press, Inc. **7.5** Adapted from Ericsson, K. A., Chase, W. G., and Faloon, S., Acquisition of a memory skill, *Science* 208 (June 1980): 1181-82. **7.6** Adapted from Bower, G. H., Analysis of a mnemonic device, *American Scientist* 58 (1970): 496-510. Reprinted by permission of *American Scientist*, journal of Sigma Xi, The Scientific Research Society. Drawing by Maura Conron. **7.7** Godden, D. R., and Baddeley, A. D., Context-dependent memory in two natural environments: On land and underwater, *British Journal of Psychology* 66 (1975): 325-31. Used by permission of the British Psychological Society and the author. **7.11** Adapted from Bahrick, H. P., Semantic memory content in permastore: Fifty years of memory for Spanish learned in school, *Journal of Experimental Psychology: General* 113 (1984): 1-35. **7.12** Orne, M. T., The mechanisms of hypnotic age regression: An experimental study, *Journal of Abnormal and Social Psychology* 58 (1951): 277-99. Copyright 1951 by American Psychological Association. **7.13** From *Scientific American* "The Anatomy of Memory" by M. Mishkin and T. Appenzeller, vol. 256, pp. 80-89. Copyright © 1987 by Scientific American. **7.14A** From *Fundamentals of*

Human Neuropsychology, 2nd ed., by B. Kolb and I. Q. Whishaw, Figure 20-5, p. 485. San Francisco: W.H. Freeman and Company. Copyright © 1980, 1985. **7.14B** Milner, B., Corkin, S., and Teuber, H. L., Further analysis of the hippocampal amnesic syndrome: Fourteen-year follow-up of H.M., *Psychologia* 6 (1968): 215-34.

Chapter 8: **8.1** Illustration by Marjorie Torrey; from Lewis Carroll's *Alice in Wonderland*, illustrated by Marjorie Torrey. Copyright © 1955 by Random House, Inc. Reprinted by permission of Random House, Inc. **8.3** Reprinted with permission from *Science* Mental rotation of 3-D objects by R. N. Shepard and J. Metzler, vol. 171, pp. 701-703. Copyright © 1971 American Association for the Advancement of Science. **8.4** Adapted from Kosslyn, S. M., Ball, T. M., and Reisser, V. J., Visual images preserve metric spatial information: Evidence from studies of image scanning, *Journal of Experimental Psychology: Human Perception and Performance* 4 (1978): 47-60. Copyright 1978 by the American Psychological Association. Drawing by Maura Conron. **8.9** Collins, A. M., and Loftus, E. F., A spreading activation theory of sematic processing. *Psychological Review* 82 (1975): 407-28. Copyright 1975 by the American Psychological Association. **8.15** From Bootzin, R., et al. *Psychology Today* Fourth Edition. Copyright © 1972 the McGraw-Hill Companies. Reproduced with permission of the McGraw-Hill Companies. **8.20** Scheerer, M., Goldstein, K., and Boring, E. G., A demonstration of insight: The horse-rider puzzle, *American Journal of Psychology* 54 (1941): 437-38. Copyright © 1941 by Board of Trustees of the University of Illinois, used with permission of the University of Illinois Press. **8.21** Drawing by Maura Conron. **8.22** Adapted from Duncker, K., On problem solving, *Psychological Monographs*, Whole No. 270 (1945): 1-113. **8.23** Engraving by Walter H. Ruff; courtesy The Granger Collection. **8.24** Adapted from Suls, J. M., A two-stage model for the appreciation of jokes and cartoons, in Goldstein, J. H., and McGhee, P. E. (Eds.), *The Psychology of Humor.* New York: Academic Press, 1972, p. 85. Reprinted by permission of the publisher and the author. **8.25** Reproduced from Lewis Carroll's *Alice in Wonderland*, original illustrations by John Tenniel; in color for this edition by Martina Selway. Secaucus, N. J.: Castle Books.

Chapter 9: **9.3** Reproduced from Lewis Carroll's *Alice in Wonderland*, original illustrations by John Tenniel; in color for this edition by Martina Selway. Secaucus, N. J.: Castle Books. **9.4** Courtesy Sharon Armstrong. **9.11** Drawing by Maura Conron. **9.12** Drawing by Frank Forney. **9.13** Adapted from Slobin, D. I., Grammatical transformation and sentence comprehension in childhood and adulthood, *Journal of Verbal Learning and Verbal Behavior* 5 (1966): 219-27. Used by permission of Academic Press. **9.14** Drawing by Maura Conron. **9.16A** Photograph by Philip Morse, University of Wisconsin. **9.16B** Reprinted with permission from Eimas, P. D., Siqueland, E. R., Jusczyk, P. and Vigorito, J. Speech perception in infants, *Science* 171 (1971): 303-306. Copyright © 1971 by the American Association for the Advancement of Science. **9.17** Drawing by Maura Conron. **9.18** Courtesy of Roberta Golinkoff. **9.20** Brown, R., Cazden, C., and Bellugi-Klima, U., The child's grammar from 1 to 3, in Hill, J. P. (Ed.), *Minnesota Symposium on Child Psychology* by The University of Minnesota Press, Minneapolis. Copyright © 1969 by the University of Minnesota. **9.22** Drawing by Maura Conron. **9.23** Photographs courtesy AP/Wide World Photos. **9.24** Frishberg, N., Arbitrariness and iconicity: Historical change in American Sign Language, *Language* 51 (1975): 696-719. **9.25** Drawings courtesy Noel Yovovich. **9.26** Drawings courtesy Robert Thacker. **9.28** Marler, P. R., A comparative approach to vocal learning: Song development in white crowned sparrows, *Journal of Comparative and Physiological Psychology Monograph* 71 (May 1970): (No. 2, Part 2), pp. 1-25. Copyright 1970 by the American Psychological Association. Reprinted by permission of the author. **9.29** Adapted from Johnson, J., and Newport, E., Critical period effects in second language learning: The influence of maturational state on the acquisition of English as a second language, *Cognitive Psychology* 21 (1989): 60-99. Copyright 1989 by Academic Press, Inc. Reprinted by permission of the publisher and authors. **9.30** Adapted from Newport, E., Maturational constraints on language learning, *Cognitive Science* 14: 11-28.

Chapter 10: **10.1A** Adapted from Keeton, W. T., and Gould, J. L., *Biological Science*, 4th ed. New York: W. W. Norton & Company, 1986. Copyright © 1986, 1980, 1979, 1972, 1967 by W. W. Norton & Company, Inc. Used with permission. **10.1B** Photograph courtesy of John Sparks, BBC (Natural History). **10.2** Photograph © M. P. Kahl/DRK. **10.3** Barnett, S. A., 1963. *The Rat: A Study in Behavior*. Chicago: The University of Chicago Press. Copyright © 1963 by Aldine Publishing Co. Reprinted by permission of the University of Chicago Press. **10.4** Photograph by Hans Reinhard, © Bruce Coleman, Inc., 1988. **10.5A** Photograph by Rod Williams, © Bruce Coleman, Inc., 1991. **10.5B** Kevin Schafer, Corbis. **10.6A** Courtesy of L. T. Nash, Arizona State University. **10.6B** Courtesy of Bruce Coleman.

10.7A © Allan D. Cruikshank, 1978/Photo Researchers. **10.7B** © J. Messerschmidt/Bruce Coleman. **10.8** © 1987 Garry D. McMichael/Photo Researchers. **10.9A** Photograph by Philip Green. **10.9B** Photograph by Bob and Clara Calhoun/Bruce Coleman. **10.9C** Photograph by Jeff Foott/Bruce Coleman. **10.10** From Klopfer, *An Introduction to Animal Behavior: Ethology's First Century*, Copyright © 1974. Reprinted by permission of Prentice-Hall, Inc., Upper Saddle River, NJ. **10.11** Photograph © Rudie H. Kuiter, Oxford Scientific Films. **10.12** Adapted from Keeton, W. T., and Gould, J. L., *Biological Science*, 4th ed., New York: W. W. Norton & Company, Inc., 1986. Copyright © 1986, 1980, 1979, 1972, 1967 by W. W. Norton & Company, Inc. **10.13** Bermant, G., and Davidson, J. M., *Biological Bases of Sexual Behavior*. New York: Harper & Row, 1974. In turn adapted from data of Davidson, J. M., Rodgers, C. H., Smith, E. R., and Bloch, G. J., Relative thresholds of behavioral and somatic responses to estrogen, *Physiology and Behavior* 3 (1968): 227-29. Copyright 1968, Pergamon Press, PLC. **10.14A** Photograph by Francisco J. Erize/Bruce Coleman. **10.14B** Photograph © Jim Clare, Partridge Films Ltd./Oxford Scientific Films. **10.15A** John Shaw/Bruce Coleman. **10.15B** Courtesy of Ian Wyllie, Monks Wood Experiment Station. **10.16B** © Walt Disney Productions. **10.17** Wayne Lankinen/Bruce Coleman. **10.18** Georg D. Lepp/Bio-Tec Images. **10.19** Photograph by P. Craig-Cooper, Nature Photographers, Ltd.

Chapter 11: **11.1** Asch, S. E., Studies of independence and conformity: A minority of one against a unanimous majority, *Psychological Monographs* 70 (9, Whole No. 416), 1956. Copyright 1956 by the American Psychological Association. **11.2, 11.3, 11.4** Drawings by Maura Conron. **11.5** © Paul Ekman, 1971. **11.6** From *Psychology of Facial Expression* by J. A. Russell and J. M. Fernandez-Dols. Copyright © 1997 by Cambridge University Press. Reprinted with permission of Cambridge University Press. **11.7** Ekman, P., and Friesen, W. V., *Unmasking the Face.* Englewood Cliffs, N.J.: Prentice-Hall, 1975. Reprinted by permission of the author. **11.8** AP Photo/Eric Risberg.

Chapter 12: **12.1** Drawing by Maura Conron. **12.4** Leonardo da Vinci's *La Jaconde* (Mona Lisa), Louvre, Paris; photograph courtesy of Service Photographique de la Reunion des Musées Nationaux. **12.5 and 12.6** Copyright 1965 by Stanley Milgram. From the film *Obedience*, distributed by the Pennsylvania State University, PCR.

Chapter 13: **13.1** From *Biological Science*, Sixth Edition by James Gould and William T. Keeton. Copyright © 1996, 1993, 1986, 1980, 1979, 1978, 1972, 1967 by W. W. Norton & Company, Inc. Reprinted by permission of W. W. Norton & Company, Inc. **13.2** Liebert, R. M., Poulos, R. W., and Strauss, G. D., *Developmental Psychology*, Fig. III-10, p.81. Englewood Cliffs, N. J.: Prentice-Hall, Inc., 1974. Originally adapted from H. M. Halverston, printed by The Journal Press, 1931. Photographs by Kathy Hirsh-Pasek. **13.3** Conel, J. L., *The Postnatal Development of the Human Cortex*, vols. 1, 3, 5. Cambridge, Mass.: Harvard University Press, 1939, 1947, 1955. **13.4** Tanner, J. M., Physical growth, in *Carmichael's Manual of Child Psychology*, 3rd ed., vol. 1, Mussen, P. H., ed., Fig. 6, p. 85. New York: John Wiley & Sons, 1970. Copyright 1970 by John Wiley & Sons. **13.5** Shirley, M. M., *The First Two Years: A Study of Twenty-five Babies*, vol. II. University of Minnesota Press, Minneapolis. © 1933, 1961, University of Minnesota Press. **13.6** Photograph courtesy of M. M. Grumbach. **13.7** From *Biological Science*, Sixth Edition by James Gould and William T. Keeton. Copyright © 1996, 1993, 1986, 1980, 1979, 1978, 1972, 1967 by W. W. Norton & Company, Inc. Reprinted by permission of W. W. Norton & Company, Inc. **13.8** Photograph by Victor Englebert/Photo Researchers. **13.9** Courtesy Dr. Mark Rosenzweig. **13.10** Photographs by Doug Goodman 1986/Monkmeyer. **13.11 and 13.13** Photographs by Chris Massey. **13.12** Photograph by Ed Boswell. **13.14** Piaget, J., and Inhelder, B., *The Child's Conception of Space.* Humanities Press International Inc., Atlantic Highlands, N.J., 1967. Adapted by permission of the publisher and Routledge & Kegan Paul Ltd. Drawing by Maura Conron. **13.15** Drawing by Maura Conron. **13.16** Photographs courtesy of Phillip Kellman. **13.17** Kellman, P. J., and Spelke, E. S., Perception of partially occluded objects in infancy, *Cognitive Psychology* 15 (1983): 483-524. Copyright 1983 by the American Psychological Association. Adapted by permission of the author. **13.18** Adapted from Baillargeon, R., Object permanence in 3½- and 4½-month-old infants, *Developmental Psychology* 23 (1987): 655-64. **13.19** Photographs courtesy of Adele Diamond. **13.20** Starkey, P., Spelke, E. S., and Gelman, R., Detection of intermodal numerical correspondences by human infants, *Science* 222 (1983): 179-81. Drawing by Maura Conron. **13.21** Figure 2.3 on p. 31 of Johnson, M. H. and Morton, J., *Biology and Cognitive Development: The Case of Face Recognition*. Copyright © 1991 by Blackwell Publishers. Reprinted by permission of Blackwell Publishers. **13.22** Photographs courtesy of Helene Borke. Borke, H., Piaget's mountains revisited: Changes in the egocentric landscape, *Developmental Psychology* 11

(1975): 240-43. **13.23** Photographs courtesy of Kimberly Canidy. **13.24A** A. Frederic B. Siskind ©. **13.24B** Photograph by Ray Ellis/Photo Researchers. **13.24C** Photograph by Chris Massey. **13.25** Case, R., 1978. Intellectual development from birth to adulthood: A neo-Piagetian interpretation, in Siegler, R., (Ed.), *Children's Thinking: What Develops*. Hillsdale, N. J.: Lawrence Erlbaum Associates, Inc. Reproduced by permission of Lawrence Erlbaum Associates, Inc.

Chapter 14: **14.1** Photograph by Martin Rogers/Stock, Boston. **14.2** Photograph by Suzanne Szasz. **14.3** Photograph by Nina Leen/Life Magazine, © Time Warner, Inc. **14.5** Ainsworth, M., Blehar, M., Waters, E., and Wall, S., 1978. *Patterns of Attachment*, p. 34. Hillsdale, N. J.: Lawrence Erlbaum Associates, Inc. Reproduced by permission of Lawrence Erlbaum Associates, Inc. Drawing by Maura Conron. **14.7** Photographs courtesy Kathy Hirsh-Pasek. **14.8, 14.9, and 14.10** Courtesy Harry Harlow, University of Wisconsin Primate Laboratory. **14.11** Photograph by Michael Heron/Woodfin Camp. **14.12** Kohlberg, L., Development of children's orientation towards a moral order in sequence in the development of moral thought, *Vita Humana* 6 (1963): 11-36. Adapted by permission of S. Karger AG, Basel. **14.15** Tanner, J. M. Physical growth in Damon, ed. *Carmichael's Manual of Child Psychology*, 5th Edition. Copyright © 1998 by John Wiley & Sons, Inc. Reprinted by permission of John Wiley & Sons, Inc. **14.16A and 14.16B** *Left* Photograph by David Reed/Corbis. *Right* Photograph © Bill Gillette/Stock Boston. **14.17A** T. Lowell/Black Star. **14.17B** © Spencer Grant/The Picture Cube. **14.17C** © Timothy Ross/The Image Bank.

Chapter 15: **15.3** Figure 16.1 from Anastasi, A. *Differential Psychology*, 3/e, 1958. Copyright Macmillan College Publishing Co. Reprinted by permission of Prentice Hall, Upper Saddle River, N J. **15.4** Courtesy H. Douglas Pratt. **15.7** Simulated items similar to those in the Weschler Adult Intelligence Scale: Third Edition. Copyright © 1997 by The Psychological Corporation. Reproduced by permission. All rights reserved. "Weschler Adult Intelligence Scale" and "WAIS" are registered trademarks of The Psychological Corporation. **15.8** SAT materials selected from *10 SATs*, College Entrance Examination Board, 1983. Reprinted by permission of Educational Testing Service and the College Entrance Examination Board, the copyright owners. Permission to reprint SAT materials does not constitute review or endorsement by Educational Testing Service or the College Board of this publication as a whole or of any other questions or testing information it may contain. **15.9** From the Raven Standard Progressive Matrices. **15.12** Jones, H. E., and Kaplan, O. J., Psychological aspects of mental disorders in later life, in Kaplan, O. J. (Ed.), *Mental Disorders in Later Life*, 72. Stanford, Calif.: Stanford University Press, 1945. Adapted by permission of Stanford University Press. **15.10** Brody, N., *Intelligence*, 2nd Ed. New York: Academic Press, 1992. **15.13** Selfe, S. *Nadia: A Case of Extraordinary Drawing Ability in an Autistic Child*. New York: Academic Press, 1977. Reproduced by permission of Academic Press and Lorna Selfe. **15.14** Courtesy Photofest. **15.15** Based on Winchester, A. M., *Genetics*, 5th ed. Boston: Houghton Mifflin, 1977. **15.16** Photographs courtesy of Dr. Franklin A. Bryan. **15.18** Drawing by Maura Conron.

Chapter 16: **16.1** Lanyon, R. I. *Personality Assessment*, 3/e. Copyright © 1996 by John Wiley & Sons, Inc. Reprinted by permission of John Wiley & Sons, Inc. **16.3** From *Journal of Abnormal and Social Psychology*, Toward an adequate taxonomy of personality attributes: replicated factor structure in peer nomination personality rating by W. T. Norman, vol. 66, p. 5770. Copyright © 1963 by American Psychological Association. Adapted with permission. **16.4** Eysnck, H. J., and Rachman, S., *The causes and cures of neurosis*, p. 16. San Diego, Calif.: Robert R. Knapp, 1965. **16.5** The Bettmann Archive. **16.6A** Wilfong Photographic/Leo de Wys, Inc. **16.6B,C** Photographs by H. Reinhard/Bruce Coleman.

Chapter 17: **17.3** "Hierarchy of Needs" from *Motivation and Personality* 3/e by Abraham H. Maslow. Copyright 1954, 1987 by Harper & Row, Publishers, Inc. Copyright © 1970 by Abraham H. Maslow. Reprinted by permission of Addison Wesley Educational Publishers Inc.

Chapter 18: **18.1** Negative #31568. Courtesy Department of Library Services, The American Museum of Natural History. **18.2** William Hogarth's *The Madhouse, 1735/1763*; courtesy The Bettmann Archive. **18.3** © Stock Montage, Inc. **18.5** Photograph by Bill Bridges/Globe Photos. **18.7** Nicol, S. E., and Gottesman, I. I., Clues to the genetics and neurobiology of schizophrenia, *American Scientist*, 71 (1983): 398-404. Reprinted by permission of *American Scientist*, journal of Sigma Xi, The Scientific Research Society. **18.8** Data from Faris, R. E. L., and Dunham, H. W., *Mental Disorders in Urban Areas*. Chicago: University of Chicago Press, 1939. Adapted by permission of the author. **18.10** Rosenthal, N. E., Sack, D. A., Gillin, J. C., Lewy, A. J., Goodwin, F. K., Davenport, Y., Mueller, P. S., Newsome, D. A., and Wehr,

T. A., Seasonal affective disorder: A description of the syndrome and preliminary findings with light therapy. *Archives of General Psychiatry* 41 (1984): 72-80. Copyright 1984, American Medical Association. **18.11** Stone, A., Mental health and law: A system in transition, U.S. Department of Health, Education and Welfare, #75176, p. 7, 1975. **18.12** Hare, R. D., Temporal gradient of fear arousal in psychopaths, *Journal of Abnormal Psychology* 70 (1965): 442-45.

Chapter 19: **19.1A** Courtesy Historical Pictures Service. **19.1B** Courtesy National Library of Medicine. **19.1C** Culver Pictures. **19.5** Photograph by James D. Wilson/Woodfin Camp. **19.7** Gibbons R. D., Hedeker, D., Elkin, I., Waternaux, C., Kraemer, H. C., Greenhouse, J. B., Shea, M. T., Imber, S. D., Sotsky, S. M., Watkins, J. T., Some conceptual and statistical issues in analysis of longitudinal psychiatric data. Application to the NIMH treatment of Depression Collaborative Research Program dataset. *Archives of General Psychiatry*, 50 (1993), 739-50.

TABLES

14.1 Adapted from Kohlberg, L., Classification of moral judgment into levels and stages of development, in Sizer, Theodore R., *Religion and Public Education*, pp. 171-73. Copyright © 1967 Houghton Mifflin Company. Used with permission. **14.2** Erikson, E. H., *Childhood and Society*. New York: W. W. Norton & Company, Inc., 1963. Adapted by permission. **15.2** Adapted from Mental Retardation Activities of the U. S. Department of Health, Education, and Welfare. Washington, DC: United States Government Printing Office, 1963, p. 2. Score interval data from a classificatory system formerly recommended by the American Association for Mental Deficiency. **15.3** Bayley, N., Mental growth during the first three years, *Genetic Psychology Monographs* 14 (1933): 1-92. Reprinted with permission of the Helen Dwight Reed Educational Foundation. Published by Heldref Publications, 4000 Albemarle St. N.W., Washington, D.C. 20016. **15.4** Wechsler, D., *The Measurement and Appraisal of Adult Intelligence*, 4th ed. Baltimore, Md.: The Williams & Wilkins Co., 1958. Table adapted from the Manual for the Wechsler Adult Intelligence Scale. **16.3** Norman, W. T., Toward an adequate taxonomy of personality attributes: Replicated factor structure in peer nomination personality ratings, *Journal of Abnormal and Social Psychology* 66 (1963): 577. Copyright 1963 by the American Psychological Association. Adapted by permission of the author.

UNNUMBERED PHOTOS AND ART

(Chapter 1 Opener) Detail of Michelangelo's *Profile with Fantastic Head-Dress*, courtesy Ashmolean Museum, Oxford, England. **9** Two illustrations from *Where the Wild Things Are*, written and illustrated by Maurice Sendak. Copyright 1963 by Maurice Sendak. Reprinted by permission of Harper-Collins Publishers. **10** Pablo Picasso, *The Dream*, 1932; Scala/Art Resource. **11** *Top* Courtesy of Archives of the History of American Psychology–University of Akron. *Bottom* The Warder Collection. *(Part Opener I)* Detail of *The Battle of the Melvian Bridge*, Stanze di Raffaello, Vatican Palace, Vatican State; courtesy Scala/Art Resource. **16** Courtesy National Library of Medicine. **27** Photofest. **33** Courtesy of The Natural History Museum, London. **37** Photograph by M. Sakka, courtesy Musée de l'Homme et Musée Depuytren, Paris. **52** Photograph by David M. Phillips/Visuals Unlimited. **54** Courtesy National Library of Medicine. **59** *Left* Photograph by B. Malkin/Anthro-Photo. *Right* Buddy Mays/Corbis. **67** Courtesy of Department of Psychology, University of Pennsylvania. **72** Gift of Mrs. George von Lengerke Meyer. Courtesy Museum of Fine Arts, Boston. **75** Photograph by Jane Burton, © 1987, Bruce Coleman, Inc. **78** Photofest. **82** Peter Brueghel the Elder, *The Peasants' Wedding*, 1568, Kunsthistorisches Museum. Photograph © Erich Lessing/Art Resource, NY. **90** Photograph by Jane Carter. **91** *Left* Courtesy Naturhistorisches Museum, Wien. *Center* Courtesy Museo del Prado. *Right* AP Photo/Laurent Rebours. **92** Courtesy National Library of Medicine. **98** Photograph by Grant Leduc/Monkmeyer. **104** Photographs by Takahisa Hirano/Nature Production. **105** *Jacob's Ladder*, from the Lambeth Bible; courtesy the Archbishop of Canterbury and the Trustees of

Lambeth Palace Library. **106** Salvador Dali, *The Grand Paranoic*, 1936, oil on panel, 62 x 62 cm.; collection Museum Boymans-van-Beuningen, Rotterdam. **109** *Left* AP Photo. *Middle* Photograph by Guy Sauvage/Agence Vandystadt/Photo Researchers. *Right* Photograph courtesy of Photofest. **118** Photograph by Bette Splendens/Oxford Scientific Films. **119** Corbis-Bettmann. **126** Courtesy of the Museum of the City of New York. **128** The Granger Collection. **131** Photograph by Nina Leen/Life Magazine, © Time Warner. **133** Photograph © Hank Morgan. **138** Photograph by Erika Stone. **140** Courtesy Psychology Department, University of California, Berkeley. **148** Courtesy of Animal Behavior Enterprises, Inc. **150** Photographs by Lincoln P. Brower. **152** Courtesy of Animal Behavior Enterprises, Inc. **159** The Warder Collection. *(Part Opener II)* Detail from Raphael's *School of Athens*, 1505, Stanza della Segnatura, Vatican; courtesy Scala/Art Resource, New York. **170** Courtesy National Portrait Gallery, London. **171** Detail from *The Bermuda Group* by John Smibert; courtesy Yale University Art Gallery; gift of Isaac Lothrop of Plymouth, Mass. **173** Culver Pictures, Inc., New York. **174** Photographs courtesy National Library of Medicine. **182** Photograph by Ed Reschke. **187** Photograph © RDR Productions, 1981; Rex Features USA. **191** Courtesy National Library of Medicine. **192** Courtesy Dr. David D. Yager and Michael L. May; © The Company of Biologists Limited. **206** Courtesy National Library of Medicine. **203** Photographs by Fritz Goro/Life Magazine, © Time Warner, Inc. **207** Courtesy of Department of Psychology, University of Pennsylvania. **218** Claude Monet, *Terrace at Sainte-Adresse*, oil on canvas, 38⅝ x 51⅛"; reproduced by permission of the Metropolitan Museum of Art, New York; purchased with special contributions and purchase funds given or bequeathed by friends of the Museum, 1967. **223** © Globus Studios/The Stock Market. **228** Photograph by Paul Haller. **231** Salvador Dali's *The Trojan War*, courtesy Esquire. **247** © Jeff Zamba/Allstock/PNI. **248** Courtesy E. J. Gibson. **251** Photograph courtesy of Department of Psychology, Swarthmore College. **262** Photograph by Kathy Hirsh-Pasek. **264** The Kobal Collection. **267** Detail of *Netherlandish Proverbs* by Pieter Brueghel, 1559; courtesy of Gemaldegalerie, Staatliche Museen Preuischer Kulturbesitz, Berlin. **268** Paul Cezanne, *The Cardplayers*; courtesy The Metropolitan Museum of Art, bequest of Stephen C. Clark, 1960. **274** Photofest. **282** Photograph by Suzanne Szasz. **283** Marc Chagall, *I and the Village*, 1911, oil on canvas, 63⅝ x 59⅝" (192.1 x 151.4 cm); collection, The Museum of Modern Art, New York, Mrs. Simon Guggenheim Fund. **284** *Top* Corbis-Bettmann. *Bottom* AP Photo/John Gap III. **286** Salvador Dali, *The Persistence of Memory*, 1931, oil on canvas, 9½ x 13"; Collection, The Museum of Modern Art, New York; given anonymously. **293** Nikita Krushchev (Corbis-Bettmann); Mohammed Ali (The Everett Collection/ABC); Golda Meir (Corbis-Bettmann); Anwar El-Sadat (William Karel/Sygma); Betty Ford (Tony Korody/Sygma); Patty Hearst (Corbis-UPI/Bettmann); Mary Lou Retton (AP Photo); Nancy Reagan (AP Photo/Dennis Cook); Boy George (Photofest); Michelle Kwan (AP Photo/Damain Dovarganes); Timothy McVeigh (AP Photo/David Longstreath); Colin Powell (AP Photo/Greg Gibson). *Bottom* Marslan-Wilson, W. D., and Teuber, H. L., Memory for remote events in anterograde amnesia: Recognition of public figures from news photographs, *Neuropsychologia* 13 (1975):353-64. **302** *Top* Rembrandt's *Aristotle with a Bust of Homer*, oil on canvas, 56½ x 53¾"; courtesy The Metropolitan Museum of Art, purchased with special funds and gifts of friends of the Museum, 1961. *Bottom* Pablo Picasso, *Portrait of Ambroise Vollard*, 1909, Pushkin Museum, Moscow; courtesy Scala/Art Resource. **323** *Left* Courtesy of Lifesmith Classic Fractals. *Right* Courtesy Harold Cohen. Photograph © Becky Cohen. **326** Adam Nadel/AP Photo. **328** © 1998 by Sidney Harris. **331** From a British National Theatre production of *Galileo* by Bertolt Brecht; photograph by Zoe Dominic. **338** *Figure 14*, Alfredo Castañeda, 1982. Courtesy Mary-Anne Martin/Fine Art, New York. **346** Pieter Brueghel the Elder, *Trumbau zu Babel (Tower of Babel)*; courtesy Kunsthistorisches Museum, Vienna. **347** Photograph by Leonard McCombe/Life Magazine, © Time Warner, Inc. **348** William Blake, *Adam Naming the Beasts*, courtesy The Stirling Maxwell Collection, Pollok House, Glasgow Museums & Art Galleries. **349** Henri Rousseau, *The Sleeping Gypsy*, 1897, oil on canvas, 51" x 6'7"; collection, The Museum of Modern Art, New York. Gift of Mrs. Simon Guggenheim. **353** By permission from *Merriam-Webster's Collegiate® Dictionary* Tenth Edition. Copyright © 1998 by Merriam-Webster Incorporated. **354** Reproduced from Lewis Carroll's *Alice in Wonderland*, original illustrations by John Tenniel; in color for this edition by Martina Selway. Secaucus, N.J.: Castle Books. **356** Tim Wright, Alissa Crandall, and Wolfgang Kaehler/Corbis. **358** Reproduced from Lewis Carroll's *Alice in Wonderland*, original drawings by John Tenniel; in color for this edition by Martina Selway. Secaucus, N.J.: Castle Books. **366** Drawing by Maura Conron. **377** Reproduced from *Higglety Pigglety Pop! or There Must Be More to Life* by Maurice Sendak, New York: HarperCollins. Copyright M. Sendak. **395** Lewis Carroll's *Through the Looking Glass*, illustration by John Tenniel, courtesy of General Research Division, The New York Public Library, Astor, Lenox, and Tilden Foundations. **371, 372** Photographs by Erika Stone. **379** Photograph by Roberta

Intrater. **388, 389** Courtesy of The Perkins School for the Blind. **393** Photographs courtesy of Herbert Terrace. *(Part Opener III)* Detail from Auguste Renoir's *Le Moulin de la Galette*, 1876, Louvre, Paris; photograph © R.M.N. **406** *Top* Painting by John Michael Wright; courtesy The Granger Collection. *Bottom* Painting by J. Collier; courtesy of The National Portrait Gallery, London. **407** *Top* Photograph © Norbert Wu/Allstock/PNI. *Bottom* Brian M. Rogers/Biofotos. **408** Photographs by Nina Leen. **410** Stouffer Productions/Animals Animals. **412** Photograph © Manfred Danegger. **414** Photograph © I. Eibl-Eibesfeldt. **417** Photograph by John Wightman/Area London, Ltd. **419** Courtesy of R. Thornhill, University of New Mexico. **422** Photograph by Robert W. Hernández/The National Audubon Society Collection/Photo Researchers. **425** Courtesy of The Motion Picture and Television Photo Archive. **426** Photograph © Zefa Germany/The Stock Market, 1994. **429** *Left* © 1978 Tom McHugh/Photo Researchers. *Right* © Luis Castaneda/The Image Bank. **430** Photograph by Benny Ortiz. **431** *Top* Photograph by Bob Peck, Academy of Natural Sciences, Philadelphia. *Bottom* Courtesy of Dorothy Cheney. **435** AP Photo/J. Pat Carter. **436** Photofest. **442** *Top left* Photograph by Michael Cooper/Stratford Festival. *Top right* Photofest. **443** *Top* Courtesy Swarthmore College. *Bottom* Photographs by William Vandivert. **444** *Top* The Kobal Collection. *Bottom* Photograph by Burt Glinn, © 1964/Magnum Photos. **446** *Left* © Sylvia Johnson/Woodfin Camp. *Right* © Susan McElhinney/Woodfin Camp. **448** *Top* Courtesy of DeBeers. *Bottom* Courtesy of Best Foods Baking Group. **449** Frontispiece from *The Wonderful World of American Advertising, 1865-1900*, by Leonard de Vries and Ilonka van Amstel. Chicago: Follett, 1972. **450** Courtesy of the U.S. Army. **452** *Top left* Paul Fusco/Magnum Photos, Inc. *Top center* Rex Features USA. *Top right* James Foote/Photo Researchers. *Bottom* Michael Probst/UPI Bettman Newsphotos. **454** From the 1993 film *Much Ado About Nothing*; photograph by Clive Coote. **456** British poster, 1900, John R. Freeman collection; by courtesy of the Board of Trustees of the Victoria and Albert Museum. **459** AP/Wide World Photos. **461** The Kobal Collection. **464** Photograph © Mark Mirko/Palm Beach Post. **465** Photograph by Suzanne Szasz. **466** Photofest. **467** Photograph by S. C. Delaney/EPA. **471** © Lee Snider/Photo Images; courtesy New York Gilbert & Sullivan Players. **475** Photograph by Michael Nichols/Magnum Photos. **476** Constantine Manos, © 1968/Magnum Photos. **482, 485** Photographs by Suzanne Szasz. **486** Photofest. **492** Magnum Photos. **493** Edward Burne-Jones, *The Star of Bethlehem*; courtesy of Birmingham Museums and Art Gallery. **495** Roger Brown, *The Streetlight*, 1983; private collection, New York; courtesy of Phyllis Kind Gallery, New York/Chicago. **497** Jacopo Bassano's *The Good Samaritan*; courtesy The National Gallery, London. **498** AP Photo/Khalil Senosi. **501** Grant Wood, *American Gothic*, 1930, oil on beaver board, 76 x 63.3 cm' Art Institute of Chicago, Friends of American Art Collection; photograph © 1990, The Art Institute of Chicago. All Rights Reserved. **502** *Left* Yann Arthus-Bertrand/Corbis. *Right* Kevin R. Morris/© Corbis. **503** Photofest, NY. **504** Henry Fuseli, *Titania Awakes*, 1793-94, oil on canvas, 169 x 135 cm; courtesy Kunsthaus Zürich. **505** *Top* © Martha Swope/Martha Swope Photography, Inc. *Bottom* Jean-Auguste-Dominique Ingres, *Roger et Angelique*, 1819, Louvre, Paris; © R.M.N. **506** © Sonlight/Stock South/PNI. **507** Photograph by Gale Zucker/Stock, Boston. **508** Photograph by G. Frank Radway. **510** *Top* The Kobal Collection. *Bottom* Photograph by Dan Budnick/Woodfin Camp. **511** UPI/Bettmann. **518** © Aneal Vohra/Unicorn Stock Photos. **519** Jean-Antoine Gros, *Napoleon on the Battlefield of Eylau*, February 19, 1807, 1808. Louvre, Paris. Photography courtesy Scala/Art Resource, NY. **522** *Top* Photograph by Michael Sheil/Black Star. *Bottom* © Detroit Free Press, 1988, Pauline Lubens/Black Star. **524** Photograph by Eamonn McCabe, The Observer. **525** Dave Gleiter/FPG International. **527** Photograph by Carlo Bevilacqua; courtesy Istituto Geografico DeAgostini, Milan. *(Part Opener IV)* John Singer Sargent, *Carnation, Lily, Lily, Rose*, 1885-86; courtesy Tate Gallery, London/Art Resource. **536** Photograph courtesy of Kathy Hirsh-Pasek. **537** Photograph by Kenneth Garrett 1984/Woodfin Camp. **543** Detail from Michelangelo's *Creation of Eve*, Sistine Chapel; courtesy Scala/Art Resource. **544** *Bottom* © David Strick/Outline. **546** Gerhard Ter Borch's *Portrait of Helena van der Schalke*; courtesy Rijksmuseum, Amsterdam. **548** Photograph by Steve Skloot/Photo Researchers. **549** Photograph by Yves DeBraine/Black Star. **533** Photograph courtesy Smith College Archives. **569** Benainous, © Gamma. **568** Photographs by Kathy Hirsh-Pasek. **570** Reproduced from S. D. Thomas, *The Last Navigator*. New York: Holt, 1987. Reproduced by permission of Henry Holt & Company, Inc. **576** *Top* Mary Cassatt, *Mother and Child*, 1890; courtesy of the Wichita Art Museum, the Roland P. Murdock Collection. *Bottom* Photograph by Suzanne Szasz. **580** Photograph by J. Blyenberg/Leo de Wys. **583** Photo Researchers. **584** Photograph © 1993 Stephen Shames/Matrix. **589** Photographs courtesy of George Gleitman. **590** © Spencer Grant/Stock Boston. **591** Photograph by Erika Stone. **592** © Nancy Richmond/The Image Works. **595** Photograph by Suzanne Szasz. **596** Photograph by Roberta Grobel Intrater. **599** © Martha Swope/Martha Swope Photography. **600**

NAME INDEX